A Treatise on

INTERNATIONAL CRIMINAL LAW

Volume I

CRIMES AND PUNISHMENT

A Treatise on

INTERNATIONAL CRIMINAL LAW

Volume I

CRIMES AND PUNISHMENT

Compiled and Edited by

M. CHERIF BASSIOUNI

Professor of Law
DePaul University
Chicago, Illinois
Guest Scholar Woodrow Wilson International Center for Scholars, 1972
Visiting Professor of Law, New York University, 1971
Fulbright-Hays Visiting Professor of International Criminal Law,
Albert Ludwig University, Freiburg, Germany, 1970

and

VED P. NANDA

Professor of Law
Director of International Legal Studies
University of Denver
Denver, Colorado

CHARLES C THOMAS • PUBLISHER
Springfield • Illinois • U.S.A.

Published and Distributed Throughout the World by
CHARLES C THOMAS • PUBLISHER
Bannerstone House
301–327 East Lawrence Avenue, Springfield, Illinois, U.S.A.

© 1973, by CHARLES C THOMAS • PUBLISHER

ISBN 0–398–02555–X (cloth)
ISBN 0–398–02557–6 (paper)

Library of Congress Catalog Card Number: 72–79181

*With THOMAS BOOKS careful attention is given to all details of
manufacturing and design. It is the Publisher's desire to present books
that are satisfactory as to their physical qualities and artistic possibilities
and appropriate for their particular use. THOMAS BOOKS will be true
to those laws of quality that assure a good name and good will.*

Printed in the United States of America

BB-14

CONTRIBUTORS

S.K. Agrawala

Professor of International Law; Head of the Department of Law, University of Poona, Poona, India.

M. Cherif Bassiouni

Professor of Law, DePaul University, Chicago, Illinois.

J.M. van Bemmelen

Emeritus Professor of Law, University of Leyden, Netherlands.

Douglas Besharov

Assistant Corporation Counsel, City of New York; Adjunct Assistant of Law, New York University, New York, New York.

Remigiusz Bierzanek

Professor of International Law, University of Warsaw, Warsaw, Poland.

Denise Bindschedler-Robert

Professor of International Law, The Institute of High International Studies, Geneva, Switzerland.

William E. Butler

Reader in Comparative Law, University College, London, England.

J.Y. Dautricourt

Judge; Professor of Law, University of Louvain, Brussels, Belgium.

Yoram Dinstein

Professor of International Law, The University of Tel Aviv, Tel Aviv, Israel.

Perry Gulbrandsen

Attorney at Law, Chicago, Illinois.

Hans-Heinrich Jescheck

Professor of Criminal Law, Albert Ludwig University; Director, the Max-Planck Institute for Foreign and International Criminal Law, Freiburg, Germany.

Andrew Lee

Dean and Professor of Law, University of Soochow, Taipei, Taiwan, The Republic of China.

W. Thomas Mallison, Jr.

Professor of Law, George Washington University, National Law Center, Washington, D.C.

Jean Mirimanoff-Chilikine

Attorney at Law; Legal Adviser, Legal Department of the International Committee of the Red Cross, Geneva, Switzerland.

G.O.W. Mueller

Professor of Law, New York University; Director, Criminal Law Education and Research Center, New York, New York.

Fritz Munch

Professor of International Law, University of Bonn, Bonn, Germany.

M. Kitili MWendwa

Chief Justice, High Court of Kenya, Nairobi, Kenya.

Ved P. Nanda

Professor of Law; Director of International Legal Studies, University of Denver, Denver, Colorado.

Jean Nepote

Secretary General, INTERPOL, Paris, France.

John C. Novogrod

Attorney at Law, New York, New York.

Bert V.A. Roling

Professor of International Law; Director, Institute of Polemology, Groningen University, Groningen, Netherlands.

Paul K. Ryu

Professor of Law, The University of Seoul, Seoul, The Republic of Korea.

Helen Silving

Professor of Law, The University of Puerto Rico, Rio Piedras, Puerto Rico.

S. Prakash Sinha

Associate Professor of .Law, University of Western Ontario, London, Canada.

Jacob W.F. Sundberg

Professor of Jurisprudence, University of Stockholm, Stockholm, Sweden.

Criton G. Tornaritis

Attorney General of the Republic of Cyprus, Nicosia, Cyprus.

Tran-Tam

Professor of Criminology, University of Minh Duc, Saigon, Republic of South Vietnam.

Martial Tricaud

Professor of International Law, University of Paris, Paris, France.

Michel Veuthey

Attorney at Law; Legal Advisor, Legal Department of the International Committee of the Red Cross, Geneva, Switzerland.

Theo Vogler

Professor of Criminal Law, University of Berlin, Berlin, Germany.

John B. Whitton

Emeritus Professor of Politics, Princeton University, Princeton, New Jersey.

Robert K. Woetzel

Professor of International Politics and Law, Boston College, Chestnut Hill, Massachusetts.

To

EARL WARREN

Chief Justice of the United States, *Retired*

and

MYRES S. McDOUGAL

Sterling Professor of International Law, Yale Law School

———————

In recognition of their contribution to the advancement of the rule of law

———————

To

EARL WARREN

Chief Justice of the United States, Retired

and

TOM C. CLARK

retired Professor of ...

In recognition of their contribution to the

advancement of the rule of law

PREFACE

It is often said that ours is a small world. Perhaps never before was such a vision clearer than when pictures taken from outer space revealed the size of the globe in relationship to the universe. The world, however, continues to be plagued by man-made ills, some of which threaten its very existence. Among such threats are forms of conduct by states and individuals which so offend the common morality of mankind that they rise to the level of international crimes. The principle of state and individual accountability for conduct affecting the world community has been established by treaties, historical precedents, and doctrine, but it is insufficiently implemented in actual practice.

Scholars, particularly Europeans, have written for the last half a century on the subject, and their work is now recognized as classic. Their contributions and that of the United Nations have been a pioneering effort. It is now felt, however, that a new direction must be given to this entire field. One way is to consider it as a distinct discipline which falls neither under classical international law nor conventional criminal law. This indeed is one of the purposes of this book.

If a general thesis can be gleaned from the many outstanding contributions in the book, it would be that there is an ever-increasing need for an effective body of international criminal law. A simple, albeit incomplete, enumeration of international crimes can be grouped under three headings and should make manifest that the preceding is not an idle conclusion of sequestered scholars; they are (1) disruptions of world peace and security of mankind, (2) violations of rules of armed conflicts, and (3) common crimes against mankind. After the doctrinal and the theoretical bases of international criminal law are explored, all of these aspects are discussed here.

Despite a deep-rooted history, international criminal law remains in a nascent and nebulous stage. Thus, many authors have expressed the position that international criminal law somehow eludes a perspicacious definition; nevertheless, this may be an overstatement. The vast amount of literature and the numerous international conventions, treaties, and resolutions of professional and scholarly organizations suggest that international criminal law is more a reality than an abstract concept. Nuremberg and Tokyo stand out as landmarks in this emerging discipline. State enforcement of sanctions to curb acts recognized as international crimes is fast becoming a useful tool in suppressing common crimes of an international character, such as piracy of the sea and air, slavery, and illicit traffic of narcotics. But international criminal law still suffers from the lack of enforcing authority.

Two main problems seem to plague the ultimate establishment and effectiveness of international criminal law. Foremost is the adamant refusal of nation-states to surrender or share their power with an international organization in certain areas determined for various reasons by each nation-state to be of vital self-interest. This recalcitrance derives from a multitude of sources. The other seminal problem is the apparent impossibility of nation-states to agree on common goals in the areas considered part of the subject matter. Even when some consensus is reached on commonly shared goals, there is disagreement on the appropriate means to achieve them.

Not the least overwhelming of all prospects are the problems of codification, draftsmanship, definitional content of the prohibited conduct, appropriate sanctions, jurisdiction, and enforcement. The perennial attempt to define "aggression" is a constant reminder of that fact.

Defining crimes and necessary sanctions are troublesome indeed, but deciding on the type of structure to implement it is equally arduous. A court system and its enforcement machinery are not likely to be easily agreed upon.

The contributing authors to this book agree, however, that we cannot afford to remain still because of these difficulties, for even if there is doubt about international criminal law, there is no doubt about international criminality. And as some of the writers suggest, our very existence may depend on the control of this type of criminality.

Several approaches and recommendations suggested herein are bold and imaginative and deserve serious consideration by scholars and statesmen everywhere.

The widest theoretical and doctrinal basis is presented by thirty-three contributing authors from seventeen countries transcending ideological lines. Their writings offer a truly international perspective and demonstrate in a tangible manner that intellectual cooperation can prevail among scholars for the attainment of world peace through the rule of law. In preparation since 1968, this project will hopefully add its contribution to legal education and to world peace, cooperation, and understanding through the rule of law.

M. Cherif Bassiouni
Ved P. Nanda

ACKNOWLEDGMENTS

The editors sincerely thank Jeanine Bisson at DePaul and Estella Zook at Denver for their painstaking efforts in preparing the copy, and gratefully acknowledge the research assistance of Britt Anderson, Stephen Everall, Georgina Landman, and Stephen Yasinow.

CONTENTS

PART ONE

SCOPE AND RESPONSIBILITY

CHAPTER I. THE SCOPE AND SIGNIFICANCE OF INTERNA-
TIONAL CRIMINAL LAW

PART TWO

CRIMES AGAINST PEACE

CHAPTER III. AGGRESSION

CHAPTER IV. INDIRECT AGGRESSION

CHAPTER V. NATIONAL AND COLLECTIVE SELF-DEFENSE

PART THREE

THE REGULATION OF ARMED CONFLICTS

CHAPTER VI. PROBLEMS OF THE LAW OF ARMED CONFLICTS
           —*D. Bindschedler-Robert*

A Treatise on

INTERNATIONAL CRIMINAL LAW

Volume I

CRIMES AND PUNISHMENT

PART ONE

SCOPE AND RESPONSIBILITY

CHAPTER I

THE SCOPE AND SIGNIFICANCE

OF INTERNATIONAL CRIMINAL LAW

Section 1. THE EXISTENCE OF INTERNATIONAL CRIMINAL LAW AND ITS EVOLUTION TO THE POINT OF ITS ENFORCEMENT CRISIS

G.O.W. MUELLER AND DOUGLAS BESHAROV

1.1. The Emergence of International Criminal Law

In answer to the question of whether there is, in fact, such a thing as international criminal law (I.C.L.), a pundit once remarked, "There must be, it is taught in universities by professors." Although the university discipline of I.C.L. can hardly be said to have meaningfully existed before 1910 on the continent [1] and 1965 in North America, [2] as an object of academic inquiry, it is as old as academic inquiry itself.

The purpose of this introduction is twofold: (1) The authors seek to justify the claim that I.C.L. does exist and that it relies on an emerging system of functions. (2) The authors assert that I.C.L. has reached a crisis in enforcement and therefore propose a model for the enhancement, expansion, and enforcement of I.C.L.

As a complex set of norms and conflict-resolving mechanisms adhered to by sovereigns within a particular jurisdictional unit, through agreement or the use of sanctions, I.C.L. is at least as old as the earliest recorded laws. When we meet the Romans in history, their jurisdictional unit is the large family, in which the sovereign, the *pater familias,* exercises full sovereign criminal law jurisdiction *(patria potestas),* including the power to impose capital punishment, with respect to any family member. But when a criminal act offends some other family, or some member thereof, the problem becomes an intersovereignty matter, or as we would call it today, a problem of I.C.L. The sovereigns of the two concerned jurisdictions had to meet and arrange for a *noxae deditio,* or surrender of the offender to the injured family. On the North American continent when we first meet the Cherokees, the same conflict situation is likewise handled as a problem of I.C.L., or interclan criminal law, for the clan was the

The authors wish to express their appreciation to Professor Paul W. Gormley for several useful suggestions.

[1] MEILI, LEHRBUCH DES INTERNATIONALEN STRAFRECHTS UND STRAFPROZESSRECHTS (1910).
[2] MUELLER & WISE, INTERNATIONAL CRIMINAL LAW (1965).

basic jurisdictional unit of criminal law, as had been the family among the Romans, as is the state in our contemporary North American system, or the nation in Europe.[3] Among the Cherokees, however, the interclan response was regulated retaliation, rather than surrender, although the latter method was not totally unknown.[4]

1.2. The Growth of the Jurisdictional Unit

As we trace mankind through recorded history we note with fascination that the jurisdictional units are becoming larger and larger, not only in terms of sheer numbers of component members but also in terms of hierarchical order. The family as a basic criminal law jurisdictional unit is replaced by the clan, the clan by the tribe or city, which, in turn, loses out to the kingdom or empire, until today, when nations are yielding some slices of their criminal law sovereignty to yet higher units, such as regional international groupings—of which the Council of Europe is an example—or world bodies like the United Nations. Naturally, the development does not proceed in an unbroken line but, rather, ordinarily suffers setbacks before it can proceed to the next higher stage.

We are justified to hypothesize, on the basis of historical observation, that the jurisdictional unit of criminal law has moved upward from narrow communal groupings to larger political organizations. In short, the jurisdictional unit of criminal law has become ever larger, both numerically, by its component members, and politically, in terms of communal organizations.

1.3. The Growth of I.C.L.

Growth marks the development of criminal law in every respect. We are quite familiar with the inflation of penal regulation as society becomes more complicated, making for an enormous increase in municipal criminal legislation within each jurisdictional unit. But equally, with the growth of trade, commerce, and all other types of communication among jurisdictional units—relations of peace and war among nations—the intensity of contact among these jurisdictional units requires and produces more and more contact—conduct norms. In other words, I.C.L. grows and grows and has not stopped growing, although not all of that law is necessarily entitled to be called I.C.L.

Indeed, at this point it becomes necessary to seek an analysis of what, so far, we have nonchalantly called I.C.L. Actually, there are two rather distinct types of conduct norms which vie for the designation I.C.L. If we think of the type of conduct norm by which ancient Romans or not

[3] *See* REID, A LAW OF BLOOD 47 (1970).
[4] *Id.* at 73–84.

so ancient Cherokees resolve interfamily or interclan disputes arising out of a commission of a public wrong by a member of one jurisdictional unit against a member of another jurisdictional unit, we are confronted with I.C.L. in the sense of an *accommodation type.* This is a conduct norm which fully recognizes the existence of two sovereigns; it simply provides for mutual assistance or accommodation in a conflict situation which arose precisely because of the existence of independent sovereign entities. We might wish to call that type of I.C.L. *adjective,* and it would include all that which today we group under such topics as conflict of criminal laws, international judicial assistance, extradition. [5]

There is, however, another quite distinct type of I.C.L. It is that part of municipal criminal law which nations have ceded for the sake of the common good of a greater community or interest and which, thus, they have entrusted for administration to a larger jurisdictional unit, without, however, giving up their own sovereignty. [6] When the sovereign states of the United States ceded that part of their sovereign criminal law juris-diction which is concerned with treason, piracy, coinage offenses, etc., to the union, they, in effect, imbued a greater jurisdictional unit with a certain amount of criminal law power. They thereby permitted the creation of a *substantive* I.C.L. applicable to and binding within all the states which formed that greater unit. What keeps the United States federal law from being truly international is simply the fact that the states did not stop at this point, but turned the new sovereign into a national one. But when international sovereigns meet and decide to cede slices of their criminal jurisdiction to a truly international community, or when they merely subject it to international scrutiny, we can speak of I.C.L. in a substantive sense. To a smaller or greater degree, this is a process that has taken place for several hundred years and has resulted in the creation of international criminal jurisdiction over piracy offenses, war crimes, and crimes against humanity, genocide, and a host of lesser international offenses provided for by treaty and convention. Most significantly, however, the emergence of international standards of human rights, on both world and regional levels, and of general or special application, has added to the growing body of international conduct norms which, because they require enforcement, qualify as substantive I.C.L. Progress in enforcing these has been much more spectacularly successful than adjudication of war criminals. Hence, we shall have to look to the experience with their implementation in order to learn something about I.C.L. enforcement in general.

That not all of these international conduct norms are prosecuted and

[5] Mueller & Wise, *supra* note 2, chs. 1 & 4.
[6] *Id.,* chs. 2, 3, & 5.

adjudicated by international agencies and tribunals does not detract from their incipient status as being substantive I.C.L. Nor should it disturb us that the differences between adjective and substantive I.C.L. on the one hand, and between suprajurisdictional but infrainternational (*e.g.* federal) and truly I.C.L. are not always clearly marked; for we are concerned with a dynamic trend rather than a solidified situation.

To summarize, I.C.L. seems to consist of (1) adjective criminal law (accommodation norms) and (2) substantive criminal law (deviant conduct regulation which sovereigns have ceded to higher authority or general international supervision).

1.4. The Relation of Adjective to Substantive I.C.L.

If so far we have hypothesized on the basis of general historical observations, we are now reaching the point where we are becoming more and more speculative. To begin with, it seems clear that among sovereigns who, or whose subjects, are in contact with each other, there is need for regulation of potential deviance and for conflict resolution. This may be accomplished through either (1) adjective or (2) substantive criminal law (unless the sovereigns wish to merge and subscribe to a common municipal criminal law).

Historical observation seems to indicate that nations are likely to begin with method (1), and only gradually utilize method (2). The greater the unity and uniformity of criminal law and its enforcement, the smaller will be the need for accommodation norms, for those were designed primarily to mediate in case there is a conflict of norms. The trend, thus, is from (1) to (2). It occurs to us that if (1) is large, then (2) is small. Possibly, (1) will decrease and (2) will increase, which simply is to say that there is more and more an explicit recognition of a basic law common to all mankind and an increasing trend toward making the standards of that law binding on all sovereigns.

1.5. Optimal Jurisdictional Units

It is often prophesied that some day there will be one world under one law and subject to uniform enforcement, *i.e.*, a single jurisdictional unit. But this is not likely to be the case in the foreseeable future, if past experience and present observation are to be our guide. Petty domestic disputes have found their enforcement jurisdiction in family-type units, which administer substantive propositions varying in content in different parts of the world, even though value divergencies tend to diminish with uniformization of life styles all over the world, occasioned by increased communication. On a somewhat higher level, assaults and larcenies, as well as most other street-type crimes, will continue to require infra-national jurisdictions for purposes of definition as well as enforcement. However, offenses affecting large-scale commerce are already finding their definition and enforcement optimum at supranational levels, while those affecting the peace and security of all mankind have their incipient ful-fillment at the world level. One might say that criminal law always seeks and ultimately finds that jurisdictional unit which can handle its definition and administration with the optimal ease and efficiency.

Viewed in this perspective, I.C.L. already is but one stratum of criminal law and enforcement which binds and aids the same individual who continues to take his smallest or more immediate conduct norms from the family or, in a technically more correct sense, from the state.

Consequently, it is not to be expected that a world agency will result as the ultimate and exclusive definitional and jurisdictional unit, rather it will be but one more of many other coexisting jurisdictional units. Naturally, as world conditions change, and thus alter the level of optimal ease and efficiency, we can expect greater or lesser resort to larger jurisdictional units.

1.6. Enforcement Sanctions of I.C.L.

On its evolutionary path, mankind has reached the point at which municipal criminal law has become a *fait accomplis* and is generally re-lied upon for the maintenance of peace and tranquility whenever other means of social conflict resolution appear inadequate. Among the com-munity of nations, however, criminal law has not yet reached the same peace-keeping position. Unquestionably, though, traditional concepts of national criminal law are gaining a certain significance with respect to the relation of nations among each other, or of individuals, insofar as their behavior affects the relations among nations.

As the subsequent chapters of this book will describe, the actual condi-tion of I.C.L., both adjective and substantive, is fairly clear. What is not nearly as clear is the role played by the sanction by which most lawyers identify a law norm as criminal in nature to begin with.

The current stage in the evolution of I.C.L. is marked by a law enforce-ment crisis, and, unless this crisis is resolved—or resolves itself in evolu-tionary fashion—the development of I.C.L. will have arrived at its terminal point—short of the goal (whatever that might be). How easy it would be to brush aside all our preceding hypotheses and speculations with a single, simple comment that none of the propositions to which we refer can be dignified as I.C.L., if they lack an effective sanction of the type that has been developed for municipal criminal law! We reject this pleasing but puerile approach. Just as sanctions and norm adherence devices in municipal law are often not found on the statute books, so too the methods of enhancing compliance to I.C.L. go beyond formal sanctions.

Just as I.C.L. and the jurisdictional unit can be understood only in terms of a dynamic development, so must we view the sanctions with which this I.C.L. is, or wishes to be, equipped. The sanctions of I.C.L.— both those protecting compliance with accommodation norms and those protecting the substantive propositions—are of a type and severity which is conditioned by the cultural and ideological common denominators of the cultures served by it. Regulated violence was the expected response in some cultures, manipulations of shame and disgrace prevailed elsewhere —and still do—while arbitration or even adjudication, with subsequent execution of judgments by force, are preferred in most Western cultures. Sanctions are beginning to play a role in regulating the relations among nations in a form comparable to the old-fashioned regulation of human beings in their relations among each other within a nation, or within other jurisdictional units. We are extremely hesitant to put these sanctions to be presently discussed in an order of ascending or descending significance, for while formal adjudication seems to be preferred in the international community of most of the so-called developed nations, the less formidable and less formal methods of coercing compliance with international conduct norms through manipulation of national or personal pride and reputation, practiced, for example, by some American Indian nations, seems to bespeak of greater culture in many respects.[7]

1.6.1. EDUCATION AND PROPAGATION. We must try to forget our lawyer bias toward formal or court-enforced sanctions. Parents and teachers could remind us that norm compliance is often easier to accomplish via education than through harsher methods. In these times of international rivalry, it is important to remember that education and propagation are forms of enforcement and implementation of norms least offensive to traditional notions of sovereignty.

1.6.2. PERIODIC REPORTING. Although national reporting on compliance is occasionally regarded as onerous, especially if national reporting is coupled with international control or supervision by an international agency, such an international system of reporting and control does exist for many spheres of what properly should be termed I.C.L., *e.g.*, through the Human Rights Commission of the United Nations.[8] In its efforts to achieve worldwide implementation of the Universal Declaration of Human Rights, for example, the United Nations, in 1953, initiated an "action programme,"

---

[7] REID, *Supra* note 3, at 64–65, 241–245.

[8] J. Carey, *Implementing Human Rights Conventions: The Soviet View*, 53 KY. L.J. 115,130 (1964).

which consisted of triennial reporting by member nations, studies and research and advisory services in the field of human rights.[9]

Effective national reporting of compliance data depends upon two factors: (1) reportability of compliance data and (2) existence of an effective receiving agency. By reportability of compliance data we mean to refer to precise standards of behavior, reported in a manner which can be verified and recorded with relative accuracy, *e.g.*, nations may be required to respond to specific questions on periodically disseminated questionnaires. By an effective receiving agency we mean an international authority which has the power to disseminate such questionnaires, urge governments to respond, calculate and evaluate such responses, and publish the resulting data. The International Law Association, in a resolution at the 1968 Buenos Aires Conference, recommended the "rational development of the system of periodic reporting governed by ECOSOC Resolution 1074C (XXXIX),"[10] and called upon the "United Nations to establish an independent committee of experts to study the reports and to make recommendations and comments thereon to the Commission on Human Rights.[11]

1.6.3. VERIFICATION OR INVESTIGATION. Information received through self-reporting is essentially unverified. For this reason and for reasons of social science methodology, other and additional sources of information may be desired.

On-the-spot investigation is probably the most efficacious means of information gathering. Such investigation could be conducted by nationals of the nations involved. U.N. correspondents or special rapporteurs might be appointed to report on local conditions,[12] *e.g.*, the United Nations Special Rapporteur on Slavery.[13] Or there might be roving international investigators similar to those employed by the International Red Cross to inspect prisoner-of-war camps.[14]

"In terms of technical qualifications," such investigators should be "academically oriented with special training and capability in the fields

[9] E. Wise, *Steps Towards the Advancement of Human Rights*, 18 W. RES. L. REV. 1548, 1565 (1967); UNITED NATIONS WORK FOR HUMAN RIGHTS 27 (U.N. Pub. Sales No. 1965. I.19); *See also* J. Humphrey, *The United Nations and Human Rights*, 11 How. L.J. 373,377 (1965).

[10] INTERNATIONAL LAW ASSOCIATION, BULLETIN OF THE 53RD CONFERENCE 15 (Buenos Aires, Aug. 25–31, 1968.)

[11] *Id.*

[12] *See* ALI, BADR-EL-DIN, INTERNATIONAL SURVEY ON STANDARD MINIMUM RULES (July 1968), published by the International Prisoners' Aid Society.

[13] U.N. Doc. E/4056/Add. 2, at 1, 2–3 (1965).

[14] *See generally* REPORT OF THE INTERNATIONAL COMMITTEE OF THE RED CROSS ON ITS ACTIVITIES DURING THE SECOND WORLD WAR (Sept. 1, 1939–June 30, 1947), Vol. 1, at 228 *seq.* (1948). During World War II more than 11,000 inspections were performed. *Id.* at 230.

of criminal law, penology, (and) research techniques."[15] A nation's co-operation with such a person would be entirely voluntary. Its grant of permission to investigate need not be a grant of right. Such permission is not without precedent. During World War I, with no treaty basis, neutral diplomats were admitted to prison camps under German and Allied administration. By 1916, there were few restrictions imposed upon these inspectors, and minute inspections were permitted.[16] These reports would be entirely routine and might be a part of a periodic examination of questions within the competence of the receiving agency.[17]

1.6.4. PUBLICATION OF DATA. While education, propagation, and reporting may have some enforcement values in themselves, they will also aid in the identification of those who through carelessness or intent do not (yet) wish to comply. At this point a "sanction" of stronger power is available, *i.e.,* publication of data.

Once the information gathered through self-reporting has been analyzed and digested, the question then becomes how to utilize this material, and in particular, whether to disclose it. There are, of course, legitimate considerations in favor of maintaining the confidentiality of information gathered by an international organization about conditions within sovereign states. It may, for example, be appropriate to prevent or delay publication of unflattering information during negotiations or during periods of good-faith attempts to implement standards.[18]

But if need be, publication of the fact of noncompliance with standards of international law may have to be resorted to. Publication of noncompliance may well be the most potent sanction for purposes of achieving compliance with international standards.[19] It can be used in such a way as to direct world public opinion in a manner capable of encouraging compliance. The mobilization of world public opinion may solidify international standards of behavior, because public knowledge that a given nation may be in violation of commonly accepted codes of behavior may result in a loss of international prestige, standing, cooperation, or political friendship.[20] This is what Dr. H. Saba, Legal Advisor to UNESCO, has

[15] ALI, *supra* note 12, at 10–11.

[16] CAHEN, CAHEN, & SALVADOR, LES PRISONIERS DE GUERRE 1914–1919, at 66 (1929).

[17] M. Ancel, *Capital Punishment Today,* INT'L COMMN JUR. REV. at 29 (June 1969).

[18] *E.g.,* arts. 14 & 22 of the International Convention on the Elimination of All Forms of Racial Discrimination. G.A. Res. 2106, 20 U.N. GOAR Supp. 47, U.N. Doc. A/6014 (1965). *See also* discussion on negotiation by Committment or Indictment chamber, herein.

[19] P. Gormley, *The Use of Public Opinion and Reporting Devices to Achieve World Law: Adoption of ILO Practices by the United Nations,* 32 ALB. L REV. 273,288 (1968); for an interesting tangent, *see* E. Debevoise, *Lessons From Organizations Like the International Commission of Jurists in Focusing Public Opinion,* 58 AM. SOC INT'L L. PROC. 143 (1964).

[20] *See, e.g.,* G. Larde, *The Changing Effectiveness of General Assembly Resolutions,* 58 AM. SOC INT'L L. PROC. 162 (1964).

called the "world sense of shame."[21] An example of the value placed on public opinion is the E.E.C. Treaty which substitutes the force of moral sanction for the very potent economic sanctions of the earlier European Coal and Steel Community.[22]

This "sense of shame," or public disapproval, may lead to other more concrete, although oblique, consequences. Short of abrogating the "rights and privileges of membership" in the United Nations, certain assistance benefits have been withheld because of noncompliance with General Assembly or Security Council resolutions. "Thus, Portugal and South Africa, in light of General Assembly resolutions, are not eligible for assistance from the United Nations Development Programs. They have also been barred from participation in the Economic Commission for Africa (ECA) and stand little or no chance of being elected to Council or Committee memberships decided by the General Assembly and the Economic and Social Council."[23] These admittedly are extreme examples, but they demonstrate the extent to which mobilized public opinion may exercise a significant impact.

1.7. The Use of Ad Hoc Groups to Secure Implementation

In particularly infamous cases, it is possible that an ad hoc study of the implementation of a specific proposition of international law in a specific country might be conducted. Such an ad hoc group or visiting mission from the receiving agency, if granted permission, could visit a nation in much the same way as the representatives from the Inter-American Commission visited the Dominican Republic in 1962 and, more significantly, in 1965. In the words of Dr. Durward V. Sandifer, U.S. member of the Inter-American Commission, "with no other sanction than publicity, the Commission has effectively established its role as guardian and critic."[24]

Permission could be refused, of course, as it was for Nicaragua and for Haiti, both in 1963.[25] This does not necessarily terminate the agency's activities. In the Haitian case, the Commission issued a report containing

---

[21] H. Saba, *The Quasi-Legislative Activities of Specialized Agencies*, 111 RECUEIL DES COURS 604 (1964 I).

[22] Treaty Establishing the European Economic Community, 4 EUROP. Y.B. 413 (1958); Treaty Establishing the European Coal and Steel Community, 1 EUROP. Y.B. 353 (1955), arts. 86 & 92.

[23] R. Falk, *On Identifying and Solving The Problem of Compliance with International Law*, 58 AM. SOC INT'L L. PROC. 1, 10 (1964).

[24] D. Sandifer, *Human Rights in The Inter-American System*, 11 HOW. L.J. 508, 521–22 (1965).

[25] For a useful description of Inter-American activities, *see* A. Thomas & A. J., Jr., *The Inter-American Commission on Human Rights*, 20 SW. L.J. 282 (1966).

communications from various Haitian citizens, containing accusations of violations of human rights.[26]

The Human Rights Commission's Ad Hoc Group of Experts investigating the plight of prisoners, and others in police custody in South Africa, went even further. After being denied permission to visit the country, they heard twenty-five witnesses and received twenty-three written statements.[27] More recently, the U.N. committee investigating the status of Arabs in Israel completed hearing testimony from Arabs and other interested parties in Arab capitals.[28] In cases where the duration of difficulties would indicate a more permanent group, hybrids could be developed, as in the proposal for a grand jury of legal experts for Namibia.[29]

One caveat should be given. Lack of impartiality was the reason provided for exclusion from both South Africa[30] and Israel.[31] Whether or not justified, these exclusions demonstrate the need for establishing a group or agency, in the words of South Africa, as to "whose bona fides and dedication to the humanitarian ideal there can be no doubt."[32]

1. 8. The Judicial Enforcement Model

Once a problem subsumable under the heading I.C.L. has been agreed upon by nations via treaty, convention, or custom, it might be deemed appropriate to utilize a judicial enforcement system, along the lines of enforcement of municipal criminal law norms.

There have been many suggestions as to the form of an international judicial enforcement agency. All involve an ultimate adjudication by some sort of international tribunal. "The past model relied absolutely on the jurisdiction and enforcement power of an international criminal court, and an executive arm of that court."[33] Newer models include such ultimate adjudication but also recognize that the procedures precedent to such adjudication may have equal if not greater influence toward implementation. Hence, our new model envisages a tristage procedure of (1) receiving and screening, (2) commitment or indictment, and (3) adjudication.

[26] *Id.* at 290; *also* PAU, Inter-American Commission on Human Rights Report on the Situation Regarding Human Rights in Haiti, OEA/Ser. L. v/II.8 (Doc. No. 5, 1963).

[27] Carey, *infra* note 53, at 311.

[28] N.Y. Times, Sept. 15, 1969, at 14, col. 1.

[29] Commission on Human Rights, *The Possibility of Establishing a Grand Jury of Legal Experts for Namibia for the Protection of Life, Personal Safety and Rights of the Inhabitants of that Territory,* U.N. Doc. E/CN. 4/979/Add. 3, at 24 (Jan. 1969).

[30] Carey, *infra* note 53, at 323.

[31] N.Y. Times, *supra* note 28.

[32] U.N. Doc. E/4340/Add. 1-E/CN. 4/942/Add. 1 (1967); *see also,* Carey, *infra* note 53, at 323.

[33] G. Mueller, *Two Enforcement Models for International Criminal Justice,* in ETUDES EN L'HONNEUR DE JEAN GRAVEN 107–115, (1959).

What follows, then, is a model for the implementation of standards of international criminal justice based upon the many proposals and the initial experience of the past thirty years in dealing with matters of dispute and nonconformance in I.C.L.

1.8.1. THE RECEIVING AND SCREENING AGENCY. As emphasized earlier, it is important that an agency capable of receiving cases and evaluating data be established. It would also be desirable that such an agency be able to gather more information than would ordinarily be available from government self-reporting or through the works of rapporteurs. Therefore, it is suggested that the agency be empowered to conduct routine inspections of actual trouble spots. In and of themselves, such inspections could have a significant effect on conditions. As the Red Cross has found:

> Visits have the advantage over other methods by the direct influence they exercise on the treatment of P.W.: some infringements of the elementary laws of humanity are too grave for a state, even though it has little concern for the respect of such laws, to dare expose before the eyes of neutral witnesses.[34]

There is ample precedent for mandatory inspection by international institutions, and it is desirable that the agency have such authority. Both the Antarctic Treaty[35] and the Space Treaty[36] provide for such inspection, as does the EURATOM Treaty[37] and the International Atomic Energy Agency Statute.[38] The latter provides for "access at all time for reactors having a potential plutonium production in excess of 60 kilograms per year."[39] Of relevance is the well-known work of the International Red Cross under the Geneva Convention. In the period from 1939 to 1947, delegates of the Red Cross carried out over 11,000 intensive visits of prisoner-of-war camps. Although some difficulties arose, they were minor when compared to the overall success of the endeavor.[40] It was also suggested earlier that a highly visible receiving agency of the sort described would receive complaints from private sources whether or not they were solicited. Under the formalized procedures envisaged, instead of attempting an informal resolution of the matter, the receiving agency would perform the function of determining which complaints merited further action. Reception of complaints from private sources, in addition to those from states, is a necessity if maximum utilization of procedures is to be desired.

[34] Red Cross Report, *supra* note 14, at 222.
[35] Dec. 1, 1959 [1961], 1 U.S.T.794, T.I.A.S No. 4780,402 U.N.T.S. 71; *also* S. Gorove, *Maintaining Order Through On-Site Inspection: Focus on the IAEA*, 18 W. RES. L. REV. 1525, 1530 (1967).
[36] Art. 12, 55 DEP'T OF STATE BULL. 953 (1966).
[37] Art. 81. Gorove, *supra* note 35, at 1530.
[38] *Id.* Statute of the I.A.E.A.
[39] *Id.*, Art. XII, para A(b).
[40] Red Cross Report, *supra* note 14, at 230.

Logic would indicate that "it is hardly reasonable to expect that states will bring before an international instance other states with which they have friendly relations. This seems to be born out of experience."[41] In the forty years of the International Labor Organization, for example, if cases under the Freedom of Association Clause are not counted, only three states have ever brought a case before the I.L.O. and then only recently and under unusual circumstances.[42] Likewise, there have been only three cases brought by states against states under the European Convention on Human Rights.[43] In 1963, the Secretary-General's Explanatory Paper on Implementation, in summarizing the arguments for and against allowing individuals and NGO's to petition, said that

> . . . the experience of the Trusteeship Council and the International Labor Organization did not bear out the fear that the right to petition would release a flood of malicious and groundless complaints which might overwhelm the permanent organ and paralyze its action.[44]

Therefore, it may be well to equip the receiving agency with the power to receive nongovernmental complaints. The experience of prisoners petitioning the Council of Europe suggests the consideration of the problem of immunity for statements made in complaints.[45]

If a highly visible receiving agency is established, even if no provision is made for the reception of individual complaints, it can be anticipated that numerous such complaints will in fact be received. This was the experience of the U.N. Commission on Human Rights. Even after the Economic and Social Council decided in 1947 that the Commission would not act on private complaints, it continued to receive large numbers of them.[46] In the last twenty years, over 60,000 such complaints were received.[47] They are kept confidential and unpublished. In a process that has been described as an "elaborate wastepaper basket"[48] the Secretariat's Division of Human Rights summarizes these complaints and sends them to the state mentioned. Any reply is submitted to the Human Rights Commission

[41] Humphrey, *supra* note 9, at 374.

[42] *Id.*, *also* Parson, *supra* note 24, at 687.

[43] McNulty, *infra* note 51, at 430.

[44] U.N. Doc. A/5411 (Apr. 29, 1963) at 20; *see* Carey, *supra* note 8, at 131.

[45] *See, e.g.*, European Agreement Relating To Persons Participating in Proceedings of the European Commission and Court of Human Rights, E.T.S. 67 (May 1969).

[46] Compare with Res. 888B (XXXIV) July 24, 1962, where ECOSOC invited NGOs with consultative status to submit comments.

[47] Parson, Donald P., *The Individual Right of Petition: A study of Methods Used by International Organizations to Utilize the Individual as a Source of Information on the Violation of Human Rights*, 13 WAYNE L. REV. 678, 689 (1967).

[48] Lyon, Peter, *A World Without Slaves*, HOLIDAY MAGAZINE (Sept. 1961) *quoted in* Carey, *supra* note 8, at 131.

with the list of complaints received.[49] In 1954, only thirteen of 9,524 such complaints were answered by member states.[50]

Perhaps if the unanswered complaints were not kept confidential, except where requested, there would be a better response. Once such responses are successfully encouraged, it might be appropriate to attempt an informal version of the negotiation and conciliation practices of the European Commission on Human Rights[51] or the International Labor Organization.[52]

> The relative success of various international organizations such as the I.L.O., the two regional human rights commissions, the High Commissioner for Refugees, and the International Red Cross in using certain procedures for the protection of Human Rights indicates the feasibility and desirability of a permanent United Nations Office with a mandate broad enough to encompass all such methods. While a number of methods for international protection of individuals have demonstrated their usefulness, those which already have been of greatest benefit to the victims of oppression and which appear to hold the most potential for development during and immediately following the 1968 International Year for Human Rights are impartial investigation, followed by negotiation, and, where necessary, publication.[53]

Precedent for this kind of semi-informal procedure can be found in an optional Protocol to the Covenant on Civil and Political Rights which provides that individuals may "communicate" with the Human Rights Commission, which, after considering the petition *in camera,* would forward its views to the state and individual concerned. The matter could also be published in the Commission's Annual Report to the General Assembly.[54]

After evaluating the complaint, including a comparison of its allegations with the information obtained through governmental reports by informal rapporteurs or inspectors, the agency would determine, *in camera* and *ex parte,* whether it would be appropriate to take further action. The European Commission on Human Rights utilizes a similar preliminary screening of petitions by a three member subcommittee without notice to the state involved. However, this subcommittee will approve a petition only if it establishes a prima facie case. Hence, very few cases reach the second stage. As of May, 1967, of the 3,128 petitions received since 1955, 2,322 were rejected de plano at the preliminary stage, and eighty-two addi-

---

[49] Carey, *supra* note 8, at 131.

[50] Parson, *supra* note 47, at 692.

[51] *See generally* A. McNulty, *The Practice of the European Commission of Human Rights,* 11 How. L.J. 430 (1965).

[52] *See* Gormley, *supra* note 19; *also,* P. Gormley, *The Emerging Protection of Human Rights by the International Labor Organization,* 30 Alb. L. Rev. 13 (1966); and J. Nafziger, *The International Labor Organization and Social Change,* 2 N.Y.U. J Int'l L. 1 (1969).

[53] J. Carey, *Procedures for International Protection of Human Rights,* 53 Ia. L. Rev. 291, 324 (1967).

[54] L. del Russo, *The International Law of Human Rights: A Pragmatic Appraisal,* 9 Wm & Mary L. Rev. 749, 753 (1968); and *see* note 47 at 697.

tional ones after communication with the responding state.[55] While this "procedural bottleneck" has been criticized as preventing the desired utilization of the Convention,[56] it must also be credited with having served a valid screening function. However, it is recommended that the first stage preliminary procedure requires only a showing of substantiality for the agency to refer the case to the committing or indictment chamber.

It is hoped that such an agency would take an active role in the formulation and proposal of new and expanded human rights standards and conventions. American grand juries have traditionally performed this task, in addition to their accusation function, and a similar service is being performed by the International Labor Organization in matters relating to that organization's jurisdiction.[57] Article 26 of the Draft Inter-American Human Rights Convention provides in part:

> The Commission shall make appropriate recommendations and, when such measures have been widely accepted, shall promote the conclusion of a special convention, or additional protocols to this Convention. . . .

1.8.2. THE COMMITMENT OR INDICTMENT CHAMBER. The concept of a commitment or indictment chamber is well known in both domestic and international law. It is found in common law countries as the grand jury and in civil law countries as the chambre d' accusation.[58] The European Commission on Human Rights fulfills such a role in relation to the European Court.[59] It has been proposed as part of the Draft Statute of the International Criminal Court[60] and exists in incipient form within a variety of human rights conventions, *e.g.*, the International Convention on the Elimination of All Forms of Racial Discrimination[61] and the Convention on Civil and Political Rights.[62]

As these conventions suggest, the Chamber would be comprised of eighteen experts of "high moral standing and acknowledged impartiality" who are elected by secret ballot for four years.[63] The Chamber would initiate the formal procedures of the convention after presentation by the receiving agency of prescreened cases.

[55] del Russo, *supra* note 54, at 963–64.

[56] Parson, *supra* note 47, at 703–04; for a critical evaluation by a judge of the European Court, *see* H. Rolin, *Has the European Court of Human Rights a Future?* 11 How. L.J. 442 (1965).

[57] P. Blamont, *Human Rights and the International Labor Organization,* 11 How. L.J. 413,414–15 (1965); *also* Gormley, *supra* note 52, at 26–35.

[58] *See generally* Mueller, *supra* note 33, at 109–115.

[59] *Id.* at 113.

[60] Art. 33.

[61] Art. 8 established a Commission on the Elimination of Racial Discrimination composed of eighteen experts; *also* Parson, *supra* note 47, at 695–97.

[62] Art. 2 (1) commits states' parties to report, and arts. 27–48 create a Human Rights Commission of eighteen, including an ultimate referral to the International Court of Justice.

[63] See *supra* note 18.

Operating in strict confidentiality, just as the agency, the Chamber could use a variety of tools in determining what action should be taken. It could request a supplemental response by the government involved or a supplemental report or evaluation by the agency. This supplemental report could include information already gathered or to be gathered by a formal inspection, to be performed by the agency.

Having once determined that the situation requires change, the Chamber would attempt an informal resolution of the case through confidential negotiations. This is the scheme under the European Convention, and experience has demonstrated that "the pressure generated before the Commission has generally been sufficient to bring the matter to successful termination."[64] For example, while a large number of petitions against the Austrian Government alleging a violation of article VI of the Convention, in that there was unequal representation of defendants on appeal, were pending before the Commission, the Austrian Parliament amended the offending legislation with a candid reference to the pending complaints.[65] Likewise, as a result of *De Becker v. Belgium* the Parliament of Belgium amended legislation which had been successfully challenged.[66] Through the good offices of the Commission, a prisoner was released because of an unlawful length of detention,[67] and in another case, monetary redress was secured.[68] However, of over 2,100 petitions filed with the Commission, only thirty have been declared acceptable for the second stage. The rest have been either rejected, struck off the list, or are still pending.[69]

Thus, although utilization of these procedures has not been as great as might have been desired, experience has indicated their great potential.

If the case cannot be settled by informal negotiation by the Chamber, it would have two alternatives open to it if further action is deemed appropriate. The Chamber could publish a report in a procedure similar to that under Article 14 of the Convention on Elimination of All Forms of Racial Discrimination. In itself, this publication would be a potent tool. The "release of a well-documented accusation . . . even though there be little or no chance of an ultimate trial" before an international court[70] will subject "the defendant to the spotlight of world opinion, the coercive psychological pressures of a respected juridical organ of organized mankind."[71]

If it deemed it necessary, the Chamber would be empowered to trans-

[64] Mueller, *supra* note 33, at 113.
[65] McNulty, *supra* note 51, at 439; *also* del Russo, *supra* note 54, at 756.
[66] 5 EUROP. Y.B. 320 (1962); also *Id.*
[67] Porschke v. Germany, 21 COLLECT. DOC. COMM'N 84 (Mar. 1967).
[68] Boeckman v. Belgium (Appl. 1727/62) 6 EUROP. Y.B. 371.
[69] Parson, *supra* note 47, at 704.
[70] Mueller, *supra* note 33, at 113.
[71] *Id.* at 112.

mit the case to an international court. This ultimate step should be reserved for only those cases deemed appropriate, although perhaps such transmittal should not be as infrequent as has been the case.[72] The alternate procedure provided by the Draft Inter-American Human Rights Convention also merits consideration. Under Article 40 (2) of the Convention, the Commission's findings can be made binding if recourse to the proposed Inter-American Court is not taken. Thus, the international court is turned into a tribunal in the nature of an appellate court.

1.8.3. AN INTERNATIONAL TRIBUNAL. The world already is fortunate enough to have an International Court of Justice. Proposals have been made to create other international tribunals whose jurisdiction would be more directly concerned with problems of I.C.L., *e.g.* an International Court of Human Rights,[73] an International Criminal Court,[74] an International Court of Habeas Corpus,[75] or a modified version of the Permanent Court of International Justice.[76] However, for whatever reasons, there does seem to exist good reason utilizing the existing facilities of the underemployed International Court at the Hague.

Although it might be envisaged to grant the adjudicating court some coercive sanctions, practical considerations would seem to favor the more flexible and less onerous sanctioning apparatus of public opinion, previously discussed. A system of "very extensive reporting and examination techniques represents the most refined procedure ever developed to give practical implement to the moral sanction of international law."[77] Indeed, as has been demonstrated throughout this report:

> Far from taking advantage of the absence of any coercive method of enforcing obedience to the principles of international law, states actually compete with each other in asserting their strict fidelity to such principles . . . [P]ublic opinion of the civilized world plays in an ever increasing degree the part of a sanctioning authority. [78]

[72] Rolin, *supra* note 56.
[73] The 1948 text of the Human Rights Convenants drafted by the Human Rights Commission of the United Nations included a prosposal for an International Court of Human Rights open to individuals as well as states. Paris Peace Conference, Gonfer. Doc. (Gen) I.B. 13, at 444–45 (1946); *see also* A. Goldberg, *The Need for a World Court on Human Rights*, 11 How. L.J. 621 (1965); *see generally* del Russo, *supra* note 54, at 757.
[74] *E.g.*, Draft Statute for an International Criminal Court, Rept. of 1953 Committee on International Criminal Jurisdiction, 9 U.N. GAOR, Supp. 12, at 23–26, U.N. Doc. A. 2645(1954).
[75] *E.g.*, L. Kutner, *World Habeas Corpus and International Extradition*, U. DET. L.J. 525 (1964); *also* KUTNER, WORLD HABEAS CORPUS (1962).
[76] *E.g.*, the Draft Convention on Political and Civil Rights, G.A. Res. 2200 (XXI) (1966).
[77] Gormley, *supra* note 52, at 47.
[78] Golt, *The Necessity of an International Court of Criminal Justice*, 157 N.Y.L.J. 4 (Feb. 24, 1967).

The Versailles Treaty attempted to establish a coercive sanction apparatus for the enforcement of international law obligations. It gave the Entente Powers the legal right to compel Germany, by force if necessary, to abide by her international obligations. The exercise of this legal right would have been but war under another name.[79]

> [A]n international law that is meant to be applied to the world powers is a contradiction in terms. It presupposes an international authority which is superior to these states. In reality, however, any attempt to enforce an international criminal code against either the Soviet Union or the United States would be war under another name. [80]

Unfortunately, even under conditions where the only sanction is publicity, it is still doubtful whether, in Jacob Blaustein's words, "any appreciable number of governments would be ready to vote for such a solution . . . let alone ratify a treaty which would subject them to the possibility of being hauled before an international tribunal by an individual or an NGO."[81]

Furthermore, the international courts already in existence have only infrequently exercised their jurisdiction. In the years 1920 through 1945, of the thirty-five cases submitted to the Permanent Court of International Justice, only nineteen were decided on the merits. In the same period, the Court rendered twenty-six advisory opinions. Between 1945 and 1965, the ICJ had only thirty-six cases submitted to it, of which only twelve were decided on the merits. During this period, only twelve advisory opinions were rendered. [82] Similarly, in the eight years the European Court and Commission on Human Rights have been in existence, a nation was judged guilty of a violation of human rights for the first time in 1969.[83]

1.9. Resolution of the Enforcement Crisis

The areas of common international concern—whether on a global or a regional level—are constantly increasing as communication and travel be-

---

[79] *See,* G. Mueller, *The United Nations Draft Code of Offenses Against the Peace and Security of Mankind. An American Evaluation,* in INTERNATIONAL CRIMINAL LAW 597, 611–613, (Mueller & Wise, ed. 1965).

[80] Schwarzenberger, *The Problem of an International Criminal Law.* CURRENT LEGAL PROB. 263,295 (1950).

[81] J. BLAUSTEIN, A CHALLENGE TO THE UNITED NATIONS AND TO OUR GENERATION, Dag Hammarskjold Memorial Lecture, Dec. 4, 1963, (Printed Pamphlet) 15,22–23; *quoted in* Carey, *supra* note 8, at 133.

[82] Gottlieb, Gerald, *The Court of Men,* 74(5) CASE & COM. 3.3 (Sept.–Oct. 1969).

[83] Austria was adjudged in violation twice during 1969. Neumeister v. Austria (1964) EUROP. CONV. ON HUMAN RIGHTS Y.B. 224; Stogmuller v. Austria, (1964) EUROP. CONV. ON HUMAN RIGHTS Y.B. 168. For a discussion of these and other European Court cases, *see* W. P. Gormley, *The Development of International Law Through Cases From the European Court of Human Rights: Linguistic and Detention Disputes,* 2(2) OTTAWA L.R. 382(1968).

come easier. With recognition of this increase will come a realization of the need for more and larger jurisdictional units, and ultimately, the appreciation that such larger units do exist.

We are now in the midst of an enforcement crisis. There is a gap between the apprehension of the larger international concern and the fashioning of appropriate responses. Surely, if the past is any guide, there will be a response in the nature of the creation of new jurisdictional units at optimal efficiency and effectiveness, to operate internationally. But as long as sovereign nations refuse to show a greater willingness to cede substantial portions of national sovereignty to the larger unit, progress will remain tied to hope, not action. At the moment it is utopian to expect an accelerated evolution of I.C.L. containing real coercive or compliance powers.

Reluctantly, we must acknowledge that for the foreseeable future, reliance will have to be placed on the traditionally less criminal and much more civil and urban, though also more subtle, appeal to the sense of injustice of all mankind, the pride of nations, and the competition for prestige and honor. These appeals have always worked well to spur men to combat. Can these appeals not work when men are called to gird for peace?

Section 2.   INTERNATIONAL CRIMINAL LAW—A SEARCH FOR MEANING

PAUL K. RYU AND HELEN SILVING

2.1. Introduction

Efforts at formulating rational bases for an I.C.L. are obfuscated by a failure of the "international community" and its interpreters to recognize the sui generis nature of criminal law. Often standards of international law developed in contractual, commercial, or torts context are indiscriminately applied to I.C.L. It is hence important to stress that the very desirability of attaining an internationally valid system of criminal law is predicated upon the soundness of the policy it purports to enforce in the specific context of criminal law.

International law has grown out of the custom of nations. A nation may have a duty to abide by the principles laid down by such custom. In the field of private law such custom may also prove perfectly appropriate. But when in the international community a problem arises on the level of criminal law, it is necessary to consider the distinctive aspects of the latter's modern constitutional development: custom as a source of law is not acceptable in criminal law matters. There is need for conscious, purposive, goal-directed law-creation by the international community, involving its "legislative" processes with orientation to the future. For this, agreement of all parties is of the essence. Is such agreement possible given present international conditions?

The world today is widely split along ideological lines. It would be dangerous indeed to permit the diverse ideologies to be projected on the international scene in the course of enforcement of a would-be international criminal justice, with individual life and freedom at stake. We may well talk of an international penal code, but if this is to mean a code defining universal penal offenses affecting individuals, caution is wisdom.

There is, however, a field of criminal law in which collaboration of peoples of diverse ideologies is not foreclosed. As regards certain constitutional limitations upon penal legislation, there is often at least a verbal agreement among nations. We should focus our efforts on developing this segment of constitutional criminal law, in the hope that this may later lead to a breaking of new ground in other areas.

Though we have thus submitted a preview of our conclusions, we feel that we should not pass over in silence other potential branches or meanings of I.C.L. It is, of course, but a terminological question whether we choose to speak of a comprehensive area of law to be called I.C.L., subdividing it into several "branches," or prefer discourse in terms of the several meanings[1] of I.C.L. We have chosen to use the symbol I.C.L. in the sense of an internationally valid criminal law or, more precisely, an international law dealing with criminal matters. As thus used, this symbol may represent three potential meanings to be discussed here. We shall thereafter indicate the difficulties encountered when trying to reach a concordance of meanings for current concepts of the world's penal laws, even those apparently accepted universally. Finally, we shall submit suggestions regarding those topics of the world's criminal laws to which international constitutional limitations may most fruitfully be applied.

2.2. The Several Meanings of I.C.L.

Among the various potential meanings of I.C.L., three indicate comprehensive topics of contemporary relevance.

2.2.1. I.C.L. ADDRESSED TO STATES. States, as primary subjects of international law, may conclude treaties whereby they agree to apply "sanctions" to an offending state party, or sanctions against states may develop by way of international custom. The body of law thus evolving may be called I.C.L. Language usage, however, does not assign that symbol to this type

[1] *See, e.g.,* Schwarzenberger, *The Problem of an International Criminal Law,* 3 CURRENT LEGAL PROB. 263 (1950), reproduced in INTERNATIONAL CRIMINAL LAW 3 (Mueller & Wise ed. 1965), suggesting six meanings of the term.

of construct. The reason for this may be thought to lie in the nature of the sanctions applied to states or in the absence of general confidence in their efficacy or in the lack of anticipation of their use. But international sanctions against states are not per se distinctive. Even war, which might be considered an ultimate sanction in international relations,[2] compares with the normal execution processes of national laws, capital punishment, imprisonment, and property seizures; economic sanctions against states resemble fines imposed by national legislation. Nor is confidence in the efficacy of national law sanctions at present as marked as it was in former days: it is certainly not substantial enough to afford a basis for distinguishing these sanctions essentially from those of international law. Finally, in view of the prevalent tolerance of more or less violent national protest movements, anticipation that national sanctions will be applied to an offender is no longer sufficiently firm to supply the distinguishing feature. When we take into account historical practices of national communities, the contemporary international law of sanctions against states appears even less sui generis. Suffice it to recall the methods whereby the *Magna Carta* was concluded and made operative[3] or the way the anarchical institution of sanctuary evolved.[4] True, the test of sanctionability in international law is still defeat, but so was the test of execution in the days of ordeal. The difference might lie in the fact that those who used ordeal as a test believed in its rationality, whereas victory is not associated with rationality in our times.

In the last analysis, reluctance to apply the term "international criminal law" in referring to the incoherently operating sanctions against states is a matter of tacit convention grown out of discontent with the total system of these sanctions. This discontent, in turn, might be traceable to a wish, whether conscious or unconscious, to transform international law into a genuine universal, egalitarian, and humanitarian law, a law of peace. We have a vague feeling that this might be achieved if we succeeded in piercing the corporate veil of the nation-states which are at present the proper subjects of international law. We dream of a world government based on the dignity and equality of all men, endowed with a coherent and effective world system of adjudication and enforcement, guaranteeing evenhanded impartial justice. The international government at present in effect is far removed from this ideal. Were it to serve as a pattern of further development of international cohesion, the end result would hardly

---

[2] On war as a "sanction" of international law, see H. KELSEN, PRINCIPLES OF INTERNATIONAL LAW 25–27 (R. W. Tucker ed. 1966).

[3] The Magna Carta imposed upon violation of its terms by the king the sanction of "rebellion." *See* art. 61 of that Document.

[4] On the institution of "sanctuary," *see* Silving, *Sanctuary*, in ENCYCLOPAEDIA BRITANNICA (1966).

be a democratic world order. Power politics, ideological clashes, competing nationalistic ambitions, propaganda wars, and struggles for dominion over men's minds, with some modicum of balance dictated by fear of total destruction in an atomic age, these are the characteristic features of our incipient world state. Perhaps its most salient institution is the "veto power" of specially favored nations.

On the other hand, realistic confidence in the utility and feasibility of a more modest "world government" pattern increases with declining reliance on the efficacy and operational expectability of balanced justice of national government systems. Social injustices, corruption, suppression of freedom, observable in many national systems, and the rising vigor throughout the world of protest movements shaking national government structures, along with the erratic character of these movements, may indeed help to prepare people for a world public order. As "establishments" crumble in every sphere of "authority"—religious, political, academic, and educational—and as attacks on "authority" lose all sense of direction, mere "authority" being their invariable object, we may be heading for new constructs and novel symbols, both of "authority" and of "revolution."

Of course, once we achieve a world state, even federal, sanctions against states will become at best secondary. However, they need not disappear entirely. Sanctions against collective bodies, *e.g.*, corporations and political parties, are well known in national criminal laws.[5]

The term "international criminal law" may be also used in the sense of an international law either requiring states to adopt certain crime concepts within their national penal legislation, *e.g.*, to punish certain types of offenses, or imposing limitations upon certain national penal laws or procedures. As will be shown, we regard the latter type of I.C.L. as its most significant category at this time. We will hence deal with it under a separate heading, "I.C.L. of Minimum Standards."

2.2.2. I.C.L. OF INDIVIDUAL RESPONSIBILITY. It may well be but a reflection of our innermost yearning for a universal law of mankind that we are already at this state confining the symbol "I.C.L." to constructs in which international law, whether contractual or customary, appears as the source of individual responsibility and individual right. In fact, this term is mostly used at present to designate a type of law whereby individuals are personally held to account for violations of the international order.[6] In

---

[5] A declaration by the Federal Constitutional Court of the Federal Republic of Germany that a political party is "unconstitutional" (art. 21 of the Basic Law) is for all intents and purposes a "sanction." At any rate, it puts into operation ordinary criminal law sanctions. *Compare* GERMAN PENAL CODE §§ 84, 85, 86, 86a, *as amended* by the Eighth Penal Law Amendment Act of June 25, 1968 (BGB1 I 741) and the First Act on the Reform of Criminal Law of June 25, 1969 (BGB1 I 645).

[6] On the development of this notion, *see* H. JESCHECK, LEHRBUCH DES STRAFRECHTS ALLGEMEINER TEIL 83–89 (1969).

Germany, there is now in use with regard to such type of law a term coined by Beling, "criminal law of nations" (*Völkerstrafrecht*).[7] In so-called criminal law science, much concern has been shown with questions such as whether international law is or could be a direct or indirect source of crime constructs belonging to the *Völkerstrafrecht* category or what was the status or source of authority of tribunals adjudicating them.[8] Questions of this type cannot be resolved by science unless this term is used in a very specific sense for which there is no modern pattern in Anglo-American usage.[9] However, they require resolution, for on it depends the problem of justification of I.C.L. in a democratic criminal law system.

The London Charter of August 8, 1945,[10] which afforded a legal basis for the Nuremberg Trials, formulated three categories of international law crimes for which individuals were to be called to answer: crimes against peace, war crimes, and crimes against humanity.[11] All these crime categories were vulnerable in the light of strict legality principles as elaborated in conventional constitutional laws of the civilized world. Of the two sources of international law, treaties and customary law, only the former could conceivably serve as a proper indirect basis for individual criminal responsibility, though either could serve as a basis of exemption.[12] International customary law, as any customary law, does not satisfy the postulate that crime be referable to a *lex scripta* of definite and certain content.[13] A treaty might create or at least originate an international crime, provided that the country whose national is to be held responsible is a party to it[14] and that all safeguards of the rule of law, such as advance notice to the offender and proper guidance to the adjudicator, are afforded. At the present stage of international law development and in view

[7] BELING, DIE STRAFRECHTLICHE BEHANDLUNG DER EXTERRITORIALITÄT 40 (1896). Beling, however, did not believe in a "Völkerstrafrecht" imposing individual responsibility.

[8] *See* JESCHECK, *supra* note 6, at 84–87.

[9] On the so-called "science of law" see Ryu & Silving, *Toward a Rational System of Criminal Law,* 32 REV. JUR. U.P.R. 119 (1963); SEOUL NAT. U.L. REV. (1962).

[10] 82 U.N.T.S. 279, originally signed by the United States, France, the United Kingdom, and the Soviet Union and adhered to prior to the Nuremberg Trials by nineteen states. *Cf.* INTERNATIONAL CRIMINAL LAW, *supra* note 1, at 227.

[11] Art. 6 of the Charter.

[12] The "legality principle" serves protection of the accused in criminal law. It does not apply where it would limit an exemption or mitigation ground. Consult H. SILVING, CONSTITUENT ELEMENTS OF CRIME 68–69,76 (1967).

[13] "War crimes" have been said to be based on old international customary law. *See* H. KELSEN, *Supra* note 2, at 151 n. 161 and 213–217; JESCHECK, *supra* note 6, at 85. In this regard, contrast particularly the liberal use of custom as a source of law within art. 1 of the SWISS CIVIL CODE, with its total exclusion within art. 1 of the SWISS FEDERAL PENAL CODE.

[14] Though this requirement would seem to be elementary, it may not be sufficient, at least where the crime is committed outside of the territory of the national state of the defendant.

of the contemporary processes of treaty-making, one might also insist on having the terms of such a treaty reenacted in the form of penal statutes of the country whose national is to be held responsible. A general incorporating clause, even constitutional,[15] should not be deemed sufficient, for the methods of concluding and ratifying treaties are not comparable to enactment by the legislative process with full representation. These postulates of democratic criminal law are part of the civil rights of the individual called to account, of which he ought not to be deprived even by "the endorsement of the 'quasi-totality of civilized states' acting through the United Nations War Crimes Commission before the trial" or confirmation by "the UN General Assembly afterwards."[16] Nor could the defects of the "international law crimes" promulgated by the London Charter be cured by their being "laid down in [it] and elaborated in the Judgment of the Court which received the unanimous confirmation of the international community acting through the United Nations in the General Assembly Resolution (95) of December 11, 1946."[17] International law commentators who propagate a policy of invasion of constitutional criminal law principles by and in the name of international law majorities or, indeed, by unanimous consent of the international community unwittingly play a dangerous game.

Though not legitimate when judged by conventional conceptions of criminal justice, [18] "Nuremberg justice" was justifiable in the light of a

[15] The Constitution of Weimar Republic 1919, art. 4, and following it, the Basic Law of the Federal Republic of Germany, art. 25, contain such an incorporation clause. Art. 25 of the latter (the Bonn Constitution) declares: "The general rules of international law are a constituent part of federal law. They have primacy over statute and create rights and duties directly for the inhabitants of the federal territory." Of course, art. 4 of the Weimar Constitution did not seem to apply to rules which Germany had not hitherto expressly recognized; nor did it establish a primacy over ordinary statutes. *See* ANSCHÜTZ, DIE VERFASSUNG DES DEUTSCHEN REICHS (10th ed. 1929), *comment* to art. 4. Art. 25 of the Bonn Constitution is believed to be applicable to future rules. But it is often controversial whether certain principles, *e.g.*, those of the European Convention for the Protection of Human Rights and Basic Freedoms (Act of July 8, 1952, BGB1. II 685), belong to the category of general rules of international law. *See* GIESE & SCHUNCK, GRUNDGESETZ FÜR DIE BUNDESREPUBLIK DEUTSCHLAND, *Kommentar* (1962), *comment* to art. 25, at 69.

[16] Woetzel, *The Eichmann Case in International Law*, in INTERNATIONAL CRIMINAL LAW, *supra* note 1, at 354–55.

[17] *Id.*

[18] An additional element of "legality" conspicuously missing in "crimes against peace" under the London Agreement was their failure to satisfy the tenet of *nulla poena sine lege*. This has been little noticed. The "rule of law" requires that not only the crime but also the punishment be defined in advance of "crime commission." In "war crimes" and in "crimes against humanity," to the extent of their concurrence with certain crimes defined in penal codes, such as murder and assault, the penalties might be derived from those imposed upon such crimes by the national legislation. But at the time of the London Agreement, "waging a war of aggression" had no parallel in conventional codes. Preparing and publicly inciting

set of background factors that marked it as exceptional. Foremost among these factors was the enormity of the crimes at bar that made their utter unforeseeability by a normal legislator plausible, and the peculiar combination of individual and state involvement characteristic of National Socialist criminality. These crimes were authorized by, and committed in the name of the state, by individuals who, on the other hand, often utilized and manipulated the state machinery to satisfy their own yearning for personal power and their base instincts. These background factors were also present in the Eichmann Trial in Jerusalem [19] and afforded the latter a similar justification. [20] Indeed, that justification applied a fortiori to the Jerusalem Trial, since the State of Israel was not in a position to enact legislation for the protection of the Jewish people in advance of crime commission, whereas the international community of nations at least in theory could have formulated international crimes before they were committed. In any event, to follow either the Nuremberg Trials or the Eichmann Trial as "precedents," one would have to find the presence of a similar set of factors.

While the enormity of the evil committed by the National Socialists justifies its special treatment, whether in Nuremberg or in Jerusalem, this feature should not obscure due assessment of the values which criminal law in a free society ought to protect. Murder, mutilation, torture, deportation, as well as any form of participation in such acts, are evil whether they strike at a single human being or at several millions of men, women, and children. [21] Nor is the harm inflicted upon a human being ever banal. [22] This is implicit in the democratic principle of man's dignity and

---

aggressive war have recently been made crimes in Germany: §§ 80 and 80a of the GERMAN PENAL CODE, introduced by the Eighth Penal Law Amendment Act, *supra* note 5. In fact, the London Agreement simply provided in art. 27: "The Tribunal shall have the right to impose upon a defendant, on conviction, death or such other punishment as shall be determined by it to be just." It is most unfortunate that the Draft Statute for an International Criminal Code (Report of the 1953 Committee on International Criminal Jurisdiction, 9 U.N. GAOR, Supp. 12, at 23–26, U.N. Doc. A/2645 (1954)) follows the same pattern. Art. 32 of this Draft Statute provides: "The Court shall impose upon an accused, upon conviction, such penalty as the Court may determine, subject to any limitations prescribed in the instrument conferring jurisdiction upon the Court."

[19] The Attorney-General of the Government of Israel v. Adolf, the son of Karl Adolf Eichmann, District Court of Jerusalem, Criminal Case No. 40/61, *appeal dismissed* by the Supreme Court of Israel, Decision No. 336/61.

[20] Eichmann was tried under the Israeli law called "The Nazis and Nazi Collaborators (Punishment) Law, 1950," defining "crimes against the Jewish people." [5710] Sefer Ha-Hukkim 281. For translation, *See* L.S.I. 154; for explanatory note, *see* (5710) 36 *Hatza'ot Hok* 119.

[21] This should not be understood to imply that there is no room for a special crime category of "genocide," as it does not preclude penal code provisions on "crime concurrence" and "recurrence." *See* H. SILVING, *supra* note 12, at 166–197.

[22] The contention that the evil proven to have been committed by Eichmann was "banal" was advanced by H. ARENDT in her controversial "report" (*A Report on the Banality of Evil*) on the Eichmann Trial, EICHMANN IN JERUSALEM, (rev. & enlarged ed. 1964).

uniqueness. We must carefully separate the jurisdictional issue from the question of substantive legitimacy involved in criminal law, whether national or international. Where common criminality coincided with the so-called international crimes specified by the London Agreement or with crimes against the Jewish people as defined by Israeli law, objections against these crime categories based on grounds of substantive law were inapposite: to the extent of such concurrence, these crimes were neither retroactive nor otherwise constitutionally challengeable. [23] It could be argued that where a crime is charged specifically, *e.g.*, as one against humanity, when in terms of national legislation that which is actually described constitutes, for example, murder, there is a variance between the proper and the actual charge which deviates from strict legality principles. [24] However, in most cases adjudicated at Nuremberg as well as in the counts adjudged in Jerusalem the charges were multiple, so that defendants could hardly claim to have been prejudiced by a mislabeling, provided that the facts were accurately charged. [25]

Looking to the future, we must concern ourselves with the conditions under which international principles enforceable against individuals by means of criminal law can be developed without infringement upon the

[23] Prosecution of National Socialist criminals in Germany simply charged crimes as defined in the GERMAN PENAL CODE, which was never formally amended to authorize or condone the atrocities of the National Socialist era. Thus, *e.g.*, one of the most celebrated cases decided by the Bundesgerichtshof, 2 BGH St. 234 (1952) (I. Strafsenat, Jan. 29, 1952, g. K. u.a.), involved charges within the terms of § 239 of the PENAL CODE, defining "wrongful deprivation of liberty." The defense argued that the deportations of Jews in which defendants participated were ordered by the authorities in power and were thus not known by the defendants to have been "wrongful" or "illegal." The Supreme Court reversed acceptance of this defense by the Court below, stating that an authorization or condonation of such nature conflicted with basic principles recognized by all civilized nations. Said the Supreme Court with reference to the "retroactivity" argument (*supra* at 239):

> This does not mean that the conduct of the defendants is being measured by standards which did not acquire general validity until after the events, and it is not being claimed that defendants should have answered the question of right or wrong according to principles which were not or which were no longer in force at the time. That they should have ignored the few principles which are essential to men's life in a community and which belong to the inviolable essence and fundamental core of law, as is alive in the legal consciousness of all civilized nations, or that they should have failed to realize the binding force of these principles independently of any recognition by the state, cannot be accepted, particularly in the light of the fact that they had received the impressions in which such persuasions are formed at a time before National Socialism could spread its confusing and poisonous propaganda.

[24] Of course, not in all legal systems is the labeling of the charge determinative. In German law, a reviewable defect of the charge lies only where and to the extent that the charge is lacking in adequate description of a relevant independent historical event or in its reference to a particular defendant. See KLEINKNECHT-MÜLLER, KOMMENTAR ZUR STRAFPROZESSORDNUNG (4th ed. 1958), *comment* (d) to § 200 of the Code of Criminal Procedure.

[25] In the United States the federal "harmless error statute," § 269 of the Judicial Code, *as amended*, 28 U.S.C. § 391, declares not to be reversible any error which "after an examination of the entire record," appears "not [to] affect the substantial rights of the parties." In a trial of such dimensions as was the Nuremberg Trial or the Trial of Eichmann, some error was almost bound to occur. The problem would seem to be whether any such error was genuinely "prejudicial" to a defendant.

defendants' civil liberties. Such principles cannot be validly established by the methods characteristic of the common law, *i.e.*, by judicial lawmaking.[26] There is thus no magic in the creation by general convention of an international court endowed with competence to try individuals for certain violations of international law. Given the overwhelming influence of the victorious and the politically powerful in international relations at this time, such a court would have to demonstrate to the satisfaction of the world's public opinion a spirit of political impartiality which no national supreme court and certainly no organ of the United Nations has thus far exhibited. But assuming that a method could be devised to overcome this difficulty of international adjudication, substantive legality would still require that the court operate under a general law, a world code of international offenses, adopted by the community of nations in advance of the commission of the adjudicated offenses. Indeed, to be rational, the world's public order must eventually cease operating on the basis of *ad hoc* submission or consent. It should not be expected to evolve from the states' or the individual defendants' admissions of guilt in concrete cases. Psychoanalysts traced the criminality of individuals to a presence rather than an absence of a conscience and a sense of guilt.[27] A similar self-destructive attitude in a nation, reflected in self-accusations and protests, may well increase rather than reduce chances of war. Such an attitude which constitutes an unconscious temptation of the "enemy," and at the same time, indirectly contributes to the formation of a spirit of combined heroism and criminality, is reflected in such incidents as the *Green Berets*[28] and the *Song My*[29] cases.

---

[26] Even in England, the mother country of the common law, creation of crimes by the judiciary is no longer tolerated. Said Lord Goddard in *Regina v. Newland,* (1953) 2 All E.R. 1067, 3 W.L.R. 836: [I]t surely is now the province of the legislature and not of the judiciary to create new criminal offences."

[27] REIK, *Geständniszwang und Strafbedürfnis,* in PROBLEME DER PSYCHOANALYSE UND DER KRIMINOLOGIE 118 (1925); *also* THE COMPULSION TO CONFESS 306 (1959).

[28] The brief summaries of this case and of that reported in the following note do not purport to be accurate. They are based on newspaper accounts. There has been no trial in the Green Berets case and no disposition as yet in the Song My case.

In the Green Berets case, the facts (as summarized in *Newsweek,* Oct. 13, 1969, at 43–44), according to some accounts, occurred in the following manner. In May of 1969 members of the Special Forces' B-57 detachment, specializing in clandestine across-the-border forays from South Vietnam, overran a Vietcong camp and found a film indicating that one Thai Khag Chuyen, who worked for the Green Berets as an interpreter and low-level operative, was a double agent. The agent was subsequently killed, and several Green Berets were arrested. The charges against them were later dropped because the CIA insisted that a public airing of the case would jeopardize U.S. intelligence-gathering activities in Vietnam.

Our contention is not that charges such as were involved in the case should be suppressed. Indeed, they should be fully aired but not until the underlying conflict comes to an end. As these charges were dealt with in the case, the Green Berets were given no opportunity of a fair trial. In announcing dismissal of the charges, Secretary of the Army Stanley R. Resor

Of vital significance is the nature of the contents of a world's code of offenses. "Justice" is an often-used but seldom-defined concept. One of the lay commentators of the Eichmann Trial spoke of the need for criminal justice while at the same time stressing the banality of evil. [30] What does criminal justice mean if evil can be banal? [31] An international law expert assessed the possibility of compiling a minimum type of I.C.L. derived from

---

noticed: "I want to make it clear that the acts which were charged, but not proven, represent a violation of Army regulations, orders, and principles." A question necessarily arising in any lawyer's mind is, What remedy does a person thus publicly charged possess against the "defamation" implicit in that type of "dismissal"? An international lawyer will ask, Why were these charges publicly raised at this time if they could not be followed up?

In the case of Capt. John J. McCarthy, convicted of murder in Vietnam in 1968, and sentenced to hard labor for life, it is being asserted on appeal to the Army Court of Military Review that a vital defense witness "was advised by a superior officer . . . not to make his presence known to the appellant and was thus rendered unavailable to the defense at trial." This was allegedly done for fear that the witness might disclose sensitive information. In this case, the lack of publicity is claimed to have been prejudicial to the defendant. *See* N.Y. Times, Mar. 29, 1970, at 17.

[29] The charge in this case was that on March 16, 1968, American soldiers had massacred a large number of Vietnamese civilians in the village of Song My. Reactions of the American public to this event have been sharply divided and at times ambivalent. This is vividly reflected in the reports, editorial comments, letters to the editor, book reviews, etc., as, *e.g.*, published in The New York Times in various issues between 12/7/69 and 9/3/72. The salient questions are: How should those to be tried for such crimes be selected, so as to avoid a justifiable charge of arbitrary justice, indeed, of scapegoatism? By what type of tribunal should they be tried? Should they be charged and tried while the Vietnam conflict is still pending? Should "publicity" be allowed in advance of trial? In the Song My case the Court of Military Appeals declined to impose a ban on mass media of publicity though such ban was requested by both prosecution and defense. *See* N.Y. Times, Dec. 7, 1969, § E, at 3.

[30] H. ARENDT, *supra* note 22. In answer to critical attacks upon her theory of the "banality of evil," the author limited this theory to the evil committed by Eichmann. She then proceeded to distinguish that "evil" from other "evils," particularly some found described in classics of literature. She said (at 287–288):

> Eichmann was not Iago and not Macbeth, and nothing would have been farther from his mind than to determine with Richard III "to prove a villain." Except for an extraordinary diligence in looking out for his personal advancement, he had no motives at all. And this diligence in itself was in no way criminal; he certainly would never have murdered his superior in order to inherit his post. He merely, to put the matter colloquially, *never realized what he was doing* . . . . He was not stupid. It was sheer thoughtlessness—something by no means identical with stupidity—that predisposed him to become one of the greatest criminals of that period. And if this is "banal" and even funny, if with the best will in the world one cannot extract any diabolical or demonic profundity from Eichmann, that is still far from calling it commonplace.

The writers of the present article are ardent supporters of the defense of "error of law" to a charge of crime. *Cf.* Ryu & Silving, *Error of Law: A Comparative Study*, 24 U. CHI L. REV. 421 (1957). That "error of fact" constitutes a defense is commonly recognized. But, surely, Eichmann did not even contend that he acted in error of either law or fact. Instead, his defense was that while "sitting at his desk doing his things," it was none of his business that these "things" would lead to death, mutilation, etc. We fail to see that this type of crime in an age when one can destroy humanity while "sitting at a desk" is either "banal" or "funny."

[31] What, indeed, is the line of distinction between "banal" and "dramatic evil?" DOSTOEVSKY in CRIME AND PUNISHMENT expressed a "drama" underlying a plain robbery-murder.

the common ingredients of the crime constructs of the world's penal codes. [32] One might assume that such a minimum type code would represent the world's sense of justice; however, it would be difficult indeed to define the common root of even such a universal crime as murder. Moreover, is a concept of murder stripped to a minimum content still a socially meaningful construct? Yet, beyond minimum concepts there appear differences among the various ideologies of the world's legal systems. Often these ideological differences seem to be but technical distinctions, *e.g.*, variants in methods of proof, but they nevertheless affect the very essence of the respective crime categories.

2.2.3. I.C.L. DEFINING MINIMUM STANDARDS OF CRIMINAL JUSTICE. A third potential meaning of I.C.L. is suggested by the so-called international minimum standards of criminal justice. These are limitations imposed or to be imposed by international law upon the penal legislations of national governments. Such standards may be established by convention between states, whether by universal convention or by a series of regional conventions, or evolved through custom, indeed, as general principles of law recognized by civilized nations. Since they favor individuals, there is no objection on legality grounds against their creation by inchoate sources, such as custom, judicial decision, and even natural law. Because minimum standards are limitative negative notions, it is not usual to refer to them as I.C.L. In fact, it may be more appropriate to use in this context the term "international constitutional law." However, to the extent that the object of limitation is a criminal provision, there can hardly be any objection against application to such body of law of the phrase "international constitutional criminal law," for constitutional criminal law is an accepted form of referring to a branch of national law.

There is need for international constitutional minimum standards of criminal law in all areas of the administration of criminal justice: both in substantive and procedural laws, in court organization laws, and in the laws and practices of sentence enforcement. So far, there has been a greater readiness to apply international minimum standards to procedural than to substantive criminal law, [33] and within the latter, a greater preparedness

---

[32] Schwarzenberger, *supra* note 1, at 10–11.

[33] This may be noticed upon an even cursory perusal of the basic international documents of human rights, the Universal Declaration of Human Rights adopted by the United Nations on November 10, 1948 (*See* G.A. Res. 217 A(III), Nov. 10, 1948, 3 U.N. GAOR 1, Res. (A/810), at 71); the European Convention for the Protection of Human Rights and Fundamental Freedoms, signed in Rome on Nov. 4, 1950 (213 U.N.T.S. 221; Europ. T. S. No. 5); and the International Covenant on Civil and Political Rights, adopted by the General Assembly of the United Nations on Dec. 16, 1966 (G.A. Res 2200, 21 U.N. GAOR Supp. 16, at 52–58, U.N. Doc. A/6316). The first two documents are also cited and reproduced in INTERNATIONAL CRIMINAL LAW, *supra* note 1, at 170–176, 177–194. The latter document is also cited

to recognize minimum patterns of enforcement than of crime definition or sentencing. [34] With regard to constituent elements of crime, stricter standards have been required than with regard to sanctions, and within the area of crime definition, greater concern has been shown for observance of general principles laid down in "General Parts" of penal codes than for maintenance of a sound economy in selecting conduct to be made criminal. There is no rational ground for this hierarchy of preferences. Some of these preferences may be traceable to particular constellations in the conflict of patterns on the international scene at a given time period. Thus, for example, consideration of procedural matters ahead of substantive ones may be the result of different attitudes in the determinant cultures: in Anglo-American law, procedure is emphasized, since it is regarded as more significant than substance; while in laws of Roman civil law background, procedure is more readily submitted to international regulation precisely because it is deemed secondary.

As we shall show in greater detail later, among the minimum standards to be imposed by international constitutional law upon criminal justice, two principles deserve special notice: (1) the economy principle and (2) the principle of scientific rationality. These serve as fundamental guides in purging criminal concepts, both substantive and procedural.

To the extent that the state prohibits certain conduct under threat of sanction, it restrains man's freedom. Obviously, it should not be permitted to do so except where the interest of the community in barring such conduct is overwhelming and the probability of preventing it by means of prohibition or by the particular sanction that is being imposed is very high. Economy, both in making conduct criminal and in imposing particular sanctions, deserves the highest priority in the catalogue of "International Human Rights and Basic Freedoms."

Crime concepts should be geared to our modern knowledge of man, his needs and aspirations in the world of today. While taking account of man's total personality—*i.e.*, both its conscious and its unconscious components—legislators should not yield to man's rationally unsupportable demands, *i.e.*, demands based on his preconceptions and prejudices, hatreds, and vindictiveness, as particularly reflected in the crime conceptions of contemporary criminal legislations. In the latter there may be found many outmoded criminal law constructs derived from superstition or from obsolete notions of the morality or religion of past ages, which

---

and reproduced in THE UNITED NATIONS AND HUMAN RIGHTS, *Eighteenth Report of the Commission to Study the Organization of Peace* 208–225 (1968).

[34] Minimum standards of sentence enforcement are contained in the Standard Minimum Rules for the Treatment of Prisoners, adopted by the First United Nations Congress on the Prevention of Crime and Treatment of Offenders, Resolution of Aug. 30, 1955, in Report prepared by the Secretariat. *See* U.N. ECOSOC 67–73 (1956).

modern science has shown to be without support in reason. These notions indeed impede the progress of morality adapted to our time.

Economy and scientific rationality in formulating criminal proscriptions are humanitarian goals benefiting human well-being everywhere. One might, indeed, expect that they be treated as belonging to an ideology-free sphere, in which international cooperation is not precluded. Even more so may such cooperation be anticipated in the scientific approach, for in science collaboration cutting through diversity of ideologies is already current.

The law of minimum standards arises from a universal humanitarian necessity to protect man against the state, including his own. As we see it, the most important immediate function of I.C.L. is to establish such standards. Moreover, an international law of minimum standards constitutes the most likely medium of a gradual transformation of national legal systems into an international public order. It is highly improbable that states will be prepared in the near future to adopt a truly binding convention formulating a positive concept of crime against peace, enforceable against their own officials and agents and subject to the jurisdiction of a genuinely impartial international court. But the same states which will be reluctant to accept such a positive concept of superstate may well accept review of their systems of criminal justice by an international court. Once a uniform public order of limited scope is reached, its formalization into a world federal union should be substantially facilitated.

2.3. Quest for Universally Valid Concepts

Having outlined the three potential meanings of I.C.L. and stressed the significance of its third meaning, we must now take notice of the difficulties to be expected in trying to give substance to this law—a substance beyond pious declarations of principles. We must also consider what steps might be taken by jurists to promote the development of that law and, with it, a world public order.

In all its phases and forms, I.C.L., as all law, is verbal and conceptual. This does not imply that it is *merely* verbal or conceptual. It rather indicates that since I.C.L. purports to be an order of conduct of uniform application to all parties concerned, it requires communication by verbal symbols, denoting abstract ideas or concepts. However, I.C.L. has no autonomous system of symbols. [35] Its symbols are borrowed from various national legal systems, each bearing the imprint of its own history and tradition. As a result, international lawyers do not have a genuinely common language. In addition, very often they do not know that their lan-

---

[35] *Cf* Silving, *Book Review,* 43 VA. L. REV. 303 (1957).

guage is not the same. They thus talk *past* each other rather than *to* each other.

Hence, in trying to promote I.C.L., the very first task should be establishing for it an adequate system of communication, a common language. To this end, it is submitted that it is necessary to make "a thorough study of the different legal systems with a view to evolving a genuine 'comparative law'—an emancipated product of a comparison of laws, concepts and terminology, which might serve as a reservoir of future international law."[36]

Of course, it is not our contention that universal adherence to a common verbal symbol utilized to designate a variety of social meanings in different parts of the international community is utterly devoid of significance. In cases of this type, there may always be found in the various meanings of a verbal symbol some common ideological root that might be fruitfully developed. But even such potential development is predicated upon the parties' awareness of the presence of the differences in meaning.

It may be instructive to demonstrate what is meant in this context by a lack of a common language. Often an identical verbal symbol, when used in two countries, represents diverse social valuations. Language in some provisions of the Covenant on Civil and Political Rights adopted uanimously by the General Assembly of the United Nations in December 1966[37] presents manifestations of the phenomenon. It is pertinent to note that upon its face, this Covenant, where accompanied by the protocol which supplies means of enforcement, is the most advanced document of international solidarity of nations and peoples, breaking through the barriers of state sovereignty and reaching out toward fulfillment of a world state.[38]

---

[36] *Id.* at 309.

[37] Cited *supra*, note 33. There is attached to this Covenant an Optional Protocol. While the Covenant was adopted unanimously, there were for the Protocol 66 votes in favor, 2 against, with 38 abstentions. Art. 1 of this Protocol provides that a state party to the Covenant that becomes a party to the Protocol "recognizes the competence" of the Human Rights Committee created for the enforcement of the Convenant "to receive and consider communications from individuals, subject to its jurisdiction, claiming to be victims of a violation by that state party of any of the rights set forth in the Covenant." According to subsequent articles, the Committee brings the communication received from the individual concerned to the attention of the state involved and is supposed in turn to receive explanations in writing or statements clarifying the matter and the remedy, if any, that may have been taken by the state. After consideration of the matter, the Committee is to forward its views to the state party concerned and the individual. It is also to include in its report a summary of its activities, presumably including each such matter.

[38] The "sanction" provided by the Protocol, to be sure, is not as forceful as visualized by those who conceived the original Human Rights Declaration in the hope that it would be a "binding" document. However, the type of "mediation" contemplated by the Protocol has been effectively used regionally, under the terms of the European Community Convention. A good example is the much cited *Boeckmans Case*, reported in 8 J. INT'L COMMN JUR. 114–115 (1967).

Article 14(3)(g) of the Covenant reads in pertinent part thus:

"In the determination of any criminal charge against him, everyone shall be entitled . . .
(g) Not to be compelled to testify against himself. . . ."

This clause, the so-called privilege against self-incrimination, or as it is sometimes referred to in the United States, the Fifth Amendment, has an entirely different scope in civil law countries from the one it has in the common law world today. In the former, this privilege signifies that a suspect or an accused must not under any circumstances be put under oath. If he is sworn, he may lie and will not be responsible for perjury or for misleading the authorities. On the other hand, the suspect and the accused are questioned, though this is done mostly by a judge-investigator and only to a limited degree by the police. When questioned, the suspect or the accused need not answer. However, so rarely does an accused person avail himself of this theoretical right, that the latter is deemed to be highly unrealistic. [39] In Germany, it has been prominently reported in legal literature that Dr. Adams, the famed physician accused of murdering several wealthy wives, did not say a word during his entire trial in England beyond "I plead not guilty." [40]

In England and in the United States, per contra, an accused person has an absolute right to stand mute. He may plead not guilty, but need not even open his mouth to do that, for if he is silent, the plea will be entered for him. This does not also imply that if he had already confessed to the police or the prosecutor, such confession is ipso facto inadmissible, although in recent years very important safeguards have been introduced by the Supreme Court of the United States to assure that a confession is "voluntary."[41] Formerly, the rule as to the privilege against self-incrimination was the same in England and in the United States as it is now in France, Germany, or Italy. But since the end of the nineteenth century the rule has been changed and by statutes the accused has obtained what is regarded as a privilege accorded to him: he may take the stand and testify under oath—as a witness. When he so testifies, he is liable for perjury if he lies. Also, he may be cross-examined as any other witness. The accused thus has this choice: he must either preserve complete silence and not utter a word or testify as a witness, under oath, subject to perjury sanctions. It should be noted that in civil law countries he is allowed to talk freely, but that what he says does not possess the character of testimony.

[39] *See* H. SILVING, ESSAYS ON CRIMINAL PROCEDURE 118–119 (1964).
[40] *Id.*
[41] *See* SILVING, *supra* note 39, at 182–183, 261–269. For developments since 1964, see Silving, *On Police Brutality*, 37 REV. JUR. U.P.R. 279, at 286–293 (1968). But *see* Harris v. New York, 401 U.S. 222 (1971).

However, this does not bar the court from basing its findings on his declaration.

Until only recently, the rule as prevailing in civil law countries was maintained in the United States in only one state, Georgia. However, Georgia modified it in 1962, apparently in order to meet the holding of the United States Supreme Court in *Ferguson v. State of Georgia*.[42] In this case the defendant was permitted to speak as much as he wished, without being interrupted, but was not permitted to be questioned by his attorney, for this—the Georgia Court thought—would be testifying. The United States Supreme Court held that if thus interpreted to bar the defendant from being questioned by his attorney, the Georgia provision would be violative of the Fourteenth Amendment to the Federal Constitution, since it would deprive the defendant of the full meaning of assistance of counsel. But the majority of the United States Supreme Court did not find that merely barring the defendant from testifying under oath was unconstitutional. However, most American judges no doubt believe that the defendant's right to take the stand and testify under oath is a sacred and inalienable right. Indeed, in the *Ferguson* case Justices Frankfurter and Clark, concurring, expressed the view that it is a constitutional right.[43]

On the other hand, as pointed out above, civil law jurists assert that under no circumstances must a suspect or an accused be put under oath. Indeed, they contend that permitting such a person to testify under oath is state cooperation in perjury and that to punish a man for perjury committed in his own trial is cruel and unusual. How, then, are we to interpret the provision of article 14(3) (g) of the Covenant? The civil law rule may be preferable, since it limits oath-taking. Oaths, particularly in court, are objectionable, generally, and not merely in the case of an accused or a suspect.[44]

---

[42] 365 U.S. 570 (1961).

[43] The Georgia legislature apparently interpreted the *Ferguson* holding as at least favoring a grant to the defendant of a right to testify under oath, becaue it amended the provision of the GEORGIA CODE, § 38–415, confirming the defendant's right to make unsworn statements, which the jury might "believe . . . in preference to the sworn testimony in the case," but at the same time, granting him an alternative right to testify under oath. See CODE OF GA. ANNOT. § 38–415, as amended 1962 (Acts 1962, at 133, 134) Supp. 1965.

[44] Regarding other testimonial "privileges," which are not mentioned in the Covenant, there is also a basic difference in approach between civil law and common law countries. In the former countries, the privileges are more extensive and also tend to be differently structured. For example, in both civil law and common law countries there exists a "husband and wife privilege." But in the former countries, it is, as all testimonial privileges, a privilege accorded to the witness, which the witness may waive, whereas in the latter it is the privilege of the defendant, though in some laws both defendant and witness must consent to render the testimony competent. Concerning the German privilege not to testify (§ 52. CODE OF CRIMINAL PROCEDURE), see SILVING, *supra* note 39, at 144–146.

Article 14(2) of the Covenant accords to the defendant in a criminal case a presumption of innocence. [45] This presumption is universally accepted. But what is its meaning or import? [46] On this there is a disparity of interpretations in the countries which adopted the Covenant. In countries of common law tradition the very questioning of the suspect and the accused is believed to violate the adversary nature of the procedure, whereby the presumption is protected. Dealing at arms length with the prosecution is often taken to support the presumption. On the other hand, in countries of civil law background, as mentioned above, the accused is being questioned even though, in theory, he need not answer and, in fact, may lie with immunity. Theoretically there is much support for the proposition that the prosecution ought to have no interest in a conviction but should assist in finding objective truth and justice. Accordingly, there is known in civil law countries a prosecutor's appeal in behalf of the defendant. [47] Which philosophy of the presumption of innocence does the Covenant adopt as a minimum standard?

Article 14(3)(e) of the Covenant accords to everyone "[i]n the determination of any criminal charge against him" the right "[t]o examine, or have examined, the witnesses against him and to obtain the attendance and examination of witnesses on his behalf under the same conditions as witnesses against him." The wording of this provision rather suggests that it applies only to the guilt-determination stage. However, should it be read to apply also to the significant stage of sentencing, in the United States it is being violated daily. In *Williams v. New York,* [48] the United States Supreme Court held that in the sentencing process the prosecution need not produce the witnesses who testified against the defendant in a presentencing investigation conducted by a probation officer after conviction. Jurists of civil law countries might well support the opposition to the *Williams* ruling.[49] The question is, Which interpretation will be held the correct international minimum standard within article 14(3)(e)?

[45] The provision reads: "Everyone charged with a criminal offence shall have the right to be presumed innocent until proved guilty according to law."

[46] Often a scarcely noticed factor casts a shadow on the effectiveness of the presumption, to which all lawyers pay lip service, *e.g.,* in many developing countries, defendants appear handcuffed at the trial.

[47] *See, e.g.,* § 296 of the GERMAN CODE OF CRIMINAL PROCEDURE, which provides that the prosecution may avail itself of any admissible remedy also in behalf of the accused.

[48] 337 U.S. 241 (1949).

[49] In the Third International Congress on Criminology, which dealt with "Recidivism," W.H. Overbeek, representing Holland, objected to Professor Glueck's proposal that the Glueck Prediction Tables be utilized in the sentencing process. Mr. Overbeek's objections were of a constitutional nature. He stated that a judge "is not permitted to avail himself of secret documents to which the accused and his counsel have no access." In answer to these arguments, to which most lawyers of the civil law world would most probably subscribe, Professor Glueck replied simply invoking the *Williams* case and Mr. Justice Black's philosophy set

In many instances the language of the Covenant is ambiguous. For example, the Covenant prohibits imposition of a death penalty except for the most serious crimes (art. 6(2)), without explaining what may be deemed a serious crime or whether the standard of seriousness is abstract or concrete. Thus, *e.g.*, in *Chessman*, [50] which captured the sympathy of the entire world, the death penalty was imposed and executed for "kidnaping to commit robbery." [51] In itself, such kidnaping is a very serious crime. Only in *Chessman*, whatever other elements may have been involved, the kidnaping factor was trite: the victim was forced to move only twenty-two feet, from one car to another. That which seemed decisive to the California Supreme Court was that the kidnaping occurred "pursuant to a plan which purposed the commission of robberies and the infliction of bodily harm (the sex crimes)."[52] In a later case, leading Justices of the Supreme Court of the United States expressed the view that in a rape case without fatal result a death sentence is exorbitant. [53]

In addition to the ambiguity and, indeed, frequent indefiniteness of the symbols of international law, arising from being lifted in literal verbal form from different national law contexts, there obtain differences as a result of diverse social value implications in the various countries. This phenomenon may best be illustrated in relation to confessions.

Article 14(3)(g) of the Covenant, discussed above, in addition to barring compulsory self-incrimination, prohibits compulsion to confess guilt. What, however, constitutes compulsion to confess guilt is one of the most intricate definitional problems of law everywhere. Admitting confessions in court, of course, contradicts the privilege against self-incrimination. Yet, subject to certain safeguards, extrajudicial confessions are admissible in all laws except that of the Talmud. While the legal safeguards against extraction of confessions by state authorities exhibit a growing similarity in modern laws, this is not paralleled by the degree of cultural acceptance of the phenomenon of confession.

---

forth therein: "The due-process clause should not be treated as a device for freezing the evidential procedure of sentencing in the mould of trial procedure." *See* THIRD INTERNATIONAL CONGRESS ON CRIMINOLOGY, Sept. 12–18, 1955, SUMMARY OF PROCEEDINGS 174–175 (1957). It may be interesting to note that Mr. Justice Black, in his *Williams* reasoning, relied heavily on the authority of Professor Glueck and his advocacy for "tailoring the punishment to fit the offender" rather than his crime.

[50] People v. Chessman, 38 Cal.2d 166, 238 P.2d 1001 (1951), *cert. denied*, Chessman v. California, 343 U.S. 915 (1952), *rehearing denied*, 343 U.S. 937 (1952).

[51] The death penalties, of which two were imposed upon the same individual, were based on § 209 of the CALIFORNIA PENAL CODE (West's California Codes), which authorizes capital punishment where the victim of "kidnaping to commit robbery" suffers bodily harm.

[52] The Supreme Court of California found capital punishment incompatible with California Constitution. California v. Anderson 6 Cal. 3d 62.8, 100 Cal. Rpts. 152, 493 p. 2d 880 (1972), cert. denied, 92 S.Ct. 2060.

[53] Rudolf v. Alabama, 375 U.S. 889 (1963). Cf. Furman v. Georgia, 92 S.Ct. 2726 (1972).

Confessions as an institution involve the total problem of man's relationship to authority in given societies. The phenomenon is known in all Western cultures, but psychologists have vigorously questioned the reliability of confessions. In a society in which the state is looked upon as a utilitarian device, a confession which does not rationally benefit the person concerned is not expected except where the defendant neurotically projects his unresolved Oedipus complex onto the state authority. In fact, the problem of the so-called voluntariness of confessions has vexed the United States Supreme Court for a long time. The conditions imposed by that Court upon confessions have reduced their ultimate availability to a minimum. Yet, the problem of why people confess or why courts accept their confessions has not been resolved. To an observer from a civil law country, the obvious tendency in the United States to avoid confessions and simultaneous acceptance and institutionalization of guilty pleas may, indeed, appear incongruous.

In cultures in which the state is looked upon as a benevolent, forgiving parent, a confession is an act of filial loyalty which is expected. Such is the social expectation, for example, in Japan and other Far Eastern countries. There, offenders are encouraged to confess. A self-denunciation is a ground for mitigation or even remittal of punishment. [54] Once caught by the authorities, offenders normally confess. The function of lawyers is deemed to consist in pointing out to the court mitigating circumstances that would induce the court to reduce the punishment.

Of course, involuntary confessions are today barred in Japan,[55] just as they are in the United States, and in Japan, as in the United States, the prosecution must prove the voluntariness of a confession as a condition of its admissibility in evidence. [56] But despite the unavailability in Japan of guilty pleas, which play such a prominent role in this country, a confession is socially more acceptable there than it is in this country. [57]

The problem of the proper treatment of confessions on an international

[54] JAPANESE CRIMINAL CODE § 42; KOREAN CRIMINAL CODE, § 52. There is an increasing tendency in these countries to reward self-denunciation. While the present JAPANESE CRIMINAL CODE recognizes it as but a mitigation ground (§ 42), JAPANESE CRIMINAL CODE drafts, including the prominent one of 1960 (§ 50), as well as the KOREAN CRIMINAL CODE of 1953 (§ 52), treat it as a ground of remittal.

[55] Japan's Constitution of Nov. 3, 1946, art. 38, para. 2, provides: "Confession made under compulsion, torture, or threat, or after prolonged arrest or detention shall not be admitted in evidence." Art. 319(1) of the CODE OF CRIMINAL PROCEDURE in addition bars admissibility in evidence of any confession "suspected not to have been made voluntarily."

[56] For discussion of the problem of "voluntariness" of confessions in Japan, see SHIGEMITSU DANDO, JAPANESE CRIMINAL PROCEDURE 248–58 (7th ed. 1966).

[57] Although Japanese Criminal Law largely follows German patterns, it does not adopt the German approach to "confessions." In Germany a confession cannot by itself afford a mitigation ground, since this would be regarded as exercising an "inadmissible pressure upon the defendant." BGHSt., 105, at 106 (I. Strafsenat 1951).

level is not merely one of comparative law but also one of comparative cultural standards. It is such standards, rather than the pertinent law, that may shed light on phenomena such as the North Korean obstinate reliance on the confessions of the Pueblo crew made under conditions of prolonged detention. [58] Of course, in most countries today confessions thus made would be involuntary as a matter of law, *i.e.*, irrebuttably presumed to be involuntary, and thus absolutely inadmissible in any court.

"Compulsion to confess guilt" may thus have a vast variety of meanings in diverse cultures despite identity of legal provisions. Indeed, to reach uniform social results rather than merely a uniform verbal application of rules, it may be necessary to formulate special minimum standards for relations between states. For example, taking into account situations such as those which obtained in the Pueblo case, the confession of a prisoner in custody should be deemed a nullity in international law unless he is allowed, prior to confessing, to consult an attorney of his own nation and confesses in his presence.

2.4. Quest for Contents

Assuming the desirability of establishing a world public order, we must consider in what way we can contribute to its formation. As pointed out in the first section of this paper, of the three meanings of I.C.L. described there, the law of minimum standards is the most likely to gain a firmer and broader foundation in the near future, and it is from this law that we may expect evolution of an incipient world federal state, cutting across national sovereignty barriers as well as ideological diversities. Its elaboration is our most important immediate task.

As shown in section 2.2, considerable difficulties must be overcome before we can reach a genuinely meaningful body of minimum standards. These difficulties are partly of a kind that comparative lawyers, sociologists, psychologists, and anthropologists may well help to resolve. Clarification of all the potential meanings of symbols used or to be used in international sources and suggestions for an order of preference for the various meanings based on research into their operation in the respective legal systems, are some of the functions which experts may perform. But the creation of minimum standards is a lawmaking function, beyond the

---

[58] In Jan., 1968, North Korean subchasers and torpedo boats captured the American intelligence ship Pueblo and held its 82 surviving crewmen in captivity for eleven months. During this period some of the crewmen confessed to having violated North Korean waters. The Court Martial trial subsequent to their release revealed a pattern of torture that made the confessions clearly incredible and void. However, the length of detention itself would have been sufficient to invalidate these confessions. On the Pueblo Trial, see N.Y. Times, Jan. 23, 1969, at 1; *id.*, Jan. 24, 1969, at 1, 12; *id.*, Jan. 26, 1969, § 4, at 6; *id.*, Feb. 3, 1969, at 10; *id.*, Feb. 26, at 12.

authority of experts. It is to be achieved by the usual norm creating processes of international law, treaties or customary development. Yet, experts may assume an advisory role beyond merely technical consultation. They can guide lawmakers in the choice of law to be adopted.

To lay a foundation for developing minimum standards on a large scale, we must choose a comprehensive guideline of action. Such guideline must be formulated in the face of the apparently irreconcilable broad differences in the world's political ideologies. How is it possible to find a common denominator in the apparently mutually exclusive aspirations of the Free World and the Communist World? At first glance, that which is common to the two ideologies advanced by these "worlds" appears to be but a verbal symbol. Everywhere today government pretends to represent democracy, indeed, the only true democracy. Upon closer scrutiny, however, that which in some situations seems to be a sham pretense may be shown to reflect a rudiment of genuine thought content. Both the Free World and the Communist World today are, at least in their ideologies, aiming at one fundamental ultimate value, a dignity for man, the former, however, stressing its libertarian, spiritual aspects, the latter emphasizing its egalitarian economic-welfare denotations. Though, obviously, "dignity" does not mean the same within the two indicated uses, the meanings are not completely disparate. Both now seem to support such principles of modern criminal law as *nullum crimen, nulla poena sine lege* [59]; e.g., in Soviet criminal law doctrine and legislation certain principles and drafting techniques derived from civil law/criminal law science have been preserved. It will be recalled that the modern version of this "science" itself originated in Belingian efforts to establish legality.

Proceeding, then, from the universal basic belief in the dignity of man, we must first develop comprehensive fundamental principles which in our view flow from it. This we must do notwithstanding any laws to the contrary to be found in the world's penal legislation, for it is precisely minimum standards which are to limit such legislation that we aim to formulate.

A first tenet in the order of generality and significance flowing from the dignity of the offender is the economy principle, [60] which implies a minimization of the role of crime, meaning, general reduction of the func-

---

[59] On the "return to the *nulla poena* rule" in § 3 of the Basic Principles of Criminal Legislation of the USSR and the Union Republics 1958 for citation and translation see THE FEDERAL CRIMINAL LAW OF THE SOVIET UNION, in LAW OF EASTERN EUROPE. (Szirmai ed. 1959) and Bassiouni, *The Criminal Justice System of the Union of Soviet Socialist Republics and the Peoples Republic of China,* 11 REVISTA DE DERECHO PUERTORRIQUENO (1971).

On efforts in Communist China to control the analogy principle, *see* COHEN, THE CHINESE CRIMINAL PROCESS, 1949–1963, AN INTRODUCTION 336–38 (1963).

[60] Compare *supra,* § 2.2.3.

tion of criminal law to an unavoidable minimum. International law should guarantee to each individual the utmost freedom compatible with the equal freedom of others. It should function as a world constitution protecting man everywhere against prejudices of majorities without and within his own national group. This implies, firstly, that the number of crime constructs ought to be strictly limited and that for those crimes which are to be preserved, sanctions ought to be diversified with a view to an utmost minimization of suffering consistent with realization of the proper ends of criminal law. The economy principle as a guide to reducing the number of admissible crime types requires, secondly, that doubt as regards the propriety within a free society of a crime construct should always be resolved in favor of individual freedom. Unless a crime construct can be clearly shown to be absolutely necessary for the maintenance of basic protection against substantial harm, it should be eliminated. Thirdly, even should a given community need or demand per se be properly enforceable by the methods of criminal law, such methods ought not to be used unless they are provably effective: futile use of criminal law should be constitutionally barred. Implicit in this suggestion is proscription of criminal law methods wherever other methods are in substance comparably effective. [61]

Another tenet implicit in the offender's dignity is protection against imposition of irrational crime types. Perusal of contemporary legislation shows that some of our crime types simply cannot stand the test of rationality, even when this term is used to convey the notion of ordinary common sense. [62] Beyond this notion, rationality to be applied as a testing

[61] FERRI, in his famed CRIMINAL SOCIOLOGY 426 (trans. Kelly & Lisle; Smithers ed. 1917), suggested utilization of "equivalents of punishment," "*sostituiti penali*," with a view to removing the causes of crime, directing criminal tendencies toward constructive legitimate goals, and eliminating certain crime categories.

[62] An obvious example is the crime of "seduction under promise of marriage" (CALIFORNIA PENAL CODE § 268; PENAL CODE OF PUERTO RICO § 261, 33 L.P.R.A. § 967, which, amazingly, is preserved in the Official Draft of a Penal Code for Puerto Rico 1967, P. del S. 581, 5ta. Asamblea Legislativa, 3ra Sesión Ordinaria, §§ 132, 133). This crime is being utilized as a means of coercing marriage by threat of imprisonment. According to the usual rules of family law, such marriage would seem to be void, since not fulfilling the requirement of free consent on the part of the would-be husband. Of course, this crime is now disappearing from the penal codes, *e.g.*, it has been eliminated from the GERMAN PENAL CODE (former § 176, "obtaining extramarital cohabitation surreptitiously" has been repealed by the First Act on the Reform of Criminal Law, 1969, BGB1 I 645).

Another, less obvious example of a crime which "makes no sense" in a democratic state is that of "escape from prison," which actually penalizes the prisoner for loving freedom. The German Reichsgericht set forth as rationale for the legislators' leaving a prisoner's self-release immune from punishment their desire based "on humanitarian grounds to take account of man's drive for freedom." R.G.St. 3 140, 141. The Bundesgerichtshof likewise held the mere collaboration of several prisoners in their common escape immune on the same ground. BGHSt. 17 369, 374–375 (IV. Strafsenat), Decision of July 20, 1962 g. M.

On the dependence of "rationality" of crime concepts on time-bound "scientific" beliefs see Ryu, *Causation in Criminal Law*, 106 U. PENN. L. REV. 773, at 800 (1958).

standard ought to be taken to mean scientific rationality, *i.e.*, rationality in the light of the modern sciences of men such as psychology, anthropology, sociology.

Many of our crimes against morality ought to be jettisoned simply on the ground of lacking scientific rationality. But it is, of course, arguable that crimes of this type, the origins of which are traceable to religious tabus, have no place in a modern secular state.[63] Such a state is not a proper agent for promoting morality, though it should itself be governed by moral standards and restraints.

It would exceed the proper scope of this section were we to submit a comprehensive program for elimination of odd crime concepts [64] or, indeed for reconstruction of those which should be maintained. [65] Suffice it to point out that all this falls within an area in which policy-makers in I.C.L. should take an active interest for the protection of the dignity of man in the widest sense of this term.

International minimum standards ought to be formulated for the large and complex area of criminal sanctions, affording tests of their definiteness, rationality, and proportionality as to kind and extent; *e.g.*, these standards should preclude imprisonment except in cases where that sanction is genuinely unavoidable. [66] Minimum standards ought to govern also the laws of sentence execution or penitentiary laws, as well as court organization laws. [67] Finally, beyond formal termination of the process of execution, international standards should be formulated for the social protection and care of former convicts and for relief for victims of judicial and other government error.

Part of the reconstruction of crime concepts should consist in purging

[63] This, obviously, should not be taken to mean that offenses against "morality" are being in any sense condoned. Not everything that is not sanctioned by criminal law is thereby necessarily exempted from social censure.

[64] Examples of crime constructs that ought to be eliminated from modern penal codes are suggested in Ryu & Silving, *Nullum Crimen Sine Actu*, SEOUL NAT'L UNIV. L. REV. (1964); also in German, 77 ZEITSCHRIFT FÜR DIE GESAMTE STRAFRECHTSWISSENSCHAFT 173 (1965).

[65] *E.g.*, our common law construct of "burglary" requires a thorough reexamination and reconstruction. For criticism of this concept. *see* Ryu & Silving, *supra*. note 64, and Silving, *Philosophy of Source and Scope of Criminal Law*, in CRIME, LAW AND CORRECTIONS 232, 246–51 (Slovenko ed. 1966). Spanish version under the title *La Filosofia de la Parte Especial de un Código Penal*, 33 REV. JUR. U.P.R. 17, 44–51 (1964). A redeemable ingredient of this concept is that portion which constitutes "housebreaking," in the sense of a violation of the privacy of domicile. Otherwise, the "breaking" in "burglary" should constitute but an aggravation of the crime in connection with which it is committed.

[66] *Compare* Silving, *Toward a Contemporary Concept of Criminal Justice*, 4 ISRAEL L. REV. 479, 481–485 (1969).

[67] *E.g.*, "minimum standards" dictate creation of "courts of sentence execution" that would supervise conformance of the offender treatment to legality principles. *See* Silving, *"Rule of Law" in Criminal Justice*, in ESSAYS IN CRIMINAL SCIENCE 75, 130–138, 152–154 (Mueller ed. 1961).

the total area of criminal law of certain obsolete notions. There is an urgent need for an analytical inquiry into these notions, their origin and the problem of their pertinence to contemporary life contexts and to the rational aspirations of modern man. The analysis we have in mind should combine a language critique with anthropological and psychoanalytic studies. Many of our so-called moral principles which are incorporated in law are survivals of ancient beliefs and feudal notions that have become petrified in habits of social communication and are unconsciously utilized as means of mutual cross-incitement within groups. Examples of such survivals in national legislations are special provisions on duels[68] and certain rules on self-defense[69] derived from the codes of honor of medieval knighthood.

Purging concepts of the indicated type would benefit not only criminal law proper, whether national or international, but indeed the general area of international law; *e.g.*, the international law concept of self-defense, a key-concept of that law, clearly bears the imprint of "killing as of right" of feudal origin.[70] Other basic moral notions of international law require a thorough reexamination in the light of a more advanced morality of our times. That while it is immoral to kill a woman or a child or a civilian, it is heroic to kill an enemy soldier, is a carry-over from feudal crime concepts where treacherousness was contrasted with open combat. It is difficult indeed for a soldier to guess what conduct is expected from him where proper conduct is defined by a combination of feudal tenets and the realities of modern warfare techniques.[71]

Ultimately, mankind must confront the need for purging a crucial, general concept pervading international law and impeding the course of international justice: the concept of alienship. Only when this concept is overcome, will we be able to reach out for a genuine world state and international criminal justice. The Covenant on Civil and Political Rights (art. 13) has made a commendable effort to protect aliens "lawfully in the territory of a state party" against arbitrary expulsion. However, this provision but touched the surface of the problems arising from the myth

---

[68] The special provisions on dueling (§§ 201 to 210, GERMAN PENAL CODE) were repealed in Germany by the First Act on the Reform of Criminal Law, *supra* note 62.

[69] *See* H. SILVING, CONSTITUENT ELEMENTS OF CRIME 392 (1967).

[70] The privileged status accorded to self-defense in international law (*cf* SCHWARZENBERGER, INTERNATIONAL LAW, 185, 572 (3d ed. 1957), its so-called "absolute character," reflects most clearly the feudal notion of *matar con derecho* adopted from a law of the *Fuero Real* by the *Novísima Recopilación* (Ley I, t. XVII, lib. IV). *See* QUINTANO RIPOLLES COMEN-TARIOS AL CODIGO PENAL 97–98 (2d ed. 1966).

[71] On the "moral dilemmas" faced by soldiers, *see, e.g.*, Beecher, *Questions on Songmy: G.I.'s Seen Facing Moral Dilemmas in Deciding Whether to Shoot and Kill*, N.Y. Times, Jan. 1, 1970, § C, at 8.

with which history surrounded the notions of citizenship and alienship.

There is in all likelihood a close connection in origin between the concept of alienship and that of enmity: the stranger, the unknown, is feared and hated; he is thought to be an enemy.[72] Yet, it was in the alien—not in the brother or friend, deemed *quasi,* a part of the same body with oneself, one's clan—that "man discovered the idea of humanity." (Hermann Cohen).[73] The Old Testament commanded that there be one law for the resident alien and the citizen (Lev. 24:22), and Christ challenged mankind, indeed, to love the enemy (Matthew 5:44). But not long after Christ spoke, Paul invoked his Roman citizenship in quest of special privilege (Acts 22:25–29). Throughout the ages the idea of enmity inherent in alienship survived, if only under the guise of negation of citizenship.

The concept of citizenship acquired at birth without choice or merit is incompatible with the idea of the equal dignity of everyman, the brotherhood of mankind. Today, efforts are noticeable to assimilate the alien to the citizen in various, mostly regional, international law sources.[74] But until the general idea of the brotherhood of mankind penetrates deeply into our modern culture, we cannot hope to have a genuine world public order. I.C.L., as part of such order, must transcend distinctions of citizenship. Until very recently, a person discriminated against by his own state was defenseless in international law.[75] International convenants have since provided a certain measure of protection to persons in such situations. But much more needs to be done to deflate the significance of citizenship and enhance that of plain and simple humanity.[76] International minimum standards must be accepted vis-à-vis the citizen and the alien alike.

[72] *See* Konvitz, *Alien,* in Encyclopaedia Britannica (1966).

[73] *Id.*

[74] *See, e.g.,* the treaty constituting the European Coal and Steel Community signed in 1951, which requires member states to allow employment in the coal and steel industries of workers who are nationals of other member states on the same basis as their own nationals.

[75] As may be recalled, whenever a voice was raised in defense of the Jewish citizens of Germany during the National Socialist era, the answer was that these were German citizens and that no outside country had any right to interfere with the "total power" of a state over its own citizens—an argument of which one is strongly reminded when listening to the frequent indignant repudiation of intervention in foreign "civil wars" current at this time. German Jews, of course, were "citizens of Germany" only so far as their "duties" were concerned, for they had been gradually deprived of all "rights of citizenship" by the Nuremberg Laws and the Regulations issued thereunder—regulations which speak for themselves, *e.g.,* one regulation provided for the clothing ration of a Jew: yearly, one spool of thread and a needle. Nevertheless, Jewish citizens of Germany who had honorably served in the British Armed Forces were treated in England as "enemy aliens" for the purpose of the British law on disposition of "enemy property." Lowenthal v. Attorney General 1 All E.R. 295 (1946).

[76] For a proposal that the United Nations declare all stateless persons to be their direct nationals, *see* Silving, *Freedom and Citizenship,* in Freedom and Authority in Our Time, Twelfth Symposium of the Conference on Science, Philosophy and Religion 253, 259 (Bryson, Finkelstein, MacIver, & McKeon eds. 1953). This, of course, would considerably reduce the significance of citizenship and enhance that of humanity.

Of great importance for the development of a world public order is evolution of a proper structural relationship between that order and the component units, both states and individuals. It is essential to reach a proper distribution of contents and functions between the union and the component units. For example, the European Human Rights Convention, [77] which requires member states to grant to suspects and accused persons a presumption of innocence (art. 6 (2)), has been interpreted by the German Supreme Court [78] as leaving the states free to determine "what belongs to the statutory proof of guilt and how the proof of guilt is to be adduced." This, of course, allows the states considerable · freedom to manipulate the presumption. [79] Similarly, applicability of an international standard may be frustrated where a national court is authorized to classify with finality certain decisive concepts according to its own lights.[80] These are examples of the inadequacies of present international federal structures. Comparative studies of the world's federal structures should be instituted with a view to finding one best suited for a world state.

The character of the international organs that are to administer the world's "criminal justice" is comparable in importance to the problem of the individual's access to such organs. To be legally meaningful, human dignity requires implementation by an effective impartial agency, which according to our Western ideology is a court. To such court, individuals should have access directly rather than by the medium of their respective states. [81]

2.5. Conclusion

Having assumed the symbol I.C.L. to be confined to "international law dealing with criminal matters," we searched among the several potential meanings of this symbol for one that we thought could acquire a solid

---

[77] 213 U.N.T.S. 221; Europ. T. S. No. 5.

[78] Decision of the Bundesgerichtshof in Strafsachen (I. Strafsenat) of Sept. 5, 1967, g. C., BGHSt. 21 306, at 308 (1968).

[79] It is required, however, that proof be made in a properly regulated proceeding.

[80] Decision of the Bundesgerichtshof in Strafsachen (I. Strafsenat) of Jan. 19, 1965, g. H. u.a., BGHSt. 20 143, at 146–150 (1966). The issue in this case was whether the provision of § 161 of the GERMAN PENAL CODE, imposing a mandatory permanent incapacity to testify as a witness or expert under oath for cases of perjury conviction, violated art. 3 of the European Human Rights Convention ("No one shall be subjected to torture or to inhuman or degrading treatment or punishment.") The Bundesgerichtshof held that the incapacity in issue was not a "punishment" but a "security measure."

[81] Compare comment on the progress of the European Convention on Human Rights by Professor René Marcic, Written Communication, reproduced in HUMAN RIGHTS IN NATIONAL AND INTERNATIONAL LAW, *Proceedings of the Second International Conference on the European Convention on Human Rights Held in Vienna Under the Auspices of the Council of Europe and the University of Vienna, Oct. 18–20, 1965* 38–40 (Robertson ed. 1968), stressing lack of direct access of individuals to the Court as an obstacle to effective assertion of human rights under the Convention.

foundation and, indeed, could serve as a basis for a future world public order. We found in international minimum standards of criminal justice a body of law both susceptible to further development and capable of serving as a medium for acceptance of wider areas of international law. We reached the conclusion that growth of this body of law should be encouraged, and we attempted to point out the areas in which jurists and other experts could best contribute to its growth.

In our search for a meaning of comparative law concepts and of diverse value patterns, we encountered two major obstacles: (1) the ambiguity and indefiniteness of internationally used criminal law symbols and (2) polarization of social and political ideologies. Comparative law studies oriented to resolution of value conflicts and law development might help to overcome the first-mentioned difficulty. The second difficulty, on the other hand, presents an impediment of major dimension. Yet, we have been able to find a common denominator, though narrow in scope, among even the seemingly most wholly disparate ideologies of the two "worlds" into which mankind is at present divided. That common denominator on which we might build a future world order is afforded by the ultimate belief in the dignity of man, prevailing both in the Free World and in the Communist World, despite diversity of the methods suggested for its fulfillment. Minimum standards of criminal justice as means of safeguarding human dignity everywhere, imposing bars on state omnipotence vis-à-vis the individual, may serve as a vehicle of better understanding among nations and peoples. Among the minimum standards thus postulated, we laid special stress on the principles of economy and scientific rationality that ought to govern criminal law policy everywhere in the world.

In this atomic age there is hardly any room left for competition among states under the motto "Might is Right." Unless we eliminate wars, we may all perish. Cooperation is vital. It must be sought on two levels. There is need for recognition that ideological differences cannot be resolved either by fiat or by force of convictions. There is no firm basis in the value system of one community for criticizing that of another community. Hence, in ideological matters, national sovereignties must be respected. However, peaceful coexistence is predicated upon attributing to sovereignty a relative meaning and a limited scope—a scope perhaps best derived from recognition that international law, more than any other law, must be firmly supported by the authority of reason and uniform compliance.

Against this background, we might give thought to the task which concerns particularly our juristic conscience: what is the function of lawyers in the face of the described state of conflicts and opportunities? Lawyers' functions have been known to change in response to changing social needs. [82] Today, the international community of nations and peoples expects lawyers to respond to its call for elaborating a scheme of common understanding of however small initial scope, with a view to future expansion. Law is never wholly created but is always in a sense found. Nor is it ever wholly found but is always at the same time invented.

Section 3. INTERNATIONAL CRIMINAL LAW: ITS OBJECT AND RECENT DEVELOPMENTS*

HANS-HEINRICH JESCHECK

3.1. Introduction

The question of whether or not there exists an I.C.L. and the problem of establishing its content in a given case are well-known controversies. Noncontroversial, however, is the fact that a state and its citizens do not exist in and for themselves, but instead are organized in manifold ways into an international community of nations. Accordingly, the domestic criminal law of states is not concerned exclusively with internal events, but rather often produces effects reaching beyond its own national borders and the citizens of its own state. That the international community of nations itself could possess its own criminal power, from which an I.C.L. in turn could be developed, is also an idea one cannot dispute.

However differently from a juridical standpoint the present existence of an international criminal law might be assesssed by various legal scholars,[1] such differences do not detract from the value of a systematic classification of the manifold international relationships among the individual national criminal laws. These relationships, the object of our analysis here, are presented by the diverse legal obligations undertaken by the various states, by the international legal customs of nations, and by international treaties and draft conventions. Such a schematic analysis of the relationships among national criminal laws, with the assistance of scientific concepts, can then clarify the existing interrelation of all the national criminal laws. Thus, the concept of an I.C.L. here presupposed is developed to

---

[82] *Cf.* Ryu, Work Paper on *Research, Legal Education, and Training,* in THIRD GENEVA WORLD PEACE THROUGH LAW CONFERENCE (1967).

* Translated from the German by John A. St. Clair, J.D., in collaboration with Mr. Peter Sitzler and Mrs. Alice Zeidler of the Max Planck Institute for Foreign and International Criminal Law, Freiburg im Breisgau, Germany.

[1] Compare Schwarzenberger, *The Problem of an International Criminal Law,* 3 CURRENT LEGAL PROB. 293 (1950): "International law has not yet evolved a branch of criminal law of its own." with Glaser, 1970 DROIT INTERNATIONAL PÉNAL CONVENTIONNEL 16: "Il faut entendre par droit pénal international . . . l'ensemble des règles établies pour réprimer les violations des préceptes du droit international public." [Hereinafter referred to as *Ghaser*]

a great extent from the above pragmatic approach and does not depend upon a prior juridical definition of all the relevant material. We shall include within this pragmatic working hypothesis of I.C.L. all rules of a criminal nature which concern the integration of states and their citizens within the community of nations, as well as those rules which exist for the protection of this international community and its legally protected interests.

This method of proceeding offers important advantages. In the first place it facilitates the objective perception of correlations among diverse legal phenomena which have not yet been rationally classified. Further, this method of proceeding makes possible a demonstration of the reciprocal interdependence of the relevant criminal law matters, thereby allowing one to draw those reasonable conclusions which are appropriate for an accurate treatment of the subject. Finally, such an overview of the entire subject matter makes it possible to more easily recognize the juridical value of a particular rule in its spheres of application. With this pragmatic conceptualization of I.C.L. as the point of reference, various examples of its newest developments will be presented here. To be considered are (1) I.C.L. in its original sense, (2) the law of extradition and mutual international assistance in criminal matters, (3) those rules having a criminal nature which exist to protect the community of nations and its supranational interests, (4) the criminal law in the field of the European communities and (5) international criminal jurisdiction.

3.2. International Criminal Law as a Limitation of Domestic Criminal Power in Relation to Foreign Nations

I.C.L. in its original sense refers to the question of whether or not an act which was committed abroad, or by a foreigner, or which resulted in an injury to a foreign interest, is subject to the domestic criminal power (*jus puniendi*) of the prosecuting state.[2] At a time when sojourns abroad for purposes of study, business, and vacation last longer and occur even more frequently, this function of I.C.L. acquires significant practical importance. It is only after it has first been determined that the prosecuting state's criminal power exists with reference to an act having an international relationship that one must ask the narrower question regarding which state's particular criminal law should be applied to the individual case. In the majority of cases this is simply the criminal law of the state in which the prosecution occurs. In certain other instances, however, the applicable law of the prosecuting state refers to the law of another state for the specific rule to be applied to these particular facts (renvoi). Such

---

[2] *See generally* JESCHECK, LEHRBUCH DES STRAFRECHTS, General Part, 115 (1969).

an example of criminal law renvoi is found, for example, in article 6 (1) second sentence of the Swiss Criminal Code.[3]

It is clear then that I.C.L. in this original meaning does not have the primary function of defining those areas in which the prosecuting state's own criminal law rules should be applied, but instead answers the necessarily antecedent question regarding the existence and extent of this state's criminal power. That the forum state's judicial power is manifested as much by the renvoi process as by an application of its own law is well recognized in international private law. Each state itself has full authority to determine the limits of its own criminal power. It is, therefore, national rather than international law that in fact is involved. As a constituent part of the international community of nations, however, each state in making the determination of its criminal power must give due regard to the relevant international law rules, whether they are found in treaties, customary international law, or in the general legal principles which are recognized by all civilized nations.

In this connection, certainly the most important of such generally recognized legal principles is that a state may not arbitrarly subject to its own criminal power acts which either occurred abroad or were committed by a foreigner, unless there exists a meaningful point of relation which rationally connects the factual context of the act to the legitimate interests of the prosecuting state.[4] Such points of relation widely recognized in international law include the territorial principle, the registration—or flag-state—principle, the active personality principle, the protective principle, and the principle of substituted administration of criminal justice.[5]

A significant recent case of the substituted administration of criminal justice is found in the European Convention on the Punishment of Road Traffic Offences,[6] which was drafted by the Council of Europe and which was signed by several European countries on November 30,1964, but which has not yet become effective. For instances of road traffic violations this Convention establishes for the signatory states a new type of criminal power in the process by which the state where the offense occurred requests that prosecution be instituted by the state in which the offender

---

[3] The application of foreign criminal law by the national judge was proposed and exhaustively justified by the Eighth International Criminal Law Congress in 1961, meeting in Lisbon. *Cf.* Reseolution in 74 *Feitschrift für diegesante Strafrechtswissenschaft* 195 (1962). *See generally* STAUBACH, DIE ANWENDUNG AUSLÄNDISCHEN STRAFRECHTS DURCH DEN NATIONALEN RICHTER 196 (1964).

[4] *Cf.* Oehler, *Theorie des Strafanwendungsrechts,* in FESTSCHRIFT FÜR H. GRÜTZNER. AKIVELLE PROBLEM DAS INTERNATIONALE STRAFRE CHI 115 (Oehler & Pötz eds. 1970) [Hereinafter referred to as *Festschrift fur H. Grutzner*].

[5] *See generally Harvard Research in International Law: Jurisdiction with Respect to Crime,* 29 A.J.I.L. 439 (Supp. 1935).

[6] *European Treaty Series,* No. 52.

is located. In such cases the state in which the offender is located must obey a request for prosecution made according to the treaty.[7]

Of the above points of relation establishing the criminal power of a state, only the passive personality principle is not absolutely recognized by international law.[8] According to this principle, a state has the right to subject a foreigner to its criminal power, even in regard to an offense committed abroad, if as a consequence of the act one of its nationals was injured.[9] Although certainly no general international law rule now exists which directly prohibits a state from extending its criminal power to foreigners who commit offenses in another country, the international law rule prohibiting the abuse of criminal power must be considered in such instances.[10] At the very least this prohibition would bar application of the passive personality principle in those instances in which the act was not criminal according to the law of the country in which the alleged offense occurred.[11]

In the selection and application of the determinative points of relation, the existence of a fundamental difference between the Continental and the Anglo-American legal views becomes evident. In the European states, it is usual to start from the territorial principle,[12] but then to combine it with other points of relation in order to include within the criminal power of the state acts which occurred abroad, often even if the actor was also an alien.[13] The Anglo-American legal systems, on the other hand, limit

---

[7] *See generally text, infra* at notes 54 & 55.

[8] *Cf.* The *Cutting Fall* case of 1886, in which the position of the U.S.A., that the passive-personality principle was contrary to international law, was adopted over Mexico's proposed contentions. See also in this connection von Münch, I Wörterbuch des Völkerrechts 305 (Strupp-Schlochauer 1960). The binding force of international law over the formulation of the I.C.L. by the states is now assured. *Cf.* Oehler, *supra* note 4, at 111.

[9] The decision of the Permanent Court of International Justice in the 1926 *Lotus* case does *not* contain a recognition of the passive-personality principle because the exercise of the criminal power of Turkey there could have been rested on the broader meaning of the territorial principle. *Cf.* Herndl, *II* Wörterbuch des Völkerrechts 431 (Strupp-Schlochauer, 1961).

[10] *Cf.* Oppenheim-Lauterpacht, I International Law 345 (8th ed. 1955).

[11] *Cf.* Robwog, Das Problem der Vereinbarkeit des Aktiven und des passiven Personalgrundsatzes mit dem Völkerrecht 181 (1965).

[12] West Germany has also returned to the territorial principle as the main point of relation in German I.C.L. *See* § 3 of the new *General Part* of the German Criminal Code (to become effective October 1, 1973). *See generally* Jescheck, *Zur Reform des internationalen Strafrechts,* 1956 Zeitschrift für internationales Recht und Diplomatie 75; Oehler, *Das Territorialitätsprinzip,"* 83 Zeitschrift für die gesamte Strafrechtswissenschaft 80 (1971), Vogler, *Geltungsanspruch und Geltungsbereich der Strafgesetze,* 1970 Festschrift für H. Grützner 155.

[13] *See, e.g.,* the French provisions found in art. 689, *Code de Procédure pénale* (active personality principle); art. 694, *Code de procédure pénale* (protection of state principle); art. 8, *Code de l'aviation civile et commerciale* of 1955 (flag or state of registration principle).

prosecution either to offenses which were committed on their own territory or to those the consequence of which was effected within their borders, thus generally excluding prosecution for foreign offenses.[14] This difference in the fundamental conceptualization of the two systems has significant consequences for the law of extradition. The Continental states can well accept the principle of nonextradition of their own citizens because they satisfy the imperative demands of justice through prosecution according to the active personality principle of their own citizens for offenses committed abroad. The Anglo-American states, on the contrary, generally must accede to extradition of their citizens because ordinarily they are legally not able to prosecute nationals for acts done abroad.

The coexistence of multiple points of relation in I.C.L. often leads to overlappings of criminal power and to the possibility of double jeopardy. Although there seems hardly to exist a legal issue in this area of law bordering both international and criminal law which would be more suitable to regulation by convention than this, I.C.L. treaties up to the present time have come into existence only in Central and South America, where the Bustamante Code of 1928 and the Montevideo Treaty of 1940 are in force.[15] The significant Harvard Research Draft Convention on Jurisdiction with Respect to Crime[16] has received major recognition as a scholarly achievement but has never been legally adopted. Presently, however, the Council of Europe is very close to concluding the Convention on the Transfer of Proceedings in Criminal Matters.[17] This convention provides a quite flexible system of obligations to accept criminal prosecutions, and correctly gives this flexible system precedence over any rigid ranking of priorities. Moreover, this draft convention extends to the international relations of the signing nations the fundamental principle of *ne bis in idem,* which beforehand had been recognized primarily only in domestic law.[18]

Although there now exists no comprehensive treaty or convention with regard to I.C.L. as an entity, I.C.L. treaties in particular areas have none-

---

[14] *Cf.* BASSIOUNI, CRIMINAL LAW AND ITS PROCESSES, 329–330 (1969), and George, *Extraterritorial Application of Penal Legislation,* 64 MICH. L. REV. 617 (1965).

[15] The BUSTAMANTE CODE of 1928 has been in force in 15 South and Central American countries since 1936. See *Convention of Private International Law* adopted at Havana on Feb. 20, 1928, in 29 A.J.I.L. 642 (Supp. 1935).

The Montevideo Treaty has been signed by 7 South American states. See *Treaty on International Penal Law* adopted at Montevideo on Mar. 13, 1940, in 38 A.J.I.L. 122 (Supp. 1944).

[16] 29 A.J.I.L. 439 (Supp. 1935).

[17] *Cf.* Grützner, *Die Tätigkeit des Europarats auf strafrechtlichem Gebiet,* 1970. DEUTSCHE RICHTERZEITUNG 78; Grützner, DER ANDWENDUNGSBEREICH DES STRAFRECHTS: RECHTSVERGLEICHENDE ÜBERSCHT 58 (1964 mimeograph).

[18] This result is in agreement with Res. IV of the Ninth International Criminal Law Congress, which met in the Hague in 1964. *Cf.* 77 ZEITSCHRIFT FÜR DIE GESAMTE RECHTSWISSENSCHAFT 686 (1965).

theless had a major effect on the legal development. For example, the four Geneva Conventions of August 12, 1949, establish the universality principle for war crimes,[19] while in opposition to every political expectation the Genocide Convention took the territorial principle as its basis.[20] The universality principle in its traditional form is also found in article 19 of the Convention on the High Seas of April 4, 1958,[21] dealing with piracy, which, however, has not yet been ratified by Germany. In other recent conventions the signing nations have been content to merely establish a duty or obligation to punish in certain instances.[22] Occasionally also the signatory states expressly refer to the territorial or active personality principles,[23] or in other instances they explicity reserve their own viewpoint on the application of national criminal law.[24] When this occurs, the act which is made an offense in the treaty can serve as the basis of a national law prosecution according to the universality principle, but it need not necessarily be so prosecuted.[25]

There also have been some significant recent agreements contained in international treaties, with regard to both air and ship travel, which have followed the flag (state of registration) principle. The application of the criminal power of a state to its ships in foreign coastal waters is ruled by article 19 of the Geneva Convention on the Territorial Sea and Contiguous Zone of April 29, 1958, which, like the Convention on the High Seas, has not yet been ratified by Germany. In such instances of appli-

[19] *Cf.* DAHM, ZUR PROBLEMATIK DES VÖLKERSTRAFRECHTS 34 (1956).

[20] For the text of the convention, *see* 78 U.N.T.S. 277. *See also* Jescheck, *Die internationale Genocidium-Konvention,* 66 ZEITSCHRIFT FÜR DIE GESAMTE STRAFRECHTSWISSENSCHAFT 211 (1954). Glaser, *supra* note 1, at 108, assumes only a priority principle. *Cf.* the new *General Part* of the GERMAN CRIMINAL CODE (to become effective Oct. 1, 1973), which in § 6 (1) provides for the universality principle for genocide.

[21] Printed in abridgment in MUELLER-WISE, INTERNATIONAL CRIMINAL LAW 87, 215 (1965). *Cf.* Glaser, *supra* note 1, at 157.

[22] *E.g.,* art. 36, *Single Convention on Narcotic Drugs* of Mar. 30, 1961, 520 U.N.T.S. 204, and Amending Protocol of March 24, 1972, E/Conf. 63/8 and Bassiouni, *The International Narcotics Control Scheme—A Proposal* 46 ST. JOHN's L. REV. (1972); Glaser, *supra* note 1, at 138; art. 2, *International Convention for the Suppression of the Traffic in Women and Children* of Oct. 30, 1921, in the German REICHSGESETZBLATT of 1924, Part II, at 180; arts. 1 & 4 *International Convention for the Suppression of the Circulation of and Traffic in Obscene Publications* of Oct. 12, 1923, in the German REICHSGESETZBLATT of 1925, Part II, at 287.

See also Glaser, *supra* note 1, at 141; *see generally* text, at notes 89–96, *infra.*

[23] *E.g.,* art. 2, *International Convention for the Suppression of the Circulation of and the Traffic in Obscene Publications* of Oct. 12, 1923, *Supra* note 22; art. 9, *Convention for the Suppression of the Traffic in Persons and of the Exploitation of the Prostitution of Others* of Dec. 2, 1949, in 96 U.N.T.S. 272. *See also,* Nanda and Bassiouni, *Slavery: Steps Towards Its Eradication,* SANTA CLARA LAWYER 424 (1972).

[24] *E.g.,* art. 17, *International Convention for the Suppression of Counterfeitting Currency* of Apr. 20, 1929, in the German REICHSGESETZBLATT, Part II, at 913.

[25] *See, e.g.,* the GERMAN CRIMINAL CODE § 4 (3), nos. 4,7,8,9.

cation of the flag principle, the criminal power of both the state of registration and the coastal nation exist concurrently, but with the criminal
power of the flag state having precedence over that of the coastal state to
the extent the latter is not directly disturbed by the offense. The instance
of a similar concurrence of the flag and active-personality principles is
now governed by article 11 of the Convention on the High Seas, which
provides that the parties liable for a ship collision can be prosecuted
only by the flag state or the state of their nationality, thereby reversing
the precedent of the 1926 *Lotus* case. The criminal power over acts committed aboard aircraft[26] is now covered by the Tokyo Convention on
Offenses and Certain Other Acts Committed on Board Aircraft of September 14, 1963. Although this convention gives effect to the concurrence
principle,[27] the Hague Convention of 1970 establishes a duty to prosecute
or extradite on the part of the landing state and a universal jurisdiction to
prosecute.[28]

To be distinguished from the above problem of the limitation of domestic criminal power in relation to foreign states is the separate issue
of the scope of a state's domestic criminal jurisdiction.[29] Certainly, it is
true that in the majority of instances a state's criminal power will be
congruently extensive with its domestic criminal jurisdiction simply because every state, as the agent responsible according to international law
for the maintenance of public order, naturally will attempt to exercise
its criminal power by means of its own courts. There exist cases, however,
in which certain persons (*ratione personae*) or certain cases (*ratione
materiae*) are exempted from the domestic criminal jurisdiction of a state
by international treaties or customary international law, although the
substantive criminal power of the state abstractly considered, *e.g.*, resulting from the territorial or active personality principles might be present.
Such a situation is presented by the diplomatic personnel of a foreign
state, their families, and their service employees who are not citizens of
the resident state. The issue of diplomatic and consular immunity has
been newly regulated by the Vienna Convention on Diplomatic Relations
of April 18, 1961,[30] and the Vienna Convention on Consular Relations of
April 24, 1963.[31]

[26] The German adoption of this convention is found in the West German 1969 BUNDES-
GESETZBLATT, pt. 2, at 121; and 1970 *Bundesgesetzblatt*, pt. 2, at 276.
[27] [1970] 20 U.S.T. 2941, T.I.A.S. No. 6768. *Cf.* Jescheck, *Die an Bord von Luftfahrzeugen
begangenen Straftaten und ihre Folgen*, DEUTSCHE BEITRÄGE ZUM VII INTERNATIONALEN
STRAFRECHTSKONGRESS *in Athen* 216 (1957).
[28] For the text of the 1970 Hague Convention, *See* 65 A.J.I.L. 440 (1971).
[29] *See, e.g.*, Jescheck, *supra* note 2, at 116; Zlataric, *supra* note 28, at 164n. 24.
[30] 500 U.N.T.S. 95.
[31] 596 U.N.T.S. 261

The same exclusion from domestic criminal jurisdiction is presented by alien heads of state, high-ranking state officials, agents of international organizations, and state representatives at international congresses and conferences. This situation acquires great practical importance in excluding from domestic criminal jurisdiction the resident armed forces of a foreign nation. For those nations within the NATO organization this issue has been regulated by article VII of the Agreement Between the Parties to the North Atlantic Treaty Regarding the Status of Their Forces of June 19, 1951, and its supplements.[32] There exist similar agreements for those nations within the Warsaw Pact. This same type of continuing limitation of domestic criminal jurisdiction may also result from a prior military occupation by a foreign state.[33]

3.3 Extradition and International Legal Assistance in Criminal Matters

The rules regarding extradition serve as a counterpart to I.C.L. in its original sense. On the one hand, I.C.L. limits the extent of the domestic criminal power in relation to foreign states, and in the last analysis is determined by the sovereign judgment of the concerned state. Extradition, on the other hand, defines that process in which the authorities of the state in which the alleged offender is residing surrender him over to the officials of another state either for the purpose of prosecution or for the enforcement of a criminal judgment.[34]

Whether or not the specific rules governing extradition are found in an international treaty, the extradition itself always is based on an international legal transaction (*völkerrechtliches Rechtsgeschäft*) rather than alone on the sovereign judgment of the state. Although currently an *obligation* of extradition is to be derived only from international treaties,[35] the right of the state to extradite the party concerned can arise only from its national law. However, the law governing extradition as found both in international treaties and domestic legal rules is still to the utmost degree formalistically and dogmatically formulated. Possessive notions of national state sovereignty still reign supreme in the law of extradition and, consequently, even today the person to be extradited frequently is viewed merely as the object of international barter.

---

[32] 1961 BUNDESGESETZBLATT, pt. 2, at 1190; the supplementary agreement with West Germany of Aug. 8, 1959, is found in 1961 BUNDESGESETZBLATT, pt. 2, at 1218.

[33] *E.g.*, in art. 3 (2) of the *Convention on the Settlement of Matters Arising out of the War and the Occupation*, May 26, 1952, German criminal jurisdiction is excluded for all acts which had not been within German criminal jurisdiction at the time the treaty became effective. 1955 BUNDESGESETZBLATT, pt. 2, at 405. *See, e.g.*, Jescheck, *supra* note 2, at 116.

[34] *See also* SCHULTZ, DAS SCHWEIZERISCHE AUSLIEFERUNGSRECHT 15 (1953).

[35] However, Hugo Grotius in 1634 already had designated extradition as an international law obligation, the violation of which constituted a *justa causa belli* against the state of refuge; *see* De jure belli ac pacis, lib. II, Cap. XXI, §4.

This approach [to the law of extradition] contradicts the slowly forming, but increasingly supranational, legal consciousness that now boldly contrasts the idea of interstate cooperation and solidarity in battling criminality to the position of those states remaining in rigid autocracy." [36]

As a result of this retrogressive state of the law in matters of extradition, the Tenth International Congress of Criminal Law of Rome in 1969, which was to further develop the foundations laid by the Freiburg, Germany, and Syrakuse, Italy, meetings,[37] formulated a series of provisions which were designed to modernize this area of the law.[38] The most important of these proposed reforms include the following:[39]

Extradition should be granted *soll zulässig sein* whether or not there exists a treaty between the countries.[40] A prerequisite condition of reciprocity should be abolished as a legal formula of too great inflexibility.[41] The requirement that the act be criminal in both states is still retained in principle, but here with the proviso that if the petitioned state's own *ordre public* is not endangered, it may disregard this prerequisite to extradition in those cases in which those particular circumstances, such as the geographical, political, or cultural conditions of the petitioning state, which are nonexistent in the petitioned state, make punishment mandatory.[42] On the contrary, however, the prerequisite that the party to be extradited be liable to prosecution for the act in both countries (*i.e.*, that prosecution

[36] "Dieser Ausgangspunkt stimmt nicht überein mit dem langsam entstehenden, über die einzelnen Staaten hinausgreifenden neuen Rechtsbewusstsein, welches den in starrer Selbstherrlichkeit verharrenden souveränen Staaten die Idee der zwischenstaatlichen Soldarität und der Zusammenarbeit, nicht zuletzt auf dem Gebiete der Bekämpfung der Kriminalität, gegenüberstellt." Schultz, *Aktuelle Probleme der Auslieferung*, 81 ZEITSCHRIFT FÜR DIE GESAMTE STRAFRECHTSWISSENSCHAFT 199 (1969). In this regard also, *see* Bassiouni, *World Public Order and Extradition: A Conceptual Evaluation*, 1970, FESTSCHRIFT FÜR GRÜTZNER, *supra* note 28, at 10.

[37] The material and resolutions of the Freiburg meeting appeared in 39 REVUE INTERNATIONALE DE DROIT PÉNAL (1968).

[38] These proposals were based upon the General Report of Hans Schultz, *Rapport Général provisoire sur la question IV pour le-Xe Congrès international de droit pénal*, which appeared in 39 REVUE INTERNATIONALE DE DROIT PÉNAL 784 (1968).

[39] *Conclusioni del X Congresso Internazionale di Diritto Penale*, Rome, Sept. 29–Oct. 5, 1969. The German text appeared in 82 ZEITSCHRIFT FÜR DIE GESAMTE STRAFRECHTSWISSENSCHAFT 243 (1969).

[40] The opposed view is found above all in the result reached in the law of the USA. *See* Bassiouni, *International Extradition, A Summary of the Contemporary American Practice*, 39 REVUE INTERNATIONALE DE DROIT PÉNAL 497 (1968), reprinted in 15 WAYNE L. REV. (1969), and *id.*, *International Extradition in American Practice and World Public Order* 36 TENN. L. REV. 1 (1969).

[41] Here the opposed view is found above all in the present law of Germany. *See* Volger, *Aktuelle Probleme der Auslieferung*, 81 ZEITSCHRIFT FÜR DIE GESAMTE STRAFRECHTSWISSENSCHAFT 165 (1969).

[42] The relevant extradition statute of Switzerland has followed this view since 1892. *See* art. 4, *Swiss Extradition Statute*. *See generally* Markees in 39 REVUE INTERNATIONALE DE DROIT PÉNAL 747 (1968).

is barred neither by amnesty nor the statute of limitation, for example)
is here relinquished insofar as the deed is not previously subject to the
criminal power of the petitioned state. The effect of the principle of nonextradition for political delicts is excluded if the relevant offense is a
crime against humanity, a war crime or any other serious violation of the
Geneva Convention. For war crimes a statute of limitation shall never
bar extradition, even if the petitioned state itself possesses criminal power
in regard to the relevant acts. However, the extradition may be refused
in situations where it is feared that the prosecution might not satisfy the
minimum standards of justice under the rule of law. Those states which
fundamentally do not extradite their own citizens (principally the continental nations) shall be bound to institute their own prosecution upon the
request of a petitioning state. Also, quite interestingly, those states (generally the nations of the Anglo-American legal world) which follow the
principle of extradition of their own citizens are likewise bound to institute their own criminal prosecution if such an extradition is barred by
the lack of reciprocity with the petitioning state. The last of these significant proposals of the 1969 International Congress of Criminal Law in
Rome regarding extradition is that the states are to be limited to a formal
examination of the presented record in determining if the prerequisites
for extradition are present; in no case is the petitioned state to carry out
its own evidentiary process to determine if a certain suspicion of guilt
required for extradition in fact is present.[43]

Regard for some aspects included in these proposals already has resulted in drafts for new statutes and in new treaties. Thus the draft for a
new German statute on extradition, in conformity with other European
laws,[44] abandons the requirement of reciprocity as a legal prerequisite
of extradition. Similarly, the principle requiring criminality of the act
in both countries finds only a limited place in this draft. The requirement
of liability to prosecution in both countries is retained only with regard
to the statute of limitation.[45] The German-French Treaty on Extradition
of November 29, 1951,[46] further mitigates the rule of nonextradition of
nationals by placing an obligation of criminal prosecution on the petitioned state. In addition to this it excludes genocide from those political
delicts for which nonextradition is the usual role. The European Conven-

---

[43] The contrary view is reached in the U.S.A. by the requirement that "probable cause"
be present before extradition will be granted. *See* Bassiouni, *supra* note 40, at 512; Wise,
id., at 530.

[44] *Cf.* Weber, *Die Zwischenstaatlichen und innerstaatlichen Voraussetzungen des Gegen-
seitigkeitsprinzips* 58 (Diss. Albert Ludwigs Univ., Freiburg, Germany, 1962).

[45] *See generally* Jescheck, *Gedanken zur Reform des deutschen Auslieferungsgesetzes*,
ETUDES EN L'HONNEUR DE JEAN GRAVEN 77 (1969).

[46] 1953 BUNDESGESETZBLATT, pt. 2 at 152; *id.* at 1251 (1959).

tion on Extradition of December 13, 1957,[47] likewise weakens the principle of reciprocity.[48] It guarantees the right of asylum in situations where reasonable grounds exist for the assumption that although the extradition request is based on a crime punishable at common law, the offender is in reality to be prosecuted for racial, religious, national or political reasons. This Extradition Convention also substitutes for the extradition of nationals the institution of criminal prosecution by the requested state's own criminal courts. Finally, the European Convention on Mutual Assistance in Criminal Matters of April 20, 1959,[49] significantly strengthens mutual judicial assistance by abandoning the reciprocity principle and limiting the grounds for refusal of assistance to political and fiscal criminal acts or reasons of *ordre public.*[50]

The cooperative work of the European nations in the area of international criminal policy has made significant progress in the last three decades. Although extradition constituted the original means of international cooperation in criminal prosecutions, and will probably remain the chief method of international criminal assistance (at least insofar as it is an issue of extradition to the country where the offense was committed[51]), other new types of legal assistance between states, which supplement and often replace extradition, have been developed in the period following World War II. These new types of international assistance include the assumption of a criminal proceeding pending in a foreign country, the execution of foreign criminal judgments, and the supervision of offenders who have been conditionally sentenced abroad.[52]

The acceptance of a criminal prosecution pending in a foreign state was first developed in regard to road traffic offenses because here the practical necessity for new measures was obvious.[53] The European Convention on

[47] 1964 BUNDESGESETZBLATT, pt. 2, at 1371. *Cf.* Franck, *Extradition en droit pénal européen,* 1970 FESTSCHRIFT FÜR H. GRÜTZNER, *supra* note 28, at 54.

[48] *Cf.* Grützner, *Aktuelle Probleme der Auslieferung,* 81 ZEITSCHRIFT FÜR DIE GESAMTE STRAFRECHTSWISSENSCHAFT 120 (1969).

[49] 1965 BUNDESGESETZBLATT, pt. 2 at 1386.

[50] *Cf.* Mueller, *International Judicial Assistance in Criminal Matters,* in MUELLER-WISE, INTERNATIONAL CRIMINAL LAW 410 (1965).

[51] *Cf.* Schultz, *Das Ende der Auslieferung?* 1970 FESTSCHRIFT FÜR H. GRÜTZNER 146.

[56] *See generally* Grützner, *Die Zwischenstaatliche Anerkennung Europäischer Strafurteile,* 1970 FESTSCHRIFT FÜR R. HONIG 70; Vogler *Zur Tätigkeit des Europarats auf dem Gebiet des Strafrechts,* 79 ZEITSCHRIFT FÜR DIE GESAMTE STRAFRECHTSWISSENSCHAFT 376 (1967). Regarding art. 101 of the 1958 *Swiss Federal Statute* on road traffic as a precursor of the assumption of a prosecution within domestic law, *see* Schultz, *Neue Entwicklungen im sogenannten internationalen Strafrecht,* 1963 FESTSCHRIFT FÜR H. VON WEBER 314. Regarding a Scandinavian precursor to such assumption of a foreign criminal prosecution, *see* Simson, *Das Nordische Strafvollstreckungsgesetz Schwedens,* 77 ZEITSCHRIFT FÜR DIE GESAMTE STRAFRECHTSWISSENSCHAFT 167 (1965).

[53] The statistics for Austria for the year of 1963 indicate that in the peak vacation months in the Tirol area, more than 50 per cent of all automobiles involved in accidents

the Punishment of Road Traffic Offences,[54] which was signed on November 30, 1964, but up to now ratified only by France, established a special criminal power conforming to the principle of substituted administration of criminal justice, and further gives rise to an obligation on the part of the petitioned state to accept criminal prosecution when properly requested to do so by another party to the convention.[55] The second new type of international assistance in criminal matters, which correlates with this acceptance of a prosecution pending in a foreign country, is the domestic execution of foreign criminal judgments. This execution of a foreign criminal verdict in fact may have a much greater long-range impact than the acceptance of a pending foreign criminal proceeding, since the significance of the latter in practice will be limited by the principle requiring in-court oral presentation of evidence. The execution of foreign criminal judgments by the state of the offender's domicile, when combined with the extradition of an accused for prosecution by the nation where the alleged offense occurred, constitutes the paragon of a rational system for combating crime at the international level.

It is interesting to note that the preliminary stage in the development of a system of domestic execution of foreign judgments was already present in the 1964 European Convention on Road Traffic Offences. According to this treaty, in the case of a road traffic offense the state of the violation cannot only request that the state of the offender's residence institute its own criminal prosecution, it can also request the execution there of its own criminal judgment or the imposition there of an administrative fine. The culmination of this development is presented by the European Convention on the International Validity of Criminal Judgments, which was signed during the conference of European ministers of justice at the Hague on May 28, 1970.[56] This Convention is in part based on the preparatory work of the Ninth International Congress of Criminal Law, which met at the Hague in 1964, and which itself used the 1962 Freiburg, Ger-

---

were foreign. These figures have since then probably become too conservative. *Cf.* Linke, *Ein Europäisches Abkommen über die Bestrafung von Verkehrsdelikten,* 1965 ZEITSCHRIFT FÜR VERKEHRSRECHT 29.

[54] Europ. T. S. No. 52. *See also, Rapport explicatif sur la Convention, Conseil de l'Europe,* Strasbourg, 1970.

[55] *See supra,* text at notes 4–7. *See generally* K. ZIMMERLI, DAS EUROPÄISCHE ÜBEREINKOMMEN ÜBER DIE VERFOLGUNG VON ZUWIDERHANDLUNGEN IM STRASSENVERKEHR 31 (1969). This convention has particularly great importance for Germany, because acts which violate the convention now are equated to criminal acts (beforehand they were mere misdemeanors, which now are no longer criminal).

[56] *See generally* Grützner, *Die Zwischenstaatliche Anerkennung Europäischer Strafurteile,* 1969 NEUE JURISTISCHE WOCHENSCHRIFT 345; Jescheck, *Die Vollstreckung ausländischer Strafurteile in der Bundesrepublik Deutschland,* 1963 FESTSCHRIFT FÜR H. VON WEBER 325.

many, Symposium as a foundation.[57] The possibility for the execution of a foreign criminal judgment exists in regard to all foreign penal sentences, both those imposing measures of imprisonment, monetary fine, or confiscation and even those decreeing a deprivation of civil rights or authority. It is important to note that also in regard to this issue there must exist a rational point of relation between the accused and the state of attempted execution. Such a sufficient point of relation should clearly evidence the appropriateness of execution in the requested state. This would be shown, for example, if the offender resided there or if other general conditions for a more efficient social rehabilitation existed in the state which is petitioned for execution of the foreign judgment.

The acceptance of a pending foreign criminal prosecution and the execution of foreign criminal judgments are now supplanted by a third new type of international mutual assistance in criminal proceedings. Pursuant to the European Convention on the Supervision of Conditionally Convicted and Conditionally Released Offenders of November 30, 1964,[58] a state which has imposed a conditional sentence (*e.g.,* a suspended sentence, a warning sentence, a conditioned release or probation, or a suspension of prosecution subject to a condition) can ask the state of residence to undertake the supervision of the person conditionally released or sentenced. If the conditioned sentence then becomes actively enforceable, the sentencing state can request the state of residence to enforce the judgment. Finally, the state which has imposed the sentence may even transfer over to the state of residence the complete jurisdiction of the matter so that this state then has full authority and responsibility for all further proceedings. Such a transfer results in the complete integration of the entire relationship between the prosecution and the person sentenced into the legal system of another state in order to better promote the social rehabilitation of the offender.

3.4. Criminal Provisions for the Protection of International Peace, Human Rights, and other Legally Protected Interests of the Community of Nations

In that area of I.C.L. involving the crucial issues of world peace, international security, human rights, and other supranational legally protected

---

[57] *Cf. Material from the Freiburg Symposium of 1962,* in 34 Revue internationale de droit pénal (1963); the general report to the Hague Congress from Jescheck, *Les Effets internationaux des jugements pénaux,* in ix⁰ Congrès International de droit Pénal, La Hague (1964); the Resolutions of this Congress, *id.* at 484 (in English and French); and in 77 Zeitschrift für die gesamte Strafrechtswissenschaft 685 (1965) (in German).

[58] Europ. T. S. No. 51. *Cf.* Rapport explicatif sur la convention, Conseil de l'Europe, Strasbourg (1970).

interests, the judgments of Nuremberg and Tokyo remain of central importance.

In the whole of I.C.L., the criminal provisions for the protection of peace among nations have the greatest political significance. These provisions were as absolute res nova first contained in the Statutes for the International Military Tribunals of Nuremberg and Tokyo, and as such constituted the legal basis for the trial of numerous German and Japanese World War II leaders, who were sentenced in 1946 and 1948 for crimes against peace.[59] In addition, the Control Council Law Number 10 of December 20, 1945,[60] enacted a similar criminal provision for crimes against peace, which was frequently applied by the English, French, and American courts of the Occupying Powers in trials of German war criminals during the years of 1946–1949. Nonetheless, the international law validity of the principles on which the individual's criminal responsibility for aggressive war is based remains doubtful. It is true that in its Resolution of December 11, 1946, the General Assembly of the United Nations affirmed the principles and decisions of the Nuremberg statute and judgment.[61] However, in this regard one must recognize that the General Assembly possesses no inherent lawmaking authority and its resolutions constitute proof of the existence of customary international law, or a general legal principle recognized by all civilized nations, only if there also exist other independent criteria which support the conclusion that an international consensus has developed. However, *in regard to crimes against peace it is precisely such other independent criteria indicating an international recognition of the principle which do not yet exist.* Admittedly, the concept of crime against peace was adopted in the International Law Commission's 1954 Draft Code of Offences Against the Peace and Security of Mankind, but from that time to the present the authoritative committees of the United Nations have been unable to agree on this Draft Code and have found themselves particularly divided in regard to the preliminary issue of defining in an objective way the content of "aggression."[62] Although Russia in February of 1969 proposed a new definition of aggression to the Geneva special committee (it would have included *inter*

---

[59] *Cf.* Jescheck Die Verantwortlichkeit der Staatsorgane nach Völkerstrafrecht 346 (1952); Woetzel, The Nuremberg Trials in International Law 122 (1960).

[60] *Kontrollrats-Amtsblatt,* no. 3, at 50 (Jan. 31, 1945).

[61] In regard to the different interpretations of this Resolution, see Jescheck, *Etat actuel et perspective d'avenir des projets dans le domaine du droit international-penal,* 1964 Revue internationale de droit pénal, *supra* note 37, at 92.

[62] *Cf.* Triffterer, Dogmatische Untersuchungen zur Entwicklung des materiellen Völkerstrafrechts seit Nürnberg 76 (1966); Jescheck, *Die Entwicklung des Völkerstrafrechts nach Nürnberg,* 72 Schweizerische Zeitschrift für Strafrecht 224 (1957); Röling, *The Question of Defining Aggression,* 1958 Symbolae Verzijl 314, Bassiouni, *infra* Part II, Chapter I, Section 1.

alia, "*l'invasion ou l'attaque, par les forces armées d'un Etat, du territoire d'un autre Etat.*"), an objective observer must grant in light of the invasion of Czechoslovakia by troops of the Warsaw Pact on July 21, 1968, that the question from Stefan Glaser regarding this proposal is not unfair: "*Ce projet n'est-il qu'un acte du cynisme habituel ou bien une manifestation du repentir?*"[63]

The reality of the presently reigning disagreement in regard to the concept of aggression is well demonstrated by the opinion of a leading East German international law scholar, who judges the offensive war of the USSR against Finland in the winter of 1939 to be the single nonaggressive war of the World War II period, notwithstanding the fact that the USSR was expelled from the League of Nations for just this action.[64] Exactly how little Glaser's own formulation of aggression ("*l'agression consiste dans tout recours à la force dans un but illégal*"[65]) would promote agreement on this issue becomes clear if one attempts to apply it consistently to the war situation in the Middle East. In these circumstances the newly formulated criminal provisions regarding betrayal of peace in Sections 80 and 80a of the German Criminal Code must be viewed with the utmost skepticism in light of the prohibition of vagueness in article 103 (2) of the German Basic Law.[66]

Abstractly considered, the recent history of individual culpability for war crimes is the same as that of crimes against the peace. All the same, however, there exists the important difference that the criminal culpability for war crimes corresponds to ancient customary international law rules,[67] while the individual's criminal culpability for a war of aggression was newly inaugurated in 1945.[68] As a result of this correspondence to customary international law, definitions of *infractions graves,* which clearly stated the minimum standards for war crimes, were quickly accomplished in the four Geneva Conventions of August 12, 1949.[69] The *infractions graves* were then supplemented by the criminal responsibility of the individual for acts violative of the *Convention pour la protection des biens culturels en cas de conflit armée* of May 14, 1954.[70] To varying extents

[63] Glaser, *supra* note 1, at 63 n.8.

[64] *See* STEINIGER, I DER NÜRNBURGER PROZESS 17 (1957). *See also* the 1950 East German Statute for protection of peace, the preamble of which determines a priori that only the enemy can be considered as the aggressor. East German 1950 GESETZBLATT 1199.

[65] Glaser, *supra* note 1, at 65.

[66] The conclusion of Schroeder, *Der Schutz des äusseren Friedens im Strafrecht,* 1969 JURISTENZEITUNG 47, seems correct in this regard.

[67] *Cf.* DAHM, III VÖLKERRECHT 296 (1961).

[68] *Cf.* Wehberg, *Die völkerrechtliche Verantwortlichkeit von Individuen wegen Friedensbruchs im Zeitalter des Völkerbundes,* 1953 FESTSCHRIFT FÜR R. LAUN 394.

[69] *Cf.* Jescheck, *Die Entwicklung des Völkerstrafrechts nach Nürnberg, supra* note 62, at 227; *see also* Pictet, *Commentary on the Geneva Conventions* (ICRC 1952–1960).

[70] Printed in Glaser, *supra* note 1, at 505.

the states have also performed their obligation to enact the necessary penal provisions for sanctioning these defined war crimes.[71] The required provisions for supplementing the German criminal law in this area were prepared by a commission in 1966, but have not yet been legislatively enacted. The *Convention sur l'imprescriptibilité des crimes de guèrre et des crimes contre l'humanité*,[72] which the United Nations General Assembly approved on November 26, 1968, (by a majority of those nations voting, but against the votes or with the abstention of nearly all the Western states), provides for the retroactive, absolute suspension of all statutes of limitation for war crimes and crimes against humanity. Such a retroactive effect of the imposition of criminal penalties cannot be reconciled with the ex post facto principle of the rule of law in criminal matters.[73]

In its origins the concept of crimes against humanity shared the fate of crimes against the peace. The crucial difference which here existed was that those acts which were culpable as crimes against humanity were in large part already covered by the existing criminal law. However, this notion of an offense violating the minimum standards of human social existence added a new psychological and criminal law point of view.[74] A parallel to the development of positive law rules governing war crimes has occurred regarding the concept of crimes against humanity in the 1948 Convention on the Prevention and Punishment of the Crime of Genocide,[75] which served in several nations as the foundation for positive criminal law provisions penalizing the crime of genocide.[76] How little this Convention itself really has advanced I.C.L. was assessed in the now well-known sentence of Schwarzenberger that "The Genocide Convention is unnecessary when applicable and inapplicable when necessary."[77]

Substantively, however, the Convention is weakest in its failure to provide to political groups the essential protection of provisions outlawing, for example, political kidnaping and political denunciation, as is done,

----

[71] *Cf.* "Respect des Conventions de Genève, Mesures prisées pour réprimer les violations," *Rapport présenté par le Comité international de la Croix-Rouge à la XXᵉ Conférence internationale de la Croix-Rouge* (Genève 1965).

[72] Printed in Glaser, *supra* note 1 at 399.

[73] *See generally* Glaser, *supra* note 1, at 113, who also discusses in detail the changes in national laws, but does not here take a position in regard to the retroactive effect of the statute of limitations. *See also,* Graven, *Les crimes contre l'humanité peuvent-ils bénéficier de la prescription?* 81 REVUE PÉNALE SUISSE 113 (1965); Jescheck, *Le projet de convention internationale sur l'imprescriptibilité des crimes de guerre et des crimes contre l'humanité,* 37 REVUE INTERNATIONALE DE DROIT PÉNAL 513 (1966) (in addition to the other articles appearing in the latter publication).

[74] Graven, *Les crimes contre l'humanité,* 76 *Recueil des Cours (pt. 1)* 433 (1950).

[75] *Supra* note 20.

[76] *See, e.g.,* § 220a of the WEST GERMAN CRIMINAL CODE.

[77] SCHWARZENBERGER, I INTERNATIONAL LAW 143 (3rd ed. 1957).

for example, in articles 234 and 241 of the West German Criminal Code. In this connection should also be mentioned the *Convention sur l'élimination de toutes les formes de discrimination raciale,* of December 21, 1965,[78] which like the Geneva Conventions and the Genocide Convention establishes a duty of prosecution which is restricted above all by the conditional *si les circonstances l'exigent* formulation.

The legal development which has occurred as a consequence of the signing of the European Convention for the Protection of Human Rights and Fundamental Freedoms of November 4, 1950,[79] has in fact been more significant than that which followed the original definition of crimes against humanity in the Nuremberg Statute. While in the concept of crimes against humanity a criminal law protection of the minimum standards of human social existence was attempted, the European Convention for the Protection of Human Rights and Fundamental Freedoms seeks to insure, by using the means of a legally binding and directly applicable international treaty, those most important fundamental rights which have been developed in Europe as the essential element of a democratic state under the rule of law. The effects of this treaty on the political and legal formation of the member-states are quite important, not least in regard to the consequences for their criminal lay systems.[80] For example, the permission of euthanasia by the criminal law system of a member state would constitute a violation of the right to life protected in article 2 of the Convention. Moreover, according to one widely held opinion, article 2 (2a) of the Convention contracts even the right of self-defense in the legislation of the member states.[81] Article 3, which is, above all, important in regard to the enforcement of criminal verdicts, forbids inhuman or degrading punishments and all similar cruel treatment of accused or convicted individuals. Article 7 of the Convention insures the principle of *nulla poena sine lege,* but unfortunately is weakened by an acceptance in section 2 of the Nuremberg clause whereby the criminality of the act at the time of its commission "according to general principles of law recognized by the civilized nations of the world" shall be sufficient. The effect of this Convention is even greater on the law of criminal procedure. For example, in article 3 one finds a prohibition of torture, which

---

[78] *See* G.A. Res. 2106A (XX), 20 U.N. GAOR Supp. 14, at 47 (1966); 660 U.N.T.S. 195. *See also* Reisman, *Responses to Crimes of Discrimination and Genocide,* 1 Denver J. Int'l L. & Policy 29 (1971).

[79] 213 U.N.T.S. 221.

[80] *See generally* Jescheck, *L'influence du droit européen sur dévelopment du droit-pénal allemand,* 1971 Mélanges en l'Honneur de Jean Constant (to appear); Velu, *Le role du Conseil de l'Europe dans l'élaboration* du droit pénal européen, 1969 Journal des Tribunaux 721.

[81] On this issue, *see generally* Jescheck, *supra* note 2, at 232.

then in turn reappears in article 104 (1), second sentence of West Germany's *Basic Law.* The provisions of article 5 of this Convention on pre-trial detention have had immense practical significance and have now led to an extensive line of European case law.[82] Finally, the minimum conditions for a European "fair trial" are laid down in the forceful formulation of article 6 of the Convention.

Also to be considered within this broad category of criminal law rules for the maintenance of world peace and those criminal provisions relating to acts against foreign nations, which have as their object not only the protection of the national interests of the individual states as such, but in addition are resigned to preserve the foundation for a common co-existence of all mankind within a community of nations.[83] These rules are required by an international legal order because acts of aggression against foreign heads of state, members of foreign governments or diplomats, who are present in a state in their official capacity, do not merely disturb the good foreign relations of that particular state but also directly violate existing rules of international law. In another aspect, however, one should note that the criminality of those offenses which formerly were characterized in the German criminal law as acts of high treason against a foreign nation is in today's world of fundamental political diversity hardly conceivable.[84] The right of asylum, as guaranteed in article 16 (2), second sentence of the German *Basic Law,* when combined with the principle of nonextradition for political delicts, serves the cause of international peace much better than any criminal rule which carries along with it the danger of interference in the domestic political affairs of a foreign state. Criminal law safeguards against gross insults and assaults on the life and limb of all representatives of foreign nations, in combination with protection against damage or abuse of the publicly displayed flags or other symbols of national sovereignty, constitute the minimum standard of domestic criminal law protection of diplomatic intercourse required by international law.[85] Unfortunately, the corresponding protection for supranational organizations such as the United Nations, the European Community Organizations, the International Red Cross, and the International Labor Organization remains to be accomplished. The first step

[82] *See generally* Guradze, *Die Angemessenheit der Dauer der Untersuchungshaft nach Art. 5 Abs. 3 der Europäischen Menschenrechtskonvention,* 1968 NEUE JURISTISCHE WOCHENSCHIFT.

[83] *See* Schönke-Schröder, *Strafgesetzbuch,* introductory note to § 102 of the GERMAN CRIMINAL CODE (15th ed. 1970); Jescheck, *Straftaten gegen das Ausland,* 1957 FESTSCHRIFT FÜR TH. RITTLER 277. An even stronger presentation of this view is found in Dreher, *Das dritte Strafrechtsänderungsgesetz,* 1953 JURISTENZEITUNG 426.

[84] Such criminal law provisions still exist in a few national criminal law systems. *See, e.g.,* § 66 of the AUSTRIAN CRIMINAL CODE; § 153 of the GREEK CRIMINAL CODE.

[85] Such protection is found, for example, in the GERMAN CRIMINAL CODE §§ 102–104.

toward this goal was taken by Germany in its 1957 statute amending the German Criminal Code.[86] This statute extended the wide-reaching protection of many of the German criminal law provisions to the NATO powers as well as their troops stationed in Germany.[87]

Other legally protected interests of the international community of nations have been expressly recognized as such in international treaties, but have enjoyed quite different degrees of protection by I.C.L. The universality principle [88] has always been valid in regard to piracy, principally in order to make possible its prosecution by any state whatever. A duty of prosecution arising from international law, however, is a very recent phenomenon. Article 18 of the Harvard Research Draft·Convention on Piracy of 1932, [89] for example, contained only the obligation of the parties "to make every expedient use of the powers to prevent piracy," while, on the other hand, the 1958 Convention on the High Seas extends the cooperative obligations of the parties to the *"repression de la piraterie en haute mer."*[90]

Unfortunately, as a result of a too narrow definition of piracy in article five, the now important hijacking of airplanes is not covered. [91] In the meantime the International Civil Aviation Organization is in the process of preparing a specific international convention for the combatting of such air hijackings. This convention will impose a duty of prosecution on the signatory states and will further establish new rules for I.C.L.

Monetary protection presently is established by the Convention for the Suppression of Counterfeiting Currency of April 4, 1929, [92] which also imposes a duty of prosecution and which provides for the identical treatment of both foreign and domestic money. [93] In addition to classifying monetary counterfeiting in article 9 as an offense providing cause for extradition, this Convention further provides for application of the active

[86] Art. 7, 4. STRAFRECHTSÄNDERUNGSGESETZES (July 11, 1957).

[87] *Cf.* Jescheck, *supra* note 2, at 125. The 1962 draft for a new German Criminal Code, contained in §§ 480 *et. seq.*, provisions which provided that all such transnational organizations were to be given the same protection as the property and representative of a foreign state. Further, the criminal law protection of all such foreign states, transnational organizations, their properties and representatives was then uniformly and generally provided in a single section of the Code governing "criminal acts against the international community."

[88] *See* text, *supra* at notes 21–23.

[89] 26 A.J.I.L. 754 (Supp. 1932).

[90] Glaser, *supra* note 1, at 155, properly laments the fact that a robbery "on the high seas," which in § 250(3), of the present GERMAN CRIMINAL CODE is classified as aggravated robbery, in § 246 of the 1962 Draft for a new criminal code is no longer treated as an example of such an aggravated crime of robbery.

[91] *See also* Glaser, *supra* note 1, at 159.

[92] German 1933 REICHSGESETZBLATT, pt. 2 II, at 913.

[93] Accordingly, § 146 of the GERMAN CRIMINAL CODE makes foreign and domestic money identical in determining the crime of counterfeiting.

personality principle in those lands which refuse extradition of their own citizens. The Convention refuses to stipulate a general application of the universality principle, in articles 9 and 17, probably in consideration of the contrary view of the states of the Anglo-American legal world. [94] To a similar extent the Convention for the Suppression of the Traffic in Persons and of the Exploitation of the Prostitution of Others of December 2, 1949, [95] contains wide-reaching duties of prosecution against this kind of dealings; and like the Convention on counterfeiting, declares such criminal offenses to provide cause for extradition. This Convention also follows the same principle regulating the international criminal power of the signatory states as does the counterfeiting Convention. The Single Convention on Narcotic Drugs of March 30, 1961, [96] likewise creates extensive duties of criminal prosecution for the signing states. These duties to prosecute encompass even an express requirement of imprisonment or functionally equivalent punishment for serious violations of the relevant provisions. Although the the formulation of rules governing their own provisions of international criminal power is in principle left to the states, this Convention requires that in instances of serious violation each state must exercise its international criminal power according to the principle of substituted administration of criminal justice.

Even though this Convention does not expressly state that narcotic drug law violations constitute cause for extradition, extradition is recommended in such instances. Also included in this general category of those offenses regulated by treaty which are injurious to the common cultural interests of mankind are dealings in obscene publications. The International Convention for the Suppression of the Circulation of and Traffic in Obscene Publications of September 12, 1923, [97] from which Denmark has recently given notice of withdrawal, requires the signatory states to prosecute acts violative of its provisions, based on application of the territorial principle. This Convention also refers to prosecution based on the active-personality principle, but only to the extent of national legislative power.

3.5. The Criminal Law of the European Communities

The formation of the European Communities in 1951 has in the past two decades given rise to new I.C.L. problems. As the formative treaties themselves do not contain criminal provisions of their own, three different procedures are to be considered as means for the protection of the communities and for the enforcement of decisions of their authorities: (1) the

---

[94] *Cf. contra* Glaser, *supra* note 1, at 165, and Bassiouni and George *supra* note 14.
[95] *Supra* note 23, printed in Glaser, *supra* note 1, at 436.
[96] *Supra* note 22.
[97] *Supra* note 22.

community law can refer to the national legal rules of the member states; (2) the authorities of the communities themselves can impose admini- strative fines for violations of the treaty provisions, and (3) the authori- tative organs of the communities can oblige the member states to enact sanctioning provisions. [98]

A renvoi to the national law of the member states is contained in article 27 of the Statute of the Court of Justice of the Economic Com- munity (E.E.C.) and the European Atomic Community (Euratom) of March 25, 1957. [99] According to this article, each member state "*regarde toute violation de serments de témois et des experts comme le délit correspondant commis devant un tribunal national statuant en matière civile.*" This provision must be considered to be a *directly* applicable law of the member states. [100] This means that in their own right the national criminal law provisions governing perjury become applicable to violations of the statute, and this without regard to the nationality of the actor or to the situs of the act within the EWG area (this means, for example, that the perjury could have occurred at the location of the Court in Luxem- bourg or in any of the other six member states). By virtue of this direct application, article 27 at the same time replaces the domestic law provisions in regard to I.C.L. by a "territorial principle extended to the community as a whole."[101] This is likewise valid for article 194 of the Euratom Treaty. According to section 1 of this Treaty, both employees and private persons are bound to a duty of nondisclosure if they have received information which had been classified as secret by an organ of the Euratom or one of the member states. According to article 194(2), the member states are to treat any violation of this nondisclosure duty established in section 1 as a breach of their own relevant statute prohibiting disclosure of classi- fied material, and apply the criminal sanction of that law (*i.e.,* surrender of state secrets or punishment for breach of secrecy in economic matters) directly to the offender, [102] regardless of his nationality or the place where

---

[98] *Cf.* Jescheck, *Lo stato attuale del diritto penale europeo,* PROSPETTIVE PER UN DIRITTO PENALE EUROPEO 327, 339 (1968).

[99] 1957 BUNDESGESETZBLATT, pt. 2, at 1166, 1194.

[100] The same result was reached in the corresponding application of art. 194 of the treaty establishing the European Atomic Community by the German Supreme Court. See *Entscheidungen des Bundesgerichtshofs in Strafsachen* 17, 121. The treaty is found in 1957 BUNDESGESETZBLATT, pt. 2, at 1014.

[101] *See* Johannes, *Das Strafrecht im Bereich der Europäischen Gemeinschaften,* 1968 EUROPARECHT 71.

[102] Regarding the direct applicability of this provision, see *Entscheidungen des Bundesgerichtshofs in Strafsachen* 17, 121. As a result of the substantive content of the con- cept of classified material according to German law, several very difficult issues in German law result from this article of the Convention. *See generally* Johannes, *supra* note 101, at 80; PABSCH, DER STRAFRECHTLICHE SCHUTZ DER ÜBERSTAATLICHEN HOHEITSGEWALT 153 (1965).

the disclosure occurred. These provisions of article 194 of the Euratom Treaty also create in this manner a common protection principle for the entire community.

A somewhat differently formulated renvoi to the national law rule is represented by article 28 (4) of the Statute of the Court of Justice of the European Coal and Steel Community of April 18, 1951. [103] According to this provision, the Judge of the Court of Justice, in any situation involving the perjury before him of either a witness or expert, can request the Ministry of Justice of the nation of the witnesses' or expert's citizenship to impose the sanction which that national law provides for the offense.[104] Article 28(4) thus is based on the active personality principle and consequently limits the renvoi to that national law rule of the actor's nationality. This method of renvoi contains the serious gap which arises if the witness or expert is not a citizen of any of the member states.[105]

A third type of renvoi is present in article 5 of Regulation 28 of the E.E.C. Council, which involves the performance of a survey of wages. [106] In regard to the issue of criminal sanctions, this provision does look to the corresponding national law rule of the member state, but does not contain its own definitional rule determining its scope of application. This means the renvoi to national law is total, *i.e.*, also includes the national law rule in regard to I.C.L. This complete renvoi leads to results which differ to the same degree as these national law rules on the limitation of application.

The most efficient means for the accomplishment of the political and economic goals established by the organs of the European Communities is the authorities' own power of sanction. Precisely such a power of sanction is granted to the high authority in numerous articles of the E.C.S.C. Treaty providing for the imposition of administrative fines. [107] This power was more sparingly used in the E.E.C. Treaty, which contains an unambiguous grant of this power to levying fines only in article 87(2)(a), which concurs the sanction for violation of article 87(1) (prohibition of a restraint on trade) and article 86 (prohibition of an abuse of a dominant market position). This article constitutes the enabling authority for article

---

[103] 1951 BUNDESGESETZBLATT, pt. 2, at 1454.

[104] The view of Nehring, STRAFNORMEN IM ATOMENERGIERECHT 169 (1965), that this provision is not directly applicable seems wrong.

[105] *Cf.* Johannes, *supra* note 101, at 98.

[106] 1962 AMTSBLATT DER EUROPÄISCHEN GEMEINSCHAFTEN 1277. The objections of Everling, *Europäisches Gemeinschaftsrecht und nationales Recht,* 1967 NEUE JURISTISCHE WOCHENSCHAFT 470 n. 59, to the permissibility of this type of renvoi are not well founded in view of the precedence of the community law.

[107] *See, e.g.,* art. 47(3); 54(6); 58(4); 59(7); 64(6); 66(7); & Art. 68(6). *See generally* Jescheck, *Die Strafgewalt internationaler Gemeinschaften,* 65 ZEITSCHRIFT FÜR DIE GESAMTE STRAFRECHTSWISSENSCHAFT 502 (1953).

15 of Regulation 17 of the E.E.C. Council of February 6, 1962, [108] which provides for fines of up to one million monetary units of account for violations of these provisions of European cartel law. On the basis of article 87 of the E.E.C. Treaty and this Regulation of the E.E.C. Council, the Commission in its decision of July 16, 1969, levied significant fines against six members of an international quinine cartel. [109] The appeals of three of these firms from this decision were denied by the Court of Justice of the European Communities in a decision of July 15, 1970. These fines, according to article 15(2), final sentence of Regulation 17, are not of a criminal nature. The Court in this decision clearly distinguished sanctioning fines, like those levied by the Commission against the six quinine-cartel members, from mere monetary forfeits by describing the purpose of such sanctioning fines as "the prosecution of wrongful acts as well as the prevention of their repetition." [110] Because there was no mention in Regulation 17 of an applicable statute of limitations, the Court felt it lacked the authority to decide the issue regarding the period of limitation for violations of the ordinance. [111] This aspect of the decision is disappointing from a legal point of view because in earlier cases the Court had not felt so restrained in providing solutions for recognized gaps in the community law from its own inherent completeness of judicial power. [112] In this case, however, the Court refused to consider the issue, which had been raised in the challenged decision, of whether or not a general period of limitation for economic offenses could be derived from the legal systems of the member states. [113] Finally, a separate authority for the levying of administrative fines is also granted by articles 17 and 18 of Regulation 11 of the Council, [114] which is based on article 79(3), second sentence of the E.E.C. Treaty eliminating discrimination in the transport industry.

[108] 1962. AMTSBLATT DER EUROPÄISCHEN GEMEINSCHAFTEN 204.

[109] The decision is printed in 1969 AMTSBLATT DER EUROPÄISCHEN GEMEINSCHAFTEN, No. L 192, at 5.

[110] To the same effect, see the decision of the Court of Dec. 10, 1957, Rs 8/56, in DÖLLE-ZWEIGERT, RECHTSPRECHUNGSSAMMLUNG ZUM EUROPARECHT § 52f(1) (1966). This distinction naturally calls to mind the difference familiar to German law between crimes (*Straftaten*) and misdemeanors (*Ordnungswidrigkeiten*).

[111] *Accord,* Gleib and Kleinmann, *Keine Verjährung von Ordnungswidrigkeiten im europäischen Kartellrecht,* 1967 NEUE JURISTISCHE WOCHENSCHRIFT 2097.

[112] *Cf.* Judgment of the Court of July 12, 1957. Rs 7/56, 3–7/57, in Dölle-Zweigert, *supra* note 110, at § 1(1); *Entscheidung des Europäischen Gerichtshofs,* 1967 NEUE JURISTISCHEN WOCHENSCHRIFT 1197.

[113] *E.g.,* in German law there exists a 3 to 30 years' period of limitation for violations of §§ 38 & 39 of the law of Jan. 3, 1966, prohibiting restraints of competition. See art. 27(2) (1), *Gesetz über Ordnungswidrigkeiten* of May 24, 1968. Attorney General Gand's view was that the establishment of the limitation as such is a general legal principle; but in relation to the particular conditions of the community he found 5 years as just, a view which is extremely persuasive.

[114] 1960 AMTSBLATT DER EUROPÄISCHEN GEMEINSCHAFTEN 1121.

A final example of the means by which communitywide order is to be established is presented by the power of the Community Organs to place a duty by means of a directive or regulation directly on the member states to enact appropriate criminal provisions.[115] Since such criminal provisions must remain national law, the rules of the respective state's own I.C.L. validly apply to them. These latter rules must be so formulated, however, that they permit prosecution of all violations of the criminal provisions, regardless of the actor's nationality or the state in which the offense was committed. This obligation of the member states to enact appropriate national criminal laws results from the general duty in article 5 of the E.E.C. treaty to further the goals of the community. This means, for example, that the territoriality principle of the German statute of 1968 on offenses punishable by administrative fine (*Ordnungswidrigkeiten*) ought to be modified to further the purpose of the community, *i.e.*, prosecution should here be based on a community-wide territorial principle.[116]

3.6. International Criminal Jurisdiction

The conclusion to a development of I.C.L. as well as its crowning achievement would be the establishment of an international criminal jurisdiction. Such jurisdiction could be vested in an institution having a genuine supranational criminal power, or it could effectively be accomplished by means of an international body having control over the exercise by the individual states of their own criminal power.

The concept of an international criminal court having its own supranational criminal power goes back to the era of the League of Nations, a time of quite naive faith in the omnipotence of the force of law and effusive enthusiasm regarding magnificent international projects. During this period it was expected that the establishment of an international court would exert a decisive influence on the maintenance of peace and security in the world.[117] A clear expression of this belief is found in the unratified *Convention de Genève pour la création d'une Cour pénale internationale* of November 16, 1937,[118] in which the creation of an international criminal court for sentencing acts of terrorism was planned.[119]

In the period following the Nuremberg judgment, Professor Donnedieu deVabres, himself a member of the Nuremberg Tribunal and obviously sharing the doubts with respect to the ad hoc establishment of this tribunal, accordingly advocated the creation of a permanent international

---

[115] *Cf.* Johannes, EUROPARECHT 108 (1968).

[116] *Id.* at 124.

[117] The historical presentation is found in *Historical Survey of the Question of International Criminal Jurisdiction*, U.N. Doc. A/CN. 4/7.

[118] Printed in Glaser, *supra* note 1, at 241.

[119] *Cf.* Jescheck, *supra* note 59, at 117.

criminal court with its own criminal power. [120] Originally the prospects for such a court were propitious, and in 1950 the International Law Commission came out in support for such an institution. [121] Two special committees of the U.N. General Assembly in 1951 and 1953 formulated a basic statute for such a court [122]: a statute, however, which in light of the political nature of international law crimes would *ab initio* destine the court to paralysis through its two conditions precedent to exercise of the court's criminal jurisdiction. [123] According to this statute both the state of the accused's nationality and the state in which the alleged crime occurred would have to transfer ad hoc their criminal power to the international court. Although it is true that in spite of the promise of future "equality of treatment," [124] which was given at the time of the Nuremberg trials, there has been no prosecution of subsequently committed aggressive war, war crimes, or crimes against humanity; it can properly be assumed that these crimes also would never have been prosecuted by the international court because the relevant states would not have been prepared to cede their own criminal power in regard to such acts to an international court. The transfer by the interested states of their own criminal power to the international court is a totally ineffective replacement in today's politically tense and strained world for the court's own inherent criminal power. The inherent criminal power of an international court presupposes, however, a supranational integration of sovereignty presently possessed by the individual states—exactly, in other words, what in regard to crucial issues of international policies currently does not exist. But that presently the vesting of criminal power in the hands of international authorities is not totally utopian is demonstrated by the preliminary stage in this development which the decisions in regard to administrative fines of the E.E.C. Commission and the Court of Justice of the European Communities represent. [125]

The first example of the method by which an *international authority*

[120] *Cf.* U.N. Doc. A/AC. 10/21 (May 5, 1947).

[121] *Cf. Report of the International Law Commission* (2d Sess., 1950), in 44 A.J.I.L. 134 (Supp. 1950). Also noteworthy in this regard is the positive view of Oppenheim-Lauterpacht, II INTERNATIONAL LAW 586 (7th ed. 1952).

[122] Printed in Glaser, *supra* note 1, at 567; *cf.* CARJEU, PROJET D'UNE JURIDICTION PÉNAL INTERNATIONALE (1953); REEDER, THE ESTABLISHMENT OF AN INTERNATIONAL CRIMINAL COURT: SOME GENERAL PROBLEMS (1962).

[123] *Compare* here Glaser's criticisms in DROIT INTERNATIONAL PÉNAL CONVENTIONNEL 28 n.23, 201. *Les projets des Nations lines pour l'institution d'une justice pénale internationale,* 35 REVUE INTERNATIONALE DE DROIT PÉNAL 99 (1964); Romaschkin, *id.* at 42; Herzog, *id.* at 57; Quintano Ripollès, *id.* at 118; Klein & Wilkes, *id.* at 170, 235; and Glaser, *id.* at 338.

[124] *Cf.* the opinions of the three chief prosecutors of the Western states: JACKSON, II DER PROZEB: GEGEN DIE HAUPTKRIEGSVERBRECHER VOR DEM IMG IN NÜRNBERG 118 (1947); Shawcross, *id.*, vol. III, at 107; de MENTHON, *id.*, vol. IV, at 480.

[125] *See supra,* text at notes 107–114.

of control over the individual states' exercise of their own criminal power could work is presented by the line of decisions of the European Commission and the European Court of Human Rights, based on the Convention for the Protection of Human Rights and Fundamental Freedoms of November 4, 1950. [126] This line of decisions concerns nothing less than the protection of these rights guaranteed in the Convention by the means of a supranational institution. Although the rights granted in the Convention have effects beyond the fields of substantive and procedural criminal law, it is here that they have the greatest practical significance.

The system for legal protection of the rights granted in the Convention for the Protection of Human Rights and Fundamental Freedoms is constructed on two levels. Two methods of petition are provided: (1) the state complaint, in article 24, and (2) the individual complaint, in article 25 of the Convention, both of which are heard by the Commission, which consists of independent members. Both forms of petition represent innovations in existing international law. The state complaint is novel because the petitioning state need not set forth an injury to one of its own protected rights, but may also petition in order to urge the vindication of the system of common rights established in the Convention.[127] The individual complaint constitutes a unique advance for international law because, for the first time, the individual person is given a legal remedy, effective even against his own state, for vindication by an international legal institution of his fundamental human rights. [128]

If the validity of the petitioner's complaint is affirmed at the first instance by the Commission, it then has the duty of hearing the facts and endeavoring to secure an amicable settlement of the issue. [129] If this attempted amicable settlement cannot be accomplished, the second instance of the procedure established by the Convention begins, and the case is transferred to the Committee of Ministers or the Court of Human Rights. This procedure at this second instance is legal in nature, *i.e.*, it corresponds to a court proceeding, but as the consequence of the court's duty to secure an amicable settlement if possible, the proceedings are *in camera*. [130] Although the Committee of Ministers consists of national representatives to the Council of Europe, it sits in this proceeding in the

---

[126] 1952 BUNDESGESETZBLATT, pt. 2, at 686.

[127] GURADZE, DIE EUROPÄISCHE MENSCHENRECHTSKONVENTION, KOMMENTAR, Art. 24, n.1 (1968).

[128] Regarding the limitations and failures in general of this proceeding, *see* Huber, *Das Zusammentreffen der Europäischen Konvention zum Schutze der Menschenrechte und Grundfreiheiten mit den Grundrechten der Verfassungen,* GEDÄCHTNISSCHRIFT FÜR H. PETERS 375 (1967).

[129] *Convention for the Protection of Human Rights and Fundamental Freedoms,* art. 28–30.

[130] *Id.,* art. 33. *Cf.* Mosler, *Kritische Bemerkungen zum Rechtschutz system der Europäischen Menschenrechtskonvention,* 1964 FESTSCHRIFT FÜR H. JAHRREIB 289.

capacity of a legal organ of the community of member states united under the Convention for the Protection of Human Rights and Fundamental Freedoms. [131] The Committee of Ministers must decide according to the two-thirds-majority principle whether or not the Convention has been violated. If it finds a violation is stated, the violating state is then directed to take certain measures for remedying the situation which violates the Convention. [132] Within three months after the transmission of the Commission's report to the Committee of Ministers, the case can be brought before the Court of Human Rights. [133] The Court can be convened by the concerned states or by the Commission as trustee for the community of member states, [134] but not by the individual person. [135]

The Court of Human Rights has no power of cassation, but it does have the power to order the defendant state to remedy through use of its legislative power the situation which is violative of the Convention, or, if this is impossible (*e.g.*, because the effect of res judicata has intervened), the Court can order the defendant state to pay reasonable reparation to the injured party. [136]

Although up to the present time there have been only a few judgments of the Court, these have had immediate significance in the area of criminal law. For example, the Court in the Irish case *Lawless* approved political detention solely on the basis of the existence of a state of national emergency, a permissible basis according to article 15(1) of the Convention. [137] In the Belgian *de Becker* case, which concerned the apparent violation of article 10 of the Convention by a permanent deprivation of the plaintiff's right to practice the profession of journalism, the Belgium Government made the case moot by a removal of the relevant legal provision. [138] The practical significance of the decisions in regard to the length of pretrial detention [139] permissible under article 5(3) and article 6(1) of the Convention has been especially great. In the German *Wemhoff* case, which concerned an extraordinarily complicated context of "white collar criminality," the Court approved a pretrial detention of four years

---

[131] *Cf.* GOLSONG, DAS RECHTSSCHUTZSYSTEM DER EUROPÄISCHEN MENSCHENRECHTSKONVENTION 33 (1958).

[132] *Convention for the Protection of Human Rights and Fundamental Freedoms*, art. 32.

[133] *Id.* art. 45.

[134] *Cf.* GOLSONG, *supra* note 131, at 102.

[135] *Convention, supra* note 132, art. 48.

[136] *Cf.* Golsong, *Der Europäische Gerichtshof für Menschenrechte*, 1960 JURISTENZEITUNG 197.

[137] Affaire "Lawless," Arrêt du July 1, 1961, PUBLICATIONS DE LA COUR EUROPEÉNNE DES DROITS DE L'HOMME, *Serie A, Arrets et Décisions* (Strasbourg, 1961).

[138] Affaire "de Becker," Arrêt Mar. 27, 1962, *id.* (Strasbourg, 1962).

[139] *Convention, supra* note 132, arts. 5(3) & 6(1).

that was subtracted from the final six-and-one-half-year sentence. [140] However, in a second decision involving economic crime, the Austrian *Neumeister* case, the Court held a pretrial detention of three years to be a violation of article 5(3) of the Convention. [141] Further, in two other Austrian cases involving pretrial detention of approximately twenty-six months, the Court adopted the viewpoint that the issue of the length of the permissible pretrial detention can be determined only after a thorough consideration of the facts in the individual case. [142]

The area of I.C.L. is the area of superlatives. Within its sphere, the interplay of national law, international law, and now the law of supra-national communities combines with aspects of substantive, procedural, and jurisdictional law to create technical complexity of the highest degree. The issue of the limitation of a state's criminal power and the scope of the application of the substantive law brings the entire criminal law into consideration. The issues of I.C.L. in the areas of extradition and international judicial mutual assistance span the earth and create the most important means for the international battle against criminality. Through the protection by I.C.L. of the international community's precious legal values and cultural interests it contributes to the preservation of peace, security, and mankind's basic human rights, as well as to those living conditions worthy of human existence. I.C.L. in the area of European Community law is a constituent element of a new supranational order. With the creation of a genuine international criminal jurisdiction, it moves to the very border of a true world state and simultaneously necessitates the establishment of organizational and procedural models into which continental and Anglo-American legal principles are successfully combined. Finally, I.C.L. is of supreme timeliness because much of its content is only presently beginning to emerge from the original concept, and because much of its substance still awaits the transformation from idealistic utopia to working reality—but all of it possessing supreme importance for the well-being of a modern, but internationally often chaotic, world.

[140] Affaire "Wemhoff," Arrêt June 27, 1968, PUBLICATIONS, *supra* note 137 (Strasbourg, 1968). *Cf.* Guradze, *Die Angemessenheit der Dauer der Untersuchungshaft*, 1968 NEUE JURISTISCHE WOCHENSCHRIFT 2161.

[141] Affaire "Neumeister," Arrêt June 27, 1968, PUBLICATIONS, *supra* note 137 (Strasbourg, 1968). *Cf.* Liebscher, *Strafverfolgung und Menschenrechte*, 1969 JURISTISCHE BLÄTTER 465.

[142] Affaires "Stögmüller" et "Matznesser," Arrêts Nov. 10, 1969, PUBLICATIONS, *supra* note 137 (Strasbourg, 1969). *Cf.* Golsong, *Die "angemessene Dauer" der Untersuchungshaft in der Rechtsprechung des Europäischen Gerichtshofs für Menschenrechte*, 1970 FEST-SCRIFT FÜR H. GRÜTZNER 68.

Section 4. **REFLECTIONS AND OBSERVATIONS
ON INTERNATIONAL CRIMINAL LAW**

J. M. van Bemmelen

4.1. Scope and Significance

It is a rather dismal task to write about I.C.L. While there exists such voluminous literature on the subject that one might conclude that I.C.L. is already an important part of the whole system of international law, it becomes clear as soon as one remembers all the crimes committed by different states and particularly by their leaders, such as the manufacture and sale of armaments and invasions of peaceful countries, that at present I.C.L. is only in its infancy. [1]

Dr. P. H. Kooymans has recently hypothesized that "international criminal law is perhaps one of the most obscure fields of international law, which in itself is already very indistinctly circumscribed." [2] Similarly, Professor George Schwarzenberger believes that "[i]t would be unduly optimistic to assume that 'international criminal law' has now been established unequivocally as a technical term." [3]

Let us hope that there is sufficient reason to be somewhat less pessimistic and skeptical about I.C.L. In my opinion, we must look at it in the following way. Mankind is cooperative. We cooperate with each other in families, at work and play, in clubs, societies, and associations, and in governing our communities and states. All these cooperative ventures need their own rules and provide for sanctions against breaches of these rules. In communities and states, criminal law is invoked to impose sanctions for such breaches. Even sovereign states must coexist and cooperate to a certain extent to combat crime, *e.g.*, rules on extradition. Also, they must have rules governing the extraterritorial application of their own municipal criminal law, which is rarely considered permissible and even that in a limited fashion. They must make rules about how far they will recognize each other's decisions taken during the application of the

*This article is based on a series of lectures given by the author in New York University Law School when he was a visiting professor in 1969, and the editors are grateful to Professor Mueller for allowing its publication herein.

[1] *E.g.*, International Criminal Law (G Mueller & E. Wise eds. 1965) [hereinafter cited as Mueller & Wise].

[2] Published by the Calvanistic Association of Jurists, May 22, 1968 (in Dutch).

[3] 3 Current Legal Problems 263 (1950), reprinted in International Criminal Law, *supra* note 1 (page references below will be to that book).

municipal criminal law, *e.g.*, rules about the recognition and enforcement of foreign statutes of limitation and about how far they will apply the rule *ne bis in idem (autrefois acquit* and *autrefois convict)* in case there exists a foreign judicial acquitment or conviction. They enter into treaties whereby they oblige themselves to enact similar penal provisions against certain crimes. Schwarzenberger speaks of internationally prescribed municipal criminal law, *e.g.*, treaties about penalization of traffic in women. There are customary rules permitting any state to apply its municipal criminal law to certain crimes, *e.g.*, piracy and war crimes, irrespective of the location of crime or the identity of the defendant. All these kinds of I.C.L. are related to mutual help and cooperation and respect for each other.

States do not always cooperate, however. Just as individuals, they are often antagonistic to each other. They quarrel, they compete, and they make war. Some acts falling in these categories might be termed crimes according to I.C.L., and either the offending sovereign states or the responsible individuals governing these states might be punished. Schwarzenberger calls this "international criminal law in the material sense of the word."[4] In Germany it is called *Völkerstrafrechts.*[5] Vespasien Pella and Donnedieu de Vabres called this kind of law, in 1926, *droit pénal intéretatique.*[6] Glaser speaks of *droit international pénal* in contrast to *droit pénal international.*[7] Does this kind of I.C.L. in the material sense of the word already exist? The answer to this question depends on the concept of law in general and international law in particular.

While I agree with Professor H. L. A. Hart that international law deserves the title of "law,"[8] in my opinion he ought to have added that because international law lacks sanctions and is not provided with a central organ for the enforcement of its rules and does not know a legal system, no rules of change nor rules conferring judicial powers to judges or courts, international law is in no way I.C.L. in the material sense of the word.

Schwarzenberger expresses a similar opinion.

"The position is still, as it was summed up by the Committee on the Permanent Court of International Justice of the First Assembly of the League of

---

[4] *Id.*

[5] O. Triffterer, Dogmatische Untersuchungen zur Entmicklung des materiellen Völkerstrafrechts seit Nürnberg (1966).

[6] V. Pella, Actes du premier congrès international de droit pénal 430–59 (1926); V. Pella, La Criminalité collective des états et le droit pénal de l'avenir (2d ed. 1926); D. de Vabres, Droit Penal International (1926).

[7] Glaser, Droit International Penal Conventionnal (1970).

[8] The Concept of Law 95 (rev. ed. 1967).

Nations in 1920: "There is not yet any international penal law recognized by all nations."[9]

Schwarzenberger explains that

> ... only where there is a sovereign who firmly holds in his hands both the swords of war and of justice can there exist international criminal law in a true sense. As long as there are some powers who are not only in fact immune to the application of collective enforcement measures, but who in law, too, are in a privileged position by the reservation of their veto power, only paper swords of war and justice can be wielded by the international quasi-authorities of the United Nations. [10]

"In such a situation," Schwarzenberger says, "an international law that is meant to be applied to the world powers is a contradiction in terms." [11]

Not only major powers, but even small states are exempt from I.C.L., as they can commit crimes against peace and humanity without being punished according to I.C.L.

The main difficulty in I.C.L. is that major crimes against peace and humanity, such as genocide, invading and occupying peaceful countries, and annihilating whole towns populated by noncombatants, are committed by the governments of states. It is therefore understandable that the 1953 United Nations Draft Statute changed article 1 of the original Draft which established an International Criminal Court to try persons accused of crimes generally recognized under integrated law. In 1953, the words "natural persons" were substituted for "persons" as the subjects of the ICC's jurisdiction. Under article 25 of both Drafts, jurisdiction was consciously restricted to "natural persons" because it was stated that some states do not have criminal responsibility for juridical entities and its inclusion would arouse considerable controversy. [12]

The same is true for the crime of manufacturing of weapons. Hence, we must start with the municipal codes, which must forbid this manufacturing without a license of the government. This in itself would be an important step forward in the right direction, but it must be supplemented by a world authority which controls the licenses the different states issued. A world treaty on the manufacturing of weapons must not only forbid nuclear, chemical, and biological weapons but must also contain rules about the kind of small weapons that may be manufactured on behalf of the police of the municipal states. This world authority at the same time would have to decide which weapons would be necessary for a world police to control and restrain the manufacturing of weapons in

---

[9] Schwarzenberger, *supra* note 3, at 7, 23.

[10] *Id.* at 34–35.

[11] *Id.*

[12] Klein & Wilkes, *United Nations Draft Statute for an International Criminal Court: An American Evaluation,* in MUELLER & WISE, *supra* note 1, at 531.

general. It is insufficient to declare aggressive war as a crime. The whole
world must recognize that the preparation for war and the manufacture
of weapons also constitute serious crimes.

This crime—as all crimes—would be committed by individual persons
even if they were following orders of their government. Thus, the municipal codes must in first instance forbid this crime and must also be willing
to permit international control of the licenses they issue for this
manufacture.

In conclusion, history teaches us that the primary rules originated from
the fear of death, and that they only become real law when secondary
rules come into force. Our generation and those which will follow have
the obligation to create these secondary rules and to maintain them. It
is proposed to start with introducing the primary and secondary rules in
the municipal codes, because that is the way the whole body of international law has found its recognition. Treaties can prescribe these altera-
tions of the municipal codes, but it remains of great importance that the
municipal codes constitute the first barrier against international crimes.

4.2. Rules on the Applicability of Municipal Law and Assistance in Penal Matters

4.2.1. THE TERRITORIALITY PRINCIPLE IN CRIMINAL JURISDICTION. The rules
on the extent of applicability of municipal law differ from state to state,
although there are some similarities. Most states start with the territoriality
principle. But this principle of territorial jurisdiction "shows glaring
weaknesses," as is pointed out very clearly by Professor M. Cherif
Bassiouni. [13] In itself the territoriality principle is readily understandable.
It only needs to be complemented by other principles such as the personality principle (also called the active nationality principle) and the
protection principle (also called passive nationality principle), and sometimes by the universality principle. According to Schwarzenberger, the
territoriality principle

> . . . follows from the principle of the independence of states that to any extent
> to which subjects of international law are not limited by principles of inter-
> national law, they are free to determine as they see fit the territorial scope of
> their municipal criminal laws. They may limit the scope of their criminal laws
> to acts committed in their own territories and territorial waters, on ships sailing
> under their own flags or on airplanes of their own nationality. [14]

We must lay stress on the reservation Schwarzenberger makes, when
speaking of this independence of states and their freedom to determine
as they see fit the territorial scope of their municipal criminal laws. This

[13] CRIMINAL LAW AND ITS PROCESSES, 329–30 (1969).
[14] Schwarzenberger, *supra* note 3, at 5.

freedom exists only to the extent to which subjects of international law (*i.e.*, the municipal states) are not limited by principles of international law. The difficulty is that these rules recognized by I.C.L. are rather uncertain. But in 1897, in the Costa Rica *Packet* case[15] and even much earlier, it was certain that a state could not extend the territorial scope of its municipal law outside the territorial waters. The only question was, and still is, how far these territorial waters reach. Schwarzenberger recognizes that this "freedom for each state to determine as they see fit the scope of their municipal criminal laws" may result in "a wide field in which the various systems of municipal criminal law claim concurrent or conflicting jurisdiction." He says further:

> In practice the chaos that might result from such concurrent and conflicting claims is reduced to manageable proportion by one definite prohibitive rule of international law. In principle, at least, the actual exercise of criminal jurisdiction in concrete instances must take place within a state's own territory or in places assimilated to it. Within these limits it is left to every system of municipal criminal law to determine for itself whether and to what extent it applies its laws to crimes with a foreign element. It has to take into consideration internationally recognized rules, *e.g.*, the rule that it cannot extend, with certain exceptions, the applicability of its criminal law to foreign ships on the high seas. [16]

But already at the moment—and still more in the future—a state will not be free to make certain criminal laws, and it certainly will not be allowed to apply them either within or outside its own territory. The Convention on Genocide, for example, forbids a state to impose "measures intended to prevent births within the group." If, therefore, a criminal law would punish acts to thwart such measures, this law in itself would be null and void according to international law, and a state making such a law would expose itself to countermeasures taken by the states or by the United Nations.

Protocol No. 4 of September 16, 1963, adds to article 1 of the European Convention on Human Rights (1950) "[n]o one shall be deprived of his liberty merely on the ground of inability to fulfill a contractual obligation." If, therefore, one of the contracting parties makes it a crime to be unable to fulfill a contractual obligation, such a law would be contrary to the 4th Protocol. It is to be expected that in the future more of these conventions will be made and that they will influence the criminal law of all countries. Laws not in accordance with these conventions will not be applicable, neither within nor outside the territory of a state. The rules about the applicability of municipal law, in my opinion, belong really to

[15] Arbitral decision of Prof. F. de Martens, Feb. 13/25, 1897, Rev. gen. de dr. intern. public, vol. V, at 59 (1898).

[16] Convention on the High Seas, Geneva, Apr. 29, 1958; *see* MUELLER & WISE, *supra* note 1, at 215.

I.C.L. Here again I disagree with Schwarzenberger. States are not free to extend the applicability of their municipal criminal law to the territory of other countries or to the high seas and the territory of the North and South poles. They are allowed to do that only on the basis of conventions with other states.

Langemeyer in his article "Principe de territorialite" [17] stresses that in the *Ahlbrecht* decision, the special court of cassation in the Netherlands has maintained that the territoriality principle is limited by the rules of the law of nations.

On the night of January 13, 1944, a German sergeant of the German army, Ahlbrecht, shot a Dutchman, Jelis Budding, who at that moment was a prisoner of the German army. The only apparent reason for this murder was that Ahlbrecht was afraid that Budding would try to escape. After the war, Ahlbrecht was prosecuted before the Dutch special court for war criminals of Arnhem and sentenced to death. Ahlbrecht appealed to the special court of cassation in the Hague. The indictment against Ahlbrecht was founded on article 287 of the *Dutch Penal Code* (homicide) and on article 1 of the so-called B.B.S. (Royal degree on the extraordinary criminal law for collaborators and war criminals of 1943). This last article made it possible to punish the homicide with a death sentence, because the homicide was committed with a revolver procured by the enemy. The question which the special court of cassation had to decide was whether the Dutch criminal law was applicable to German soldiers and officials, who committed crimes in the Netherlands during the time of occupation.

The special court of cassation ruled that the common Dutch criminal law was not applicable to soldiers of the occupying forces and to officials of the occupying government, because Dutch courts had no basis of international law to apply the Dutch criminal law to these soldiers and officials. The special court of cassation upheld the thesis that the Dutch judicature had no judiciary force against these soldiers or officials. The only exception to this might be that the law of nations might recognize that war criminals might be prosecuted before municipal courts. The special court of cassation was of the opinion that this was the case but that the municipal law ought to contain a special provision for these war crimes committed by soldiers and officials of the occupying forces. Such a special law for war crimes committed in the Netherlands by these soldiers and officials did not exist in the Netherlands at the time of the *Ahlbrecht* case. [18]

The importance of this decision is that the territoriality principle is limited by the rules of the law of nations.

[17] G. E. Langemeyer, *Principe de territorialité, Le droit pénal international*, RECEUIL D'ÉTUDES (E. J. Brill ed. 1965).

[18] The decision in the Ahlbrecht case is published in the Dutch Series of Criminal Decisions of the Special Courts in the Netherlands, 1947, no. 747.

In this same article Langemeyer has tried to find the reasons for the so-called territoriality principle, which he does not consider as a principle but as a criterion. He concludes that there are five reasons why most countries accept the criterion and that, with some exceptions, most countries should apply their criminal law only to crimes committed within their territory. [19]

1. It is more efficacious to do so.
2. If a crime has been committed within a certain country, moral damage has been inflicted upon the juridical order of that state and must be repaired.
3. If a crime is committed within the territory of a state, it means that a concrete juridical interest has been injured, an interest which the legal system of that state considers worthwhile to protect.
4. Even in case no national interest has been hurt, there still is a reason to punish the culprit—if he is a national or an inhabitant of the state—for then there will exist no reason to prosecute for the state of which the interest is damaged.
5. The territoriality principle has the advantage for every state that the protection of its interests in foreign states will be assured in the most efficient way by the local authorities in these foreign states, at least in so far as regards crimes which universally are considered punishable.

These considerations, according to Langemeyer [20] are of a different nature. The second and the third are based on the idea that the interests of the state and its inhabitants must be protected. The fourth and fifth depend in a more indirect way on the same idea, in the sense, and the fourth aims at offering guarantees to other states, which can lead them to refrain from a too severe application of the principle with regard to nationals (Langemeyer says "Dutchmen") who in their own state have damaged foreign interests. The fifth aims to promote the realization of the idea of protection of the own interests of the state with the help of foreign judicial authorities.

In my opinion there is still a sixth reason for the territoriality principle. I refer to Desmond Morris:

> Animals fight amongst themselves for one or two very good reasons: either to establish their dominance in a social hierarchy, or to establish their territorial rights over a particular piece of gound. Some species are purely hierarchical, with no fixed territories. Some are purely territorial, with no hierarchy problems. Some have hierarchies on their territories and have to contend with both forms of aggression. We [the human species] belong to the last group; we have it

---

[19] Langemeyer, *supra* note 17, at 23.
[20] *Id.*

both ways. As primates, we were already loaded with the hierarchy system. This is the basic way of primate life. [21]

Since we are by nature prone to defending our own territory and in consequence we do not want other states to interfere with what happens within that territory, for that would mean a foreign infringement of our territory and our hierarchical system and even our homes, the territoriality principle seems valid.

4.2.2. THE NATIONALITY PRINCIPLE. Most European codes recognize the nationality principle as complementary to the territoriality principle. It certainly eliminates some of the glaring weaknesses of the latter.

The nationality principle makes the municipal law of a state applicable to its own nationals, when committing crimes abroad. It is formulated in different ways. For example, in Holland, article 5 of the *Dutch Penal Code* says

> [t]he Dutch criminal law is applicable to a Dutchman, who outside the Dutch territory in Europe has committed:
> 1. One of the offences of the Titles I and II of the second part of this code [crimes against the security of the state and against the royal dignity] and the offences of the articles 206, 237, [bigamy] etc.
> 2. An offence, which the Dutch criminal law considers a crime [misdrijf] and which is punishable according to the law of the country where it has been committed.
>
> Prosecution may also take place when the accused has obtained the Dutch nationality after the commission of the offence

Section 1933 of the New York Penal Law says: "A person who commits an act without this state which affects persons or property within this state, or the public health, morals, or decency of this state, and which if committed within this state would be a crime, is punishable as if the act were committed within this state." [22] There is a difference between the Dutch and the New York solutions. According to the *Dutch Code*, only a Dutchman who commits, for example, bigamy outside Holland is punishable according to Dutch law. In New York, bigamy probably would be considered as affecting the morals and decency of this state, but not only an inhabitant of New York but every person, even a foreigner might be prosecuted even if he had committed bigamy outside the State of New York.

Both the New York and the Dutch systems attempt to fill what Lotika Sarkar calls "gaps" in jurisdiction that the territorial principle creates. [23]

---

[21] D. MORRIS, THE NAKED APE 120 (1968).

[22] IN MUELLER & WISE, *supra* note 1, at 47.

[23] *The Proper Law of Crime in International Law*, 11 INT'L & COMP. L.Q. 462 (1962); reprinted in MUELLER & WISE, supra note 1, at 150.

This gap situation may arise as the result of a bigamous marriage, since the crime of bigamy occurs only where the second marriage takes place. Only the forum of the second celebration can prosecute, and not even the state of the matrimonial domicile, which would normally be the state most concerned, can take jurisdiction. Thus the second marriage in the case of *Re Quiros* had taken place in the United States and the matrimonial domicile was Costa Rica. The Costa Rican court held that it was unable to assume jurisdiction, as none of the acts constituting the crime of bigamy had taken place within the country. Sarkar further says:

> The Costa Rican Court of Cassation, however, mentioned that the legally indispensable prerequisite for the jurisdiction of this court in cases of crimes committed abroad was the presence of the guilty party in the country, and that presence within the country "would produce a social disturbance which justifies the intervention of the national justices." [24]

But which national system is better? Is it the Dutch one, that permits prosecution, when the accused is a Dutchman, or one who has committed bigamy abroad and has since become a Dutchman, or is it the New York system, that allows the prosecution in New York State when a person has committed bigamy outside the State of New York?

The Dutch system, the so-called active-personality principle, accepts the fact—and the same is true for England—that there are countries where bigamy is legally allowed. Obviously it would be rather inopportune to prosecute such an alien in Holland or England even if he had established a domicile there with one or two of his wives. On the other hand, the New York system has the advantage that even an alien—who, according to his own law or according to the law of the country where the bigamous marriage was celebrated, could not legally marry a second time—can be prosecuted in New York State when he takes his domicile there. This is the better solution because, otherwise, a foreigner domiciled in New York State would escape with impunity after having committed the crime of bigamy in a country where it is now allowed, whereas the New Yorker who had committed the same crime abroad might be prosecuted.

Hence, the New York system is preferable to the Dutch and English system. In Norway there is still another, rather practical, solution to this problem. There they also have the active-personality principle, but they assimilate persons who have a permanent residence in Norway. [25]

A fourth system is to be found in the *German Penal Code* in paragraphs 3 and 4:

> German criminal law applies to the deed of a German citizen, no matter whether it was committed within Germany or abroad.

[24] *Id.* at 53.
[25] ANDENAES. THE GENERAL PART OF THE CRIMINAL LAW OF NORWAY 318 (1965).

German criminal law is not applicable to a deed committed but not punishable abroad, if this deed is no offense abroad by reason of special conditions obtaining there.

A deed is committed at every place where the perpetrator has acted, or, in case of omission, where he should have acted, or where the result became, or should have become, effective.

The German criminal law is also applicable to deeds committed by foreigners within Germany. The German criminal law is applicable to offenses committed by foreigners abroad, if these are subject to punishment where committed, or if the place of commission is not subject to any criminal jurisdiction, and if

1. the perpetrators acquired German citizenship after commission of the dead, or
2. the offense was directed against the German people or against a German citizen, or
3. the perpetrator is found within Germany and is not extradited, although he could have been extradited by reason of the nature of the offense. [26]

Regardless of the law of the place of commission, the German criminal law is applicable to the following offenses committed by a foreigner abroad:

1. Offenses committed while holding a German public office or as a soldier of the German armed forces, or committed against the holder of a German public office or against a soldier of the German armed forces during the performance of his official service or with relation to such service.
2. Conduct amounting to high treason or treason against the German Federal Republic or one of her member states, as well as felonies of constitutional treason.
3. Felonies committed with explosives.
4. Traffic in children and women.
5. Betrayal of an industrial or business secret of a German enterprise.
6. Perjury in a proceeding pending before a German court or German agency competent to receive oaths.
7. Felonies and misdemeanors against coinage.
8. Unlawful narcotics traffic.
9. Traffic in obscene publications.

The German criminal law is applicable to deeds committed aboard a German ship or air vessel, regardless of the law of the place of commission. Petty misdemeanors committed abroad are punishable only when specifically provided for by statute or treaty. A punishment executed abroad must be deducted from a German punishment subsequently imposed for the same offense.

This German law certainly has some advantages. It covers nearly the

---

[26] For the text, *see* MUELLER & WISE, *supra* note 1, at 48–49.

whole range of possibilities. But like the Dutch system, it still does not go so far as the New York law that it punishes all foreigners who have committed a crime abroad which affects the "morals or decency of their own state." The New York system has the advantage of filling a gap. But on the other hand, it has the disadvantage of imposing on foreigners its own rules of morals and decency which are reflected in its criminal law.

The nationality principle is particularly of importance in cases of crimes committed abroad by a national of a country. In those cases it is often much better that the crime is tried by the judiciary of the country to which the criminal belongs and that at least there exists a possibility to execute the punishment which has been imposed by the judiciary of the *locus delicti* in the home country of the criminal.

The relative merits of these alternatives become clear in the *Drost* case. [27] Two young Dutchmen, X and Y, brutally murdered another young dutchman, Drost, in Stockholm. Before the trial in Sweden, the Dutch Minister of Justice asked the Swedish Minister of Justice to extradite X and Y to the Netherlands so that they might be tried in their home country. But the Swedish government refused to do so because of the territoriality principle and also because of the rule that all crimes committed in Sweden had to be tried in Sweden (legality principle). On January 24–27, 1966, X and Y were tried by the court of first instance in Stockholm. The court ordered a psychiatric investigation and subsequently reopened the trial on July 26 and 27. The district attorney had required that both the defendants would be trusted to the psychiatric mental hygiene service in accordance with the law on mentally disturbed patients. The court decided in conformity with this request. The district attorney had asked too that X and Y should be expelled from the country of Sweden on account of paragraphs 26 and 28 of the Foreigners Act and that they would be forbidden to reenter the country. X and Y had made a full confession about the murder. The court gave as its judgment that the defendants had committed murder, but that the reports of the psychiatrist showed that they had acted under the influence of such a serious mental disturbance, that this ought to be put on a level with insanity. According to article 5 of the *Dutch Penal Code*, it would have been possible that the defendants could have been tried in the Netherlands, for they were Dutchmen and had committed a felony under Dutch criminal law which was also punishable under Swedish law. The Dutch minister of justice wanted the defendants to be tried in Holland, particularly because he foresaw from

---

[27] A description of this case is to be found (in Dutch) in the Dutch Tijdschrift voor Strafrecht by Dr. J. Meursing, Zweedse en Nederlandse strafrechtelijke competentie. See further the Decision of the Court of Appeal in The Hague d.d. Nov. 21, 1967, Dutch Jurisprudence (Nederlandse Jurisprudentie) 1968, no. 1.

the beginning, that probably after a short time these two young men would be expelled from Sweden, and that Holland would be the only country legally and morally obligated to accept them. This fear of the Dutch minister of justice proved to be well founded. In October, 1967, within two years after they had committed the crime, both X and Y were transported to the Netherlands. Up to that moment one of them was still in the psychiatric institution in Sweden, but the other was already released on license and sold paintings that he had made during his stay in the institution.

As soon as they arrived in the Netherlands, the court of first instance ordered their apprehension. One of them, who had been transported to a house of arrest in Utrecht, which is also a psychiatric observation clinic, protested against this arrest, on the ground that he had already been tried in Sweden and that article 68 of the *Dutch Penal Code* forbids that someone who has already been convicted or acquitted in a foreign country can be retried in Holland. There is an exception to this rule, saying that in case the punishment which has been pronounced by the foreign judge has not been fully executed, there may be a new trial in the Netherlands. The Rotterdam court refused to repeal the order of arrest and the Court of Appeals in The Hague upheld this decision. The Court recognized that article 68 of the *Dutch Penal Code* spoke only of a punishment which has not been fully executed. But the Court was of the opinion that confinement in a mental institution should be deemed to be the equivalent of a sentence or fine.

Furthermore, the Court made it one of its considerations that this measure certainly had not come completely to an end in Sweden, because the Swedish authorities had asked the Dutch authorities to continue the treatment. The Court considered that the Swedish Court had ruled that the defendant was not wholly irresponsible but had decided only that he had committed his crime under the influence of a mental aberration of such serious character that it ought to be put on a level with insanity. The Hague Court of Appeal therefore decided that the decision of the Swedish Court ought not to be considered as a discharge of all prosecution (Dutch: *ontslag van alle rechtsvervolging*), which according to Article 68 of the Dutch penal code would bring with it that the defendant was no longer indictable and prosecutable in the Netherlands.

After this decision of the Court of Appeals, both the defendants put in a demurrer against the indictment, but also without success. On February 4, 1969, the Supreme Court decided that the Swedish judgment had been conviction of murder and that the sanction of commitment to a public mental health service had not come to an end in Sweden, because the Swedish government had ordered the expulsion of the defendants before the medical council had had the opportunity to propose the *Utskriving-snamorden* (a proposal to declare the defendants suitable for discharge). On the contrary, the Swedish government made the request to the Dutch government to take over the treatment. Even according to Swedish standards, the treatment had not come to an end. Article 68 of the Dutch penal code could therefore not be applied.

On March 17, 1969, the Court of Rotterdam again tried the case against the two defendants (*X* and *Y*). They were sentenced to one and a-half years in prison with deduction of their pretrial detention and they were at the same time put at the disposal of the government for treatment in an institution for psychopathic delinquents. [28]

This case shows how necessary it is that all civilized countries make new rules and conventions on extradition, execution of foreign judicial criminal decisions, transmission of prosecution, and mutual assistance in criminal matters. A desirable first step is the Benelux convention of June 27, 1962, entered into force on December 11, 1967. Benelux countries have also agreed to a convention on the execution of judicial criminal decision given in one country, which in the future can be executed in both the other states. (Benelux convention of September 26, 1968, not yet entered into force.) Furthermore, there is a project for a convention on the transmission of prosecution in criminal matters.

It seems to me that these three conventions are of importance for other countries as well. Until recently extradition and international judicial assistance were the only methods of international judicial cooperation, and even these methods were—and for the great part of the world still are—very defective and full of loopholes. They are closely connected to the territoriality principle. Only the state of the place where the crime has been committed is able to prosecute and thus the other states to which the criminal has fled have an obligation to extradite him because in most cases they themselves cannot prosecute and punish. Most times they do not want to extradite their own nationals; therefore, many countries have made a rule that they have the right to prosecute and to apply their own criminal law in case one of their nationals has committed in another country an act which is a crime according to the law of the state where the crime has been committed and at the same time a crime according to the country of which he is a national.

This system, of course, is rather ineffective, particularly because most conventions on extradition allow the extradition for only a very limited number of serious crimes.

---

[28] *See* Mueller, *International Judicial Assistance in Criminal Matters,* in MUELLER & WISE, *supra* note 1, at 410; The *Archina* case is especially interesting in comparison to the *Drost* case (p. 412).

The new Benelux conventions have set forth some significant principles:

1. The first one, on extradition, has extended the series of crimes for which extradition is to be granted. Instead of enumerating them specifically, the three countries have agreed to make extradition possible for crimes which in both countries "interested in the case" are punishable with at least six months of imprisonment. In case a prison sentence has already been pronounced in the requiring state, extradition is possible only when the sanction (punishment or measure) amounts to at least three months of detention. The principle of double incrimination is maintained.

2. They have extended even further the series of crimes for which extradition may be granted, insofar as that in case a man is extradited for a crime as mentioned under (1), he may at the same time be tried for crimes punishable with less than six months.

3. Extradition is excluded for political crimes, but the assault on the life or liberty of the Head of the State or a member of the reigning House, and desertion, will not be considered political crimes as such.

4. Crimes against fiscal laws are excluded from extradition as long as the contracting parties do not make a special convention allowing the extradition for these specifically mentioned crimes.

5. Extradition may even be granted for crimes committed outside the territory of the requesting Party, and may only be refused in case the law of the requesting Party does not allow the prosecution of such a crime (art. 6).

The High contracting Parties have upheld the principle that they do not extradite their nationals.

This last principle was one of the reasons why the Benelux countries did not content themselves with this convention on extradition and mutual judicial aid. They also entered into a convention on the possibility of mutually executing each other's sentences and decisions in criminal matters. This is a much more complicated matter than that of extradition, because there are great differences between definition and circumscription of crimes and between the punishments and measures in the contracting states. The Benelux countries have adopted the following main principles:

1. They have adhered to the principle of double incrimination, not only in abstracto but also in concreto. Nevertheless, it is possible with certain crimes to have one state prosecute and convict a person in another state, and then request the second state to execute the punishment. This execution in the requested state is of significance when the person against whom the sentence is pronounced is a national of the requested state and therefore not apt to be extradited. But there are other cases in which this possibility of an execution in the requested state may be practical, *e.g.,* when

the convict is an inhabitant (though not a national) of the requested state. It may be that he has his family there or that he is already serving another sentence in the requested country.

2. The procedure to be followed in the case of a request to execute a foreign sentence is rather complicated. The Minister of Justice of the requesting state asks his counterpart in the requested state to undertake the execution. As soon as the request is accepted by the requested state, the convention prescribes that a judge in the requested state must consider whether the request is authentic and whether the conviction can be executed. He must see if there is double incrimination, or if the crime is listed in the convention, if the condemned person has already been convicted or acquitted in another state for the same crime, and if convicted, whether he has already served his sentence. If all is in order, the judge adapts the pronounced punishment or measure to one which is applicable in his own country. There are further elaborate rules for cases in which the execution is asked of a sentence pronounced by default. In that case, the condemned person has the right to make an appeal either to the judge of the requesting state or to the judge of the requested state. If he does not specifically mention the former, the appeal will be treated by the judge in the requested state, who will try the case according to his law as if the crime had been committed in his own country.

3. The request to execute a foreign sanction, however, can be refused in the following cases:

    a. The crime is of a political character.
    b. It is a military crime.
    c. The crime has already been tried by the requested state.
    d. The crime has been committed outside the territory of the requesting state.
    e. The execution would be contrary to international obligations of the requested state.
    f. The execution concerns a sentence of deprivation of certain rights or competencies.
    g. The requested state is of the opinion that the execution would be contrary to the fundamental principles of its juridical order.

It is to be expected that this convention will be used most when the judge in the requesting state has pronounced a fine. There is already a possibility for the public prosecutor in the requesting state to ask his counterpart in the requested state to invite the condemned person to pay such a fine of his own accord. This possibility has been regulated in an earlier informal agreement of the three Benelux partners of 1964, which has come into operation by ministerial circulars of January 1965. In addition to these conventions on extradition, on mutual assistance in criminal matters and on the execution of criminal judicial decisions, there is now a project of November 1968 on the transmission of prosecution. This certainly was the most intricate and difficult subject of the three, but its adoption was facilitated by the results obtained by the other two.

Article 1 of this convention states: When somebody has committed an act for which a punishment or measure can be applied according to the law of one of the contracting parties, that party may request another contracting party to prosecute the offender in the following cases:

a. The offender is domiciled or staying in that other state;
b. The offender exercises his main profession or trade in the other state;
c. The offender is already being prosecuted there for another offense or is already serving there a punishment for another offense.

Article 2 abolishes double criminality and double jeopardy. The territoriality principle, of course, has been rendered nugatory. When the requested state accepts the transmission of the prosecution, the law of that state becomes applicable to the offense for which the transmission is asked. At that moment the requesting state loses its right to prosecution. The request *must* be refused in the following circumstances:

a. in case the conditions mentioned in articles 1 and 2 are not fulfilled;
b. in case there is already an irrevocable decision about this offense in one of the states of the contracting parties;
c. in case there is such a decision in another state and the defendant has not been subjected to any sanction;
d. in case there is such a decision in another state and the defendant has been fully subjected to the sanction.

The request *may* be refused in the following circumstances:

a. in case the offense is of a political character;
b. in case it is a military offense;
c. in case the offense has been committed outside the territory of the requesting state;
d. in case the defendant neither is a national of one of the contracting parties or an inhabitant of them; nor had his main profession or trade in one of them.

As soon as the affair is before the judge in the requested state there is no longer a possibility to refuse the request, unless it becomes clear that none of the conditions for transmission, mentioned in article 1 (a-c) has been fulfilled.

4.3. Conclusion

At present I.C.L. does not really exist. The regulations about the extent of the applicability of municipal criminal law have not yet reached this status of I.C.L. because there is no conformity in these regulations and there are no binding rules about cases of conflict. These rules can become I.C.L. only when there are conventions which require one state to yield to another state in the application of the criminal law.

Even the fact that piracy, genocide, and other crimes against humanity are almost universally recognized as crimes and that every state is able to apply its municipal criminal law to these crimes (universality principle) does not mean that these rules have attained the status of I.C.L.

As long as we do not have an international government with an international judiciary, an international attorney general and an international police force strong enough to execute the decisions of the international court, there is no I.C.L. in the material sense of the word. This does not mean that we must not try to extend our municipal criminal law to different sorts of universally recognized crimes. The world can survive only when all states forbid the manufacture and sale of weapons and are willing to recognize these acts as a crime.

The first step in this direction would certainly be that all states would agree to penalize in their own courts the manufacture and sale of weapons. This still would not be I.C.L. in the true sense of the word, but it would be a step in the right direction. On the other hand, how difficult it will be to achieve this agreement on disarmament becomes clear, by reading a recent article of Dr. Nicholas M. Poulantzas: "The Problem of 'Peaceful Purposes' Revisited." [29] He points to the difficulties inherent in the interpretation of the term "peaceful purposes or uses of outer space" in the Outer Space Treaty of January 27, 1967, and the term "prohibition of the use for military purposes of the seabed and the ocean floor and the subsoil thereof" in the Draft Treaties on this subject submitted by the USSR and the United States on March 18, 1969, and May 22, 1969, respectively to the Eighteen National Disarmament Committee.

Poulantzas expresses "serious concern" over this procedure of the two big nuclear powers to draft a Joint Treaty and thereafter to appeal to all world states to sign and ratify this treaty, which in fact represents, more or less, the agreement only of the two nuclear superpowers. Poulantzas says:

[29] Nederlands Jurisprudentie (NETHERLANDS JURISDICLE REV.) 265 (1970); see also on the doctrine of legitimacy, M. Bos, *Self-Determination by the Grace of History*, 1968 NETHERLANDS INT'L L. REV. 362; BASSIOUNI, *Self-Determination and the Palestinians*, 1971 PROCEEDINGS OF THE AMERICAN SOCIETY OF INTERNATIONAL LAW, 65 A.J.I.L. 31 (1971); Nanda, *Self-Determination in International Law*, 66 A.J.I.L. 321 (1972).

> In fact, we are guided in this way by a behavioural code drawn by the two superpowers, often with the criterion of their national interests, which world states have to follow. The danger of this procedure lies in the fact that international legitimacy in the future may be dictated only by the two superpowers of a common accord, and therefore become monolithic. [30]

In my opinion, there is no place for this "serious concern." We must be glad when in the end the two super powers find a way to avoid the destruction of the whole world, and we must hope that this will ultimately lead to a sort of federal world government complete with legislation, judiciary, administration, and police.

Section 5. SOVEREIGNTY AND INTERNATIONAL CRIMINAL LAW

M. Kitili M'Wendwa

5.1. Introduction

The lines along which International Law has developed since the emergence of the nation-state seem to insure a permanent place to the doctrine of sovereignty[1] and its concomitant, the concept of nationality. Whatever one may say with regard to international law in general, that part of it which has been called I.C.L. seems to be impeded at every step by the sovereignty of nations on the one hand and by the absence of a world legislature on the other.[2] It should be observed that the development of a world legislature itself depends on the extent of the willingness of nations to surrender some part of their sovereignty.

Every state is supposed by law to have the right to do everything that it likes to do within its own territory.* This is what, in the simplest terms, sovereignty means. [3] This right, which appears to be absolute in law,* has

---

[30] *Id.*

* EDITORS' NOTE: This statement is subject to the caveat that all states are bound by their obligations under international law.

[1] Art. 3 of the latest *Declaration on Social Progress and Development* considers "respect for the sovereignty and territorial integrity of states" as one of the primary conditions of social progress and development (U.N. MONTHLY CHRONICLE, 136 Jan. 1970).

[2] The deficiency is made up to some extent by the various Conventions signed by the Great Powers and the efforts of the International Law Commission. Details may be found in *International Criminal Law* (Mueller & Wise, eds. 1965). There are also multistate unions or organizations, *e.g.,* the East African Community which has a legislative assembly with power to pass laws and to create and punish offenses on common subjects.

[3] Some definitions of sovereignty are (1) "Sovereignty is supreme power over citizens and subjects unrestrained by the laws" (Bodin). (2) "It implies that the power of which it is used neither submits legally to the interference of any other power, nor allows its own subjects to question its omnipotence" (GROTIUS).

limitations in practice. We will not, however, go into those limitations.[4] Suffice it to say that sovereignty is still something to be reckoned with and not to be lightly ignored.

5.2. The Effects of Sovereignty on I.C.L.

The doctrine of sovereignty prevents municipal courts from enforcing I.C.L. except insofar as such law is part of municipal law. Thus, in spite of customary international law, treaties, and conventions, courts of a nation punish only those crimes which are made punishable by municipal law. Blackstone says: "International law is part of the Law of England."[5] This seems a very wide proposition but means no more than that for municipal courts, international law does not exist unless it is contained in local statutes or unless it is part of the common law. L. J. Scott stated Blackstone's proposition in modern terms in *R. v. Bottril, ex p. Keuchenmeister:* "International law is only binding on our courts insofar as it has been adopted and made part of our municipal law."[6]

The statements just quoted are from England. The position elsewhere appears to be the same, at least in countries following the common law system.

This is one consequence of the doctrine of sovereignty. No outside agency—be it the Allied and Associated Powers or the United Nations—can make law for Parliament. The law of a nation is what its legislature makes it. Some part of its law may, of course, be common law which has been recognized and enforced by courts from times immemorial.

Blackstone wrote a long time ago. Even these days it is sometimes suggested that international law is in fact part of the common law. The following are some illustrations of this view:

1. Customary international law is part of the common law (Lauterpacht).[7]

2. "Where the common law has not been 'settled,' *i.e.*, where there are no precedents, the courts will, if they can, apply the rules of international law."[8]

3. "It is quite true that whatever has received the common consent of civilised nations must have received the assent of our country, and that to which we have assented along with other nations may

---

[4] *See* I. JENNINGS, THE LAW AND THE CONSTITUTION 142–44 (3rd ed. 1943) BENTWICH & MARTIN, A COMMENTARY ON THE CHARTER OF THE UNITED NATIONS (1950); SALMOND, JURISPRUDENCE 524–31 (8th ed. 1930); KEETON, THE ELEMENTARY PRINCIPLES OF JURISPRUDENCE 21–8 (1961).

[5] *Commentaries,* IV. 5.

[6] [1947] K.B. 41, at 50.

[7] I OPPENHEIM'S INTERNATIONAL LAW 36 (5th ed. 1958).

[8] JENNINGS, *supra* note 4, at 155.

properly be called international law, and as such will be acknowledged and applied by our municipal tribunals to decide questions on which doctrines of International Law may be relevant." (*West Rand Central Gold Mining v. The King* [1905] 2 K.B. 391).

No objection can be taken to the third statement if it means, as it seems to mean, that should it be necessary for the purposes of a court case to determine what is international law on a particular subject, then that law which has been accepted by other nations and to which England has assented should be recognized by English courts as international law.

This apart, the three statements have to be read with modifications insofar as they refer to "crimes" created by I.C.L. International law is recognized and applied by municipal tribunals only insofar as it has become part of the law of the land because (1) it has come down as part of the common law, (2) it has been reenacted by the legislature, or (3) the constitution of a given state incorporates it as part of the law of the land. We know of no other case in which international law as such has been enforced by a municipal court of law.

It is an accepted principle that no person can be convicted of a criminal offense unless such an offense is created by law, *nulla poene sine legge.*[9] Section 77(8) of the Constitution of Kenya, for example, says this: "No person shall be convicted of a criminal offence unless that offence is defined, and the penalty therefor is prescribed, in a written law. . . ."
This makes it necessary that I.C.L. be enacted by Kenya Parliament before it can be enforced in Kenya.*

Municipal courts are, for understandable reasons, reluctant to convict persons of crimes unless such crimes are within not only the letter but also the spirit of municipal law. In England, for example, potentially polygamous marriages have been recognized for civil purposes (*e.g.*, inheritance, property rights, legitimacy of children), but English courts have expressed the opinion that they would not go so far as to make such marriages the basis of a prosecution for bigamy.[10] On the same principle, courts of other countries have refused to recognize discriminatory or confiscatory legislation of even friendly countries.

---

* EDITORS' NOTE: This is one interpretation; another one is that to enforce International Criminal Law that law must first be defined in such a manner so as to make it part of codified international law or recognized as a general principle of international law. In this case it is applicable to the members of the world community, but its application in municipal law will depend on the constitutional requirements of each state.

[9] This principle of legality exists at common law as well as in civil law concepts. See for these respective systems: BASSIOUNI, CRIMINAL LAW AND ITS PROCESSES 37–47 (1969); and MERLE & VITU, TRAITÉ DE DROIT CRIMINEL (1968); JESCHECK, LEHRBUCH DAS STRAFRECHT (1969).

[10] Baindail v. Baindail, 1 All E. R. 343 (1946).

The problem of conflict between an outside criminal law and the constitution of a country also arises. Even in cases where such outside laws are accepted as part of the law of the land and it has been agreed that it should be enforced by municipal courts, courts refuse to enforce such outside law if it conflicts with the constitution. This is certainly the position in countries with a written constitution. Two Kenya cases may be quoted. The three countries of East Africa (Uganda, Tanzania, and Kenya) have formed a common organization called the East African Community which administers services common to the three countries. Such services are the railways, harbors, post office, customs and excise, income tax, etc. The East African Community has its own legislature which, within the powers given to it by the Treaty, passes laws. The Community enforces them through its own legal department.

The first case was concerned with a section of the East African Customs and Transfer Tax Management Act of 1952. That Act makes it an offense for any person to obstruct any officer in the execution of his duty. Then, section 174(1) provides:

> The Commissioner may, where he is satisfied that any person has committed any offence against this Act in respect of which a fine is provided . . . compound such offence and may summarily order such person to pay such sum of money, not exceeding two hundred shillings, as he may think fit . . .

An employee of a commercial organization operating at the Nairobi Airport was held by customs authorities to have obstructed a customs officer in the execution of his duty and a fine had been imposed on him. That employee applied to the High Court for an order of certiorari and mandamus on several grounds. Several points arose and were considered by the High Court, a gist of whose judgment is contained in the following sentence.

> In the result, we hold that selection 174 of the East African Customs and Transfer Tax Management Act, 1952, is void and of no effect in Kenya being inconsistent with the provisions of the Constitution.

The second case arose from a prosecution under the Official Secrets Act (no. 4 of 1968) of the East African Community. Section 8(1) of that Act provides:

> A prosecution for an offence under this Act shall not be instituted except with the written consent of the Counsel to the Community.

The prosecution in this case had been instituted by the Attorney-General of Kenya who contended that section 8(1) of the Community's Act was a clog on the powers given to him by the Constitution of Kenya. He relied for this proposition on the following provisions of the Constitution.

26(3). The Attorney-General shall have power in any case in which he considers it desirable so to do—

(a) to institute and undertake criminal proceedings against any person before any court (other than a court-martial) in respect of any offence alleged to have been committed by that person;

. . . .

(8) In the exercise of the functions vested in him by sub-sections (3) and (4) of this section and by sections 44 and 55 of this Constitution, the Attorney-General shall not be subject to the direction or control of any other person or authority."

The High Court held that the Attorney General was correct and that section 8(1) of the Community's Official Secrets Act was a clog on the powers given to the Attorney General by the Constitution and was ipso facto invalid and of no effect in Kenya. This was in spite of the fact that the treaty between the three countries contained the following provision:

10(3). Where an Act of Parliament is inconsistent with . . . an Act of the Community enacted before it, it should not be construed so as to repeal any part of the Community, unless it makes express provision indicating the intention that it shall have effect notwithstanding the Act of . . . the Community.

Such a provision indicating the contrary intention was found in section 3 of the Constitution of Kenya which states:

If any other law is inconsistent with this Constitution, this Constitution shall prevail and the other law shall, to the extent of the inconsistency, be void.

This provision obtains because each state is sovereign and its courts enforce only its own laws, ignoring those laws which, although recognized by the state, are in conflict with the constitution which is the fundamental law of the country. The two cases quoted illustrate the principle. The position would be the same if we were dealing with I.C.L. instead of the East African Community law.

The present position may be summarized in the words of Dr. Schwarzenberger: [11]

The rise of the modern State . . . has its lesson to tell. After the princes of Europe had established their absolute power within territorially defined States, then, in the words of Hobbes, they firmly held in their hands both the swords of war and of justice. Both swords were "annexed to the Sovereign Power". In the words of the old English forms of indictment, crimes were committed "against the peace of our Lord, the King, his Crown and Dignity."

Here lies the explanation why, in the present state of world society, international criminal law in any true sense does not exist.

In the Atomic Age, most of the 'sovereign and equal' members of the United

[11] *The Problem of an International Criminal Law* 3 CURRENT LEGAL PROB. 263–296 (1950).

Nations have lost their political sovereignty and know their humble station in the international hierarchy.

In form, they all are subject to the Charter of the United Nations . . . There are, however, some powers who are not only in fact immune to the application of collective enforcement measures, but who, in law, too, are in a privileged position. By the reservation of their veto power, they have made sure that only paper swords of war and justice can be wielded against them by the international quasi-authorities of the United Nations. They are fully conscious of the fact that the real swords of war and justice are still "annexed to the Sovereign Power".

In such a situation an international criminal law that is meant to be applied to the world powers is a contradiction in terms: It presupposes an international authority which is superior to these States.[12]

Schwarzenberger is aware of the various proposals for a universal I.C.L. They, according to him, all

share the deficiency of taking for granted an essential condition of their realisation, a *sine qua non* which cannot easily be attained: the transformation of the present system of world power politics in disguise into at least a world federation."[13]

The principle of nationality flows from sovereignty. States claim the right to punish their own nationals for crimes committed abroad and also to protect them when they are outside the territory of their state. There is no uniformity of practice. Some states reserve the right to punish their nationals for any offense.[14] Some claim the right to punish their nationals for offenses committed by them before they obtained nationality.[15]

Sometimes states go even beyond the nationality principle. William Joyce was held guilty of treason although he was an alien. The link between him and the United Kingdom was that he had taken a British passport and traveled to Germany where the acts of treason were committed.[16] Eichmann was sentenced to death by an Israeli court for crimes committed against Jews in Germany long before the State of Israel came into existence.[17] In a South African case, the accused was a German national who was domiciled in South Africa and had applied for naturalization.

He committed acts in Germany against the security of South Africa. It was held that by reason of his residence in South Africa and enjoyment

---

[12] *Id.* at 295.

[13] *Id.* at 296.

[14] Section 4 of the Indian Penal Code is a very wide provision applying to "any offence." One of the illustrations to the section reads: "A, a coolie, who is a Native Indian subject, commits a murder in Uganda. He can be tried and convicted of murder in any place in British India in which he may be found."

[15] Germany and the Netherlands in INTERNATIONAL CRIMINAL LAW 62 & 64, (MUELLER & WISE ed. 1965).

[16] Joyce v. D.P.P. [1946] A.C. 346.

[17] MUELLER & WISE, *supra* note 2, at 290–365.

of its protection, the accused "owed allegiance to that state, breach whereof renders him liable to the penalties of high treason."[18]

The principle of nationality is fraught with more difficulties than the principle of sovereignty. Issues have to be resolved and some rational arrangements made for dealing with offenses in which two or more states are concerned or which are committed on the high seas—or perhaps, in outer space. The territorial principle is far better than the nationality principle. Nations must be content to let their sister nations deal with the crimes committed within their territories.

A state has never had any real difficulty in dealing with offenses committed within its own territory whether the offenders have been aliens or its own nationals unless the offenders have absconded, in which case extradition treaties have been generally useful.[19] Difficulties arise when political ideologies are allowed to interfere with law. A powerful politician sometimes flees his country, fearing a prosecution for what he regards as trumped up offenses but what the government regards as real offenses. It also happens that a scientist employed by defense service or a Foreign Office functionary who has been supplying strategic information to a foreign power escapes before he is found out. Extradition has not been known to work in these cases.[20] In the case of ordinary crimes also, extradition is sometimes refused, although the state desiring extradition may strongly feel that there is a prima facie case against the alleged offender. Here, I.C.L. should make it possible for an actual trial to be held in the country where the criminal is found. The trial may be conducted according to the law of the country where the offense was committed. This will be as good a guarantee of a fair trial as can be hoped for.

5.3. The Development and Future of I.C.L.

One cannot help feeling that Schwarzenberger is being unduly pessimistic. Some progress has been made in both prescribing and enforcing I.C.L.[21] Slave-trading and piracy have existed as international criminal offenses for a long time. Existence of at least some war crimes is generally admitted although certain aspects of the war crimes trials after the two

---

[18] *Id.* at 56: 1949(3)S.A. 1238.

[19] *See* Bassiouni, *International Extradition in the American Practice and World Public Order*, 36 TENN. L. REV. 1–40 (1969).

[20] Bassiouni, *Ideologically Motivated Offenses and the Political Offenses Exception in Extradition: A Proposed Juridical Standard for an Unruly Problem*, 19 DEPAUL L. REV. 217–269 (1970).

[21] Much of this is dubbed by Schwarzenberger "internationally postulated municipal criminal law" (*supra* note 11 at 268, 271), but this is largely a matter of definition.

world wars have been justifiably criticized.[22] The defects criticized appear to be remediable.

Clarke and Sohn suggest at least part of the problem—that relating to war and peace—can be solved by a revision of the United Nations charter.[23] Their proposals are these:

1. Instead of guaranteeing "sovereign equality" of members, article 2 should guarantee equal protection of the charter to all members, big and small. States will still retain sovereign powers "except such as are delegated to the United Nations."[24]
2. The General Assembly should have representation weighted according to population, and representation on other organs of the United Nations should be revised.[25]
3. The United Nations, instead of being, as now, a league of independent states retaining their "sovereign equality," would become a world authority equipped with adequate rights and powers of its own in the field of preventing war . . . the member nations would . . . accept definite and unprecedented limitations on their traditional freedom of action; and moreover, there would be no right of withdrawal by the ratifying nations.[26]

Such a reformed United Nations Organization will have power not merely to consider and discuss and make recommendations in regard to peace, it will be able to enact "laws" and to provide penalties for their breach.[27]

Reforms such as these will improve the position very considerably, but even if reforms on these lines were not to be agreed to, there is no reason why the age-old method of treaties and conventions should not continue to be used. The immediate aim should be to consolidate the position with regard to war crimes and to remedy the defects shown by the last set of trials. One requirement is for agreement to be reached on the list and definitions of war crimes, the composition of courts, and the venue and procedure of trials.

To summarize, sovereignty is still a real obstacle to the extension of the sphere of I.C.L. More United Nations action or multilateral conventions are necessary. Nationality of the criminal should not, as it does today, matter.

[22] *See* Prof. J. H. MORGAN, THE GREAT ASSIZE (1948), and LORD HANKEY, POLITICS TRIALS AND ERRORS (1950), especially the summary of Mr. Justice R. Pal's dissenting judgement at the Tokyo trials at 133–36.
[23] WORLD PEACE THROUGH WORLD LAW (2nd ed. 1964).
[24] *Id.*, at 6.
[25] *Id.* at XX–XXI, 25–31, 66–74.
[26] *Id.* at 203.
[27] *Id.* at 40.

The state within whose territory an offense takes place should be primarily responsible for dealing with it. Where two or more states are affected, there should be an internationally agreed code of rules for resolving the conflict of jurisdictions.

CHAPTER II

INDIVIDUAL AND COLLECTIVE RESPONSIBILITY IN INTERNATIONAL CRIMINAL LAW

Section 1. THE INDIVIDUAL AS A SUBJECT OF INTERNATIONAL LAW AND INTERNATIONAL CRIMINAL RESPONSIBILITY

CRITON G. TORNARITIS

1.1. The Position of the Individual in International Law

Every legal norm, aiming at securing harmonious living within a community, either national or international, contains commands of behavior for this purpose which could be addressed to no other than individuals or juristic persons who have to obey such commands and comply with their requirements.[1]

The person enjoying the benefit conveyed by such norm is the subject, while the matter regulated by such norm which its subject enjoys or the persons who have to obey the norm and comply with its requirements constitute the object of the norm.

No one can be the subject of a legal norm unless he is either an individual or a juristic person, while the object of a norm may also be inanimate things.[2]

In theory, therefore, the individual may be the subject not only of a norm of municipal law but also of an international law norm.

As observed by Baker,[3]

> Man's natural bond to his fellowman, however, does not disappear at the boundaries of each man's particular state, but rather is coextensive with all human society. The fundamental precepts of justice and charity, of mutual aid and respect for the interests of others, obtain just as truly among men of different states as among men of the same state. Consequently, the same intimate relationship, which exists between the domestic civil law and the natural law, also exists between natural law and international law.

---

[1] Cf. SANDERS, THE INSTITUTES OF JUSTINIAN; cf. PICARD: LE DROIT PUR 62, where the definition of law is given as "un rapport de jouissance—d'un Sujet—Sur un Objet—protegé par la Contrainte Sociale."

[2] PICARD, supra note 1, at 71, 76.

[3] Baker: The Scholastic Concept of International Law, 16 NOTRE DAME L.R. 1, 3, 4, 8–10 (1940) cited by WHITEMAN, I DIGEST OF INTERNATIONAL LAW 7.

For three centuries until World War I, the main,[4] if not the exclusive, subject of international law was considered to be the state. "It is unthinkable," said Anzilotti, "that there may exist any subjects of international rights and obligations other than the states."[5]

But such a concept was inconsistent with the reality and could not subsist for long. Toward the second half of the nineteenth century the first reactions appeared. It was Hefter who first pointed out that man, irrespective of nationality, had rights and duties inherent in human nature and he was therefore not only a subject of international law but also a member of the international community.[6] Since then there has been a growing body of legal literature regarding the legal position of the individual in international law.

Furthermore, a series of provisions and rules of international law, especially of a humanitarian nature, apply directly to the individual and aim at the protection of his life and corporal integrity (as the provisions prohibiting piracy,[7] interdicting the use of asphyctic or toxic gases,[8] regulating the use of submarines[9]), at the protection of his freedom (as those for the abolition of slavery, of slave trade and of forced labor),[10] at the safeguard of his health and prevention of abuses injurious to it,[11] at the protection of his morality,[12] and at the determination of his status and security in life (as the treaties relating to refugees and stateless persons).[13]

Since World War II the scope and province of contemporary interna-

[4] Among other subjects of international law in this respect may be mentioned the Pope, the recognized belligerents. *Cf.* Spiropoulous, *L'individu et le droit international,* 30 RECUEIL 201 (1929); Lauterpacht, *The Subjects of the Law of Nations,* 63 L.Q. REV. 438, 444, 445 (1947).

[5] *Il diritto internazionale nei giudizi interni,* at 44.

[6] POLITIS, LES NOUVELLES TENDANCES DU DROIT INTERNATIONAL 58 (1928).

[7] *Cf.* OPPENHEIM-LAUTERPACHT, 8 INTERNATIONAL LAW 608; ROUSSEAU: DROIT INTERNATIONAL, PUBLIC 216; BISHOP, INTERNATIONAL LAW 265 (2d ed. 1963).

[8] *Cf.* The Protocol of Geneva of June 17, 1925; ROSSEAU, supra note 7, at 216.

[9] *Cf.* The Protocol of London of Nov. 6, 1936; ROUSSEAU, supra note 7.

[10] *Cf.* OPPENHEIM-LAUTERPACHT, *supra* note 7, at 732; The Convention of St. Germain of Sept. 10, 1919, and the Slavery Convention of Geneva of 1926; SIBERT, I TRAITÉ DE DROIT INTERNATIONAL PUBLIC 461, 470; Convention of June 28, 1930, concerning forced labor; Conventions of May 4, 1910, Sept. 30, 1921, and Dec. 2, 1949, relating to the trade of women; SERENI, I PIZITTO INTERNAZIUNDE 261. Regarding the trade of Negroes, *cf.* SIBERT at 463.

[11] *Cf.* OPPENHEIM-LAUTERPACHT, *supra* note 7, at 982–984; SIBERT, *supra note* 10, at 483; Regulation of manufacture of stupefying drugs Conventions referred to in SERENI, *supra* note 10, at 269 n. 5; ROUSSEAU, *supra note* 7, at 216, 748.

[12] *Cf.* Convention of Sept. 12, 1923, regarding obscene publications; ROUSSEAU, *supra* note 7, at 216; SIBERT, *supra* note 10, at 489; SERENI, *supra note* 10, at 261.

[13] *Cf.* The Hague Codification Conference, 1930, adopting a number of provisions aiming at the limitation of statelessness; *cf.* OPPENHEIM-LAUTERPACHT, *supra* note 7, at 699; SIBERT, *supra note* 10, at 485 DELBEZ, PRINCIPES GÉNÉRAUX DU DROIT INTERNATIONAL PUBLIC 205; *see also* Convention of Oct. 28, 1933, regarding the refugees.

tional law has been oriented toward the direction of considering the individual as a subject of international law.

Though the state continues to be the main subject of international law, nevertheless, the man, in the very phrase of De Lapradelle, "écartant l'Etat a monté avec des institutions nouvelles au premier rang de la vie internationale."[14]

The creation of the United Nations and all its specialized agencies and the various regional organizations and a considerable number of law-making treaties opened new avenues in the international sphere for the individual, the exercise of his rights and the performance of his obligations and generally for his well-being.

With regard to human rights their internationalization started after the end of World War I with the establishment of the League of Nations when the rigidity of the concept of sovereignty was relaxed and the need for the protection of minorities contributed to bringing forward the protection of human rights.[15] Certain individual freedoms and social rights of the workmen and generally of employed persons were recognized and put under the protection of international organizations such as the International Labor Organization and the International Labor Office.[16] By article 25 of the European Convention for the Protection of Human Rights and Fundamental Freedoms, the European Commission of Human Rights, established thereby, may receive petitions from any individual claiming to be the victim of a violation by one of the contracting parties (including his own state) of the rights set forth in the Convention if the Party against which the complaint has been lodged has declared that it recognizes the competence of the Commission to receive such petitions.[17] The trend of bringing the individual directly on the international plane and not through the medium of his own state and through the mass of interstate relations has been followed in recent treaties and conventions of the United Nations.[18]

[14] De Lapradelle, *La place de l'homme dans la construction du droit international,* 1 CURRENT LEGAL PROB. 151 (1948).

[15] *Cf.* TORNARITIS, THE SOCIAL AND ECONOMIC RIGHTS UNDER THE LAW OF THE REPUBLIC OF CYPRUS 9; Guggenheim, 2 TRAITÉ DE DROIT INTERNATIONAL PUBLIC 289; DE LAPRADELLE, *supra* note 14.

[16] *See* OPPENHEIM-LAUTERPACHT, *supra* note 7, at 716; SIBERT, *supra* note 10, at 491; SERENI, *supra* note 10, at 1127; *cf.* Green, *The International Labor Organization under Pressure,* 10 CURRENT LEGAL PROB. 57; HACKWORTH, 5 DIGEST OF INTERNATIONAL LAW 30, 407 (1943).

[17] For the history of this Article, see ROBERTSON, HUMAN RIGHTS IN EUROPE 63, 112; Robertson, *The First Case before the European Court of Human Rights,* 36 BRIT Y.B. INT'L L. 343–514 (1960); de Becker v. Belgium; III YEARBOOK OF THE CONVENTION 214–54; vol. 3, at 488.

[18] See The International Convention for the Elimination of all Forms of Racial Discrimination adopted by the General Assembly of the United Nations Dec. 21, 1965, and acceded to by

International Criminal Law

But though the individual may also be a subject of international law possessing international rights and duties and though he has capacity to maintain his rights by bringing international claims, yet it does not follow that he could have all the attributes of a state, perform all its functions in the same way as a state does, nor possess the totality of international rights and duties recognized by international law as vested and performed by another international organization or entity as specified or implied in its constituent documents and developed in practice. For example, an individual cannot recognize a state, make treaties, declare war, or make peace.

1.2. The Obligations, Duties, and Responsibilities of the Individual Under International Law

So long as the individual is a subject of international law he has not only rights and interests directly derived from and protected by international law but also obligations imposed by, and enforced under international law.[19]

It has long been held that individuals were capable of violating international law, irrespective of whether their punishment was at the hands of the states or more recently of international courts.[20]

There are various norms of international law directly determining the person committing the criminal or unlawful act and providing for his punishment or other sanction for the contravention of such norms although the imposition of such punishment or sanction is left to the municipal court. Although the offense is defined by international law, that law has no means of trying or punishing the offender. The recognition of offenses as constituting crimes and the trial and punishment of criminals are left to the municipal law.[20a]

An early example of an offense under customary international law is the offense of piracy, the illicit violence committed on the high seas against persons or property by the means of a privately owned ship.[21]

In the cases of piracy, by the law of nations there has been conceded a

the Republic of Cyprus and ratified by the Convention for the Elimination of Any Form of Racial Discrimination (ratification) Law, 1967; The Convention on Political Rights of Women adopted by the General Assembly of the United Nations Dec. 20, 1952, and acceded to by the Republic of Cyprus and ratified by the Convention of Political Rights of Women (ratification) Law, 1968.

[19] Cf. Eagleton, International Organization and the Law of Responsibility, 76 RECUEIL DES COURS 322, 325 (1950).

[20] BISHOP, supra note 7, at 265; 2 GUGGENHEIM, supra note 5, at 28; cf. BRIGGS, THE LAW OF NATIONS LAWS AND DOCUMENTS 93, 579. Regarding the principle that on a subject of international law obligations are imposed, see SERENI, supra note 10, 1503.

[20a] A.C. 586, at 589 (1934).

[21] Kelsen, in 4 RECUEIL DES COURS 121, 149 (1932).

universal jurisdiction under which the person charged with the offense may be tried and punished by any state into whose jurisdiction he may come.

Another norm of international law directly binding the individual is the breach of a blockade. The vessel breaking the blockade, and ultimately her cargo, are liable to confiscation. There exists, therefore, a rule of customary international law directly affecting the individual (*i.e.*, the owner of the vessel or of the cargo who had to obey that rule or suffer the consequences of its breach).[22]

The norms of international law relating to contraband also impose an obligation on any individual, not a national of a belligerent state, not to supply goods which are contraband to any belligerent under the penalty of having the offending vessel and goods confiscated.[23]

There are also various treaties which prohibit individuals from committing certain acts, the commission of which is rendered a criminal offense in respect of which the individual may be prosecuted in one or more jurisdictions:

1. The International Convention for the Protection of Submarine Cables of 1884, which makes the intentional or negligent breaking or damaging of submarine cables punishable by the appropriate signatory power.[24]

2. The Anglo-Portuguese Commercial Treaty of 1914, which confers the protection of international law upon port and madeira so far as concerns the United Kingdom and makes it a criminal offense to import any wine or other liquor as the produce of Portugal and the island of Madeira.[25]

3. The Treaty of Washington of 1922 (not ratified) between the United Kingdom, France, Italy and Japan, relating to the use of submarines and noxious gases. Under its article 3 an individual in the service of a State who commits an act of a violation of the rules laid down in the Convention shall be deemed to have violated the laws of war and shall be tried and punished as if he had committed an act of piracy.[26]

[22] *See* Kelsen, *supra* note 21, at 153; 2 OPPENHEIM-LAUTERPACHT, *supra* note 7, at 790; 3 HACKWORTH, *supra* note 16, at 130; 2 GUGGENHEIM, *supra* supra note 15, at 424; *cf.* MONACO, MANUALE DI DIRITTO INTERNAZIONALE PUBBLICO 482.

[23] Kelsen, *supra* note 21; 3 HACKWORTH, *supra* note 16, at 29, 80 *seq.*; 2 OPPENHEIM-LAUTERPACHT, *supra* note 7, at 823; *cf.* The Declaration of London of 1909; 2 GUGGENHEIM, *supra* note 15, at 415, 416; MONACO, *supra* note 22, at 485 *seq.*

[24] McNAIR, THE LAW OF TREATIES 579 *seq.*; POLITIS, *supra* note 6, at 97; 2 HACKWORTH, *supra* note 16, at 676; and see the Report of 1951 of the International Law Commission to the General Assembly on the Draft Code of Offenses against the Peace and Security of Mankind, 7 U.N. GAOR Supp. II, U.N. Doc. A/2136(1952).

[25] McNAIR, *supra* note 16, at 579.

[26] McNAIR, *supra* note 16, at 579. Kelsen, *supra* note 21, at 151; *see* ROUSSEAU, *supra* note 7, at 422, where he calls these acts "piraterie par analogie;" POLITIS, *supra* note 6, at 98; 2 HACKWORTH, *supra* note 16, at 691. In this connection reference may be made to the Nyon arrangement signed on Sept. 14, 1937, by representatives of Great Britain, Bulgaria, Egypt, France, Greece, Roumania, Turkey, and the USSR in connection with submarine attacks in the Mediterranean against merchantships not belonging to the conflicting parties in Spain; *see* ROUSSEAU, *supra* note 7, at 422; 1 HACKWORTH *supra* note 16, at 692 *seq.*

4. The Treaty of Versailles, by article 227, of which the former Emperor of Germany was to be charged for committing offenses against the international morality and breach of the sanctity of treaties. It was also considered by that Treaty that acts against the laws and the customs of war were international crimes for which sanctions were imposed (article 228). Similar provisions were included in the other treaties of peace after the First World War, except that of Lausanne. This system was completed in the Treaty of Sèvres (not ratified), whereby the Turkish Government undertook to deliver to the allied powers the persons responsible for the organized massacres in Turkey (article 230), for the trial of whom the Society of Nations were to establish an appropriate Court.[27]

5. The Geneva Conventions of 1949 which impose direct obligations on individuals and sanctions for the contravention of any of them.[28]

From what has been said, it appears that by both the customary and the conventional international law obligations are imposed directly on the individual,[29] the breach of which renders him personally responsible and entails for him such punishment or other sanction as may either be defined by the international law or left to be determined by the municipal law.

However, the incipient beginnings of I.C.L. have been more sharply brought into focus as a result of World War II, owing to the extensive and unprecedented atrocities committed during that war.

At least six different meanings have been attributed to the term "inter-

[27] *See* POLITIS, *supra* note 6, at 111; Kelsen, *supra* note 21, at 154. The German Emperor was not tried under art. 227 of the Treaty of Versailles, because the Government of the Netherlands, where he had been given asylum, refused to deliver him; *see* 2 OPPENHEIM-LAUTERPACHT, *supra* note 7, at 569 n.3, 719.

[28] See The Geneva Convention for the Amelioration of the Condition of the Wounded and Sick in Armed Forces in the Field of Aug. 12, 1949, especially art. 49, 50, & 53; The Geneva Convention for the Amelioration of the Condition of Wounded, Sick, and Shipwrecked Members of Armed Forces at Sea of Aug. 12, 1949, especially art. 50 & 51; The Geneva Convention relative to the Treatment of Prisoners of War of Aug. 12, 1949, especially art. 129 & 130; The Geneva Convention relative to the Protection of Civilian Persons in Time of War, especially arts. 146 & 147.

All these Conventions were acceded to by the Republic of Cyprus and ratified by Law 40 of 1966. In England, *see* The Geneva Conventions Act, 1957; *cf.* Gutteridge, *The Geneva Convention of 1949*, 26 BRIT. Y.B. INT'L L. 294–326 (1949); Lauterpacht, *The Limits of the Operation of the Law of War*, 30 BRIT. Y.B. INT'L. L. 206 (1953); *Geneva Conventions at* 213; Jean Graven, *Les Crimes contre l'humanité*, I RECUEIL (1950).

[29] As observed by Kelsen, *supra* note 21, at 154, such obligation may be imposed either by providing directly for the person responsible who is to suffer the consequences of its breach or by providing for the persons who have to perform the acts required for the fulfillment of the obligation. The obligation may also be defined by the international law but the sanction for its contravention be left to the State, of which the person responsible is an organ. *Cf.* art. 26 of the Hague Relations, 1907, imposing on the commander of a besieging force, in case of a proposed bombardment, the duty to notify his intention to resort to such bombardment; *see* 2 OPPENHEIM-LAUTERPACHT at 420.

national criminal law."[30] However, in the context of this section, this expression is used in its material sense, that of dealing with international crimes which can be committed only by subjects of international law.

As has been pointed out in contemporary international law, the individual has become a direct subject of some international obligations. This has occurred particularly in the criminal field. Regarding certain offenses, particularly those recently provided by international conventions such as the Genocide Convention and the Draft Code of Offenses against the Peace and Security of Mankind prepared by the International Law Commission, with which I shall deal later, the individual is the solely responsible subject for the commission of international crimes. But the individuals may also be responsible for international offenses committed by them as instrumentalities of states, or with the abetment or incitement of states.

As observed by Oppenheim-Lauterpacht,

> The State and those acting on its behalf bear criminal responsibility for such violations of international law as by reason of their gravity, their ruthlessness and their contempt for human life place them within the category of criminal acts as generally understood in the law of civilized countries ...

> Yet it is impossible to admit that the individuals, by grouping themselves into States and increasing immeasurably their potentialities for evil, can confer upon themselves a degree of immunity from criminal liability and its consequences which they do not enjoy when acting in isolation. Moreover, the extreme drastic consequences of criminal responsibility of States are capable of modification in the sense that such responsibility is additional to and not exclu-

---

[30] *The criminal international law—droit pénal international* relating to offenses having a foreign element in them either as regards the accused or the victim, or the place of their commission or their eventual effects *see* MAITLAND KONQUI, L'INFRACTION DITE INTERNATIONALE EN DROIT CRIMINAL FRANCAIS (1962) should be distinguished from the *I.C.L.—droit international penal* which deals with international crimes or offenses against the law of nations. Regarding the second, some writers use the expression *interstate criminal law—droit pénal interètatique* (*cf.* Pella, *Towards an International Criminal Court,* 44 A.J.I.L. 55–56 (1950)). Schwarzenberger attributes six different meanings to the term "international criminal law." It may relate to the territorial scope of municipal criminal law or be considered with internationally authorized municipal criminal law or mean criminal law common to civilized nations or may signify international cooperation with the administration of municipal criminal law or, finally, international criminal law in the material sense of the word which deals with international crimes committed by the subjects of international law; *see* Schwarzenberger, *International Criminal Law,* 3 CURRENT LEGAL PROB. 263, 264–70 (1950). Regarding the question of the extraterritorial operation of the municipal criminal law, compare *Joyce v. Director of Public Prosecutions* A.C. 347 (1946), and for this question coupled with the jurisdiction of the trial court, compare *Eichmann's Case; see* Schwarzenberger, *The Eichmann Judgment,* 15 CURRENT LEGAL PROB. 23, 248 (1962); Green, *The Eichmann Case,* 23 MODERN L. REV. 507 (1960); Fawcett, *The Eichmann Case,* BRIT. Y.B. INT'L L. 181–215 (1962); Green, *The Maxim Nullum Crimen sine Lege and the Eichmann Trial,* 38 BRIT. Y.B. INT'L L. 457–71 (1962).

sive of the international criminal liability of the individuals, guilty of crimes committed in violation of international law.[31]

The question of offenses against international law and generally of substantive I.C.L. is closely connected with the question of the machinery whereby offenders would be punished and especially with the manner in which international criminal jurisdiction is to be exercised.

A considerable advance has been made in both the above spheres during and after World War II, with the establishment of the International Military Court for the Trial of the Major War Criminals at Nuremberg and its judgment.

After preparatory work[32] an Agreement "for the Prosecution and Punishment of the Major War Criminals of the European Axis" was signed on August 8, 1945, by the United States, the Provisional Government of France, the United Kingdom, and the Union of Soviet Socialist Republics

[31] 38 BRIT. Y.B. INT'L L. 355–57. There is however, a second school of thought, mainly represented by the Saldana and Pella that the state continues to be the responsible subject; *see* DALLOZ, 2 ENCYCLOPÉDIE–DROIT INTERNATIONAL, under the heading "Infractions Internationales" at 187, while a third view held by Professor Dautricourt is that whenever an international offense is committed, the individual is the subject of the criminal responsibility while the state bears the civil responsibilty in connection therewith. *See* Garcia-Amador, *State Responsibility*, 49 AJIL 345–46 (1955).

[32] See the first inter-Allied Declaration on war crimes signed at St. James Palace, London, on Jan. 13, 1942, by representatives of nine countries, in which the acts of violence of Germany, her allies and associates were noted and reference was made to the Convention signed at the Hague in 1907 regarding the laws and customs of land warfare. It was declared that among the principal aims of the signatories was the "punishment through organized justice, of those guilty or responsible for these crimes, whether they have ordered them, perpetrated them or participated in them."

A "Declaration of German Atrocities" signed by President Roosevelt, Prime Minister Churchill, and Premier Stalin was released to the Press in Moscow on Nov. 1, 1943, whereby it was solemnly declared that at the time of the granting of any armistice which was to be set up in Germany, those German officers and members of Nazi party who had been responsible for, or had taken part in, the atrocities described therein, massacres and executions would be sent back to the countries in which their abominable deeds were committed in order that they might be judged and punished according to laws of those liberated countries and of the free governments created therein. A commission was set up by a conference convened at the British Foreign Office on Oct. 23, 1943, which later adopted the shorter title of the United Nations War Crimes Commission, composed of representatives of seventeen countries. It commenced its meetings in London on Jan. 11, 1944, and completed its work on Mar. 31, 1948.

The Commission prepared a list of war criminals and recommendations to the member governments on various problems relating to their apprehension, trial, and punishment. The Commission published a 15-volume series called *Law Reports on Trials of War Criminals*, London, 1948–1949, containing objects and history of certain important and representative war crimes trials held in national courts.

A Far Eastern and Pacific Sub-Commission as a branch of the United Nations War Crimes Commission was established later, in which 10 countries were represented. It met at Chungking and subsequently at Nanking, China, beginning on Nov. 29, 1944, and terminating on Mar. 31, 1947.

"acting in the interests of all the United Nations." The Agreement provided in article I for the establishment, after consultation with the Control Council of Germany, of an "International Military Tribunal for the trial of war criminals whose offenses have no particular geographical location whether they be accused individually or in their capacity as members of organizations or groups or in both capacities." It was further provided that the jurisdiction or the powers of any national or occupation court established or to be established in any Allied Territory for the trial of war criminals would not be prejudiced (art. 6) and that any government of the United Nations could adhere to the agreement by notice to the United Kingdom (art. 5). The Agreement came into force on its signing and subsequently it was adhered to by nineteen other countries, and the Charter of the Tribunal was annexed to the above Agreement.[33]

In accordance with article 6 of the Charter, the Tribunal established by the Agreement for the trial and punishment of major war criminals of the European Axis countries was given the power to try and punish persons who, acting in the interests of the European Axis countries, whether as individuals or as members of organizations, committed any of the following crimes:

(a) crimes against peace: namely planning, preparation, initiation or waging of war of aggression, or war in violation of international treaties, agreements or assurances, or participation in a common plan or conspiracy for the accomplishment of any of the foregoing;
(b) war crimes: namely violations of the laws or customs of war, including murder, ill-treatment or deportation to slave labour or for any other purpose of civilian population of or in occupied territory, murder or ill-treatment of prisoners of war or persons on the seas, killing of hostages, plunder of public or private property, wanton destruction of cities, towns or villages, or devastation not justified by military necessity;
(c) crimes against humanity: namely murder, extermination, enslavement, deportation and other inhumane acts committed against any civilian population, before or during the war, or persecutions on political, racial, or religious grounds in execution of or in connection with any crime within the jurisdiction of the Tribunal, whether or not in violation of the domestic law of the country where perpetrated.

The official position of defendants, whether as heads of state or responsible officials in governmental departments, should not be considered as absolving them from responsibility or mitigating punishment (art. 7), nor the fact that the defendant acted pursuant to orders of his government or of a superior should free him from responsibility but might be con-

[33] Cmd 6668; *see also* the Agreement and the Charter at the Trial of German Major War Criminals, Proceedings of the International Military Tribunal sitting at Nuremberg, 1950, at 548–49, 550–55; U.S. EAS 472.

sidered in mitigation of punishment if the Tribunal determined that justice so required (art. 8).

The Tribunal was given authority to declare "criminal" a group or organization to which the convicted individual belonged (art. 9).

In such a case the competent national authority of any signatory was given the right to bring individuals to trial for membership therein before national, military, or occupation courts. In such trials the criminal nature of the group or organization should not be questioned (art. 10), and such person might be charged before any such court with a crime other than membership of such group or organization and be punished independently of and in addition to the punishment imposed for participation in the criminal activities of such group or organization (art. 11).

The Tribunal consisted of four judges and four alternates. Each signatory of the agreement appointed one judge and one alternate. Provision was also made for the appointment by each signatory of a chief prosecutor.

As indictment was brought against twenty-four German major war criminals and six groups or organizations on October 18, 1945, one of the defendants committed suicide and the trial of another defendant was postponed by the Tribunal. The trial opened on November 20, 1945, and final arguments were concluded on August 31, 1946.

The Tribunal delivered its judgment on September 30 and October 1, 1946: three of the defendants were acquitted (Schacht, von Papen, and Fritzche) and the remaining nineteen defendants were found guilty on one or more counts of the indictment; three of the groups or organizations were found criminal; those who remained members thereof after September 1, 1939, were found guilty. [34]

The Tribunal by its frequent references to international law, to the treaties governing the conduct of war, to the amenability of individuals to international law and to the responsibility of individuals under international law seems to have indicated that the substantive law which it applied was international law and not a new internationally enacted system of municipal law. [35]

It pointed out that the Tribunal had to administer the law of the Charter which is "decisive and binding upon the Tribunal."

> The making of the Charter was the exercise of the sovereign legislative power by the countries to which the German Reich unconditionally surrendered;

---

[34] See the judgement of the Tribunal, Cmd 6967 (1946); 41 A.J.I.L., 172–333 (1947); · Trial of German Major War Criminals, *supra* note 33, at 411–547 (including the dissenting judgement of the Russian judge Nikitchenku).

[35] *Cf.* Finch, *The Nuremberg Trial and International Law*, 35 41 A.J.I.L. 20 (1947). *See also* Viscount Maugham (formerly L.C.) U.N.O. and War Crimes, 1951, and the last chapter ("Postscript") of the book contributed by Lord Hankey, in which the legal and political aspects of punishment of war criminals are respectively discussed.

and the undoubted right of these countries to legislate for the occupied territories has been recognized by the civilized world. The Charter is not an arbitrary exercise of power on the part of the victorious nations but in the view of the Tribunal, as will be shown, it is the expression of international law existing at the time of its creation; and to that extent it is itself a contribution to international law."[36]

Further, the Tribunal rejected the submission of the defendants that a fundamental principle of all law—international and domestic—that *Nullum crimen sine lege, nulla poena sine lege* had not been observed inasmuch as the defendants were well aware that they were acting in defiance of international law when they carried out their designs of invasion and aggression.

In the judgment it was also emphasized that the individuals were liable under international law for the commission of international crimes.

That international law imposes duties and liabilities upon individuals as well as upon states has long been recognized. In the recent case *Ex parte Quirin* (1942, 317 U.S. 1) before the Supreme Court of the United States, persons were charged during the war with landing in the United States for the purposes of spying or sabotage. The late Chief Justice Stone, speaking for the Court said:

> From the very beginning of its history the Court has applied the law of war as including that part of the law of nations which prescribes for the conduct of war, the status, rights and duties of enemy nations as well as enemy individuals.[37]

Crimes against international law are committed by men, not by abstract entities, and only by punishing individuals who commit such crimes can the provisions of international law be enforced.

On the other hand the very essence of the Charter is that individuals have international duties which transcend the national obligations of obedience imposed by the individual State. He who violates the law of war cannot obtain immunity while acting in pursuance of the authority of the State if the State in authorizing action moves outside its competence under international law.[38]

From these extracts of the judgment of the International Military Tribunal at Nuremberg it clearly emerges that the individual himself can be held responsible for crimes against international law.[39]

Following the wake of the European precedent, on April 3, 1946, the Far Eastern Commission, sitting at Washington, adopted a general policy

---

[36] Judgment in the Trial of German Major War Criminals, *supra* note 33, at 433–444.
[37] Judgment, *supra* note 33, at 446–47.
[38] Judgment, *supra* note 33, at 447.
[39] For the Nuremberg Trial, see MERLE, LE PROCES DE NUREMBERG ET CHATIMENT DES CRIMINELS DE GUERRE (1948); Kelsen, *Will the judgment in the Nuremberg Trial constitute a Precedent in International Law?* I INT'L L. Q. 153–77 (1947); Lauterpacht, *The Law of Nations and Punishment of War Crimes,* 21 BRIT. Y.B. INT'L L. (1944), where there is reference to the literature on the matter.

decision on the "Apprehension, Trial, and Punishment of War Criminals in the Far East." [40] Subsequently the Supreme Commander on April 26, 1946, issued General Order No. 20 (whereby previous general orders were suspended), which contained the Charter of a Tribunal to try and punish Far Eastern war criminals who as individuals or as members of organizations were charged with offenses, including crimes against peace, which were specifically described in the Charter. [41]

An International Military Tribunal for the Far East was established under the Charter, before which twenty-eight major Japanese war criminals were indicted on April 29, 1946. The trial started on May 3, 1946, and closed on April 16, 1948. The judgment of the Tribunal delivered between November 4 and 12, 1948, [42] restated the position that individuals could be held responsible for war crimes.

The individual responsibility for war crimes has also been held in the Nuremberg Trials (or subsequent proceedings,[43] as they were called) and in various cases tried by military tribunals of various countries. [44]

In a number of such cases it was held that the law of war is addressed not only to combatants and public authorities of a state but to anybody, including civilians, regardless of status or nationality, who assists or participates in violation thereof. [45]

By Resolution 95(1) adopted on December 11, 1946, the General Assembly of the United Nations noted the Agreement for the establishment of an International Military Tribunal signed on August 8, 1945, and the annexed Charter and the fact that similar principles had been adopted in the Charter of the International Military Tribunal for the Far East proclaimed on January 18, 1946, and affirmed "the principles of international law recognized by the Charter of the Nuremberg Tribunal and the judgment of the Tribunal." The General Assembly on November 21, 1947, by its Resolution 177(II), directed the International Law Commission (1) to formulate the Nuremberg principles and (2) to prepare a draft code of offenses against the peace and security of mankind, indi-

[40] *See* text in WHITEMAN, *supra* note 3, at 965.

[41] See art. 5 of the Charter, as set out, and other articles, as described in WHITEMAN, *supra* note 3, at 971. For this Charter as amended, see *Trial of Japanese War Criminals* 39 (Dep't State Pub. 2613, 1946).

[42] Summary of the Tribunal's judgment: *see* WHITEMAN, *supra* note 3, at 973.

[43] The twelve trials under Control Council Law 10 before the American Tribunals set up at Nuremberg under Ordinance 7 during the years 1946 to 1948.

[44] *See* WHITEMAN, *supra* note 3, at 934; *cf.* R.R.R., *The Municipal and International Law Basis of Jurisdiction over War Crimes*, 28 BRIT. Y. B. INT'L. L. 382 (1951)

[45] *See* Report of the Deputy Judge Advocate for War Crimes, European Command, June 1944 to July 1948, at 46–49, para. 5, cited in 2 WHITEMAN, *supra* note 3, at 940; but *cf.* Efstathiades: Παραβιάσεις ὑπό του ἀτόμον κανόνων διεθνους δικαίον, in Τόμος πρός τιμήν Κωνσταντίνου Τριανταφυλλοπούλου, at 72, 86.

cating clearly the place to be accorded therein to the said principles. [46]

The International Law Commission, without expressing any opinion on the legal character of the Nuremberg principles and especially whether the Charter was the expression of international law existing at the time and whether aggression and war crimes were already crimes under international law at the outbreak of World War II, [47] formulated the following seven principles:

1. Any person who commits an act which constitutes a crime under international law is responsible therefor and liable to punishment.
2. The fact that the international law does not impose a penalty for an act which constitutes a crime under international law does not relieve the person who committed the act from responsibility under international law. [48]
3. The perpetrator of an international crime is not relieved from responsibility under international law on the ground that he acted as head of state or responsible government official.
4. The fact that a defendant acted under orders of a superior could not free him from responsibility provided a moral choice was in fact possible to him. [49]
5. A defendant has the right to a fair trial.
6. Three international crimes, namely crimes against peace, war crimes, and crimes against humanity, are defined. [50]
7. Complicity in a crime against peace, war crime, or crime against humanity is a crime under international law.

[46] *See* G.A. Res. 177(11) (1947). For the history of the resolutions, see the memorandum of the Secretary-General entitled *The Charter and Judgment of the Nuremberg Tribunal: History and Analysis* (U.N. Doc. A/CN 4/5, at 11–33).

[47] For the various discussions at the International Law Commission and at the Sixth Committee, see Yuen-Li-Liang, *Notes on Legal Questions Concerning the United Nations*, 45 A.J.I.L. 514 (1951); Johnson, *Code of Offenses Against the Peace and Security of Mankind*, 4 INT'L & COMP. L. Q. 446–49 (1955); Parry, *Some Considerations upon the Contents of a Draft Code of Offenses against the Peace and Security of Mankind*, 3 INT'L & COMP. L. O. 208, 212, 213 (1950).

[48] It seems that the Commission implied first that international law may impose duties on individuals directly without any interposition of internal law and secondly that international law held supremacy over internal law. See Yuen-Li-Liang, *supra* note 47, at 519.

[49] See U.N. Doc. A/1316 at 12. The proviso did not exist in art. 8 of the Charter, but the International Law Commission based itself on a passage in the Judgment of the Nuremberg Tribunal; *see* Yuen-Li-Liang, *supra* note 47, at 521.

[50] Regarding crimes against humanity, the Commission widened its scope by no longer requiring them to be committed "before or during war"; *see* Johnson, *supra* note 47, at 450; *cf. generally* on Nuremberg Trials, *The Nuremberg Trials and Objection to Military Service in Viet Nam*, in PROCEEDINGS OF THE AMERICAN SOCIETY OF INTERNATIONAL LAW at its Sixty-Third Annual Meeting at Washington, Apr. 24–26, 1969, at 140–178.

By a resolution of the General Assembly the member states would be invited to furnish their observations on the formulation of those principles and the International Law Commission would be requested, in preparing the draft code of offenses against the peace and security of mankind, to take account both of such observations and of observations made by delegations during the Fifth Session of the General Assembly. [51] The government's comments on the formulated principles were submitted, [52] but no further discussion on that matter was made before the International Law Commission. [53]

The International Law Commission parallel to the formulation of the principles of international law recognized in the Charter and the Judgement of the Nuremberg Tribunal embarked upon the second task entrusted to it by the aforementioned Resolution of the General Assembly of the United Nations 177(II), *i.e.*, the preparation of a Draft Code of Offenses against the peace and security of mankind with a clear indication of the place to be accorded to such principles.

The International Law Commission appointed for this purpose a special rapporteur, Professor Spiropoulos, [54] and had before it the valuable memorandum of the Roumanian Professor Vespasian Pella [55] which was prepared under the auspices of the Secretariat of the United Nations. The Commission held six sessions in this respect, [56] and at its sixth session, held in Paris in June and July, 1954, adopted the Draft Code of Offenses Against Security of Mankind, which did not differ substantially from its previous draft code adopted at its third session in 1951. [57]

The Draft Code is not an International Criminal Code but deals only with offenses against the peace and security of mankind, which according to the Commission "contain a political element and which endanger or disturb the maintenance of international peace and security," and not with offenses *communis juris*, such as piracy, slave trade, interference with submarine cables, and traffic in dangerous drugs. [58] Such offenses may be

[51] 5 U.N. GAOR 604, 320th meeting, (Dec. 12, 1950).

[52] A/CN4/45.

[53] See 36 Brit. Y.B. Int'l L. 394 (1960).

[54] *See* Spiropoulos Report of 1950 in A/CN 4/25, Spiropoulos Second Report in A/CN 4/44, and Spiropoulos Third Report in A/CN 4/85.

[55] *See* Pella's memorandum in A/C 4/39 and *cf.* Kuhn, *The Pella Memoranda Relating to International Crimes and Criminal Jurisdiction*, 46 A.J.I.L. 129 (1952).

[56] II Yearbook of the International Law Commission 1954.

[57] The text of the Draft Code of 1954 is set out in the Appendix to Johnson, *supra* note 47, at 466–68. For the previous Draft Code, see Wright, *Proposal for an International Criminal Court*, 46 A.J.I.L. 70–72 (1952); Fenwick, 46 A.J.I.L., 98–100; Potter, *Offenses against the Peace and Security of Mankind*, 46 A.J.I.L. 101–102; Parry, *supra* note 47, at 208–227. For a critique of the Code, see Johnson, *supra* note 47, at 454–65.

[58] *See* Parry, *supra* note 47, at 211 & n.17; Fenwick, *supra* note 57, at 99.

committed either in peace or war or against another state or its citizens or against one's own state or its citizens. [59]

Although the International Law Commission in the Draft Code is dealing with offenses against the peace and security of mankind if committed by the authority of a state [60] or such authorities or individuals, [61] the Commission had in mind mainly the criminal responsibility of the individual by referring to the well-known passage in the judgment of the Nuremberg Tribunal to the effect that "crimes against international law are committed by men, not abstract entities, and only by punishing individuals who commit such crimes can the provisions of international law be enforced." [62]

While the Draft Code was intended to provide for offenses against peace and security of mankind a novel provision not encountered in any other international instrument, it could be argued that paragraph (10) of article 2 covers more or less the same ground, with some changes, as that covered by article II of the Genocide Convention. [63]

Genocide was declared as "a crime under international law which the civilized world condemns" by Resolution of the General Assembly of the United Nations 96(I) and the Genocide Convention was adopted by the Assembly on December 6, 1948.

The Convention defines as genocide the acts specified in article II if committed with intent to destroy the whole or in part a national, ethnical, racial, or religious group—such as killing or causing serious bodily or mental harm to members of the group or deliberately inflicting on the group conditions of life calculated to bring about its total or partial physical destruction or imposing measures intended to prevent births within the group or forcibly transferring children of the group to another. The Convention renders punishable the actual perpetration of such acts as well as acts of conspiracy, incitement, attempt, and complicity. It is laid down that not only private persons are punishable for the crime of genocide but public officials too. While the main sanction of the Convention lies in the undertaking of the parties thereto to enact legislation to implement the Convention and to provide for the punishment of the offenders by the national courts of the state within the territory of which the genocide has been committed, the possibility is left open for the even-

[59] *See* Parry, *supra* note 47, at 219.
[60] *See* paras. 1 to 9 of art. 2 of the Draft.
[61] *See* paras. 10 and 11 of art. 2 of the Draft.
[62] *See* para. 58(c) of the *Report of the International Law Commission* relating to its Third Session (A)/1858) and *cf.* the provisions of arts. 1, 3, & 4 of the Draft.
[63] *Cf.* Johnson, *supra* note 47, 464.

tual jurisdiction of an international penal tribunal agreed by the parties (art. 6.) [64]

The International Court of Justice in its Advisory Opinion on the Convention confirmed that . . .

> . . . the principles underlying the Convention are principles which are recognized by the civilized nations as binding on states even without conventional obligation. . . . In such a convention the contracting states do not have any interests of their own; they merely have, one and all, a common interest, namely the accomplishment of those high purposes which are the raison d'etre of the Convention. Consequently, in a contravention of this type one cannot speak of individual advantages or disadvantages to states. . . .[65]

Finally, aircraft hijacking is a contemporary addition to the list of international and national crimes and the necessity for its control on international and national levels is being realized by states.

Although aircraft hijacking may be a form of piracy, nevertheless it is not "piracy" in the classical sense or as defined in article 15.1(b) of the Geneva Convention on the High Seas, 1958, under which, piracy consists of the commission of any illegal act of violence, detention, or any act of depredation committed for private ends by the crew or the passengers of a private aircraft and directed against an aircraft, persons, or property in a place outside the jurisdiction of a State. [66]

Aircraft piracy was defined as "any seizure or exercise of control by force or violence or threat of force or violence and with wrongful intent of an aircraft in flight in air commerce" [67] and essentially consists in the taking or conversion to private use of an aircraft as a means of transportation and forcibly changing its flight plan to a different destination. [68]

The Tokyo Convention of 1963, which went into effect on December 4, 1969, without declaring the "unlawful seizure of aircraft" in flight as an offense, recognizes its illegality and imposes on the contracting parties

---

[64] *Cf.* WHITEMAN, *supra* note 3, at 848; for the repercussions of the Convention with regard to the *United States Constitution, cf. id.* at 865. The Genocide Convention entered into force on Jan. 12, 1951; BISHOP, *supra* note 7, at 475. For bibliography on the Convention, *cf. id.* at 476 n.54.

[65] *Reservations to the Convention of Genocide, Advisory Opinion;* I.C.J. REP. 15, 23 (1951).

[66] *Cf.,* *supra* note at 716; as to Geneva Conference on the Law of the Sea, compare *The Conclusions of International Conferences,* 35 BRIT. Y.B. INT'L L. 16–33 (1959). By § 4 of the Tokyo Convention Act, 1947, art. 15 of the Geneva Convention on the High Seas, 1958, is declared to be part of the law of nations applicable to the United Kingdom.

[67] *Cf.* 49 U.S.C. para. 1472(i)(2) & para. 1301(4).

[68] *Cf. Aircraft Hijacking:Its Cause and Cure,* 63 A.J.I.L., 695 (1969). *see also* art. 11 of the Tokyo Convention which provides for the case "where a person on board unlawfully commits an act of interference, seizure, or other wrongful exercise of control of an aircraft on flight or where such an act is about to be committed."

the duty of restoring the aircraft and cargo to the lawful owners and facilitating the resumption of the interrupted flight. [69]

At the Fourth Biennial Conference of World Peace Through Law at Bangkok, Thailand, some 1500 lawyers from 114 countries, as members of the World Peace Through Law Center of Geneva, unanimously adopted various resolutions dealing with crucial issues designed to promote world peace. Among them, Resolution 13 relates to aircraft hijacking. As a result of that Resolution, a Convention to deter aircraft hijacking was drafted and circulated among the members of the Center. [70]

A subcommittee of the Legal Committee of the International Civil Aviation Organization on the other hand drafted a convention implementing the Tokyo Convention relating to prosecution and extradition of persons committing the offense as defined thereunder. [71]

The General Assembly of the United Nations at its Twenty-fourth Session by its Resolution on forcible diversion of civil aircraft in flight [72]

1. Called upon member states to take appropriate measures to ensure that their respective national legislations provide for adequate measures against all kinds of acts of unlawful interference with, seizure of, or other wrongful exercise of control by force, or threat of force, over civil aircraft on flight.
2. Urged such states to prosecute the persons committing such acts.
3. Urged full support for the efforts of the International Civil Aviation Organization for the preparation and implementation of a convention providing, *inter alia,* for making the unlawful seizure of such aircraft a punishable offense.
4. Invited the member states to ratify the Tokyo Convention.

In 1970 the Hague Convention for the Suppression of Unlawful Seizure of Aircraft elaborated the obligation to extradite or punish hijackers.

Closely linked with the codification of international crimes and par-

[69] *See* the text of the Convention issued by the International Civil Aviation Organization and its art. 1, 1(b), & 11. In England, the Convention was ratified by the Tokyo Convention Act, 1967; *cf. Extradition–An Answer to Hijacking,* 119 NEW L. J., 851 (1969).

[70] *See* Pamphlet Series No. 13, Dec. 1969, of the World Peace Through Law Centre under the heading *Convention to Deter Aircraft Hijacking.*

[71] *Cf. Hijacking of Aircraft,* 119 NEW L. J. 281 (1969). In the Draft Convention the offense of hijacking is defined in the following terms:
Any person who on board an aircraft in flight—
(a) Unlawfully, by force or threat thereof, interferes with, seizes or otherwise wrongfully exercises control of that aircraft in order to change its itinerary; or
(b) attempts to perform such an act; or
(c) is an accomplice of a person who performs or attempts to perform such an act,
shall be guilty of a penal offense.

[72] Res. 2551 (XXIV) (Dec. 12, 1965).

ticularly of offenses against peace and security of mankind is the question of exercise of criminal jurisdiction with respect to such offenses.

Is the contemplated Code to be administered through an international tribunal, through national tribunals, or through both? [73]

It is a settled principle that a state can exercise criminal jurisdiction in respect of offenses committed on its territory (the principle of territoriality) and as far as its nationals are concerned for offenses committed by them anywhere (principle of active nationality). It has also been maintained that the state's criminal jurisdiction extends also to offenses committed against its own nationals (principle of passive nationality) or over offenders on the ground that the offense was prejudicial to the vital interests of the state (protective principle).

But there is a more comprehensive principle, that of universality, through which a state could claim jurisdiction over an offender irrespectively of the place of the commission of the offense or of the nationality of the offender in cases of offenses not committed in the territory of any particular state, such as piracy, an offense committed on the high seas, or under certain international conventions such as the Genocide Convention, 1948, and 1949 Geneva Conventions and the 1954 Hague Convention. [74]

It is significant how the chief French prosecuting counsel argued the question of the jurisdiction of the International Military Court at Nuremberg:

> The principle of territorial application of penal laws, he said, gives to every State the right to punish crimes committed on its territory. The application of the territorial principle covers the violations of international law in territories subject to military occupation; these violations are the chief source of war crimes. But the crimes committed by the defendants were not directed against any given State, in any occupied territory. All the States which were occupied and temporarily enslaved by their Armed Forces have been equally victims both of the illicit war which they launched and of the methods used by them in the conduct of this war.
>
> There is, therefore, no State which could legitimately claim the privilege of trying these criminals. Only an International Tribunal emanating from the combined United Nations, which were yesterday at war with Germany, can rightly claim this privilege. . . . There is, therefore, nothing new from a juridical point of view in the principle of justice which you are called upon to render.[75]

The need for an international criminal jurisdiction was recognized by the General Assembly of the United Nations in a resolution adopted in

[73] *Cr.* Parry, *supra* note 47, at 217; for an historical review of the matter, *see* Wright, *supra* note 57, at 61, 63.

[74] Carnegie, *supra* note at 403, 407.

[75] Trial of the German Major War Criminals, H.M.S.O., 1946, pt. 4, at 340, cited by Carnegie, *supra* note 74, at 414.

1948, in which it was stated in the preamble that in "the course of development of the international community, there will be an increasing need for an international judicial organ for the trial of certain crimes under international law."[76] In the same resolution the General Assembly requested the International Law Commission to study the desirability and possibility of establishing an international criminal organ "for the trial of persons charged with genocide or other crimes over which the jurisdiction will be conferred upon that organ by international conventions."[77]

The International Law Commission after consideration decided that the establishment of an international criminal court was desirable and that it was possible.[78]

The General Assembly at its fifth session in 1950 discussed the conclusions of the International Law Commission, but the majority preferred not to take any side on the matter in abstracto, until a concrete Draft Statute of the Court was laid before the Assembly. By Resolution 489(V) of December 1950, the General Assembly decided to set up a committee of representatives of seventeen member states "for the purpose of preparing one or more preliminary draft conventions and proposals for the establishment and the statute of an international court."[79]

The Committee was convened at Geneva on August 1, 1951, and concluded its work on August 31, 1951. It produced a Draft Statute of the Court accompanied by a Report to the General Assembly explaining the general purpose and commenting upon the detailed provisions of the proposals.[80]

In this respect, reference may be made to the Geneva Supplementary Convention signed at Geneva on November 16, 1937; ten of the signatories of the main Convention signed at Geneva on the same day and dealing with acts of terrorism, agreed to the creation of an International Criminal Court to which the parties would be entitled to hand over the accused if they decided not to extradite them or to try them before their own courts. Those Conventions have not yet entered into force.[81]

---

[76] G.A. Res. 260 B(III) (3rd Sess.) 3 U.S. GAOR 177 (1948).

[77] *Id.*

[78] U.N. Doc. A/1316.

[79] 5 U.N. GAOR 977–78; *cf.* Green, *United Nations General Assembly* 1950, 4 I.C.L.R. (1951).

[80] See the Draft Statute for an International Criminal Court prepared by the Committee on International Criminal Jurisdiction, in its relative Report, 7 UN. GAOR, Supp. 11, at 21–25, U.N. Doc. A/2136 (1952), and 46 A.J.I.L. 1–11 (1952), *Official Documents* 1–11; *cf.* FINCH, *Draft Statute for an International Criminal Court* 46 A.J.I.L.; Yuen-Li-Lang, *supra* note 47, at 73; regarding the competence of the Court, *id.* at 76–82, and its organization at 82–88.

[81] OPPENHEIM-LAUTERPACHT, *supra* note 7, at 710. For an analysis see 19 BRIT. Y.B. INT'L L. 217 (1938).

Section 2.   THE POSITION OF THE INDIVIDUAL IN AN INTER-
NATIONAL CRIMINAL LAW

S. Prakash Sinha

2.1. Introduction

Common sentiments of condemnation toward the violation of penal law,
have led certain writers to view the objective of criminal law too narrowly, as being primarily the punishment of the offender and no more. [1]
However, it seems that the objective of a criminal law is not limited to
the punishment of individuals, it includes, in addition, the protection of
individuals, both procedural and substantive. Criminal justice thus conceived in both of these aspects shapes the content of a criminal law.
The concern in this context is with the conduct of the individual and not
with that of the states, although the relevance of states to the treatment
of the individual is in no way denied. Thus, it is the crimes of individuals,
and not those of the states, which are of concern to the problem of an I.C.L. [2]

When the problem is approached in the sense stated above, one is confronted with an equivocation of the term "international criminal law," or
certainly a plurality of its meaning. For example, one observer points out
at least six meanings in which it is used, the territorial scope of municipal
criminal law, the internationally prescribed municipal criminal law, the
internationally authorized municipal criminal law, the municipal criminal
law common to civilized nations, the international cooperation in the

---

[1] Professor Mueller talks only of punishment of the wrongdoer while discussing "[t]he
aims of international penal law," and then proceeds to enumerate the subpurposes of "the
ultimate purpose of *absolute prevention*." Mueller, *The United Nations Draft Code of
Offences Against the Peace and Security of Mankind: An American Evaluation*, in International Criminal Law 597,618–19 (G. Mueller & E. Wise eds. 1965); *cf*. C. Bassiouni,
Criminal Law and Its Processes 5–11(1969).

[2] It is largely in this sense that Professor Schwarzenberger has explored the problem
de lege lata in his celebrated article on the subject, but it is unfortunate that in his reflections on the problem of international criminal law *de lege ferenda* he should confuse the
problem of the criminal conduct of the individual with the problem of the comparable
conduct of the states. Consequently, he is led to the conclusion that "[i]n such a situation
an international criminal law that is meant to be applied to the world powers is a contradiction in terms. It presupposes an International authority which is superior to these
states. In reality, however, any attempt to enforce an international criminal code against
either the Soviet Union or the United States would be war under another name. Thus,
proposals for a universal international criminal law fall into the category of the one-way
pattern for the reorganization of the international society." G. Schwarzenberger, *The
Problem of International Criminal Law*, in International Criminal Law 3, 35–36 (G.
Mueller & E. Wise eds. 1965).

administration of municipal criminal justice, and the material sense of the term which relates to acts striking at the very root of the international society.[3] However, for the purpose of observing the individual's position in an I.C.L. it is useful, and probably sufficient, to examine (1) international law with respect to crimes of the individual and (2) international legal arrangements for procuring his due punishment for his acts generally regarded as criminal, and for protecting him from persecution for having exercised those options of his political and private life which are generally regarded as legitimate. (A precise and comprehensive formulation of international legal standards for determining universally the legitimacy of these options has not yet been achieved. However, the European legal régime for human rights illustrates one approach to that formulation.)

2.2. International Law With Respect to Crimes of the Individual

Two issues immediately arise in exploring international law with respect to crimes of the individual: (1) What is the juridical position of the individual in international law, in other words, does this law regard the individual as its subject and, therefore, concern itself with his acts and his protection? and (2) Does this law contain a body of I.C.L.?

The law of nations, later to be called international law,[4] referred to the common law of all nations in its older meaning of the ancient Jewish, Greek, and Roman law,[5] and not yet to a distinct system of law.[6] The idea of a universal state emerged with the conquest of neighbors, producing the idea of *pax romana* whereunder the Romans would rule the world. The common principles of all nations provided the guidance needed for governing the relations of peoples and, later, of states.[7] The law of nations, or the *jus gentium*, was thus a law of individuals and their associations in various forms, including the form of the ancient states. Its basis was found in natural reason[8] and it was recognized as applying to relations between different peoples without requiring legislative recognition.

In the classical period of Roman law, *jus civile* governed the Romans and

---

[3] G. Schwarzenberger, *supra* note 2, at 4–14.

[4] The term "international law" first appeared in Jeremy Bentham's introduction to his book *An Introduction to the Principles of Morals and Legislation* (1789).

[5] J. SELDEN, DE JURE NATURALI ET GENTIUM JUXTA DISCIPLINAM EBRAEORUM (1695) C. PHILLIPSON, THE INTERNATIONAL LAW AND CUSTOM OF ANCIENT GREECE AND ROME (1911).

[6] R. REDSLOB, HISTOIRE DES GRANDS PRINCIPES DU DROIT DES GENS DEPUIS L'ANTIQUITÉ JUSQU' À LA VEILLE DE LA GRANDE GUERRE 108 (1923); A. PILLET, DÉS PERSONNES MORALES EN DROIT INTERNATIONAL PRIVÉ 301 (1914).

[7] See V.R. Idelson, *The Law of Nations and the Individual*, 30 THE GROTIUS SOCIETY TRANSACTIONS FOR THE YEAR 1944, at 50, 51 (1945).

[8] For the correspondence of the meanings of *jus gentium* and *jus naturale*, see F.K. VON SAVIGNY, I SYSTEM DES HEUTIGEN RÖMISCHEN RECHTS 414 (1840–49).

jus gentium referred to the special status granted to foreigners in Rome.[9] This appears to be the first instance in the Western world, of a legal relationship with foreigners. [10] A triple distinction of law is made in the Justinian compilation where the civil law, the law of nations, and the law of nature compose the scheme of law. The medieval Christian theologians seem to have later adopted this distinction in constructing their own ecclesiastical, or canon, law. Unlike the Roman law, the law of nature of these theologians postulated the existence of a higher authority than man and his legal systems.[11] The law of nations was considered to be man-made law of superhuman origin. [12] At least partly, it grew from the positive law of human legislators, a fact which was first pointed out by Abélard and the French scholars of canon law in the twelfth century. The juristic thought of the later middle ages, notably at the beginning of the fourteenth century, viewed the law of nature as common to all peoples; it applied certain principles of the law of nations in both domestic affairs as well as in relations with other peoples; [13] and it distinguished the civil law from both the law of nature and the law of nations. Until the twelfth century, the view prevailed in the Western World that the Roman custom, the *consuetudo communis,* applied throughout the known world. The emperors of the West were regarded by the medieval lawyer as lawgivers, not only for the Occident but for the entire world, for the *universus orbis.*[14] From the twelfth century onward, the Imperial power began to abate as the universal lawgiver. Rulers claimed exemption from the Emperor's authority on legal grounds, such as prescription, privilege granted by the Emperor, ancient custom, and even assumption of irregular titles. Eventually, the Holy Roman Empire broke up, giving the final truth to the popular saying that it was neither holy, nor Roman, nor an empire. It was in the spirit of these times that Bartolus wrote, *Civitates non recognoscunt superiorum*

[9] A.F.J. THIBAUT, SYSTEM DES PANDENKTENRECHTS 7 (Lindley's trans. 1855).

[10] *Cf.* P. Guggenheim, *The Birth of Autonomous International Law,* in INTERNATIONAL LAW IN A CHANGING WORLD 80 (C. Jenks 1963).

[11] Thus, St. Augustine maintained in the fourth century that law eternal, or the law of nature, took precedence over temporal and secular law. St. Isidore, the Bishop of Seville in the sixth century, wrote in the fifth book of his *Etymologies* that the origin of the law of nature rested in the natural instincts of man and not in any human legislative system.

[12] This was the contention of certain medieval writers, such as St. Isidore in the sixth century, Gratian's decree published about 1140, St. Thomas Aquinas, and various other writers of the late thirteenth century.

[13] These rules were applied in relation to all other peoples, Christian or non-Christian. Three centuries later, Grotius elaborated the notion into a concept that the application of the law of nations was not limited to Christendom alone. H. Grotius, *Mare Liberum (1609)* in THE CLASSICS OF INTERNATIONAL LAW 11 (R. van Deman Magoffin transl. (1916).

[14] Contemporary practice supported this notion. For example, King Robert of Sicily invoked *pandacts* and *codax* no less than 20 times in his instructions to his legates to the Pope in 1319. See P. Guggenheim, *supra* note 10, at 84.

[states do not recognize a higher authority than their own], and Balde stated, "*Rex in regno suo est imperator regni* [the king, in his kingdom, is emperor of that kingdom]."[15] With the fall of the Roman Empire a feudal system of authority emerged in Europe. There grew a world of warrior, priest, free farmer, serf, and the local trader. By the beginning of the seventeenth century, Western man had colonized the New World and moved eastward in quest of further trade. He also searched for a new ordering of the system of authority to control the rich life of this trade and intercourse. He found it not in a Roman state but in the nation-state. At first the warrior chief became the sovereign, but soon an impersonal sovereign emerged to take his place. It was the modern state. The state was sovereign. It was impersonal. It was separate from its prince, separate even from its government. It was a juridical entity by itself.[16] The final step in the emergence of the modern system of states is represented by the Peace of Westphalia of 1648.[17] From the viewpoint of that system, the world was carved into various states.[18] The new states took shape along the Aristotelian concept of the *civitas perfecta*, that the state was self-sufficing. The civil law and the law of nature provided them their legal foundation. The law of nations provided them the governing principle for the juridical relations among states. It thus faded out of civil law and emerged as a law applicable exclusively to the interstate relations. It was newly conceived. Its content developed along new lines.[19]

[15] *id.*

[16] K.S. CARLSTON, LAW AND STRUCTURES OF SOCIAL ACTION 132–133 (1956).

[17] L. Gross, *The Peace of Westphalia, 1648–1948,* 42 A.J.I.L. 20 (1948).

[18] As Professor Carlston has stated, although the structure of the world was so compartmentalized, neither the social action of the world could be so compartmentalized nor was one state able to achieve authority over all social action. The system thus failed to provide the necessary means of control for the social action of the world society even under the conditions of the world of 1648. CARLSTON, *supra* note 16, at 133.

[19] Vitoria (1480–1546) had advanced the new concept of the community of nations, the *societas gentium,* which obeyed one law, the *jus gentium.* This law was either equated with or derived from the law of nature. In 1612, Suarez (1548–1617) viewed the law of nations as independent of the law of nature in certain respects. In 1625, Grotius (1583–1645) distinguished it completely from the law of nature and asserted its fully autonomous status, although he does not seem quite clear as to what rules belong to which laws. Later, particularly in the eighteenth century, the law of nations was claimed to prevail over the law of nature. Jurists, such as Christian Wolff (1679–1754) of Germany and Emerich de Vattel (1714–1767) of Switzerland, stripped the law of nature of its legal imperative and confined it to its moral influence, and Otto von Gierke (1841–1921) of Germany held that the role of the law of nations was independent of the civil law and the law of nature. Finally the legal historians of the nineteenth century expounded that a legal system is valid to the extent of its effectiveness. That gave birth to the contemporary theory of positive law. International law is valid if it conforms to the actual practice of states. *See* F. DE VITORIA, DE INDIS ET DE IVRE BELLI REFLECTIONES (1557) (E. Nys ed. 1917); F. Suarez, *De legibus, ac Deo Legislatore* (1612), ch. XIX, ss. 1, 2, in CLASSICS OF INTERNATIONAL LAW, 1944; H. GROTIUS, DE JURE BELLI AC PACIS TRES (1625), Prolegomena

In this international law, the position of the individual is not the same as in the earlier *jus gentium*. Although it is the collections of individuals which compose entities of the social structures called states and although the international activity of states in our times shows an increasing concern for the well-being of the individual, [20] it is nevertheless true that the state exists not merely in the abstract and symbolic terms but in the behavioristic and concrete sense, and the individual finds his place under the system of international law only through membership in the state. The states, not individuals, are governed by this law, although there is a tendency to extend its application to certain international organizations

(corresponding to §§ 40 and 41 of the translation by F.W. Kelsey). Ch. I, § XIV, in CLASSICS OF INTERNATIONAL LAW 1913; C. Wolff, INSTITUTIONES JURIS NATURAE ET GENTIUM, in QUIBUS EX IPSA HOMINUS NATURA CONTINUO NEXU OMNES OBLIGATIONES ET JURA OMNIA DEDUCUNTUR, ch. II, 12 (1769); E. de Vattel, *Le droit des gens; ou, Principes de la loi naturelle appliqués à la conduite et aux affaires des nations et des souverains* (1785), Preliminaires, §§ 26, 27, in CLASSICS OF INTERNATIONAL LAW (1916); O.F. von Gierke, *Die grundbegriffe des staatsrechts und die neuesten staatsrechtstheorien, Unveränderter abdruck der* in *der Zeitschrift für die gesamte staatswissenschaft* (1915). Thus, when the first foundations of the newly conceived law of nations were being laid, it was generally accepted that nature had given man universally valid inherent rights, which could be discovered through right reason. This law which nature gave man was a higher law to which all mankind was subject. At first it was thought that this higher law rested directly upon the conscience of rulers as individuals and thence upon states. Later, when the state itself was given juridical personality, the law of nations became that branch of the law of nature which applied to the society of states. This conception of the law of nations had profound influence on it in its early formative stages in the seventeenth and the eighteenth centuries. But since it was impossible to found an objective legal system upon so subjective a basis as a revealed law of nature, it gave way in the nineteenth century to the positivist approach, according to which what is law and what should be law are not necessarily the same thing. What the international law is can be discovered only by an examination of the practice of states and the principles upon which this practice is based. The validity of this law is sought in the common consent of states. Substantial uniformity of practice becomes evidence of the existence of the convergence of the wills of the states, which produces a rule that binds a state without reference to its particular consent. Scientific methodology has been used to develop the content of the principles of international law along these lines. International law is created by a general recognition among states of a certain practice as obligatory. It is customary. S.P. Sinha, *New Nations and the International Custom*, 9 Wm. & Mary L. Rev. 788, 790–792 (1968).

[20] For an outstanding example, see the arrangements made by certain European states by international agreements in the human rights area to give the individual access to a legal system which prevails beyond the periphery of his state. Convention for the Protection of Human Rights and Fundamental Freedoms, signed in Rome on Nov. 4, 1950, 213 U.N.T.S. 222; the Protocol to the Convention for the Protection of Human Rights and Fundamental Freedoms, signed in Paris on Mar. 20, 1952, 213 U.N.T.S. 262. *See also* H. GURADZE, DER STAND DER MENSCHENRECHTS IM VÖLKERRECHT (1956). The Convention grants eleven civil rights and establishes a European Commission of Human Rights with power to consider alleged breach of the Convention by a party to the Convention and to receive petitions from any person, nongovernmental organization, or groups of individuals claiming to be the victim of a violation by a party of the rights set forth in the Convention. The Convention also establishes a European Court of Human Rights with a view to insuring the observance of its provisions.

which are in the nature of an international person because "its members, by entrusting certain functions to it, with the attendant duties and responsibilities, have clothed it with the competence required to enable those functions to be effectively discharged." [21]

Various theories have been advanced to explain the individual's position in international law. Thus, he has been regarded as an object of international law, since he possesses no rights and duties under this law, but derives benefits from it and endures its burdens as an incidence of the rights and duties which his state possesses under this law. [22] He has been

[21] The Advisory Opinion of the International Court of Justice, Apr. 11, 1949, on *Reparations for Injuries Suffered in the Service of the United Nations,* 1949 I.C.J.R. 174.

[22] Heilborn is supposed to be the first theorist to propound the object theory of the individual. See P. Heilborn, Das System des Völkerrechts 58–211 (1896). Other proponents of this theory include D. Anzilotti, Cours di Diritto Internazionale, Vol. I, 113, 121 (3d ed. 1928); D. Anzilotti, Cours de droit international 132–136 (1929); A.S. de Bustamente, Droit international public, Vol. I, 4, 9, 136 (1934); E.M. Borchard, Diplomatic Protection of Citizens Abroad, 16, 18, 29, 354, 355 (1915); A. Cavaglieri, Corso di Diritto Internazionale 110, 254 (1925); A. Cavaglieri, *Règles générales du droit de la paix* 26 Recueil dies Cours 319 (1929); F.C.R. Despagnet, Cours de droit international public 79, 361 (3d ed. 1905); C. Diena, Principi di Diritto Internazionale 260 (2d ed. 1914); C.G. Fenwick, International Law, 32, 86, 189 (2d ed. 1934); R. Foignet, Manuel élémentaire de droit international public 1, 57 (14th ed. 1929); Sc. Gemma, Appunti di Diritto Internazionale 55, 161 (1923); J.W. Garner, Recent Developments in International Law 25 (1925); P. Heilborn, Grundbegriffe des Völkerrechts 88, 95 (1912); P. Heilborn, *Die Subjekts des Völkerrechts,* 2 Strupps Wörterbuch des Völkerrechts und der Diplomatie 684 (1925); A.S. Hershey, Essentials of International Public Law 92 (1912); A. Hold-Ferneck, I Lehrbuch des Völkerrechts 251 (1930); T.E. Holland, Lectures on International Law 1, 55, 61 (1933); M.O. Hudson, Cases on International Law 17, 20 (2d ed. 1936); C.C. Hyde, International Law Chiefly as Interpreted and Applied by the United States, Vol. I, 1, 21, 33 (2d ed. 1945); Hammarskjöld, *La neutralité en général,* 3 Bibliotheca Visseriana 53, 113 (1924); G. Jellinek, System der subjektiven öffentlichen Rechts 324 (2d ed. 1905); R. Knubben, Die Subjekte des Völkerrechts 487 (1928); E. Kaufmann, Das Wesen des Völkerrechts und die Clausula Rebus sic Stantibus 140–144 (1911); E. Kaufmann, *Régles génerales du droit de la paix,* 54 Recueil des Cours 320 (1935); H. Kraus, *Systéme et fonctions de traités internationaux,* 50 Recueil des Cours 317 (1934); T.E. Lawrence, The Principles of International Law 72 (6th ed. 1915); J. de Louter, Le droit international public positif, Vol. I, 1, 11, 160, 163, 168, 259 (1920); *id.,* Vol. II, 1; Meier, Der Staatsangehörige und seine Rechte 20 (1927); J.B. Moore, A Digest of International Law, Vol. I, 17 (1906); Nielson, International Law Applied to Reclamations 8 (1933); L. Oppenheim, International Law, Vol. I, 2, 17–19, 456–463 (6th ed. 1915); W.G.F. Phillimore, *Droits et devoirs fondamentaux des états,* 1 Recueil des Cours 26, 33 (1923); R. Redslob, Histoire des grands principes du droit des gens depuis l'antiquité jusqu' à la veille de la grande guerre 13–15, 538–543 (1923); L. Renault, *De l'application de droit pénal aux faits de guerre* 25 Revue générale de droit international public 5, 29 (1918); K. Strupp, *Les règles générales du droit de la paix,* 47 Recueil des Cours 456, 536 (1934); P. Schoen, *Zur Lehre von den Subjekten des Völkerrechts,* 23 Zeitschrift für Völkerrechts 418, 436 (1939); G. Schwarzenberger, A Manual of International Law 35, 53 (1947); G. Schwarzenberger, International Law 75, 78, 161 (2d ed. 1949); H. Triepel, Völkerrecht und Landesrecht 13, 21, 259, 329 (1899); H. Triepel, *Les rapports entre le droit interne et*

regarded not merely as an object of this law but also its final end, [23] its beneficiary, [24] and its potential subject. [25] He has even been suggested as the subject of international law when states enforce this law upon him as part of their municipal law, [26] or when he receives benefits as a national of a member state of the international community, [27] or when obligations are imposed on him both by national and international laws as in instances involving slave trade, carriage of contraband, piracy, breach of blockade, damage to submarine cables, and so on,[28] or when international law is

---

la droit international, 1 RECUEIL DES COURS 81 (1923); H. TAYLOR, A TREATISE ON INTERNATIONAL PUBLIC LAW, 211 (1901); ULLMANN, VÖLKERRECHT, 88, 253, 311, 344 (2d ed., 1908); C. de Visscher, *La responsibilité des etats,* 2 BIBLIOTHECA VISSERIANA 87 (1923); G.-A. Walz, *Les rapports du droit international et du droit interne,* 61 RECUEIL DES COURS 387, 409 (1937); WILLIAMS, CHAPTERS ON CURRENT INTERNATIONAL LAW AND THE LEAGUE OF NATIONS 5 (1929); A ZORN, GRUNDZÜGE VÖLKERRECHTS 26 (2d ed. 1903).

[23] H.W. Briggs, *Remarks,* 40 PROCEEDINGS OF THE AMERICAN SOCIETY OF INTERNATIONAL LAW 40 (1946); F.S. Dunn, *The International Rights of Individuals,* 35 PROCEEDINGS OF THE AMERICAN SOCIETY OF INTERNATIONAL LAW 14 (1941); C. EAGLETON, THE RESPONSIBILITY OF STATES IN INTERNATIONAL LAW 221 (1928); J.W. Garner, *La reconstruction de droit international,* 28 REVUE GÉNÉRALE DE DROIT INTERNATIONAL PUBLIC 413 (1921); P. Heilborn, *supra* note 22, at 685; J. DE LOUTER, I LE DROIT INTERNATIONAL PUBLIC POSITIF 160, 259 (1920); J.H. RALSTON, DEMOCRACY'S INTERNATIONAL LAW 10 (1920); S. Séfériadès, *Principes généraux du droit international de la paix,* 34 RECUEIL DES COURS 181 292 (1930); SCHWARZENBERGER, MANUAL 35; K. STRUPP, WÖRTERBUCH DES VÖLKERRECHTS UND DER DIPLOMATIE 685 (1925).

[24] BORCHARD, DIPLOMATIC PROTECTION 18; H.W. BRIGGS, THE PROGRESSIVE DEVELOPMENT OF INTERNATIONAL LAW 29 (1947); A.V. Freeman, Remarks, 35 PROCEEDINGS OF THE AMERICAN SOCIETY OF INTERNATIONAL LAW 19 (1941); GAREIS, VÖLKERRECHT 148 (1901); HYDE, INTERNATIONAL LAW, Vol. I, 36–40, Vol. II, 873; Kraus, *supra* note 22 at 373, 379; E. Kaufmann, *supra* note 22 at 324; A.G.J.A. MÉHRIGNHAC TRAITÉ DE DROIT PUBLIC INTERNATIONAL, Vol. II, 69 (1907); K. Strupp, *supra* note 22, at 263; SCHWARZENBERGER, INTERNATIONAL LAW 75–77; G. Salvioli, *Les règles générales du droit de la paix,* 46 RECUEIL DES COURS 4, 41 (1933); G.-A. Walz, *supra* note 22, at 381.

[25] ANZILOTTI, COURS 1, 41, 111, 121; S. Basdevant, *Règles générales du droit de la paix,* 58 RECUEIL DES COURS 475, 528 (1936); A. Cavaglieri, *I soggetti del diritto internazionale,* 17 REVISTA DI DIRRITTO INTERNAZIONALE 18, 18–32, 169–187 (1925); S. ROMANO, CORSO DI DIRITTO INTERNAZIONALE 71 (1929); G. Streit, *La conception du droit international privé,* 20 RECUEIL DES COURS 35 (1927); J. SPIROPOULOS, L'INDIVIDU EN DROIT INTERNATIONAL 33, 66 (1928); STRUPP, GRUNDZÜGE 1, 103; M. Siotto-Pintor, Les sujects du droit international autres que les états, 41 RECUEIL DES COURS 251, 267, 274 (1932); K. Strupp, *supra* note 22, at 463, 465; P. Schoen, *supra* note 22, at 411–448; SCHWARZENBERGER, MANUAL 1, 35.

[26] C. Bilfinger, *Les bases fondamentales de la communauté der états,* 63 RECUEIL DES COURS 133, 134 (1938); G. Diena, *L'individu devant l'autorité judiciaire et le droit international,* 16 REVUE GÉNÉRALE DE DROIT INTERNATIONAL PUBLIC 57 (1909).

[27] GAREIS, VÖLKERRECHT 148–152; MÉRIGNHAC, TRAITÉ, Vol. II, 171; F. VON LISZT, VÖLKERRECHT 112 (4th ed. 1906); A.P.O. RIVIER, PRINCIPES DU DROIT DES GENS, Vol. I, 13 (1896).

[28] A. Adler, *Über die Verletzung völkerrechtlicher Pflichten durch Individuem,* 1 ZEITSCHRIFT FÜR VÖLKERRECHT 614, 614–618 (1907); H. Rehm, *Untertanen als Subjekts völkerrechtlicher Pflichten,* 1 ZEITSCHRIFT FÜR VÖLKERRECHT 53, 53–55 (1907).

enforced against both the state and its individuals,[29] or when international bodies recognize the individual as having a standing before them,[30] or when criminal violations of the international laws of war and humanity are involved. There are yet additional situations where the individual has been treated as more than an object of international law.[31] In theory, the perception of the position of the individual in international law has followed the conception of the relationship between municipal law and international law. According to the monist conception, the two laws are constituent of the same legal order. Consequently, national courts can apply international law without requiring its specific transformation into municipal law. According to the dualist conception, the two laws represent two distinct systems of law. Consequently, international law has to be transformed into municipal law before national courts can apply it.

[29] G.-A., Walz, *supra* note 22, at 381, 443.

[30] VON LISZT, VÖLKERRECHT 41, 144; W. SCHÜCKING, DER STAATENVARBAND DER HAAGER KONFERENZEN 141 (1912).

[31] *See* B. AKZIN, LES PROBLÈMES FONDAMENTAUX DU DROIT INTERNATIONAL PUBLIC 121 (1929); S. Basdevant, *supra* 25, at 528; C. Berazowski, *Les sujets non-souverains du droit international,* 65 RECUEIL DES COURS 5, 6–20 (1938); H.H.L. Bellot, *War Crimes and War Criminals,* 36 CANADIAN LAW TIMES 754, 876 (1936); H.H.L. Bellot, *War Crimes, Their Prevention and Punishment,* 2 TRANSACTIONS OF THE GROTIUS SOCIETY 31 (1916); E. BAUER, DIE KRIEGSVERBRECHER VON GERICHT (1945); C.A.H. Bartlett, *Liability for Official War Crimes,* 35 L.Q. REV. 177 (1919); A. Cavaglieri, *supra* note 25, at 18, 169, 186; J. DUMAS, LES SANCTIONS PÉNALES DE CRIMES ALLEMANDS (1916); F.S. Dunn, *supra* note 23, at 14; G.J. Ebers, Remarks, 1926 MITTEILUNGEN DER DEUTSCHEN GESELLSCHAFT FÜR VÖLKERRECHT 38; C. Eagleton, *The Individual in International Law,* 40 PROCEEDINGS OF THE AMERICAN SOCIETY OF INTERNATIONAL LAW 22 (1946); G.A. Finch, *The Nuremberg Trial and International Law,* 41 A.J.I.L. 20 (1947); J.W. Garner, *Punishment of Offenders Against the Laws and Customs of War,* 14 A.J.I.L. 70 (1920); J. Hostie, *Examen de quelques règles du droit international dans le domaine des communications et du transit,* 40 RECUEIL DES COURS 403, 488 (1932); J. Hostie, *Les affaires de communication devant la Cour Permanente de Justice Internationale,* 22 REVUE DE DROIT INTERNATIONAL 105, 138 (1938); E. Hambro, *Individuals Before International Tribunal* 35 PROCEEDINGS OF THE AMERICAN SOCIETY OF INTERNATIONAL LAW 22 (1941); N. Hall, *The Individual in International Organization,* 28 AMERICAN POLITICAL SCIENCE REVIEW 276 (1934); H. Isay, Remarks, 1926 MITTEILUNGEN DER DEUTSCHEN GESELLSCHAFT FÜR VÖLKERRECHT 98; H. Isay, *Die Zuständigkeit der Gemischten Schiedsgerichte,* 53 JURISTISCHE WOCHENSCHRIFT 596 (1924); P.C. JESSUP, A MODERN LAW OF NATIONS, 9 (1948); M. St. Korowicz, *La personnalité international de l'individu d'après la Convention relative à la Haute Silésie (1922–1937),* 6 REVUE INTERNATIONAL FRANÇAISE DE DROIT DES GENS 5, 23 (1938); M. LACHS, WAR CRIMES, AN ATTEMPT TO DEFINE THE ISSUES, (1945); A.D. McNAIR, "Collective Security, 17 *British Yearbook of International Law* 150 (1936); A. Mérignhac, *De la sanction des infractions au droit des gens commises, au cours de la guerre européenne, par les empires du centre,* 24 REVUE GÉNÉRALE DE DROIT INTERNATIONAL PUBLIC 5 (1917); A.G.J.A. Mérignhac & E. Lamonon, LE DROIT DES GENS ET LA GUERRE DE 1914–1918, Vol. II, 563 (1921); Musso, L'INDIVIDUO E LE MINORANZE COME SOGGETTI DEL DIRITTO INTERNAZIONALE 32 (1938); PALLIERI, DIRITTO INTERNAZIONALE PUBBLICO, 277 (1937); ROMANO, CORSO 71; Rocco, SISTEMA DI DIRITTO INTERNAZIONALE 32 (1938); S. Rundstein, *L'arbitrage internationale en matière privée,* 23 RECUEIL DES COURS 329, 347, 363 (1928); P. Schoen, *supra* note 22, at 411; M. Siotto-Pintor, *supra* 25, at 346.

Corresponding to these conceptions of the relationship between these two laws, three main thoughts have appeared to describe the individual's position in international law.

1. From the dualist conception it is deduced that international law has states as its subjects, whereas municipal law has individuals as its subjects. The rules of international law relating to the interests of individuals are addressed to the states having jurisdiction over them and not to the individuals themselves. When international law contemplates a right and procedural ability for the individual, it is in fact authorizing his state to confer these on him. Or, when this law contemplates a duty and procedural amenability for him, it is in fact directing his state to enforce these upon him. International agreements may confer these to him, but that is only an expression of them and is solely dependent on the will of the party states and is not sufficient to make the individual a subject of international law. [32] It may even be that it is not inherent in the nature of international law that individuals cannot have attributes of rights, duties, procedural ability, and amenability directly under this law but, it is pointed out, possession of these attributes in this manner is not actually the case.[33]

2. From the monist conception it is deduced that both states and individuals are subjects of international law. Individuals are direct subjects of this law when it specifies them as such, and they are its indirect subjects when it leaves it up to the municipal law to determine the subject individuals. [34] What makes individuals its subject is the fact that their conduct is regulated by international law, for the violations of which they are held responsible before an international court and to uphold which they have a right to proceedings before such a forum.[35] If there are rules of international law which apply directly to them and give them access to international tribunals, that is sometimes considered sufficient to make the

[32] ANZILOTTI, COURS DE DROIT INTERNATIONAL 134; G. Sperdutti, *L'individu et le droit international*, 90 RECUEIL DES COURS 727, 849 (1956); T GIHL, FOLKRÄTT UNDER FRED 31 (1956).
[33] G. SCHWARZENBERGER, INTERNATIONAL LAW, Vol. I, 140, 155 (3d ed. 1957); G. Schwarzenberger, *The Protection of Human Rights in British State Practice*, 1 CURRENT LEGAL PROBLEMS 152, 153 (1948).
[34] H. KELSEN, GENERAL THEORY OF LAW AND STATE 59, 65, 83, 347 (A. Wedberg transl 1945). H. KELSEN, PRINCIPLES OF INTERNATIONAL LAW 96, 114, 124, 126 (1952).
[35] A. VON VERDROSS, VÖLKERRECHT 128 (4th rev. ed. 1959). ["Subjekte des Völkerrechts sind jene Personen, deren Verhalten unmittelbar von der Völkerrechtsordnung geregelt wird."]; S. SEGAL, L'INDIVIDU EN DROIT INTERNATIONAL POSITIF 57, 168 (1932); J. SPIRO-POULOS, L'INDIVIDU EN DROIT INTERNATIONAL 21, 32 (1928); J. Spiropoulos, *L'individu et le droit international*, 30 RECUEIL DES Cours 195, 200 (1929); J. Spiropoulos, TRAITÉ THEORIQUE ET PRATIQUE DE DROIT INTERNATIONAL PUBLIC 42–46, 127 (1933). It is important in this connection to bear in mind Verdross' distinction between the traditional international law and "Staatengemeinschaftsrecht." VON VERDROSS, VÖLKERRECHT 155.

individuals subjects of this law.[36] Sometimes a *dédoublement fonctionnel* is suggested, namely that to the extent that international law does not have the necessary organs for its enforcement it uses the judicial and executive organs of the state for this purpose, and when the individual enforces his rights and accounts for his duties under international law before the municipal organs in this manner he is in fact a subject under international law. [37] The individual is sometimes regarded as a subject of rights under international law even if he lacks the capacity to enforce these before an international court. [38] It is the direct link between the person and the legal system which is considered crucial to personality under a legal system, and the link between the individual and international law is established by his internationally created rights. These rights may be perfect, as when they can be enforced by him before an international tribunal; or imperfect, as when they can be enforced by him only before a municipal court.[39] Some observers view the individual as subject of international law when his international right is combined with his international procedural ability, or his international duty with his international procedural amenability. [40] Some see his international personality in his right to send petitions directly to an international organ. [41] For some it is sufficient that he is a subject of rights and duties, regardless of the fact that he does or does not possess international procedural ability and amenability.[42] According to another viewpoint, the abilities (*Fähiokeiten*) which a subject of international law possesses include the ability to conclude international agreements (*Ceschäftsfähigkeit*), the ability to commit international delicts (*Deliktsfähigkeit*), and the ability to be a party before an international organ (*Parteifähigkeit*), but in order for the individual to be a subject of this law it is not necessary that he possess all

---

[36] C. ROUSSEAU, DROIT INTERNATIONAL PUBLIC 215 (1953).

[37] G. SCELLE, PRÉCIS DE DROIT DES GENS, Vol. I, 43, 54, 56, 217; Vol. II, 10, 319, 450 (1932–1934); G. SCELLE, MANUEL DE DROIT INTERNATIONAL PUBLIC 21 (3d ed. 1948). *See also* P. GUGGENHEIM, TRAITÉ DE DROIT INTERNATIONAL PUBLIC Vol. I, 171, 201–214, 283–284, 305, 310 (1953–1954). For an analysis and criticism of the theory of *dédoublement fonctionnel*, see P.H. FISCHER, DAT EUROPAEISKE KUT OG STALFAELLESSKAB 133 (1957).

[38] H. LAUTERPACHT, INTERNATIONAL LAW AND HUMAN RIGHTS 21, 27, 38, 54 (1950).

[39] G. TÉNÉKIDÈS, L'INDIVIDU DANS L'ORDRE JURIDIQUE INTERNATIONAL 1, 215, 219, 223, 237, 238 (1933).

[40] Ross, TEXTBOOK 17, 24, 110; M. SIBERT, TRAITÉ DE DROIT INTERNATIONAL PUBLIC, Vol. I, 95–98 (1951); J. ROCHETTE, L'INDIVIDU DEVANT LE DROIT INTERNATIONAL 47, 52 (1956); C. Th. Eustathiades, *Les sujets du droit international et la responsibilité internationale*, 84 RECUEIL DES COURS 397, 412, 509, 514–516, 546–566 (1953).

[41] M. St. Korowicz, *The Problem of the International Personality of Individuals*, 50 A.J.I.L. 533, 554, 557, 561–562 (1956).

[42] M. GRASSI, DIE RECHTSSTELLUNG DES INDIVIDUUMS IM VÖLKERRECHT 87, 89, 269–299 (1955).

these abilities. It is sufficient that he has rights under this law which he can enforce before an international organ and has duties for which he can be held responsible.[43]

Three, it is maintained that the subject of law is the one who can be submitted to its rules permitting or prohibiting certain acts, that this is possible only as to the *volontés consciente,* that man is the only being with voluntary conscience, and that, therefore, only individuals and not states are subjects of international law.[44] It is *l'agent juridique* who is the subject of law, on whom the positive law confers the competence of producing or modifying the juridical situations.[45] Therefore, those individuals are subjects of international law who have powers and obligations with respect to the interests which are the concern of this law.[46]

The agony of theorizing as variously as above about the status relationship of the individual to international law has been a result of the individual's assertiveness in the international legal system. Unlike early stages of international law when the legal attributes of the individual on the international plane were practically nonexistent, this century witnesses a steady growth of his contact with this legal system through creation of his rights, duties, right to petition, procedural ability, and procedural amenability. Thus, in addition to enjoying rights and privileges as a diplomatic envoy, a head of state, or a member of military forces abroad, or through the operation of the rule of the international minimum standard of justice for the treatment of aliens, the individual has gained international rights through minority treaties, trusteeship system of the United Nations, International Labor Organization, and Office of the United Nations High Commissioner for Refugees. He is made responsible for war crimes, genocide, crimes against humanity if these at the same time constitute war crimes, crimes against peace if these at the same time constitute war crimes, offenses against the peace and security of mankind, slavery, piracy, breach of blockade, carriage of contraband, and so on.[47] His right to petition is

---

[43] R. KNUBBEN, DIE SUBJEKTE DES VÖLKERRECHT, HANDBUCH DES VÖLKERRECHTS 241–242, 276, 485–487, 489, 512, 516 (1928).

[44] L. DUGUIT, TRAITÉ DE DROIT CONSTITUTIONNEL 319, 324 (2d ed. 1921); M. Réglade, *Perspectives qu'ouvrent les doctrines du Dóyen Duguit pour un renouvellement de l'étude de Droit International Public,* 37 *Revue générale de droit international public* 381, 396, (1930).

[45] G. SCELLE, MANUEL DE DROIT INTERNATIONAL PUBLIC 507 (3d ed. 1948).

[46] H. KRABBE, *Die moderne Staatsidu* [translated as *The Modern Idea of the State*] 242–243 (1927).

[47] For war crimes, *see* arts. 46, 50, 52, & 56 of the Hague Convention of 1907; arts. 2, 3, 46, & 51 of the Geneva Convention of 1929; art. 6(b) of the Charter establishing the International Military Tribunal, annexed to the Agreement concluded in London on Aug. 8, 1945; I INTERNATIONAL MILITARY TRIBUNAL, TRIAL OF THE MAJOR WAR CRIMINALS BEFORE THE INTERNATIONAL MILITARY TRIBUNAL 8, 64 (1947–1949); *see also* the 4 Geneva Conventions of 1949, namely, Convention I, arts. 49–50; Convention II, arts. 50 & 51; Con-

found in the Minorities System of the League of Nations,[48] in the German-Polish Convention of May 15, 1922, concerning the minorities in Upper Silesia,[49] in the Resolution of the Council of the League of Nations of May 17, 1920, concerning the inhabitants of the Saar,[50] in arrangement of 1925 by the Council of the League of Nations concerning inhabitants of the Free City of Danzig,[51] in an agreement concluded in 1954 by the United Kingdom, the United States of America, Italy, and Yugoslavia concerning the inhabitants of the Free Territory of Trieste,[52] in the mandates of the Council of the League of Nations in 1923,[53] in the Charter of the United

---

vention III, arts. 129–130; Convention IV, arts. 146–147. For genocide, *see* G.A.R. 96 (I), 1946–47 YEARBOOK OF THE UNITED NATIONS 255; the Convention on the Prevention and Punishment of the Crime of Genocide, adopted by the G.A.R. 260 (III) A, 1948–49 YEARBOOK OF THE UNITED NATIONS 959–960. For crimes against humanity, *see* G.A.R. 95 (I), 1946–47 YEARBOOK OF THE UNITED NATIONS 254. For crimes against peace, see G.A.R. 95 (I), 1946–47 YEARBOOK OF THE UNITED NATIONS 254. As to offenses against the peace and security of mankind, the draft prepared by the International Law Commission in this connection (first draft in 1951, second draft in 1954) was postponed for consideration by the General Assembly until after the problem of defining aggression is solved. For slavery, see Peace Treaty of Paris, 1814, between France and England; the International Slavery Convention of 1926, UNITED NATIONS PUBLICATION, 1951, XIV, 2, 12; the Supplementary Convention of 1957, UNITED NATIONS PUBLICATION, 1957, XIV, 2, 19; the Convention for the Suppression of the Traffic in Persons and of the Exploitation of the Prostitution of Others, 1948–49 YEARBOOK OF THE UNITED NATIONS 608; *see also* L. Oppenheim, INTERNATIONAL LAW, 732 (8th ed., H. Lauterpacht ed. 1955). For piracy, *see* LEAGUE OF NATIONS PUBLICATIONS, V. Legal V.5 (C48.M25, 1926, V.), (C.P.D. I, 58); LEAGUE OF NATIONS PUBLICATIONS, V. Legal 1927, V.I (C.196.M.70, 1927, V., 273–279), (C.P.D. I, 95 (2)); LEAGUE OF NATIONS DOC. A 133, 1927, V; Harvard Research in International Law, 26 A.J.I.L. 743–1031 (Supp. 1932); Report of the International Law Commission, Eighth Session, 1956, U.N. Doc. A/3159, 28; U.N. Doc. A/Conf. 13.40, 78, 84; U.N. Doc. A/Conf. 13/C2/L80; U.N. Doc. A/Conf. 13/38, 21, 22, 137; U.N. Doc. A/CN 4/L59/Add. 1, 11; U.N. Doc. A/CN4/SR326; U.N. Doc. A/CN4/L68/Add. 3, 14; 1955 YEARBOOK OF THE INTERNATIONAL LAW COMMISSION, Vol. I, 265; Art. 14–21, Convention on the High Seas, Apr. 25, 1958, 450 U.N.T.S. 82.

[48] U.N. Doc. E/CN4/Sub.2/6, Report of the Secretary-General on the International Protection of Minorities under the League of Nations; LEAGUE OF NATIONS DOC. C.8M.5.1931, I, 2d ed. 7 ff. The System was terminated with the dissolution of the League of Nations. U.N. Doc. E/CN4/367, and Add. 1.

[49] *League of Nations Doc.* C.L. 110, 1927, I Annex, 64–87.

[50] Procès-Verbal of the Fifth Session of the Council, 1920, 25–29, 191; LEAGUE OF NATIONS DOC. I/23071/27099, Annex A.

[51] LEAGUE OF NATIONS OFF. J. 863, 950 (1925).

[52] U.N. Doc. S/3301, Annex II; Special Statute, Art. 8; Regolamente del Comita Misto Italo-Jugoslavo previsto dall'art. 8 dello Statuto speciale (allegato II del Memorandum d'intesa del 5 ottobre) Roma, Feb. 16, 1955.

[53] LEAGUE OF NATIONS DOC. C.P.M. 38 (1), (Publication No. VI.A.Mand.1927 VI. A.3), also in LEAGUE OF NATIONS OFF. J. 989 (1926); LEAGUE OF NATIONS DOC. C.P.M. 558 (1), also in C.545.M.194, 1927, VI (Publication No. VI.A. Mand. 1927, VI.A.10), 176–178. The provision for petitions, however, is not included in the Peace Treaties concluded after World War I, or the Covenant of the League of Nations, or the arrangements made with the Mandatory Powers.

Nations which provides that the Trusteeship Council may accept petitions and examine them in consultation with the administering authority,[54] in the procedures of the International Labor Organization,[55] and in the European Convention of 1950 for the Protection of Human Rights.[56] Additional instances may perhaps be found. For instances of the individual's procedural ability on an international plane, one might point to the attempt made for the establishment of an International Prize Court by the XII Hague Convention of October 18, 1907,[57] which was never ratified, to the Central American Court of Justice, established on December 20, 1907, and dissolved on March 12, 1918,[58] to the Mixed Arbitral Tribunals established by the Peace Treaties following World War I,[59] and to the Upper Silesian Arbitral Tribunal established by a convention between Germany and Poland concluded in Geneva on May 15, 1922.[60] His procedural amenability on an international plane is illustrated by the European Commission of the Danube, established in 1856 and abolished in 1938,[61] which

[54] Art. 87, UNITED NATIONS CHARTER, U.S. T.S. 993.

[55] INTERNATIONAL LABOR OFFICE, CONSTITUTION OF THE INTERNATIONAL LABOR ORGANIZATION AND STANDING ORDERS OF THE INTERNATIONAL LABOR ORGANIZATION, (1958). The Standing Orders Concerning the Procedure for the Discussion of Representatives were adopted by the Governing Body on Apr. 8, 1932. It may be pointed out that petitions are accepted under these procedures from industrial associations and not from private persons.

[56] Art. 25 of the Convention for the Protection of Human Rights provides that the European Commission of Human Rights "may receive petitions . . . from any person, nongovernmental organization or group of individuals claiming to be the victim of a violation by one of the high contracting parties of the rights set forth in this Convention," provided that this party has recognized the Commission's competence to receive such petitions. 213 U.N.T.S. 222. The Convention was signed in Rome on Nov. 4, 1950, and came into effect on Sept. 3, 1953.

[57] I THE PROCEEDINGS OF THE HAGUE CONFERENCES, THE CONFERENCE OF 1907, at 660–671.

[58] This Court was established by the Convention for the Establishment of a Central American Court of Justice, Dec. 20, 1907, 2 A.J.I.L. 231 (Supp. 1908). For a review of its activities, see M.O. Hudson, *The Central American Court of Justice*, 26 A.J.I.L. 759 (1932).

[59] Art. 304 of the Treaty of Versailles; art. 256 of the Treaty of St. Germain; art. 188 of the Treaty of Neuilly; art. 239 of the Treaty of Trianon; and art. 92 of the Treaty of Lausanne. For texts, *see* P.F. SIMONSON, PRIVATE PROPERTY AND RIGHTS IN ENEMY COUNTRIES AND PRIVATE RIGHTS AGAINST ENEMY NATIONALS AND GOVERNMENTS UNDER THE PEACE TREATIES WITH GERMANY, AUSTRIA, HUNGARY, BULGARIA, AND TURKEY 280–289 (1921).

[60] G. KAECKENBEECK, THE INTERNATIONAL EXPERIMENT OF UPPER SILESIA App. III, at 567–822 (1942).

[61] It was established by the Treaty of Paris, Mar. 30, 1856. *See also* COMMISSION EUROPÉENNE DU DANUBE ET SON OUEVRE DE 1856 à 1931, (1931); COMMISSION EUROPÉENNE DU DANUBE—UN SIECLE DE COOPERATION INTERNATIONALE SUR LE DANUBE, 1856–1956). It was abolished by the Treaty of Sinaia, Aug. 18, 1938. *See* GREAT BRITAIN MISCELLANEOUS TREATIES, Vol. 6, No. 176 (Cmd. No. 5946). By the Treaty of Belgrade, Aug. 18, 1948, a new régime was established for the Danube, but this treaty did not confer any jurisdictional powers on the river commission established by it. 33 U.N.T.S. 181.

had powers over the individuals navigating on the river, by the International Military Tribunal of Nuremberg, established by the London Agreement of August 8, 1945, among the United Kingdom, France, the United States of America, and the Union of Soviet Socialist Republics, which tried individuals for certain acts of international character,[62] and by efforts made, although without success, to establish a permanent international criminal court with jurisdiction over the individual, as, for example, contemplated in the Convention for the Prevention and Punishment of Terrorism and in the Convention for the Creation of an International Criminal Court adopted at the Geneva Conference of November, 1937,[63] and in the two Draft Statutes for an International Court prepared by a committee of the United Nations General Assembly in 1951[64] and 1953.[65] Further illustrations of the individual's international procedural ability and amenability are found in the laws of the European Coal and Steel Community, the European Economic Community, and the European Atomic Energy Community.[66] The Paris Convention of December 20, 1957, established a security control system for nuclear energy among the seventeen member states of the Organization for European Economic Cooperation, which applies to individual undertakings in addition to governments and whereunder the individuals have access to the Tribunal created by the Conven-

---

[62] International Military Tribunal, TRIAL OF THE MAJOR WAR CRIMINALS BEFORE THE INTERNATIONAL MILITARY TRIBUNAL, NUREMBERG, NOVEMBER 14TH, 1945–OCTOBER 1ST, 1946, Vols. 1–42 (1947–49). *See also* R.K. WOETZEL, THE NUREMBERG TRIALS IN INTERNATIONAL LAW, (1960). The International Military Tribunal for the Far East (The Tokyo Tribunal) is not considered an international tribunal since it was not set up by a treaty among states but, instead, by a special proclamation made by the Supreme Commander for the Allied Powers. In fact, the true international character of the Nuremberg Tribunal is somewhat diminished by the fact that the conquering powers did in conquered Germany jointly what a conquering power could do in a conquered country, which is essentially a matter of the municipal law of the conquering state. See also G. Schwarzenberger, *supra* note 2, at 30–31.

[63] LEAGUE OF NATIONS DOC. C.94, M.47, 1938, V.

[64] U.N. Doc. A/AC.48/4.

[65] YEARBOOK OF THE UNITED NATIONS 430 (1954).

[66] Treaty Establishing the European Coal and Steel Community, signed in Paris on Apr. 18, 1951, 1 EUROPEAN YEARBOOK 359–428; Protocol on the Code of the Court of Justice, signed in Paris on Apr. 18, 1951, 1 EUROPEAN YEARBOOK 435–350; Treaty Establishing the European Economic Community, signed at Rome on Mar. 25, 1957, 4 EUROPEAN YEARBOOK 413–587; Protocol on the Statute of the Court of Justice of the European Economic Community, signed at Brussels on Apr. 17, 1957, 5 EUROPEAN YEARBOOK 439–453; Treaty Establishing the European Atomic Energy Community, signed at Rome on Mar. 25, 1957, 5 EUROPEAN YEARBOOK 455–559; Protocol on the Statute of the Court of Justice of the European Atomic Energy Community, signed at Brussels on Apr. 17, 1957, 5 EUROPEAN YEARBOOK 571–587; Convention Relating to Certain Institutions Common to the European Communities, signed at Rome on Mar. 25, 1957, 5 EUROPEAN YEARBOOK 587; Regulation No. 17 of Feb. 6, 1962, regarding the application of the European Economic Community Treaty, 1962 JOURNAL OFFICIEL DES COMMUNAUTÉS EUROPÉENNES 204.

tion.[67] A system for international control of armaments was created in 1954 among the member states of the Western European Union and an international tribunal was established in 1957 to handle claims for compensation brought by the individuals against the Union.[68] The International Center for Settlement of Investment Disputes was established by a Convention of March 18, 1965, under the auspices of the International Bank for Reconstruction and Development, whereunder facilities are provided for conciliation and arbitration of investment disputes between states and the nationals of other states.[69] The international civil servant enjoys access to the international administrative tribunals, namely, the Administrative Tribunal of the International Labor Organization,[70] the United Nations Administrative Tribunal,[71] the Court of the European Communities,[72] and the International Court of Justice.[73]

The above evidence of the individual's rights, duties, procedural ability, and procedural amenability on the international plane indicates the extent of his contact with the contemporary international legal order. Certain particular international legal orders have made him their subject through international agreements among the constituent states of these legal orders. However, it cannot be deduced from the evidence of his position as a subject of these particular international legal orders that he has become a subject of international law in general. He relates to this law only through his membership in his state, which is a subject of this law. Generally speaking, therefore, international law governs relations among states and not acts of individuals, criminal or not.

However, it would be unwarranted from the above discussion of the individual's position in international law to infer an a priori assumption that this law cannot possibly contain a body of I.C.L. as long as the individual

[67] 5 EUROPEAN YEARBOOK 283.

[68] Convention concerning measures to be taken by the member states of Western European Union in order to enable the Agency for the Control of Armaments to carry out its control effectively, and making provision for due process of law in accordance with Protocol No. IV of the Treaty of Brussels, as modified by the protocols signed at Paris on Oct. 23, 1954, 5 EUROPEAN YEARBOOK 245.

[69] 4 INTERNATIONAL LEGAL MATERIALS 532 (1965).

[70] LEAGUE OF NATIONS OFF. J., SPEC. SUPP. 194, at 282. Art. II (5) of the Statute of the Administrative Tribunal of I.L.O. provides for arrangements which open the Tribunal, since 1949, to the officials from other international organizations. See STATUTE AND RULES OF THE COURT OF THE ADMINISTRATIVE TRIBUNAL (1954). These arrangements have been made with W.H.O., I.T.U., U.N.E.S.C.O., W.M.O., F.A.O., C.E.R.N., G.A.T.T. See *Minutes of the 138th Session of the Governing Body, Geneva, March 11th to 15th*, at   56 (1958).

[71] Res. 351 (IV), U.N. Doc. AT/11/Rev. 1.

[72] See art. 40 of the European Coal and Steel Community Treaty; arts. 179 & 215 of the European Economic Community Treaty; arts. 179 & 188 of the European Atomic Energy Community Treaty.

[73] Art. 7, Staff Regulation for the Registry of the International Court of Justice, 1946–47 I.C.J. YEARBOOK 66–71.

remains less than a full-fledged subject of this law. Therefore, the second issue, raised at the beginning of this section, needs to be examined. That issue is whether customary international law contains a body of I.C.L. The inquiry here is not that there is or is not anything inherent in the nature of international law which precludes the emergence and growth of such a body of rules, or that international law ought or ought not to contain such rules, but whether this law does in fact contain such rules.

The issue was examined in 1920 by the League of Nations Advisory Committee of Jurists at the Hague. The Advisory Committee noted in its Annex 23 to its Draft Scheme for the Establishment of a Permanent Court of International Justice that "there is not yet any international penal law recognized by all nations."[74] This observation of the Advisory Committee seems as true today as it was in 1920. The practice of states since 1920 does not show that states have adopted generally applicable principles, with the conviction that they are legally bound by these, relating to the crime treatment of the individual, both as to his punishment and as to his procedural and substantive protection in this regard. Evidence, thus, does not exist for an I.C.L. as part of customary international law. It may be pointed out additionally that such rules or principles concerning the crime treatment of the individual have not appeared in the practice of international courts and tribunals either,[75] largely because to the extent these bodies apply international law such rules are not found in this law.

We have so far explored the problem of I.C.L., and the individual's position in it, in the first of its two conceptions outlined at the beginning of this article. The second conception is in terms of international legal arrangements made for the crime treatment of the individual, the term "crime treatment" being used here to include both aspects of the relevant treatment, namely punishment for his acts generally regarded as criminal and protection from persecution for having exercised those options of his private and political life which are generally regarded as legitimate.

2.3. Crime Treatment of the Individual Through International Legal Arrangements

These arrangements relate to (1) procuring punishment of the individual for his crime and (2) protecting him from persecution.

2.3.1. PUNISHMENT. International arrangements which relate to the procuring of due punishment of the individual for his crime may be classified as

---

[74] The Committee recommended that "if it were possible to refer certain crimes to any jurisdiction, it would be more practical to establish a special chamber in the Court of International Justice." LEAGUE OF NATIONS, I THE RECORDS OF THE FIRST ASSEMBLY, MEETINGS OF THE COMMITTEES 588, 589 (1920).

[75] G. Schwarzenberger, *supra* note 2 at 16–20.

being of three main types: (1) those relating to the substance of the crime, (2) those relating to the procedure for obtaining punitive jurisdiction over him, and (3) those relating to the institutions for apprehending him and making a judicial decision of his crime.

2.3.1.1. *Substance of the Crime.* Ordinarily, crimes are defined by municipal laws. However, treaties have given definition to certain acts of the individual and have treated these as criminal acts which make him liable for punishment under those treaties. Some of these crimes have been discussed above,[76] and include war crimes, crimes against peace, offenses against the peace and security of mankind, slavery, piracy, and so on.

2.3.1.2. *Procedure for Obtaining Punitive Jurisdiction.* Extradition treaties provide legal arrangement between party states for bringing the fugitive within the jurisdiction of the courts which would make the judicial decision as to his alleged crime. A network of extradition treaties exists among states to provide for the international rendition of fugitives accused or convicted of crimes, with the exclusion, generally, of political offenders.

2.3.1.3. *Institutions.* The institutions established by agreement of states in this connection include (1) those for apprehending the accused and (2) those for making a judgment of his crime. The former is exemplified by the International Criminal Police Commission, commonly known as Interpol.[77] Instances of the latter have been discussed above[78] and include the International Military Tribunal of Nuremberg. Efforts, unsuccessful thus far, have been made for creating a permanent international criminal court. For example, the League of Nations Advisory Committee, mentioned above, suggested in 1920 that a special chamber for this purpose might be established in the Court of International Justice.[79] The Geneva Conference in November, 1937, contemplated such a court in the Convention for the Prevention and Punishment of Terrorism and the Convention for the Creation of an International Criminal Court.[80] Such a court was also conceived in the two draft statutes prepared by a committee of the United Nations General Assembly in 1951[81] and 1953[82]

2.3.2. PROTECTION. The problem of protection of the individual from perse-

---

[76] See *supra,* text accompanying note 47.

[77] See A.J. FORREST, INTERPOL (1955); M. SICOT, A LA BARRE DE L'INTERPOL (1961); U.S. Congress, House, Committee on the Judiciary, *Report of a Special Subcommittee on the International Court of Justice and the International Criminal Police Organization* (1959).

[78] See *supra,* text accompanying notes 62 to 65.

[79] League of Nations, I THE RECORDS OF THE FIRST ASSEMBLY MEETINGS OF THE COMMITTEES 588, 589 (1920).

[80] LEAGUE OF NATIONS DOC. C.94, M.47, 1938, V.

[81] UN Doc. A/AC. 48/4.

[82] *Yearbook of the United Nations* 430 (1954).

cution relates to two types of persecution: (1) persecution by other citizens and (2) persecution by the state. The problem of persecution by other citizens may probably be met adequately by the municipal law of the state itself. The problem of persecution by the state becomes a matter (1) of providing international legal standards for a due process of law and (2) of protecting the individual from persecution by his state for having exercised legitimate options of his private and political life. International law as to (1) has been limited only to making a provision for the international minimum standard of justice in the treatment of aliens. As to (2), there has as yet been no precise and comprehensive formulation of international legal standards for determining the legitimacy of these options and for protecting the individual for having exercised these, although the European legal regime for human rights provides one example of efforts in that direction. The problem has appeared on the international plane generally as a problem of asylum. For the purpose of an overall view, asylum may be classified as (1) territorial and (2) nonterritorial.

2.3.2.1. *Territorial Asylum.* Asylum is territorial when granted upon the territory of the state of refuge to a fugitive coming from another state. Generally speaking, international legal arrangements for territorial asylum are found (1) in customary international law which grants the state an exclusive territorial jurisdiction within its boundaries and the right to admit aliens on its territory as a consequence of this jurisdiction; and (2) in exception from extradition of persons accused of political offense by virtue of a provision therefor in extradition treaties, which are entered by states in order to vary the rule of customary international law mentioned in (1) for the purpose of apprehending criminals and bringing them to justice. There has been an interesting departure on the part of states in this connection to treat asylum as a human right of the individual, although of no legal significance.[83] As to one type of persons seeking asylum, namely the

[83] The Charter of the United Nations, 1945, and the Universal Declaration of Human Rights, 1948, introduce the notion of the individual's fundamental freedoms and human rights in the international system. However, the Charter does not specify asylum as a human right, just as it does not specify any other human right. It also does not provide a specific machinery to insure the observance of human rights, nor are the provisions of the Charter in this regard sufficiently precise to permit effective implementation of these rights. The Declaration, on its part, pronounces for everyone the right to seek and enjoy in other countries asylum from persecution, but not the right to be granted it. Moreover, the Declaration does not create any legal obligation for states, although its full importance cannot be judged merely on the touchstone of its legal character. The International Covenant on Economic, Social, and Cultural Rights, the International Covenant on Civil and Political Rights, and the Optional Protocol to the International Covenant on Civil and Political Rights, adopted in 1966, do not contain a right of asylum. Nor is a right of asylum included in the European Convention of Human Rights, 1950. Therefore, it cannot be said that the individual has a human right of asylum of any legal significance.

international political refugee, that is to say, a person who has been forced to leave or stay out of his state of nationality or habitual residence for political reasons arising from events occurring between that state and its citizens which make his stay there impossible or intolerable and who has taken refuge in another state without acquiring a new nationality, certain international legal arrangements have been made to provide for him rights and the protection of asylum.[84] Among the treaties concerning the refugee,[85] there are two instruments of most current importance, namely the Convention Relating to the Status of Refugees of July 28, 1951,[86] and the Statute of the United Nations Office of the High Commissioner for Refugees of December 14, 1950.[87]

[84] For a survey of international efforts to assist refugees, *see* United Nations Department of Social Affairs, *A Study of Statelessness*, Pt. I, at 34–41, UNITED NATIONS PUBLICATION 1949, XIV, 2; J.L. Rubenstein, *The Refugee Problem*, 15 INT'L AFF. 716 (1936); E. Reut-Nicolussi, *Displaced Persons and International Law*, 73 RECUEIL DES COURS 5 (1948); W. Rothholz, *Der Bergriff der 'protection juridique et politique,'* in 1950 ARCHIVES DES VÖLKER-RECHTS 404; P. Weis, *The International Status of Refugees and Stateless Persons*, 83 JOURNAL DU DROIT INTERNÂTIONAL 4, 8 (1956); P. Weis, *The International Protection of Refugees*, 48 A.J.I.L. 193, 207 (1954); P. Weis, *The Concept of the Refugee in International Law*, 87 JOURNAL DU DROIT INTERNATIONAL 928, 930 (1960); F. Morgenstern, *The Right of Asylum*, 26 BRIT. Y.B. INT'L L. 327, 354 (1949); E. Reale, *Le droit d'asile*, 63 RECUEIL DES COURS 469, 562 (1938); G.J. van Heuvan Goedhart, *The Problem of Refugees*, 82 RECUEIL DES COURS 265, 271 (1953); F. Schnyder, *Les aspects juridique actuels de problème des rèfugiés*, 114 RECUEIL DES COURS 339, 35, 393 (1965); J.H. SIMPSON, THE REFUGEE PROBLEM (1939); TURPIN, L'ASILE POLITIQUE (1937); R.Y. Jennings, *Some International Law Aspects of the Refugee Question*, 20 BRIT. Y.B. INT'L L. 98 (1939); L.B. KOZIEBRODZKI, LE DROIT D'ASILE 128 (1968); A. GRAHL-MADSEN, I THE STATUS OF REFUGEES IN INTERNATIONAL LAW 9 (1966); P. FRINGS, DAS INTERNATIONALE FLÜCHTLINGS-PROBLEM 1919–1950, at 15 (1951); M. HANSSON, FLYKTNINGSPROBLEMET OG FOLKEFOR-BUNDET 5 (1938); L.W. Holborn, *The Legal Status of Political Refugees, 1920–1938*, 32 A.J.I.L. 680 (1938); INSTITUT FÜR BESATZUNGSFRAGEN, DAS DP-PROBLEM 4 (1950); I. JOKSIMOVIC, LE STATUT JURIDIQUE DES RÉFUGIÉS POLITIQUES ET DES APATRIDES SELON LE NOUVEAU DROIT INTERNATIONAL 61 (1951); R. NATHAN-CHAPOTOT, LES NATIONS UNIES ET LES RÉFUGIÉS 42 (1949); W. von Schieden, *Die Flüchtlingshilfe des Völkerbundes*, in HANDBUCH 219 (1960); J.M. THOMASHEFSKY, THE DEVELOPMENT OF INTERNATIONAL PRO-TECTION OF REFUGEES 11 (1949); J. VERNANT, THE REFUGEE IN THE POST-WAR WORLD 24 (1953); M. Vichniac, *Le statut international des apatrides*, 43 RECUEIL DES COURS 115, 189 (1933).

[85] Treaties concerning the refugee may be classified as those (1) concluded for the benefit of refugees and dealing with their status in general, (2) concluded for the benefit of refugees and dealing with certain special matters relating to them, (3) on the right of asylum, (4) concerning stateless persons, (5) of general application but containing provisions for refugees, (6) applicable to nationals of the contracting states but extended in application to refugees, (7) of general application to all persons within their scope, national or other, (8) establishing certain international bodies, and (9) having a certain bearing on refugees. See GRAHL-MADSEN, I STATUS OF REFUGEES 32. Treaties in group (1) include Arrangement with Regard to the Issue of Certificates of Identity to Russian Refugees, July 5, 1922, 13 L.N.T.S. 237; Arrangement Relating to the Legal Status of Russian and Armenian Refugees, June 30, 1928, 89 L.N.T.S. 53; Convention Relating to the International Status of Refugees, Oct. 28, 1933, 159 L.N.T.S. 199; Convention Con-

cerning the Status of Refugees Coming from Germany, Feb. 10, 1938, 192 L.N.T.S. 59; Convention Relating to the Status of Refugees, July 28, 1951, 189 U.N.T.S. 137, including the Protocol Relating to the Status of Refugees, Jan. 31, 1967, 6 INTERNATIONAL LEGAL MATERIALS 78. Treaties in group (2) include London Agreement Relating to the Issue of a Travel Document to Refugees, Oct. 15, 1946, *U.N.T.S.* 73; Hague Agreement Relating to Refugee Seamen, Nov. 23, 1957, 7 INT'L & COMP. L. Q. 344; European Agreement on the Abolition of Visas for Refugees, Apr. 20, 1959, 376 U.N.T.S. 85; Agreement on the Movement of Refugees Between France and Switzerland, Apr. 12, 1960, 1960 JOURNAL OFFICIEL DE LA RÉPUBLIQUE FRANÇAISE 6143; the German-Swiss Agreement on Abolition of Visas for Refugees, May 15, 1962; various agreements dealing with the resettlement of refugees concluded between the International Refugee Organization and certain states; and the Agreement between the United Nations High Commissioner for Refugees and the Government of the Federal Republic of Germany Concerning Payments in Favor of Persons Damaged by Reason of Their Nationality, Oct. 5, 1960. Treaties in group (3) include the Havana Convention on Asylum, adopted by the Sixth International Conference of American States, Feb. 20, 1928, 132 L.N.T.S. 323; the Montevideo Convention on Political Asylum, adopted by the Seventh International Conference of American States, Dec. 26, 1933, M.O. HUDSON, VI INTERNATIONAL LEGISLATION 607 (1931–1950); the Montevideo Treaty on Political Asylum and Refuge, Aug. 4, 1939, HUDSON, 8 INTERNATIONAL LEGISLATION 404; the Caracas Convention on Territorial Asylum, adopted at the Tenth International Conference of American States, Mar. 28, 1964, *Tenth International Conference, Caracas, Venezuela, Mar. 1–28, 1954.* Treaties in group (4) include those concluded for defining or improving the status of stateless persons, such as the Cenvention Relating to the Status of Stateless Persons, Sept. 28, 1954, 360 U.N.T.S. 117; and those eliminating or reducing statelessness, such as the International Convention on Certain Questions Relating to the Conflict of Nationality Laws, Apr. 12, 1930, including its three protocols, 179 L.N.T.S. 89; the United Nations Convention on the Reduction of Statelessness, Aug. 30, 1961, 11 INT'L & COMP. L. Q. 1090; the European Convention on Reduction of Cases of Multiple Nationality and Military Obligations in Cases of Multiple Nationality, May 5, 1963, 43 Europ. T.S. Treaties in group (5) include the Geneva Convention Relating to the Protection of Civilian Persons in Time of War, Aug. 12, 1949, particularly art. 44, 75 U.N.T.S. 287; Protocol to the Consular Convention between Sweden and the United Kingdom, Mar. 14, 1952, 202 U.N.T.S. 157; most of the extradition treaties which exclude political offenses from extraditable crimes, such as the European Convention on Extradition, Dec. 13, 1957, 359 U.N.T.S. 273; the European Convention on Mutual Assistance in Criminal Matters, Apr. 20, 1959, 30 Europ. T.S.; the European Convention on the Supervision of Conditionally Sentenced or Conditionally Released Offenders, Nov. 30, 1964, 51 Europ. T.S. Treaties in group (6) include the Universal Copyright Convention, Sept. 6, 1952, 216 U.N.T.S. 176; the European Interim Agreement on Social Security Schemes Relating to Old Age, Invalidity and Survivors, and Protocol thereto, Dec. 11, 1953, 13 Europ. T.S., 218 U.N.T.S. 211; the European Interim Agreement on Social Security Other Than Schemes for Old Age, Invalidity and Survivors, and Protocol thereto,, Dec. 11, 1953, 14 Europ. T.S., 218 U.N.T.S. 255; the European Social Charter, Oct. 18, 1961, 35 Europ. T.S.; the International Labor Organization Convention Concerning Equality of Treatment of Nationals and Non-Nationals in Social Security, June 28, 1962, *ILO Convention* 118. Treaties in group (7) include the ILO Conventions on Migration for Employment, June 28, 1939, and July 1, 1949, 75 U.N.T.S. 5; the European Convention for the Protection of Human Rights and Fundamental Freedoms, Nov. 4, 1950, and Protocols thereto, 213 U.N.T.S. 221; the Convention on the Recovery Abroad of Maintenance, June 20, 1956, 268 U.N.T.S. 3; and the various treaties concluded since 1950 by many European states concerning refoulement. Treaties in group (8) include the Charter of United Nations, June 26, 1945, U.S. T.S. 993; the Constitution of the International Refugee Organization, Dec. 15, 1946, 18 U.N.T.S. 3; the Statute of the Office of the United Nations High Commissioner for Refugees, adopted by the United Nations General Assembly on Dec. 14, 1950, Annex to A/RES/428 (V);

2.3.2.2. *Nonterritorial asylum.* Asylum is nonterritorial when accorded in embassies or legations, consulates, public vessels in foreign waters, military camps abroad, or aircraft in the territory of another state. It is accorded outside the territory of the state granting asylum. The most usual form of this type of asylum has been diplomatic asylum. The grant of such asylum does not find support in customary international law, for (1) it cannot be justified on a principle of exterritoriality of the diplomatic premises, since this principle is no longer accepted for explaining diplomatic immunities; (2) it cannot be justified on the basis of diplomatic privileges of the diplomat according it, since a right to interfere with the territorial jurisdiction of the host state through according diplomatic asylum to its fugitives is not generally regarded as necessary for providing that freedom and security to the diplomat which is necessary for discharging the diplomatic function and (3) it cannot be justified on the basis of international custom, since the evidence of the practice of states does not reveal a concordantly general practice to the effect and its acceptance by them as obligatory. Its justification, therefore, can come only from treaties. Practically all the important treaties in this regard have been adopted among the Latin American states, and include the Treaty on International Penal Law signed in Montevideo on January 23, 1889, the Convention on Asylum signed in Havana on February 20, 1928, the Convention on Political Asylum signed in Montevideo on December 26, 1933, the Treaty on Political Asylum and Refuge signed in Montevideo on August 4, 1939, and the Convention on Diplomatic Asylum signed in Caracas on March 28, 1954.[88] It is significant to note that the two of these treaties which have received most wide ratification of all, namely the Havana Convention of 1928 and the Montevideo Convention of 1933, make a state's right to accord diplomatic asylum dependent on a preexisting custom, treaty, or legislation, and those treaties which declare the right as such have not received general ratification.

Thus, an exploration of the individual's position in I.C.L. is governed by the content of what is denoted by the term "international criminal law." The term may denote (1) customary international law with respect

---

the European Convention for the Protection of Human Rights and Fundamental Freedoms, Nov. 4, 1950, 213 U.N.T.S. 221; the Treaty of Rome establishing the European Economic Community, Mar. 25, 1957, 298 U.N.T.S. 11. Treaties in group (9) include the Convention on the Privileges and Immunities of the United Nations, Feb. 13, 1946, 1 U.N.T.S. 15; the Revised General Act for the Pacific Settlement of International Disputes, Apr. 29, 1957, 320 U.N.T.S. 243; and various consular conventions, such as the Vienna Convention on Consular Relations, Apr. 24, 1963, U.N. Doc. A/CONF.25/12.

[86] 189 U.N.T.S. 137.

[87] A/RES/428/V

[88] These treaties have been collected in Pan American Union, *T.S. No. 34, Inter-American Treaties and Conventions on Asylum and Extradition* (1967).

to the crimes of the individual and (2) international legal arrangements for the crime treatment of the individual although other meanings may be ascribed to it. I.C.L. in the sense of the former is nonexistent. In the sense of the latter, it comprehends a wide range of legal arrangements on the international plane for procuring due punishment of the individual for his crime and for protecting him from persecution.

Section 3. STATE RESPONSIBILITY IN INTERNATIONAL CRIMINAL LAW

FRITZ MUNCH

3.1. Punishability of a State and War

This section will discuss only one of the many aspects of I.C.L. as it deals with the question of whether states as such, not their subjects, organs, or leaders, can be punished for international crimes. Punishment is to be distinguished from sanctions, understood as measures of direct coercion applied in order to stop illegal behavior, and from obligations to restore the status quo ante or to pay damages.

A penalty is, as canon law has it, the privation of some good, inflicted by legitimate authority for the correction and punishment of delinquency.[1] It is, therefore, an additional reaction to the disturbed order, which is not satisfied with restoration but seeks more from the perpetrator. Thus it discriminates, at least for some time, against the culprit.

There have been, in the past, doctrines and even texts on the punishment of communities and political units. Barbarossa menaced Italian lords and cities with fines (Feud. Lib. II Tit. 53 pr. *si quis vero ausu*); canon law has even now the *interdictum personale generale* and *locale generale* (can. 2269 *et seq.*, 2291 1).[2] Modern international law has abandoned these concepts with few exceptions. Proposals for collective penalties did not have much success in modern times.

The first notions of war as depicted in the Old Testament show it as an evil sent by God to punish people for their sins.[3] This early concept recurs in legal works,[4] and even a passage in the Potsdam Protocol of August 2,

---

[1] This translation of can. 2215 is taken from H.A. AYRINHAC, PENAL LEGISLATION IN THE NEW CODE OF CANON LAW 54 (1920).

[2] On the history and interpretation of these collective penalties, See HINSCHIUS, 5 SYSTEM DES KATHOLISCHEN KIRCHENRECHTS 19, 518 (1895); G. MICHIELS, 3 DE DELICTIS ET POENIS, COMMENTARIUS LIBRI V CODICIS JURIS CANONICI 278 (1961).

[3] *E.g., Isaiah* 3:25, 5:24, 9:10; *Jeremiah* 1:15–16, 4:16, 5:15; *Habakkuk* 1:12.

[4] c. 49 C. 23 Q. 5 § Puniuntur; Giovanni di Legnano, De Bello, de Represaliis et de Duello (*ca.* 1390) 209, 226 (transl. Brierly, Holland ed. reprint 1964).

1945, reflects the idea that wars punish people for their wrongful conduct.[5] It is interesting to note the extent to which discussion on legitimacy of war is tied up with that of punishment[6] the common problem being to find exceptions to the Fifth Commandment.

A corollary of the punitive war theory is that an invader or aggressor is the instrument of the will of God[7] and thus two possible justifications for *bellum justum* can be derived: (1) the command of God[8] and (2) the punishment of notoriously wicked people.[9] These two justifications are often intertwined.[10]

The argument for the justification for war gradually restricts itself to punishment of wrongs done to the warring prince himself or to his friends and allies, that is to say, that the principle of general intervention dwindles away.[11] Still the purposes of war can be seen as not only to repair wrongs and to recover damages, but also to seek revenge.[12] Revenge is then a motive for going to war, for war activities (devastation, occupation), and for peace terms.

[5] II. A. 3: "The purposes of the occupation of Germany are
(ii) To convince the German people that they have suffered a total military defeat and that they cannot escape responsibility for what they have brought upon themselves, since their own ruthless warfare and the fanatical Nazi resistance have destroyed German economy and made chaos and suffering inevitable."

[6] It is still so in GROTIUS, DE JURE BELLI AC PACIS, lib. II cap. XX §§ 38 [Hereinafter referred to as Grotius]

[7] *Isaiah* 10:5–7; this brought Luther to write: "Praeliari adversus Turcas est repugnare Deo visitanti iniquitates nostras per illos," Assertio omnium articulorum etc., 1520, art. 34, Weimar edition of Luther's Works, vol. 7, at 140; see also RESOLUTIONES DISPUTATIONUM DE INDULGENTIARUM VIRTUTE (1518) on his 5th thesis, *id.* vol. 1, at 535. He mitigated, however, the radicalism of this position in the German version of the ASSERTIO (Grund und Ursach aller Artikel etc., vol. 7, at 442 (1521) and tried to explain it away in his pamphlet VOM KRIEG WIDER DIE TURKEN (Sept. 10, 1528), vol. 30 II, at 108 (1528). About his further opinions v. Hermann Kunst, Martin Luther, und der Krieg, at 27 (1968).

[8] AMBROSIUS, DE CAIN ET ABEL, lib. 2 cap. 4 as quoted after c. 49 C. 23 q. 5, § Per scientes and § Cum ergo; c. 2 C. 23 q. 2; c. 9 C. 23 q. 5 § Quasdam; GENTILI, DE JURE BELLI, lib. I cap. 8 (1612). VITORIA, Relectio VI DE JURE BELLI § 13 in fine seems to avoid this point [hereinafter referred to as Gentili and Vitoria].

[9] Gentili, *supra* note 8, cap. 25; Grotius, *supra* note 6, lib. II cap. XX § 40, 3 & 4.

[10] Thomas Aquinas, SECUNDA SECUNDAE q. XL art. 1 c. ad primum: " ... ex zelo justiciae quasi ex auctoritate Dei." This has been taken over by Stanislaus de Scarbimiria, SERMO DE BELLIS JUSTIS Ludwik Ehrlich Ed. (ca. 1410): Polski wyknd prawa wojny XV wieku, § 1, *see also* §7: "propter zelum legis divinae." Legnano *supra* note 4, at 224.

[11] PIER. BELLI, DE MILITARI ET BELLO (1563), Pars II Tit. § 9; Vitoria *supra* note 8, § 13; Ayala, DE JURE ET OFFICIIS BELLICIS ET DISCIPLINA MILITARI (1582), lib I cap. 2 § II [hereinafter referred to as Ayala]; with particular emphasis VATTEL, LE DROIT DES GENS (1758), lib. III cap. III § 41 in fine. It is not necessary here to take sides in the discussion between C. van Vollenhoven (GROTIUS & GENEVA, BIBLIOTHECA VISSERIANA, vol. VI no. 13 p. 21) and BEAUFORT (LA GUERRE COMME INSTRUMENT DE SECOURS OU DE PUNITION, 1933) on the position of Grotius and his predecessors regarding this point. Beaufort, at all events, quotes a number of authors and summarizes others: *see* 22, 29, 55, 71, 111, 118, 120, 148, 151, 179. For Grotius, see *supra* note 6, lib. II, cap. XX, cap. XX § 40, 1 & 4.

[12] Vitoria *supra* note § 19; Gentili, *supra* note 8, lib. III cap. 2.

As one moves through history, writers evidence the realization that the justice of a war is often hard to determine. It is significant to note how the older texts already discuss the bona fides of the simple subject or soldier of a warring prince exempting him from sharp examination and giving him the benefit of doubt.[13] The concept of "just" is later applied to both sides.[14] Furthermore it must have become evident that the just side is not necessarily the victor. In the end, war is simply a tool of politics without any moral or legal implications, and the last century has stood under Clausewitz' very sober formula that war is the continuation of politics with different means.[15]

There is today a curious reversal of this tendency. *Jus contra bellum* signifies that warfare is allowed only in self-defense. But sanctions, even military ones, are called for against states which behave "badly," *e.g.*, practice racial discrimination.

The question whether the peace terms could imply punitive conditions seems not to have attracted much attention as long as war itself was a punitive instrument. But in the second half of the eighteenth century, the question comes to the fore with a curious uncertainty. Wolff maintains the right to punish by war,[16] but penalty demanded is restricted to confiscation of property and to abolition of certain rights.[17] Some penalties are inapplicable against states.[18] Vattel speaks about punishment at many places; he vaguely wants to see it administered with measure,[19] and his motive seems to be to obtain security; in other terms, punishment serves what is called special prevention. The writer C.W.F. Duman, however, in his 1775 work, opposed fiercely an idea of punishment, even of individuals.[20]

[13] They are guided by St. Augustinus c. 4 C. 23 q. 1 in fine; John of Fribourg, lib. II Quaestionum casualium Tit. V q. LXXIII, quoted after an Utrecht treatise from about 1419/20 (H. Stehkamper, Ein Utrechter kanonistischer Traktat uber Kriegsrecht (1419/1420), Zeitschrift der Savigny-Stiftung fur Rechtsgeschichte, Kanonistische Abteilung, vol. 47, at 256); Vitoria *supra* note 8, § 25, el and 32 in fine; Ayala *supra* note II, lib. I § 31.

[14] Vattel (*supra* note II, lib. III cap. III § 39, 40) is not the first to say so. Vitoria, with some hesitation, admitted it to the benefit of the party which was in excusable error about the justice of her war, *supra* note 8, § 27, 32; Ayala *supra* note H, lib. I, cap. 2 § 34 and Gentili *supra* note 8, lib. I cap. 6 quoting two authors and Pope Pius II Piccolomino.

[15] Clausewitz, Vom Kriege, title of § 24 of ch. 1. About the abandon of *bellum justum*, see Kunz, *Bellum justum and bellum legale*, 45 A.J.I.L. 531 (1951); *see also* Schwarzenberger, 2 International Law 38 (1968).

[16] Chr. Wolff, Jus gentium methodo scientifica pertractatum, § 580, 616, 639 (1764)—there is a discrepancy between §§ 616 & 636 about punitive war against generally criminal peoples.

[17] *Id.* § 581.

[18] *Id.* § 789.

[19] *Id.* lib. II § 52, 53, 69, 70; lib. III § 5, 28, 41, 185, 201.

[20] At the end of his "Lettre a l'Editeur" and in his notes to lib. I § 169, L. II § 7 & 52, lib. III § 28, 41, 185.

Diplomatic practice during the nineteenth century seems to abandon the idea of punitive peace terms. The treatment of France after the Napoleonic Wars and the conservation of the Kingdom of Saxony,[21] in spite of reasons which could have been alleged in favor of harsher conditions, seem to inaugurate an era where war and peace are considered under strictly political aspects.[22]

It is interesting still to follow the public discussions on the annexation of Alsatia and Lorraine by Germany at the end of the War of 1870. There was, at that time, a majority opinion placing upon France the fault for the outbreak of the war. A mass of pamphlets and articles argued pro and con from the history of the annexed territories, from the nationality of its inhabitants, or claimed a plebiscite. G. Rolin-Jaequemyns, trying to bring the discussion back to the field of international law, affirmed the right of the victorious state to set the peace conditions according to its security interests, but he also, rather surprisingly, mentioned that France must suffer a penalty.[23] Padelletti[24] was the one who spoke out the modern point of view: whatever were her motives, France, by signing and ratifying the peace treaty, has disposed validly of the territories in favor of Germany; the treaty of cession is the only important and sufficient title.[25]

G. Rolin-Jaequemyns was still under some influence of natural law, and he asked the question concerning *bellum justum* or *injustum*. He was not alone among his contemporaries and colleagues of the early Institut de droit international; Lorimer[26] and P. Fiore[27] confessed openly their adherence to natural law. But as a whole this tendency disappeared, and for some time the idea of punitive peace terms was subsumed into the domain of popular politics and sheer propaganda.

3.2. Responsibility and Punishment of States

A certain change came with the two great wars of the present century. Full responsibility was placed on the aggressor states. Penal responsibility

[21] It is true that after the Hundred Days the Saar and Savoy were separated from France, and that Saxony suffered heavy territorial losses in favor of Prussia; but the motives seem to have been political ones.

[22] *See* recently H.A. KISSINGER, A WORLD RESTORED: METTERNICH, CASTLEREAGH AND THE PROBLEMS OF PEACE 1812-22, at 138 & especially 139; Schwarzenberger, 2 INTERNATIONAL LAW 759 (1968).

[23] REVUE DE DROIT INTERNATIONAL 1870, at 696; 1872, at 509, 515 (his formula has been followed by his contemporary P. FIORE in DIRITTO INTERNAZIONALE CODIFICATO (5th ed. 1959); on the other hand, *id.* 1870 at 697; 383; 537; 1872 at 517 n. 1.

[24] *Id.* 1871, at 495.

[25] See also P. Fiore *supra* note 22 § 1960.

[26] LORIMER, 1 THE INSTITUTES OF THE LAW OF NATIONS 1, 19, 22 (1883).

[27] *Supra* note 22. § 3, and more forcefully for a Christian version of natural law in NUOVO DRITTO INTERNAZIONALE PUBBLICO 30, 41 (1865). There also, at 379, he discusses *bellum justum*.

was claimed not only for those who had contravened the laws of warfare, but for those who had politically led states into war.

C. van Vollenhoven is guilty of an understatement when he writes that during the twentieth century—we must add: up to 1925 when he held his lectures at Columbia—nothing had been published on punishment of states.[28]

Suggestions for such punishment had been made by the pacifist movement[29] and also in some legal studies. Merignhac, in 1917,[30] had devoted some phrases to the problem, but with a negative conclusion, likewise Strupp in 1920.[31] V. Pella has been particularly active since 1920 in advocating penal responsibility of states and the establishment of an international criminal court; and his initiative, together with that of H. L. Bellot, brought about discussions and resolutions in several private scientific associations.[32] The idea of arraigning states before an international court in criminal proceedings found expression in opinions uttered and in regulations drafted for such a court;[33] the most explicit draft of that sort seems to have been that of Q. Saldana of 1925.[34]

[28] *Supra* note 11, at 21. One very casual and hypothetical remark occurs in BELING, DIE STRAFRECHTLICHE BEDEUTUNG DER EXTERRITORIALITAT 41 (1896): If ever there should be a penal law against states, the penalties would be fines, imposed cessions of territory, or dissolution.

[29] A Fabian Committee had one in *International Government* 253 (1916), in *The Framework of a Lasting Peace* 115 (1917), and in Entwurf eines Volkervertrages, 3 INTERNATIONALE RUNDSCHAU 620, at § 17. (1917). See further Arthur Muller, *Ideen zu einem Volkerstrafrecht*, in DOKUMENTE DES FORTSCHRITTS 118, 121 (July 1915); R. Broda *id.* at 129 (Oct. 1915); G. Grosch, *Volkerrechtliche Delikte und ihre Bestrafung*, in DIE FRIEDENS-WARTE 254 (1912) speaks in fact only about what we are used to call sanctions, *i.e.*, measures to stop illegal behavior; the same is true about the proposal to institute an international "prosecutor," by Baron E. Palmstierna, *An International Police, in Organisation Centrale pour une Paix durable*, 3 RECUEIL DES RAPPORTS 137 (1917). More research would be needed to verify in what category come the authors and collective projects mentioned by V. Pella in his report to the Interparliamentary Union (Compte Rendu de la XXIII Conference 1925) at 206.

[30] 24 REVUE GENERALE DE DROIT INTERNATIONAL PUBLIC 48.

[31] Strupp, Das volkerrechtliche Delikt (Handbuch des Volkerrechts, III la) at 217. He mentions as contemporaneous advocates of state punishment Ansaldi and Olivi.

[32] The problem was always implied in a broader subject; so the International Law Association, in 1922 & 1926, considered proposals for a Permanent International Criminal Court (Report of the 31st Conference, at 63–86, Report of the 34th Conference, at 106–225, 279–309), the Interparliamentary Union in 1925 the crime of aggressive war (Report of the 23rd Conference, at 205–242, 409, 415, 468—on a suggestion by V. Pella on the 22d Conference, Report at 328), the Premier Congres International de Droit penal, 1926, the punishment of corporate bodies (Rapports preparatoires at 181–280, Actes du Congres at 367–480, 554–579, 584–602, 634), Deuxieme Congres etc. 1929, Actes du Congres, at 76, 135, 607–669.

[33] All this is summarized in the U.N. Memorandum: *Historical Survey of the Question of International Criminal Jurisdiction* (A/CN. 4/7/rev. 1), *see also* appendices.

[34] Printed as appendix to Saldana's The Hague lecture: La Justice penale internationale, 10 RECUEIL DES COURS and in ACTES DU PREMIER CONGRES INTERNATIONALE DE DROIT PENAL (1926); see especially 403 & 408 resp. 642 & 645.

Officially, however, there was no trace of punishment of states. The treaties which closed World War I may have been resented as vindictive, and reparation claims were based on an explicit admission of responsibility, but Part VII of the Versailles Treaty (art. 227–230), inscribed "Penalties," concerns only individuals. Nor did the work on the Statute of the Permanent Court of International Justice lead to any fundamental innovation in the orbit of international jurisdiction.

Since World War II, being far more intense than its predecessor, it was natural to hear voices taking up the former plans to institute international criminal jurisdiction. In fact, this time the inhibitions against penal responsibility of political leaders for the outbreak of war, which in 1919 had been voiced particularly by the American Peace Delegation,[35] were overcome. As to penal responsibility of states as such, there was an interesting article by M. Muszkat (now in Tel Aviv) and the suggestion of J. Sawicki[36] to impose the cession of Eastern Germany to Poland as an outright penalty.

While the doctrinal opinions voiced[37] are far too numerous, it will suffice for our present purpose to note that the outcome has been insignificant. In the official field, again, the outcome is nil. When the Genocide Convention of 1948 was prepared in the United Nations, there was a mention of criminal responsibility extending to states, government, organs, or authorities in a British amendment to the draft.[38] In the somewhat confused negotiations that followed, protests emerged;[39] and in the end, the amendment was withdrawn insofar as it concerned states.[40] When the United Nations Committees on International Criminal Jurisdiction continued to consider the institution of an international criminal court, it was clear that this court was intended to judge individuals only.[41] Consideration of that item was

[35] See U.N. Doc. A/CN. 4/7 Rev. 1, at 52; *Memorandum of Reservations* etc., 14 A.J.I.L. 127–151 (1920).

[36] 25 REVUE DE DROIT INTERNATIONAL, DE SCIENCES DIPLOMATIQUES ET POLITIQUES 31–42 (1947).

[37] Muszkat & Sawicki are not complete; one would have to consult H. VON WEBER, INTERNATIONALE STRAFGERICHTSBARKEIT (1934); C.A. POMPE, AGGRESSIVE WAR AN INTERNATIONAL CRIME (1953) especially at 171; DAHM, ZUR PROBLEMATIK DES VOLKERSTRAFRECHTS (1956); QUINTANO RIPOLLES, 1 TRATADO DE DERECHO PENAL INTERNACIONAL Y INTERNACIONAL PENAL 218–221 (1955); GERH. HOFFMANN, STRAFRECHTLICHE VERANTWORTUNG IM VOLKERRECHT 34 (1962).

[38] 3 U.N. GAOR, 6th Comm., Doc. A/C. 6/236 & Corr. 1.

[39] *Id.* Summary Records, 93rd & 95th meetings: Chaumont at 320, 344; Kaeckenbeeck at 338, 345; Perez Peroso at 345; *see also* Morozov 104th meeting, at 441.

[40] *Id.* Fitzmaurice at 346; see also at the end of the 103rd meeting, at 440, when he described the international responsibility of states as "civil, not criminal."

[41] U.N. Doc. A/2136 para. 87 and Annex, Draft Statute arts. 1 & 25; A/2645, Annex. An account is given in REVUE DE DROIT INTERNATIONAL, DE SCIENCES DIPLOMATIQUES ET POLITIQUES (Sottile), vols. 35–38 by V. Pella and vols. 38–41 by J. Graven.

finally postponed until a definition of aggression could be formulated.[42]
3.2.1 DE LEGGE FERENDA. Curiously enough, all these debates seem to consider penal responsibility of states as a point of lex ferenda, the scope of which is broad enough to cover extreme utopias, but is free from preconceived dogmas and theoretical constructions. Therefore, one need not resolve the problem[43] of whether corporations (moral or juridical persons) can meet the prerequisites for criminal guilt. The question is whether society is better protected if corporate bodies can be punished as such, and whether evil is done by hurting those members of such body as are in no way guilty themselves. Likewise, theorems on sovereignty[44] must not stand in the way of rational consideration.

Few partisans of criminal responsibility of states have gone far enough to consider in detail what penalties there could be. Sometimes they propose sanctions, but sanctions are measures calculated to stop illegal behavior. There still remains reparation due for the damage incurred. But all this is not new, and many of the plans, therefore, are merely procedural: the application of reprisals and the obtention of damages is formalized.

V. Pella shrinks from what really would be a penalty: dissolution of the guilty state or annexation in whole or in part.[45] This proviso was derived from the territorial guarantee in article 10 of the League of Nations Covenant and is expressed in article 15 (al.2) of the Protocol of Geneva, February 10, 1925.[46]

Lastly, to insist on the absence of a superior organization wielding authority over the states does not alter one from maintaining the penal responsibility of states in abstracto. As international society stands now, states could very well, by convention and/or developing custom, submit themselves to penal sanctions and to appropriate proceedings before some council or court.

[42] G.A. Res. 1187 (XII) (1957).

[43] It was hotly debated at the Deuxieme Congres International de Droit penal in 1929. It is interesting to note that every argument pro et contra seems to have been exhaustively debated already in the Middle Ages. See O. v. Gierke as quoted *supra* note 2. V. Pella invoked the Germanic theory of corporate bodies; moreover, he announced studies on collective psychology. The present writer does not know of sufficient support from that side; Myerson in the last two chapters of *Germany's War Crimes and Punishment: The Problem of Individual and Collective Criminality* 237, (1944) speaks about guilt consisting in creating or maintaining the psychological climate producing the crimes against peace and humanity.

[44] Dear to the members of the Communist Bloc during the debate on international criminal jurisdiction. It must be seen whether the ideas of international *jus cogens* or the Brezhnev Doctrine will change this attitude.

[45] Interparliamentary Union, 23d Conference, Report at 225. See what Beling had said as far back as 1896, *supra* note 28, on appropriate penalties.

[46] See MANLEY O. HUDSON, THE GENEVA PROTOCOL 85 (1925): the protocol becomes the guarantee of the aggressor.

Therefore, we may summarize this outlook on lex ferenda by stating that penal responsibility of states would not be unthinkable.[47] But there are tendencies in the present world which seem to run against it. Punishment is more than repression of actual illegal behavior and more than reparation, even more than measures of precaution against recurring breaches of law. Punishment is an extra burden or damage inflicted on the guilty. Punishment is a discrimination, material and moral, administered on the strength of tradition and empiricism. At present, all endeavors to define aggression and to codify the rules of peaceful coexistence tend to condemn every sort of political, economic, and moral pressure on fellow states; the equality and full integrity of all states being the advocated principles.

Punishment of states, however, would in fact result in collective punishment of a state's subjects, and often of the foreign inhabitants. The tendency of the Nuremberg Courts, though, has been hostile to the principle of collective punishment, and Myerson[48] tries to mitigate his theses by permitting individuals to escape from the judgment on the collectivity.

On the other hand, it would not be a valid argument contrast to point to the medieval, even antique, origin of collective responsibility.[49] The old theologians often have held sounder and more natural opinions than modern laics. But this writer is not aware of confederal or federal constitutions providing for more than coercive measures against member states in case of federal intervention, and he does not know of penalties in the stricter sense in the system of supervision of public law bodies subordinate to the state. Therefore, it seems that the idea of penal responsibility of public corporate bodies, especially of states, does not recommend itself.

3.2.2. LEX LATA. There is, nevertheless, the question of lex lata. The problem presents itself in this form:

There is no penalty for states sub verbo I.C.L. Many writers omit any mention of it; others reject the idea.[50] The discussion on introducing punishment of states has been summarized, in the specialized writings, as con-

---

[47] In this sense already H. von Weber *supra* note 37, at 95; BROWNLIE, INTERNATIONAL LAW AND THE USE OF FORCE BY STATES 150 (1963); Dahm *supra* note 37, at 5; Gerh. Hoffman *supra* note 37, at 33, 39.

[48] *Supra* note 43, at 225, 233. Even Molotov did not charge the German people with the attack on Russia in his broadcast speech of (June 6, 1941) (Keesing at 5095), and Kruschtschew condemned collective measures against ethnic groups which had indulged in collaboration with the Germans (speech of Feb. 25, 1956).

[49] *See* O. v. Gierke as quoted *supra* note 2, and St. Glaser *infra* note 50.

[50] POLITIS, LES NOUVELLES TENDANCES DU DROIT INTERNATIONAL 127 (1962); PERSONNAZ, LE REPARATION DU PREJUDICE EN DROIT INTERNATIONAL PUBLIC 302 (1939); Stefan Glaser, *L'Etat en tant que personne morale est-il penalement responsable?* 29 REVUE DE DROIT PENAL ET DE CRIMINOLOGIE 451 (1948/49) and *Responsabilité pour la participation*

firming the principle of individual as against collective responsibility.[51] The partisans of punishment of states in a manner different from traditional arbitral and judicial procedure[52] seem to be in a minority.

But one could still try to analyze the law of international delinquencies and ask whether the consequences imply a punitive element. The point is difficult to elucidate because international delinquency traditionally comprises a breach of international conventions as well as violation of general international law. Nevertheless many writers have been under the impression that on occasion the damages awarded have had a punitive character or at least resemble penalties.[53] The most specialized study on damages in international law, however, quotes many cases in which punitive damages have been discarded, and its authoress, Marjorie Whiteman, sums up by stating that punitive damages occur rarely and then only reluctantly.[54]

The most renowned cases are *Manouba*, *Carthago*, and the *Corfou Channel*, where the constatation of the wrong by the tribunal has been con-

---

à une guerre-crime, 24 REVUE DE SCIENCE CRIMINELLE ET DE DROIT PENAL COMPARE 601 (1969); Schwarzenberger, *The Problem of an International Criminal Law*, 3 CURRENT LEGAL PROBLEMS 279, 295 (1950); POMPE, AGGRESSIVE WAR AN INTERNATIONAL CRIME 173, 396 (1953); Kr. Skubiszewski, *La frontiere polono-allemande en droit international*, 61 REVUE GENERALE DE DROIT INTERNATIONAL PUBLIC 225 (1957)—polemizing against Muszkat and Sawicki; Drost, 1 THE CRIME OF STATE 291, 296 (1959); TUNKIN, DAS VOLKERRECHT DER GEGENWART, THEORIE UND PRAXIS 219 (1963)—but with an exception ad hoc against an aggressor, at 231.

[51] H. de Touzalin, *Reflexions a propos du delit d'appartenance etc.*, 4 REVUE DE DROIT PENAL MILITAIRE ET DE DROIT DE LA GUERRE 133, 154 (1965); PLANZER, LE CRIME DE GENOCIDE 127 (1956); W. J. Ganshof van der Meersch, *Justice et droit international penal, allocution of Jan. 9, 1961*, 76 JOURNAL DES TRIBUNAUX 539 (1961); G. del Vecchio, *Der Staat als Verbrecher*, ARCHIV FUR RECHTS—UND SOZIALPHILOSOPHIE 161 (1965).

[52] Apart from V. Pella, Bellot, Saldana, Muszkat and Sawicki, Quintano Ripolles quoted *supra* notes 32–37, *see* DONNEDIEU DE VABRES, LES PRINCIPES MODERNES DU DROIT PENAL INTERNATIONAL 427, (1928); Salvioli, *La responsabilite des Etats et la fixationdes dommages et interets par les tribunaux internationaux*, 28 RECEUIL DES COURS 236 n.1 (1929); Bustamante & Sirven, 4 DROIT INTERNATIONAL PUBLIC 7, 42 (1937); Ago, *Le delit international*, 68 RECEUIL COURS 524 (1939); Oppenheim, 1 INTERNATIONAL LAW (Lauterpacht § 156b 1955); TRIFFTERER, DOGMATISCHE UNTERSUCHUNGEN ZUR ENTWICKLUNG DES MATERIELLEN VOLKERSTRAFRECHTS SEIT NÜRNBERG 155, 221 (1966).

[53] ANZILOTTI, CORSO DI DIRITTO INTERNAZIONALE 425 (4th ed.); Eagleton, *Measure of Damages in International Law*, 39 YALE L.J. 62 (1929); Personnaz *supra* note 50, at 272; SCELLE, MANUEL ELEMENTAIRE DE DROIT INTERNATIONAL PUBLIC 714, 716 (1943); BISSONNETTE, LA SATISFACTION COMME MODE DE REPARATION EN DROIT INTERNATIONAL 8, 37, 121, 128, 146 (1952); Oppenheim *supra* note 52. § 156a; Garcia Amador in I.L.C. Report on International Responsibility, A/CN/4/96 at 130 (Basis of Discussion VI 2); MONACO, MANUALE DI DIRITTO INTERNAZIONALE PUBBLICO 378 (1960); MORELLI, NOZIONI DI DIRITTO INTERNAZIONALE 209 (6th ed. 1963); Schule, Genugtuung, in Strupp-Schlochauer, 1 WORTERBUCH DES VOLKERRECHTS; Tunkin at 220; Dahm *supra* note 37, at 9.

[54] WHITEMAN, 1 DAMAGES IN INTERNATIONAL LAW 137, 154, 264, 571, 717; *id.* Vol. II, at 903, 1004; *id.* Vol. III, at 1652, 1874, 1984 (1937); 8 DIGEST OF INTERNATIONAL LAW 1214.

sidered to be a sufficient sanction.[55] Doubtful is the meaning of the "material amend" of 25,000 in the *I'm alone* case.[56] The sum is explicitly not awarded for ship and cargo; it seems to be rather a compensation for the disgrace done to the flag. Whether such compensations are moral damages or outright penalties, rest in last resort on an a priori determination. One incident resembles military aggression, which is what punishment of states really is meant to sanction. In the *Naulilaa* case[57] penal damages to the amount of two billion goldmarks were asked for by, and denied to, Portugal.

Somebody has argued that the terms of reference of the arbitral tribunals were too strict to allow penalties to be pronounced. It would be difficult to verify the weight of this argument. At all events, the gap between international responsibility as understood in the last 150 years and the new ideas about criminal responsibility of states seem still to be wide open. Some writers[58] compare the first to the "civil responsibility" of municipal law; it has not changed its character, although it may carry some extension of moral damages.[59]

Nevertheless, one might ask whether the reparation problems relative to World War II do not show, at least in some aspects, a different tendency. This writer is inclined to give a negative answer.

As long as peace treaties were considered only from a political point of view,[60] war indemnities were not necessarily based on legal motives. The Peace Treaties of 1919/1920 stipulated a responsibility for damages caused by the war,[61] but war was not considered a delinquency at that time, and the articles in question read rather like political motivations for the constitution of a debt. Singularly enough, the Peace Treaties of 1947[62] abstain from explicit proclamations of guilt, although the Briand-Kellogg pact could have given a technical basis. But the authors of these treaties fixed an amount of reparations below any sum that could correspond to effectively caused damages.[63] The Peace Treaty with Japan, of August 9,

---

[55] 6 *Reports on International Arbitral Awards.* I.C.J. Rep. 36 (1949. See Schwarzenberger, International Law 658 (3d ed. 1957).

[56] 3 *Reports on International Arbitral Awards* 1609, 1618.

[57] *Id.* Vol. II, at 1035, 1074.

[58] Donnedieu de Vabres *supra* note 52, at 429; Fitzmaurice see *supra* note 40; St. Glaser, 29 Revue de droit penal et de criminologie 451 (1948/49).

[59] The formula by which O'Connell, International Law 1029 (1965) sums up the matter may seem somewhat baffling after all this discussion: ". . . damages are the only means known to international law for the punishment of delinquency."

[60] See *supra* § 3.1.

[61] Versailles art. 231, St. Germain art. 177, Trianon art. 161, Neuilly art. 121, Sèvres art. 231, the latter two using milder language.

[62] With Italy art. 74, Hungary art. 23, Bulgaria art. 21, Rumania art. 23, Finland art. 23. R. Castillon, Les Réparations allemandes, deux expériences 1919–1932, 1945–1952, at 79 & 167 (1953) stresses the difference between the principles that underlie reparations in 1919 & 1947.

[63] R. Castillon, *supra* note 62, at 79, 150.

1951, reduces reparations to very limited categories of damage,[64] similar to the treaties ending World War I which hesitated to draw the full consequences from the principle of responsibility.[65] Taken as a whole, all these instruments do not seem to impose punitive damages; the idea of punishment disappears behind an endeavor to construct what some have called "civil" responsibility.[66]

Is the case of Germany a different one? Again this writer would hesitate to say so. Of course, the Allies instituted, at the beginning of the postwar period, a harsh occupation regime, as shown in a curious passage of the Potsdam Protocol quoted in note 5. But as even violations of the rules on military occupation rarely meet sanction, it seems futile to look for justification for what the Allies did or proclaimed in the early texts of 1945. Taking the texts as they are, their objectives appear to be two: (1) a secure future and (2) an equilibrium within Europe.[67] After some years, any idea of discriminating against Germany had disappeared; the Federal Republic and the Democratic Republic being treated by their respective sponsors as sovereign entities and the reparation problem being shelved.[68]

The excesses of the Nazi regime against the Jews have not led to punitive measures against the German State. The payments arranged by the German-Israeli agreement of October 9, 1952,[69] are reparations for real damage and restitutions for looted property. This is clear not only from the very words of the preamble and of Protocol 1 between the German Government and the Conference of Jewish Material Claims[70] but also from the documents that have led to these arrangements.[71] The sole problem was to substitute the State of Israel (and, for the preceding period, the Claims Conference) for individual Jews whose claims could not be taken up by anybody legitimated according to positive law.

It would be difficult to argue that from the point of view of popular

[64] In art. 14, to occupation damages, and in art. 16, to undue hardships to prisoners.

[65] In the treaties of Versailles, St. Germain, and Trianon, the articles quoted *supra* note 61 are followed by articles and annexes which declare full reparation impossible. The categories of damages retained for reparation concern in part violations of *jus in bello*, i.e., that they have insofar a valid legal basis.

[66] *See supra* note 58.

[67] *See e.g.*, the Potsdam Protocol, II B §§ 11 & 12.

[68] The Soviet Union signed even a protocol of Oct. 22, 1953, with the authorities of her occupation zone abolishing reparations.

[69] U.N.T.S. 162, at 205.

[70] *Id.* at 270.

[71] Israeli Ministry for Foreign Affairs, documents relating to the agreement between the Government of Israel and the Government of the Federal Republic of Germany, 1953: Letter of Sept. 20, 1945, from Dr. Weizmann, §§ 3 & 5, at 10; Israel note of Jan. 16, 1951, at §§ 2, 4, 8, at 13; Israel note of Mar. 12, 1951, § 6, at 20 always insisting that the evil done cannot be redressed, but the only thing left is material reparation. Here also this reparation is far below the material damage done—see pp. 35 & 40 the notes of the United States and France of July 5, 1951. Therefore the damages are certainly not punitive.

politics the postwar treatment of Germany and her Allies shows punitive elements and that there is a beginning of *opinio juris*. What victors do to the vanquished is no proof of international law. For such proof one would seek a general consensus established freely after peace has been found. Such a consensus is still lacking.

3.3. Conclusion

The introduction of criminal responsibility in a sense analogous to municipal penal law would not be impossible, but it would ask for the participation of the whole community of states, just as punishment in municipal law is an interest of the whole community and administered in modern times by its constituted organs. It could not be entrusted to the wronged state or to interested groups as may assemble in a peace congress. It would presuppose a change in the constitution of the community of states, and not only the institution of a tribunal by, for example, the United Nations.

Moreover there would be need for a consensus on the fundamental problem of collective responsibility. It lacks support in the current doctrines of today; going back to the germanic and, in part, canon law theories of the Middle Ages would demand a clear and outright decision by the community of states.

3.4. Editors' Note on the Codification of State Responsibility

The International Law Commission issued its third report on State Responsibility March 5, 1971, (A/Cn. 41 246) entitled: *The Internationally Wrongful Act of the State, Source of International Responsibility*. This ninety-four-page report explains and comments upon the prepared codification of state responsibility for wrongful acts. Concerning every aspect of wrongful conduct it does not draw a distinction between a tort and a crime. The absence of such a distinction is predicated on the assumption that a wrongful act subjects a state to responsibility under international law regardless of the focus or label attached to reparations. The report does not cover reparations but seeks to codify four basic principles as follows:

> Article I *Principle attaching responsibility to every internationally wrongful act of the State.*
> Every internationally wrongful act of a state involves the international responsibility of that state.
> Article II *Conditions for the existence of an internationally wrongful act.*
> An internationally wrongful act exists when (1) conduct consists of an action or omission attributed to the state in virtue of international law and (2) that conduct constitutes a failure to comply with an international obligation of the state.

Article III *Subjects capable of committing internationally wrongful acts.*
Every state is capable of being considered as the author of an internationally wrongful act.

Article IV. Irrelevance of municipal law to the characterization of an act as internationally wrongful.

The municipal law of a state cannot be invoked to prevent an act of that state from being characterized as wrongful in international law.

PART TWO

CRIMES AGAINST PEACE

CHAPTER III

AGGRESSION

Section 1. THE DEFINITION OF AGGRESSION IN INTERNATIONAL LAW: THE CRIME AGAINST PEACE.

M. CHERIF BASSIOUNI

1.1. Introduction

The notion of aggression was known as far back as the early days of Greece.[1] In the twentieth century, it has been a recurrent theme among international lawyers, who have tried to determine the merits of the concept and its usefulness to the development of world order.[2] The term "aggression," as a legal concept in international law, began to develop meaningfully during the era of the League of Nations, which sought to control the limits of the legal license to engage in war.[3] These efforts have continued to the present in the United Nations where a Special Committee on the Question of Defining Aggression[4] is at work to produce an internationally agreed-upon definition. (See, in text below, its latest report.)

Most of the problems of aggression arise from the attempt to define it. Some feel there must be a juridically enforceable definition to enable the United Nations to exercise its control over state action transgressing the prohibition against aggression. Others, however, feel that a definition should be only a starting point, because no definition can be all inclusive and still remain flexible enough to be adapted to future needs. Some even consider that no workable definition can be arrived at and that the idea should be dropped altogether.

This introductory note will retrace the development of the concept of aggression since World War I and discuss the relevance of the past to the present and the future. Soviet conceptions of aggression will be alluded to but will be covered in detail in section 2 and indirect aggression is discussed in Chapter IV.

1.2. From World War I to World War II

After World War I had ended, there were various indications that the

---

[1] BROWNLIE, INTERNATIONAL LAW AND THE USE OF FORCE BY STATES 1–65 (1963).
[2] STONE, AGGRESSION AND WORLD ORDER 1 (1958).
[3] *Id.* at 15.
[4] VI U.N. MONTHLY CHRONICLE 56 (May 1969).

waging of aggressive war would not be tolerated. During the war itself, various peace plans were brought forth and the formation of the League of Nations was an integral part of the peace settlement. There was an effort made to give a legal significance to the concept of war guilt.[5] Brownlie lists the following as a reply of the Allies to the Bulgarian Delegation at the Peace Conference dated November 3, 1919.

> Bulgaria will undoubtedly have heavy liabilities to bear. These will not, however, be the result of the Conditions of Peace, but of the war of aggression in which she voluntarily took part . . . in a spirit of domination and conquest. Bulgaria has failed in a scheme undertaken contrary to the law of nations and of liberty, in the hope of illicit territorial and material gains.[6]

This quotation is indicative of the spirit with which the Allies entered the Peace Conference. They truly believed this to have been the "war to end all wars."

This aim was to be further carried out in the League of Nations. While the only explicit reference to aggression is to be found in article 10, later inferences to the concept were made in discussions of other articles of the Covenant. Article 10 reads:

> The members of the League undertake to respect and preserve as against external aggression the territorial integrity and existing political independence of all members of the League. In case of any such aggression or in case of any threat or danger of such aggression the Council shall advise upon the means by which this obligation shall be fulfilled.[7]

Article 10, however, tended to lose significance in light of the primary concern of the time, banning war. The importance of the concept of aggression had not yet emerged. Even when the notion of aggression began to come to the fore it was through article 11, which empowered the Council to intervene in the event of war, threat of war, or to bring a cease-fire to hostilities already started, that it gained recognition.[8] In this respect the idea arose that the refusal of a country to comply with a directive of the Council, particularly as to cease-fire, might come to be considered aggression. This notion was endorsed by Professor Quincy Wright[9] but rejected by Julius Stone.[10]

Further attempts to expand and define what constituted aggression were made by the Geneva Protocol draft of 1924 and The Locarno Treaties of 1925. The Protocol attempted to establish a presumption of aggression,

---

[5] BROWNLIE, *supra* note 1, at 51.

[6] *Id.* at 52.

[7] STONE, *supra* note 2, at 27.

[8] *Id.* at 28.

[9] Q. Wright, *The Concept of Aggression in International Law*, 29 A.J.I.L. 381 (1935); *also* Wright *The Prevention of Aggression*, 50 A.J.I.L. 532 (1956).

[10] STONE, *supra* note 2, at 28 n.4.

in the absence of a decision of the Council, where hostilities have broken out and a state has refused to submit the dispute to a peaceful settlement, or to comply with an award or Council recommendation, or has refused or broken an armistice proposed by the Council.[11] However, the Protocol did not receive approval when it came before the Council and never came into effect. The treaties concluded at the Locarno Conference between Germany, Belgium, France, Great Britain, and Italy provided that these countries "will in no case invade each other or resort to war against each other." unless it is in the "exercise of the right of legitimate defense" or "action as a result of a decision taken by the Assembly or by the Council of the League of Nations."[12]

These and other agreements and the temperment of the times led to the signing of the General Treaty for the Renunciation of War signed August 27, 1928, and better known as the Kellogg-Briand Pact. The provisions of the treaty are expressed briefly as follows:

Article I—The high contracting parties solemnly declare in the names of their respective peoples that they condemn recourse to war for the solution of international controversies, and renounce it as an instrument of national policy in their relations with one another.

Article II—The high contracting parties agree that the settlement or solution of all disputes or conflicts of whatever nature or of whatever origin they may be, which may arise among them, shall never be sought except by pacific means.[13]

Sixty-three countries have ratified or adhered to this instrument and since it contains no provision for renunciation or lapse, at least one author feels it is still in force.[14] However, the hopes of the signatories of the pact, whether real or fancied, were shattered by the realities of World War II. The Pact was, however, the subject of discussion in numerous debates prior to 1939, and was affirmed in several treaties of that period. The potency of the Pact was also affirmed by the Nuremberg Tribunal of 1946.[15] Brownlie is still an advocate of the pact and states: "The General Treaty for the Renunciation of War at present stands together with the United Nations Charter as one of the two major sources of the norm limiting force by states. It is parallel to and a complement to the Charter."[16]

In February 1933, the Soviet Union made its initial contribution to the definition of aggression. They did so by offering a draft resolution which has remained virtually unchanged to date. This definition is characterized as a major "contribution towards confirming and developing the principle

[11] BROWNLIE, *supra* note 1, at 70.
[12] *Id.* at 71.
[13] *See, e.g.,* FERRELL, PEACE IN THEIR TIME (1968).
[14] BROWNLIE, *supra* note 1, at 75.
[15] *Id.* at 80.
[16] *Id.* at 91.

of banning wars of aggression," by Evgeny N. Nasinovsky, Legal Advisor
of the Permanent Soviet Mission to the United States.[17] The proposal reads
as follows:

1. The aggressor in an international conflict shall be considered that state
which is the first to take any of the following actions:

    a. Declaration of war against another state.
    b. The invasion by its armed forces of the territory of another state without
       declaration of war.
    c. Bombarding the territory of another state by its land, naval, or air forces
       of another state.
    d. The landing in, or introduction within the frontiers of another state, of
       land, naval, or air forces without the permission of the government of
       such a state, or the infringement of the condition of such permission,
       particularly as regards the sojourn or extension of area.
    e. The establishment of a naval blockade of the coasts or ports of another
       state.

2. No consideration whatsoever of a political, strategic or economic nature,
including the desire to exploit natural riches or to obtain any sort of advantages
or privileges on the territory of another state, no references to considerable
capital investments or other special interest in a given state, or to the alleged
absence of certain attributes of state organization in the case of a given
country, shall be accepted as justification of aggression as defined in Clause 1.

In particular, justification for attack cannot be based upon:

A. The internal situation in a given state, as for instance:

    a. Political, economic or cultural backwardness of a given country.
    b. Alleged maladministration.
    c. Possible danger to life or property of foreign residents.
    d. Revolutionary or counterrevolutionary movements, civil war, disorders,
       or strikes.
    e. The establishment or maintenance in any state of any political, economic,
       or social order.

B. Any acts, laws, or violations of a given state, as for instance:

    a. The infringement of international agreements.
    b. The infringement of the commercial, concessional, or other economic
       rights or interests of a given state or its citizens.
    c. The rupture of diplomatic or economic relations.
    d. Economic or financial boycott.
    e. Repudiation of debts.
    f. Nonadmission or limitation of immigration, or restriction of rights or
       privileges of foreign students.
    g. The infringement of the privileges of official representatives of other
       states.
    h. The refusal to allow armed forces transit to the territory of a third state.
    i. Religious or antireligious measures.
    j. Frontier incidents.

3. In the case of the mobilization or concentration of armed forces to a con-

---

[17] Nasinovsky, *The Impact of 50 Years of Soviet Theory and Practice on International Law*
Am Soc'y Int'l L. Proc. 189 (1968).

siderable extent in the vicinity of its frontiers, the state which such activities threaten may have recourse to diplomatic or other means for the peaceful solution of international controversies. It may at the same time take steps of a military nature, analogous to those described above, without, however, crossing the frontier.[18]

Following this proposal by the Soviets, the Committee on Security Questions drew up a draft, similar to that proposed by the Soviet Union,[19] and presented it to the Political Committee for their consideration. But as various nations took up their expansive activities, the interest in the definitional problem waned. This lapse of interest began with Japan's seizure of Manchuria and closed with the German and Japanese initiatives of World War II.[20]

The League's actions in this time were mainly concerned with the task of separating the combatants after the conflicts had begun. In so doing, it addressed itself to both parties as if each were at fault. Only after hostilities had been stopped would the Council decide who was to blame.

1.3. The United Nations Charter

The necessity of focusing attention on the Charter of the United Nations is made more obvious by a reading of the authorities on the topic. All have found it necessary to refer to the Charter in their discussions of "aggression" and "war." However, those who drafted the Charter did not limit themselves to the use of these words. The "threat or use of force" is likewise prohibited. These words were not arrived at by chance, but clearly by choice.

> The development from the words of the Kellogg-Briand Pact to the wording of the Charter was deliberate. It had soon been realized after the adoption of the Kellogg-Briand Pact that the association of the word "war" with a technical condition or states meant that states might contend that their use of force, since it fell short of "war" did not violate the prohibition of the Pact. The words of Article 2(4) of the Charter were intended to fill this gap. What was now prohibited was the deliberate initiation of a situation of force. Henceforth, there was to be no room for the argument about whether or not the hostilities amounted to war.[21]

Clearly, the Charter had to do more than separate the combatants, for in this atomic age, after the initial use of force there may no longer be any combatants to separate, much less anyone to separate them. While the Charter does not set out any definitions, it has more clearly set out

---

[18] STONE, *supra* note 2, at 34–35.

[19] STONE, *supra* note 2, at 35, Soviet para. 1(d) was omitted, and inserted was a paragraph labeling the support of "Armed bands" as aggression.

[20] *Id.* at 36.

[21] E. Lauterpacht, *The Legal Irrelevance of the State of "War,"* AM. SOC'Y INT'L L. PROC. 62 (1968).

criteria by which the conduct of nations can be regulated. Before beginning a discussion of the pertinent articles of the Charter, it might be best to set them out.

> Article 2—The organization and its members, in pursuit of the purposes stated in article I, shall act in accordance with the following principles:
>
> . . . (4) All members shall refrain in their international relations from the threat or use of force against the territorial integrity or political independence of any state, or in any other manner inconsistent with the purposes of the United Nations.
>
> Article 39—The Security Council shall determine the existence of any threat to the peace, or act of aggression, and shall make recommendations, or decide what measures shall be taken in accordance with articles 41 and 42 to maintain or restore international peace and security.
>
> Article 51—Nothing in the present Charter shall impair the inherent right of individual or collective self-defense if an armed attack occurs against a member of the United Nations, until the Security Council has taken measures to maintain international peace and security. Measures taken by the members in the exercise of this right of self-defense shall be immediately reported to the Security Council and shall not in any way affect the authority and responsibility of the Security Council under the present Charter to take at any time such action as it deems necessary in order to maintain or restore international peace and security.

In reading these articles, they must be examined carefully. The prohibition of article 2 (4), for example, does not prohibit the use of force by states in their international relations. What it prohibits is the use of force in a manner inconsistent with the purposes of the United Nations; or the use of force against (1) the territorial integrity or (2) the political independence of any state. It makes no difference whether that state is a member or not.[22]

It is also argued that the threat or use of force employed consistently with the purposes of the Charter, and not directed against the "territorial integrity or political independence," may be condoned as not forbidden by the Charter.[23] At the very least, Stone feels that there is no need to read in to article 2 (4) the exclusion of all resort to force except in self-defense or under the authority of the United Nations.

Also to be noted is that where the League forbade "the resort to war," the Charter prohibits "the threat or use of force." As has been stated before, the use of force without actual declaration of war has developed into a fine art. This change in terminology is justified, since the squabble over the technical state of war is easily avoidable. The prohibition remains as to the essence of war, *i.e.*, the use of force.[24]

---

[22] BENTWICH & MARTIN, COMMENTARY ON THE CHARTER OF THE UNITED NATIONS 13 (1969); also STONE, *supra* note 2, at 43.

[23] *Id.* STONE, at 43.

[24] BENTWICH & MARTIN, *supra* note 22, at 14.

The text of article 39 left the term "aggression" undefined and gave equal weight to the "threat to the peace, breach of the peace, or act of aggression." It was hoped that article 2 (4) would satisfactorily prohibit a use of force unless it was "consistent with the purposes of the United Nations." Should a "threat to the peace, breach of the peace, or act of aggression" take place, it is left in the hands of the Security Council to determine its existence and what sanctions would be used to end it. When the Charter was drafted, it was felt that (1) no definition of aggression could be established that could cover every possible case and (2) it was best to let the Security Council decide what had happened and what actions to take.[25] Both reasons fall short of their objective.

The failure of this plan is certainly not surprising, and it was obvious even then that the Great Power veto could paralyze this process, "Then as now, it was apparent that if use of the Great Power veto paralysed Security Council action, none of these terms could be given meaning in the particular case, and that means other than legal coercion under the Charter would have to be used."[26] The effects of this paralysis are all too obvious.

Article 51 recognizes that the right to self-defense is inherent in every state. This theory is well founded in international law, but is limited to states which have been "attacked." The Charter widens the principle in that it speaks both of individual and collective self-defense. This takes into consideration that there are many alliances for mutual self-defense which operate on the basis that aggression committed against one of the allies is aggression against all of them. Whether as a matter of legal principle it is justifiable to extend the "inherent" right of self-defense to attacks on third parties is questionable, but the wording of the Charter leaves no doubt that members are free to retaliate by way of self-defense to attacks made on their allies.[27]

The relation of the concept of self-defense to that of aggression is immediately obvious when applied to a practical problem such as the Vietnam conflict. It then becomes apparent that what is claimed to be collective self-defense by the United States[28] becomes aggression when viewed by the Viet Cong and the North Vietnamese.[29] The same applies to the Palestinian and Arab-Israeli conflict.

---

[25] *Id.* at 88.

[26] STONE, *supra* note 2, at 44.

[27] BENTWICH & MARTIN, *supra* note 22, at 108.

[28] *The Legality of the U.S. Participation in the Defense of Viet Nam*, 54 DEP. STATE BULL. 474 (1966); 60 A.J.I.L. 565 (1966).

[29] Wright, *Legal Aspects of the Vietnam Situation*, 60 A.J.I.L. 755 (1966).

1.4. The Security Council and The General Assembly

As it was originally conceived in San Francisco after the War, there was no need for any further mention of aggression than that proposed in article 39. Of the two main branches of the United Nations, the Security Council was designated as the peace enforcement branch, which could, within the United Nations Charter, exercise military sanctions to bring an end to hostilities. The General Assembly, as originally conceived, was relegated to a position of secondary importance and had no power to put an end to a conflict, save the passing of a resolution condemning the actions and thereby acting as an expression of world opinion.

However, **as time** passed, the world began to see that the Great Powers veto was paralyzing the Security Council and that if the trend continued, the United Nations would go the way of the League before it. The problem is thus stated,

> . . . a permanent member which has committed or is about to commit aggression, or is in league with the aggressor, can lawfully use its right to veto: it can stop the Council from finding there has been an act of aggression. Here, precisely, lies one of the fundamental weaknesses of the Charter.[30]

It is in the light of the draftsmen's refusal to formulate advance criteria of "aggression" and the failure of the Security Council in determining "a threat to the peace, breach of the peace, or act of aggression" in a particular case, that the contemporary drive in the General Assembly to formulate other criteria is to be understood.[31] Realizing this, it is easier to appreciate the hope that the Assembly, lacking as it does the legal power of binding determination, and action vested in the Security Council, should attempt to build up by the effect of uniformly accepted definition of "aggression" a foundation for securing future compliance with its resolutions.

When the full paralysis of the Security Council was achieved in August, 1950, the General Assembly shortly thereafter sought to obtain for itself more influence in situations where it formerly would have been powerless. The action of the Assembly took several forms in its attempt to assume some of the derelict functions of the Security Council. Two of these were the establishment of the "Little Assembly," and more successfully the Uniting for Peace Resolution of November 3, 1950.[32] It was also during this period that the members of the United Nations began to press for a definition of "aggression." Since the Security Council could no longer

[30] BENTWICH & MARTIN, *supra* note 22, at 88.

[31] Kluski, W.W. *The Soviet System of Collective Security Compared with the Western System* 44 A.J.I.L. 453 (1950); Wright, *The Prevention of Aggression,* 50 A.J.I.L. 518, (1956).

[32] STONE, *supra* note 22, at 184.

determine, without definition, when aggression occurred, it was felt that the General Assembly should determine, by definition, what criteria should be used in determining aggression. While the Assembly had no powers of legal compulsion in this area, it was hoped that through the voluntary cooperation of members, the definition would acquire the force of law.[33]

This is still the hope of some authors who talk about the force of such a method of enforcement. Professor Hazard has recently stated:

> Law based on custom widely accepted and respected may appear indefinite to the Romanist trained legal mind, but it has remarkable strength because it is firmly rooted in the mores of the community. It is obeyed and not flouted as the dictate of some far away authority creating norms for which there is no general acceptance among the peoples of a given region.[34]

From this setting the quest for a definition began when in the First Committee of the General Assembly, on November 6, 1950, the Soviet Union revived its draft definition of 1933.

1.5. The Continued Search for a Definition

The only real change in the Soviet definition was the substitution of the word "attacker" for that of "aggressor." By a resolution of November 17, 1950, the General Assembly decided to refer this proposal of the Soviets concerning the definition of the notion of "aggression" to the International Law Commission. The Commission failed to agree on a definition but decided to include in the Draft Code of Offenses any act of aggression and any threat of aggression. During the Sixth Session of the Assembly the Sixth Committee discussed the report of the Commission on the question. There was still no agreement on a definition or even on the desirability and possibility of defining aggression.

By a resolution of January 31, 1952, the General Assembly decided to include aggression on the agenda of the Seventh Session and instructed the Secretary-General to submit a report on the subject. The recitals to this resolution stated that although the crime of aggression may be inferred from the circumstances peculiar to each case, it is possible and desirable to define aggression by reference to the elements which constitute it and also that it would be of definite advantage if directives were formulated for the future guidance of such international bodies as may be called upon to determine the aggressor. The Sixth Committee subsequently examined the problem in 1952, 1954, and 1957 and in Special Committees in 1953 and 1956.[35]

---

[33] *Id.* at 46.

[34] Hazard, *Why Try Again to Define Aggression*, 62 A.J.I.L. 702 (1968).

[35] BROWNLIE, *supra* note 1, at 353–357; STONE, *supra* note 2, at 47–77.

Further consideration of the problem was put off again and again over the next decade until in September 1967 the Soviet Union again proposed that further meetings be held to establish the "much needed" definition.[36]

The Special Committee on the Question of Defining Aggression was established by the General Assembly in Resolution 2330 (XXII) of December 18, 1967. Thirty-six member nations were appointed by the President of the Assembly to serve on the Committee.[37] During the latest session, no definite decisions were made, but three main draft proposals have been submitted for consideration by the members of the Committee.

The first of these was a proposal by the USSR which would have the General Assembly declare that "armed aggression (direct or indirect) is the use by a state, first of armed force against another state contrary to the purposes, principles, and provisions of the Charter of the United Nations."[38]

Other provisions state that an act of aggression would be considered to have been committed by the state first declaring war and when certain acts were committed first without a declaration of war. These acts would include the use of any weapons of mass destruction; bombardment of territory or an attack on land, sea, or air forces of a state; invasion, military occupation, annexation, or blockade.

The draft also calls for a statement of what constitutes indirect aggression. This would include the use by a state of armed force by sending armed bands, mercenaries, terrorists, or others to the territory of another state and engagement in other forms of subversive activity involving the use of armed force with the aim of promoting internal upheaval in another state or a reversal of policy in favor of an aggressor.

The Soviet draft would have the Assembly declare that no territorial gains or special advantages resulting from armed aggression should be recognized. It further stated that "nothing in the foregoing shall prevent the use of armed force in accordance with the Charter of the United Nations, including its use by dependent peoples in order to exercise their inherent right of self-determination" in accordance with the General Assembly resolution on the ending of colonialism.[39]

The second proposal was sponsored by Colombia, Cyprus, Ecuador, Ghana, Guyana, Haiti, Iran, Madagascar, Mexico, Spain, Uruguay, Uganda, and Yugoslavia. This thirteen-power draft consisted of seven

[36] VII U.N. MONTHLY CHRONICLE 42 (Mar. 1969).

[37] *Id.* These are Algeria, Australia, Bulgaria, Canada, Columbia, Congo, Cyprus, Czechoslovakia, Ecuador, Finland, France, Ghana, Guyana, Haiti, Indonesia, Iran, Iraq, Italy, Japan, Madagascar, Mexico, Norway, Romania, Sierra Leone, Spain, Sudan, Syria, Turkey, Uganda, USSR, United Arab Republic, United Kingdom, the United States, Uruguay, and Yugoslavia.

[38] VII U.N. MONTHLY CHRONICLE 79 (Apr. 1969).

[39] *Id.*

preambles and ten operative paragraphs. It would have the General Assembly declare that "for the purpose of this definition, aggression is the use of armed force by a state against another state, including its territorial waters or air space, or in any way affecting the territorial integrity, sovereignty, or political independence of such state" save in self-defense or when undertaken by or with the authority of the Security Council.[40]

The draft stipulated that the inherent right of individual or collective self-defense of a state could be exercised only in case of armed attack by another state and that any measures which the state might take in the exercise of such right should be reasonably proportionate to the armed attack against it.

Other operative paragraphs would have the General Assembly declare that enforcement action of use of armed force by regional arrangements or agencies might be resorted to only if there was a decision to that effect by the Security Council.

In accordance with the foregoing and without prejudice to the powers and duties of the Security Council, any of the following acts when committed by a state first against another state in violation of the Charter should constitute acts of aggression:

1. Declaration of war by one state against another state.
2. The invasion or attack by the armed forces of a state, against the territory of another state, or any military occupation, however temporary, or any forcible annexation of the territory of another state or part thereof.
3. Bombardment by the armed forces of a state against the territory of another state, or the use of any weapons, particularly weapons of mass destruction, by a state against the territory of another state.
4. The blockade of the coasts or ports of a state by the armed forces of another state.

Further, when a state was a victim on its own territory of subversive and/or terrorist acts by irregular, voluntary, or armed bands organized or supported by another state, it might take all reasonable and adequate steps to safeguard its existence and institutions, without having recourse to the right of self-defense against the other state under article 51 of the Charter. The territory of a state was to be considered inviolable and could not be the object, even temporarily, of military occupation or of other measures of force taken against it by another state on any grounds, and territorial acquisitions obtained by force are inadmissible.

It was further proposed that armed aggression should constitute a crime against international peace, giving rise to international responsibility, and finally the draft also would have the General Assembly state that none of the preceding paragraphs might be interpreted as limiting the scope of

[40] *Id.*

the Charter's provisions concerning the rights of peoples to self-determination, sovereignty, and territorial integrity.[41]

The third proposal was sponsored by Australia, Canada, Italy, Japan, the United States, and the United Kingdom. It stated that aggression was applicable

> . . . without prejudice to a finding of a threat to the peace or breach of peace, to the use of force in international relations, overt or covert, direct or indirect, by a state against the territorial integrity or political independence of any other state or in any other manner inconsistent with the purposes of the United Nations.[42]

This six-power draft stipulated that "aggression" was a term to be applied by the Security Council "when appropriate in the exercise of its primary responsibility for the maintenance of international peace and security" under the relevant articles of the Charter.

Turning to the right of self-defense, they stated that the use of force "in the exercise of the inherent right of individual or collective self-defense, or pursuant to decisions of, or authorization by, competent United Nations organs or regional organizations consistent with the Charter of the United Nations" did not constitute aggression.

The draft stated that the use of force by a state which may constitute aggression includes a use of force by a state:

    A. In order to:
       1. Diminish the territory or alter the boundaries of another state.
       2. Alter internationally agreed lines of demarcation.
       3. Disrupt or interfere with the conduct of the affairs of another state.
       4. Secure changes in the government of another state.
       5. Inflict harm or obtain concessions of any sort.
    B. By means such as:
       1. Invasion by its armed forces of the territory under the jurisdiction of another state.
       2. Use of its armed forces in another state in violation of the fundamental conditions of permission for their presence, or maintaining them there beyond the termination of permission.
       3. Bombardment by its armed forces of territory under the jurisdiction of another state.
       4. Inflicting physical destruction on another state through the use of other forms of armed forces.
       5. Carrying out deliberate attacks on the armed forces, ships, or other aircraft of another state.
       6. Organizing, supporting, or directing armed bands or irregular or volunteer forces that make incursions or infiltrate into another state.
       7. Organizing, supporting, or directing violent civil strife or acts of terrorism in another state.

[41] *Id.* at 79–80.
[42] *Id.* at 80.

8. Organizing or supporting or directing subversive activities aimed at the violent overthrow of the government of another state.[43]

Over the years the categories of definitions proposed has generally been classified into three general types: enumerative, general, and mixed. The enumerative definitions set out concrete acts or situations in which aggression is said to exist. The general and abstract definitions seek to set out in broad terms what the elements of the offense are. The mixed definitions seek to offer the best of both worlds by setting out an abstract definition in the first clause, together with a list of concrete aggression situations to assist in the understanding of the general formula.[44]

Interestingly enough the three latest proposals fall within the category of "mixed" definitions. It would seem to be an indication that some progress has been made, as the Soviets have, until recently, always stayed with their enumerative definition and the Western Powers have tended to rely on the general form of definition.

This, of course, is not to say that the "mixed" definition is the best or most appropriate or without problems of its own. There are still obstacles to be overcome which are to be found in any attempt at definition and which proponents of "definition" have been facing since the League.[45] The problem with mixed definitions is best stated by Julius Stone:

> If the abstract definition in the general clause could be self-applying, the list of acts or situations would be unnecessary; and it is not, in any case, really a part of the definition. Its inclusion manifests doubt as to the adequacy of the definition in the general clause and seeks to ensure that it will at least extend to the list of acts or situations.[46]

Apparently, both the general and the enumerative definitions have lost favor. As for a purely enumerative definition, the Yugoslav delegate at the 1956 Special Committee said, "A purely enumerative definition was now rejected by all the member states."[47] Nor has there been much support for general definitions.[48]

The main motives behind the latest "mixed" definitions seem to be concerned less with providing a definition and more with seeking to exclude, in their proposed enumerations of "acts of aggression," those activities which the proposer regards as particularly menacing to their own special interests.

The latest Soviet draft, it will be noted, is particularly weak in its abstract definition, and quite noticeably strong in its enumerative listing.

---

[43] *Id.*

[44] STONE, *supra* note 2, at 80.

[45] WORLDMARK ENCYCLOPEDIA OF THE NATIONS: THE UNITED NATIONS 126 (1967).

[46] STONE, *supra* note 2, at 80.

[47] *Id.* at 81 n.13.

[48] BROWNLIE, *supra* note 1, at 355.

This reflects the Soviet preference since 1933. The main drive of Soviet definitions has been and still is concerned with the prohibition of the declaration of war and armed invasion of territory. Further, the Soviet expansionary gains of the postwar period have aided in isolating her from her age-old fear of invading land armies from Europe by the use of the satellite nations as a buffer zone. The Soviet desire to maintain this front is witnessed by the quick action to reestablish an acceptable government in Czechoslovakia under the questionable Brezhnev Doctrine.

The Soviets have also been quick to adopt the proposals for inclusion of "indirect aggression" in the definition of aggression, since it was first espoused by certain Arab, African, and South American countries with which it sought favorable relations at the time. They have also sought to deny in their definition any recognition to a country which has gained territory through the use of armed aggression. This, of course, with obvious reference to the desire to condemn the territorial gains of Israel achieved in their conflict with the Arab States in 1967. To this extent Resolution 247 of November 22, 1967, found worldwide support against "acquisition of territory by use of force."

The draft of the thirteen powers also reflects their special interests. Of primary import to these lesser powers is the preservation of their territorial integrity along with the condemnation of indirect aggression, which, when perpetrated, would usually be directed against them.

The third draft was no less a subject of the special interests of the involved states. The most important point in this definition is the preservation of the "inherent right of individual or collective" self-defense—the principal which the United States has evoked in almost every instance of its intervention within the past twenty years.[49] It further enumerates acts which should be considered aggression which the United States has listed as reasons justifying involvement in the Viet Nam conflict, such as an attempt "to alter internationally recognized lines of demarcation" or "disrupt or interfere with the conduct of the affairs of another state."[50]

This commentary is not meant to decry the motives of nations in their actions concerning the definition of aggression. It is merely stating a political fact of life that a state can be expected to act in any international organization in a manner most suited to its own interests.

One question which is raised by this discussion, is whether it is sensible to search for criteria consisting of simple factual elements such as the armed crossing of a frontier, declaration of war, bombardment of land or vessels, or threat or use of force, since the advent of mass destruction technology.

[49] Barnett, *U.S. Involvement in Foreign Civil Strife Since World War II*, Am. Soc'y Int'l. L. Proc. 72 (1961).

[50] *The Legality of the U.S. Participation of the Defense of Viet Nam, supra* note 28, at 565–75.

1.6. Summary of Proposals Before the United Nations on Defining Aggression as of June, 1971

USSR Proposal

1. Armed aggression (direct or indirect) is the use by a state, first, of armed force against another state contrary to the purposes, principles, and provisions of the Charter of the United Nations. (para. 1)

Thirteen-Power Proposal

2. For the purpose of this definition, aggression is the use of armed force by a state against another state, including its territorial waters or air space, or in any way affecting the territorial integrity, sovereignty, or political independence of such state, save under the provisions of paragraph 3 hereof or when undertaken by or under the authority of the Security Council. (para. 2)

Six-Power Proposal

II. The term "aggression" is applicable, without prejudice to a finding of threat to the peace or breach of the peace, to the use of force in international relations, overt or covert, direct or indirect, by a state against the territorial integrity or political independence of any other state, or in any other manner inconsistent with the purposes of the United Nations. Nations. . . . (para. II)

Texts Proposed in the Working Group

(i) Aggression is the use of armed force by a state against the territorial integrity [including the territorial waters and airspace] [or sovereignty] or political independence of another state, or in any other manner inconsistent with the purposes of the United Nations.

(ii) Aggression is the use of armed forces by a state against another state, or in any way affecting the territorial integrity [including the territorial waters and airspace] [or sovereignty] or political independence of such state.

(b) There is general agreement that the concept of "priority" or "first use" should be introduced into the definition; however, there are two ways of doing this:

(1) Specific mention, as in the USSR draft (paragraph 1) and thirteen-power draft (paragraph 5).
(2) Reference to this factor in a formulation of the kind found in paragraph 5 of the Working Group's report, which reads:

In determining whether force was used by a state in order to act against the territorial integrity or political independence of another state, or in any manner inconsistent with the purposes of the United Nations, due weight shall be given to the question which of those states first used force.

(c) There is general agreement that it is essential to include in the definition a reference to the legitimate uses of force in accordance with the Charter.

USSR Proposal

6. Nothing in the foregoing shall prevent the used of armed force in accordance with the Charter of the United Nations, including its use by dependent peoples in order to exercise their inherent right of self-determination in accordance with General Assembly Resolution 1514 (XV). (para. 6)

Thirteen-Power Proposal

3. The inherent right of individual or collective self-defense of a state can be exercised only in case of the occurrence of armed attack (armed aggression) by another state in accordance with article 51 of the Charter.

4. Enforcement action or any use of armed force by regional arrangements or agencies may only be resorted to if there is decision to that effect by the Security Council acting under Article 53 of the Charter. (paras. 3 & 4)

Six-Power Proposal

III. The use of force in the exercise of the inherent right of individual or collective self-defense, or pursuant to decisions of or authorization by competent United Nations organs or regional organizations consistent with the Charter of the United Nations, does not constitute aggression. (para. III)

Texts Proposed in the Working Group

(i) The use of armed force in accordance with the Charter to maintain or restore international peace and security, or in the exercise of the inherent right of individual or collective self-defense, does not constitute aggression.

(ii) The use of armed force in accordance with the Charter to maintain or restore international peace and security, or in the exercise of the inherent right of individual or collective self-defense, does not constitute aggression.

The inherent right of individual or collective self-defense of a State can be exercised only in case of the occurrence of armed attack (armed aggression) by another State in accordance with article 51 of the Charter.

Enforcement action or any use of armed force by regional arrangements or agencies may only be resorted to under article 53 of the Charter.

(d) There is general agreement that the nonexhaustive list of the most common cases of aggression should be preceded by a statement to the effect that the enumeration is made without prejudice to the authority vested in the Security Council by the Charter.

USSR Proposal

2. In accordance with and without prejudice to the functions and powers of the Security Council.

Thirteen-Power Proposal

3. In accordance with the foregoing and without prejudice to the powers and duties of the Security Council, as

Six-Power Proposal

I. Under the Charter of the United Nations, "aggression," is a term to be applied by the Security Council when

3. In addition to the acts listed above, other acts by states may be deemed to constitute an act of aggression if in each specific instance they are declared to be such by a decision of the Security Council. (paras. 2 & 3)

provided in the Charter. . . . (para. 5)

appropriate in the exercise of its primary responsibility for the maintenance of international peace and security under article 24 and its functions under article 39. (para. I)

(e) There are two views on the inclusion of the concept of "declaration of war" among the typical acts of aggression:

(1) "Declaration of war" should be included among typical acts of aggression.

(2) A statement should be included before the listing of typical acts indicating that the acts included in the list constitute aggression whether or not they are accompanied by a declaration of war.

(f) There is general agreement on the desirability of including in the list of typical acts of aggression the following cases:

Invasion of the Territory of Another State

USSR Proposal

(c) Invasion or attack by the armed forces of a state against the territory of another state, military occupation or annexation of the territory of another state or part thereof. (para. 2.B.c.)

Thirteen-Power Proposal

(b) The invasion or attack by the armed forces of a state, against the territories of another state, or any military occupation, however temporary, of any forcible annexation of the territory of another state or part thereof. (para. 5.b)

Six-Power Proposal

(1) Invasion by its armed forces of territory under the jurisdiction of another state. (para. IV.B.1)

Bombardment of the Territory of Another State

USSR Proposal

(b) Bombardment of or firing at the territory and population of another state. . . . (para. 2.B.b)

Thirteen-Power Proposal

(c) Bombardment by the armed forces of a state against the territory of another state. . . . (para. 5.c)

Six-Power Proposal

(3) Bombardment by its armed forces of territory under the jurisdiction of another state. (para. IV.B.3)

Attack on the Armed Forces, Ships, or Aircraft of Another State

USSR Proposal	Thirteen-Power Proposal	Six-Power Proposal
(b) . . . or an attack on its land, sea, or air forces. (para. 2.B.b)		(5) Carrying out deliberate attacks on the armed forces, ships, or aircraft of another state. (para. IV.B.5)

Indirect Use of Force

(g) There is general agreement that reference should be made in the definition to the problem of armed bands of irregular forces; however, there is no agreement on how to do this.

USSR Proposal	Thirteen-Power Proposal	Six-Power Proposal
C. The use by a state of the armed force by sending bands, mercenaries, terrorists, or saboteurs to the territory of another state and engagement in other forms of subversive activity involving the use of armed force with the aim of promoting an internal upheaval in another state or a reversal of policy in favor of the aggressor shall be considered as an act of indirect aggression. (para. 2.C)	7. When a state is a victim in its own territory of subversive and/or terrorist acts by irregular, volunteer, or armed bands organized or supported by another state, it may take all reasonable and adequate steps to safeguard its existence and its institutions, without having recourse to the right of individual or collective self-defense against the other state under article 51 of the Charter. (para. 7)	(6) Organizing, supporting, or directing armed bands or irregular or volunteer forces that make incursions or infiltrate into another state. (7) Organizing, supporting or directing violent civil strife or acts of terrorism in another state. (8) Organizing, supporting or directing subversive activities aimed at the violent overthrow of the government of another state. (para. IV.B.6, 7, 8)

Text Proposed in the Working Group

The following text was proposed in the Working Group to replace paragraph IV.B, 7, 8 of the six-power proposal:

The sending by a state of armed bands of irregulars or mercenaries which invade the territory of another state in such force and circumstances as to amount to armed attack as envisaged in article 51 of the Charter.

3. Points on Whose Inclusion There Is No Agreement

(a) Recognition of the fact that the power of decision to use force is centralized in the United Nations and consequences of the application of this principle in the activities of the regional agencies in accordance with article 53 of the Charter.

(b) Application of the definition to political entities other than states.

(c) Inclusion of the use of weapons of mass destruction as a typical case of aggression.

(d) Naval blockade as a typical case of aggression.

(e) Question of maintaining armed forces in another state.

(f) Principle of proportionality.

(g) Inclusion of the concept of "aggressive intent."

(h) Inclusion in the definition of the legal consequences of aggression, fundamentally of the following:

  (i) Aggression is a crime against peace and commission of this crime entails international responsibility;

  (ii) There exists an obligation not to recognize the occupation and acquisition of territory by force.

(i) Inclusion in the definition of the question of the right of peoples to self-determination of.

178 International Criminal Law

1.7. Conclusion

The history of the concept of aggression from the time of the League of Nations down to the present day in the Vietnam and Arab-Israeli conflicts has been marked with few successes. The future does not look to be much more promising if the goal remains that of molding the rules to fit our own purpose. The United Nations has been rendered ineffective for this very reason.

Many have felt over the years that the starting point in the investigation should be that of establishing a definition so that the international body that would decide on a violation would have advance criteria on which to base its judgment. It is, however, unrealistic at this time to expect a definition of any kind to be a reliable tool due to the fact that there is no international body that could successfully enforce its judgment. The realistic position is that taken by Professor Sohn. "A definition of aggression is not a panacea. It is but one of the many steps which need to be taken if we really want peace. The rule of law in world affairs can only be achieved through gradual extension to many fields."[51]

If the proper steps are taken in the future, a definition of aggression may not be needed at all. The proper steps might be the establishment of a permanent Tribunal composed of internationally renowned jurists to whom countries must submit all grievances and accept the decision of the court as final. Such a judge would not need a definition, but could make his decision fair and equitable based on the facts of each case. The lesson of Nuremberg is that such a decision is possible without advance criteria. Perhaps someday the International Court of Justice might assume this role.

But what of the present? What can be done now? Despite its inadequacies, we do have the United Nations. On occasion it has come up with a fair appraisal of an international dispute and helped somewhat to smooth over what could have been a major confrontation. Such an incident was the U-2 affair of 1960 after the Soviet Union requested the Security Council to brand the instrusion over their territory as "aggressive acts."[52] The resolution was defeated, however, by a vote of 2 for, 7 against, and 2 abstentions.[53] Such a conclusion would seem warranted based on interpretation of "aggression" as that term is understood under the Charter. Under the Charter "such an act involves actual threat or use of armed force under article 39; or an 'armed attack' justifying individual or collective self-defense under article 51."[54]

[51] L. Sohn, *The Definition of Aggression*, 45 Va. L. Rev. 700 (1959).
[52] Wright, *Legal Aspects of the U-2 Incident*, 54 A.J.I.L. 836 (1960); *also* Lissitzyn, *Some Legal Implications of the U-2 and RB-47 Incidents*, 56 A.J.I.L. 135 (1962).
[53] Poland and the USSR voted in favor of the resolution, and Tunisia and Ceylon abstained.
[54] Wright, *The U-2 Incident*, *supra* note 52, at 846.

This is not to say that the United States was without fault in this incident. The United States was guilty of a violation of international law, but this act could not be characterized as "aggression."[55]

Thus, it can be argued that today we still have the United Nations and, through it, hope for the future.

Finally, what of the past? Has the dream of Kellogg-Briand of the outlawry of war been forever cast aside?[56] Has the labor of so many for so long been to no avail? Or would the world have been in a worse condition had it not been for those who devoted their lives and efforts to the ideal of peace? Along that arduous road another milestone might have been attained if the draft code of offenses against the peace and security of mankind had been adopted. Its existence, however, is illustrative of the continuing efforts made to preserve minimum world order.[57] As such, it is hereby appended.

APPENDIX I

Text of the Draft Code of Offenses against the Peace and Security of Mankind adopted by the International Law Commission at its sixth session, held in Paris in June and July, 1954. [9 U.N. GAOR, supp. 9, at 11–12, U.N. Doc. A/2693 (1954)]

Article 1

Offences against the peace and security of mankind, as defined in this Code, are crimes under international law, for which the responsible individuals shall be punished.

Article 2

The following acts are offences against the peace and security of mankind:

(1) Any act of aggression, including the employment by the authorities of a State of armed force against another State for any purpose other than national or collective self-defence or in pursuance of a decision or recommendation of a competent organ of the United Nations.

(2) Any threat by the authorities of a State to resort to an act of aggression against another State.

(3) The preparation by the authorities of a State of the employment of armed force against another State for any purpose other than national or collective self-defense or in pursuance of a decision or recommendation of a competent organ of the United Nations.

(4) The organisation, or the encouragement of the organisation, by the authorities of a State, of armed bands within its territory or any other territory for incursions into the territory of another State, or the toleration of the organisation of such bands in its own territory, or the toleration of the use by such armed bands of its territory as a base of operations or as a point of departure for incursions into the territory of another State, as well as direct participation in or support of such incursions.

(5) The undertaking or encouragement by the authorities of a State of activities

[55] *Id.* at 583.
[56] *Supra* note 13.
[57] McDougal and Feliciano, Law and Minimum World Public Order (1960).

calculated to foment civil strife in another State, or the toleration by the authorities of a State of organized activities calculated to foment civil strife in another State.

(6) The undertaking or encouragement by the authorities of a State of terrorist activities in another State, or the toleration by the authorities of a State of organised activities calculated to carry out terrorist acts in another State.

(7) Acts by the authorities of a State violation of its obligations under a treaty which is designed to ensure international peace and security by means of restrictions or limitations on armaments, or on military training, or on fortfications, or of other restrictions of the same character.

(8) The annexation by the authorities of a State of territory belonging to another State, by means of acts contrary to international law.

(9) The intervention by the authorities of a State in the internal or external affairs of another State, by means of coercive measures of an economic or political character in order to force its will and thereby obtain advantages of any kind.

(10) Acts by the authorities of a State or by private individuals committed with intent to destroy, in whole or in part, a national, ethnic, racial or religious group as such, including:

  (i) Killing members of the group;
 (ii) Causing serious bodily or mental harm to members of the group;
(iii) Deliberately inflicting on the group conditions of life calculated to bring about its physical destructions in whole or in part;
 (iv) Imposing measures intended to prevent births within the group;
  (v) Forcibly transferring children of the group to another group.

(11) Inhuman acts such as murder, extermination, enslavement, deportation or persecutions, committed against any civilian population on social, political, racial, religious or cultural grounds by the authorities of a State or by private individuals acting at the instigation or with the toleration of such authorities.

(12) Acts in violation of the laws or customs of war.

(13) Acts which constitute:

  (i) Conspiracy to commit any of the offences defined in the preceding paragraphs of this article, or
 (ii) Direct incitement to commit any of the offences defined in the preceding paragraphs of this article; or
(iii) Complicity in the commission of any of the offences defined in the preceding paragraphs of this article; or
 (iv) Attempts to commit any of the offences defined in the preceding paragraphs of this article.

Article 3

The fact that a person acted as Head of State or as responsible government official does not relieve him of responsibility for committing any of the offences defined in this code.

Article 4

The fact that a person charged with an offence defined in this code acted pursuant to an order of his Government or of a superior does not relieve him of responsibility in international law if, in the circumstances at the time, it was possible for him not to comply with that order.

APPENDIX II

Excerpts From Declaration on Principles of International Law
Concerning Friendly Relations and Cooperation
Among States in Accordance With the Charter of
the United Nations [G.A. Res. 2625 (XXV) (Nov. 4, 1970)]

[H]aving considered the principles of international law relating to friendly relations
and co-operation among States,

1. *Solemnly proclaims* the following principles:

   (a) The principle that States shall refrain in their international relations from
   the threat or use of force against the territorial integrity or political independence of any State, or in any other manner inconsistent with the purposes
   of the United Nations,

   (b) The principle that States shall settle their international disputes by peaceful
   means in such a manner that international peace and security and justice are
   not endangered,

   (c) The duty not to intervene in matters within the domestic jurisdiction of any
   State, in accordance with the Charter,

   (d) The duty of States to co-operate with one another in accordance with the
   Charter,

   (e) The principle of equal rights and self-determination of peoples,

   (f) The principle of sovereign equality of States,

   (g) The principle that States shall fulfil in good faith the obligations assumed by
   them in accordance with the Charter,

so as to secure their more effective application within the international community,
would promote the realization of the purposes of the United Nations,

2. *Declares* that:

In their interpretation and application the above principles are interrelated and
each principle should be construed in the context of the other principles.

Nothing in this Declaration shall be construed as prejudicing in any manner the
provisions of the Charter or the rights and duties of Member States under the Charter
or the rights of peoples under the Charter, taking into account the elaboration of
these rights in this Declaration.

3. *Declares further* that:

The principles of the Charter which are embodied in this Declaration constitute
basic principles of international law, and consequently appeals to all States to be
guided by these principles in their international conduct and to develop their mutual
relations on the basis of the strict observance of these principles.

Section 2. SOVIET CONCEPTS OF AGGRESSION

WILLIAM E. BUTLER

2.1. Introduction

The search for a means of regulating the use of force in the international system since World War I has, in part, been one of attempting to identify and precisely delineate the types of coercion considered to be "aggressive." Seventy years into the twentieth century a satisfactory definition has yet to be formulated; in fact, many governments, statesmen, and jurists continue to harbor profound doubts about the efficacy or desirability of devising one.[1]

One of the more interesting and perhaps paradoxical elements in this quest is found in the role of the Union of Soviet Socialist Republics. Widely regarded in the interwar era as the illegitimate offspring of World War I and in the post-1945 era as the pariah of the international community, the Soviet government nevertheless has been the leading proponent of defining aggression, and its numerous proposals have occupied a central place in jurisprudential discussions of the issue during the past four decades.

2.2. Early Soviet Attitudes: 1917–32

Force, exploitation, influence, war, coercion—these notions figured prominently in Lenin's analyses of international relations prior to, during, and following World War I. All were believed to be endemic to a system which Lenin characterized as "imperialism—the highest stage of capitalism" in his classic work bearing that title.

Philosophically at least, it would have been absurd in Lenin's view to characterize the resort to force by states as "illegal," since the interests of the ruling classes and the dynamics of the international system were believed to make the use of force unavoidable. Although Lenin had little to say in his writings about international law in the sense we understand that term today, one may suppose that, at least before the 1917 Revolution, he would have held international law in low esteem as an effective independent restraint on the actions of capitalist states. This same impression of international law may well have been dominant after the October Revolution, but the Soviet Government nonetheless found it advantageous to insist that foreign states comply with their international legal obligations. Thus, while the coercive nature of the international

---

[1] One of the most thoughtful and imaginative inquiries into the subject is J. STONE, AGGRESSION AND WORLD ORDER: A CRITIQUE OF UNITED NATIONS THEORIES OF AGGRESSION (1958).

order was uppermost in the perceptions of the Bolshevik leadership, the term "aggression" was not widely used in early Soviet media as either a moral or a legal pejorative.[2]

The concept of aggression is widely regarded to have first received juridical status in article 10 of the League of Nations Covenant,[3] although the Covenant did not attempt to define aggression. The Soviet Government—remaining outside the League and being deeply suspicious of the principle of collective security as practiced by the major powers in the 1920's—was initially pessimistic about achieving an acceptable definition. Commenting upon a draft treaty of mutual assistance prepared by the Third Committee of the League Assembly, the USSR

> . . . denied the possibility of determining in the case of every international conflict which state is the aggressor and which is the victim. There are, of course, cases in which a state attacks another state without provocation, and the Soviet Government is prepared in its conventions with other governments, to undertake, in particular cases, to oppose attacks of this kind undertaken without due cause. But in the present international situation, it is impossible in most cases to say which party is the aggressor. Neither the entry into foreign territory nor the scale of war preparations can be regarded as satisfactory criteria. Hostilities generally break out after a series of mutual aggressive acts of the most varied character. For example, when the Japanese torpedo boats attacked the Russian fleet at Port Arthur in 1904, it was clearly an act of aggression from a technical viewpoint, but, politically speaking, it was an act caused by the aggressive policy of the Tsarist Government toward Japan, who, in order to forestall the danger, struck the first blow at her adversary. Nevertheless, Japan cannot be regarded as the victim, as the conflict between the two states was not merely the result of the aggressive acts of the Tsarist Government, but also of the imperialist policy of the Japanese government towards the peoples of China and Korea.[4]

The preference for bilateralism expressed in the preceding excerpt was

[2] A volume published in 1958 and devoted to Lenin's writings on international law and relations contained profuse references to "aggression" in the index, but in each case the text used expressions such as intervention, plunder, force, annexation, and robbery. In no case was the word "aggression" used. See I. KUL'KOV (comp.), LENIN O MEZHDUNARODNOI POLITIKI AND MEZHDUNARODNOM PRAVE (1958).

[3] Art. 10 of the Covenant provided:

> The Members of the League undertake to respect and preserve as against external aggression the territorial integrity and existing political independence of all members of the League. In case of any such aggression or in case of any threat or danger of such aggression the council shall advise upon the means by which this obligation shall be fulfilled.

[4] Note of Mar. 12, 1924. Curiously, this paragraph is omitted from the excerpt of the Note published in a volume commemorating fifty years of Soviet efforts to achieve disarmament. See K. NOVIKOV (ED.), 50 LET BOR'BY SSSR ZA RAZORUZHENIE: SBORNIK DOKUMENTOV 47 (1967). The full English text may be found in the Minutes of the 3rd Committee, Records of the 5th Assembly. LEAGUE OF NATIONS OFF. J., Spec. supp. 26, at 138.

the pattern followed in Soviet practice.[5] Six security treaties were concluded during 1925–27 in reaction to the draft Geneva Protocol and the Locarno treaty.[6] Three of these (Turkey, Afghanistan, Persia) bound the parties to abstain from "attacks," one (Lithuania) employed the expression "aggressive actions," and one (Germany) merely referred to attacks by a third party. The treaties with Afghanistan and Persia also prohibited participation in economic or financial boycotts directed against either party, but these provisions were not linked expressly with the concept of armed attack.

A brief flirtation with multilateralism occurred in connection with the Kellogg-Briand pact of August 27, 1928.[7] Much to its annoyance, the Soviet Government had been excluded from the negotiations leading to the treaty. When on the day of its signature the French Government tendered an invitation to the USSR to adhere to the pact,[8] no time was lost. The decision to adhere and the formal act of ratification were both approved by the USSR on August 29. By August 31, the act of adhesion had been transmitted to the French Government accompanied by a lengthy explanation of Soviet anxieties about certain weaknesses in the treaty; no complaint was made of the failure to define or even mention aggression.[9] When ratifications of the pact were, in the Soviet view, un-

[5] We exclude from consideration here the series of agreements contracted by the RSFSR from 1920–22 which laid the basis for normal relations with neighboring states. Whether treaties of peace or of friendship, they generally contained reciprocal military guarantees against future attacks, pledged mutual policies of nonintervention, and undertook to curtail the actions of various illicit groups or bands. None of these agreements purported to define aggression.

[6] See the treaties with Turkey (1925), Sbornik deistvuiushchikh dogovorov, soglashenii i konventsii, zakliuchennykh SSSR s inostrannymi gosudarstvami [hereinafter cited as SDD] III, 9–10; LNTS, CLXXI, 353–57; Germany (1926), SDD, IV, 16–18; LNTS, LIII, 392–96; Afghanistan (1926), SDD, IV, 38–42; LNTS, LIV, 155–76; Lithuania (1926), SDD, IV, 19–22; LNTS, LX, 145–59; Persia (1927), SDD, IV, 23–26; LNTS, CXII, 275–96. A treaty of nonaggression and neutrality signed with Latvia on Mar. 9, 1927, was never ratified. A second Soviet-Afghan treaty of June 24, 1931, contained essentially the same provisions regarding aggression as that of 1926. See SDD, VII, 3–5; L.N.T.S., CLVII, 371–81. The 1931 treaty was extended by a Protocol of Dec. 18, 1955, and remains in force. See Vedomosti verkhovnogo soveta SSSR (1956), No. 16, item 349; U.N.T.S., CCLIX, 101–109.

[7] L.N.T.S., XCIV, 57.

[8] See the TASS communication on the official invitation to adhere to the pact and the memorandum of Litvinov's conversation with the French ambassador to the USSR. Dokumenty vneshnei politiki SSSR, XI, 487–91.

[9] *Id.* at 493, 503. The rapidity with which the ratification process was accomplished apparently caused some concern, for on Sept. 18, 1928, a TASS dispatch noted: "The resolution was passed by the presidium in the interval between two sessions of the Central Executive Committee and, according to the Constitution, such a resolution is an act substituting for the decision of the committee itself. Regarding international treaties concluded by Russia as well as acts of adhesion, a resolution of the presidium is an act of ratification." Quoted in M. Graham, *The Soviet Security Treaties*, XXII A.J.I.L.

duly tardy, a Protocol for Putting into Force the Treaty for the Renunciation of War was signed at Moscow on February 9, 1929, by the USSR and most of its immediate neighbors.[10]

Progress was made toward a more precise definition of aggression in four bilateral nonaggression treaties contracted by the USSR in 1932 with Finland, Latvia, Estonia, and Poland. The Soviet-Finnish treaty provided in article 1(2) that "any forcible action violating the integrity or territorial inviolability or the political independence of the other High Contracting Party, even if such should be committed without declaration of war and avoids [warlike] manifestations, shall be considered to be an aggression." [*napadenie*][11]

The treaty signed with Latvia a fortnight later contained a different formulation. The parties bound themselves to "refrain from any act of aggression [*napadenie*], as well as from any forcible actions . . . irrespective of whether such aggression or similar actions were undertaken individually or jointly with other powers or with or without a declaration of war."[12] Virtually identical wording is found in the Soviet-Estonian treaty.[13]

The Soviet-Polish treaty obliged the parties "to refrain from aggressive [*agressivnye*] actions or attacks [*napadeniia*]" in their relations, juxtaposing the expressions "aggression" and "attack" in still another manner.[14]

---

[10] SDD, V, 8–10; LNTS, LXXXIX, 369–75.

[11] Art. 2. SDD, VII, 21–24; LNTS, CLVII, 393–99. There are in fact two Russian terms used in connection with aggression. The first, and more commonly used in Soviet treaty practice, is *napadenie*, defined as a "rapid, swift action undertaken against someone or something for the purpose of seizure, inflicting losses, damage, etc." Used in this sense, it is a morally and legally neutral expression, which one would ordinarily translate into English as "attack." In its negative aspect, *nenapadenie*, or "nonattack," the term normally appears in Soviet treaties and draft proposals and often is translated as "nonaggression." The Russian word *agressiia*, claimed by Russian dictionaries to derive from the Latin *aggressio*, is defined as an "attack [*napadenie*] of one state against another for the purpose of seizing territory, destroying or limiting its independence, suppressing democracy, or imposing reactionary regimes." Always translated into English as "aggression," this term clearly connotes moral and legal disapproval. In condemning aggression as an international crime, Soviet jurists nearly always speak of "*agressiia*" and not *napadenie*, the latter being the narrower and more neutral term. On the etymological origins of aggression, see Stone, *supra* note 1, at 15–21.

[12] Art. 1. SDD, VII, 6–8; L.N.T.S., CXLVII, 113–26. This phraseology illustrates the problem of translation discussed in the preceding note. If *napadenie* is translated as "attack," then clearly other forcible actions are being equated to an attack. Translating *napadenie* as "aggression" suggests that "other forcible actions," though proscribed, are not acts of aggression.

[13] SDD, VII, 32–34; L.N.T.S., CXXXI, 297–307.

[14] SDD, VII, 12–15; L.N.T.S., CXXXVI, 41–53. The Soviet-French nonaggression pact of Nov. 29, 1932, stipulated the parties would not resort to "war, nor to any aggression [*napadenie*] on land, sea, or air . . . ." SDD, VII, 27–29; L.N.T.S., CLVII, 411–19.

2.3. The Soviet Definition of 1933

On February 6, 1933, the Soviet delegation to the League of Nations disarmament conference submitted an enumerative draft definition of aggression that, with certain modifications to be discussed below, has served as the basis of all Soviet drafts on this subject and, indeed, of most international discussions of the issue. Under this proposal,

1. The attacker in an international conflict shall be considered that state which is the first to take any of the following actions:

a. Declaration of war against another state.

b. The invasion by its armed forces of the territory of another state without declaration of war.

c. Bombarding the territory of another state by its land, naval, or air forces or knowingly attacking the naval or air forces of another state.

d. The landing in, or introduction within the frontiers of another state of land, naval, or air forces without the permission of the government of such state, or the infringement of the condition of such permission, particularly as regards the duration of sojourn or extension of area.

e. The establishment of a naval blockade of the coast or ports of another state.

2. No considerations whatsoever of a political, strategic, or economic nature, including the desire to exploit natural riches or to obtain any sort of advantages or privileges on the territory of another state, no references to considerable capital investments or other special interests in a given state, or to the alleged absence of certain attributes of state organization in the case of a given country, shall be accepted as justification of aggression as defined in clause 1.

In particular, justification for attack cannot be based upon:

A. The internal situation in a given state, as for instance:

a. Political, economic, or cultural backwardness of a given country.

b. Alleged maladministration.

c. Possible danger to life or property of foreign residents.

d. Revolutionary or counterrevolutionary movements, civil war, disorders, or strikes.

e. The establishment or maintenance in any state of any political, economic, or social order.

B. Any acts, laws, or regulations of a given state, as for instance:

a. The infringement of international agreements.

b. The infringement of the commercial, concessional, or other economic rights or interests of a given state or its citizens.

c. The rupture of diplomatic or economic relations.

d. Economic or financial boycott.

e. Repudiation of debts.

f. Nonadmission or limitation of immigration, or restriction of rights or privileges of foreign residents.

g. The infringement of the privileges of official representatives of other states.

h. The refusal to allow armed forces transit to the territory of a third state.

i. Religious or antireligious measures.

j. Frontier incidents.

3. In the event of the mobilization or concentration of armed forces to a considerable extent in the vicinity of its frontiers, the state which such activities threaten may have recourse to diplomatic or other means for the peaceful soluton of international controversies. It may at the same time take steps of a military nature, analogous to those described above, without, however, crossing the frontier.

This definition, as modified in the Politis Report,[15] was embodied in a Convention defining aggression [*agressiia*], signed at London on July 3, 1933,[16] and a substantially identical Convention, also signed at London, on July 4, 1933.[17] A Soviet-Lithuanian treaty of July 5, 1933, contained the same definition.[18]

The differences in style and substance between the original Soviet proposal of February 6 and the Politis Report indicate how deeply the original formulation was indebted to Soviet experience during the first sixteen years of statehood. To be sure, some modifications were technical in nature, *e.g.*, the addition to article 1(b) of "invasion . . . *with or* without declaration of war" or the replacement in article 1(c) of "bombarding" by "attacking." The provisions of 1(d), however, which obviously were aimed at the kind of intervention employed by Western Powers and Japan during the Russian revolution and civil war, were deleted from the Politis Report in favor of a proscription against aid to certain invasions by armed bands. Similarly, in article 2 the subsidiary clause descriptive of political, strategic, or military considerations was eliminated, as was the reference to "possible danger to life or property of foreign residents" not being a justification for an attack. The heading of article 2(B) was changed in the Politis Report to read "The international conduct of a state," and examples (f) through (i), also drawn largely from Soviet experience, were deleted.

The general Soviet approach to defining aggression also was distinctive. In place of a flexible definition to be evaluated in each case by a duly

[15] The Soviet draft of Feb. 6, 1933, was discussed and revised in the General Commission of the General Disarmament Conference (Committee on Security Questions), for which Mr. Politis acted as rapporteur. The conventions defining aggression expressly incorporated the definition "as explained in the report dated Mar. 24, 1933, of the Committee on Security Questions . . . ."

[16] Ratified by Rumania, Poland, USSR, Afghanistan, Persia, Latvia, Estonia, Turkey, and Finland. The same states ratified the Declaration annexed to art. 3 of the Convention, which contained §§ 2(A) & (B) of the Soviet draft as amended by the Politis Report. L.N.T.S., CXLVII, 67–77.

[17] Ratified, with a declaration identical to that cited in note 16 *supra*, by Czechoslovakia, Rumania, USSR, Yugoslavia, and Turkey. L.N.T.S., CXLVIII, 211–19.

[18] L.N.T.S., CXLVIII, 79–85.

authorized international body, the Soviet definition rejected the notion of provocation and excluded the use of force in general. In the Soviet view, the first state to employ force beyond its frontiers must be considered the aggressor.[19]

This approach has obvious intrinsic merit, but at the time it must have been attractive to the Soviet government for other reasons as well. The USSR was not a major military power during the interwar era, and moreover, it had been the object of various military measures—including armed intervention, blockade, and partisan warfare—from its very inception until the proposal of 1933. The ideological myth of unified capitalist encirclement did nothing to allay Soviet apprehensions; indeed, growing militarism in Germany and Japan seemed to confirm them. Under these circumstances it was natural for the Soviet Government to prefer an approach proscribing all offensive use of force or coercion without invoking the discretionary judgments of agencies under the control of non-socialist powers. Thus, the Soviet proposal would have promoted collective security, characterized as illegal the kinds of force previously applied against the USSR, condemned such use of force against other states where a similar social transformation might occur, and ensured that characterizations of aggression could not be withheld arbitrarily by an agency in which the offending powers were predominant. While self-defense by no means was excluded, the list of acts not justifying an attack would have created a very high threshold before the right of self-defense could be lawfully invoked.

The Soviet Union contracted other treaties of nonaggression after 1933, but none incorporated an enumerative definition of aggression. The Soviet-Italian treaty of friendship, nonaggression, and neutrality, signed only two months after the multilateral aggreements concluded at London, reverted to the formulations of the Soviet security pacts of the 1920's.[20] Equally opaque provisions were to be found in the Franco-Soviet[21] and Czechoslovak-Soviet[22] mutual assistance pacts of 1935, the Sino-Soviet

[19] The Soviet representative at the League Conference for the Reduction and Limitations of Armaments declared:

> The definition and establishment of an act of aggression must leave as little opening as possible for subjective feelings and judgements. Still more, the complete definition must, as far as possible, exclude any possibility of subjective interpretation, and the more automatic the establishment of the aggressor, the better for the work of peace.

League of Nations, Records of the Conference for Reduction and Limitation of Armaments, ser. D. vol. V, 49.

[20] SDD, VIII, 8; L.N.T.S., CXLVIII, 319.
[21] SDD, IX, 45; L.N.T.S., CLXVII, 395.
[22] SDD, IX, 49; L.N.T.S., CLIX, 347.

nonaggression treaty of August 19, 1937,[23] and the German-Soviet non-aggression pact of August 23, 1939.[24]

2.4. Soviet Postwar Attitudes: 1945–70

Soviet attitudes toward defining aggression seemed to have undergone an abrupt change when, during the drafting of the Charter of the Nuremburg Tribunal, the Soviet delegate opposed a definition introduced by the American delegation which was based largely upon the Soviet draft of 1933. Such a definition, the Soviet delegate declared, was unnecessary, and the conference was not a competent body to prepare one in any event.

The same attitude apparently prevailed at the San Francisco Conference of 1945. Both Bolivia and the Philippines sought to introduce enumerative definitions of aggression based upon the Soviet model of 1933, but there is no evidence of Soviet support for their initiative or of Soviet disagreement with the majority conclusion of the Third Committee of the Third Commission that a preliminary definition of aggression went beyond the possibilities of the Conference.[25]

The debate over defining aggression was renewed in 1950 in response to the events in Korea, the stalemate in the Security Council after the Soviet representative returned to exercise his prerogative to veto peace-keeping matters, and the corresponding move to place larger responsibilities for peace-keeping upon the General Assembly. In November of that year the USSR introduced in the First Committee of the General Assembly a draft definition incorporating article 2(5) of the London conventions but otherwise identical in every respect to that proposed in February 1933. The Soviet draft was referred to the International Law Commission which, after eleven meetings in 1951, reported in favor of a "general and abstract definition" because an enumerative definition could not be exhaustive and might therefore limit the freedom of judgment of competent organs.[26] In all, the question of defining aggression was discussed at General Assembly sessions V (1950), VI (1951), VII (1952), IX (1954), XII (1957), and XIV (1959), as well as in special committees created for that purpose in 1953 and 1956. Little progress was made, however, despite the sentiment

[23] L.N.T.S., CLXXXI, 101.

[24] L. SHAPIRO (ed.), SOVIET TREATY SERIES, II, 208. Confidence in the Soviet approach to defining aggression was scarcely enhanced by the attack upon Finland in 1939 and Molotov's speech to the Supreme Soviet of the USSR on Oct. 31, 1939, in which he declared that the concepts of aggression and aggressor "had acquired new meaning, for since the liquidation of Poland, France and England were the aggressors."

[25] 12 U.N. C.I.O. Docs. 505. The definitive Soviet history of the San Francisco Conference does not mention these events at all. See S. KRYLOV, ISTORIIA SOZDANIIA ORGANIZATSII OB"EDINENNYKH NATSII (1960).

[26] Report of the International Law Commission 9. U.N. Doc. A/C.1/108

recorded in a 1952 General Assembly resolution as to the possibility and desirability of defining aggression.

The criticisms voiced by many Latin American states against the omission of "indirect aggression" from the Soviet draft were sufficiently consequential to persuade the Soviet delegation to submit a revised draft definition to the special committee formed in 1953. The revisions took the form of additions to the 1950 draft, which otherwise was retained intact.

Paragraphs 2 and 3 of the 1950 draft were renumbered 6 and 7, respectively, and the following text introduced as paragraphs 3–5:

3. An act of indirect aggression *[agressiia]* committed by a state included:
   a. Encouraging subversive activity against another state (terroristic acts, sabotage, etc.)
   b. Promoting the stirring up of civil war in another state.
   c. Promoting an internal coup in another state or a change in policy to please the aggressor.

4. An act of economic aggression was one of the following first committed by a state:
   a. Undertaking measures of economic pressure violating the sovereignty of another state or its economic independence or threatening the basic principles of economic life of such state.
   b. Undertaking measures with respect to another state which prevent the exploitation by it of its own natural wealth or the nationalization of such wealth.
   c. Subjecting another state to economic blockade.

5. An act of ideological aggression by a state is:
   a. Encouraging war propaganda.
   b. Encouraging propaganda for the use of atomic, bacteriological, chemical, or other types of weapons of mass destruction.
   c. Promoting the propaganda of fascist-nazi views, racial or national exclusiveness, or hatred or disparagement toward other peoples.

In addition to the acts enumerated above, the Soviet draft declared that any other acts considered by the Security Council to be an attack or an act of economic, ideological, or indirect aggression would qualify as aggression.[27]

While it cannot be doubted that the revisions embodied in the 1953 Soviet draft were strongly influenced by the views of smaller powers expressed during Assembly debates, they must also be viewed against broader developments in Soviet foreign policy at the time. Even in the

[27] A Russian text of the Soviet draft appears in V. SOBAKIN (comp.), SOVREMENNOE MEZHDUNARODNOE PRAVO: SBORNIK DOKUMENTOV 592 (1964). Divergent translations of the 1933, 1950, & 1953 Soviet drafts led some observers, including Professor J. Stone, to speculate about the significance of "curious changes" in the 1950 & 1953 drafts. In fact, the Russian texts in these respects were identical in all three cases, again pointing to the problem of translating *napadenie* and *agressiia*. See Stone, *supra* note 1, at 47.

months prior to Stalin's death in early March 1953, there were indications that the policy of identifying "nonaligned" states with the imperialist bloc was being seriously reconsidered. Espousing Latin American sentiments against forms of indirect aggression was a positive, yet low-key, move in that direction. Perhaps of greater importance were the signs of instability in Eastern Europe and the election of an administration in the United States rhetorically committed to "liberating communist satellites." In this period predating nuclear stalemate, when the USSR was confronted with economic boycott in the West and "wars of words" were waged fiercely over the airwaves, the definition and proscription of indirect, economic, or ideological aggression might have been viewed from the Soviet side as a potentially useful undertaking.

The rationale of the Soviet approach to defining aggression has remained essentially unchanged from 1933–70, although the 1953 additions to the Soviet draft represented a partial compromise with principle. Dovgalevskii had argued in introducing the first Soviet draft that its purpose was to place security on a sound basis: "No system of security against aggression is efficacious in the absence of a clear idea regarding aggression. A definition would serve as a guide for a group of states and reduce the danger of regional agreements assuming the character of alliances against third parties."[28] The Soviet representative insisted in the 1953 special committee that aggression must be defined if the United Nations was to pursue the objective of preventing acts of aggression: "It would be impossible to forestall warlike acts unless the notion of aggression was clearly defined."[29] More recently, Soviet jurists have noted that an agreed definition would provide a legal basis for establishing the existence of acts contrary to *jus cogens* and would contribute to the progressive development of international law.[30]

The proponents of the Soviet draft definition continued to stress its two distinctive features. First, the Soviet definition was enumerative, *i.e.*, it listed those acts whose commission would be considered aggression. In the versions of 1933 and 1950, the list of acts of aggression was deemed by Soviet diplomats to be exhaustive, although representatives of other countries found it relatively easy to postulate instances of aggression not encompassed by the Soviet draft. Assertions by the Byelorussian delegate Kiselev during debates in the First Committee of the General Assembly that the USSR draft "enumerated all acts which could be termed aggres-

[28] Report of the Committee on Security Questions, League of Nations, May 24, 1933. Conf. D./C.G.108. Conf. Doc., Vol. I, at 679.

[29] P. Morozov, in the Summary Records of the 8th Meeting of the Committee, Apr. 2, 1962. A/AC.91/SR.8.

[30] See the Report of the Special Committee on the Question of Defining Aggression. GAOR (XXV), Doc. A/8019.

sion" were compromised later in that same session by the admission that the draft "did not list all possible eventualities of aggression."[31] With the submission of the 1953 version, which left open the listed acts of aggression to be supplemented by competent organs when necessary, the USSR abandoned once and for all the notion of an exhaustive enumerative definition.

A second feature of the Soviet draft was the great emphasis placed upon first resort to force as the inculpatory act. The reasoning underlying that premise was uncomplicated, and therein, in the Soviet view, lay its virtue. If the object of defining aggression was to prevent, or at least inhibit, the unlawful use of force, then in every case the first state to employ force would be the aggressor—irrespective of provocation, intention, etc. While admittedly there could be some difficulty in ascertaining which party to a conflict first resorted to force, that was a question of fact, and the principle of prior use was held to be far more objective than any other.

Provocation was said to be too subjective to assess fairly. Were provocation to justify the use of force, Litvinov prophesied that "an aggressor will never be found in any armed conflict, and that only mutually aggressive defensive parties will be established, or, worse still, the defense party will be considered the aggressor, and vice versa.[32] The notion of "aggressive intent" was similarly suspect. Apart from its ambiguity, proof of absence of intent would presumably permit the perpetrator to escape the legal consequences of its actions.[33]

The use of force in response to a threat of other anticipatory forcible action to prevent an imminent aggression also would not have been permissible under the Soviet draft. This position was especially important to the USSR during the early stages of the cold war, when the United States held a clear nuclear superiority and there was talk in some quarters of a

[31] See the remarks of Kiselev & Zarubin during the 385th meeting of the First Committee of the General Assembly. GAOR (V), Doc. A/C.1/608. Baginian later contended that even in 1933 the Soviet draft was not intended to be exhaustive. See K. BAGINIAN, AGRESSIIA— TIAGCHAISHEE MEZHDUNARODNOE PRESTUPLENSE: K VOPROSU OB OPREDELENII AGRESSII 19 (1955).

[32] LEAGUE OF NATIONS, II CONFERENCE FOR THE REDUCTION AND LIMITATION OF ARMAMENTS, ser. B, at 237.

[33] Soviet reasoning on this point is less than persuasive. The Soviet definition was said to embrace the notion of "aggressive intent" because an "aggressive action includes an aggressive intention." International law is said to proceed from "the presumption that a state as a social organism is capable of guiding its actions and of consciously pursuing its goals and that a state may not be nonimputable." Aggression, therefore, may be committed only by a state intentionally, but to include intention in the definition would create the impression that proof of absence of intent would enable the offending state to escape legal responsibility. BAGINIAN, *supra* note 31, at 59.

nuclear strike to forestall once and for all an "inevitable" communist takeover of the world.[34]

While the additions inserted in the 1953 draft made it politically more appealing to the less-developed countries of the United Nations, they also compromised the principles so long defended in the original version. The principle of prior use of force could not be applicable to ideological aggression for both conceptual and practical reasons; *i.e.,*. verification would be virtually impossible and the enumerative clauses were much vaguer than those appertaining to armed attack. Also, the claim to an exhaustive enumerative definition was abandoned by empowering competent organs to find nonlisted cases of aggression.

It is of more than passing interest that, in contrast to the network of bilateral and multilateral treaties containing enumerative definitions of aggression contracted by the USSR in the 1930's, not one has been concluded since World War II even within the socialist bloc. Articles 3 and 4 of the Warsaw Pact, for example, refer to the "threat of an armed attack" [*napadenie*] or "an armed attack in Europe" without further explication,[35] and the various bilateral treaties of assistance among the socialist countries are just as vague.[36] It may be argued that an aggressive attack by socialist countries upon one another is inconceivable (through hostilities along the Sino-Soviet frontier belie this), but the absence of a definition of armed attack, were it to come from "the West," could cause difficulties in determining whether the assistance obligations under the treaties of friendship were operable or not.[37]

From 1953 to 1968, discussions of defining aggression proceeded fitfully, without material result. Indeed, from 1959 to 1967, there was no activity whatsoever, the special committee charged with this matter having met only to adjourn to a future date. Even in resolving to adjourn, the committee's deliberations could not have encouraged those who genuinely believed in the efficacy of defining aggression, for at the 1965 session the United States was excoriated thoroughly for "aggression" in Vietnam and in 1968 the USSR similarly treated for its actions in Czechoslovakia.

[34] See Baginian, *id.* who stressed that the "threat of force" by one state would be used as a pretext for individual capitalist states to use armed force without the risk of being declared an aggressor.

[35] Russian text in SOBAKIN, *supra* note 27, at 37.

[36] See, *e.g.,* the Soviet-Czechoslovak treaty of friendship of May 6, 1970. IX INT'L LEGAL MATERIALS 655. However, in art. 6 of that Treaty the parties declare that the Munich Agreement of Sept. 29, 1938, was attained under threat of aggressive war and the use of force against Czechoslovakia, and therefore void from its inception.

[37] Little is said these days of the fate of the London conventions of 1933, but at least two Soviet jurists regard them as still in force. *See* V. Durdenevskii & G. Osnitskaia, *Non-Aggression Pacts—Means of Averting Aggression,* 5 INT'L AFF. 39–43 (1959).

Influenced by the scale of American involvement in Vietnam and by the Arab-Israeli war, Soviet interest in defining aggression became considerably more intense in 1967. In September of that year, the USSR proposed a new Special Committee on the Question of Defining Aggression be established, and the General Assembly so resolved in December.[38]

Considerable attention also was given to the task of defining aggression at the eleventh meeting of the Soviet Association of International Law held from January 31–February 2, 1968. Reports were delivered by L.I. Savinskii on "U.S. Aggression in Vietnam—An International Crime," by V.I. Lisovskii on "Israeli Aggression Against the Arab States—An International Crime," and by V.I. Lazarev "On Defining the Concept of Aggression." M.K. Korostarenko spoke on the interrelationship of the concepts of aggression and intervention.

Although the full texts of the reports have not yet been published, it is clear that Lazarev doubted the usefulness in modern conditions of the 1953 Soviet draft definition and advocated a definition which would separate the prohibition against armed attack from less tangible forms of aggression or intervention. Judging from the summary of discussion at the meeting, his view found considerable, but by no means unanimous, support among other jurists. L.A. Modzhorian, N.M. Minasian, Korostarenko, and A.K. Adzharov were all generally agreed that the 1953 draft was obsolete, but there were differences of opinion as to what constituted armed aggression. Adzharov doubted that any single definition of armed aggression also could embrace economic and political "aggression," even though the latter might constitute a violation of international law. Minasian also was sympathetic to this view, but he believed a declaration of war not immediately followed by an armed attack was nevertheless an act of aggression. Korostarenko urged that the concept of armed attack must embrace "concealed intrusion" by a state using the "struggle of little peoples" or inciting or organizing civil war or intervention.

I.P. Blishchenko, on the other hand, expressed concern that the 1953 Soviet draft not be discarded. Even were one to concentrate upon defining armed aggression, he urged, this did not diminish the necessity for further doctrinal development of other types of aggression. D.B. Levin appeared to side with Blishchenko in recommending that the concept of force referred to in article 2(4) of the United Nations Charter be interpreted broadly and extended to political and economic force. But Levin also recognized that all measures of political and economic influence of one

[38] G.A. Res. 2330 (XXII), Doc. A/6716. For the Soviet proposal and explanatory statement, see U.N. Doc. A/6833, Sept. 22, 1967. For a summary and critique of the problem of defining aggression prior to the Soviet initiative, see John N. Hazard, *Why Try Again to Define Aggression?* LXII A.J.I.L. 701–10 (1968).

state upon another are not unlawful and declared it to be the task of the Soviet science of international law to establish criteria for distinguishing lawful and unlawful use of such influence.[39]

Lazarev's approach seems to have been most reflective of official views, for at the first meeting of the thirty-five-member Special Committee in June–July, 1968, the USSR favored, with other Committee members, giving priority to defining armed aggression. The Committee further agreed that the definition should include both a general definition of armed aggression and an enumeration of characteristic acts, standards for clearly distinguishing between aggression and legitimate self-defense, a proviso stressing the exclusive powers of the United Nations Security Council to determine the existence of acts of aggression pursuant to article 39 of the Charter, and a stipulation concerning the legal responsibility of the aggressor.[40]

In February 1969, less than six months after the armed forces of some members of the Warsaw Pact had entered Czechoslovakia, the Soviet representative on the Special Committee introduced a new draft definition of aggression as follows:

1. Armed aggression (direct or indirect) is the use by a state, first, of armed force against another state contrary to the purposes, principles, and provisions of the Charter of the United Nations.

2. In accordance with and without prejudice to the functions and powers of the Security Council:

   A. Declaration of war by one state, first, against another state shall be considered an act of armed aggression.

   B. Any of the following acts, if committed by a state first, even without a declaration of war, shall be considered an act of armed aggression:
   a. The use of nuclear, bacteriological, or chemical weapons or any other weapons of mass destruction.
   b. Bombardment of or firing at the territory and population of another state or an attack on its land, sea, or air forces.
   c. Invasion or attack by the armed forces of a state against the territory of another state, military occupation or annexation of the territory of another state or part thereof, or the blockade of coasts or ports.

   C. The use by a state of armed force by sending armed bands, mercenaries, terrorists, or saboteurs to the territory of another state and engagement in other forms of subversive activity involving the use of armed force with the aim of promoting an internal upheaval in another state or a reversal of policy in favor of the aggressor shall be considered an act of indirect aggression.[41]

[39] The reports and subsequent discussion are summarized in SOVETSKII EZHEGODNIK MEZHDUNARODNOGO PRAVA 1968, at 355–60 (1969).

[40] *See* V. Chkhikvadze & O. Bogdanov, *Definition of Aggression—An Important Instrument in the Struggle for Peace,* 7 INT'L AFF. 27–32 (1969).

[41] U.N. Doc. A/AC.134/L.12. Reproduced in VIII INT'L LEGAL MATERIALS 661.

It was stipulated further that other acts by states may be declared by the Security Council in each specific case to constitute an act of aggression. However, the draft would not prevent the use of armed force in accordance with the United Nations Charter, "including its use by dependent people in order to exercise their inherent right of self-determination in accordance with General Assembly Resolution 1514(XV)." No territorial gains or special advantages resulting from armed aggression were to be recognized. The draft also treated the problem of legal responsibility for committing an act of aggression, holding that individual persons shall be criminally liable and states shall bear material and political responsibility.

Despite some new trappings and internal reorganization, it will be noted that the Soviet definition of armed aggression is substantially that proposed in 1933–53. The only omission from the 1933 version (para. 1) is the latter half of subclause (d) on infringement of conditions of permission to introduce forces within another's territory.[42] The 1933–53 provision on armed bands is relegated to indirect armed aggression, but otherwise retained intact.[43] The enumerative component of the definition does not purport to be exhaustive, as in the case of the 1953 draft, and the principle of proscribing first use of force is preserved, unimpaired.

Of the innovations introduced in the 1969 draft, the general definition of aggression inserted as paragraph 1 and the addition of clause 2(B)(a) on weapons of mass destruction are likely to receive the broadest support. The former is the logical consequence of abandoning an exhaustive enumerative approach, whereas the latter is somewhat belated recognition of modern technological developments. Of greater concern, however, must be the clause on the use of force by dependent peoples. On this point, the comparatively precise definitional formulations give way, for there is no restriction upon the kinds or uses of force to be employed by dependent peoples in pursuance of this "just" purpose nor is there an agreed definition of "self-determination," "dependent," or "peoples."[44]

[42] The reasons for this omission are not clear. It could relate to Czechoslovakia, where the Soviet Union has some forces stationed. As recently as 1967, some Soviet jurists had described the illegal introduction of one state's armed forces into another by way of invited occupation as aggression, citing actions of the United States in Panama, Lebanon, and the Dominican Republic, of the United Kingdom in Cyprus and Jordan, and of France in Gabon. *See* V. CHKHIKVADZE, et al (ed.), II KURS MEZHDUNARODNOGO PRAVA V SHESTI TOMAKH 125.

[43] The 1970 Report of the Special Committee on the Question of Defining Aggression agreed to delete "indirect" aggression from the proposed draft of armed aggression, presumably because agreement on a definition would have been impossible in the near future.

[44] The Soviet clause on dependent peoples can scarcely be regarded as a novelty, for the Soviet position on this issue has long been well-known. Even though the 1953 and earlier Soviet drafts said nothing about colonial or civil wars, Soviet jurists held that only

2.5. Concluding Observations

It is especially noteworthy that the Soviet draft definitions of aggression have emanated exclusively from official governmental sources. The role of the academic jurist in developing the drafts, apart from vigorously defending them in doctrinal writings, is obscure. Assuredly, academic jurists have not circulated their own draft definitions independently, and the few articles and monographs devoted to the subject in the USSR are largely repetitive of governmental views expressed in the relevant bodies of the United Nations. Perhaps the most innovative aspect of doctrinal writings has been the "catalogues" of alleged aggressions committed by "imperialist" states,[45] but the arbitrary manner in which such characterizations are expressed can hardly be reassuring to Western governments already deeply suspicious of Soviet motives in seeking to define aggression.

The 1968 meeting of the Soviet Association of International Law is most interesting in this connection. It is unclear whether the government had a final version of the 1969 draft definition at that time and was both informing the assembled gathering and inviting comments or whether the drafting process was still underway and the reactions of Soviet jurists to a possible change of approach were being solicited. In fact, most of the views reported seem to have been accommodated in the 1969 draft.

If international agreement is reached upon a definition of armed aggression—as now seems within the realm of possibility—it will be interesting to see whether Soviet doctrine characterizes other forms of aggression in the sweeping terms of the past or whether attention is given to delineating more precisely between aggression and intervention.

---

attacks first committed by *states* which were independent subjects of international law fell within the definition. The Korean War was given as an example of a civil war (Baginian, *supra* note 31 at 26–40). Soviet doctrinal views on who may be a subject of international law have changed since 1955; many Soviet jurists believe that peoples fighting for national liberation are subjects of international law for certain purposes.

[45] *See, e.g.,* K.A. BAGINIAN, NARUSHENIE IMPERIALISTICHESKIMI GOSUDARSTVAMI PRINTSIPA NEVMESHATEL'STVA (1954). A more constructive treatment by the same author ·is BOR'BA SOVETSKOGO SOIUZA PROTIV AGRESSII (1959).

CHAPTER IV

INDIRECT AGGRESSION

Section 1. CIVIL STRIFE AND INDIRECT AGGRESSION

JOHN C. NOVOGROD

1.1. Indirect Aggression and the Postulate of Peaceful Change

The conception of world order projected by the United Nations Charter is based on the fundamental principle that any change in the structure of power in the world arena should be conducted in a peaceful and orderly manner so as not to waste human or natural resources.[1] To this end, the Charter requires its members to settle their disputes by peaceful means[2] and to refrain from the threat or use of force against the territorial integrity or political independence of any state.[3] Under the Charter's framework for the regulation of coercion, force lawfully may be employed only in the exceptional circumstances of individual or collective self-defense[4] or pursuant to Security Council authorization.[5] Violative, there-

This author has benefited from the critical comments and generous advice of Captain William O. Miller, JAGC, USN, Commander Richard L. Fruchterman, JAGC, USN, Lieutenant Norman A. Wulf, JAGC, USNR; Lieutenant William F. Newton, JAGC, USNR of the Office of the Judge Advocate General, Department of the Navy; and Harry Almond, Esq., Office of the General Counsel, Department of Defense. The responsibility for the views expressed herein is, of course, solely that of the author.

[1] In the context of contemporary nuclear technology, peaceful change must be regarded as indispensable. For excellent treatment of the "postulate of peaceful change," see BLOOM-FIELD, EVOLUTION OR REVOLUTION?: THE UNITED NATIONS AND THE PROBLEM OF PEACEFUL TERRITORIAL CHANGE 9–20, 60–68, 131–41 (1957); CRUTTWELL, A HISTORY OF PEACEFUL CHANGE IN THE MODERN WORLD (1937); Dunn, *Peaceful Change Today*, 11 WORLD POLITICS 278–79 (1959).

[2] U.N. Charter, art. 2(3), provides:

> All members shall settle their international disputes by peaceful means in such a manner that international peace and security, and justice, are not endangered.

[3] U.N. Charter, art. 2(4), reads:

> All members shall refrain in their international relations from the threat or use of force against the territorial integrity or political independence of any state, or in any other manner inconsistent with the purposes of the United Nations.

[4] U.N. Charter, art. 51, provides in part:

> Nothing in the present Charter shall impair the inherent right of individual or collective self-defense if an armed attack occurs against a member of the United Nations, until the Security Council has taken measures necessary to maintain international peace and security.

[5] Pursuant to Security Council authorization, enforcement action involving the use of force may be taken by the United Nations itself (U.N. Charter, art. 42) or by regional organizations (U.N. Charter, art. 53).

fore, of the postulate of peaceful change, as it is reflected in the normative structure of the Charter, is unilateral change through violent modes
of coercion across national boundaries.

Peaceful change as a binding norm must be the cornerstone of a world
order in which there will be the maximum promotion of peaceful relations between states and the minimum resort to international violence.
Freedom from the expectation of unauthorized violence is an indispensable step toward the optimum allocation of basic values (such as health,
safety, education, comfort, and skill) in the larger effort to secure and
protect the fundamental dignity of man.[6] Unfortunately, in a world
marked by revolutionary change with respect to all values, the conception
of world order projected by the Charter is not meeting full acceptance
in our still decentralized world community. Despite the Charter's attempt
to delimit legitimate recourse to international violence, states nonetheless
continue to pursue their value goals by means of impermissible coercion
applied against other nations through all the major instruments of state
policy (military, diplomatic, ideological, and economic).[7]

Rather than overt, classical armed aggression across national boundaries, however, external attack disguised as internal change has become
a most dangerous and pervasive phenomenon in the world arena. An internally unstable or weak territorial policy may easily become the victim
of covert modes of aggression employed by a hostile foreign state. These
subtle, yet effective, methods of destroying a state's political independence have been labeled indirect aggression, since the aggressor does
not use its own armed forces, but achieves its purpose through armed
and/or unarmed persons performing hostile acts inside another state, os-
tensibly on their own initiative and resources.[8] Externally fomented and

[6] An explanation and discussion of these "values" may be found in McDougal & Lasswell,
The Identification and Appraisal of Diverse Systems of Public Order, 53 A.J.I.L. (1959).
See also McDougal, *Perspectives for an International Law of Human Dignity*, Am. Soc'y
Int'l L. Proc. 107 (1959).

[7] *See* McDougal & Feliciano, Law and Minimum World Public Order 27–36, 190–96
(1961).

[8] *See* Report of the Secretary-General, *Questions of Defining Aggression*, 7 U.N. GAOR
Annexes, Agenda Item No. 54, at 50, U.N. Doc. A/2211 (1952) [hereinafter cited as
Report of the Secretary-General]; Kelsen, *Collective Security Under International Law*
[1954] U.S. Naval War College, In't L. Studies 64 (1957). The term "indirect aggression"
is descriptive of a particularized mode of coercion and will be used interchangeably with
such terms as "external attack disguised as internal change," "external fomentation and
support of civil strife," "the exercise of coercion through the medium of internal rebel
groups." In considering the problem of indirect aggression, it is relevant to note that, as
one commentator observes, it "is a matter of common knowledge that in every social upheaval the party attacked claims that the trouble has been stirred up by outside agents
and agitators." Edwards, The Natural History of Revolution 24 (reissued 1965).

abetted domestic conflict[9] is presently one of the major strategies by which states seek the extension of their values at less exorbitant costs than would be entailed by use of overt armed aggression.[10] This link between civil strife and indirect aggression must be recognized as an ominous development in the world power process. In an international system characterized by intense ideological rivalry and high expectations of violence, strife which upsets domestic tranquillity can radiate severe shock waves potentially destructive of the more comprehensive world public order.[11]

In view of this disquieting reality, it is scarcely novel to suggest that the most important challenge to national as well as global decision-makers is to perfect and practice the skills of international conflict management.[12] As our world community becomes progressively more centralized—a course indispensable to survival in an era threatened by nuclear extinction—it may be possible, through strengthened measures of collective security, to prevent potential breaches of the public order before they have erupted into overt military violence. Pending the realization of this still utopian capability, however, international scholars may play a useful role in conflict prevention by assisting, through the identification of the common interests of mankind and detailed analysis of past trends in decision, in the formulation of norms which will be consensually applied by large and small powers alike.[13] It is to be hoped that the emergence of a central core of norms, intended to protect the minimum security requirements of the individual members of the world community, will be increasingly invoked and applied, and thus act as a centripetal force acquiring additional, more sophisticated norms of a consensual nature.

[9] In this section, the terms "domestic conflict," "domestic violence," "internal strife," and "civil strife" will be used synonymously and interchangeably as all-inclusive terms describing internal ". . . attempts to change by violence, or threat of violence, a government's policies, rules, or organization." Eckstein, *Toward the Theoretical Study of Internal War*, INTERNAL WAR: PROBLEMS AND APPROACHES 1 (Eckstein ed. 1964).

[10] The covert nature of indirect aggression makes its exercise less dangerous both in a political sense (*i.e.*, less possibility of such activity being discovered and censured) and in a material sense (*i.e.*, less expensive in terms of men, money, and equipment). *See* BLOOMFIELD, THE UNITED NATIONS AND U.S. FOREIGN POLICY 84 (rev. ed. 1967); SPANIER, WORLD POLITICS IN AN AGE OF REVOLUTION 214–27 (1967); STRAUSZ-HUPE *et al.* PROTRACTED CONFLICT: A CHALLENGING STUDY OF COMMUNIST STRATEGY 53–66 (1959).

[11] This point is well made in Rosenau, *Internal War as an International Event*, in INTERNATIONAL ASPECTS OF CIVIL STRIFE 45 (Rosenau ed. 1964). *See also*, CALVOCORESSI, WORLD ORDER AND NEW STATES 101 (1962); Deutsch *External Involvement in Internal War*, in Eckstein, *supra* note 9, at 100; OSGOOD & TUCKER, FORCE, ORDER, AND JUSTICE 159 (1967).

[12] *Cf.* remarks of Professor Muller in AM. SOC'Y. INT'L L. PROC. 111 (1963). *See also* in this regard, BOULDING, THE ROLE OF LAW IN THE LEARNING OF PEACE, *id.*, at 92.

[13] For an inspiring challenge to scholars, *see* McDougal & Lasswell, *supra* note 6, at 28–29.

Inspired largely by the judgments of the Nuremberg and Tokyo tribunals, there has been evidenced, both in the work of specialized organs of the United Nations and in the writings of jurists, substantial and continuing interest in the development of an I.C.L.[14] The Nuremberg and Tokyo judgments provide some guide—however general—both to the type of conduct deemed criminal and to the quantum of punishment that may be expected with regard to classical, armed aggression across state lines.[15] Although no tribunal has ever determined the criminality of indirect aggression, both the General Assembly[16] and the International Law Commission[17] have deemed such conduct to be an international crime. Lest the world community be lulled into believing that the mere labeling of indirect aggression as an international crime will be a panacea for its troubles, attention might well be turned to this covert form of coercion with a view toward clarifying its delictual and criminal content. Before commencing such an analysis, this section will offer a brief description of the process of indirect aggression and a clarification of the relevant community policies at stake in such a process.

1.2. The Process of Indirect Aggression

An understanding of the major features of the process of indirect aggression is relevant to this inquiry. While similar in many respects to the process of overt, classical armed attack, the process of indirect aggression is of greater complexity, owing not only to its intrinsically covert character but also to the participation of a third major actor, *i.e.* the rebel forces in the target state. The following descriptions take into account the varied and changing features of the process of indirect aggression by briefly describing the participants in the process, the objectives sought by the

[14] For a fine collection of documents and articles reflecting the broad community interest in "international criminal law," see INTERNATIONAL CRIMINAL LAW (Mueller & Wise eds. 1965). For further inquiries into this subject, *see* Murray, *The Present Position of International Criminal Justice*, 36 TRANS. GROT. SOC'Y 191 (1951); Radin, *International Crimes*, 32 IOWA L. REV. 33 (1946); Schick, *International Criminal Law—Fact and Illusions*, 11 MOD. L. REV. 290 (1948); THORNEYCROFT, PERSONAL RESPONSIBILITY AND THE LAW OF NATIONS (1961).

[15] For the text of the Nuremberg Judgment, see NAZI CONSPIRACY AND AGGRESSION— OPINION AND JUDGMENT, U.S. Gov't Print. Off. (Washington 1947) [hereinafter cited as *Nazi Conspiracy and Aggression*]. The text of the Judgment may also be found in 41 A.J.I.L. 172 (1947). For a text of the Judgment of the Tokyo Tribunal, *see* SOHN, CASES AND MATERIALS ON UNITED NATIONS LAW 904 (1956). It is interesting to note that Germany's coercive activities with respect to Austria and Czechoslovakia—conduct analagous to modern-day indirect aggression—were deemed by the Nuremberg Tribunal to constitute "aggressive action" as opposed to "aggressive war." See NAZI CONSPIRACY AND AGGRESSION 16, 21–27, 119, 136, 153.

[16] See text accompany note 118 *infra*.

[17] See text accompanying note 121 *infra*.

aggressor state, the strategies employed by the aggressor state, the particular geophysical and temporal situations which may characterize the process of indirect aggression, and finally, the general conditions obtaining in the world arena under which the process of indirect aggression takes place.

1.2.1. PARTICIPANTS. As in any process of international coercion, the nation-state is the primary participant in the more particularized process of indirect aggression. The initial points of focus, then, are the aggressor and target states, although the former may have acted in concert with other states through a regional organization.[18] Since the setting of indirect aggression is domestic conflict in the target state, groups and entities within the target state also are important participants. For example, depending upon the particular factual circumstances, provinces or sub-states in federated systems may play a role in the process of indirect aggression.[19] Moreover, in that the very nature of indirect aggression involves a medium through which the outside state pursues its unlawful objectives, the rebellious forces inside the target state must be listed as a prime participant.[20] Finally, historical examples may be cited in which transnational political parties,[21] religious organizations,[22] patriotic emigrees,[23] and even tribal groups[24] have played a significant part in the process of indirect aggression.

[18] *See, e.g.,* the allegations made by France before the First Committee to the effect that the League of Arab States was supplying financial assistance to the Algerian rebels. 12 U.N. GAOR 1st Comm., 913th Mtg., U.N. Doc. A/C.1/SR.913 (1957).

[19] An obvious illustration of the role a province can play is that of Biafra in the recent Nigerian strife. *See generally* Baker, *The Emergence of Biafra: Balkanization or Nation-Building,* 12 ORBIS 518 (1968); Garrison, "Biafra vs. Nigeria: The Other Dirty Little War," *N.Y. Times Magazine* 44 (Mar. 31, 1968).

[20] *See generally* CROZIER, THE REBELS: A STUDY OF POST-WAR INSURRECTIONS (1960); PARET & SHY, GUERRILLAS IN THE 1960's (rev. ed. 1966).

[21] In the conflict in South Vietnam, for example, the People's Revolutionary Party (PRP) of South Vietnam is substantially controlled by the Lao Dong Party of North Vietnam. The PRP controls the military and political affairs of the National Liberation Front of South Vietnam. *See* Carver, *The Faceless Viet Cong,* 44 FOREIGN AFF. 347, 361–70 (1966); Honey, *North Vietnam's Workers' Party and South Vietnam's People's Revolutionary Party,* 25 PACIFIC AFF. 375 (winter 1962/63); PIKE, VIET CONG 136–53 (1966); SCIGLIANO, SOUTH VIETNAM: NATION UNDER STRESS 146–47 (1964). The role of transitional political parties in civil strife in the Americas is particularly apparent. *See,* in this regard, O.A.S. Special Consultative Committee on Security, *Initial General Report—1962,* O.A.S. OFF. REC. OEA/Ser. L/X/II.2, Rev. 2 (English).

[22] The best contemporary illustration of the role religious organizations have played in the process of indirect aggression may be found in the Vietnamese domestic strife. *See* Pike, *supra* note 21, at 201–04.

[23] Again in the context of the conflict in South Vietnam, it is well established that, in the years 1956 to 1960, Lao Dong Party cadres, comprised primarily of indigenous southerners, were sent by North Vietnam into the South "with directions to build a political-paramilitary organization." HULL & NOVOGROD, LAW AND VIETNAM 31–32 (1968). *See*

1.2.2. OBJECTIVES. External attack through the medium of rebellious internal groups in the target state may, at least in theory,[25] be initiated for the purpose of securing various objectives.[26] These objectives may be of the most comprehensive nature, such as the replacement of the target state's governmental elite with a new set of decision-makers who share a conception of world order similar to that of the aggressor state.[27] An equally comprehensive objective would be the secession of a province or substate from the political control or authority of the target state.[28] Objectives of a less comprehensive nature might entail the modification of the expectations of the target state's governmental elite in order that their future behavior conform more closely to the policies of the aggressor state.[29] Specific and commonly proclaimed objectives which, depending upon the factual configuration of the particular conflict, would be of a greater or lesser comprehensiveness include the elimination of residual colonialism, the eradication of racism, and the promotion of self-determination.[30]

1.2.3. STRATEGIES. The modalities of coercion to which the target state is subjected may be selectively employed, singly or in combination, to effect the desired objective. In the process of indirect aggression, it will be re-

---

also Honey, *The Origins of the Vietnam War,* in VIETNAM: SEEN FROM EAST AND WEST 21, 27 (Ray ed. 1966).

[24] *See generally* Mazrui, *Violent Contiguity and the Politics of Retribaliation in Africa,* 23 J. INT'L AFF. 89 (1969). *Cf.* arts. 5 & 6 of the Agreement between the United Kingdom and Nejd Regarding Certain Questions Relating to the Nejd-Transjordan Frontier (Nov. 2, 1925), 121 BRITISH AND FOREIGN STATE PAPERS 818; Agreement between Iraq and Nejd to Secure Good Relations in Frontier Matters (Nov. 1, 1925); *id.* at 950.

[25] Distinguishing between the proclaimed and the real objectives of a state exercising coercion is, of course, a well-recognized problem. For this reason, it has been argued that "the effect of the act, rather than the intention of the aggressor, should be the decisive factor in determining aggression. . . ." Remarks of Mr. Adamiyat (Iran), U.N. 9 GAOR, 6th Comm., 416th mtg., at 104, U.N. Doc. A/C.6/SR.416 (1954).

[26] The objectives of a state exercising coercion, however, are of cardinal importance in determining the lawfulness of its actions. As McDougal and Feliciano point out, *supra* note 7, at 197, "a certain degree of coercion is inevitable in states' day-to-day interactions for values. Fundamental community policy does not seek to reach and prohibit this coercion, as indeed it cannot without attempting to impose moral perfection, not to mention social stagnation, on humanity." *See also Trial of Von Leeb,* 12 LAW REPORTS OF TRIALS OF WAR CRIMINALS 67 (1949).

[27] This would appear to be the objective of North Vietnam with respect to its participation in the civil strife in the South. *See generally,* Honey, *North Vietnam's Workers' Party and South Vietnam's People Revolutionary Party, supra* note 21.

[28] France, Tanzania, Zambia, Gabon, and the Ivory Coast all lent some form of assistance to Biafra—by way of materiel or recognition of its independence—in that province's attempt to secede from Nigeria.

[29] For elaboration and analysis, see Lasswell, *Political Factors in the Formulation of National Strategy,* 6 NAVAL WAR COLL. REV. 19, 34–35 (1954).

[30] See text accompanying notes 51–54, 59–75 *infra.*

called, the aggressor state does not employ its own military instrument
but exercises varying intensities of coercion through the medium of rebel
groups in the target state. Thus, the ideological, diplomatic, and economic
instruments assume heightened importance in this context, while the
military instrument plays a significantly less prominent role.[31] Strategies
commonly employed include providing financial assistance, war material,
and irregulars to the rebels in the target state. Often tactical, organizational, and doctrinal guidance is provided as well. At the same time, the
skillful use of the ideological instrument, in the form of hostile propaganda, may have the effect of significantly altering the expectations and
allegiance of the citizens of the target state toward their government.
Rebel leaders, moreover, might receive, in the territory of the aggressor
state, training in sabotage, subversion, and the techniques of coup d'état.
Additionally, the aggressor state may permit the use of its territory by
the rebel forces as a sanctuary, a base of operations, or as a place of
refuge in case of tactical defeat.

1.2.4. SITUATIONS. The situation in which the exercise of indirect aggression takes place may be considered first in reference to the particular
character of the civil violence in the target state. The violence, for example, may take the form of colonial or secessionary strife, domestic
conflict in one half of a cold-war-divided nation, or the breakdown of
internal law and order in an established state.[32]

Secondly, the temporal duration of the external assistance to internal
rebel groups is also relevant to an understanding of indirect aggression.
Sporadic or relatively shortlived external assistance must be viewed quite
differently from assistance which has become practice. A sustained activity has a greater impact on world order and raises a different set of
expectations both within the target state and the world community in
general.[33]

Thirdly, the relative priority between the initiation of the internal violence and the commencement of external assistance is a further consideration. External assistance provided to the rebels in an already ongoing domestic struggle is qualitatively far different from the fomenting of
civil strife in a domestically peaceful state.[34]

[31] See generally *Report of the Secretary-General* 71–75; 1956 Special Committee on the
Question of Defining Aggression, *Report*, 12 U.N. GAOR, Supp. 16, at 7–8, U.N. Doc.
A/3574 (1957) [hereinafter cited as *1956 Special Committee Report*].

[32] For an excellent discussion of the relevance of the particular type of conflict in a
decision as to the permissibility of intervention in civil strife, *see* Moore. *The Control of
Foreign Intervention in Internal Conflict*, 9 VA. J. INT'L L. 205, 254–94 (1969).

[33] This point has been made with respect to the use of the ideological instrument by
MURTY, PROPAGANDA AND WORLD PUBLIC ORDER 48 (1968).

[34] Although this distinction would appear to have no relevance in a determination as

1.2.5. CONDITIONS. The general conditions obtaining in the world arena under which the process of indirect aggression takes place embrace all the components of the world power process that are relevant in respect to any unlawful resort to coercion. Two features, however, appear to be of special relevance in relation to this more particularized modality of coercion.

1.2.5.1. *The Continuing Likelihood of Civil Strife.* In a study completed in 1961, Professor Huntington predicted that internal strife appeared to be "the most probable future form of nonstrategic instability. . . ."[35] Lamentably, the persistent and widespread occurrence of domestic conflict of the past ten years suggests that this prediction will continue to be an accurate forecast of the type of violence likely to erupt in the forseeable future.[36] The principle locus of that violence, of course, will be in the developing states.[37] In the first place, the process of decolonization often is itself violent, as demonstrated by the histories of Vietnam, Indonesia, Algeria, Kenya, and Cyprus. Many of the newly independent states thus have a revolutionary or quasi-revolutionary heritage. Even absent such a heritage, the lack of a tradition of peaceful constitutional change leaves the process of political transition in the new states highly susceptible to violence.[38]

Secondly, the insufficiently centralized authority structures in many of the developing states often do not permit the governing elite to prevent or control a violent challenge to their incumbency.[39] The lack of both

to the lawfulness of the conduct in question, a future tribunal might take it into account in determining criminality or, once that had been decided, the quantum of punishment.

[35] HUNTINGTON, INSTABILITY AT THE NON-STRATEGIC LEVEL OF CONFLICT 17 (Institute for Defense Analysis, Study Memorandum No. 2, 1961). *See generally* Sanger, "The Age of Insurgency," Foreign Service Institute, Wash., D.C. (Memo., n.d.).

[36] *Cf.* McNAMARA, THE ESSENCE OF SECURITY 145 (1968). Professors Leiden & Schmitt forecast that "the last third of the twentieth century promises to be a period of almost constant revolutionary turmoil. . . ." LEIDEN & SCHMITT, THE POLITICS OF VIOLENCE: REVOLUTION IN THE MODERN WORLD 212 (1968).

[37] *See* BLACK, THE DYNAMICS OF MODERNIZATION 166 (1966), who predicts the likelihood of "ten to fifteen revolutions a year for the foreseeable future in the less-developed societies."

[38] This point is developed by Huntington, "Patterns of Violence in International Politics," CHANGING PATTERNS OF MILITARY POLITICS 39 (Huntington ed. 1962). See also Deutsch, *Social Mobilization and Political Development,* 55 AM. SOC. SCI. REV. 493 (1961); LERNER, THE PASSING OF TRADITIONAL SOCIETY (1958).

[39] It is often the case, especially in the newly independent African state, that the national army presents a significant threat to the authority of the incumbent government. For differing views, see Coleman & Price, *The Role of the Military in Sub-Saharan Africa* in THE ROLE OF THE MILITARY IN UNDERVELOPED COUNTRIES 359 (Johnson ed., 1962); Feit, *Military Coups and Political Development: Some Lessons from Ghana and Nigeria,* 20 WORLD POLITICS 179 (1967/68); GUTTERIDGE, MILITARY INSTITUTIONS AND POWER IN THE NEW STATES (1965).

effective power and a political myth underscoring the legitimacy of the
established government create conditions of potential or quasi-anarchy.[40]

Thirdly, the process of modernization, with its wrenching effect on the
traditional society, is a factor conducive to the outbreak of internal disorder. Indeed, there is much evidence to support the proposition that
political stability is inversely proportional to the rate of modernization.[41]
The breakdown of traditional loyalties and beliefs, the gap between
"value expectations" and the society's apparent "value capabilities,"[42]
and the short-run exacerbation of long-standing social and economic
inequalities[43]—all caused by a rapid and pervasive process of modernization—combine to make domestic violence endemic to the developing
state.

1.2.5.2. *High Level of Foreign Interest in Domestic Violence.* Internal
strife, when considered in light of the contemporary world power process, has rightfully become a major concern of all who desire and seek
a stable world public order. Understandably, the two opposing systems
of public order and the resulting bipolorization of the world community[44]
have generated pressures which, in spite of the considerable bloc erosion

[40] For a discussion of the relationship of a political myth to effective control by an incumbent government, *see* LASSWELL & KAPLAN, POWER AND SOCIETY: A FRAMEWORK FOR
POLITICAL INQUIRY 116–17 (1950). *See also* Janos, *Authority and Violence: The Political
Framework of Internal War,* in Eckstein, *supra* note 9, at 130. MERRIAM, POLITICAL POWER
102 (1934); MOSCA, RULING CLASS 70, 97 (1939); Parsons, *Some Reflections on the Place
of Force in the Social Process,* in Eckstein, *supra* note 9, at 33, 43–47. The process of loss
of authority has been described as a type of power deflation by Johnson, REVOLUTIONARY
CHANGE 30–32 (1966).

[41] *See* HUNTINGTON, POLITICAL ORDER IN CHANGING SOCIETIES 45 (1968): "Not only
does social and economic modernization produce political instability, but the degree of
instability is related to the rate of modernization." See also THE POLITICS OF THE DEVELOP-
ING AREAS (Almond & Coleman eds. 1960); Olson, *Growth as a Destabilizing Force,* 23 J.
ECON. HISTORY 550 (1963).

[42] For an excellent discussion of the concepts of "value expectations" and "value capabilities," see Gurr, *Psychological Factors in Civil Violence,* 20 WORLD POLITICS 245, 257–63
(1967/68). Other psychosociological approaches to the study of the causes of internal
strife include Amann, *Revolution: A Redefinition,* 77 POL. SCI. Q. 36 (1962); Bernard,
Where is the Modern Sociology of Conflict? 56 AM. J. SOCIOLOGY 11 (1950/51); Davies,
Toward a Theory of Revolution, 27 AM. SOCIOLOGY REV. 5 (1962); Gottschalk, *Causes of
Revolution,* 50 AM. J. SOCIOLOGY 1 (1944); Hooper, *The Revolutionary Process: A Frame of
Reference for the Study of Revolutionary Movements,* 28 SOCIAL FORCES 270 (1950);
Nieburg, *The Threat of Violence and Social Change,* 56 AM. POL. SCI. REV. 870 (1962);
SOROKIN, THE SOCIOLOGY OF REVOLUTIONS (1925); Stone, *Theories of Revolution,* 18 WORLD
POLITICS 159 (1965/66).

[43] *See* Huntington, *supra* note 41, at 56–59, for a discussion of the effect of modernization
on social and economic inequalities. *See also* Russett, *Inequality and Instability: The Relation
of Land Tenure to Politics,* 16 WORLD POLITICS 442 (1963/64).

[44] *See, e.g.,* HERZ, INTERNATIONAL POLITICS IN THE ATOMIC AGE 76–95 (1959); Lasswell,
The Conditions of Security in a Bi-Polarizing World, [1950] AM. SOC'Y INT'L L. PROC. 3.

in the last decade,[45] have made the powerful nations vitally concerned with the outcome of civil strife in smaller states.[46] The crucial mixture of the ideological and political confrontation between the two power blocs has made this concern a fact of international life.[47] If the causes of domestic violence generally are found in the social, economic, and political structures of the disrupted state,[48] the outcome of that strife very frequently has a profound influence on the allocation of power in the world community.[49]

When inspired by conceptions of public order which compel action, this high level of foreign interest in the outcome of domestic violence has a potentially adverse impact on the stability of the international system.[50] Presently, wide differences of view exist among the members of the world community with respect to the legitimate uses of violence. The Soviet Union, Communist China, and the Afro-Asian states, to take an obvious and extreme example, have declared their support for "wars of national liberation." In Communist theory, a war of national liberation is a just war prosecuted against, *inter alia,* the continuing illegality of colonialism:

> The people of a dependent or colonial country preserve the right to counter-action to an imperialist aggression for the duration of the whole period of annexation of the given country or part of its territory. At any moment the oppressed people, living on the territory annexed by the imperialist state, have the right to launch a national liberation struggle against this imperialist state.[51]

The official *Soviet Manual on International Law* explicitly gives approval

[45] For discussion and analysis, *see* POLYCENTRISM: GROWING DISSIDENCE IN THE COMMUNIST BLOC? (Bennet, ed. 1967); BRZEZINSKI, THE SOVIET BLOC: UNITY AND CONFLICT (1961); IONESCU, THE BREAK-UP OF THE SOVIET EMPIRE IN EASTERN EUROPE (1965).

[46] See Huntington, *supra* note 35, at 27: "In the 1960's the world powers are interested, to a greater or lesser degree, in the composition of every other government in the world."

[47] *Cf.* MacPherson, *Revolution and Ideology in the Late Twentieth Century,* in *Revolution* 139 (Friedrich, ed. 1966).

[48] In addition to the authorities cited in note 42 *supra,* see *generally* Feldman, *Violence and Volatility: The Likelihood of Revolution,* in Eckstein, *supra* note 9, at 111; Pye, *The Roots of Insurgency and the Commencement of Rebellions, id.* at 157.

[49] For an analysis of the effect of revolution on the world power process, see SETON-WATSON, NEITHER WAR NOR PEACE: THE STRUGGLE FOR POWER IN THE POSTWAR WORLD 103–209 (1960).

[50] *See generally* Beloff, *Reflections on Intervention,* 22 J. INT'L AFF. 198 (1968); Scott, *Internal Violence as an Instrument of Cold Warfare,* in Rosenau, *supra* note 11, at 154; Young, *Intervention and International Systems,* 22 J. INT'L AFF. 177 (1968).

[51] Sharmanazashvili, *Colonial War—A Serious Violation of International Law* 60 (1957), quoted from Ginsburg, *Wars of National Liberation and the Modern Law of Nations—the Soviet Thesis,"* in THE SOVIET IMPACT ON INTERNATIONAL LAW 66, 76 (Baade, ed. 1965). *See also* Commission of the Central Committee of the C.P.S.U., HISTORY OF THE COMMUNIST PARTY OF THE SOVIET UNION (BOLSHEVIKS), SHORT COURSE 167–68 ([B] ed. 1939), which makes the point that wars of liberation are waged "to defend the people from foreign attack" and "to liberate the people from capitalist slavery" as well as to eradicate colonialism.

to the support of wars of national liberation, on the theory that the
colonial regime lacks legitimacy and thus lawfully may be subverted:

> History contains many examples of just and unjust wars. A just war is a non-
> predatory, liberatory war. Its aim is the defense of a people against external
> attacks and attempts to enslave it. Just wars include defensive wars and wars
> of national liberation. All progressive mankind sympathizes with such wars
> and supports those fighting for freedom and independence.[52]

Similarly, the Afro-Asian states, in their continuing attempt to eliminate colonialism and racism, also have urged support for liberation movements.[53] Julius Nyerere, the President of Tanzania, expressed widely held
sentiments when he urged a forceful response should Portugal continue
in its refusal to decolonize:

> . . . then Africa will have to pursue this battle on her own, or with what
> allies she can find. Our own weakness means that we shall have only one way
> of doing that—by supporting guerrilla warfare until, after suffering and de-
> struction, Portugal wakes up to her own realities.[54]

To those seeking a genuine and lasting world order, these declarations
of support for liberation movements must be viewed as having the practical effect of weakening the protective prescriptions of article 2(4) of
the United Nations Charter,[55] at least with respect to states which do not
exhibit ideological conformity.[56] That a stable international system must
be built on neutral principles—standards of conduct binding on all states
irrespective of ideology—requires no new emphasis.

[52] ACADEMY OF SCIENCES OF THE USSR, INSTITUTE OF STATE AND LAW, INTERNATIONAL
LAW 402 (n.d.).

[53] *See, e.g., The Decolonization Resolution Adopted at the Summit Conference of African
States at Addis Ababa, Ethiopia,* in May, 1963, in THE IDEOLOGIES OF THE DEVELOPING
NATIONS 207 (Sigmund ed. 1967). For an analysis of the Afro-Asian position on wars of
national liberation, *see* Falk, *The New States and International Legal Order,* 118 HAGUE
RECUEIL DES COURS 1, 64–67).

[54] Nyerere, *Rhodesia in the Context of Southern Africa,* 44 FOREIGN AFF. 373, 377–78
(1966).

[55] It is difficult, in this connection, to understand Professor Hoffman's statement that
indirect aggression does "not fall squarely under the prohibition of the 'new' international
law of the Charter. . . ." Hoffman, *International Law and the Control of Force,* in THE
RELEVANCE OF INTERNATIONAL LAW 21, 28 (Deutsch & Hoffman eds. 1968). See text
accompanying notes 117–164 *infra.*

[56] Although the United States does not publicly proclaim a similar ideology, the involvement of the Central Intelligence Agency in the 1954 overthrow of Arbenz by Castillo-Armas
in Guatemala, and in the 1961 Bay of Pigs invasion, reveals that the United States, upon
occasion, will assist the rebels attempting to overthrow a government espousing policies
antithetical to U.S. interests. *See generally* BARNET, INTERVENTION AND REVOLUTION: THE
UNITED STATES IN THE THIRD WORLD 225–51 (1968); WISE & ROSS, THE INVISIBLE GOVERN-
MENT (1964).

1.3. Clarification of Community Policies

If international law is to have a restraining influence on the resort to international violence, its function must be to protect those primary values—or fundamental community policies—most widely shared by the participants in the world power process. Even in a world arena divided by competing systems of public order, there remain certain basic shared interests indispensable to a tolerable survival. The community policies at stake in an analysis of the delictual and criminal content of external attack disguised as internal change appear to be world order, self-determination, and human rights.

1.3.1. WORLD ORDER. The overwhelming common interest in securing and protecting basic human values requires that the postulate of peaceful change be an accepted and controlling norm in the world community. Covert attack through the medium of internal rebel groups threatens the attainment of a stable world public order in two major ways. First, the fomentation of civil strife from without and/or external assistance to rebel groups undeniably may entail as comprehensive a destruction of values as a classical armed attack across national boundaries. Indeed, as Dr. Pompe has argued:

> Through indirect action, via secret agents or internal groups supported by outside propaganda . . ., money, arms, and, at the critical moment of the disturbances by direct intimidation and political pressure, a state can put an end to the independent existence of another as effectively as with the classical, external, military aggression.[57]

Secondly, in a world arena characterized by an intense ideological rivalry and high expectations of violence, externally sponsored or supported domestic violence may provoke competitive participation by other states.[58] As an internal conflict becomes increasingly internationalized the possibility of a Great Power confrontation incinerating the globe becomes correspondingly greater.

1.3.2. SELF-DETERMINATION. In broadest statement, self-determination may be defined as the genuine self-direction of a people in establishing their own internal public order, no matter what form that public order may take, nor what internally applied policies it may pursue.[59] Although

---

[57] POMPE, AGGRESSIVE WAR: AN INTERNATIONAL CRIME 53 (1953).

[58] Because of the commonly shared reluctance to risk the horrors of nuclear warfare, today's Great Power confrontations are rarely direct. Instead, the confrontations are manifested in the internal strife of a third state, especially in strife heavily imbued with ideological overtones. *See* Falk, *Janus Tormented: The International Law of Internal War,* in Rosenau, *supra* note 11, at 185.

[59] *See, e.g.,* COBBAN, NATIONAL SELF-DETERMINATION 45–46 (1945), who defines self-determination as "the right of a nation to constitute an independent state and determine its

in neither of its two appearances in the United Nations Charter could it be deemed an operative right,[60] the principle of self-determination nonetheless has been given substance by United Nations practices.[61] Invoked by virtually every colony seeking its independence from the mother country, self-determination has been affirmed in many General Assembly resolutions,[62] most notably in the 1960 Declaration on the Granting of Independence to Colonial Countries and Peoples:

> All peoples have the right of self-determination. By virtue of that right they freely determine their political status and freely pursue their economic, social, and cultural development. . . .[63]

The policy of self-determination, however, should not be so narrowly conceived as to limit its application to colonial peoples. Self-determination is as much at stake in such situations as Czechoslovakia (1968)[64] and South Africa[65] as it is in Angola, Mozambique, and the other remaining colonial territories.

---

own government for itself." *See also* Wright, *International Law and Civil Strife* [1959] Am. Soc'y Int'l L. 145, 147: "Each state has the right, as an attribute of its sovereignty, to establish its form of government of economy and of ideology and to change those forms even by revolutionary methods. . . ." For the Soviet view, *see* Lenin, On the Right of Nations to Self-Determination (1914); Stalin, Marxism and the National and Colonial Question (2d ed. 1936).

[60] In both art. 1 & 55, the phrase "respect for the principle of equal rights and self-determination of peoples" is referred to as a standard to which the United Nations should adhere when achieving its "Purposes" (art. 1) and when promoting "International Economic and Social Cooperation" (art. 55). *See* Report of Rapporteur of Committee 1 to Commission I, Doc. 944, I/1/34(1), at 10; 6 U.N.C.I.O. 455 (1945); Goodrich & Hambro, Charter of the United Nations: Commentary and Documents 95–96 (2d ed. 1949); Kelsen, The Law of the United Nations 50–53 (4th ed. 1964).

[61] *See generally* Report of the Secretary-General on the Work of the Organization, 25 U.N. GAOR, Supp. 1, at 83–101, U.N. Doc. A/800, (1970). For development and differing views, see Eagleton, *Self-Determination in the United Nations*, 47 A.J.I.L. 88 (1953); Jacobson, *The United Nations and Colonialism: A Tentative Appraisal*, in The United Nations Political System 302 (Kay, ed 1967); Johnson, Self-Determination Within Nations (1967); Kohn, *Nationalism in the United Nations*, in The United States and the United Nations 42 (Gross, ed. 1964); Shukri, The Concept of Self-Determination in the United Nations (1965).

[62] For a study of the legal status of these resolutions, see Asamoah, The Legal Significance of the Declarations of the General Assembly of the United Nations 163–85 (1966).

[63] G.A. Res. 1514 (XV), 15 U.N. GAOR, Supp. 16, at 66–67, U.N. Doc. A/4684 (1960). *See* Schwelb, Human Rights and the International Community 132 (1964), who argues that Resolution 1514 reflects contemporary international law with respect to the right of self-determination. *See also* Report of the Special Committee on the Situation with Regard to the Implementation of the Declaration on the Granting of Independence to Colonial Countries and Peoples, 24 U.N. GAOR, Supp. 23, U.N. Doc. A/7623/Rev. 1 & Supp. 23A, U.N. Doc A/7623/Rev. 1 & Add. 1 (1969).

[64] See Pravda article (Sept. 25, 1968) containing the argument justifying the Soviet armed intervention with other Warsaw Pact countries in Czechoslovakia. 7 Int'l Legal

Self-determination, it has been seen, is oftentimes the proclaimed objective of an outside state providing assistance to rebellious internal groups in the target state. Especially common, in this regard, is the invocation of the right of self-determination accompanying assistance from Afro-Asian states to rebels in anti-colonial strife,[66] and accompanying aid from the Soviet Union[67] and Communist China[68] to the "freedom fighters" in wars of national liberation. Whether the policy of self-determination should be permitted to justify a course of action inherently destructive of world order is questionable indeed.[69] Moreover, it is clear that all internally organized resistance to an incumbent elite cannot be regarded as a manifestation of self-determination.[70] The majority of African states, for example, vehemently would argue that the principle of self-determination is inapplicable where foreign domination is not the issue, a view obviously reflecting the fear on the part of African elites of successful secessionary movements.[71] Finally, it appears beyond argument that self-determination itself may be threatened if a foreign state should assist a rebel group not reflecting the genuine demands of the majority of the people. Coercive strategies initiated from without can thus result

---

MATERIALS 1323 (1968). For a discussion of the relationship between this argument, which has become known as the Breshnev Doctrine, and the U.S. attitude toward regimes not exhibiting ideological conformity, see Franck & Weisband, *The Johnson and Breshnev Doctrines: The Law You Make May Be Your Own*, 22 STAN. L. REV. 979 (1970); Miller, *Collective Intervention and the Law of the Charter*, 22 NAVAL WAR COLL. REV. 71, 93, (1970).

[65] *Cf.* REPORT OF THE SPECIAL COMMITTEE ON THE POLICIES OF APARTHEID OF THE GOVERNMENT OF THE REPUBLIC OF SOUTH AFRICA, 24 U.N. GOAR, Supp. 25 U.N. Doc. A/7625/Rev. 1 (1969).

[66] See the discussion of the African Liberation Coordination Committee's support of "freedom fighters" in Sanger, *Toward Unity in Africa*, 42 FOREIGN AFF. 269, 277–80 (1963–64).

[67] For discussion and analysis, *see* Gibert, *Wars of Liberation and Soviet Military Aid Policy*, 10 ORBIS 839 (1966–67).

[68] See generally Tsou & Halperin, *Mao Tse-tung's Revolutionary Strategy and Peking's International Behavior*, 59 AM. POL. SCI. REV. 80 (1965). *See also* HINTON, COMMUNIST CHINA IN WORLD POLITICS 56–61 (1966); Katzenbach & Hanrahan, *The Revolutionary Strategy of Mao Tse-tung*, 70 POL. SCI. Q. 321 (1965).

[69] For the U.S. view on the relationship of art. 2(4) of the Charter, self-determination, and wars of national liberation, see Rusk, *Address*, [1965] AM. SOC'Y INT'L L. PROC. 247, 249–51.

[70] *Cf.* Moore, *The Lawfulness of Military Assistance to the Republic of Viet-Nam*, 61 A.J.I.L. 1, 31 (1967).

[71] Thus the Organization of African Unity supported Nigeria in its effort to reunify the country. For a discussion, *see* Mazrui, *supra* note 24, at 99–104. It is ironic, although understandable, that the African elites, having been staunch defenders of the principle of self-determination during the anticolonial movement, deny the further application of the principle once independence has been attained. *See generally* EMERSON, SELF-DETERMINATION REVISITED IN THE ERA OF DECOLONIZATION 28–30 (1964).

in as thorough a denial of self-determination as does colonialism or a repressive government.

1.3.4. HUMAN RIGHTS. Long-standing international concern for at least minimum human rights has been reflected in authoritative prescription permitting "humanitarian intervention" under exceptional circumstances.[72] It has been only in the years since World War II, however, that the concern, energy, and intelligence of mankind has been focused with determination on securing and protecting a dignified human existence for all men.[73] Correctly perceiving the link between the protection of human rights and the maintenance of world order, the 1948 Universal Declaration of Human Rights declared that the "recognition of the inherent dignity and of the equal and inalienable rights of all members of the human family is the foundation of freedom, justice, and peace in the world. . . ."[74]

Open contempt and disregard of human rights by a repressive regime may provoke domestic violence which, in view of the contemporary world power process, could become virtually indistinguishable from international conflict. Recent events in Africa serve to illustrate that blatant violations of human rights, *e.g.,* discrimination on the basis of race, inspire external assistance to rebel groups in the oppressed society.[75] In this regard, as with the policy of self-determination, an ultimate issue

---

[72] *See generally* LAUTERPACHT, INTERNATIONAL LAW AND HUMAN RIGHTS, 32 (1950); Lillich, *Forcible Self-Help by States to Protect Human Rights,* 53 IOWA L. REV. 325 (1967); McDougal & Reisman, *Comment,* 3 INT'L LAWYER 438 (1969); OPPENHEIM, INTERNATIONAL LAW 347 (1905); STOWELL, INTERVENTION IN INTERNATIONAL LAW 51–277 (1921).

[73] For development, *see* INTERNATIONAL COMMISSION OF JURISTS, THE RULE OF LAW AND HUMAN RIGHTS: PRINCIPLES AND DEFINITIONS (1966); McDougal, Lasswell, & Chen, *Human Rights and World Order,* 63 A.J.I.L. 237 (1969); MOSKOWITZ, THE POLITICS AND DYNAMICS OF HUMAN RIGHTS (1968); *Panel: The United Nations and Race: Will U.N. Law Affect Victims of Racial Discrimination and Oppressors?* [1970] AM. SOC'Y INT'L L. PROC. 106; Schwelb, *Civil and Political Rights: The International Measures of Implementation,* 62 A.J.I.L. 827 (1968); *Symposium on the International Law of Human Rights,* 11 HOW. L.J. 253 (1965).

[74] G.A. Res. 217A (III), 3 U.N. GAOR 71–77, U.N. Doc. A/810 (1948). For analysis, *see* Sohn, *The Universal Declaration of Human Rights,* 8 J. INT'L COMM. JURISTS 16 (1968). *See also,* the Convention on the Prevention and Punishment of the Crime of Genocide, 78 U.N.T.S. 277 (1951); International Covenant on Civil and Political Rights, G.A. Res. 2200 (XXI), 21 U.N. GAOR, Supp. 16, at 52–58 (1966); International Convention on the Elimination of All Forms of Racial Discrimination. 20 U.N. GAOR, Supp. 14, at 47, U.N. Doc. A/6014 (1965). For a further listing of international treaties and Declarations concerning human rights, *see* McDougal, Lasswell, & Chen, *supra* note 73, at 261 n.6.

[75] For a discussion of the effect of deprivations of human rights on world order, see McDougal & Reisman, *Rhodesia and the United Nations: The Lawfulness of International Concern,* 62 A.J.I.L. 1, 5–13 (1968). *See also,* Special Committee on the Policies of Apartheid of 'the Government of the Republic of South Africa, *Report,* 23 U.N. GAOR, Annexes, Agenda Item No. 31, at 31, U.N. Doc. A/7254 (1968).

arises as to the relative importance of maintaining world order and maximizing human rights. In further parallelism with the policy of self-determination, it is clear that external assistance to rebel groups demanding a totalitarian system of internal public order scarcely may be said to maximize human rights.

1.4. Trends in Decision

The process of indirect aggression, it will be recalled, is the exercise of coercion through the medium of rebel groups in the target state. While the strategies employed by aggressor states no doubt have become more refined in recent decades, the problem of outside interference in the internal affairs of states is scarcely a modern phenomenon. Indeed, history reveals that statesmen and jurists have struggled with difficult legal and policy issues arising from interstate coercion analogous to indirect aggression long before the rise of the modern nation-state system.[76] Pre-Charter efforts to regulate interstate coercion were based on the dichotomous structure of war and peace. As a result, the customary law doctrine of nonintervention was developed as a general norm governing state conduct in time of peace, while the law of neutrality applied in time of war.[77] The prescriptions of the Charter, in contrast to the one-dimensional doctrine of nonintervention, attempt to regulate the whole range of intensities of coercion—from the application of highly intense coercion traditionally categorized as "war" to the lesser intensities of coercion commonly referred to as "measures short of war."[78] Under either framework, however, what is sought to be proscribed is externally applied coercion, the objective of which is the loss by the target state of effective control over an area under its jurisdiction (*i.e.*, impairment of territorial integrity) or of freedom of decision-making by its internal elite (*i.e.*, impairment of political independence). Since the objective of externally fomented or abetted internal strife is impairment of the territorial integrity or political independence of the target state (or both), indirect aggression would appear to be in direct violation of both the doctrine of nonintervention and the prescriptions of the Charter.

1.4.1. PRE-CHARTER PRACTICE UNDER THE DOCTRINE OF NONINTERVENTION. In general statement, the doctrine of nonintervention provides that no state may interfere in the affairs of another state in derogation of the

[76] For discussion and historical examples, *see* THOMAS & THOMAS, NON-INTERVENTION: THE LAW AND ITS IMPACT IN THE AMERICAS 3–5 (1956).

[77] The confusion engendered by this dichotomy is discussed and an alternative conception is offered in McDOUGAL & FELICIANO, *supra* note 7, at 97–120.

[78] *Id.* at 125. It should not be inferred, however, that the doctrine of nonintervention no longer constitutes authoritative prescription. See text accompanying notes 128–137 *infra*.

latter's sovereignty.[79] Premised on the sovereign equality of all states,[80] the doctrine recognizes that every state possesses the freedom to establish and maintain its own internal public order, and to exercise exclusive jurisdiction over its own territory, without external interference.[81] Despite this categorical formulation, the doctrine of nonintervention contains considerable ambiguity. There is, for example, little agreement on precisely what acts constitute intervention, *i.e.*, the violation of the norm.[82] Some jurists contend that intervention is limited to the interference by one state in the *internal* affairs of another against its will;[83] others take the position that the term applies when one state intervenes *by use of force* in the affairs of another state,[84] and still others apply the term to *any involvement*, including by diplomatic means or hostile propaganda, in the internal or external affairs of another state.[85] Out of this conceptual disorder, however, one point emerges clearly: in view of the effectiveness of the economic, political, and ideological instruments in impairing a state's territorial integrity or political independence, a concept of intervention limited to the direct use of physical force would be dangerously

[79] See generally CALVO, LE DROIT INTERNATIONAL THEORIQUE ET PRATIQUE 110 (1896); I. HYDE, INTERNATIONAL LAW CHIEFLY AS INTERPRETED AND APPLIED BY THE UNITED STATES 245 (1945); SVARLIEN, AN INTRODUCTION TO THE LAW OF NATIONS 123–24 (1955).

[80] For an analysis of the development of the principle of the equality of states, *see* JESSUP, THE MODERN LAW OF NATIONS 37 (1958). *See also* DICKENSON, THE EQUALITY OF STATES IN INTERNATIONAL LAW, AM. SOC'Y INT'L L PROC. 147, 156 (1963); KOOIJMANS, THE DOCTRINE OF THE LEGAL EQUALITY OF STATES (1964); I SCHWARZENBERGER, INTERNATIONAL LAW 35–36 (3d ed. 1957); Weinschel, *The Doctrine of the Equality of States and Its Recent Modification*, 45 AJ.I.L. 412 (1951); art. 2(1) of the U.N. Charter states that the Organization "is based on the principle of the sovereign equality of all its members." For a canvassing of the conventional law and scholarly works on the subject, *see* 5 Whiteman, DIGEST OF INTERNATIONAL LAW 134–54 (1965).

[81] See FRIEDMANN, INTERVENTION, CIVIL WAR AND THE ROLE OF INTERNATIONAL LAW 67 (1965): "The most basic principle of international law is the equal claim to integrity of all states, regardless of their political or social ideology." See also Wright, *supra* note 59, at 147–48. Simply put, the doctrine of nonintervention is intended to protect a state's sovereignty and independence. *See generally* van Kleffens, *Sovereignty in International Law*, 82 RECUEIL DES COURS 5 (1953).

[82] For a discussion of this point, *see* I BONFILS, MANUAL DE DROIT INTERNATIONAL PUBLIC 156 (4th ed., Fauchille 1905); BRIGGS, THE LAW OF NATIONS 960 (2d ed. 1952); Fenwick, *Intervention: Individual and Collective*, 29 A.J.I.L. 645 (1945); GROB, THE RELATIVITY OF WAR AND PEACE 227 (1959); LAWRENCE, PRINCIPLES OF INTERNATIONAL LAW 125 (5th ed. 1913); Sanders, *Sovereignty and Interdependence in the New World*, 43 DEPT. STATE BULL. 155, 171 (1948).

[83] I WESTLAKE, INTERNATIONAL LAW 304–05 (1904).

[84] See, e.g., KELSEN, PRINCIPLES OF INTERNATIONAL LAW 74 (2d rev. ed., Tucker 1966) who defines intervention as "dictatorial interference" and then states that "dictatorial" involves the threat or use of force. For similar views, *see* BRIERLY, THE LAW OF NATIONS 247 (2d ed. 1938); HERSHEY, ESSENTIALS OF INTERNATIONAL LAW 236 (1935); Lawrence, *supra* note 81, at 124; I OPPENHEIM, INTERNATIONAL LAW 305 (8th ed., Lauterpacht 1955).

[85] See HODGES, THE DOCTRINE OF INTERVENTION 1 (1915). For an analysis of this view, *see* Winfield, *The History of Intervention in International Law*, 3 BRIT. Y.B. INT'L L. 130, 141 (1922/23).

restrictive and not in accord with reasonable community expectations.[86]

This conclusion appears to be substantiated by customary authoritative prescription which has long imposed the following duties on all states. Based on the obligation to respect the independence of other nations,[87] every state has the duty to prevent on its territory the commission of hostile and injurious acts against other states.[88] Moreover, since it is within the sovereign powers of a state to exercise complete control and jurisdiction over all activities taking place on its territory,[89] the failure to exercise due diligence—whether by design or by carelessness—in preventing the commission of acts injurious to other states is deemed delictual under customary prescription.[90] Thus, not only must a state refrain from organizing or supporting on its territory armed bands operating against the government of another state,[91] but it must also police its frontiers to insure that its territory is not being used by such bands as a base of operations.[92] Professor Kelsen expresses this duty quite succinctly:

[86] Thus McDougal & Lasswell, *supra* note 6, at 21, ask rhetorically: "Are the principles of nonintervention fashioned to catch the more subtle modalities of coercion or only the cruder physical forms?" *See also* EAGLETON, INTERNATIONAL GOVERNMENT 83–84 (3d ed. 1957).

[87] *See* FENWICK, INTERNATIONAL LAW 249–50 (3d ed. 1948); LAUTERPACHT, RECOGNITION IN INTERNATIONAL LAW 229 (1947).

[88] *See generally* Curtis, *The Law of Hostile Military Expeditions as Applied by the United States*, 8 A.J.I.L. 1, 5, 34 (1914); Fitzmaurice, *The General Principles of International Law Considered from the Standpoint of the Rule of Law*, 92 RECUEIL DES COURS 5, 175–76 (1957); I OPPENHEIM, *supra* note 84, at 292–93. *See also Island of Palmas* case (United States v. Netherlands) (1828) in *Hague Court Reports* 84 (2d ser. 1928).

[89] *See* STORY, CONFLICT OF LAWS 18 (8th ed. 1883): "Every nation possesses an exclusive sovereignty and jurisdiction within its own territory." *See also* DE VISSCHER, THEORY AND REALITY IN PUBLIC INTERNATIONAL LAW 331 (rev. ed. 1968); FAUCHILLE, TRAITÈ DU DROIT INTERNATIONAL PUBLIC 3–10 (8th ed. 1925).

[90] For detailed discussion, *see* EAGLETON, THE RESPONSIBILITY OF STATES IN INTERNATIONAL LAW 88–92 (1928); Garcia-Mora, *International Law and the Law of Hostile Military Expeditions*, 27 FORD. L. REV. 309, 320–25 (1958–59); Thomas & Thomas, *supra* note 76, at 217; WRIGHT, INTERNATIONAL LAW AND THE UNITED NATIONS 97–98 (1960). *See further*, dissent by Judge Moore in the case of the S.S. "Lotus," P.C.I.J., ser. A,No. 10 at 88–89 1927): "It is well settled that a state is bound to use due diligence to prevent the commission within its dominion of criminal acts against another nation or its people." For further elaboration, *see Alabama Claims* case, 4 *Papers Relating to the Treaty of Washington* 49 (1872); United States v. Arjona, 120 U.S. 479, 488 (1887). If a state tolerates or fails to exercise due diligence in preventing the commission of such acts, there arises "a presumption of governmental complicity which amounts to an international delinquency." Garcia-Mora, *supra*, at 311.

[91] *See* Brownlie, *International Law and the Activities of Armed Bands*, 7 INT'L & COMP. L.Q. 712, 734 (1958); Curtis, *supra* note 88, at 34; II HACKWORTH, DIGEST OF INTERNATIONAL LAW 336–42 (1941); I Oppenheim, *supra* note 84, at 293.

[92] LAUTERPACHT, REVOLUTIONARY ACTIVITIES BY PRIVATE PERSONS AGAINST FOREIGN STATES 105, 121 (1928). *See also* Curtis, *supra* note 88, at 1; GARCIA-MORA, INTERNATIONAL RESPONSIBILITY FOR HOSTILE ACTS OF PRIVATE PERSONS AGAINST FOREIGN STATES, 114 (1961); III Hyde, *supra* note 79, at 2254.

. . . states are obliged by general international law to prevent certain acts injurious to other states from being committed on their territories, and if prevention is not possible, to punish the delinquents and force them to repair the damage caused by the delict. Such injurious acts are, for example, . . . hostile expeditions organized in the territory of the state and directed against the territorial integrity of a foreign state or intended to overthrow the legitimate government of another state.[93]

An examination of pre-Charter treaties and conventions supports the conclusion that general community opinion has condemned the encouragement or toleration by a state on its territory of hostile armed bands operating against another state. In the 1920 Treaty of Peace between Lithuania and Russia, for example, the parties agreed not

. . . to permit on their territory the formation and sojourn of governments, organizations or groups, who have for their object armed warfare against the other contracting party, and similarly not to permit within their territories the recruiting and mobilization of effectives for the armies of such governments, organizations, or groups, and the sojourn of their representatives and officials.[94]

In a similar vein, the 1933 London Conventions for the Definition of Aggression, signed or acceded to by twelve states, included, *inter alia*, as an act of aggression:

Provision of support to armed bands formed in its territory which have invaded the territory of another state, or refusal, notwithstanding the request of the invaded state, to take, in its own territory, all the measures in its power to deprive those bands of all assistance and protection.[95]

The 1934 Protocol Annex to the Pact of the Balkan Entente[96] and the 1937 Saadabad Pact[97] either incorporate, or contain provisions similar to, the above cited definition of aggression in the 1933 London Conventions.

[93] Kelsen, *supra* note 84, at 205–06. Oppenheim, *supra* note 84, at 292–93, contends that states "are under a duty to prevent and suppress such subversive activities against foreign governments as assumes the form of armed hostile expeditions, or attempts to commit common crimes against life or property."

[94] Art. IV. 113 *British and Foreign State Papers* 1121. For citations of treaties containing similar provisions, *see* Brownlie, *supra* note 91, at 720 n.44.

[95] Art. 2(5). 147 L.N.T.S. 67; 148 L.N.T.S. 79; 148 L.N.T.S. 211; 27 A.J.I.L. 192, 194, 195 (Supp. 1933); VI HUDSON, INTERNATIONAL LEGISLATION 410, 414, 415, 416 (1932–34). Art. 2(5) of these Conventions is based on art. 1(5) of the 1933 draft "Act Relating to the Definition of the Aggressor" (commonly known as the Politis Report) adopted by the Committee on Security Questions of the General Commission of the League of Nations Disarmament Conference. For the text of art. 1(5), *see* Report of the Secretary-General, *supra* note 8, at 35.

[96] Art. 1 of the Protocol Annex expressly incorporates the definitions of aggression contained in the 1933 London Conventions. 153 L.N.T.S. 156; VI Hudson, *supra* note 95, at 633.

[97] Art. 7 of the Saadabad Pact, although it does not refer explicitly to armed bands, proscribes the encouragement or toleration of activities of such bands in the signatory states. 190 L.N.T.S. 21; VII HUDSON, INTERNATIONAL LEGISLATION 822 (1935–37).

Moreover, customary authoritative prescription placed states under an obligation not to participate in terrorist activities taking place in another state. Conceptually, the duty of a state neither to encourage nor tolerate on its territory terrorist activities directed against another state is based on the identical premises as the general duty to repress the activities of armed bands.[98] Considerable attention was given during the period of the League of Nations to the problem of controlling the export of terrorism. In a 1934 resolution, for example, the Council of the League of Nations stated, after the assassination of the King of Yugoslavia in Marseilles by terrorists who allegedly had been conducting similar activities on Hungarian territory, that

> . . . it is the duty of every state neither to encourage nor tolerate on its territory any terrorist activity with a political purpose;

> That every state must do all in its power to prevent and repress acts of this nature and must for this purpose lend its assistance to governments which request it. . . .[99]

Incorporating the proposals contained in a 1936 Report of the Committee of Experts of the League of Nations,[100] the Convention for the Prevention and Punishment of Terrorism, signed by twenty-three states in Geneva in 1937, reaffirmed

> . . . the principle of international law in virtue of which it is the duty of every state to refrain from any act designed to encourage terrorist activities directed against another state and to prevent the acts in which such activities take shape. . . .[101]

It appears beyond argument that where it can be demonstrated, as Professor Friedmann has written, "that an individual committed an act of terrorism on the instructions and with the direct support of a foreign government, the latter should clearly be held responsible."[102]

States are bound, furthermore, not to conduct hostile propaganda against another state. Understandably, in a process of coercion not dependent upon the direct application of violence, the manipulation by the ideological instrument of the opinions and attitudes of a target state's population is a particularly effective strategy.[103] However, insofar as the

[98] *See* STARKE, AN INTRODUCTION TO INTERNATIONAL LAW 96 (6th ed. 1967).

[99] Quoted from II Hackworth, *supra* note 91, at 336.

[100] For text of the proposals, *see* Friedmann, *Some Impacts of Social Organization on International Law*, 50 A.J.I.L. 475, 494 n.53.

[101] Art. 1(1). VII Hudson, *supra* note 97, at 862, 865.

[102] Friedmann, *supra* note 100, at 494. *See also* Blum, *The Beirut Raid and the International Double Standard: A Reply to Professor Richard A. Falk*, 64 A.J.I.L. 73,76–87 (1970).

[103] For development, *see generally* BARTLETT, POLITICAL PROPAGANDA 5–6 (1940); Lasswell, *Propaganda* 12 ENCYCLOPEDIA OF THE SOCIAL SCIENCES 521, 522 (1934); Lasswell, *The Strategy of Soviet Propaganda*, in PROPAGANDA IN WAR AND CRISIS 27 (Lerner ed 1951); RIEGEL, MOBILIZING FOR CHAOS: THE STORY OF THE NEW PROPAGANDA 7 (1935).

ideological instrument is utilized for the purpose of undermining the political independence of the target state, it is a delict under customary prescription.[104] It has long been accepted that a state is under a duty to refrain from inciting the populace of another state to revolt or in any other manner disobey its government:

> The right of every state to govern itself freely under a constitution of its own choice is violated by any attempt on the part of a foreign state to influence its political life through forceful measures, through hostile propaganda, and, especially, through incitement of its population to revolt. For such acts on the part of its government the state must assume responsibility, whether they be committed by government organs directly or with their active encouragement or support.[105]

This duty is reflected in article 1 of the 1936 Convention Concerning the Use of Broadcasting in the Cause of Peace in which the parties undertook

> . . . to stop without delay the broadcasting within their respective territories of any transmission which . . . is of such a character as to incite the population of any territory to acts incompatible with the internal order of the security of a territory of a high contracting party.[106]

Of similar import are the 1937 and 1940 South American Regional Agreements on Radiocommunications, wherein the parties pledged to take the necessary steps to "ensure their propagation through broadcasting ideas which might threaten the sovereignty and integrity of states shall be avoided."[107] Contrarily, it is also accepted (at least among democratic nations) that a state has no duty, apart from an obligation under a treaty, to suppress hostile propaganda on the part of private individuals.[108]

[104] See Glahn, *The Case for Legal Control of "Liberation" Propaganda*, in INTERNATIONAL CONTROL OF PROPAGANDA 115, 122–35 (Havighurst ed. 1967); Lauterpacht, *Revolutionary Propaganda by Governments*, 13 TRANS. GROT. SOC'Y 143, 145–46 (1928); MANNING, COMMENTARIES ON THE LAW OF NATIONS 13 (rev. ed. 1875); MARTIN, INTERNATIONAL PROPAGANDA 60 (1958); Murty, *supra* note 33, at 93–127; Thomas & Thomas, *supra* note 76, at 273–81; Van Dyke, *The Responsibility of States for International Propaganda*, 34 A.J.I.L. 58, 73 (1940); WHITTON & LARSON, PROPAGANDA–TOWARDS DISARMAMENT IN THE WAR OF WORDS 95 (1963). Wright, *Subversive Intervention*, 54 A.J.I.L. 521, 530–35 (1960).

[105] Preuss, *International Responsibility for Hostile Propaganda Against Foreign States*, 28 A.J.I.L. 649, 652 (1934). *See also* O'Brien, *International Propaganda and Minimum World Public Order*, in Havighurst, *supra* note 104, at 151.

[106] 186 L.N.T.S. 303; VII Hudson, *supra* note 97, at 409.

[107] Quoted from Martin, *supra* note 104, at 83. For a discussion of the attempts to control propaganda by agreement, on both the bilateral and multilateral level, *see id.* at 62–108; LeRoy, *Treaty Regulation of International Radio and Shortwave Broadcasting*, 32 A.J.I.L. 729 (1938).

[108] State suppression of propaganda hostile to another state by private individuals is considered to place in jeopardy both the right of free speech and the right of freedom of communication across national boundaries. See Wright, *supra* note 104, at 530, 532 n.34 for discussion. *See also* Newhouse, *The Constitution and International Agreements or Unilateral*

Finally, the doctrine of nonintervention prohibits a state from assisting the rebels of another state during ongoing civil strife. Under customary prescription, outside states owe complete respect to the incumbent government and must not incite its citizens to revolt nor support them in any way once a rebellion has begun and before belligerency has been recognized.[109] These principles have been codified in such documents as the 1900 Regulation on the Rights and Duties of Foreign Powers in Case of Insurrectional Movements Against the Established and Recognized Government,[110] the 1928 Havana Convention on the Duties and Rights of States in the Event of Civil Strife,[111] and the 1957 Protocol to the Havana Convention.[112] Taken together, these documents make it unlawful for the signatories to organize, train, or tolerate in their territories military expeditions against the legitimate government of another state; provide war material, munitions, or financial assistance to the rebels; and finally, to fail to disarm and intern rebel forces coming into their territories.[113]

The pre-Charter practice under the doctrine of nonintervention clearly condemned all activities carried on or tolerated by state authorities for

---

Action Curbing "Peace-Imperiling" Propaganda, in Havighurst, *supra* note 104, at 68; Van Alstyne, *The First Amendment and the Suppression of Warmongering Propaganda in the United States: Comments and Footnotes, id* at 92. *See further,* Lauterpacht, *supra* note 104, at 126; Murty, *supra* note 83, at 109–114. But *see* Whitton & Larson, *supra* note 104, at 7.

[109] For an exposition of the customary and conventional law on this point, *see* Beale, *The Recognition of the Cuban Belligerency,* 9 HARV. L. REV. 406 (1896); Borchard, *"Neutrality" and Civil Wars,* 31 A.J.I.L. 304 (1937); Fawcett, *Intervention in International Law,* 103 HAGUE RECUEIL DES COURS 343 (1961); Garner, *Questions of International Law in the Spanish Civil War,* 31 A.J.I.L. 66 (1937); Novogrod, *Internal Strife, Self-Determination, and World Order,* 23 J.A.G.J. 62 (Dec. 1968–Jan. 1969); O'Rourke, *Recognition of Belligerency and the Spanish Civil War,* 31 A.J.I.L. 226, 227 (1937); ROUGIER, LES GUERRES CIVILES ET LE DROIT DES GENS (1903); Thomas & Thomas, *supra* note 76, at 215–40; Wehberg, *La Guerre Civile et le Droit International,* 63 HAGUE RECUEIL DES COURS 7 (1938).

[110] Art. 2. SCOTT, RESOLUTION OF THE INSTITUTE OF INTERNATIONAL LAW 157 (1916).

[111] Art. 1. 46 Stat. 2749 (1930); U.S.T.S. No. 814; IV HUDSON, INTERNATIONAL LEGISLATION 2416 (1928–29).

[112] Arts. 1–5. 284 U.N.T.S. 201. For citations to U.S. legislation implementing the 1928 Convention and its Protocol, *see* 5 Whiteman, *supra* note 80, at 275.

[113] Customary prescription—which, upon request, permitted assistance solely to the incumbent government until belligerency was recognized, at which time the rules of neutrality became applicable—is coming under increasing attack as being overly protective of the status quo. *See generally* Barnet, *supra* note 56, at 257–85; Falk, *supra* note 58; Farer, *Intervention in Civil Wars: A Modest Proposal,* 67 COLUM. L. REV. 266 (1967); Farer, *Harnessing Rogue Elephants: A Short Discourse on Foreign Intervention in Civil Strife* 82 HARV. L. REV. 511 (1969); Franck & Rodley, *Legitimacy and Legal Rights of Revolutionary Movements with Special Reference to the Peoples' Revolutionary Government of South Viet Nam,* 45 N.Y.U.L. REV. 679 (1970); Friedmann, *Law and Politics in the Vietnamese War: A Comment,* 61 A.J.I.L. 776 (1967); Moore, *supra* note 32, at 315–18. For deeper inquiry into the policy issues arising from the unilateral interventions in the Vietnamese strife, *see* the collection of articles in FALK, THE VIETNAM WAR AND INTERNATIONAL LAW (Vol. I, 1968; Vol II, 1969).

the purpose of impairing the territorial integrity or political independence of another state. Indeed, article X of the Covenant of the League of Nations may be viewed as supplementing the customary duty of nonintervention:[114]

> The members of the League undertake to respect and preserve as against external aggression the territorial integrity and political independence of all members of the League. . . .[115]

Moreover, it is fair to conclude that during the League period neither the concept of intervention nor the idea of aggression was limited strictly to the direct use of physical force. Writing in 1921, Lord Stowell correctly viewed the encouragement or toleration by a state on its territory of the operations of an armed band against another state as a constructive attack.[116] Thus it is not unreasonable to view indirect aggression as violative both of the customary duty of nonintervention as well as of the League Covenant.

1.4.2. PRACTICE UNDER THE UNITED NATIONS CHARTER. United Nations practice would appear to confirm the conclusion that impermissible coercion need not involve the direct use of physical force. While the Charter does not contain the term "indirect aggression," it does obligate the members of the United Nations, in article 2(4), to

> . . . refrain in their international relations from the threat or use of force against the territorial integrity or political independence of any state, or in any other manner inconsistent with the purposes of the United Nations.

An examination of the practice under the Charter, it is submitted, reveals that the proscriptions of article 2(4) have been interpreted, for various purposes and in varying contexts, to include indirect aggression.

Several general pronouncements of the General Assembly strongly condemn resort to indirect aggression. In its 1949 Essentials of Peace Resolution, the General Assembly branded as unlawful

> . . . any threats or acts, direct or indirect, aimed at impairing the freedom, independence, or integrity of any state, or at fomenting civil strife and subverting the will of a people in any state.[117]

In similar manner, the Assembly, in its well-known Peace Through Deeds Resolution, condemned "the intervention of a state in the internal affairs of another state for the purpose of changing its legally established government by the threat or use of force . . ." and reaffirmed that

[114] *See* BOWETT, SELF-DEFENCE IN INTERNATIONAL LAW 29 (1958).
[115] Text of the Covenant of the League of Nations may be found in 15 A..J.I.L 4 (Supp. 1921).
[116] Stowell, *supra* note 72, at 373–78.
[117] G.A. Res. 290 (IV), 4 U.N. GAOR, 13, U.N. Doc. A/1159 (1949).

. . . whatever the weapons used, any aggression, whether committed openly, or by fomenting civil strife in the interest of a foreign power, or otherwise, is the gravest of all crimes against peace and security in the world.[118]

More recently, the General Assembly again condemned indirect aggression by declaring in a 1965 Resolution that

. . . no state shall organize, assist, foment, finance, incite, or tolerate subversive, terrorist, or armed activities directed toward the violent overthrow of the regime of another state, or interfere in civil strife in another state.[119]

Moreover, authoritative pronouncements of the International Law Commission emphatically outlaw indirect aggression. In its Draft Declaration on the Rights and Duties of States, the Commission reaffirmed the general duty of non-intervention and imposed upon states the specific duty

to refrain from fomenting civil strife in the territory of another state, and to prevent the organization within its territory of activities calculated to foment such civil strife.[120]

Of particular interest, however, is the Draft Code of Offenses Against the Peace and Security of Mankind in which, *inter alia*, support for armed bands operating against another state, fomentation of civil strife, and encouragement of terrorist activities in another state are listed as "crimes under international law, for which the responsible individuals shall be punished."[121]

[118] G.A. Res. 380 (V), 5 U.N. GAOR, Supp. 20, at 13, U.N. Doc. A/1775 (1950).

[119] "Declaration on the Inadmissibility of Intervention in the Domestic Affairs of States and the Protection of their Independence and Sovereignty." G.A. Res. 2131 (XX), 20 U.N. GAOR, Supp. 14, at 11, U.N. Doc. A/6014 (1965). The text of G.A. Res. 2131 (XX) may also be found in 60 A.J.I.L. 662–64 (1966).

[120] Art. 4. International Law Comm'n, Report, 6 U.N. GAOR, Supp. 10, at 10, U.N. Doc. A/925 (1949). For debates within the Commission on the Draft Declaration, *see* Y.B. INT'L L. COMM'N 60 (1949). *See also* Kelsen, *The Draft Declaration on Rights and Duties of States: Critical Remarks*, 44 A.J.I.L. 259 (1950). *See further*, draft art. 225 "Duty Not to Foment Civil Disturbances in Other States," and commentary thereto in *Preparatory Study Concerning a Draft Declaration on the Rights and Duties of States* (Memorandum submitted by the Secretary-General), U.N. Doc. A/CN.4/2, at 123–24 (1948).

[121] *See International Law Comm'n*, Report, 9 U.N. GAOR, Supp. 9, at 11, U.N. Doc. A/2693 (1954), in which the following are considered offences:

Art. 2(4)—The organizations, or the encouragement of the organization, by the authorities of a state, of armed bands within its territory or any other territory for incursions into the territory of another state, or the toleration of the organization of such bands in its own territory, or the toleration of the use by such armed bands of its territory as a base of operations or as a point of departure for incursions into the territory of another state, as well as direct participation in or support of such incursions.

Art. 2(5)—The undertaking or encouragement by the authorities of a state of activities calculated to foment civil strife in another state, or the toleration by the authorities of a state of organized activities calculated to foment civil strife in another state.

Art 2(6)—The undertaking or encouragement by the authorities of a state of terrorist activities in another state, or the toleration by the authorities of a state of organized activities calculated to carry out terrorist acts in another state.

For commentary on the Draft Code, *see* Fenwick, *Draft Code of Offenses Against the Peace and Security of Mankind*, 46 A.J.I.L. 98 (1952); Johnson, *The Draft Code of Offences*

Community fear of the effectiveness of indirect aggression has manifested itself clearly in the efforts within the United Nations to define aggression. Many delegates to the International Law Commission[122] and to the Special Committee on the Question of Defining Aggression,[123] for example, have offered draft definitions of aggression which either specifically cover, or are sufficiently broad to cover, the indirect use of force such as encouraging or tolerating armed bands, fomenting civil strife, and planting fifth columnists.[124] In all three forums, it was argued that any useful definition of aggression must include the indirect or hidden use of force.[125] An accurate summary of this general position was given in the Report of the 1956 Special Committee:

> Any state that encouraged and assisted groups of the people of another state to take up arms against its own government was no less guilty than if it had itself taken part in an armed attack.[126]

As a recent expression of community condemnation of indirect aggression, a draft proposal submitted in 1969 by Australia, Canada, Italy, Japan, the United States, and the United Kingdom lists as aggression the following activities:

> 1. Organizing, supporting, or directing armed bands or irregular or volunteer forces that make incursions or infiltrate into another state.
>
> 2. Organizing, supporting, or directing violent civil strife or acts of terrorism in another state.

Against the Peace 4 INT'L C. & COMP. L.Q. 445 (1955); Parry, *Some Considerations Upon the Content of a Draft Code of Offences Against the Peace and Security of Mankind,* 3 INT'L L.Q. 208 (1950); Potter, *Offenses Against the Peace and Security of Mankind.* 46 A.J.I.L. 101 (1952).

[122] *See, e.g.,* the proposals of Mr. Yepes (Colombia), Mr. Hsu (China), and a Mr. Cordova (Mexico) in International Law Comm'n, Report, [1951] II Y.B. INT'L L. COMM'N 123, 132.

[123] *See, e.g.,* the Soviet draft definition and the Chinese, Mexican, & Bolivian working papers in Special Committee on the Question of Defining Aggression, Report, U.N. GAOR, Supp. 11, at 13–15, U.N. Roc. A/2638 (1954). [Hereinafter cited as *1953 Special Committee Report*]. *See also* the draft definitions of Mexico, Paraguay, Iran and Panama, China, and the Soviet Union in *1956 Special Committee Report* at 26–33.

[124] For the best study of the U.N. efforts to define aggression and, in that context, of the problem presented by the concept of indirect aggression, see STONE, AGGRESSION AND WORLD ORDER 54, 58–61, 66–68, 85, 111 (1958).

[125] *See, e.g.,* remarks of Mr. El Khoury (Syria) and Mr. Hsu (China) in [1951] I Y.B. INT'L COMM'N 109. For views expressed in the Sixth Committee, *see, e.g.,* remarks of Mr. Ammoun (Lebanon), Mr. Chaudhuri (India), Mr. Crepault (Canada), Mr. Fitzmaurice (United Kingdom), Mr. Roling (Netherlands), and Mr. Sastroamidjojo (Indonesia) in *Report of the Secretary-General* at 72–73. *See further,* remarks of Mr. Adamiyat (Iran) & Mr. de Machena (Dominican Republic) in *1953 Special Committee Report* 10–11; *1956 Special Committee Report* 8; Special Committee on the Question of Defining Aggression, Report, 23 U.N. GAOR, Agenda Item No. 86, at 22–23, U.N. Doc. A/7185/Rev. 1 (1968).

[126] *1956 Special Committee Report* 8.

3. Organizing, supporting, or directing subversive activities aimed at the violent overthrow of the government of another state.[127]

The work of the Special Committee on Principles of International Law Concerning Friendly Relations and Cooperation Among States may be interpreted as clearly condemning indirect aggression.[128] Since its establishment in 1963, the Special Committee has consistently reaffirmed the following principles: (1) states shall refrain from the threat or use of force against the territorial integrity or political independence of any state[129] and (2) states have a duty not to intervene in matters within the domestic jurisdiction of any other state.[130] During the formulation of the first principle, several delegations offered proposals in which the prohibition of "force" included not only armed force, but in addition, the indirect use of force such as fomenting civil strife in another state,[131] organizing armed bands for incursions into the territory of another state,[132] as well as "other forms of pressure, which have the effect of threatening the territorial integrity or political independence of any

[127] Special Committee on the Question of Defining Aggression, Report, 24 U.N. GAOR, Supp. 20, at 8–9, U.N. Doc. A/7620 (1969). For a defense of this draft proposal, see Statement by Stephen M. Schwebel, United States Representative to the United Nations Special Committee on the Question of Defining Aggression, July 22, 1970, U.S. Information Service Press Release, *see also* excerpts of the report *supra* in Ch. III, § 1 in text.

[128] *See* text of the resolution and annex *supra* in ch. 6, § 1, App. 1, on the work of the Special Committee on Friendly Relations, *see generally* Houben, *Principles of International Law Concerning Friendly Relations and Cooperation Among States*, 61 A.J.I.L. 703 (1967); McWhinney, *The "New" Countries and the "New" International Law: The United Nations' Special Conference on Friendly Relations and Co-Operation Among States*, 60, A.J.I.L. 1 (1966).

[129] *See generally* Special Committee on Principles of International Law Concerning Friendly Relations and Co-Operation Among States, Report, 20 U.N. GAOR, Annexes, vol. III, Agenda Items Nos. 90 & 94, at 83–129, U.N. Doc. A/5746 (1965); 1966 Special Committee on Principles of International Law Concerning Friendly Relations and Co-Operation Among States, Report, 21 U.N. GAOR, Annexes, vol. III, Agenda Item No. 87, at 29–48, U.N. Doc A/6230 (1966).

[130] *See generally* Sixth Committee, Report, 20 U.N. GAOR, Annexes, Vol. III, at 143, 149, U.N. Doc. A/6165 (1965); 1966 Special Committee Report, *supra* note 129, at 64–77.

[131] *See* para. 4 of the proposal by the United Kingdom, [1965] Special Committee Report, *supra* note 129, at 84. After stating that the "... prohibition of the threat or use of force embraces both the direct and indirect use of force," the U.K. draft states that ". . . every state is under a duty to refrain from fomenting civil strife or committing terrorist acts in another state, or from tolerating organized activities directed toward such ends." See also para. 2(d)(ii) of the joint proposal of Italy and the Netherlands, 1966 Special Committee Report, *supra* note 129, at 31.

[132] *See* para 2(b) of the joint proposal of Australia, Canada, the United Kingdom, and the United States which provides that every "state has the duty to refrain from organizing or encouraging the organization of irregular or volunteer forces or armed bands within its territory or any other territory for incursions into the territory of another state . . . ." 1966 Special Committee Report, *supra* note 129, at 30. See also para. 2(d)(i) of the joint proposal of Italy and the Netherlands. *Id.* at 31.

state."[133] Similarly, with respect to the second principle, proposals included such prohibited conduct as interference in civil strife in another state,[134] pressure by one state to change the social or political order in another,[135] or the organization of terrorist activities directed against another state.[136] Wide acceptance of the general thrust of these proposals may be seen in the Draft Declaration adopted by the Special Committee on May 2, 1970, which, in its formulation of the above principles, included the duty to refrain from the most commonly feared manifestations of indirect aggression.[137]

Specific cases arising within the United Nations serve further to illustrate that community opinion has condemned indirect aggression as impermissible coercion. In the 1947–48 Greek situation, for example, a Commission of Investigation[138] (established by the Security Council) and a Special Committee on the Balkans[139] (established by the General Assembly) both supported the Greek Government's allegations that Albania, Bulgaria, and Yugoslavia had been supplying indigenous guerrilla forces with military aid and had been permitting the use of their territories for staging areas for subversive operations against the incumbent government.[140] After a Soviet veto paralyzed the Security Council, the General Assembly, in a 1948 resolution, condemned these activities by stating that ". . . the continued aid given by Albania, Bulgaria, and Yugoslavia to Greek guerrillas endangers peace in the Balkans, and is inconsistent with the purposes and principles of the Charter of the United Nations."[141]

---

[133] *See* para. 2(b) of the proposal by Ghana, India, and Yugoslavia in [1965] Special Committee Report, *supra* note 129, at 85. *See also* para. 4 of the Czechoslovakian proposal. *Id.* at 84.

[134] *See* para. 2 of the joint proposal by India, Lebanon, the United Arab Republic, Syria, and Yugoslavia in 1966 Special Committee Report, *supra* note 129, at 65.

[135] *See* Czechoslovakian proposal in [1965] Special Committee Report, *supra* note 129, at 109.

[136] *See* para. 3(d) of the Yugoslav proposal in [1965] Special Committee Report, *supra* note 129, at 109; para. 2 of the joint proposal of India, Lebanon, The United Arab Republic, Syria, and Yugoslavia in 1966 Special Committee Report, *supra* note 129, at 65; para. 2c of the joint proposal by Australia, Canada, France, Italy, the United Kingdom, and the United States. *Id.* at 65.

[137] *See Draft Declaration on Principles of International Law Concerning Friendly Relations and Co-Operation among States,* 7 U.N. Monthly Chronicle 62, 64–66 (1970).

[138] *See* Commission of Investigation Concerning Greek Frontier Incidents, Report to the Security Council, 2 U.N. SCOR, Spec. Supp. 2, vol 1, at 106–09, U.N. Doc. S/360/Rev. 1 (1948).

[139] *See* United Nations Special Committee on the Balkans, Report, 3 U.N. GAOR, Supp. 8, at 28 U.N. Doc. A/574; Supp. 8A, at 9, U.N. Doc. A/644 (1948).

[140] Letter from Mr. Aghnides, the Acting Chairman of the Greek delegation to the United Nations, to the Secretary-General, and enclosed memorandum, U.N. SCOR, Supp. 10, Annex 16, U.N. Doc S/203, at 169 (1946).

[141] G.A. Res. 193 (III), "threats to the political independence and territorial integrity of

Also of interest is the 1948 Czechoslovakian question which involved highly effective political infiltration and threats of force by the Soviet Union resulting in a successful coup d'etat by the Czech Communist party. Charges that the activities of the Soviet Union were in violation of article 2(4) of the Charter were made by the former permanent representative of Czechoslavia to the United Nations.[142] Although a Soviet veto prevented Security Council action on the matter, the debates within the Council clearly reveal the consensus that the activities of the Soviet Union, if proven, would indeed have constituted serious 'violations of the Charter.[143]

The response by the United Nations to the 1958 Lebanese situation is also instructive. The Lebanese representative complained his country was the victim of indirect aggression waged by the United Arab Republic (Egypt and Syria) consisting of "infiltration of armed bands from Syria," "participation of [UAR] nationals in acts of terrorism and rebellion" in Lebanon, "the supply of arms from Syria to individuals and bands in Lebanon," and "the waging of a violent radio and press campaign in the [UAR] calling for strikes, demonstrations; and the overthrow of the established authorities in Lebanon. . . ."[144] Although both the UAR and

---

Greece." 3(1) U.N. GAOR, Plenary Mtgs. (Pt. 2), Resolutions at 18 U.N. Doc. A/728 (1948). Dr. Higgins has argued that when G.A. Res. 193 (III) and subsequent U.N. action with respect to the Greek case are read in light of the "Peace through Deeds" Resolution, "there can be little doubt that the actions of Yugoslavia, Albania, and Bulgaria constituted, 'indirect aggression'; or, more precisely, that these indirect forms of aid to rebels in another state constituted impermissible coercion." HIGGINS, THE DEVELOPMENT OF INTERNATIONAL LAW THROUGH THE POLITICAL ORGANS OF THE UNITED NATIONS 191 (1963). *See further,* Black, *Greece and the United Nations,* 63 POL. SCI. Q. 551 (1948); HOWARD, *The Greek Question in the Fifth Session of the General Assembly of the United Nations,* 24 DEP'T STATE BULL. 333 (1951); MILLER, WORLD ORDER AND LOCAL DISORDER: THE UNITED NATIONS AND INTERNAL CONFLICTS 174–80 (1967); *Threats to the Political Independence and Territorial Integrity of Greece,* in [1948–49] Y.B. UNITED NATIONS 28, 243.

[142] *See* letter dated Mar. 15, 1948 from Mr. Santa Cruz, the permanent representative of Chile to the United Nations addressed to the Secretary-General in which Mr. Jan Papanek, the former permanent representative of Czechoslovakia, is quoted as follows: "The political independence of Czechoslovakia, a member of the United Nations, has thus been violated by the threat of use of force of another member of the Unitd Nations, the Union of Soviet Socialist Republics, in direct infringement of para. 4, art. 2, of the Charter." 3 U.N. SCOR, Supp. (Jan.-Mar.) at 34, 35, U.N. Doc. S/696 (1948).

[143] *See, e.g.,* remarks of Mr. Santa Cruz (Chile), 3 U.N. SCOR, 268th mtg., at 103 (Jan.–Mar. 1948; remarks of Mr. Papanek, *id.,* 272d mtg., at 175–91; remarks of Mr. Cadogan (United Kingdom), *id.* at 191–96; remarks of Mr. Parodi (France), *id.,* 273d mtg. at 206–08; remarks of Mr. Austin (United States), *id,* at 225–29; remarks of Gen. McNaughton (Canada), *id.,* 276th mtg., at 271–75; remarks of Mr. El-Khouri (Syria), *id.* at 275–78.

[144] Letter dated May 22, 1958, from Mr. Azkoul, a representative of Lebanon, to the President of the Security Council, 13 U.N. SCOR, Supp. (Apr.–June) at 33, U.N. Doc. S/4007 (1958). *See also,* statement of Mr. Malik (Lebanon) in 13 U.N. SCOR, 823rd mtg., at 1, 14, 20, U.N. Doc. S/PV.823 (1958).

Soviet delegates argued that no tangible evidence was produced to support the Lebanese charges, implicit in their argumentation was the recognition that such conduct was unlawful.[145] Many Western delegations, moreover, took the position that the activities of the UAR constituted a violation of article 2(4) of the Charter.[146] Indeed, that such conduct must be viewed as unlawful appears to be confirmed—if somewhat obliquely—by General Assembly Resolution 1237 (ES-III), which called upon all members of the United Nations to ensure that their conduct "by word and deed" conformed to the principles of "mutual respect for each other's territorial integrity and sovereignty" and of "strict noninterference in each other's internal affairs."[147]

The treatment of particular cases arising within the Organization of American States further confirms the conclusion that the world community has proscribed the external fomentation and support of civil strife as constituting impermissible coercion.[148] The Council of the Organization of American States, acting provisionally as Organ of Consultation, has assumed jurisdiction over many complaints involving charges of indirect aggression and, when such charges have been proven, has issued strong condemnations of such conduct.[149] Practice under the OAS Charter and the Rio Treaty of Reciprocal Assistance reveals the widely shared expectation that impermissible coercion need not include the direct use of physical force.[150]

[145] *See* statement of Mr. Loutfi (United Arab Republic), *id.* at 22, 29, 32; *see* statement of Mr. Sobolev (Soviet Union), *id* at 36, 37.

[146] *See, e.g.,* remarks of Mr. Jamali (Iraq), 13 U.N. SCOR, 824th mtg., at 35, 40–41, U.N. Doc. S/PV.824 (1958); remarks of Mr. de Vaucelles (France), *id.* at 44–46; remarks of Mr. Lodge (United States), *id*, at 47–49; remarks of Mr. Dixon (United Kingdom), *id.* at 50–54.

[147] 14 U.N. GAOR (Emer. Sess. 3), Supp. 1, U.N. Doc. A/3905 (1958). *See further,* Higgins, *supra* note 141, at 193–94; Miller, *supra* note 141, at 183–85.

[148] *See generally* FENWICK, THE ORGANIZATION OF AMERICAN STATES: THE INTER-AMERICAN REGIONAL SYSTEM 237–46 (1963); Thomas & Thomas, *supra* note 76, at 189–95; THOMAS & THOMAS, THE ORGANIZATION OF AMERICAN STATES 298–371 (1938).

[149] *See, e.g.,* the 1950 Haiti-Dominican Republic Case in PAN AMERICAN UNION, INTER-AMERICAN TREATY OF RECIPROCAL ASSISTANCE—APPLICATIONS, vol. I, 1948–1959, at 130–31 (1959); the 1950 Dominican Republic-Cuba case, *id.* at 130–135; the 1955 Costa Rica-Nicaragua case, *id.* at 176; the 1960 Venezuela-Dominican Republic Case in PAN AMERICAN UNION, INTER-AMERICAN TREATY OF RECIPROCAL ASSISTANCE—APPLICATIONS, vol. II, 1960–1964, at 8–9 (1964); the 1963 Venezuela-Cuba case, *id.* at 185–88. For an analysis of these cases as well as a discussion of other similar controversies which were considered by the Organization of American States, *see* the authorities cited in note 148, *supra. See also,* 5 Whiteman, *supra* note 80, at 279–81.

[150] The American Republics have long been aware of the dangers of indirect aggression. For example, at the Second Meeting of Consultation of American Ministers of Foreign Affairs, held in Havana in 1940, the recognition of the efficacy of the indirect use of force

1.4.3. APPRAISAL. The burden of history since World War II is that through a subtle manipulation of its political, ideological, and economic instruments, a state need not resort to its military instrument to destroy, or severely impair, another state's territorial integrity or political independence.[151] The Greek crisis, to cite only one example, reveals the deep community concern as well as recognition that indirect aggression is a form of concern as dangerous as a classical, armed invasion.[152] Community expectations as to the impermissibility of such coercion has been reflected clearly in both customary prescription and practice under the United Nations Charter. Customary prescription branded as unlawful activities carried on or tolerated by a state on its territory which were calculated to be injurious to another. United Nations practice has condemned indirect aggression as being contrary to the purposes and principles of the Charter. More specifically, indirect aggression must be deemed violative of the postulate of peaceful change. Indeed, to argue that direct and indirect aggression could not equally be violations of article 2(4) of the Charter would be to make a fetish of literalism.[153]

Some observers may argue that the existence of a genuine community consensus as to the impermissibility of external assistance to internal rebel groups is open to doubt in view of the Soviet Bloc/Afro-Asian support for wars of national liberation. Such an argument is entirely un-

---

was made manifest in a resolution which obligated the American governments to adopt measures

> . . . to prevent and suppress any activities directed, assisted, or abetted by foreign governments, or foreign groups or individuals which tend to subvert the domestic institutions, or to foment disorder in their internal political life, or to modify by pressure, propaganda, threats, or in any other manner, the free sovereign rights of their peoples to be governed by their democratic systems.

Res. VI, Final Act, Second Meeting of Ministers of Foreign Affairs of the American Republics, Havana, July 21–30, 1940, 30 A.J.I.L. 1, 9 (Supp. 1941).

[151] *Cf.* Higgins, *supra* note 141, at 189: "The framers of the Charter were primarily concerned with the problem of 'armed attack' and it is only the unhappy events of the last fifteen years which have strongly focused attention on the problem of "indirect aggression.'" For the fullest discussion of all the post-World War II cases involving charges of indirect aggression, see Thomas & Thomas, *The International Law of Indirect Aggression and Subversion,* prepared for the United States Arms Control and Disarmament Agency, Contract No. ACDA/6C-41, at 109–26, 162–93, 229–57, 349–60, 405–12 (1966).

[152] *Cf.* the remarks of Sir Gerald Fitzmaurice criticizing certain draft definitions of aggression during U.N. Sixth Committee debates: "Armed attack from the outside and subversion from within [are] all part of one and the same process, and it would be useless to adopt a definition which included the former while omitting the latter. 6 U.N. GAOR, 6th Comm, at 166, U.N. Doc. A/C.6/SR.281 (1951–52).

[153] In this connection, it may be argued that if art. 2(4) is to play a meaningful role in delimiting the resort to coercion in the world arena, at least some forms of indirect aggression must be included in the definition of force. *See* Hull & Novogrod, *supra* note 23, at 118. *See also,* Röling, *On Aggression, On International Criminal Law, On International Criminal Jurisdiction,* 2 NEDERLANDS TIJDSCHRIFT VOOR INTERNATIONAL RECHT 167, 172 (1955).

persuasive. In the first place, it must be understood that these nations do not take the position that external support for rebellious internal groups is per se lawful. On the contrary, the Soviet Bloc and Afro-Asian states consistently affirm the principle of nonintervention,[154] but consider support for wars of national liberation as an exception to the general norm based, in their view, on the higher right of self-determination.[155] Moreover, these states would not admit the lawfulness of external support to hypothetical rebel groups within their borders. Indeed, the constitutive charters of the Warsaw Pact[156] and the Organization of African Unity[157] make nonintervention a central norm governing intraregional affairs. It is also relevant to note, finally, that the newly independent states fully realize the interrelationship of nonintervention and state security, and thus, upon occasion have characterized that principle as a logical extension of self-determination.[158] Hence, while there is dis-

[154] *See* McWhinney, *supra* note 128, at 21–25. *See also,* the Sino-Indian agreement of Apr. 29, 1953, (commonly referred to as the *Panch Shila*) on "Trade and Intercourse between the Tibetan Region of China and India" in which the 5 principles of coexistence were spelled out: mutual respect for territorial integrity and sovereignty; nonaggression; noninterference in internal affairs; equality and mutual advantage; and peaceful coexistence. For discussion, *see* McWhinney, *Peaceful Coexistence and Soviet-Western International Law* 30–51 (1964); Ramundo, Peaceful Coexistence: International Law in the Building of Communism 28–32 (1967); Tunkin, *Coexistence and International Law,* 95 Hague Recueil 1 (1958). For a discussion of the Afro-Asian views on nonintervention and "peaceful coexistence," *see generally* Kahin, The Asian-African Conference, Bandang Indonesia, *April 1955* (1956).

[155] Thus, Mr. Anguelov (Bulgaria) argued in the U.N. Sixth Committee:

> . . . a state should not be permitted, under cover of the principle of nonintervention, to avoid obligations arising out of other principles of international law which had the character of *jus cogens.*

Mr. Anguelov then cited examples such as genocide, apartheid, and "various other colonialist or neo-colonialist practices" with respect to which nonintervention could not be invoked. 18 U.N. GAOR, Sixth Comm., 807th mtg., at 140, U.N. Doc. A/C.6/SR.807 (1963). To the same effect, *see* the statement by Mr. Vanderpuye (Ghana) quoted in McWhinney, *supra* note 128, at 24; and the remarks of Mr. N'Diaye (Mali) in 20 U.N. GAOR, Sixth Comm., 882d mtg., at 248, 249–50, U.N. Doc. A/C.6/SR.882 (1965). For a discussion of how the doctrine of nonintervention, in communist theory, is applicable only after "liberation," see Ramundo, *supra* note 154, at 87–103, 155–58.

[156] The fifth preambular paragraph of the Warsaw Pact reaffirms "the principles of respect for the independence and sovereignty of states and of noninterference in the internal affairs. . . ." Text of the Warsaw Pact may be found in 49 A.J.I.L. 194, 195 (Supp. 1955).

[157] The signatories of the Charter of the Organization of African Unity, in art. III (principles), affirmed their adherence to the principle of "noninterference in the internal affairs of states." Text of the O.A.U. Charter may be found in 58 A.J.I.L. 873 (1964).

[158] Professor McWhinney, in discussing the course of debates within the U.N. Special Committee on Friendly Relations, has written, *supra* note 128, at 23: "it was contended that the principle of nonintervention had a special importance for the smaller countries and particularly those which had emerged from colonial domination, its observance being the guarantee of their sovereignty and of their independent development, the principle of nonintervention thus complementing the principle of self-determination."

agreement within the world community as to whether there are permissible exceptions to the principle of nonintervention, all states are in accord that, in general, external assistance to internal rebel groups is unlawful under the normative structure of the Charter.

Branding indirect aggression as impermissible coercion is entirely in accord with community efforts to secure a genuine and lasting world order. External attack disguised as internal change is, as concerned observers have noted, "just as inimical to minimum world public order as any other mode of attack."[159] Nice distinctions between direct and indirect use of force or between military and nonmilitary coercion begin to blur when the objective and consequence of these strategies are the impairment or destruction of a target state's territorial integrity or political independence. For these reasons, the exercise of coercion through the medium of internal rebel groups may leave the target state no choice—even though it has not been subjected to a classical armed invasion—but to invoke the right of self-defense and to employ its military instrument against the aggressor state in order to preserve its territorial integrity and political independence.[160] In view of the realities of the contemporary world arena, few statesmen or jurists would insist that a state be the victim of classical armed attack before it lawfully could exercise responding coercion against the aggressor state.[161]

---

[159] McDougal & Feliciano, *supra* note 7, at 192 n.164. As Professor Roling has commented, a reasonable interpretation of the "Peace through Deeds" Resolution is that "attack is attack whatever the weapons used, and whether openly or otherwise." Roling, *The Question of Defining Aggression, in* SYMBOLAE VERZIJL 314, 223, (1958).

[160] The central issue raised by this assertion is whether the clause "if an armed attack occurs" in art. 51 of the U.N. Charter has restricted the customary right of self-defense by conditioning the exercise of the right upon the occurrence of an armed attack. Some scholars take the position that art. 51 is constitutive in character and that, therefore, self-defense has been restricted. *See* BROWNLIE, INTERNATIONAL LAW AND THE USE OF FORCE BY STATES 271–73 (1963); Kelsen, *supra* note 60, at 914; Jessup, *supra* note 80, at 165–66; Kunz, *Individual and Collective Self-Defense in Article 51 of the Charter of the United Nations,* 41 A.J.I.L. 872, 878 (1947). The majority of scholars, however, are of the view that art. 51 has not restricted the customary right of self-defense which thus would be available to counter indirect modes of aggression. *See, e.g.,* Bowett, *supra* note 114, at 184–93 (1958); Green, *Armed Conflict, War and Self-Defense,* 6 ARCHIV DES VOLKERRECHTS 387, 433 (1956–57); Higgins, *The Legal Limits to the Use of Force by Sovereign States: United Nations Practice,* 37 BRIT. Y.B. INT'L L. 269, 299–308 (1961); Hull & Novogrod, *supra* note 23, at 111; McDougal & Feliciano, *supra* note 7, at 200–02, 233–41; Moore, *supra* note 70, at 7–13; Stone, *supra* note 124, at 92–101; Waldock, *The Regulation of the Use of Force by Individual States in International Law,* 81 HAGUE RECUEIL DES COURS 454, 475–99 (1952). In order to be lawful, however, a forceful response must conform to the requirement of proportionality and thus must be of a quantum sufficient only to counter the threat posed. In the context of indirect aggression, this is a major consideration because of the covert nature of the attack. *See* Bowett, *supra* at 24.

[161] Thus Bowett, *supra* note 114, at 192 argues that it "is well recognized that an armed attack is by no means the only form of aggression, of imperiling a state's rights so that it

In a world arena pervaded by tension and deep antagonisms, the furtherance of self-determination or human rights at the expense of world
order may result in enduring nuclear ruin. While the proponents of human
dignity sympathize with the plight of black populations in the remaining
colonial territories and in the racist-oriented regimes in Southern Africa,
any attempt to alter the status quo through externally applied coercion
runs counter to the Charter's overriding emphasis on peaceful change.[162]
Thus, the Soviet Bloc/Afro-Asian support for wars of national liberation
must be deemed inimicable to the conception of world order projected
by the United Nations Charter. By similar reasoning, it is difficult to
approve of the General Assembly resolutions authorizing external assistance to rebel groups in various African colonial territories and countries.[163]
These resolutions are manifestations of short-term expediency and must
lead, in the long run, to greater destruction of values than are caused by
the evils the policy of self-determination is intended to eliminate. It is,
in any case, highly questionable that the private choice of individuals and
the protection of their inherent dignity can be furthered by externally
applied coercion, particularly if the result of such coercion is the replacement of one set of repressive internal elites with another.[164]

---

may be compelled to resort to the exercise of a right of self-defence." Even Brownlie, *supra*
note 160, at 279, 373, and Kelsen, *supra* note 8, at 88—both of whom take a restrictive
view of art. 51—admit that if the aggressor state exercises some control over the rebels
in the target state, indirect modes of aggression may amount to an armed attack. *Contra,*
Falk, *International Law and the United States Role in Viet Nam: A Response to Professor
Moore,* 76 YALE L.J. 1095, 1125, 1140–43. Further, a thirteen-power draft, submitted in
the 1969 Special Committee on the Question of Defining Aggression, provided that when
a state is the victim of an indirect use of force, "it may take all reasonable and adequate
steps to safeguard its existence and institutions, without having recourse to the right of
individual or collective self-defense against the other state under art. 51 of the Charter. . . ."
See the Report of the Special Committee, *supra* note 127, at 8.

[162] A major problem confronting those who seek a stable world order is the extent to
which the Afro-Asian states will accept and abide by both the traditional international law
and the law of the Charter restricting the unilateral resort to coercion in cases where self-
determination and human rights are at stake. See, in this regard, Professor Falk's discussion
of the 1961 Goa incident in Falk, *supra* note 53, at 53–57.

[163] *See, e.g.,* G.A. Res. 2307 (XXIII) in which an appeal was made "to all states and
organizations to provide appropriate moral, political, and material assistance to the people
of South Africa in their legitimate struggle for the rights recognized in the Charter. . . ."
23 U.N. GAOR, Supp. 18, at 58, U.N. Doc. A/7218 (1968). For further citations to other
General Assembly Resolutions calling for military assistance to internal rebel groups, *see*
Moore, *supra* note 32, at 267 n.135–37, 288 n.177, 289 n.178–80.

[164] *Cf.* the statement by Mr. N'Diaye (Mali) *supra* note 155, at 248: "An intervention . . .
which consisted in an attempt to modify the regime of another state or prevent it from
changing its constitutional structures in accordance with the wish of its people must be
considered a flagrant violation of the self-determination of peoples. . . ."

1.5. Indirect Aggression as an International Crime

That the resort to international violence may be not only unlawful, but criminal as well, is fully in accord with contemporary community expectations.[165] It would indeed be difficult—in view of the explicit acceptance of the Nuremberg Principles as authoritative prescription by the General Assembly,[166] the International Law Commission,[167] and numerous individual states[168] and jurists[169]—to argue that a state's policy-making elite are not subject to possible trial and criminal punishment for the unlawful resort to coercion. The Nuremberg Charter defined "crimes against the peace," for which major German war criminals were held individually responsible, as the

> . . . planning, preparation, initiation, or waging of a war of aggression, or a war in violation of international treaties, agreements, or assurances, or participation in a common plan or conspiracy for the accomplishment of any of the foregoing. . . .[170]

[165] The Nuremberg Tribunal, after examining the Pact of Paris, and subsequent state practice, concluded that "[a]ll these expressions of opinion, and others that could be cited, so solemnly made, reinforce the construction which the Tribunal placed upon the Pact of Paris, that resort to war of aggression is not merely illegal, but is criminal." NAZI CONSPIRACY AND AGGRESSION 52. *See also,* I Oppenheim, supra note 84, at 355: "The state, and those acting on its behalf, bear criminal responsibility for such violations of international law as by reason of their gravity, ruthlessness, and their contempt for human life place them within the category of criminal acts generally understood in the law of civilised countries."

[166] *See* G.A. Res. 95(I) which affirmed "the principles of international law recognized by the Charter of the Nuremberg Tribunal and the judgment of the Tribunal. . . ." 1(2) U.N. GAOR, Resolutions, at 188 (1946). *See also,* G.A. Res. 177 (II), in which the International Law Commission was directed to formulate the principles of international law recognized in the Nuremberg Charter and Judgment. 2 U.N. GAOR, Resolutions, at 111 (1947).

[167] See *Formulation of the Nuremberg Principles,* in International Law Comm'n, Report, 5 U.N. GAOR, Supp. 12, at 11, U.N. Doc. A/1316 (1950). For an analysis of the Nuremberg Principles, *see* Pompe, *supra* note 57, at 309–38; Spiropoulos, *Formulation of Nurnberg Principles,* [1950] II Y.B. Int'l L. Comm'n 181.

[168] For a canvassing of state practice with respect to the acceptance of the Nuremberg Principles, *see* Brownlie, *supra* note 160, at 175–88.

[169] *See* McDougal & Feliciano, *supra* note 7, at 165: "Perhaps few will doubt that the present corpus of authoritative myth permits the punishment of individual persons responsible for impermissible recourse to violence. . . ." For further authority, *see, e.g.,* Academy of Sciences of the USSR, Institute of State and Law, *supra* note 52, at 402–03; Bowett, *supra* note 114, at 266–68; CASTREY, THE PRESENT LAW OF WAR AND NEUTRALITY 83–84 (1954); Jessup, *supra* note 80, at 161; Korovin, *The Second World War and International Law,* 40 A.J.I.L. 742, 748 (1946); Lauterpacht, *supra* note 72, at 6, 42–45; REDSLOB, TRAITÉ DE DROIT DES GENS 229 (1950); SCELLE, MANUEL DE DROIT INTERNATIONAL 964 (1948); Sperduti, *L'Individuo nel Diretto Internazionale* 166 (1950), *reviewed in* 46 A.J.I.L. 756 (1952); Waldock, *supra* note 160, at 485. Brownlie, *supra* note 160, at 192–94, makes the same argument and cites additional authority at 194 n.1. *See* Wright, *The Law of the Nuremberg Tribunal,* 41 A.J.I.L. 38, 42 n.14, for still further authority supporting the criminality of "aggressive wars."

[170] Text of the Nuremberg Charter may be found in 9 A.J.I.L. 257, 258 (Supp. 1945).

The state conduct under scrutiny at Nuremberg involved the direct use of physical force of the greatest intensity and magnitude, employed for the purpose of achieving patently expansionist objectives. For this reason, the Tribunal apparently considered it unnecessary to devise a sophisticated definition of "war of aggression." Instead, the Tribunal simply concluded

> . . . that certain of the defendants planned and waged aggressive wars against ten nations, and were therefore guilty of this series of crimes. This makes it unnecessary to discuss the subject in further detail, or even to consider at any length the extent to which these aggressive wars were also "wars in violation of international treaties, agreements, or assurances."[171]

In view of the lack of guidance afforded by the Nuremberg Judgment as to what state conduct, other than the most outrageous, is to be considered criminal, the impartial observer is led to question whether the indirect use of force, such as in the case of external fomentation and support of civil strife, may also be deemed an international crime for which the responsible officials may be punished.

In answering this question, the concept of an international crime assumes central importance. Preliminarily, it should be understood that not every violation of international law by a state is an international crime for which its leaders may be subjected to potential criminal punishment. Indeed, the Nuremberg Tribunal, as a memorandum submitted by Secretary-General of the United Nations points out, made

> . . . a distinction between illegality and criminality; a criminal act is certainly an illegal act, but not every illegal act is criminal. An international crime is something more than merely a violation of international law.[172]

Neither the Nuremberg Charter nor Judgment contains a definition of an international crime, most probably because it was believed that Germany's conduct so clearly fit within whatever definition might be formulated.

In municipal law, it is generally accepted that the "essence of a criminal act, as distinguished from a contractual or tortious wrong actionable at the instance of the injured party, is the fact that it injures and is punishable by the community at large."[173] The pertinent question, then, is

---

[171] NAZI CONSPIRACY AND AGGRESSION 46. *See also* the International Law Commission's discussion of this point under Principle VI in *Formulation of the Nuremberg Principles, supra* note 167.

[172] *The Charter and Judgment of the Nuremberg Tribunal: History and Analysis,* (Memorandum submitted by the Secretary-General), U.N. Publications Sales No. 1949. V.7 (1949).

[173] II OPPENHEIM, INTERNATIONAL LAW 192 (7th ed. Lauterpacht 1952). *See also,* I DROST, THE CRIME OF STATE 283 (1959); Johnson, *supra* note 121, at 458–60; Kelsen, PEACE THROUGH LAW 117 (1944).

whether a particular act results in a deprivation in private values (tort) or in a deprivation of the public order (crime).[174] In applying this standard to state conduct in the international arena, however, the distinction between private values and public order is much more difficult to perceive. In a world arena characterized by multiplying interdependencies with respect to all values, a value deprivation on one side of the globe increasingly effects a concomitant loss on the other side.[175] This observation, though scarcely novel, would appear to be especially valid in regard to value deprivations effected through the use of coercion directed against a state's territorial integrity or political independence. In such cases, the state conduct in question virtually always will be "of such nature that the security of all states would be imperilled. . . ."[176]

For purposes of assessing the criminality of the unlawful resort to coercion, there is no reason in logic or policy to distinguish between direct or indirect use of force. Rather than placing special relevance on the use of the military instrument, inquiry should be directed toward the objectives for which the coercion had been exercised, irrespective of the particular instrument of state policy employed. In short, the critical question is whether the coercion had been directed against the basic values of the territorial integrity or political independence of the target state—values which, in the last analysis, a system of I.C.L. must protect if it is to be viable.[177] If for no other purpose, criminal responsibility should be attributed to a state's official elite who would employ the instruments of state policy, singly or in whatever combination, against such basic values of another state.

Viewed from these perspectives, it is reasonable to conclude that a future tribunal appropriately may characterize the external fomentation and support of civil strife as criminal conduct and may subject the responsible state leaders to individual criminal punishment. Such a characterization appears to be in consonance with widespread community fears that indirect aggression is as competent as armed invasion in destroying a state's

[174] See Lasswell & Donnelly, *The Continuing Debate over Responsibility: An Introduction to Isolating the Condemnation Sanction* 68 YALE L.J. 869, 878 (1958–59).

[175] *Cf.* McDougal, *The Impact of International Law Upon National Law: A Policy-Oriented Perspective* in STUDIES IN WORLD PUBLIC ORDER 165 (McDougal *et al.* 1960).

[176] Baron Descamps in debates concerning plans for the establishment of the Permanent Court of International Justice within the Advisory Committee of Jurists. *Proces Verbaux of the Proceedings of the Committee* 498 (June 16–July 24, 1920).

[177] In this regard, Professor Pella has written that, "in order to protect the peaceful *existence of the international community,* [international] criminal law should punish all acts which endanger peaceful relations between states." Memorandum presented by the Secretariat (prepared by Professor Vespasien V. Pella) in [1950] II Y.B. INT'L L. COMM'N 278, 295. (Informal translation). *See also* Professor Parry's classification of international crimes in Parry, *supra* note 121, at 221–23.

territorial integrity or political independence. Moreover, the General Assembly, it will be recalled, branded the fomentation of civil strife as "the gravest of all crimes against the peace and security in the world."[178] In like manner, the International Law Commission, in articles 2(4), 2(5), and 2(6) of its Draft Code of Offenses Against the Peace and Security of Mankind, made the support of armed bands, the fomentation of civil strife, and the encouragement of terrorist activities in another state crimes for which the responsible state officials could be punished.[179]

Still, it cannot reasonably be said that all coercion exercised through the medium of internal rebel groups constitutes an international crime. The various modalities of indirect aggression may be viewed on a continuum of ascending degrees of coercion ranging from the mildest degree of coercion at the lower end (such as providing a small quantity of technical advisers to the rebel forces) to the most intense degree of coercion at the upper end (such as supplying rebel forces with arms, war material, or "volunteers"). Conduct falling on the lower end of the continuum might reasonably be viewed simply as a violation of international law, whereas conduct falling on the upper end might be considered an international crime as well.[180] It is scarcely necessary to add that the determination of the dividing line between merely unlawful conduct and criminal conduct is no simple task.

Some observers would argue, nevertheless, that adherence to the principle of *nullum crimen sine lege* requires a preexisting standard by which to determine the criminality of indirect aggression.[181] It would be somewhat ironic, however, if precise advance criteria, formulated to satisfy a principle of justice, could serve to bring about an unjust result. The determination of criminality, like the determination of impermissibility, can be made only after an examination of all the relevant facts of the partic-

---

[178] See text accompanying note 118 *supra.*

[179] See text accompanying note 121 *supra.*

[180] To be sure, the objectives of the aggressor state must remain the key factor in determining the criminality of a particular exercise of coercion. See text accompanying note 177, *supra.* However, it is difficult to imagine that the world community, in view of contemporary realities, is prepared to characterize certain very low level nonmilitary coercion as criminal.

[181] *See, e.g.,* Borchard, *International Law and International Organization,* 41 A.J.I.L. 106, 107 (1947); Ehard, *The Nuremberg Trial Against the Major War Criminals and International Law,* 43 A.J.I.L. 223, 231–44 (1948); *Postscript by Lord Hankey,* in U.N.O. AND WAR CRIMES, 110, 120 (Maugham 1951); PAL, INTERNATIONAL MILITARY TRIBUNAL FOR THE FAR EAST 11–37 (1953); SMITH, THE CRISIS OF THE LAW OF NATIONS 46 (1947). For a discussion and analysis of these opinions, *see* NAZI CONSPIRACY AND AGGRESSION 49; STONE, LEGAL CONTROLS OF INTERNATIONAL CONFLICT 325–29, 359–61, 368–71 (1954); Wright, *supra* note 169, at 44–48, 58–59. *See generally* HALL, GENERAL PRINCIPLES OF CRIMINAL LAW 20–27 (1947); I WHARTON, A TREATISE ON CRIMINAL LAW 41–42 (8th ed. 1880).

ular case in detailed context.[182] An a priori standard—divorced as it must be from specific operational facts—necessarily would be on a high level of abstraction. Since no set of advance criteria can be self-applying,[183] a future tribunal would be forced to interpret such a standard in the light of the specific factual situation before it. Not only might the standard, even if it were correctly applied, be too restrictive (thus eliminating potentially criminal conduct) or too flexible (thus potentially covering conduct not widely considered criminal), but it might be misapplied by the Tribunal resulting in an incorrect decision clearly not in accord with justice. Common sense dictates the conclusion that the lack of certainty as to a correct decision makes an a priori standard at best illusory, and, at worst, potentially destructive of justice.[184]

Nor can it reasonably be argued that the lack of precise advance criteria would ipso facto be violative of accepted principles of justice. It would appear that justice would not be infringed if the conduct declared criminal for the first time was clearly unlawful when committed. Professor Kelsen, for example, has argued that a

> . . . retroactive law providing individual punishment for acts which were illegal though not criminal at the time they were committed, seems . . . to be an exception to the rule against ex post facto laws.[185]

The *Llandovery Castle* case may be read as supporting this line of reasoning.[186] Hence, punishments for qualitatively grave violations of the law ". . . may be fixed . . . retroactively, since the principle or norm establishing their illegality already existed at the time of their commission."[187]

---

[182] See McDougal & Feliciano, *supra* note 7, at 151–55, and Stone, *supra* note 124, at 15–26, 81, 151–57, for incisive criticism of what have been, at least to the present, fruitless efforts to define aggression. It is submitted that the thrust of their arguments may be applied to efforts to formulate a preexisting standard of criminality. It will most likely be the case, however, that an examination in full context of the state conduct in question will serve to establish both its unlawfulness and its criminality. For a policy-oriented method of analysis of alleged initiating coercion, *see* McDougal & Feliciano, *supra* at 167–206.

[183] See Stone, *supra* note 124, at 24–26.

[184] It may be further noted in this connection, that as our world community progressively becomes more centralized, the standard for proper international behavior will become gradually more stringent as a higher degree of restraint is expected on the part of all states. Any threshold of criminality to be applied by means of a mechanical test formulated at present may thus be regarded as dangerously high in the future.

[185] Kelsen, *Will the Judgment in the Nuremberg Trial Constitute a Precedent in International Law?*, 1 INT'L & COMP. L.Q. 153, 165 (1947). *Cf.* Joyce v. Director of Public Prosecutions, 1 All E. R. 186, 189 (1946).

[186] Text of this decision by the German High Court may be found in 16 A.J.I.L. 708 (1922).

[187] WOETZEL, THE NUREMBERG TRIALS IN INTERNATIONAL LAW 114 (1962). Professor Woetzel, in respect to the problem of whether principles of justice would be violated in punishing individuals for conduct illegal, but not criminal, at the time of commission argues:

> Whether or not an injustice is worked would depend on a variety of circumstances: if the act

Questions of justice aside, it may be predicted that an advance description of specific coercive acts punishable as international crimes will have little, if any, positive effect on the quest for a lasting world order. Considered realistically, the prospects of the unlawful resort to coercion decreasing upon the adoption of precise criteria by which to determine criminality are not encouraging. It surely must be realized, in this connection, that

> . . . the judicial attribution of criminal responsibility can . . . be carried out only after the termination of violence, and only upon the assumption that the state identified as having unlawfully exercised coercion has been so far forcefully subdued as to permit the arrest and seizure of its leaders and top policy-makers.[188]

Since it scarcely can be expected that the official elite of an aggressor state would resort to coercion if victory were not confidently predicted, the certain knowledge that the coercion employed will be characterized as criminal—thus making the elite subject to potential punishment—will have a minimal deterrent effect.[189]

In the final analysis, stigmatizing state conduct as an international crime serves no purpose other than to permit the punishment of the responsible state leaders. With regard to the peace enforcement role of the United Nations, for example, both the General Assembly[190] and the Security Council[191] may act to restore the peace without a finding that

---

> was a heinous violation of international law; if it was recognisable as such to the individual; if he could reasonably be expected to know that it was punishable; and if he intended to do the thing he did which was in violation of his duties and obligations under international law. If all these conditions are met in a particular case, then it would not only be just to hold the individual criminally responsible for his misdeed, it would be an injustice not to do so. There could be no violation of the maxim *nullum crimen, nulla poena* in such a case.

Id. at 115–16.

[188] McDougal & Feliciano, *supra* note 7, at 165.

[189] *Cf.* the argument of Fenwick, *The Problem of Moral Disarmament,* 41 A.J.I.L. 112, 114, (1947), to the effect that future aggressors, taking advantage of both the newer weapon systems and careful planning, could attain their objectives "before the international community had come to a decision to take action." *See also* note 192 *infra.*

[190] Thus the General Assembly took action in the 1950 Korean crisis without a determination that North Korea had committed an international crime. *See, e.g.,* the "Uniting for Peace" Resolution (377V), 5 U.N. GAOR Supp. 20, U.N. Doc. A/1481 (1950). For discussion, *see* Kelsen, *supra* note 60, at 953–90; Stone, *supra* note 124, at 152–53. *See generally,* Peterson, *Uses of the Uniting for Peace Resolution Since 1950,* 13 INT'L ORG. 219 (1959).

[191] *See* arts. 39, 41, and 42 of the U.N. Charter which authorize the Security Council to "determine the existence of any threat to the peace, breach of the peace, or act of aggression (art. 39) and to recommend either nonforceful measures (art. 41) or forceful measures (art. 42) to implement its decisions, all of which may be carried out without a finding that an international crime had been committed. *See* Stone, *supra* note 124, at 152, who correctly points out that the Security Council can be activated without even an undefined notion of aggression.

an international crime had been committed. Because the individual parties to a conflict would be more likely to submit to amicable modes of settlement, it is reasonable to believe that the peace enforcement machinery of the United Nations would have a greater chance of meeting success if the criminality of the coercion in question had not been determined.[192] With respect to the target state itself, no statesman or jurist would claim that a state need be the object of an international crime before it may enlist the aid of a supranational organization,[193] seek reparation from the aggressor state for the damage suffered,[194] or before, in the last resort, it may exercise responding coercion in self-defense.[195]

1.6. Conclusion

It is consistent with both contemporary community expectations and fundamental policy that the exercise of coercion through the medium of rebel groups in the target state—the external fomentation and support of civil strife—is not only unlawful, but may be criminal as well. When the world community becomes sufficiently centralized to permit the effective monopoly of force by a universal supranational organization, a system of I.C.L.—with, conceivably, an international criminal code and an international criminal court[196]—will have a greater restraining influence

[192] *See* Stone, *supra* note 181, at 328: "Since guilt can only be brought home to the defeated, national leaders (insofar as they give thought to it at all) are not so much deterred, as warned that they must present any war which they contemplate in a favourable light, and (even more important) make sure winning it."

[193] See text accompanying notes 190 & 191 *supra*.

[194] *See Factory at Chorzow Case*, Merits, P.C.I.J. ser. A., No. 17, at 29 (1928); "It is a principle of international law, and even a general conception of law, that any breach of an engagement involves an obligation to make a reparation." *See also* Brownlie, *supra* note 160, at 133–49; Bruck, Les Sanctions en Droit International Public 240–41 (1933); Castren, *supra* note 169, at 80; Cheng, General Principles of Law as Applied by International Courts and Tribunals 169 (1953); Jenks, The Prospects of International Adjudication 543–44 (1964); Kelsen, *supra* note 173, at 90; Lauterpacht, The Function of Law in the International Community 117 (1933); I Oppenheim, *supra* note 84, at 352–54; Wright, *The Prevention of Aggression*, 50 A.J.I.L. 514, 527, (1956).

[195] The right of self-defense may be invoked to protect the basic values of a state— *i.e.*, its territorial integrity and political independence—against unlawful coercion which may or may not amount to an international crime. It should be noted that art. 51 does not condition the exercise of self-defense upon the occurrence of an international crime. *See* note 4 *supra*.

[196] *See* U.N. Draft Statute for an International Criminal Court in 1953 Committee on International Criminal Jurisdiction, *Report* 9 U.N. GAOR, Supp. 12A, at 23–26, U.N. Doc. A/2645 (1954). For further studies prepared under the auspices of the United Nations, *see* Alfaro, *Report on the Question of International Criminal Jurisdiction*, [1950] II Y.B. Int'l L. Comm'n 1; Sandstrom, *Report on the Question of International Criminal Jurisdiction, id.* at 18; U.N. Secretariat, *Historical Survey of the Question of International Criminal Jurisdiction*, Doc. A/CN.4/7/Rev. 1 (1949). *See generally* Bridge, *The Case for an International Court of Criminal Justice and the Formulation of International*

upon state conduct than it ever could at present.[197] Until such a community monopoly of force is achieved and appropriate international institutions for the implementation of authority are created, labeling indirect aggression as an international crime, without a post hoc determination of criminality on the particular facts of the case, is at once illusory and potentially detrimental to the disposition of justice and the quest for world order.

Section 2. AGGRESSIVE PROPAGANDA

John B. Whitton

2.1. Introduction

In 1792, when the French revolutionary armies were preparing to invade the Low Countries, Dumouriez proclaimed to the Belgians:

> Our armies are at your frontiers. They bring war to tyrants, liberty to citizens. Take a stand! Wake up, Belgian lion! People of Belgium, we vow to make you free.[1]

In a somewhat similar vein, the Venezuela radio in 1959 beamed this message to Santo Domingo:

> Dominican people! However powerful a tyranny may appear, it cannot withstand the action of a people united and determined to recapture their freedom.[2]

In response, the Dominican radio answered:

> Arise, Venezuelans! Take up the arms which your strength gives you, and use them against him who oppresses, enslaves, and confuses you in order to sustain himself in power.[3]

Criminal Law, 13 Int'l & Comp. L.Q. 1255 (1964); Pella, *Toward an International Criminal Court,* 44 A.J.I.L. 37 (1950); Wright, *Proposal for an International Criminal Court,* 46 A.J.I.L. 60 (1952).

[197] Stone, *supra* note 181, at 327, who, writing in reference to the draft Code of Offenses against the Peace and Security of Mankind and the Draft Statute for an International Criminal Court, contends that insofar "as the Code and the Statute succeed of adoption and ratification, they would remove from the Nuremberg principles the stigma both of unilateral enunciation by the victors, and (for future wars) of *ex post facto* application." Stone's point with respect to the adoption and ratification of the draft Code is of relevance in view of the fact that several jurists are of the view that portions of the draft Code are *de lege ferenda. See, e.g.,* Bowett, *supra* note 114, at 46 (arts. 2(5) & 2(6)); Brownlie, *supra* note 160, at 212; Pompe, *supra* note 57, at 340, 353.

[1] A. Sorel, L'Europe et la Révolution Française, Vol. II, at 481, Vol. IV, at 164.

[2] From the "Continental Radio," Mar. 2, 1959, cited by J. Whitton & A. Larson, Propaganda, Disarmament in the War of Words 4 (1963). (Cited hereafter as Whitton-Larson).

[3] From the "Dominican Voice," Aug. 25, 1955, *id.*

These examples illustrate the play of aggressive international communication, the subject of this chapter. What is propaganda? Under what circumstances does it constitute a danger to world peace? When is it a violation of accepted rules and principles of international law? If a violation, is it held to be aggression? Finally, what can be done about it?

The media employed by nations for purposes of persuasion are numerous and of varying effectiveness. Before the invention of printing, propaganda was a matter of personal effort. With the development of postal systems, letters could be utilized to considerable effect, but writings only became of major importance with the invention of printing. But given the censorship powers of governments and their control of frontiers, transnational communication has evolved into a fine art and special science with the invention of telecommunication, of which radio broadcasting has proved to be the most useful and effective means of mass persuasion.

By the term "propaganda" is meant the communication of facts, fiction, argument, and suggestion, often with the purposeful suppression of inconsistent material, with the hope and intention of implanting in the minds of the "target" audience certain prejudices, beliefs, or convictions aimed at persuading the latter to take some action serving the interest of the communicator.[4] In Murty's words, "the main objective of ideological warfare is to develop among the audience perspectives and attitudes which accord with the strategists' policies."[5] On the domestic front the tobacco manufacturer, armed with statistics, claims that his cigarettes have less tar and less nicotine than those of a competitor; the candidate for office attacks his opponent's record and plays up his own. In each case the intended result is some action on the part of the recipient serving the communicator's interests—in one case the purchase of a product, in the other a favorable vote. In the field of foreign affairs, a government radio demeans the motives of the enemy in an attempt to weaken its morale or disparage its image among neutrals.

This process of persuasion, which sometimes amounts to actual coercion when accompanied by credible threats of grave injury, has been characteristic of the actions of governments since the first collectivity was

---

[4] M. McDougal & F. Feliciano, Law and Minimum World Public Order, 29 (1961). The use of the ideological instrument commonly involves the selective manipulation and circulation of symbols, verbal or nonverbal, calculated to alter the patterns of identifications, demands, and expectations of mass audiences in the target state, and thereby to induce or stimulate politically significant attitudes and behavior favorable to the initiator state. It includes, in combination with other instruments, all the techniques of propaganda, infiltration, subversion, and *coup d'état* which have been refined and developed to such high efficiency as to have given rise to repeated proposals to condemn their use for certain objectives as a distinct form or mode of aggression.

[5] B. Murty, Propaganda and World Order, 25 (1968).

organized. In the primitive tribe the leader may urge his followers into battle by cajoling or threatening them, or direct his appeals to the hostile tribe across the river, demanding some concession in peace or surrender in war. Moses used his rhetoric to induce his people to follow him to the Promised Land. Young men all over Europe were recruited for the Crusades by priests and other leaders with impassioned appeals and threats. Ideological campaigns played a key role in the preparation of the French and the American revolutions; both great movements were inspired by Jean-Jacques Rousseau and Thomas Paine. Nor should we underestimate the influence of *Uncle Tom's Cabin* in the long fight against slavery, especially the actual outbreak of the American Civil War. Throughout that conflict the atrocity story was used by both sides to inspire soldiers in the field and stiffen morale at home. The South stressed the cruelties of Sherman's March to the Sea, while the North publicized the sufferings of its soldiers at Andersonville Prison. Fortunately or unfortunately the Battle of Gettysburg could not be exposed to a horrified home population "in living color."

This story of atrocity propaganda is familiar to all students of the two world wars, and in fact of most any war. But the international lawyer can do little about such situations until the war is over. His immediate and most pressing problem concerns hostile communications in time of "peace." In periods of what is known as peace the propagandist may launch ideological attacks against a foreign sovereign hoping to encourage some terrorist to make an assassination attempt. Or, as a long-range program, the objective may be the creation of such a general atmosphere of doubt and discontent, such a sense of privation and oppression, as to engender an intense desire for change, with revolution and a new regime as the ultimate end. Lenin and Trotsky had to prepare the ground for 1917 through an extended campaign of subversion by means of letters, personal contact, and the organization of secret cells, plus underground intrigues of every kind. Today their work would be much easier; they could utilize the shortwave transmitter from across the frontier, and even on home territory the clandestine radio hidden in a cellar.

Ever since its first use as a weapon of power, hostile propaganda employed by one nation against another has been deeply resented and vigorously resisted. This reaction takes many forms. It may start with mere diplomatic protest and response in kind and go all the way to resort to force or even war. England actually declared war on Revolutionary France in 1793, it is asserted, because of France's persistent campaign of subversion, considered dangerous to the monarchy. At least it provided the leaders with a convenient pretext for a war believed to be in the national interest.[6] And when in 1914 the Austro-Hungarian Empire declared war on Serbia, thereby unleashing that great conflict, a major objective was to punish the Serbians for their long-continued irredentist intrigue and propaganda in Bosnia and Herzegovina. Much of this campaign was terroristic in nature, and was considered a contributing cause of the assassination of Archduke Ferdinand at Sarajevo.[7]

No self-respecting government will sit idly by as its leaders are libeled by the foreign press, or when a radio signal from across the frontier calls on its people to overthrow the government and even summons them to destroy their leaders. At the worst, the consequence may be armed conflict; at the least, poisoned relations between the hostile governments, thus making it impossible to settle the underlying issues peaceably. In fact, hostile communications can be both cause and effect of international friction, but more often an effect. Any intensive prolonged period of psychological warfare is a reliable symptom of an abnormal situation. If two governments are engaged in mutual slander over the media, this is often but the reflection of serious tension that divides them, perhaps a grave dispute of which ideological warfare is a contributing cause as well as a natural consequence. Thus, of course, the best way to deal with a campaign of mutual invective is to attack the cause of the misunderstanding or dispute. For instance, during the recent boundary dispute between Communist China and Soviet Russia, the violent press and radio attacks issuing from both sides were greatly attenuated once the parties had agreed to begin negotiations for a compromise. But this does not always follow. There may be no specific dispute at issue between the parties; or if one does exist, it may not be susceptible to peaceful settlement. So long as the present ideological rift continues between Communist China and Soviet Russia, it is not likely that a satisfactory settlement of the boundary controversy would end the mutual recrimination over the press and the airwaves.[8]

Consider also the Communist propaganda disseminated from Moscow following the Russian Revolution and which ever since has been the object of repeated protests from many countries, particularly from England and the United States. This ideological warfare will not cease until Soviet Russia has abandoned its hopes and plans for the universal spread of

---

[6] *Annual Register,* vol. 35, at 128 (1793).

[7] WHITTON-LARSON at 2, 31.

[8] J. WHITTON, THE PROBLEM OF CURBING INTERNATIONAL PROPAGANDA, A symposium on international control of propaganda, reprinted in a book by the same title edited by Havighurst [hereinafter referred to as Symposium]. 31 LAW & CONTEMP. PROB., 620 (1966).

Communism and has agreed to a policy of live and let live. Also, when a nation is frankly engaged in a crime against the peace, using intellectual coercion as a weapon of power in addition to other means, we see another case of *silent enim legis inter arma.* When Hitler was determined to bring down Schuschnigg and to seduce the Saar and Alsace-Lorraine, there was no hope that the "indirect aggression" by the Nazis would cease before those conquests had been consummated. The world had to wait until the war was over and the Nazis had been conquered before the war-mongering could be officially condemned and the perpetrators punished.

2.2. Propaganda Recognized as a Danger to Peace—Efforts to Curb

That hostile propaganda can be a grave danger to the peace of nations has been recognized for many years. But the extent of the danger did not become evident until modern times, not until propaganda had become an official weapon of power. It was first developed in time of war and then established as a regular arm of governmental power in both peace and war. This new concept with its implementation dates from World War I. In peacetime, the first great ideological campaign was launched in Moscow, and spread to other countries until now all countries consider ideological pressures to be a legitimate branch of government. (The considerable propaganda effort made by the French Revolutionists, the object of widespread protest at the time, especially in Britain, was in comparison rather sporadic, and only of temporary duration.)[9] The democratic nations, in response to Moscow, have also recognized, very tardily, the value of propaganda.

Today all governments and all students of world politics are alive to the evils of hostile international communication. Since the early days of the League of Nations, repeated attempts have been undertaken to prevent control and even outlaw the worst forms of ideological coercion.[10] Innumerable meetings called by the League of Nations and later the United Nations have debated the matter at great length and in considerable depth. These deliberations were characterized by an excessive optimism as to the chances for rapid progress in the matter, and by some exaggerated reliance on the potentialities of new treaties. To deal with the problem, impressive international meetings have been convoked, notably the 1936 conference on radio broadcasting and peace,[11] the United Nations Conference on Freedom of Information and the Press in 1948,[12] and a number of Latin-American conferences.[13] These efforts have

[9] WHITTON-LARSON, at 16, 25.
[10] Reviewed in WHITTON-LARSON, at 69 *passim.*
[11] *Id.* at 70, 125.
[12] *Id* at 199 *passim.*
[13] *Id.* at 101, 127.

produced many admirable resolutions and several treaties. Also, there have been a number of reunions of the media where representatives of press and radio have passed excellent resolutions and drafted impressive codes of conduct for communicators, the latter phathetically impotent in countries where the press is an arm of government or rigidly controlled by official sources. Very early in this movement the Rumanians would have made war propaganda something akin to piracy, thus permitting the punishment of the individual offender by any nation obtaining jurisdiction.[14] Meanwhile, Moscow clamored for the condemnation of propaganda for war and the punishment by each state of the guilty. Nor should it be forgotten that many states, including Soviet Russia, have provided in their criminal law for the prosecution of individuals found guilty of war propaganda and other types of hostile communications, including that likely to involve the nation in trouble with foreign countries.[15]

What is there to show for all this effort? The war of words still goes on. Egypt continues to incite the Arab states to destroy Israel. Moscow still utilizes the airwaves and the press for tactics of intervention wherever it finds such activities opportune. The United States has turned to the airwaves to justify its invasion of Cuba at the Bay of Pigs and to rationalize its long struggle in Vietnam. New states campaign through violent communications against real or imagined ills in foreign lands, relying on the weapon of propaganda to advance their ideological and political purposes whenever they consider it feasible.[16]

Despite all the difficulties present, now so apparent after years of frustration, the international lawyer can still play a useful role in the field

[14] Pella, *Un Nouveau Délit: la Propagande pour la Guerre d'Aggression*, REVUE DE DROIT INTERNATIONAL, 174 (1929).

[15] L. J. MARTIN, INTERNATIONAL PROPAGANDA, ITS LEGAL AND DIPLOMATIC CONTROL 109 (1958).

[16] W. O'Brien, *International Propaganda and Minimum World Public Order*, in SYMPOSIUM *supra* note 8, at 594, 599. But even the more skeptical writers in the field feel that some progress has been made. William V. O'Brien writes:

> In summary, therefore, no state or individual purporting to respect international law could contend that there is an unlimited right to engage in international propaganda. It should be emphasized that this in itself is a sign of progress. The same statement could not have been made with equal confidence in, say, 1914.

On the other hand, this same writer is pessimistic with respect to our expectations about future observances of prescriptions against hostile communications.

> It is submitted that expectations are, first, for only intermittent, variable and marginal observance of these legal prescriptions. But, perhaps, more important, one anticipates that the states as they violate these norms do not appear to be conscious of doing wrong. In many instances, on the contrary, states manifestly engage in technically illegal propaganda with a feeling of rectitude ranging from a conviction that they have a right to disseminate their propaganda to the belief that they have a duty to do so in the interests of mankind as well as for their own interests. *Until this kind of attitude is altered it would seem impossible successfully to deal with the problems of international legal regulation of propaganda.* (Italics added)

here under study. First, he may point out the rules of law already available to the aggrieved victim state and the appropriate world organization when propaganda dangerous to peace occurs. Second, he may suggest improvements in the law, and point out the possibility of sanctions for the purpose of dissuading or even of punishing the offender. He may also stress the availability of other remedial procedures. But in a single chapter more attention must be devoted to the lex lata than to the lex ferenda. Some problems of great significance may have to be suggested rather than given thorough analysis. Another matter concerns the dilemma facing the "free" states that find it difficult to impose on their media effective curbs in the interest of better relations with other nations—*e.g.*, laws against the publication of false news, hostile attacks on foreign heads of states, and messages inciting people to revolt and even war—without making unacceptable inroads on those basic human rights, freedom of speech and of the press. So far as this problem confronts the United States, it has been admirably elucidated in recent studies by Newhouse, Van Alstyne, and others.[17]

2.3. Propaganda as Aggression

Although scholars and diplomats, within the United Nations and elsewhere, have thus far failed in their effort to draft a definition of the term "aggression," it is suggested that if and when a text is agreed upon, it should include certain categories of hostile transnational propaganda, but within strictly defined limits. This problem is concerned mainly with two categories of hostile communications: (1) propaganda for war and (2) subversive propaganda. Also (although these matters cannot be dealt with here for lack of space) propaganda promoting assassination, terrorism, and genocide should be categorized in the same manner as the above offenses, under the doctrine of incitement, discussed below, and treated as such.

2.3.1. PROPAGANDA FOR WAR. Propaganda for war may be defined as a direct attempt, usually by organized and concerted pressures, to shape the minds of the masses in a particular nation in the direction of transnational conflict by force of arms or other methods of forceful coercion. It was defined by a League of Nations special committee as follows:

> . . . direct public propaganda urging the state to be the first to commit, contrary to its international understandings, any one of the following acts: a) declaration of war upon another state; b) invasion by its armed forces, even without declaration of war, of the territory of another state; c) attack by its land, naval, or air forces, even without declaration of war, upon the territory,

[17] *Id.* at 506–52.

vessels, or aircraft of another state; d) naval blockade of the coasts or parts of another state; e) assistance, given to armed bands, organized in its territory, which have invaded the territory of another state, or refusal, in spite of the request of the invaded state, to take in its territory all possible steps to deprive the aforesaid bands of all assistance or protection.[18]

This would include, in the category of war propaganda, agitation in favor of armed bands aiming to overthrow a foreign regime with whom one is technically at peace. This matter is dealt with elsewhere under the heading of subversive propaganda.

Ideological agitation for war, also called "warmongering," and, by some, "indirect aggression," occurs in several specific types which may at times be found to overlap. There is the organized campaign directed by decision-makers to the home population in an effort to provoke them to support a war of aggression, as was done by the Nazis and the Japanese in World War II. At other times, the pressure is applied to a foreign people or its leaders in an endeavor to incite an aggressive war against a third state, for example, Hitler, inciting the Italians against France. Another type of warmongering is that emphasized at the war-crime trials at Nuremburg—a campaign of divisive and subversive propaganda directed to leaders and masses of a foreign nation marked for conquest, the objective here being to divide and weaken the victim. Another distinction turns on the identity of the author of the campaign for war. The responsible party may be the government itself, which is the usual case and the one most ominous for the cause of peace. Or the source may be a pressure group, or a political party making the embarking on a new war one of its campaign slogans. More rarely it may be an influential publicist, as illustrated by the persistent efforts of a prominent U.S. newspaper at the end of the century to embroil the United States in a war with Spain.

The most extraordinary case of hostile propaganda is that for which certain of the Nazi leaders were found guilty at Nuremburg, but it should be noted that this propaganda was only part of their crimes.[19] They were, it must be noted, part and parcel of the Nazi machine. Any punishable acts of propaganda by genuine private individuals outside the ring of government leaders would be rare indeed. Numerous examples of incitement by governments can be culled from current press, radio, and television communications in troubled areas. Such pressures are sometimes the prelude to an actual outbreak of war, *e.g.*, Hitler's propaganda to Poland. But should not the term "aggression" also include hostile communications engaged in by combatants in the course of an aggressive war? These are often the most virulent types of propaganda, and are often based on false-

[18] L.O.N. *IX Disarmament* 1933, 1–4, at 702 (1935).
[19] WHITTON-LARSON, at 76.

hood, even sheer invention. If waging of an aggressive war is an international crime, as decided at Nuremburg and now generally recognized, this act is not confined to military, economic, and political capabilities; it should also include the ideological arm. Ideological pressures addressed to a neutral state by the aggressive decision-makers, urging the latter to join in the conflict against the enemy, should certainly be included.

When one addresses himself to the question at hand, namely, whether propaganda for war within certain limits is to be categorized as aggression, one should inquire into the nature of aggression itself, and ask why, on the basis of hundreds of years of experience, aggressive war has finally been held by nations to be unlawful, its practice condemned and authors punished. It is clear that the same reasons that have led statesmen, tribunals, and scholars to "outlaw aggressive war" are pertinent to the proper categorization of communications from author to target delivered with an intent to induce armed conflict. Putting it in the simplest terms, if the waging of armed conflict, except in legitimate self-defense or when carried out under the authority of a regularly constituted international organization, is now held to be a violation of accepted rules and principles of the law of nations, this is due to a higher norm based on the fundamental and essential needs and requirements for the maintenance of a peaceful and workable international community (such as it is). As in the case of the basic norm *pacta sunt servanda*, no society or community, without going into the academic controversy over the "correct" definition of those terms, can long exist without the general acceptance of the empire of this norm, and at least a degree of reverence for and compliance therewith. Respect for agreements is the *sine qua non* of community existence in family, city, nation, and international order.[20] These same considerations apply to the rules against aggressive war. And they apply as well to incitements designed to cause such a war, in short to warmongering communications. But here the *point névralgique* is not the mere categorization of propaganda for war as aggression, but the isolation and analysis of the factors governing the application of the norm to a particular case. Not every campaign of propaganda should be interpreted as aggression, which may be answered legally by the use of force in self-defense. So boundary lines must be drawn: between major and minor coercion, between persuasion and coercion, between the permissible and the impermissible matters.[21] But one wonders how, in our decentralized and unorganized international order, such subtle and complicated rules can be effectively interpreted and if, *mirabile dictu*, such interpretation is achieved in a particular case, how the rules are to be enforced. Who

[20] Whitton, *La Règle "Pacta Sunt Servanda,"* 49 RECUEIL DES COURS, 151 (1935).
[21] MURTY, supra note 5, at *passim.*

will enforce sanctions? *Quis custodiet ipsos Custodes?* Finally, it seems clear that given the primitive character of our international community, the enforcement of these rules must rest on very precarious bases. Enforcement can be achieved only if the victim of the aggression happens to win the war and has sufficient strength and willpower left at the end of the conflict to institute the required administrative and judicial proceedings, as was done at Nuremburg and in Tokyo. Perhaps a plan for a war-crimes tribunal, available for use in future wars, including a system of rules of substance and procedure, with a method for the choice of judges could be worked out in detail by the United Nations.

That the dangerous character of hostile propaganda among the nations has been generally recognized and its aggressive nature understood is demonstrated by the number and persistence of the efforts to condemn and outlaw its use.

In this century, the work of the two great international organizations, the League of Nations and the United Nations, is most significant. Early in its history the League became cognizant of the problem. In May, 1931, the League Assembly took official notice of the matter when it came to consider the Preliminary Draft of the General Convention to Improve the Means of Preventing War, which declared "there are circumstances in which aggressive propaganda against a foreign power may take such offensive forms, and assume such a threatening character as to constitute a real danger to peace."[22] Also, in 1932, the Legal Committee of the abortive Conference for the Reduction and Limitation of Armaments strongly recommended the prohibition of war propaganda, but this proposal was opposed by a majority of the delegates, including those from Britain and the United States.[23] The most notable accomplishment in this period was the adoption of the Convention Concerning the Use of Broadcasting in the Cause of Peace, one of whose articles bound the parties "to insure that their transmissions do not constitute an incitement to war, or to acts likely to lead to war."[24] This treaty was ratified by a few states and is still in force, although never utilized.

Similar efforts have been witnessed since the founding of the United Nations, and the antiwarmongering resolution passed by the General Assembly in 1947 is particularly noteworthy. It reads in part:

> The General Assembly . . . (1) condemns all forms of propaganda, in whatever country conducted, which is either designed or likely to produce or encourage any threat to the peace, breach of the peace, or act of aggression.[25]

[22] L.O.N., VII *Political*, Doc. A.14.1931.VII.8 at 32, 43 (1931).
[23] *Supra* note 18. 1–4, at 702.
[24] 32 A.J.I.L., 113 (1938).
[25] G.A. Res. 110(II).

Also, the United Nations Conference on Freedom of Information and of the Press listed in 1948 as one of its basic objectives "to combat forces which incite to war, by removing bellicose influences from media of information." And Resolution 2, adopted at the Conference by an overwhelming majority:

> Condemns solemnly all propaganda either designed or likely to provoke or encourage any threat to the peace, breach of the peace, or act of aggression, and all distortions or falsification of news through whatever channels, private or governmental, since such activities can only promote misunderstanding and mistrust between the peoples of the world and thereby endanger the lasting peace which the United Nations is consecrated to maintain.[26]

The General Assembly passed another resolution against propaganda for war in 1950, reaffirming the earlier action and condemning all propaganda against peace, including incitement to conflicts or acts of aggression.[27] Also, in October 1961, the Third Committee of the General Assembly adopted articles 19–26 of the International Covenant on Civil and Political Rights, of which article 20(1) obligates the parties to prohibit all war propaganda as well as "any advocacy of national, racial, or religious hatred that constitutes incitement to discrimination, hostility, or violence."[28]

These resolutions are admirable in tone and content, although replete with problems of definition if their application ever came before a court or international agency. Most of the texts amount merely to condemnation of evils and exhortation to good conduct, and while the above-mentioned Covenant has teeth in it, since it obligates the states concerned to *prohibit* certain types of propaganda, it has yet to be adopted by the General Assembly, with actual ratifications far in the distance. Nevertheless, here is ample evidence of the deep concern of the international community with respect to the dangers of hostile international communication.

A major obstacle to progress here is the inability of states such as the Soviet Union and the United States to find a compromise between their individual positions that would be both acceptable to the respective decision-makers and be at the same time of some practical utility. This impasse still exists, although in 1962 it seemed for a moment that the two parties with their adherents had found a *terrain d'entente*. At the Conference of the Eighteen Nation Committee on Disarmament, the Committee of the Whole Conference adopted unanimously a declaration of considerable significance. Recalling the early resolution of the General

---

[26] Whitton, *United Nations Conference on Freedom of Information and the Movement Against International Propaganda*, 43 A.J.I.L. 73–87 (1949).

[27] YEARBOOK OF THE UNITED NATIONS, 1951, at 203–204.

[28] 16 U.N. GAOR, 3d comm. (1961).

Assembly condemning war propaganda, it called on all states "to adopt, within the limits of their constitutional system, appropriate practical measures, including measures in a legislative form in the case of states which consider such form appropriate, with a view to giving effect to this declaration against war propaganda." But when the declaration came before the plenary session, the Soviet delegate introduced an amendment of such character as to bring about its immediate rejection by the West. The Soviet amendment called on the parties to enact legislation declaring war propaganda "in any form a grave crime against peace and humanity and providing for severe penalties against persons guilty of conducting such propaganda, including their immediate removal from all official posts, the loss of all ranks and titles and their criminal prosecution." Another article in the Soviet amendment was the proposed condemnation of incitement to the use of force against peoples which have embarked on the course of national liberation and independent development as "at variance with the United Nations Declaration on granting of independence to colonial countries and peoples."[29] The reaction to such proposals among the delegates of Western nations can be easily imagined. Thereafter all discussion of war propaganda disappeared from the deliberations.

But even if, without the Soviet amendment, the original resolution had been adopted, it would have been a long road indeed to its effective implementation. If a treaty conceived in these terms had been submitted to the U.S. Senate, given the attitude of that body toward the Genocide Convention and the Connally Amendment, its prompt ratification by the United States could hardly be anticipated. This pessimistic view is borne out by the attitude of the U.S. representative in 1966 before the United Nations General Assembly Special Committee on Principles of International Law Concerning Friendly Relations and Cooperation among States. The United States voted against a Czechoslovakian proposal, which read as follows:

> Any propaganda for war, incitement to or fomenting of war and any propaganda for preventive war and for striking the first nuclear blow shall be prohibited. States shall take, within the framework of their jurisdiction, all measures, in particular legislative measures, in order to prevent such propaganda.

Besides the United States, the United Kingdom and other Western states strongly opposed this draft.[30]

Despite the failure of the United Nation members to agree on an exact formula to condemn and punish propaganda for war, there is evidence,

[29] MURTY, *supra* note 5, at 235–37.
[30] *Id.* at 237–38.

in this persistent effort to eliminate this kind of hostile conduct by nations, of a clear understanding of its aggressive character and a continued hope that it may be eliminated or at least controlled.

That propaganda for war should be encompassed within the definition of aggression is suggested by another line of thought. If a particular resort to force (within certain exceptions now generally recognized) is definitely held to be aggression, then propaganda in favor of such acts of force must also be interpreted as aggression. This follows from the rules and principles of incitement. This concept is found in all systems of law. It is in force in the domestic law of all nations, and thus applies to the present situation under the familiar definition of sources of international law, general principles of law, as set forth in the statute of the International Court of Justice. Thus under the common law system:

> Solicitation is a distinct common law misdemeanor in which the act forbidden consists of the accused person's oral or written efforts to activate another to commit a criminal offense.[31]

The gist of the offense is the incitement factor which is defined in contemporary American criminal law as: "When a person commands, encourages, or requests another to commit an offense with the intent that said offense be committed."[31a]

In some states the instigator of such acts is held as an accomplice. This is true under the Soviet system.[32] In Germany, as an example of the civil law, a person who intentionally induces another by threats, gifts, abuse of authority, trickery, or any other means to commit a crime is punishable as an instigator.[33] Incitement to commit a crime is likewise punishable under other European penal codes, *e.g.*, those of Belgium, the Netherlands, and France.[34] Thus, as a leading authority on the international law of propaganda has put it:

> In order effectively to control the use of transnational violence, punishment should extend not only to actual use of the military instrument but also to all acts done with the intention of promoting, and capable of contributing substantially to the success of, the military strategy of aggression.[35]

The illegality of propaganda for war and its qualification as aggression rests on even firmer ground. The great war-crimes tribunals set up after World War II have authoritatively established that aggressive war is a crime against the law of nations, and punishable with the severest pen-

---

[31] CLARK & MARSHALL, LAW OF CRIMES, 194 (6th ed. 1958).
[31a] BASSIOUNI, CRIMINAL LAW AND ITS PROCESSES, 169 (1969).
[32] WHITTON-LARSON, at 73.
[33] GERMAN PENAL CODE, § 48.
[34] WHITTON-LARSON, at 73.
[35] MURTY, *supra* note 5, at 151.

alties, and have included incitement to such war as part and parcel of the principal crime. These trials stand as a clear demonstration that propaganda for war has been outlawed. Murty, after an exhaustive analysis of the war crimes trials at Nuremberg and Tokyo, concludes that the use of the ideological instrument to further the preparation and waging of aggressive warfare will be held illegal in the future. In his words:

> A person who, having power to shape or influence the policies of his state, plans or conspires to use a strategy of violence for purposes of aggression, or joins such conspiracy, and participates in the operation of ideological strategy— whether to make the necessary psychological preparations at home, or to undermine the will to resist of the people of the state which is intended to be or is actually the victim—will be held guilty of a crime against peace.[36]

(The author adds the caveat that the use of such instrument remains permissible to promote a strategy of self-defense carried out even by means of violence.)

2.3.1. SUBVERSIVE PROPAGANDA AS AGGRESSION. Subversive propaganda may not be as blatant and as obviously dangerous as the rarer category of propaganda for war, but it has proved to be a greater menace to the peace than any manifestation of ideological coercion among the nations. One reason for this today is the impassioned conviction of the governing elites in many new or transformed nations that they have a right to campaign against what they conceive to be wrongs in other countries. Referring to these elites, one writer states: "They further assume the necessity and rectitude of preserving their own systems and of advancing their political interests and ideological causes through the use of the ideological instrument, their strongest instrument of foreign policy."[37]

The objective of such efforts is ordinarily to create and intensify violence within the target country, stir up domestic strife, set class against class, turn the people against their government, and if possible overthrow the existing regime. Subversive propaganda is found in four categories which may, however, overlap to a greater or lesser degree.

2.3.2.1. *Ordinary Subversive Propaganda.* Here the objective of the communicator is to weaken the target country in order to achieve some special objective in the field of power politics. By causing disruption within the victim country, especially by threatening the downfall of the existing regime, the communicator may hope to obtain some concession, or perhaps weaken the nation in some other way to serve the sender's national interest. Sometimes a campaign of subversion may be launched in retaliation, as in the case of the mutual radio attacks between Santo Domingo

---

[36] *Id.*
[37] O'Brien, *supra* note 16, at 598.

and Haiti in 1950, finally settled by the Organization of American States.[38]
Another instance of this type of propaganda is furnished by the Baghdad
radio appeal of July 20, 1958, directed to the people of Jordan, reported
as follows:

> Revolt against the tyrant and imperialist agent, the traitor and grandson of a
> traitor! Revolt against the criminal who desecrated our soil! Revolt against
> the puppet of the British and Zionism and break the shackles with which you
> were fettered by the man king. Revolt, as your fathers and forefathers did be-
> fore you, against the oppressors and tyrants.[39]

2.3.2.2. Irredentist Propaganda. This term is derived from the word
"irredentist," referring to a member of an Italian association prominent
in 1878 for its struggle for the "redemption," or incorporation into Italy,
of certain neighboring territories. Cavour's military campaign, buttressed
by impassioned patriotic appeals, finally brought about the unification
of Italy. The most famous of all irredentist movements was that carried
out by Serbia in Bosnia and Herzegovina, leading to the outbreak of
World War I. Similar campaigns were launched by the Nazis in the
Sudetenland, Czechoslovakia, and by the Italians in Southern Tyrol before
World War I.

2.3.2.3. Revolutionary Propaganda. The ideological warfare may aim not
only to overthrow a given regime but also to substitute therefor a new
way of life, a new philosophy of government, and a political, economic,
and social system espoused by the communicator. Thus the French Revolutionaries strove to spread their doctrines throughout Europe.[40] The
propaganda of the Soviets from the beginning, and later that of the
Chinese Communists, is similar. Notable is the Bucharest Declaration
issued in 1960 by the International Communist Conference. Although
couched in terms of peaceful coexistence, this declaration contains a
directive to Communist leaders throughout the world to work for the
violent overthrow of any government in appropriate and feasible cases.[41]
Castro has carried on active ideological warfare of a revolutionary-
subversive character in many Latin American states.

2.3.2.4. Liberation Subversion. (This kind of coercion may be part and
parcel of a revolutionary movement, but not necessarily.) Its nature and
purpose were well described by Von Glahn as follows:

> "Liberation" propaganda has as its object the arousal and abetment of tend-

---

[38] ANNALS OAS 134, 217–219, 326 (1949).
[39] *Id.* at 90.
[40] C. BRINTON, A DECADE OF REVOLUTION 1789–1799, at 186–89 (1934); WHITTON-
LARSON, at 16.
[41] N.Y. Times, June 28, 1960, at 12; *id.,* June 29, at 32.

encies toward an outbreak of revolutionary violence in another country. The purpose of such violence may be assumed to be the creation of radical domestic changes, such as a termination of colonial status, the elimination of legal racism, the ending of "neo-colonialism," or simply the replacement of one governing elite by another. Liberation propaganda is thus connected most intimately with the manifest inability of the existing world community to legislate peaceful change. Since ruling elites in many instances are opposed to the coming of such change, a situation is created in which outside assistance appears to be necessary or desirable to effect the change. Again, since what might be termed rebellion of the mind must precede rebellion by arms, liberation propaganda occupies a vital position in the forcible production of domestic change.[42]

Evidence of the existence of a binding rule of international law proscribing the use by governmental elites of subversive propaganda is derived from an analysis of diplomatic practice going back as far as the French Revolution. On numerous occasions the use of such ideological warfare has been the object of strong protests on the part of the target state. In such cases the communicator, in answer to protests on the part of the aggrieved state, has resorted to various defenses: denial of the basis for the charge, non-responsibility for the particular communication, lack of means to suppress such acts, pleas of self-defense against abuses by the other side, etc., but for us the important point is the absence of any denial by the parties that the rule of law exists. Thus the essential *convictio juris* required for the creation of a rule through "custom" appears to have been established.

During the French Revolution the new regime tried, in official decrees and by means of the press, as well as through the dispatch of its agents or "missionaries" throughout Europe, to engender revolt and bring about the substitution of the new order for the existing monarchies. From the vigor, universality and consistency of the resulting reaction it is clear that such conduct by France was considered generally not only dangerous but also illegal. The French Government—under severe pressure, it is true—was induced to withdraw its offending decrees and to bind itself by formal promises not to interfere further in the internal affairs of other states.[43] In the many diplomatic exchanges of the period we find repeated assertions, never denied, that the conduct of the French Government and its agents was an infraction of accepted principles and norms of the law of nations. Pitt, for instance, declared that the French disclaimer against any intent to stir up an insurrection in foreign countries was made "upon the express ground (stated in the paper) that such

---

[42] G. von Glahn, in Symposium 553 (1966).
[43] Brinton, *supra* note 40, at 186–89.

interference, and such attempts, would be a violation of the law of nations."[44]

In 1816, when a dispute arose between Turkey and Russia because the Tsar was fomenting an uprising of Christians in the Balkans, all sides finally paid homage to the rule of law forbidding such intrigues.[45] The widespread protests against propaganda sent from France during their 1830 revolution led to such vigorous protests that the French Government felt obliged to declare that it would do nothing of a character to disturb the domestic peace of nations. All parties appear to have accepted the view that the French disavowal, as well its subsequent repression of subversive maneuvers on or from French soil, were in conformity with accepted rules of law.[46] And during the half century preceding the Balkan Wars, when many powers were striving to undermine the authority of the Ottoman Empire, as the underground activity came to light it was considered prudent to deny the charges and disavow the agents. There was never any question about the existence of a legal proscription against such activities.[47] Also, in the exchange of notes after Sarajevo and the answer to the Austrian ultimatum, Serbia agreed to a number of extreme measures to suppress subversive propaganda. One finds in the exchange of notes between the parties as well as in their general conduct, a clear acceptance of the view that no nation is legally permitted to indulge in propaganda hostile to the very existence of a friendly government.[48]

Between the two world wars there were many protests against Soviet propaganda throughout the world. For instance, the United States withheld recognition of the Soviet government for many years in part because of the latter's alleged subversive activity, Washington claiming "that the Soviet Government had failed to respect the right of this nation to maintain its own political and social order without interference by organizations conducting in or from Soviet territories activities directed against our institutions."[49] (This attitude was in accord with an early precedent; President Jackson, referring to Mexico, which had protested against alleged American intrigues, declared that "any act on the part of the government of the United States, which would tend to foster a spirit of resistance to her government and laws, whatever may be the character or form . . . would be unauthorized and highly improper.")[50] Many

---

[44] WHITTON-LARSON, at 97.

[45] WHITTON-LARSON, at 85–86, 98.

[46] Van Dyke, *The Responsibility of States for International Propaganda*, 34 A.J.I.L. 62 (1940).

[47] *Id* at 64.

[48] S. FAY, THE ORIGINS OF THE [FIRST] WORLD WAR, ch. VII (2d ed. 1931).

[49] (Note) *Concerning a Russian Pledge*, 29 A.J.I.L. 656 (1935).

[50] United States, *Executive Documents*, 1836–1837, vol. 1, doc. 2, at 60.

other governments have protested against Soviet incitements and agitations for revolt, and in answer to such protests, Moscow has never denied the existence of the rule in question. Even Hitler, who also was the object of strong reactions against his use of subversion, never denied the validity of the rule upon which the victim states based their protests, although his advisors, like those of Moscow, were never at a loss to find legal defenses for such actions.

Further evidence of the strength and persistence of the norm in question, and of the general belief in its validity in the world today, is found in the deliberations of various organs of the United Nations. As evidence of the existence of a rule, based on custom, under which subversive propaganda is held to be a violation of the law of nations, we may refer to the numerous projects, resolutions, and conventions (the last mainly projected, but a few actually ratified) that have been directed against such practices by various organs of the United Nations, from special commissions to the General Assembly itself.[51] Underlying all these efforts there appears to be a clear conception of the dangerous character of incitements to revolt, and a general recognition of their illegality.

Thus in 1947, the General Assembly resolved unanimously to condemn all propaganda "either designed or likely to provoke or encourage any threat to the peace, breach of the peace, or act of aggression."[52] While broad enough to include both warmongering and subversive propaganda, this formula is obviously too vague to lend itself to practical application. Another imprecise formulation pertinent to the matter of subversion is that found in article 22 of the 1948 Draft Declaration of the Rights and Duties of States, voted by the International Law Commission. It concerns the responsibility of a state with relation to the use of its territory in actual preparation for subversive actions abroad. It would clearly entail extremely broad duties for any state. Investing the state with indirect responsibility for subversion in another country, it reads as follows:

> It is the duty of every state to assure that, within its territory, no activities are organized for the purpose of fomenting civil strife within the territory of another state.[53]

In 1949, by a vote of 53 to 5, the General Assembly passed a resolution of a quite different character, since the wrongful act envisaged is actual participation of a state in transnational subversive acts. It calls on all nations "to refrain from any threats or acts, direct or indirect, aimed at impairing the freedom, independence, or integrity of any state, or at fo-

[51] WHITTON-LARSON, at 99.
[52] YEARBOOK OF THE UNITED NATIONS, 1947–1948, at 91–93, res. 110 (II).
[53] A/CN.4/2, Dec. 15, 1948, at 123.

menting civil strife and subverting the will of the people of any state."[54]
The responsibility here is direct rather than indirect. While difficult to
apply to borderline cases, this norm would certainly outlaw such acts as
Hitler's irredentist appeals to both the Sarrois and the Sudetenland. The
principles underlying the last two formulations are combined in the 1952
Draft Code of Offenses Against the Peace and Security of Mankind. It
proscribes:

> The undertaking or encouragement by the authorities of a state of activities
> calculated to foment civil strife in another state, or the toleration by the au-
> thorities of a state of organized activities calculated to foment civil strife in
> another state.[55]

Here the responsibility of the governing elite is both direct and indirect.
Another significant article in this projected code condemns "conspiracy,
direct incitement, complicity, or any attempt to commit any of the offenses defined in the preceding paragraphs of this article." This text has
been severely criticized in U.N. debates and elsewhere as a vain attempt
to impose sweeping prohibitions on most any type of interference in the
internal affairs of a state and as an unreasonable extension of accepted
rules of nonintervention.

Another significant resolution along similar lines is the General Assembly's Peace Through Deeds Resolutions, (1950), recognizing that
"fomenting of civil strife in the interests of a foreign power" might under
certain conditions fall into the general category of "aggression."[56] Also,
more recently, the General Assembly voted 109 to 0, with one abstention,
a resolution condemning all forms of intervention in any state, and this
included subversion and terrorism. Particularly important for our purposes was the statement that no country was to "organize, assist, foment,
finance, incite or tolerate subversive, terrorist, or armed activities directed
towards the violent overthrow of the regime of another state, or interfere
in civil strife in another state."[57]

These prolonged and at times impassioned U.N. debates involving so
many diplomats and international lawyers reflect the deep concern felt
in the international community with respect to subversive mass communications and a clear recognition of the latter as a serious menace to world
peace. These U.N. efforts constitute a serious, although thus far unsuccessful, attempt to place the authority of the world organization behind
rules designed to meet these dangers. In making this effort, the experts
have been on firm ground, able to rely as they are on strong authority,

---

[54] YEARBOOK OF THE UNITED NATIONS, 1950, at 344, res. 290 (IV).
[55] *Id.* at 842 (1952).
[56] Res. 380 (V), Nov. 17, 1950; MURTY, *supra* note 5, at 164–65.
[57] 60 A.J.I.L. 650 (1966).

some of it of ancient origin. We refer here not only to the long series of precedents in the field of customary international law, just mentioned, but also to the gamut of obligations set forth in bilateral treaties, and even a few multilateral treaties. Numerous accords designed to curb subversive propaganda or prohibit its use have been contracted in the past. Some date from the period of the French Revolution and the subsequent Napoleonic epoch. Other accords of this nature are scattered throughout the nineteenth century, *e.g.*, the treaty between Serbia and Austria-Hungary in 1881, renewed in 1889.[58] As early as March 1918, in the ill-fated peace treaty of Brest-Litovsk, Soviet Russia and the Central Powers agreed to refrain from official propaganda.[59] After World War I, Soviet Russia entered into over a score of treaties with Britain, France, and the United States and other states promising to refrain from subversive communications. The treaty with the United States known as the Roosevelt-Litvinov accord, contained in an exchange of notes on the occasion of the recognition of Russia, is one of the most sweeping of these treaties. It obligates the USSR and the United States to refrain from carrying on propaganda as specified in the agreement and to restrain in this matter all persons in governmental service, all governmental organizations, and all organizations under governmental control, including those receiving financial assistance from government.[60]

One early postwar treaty was that signed in 1923 between Spain, France, and Britain with respect to Tangier, notably article 10, which states: "Any agitation, propaganda or conspiracy against the established order in the French or Spanish zone of Morocco is forbidden from the zone of Tangier. Similar agitation against any foreign state is also forbidden."[61] Several Pan American conventions include similar provisions. Thus, in article 16 of the 1948 Bogota Charter of the Organization of American States, it is stated that "No state may use or encourage the use of coercive measures of an economic or political character in order to force the sovereign will of another state and obtain from it advantages of any kind."[62] Under this charter, propaganda could be considered an act of aggression against all American states. Also, at the Caracas Conference of American States held in 1954, a Declaration of Solidarity was approved condemning the activities of the international Communist movement as constituting intervention in American affairs. It expressed the determination of American states to take the necessary measures to protect their

[58] A.F. PRIBRAM, THE SECRET TREATIES OF AUSTRIA-HUNGARY 51, 137, (1920).

[59] L. SHAPIRO, ed., I SOVIET TREATY SERIES, 1917–1928, at 4 (1950).

[60] *Supra note* 49. These accords have been summarized by Martin, *supra* note 15, at ch. 5.

[61] de Martens, 13, NOUVEAU RECUEIL GÉNÉRAL DE TRAITÉS 246, 249 (1925).

[62] Pan-American Union, *Law and Treaty Series No. 23,* CHARTER OF THE OAS 26–27 (1948).

political independence against such intervention and declared that the
domination of the political institutions of any American state by the Communist movement would constitute a threat to the sovereignty and political independence of all American states.[63]

Nor should it be forgotten that the provisions of the U.N. Charter may
be invoked to deal with the use of subversive propaganda between nations. Such activities would constitute a violation of the agreement of
the signatories of the Charter to live together in peace as good neighbors,
if as we maintain, propaganda is considered a type of aggression and is
thus outlawed under Charter articles concerned with aggressive war.

These accords, especially those of which Moscow probably was a reluctant party, have been widely violated. On the other hand, they have often
been cited as law by states' victims of hostile ideological warfare, and the
validity of the rules of law they represent have never been denied. Thus
they are always available in appropriate cases of abuse of the airwaves
or in the press, to be utilized by the aggrieved target state or by the
United Nations if dealing with cases of dangerous use of propaganda.

It seems clear, from the foregoing analysis, that the illegality of subversive ideological warfare is proscribed by the existing law of nations.
It is illegal, but can it also be classed as "aggression"? The question is
important: if the governing elite of a given state can be proven to be
guilty of a clear attempt through propaganda to overthrow a "friendly"
foreign regime in time of peace, and the United Nations should declare
this to be equivalent to aggression, that body would be authorized to
deal with it under the Charter with the same authority as if it were actually a case of illegal war. Also, the victim of such attacks, the target state,
would be justified under certain circumstances in retaliating by resorting
itself (within strict limits) to propaganda otherwise illegal and even to
the legal employment of force to silence the offender. Also, if it is a case
of offensive radio propaganda, the target state would be justified if it
resorted to jamming in self-defense. The rights and duties of the parties
in case of aggression are dealt with in other chapters of the present work.

It is highly significant for our purposes that there have been many efforts, official and nonofficial, to include subversion within the accepted
definition of aggression, still under study by the United Nations. The
first debate along these lines was initiated in 1953, when the Soviet Union
proposed that the term "aggression" should be drafted so as to include
within its purview the encouragement of war propaganda, propaganda in
favor of the use of weapons of mass destruction, and the propagation of

---

[63] 10th Inter-American Conference, Caracas, 1954, *Report of the U.S. Delegation* (Dept.
of State Publ. 5692), 9, 156 (1955).

racial and national exclusiveness, hatred and contempt of other peoples and Fascist-Nazi views.[64] This proposal was attacked as incomplete on the one hand and, on the other, as too sweeping. It was also disparaged as a mere example of Soviet propaganda. A more limited and more realistic proposal was that introduced by the Chinese delegation; it would have defined incitement from abroad to civil strife as a type of aggression.[65] Subsequent efforts along these lines have been concerned mainly with subversive propaganda, also referred to as "indirect aggression," "liberation propaganda," and "ideological warfare." Thus in the Peace Through Deeds Resolution of the General Assembly (1950), we note a recognition that "fomenting of civil strife in the interests of a foreign power" is a pattern of aggression.[66] And in the Draft Code of Offenses Against the Peace and Security of Mankind (1952), article 2(5) characterizes "activities calculated to foment civil strife in another state" as a crime against the peace and the security of mankind.[67] The extended debates on this subject within the walls of the United Nations have been carefully analyzed by Pompe, Julius Stone, and others. Thus far the effort to define aggression has failed.[67a] O'Brien explains this failure as follows:

> Efforts at more systematic and generally acceptable definitions of aggression, have, notoriously, been thwarted by, among other things, ideological and political differences and the reluctance of states to agree in advance to definitions of aggression which might restrict them inordinately to the detriment of their vital interests.[68]

In our view, subversive propaganda, when it occurs with sufficient intensity, should be considered to be aggression and treated as such. We are concerned here with a type of illegal intervention which, as we have already emphasized, can be not only a mortal menace to the regime under attack, but also a grave danger to world peace. For as Von Glahn has said, "It seeks to dissolve the basic cement of loyalty that binds a citizen to his government and to his community."[69] The gravity of such antisocial acts, directly and indirectly in conflict with the most sacred right of sovereign independence, has been stressed by Quincy Wright, arguing that "civil warmongering" must be prohibited because ideological incitement and provocation are calculated to cause the target state to respond

[64] MURTY, *supra* note 5, at 160.
[65] *Id.* at 162–63.
[66] *Supra* note 56.
[67] *Yearbook of the United Nations, 1952,* at 842; International Law Comm. Report 7 U.N. GAOR, U.N. Doc. A/2693 (1954).
[67a] C. POMPE, AGGRESSIVE WAR: AN INTERNATIONAL CRIME (1953); J. STONE, AGGRESSION AND WORLD ORDER (1958).
[68] *Id.* at 591.
[69] *Id.* at 554.

by resorting to force in an effort to silence the offender. He also points out that a subversive campaign against a particular regime might so weaken it as to tempt a third state to commit an aggression against it.[70] The determination of an aggressor in such cases may be extremely difficult, even if the Security Council succeeded in reaching an agreed determination in the case. Of course, the coercion must be of a certain degree of gravity; minor coercion could be disregarded. Murty has offered valuable suggestions as to the delimination of major and minor coercion. This, he writes, would require a careful consideration of all the basic factors.

> In reference to any situation, the expected outcome is to be ascertained . . . by reference to the participants, the audience, the objectives, the characteristics of the situation, the base values at the disposal of those operating the strategy, and the various strategies employed. And community regulation must vary according to whether the expected outcome is major or minor coercion, and whether it is permissible or impermissible coercion.[71]

The major element in this determination is the degree of danger caused the target state in the actual circumstances of the case. Some, drawing on American constitutional law, would invoke here the doctrine of clear and present danger.[72] But this doctrine, which provides no easy criterion for deciding domestic disputes over freedom of speech, would be faced with immense difficulties when applied in the international field where its interpretation and application are in the hands of the most elementary legislative and judicial agencies. But the same weaknesses obtain when the case is one of direct aggression involving the crime of aggressive war; these rules were nevertheless effectively interpreted and inforced at Nuremberg, Tokyo, and other postwar trials. Luckily for the world, however, the aggressor was defeated in that war. (Otherwise, little would have been heard of postwar trials for aggressive war and one of its elements, ideological aggression.)

From earliest times, verbal and written attacks by one individual against another have been strongly resented by the victim, resulting quite commonly in physical violence and death. Hence in all social groups the community finds it imperative to initiate measures to prevent such conflicts and when they occur, to make provision for appropriate sanctions. The first step comes when the head of the tribe forbids dueling. Then, as the community matures, the equivalent of modern laws of libel and slander evolve. The duel is ultimately abolished by law and in its stead the aggrieved is enabled to sue for damages, or to set in motion certain

---

[70] Q. Wright, *The Crime of "War Mongering,"* 42 A.J.I.L. 128–136 (1948).

[71] Murty, *supra* note 5, at 220 *passim.*

[72] *Supra* note 70.

criminal procedures against the offender. Finally there emerge in advanced civilizations sophisticated remedies such as the action for group libel and even, in some states, a right of reply. All these remedies have as their basic *raison d'être* not so much the protection of the individual as the elementary need to safeguard society, by preventing intolerable and costly breaches of the peace.

In the international community similar imperatives have motivated the many efforts, already outlined in this chapter, to protect both the individual state and the international community from the consequences of libel, slander, false news, verbal attacks on state leaders, and incitements to assassination, terrorism, and revolt.

These efforts are a development of the twentieth century, especially during the period following World War I. But only in the last twenty years have publicists begun to devote much attention to these problems. These writers have not only described and decried the evils of hostile international communications, they have also stressed those rules and principles already available and have proposed preventive and remedial measures whereby the attendant evils and dangers might be attenuated.[73]

On the following pages we shall briefly analyze these "remedies" and offer certain criticisms, both favorable and unfavorable. In a community such as the world of nations, the only available "legislation" (to use that term loosely) has come through the treaty-making process. What are the chances for real progress today through this method, for which there are, as we have seen, numerous models and precedents?

2.4. Remedies for Propaganda

2.4.1. TREATY LAW. Past experience with general treaties to control hostile international communications is not encouraging. Unfortunately, there appears to be little chance for widespread acceptance at present of such a convention. Free states veer away from the very prohibitions that are the most essential, for fear of their possible incursions on freedom of speech and of the press. Also, agreement between free states and closed states is difficult because they are not in a position of equality. The free states lack effective methods of controlling their press and radio, while in closed states the press *is* the state. This means that hostile propaganda originating in the closed state ipso facto entails the responsibility of the governing elite, while in a free state whose press or radio is accused of violation of accepted precepts in this field, the government may deny responsibility by invoking well-known doctrines of the irresponsibility of states for the acts of private persons. Difficult and delicate problems of

---

[73] For bibliography, see WHITTON-LARSON, at 277–94.

responsibility arise when the state possesses a degree of control over the media through a process of licensing and subventioning. These problems cannot be dealt with here. When the Soviet Union accepted treaty proscriptions against propaganda, it contrived to incite foreign peoples to revolt through propaganda by political parties falsely alleged to be independent, a transparent pretext which has fooled no one.

Although many drafts and models of ideal treaties are available, the result of years of effort by leading scholars and learned commissions, there is a general feeling that chances for success in this direction today are small indeed. In his remarkable report as United Nations Rapporteur on Freedom of Information, Mr. Salvador P. Lopez concluded in 1953, "It is not feasible, for the present at least, to seek the outright prohibition and suppression of hostile propaganda and of false or distorted information by means of international legislation." He added, "It would be unrealistic at the present time to attempt to draw up a convention which would bind individual states to introduce legislation aimed at the suppression of objectionable reports."[74]

It is a familiar observation about treaties that the larger the number of nations participating, the more diluted the content of the treaty is apt to be. Since the object of a multilateral treaty is to attain the signatures of all the participants, the attempt to satisfy everyone tends to drive the content of the treaty to the lowest common denominator. On the other hand, the influence of a draft treaty, or of a general treaty even with few adherents, may be considerable. This has been true of the notable 1936 treaty governing communications by radio. Although ratified by only a handful of states and never applied, it stands as a model, a kind of authoritative code of good conduct, which can be invoked by victims of slander and other attacks over the airwaves. Hence its historical significance and moral influence should not be underestimated. Von Glahn argues that this treaty should be renegotiated to cover subversive propaganda, with amendments and additions to remedy certain gaps and deficiencies. Although, as he admits, a number of states, including those of the Communist Bloc, would eschew such a convention, if a sizable number of states should adhere, its effects, he maintains, would be substantial. It would put all states on notice that subversion is a violation of the law of nations and that retaliation or reparation, or both, would be legitimate. It would, he claims, reinforce in the most authoritative way the principle of nonintervention in a vital area.[75] It seems true, also, that a treaty banning propaganda for war, even if binding on a small number of states,

---

[74] Lopez, *Freedom of Information,* 16 U.N. ECOSOC, Supp. 12, at 15, U.N. Doc. E/2426 (1953).

[75] Von Glahn, in Symposium at 579.

would be useful for its moral influence generally and at the end of an aggressive war to which the propaganda had contributed would be available as an authority for a war-crimes tribunal.

A major reason for the failure of general treaties in this field, we believe, is that too much has been attempted. The scope of the planned proscriptions has been too broad. The proposed restrictions have purported to encompass both governmental and private media. The inclusion in the treaty of the private, nongovernmental press and radio delights the closed states but frightens off the free states whose decision-makers fear the restrictions on free speech and free press that such a treaty would entail. It would be more realistic to limit the prohibitions of international libel and slander to government communication. Here the restrictions and curbs would not ordinarily involve freedom of the press, as they purport to limit the speech of governments, not individuals. And there is also a more important consideration, namely, that in the vast majority of disputes over hostile communications, it is the government itself that is responsible. In the French Revolution, it was the new governing elite that was attempting to incite all Europe to revolt. As for the Russian Revolution, the offender has been Radio Moscow, the official government voice.

In modern times Goebbels, "Lord Haw-Haw," Radio Cairo, all represented the governing elite. And when the United States has been accused by Moscow of subversive tactics by radio, it is not the Columbia Broadcasting System or the American Broadcasting Company that is the target of complaints, but the Voice of America. (Just recently the United States Government has admitted that for many years Radio Free Europe and Radio Liberty, long the object of protests from Moscow have been secretly subventioned by the CIA.[75a]) In short, the cases of aggressive international propaganda, whether warmongering or subversive, which have created the greatest dangers in the past have been organized, subventioned, and implemented by governments and governmental agencies.

It may be added that a general treaty limited to the states of the same region, for instance the states of the American continent, or to regimes of a similar philosophy of government and way of life would have a greater chance of being accepted, and if ratified, to be effective in a crisis. An antipropaganda treaty for the Arab states, or encompassing free democracies everywhere, or regimes of Southeast Asia with similar forms of government, would have a reasonable chance for positive action in time of need. On the other hand, it must be admitted that many of the worst cases of hostile propaganda in the past have arisen between states of

[75a] N.Y. Times, Mar. 7 & 15, 1971.

different regions—also, between states of very different philosophies of government.

Some have advocated bilateral treaties designed to curb mutual attacks by press or radio. At first sight, this "remedy" does not appear to hold much promise. One immediately thinks of the scores of treaties signed by Soviet Russia between the wars, notably the Roosevelt-Litvinov accord, the *quid pro quo* for U.S. recognition of the new Russian regime, and the widespread violation and virtual desuetude of these agreements. Between friendly states, no such accord is necessary. If the two parties are in disaccord or on unfriendly terms, they cannot be expected to agree just then in such a delicate matter. At such a time their mutual verbal attacks may become more and more frequent and even violent, but once the matter of issue is settled, the propaganda usually ceases. At this juncture a non-propaganda accord may be accepted and even ratified, but in all likelihood it is no longer needed. It might still be useful, however, if the international situation, especially relations between the two parties concerned again became aggravated, for at such a time the existence of solemn obligations binding the parties to avoid false reports, hate propaganda, and verbal attacks on the high officials of the rival regime might have a moderating effect. Also, it could be cited by an aggrieved state presenting a diplomatic protest to the offender, or appealing to the United Nations and to world opinion in general.[76]

We believe that the best way to deal with a controversy over objectionable propaganda is through the regular machinery of the appropriate international organization. A promising example of this procedure is offered by the settlement of the dispute between two of its members by the Organization of American States.

In 1949, a dispute arose between the Republic of Santo Domingo and Haiti, the latter claiming to be the victim of "moral aggression." One of its former colonels, taking refuge in Santo Domingo, had made broadcasts of an "extremely vulgar and provocative nature offensive to the President of the Republic of Haiti," aimed at the overthrow of the Haitian

---

[76] The following general observation concerning treaties governing propaganda is pertinent at this point.

> One of the lessons that is being taught with increasing cogency by experience in international law is this: a treaty is apt to be no better than the administrative arrangements that are set up to see that it is carried out. The idea that nations can sign an agreement binding them to certain standards of conduct, and then simply go away and leave it in the expectation that the objectives of the treaty will automatically flow from the agreement, is increasingly coming into question. By contrast, the more successful treaties appear to be those which are accompanied by the creation of some kind of commission which has the full time responsibility of overseeing their execution, settling the disputes they engender and making recommendations on keeping the treaties up to date. An example of this kind of treaty is the agreement between Canada and the United States governing problems arising between the two countries along their common boundary—an agreement which was wisely accompanied by the creation of a mixed U.S.–Canadian Commission which continues to give the treaty everyday meaning. WHITTON–LARSON, at 231-232.

Government, thus constituting "moral aggression." After the matter had been submitted to the Council of Consultation of the Organization of American States, the two states settled the matter amicably, agreeing not to tolerate in their respective territories the activities of any individuals, groups, or parties, national or foreign, that had as their object the disturbance of the domestic peace of either of the two neighboring republics or of any other friendly nation. In April 1950, the OAS Council called upon the governments of "Haiti and the Dominican Republic to avoid any systematic and hostile propaganda against one another or against any American country."[77] The United Nations already has authority under its Charter to deal with such a situation, treating it as a threat to the peace, brought before the Security Council under article 36 or 39, or submitted to the General Assembly under article 10 or 14. Its competence and authority in such matters could be strengthened through several additional procedures, one of which is already in operation for a few states.[78] These are monitoring by the United Nations, the right of reply, and the extension of the U.N. broadcasting station.

2.4.2. MONITORING. President Eisenhower, referring to the evils of radio propaganda, created considerable interest in the potentialities of a monitoring system when he personally appeared before the U.N. Assembly in 1958 to make a notable proposal. He said as follows:

> I believe that this Assembly should reaffirm its enunciated policy and should consider means for monitoring the radio broadcasts directed across national frontiers in the troubled Near East area. It should then examine complaints from these nations which consider their national security jeopardized by external propaganda.[79]

The reasoning underlying this proposal is as follows: if an official agency of the world organization, monitoring the radio broadcasts of the world, discovers and records offensive messages, this would consitute the most authoritative evidence possible of breaches of international etiquette and even violations of generally accepted rules of international conduct. This evidence could be cited by victim states resentful of slander, for example, or fearing the possible consequences of subversive campaigns, and made a part of diplomatic protests presented to the offering government or cited before the appropriate organ of the United Nations. Also, the target state resorting to jamming and retaliation, or both, or other measures of self-help could thus rely on the best evidence to justify such actions on the ground of legitimate self-defense. Also, it is hoped that the knowledge

[77] WHITTON-LARSON, at 130.
[78] *Id.* pt. III.
[79] 7–10 U.N. GAOR, Plenary Meetings & Annexes (Emer. Sess. 3) (1958).

that its offensive communications may thus be exposed to world opinion and censure would have on any nation tempted to abuse the power of press and radio a healthy preventive or moderating influence. But the virtues of the Eisenhower monitoring proposal should not be exaggerated. Often there is really little secret about the misuse of the radio by aggressive governments; the virulent radio campaigns from Cairo or Havana are well known and often reported in foreign newspapers.[80] This publicity given ideological warfare seems to have little influence in preventing or curbing them even though the victim state already has the necessary evidence needed for diplomatic protests or an appeal to the United Nations or the OAS.

A realistic proposal for U.N. action in this field was that made by Salvador P. Lopez, Rapporteur on Freedom of Information for the Economic and Social Council. He said as follows:

> It would be useful, if with the cooperation of the profession, an annual survey were made of the general situation with regard to the dissemination of false or distorted information on international affairs. In cases where there is damage or harm to international understanding, an investigation might be made with a view to recommending corrective or disciplinary action. Cases requiring governmental action should, of course, be brought promptly to the attention of the Economic and Social Council. Where, moreover, the Council considers a report likely to provoke or encourage a breach of the peace or an act of aggression, it could "furnish information to the Security Council" under article 65 of the Charter.[81]

A somewhat similar suggestion was offered by Chester Bowles in an article on the African situation. As part of a comprehensive agreement to aid the new states of that continent, he proposed:

> A pledge by all nations to refrain from agitating propaganda within Africa to end all efforts at direct or indirect subversion. The United Nations could be authorized to investigate all charges of violation and to report to the General Assembly.[82]

2.4.3. RIGHT OF REPLY. Another "remedy" was proposed at the United Nations by the French representative, taking the form of a treaty later ratified by a few states. This is the Right of Reply, modeled after a similar remedy found in French domestic law and in a score of other countries, including some parts of the United States.[83] This provides detailed

---

[80] When Whitton and Larson were preparing their chapters on subversive propaganda, they had little difficulty in amassing a large dossier of examples of offensive communication of this kind, a number of which were reproduced in their final text.

[81] *Supra* note 79, at 19.

[82] Bowles, *Great Challenge to the U.N.–Africa*, N.Y. Times Magazine, Aug. 21, 1960, at 15, 108.

[83] I *Freedom of Information, supra* note 74, at 245–253; WHITTON-LARSON, at 187–194.

procedures whereby any party victim of a communication abroad claimed to be offensive may issue an official reply, stating its own version of the facts. The state in which the offensive message originated is required to publish the reply, but in case the latter fails to do so, publication is effected by the Secretary-General of the United Nations. The value of this proposal has been summarized as follows:

> The theoretical advantages of the right of reply have been generally supported by analogy from right of reply in domestic legislation, and indeed it is possible to make out a persuasive case for the appropriateness of this remedy as between nations. It is argued that the remedy is found, not in the attempt to punish the offender, but in the nature of the assistance rendered the victim, and that therefore the general interest—concern for peaceful international relations—is brought into harmony with the individual right of free expression. Thus, given general application, the right of correction could offer within the offending nation, including a dictatorship if it would accept such a remedy, an opportunity to an injured power to answer officially inspired campaigns against it or its leaders. And, on the other hand, it could give considerable satisfaction even to a dictatorship considering itself unjustly attacked by the free press in the democracies. This is particularly significant, since the governments of such free countries, because of constitutional guarantees of freedom of the press, have often found themselves unable to do more than express regrets—hardly a satisfactory remedy for the aggrieved government.[84]

While in principle the right of reply offers many advantages as a means of curbing harmful communications, as a practical matter it is beset with many difficulties. This is a delicate and complex procedure that has not always been effective even as domestic law. Whether in our international community, so weak in terms of organized and tried agencies for administrative and judicial procedures, it could be made to function effectively, could only be determined on the basis of practical experience. Thus far, ratified by only a few states, the treaty for a right of reply has become virtually a dead letter. One of its parties, however, could establish an invaluable precedent if, faced with some extreme charge of misconduct, for instance, or some false and scandalous story considered harmful to the national honor, it should invoke the treaty and demand the right to refute the accusation.

2.4.4. A NOTE ON THE LITERATURE. Before concluding this short examination of proposals for possible controls over objectionable international communication, it might be useful to review briefly the trends in the literature dealing with this subject. We may note an interesting analogy between such writing and the literature on the law of war. In the nineteenth century the jurists, positivists of the old school, were largely con-

[84] *Id.* at 192.

tent to present an exposé of the existing rules and principles concerning war and neutrality. It was only in the twentieth century that there developed the first extensive movement to prevent and outlaw war, defining aggression and proposing the necessary machinery for organized sanctions, through "remedies" designed to place the resort to organized force by nations under "the rule of law." Similarly, the first writing on transnational propaganda sought to assemble and analyze the rules and principles which already constituted an impressive body of theoretical controls through law. (Lauterpacht, Preuss, Van Dyke, Quincy Wright, Pella, and the present writer were among the first authors in this category.)[85] Then followed an invaluable work of documentation, assembling and classifying the precedents, covering both national and international administration, law, and practice, including diplomatic exchanges.[86] (L. John Martin; Terrou and Solal, compilations by United Nations.) This literature was enriched by further monographs, distinguished by a new trend, the proposal of so-called remedies, new treaties, laws, and administrative procedures.[87]

Many of the proposals for remedial procedures were presented before official U.N. commissions (on radio communication, on freedom of information, on bill of rights, the definition of aggression, or as part of efforts to draft treaties on these matters). Finally, in more recent studies, these "remedies" have been closely analyzed and subjected to criticism. These recent contributions have served to give us a more realistic understanding of the delicate problems faced by individuals, and by organizations, both world and national which are working for reform. The complexity of the problem and the need for continued effort but at the same time the necessity for a realistic understanding of practical difficulties which any proposer of remedial procedures must face were discussed at a symposium held at Duke University Law School in 1966, the results of which have since been published. Another major contribution in this direction is the monograph by Professor Murty, in his recent book, *Propaganda and World Public Order*. Professor Falk has also contributed significant essays in this same field.[88]

These recent writers warn us against the familiar pitfalls which plague the international lawyer as he proposes for the international community certain procedures and agencies which may work reasonably well as between individual subjects of law, but are sometimes of doubtful relevance

[85] Bibliography in Whitton-Larson, at 277–94.

[86] *Id.*

[87] *See especially* Murty *supra* note 5 *passim. Also,* von Glahn, O'Brien, Falk, & Whitton in Symposium, *supra* note 8; Whitton-Larson, pt. III.

[88] Falk, *Legal Order in a Violent World* 354–373 and *On Regulating International Propaganda: A Plea for Moderate Aims* 622–34, in Symposium.

for relations between states. Thus a right of reply, difficult enough when applied in France or the state of Nevada, may be too sophisticated for the primitive "community" of nations. We are warned, too, against accepting proposals for general principles or norms such as "propaganda for war is forbidden" without noting the difficulties involved in any workable definition of such a concept. Also, one is cautioned in general against the subtleties involved in any attempt to proscribe "ideological coercion." It is, of course, obvious that not all ideological coercion can be ruled out as illegal. But just where is the line separating impermissible from permissible coercion? Just where is the frontier to be drawn dividing persuasion from coercion? Or, for that matter, what is the distinction between information, education, and propaganda? Professor Murty's study offers invaluable suggestions in these matters. In the long effort by experts, when proposals were optimistically offered to outlaw the dissemination of "false news," was there sufficient recognition of the difficulty of determining just what is "true"? May mere rumors be published? Is the publication of reports of intolerable social conditions in a foreign country an unfriendly act, when the accounts represent the simple truth? If unfriendly, are such reports illegal, when the natural consequences thereof may be to incite local populations to violence or even revolt? In this order of ideas, Murty and Falk have suggested that propaganda may at times be considered as a sort of international legislation.[89] If in a certain state particularly unjust and inhuman conditions persist without remedy, not all efforts at mass persuasion from across the frontier are to be condemned. Whether originating in a world organization such as the United Nations or the OAS, or in a foreign nation, an exposure of the facts and the voicing of criticism should be encouraged as a sort of international lawmaking, *faute de mieux*. This is essential, even inevitable, in a world devoid of effective methods of peaceful change and without the means for the imposition of sanctions. The press can demand and even facilitate badly needed reforms in foreign countries where minorities are victims of intolerable abuses, especially if sacred principles of human rights are violated. In a decentralized society such as the world "community," lacking effective remedial procedures, the foreign press, radio, and television may attack from abroad intolerable conditions of apartheid or, even worse, of genocide, if found to exist in a particular nation. In such situations the guilty government would have no legitimate complaint. Nor could it appeal with justification to outmoded doctrines of sovereign independence.

2.5. Conclusions

The problem of vituperation and prevarication carried on by means of

[89] MURTY, *supra* note 5, at 174; Falk, *supra* note 88.

press, platform, radio, and television remains unsolved and may become worse with the increasing use of television, particularly of satellites for intercommunication. Some authorities have lost their early enthusiasm for new legislative and/or administrative schemes for prevention of abuses, and look rather to more modest reforms, the effects of which can only be realized over a considerable space of time. Some, for example, stress certain measures designed to assure a greater degree of freedom of information as the best means of countering propaganda. A great deal of the effort made over the years in the United Nations in the field of freedom of information has been inspired by the conviction that if the media were free, with adequate sources in the way of supplies of paper and ready access to the news, the results would be a great contribution to mutual understanding. It has been remarked rather loosely that "the best remedy for propaganda is more propaganda."[90] A worldwide broadcasting station under the auspices of the United Nations, some have argued for years, would guarantee to peoples around the globe that they were getting the straight news, so that they could judge for themselves the value of false charges injurious to nations and individuals who are victims of dangerous propaganda.

A recent example points up the real potentialities of this proposal. On the twenty-fifth anniversary of the founding of the United Nations, a great effort was made to broadcast by both radio and television the speeches of President Nixon and other world leaders to all nations, the addresses being translated into many languages.[91]

With regard to the role of the United Nations, it should not be forgotten that the abuses in the use of the media, if of sufficient gravity, can always be dealt with by the Security Council and General Assembly as breaches of the peace, and action under the Charter taken accordingly. The success of such a plan with respect to states where freedom of speech and press are anathema to the governing elite is obviously very doubtful. Also, in those cases where the offending communicator is a private individual or a newspaper, it is proposed that the government exercise adequate controls, especially through local legislation outlawing the publication of false news, incitements to aggressive war to be undertaken by the home state or some foreign regime. Many states already have such legislation, a compilation of which has been made by L. John Martin and U.N. experts.[92] Such legislation has proved useful in the prosecution of

---

[90] J. Vinson, in Dennis v. U.S., 341 U.S. 494 (1951), at 503, said that "propaganda will answer propaganda." But he cautioned that the societal value of speech must, on occasion, be subordinated to other values and considerations. WHITTON-LARSON, at 246–247.

[91] N.Y. Times, Oct. 25, 1970.

[92] Martin, *supra* note 15, at 109–163 & nn. 1–119; Fernand Terrou & Lucien Solal, *Legislation for Press, Film and Radio,* United Nations, ECONOMIC AND SOCIAL COUNCIL, PUBLICATION No. 607, (1951).

verbal attacks on heads of friendly states and on resident foreign diplomats. The further development of this type of legislation has been strongly
recommended. But since the most lethal libel and slander issue from
official propaganda bureaus occasionally camouflaged as "Departments
of Information," domestic legislation as a "remedy" cannot be expected
to cope with the most urgent problems at hand.

At all events, no effort must be spared to impress on government elites,
as well as the directors of great radio chains and influential newspapers
and other media, their tremendous responsibility in this matter—that
world peace may depend on whether they use the media for greater
mutual understanding and peace, or toward hatred, aggression, and war.
Their duties here are clear. They have been defined and set forth again
and again in codes of ethics for the media. We will close this chapter by
reproducing several articles from one such code.[93]

SUBVERSIVE PROPAGANDA

It is the duty of the communicator to refrain from disseminating material,
whether true or false, which is designed or is of a nature to disrupt peaceful
relations existing between a friendly foreign government and its citizenry,
or to foment a rebellion against the government by the use of force. With
respect to radio broadcasting, the agency in control of the station in question
must prohibit, and, if the occasion arises, stop without delay the broadcasting
to a foreign country of any transmission which to the detriment of good international understanding is of such a character as to incite the population to
acts incompatible with the internal order or the security of such foreign state.

This article does not purport to prohibit popular manifestations of mere moral
support on the soil of one state favoring an insurrectory movement in another
state, provided that the communicator is not disseminating propaganda in direct
connection with the commission of an overt act of support to such insurrection,
notably the preparation of armed bands which are planning to cross the
frontier to give armed aid to the movement. Radio broadcasts beamed or
directed to persons in a foreign country urging them to rebel against their
government are particularly harmful to good international relations and a real
danger to peace.

WARMONGERING

It is the duty of communicators to avoid the dissemination of any material
which is of a nature, whether so designed or not, to incite or provoke the
decision-makers of a given state, or the people therein, to threats or acts of
aggression against another state with whom it is at peace. This includes the
use of words, signs, symbols, or any visible or audible representensations which
are likely to promote feelings of enmity or hatred, or promote a war-spirit,
between different peoples. Incitement to threats or acts of aggression is not the
less reprehensible if it fails of its object. It is immaterial that such warmongering

[93] WHITTON-LARSON, at 261–63.

propaganda employs argument based on fact, if the motive be malicious. It is particularly dangerous to international peace for a commentator to make false charges of aggression alleged to have been prepared or committed by a foreign government or its people.

COMMUNICATION IN TIME OF CRISIS

In time of grave international tension, particularly when an international crisis occurs during which peace is seriously endangered, communicators should be especially careful not to diffuse unsubstantiated reports of inflammatory comment of a nature to cause alarm or panic either among governmental leaders or their citizenry. At such times particular care should be taken to verify the sources of all news stories and reports, and also to avoid publicizing matter based on unfounded rumor. At the very least, rumor should be clearly identified as such.

REMEDIES

In the event of a violation by a communicator of any of the principles set forth in this code, an aggrieved party, or a government acting on its behalf, may, through resort to one or more of the following remedies, seek reparation for the injury suffered. It is the duty of the state in which the offending communication originates to give satisfaction to the complaining party through cooperation in the operation of such remedies.

1. Rectification by the offending medium itself of a communication which is false or erroneous, defamatory, subversive, or warmongering, or otherwise harmful to good international relations.
2. Operation of a right of reply in accordance with domestic or international law, or both, where such a right is in effect for the interested parties.
3. Apology by the government of the state in which the offense occurs, offered to the offended government after request by the latter.
4. Punishment of the offending communicator in accordance with constitutional law and procedures. If the communication complained of is a defamatory attack on a resident of the complaining state, the proper remedy may be an action for damages pursued in the court of the state in which the offense took place.
5. Award and payment of damages where appropriate.
6. Submission of the matter to the United Nations or other appropriate international body after complaint and failure to obtain adequate satisfaction, for investigation, report, and such other action as may be appropriate in the circumstances in accordance with the provisions of the charters of such organizations and with existing precedents.
7. In case of a dispute involving a question of international law, submission of the matter to the International Court of Justice, unless the parties agree upon some other mode of settlement.

CHAPTER V

NATIONAL AND COLLECTIVE SELF-DEFENSE

Section 1. A SURVEY OF SELF-DEFENSE IN INTERNATIONAL LAW

Yoram Dinstein

1.1. Introduction

The international legal system has always been characterized by a remarkable reliance on self-help as a remedial method of response by one state to a wrong inflicted on it by another.[1] Legitimate self-help, under international law, can manifest itself in nonforcible measures, such as the break of diplomatic relations or a declaration of a member of the diplomatic staff as *persona non grata*. However, under international law, permissible self-help can also be reflected in forcible measures. It is this latter form of self-help which is termed "self-defense."

Self-defense, consequently, is one form of self-help.[2] Self-defense can be defined as a legitimate use of counterforce in the relations between states; it is authorized by way of a response, in special circumstances, to certain breaches of international law involving illegal use of force.

The term self-defense is not to be confused with similarly sounding phrases, like self-protection and self-preservation. These in general merely signify motives or mitigating circumstances invoked to justify recourse by a state to force. Such motives may or may not steer an actual course of action within the orbit of self-defense. It is only when they do that they are vindicated by international law.

Self-defense as a sociolegal phenomenon has been known to mankind since the dawn of history. Not surprisingly, therefore, it has been endorsed by scholars—as a concept applicable to the relations between states—from the very genesis of modern international law.[3] But as long as an overall licentiousness in the use of force in the international arena was taken for granted, the concern with self-defense was in effect a pure

---

[1] Kelsen says about general international law that it is "characterized by the legal technique of self-help." KELSEN, GENERAL THEORY OF LAW AND STATE 339 (1961).

[2] "Self-defense is a kind of self-help." KELSEN, PRINCIPLES OF INTERNATIONAL LAW 16 (1st ed. 1952).

[3] For a detailed analysis of the writings of the "fathers of international law, *see* Weightman, *Self-Defense in International Law*, 37 VA. L. REV. 1095 (1951).

exercise in semantic ritual. As long as uninhibited resort to force was considered acceptable for any state for any reason on earth—including self-assertion or self-aggrandizement—self-defense per se could not acquire genuine legal connotations. Thus self-defense did not make legal sense, or come to be established as an institution in the realm of international law, until the use of force had been proscribed, as a rule, in the relations between states,[4] and it is only when the mantle of general permissiveness in terms of resort to force was removed that self-defense emerged as an independent right. The selfsame illegality of the original use of force that prompted it created the need and laid the legal groundwork for the use of responsive counterforce by way of remedy.

Frequently, self-defense is referred to as an "inherent right."[5] Thus, prior to the signature of the 1928 Kellogg-Briand Pact of Paris for the Renunciation of War, the United States sent identical notes to a number of countries, stating:

> There is nothing in the American draft of an antiwar treaty which restricts or impairs in any way the right of self-defense. That right is inherent in every sovereign state and is implicit in every treaty.[6]

The use of the term "inherent" to describe the right of self-defense is, however, unwarranted.[7] Inasmuch as self-defense is a right (namely, an interest protected by law), it is based on, and derived from, international law. The adjective "inherent" appears, in this context, to be an anachronistic residue from the era when international law was swayed by ecclesiastical doctrines. One can detect here the projection of a concept according to which human, imperfect, legal systems obtain their norms from an eternal, immaculate *jus naturale*. "Inherent" rights and duties are predicted on the premise that the human reasoning power, if properly applied, can grasp transcendental truths which are divinely inspired—a sort of plucking the fruit from the tree of knowledge. But as our trust in metaphysics has diminished over the centuries, we expect rights and duties to be validated within the confines of the legal system in which they operate.

Of course, it is arguable that the right of self-defense is inherent not in an imponderable and superior legal system, but in a broad basic tenet of positive international law itself. If that is the case, the fundamental

---

[4] *See* Giraud, *La Théorie de la Légitime Défense*, 49 RECUEIL DES COURS DE L'ACADÉMIE DE DROIT INTERNATIONAL 691, 715 (1934); Kunz, *Individual and Collective Self-Defense in Article 51 of the Charter of the United Nations*, 41 A.J.I.L. 872, 876 (1947).

[5] *See, e.g.*, art. 51 of the Charter of the United Nations, discussed *infra*. It is well worth mentioning here that in the French text of the article, the version used is "droit natural."

[6] *Papers Relating to the Foreign Relations of the United States* 34, 36 (1928–I).

[7] *See*, in particular, KELSEN, THE LAW OF THE UNITED NATIONS 791–792 (1950).

principle involved would probably pertain to the "sovereignty" of the state.[8] "Sovereignty," however, is a relative term with everchanging meaning and no clearly established attributes.[9] Thus, it was once believed that a total license for states to use force against one another is inherent in "sovereignty." International law has gone through a veritable metamorphosis in this respect, and still states have not ceased to claim or enjoy "sovereignty." The existing right to respond with counterforce in self-defense is no more sacrosanct or immutable than the earlier right to initiate the use of force.

Occasionally, a sweeping statement is made that, as in the words of the International Military Tribunal for the Far East, "Any law, international or municipal, which prohibits recourse to force, is necessarily limited by the right of self-defence."[10] But whereas this proposition may have always been true in regard to domestic law, and is currently accurate also in respect of international law, it is safer to refrain from advancing axiomatic postulates that purport to cover future developments in international law for all time. As we shall see, self-defense on the part of legal entities, *i.e.,* states, is not exactly the same as it is on the part of physical beings. Consequently, irrespective of the intrinsic need of flesh-and-blood to secure the right of self-defense, it is not beyond conceiving that states will one day dispense completely with forcible measures of self-help in favor of some central authority. That is not to say that at this moment in history self-defense is of diminishing import in international affairs. On the contrary, far from receding, self-defense may even be gaining ground at present in the international reality. But what is and was, will not necessarily be.

1.2. The Law of the Charter

The Charter of the United Nations clearly forbids the use of force in the relations between states.[11] At the same time, the right of self-defense is enshrined in article 51 of the Charter, which proclaims:

[8] *See* Schwarzenberger, *The Fundamental Principles of International Law,* 87 RECUEIL DES COURS DE L'ACADÉMIE DE DROIT INTERNATIONAL 195, 339 (1955).

[9] On the relative sense of "sovereignty," *see* Dinstein, *Par in Parem Non Habet Imperium,* 1 ISRAEL L. REV. 407, 419 (1966).

[10] Judgment of the International Military Tribunal for the Far East (mimeographed) 67–68.

[11] Art. 2, para. 4, of the Charter states:

All members shall refrain in their international relations from the threat or use of force against the territorial integrity or political independence of any state, or in any other manner inconsistent with the purposes of the United Nations.

On the proper interpretation of this clause, *see* Schwarzenberger, THE LAW OF ARMED CONFLICT 51 (1968). Admittedly, para. 4 of art. 2 relates only to U.N. members, but para. 6 extends the scope of the proscription on the use of force by stipulating: "The Organization shall ensure that states which are not members of the United Nations act

> Nothing in the present Charter shall impair the inherent right of individual or collective self-defense if an armed attack occurs against a member of the United Nations, until the Security Council has taken measures necessary to maintain international peace and security. Measures taken by members in the exercise of this right of self-defense shall be immediately reported to the Security Council and shall not in any way affect the authority and responsibility of the Security Council under the present Charter to take at any time such action as it deems necessary in order to maintain or restore international peace and security.[12]

The concept of "self-defense," as pronounced in article 51, is extremely controversial. It is, however, easier to perceive the meaning of that provision when notice is taken of the conspicuous absence from the test of two very significant and commonly employed terms, namely "war" and "aggression."

1.3. Interceptive Self-Defense

"Aggression" is a very broad term which has come to mean different things for different people; aggressive war being only one form of aggression. The expression "armed attack"—used in article 51—is more limited in scope than aggression. Aggression alone, but not armed attack, covers, *inter alia,* a mere threat of war, in which case, response by way of self-defense would be anticipatory in character.[13] A mere threat not being equal to an actual armed attack, preventive countermeasures are not justified as self-defense under article 51. Admittedly, there is a strong school of thought which adheres to the view that the article only emphasizes explicitly one type of legitimate self-defense (*i.e.,* turning back an armed attack) without negating other types preexisting under customary international law (*i.e.,* resistance to aggression in all its manifestations).[14]

---

in accordance with these principles so far as may be necessary for the maintenance of international peace and security." Kelsen draws the conclusion that the meaning of the latter provision is that "the Charter claims to be valid for states, not contracting parties to this treaty." Kelsen, *supra* note 2, at 348.

[12] Art. 51 refers only to members of the United Nations. But, as pointed out by Kelsen,

> if article 2, paragraph 6, is to be interpreted to mean that the obligation to refrain from threat and use of force is imposed also upon non-member states, it may be assumed that the right of self-defence as stipulated in Article 51 cannot be denied to non-members.

KELSEN, THE LAW OF THE UNITED NATIONS 793 (1950).

[13] On anticipatory self-defense, *see* BROWNLIE, INTERNATIONAL LAW AND THE USE OF FORCE BY STATES 225–226 (1963).

[14] *See* BOWETT, SELF-DEFENSE IN INTERNATIONAL LAW 187–192 (1958); McDOUGAL & FELICIANO, LAW AND MINIMUM WORLD PUBLIC ORDER 232–241 (1961); STONE, AGGRESSION AND WORLD ORDER 44 (1958); Waldock, *The Regulation of the Use of Force by Individual States in International Law,* 81 RECUEIL DES COURS DE L'ACADÉMIE DE DROIT INTERNATIONAL 451, 498 (1952).

But such an interpretation is simply not in keeping with the letter and the spirit of the Charter, and most authorities reject it.[15]

All the same, it is submitted that the expression "armed attack" goes beyond the cut-and-dried cases of commencement of hostilities. Suppose that the DEW line sends electronic warnings to the effect that intercontinental ballistic missiles have been launched by state *A* against the United States. Suppose further that the Strategic Air Command reacts instantly, and directs bombers cruising in routine holding patterns to blast military targets in state *A* during the quarter-of-an-hour-or-so interval before the missiles strike home. Will it be said that since, technically speaking, the SAC planes attacked first, the United States did not engage in self-defense authorized by the Charter? Or, for that matter, suppose that the Japanese bombers en route to Pearl Harbor had been intercepted and shot down—before they actually managed to change the balance of power in the Pacific. Would that have put the blame for initiating an armed attack on the United States?[16]

It is quite obvious that an actual armed attack may be initiated before the first shot has been fired. It is the embarkation on an irreversible course of inevitable action—the crossing of the Rubicon rather than the actual fighting—that casts the die and consummates the armed attack. Common sense requires that response to this attack at its inception be regarded as legitimate self-defense conforming to the law of the Charter. It is inconceivable that the defending state should have to sustain and absorb a devastating—perhaps an overwhelming—strike merely to prove a legal point. To all intents and purposes, self-defense in such circumstances is not anticipatory; it is just miraculously early.

1.4. The Options of Self-Defense

In view of the fact that under the Charter, self-defense is authorized in response to an "armed attack," and to it alone, it is important to note that the term "armed attack" need not be confined to an all-out onslaught by the bulk of the armed forces of one state against another. Small-scale armed attacks are still armed attacks.[17] By the same token, self-defense

---

[15] *See* BECKETT, THE NORTH ATLANTIC TREATY 13 (1950); KELSEN, THE LAW OF THE UNITED NATIONS 797–798 (1950); Kunz, *supra* note 4, at 877–878; MANUAL OF PUBLIC INTERNATIONAL LAW 767 (Sørensen, ed. 1968); 2 OPPENHEIM, INTERNATIONAL LAW 156 (7th ed., Lauterpacht 1952); POMPE, AGRESSIVE WAR, AN INTERNATIONAL CRIME 100 (1953); Wehberg, *L'Interdiction de Recours à la Force,* 78 RECUEIL DES COURS DE L'ACADÉMIE DE DROIT INTERNATIONAL 7, 81 (1951).

[16] The Pearl Harbor example was adduced in debates in the United Nations. See 5 WHITEMAN, DIGEST OF INTERNATIONAL LAW 867–868 (1965).

[17] "If 'armed attack' means illegal armed attack, it means, on the other hand, any illegal armed attack, even a small border incident." Kunz, *supra* note 4, at 878.

takes more than one form. After all, the expression "self-defense" by itself is not descriptive. It is a label that we attach to a certain rightful course of action involving counterforce and undertaken by states in appropriate cases. Like its counterpart term ("armed attack") self-defense is not restricted to extended contests and total engagements.

Suppose that a patrol of state *B*, moving along its border, is subjected to intense fire from state *A* and suffers heavy casualties. The following categories of counterforce in self-defense are permissible under article 15 (until the Security Council has taken the necessary measures to restore the peace): reaction, reprisal, execution, and war. A brief explanation of each follows.

1.4.1. REACTION. The first category is somewhat elusive in shape, since very few lawyers, as distinct from soldiers, take special cognizance of it. For lack of a better name, it may be termed "reaction." The idea is countering force with force on the spot and on the spur of the moment. In our example, fire would be returned by the patrol, and possibly by immediately supporting units in that sector of the line. The significant characteristic of "reaction" is that the exchange of fire closes the incident and does not involve other units at other times.

1.4.2. REPRISAL. Reprisal means using force in retaliation for a previous armed attack by another state, when no other redress has been obtained. Reprisal is to be distinguished from mere "reaction" in that an altogether different incident develops, either with a separate unit or at another time or both. In our example, say that fire would be opened by troops of state *B* at a later date on an enemy patrol, or that a military base from which the assailants came would be struck. Reprisal, nonetheless, is still limited in its scope, inasmuch as the response does not entail use of force *à l'outrance,* and (as laid down by the 1928 Arbitral Award in the *Nauliaa* case between Portugal and Germany[18]) has to be proportional to the initial, illegal use of force by the other side.[19]

It is true that many international lawyers firmly believe that reprisal does not fall within the ambit of legitimate self-defense under article 51 of the Charter,[20] and this point of view has been upheld by a number of U.N. resolutions.[21] There are authorities, however, who take the reverse

---

[18] 2 REPORTS OF INTERNATIONAL ARBITAL AWARDS 1011, 1026–1028. For a clear exposition of the *Naulilaa* case, *see* BRIERLY, THE LAW OF NATIONS 400–402 (6th ed., Waldock 1963).

[19] *See* 2 OPPENHEIM, *supra* note 15, at 141.

[20] *See particularly* Brownlie, *supra* note 13, at 281 (and authorities cited there).

[21] For a recent example, *see* S.C. Res 270, (para. 4 Aug. 26, 1969). *See also* S.C. Res. 188, para 1, (Apr. 9, 1964).

position,[22] and in any event the facts of life established that states regard reprisals as far from *passé*. Indeed, all major Powers have had recourse to reprisals in recent years, to wit, the United States in the Gulf of Tonkin,[23] the United Kingdom in Danaba,[24] France in Sakhiet,[25] and the Soviet Union in the Chinese border incidents.[26]

Not surprisingly, therefore, Falk reaches the conclusion that clarity on the doctrinal level that a state "is not entitled to exercise a right of reprisal in modern international law" merely serves "to discredit doctrinal approaches to legal analysis."[27] International law is created and determined in the practice of states, and not by lawyers—regardless of their erudition and expertise—or even by misguided resolutions of nonlegislative bodies. Efforts to institute textbook tenets of international law, confusing the lex lata with the lex ferenda and widely ignored by states, only serve to perpetuate the layman's belief that the international legal system is a chimerical notion.

Even in terms of sheer rationality, since—as shown below—war is generally accepted as a legitimate form of self-defense (in response to an armed attack), it is incomprehensible that the use of a lesser weapon— a part rather than the whole—should be found objectionable. If war, the ultimate weapon, is allowed in self-defense under article 51 of the Charter, a fortiori so are measures short of war, more specifically reprisals.

1.4.3. EXECUTION. The third category of self-defense is, again, not always recognized as an independent mode of counteraction. Occasionally it is called "necessity,"[28] but it seems preferable to use a different term, such as "execution," the employment of force within the territory of another state, directed against individuals in retribution for acts committed by them—on their own responsibility—without the complicity of the government concerned. "Execution" is similar to reprisal, except that it is not addressed against a government, and would usually take place when the said government is unable or unwilling to control the situation along the border.[29] In our example, say that the patrol of state *B* is attacked not by regular troops of a neighboring country but by a band of ma-

---

[22] *See, e.g.,* MANUAL OF PUBLIC INTERNATIONAL LAW 754 (Sørensen ed. 1968): "armed reprisals that are taken in self-defence against an armed attack are permitted." *See also* COLBERT, RETALIATION IN INTERNATIONAL LAW 202–203 (1948).

[23] *See* 14 KEESING'S CONTEMPORARY ARCHIVES 20241 (1964).

[24] *Id.* 11 KEESING'S 15502 (1957).

[25] *Id.* 16203 (1958).

[26] *Cf.* 17 KEESING'S 23314 (1969).

[27] Falk, *The Beirut Raid and the International Law of Retaliation,* 63 A.J.I.L. 415, 430 (1969).

[28] *See* 1 Oppenheim, *supra* note 15, at 298–299 (8th ed., Lauterpacht 1955).

[29] *See* FENWICK, INTERNATIONAL LAW 274 (4th ed. 1965).

rauders unaided by the authorities (obviously, if the marauders were abetted by the authorities, the legal position in respect of governmental responsibility would be equated to the use of regular troops). "Execution" would take place, for instance, by sending an expeditionary force to wipe out a saboteur's camp across the border. In a sense, state *B* is acting in lieu of state *A*.[30]

The most famous historical precedent for this type of self-defense is to be found in the *Caroline* case.[31] In 1837, during the McKenzie Rebellion in Canada, a large number of Canadian insurgents, as well as unauthorized American citizens who sympathized with their cause, took over an island on the Canadian side of the Niagara River. The steamboat *Caroline* was used for transporting men and materials from the American bank of the river to the rebel-held island. When British protests failed to stop the line of supplies, a British unit crossed the American border in the dark of the night, boarded the vessel and sent her drifting to the Falls. In the course of the incident, several American citizens were killed and injured. The United States lodged a protest with the British Government for violating American sovereignty, but the British claimed to have acted in self-defense. In his correspondence with British envoys with regard to the incident (in 1841 and then again in 1842), Secretary of State Webster maintained that for the British assertion of self-defense to be accepted, it had to be shown that there existed "a necessity of self-defense, instant, overwhelming, leaving no choice of means, and no moment for deliberation.[32] Furthermore, according to Webster, the action taken must involve "nothing unreasonable or excessive; since the act, justified by the necessity of self-defence, must be limited by that necessity, and kept clearly within it."[33]

The British reply finally satisfied the United States, and the case was closed. But Webster's criterion made history and came to be looked upon as transcending the specific circumstances of the episode—meaning the issue of "execution"—and is considered applicable to self-defense in general.[34] Even in our own time, the International Military Tribunal in Nuremberg applied Webster's words as a basis for evaluating—and reject-

---

[30] Hyde says about the *Caroline* case: "the British force did in one sense that which the United States itself would have done, had it possessed the means and disposition to perform its duty." I HYDE, INTERNATIONAL LAW 240 (2d ed. 1945).

[31] *See* Jennings, *The Caroline and McLeod Cases*, 32 A.J.I.L. 82–89 (1938).

[32] 29 BRITISH AND FOREIGN STATE PAPERS 1129, 1138 (1840–1841). *See also* 30 *id.* at 194 (1841–1842).

[33] Same as in previous note.

[34] Jennings *supra* note 31, at 92) calls the *Caroline* case the "*locus classicus* of the law of self-defence." *See also* CHENG, GENERAL PRINCIPLES OF LAW 87 (1953).

ing—the German allegation that the invasion of Norway had come under the aegis of self-defense.[35]

1.4.4. WAR. War as self-defense denotes a full-scale use of counterforce, which is total in character. Even though it is sometimes hard to perceive war as a legitimate, rightful measure, there is no question that, as stated by Jessup, "A forcible act of self-defense may amount to or may result in war."[36] To surmount the psychological difficulty, Kelsen propounds the distinction between war (a delict) and counterwar (a sanction), and says, "War and counterwar are in the same reciprocal relation as murder and capital punishment."[37] But it is important to bear in mind that, regardless of appellation, in real terms—from the viewpoint of human suffering—war is war, whether it is a delict or a sanction.

Unlike reprisal, war—once launched—does not at all have to be proportional to the original use of force by the enemy. Indeed, once war starts, "no moral or legal duty exists for a belligerent to stop the war when his opponent is ready to concede the object for which war was made."[38] Hence, forcible measures undertaken at the outbreak of war for self-defensive purposes may assume an offensive character as soon as it is militarily feasible.[39] It is of the essence of war that (subject to the rules of conduct in warfare, *i.e.*, the *jus in bello*) everything is permitted in it to bring about the overall collapse of the enemy.[40] By way of illustration, after Pearl Harbor the United States could, and did, seek unconditional surrender of the enemy, and not merely retribution for the severe blow to its naval power.

Inasmuch, however, as war is the ultimate means of destruction, it is clear that not every isolated instance of an armed attack by one state gives a right to the other party to plunge into all-out war in self-defense. It is especially here that Webster's yardstick may be relied upon for measuring the justifiability of self-defense. Yet, if his words are to be accepted literally, it will become virtually impossible to vindicate war in response to an isolated use of illegal force. Presumably, he derived his high standards from the general principles of Anglo-American domestic criminal law pertaining to self-defense. But, if so, this can only prove the danger ingrained in analogies from the domestic to the international legal

[35] 1 TRIAL OF THE MAJOR WAR CRIMINALS (IMT) 207.

[36] JESSUP, A MODERN LAW OF NATIONS 163 (1950).

[37] Kelsen, *supra* note 2, at 28.

[38] 2 Oppenheim, *supra* note 15, at 225.

[39] *See* Cheng, *supra* note 34, at 99.

[40] Levontin says about war: "It is unlimited in object in the sense that every year war may be regarded, potentially, as undertaken with a view to the total subjugation or *debellatio* of the enemy. This is the chief distinction between war and reprisals." LEVONTIN, THE MYTH OF INTERNATIONAL SECURITY 63–64 (1957).

system. When a man is assaulted, and his life imperiled, one can say that there is no moment for deliberation and no choice of means. But when an isolated act of illegal force is committed against a state, there is sufficient room for deliberation, and anyhow in a well-organized country the front-line command will not unleash full-scale war (as distinct from "reaction" or reprisal), by way of self-defense, without first getting a green light from army headquarters or, better still, from the government. This is a process that takes more than a few instants, and particularly in a democratic state—where the wheels of government turn slowly—may, indeed, consume a long time. Jessup has the following opinion:

> Telegraphic or radio communication between the officer and his superiors can be taken as a counterpart of the impulses in the nervous system of the individual whose brain instructs his arm to strike.[41]

But in the international arena, response to pressure is not reflexive; it is engendered, instead, by the contemplation and deliberation disqualified by Webster.

It is submitted that Webster's test has to be reconstituted so that war in self-defense be permitted in response to an isolated instance of armed attack, when justified by a reasonable combination of urgency and necessity. The question whether this reasonable combination exists depends, of course, on the merits of each individual case. There are two separate elements welded together here: urgency and necessity. From the standpoint of urgency, war cannot be initiated in self-defense several years after an isolated case of illegal use of force by another state. From the viewpoint of necessity, if a single rifle shot is fired by an armed soldier across the border from state *A* to state *B*, and hits a tree, state *B* is scarcely in a position to respond with war. Things are not the same, however, when a thousand cannons are thundering, and one can say that, in this regard, quantity may turn into quality.

1.5. Self-Defense as a Right

It should be pointed out that recourse to war in self-defense is a right, not a duty. Granted, the assertion is made at times that self-defense is not just a duty, but a sacred duty.[42] This, however, is just a reflection of a holier-than-thou approach which expects the victim of an armed attack to risk total annihilation for the glory of conceptualism. Positive international law lays down no such obligation, and, consequently, when a

---

[41] Jessup, *supra* note 36, at 164.

[42] Thus, Suarez states: "I hold that defensive war not only is permitted, but sometimes is even commanded." 2 Suarez, *Selections from Three Works* 802 (CLASSICS OF INTERNATIONAL LAW (1944). Vattel goes even farther: "Self-defense against an unjust attack is not only a right which every nation has, but it is a duty, and one of its most sacred duties." 3 Vattel, *The Law of Nations* 246 (CLASSICS OF INTERNATIONAL LAW 1916).

state is entitled to resort to war by way of self-defense, it does not necessarily have to exercise that right. It may very well choose not to respond to force by counterforce, owing to the military supremacy of the attacking country.

The state subjected to an armed attack may also deem it adequate to respond with less rather than with more force, by embarking upon reprisal. However, the choice—or, if you please, the option—between war and reprisal is legitimately allowed only to the state under attack and not to the aggressor state. Once a state has used force in a way justifying—in the light of reasonable urgency and necessity—response by war as self-defense, all systems are "go" and it cannot demand that the state subjected to attack diminish the quantum of counterforce so as to respond merely with reprisal and not with war. Thus, after Pearl Harbor, the United States had an option: to respond with war or with reprisal. But the Japanese did not have a similar option (even had they desisted from further hostilities). This is important to remember in relation to a possible thermonuclear strike that is not followed by other military moves: the option to respond or not to respond with war is given to the state smarting under the attack and to it alone; otherwise it would be exposed to what Herman Kahn calls "postattack blackmail."[43]

1.6. Collective Self-Defense

Article 51 refers not only to "individual" self-defense, *i.e.*, a right exercised by a single state, but also to "collective" self-defense. Curiously enough, the legislative history of the drafting of the article demonstrates that at its inception the whole clause pertaining to self-defense was inserted into the Charter with a view to giving the imprimatur of the United Nations to regional arrangements (such as the inter-American security structure) dealing with mutual defense.[44] Evidently, in its final and present form, article 51 has become the cornerstone of the modern law of self-defense in general; but the particular type of "collective" self-defense still comes under the aegis of the provision. The choice of the term "collective" self-defense leaves something to be desired. From the strictly purist standpoint, there is no collective *self*-defense unless a number of states (*B, C,* and *D*) are being subjected simultaneously to an armed attack (by state *A*), and respond jointly with counterforce.[45] The

---

[43] KAHN, ON THERMONUCLEAR WAR 171 (1960).

[44] *See* GOODRICH, HAMBRO & SIMONS, CHARTER OF THE UNITED NATIONS 342–344, 348 (3d ed. 1969).

[45] See Bowett, *supra* note 14, at 207; KELSEN, THE LAW OF THE UNITED NATIONS 792 (1950); Kunz, *supra* note 4, at 875; STONE, LEGAL CONTROLS OF INTERNATIONAL CONFLICT 245 (1954); Tucker, *The Interpretation of War Under Present International Law,* 4 INT'L L.Q. 11, 29 (1951).

thrust of the issue of collective self-defense relates, however, to the more complicated case where state *B* alone is attacked by state *A*, and state *C* rushes to the rescue of state *B* (under a regional or other mutual defense arrangement). Such assistance to state *B*—though, of course, not to state *A*—is undoubtedly permitted under the Charter.[46] But, from an analytical outlook, can it really be considered *self*-defense? In our opinion the answer is positive.[47] An armed attack is like cancer in the body politic of the family of nations. History has shown time and again that (particularly when Big Powers are involved), unless premeditated aggression is checked at the outset—by the concerted action of actual as well as potential victims—it has a built-in tendency to escalate rapidly and to affect one state after another. The self-interest of the country that expects to be next on the list in the path of an armed attack compels it to become its brother's keeper. This, if no other, was the moral of World War II; and this is the concept that lies at the root of the whole Charter. *Faute de mieux*, and so long as genuine collective security does not materialize on the international scene, collective self-defense is the only insurance policy obtainable against an armed attack.

1.7. The Role of the Security Council

The justification of self-defense has always been regarded as a convenient excuse for resort to war, and more often than not, in modern times, states have initiated armed attacks while cynically brandishing the banner of self-defense.[48] Even the most brutal armed attack of the century, World War II, was instigated by Nazi Germany in an incredible and ludicrous pretext of response to Polish attacks.[49] It goes without saying, almost, that if each and every state were entitled to be the final and exclusive arbiter of its own action and were authorized to cloak it at will or whim with the disguise of self-defense, the very distinction between the use of illegal force and legitimate counterforce would have become illusory. Self-defense as a remedial institution draws its legal lifeblood from the antithetical existence of the delictual conduct which it is supposed to counter. As the judgment of the Nuremberg Military Tribunal

---

[46] *See* McDougal & Feliciano, *supra* note 14, at 248–252; MANUAL OF PUBLIC INTERNATIONAL LAW 768–769 (Sørensen ed. 1968); 2 Oppenheim, *supra* note 15, at 155.

[47] This opinion is supported by many authorities. *See* Goodhart, *The North Atlantic Treaty of 1949*, 79 RECUEIL DES COURS DE L'ACADÉMIE DE DROIT INTERNATIONAL 187, 203 (1951); McDougal & Feliciano, *supra* note 14, at 248–252; 2 Oppenheim, *supra* note 15, at 156.

[48] *See* DINSTEIN, THE DEFENCE OF "OBEDIENCE TO SUPERIOR ORDERS IN INTERNATIONAL LAW 137 (1965); Wright, *The Outlawry of War*, 19 A.J.I.L. 76, 89 (1925).

[49] The Nazis even went to the trouble of simulating a fake attack on a German radio station at Gleiwitz, near the Polish border. *See* SHIRER, THE RISE AND FALL OF THE THIRD REICH 518–520 (1960).

in the *Ministries* case proclaims, "there can be no self-defense against self-defense."[50] At least one state in an international conflict is bound to to be delinquent. Self-defense requires as an antecedent a breach of international law to which it responds.

At the same time, the whole essence of self-defense is self-help. That is to say, the facts of international life at present are such that a state subjected to an armed attack cannot reasonably expect an effective police force to intervene on its behalf and to save it from dire consequences. The state has to take the field on its own, and it has to act without undue loss of time.

As a result, it is imperative to distinguish in this context between two separate stages.[51] In the first instance, it is clear that the question whether the merits of a given case justify recourse to self-defense is left to the decision of the state under attack. That state, and it alone, determines initially whether the occasion calls for the use of forcible measures in self-defense. But the state acts at its peril. In the second and final stage, it is the international community that reviews the whole series of events and conclusively resolves whether the forcible measures objectively constituted self-defense, or perhaps an actual armed attack was carried out masked as self-defense. The judgment of the International Military Tribunal in Nuremberg espoused the two-step approach in these words:

> It was further argued that Germany alone could decide, in accordance with the reservations made by many of the Signatory Powers at the time of the conclusion of the Kellog-Briand Pact, whether preventive action was a necessity, and that in making her decision her judgment was conclusive. But whether action taken under the claim of self-defense was in fact aggressive or defensive must ultimately be subject to investigation and adjudication if international law is ever to be enforced.[52]

The International Military Tribunal for the Far East rephrased the same idea as follows:

> The right of self-defense involves the right of the state threatened with impending attack to judge for itself in the first instance whether it is justified in resorting to force. Under the most liberal interpretation of the Kellogg-Briand Pact, the right of self-defence does not confer upon the state resorting to war the authority to make a final determination upon the justification for its action.[53]

[50] 14 Trials of War Criminals Before the Nuernberg Military Tribunals (NMT) 329. The phrase is actually borrowed from Wharton *id.*, note).
[51] On the two-stage process see in particular 2 Oppenheim, *supra* note 15, at 187–188.
[52] 1 Trial of the Major War Criminals (IMT) 208.
[53] Judgment of the International Military Tribunal for the Far East (mimeographed) 68.

The Charter, too, adopts the two-stage process of determination of recourse to self-defense.[54] In conformity with article 51, the state employing counterforce acts at its own discretion, but also at its own risk. Its action must be immediately reported to the Security Council, where a review of all the circumstances de novo is possible. The Council may take all necessary measures to maintain or restore international peace or security. Which is to say that the Council may retrospectively sanction the conduct of the state engaged in self-defense; yet by the same token, it may decide that the state in question in fact tried to conceal an armed attack behind the camouflage of self-defense, and take steps accordingly.

Unfortunately, the state of affairs in the United Nations, after a quarter of a century of existence, is such that the Council is hamstrung by the abuse of the veto power and by the record of its less than effective way of handling various international conflicts. On more than one occasion in the past, it failed to discharge its responsibilities under the Charter, and declined to act to restore or maintain international law and order. Indeed, it seems at times to corroborate Pascal's pessimistic outlook: "unable to make what is just strong, we have made what is strong just." In the absence of authoritative decisions by the Council, the ultimate determination of the merits of the plea of self-defense is necessarily entrusted today to a frustrated world public opinion. The machinery, evidently, is not so sophisticated; but the product, perhaps, is also less sophistical.

Section 2. A CONTEMPORARY APPRAISAL OF OFFENSIVE WEAPONS, SANCTIONS, AND WORLD PUBLIC ORDER

W. Thomas Mallison, Jr.

Writing from the perspective of ten years after the quarantine interdiction of "offensive weapons and associated material to Cuba," it is appropriate to relate the fundamentals of the 1962 study to contemporary events.[1] The military measures of the U.S. Government were then appraised as amounting "to the least possible use of the military instrument." It was also concluded that "Any lesser use would have amounted to abandonment of the military instrument and exclusive reliance upon noncoercive procedures which most certainly would have been ineffective without supporting military power." This nonviolent and defensive use

---

[54] *See particularly* 2 Oppenheim, *supra* note 15, at 159.

[1] Mallison, *Limited Naval Blockade or Quarantine-Interdiction: National and Collective Defense Claims Valid Under International Law*, 31 Geo. Wash. L. Rev. 335–398 (1962).

of naval power was probably the principal success of American military policy in the 1960's.

The central juridical conclusion of the 1962 study was that the defensive military measures of the United States and the Organization of American States were justified under the international law criteria concerning national and collective self-defense. In view of the nuclear capabilities and range of the missiles which were being placed in Cuba, combined with the characteristics of the measures employed by the United States and the OAS, it was concluded specifically that both the requirements of actual necessity for defense and reasonable proportionality in responding coercion were met. One of the preeminent reasons for these conclusions is that the national and regional defensive measures were fully consistent with the value objectives of the world community. These objectives are still to maintain minimum world order while striving to build an optimum order system. The technique of limited naval blockade served these objectives by "de-escalating" the confrontation between the Soviet Union and the United States. National and regional measures which claim to be defensive while they actually subvert world order should be viewed with as much suspicion in 1970 as in 1962.[2]

It is appropriate to apply the juridical analysis of the limited naval blockade to the facts of the Middle East conflict situation which is the most dangerous one in the present world. It is particularly important to make such an appraisal concerning the weapons which are in use in the Middle East today, since some are equating them to those at issue in the Cuban crisis.

One of the principal factual elements involved in the placing of the Soviet missiles in Cuba in October 1962 was that they were offensive weapons with the most destructive characteristics. As President Kennedy pointed out in his address of October 22, 1962, the range of the medium-range ballistic missiles being placed in Cuba was more than 1,000 nautical miles and extended to Washington, D.C., the Panama Canal, and Mexico City. The not completed intermediate-range ballistic missiles would have had a range more than twice as far and would have included Hudson Bay, Canada, and Lima, Peru. In addition to range, the nuclear capability of the Soviet missiles in Cuba made it necessary to classify them as offensive weapons without equivocation.

The SAM (surface-to-air) missiles presently in the Suez Canal area have only the tactical objective and capability of attacking the Israeli

---

[2] In criticism of the present study as first published in 1962, Professor Falk has alleged "the patriotic habits of jurists" and "the nationalization of truth" without inquiry concerning the relation between national and world community objectives. FALK, LEGAL ORDER IN A VIOLENT WORLD 49 (1968).

aircraft used in missions over Egyptian territory in the Canal vicinity. There is no way in which they could be used to attack Tel Aviv, and they have no nuclear capability. Even if it should be assumed with a total lack of realism that they had a nuclear capability, it must be noted that their use with nuclear warheads would result only in an increased destruction of civilian as well as military targets in the Suez Canal area.

In order to provide an adequate factual context, it is also necessary to examine the characteristics of the aircraft supplied by the United States to the State of Israel. The *Washington Post* recently described the two major types of aircraft involved in the following terms:

> Practically all the American-supplied F-4s [Phantoms] and A-4s [Skyhawks] fly as bombers for Israel, not as fighter planes to combat other aircraft. The French-supplied Mirage 3C flies over these bombers as the fighter cover.
>
> Also, Israel earlier this year flew deep-penetration bombing raids into Egypt as distinguished from hitting Egyptian defenses along the Suez Canal.
>
> In military textbook terms, then, the Israeli F-4s and A-4s are indeed offensive weapons. Israel itself has the American equivalent of the SAM-3 on guard—the American Hawk anticraft missile, which has a range of twenty-two miles.[3]

The same source has provided the following particulars on the Phantom:

> The plane can fly at more than 1,600 miles per hour and has a range in excess of 1,600 nautical miles. Most importantly, the craft is extremely rugged and can carry more than 15,000 pounds of bombs and sophisticated air-to-ground missiles, including the antiradar missile, Shrike, which the United States is also supplying to the Israelis.[4]

The range of a SAM missile is simply not comparable to that of a Phantom. The Phantom has demonstrated its capability to carry out bombing attacks all over the United Arab Republic. It also has the capability of extending such attacks from presently existing Israeli bases into the Libyan Arab Republic to the west and into Iran to the east. In addition, its bomb load is fully capable of including nuclear weapons and thereby causing widespread death and destruction in territory far removed from the State of Israel.[5] In view of the capabilities as well as the demonstrated use of the Phantoms, it is not possible to classify them as anything except offensive weapons. If the Phantoms, or even the Sky-

[3] Washington Post, Sept. 14, 1970, at A 20, col. 4.

[4] *Id.*, Sept. 9, 1970, at A 16, col. 2. N.Y. Times, Feb. 15, 1970, at § 4, p. 1, cols. 3–5 provides a comparative table which sets forth the much greater speed, combat radius, and bomb load of the Phantom in comparison with that of Russian and French supplied aircraft.

[5] The Government of Israel denies that it has a nuclear capability. *See, e.g.,* N.Y. Times, July 19, 1970, at 66, col. 1.

hawks, should have some kind of defensive capability, it has not been demonstrated thus far in the Middle East War.

It is not possible, consequently, to avoid the conclusion that the American aircraft now supplied to the State of Israel[6] are closely analagous to the Soviet missiles in Cuba in 1962 and that the defensive SAMs now supplied by the Soviet Union to the United Arab Republic are not. It follows that the United Arab Republic has the authority under the doctrines concerning lawful defense to use proportionate defensive measures against the Israeli air attacks. The UAR is also entitled to ask for and to receive the assistance of the Soviet Union.[7] There can be no doubt concerning the actual necessity of such a defense in response to the aggressive Israeli air war. The doctrine of proportionality permits the use of defensive measures analogous to those employed in attack, including, for example, the use of deep-penetration air attacks. The same doctrines provide ample justification for the use of such modest defensive weapons as the SAM missiles.[8]

The contemporary world community is characterized by a decentralized decision-making process. National claims to exercise self-defense are, nevertheless, subject to review at both the regional and international levels. At the time of the Cuban quarantine-interdiction, the self-defense claim of the United States was, in effect, reviewed and approved by the Council of the Organization of American States. The regional determination was, in turn, reviewed and approved by the tacit agreement between President Kennedy and Chairman Khrushchev which removed the Soviet missiles from Cuba. The result of this decisional process was reduction of the conflict situation and an avoidance of nuclear confrontation between the United States and the Soviet Union. There is, unfortunately, no assurance that decision-makers will always act in such a rational manner to preserve the objectives of the world public order system as did President Kennedy and Chairman Khrushchev in 1962.

[6] During the controversy concerning truce violations in the Suez Canal area in Sept. 1970, the U.S. Government agreed to sell Israel 16 to 18 additional Phantoms. *Washington Post*, Sept. 9, 1970, at 1, cols. 7, 8.

[7] For the Zionist view of the role of the Soviet Union in the Middle East, *see* Eugene V. Rostow, NATO-Soviet Confrontation in the Middle East in Hearings on the Near East Conflict Before the Subcommittee on the Near East of the House Committee on Foreign Affairs, 81st Cong., 2d Sess., at 312 (1970). Professor Rostow characterizes the military role of the Soviet Union in Egypt as "act of blindness or recklessness on the part of the Soviet leadership which has no parallel in Soviet policy since the attack on Korea, or the Cuban missile crisis." *Id.* at 314. For an analysis from a different perspective, *see* Mallison, *United States Law and International Law which Is Applicable to the Middle East Conflict.* Id. at 373.

[8] Both necessity and proportionality have the requirement of reasonableness in the particular factual context. *See* McDOUGAL & FELICIANO, LAW AND MINIMUM WORLD PUBLIC ORDER 229–30, 241–44 (1961).

There is an urgent need to improve the process of decision and the sanctions available for enforcement. As a first step, an impartial fact-finding body should be created on a permanent basis. Such a body acting on behalf of the organized world community could make a significant contribution by ascertaining the specific military facts involved in particular conflict situations. This fact-finding should make it possible to draw the necessary distinctions between Soviet offensive missiles in Cuba and Soviet defensive missiles in the Suez Canal area. It could also determine whether or not a given truce agreement has been violated and, if so, the character and extent of the violation. Such an institutionalization of fact-finding would not, of course, automatically resolve conflict situations. It could, however, establish the facts impartially, in contrast to the sometimes highly emotionalized claims of participants and so promote more rational and value-conserving decisions.

A substantial improvement in the sanctions process would be provided by the creation of a permanent international criminal court.[9] Such a court could be given jurisdictional authority to try individuals, including the officials of national states, who make decisions which are in flagrant violation of the provisions of the U.N. Charter and especially those provisions concerning the requirements for lawful national and collective defense. The precedent of the principal Nuremberg Trial before the International Military Tribunal[10] as well as subsequent war-crimes trials both in Europe and in Asia have had a very great influence upon contemporary attitudes. It is now widely recognized that they constitute a substantial improvement in ICL in terms of both the substantive law applied and the detailed requirements of fair and impartial procedures. The substantive law included the basic jurisdictional conception that the crimes were committed against the common humanity of all and not against the victims alone.[11] The procedural law involved the requirement of adequate counsel for each defendant; this included lawyers who were Allied nationals as well as German ones. In referring to the trials conducted by the Allied Powers following World War II, the late Judge Lauterpacht made this appraisal:

> The stature of those tribunals is bound to grow with the passage of time and their judgments will be increasingly regarded as a weighty contribution to international law and justice. These judgments—perhaps more than anything else—give a complexion of reality to any attempt at a scientific exposition of

[9] Approval of the proposal to establish such a court combined with pertinent criticism appears in McDougal & Feliciano, *id.* at 708–09.

[10] The Trial of the Major War Criminals Before the International Military Tribunal, 42 vols. (1947–1949).

[11] 1 *id.* 226–28, 232–38.

the law of war, which never before in history wos so widely and so ruthlessly disregarded as in the Second World War. In that perspective the occasional criticisms of these courts as having been tribunals set up by the victor acting as judge in his own cause must be deemed to be of limited importance.[12]

The proposals for an international criminal court are designed to obviate two of the principal criticisms directed at the Nuremberg Trial: (1) that the Tribunal was ad hoc and (2) that it was established by the victors alone. An international criminal court should be a standing tribunal which is established by a consensus that is representative of the world community as a whole. Such a tribunal should maintain the substantive and procedural improvements made at Nuremberg as an indispensable step toward further progress. It is essential in the creation of a criminal court that its statute reflect the overriding community policy against change through the use or threat of coercion and violence which is manifested so unequivocally in the United Nations Charter. Under a statute of this kind, defensive measures such as the limited naval blockade by the United States in 1962 and the contemporary measures of the UAR along the Suez Canal would continue to receive the full support of international law. The self-defense which article 51 of the U.N. Charter characterizes as "inherent" is indispensable to the maintenance of even a minimum order system. The task of establishing optimum order is dependent upon the willingness of the world community to apply the criteria of law to solve international conflicts.

[12] 2 Oppenheim-Lauterpacht, International Law: Disputes, War and Neutrality v (7th ed. 1952).

PART THREE

THE REGULATION OF ARMED CONFLICTS

CHAPTER VI

PROBLEMS OF THE LAW OF ARMED CONFLICTS*

Section 1. SOME TERMINOLOGICAL REMARKS

DENISE BINDSCHEDLER-ROBERT

The choice of the term "law of armed conflicts" instead of the traditional expression "laws of war" (*jus in bello*) should reflect the applicability of this set of rules, at least in part, not only to cases of international war in the formal sense[1] but also to armed conflicts which are not formally defined as wars. The new expression, adopted in recent works,[2] reflects a visible evolution which found its first legal expression in the Geneva Conventions of 1949.[3]

The laws of war in their traditional and broadest sense include different groups of rules: rules concerning war on land, sea, and air; rules concerning the protection of victims of war; rules regulating the occupation of enemy territory; rules of economic warfare, and certain rules relating to the law of treaties. One might even add the rules on neutrality, a legal status intimately connected with the state of war. In practice, even today these rules as a whole apply only in the case of war in the formal sense and it is from the application of these rules as a whole that the presence of a state of war is deduced. One may, therefore, quite legitimately continue to use the expression "laws of war" to designate this set of rules as a whole. Besides, it is difficult to find an adequate terminological equivalent for economic "war" even though certain rules of economic warfare

---

* Report of the Conference on Contemporary Problems of the Law of Armed Conflicts [Geneva: 15–20 Sept. 1969]. Reprinted with permission of the Carnegie Endowment for International Peace, New York, 1971 (also chapter VII, section 1, 2.5 and 4.1 by the same author).

[1] *See* §2.2 *infra.*

[2] G. SCHWARZENBERGER, INTERNATIONAL LAW AS APPLIED BY INTERNATIONAL COURTS AND TRIBUNALS, vol. 2: THE LAW OF ARMED CONFLICT (1968); *and Réaffirmation et développement des lois et coutumes applicable dans les conflits armés,* REPORT OF THE ICRC TO THE XXIst INTERNATIONAL CONFERENCE OF THE RED CROSS (1969).

[3] Art. 2, para. 1, 2 (common to all four Conventions):

In addition to the provisions which shall be implemented in peacetime, the present convention shall apply to all cases of declared war or any other armed conflict which may arise between two or more of the high contracting parties, even if the state of war is not recognized by one of them. The convention shall also apply to all cases of partial or total occupation of the territory of a high contracting party, even if said occupation meets with no armed resistance.

may also apply in the absence of war in the formal sense of the term. It is thus impossible to avoid certain terminological inconsistencies.

Another inconsistency exists because the term "laws of war" also applies to a part—admittedly the most important one—of the above-mentioned set of rules: that group of rules whose purpose is to "regulate warfare and attenuate its rigours in so far as military necessities permit."[4] These rules are traditionally called "laws and customs of war,"[5] and they are the rules which we shall call "laws and customs of armed conflict."[6] We will be concerned particularly, though not exclusively, with the application of these rules in those cases where there is no formally declared war. In addition, these "laws of war" in the narrower sense, or "laws and customs of war," are in turn subdivided into two branches. The first is the laws of war in a still narrower sense—properly called the laws of armed conflict—which is also called the Law of The Hague,[7] and which "lays down the rights and duties of belligerents in conducting operations and limits the method of warfare."[8] The term "Law of The Hague" encompasses not only the Conventions concluded at The Hague but also international customary law relating to the same subject.[9] The other subdivision is the humanitarian law or Law of Geneva,

[4] J. Pictet, *The Need to Restore the Laws and Customs Relating to Armed Conflicts*, REVIEW OF THE INTERNATIONAL COMMISSION OF JURISTS 23 (Mar. 1969).

[5] Thus the IInd Hague Convention of July 29, 1899, respecting the Laws and Customs of War on Land, with its annexed regulation; and the IVth Hague Convention of Oct. 18, 1907, bearing the same title. *See also* 1 COMMENTAIRE DES CONVENTIONS DE GENÈVE DE 1949 394 (Pictet ed. 1952).

[6] This follows the terminology used in *Réaffirmation et développement des lois et coutumes, Report of the ICRC, supra* note 2.

[7] There is no contradiction between this statement and the use of the Hague Conventions as an illustration of the "laws and customs of war." The Hague Conventions regulate matters—the status of prisoners-of-war and the law of occupation—which have been dealt with and regulated anew in the Geneva Conventions, so that at present the "Law of The Hague" is really the law regulating the conduct of hostilities. This remark applies to the majority of the Conventions adopted by the Conference of 1907 and also to the Hague Convention of May 14, 1954, for the Protection of Cultural Property in the Event of Armed Conflict, 249(3511) U.N.T.S. 240.

[8] Pictet, *supra* note 4, at 23.

[9] The second Peace Conference (1907) adopted fourteen Conventions. Among them we shall mention the IVth Hague Convention of Oct. 18 and particularly the regulations annexed to it: Regulations Concerning the Laws and Customs of War on Land; also, as relevant to our subject, Convention III relative to the Opening of Hostilities; Convention IX respecting Bombardment by Naval Forces in Time of War; Convention X for the Adaptation to Maritime Warfare of the Principles of the Geneva Convention, revised by Geneva Convention II of 1949 for the Amelioration of the Condition of Wounded, Sick, and Shipwrecked Members of Armed Forces at Sea; and the Declaration Prohibiting the Launching of Projectiles or Explosives from Balloons. Seven of these instruments relate to war on sea and two to neutrality. The Conference also expressed the wish that the question of elaborating regulations concerning the laws and customs of war on sea would be on the agenda of the third Peace Conference; as is known, that conference never took

which "is designed to ensure respect, protection, and humane treatment of war casualties and noncombatants."[10]

The expression "humanitarian law" also needs clarification. It certainly does not mean that only rules specifically designated humanitarian have a humanitarian character; as follows from the definition above, laws and customs of armed conflicts as a whole aim at limiting the use of violence.[11] Besides, the demarcation line between the Law of The Hague and the Law of Geneva is unstable[12] and sometimes difficult to trace;. on the one hand, the Hague Convention contains stipulations which now come within the purview of the Law of Geneva, while on the other hand, the Law of Geneva also contains certain stipulations which are, in fact, rules relating to the conduct of hostilities.[13] It has been suggested that one possible criterion of delimitation is the nature of the rights conferred by the relevant legal rules, and it has been pointed out that the Law of Geneva (the humanitarian law) confers subjective rights on individuals in respect of states, whereas the Law of The Hague applies only to states.[14] The first part of this remark is correct, but the second must be qualified in that the Law of The Hague, as well as the Law of Geneva,[15] imposes direct per-

---

place. In 1954 the Convention on the Protection of Cultural Property in the Event of Armed Conflict was signed. The Conventions which have not been signed at The Hague and which are relevant to the present discussion are essentially the Declaration of St. Petersburg of 1868 Prohibiting the Use of Explosive Bullets and Projectiles Charged with Inflammable Substances and the Geneva Protocol of June 17, 1925, for the Prohibition of the Use in War of Asphyxiating, Poisonous or Other Gasses, and of Bacteriological Methods of Warfare, 94 L.N.T.S. 65.

[10] Pictet, *supra* note 4, at 23. The "Law of Geneva" is actually represented by the four Conventions of Aug. 12, 1949: Geneva Convention for the Amelioration of the Condition of the Wounded and Sick in Armed Forces in the Field (Convention I); Geneva Convention for the Amelioration of the Condition of Wounded, Sick, and Shipwrecked Members of the Armed Forces at Sea (Convention II); Geneva Convention Relative to the Treatment of Prisoners of War (Convention III); Geneva Convention Relative to the Protection of Civilian Persons in Time of War (Convention IV).

[11] One can claim that almost all the laws of war have this characteristic; the law of war on sea (contraband) and that of economic warfare, for instance, aim at limiting the rights which the belligerents may assume in respect of private property.

[12] *See supra* note 7.

[13] This is the case each time that an object or person is declared to be a prohibited target. Thus, in Convention I the clauses concerning fixed medical establishments and mobile units which may "in no circumstances be attacked" (art. 19) and in Convention IV the clause concerning the civilian hospitals which also "may in no circumstances be the object of attack" (art. 18).

[14] H. Knitel, *Le Rôle de la Croix-Rouge dans la protection internationale des droits de l'homme*, 19 OESTERREICHISCHE ZEITSCHRIFT FÜR OFFENTLICHES RECHT (1969).

[15] In each of the four Conventions there are common stipulations concerning the prosecution of serious infractions of which these Conventions give lists that are nearly identical: Convention I, arts. 49, 50; Convention II, arts. 50, 51; Convention III, arts. 129, 130; and Convention IV, arts. 146, 147. There is no doubt that these serious infractions constitute war crimes punishable as such even if one of the contracting parties has not fulfilled its

sonal obligations on individuals, as shown by the trials of war criminals which took place after World War II. Another more cynical distinction can be made by saying that the Law of The Hague essentially regulates the limits within which it is permissible to inflict casualties and to destroy property, while the humanitarian law regulates conduct toward the victims of armed conflicts whether they be wounded or persons who have fallen into the power of the enemy. It thus becomes clear that while the quintessence of the laws and customs of armed conflicts as a whole is humanitarian and consequently is part of the humanitarian law in its broad sense,[16] the Law of Geneva, by virtue of its aim and its legal structure, comes more particularly within the purview of Human Rights;[17] the Law of Geneva, however, applies to the case of armed conflicts, whereas specifically designated Human Rights are applicable mainly, though not always, in times of peace.[18]

Section 2. THE LEGITIMACY AND PRACTICABILITY OF A LAW OF ARMED CONFLICTS AND OF ITS REVISION

On occasions the legitimacy of the very existence of the laws of war has been denied or their utility hotly disputed.[19] Such an attitude, naturally, questions the effort of reformulating these laws.

2.1. The Legitimacy of a Law of Armed Conflicts

The prohibition of the use of force in the Charter of the United Nations has sometimes led to the conclusion that it is no longer legitimate to establish rules for regulating what must in all cases be considered a crime.

---

duty to publish adequate penal rules. The penal competence of states is international, *i.e.*, it applies to all crimes wherever and against whomever they have been committed. *See* Pictet, 1 *Commentaire, supra* note 5, at 406.

[16] Pictet, *Laws and Customs Relating to Armed Conflicts, supra* note 4, at 22; Pictet, LES PRINCIPES DE DROIT INTERNATIONAL HUMANITAIRE 8 (1966) Knitel, *supra* note 14, at 6.

[17] However, it is also within the framework of Human Rights that the United Nations has begun to pay attention to the rules concerning the conduct of hostilities. See *Final Act of the International Conference on Human Rights* (1968), Res. XXIII, at 18; 23 G.A. Res. 2444(Dec. 19, 1968). But the Covenants on Human Rights of 1966 and particularly the Covenant on Economic, Social, and Cultural Rights recognize only subjective and individual rights. This is also the case with the European Convention on Human Rights.

[18] PICTET, *supra note* 16, at 10. The European Convention on Human Rights allows the contracting parties to take derogatory measures "in time of war or other public emergency threatening the life of a nation" (art 15). The United Nations' Covenant on Civil and Political Rights contains a similar article, but the mention of war is omitted in that article: "In time of public emergency which threatens the life of the nation and the existence of which is officially proclaimed. . . ." (art. 4).

[19] See the various opinions offered in Kunz, *The Chaotic Status of the Laws of War and the Urgent Necessity for their Revision,* 45 A.J.I.L. 37 (1951); Nurick, *The Distinction Between Combatant and Noncombatant in the Law of War,* 39 A.J.I.L. 680 (1945).

According to this conception the aggressor would have no rights, while whoever acts in self-defense would have unlimited rights. It is clear that the law of armed conflicts would no longer have a place within this theory.

This approach is not new: it underlies the theory of the *bellum justum*.[20] However, as international law developed, one of the main hindrances in its application to relations between belligerents soon appeared: the absence of an authority to make a binding decision as to which of the belligerents was waging a just war. While Grotius was still drawing certain practical (though rather unimportant) conclusions from the theory of just war,[21] Vattel noted that since nobody could decide which party was just, it must finally be admitted that war is lawful for both sides and that the effects of war are the same for the two parties to the conflict.[22]

On the occasion of a breakdown in the system of collective security, when the United Nations is unable to determine the aggressor, the situation in the United Nations is the same as that under classical international law described by Vattel. In reality, such situations within the United Nations are not exceptions, but rather the rule.[23] In these cases, it would be impossible to deny the legitimacy of the law of armed conflicts. Furthermore, the creation of the United Nations has not put an end to the work of codifying the law of war, as the Geneva Conventions of 1949 and the Hague Convention of 1954 testify; they expressly apply "to all cases of declared war or of any other armed conflict which may arise

[20] Although the theory of just war is different from that of collective security.

[21] H. Grotius, *De Jure Belli Ac Pacis Libri Tres*, in THE CLASSICS OF INTERNATIONAL LAW bk. I, ch. II (English trans. 1964). But Grotius already recognized that a war could be *subjectively* just for both sides (*bellum utrimque justum*), and that such a just war was the official war between states (*bellum solemne*). *Id.* bk. II, chs. I & XXII; bk. III, ch. III.

[22] And as it equaly possible that either of the parties may be in the right, and as, in consequence of the independenc of nations, no on can decide between them—the condition of the two enemies is the same, so long as the war lasts. Thus, when a nation, or a sovereign, has declared war upon another sovereign . . . their war is what, among nations, is called a lawful war, in due form; and its effects are, by the voluntary law of nations, the same on both sides, independently of the justice of the cause. . . ." (Vattel, *Le Droit des gens; ou, Principes de la loi naturelle appliqués à la conduite et aux affairs des nations et des souverains*, THE CLASSICS OF INTERNATIONAL LAW, bk. III, ch. IV, para. 68).

[23] It is only in respect to Korea that the Security Council designated the aggressor (North Korea). The General Assembly's condemnations of the Soviet Union (in respect to Hungary) and of the Peoples' Republic of China (in respect to Korea) were only recommendations and hence were not obligatory, even though they might have had certain legal effects. *See* Virally, *La Valeur juridique des recommandations des organisations internationales*, 2 ANNUAIRE FRANCAIS DE DROIT INTERNATIONAL 66 (1956); R. L. Bindschedler, *La Delimitation des competences des Nations Unies*, 108 RECUEIL DES COURS DE L'ACADEMIE DE DROIT INTERNATIONAL 344–49 (1963).

between two or more high contracting parties. . . ."[24] Regrettably, there can be no doubt that war as a contemporary phenomenon remains with us.[25]

Other writers feel that it is immoral to admit the existence of the law of armed conflicts because this confers a certain legitimacy upon war and detracts from the only real task, its abolition.

An easy reply is that one must do the one thing without neglecting the other. The legitimation of war by the law of armed conflicts is based on a confusion between the *jus ad bellum* and the *jus in bello*. The principle of this distinction is not a peculiarity of the laws of war; not infrequently the law regulates de facto situations which are illegally created.[26] The unlawfulness or immorality of the resort to force does not negate the legitimacy of the law of armed conflicts which seeks to lessen the consequences of the inability of the international community to prevent the use of force.

It is exactly to the latter point that still another objection has been raised: precisely because the law of armed conflicts has the effect mentioned, it would encourage the use of force. It is possible to argue that the "balance of terror" in the postwar period, between the two great powers possessing nuclear weapons, has helped to prevent a generalized war. However, apart from this particular situation, history does not seem to show that anticipation of the horrors of war has any inhibitory effect.[27] The "balance of terror" theory risks, then, becoming a game in which civilization itself is at stake.

2.2. The Practicability of the Law of Armed Conflicts

Finally, there are a number of realistic and somewhat sceptical people who think that the whole question is futile: states would discard the most

[24] Geneva Conventions of 1949 for the Protection of Civilian Persons in Time of War, art. II (common article) and Hague Convention of 1954 on the Protection of Cultural Property in the Event of Armed Conflict, art. 18. This last convention was concluded under the auspices of UNESCO.

[25] *See* P. GUGGENHEIM, 2 TRAITE DE DROIT INTERNATIONAL PUBLIC 304–305 (1967); M. Kaplan & N. Katzenbach, *Resort to Force: War and Neutrality,* in 2 THE STRATEGY OF WORLD ORDER: INTERNATIONAL LAW 276–303 (R. Falk & S. Mendlovitz eds. 1966); Schwarzenberger, *From the Laws of War to the Law of Armed Conflict,* 21 CURRENT LEGAL PROB. 239 (1968); Academy of Sciences of the U.S.S.R., 5 KURS MEZHDUNARODNOGO PRAVA (A course in international law) (1969); J.P.A. Francois, *Reconsideration des principes du droit de la guerre,* 48 ANNUAIRE DE L'INSTITUT DE DROIT INTERNATIONAL (Session de Neuchâtel), bk. II, at 178–263 (1959).

[26] Civil law, for instance, derives certain legal consequences from the mere fact of Possession, whatever the title to it may be. *See* M. BOTHE, STREITKRAFTE, INTERNATIONALER ORGANISATIONEN 91 (1968). In this case the law fulfills not an attributive function but a function of pure regulation.

[27] E. SPETZLER, LUFTKRIEG UND MENSCHLICHKEIT: DIE VÖLKERRECHTLICHE STELLUNG DER ZIVILPERSONEN IM LUFTKRIEG 204–205 (1956).

ingenious law of armed conflicts if they thought that it was in their interest to do so and, moreover, modern methods of destruction are so powerful that any regulation would be predestined to remain illusory; only fear of countermeasures, not the existence of laws, could prevent the belligerents from committing the worst excesses. Consequently, any attempt to regulate modern war would be only a delusion.[28]

Considering the effects of modern weapons, this appraisal of the situation carries considerable weight; it is, however, based on the idea that total war, *i.e.*, the utilization of means of mass destruction on a large scale, is inevitable. But, as has been pointed out,[29] this is not a matter of making predictions, and the basic question is whether humanitarian aims are best served by elucidating as far as possible the limits of lawful behavior, or by abandoning any attempt in that direction? The question is tautological.

Furthermore, the present world situation is characterized by the existence of conflicts which are limited, not only geographically but also with respect to the aims of the belligerents and the means used by them. Such conflicts are amenable to restrictive regulations; the belligerents are acting in a (relatively) peaceful environment and cannot completely ignore international public opinion, which is often quickly alarmed, nor can they ignore the political interests of third states or the pressures which the latter can exercise to force them to adopt attitudes which conform to international rules. The fact that compliance with the law depends on such external considerations or on the belligerents' appraisal of their own interests rather than on purely humanitarian considerations does not deprive the rule itself of its legal or humanitarian character, the latter being purely objective. Moreover, the cases in which the law of armed conflicts has been violated or disregarded, in the process of escalation, reprisals, and counterreprisals, do not give a complete picture of reality; we must also consider those cases—admittedly less spectacular—which do conform to the law.

True, the threat of total war, unlimited in its aims and means, remains suspended like the sword of Damocles over our heads, and the above considerations may seem to establish a paradoxical dichotomy between the "limited wars" to which the law of armed conflicts would be applicable and the "great wars" to which it would not be applicable. Such a dichot-

---

[28] Nurick, *The Distinction Between Combatant and Noncombatant, supra* note 19, at 682, 693; H.A. Smith, *Modern Weapons and Modern War,* 9 Y.B. WORLD AFFAIRS 222 (1955); Baron von der Heydte, *Le Probleme que pose l'existence des armes de destruction massive et la distinction entre les objectifs militaires et non militaires en general,* 52 ANNUAIRE DE L'INSTITUT DE DROIT INTERNATIONAL, bk. II (1969), *id., Observations de M. Erik Bruel,* at 101–102; for a more balanced approach *see id., Observations de M. Emile Giraud,* at 111.

[29] Kaplan & Katzenbach, *supra* note 25, at 305.

omy, indeed, could not fail to affect the obligatory character of the law of armed conflicts in general. However, in reality it rather boils down to the acknowledgment that a generalized conflict or a conflict between the two great nuclear powers risks immediate degeneration into a total war, which would mean the collapse of the entire international legal order. This sort of catastrophe is capable of engulfing civilization and has fundamentally always threatened it. The existence of rules for the conduct of hostilities is certainly no guarantee that such a catastrophe would not occur; their existence, however, may contribute to the creation of certain mental habits—a "mental set"[30]—whose influence may be substantial. It also assures the availability of standards of reciprocal conduct to which we may expect the belligerents to adhere, whereas in the absence of any rules, the established standards of conduct would be considerably lower.

For these reasons, there is a growing conviction that the law of armed conflicts is not only legitimate, but also that it is possible and indeed necessary to reexamine and "restore" it.[31] The first question to be considered

[30] R. TUCKER *et al.*, PROPOSAL FOR NO FIRST USE OF NUCLEAR WEAPONS: PROS AND CONS 1–4 (1963).

[31] Kunz, *supra* note 19, at 37; Kaplan & Katzenbach, *supra* note 25, at 276–303; Pictet, *supra* note 4; Schwarzenberger, *Neo-Barbarism and International Law*, 22 Y.B. WORLD AFFAIRS 191 (1968). Several institutions are dealing with the question of the restoration of the law of armed conflicts. The Red Cross first approached this question from the point of view of the protection of the civilian population and the application of the laws of war to noninternational conflicts.

Now they are approaching it from a more general point of view. At the New Delhi International Conference of the Red Cross, the ICRC presented a draft of rules to limit the risks incurred by the civilian population in time of war, but this draft was not approved by the governments, particularly because of its art. 14, the adoption of which would have signified the prohibition of nuclear weapons. In 1965, the Vienna International Conference adopted Resolution XXVIII affirming four important principles relating to the conduct of hostilities. These principles were reaffirmed by a resolution of the International Conference on Human Rights in Teheran (1968) and—except for the last principle—by G.A. Res. 2444 (XXIII) of Dec. 19, 1968. The International Conference of the Red Cross in Istanbul (Sept. 1969) had before it a report on "Réaffirmation et développement des lois et coutumes applicable dans les conflits armés" which embodied the results of the discussions of a commission of experts, and they also considered another report on "Protection des victimes des conflits non internationaux." The Institut de Droit International has also considered this question and has had before it several reports of J.P.A. Francois *Reconsideration des principes du droit de la guerre*, 48 ANNUAIRE DE L'INSTITUT DE DROIT INTERNATIONAL, bk. II (1959) [hereinafter cited at ANNUAIRE]; the Francois report on *l'Egalité d'application des règles du droit de la guerre aux parties à un conflit arme*, 50 ANNUAIRE, bk. I, II, (1963); and the von der Heydte report on *Le Problème que pose l'existence des armes de destruction massive et la distinction entre les objectifs militaires et non militaires en général*, 52 ANNUAIRE, bk. II (1969). At its session in Hamburg (1960) the International Law Association examined the problems of an armed force of the United Nations, and at its session in Brussels (1962) the question of arms was discussed on the basis of the report of G. Schwarzenberger, *Self-Defense under the Charter of the United Nations and the Use of Prohibited Weapons*, INTERNATIONAL LAW ASSOCIATION REPORT 192 (1962). Finally, the United Nations has dealt with the problem of restoring the law of armed conflicts either from the point of

is a question *de lege lata.* We notice that the rules applicable to the conduct of hostilities—with the exception of the Geneva Protocol of 1925 and the Hague Convention of 1954 on Protection of Cultural Property in the Event of Armed Conflict—are rather old and were formulated at a time when current technical developments were not even imagined. An examination of what remains of these rules is therefore necessary to discover whether the principles deduced from them are still valid. The second question is *de lege ferenda:* on the one hand, after certain principles have been deduced, precise rules must be formulated for their application so that their implementation no longer depends on the unilateral interpretation of states; on the other hand, new rules must be made either to replace norms which are obsolete or questionable or to regulate matters which have not yet been, or are no longer, regulated.

Reconsideration and revision of the law of armed conflicts, particularly the laws and customs regulating the conduct of hostilities, is not an easy matter; it is made more difficult by the divergence of military interests of states in relation to their political situation and the power at their command. Moreover, the belligerents' interest in restraining their own freedom of action is always subject to what they consider to be military necessities. Although in 1949 and 1954 it was possible to adopt modernized and detailed rules for the protection of victims of war, and of cultural property, it would be considerably more difficult to establish new rules to conform to present-day conditions. Just as the verbal prohibition of war did not succeed in preventing war, a new codification will not succeed in compelling recognition if it remains purely declaratory. A new codification must admit certain realities and correspond to the reciprocal interests of the belligerents, but it must also be accompanied by the recognition of ethical concepts based on certain human values. These values must be independent of the ideological and political aims used to justify recourse to violence, and they must even apply to those who would trample them underfoot.

---

view of the prohibition of certain weapons or from the point of view of human rights. See G.A. Res. 1653 (XVI) of Nov. 24, 1961, on the illegality of the use of nuclear weapons; Res. 2162 B (XXI) of Dec. 5, 1966, on the prohibition of chemical and bacteriological weapons; and, again, Res. 2444 (XXIII) of Dec. 19, 1968, on human rights in armed conflicts; this last resolution requests the Secretary-General to report on the steps to be taken to secure the wider application of existing humanitarian rules and to study the need for additional humanitarian international conventions. On Oct. 10, 1967, the Secretary-General presented a report on *Effects of the Possible Use of Nuclear Weapons and the Security and Economic Implications for States of the Acquisition and Further Development of these Weapons,* U.N. Doc. A/6858; in the near future he will present another report on chemical and bacteriological weapons. The negotiations concerning disarmament are closely connected with the question of the prohibition of certain weapons, but they differ from the law of armed conflicts in that they are essentially concerned with the question of the manufacturing, the possession, and possibly, the location of weapons.

Section 3. LAWFUL AND UNLAWFUL OBJECTIVES

3.1. The Laws of Humanity and the Necessities of War

1. As has been pointed out by Schwarzenberger,[1] it is possible to see the law of armed conflicts as the simple result of a "tug-of-war" between two contradictory forces: the need for an ethical standard of civilization, and the requirements of war itself. These are, however, what may be called the sociological sources of law; neither factor is by itself a source of positive law, and it is to such formal sources of law that we must turn to determine the existence of rules and their content.

The emergence of the standard of civilization may be observed in the evolution of the laws and customs of war from antiquity to the seventeenth century: the assertion of certain religious, moral, and humanitarian values relating to the protection of the individual's life, health, and property. While still in its embryonic state, this standard reflected changing influences exerted by the great religions and philosophies on the concept of man and, consequently, of his behavior toward his enemy, combatant or noncombatant.[2] In the nineteenth century the standard of civilization was explicitly asserted in the text of conventions—first, in the Declaration of St. Petersburg, which refers to the "laws of humanity,"[3] then in the final Protocol of the Brussels Conference of 1874,[4] and later in the famous de Martens clause included in the preambles to Hague Convention II of 1899 and Hague Convention IV of 1907.[5] Resolution 1653 (XVI) of the United Nations General Assembly, of 24 November 1961, on the illegality of the use of nuclear weapons *incorporates the sense of these declarations;* according to its text, "the laws of humanity" prohibit

---

[1] Schwarzenberger, *Self-Defense under the Charter of the United Nations*, INTERNATIONAL LAW ASSOCIATION REPORT 192–200 (1962).

[2] On the history of the laws of war, *see* J.F.C. FULLER, THE CONDUCT OF WAR 1789–1961 (1961); Coursier, *l'Evolution du droit international humanitaire*, 99 RECUEIL DES COURS, bk. I, at 357 (1960); Mahmassani, *The Principles of International Law in the Light of Islamic Doctrine, id.,* vol. 117, bk. I, at 205 (1966).

[3] "That the progress of civilization should have the effect of alleviating, as much as possible the calamities of war. . . . That this object (*i.e.,* the weakening of the military forces of the enemy) would be exceeded by the employment of arms which uselessly aggravate the sufferings of disabled men, or render their death inevitable; that the employment of such arms would, therefore, be contrary to the laws of humanity. . . ."

[4] The Brussels Conference of 1874 did not go beyond drafting an international declaration concerning the laws and customs of war; this project was not ratified, but it served as a basis for the Hague Convention (II) of 1899.

[5] "Until a more complete code of the laws of war has been issued, the high contracting parties deem it expedient to declare that, in cases not included in the regulations adopted by them, the inhabitants and the belligerents remain under the protection and the rule of the principles of the law of nations, as they result from the usages established among civilized peoples, from the laws of humanity, and the dictates of the public conscience."

causing unnecessary human suffering as well as indiscriminate suffering and destruction.

Even though, as has already been pointed out, the "laws of humanity" do not themselves create formal rules, they may, nevertheless, have certain legal effects. They certainly may supply a principle of interpretation not only for the conventions in which they appear, but also for the law of armed conflicts in general, to the extent that the individual or his property is exposed to the acts of a belligerent. We may even consider that the "laws of humanity" constitute an exception to the lawfulness of measures which in themselves are permissible but which would be contrary to these humanitarian principles and that the "laws of humanity," therefore, play a role similar to the notion of the abuse of power.[6]

2. Military necessities appear to be the antithesis of the laws of humanity. The concept of military necessities may be greatly extended: it may imply that any act or measure that influences the course of hostilities in favor of one of the belligerents, either immediately or in the future, may be justified on that account. This is tantamount to saying that military necessities are directly opposed to any legal obligation that limits the freedom of action of the belligerents.[7] This calls into question the definition of the aims which may legitimately be pursued in a war and, consequently, the definition of lawful objectives.[8] The motive of "military necessities," then, becomes acceptable only within the framework of international law and, consequently, only in so far as it is accepted as a "necessity of war" by the legal rule itself.[9] This idea, incidentally, is subscribed to by writers,[10] as well as by manuals for the use of armies.[11] It is

---

[6] In the Corfu Channel case the International Court of Justice founded their decision on the obligations of Albania—which consisted of notifying shippers of the existence of a minefield, and warning them of danger—"not on the Hague Convention of 1907, which is applicable in time of war, but on certain general and well-recognized principles, namely: humanitarian considerations, even more exacting in peace than in war, and two other principles of international customary law."

[7] *See The Trial of A.F.A. Krupp von Bohlen, Hallbach, and Eleven Others,* 9 TRIALS OF WAR CRIMINALS BEFORE THE NUREMBERG MILITARY TRIBUNAL 1347 (1950) (hereinafter cited as *The Krupp Trial*):

> It is an essence of war that one or the other side must lose, and the experienced generals and statesmen knew this when they drafted the rules and customs of land warfare. In short these rules and customs of warfare are designed specifically for all phases of war. They comprise the law for such emergency. To claim that they can be wantonly—and at the sole discretion of any one belligerent—disregarded when he considers his own situation to be critical, means nothing more or less than to abrogate the laws and customs of war entirely.

[8] Meyrowitz, *Reflections on the Centenary of the Declaration of St. Petersburg,* 93 INTERNATIONAL REVIEW OF THE RED CROSS 621 (1968): ". . . the point of impact of incidence on the law of war is the problem of the delimitation of legitimate targets for hostile acts."

[10] *See* Schwarzenberger, *supra* note 1, at 192: "To the extent to which rules of warfare effectively limit wartime sovereignty, but do not contain any express reservation in favor of the necessities of war, these necessities of war must be ignored." E. CASTREN, THE PRESENT LAW OF WAR AND NEUTRALITY 65–6 (1954); J.M. SPAIGHT, AIR POWER AND WAR

also to be found in the decisions of the war crimes tribunals established after World War II.[12] It must be remembered that "military necessities" should be interpreted in a strict sense and not merely as a convenient rationalization.[13] In integrating the notion of military necessities with the law itself, in domesticating it, the law of armed conflicts thus succeeds in combining that notion with the humanitarian principle.[14] The compromise between the two principles is made when the rule itself is being created.[15]

3.2. The Distinction Between Lawful and Unlawful Objectives—Is It Still Valid?[16]

The relation between the problem of distinction between lawful and unlawful objectives and that of distinction between lawful and unlawful weapons and methods of warfare is sufficiently clear. When the Hague Regulations assert (art. 22) that "the belligerents have not an unlimited right as to the means they adopt for injuring the enemy," they limit weapons and methods of fighting as well as objectives, since the destruction of a particular objective may in itself be "a means" of injuring the enemy. This principle can also be deduced from the list of prohibitions contained in Article 23.[17] On one hand, it is clear that if all distinctions between objectives are abolished, the question as to the lawfulness or unlawfulness of methods of warfare and of weapons loses part of its importance; this is true in the case of weapons and methods of mass destruction, as well as of so-called "blind weapons," whose accuracy of fire is insufficient or

---

RIGHTS 267–272 (3d ed. 1947). Spaight admits that the bombing of whole zones of territory, although illegal in itself, becomes legal when it is the only means available. Thir conception seems to extend unduly the notion of the measure "imperatively demanded by the necessities of war."

[11] *See, e.g.,* U.S. DEPT. OF THE ARMY, THE LAW OF LAND WARFARE, FIELD MANUAL 27–10, para. 1 (1956) (hereafter cited as U.S. Army Field Manual), MANUAL DES LOIS ET COUTUMES DE LA GUERRE POUR L'ARMEE SUISSE, para. 3 (1963) (hereafter cited as Swiss Army Manual).

[12] *The Hostages Case* in II TRIALS OF WAR CRIMINALS BEFORE THE NUREMBERG MILITARY TRIBUNAL 1352–1354 (1950).

[13] J.L. KUNZ, KRIEGSRECHT UND NEUTRALITÄTRECHT 27 (1935).

[14] U.S. Army Field Manual, para. 2.

[15] *See* the Preamble of the Declaration of St. Petersburg: ". . . this commission having fixed by common accord the technical limits within which the necessities of war ought to yield to the demands of humanity. . . ."

[16] Cmd. Paper 2201, *Draft Rules on Aerial Warfare* 15 (1925) (hereafter cited as *The Hague Rules*). These rules were established in 1923 at The Hague by a commission of Jurists; *Draft Rules for the Limitation of the Dangers Incurred by the Civilian Population in Time of War,* REPORT OF THE INTERNATIONAL COMMITTEE OF THE RED CROSS TO THE XIXTH INTERNATIONAL CONFERENCE OF THE RED CROSS (1957) (hereafter cited as *Draft Rules*); von der Heydte, *Le Problème que pose l'existence des armes de destruction massive,* 52 ANNUAIRE DE L'INSTITUT DE DROIT INTERNATIONAL, bk. II (1969).

[17] *See* IV Hague Convention (1907).

whose effects are uncontrollable.[18] On the other hand, if these same weapons are declared legal, the distinction between objectives vanishes. However, the two questions are not identical, and it is necessary to treat them separately, starting with the distinction between lawful and unlawful objectives, the fundamental principal, and the one with the most far-reaching consequences.

We find here again, more specifically, the theory of total war.[19] As far as the question of objectives is concerned, this theory is based on two sorts of considerations: (1) the idea that the enemy state is a fortress whose defenders should be weakened physically as well as morally and (2) the acknowledgment that modern weapons, particularly nuclear weapons, do not permit distinctions between objectives. The distinction between combatants and noncombatants[20] is becoming emasculated for two reasons: (1) the whole population is involved in the war effort because of the necessities of modern war and (2) with modern weapons it becomes practically impossible to maintain the distinction. The Anglo-American theory of naval and economic warfare is thus transposed, by virtue of the considerations of the first category, to the war on land[21]—on the basis of the analogy with naval blockade[22]—and this transposition is in turn made possible and topical by the appearance of long-range aviation and rockets. In this situation the norms of traditional law relating to the distinction between military and nonmilitary objectives, and between the armed forces and the civilian population, have been abolished or at least have become irrelevant.

As has been mentioned, this theory unfortunately seems to infer from the possibility of total war its certainty and even its legitimacy; but the

[18] For the distinction between "blind weapons" and weapons of mass destruction *see* von der Heydte, *supra* note 16, at 61.

[19] E. Spetzler, Luftkrieg und Menschlichkeit 195 (1956). In the inquiry provided by von der Heydte, this theory was upheld by Bruel & Giraud. *See* von der Heydte, *supra* note 16, at 101 & 111. The German conception of total war referred not to hostilities, but to the treatment of occupied countries. *See* Cmd. Paper 6964, *Nuremberg Judgement* 44 (1946).

[20] In contradistinction to the Hague Regulations, we prefer to reserve the term "belligerents" to states or other entities involved in armed conflict and call combatants all those who participate in the fighting, lawfully or not.

[21] Air warfare is not a special category; in so far as aerial operations aim at terrestrial objectives they are subject, in principle, to the rules of war on land, but only to the extent that the vector of the aerial weapons does not require special rules. Swiss Army Manual, supra note 11, at para. 44.

[22] Von der Heydte, *supra* note 16 *id., Observations de M. Emile Giraud,* at 117. The extension of the Anglo-American theory of naval and economic blockade to air warfare by the British in World War I may be partly accounted for by the same geographical, and consequently, strategic situation. *See* J. Stone, Legal Controls of International Conflict 624 (1954).

observations on which this theory rests merit a detailed examination. They compel one to ask whether in existing law (not in the hypothetical future behavior of the belligerents) the fundamental distinction between lawful and unlawful objectives has lost any legal ground (apart from a few categories of persons or kinds of property enjoying a special protection) and whether it is possible to reestablish or at least to reaffirm this distinction.

Certainly the evolution of sociological and technical conditions—the creation of great mechanized armies and the development of new weapons—has affected the basis on which the Hague Rules rest.[23] As Schwarzenberger has pointed out, this fact by itself is not capable of affecting the validity of the rule, although it may call into question its effectiveness. The question *de lege lata* may be reduced to the following problem: Has the old rule been abrogated by customary law?[24] Has it become obsolete? Those who believe that it has can point out that the Allies obviously did not invoke the notion of reprisals to justify the destruction of the economic infrastructure of Germany and the terror bombings,[25] that the International Military Tribunal of Nuremburg avoided expressing an opinion on the question of indiscriminate bombings, and that all of the post-war Conventions and the ICRC Draft Rules of 1956 themselves were conceived in terms of quasi-total war.[26]

However, others have noted that the truth of these matters was more complex. While the Anglo-French Declaration of September 2, 1939,[27] may be considered canceled by later expressions of the will of these states, and, while neither Allied raids nor the use of nuclear bombs was justified on the basis of the law of reprisals, the Allies recognized the legal value of

[23] Schwarzenberger, *supra* note 1, at 214; Meyrowitz, *supra* note 8, at 551. Meyrowitz considers that this evolution has brought about a "qualitative mutation of the war"; on the contrary, Spetzler considers that the differences are a question of degree, *see* Spetzler, *supra* note 19, at 198.

[24] Schwarzenberger, *supra* note 1, at 214.

[25] The British Director of Oct. 29, 1942, on air warfare, attached to the "Draft Rules," *supra* note 16, made a distinction between countries occupied by the enemy and enemy countries: in countries of the first group, bombings were limited to military objectives and intentional bombings of civilian populations were prohibited; in enemy countries these limitations were not applicable for "consequent upon the enemy's adoption of a campaign of unrestricted air warfare, the Cabinet have authorized a bombing policy which includes the attack on enemy morale. . . ." This argument is based on the notion of *tu quoque* rather than on that of reprisals. The maintenance of the distinction between military and civilian objectives for occupied countries—*i.e.*, friendly countries—is accounted for by political reasons and does not say anything about the maintenance of that notion in the legal sense.

[26] Schwarzenberger, *supra* note 1, at 214; *id.*, 2 INTERNATIONAL LAW AS APPLIED BY INTERNATIONAL COURTS AND TRIBUNALS: THE LAW OF ARMED CONFLICT 151 (1968).

[27] According to this Declaration only "strictly military" objectives would be bombed. Germany made a similar declaration. *See* J.F.C. FULLER, THE SECOND WORLD WAR 221 (1948).

the distinction between civilian and military objectives; thus, when American airmen were executed in Japan, the American government protested that its flyers were ordered to bomb only military objectives.[28] Germany, on her part, denied the legality of the Allied bombing raids and invoked the notion of reprisals to justify her own bombing raids.[29] The same distinction between lawful (military) objectives and unlawful (civilian) objectives has been asserted by both sides in the Korean war, the Vietnam war, and the Nigerian-Biafran war; each belligerent party has periodically accused the other of having bombed non-military objectives and the accused party has denied the facts without calling into question the cogency of the distinction.[30] It is therefore impossible to infer the generalized disappearance of the *opinio juris* on the legal character of this distinction.[31] Nor can such a conclusion be inferred from postwar jurisprudence[32] or conventions whose purpose was to protect certain persons or objects under all circumstances, not to express an opinion on the validity of rules for the conduct of hostilities generally; moreover, these conventions did recognize the notion of military objectives. However, if a rule limiting the freedom of action of states begins to be questioned as obsolete, and is not replaced by another limitative rule, the doubt concerning the existence of the *opinio juris*, or even the affirmation of another *opinio juris* by certain states, may make the validity of the rule at least dubious. The negative proof of the nonemergence of a different *opinio juris* is not sufficient to confirm its validity.

We believe, however, that it is possible to prove that the *opinio juris* concerning the legal distinction between lawful and unlawful objectives is indeed permanent. Some of the facts mentioned above already point to this conclusion. Let us recall the opinion expressed by states or other entities involved in recent conflicts. These opinions are confirmed by army

[28] SPAIGHT, *supra* note 10, at 59.

[29] FULLER, *supra* note 27, at 221; SPAIGHT, *supra* note 10, at 259; Spetzler, *supra* note 19, at 223; STONE, *supra* note 22, at 625. As far as World War I is concerned, *see* Nurick, *The Distinction Between Combatant and Noncombatant*, 39 A.J.I.L. 680 (1945).

[30] Von der Heydte, *supra* note 16, at 17–18.

[31] *Id.*

[32] The Nuremberg Tribunal and other military tribunals have condemned arbitrary and unnecessary destruction and have based their decisions on the principle prohibiting causation of unnecessary human suffering and destruction rather than on the principle of drawing a distinction between objectives. *See* Cmd. Paper 6964, *Nuremberg Judgement, supra* note 19, at 45; *The Hostages Case, supra* note 12; *The Shimoda Case*, 8 JAPANESE ANNUAL OF INT'L L. 240 (1964). The decision of the District Court of Tokyo in the Shimoda case is explicit: ". . . the concept of total war is not advocated in such a vague meaning as stated above, and there was no actual example of such a situation. Accordingly, it is wrong to say that the distinction between military objective and nonmilitary objective has gone out of existence because of total war." Of course, this court is not an international tribunal, but the sentence has been very carefully motivated and has attracted much attention.

manuals, all of which draw a distinction between military and nonmilitary objectives.[33]

Besides, the United Nations itself—and, consequently, the member states—has repeatedly expressed the idea that the civilian population is not a lawful objective. Three important resolutions must be mentioned here: (1) Resolution 1653 (XVI) of November 24, 1961, on the legality of the use of nuclear weapons, which in its preamble deduces the illegality of these weapons from the prohibition against unnecessary human suffering and from the fact that these weapons cause indiscriminate suffering and destruction to mankind; (2) Resolution 2162 B (XXI) of December 5, 1966, on chemical and bacteriological weapons (the question of the Geneva Protocol), which states in its preamble that weapons of mass destruction are "incompatible with the accepted norms of civilisation" and asserts "that the strict observance of the rules of international law on the conduct of warfare is in the interest of maintaining these standards of civilisation"; and (3) Resolution 2444 (XXIII) of December 19, 1968, with respect to human rights in armed conflicts, which "adopts as its own" Resolution XXVIII adopted by the XXth Conference of the Red Cross (Vienna, 1965) and which reiterates the following principles:[34] the choice of means for injuring the enemy is not unlimited, attacks against the civilian population as such are prohibited, and a distinction must be made at all times between combatants and the civilian population. These resolutions concentrate mainly on the protection of the civilian population and do not expressly mention military objectives; nevertheless, one may infer from them not only the rule forbidding the enemy to attack the civilian population (prohibition of terror bombing) or to endanger it by the use of weapons of mass destruction, but also the fundamental idea that not all aims are lawful. True, the resolutions of the General Assembly are not legally binding,[35] but one can see in them (though propaganda may play a part in the speeches and the votes) the expression of the general opinion of states on this subject, particularly if a given resolution has been adopted unanimously, as was the case with

[33] U.S. Army Field Manual, *supra* note 11, para. 42, states that bombardments from the air of combatant troops, defended places, "or other legitimate military objectives" are not prohibited. Para. 221 of the same law establishes the fundamental distinction between combatants and noncombatants; para. 221 (b) provides that direct attacks against noncombatants and attacks for the purpose of terrorizing are forbidden. *See also* Swiss Army Manual, *supra* note 11, paras. 25, 26.

[34] Except the fourth principle, according to which the general principles of the laws of war apply to nuclear weapons. The Soviet Union opposed the inclusion of this principle because it considered that the latter presupposed the legitimacy of nuclear weapons. U.N. Docs. A/C.3/SR.1633 (Dec. 9, 1968) and A/C.3/SR.1634 (Dec. 10, 1968).

[35] *See* von der Heydte, *supra* note 16, at 44–45.

Resolution 2444.[36] Finally, the great majority of writers, while recognizing that it is difficult at present to apply the distinction between lawful and unlawful objectives, believe that it continues to be legally valid.[37]

Even if one can establish that the necessity to draw a distinction between lawful and unlawful objectives is admitted quasi-unanimously, this distinction has no value if the law does not offer any means of determining which objectives are lawful and which are not. However, despite the uncertain practical value of the distinction, we find two categories whose legality or illegality is generally agreed upon. Thus the uncertainty relates only to the intermediate categories; even there it is possible to abstract certain implicit points of view which, together with the general principles of the law of armed conflicts, should allow us to arrive at a reasonable evaluation.

Nevertheless, the fact that it has been necessary to treat this question at great length already shows that the principle is fairly fragile. The propensity of conflicts to expand to total war tends to undermine theoretical and practical foundations of the principle and causes uncertainty in its interpretation. Given this situation one could ask, *de lege ferenda,* whether we should abandon attempts to humanize conflicts by defining military objectives and instead should commit ourselves to another method, that of special protection. This method would be aimed at protecting an important part of the civilian population by developing a large-scale system of safety zones, already envisaged in the Geneva Conventions,[38] and giving up the attempt to limit destruction outside these zones. Because only specially protected and marked objectives would be protected from attacks and destruction, this would clearly represent a reversal of the general principle of distinction between objectives.

Considerable problems are raised by the creation of such zones.[39] Their existence would presuppose agreements concluded before the war began.

---

[36] G.A. Res. 1653 (XVI) of Nov. 24, 1961, adopted by 55 votes to 20, with 20 abstentions, declared the usse of nuclear weapons a violation of the Charter and "contrary to the laws of humanity."

[37] L. OPPENHEIM, 2 INTERNATIONAL LAW 524 (H. Lauterpacht ed. 1952); SPAIGHT, *supra* note 10, at 277; PICTET, LES PRINCIPES DE DROIT INTERNATIONAL HUMANITAIRE 52–53 (1966); R. L. BINDSCHEDLER, DAS VOLKERRECHT UND DIE NUKLEARWAFFEN, MELANGES FRAGISTAS 494 (1968); Skubiszewski, *Use of Force by States, Collective Security, Law of War and Neutrality.* MANUAL OF PUBLIC INTERNATIONAL LAW 801, 803, 822 (M. Sorensen ed. 1968).

[38] Convention I, art. 23 (hospital zones and localities); Convention IV, art 14 (hospital and safety zones and localities); art. 15 (neutralized zones). It is Convention IV, art. 14 which would be used as a model. *See* the review of the history of the article and its analysis in 4 COMMENTAIRE DES CONVENTIONS DE GENEVE 1949, at 129 (J. S. Pictet ed. 1956).

[39] These difficulties are already brought out, to a certain extent, by the Draft Agreement annexed to Convention IV, but the zones envisaged there do not correspond to this more radical conception.

Care would have to be exercised to see that the neutralization of certain territories did not entail any strategic advantages for one of the belligerents, that these zones would be able to become economically self-sufficient, that they could not be used for communications, and finally, that a system of international control be created to guarantee that the zones would not be used for military advantage.

It is doubtful that this would be a practicable alternative, and it seems that a solution *de lege ferenda,* based on the general principle that civilian objectives are not legitimate objectives, would be no more difficult to establish and would be preferable because it would assert that there are limits to the display of violence. Besides, the use of weapons of mass destruction, which call into question the practicability of the distinction between objectives, would also endanger the system of zones.

The first task, then, in codifying the law of armed conflicts would be to reconfirm the existing principle and then to delimit exactly its proper meaning by defining lawful objectives.[40] This, in fact, would not amount to the creation of new rules, but would constitute an assertion of an existing principle and an explanation of its contents, *i.e.,* the "restoration"[41] of the law in force. Moreover, the formulation of this principle within the context of a convention would place these rules on a new legal basis and make them largely independent of a unilateral interpretation by any belligerents.

An agreed definition of lawful objectives and also a regulation of the means of warfare are indispensable if one really wishes to succeed in limiting the aims which the belligerents may rightfully pursue in conducting hostilities.[42]

3.3. The Definition of Lawful Objectives

3.3.1 THE FUNDAMENTAL CONCEPTION. The distinction between lawful and unlawful objectives does not necessarily correspond to the distinction between military and nonmilitary objectives, and one may ask if, in fact, its content is not summed up in the assertion that the civilian population is not a lawful objective. The distinction between material objectives would thus be irrelevant.[43] It may, however, be pointed out in this

---

[40] In effect, there is a presumption, based on the notion of the use of force as an exception, which favors the fundamental immunity of persons and objects; it is, therefore, necessary to define the exceptions.

[41] This term has been used by Pictet, *Laws and Customs Relating to Armed Conflicts,* REVIEW OF THE INTERNATIONAL COMMISSION OF JURISTS 22 (Mar. 1969).

[42] Meyrowitz, *supra* note 8, at 553–554.

[43] Schwarzenberger, *supra* note 1, at 217. One may also notice that several General Assembly resolutions on the subject do not refer to material objectives, but only to the civilian population and to destruction generally. On the other hand, the Assembly of the League

connection that since civilians are necessarily located somewhere, the immunity of the civilian population cannot fail to involve material objectives,[44] be they localities where that population is concentrated or installations indispensable for its existence. Thus, we must return to the notion of an objective that includes material objects (or localities) as well as individuals, and at the same time, we are brought back to the notion of civilian material objects, *e.g.*, schools or civilian hospitals, unlawful as such, however widely one may extend that notion.

On the other hand, it is sometimes asserted that the lawful objective is characterized only by the direct or indirect military importance which its destruction represents.[45] It is clear that if the military interest were dependent on the unilateral appraisal of the belligerents, the notion of military necessities in its widest sense would be reintroduced in a still more virulent form and would legitimate any destruction; for this reason the ICRC, in its 1956 Draft Rules, proposed to make this notion objective by using the term "generally acknowledged to be of military importance."[46] It seems indeed indispensable to preserve an element of objectivity in the definition of military objectives by distinguishing them from civilian objectives, and efforts at legal clarification must focus on that qualification.

Another problem is whether part of the definition of a military objective is that military advantage be derived from its destruction. The Hague Regulations as well as the Draft Rules of the ICRC and the draft resolution presented to the Institut de Droit International[47] all stipulate that the destruction should procure an "immediate," "distinct," or "substantial" military "advantage"; the terminology of the Draft Rules, followed by von der Heydte, add the expression "in the circumstances prevailing at the time," taking into account "mixed objectives which may have an occasional military importance only."[48] The necessity of proving the military advantage resulting from destruction may actually be a supplementary condition of the legality of the destruction in the prevailing circumstances. Particularly, in defining "mixed" objectives, it will be necessary to consider possible variations of their character. It does

---

of Nations stated in its Declaration of Sept. 28, 1938, that not only was the bombing of civilians unlawful, but also it was unlawful to bomb anything other than identifiable military objectives. *See* League of Nations Assembly Doc. A.69.1938, IX (Sept. 28, 1938).

[44] This is clearly pointed out in Schwarzenberger, *supra* note 1, at 217.

[45] Von der Heydte, *supra* note 16, *Observations de M. Emile Giraud* at 117–118; and STONE, LEGAL CONTROLS OF INTERNATIONAL CONFLICT, *supra* note 22, at 631.

[46] *Draft Rules*, *supra* note 16, art. 7, para. 2, at 66.

[47] Von der Heydte, *supra* note 16, at 181.

[48] *Draft Rules*, *supra* note 16, at 70–71.

not seem that the preceding remarks have any practical bearing; they nevertheless make it easier to define military objectives.

One may also ask whether a general definition of military objectives is really necessary or whether it would not be better to specify the objectives considered as military. A legally binding list of these objectives would have the great merit of reducing to a minimum the margin of uncertainty. On the other hand, if such a list were accompanied by an equally binding general definition, there might be controversies about its interpretation. Such a definition would also cover objectives not mentioned in this list. Admittedly, this definition should have a subsidiary character.

It must then be decided which categories of objectives—military, civilian, or both—should be included in the list. Logic argues that only military objectives should be mentioned,[49] the presumption being in favor of qualifying all possible objectives as civilian ones. However, mentioning certain civilian objectives as examples would dissipate all doubts about their qualification.

On the other hand, it is obviously impossible to specify military objectives without first having some notion of what the term means; this specification thus presupposes some sort of definition. However, it may be easier to first consider arguments for or against the inclusion of certain objectives in the category of military objectives, and then to try to infer a definition from these arguments.

As previously stated, the term "objective" in its widest sense refers to individuals as well as objects. Those two categories, however, raise problems which are so different that we must treat them separately as much as possible.[50] The remarks below concentrate mainly on the definition of material objectives; as far as individuals are concerned, we shall explore only the notion of "quasi-combatants."

3.3.2. The Specification of Material Military Objectives. These objectives are not always intrinsically military objectives. They are often civilian objectives which have been converted into military objectives by their occupation or by the use made of them; they may just as easily be reconverted into civilian objectives (dwellings, schools, etc.). These objectives are found mainly in the zone of military operations. The fact that a particular locality is being defended creates a presumption that it

---

[49] It is easier to define military objectives than civilian ones.

[50] *The Hague Rules* of 1923 and the *Draft Rules* of the International Committee of the Red Cross contain only negative rules concerning the prohibition of attacking civilian populations (and private property or property destined only for civilian use). *The Hague Rules, supra* note 16, art. 22; *Draft Rules, supra* note 16, art. 6.

is a purely military objective, and in such a case there is no obligation to spare buildings except to the extent made possible by circumstances.[51]

The most difficult question is that of the delimitation of secondary military objectives as far as strategic bombing is concerned. In this case we are not dealing with objectives directly used for fighting, but with objectives which are economically relevant to the conduct of the war.

As will be recalled, no matter what the lawful aim of the war itself may be, the lawful objectives "in war,"[52] *i.e.*, in the course of the conduct of hostilities, are delimited by the laws of war. These objectives are identified on the basis of the idea that war is essentially an armed contest. This is the only concept which is not beyond the pale of the law and which safeguards a minimum standard of civilization. This concept is also a realistic one because even today enemies are, in the end, defeated by armies,[53] and it would be an oversimplification to think that indiscriminate destruction necessarily brings military victory nearer. Unrestricted freedom of indiscriminate destruction prevents the singling out of those objectives which are really decisive. Military experts today admit that the results of Allied bombing raids on Germany fell very much short of expectations, that they did not become effective until they concentrated on sources of energy and transport, and that the brutality of that form of warfare, far from shattering the enemy's morale, may even have encouraged a spirit of resistance which prolonged the war.[54] The use of strategic nuclear weapons could undoubtedly alter this picture, but only at the price of making war exceed the bounds of a category regulated by law.[55]

It is, therefore, out of the question to consider as warlike any and every activity that might be suspected of even the remotest influence on

---

[51] The Hague Regulations of 1907, art. 27. We must distinguish between undefended localities in the zone of military operations, which may be occupied without striking a blow, and "open towns" located toward the rear of the zone of military operations; a unilateral declaration that a town is "open" cannot bind the other belligerent, for such a declaration may present unilateral advantages. This suggestion resembles that of Jennings, *Open Towns,* 2 BRIT. Y.B. INT'L L. 258–64 (1945). The installation of antiaircraft defenses in a town does not make it a defended town.

[52] Meyrowitz, *supra* note 8, at 550–551.

[53] Von der Heydte, *supra* note 16, at 21–22, points out that, during the discussion in the Special Political Committee of the United Nations General Assembly, in order to prove the unlawfulness of the 50-megaton bomb, its lack of either defensive value or military importance was stressed.

[54] FULLER, *supra* note 27, at 313. As far as the question of the strategic bombing of Japan is concerned, *see id.,* at 384. On the effect of nuclear bombing, *see id.,* at 392; SPETZLER, *supra* note 19, at 286, 320, 363. SPAIGHT, *supra* note 10, at 271. This last scholar is of a different opinion.

[55] G.A. Res. 1653 (XVI) of Nov. 24, 1961: ". . . b) The use of nuclear and thermonuclear weapons would exceed even the scope of war. . . ."

the course of hostilities, even if that suspicion may be proved.[56] Consequently, it would be out of place to utilize the analogy of the blockade
in this context, or even the lists of contraband employed in maritime and
economic warfare; these institutions do not envisage the destruction of
goods, but the prohibition of exporting them to enemy territory.

Only activities closely connected with military operations may reasonably be considered in the delimitation of those objectives which are intrinsically military. "It is the special, not the general, war potential of the
enemy that is still the objective."[57]

Now, what does a modern army need for the conduct of operations?
Essentially, weapons and munitions, means of transport, and motor fuel.
The installations used directly for the production of these goods or for
their servicing may consequently be assimilated to the products themselves and thus constitute military objectives. Moreover, it is necessary
to transport these products to the front: consequently, transport installations and communication lines also acquire at least a partial military
character. The difficulty consists in the definition of the character of
those installations used for both military and civilian production, *i.e.*,
"mixed" objectives. A reasonable interpretation would be based on the
relative importance of those two kinds of production.

The list contained in the Draft Rules gives a valid idea of what may be
considered a military objective from the point of view of strategic bombing[58] (except, of course, the objectives which are intrinsically military).
A partial list of the Rules is presented here:

6. Those lines and means of communication (railway lines, roads, bridges,
   tunnels, and canals) of fundamental military importance.
7. The installations of broadcasting and television stations, and telephone and
   telegraph exchanges of fundamental military importance.
8. Industries of fundamental importance for the conduct of the war:
   (a) industries for the manufacture of armaments such as weapons, munitions, rockets, armoured vehicles, military aircraft, fighting ships, including
   the manufacture of accessories and all other war material;
   (b) industries for the manufacture of supplies and material of a military

---

[56] Geneva Convention III, art. 50 contains a list of activities which prisoners of war may
pursue; it follows from this that certain activities have an intrinsically civilian character (*e.g.*,
agriculture), while the character of other activities is determined by the product or destination of the product of the activity (*e.g.*, construction, transportation).

[57] SPAIGHT, *supra* note 10, at 277; Swiss Army Manual, supra note 11, para. 26, recognizes
as military objectives plants, factories, and establishments "directly related to the activity
of the armed forces."

[58] Von der Heydte, *supra* note 16, at 18; the list contained in the *Hague Rules* appears,
on the contrary, too vague: ". . . factories constituting important and well-known centers
engaged in the manufacture of arms, ammunition, or distinctively military supplies: lines
of communication or transportation used for miltary purposes." Cmd. Paper 2201, art. 22(2).

character, such as transport and communications material, equipment for the armed forces;

(c) factories or plants which constitute other centers of production and manufacturing fundamentally important for the conduct of war. This includes the metallurgical, engineering, and chemical industries, which are essentially military;

(d) storage and transport installations whose basic function is to serve the industries referred to in (a) (c);

(e) installations providing energy mainly for national defence, *e.g.*, coal, other fuels, or atomic energy, and plants producing gas or electricity mainly for military consumption.

9. Installations constituting experimental research centers for the development of and experimentation with weapons and war material.

We shall limit ourselves to the following observations: it would no doubt be necessary to add to the number of "unconditional" objectives, installations for the production of motor fuel, including oilfields, and to add railway stations to the means of communication. Motor fuel and transport are really the mainspring of war.[59] For this reason one may also ask whether the term "lines and means of communication of fundamental military importance" is not too restrictive, since one will have to deal almost always with mixed objectives, the civilian importance of which may be no less essential.[60]

The harvests and the factories producing foodstuffs are not included in the list, and rightly so. Not only is it difficult to distinguish what is destined for the army from what is not, but also inclusion of these items would mean, in fact, starving out the civilian population because the products destined for the population would then certainly be requisitioned.[61] More importantly, waterworks, which also supply civilians, should be spared.

3.3.3. PERSONNEL AS A MILITARY OBJECTIVE: THE QUASI-COMBATANTS. The principle that armed forces are the only legitimate human objectives[62] and that civilians in groups (civilian population) or individually are not, is so well established that it is unnecessary to dwell on it.[63] However, it has been pointed out that without workers, military installations could

[59] *See supra* notes 52–54 and the accompanying text.

[60] *The Hague Rules,* supra note 16, art. 6, para. 2, prohibits attacks against "installations or means of transport which are for the exclusive use of . . . the civilian population." There is a subtle distinction here which is, perhaps, not entirely free from contradiction.

[61] Geneva Convention III, art. 50, includes agriculture in the list of occupations having a civilian character. *See supra* note 56.

[62] One particular question is whether noncombatants in the armed forces may be attacked. The list annexed to art. 7 of the *Draft Rules* of 1957 excepts those "who obviously take no active . . . part in hostilities." The issue is, however, controversial.

[63] *Draft Rules,* supra note 16, art. 6, para. 1.

not function; hence these workers have been called "quasi-combatants." It is quite generally admitted that the civilians who happen to be within military objectives incur a risk connected with those objectives[64] and that their presence does not confer any immunity whatsoever on the objective.[65] If the above notion implies that these workers—wherever they may be and at whatever moment—are lawful objectives,[66] then the immunity of the civilian population as such is brought into question, for it is impossible to draw distinctions between civilians. This is an entirely new concept and one which must be fought energetically. It creates a class of nonprivileged combatants whose activities, nevertheless, are not considered lawful, and it fails to account for the fact that workers are engaged in activities useful to the war only as long as war installations to that end exist. The lawful objectives to be destroyed are those installations rather than an elusive and easily replaceable labor force.

3.3.4 THE OBLIGATION TO TAKE PRECAUTIONS. The power of certain modern weapons and methods of warfare may make illusory the distinction between armed forces and civilians, between military and nonmilitary material objectives. As a general rule belligerents must take necessary precautions to adapt weapons and methods to the objective attacked, according to the principle of proportionality, and they must make sure that the objective to be attacked is really a military objective.[67] Target-area bombing must be evaluated from this point of view.

Certain publicists, it is true, consider that target-area bombing has become a normal and legitimate method of warfare.[68] This, however, is tantamount to neglecting the principle of proportionality and thus it calls into question the distinction between lawful and unlawful objectives. It follows, therefore, that such bombing is admissible only in zones of military operations (even here a distinction must be made between defended and nondefended localities) and zones where military objectives are contiguous and cover a considerable part of the relevant territory.[69]

---

[64] Schwarzenberger, *supra* note 1, at 217; SPAIGHT, *supra* note 10, at 43; Hague Convention IX respecting Bombardment by Naval Forces, art. 2, para. 2.

[65] *Draft Rules,* supra note 16, art. 6, para. 3. This is explicitly stated by the Swiss Army Manual, *supra* note 11, para. 26. The presence of the civilian population in defended localities is, then, not an obstacle to their bombardment. The Hague Regulations, *supra* note 16, arts. 26, 27. This should answer the question raised by von der Heydte, *supra* note 16, at 171, 182–183.

[66] STONE, *supra* note 22, at 629.

[67] U.S. Army Field Manual, paras. 3, 41; Swiss Army Manual, supra note 11, para. 26; *Draft Rules,* arts. 8–10.

[68] SPAIGHT, *supra* note 10, at 271; STONE, *supra* note 22, at 629.

[69] *Draft Rules, supra* note 16, art. 10, forbids the bombing of zones where military objectives are at a distance from one another.

3.3.5. THE MILITARY IMPORTANCE OF THE DESTRUCTION. This condition, mentioned previously,[70] is the expression of the principle which prohibits the causing of unnecessary destruction and human suffering. Hence, the military importance of the objective would have to be rather substantial in order to be proportionate to the amount of destruction.[71] While military importance does not necessarily have to be immediate, it must not be hypothetical.[72] The destruction of civilian objectives which have become military ones by occupation or use, or the destruction of mixed objectives, would of necessity be subject to closer scrutiny than the destruction of intrinsically military objectives; the latter are presupposed to be of military importance. And, objectives situated in the hinterland would have to be scrutinized more closely than those located in the zone of fighting.

Section 4. NEUTRALITY IN ARMED CONFLICTS

M. CHERIF BASSIOUNI

The scope of this section is limited to the rights and duties of neutrals and belligerents, and the interaction of these parties under the general tenets of neutrality law in wartime situations.

At the beginning of the twentieth century, neutrality was generally understood to be

> . . . the legal position of a state which remained aloof from a war between two other states or groups of states while maintaining certain rights towards the belligerent and observing certain duties prescribed by customary law or by international conventions or treaties.[1]

Although most nations of that era would have accepted this definition of neutrality, there would not have been a clear concensus on exactly what constituted that "legal position."

While most nations in 1900 had their own individual notion of neutrality law, it remained nothing more than a vague nebulous composite that had grown in an awkward and unruly manner from the customary and unilateral actions of nations in the stress of war situations. Neutrality was devoid of international agreement and met with varying interpretations, even by the same nation, depending upon its position in a conflict—belligerent or neutral. This neutrality, as it was loosely constructed, was not

---

[70] *Supra* note 59.

[71] Here again we return to the notion of proportionality.

[72] *Draft Rules, supra* note 16, art. 7, para. 3; von der Heydte, *supra* note 16, at 208. Both of these reports convey this idea by the words, "in the circumstances ruling at the time."

[1] FENWIK, INTERNATIONAL LAW 716–749 (4th ed. 1965).

an ancient concept and was not even enunciated in international relations until the late Middle Ages. Before that time, belligerents worked under the theory that any nation not an ally was an enemy. Impartiality was deemed to be nonexistent. Grotius in 1625 was the first to approach the traditional concept of neutrality, but his neutrality knew nothing of impartiality. He saw neutrality as a nation doing nothing to aid a belligerent engaged in a wicked cause while doing all possible to avoid hampering a nation fighting for a just cause.[2]

It was not until the wars of the eighteenth century that nations began to respect the position of neutral territory and shipping as having distinctive qualities. There was not, however, any common agreement as to exactly what these qualities might be.[3] It is because of this common lack of definition and the resultant problems that were evidenced throughout the wars of the eighteenth and nineteenth centuries that the movement for international agreement in this area reached its fruition in the Hague Conference of 1907.

Although the Hague Conventions were signed over sixty years ago, they remain the most extensive attempt at codification of neutrality law. The provisions of these Conventions are divided into seven broad categories.

The forty-four nations that assembled at the Hague in 1907 represented the then significant nations of the world. Thirteen Conventions eventually grew out of this conference and two of these, conventions V and XIII dealt with the problems of neutrality. The former was devoted to neutrality in land warfare, while the latter embraced naval neutrality.[4] As a result of these agreements, international law on neutrality can be roughly subdivided into the following general categories.

4.1. The Inviolability of Neutral Territory

In articles 1 thru 5 of Convention V, the Hague signatories clearly expounded the sanctity of neutral territory. Belligerents could not move troops or munitions across neutral territory; neutral territory could not be used as a base of operations; corps of combatants could not be formed nor could recruiting occur within neutral territory.[5] The inviolability of neutral territory was quickly extended to the sea and the air. Convention XIII saw prohibition against search and seizure in neutral waters and limitations on the use of neutral ports.[6] Although air power was still a

---

[2] Hackworth, 7 DIGEST OF INTERNATIONAL LAW 345 (1943).

[3] Oppenheim, II INTERNATIONAL LAW 627 (7th ed., H. Lauterpacht ed. 1952).

[4] See Appendices II & III, and for the application of neutrality to naval warfare, see MALLISON, NAVAL WARFARE, ch. II, § 3.

[5] SCOTT (ed.), THE REPORTS OF THE HAGUE CONFERENCES OF 1899 and 1907, at 532 (1917).

[6] PFANKUCHEN, A DOCUMENTARY TEXTBOOK IN INTERNATIONAL LAW 872 (1940).

fantasy in 1907, later generations included restrictions on its use in the traditional understanding of neutral rights. The establishment of air-fields, the fueling of planes, and the indiscriminate use of a neutral's airspace, all became accepted as violations of neutral territory.[7] Belligerents were therefore obligated to respect the rights of neutral nations and to abstain in neutral territory—land, water, or airspace—from any act which would, if knowingly permitted by any nation, constitute a violation of neutrality. The inviolability of territory is not merely a neutral right, but is the right of every sovereign nation. It is so greatly emphasized, however, in this area because it is usually the crux of a nation's struggle to maintain her neutrality. Neutrality often becomes focused on a nation's striving to maintain her territorial integrity.[8]

4.2. Impartiality

Impartiality is the cornerstone of the traditional doctrine of neutrality. It is the tightrope which the neutral chooses to walk; a fall to one side or the other is so devastating that the crippled neutral will not be able again to ascend the ladder to the lofty heights of detachment that neutrality requires. The Hague Conventions called for impartiality to be exercised by a neutral in regulating the use of its territory in any form.[9] A neutral power had to apply total impartiality to the belligerents in regard to any conditions, restrictions, or prohibitions made by it in regard to the admission into its ports, territorial waters, and territory. Public officers of neutral nations should also avoid all actions which might impute nonimpartial motives not only to themselves but more particularly to the neutral nation.[10] The obligation to avoid favoritism is so exacting that the neutral violates his status by giving assistance to any side, no matter how limited. A violation also occurs even though the same assistance was offered to both opponents at the same time.[11] All enforcement actions by the neutral must be as vigorously pursued against one belligerent as against another. Failure to secure equal enforcement actively aids the belligerent who is more leniently treated and violates the neutral's obligation of impartiality.[12]

4.3. The Response of a Neutral to Violations of Its Neutrality

While neutrality is basically a negative theory predicated upon the noninvolvement of one nation in the affairs of another, it does impose its

[7] Whiteman, II Digest of International Law 215 (1968).
[8] Hackworth, *supra* note 2 at 357.
[9] Scott, *supra* note 5, at 534.
[10] Hackworth, *supra* note 2, at 375.
[11] Whiteman, *supra* note 7, at 180.
[12] Oppenheim, *supra* note 3, at 675.

positive obligations, as well, upon a would-be advocate. Neutrals must take positive action in certain areas to force violators to adhere to the rights that a neutral must enjoy. There is no general agreement on what degree of force can or must be used, but most authorities will at least recognize a right to use force, if not an obligation to do so, in certain qualified circumstances. In article 10, Convention V, of the Hague Conventions, the conferees recognized that "The fact of a neutral power resisting, even by force, attempts to violate its neutrality cannot be regarded as a hostile act."[13] The Hague conference further held that a neutral had to use force to intern any troops or ships which violated its territory. While some commentators feel that force should be used only under extraordinary circumstances such as the violation of territorial integrity,[14] others find a broader justification for imposing an obligation of using force to respond to such violations.[15] Secretary of State Robert Lansing wrote:

> When the acts of belligerents seriously infringe the rights of neutrals, a neutral government cannot permit such acts to be passed over in silence. It is a duty which a government owes to its citizens and for which it was established to protest against such violations and to endeavor to prevent their repetition.[16]

The response to such violations, however, must be most cautious to avoid infringement of its obligation of impartiality. Where the treatment of a belligerent is discriminatory or directly hostile but it is a retaliatory action adopted by the neutral because of previous injury by an illegal act of the belligerent, such action is justified and is not therefore deemed a violation of the neutral's duty of impartiality.[17] The obligation of force which a nation must employ is limited, however, by the relative strength of that nation. No obligation beyond the physical power of the neutral is imposed. Thus a small state is not called upon to intervene forcibly between the contending belligerents to insist upon the honoring of their neutral rights.[18]

4.4. Measures Which a Neutral May Employ in Advance to Prevent Violations of Its Neutrality

When a war has erupted which could conceivably involve a neutral, that nation need not wait for a violation before she enforces her rights. International law recognizes a neutral's rights to take prior measures

[13] Scott, *supra* note 5, at 534.
[14] Whiteman, *supra* note 7, at 175.
[15] Hackworth, *supra* note 2, at 385.
[16] *Id.* at 362.
[17] *Id.* at 364.
[18] *See, e.g.,* Fenwick, *supra* note 1.

which might deter a belligerent from chancing a violation of a given nation's neutral position. How extensive may a neutral's preparations be?

A neutral state, adjacent to a theater of war, has the right to mobilize a portion of its military force to secure the sanctity of its borders, to prevent belligerent troops from utilizing its soil, and to intern such troops as may have entered its soil.[19] The Hague Conference on Naval Warfare elevated this right into that of duty. A neutral had to exercise such surveillance and employ such force as was at his disposal to enforce his obligations under the Convention. The neutral must prevent the fitting-out and sailing of ships designed to commit hostile acts of war; it must prevent the misuse of its ports, and it must insure the integrity of its territorial waters. A neutral was bound to invoke "every means at its disposal" to enforce these rights once a state of war had been declared.[20] The neutral's right of self-defense further permitted neutral vessels to arm themselves, and neutral nations could also lay mines in their territorial waters provided that such mines were not laid in a manner which would be violative of the neutral's right of impartiality.[21]

4.5. Infringement of Privilege That Must Be Accepted by a Neutral

When a nation embraces neutrality, its obligations fall under two general duties: (1) impartiality and (2) the submission to certain actions by the belligerent to insure her belligerent privileges. The acquiescence referred to in a later category focuses upon the problem of neutral shipping.[22] A neutral country must tolerate certain acts on the part of belligerents which, in the time of peace, she would not allow. The belligerent claims the right to prevent the neutral from contributing anything to its opponent's ability to resist longer or more effectively. Therefore, the neutral must tolerate the visit and search of its private vessels and their seizure for the carriage of contraband, for violations of a just blockade, on grounds of unneutral service, or the illegal exercise of certain forms of military authority. A belligerent is also free to exercise military authority over neutral persons and property in the belligerent's own territory or in occupied territory.[23]

4.6. Situations Which Do Not Impose a Duty Upon a Neutral for Positive Action

A neutral nation's vigilance in safeguarding its neutrality is restricted within definite metes and bounds. A neutral has no duty to restrict cer-

[19] Whiteman, *supra* note 7, at 185.
[20] Pfankuchen, *supra* note 6, at 877.
[21] Whiteman, *supra* note 7, at 187.
[22] Oppenheim, *supra* note 3, at 673.
[23] Hackworth, *supra* note 2, at 360.

tain individual actions. Unless there is the presence of a totalitarian state, and even in those instances, it is nearly impossible to control the outpouring of sentiment on the part of nations for one side or the other. This liberty extends to the press, while a vast number of authorities would hold that even the state has the right to express its sympathy toward one side and criticize their opponent without violating its neutral status.[24] The neutral is further absolved from the obligation of preventing persons from crossing its frontiers, separately, to offer their services to a belligerent. There is no obligation for the neutral to restrict the use of its public communications. The wounded and sick of a belligerent are allowed to pass over neutral territory, while escaped prisoners of war are to be left at liberty in a neutral country.[25]

Finally, the most controversial aspect of this subtopic has to do with a neutral's position in relation to the supplying of arms to belligerents. Most authorities find that the direct supply of a belligerent by a neutral government is a violation; difficulty arises, however, over the question of the right of the private citizen in a neutral country to supply a belligerent with materiel of war. The municipal law of most neutrals prohibits its nationals from engaging in such activity, but under international law, "A neutral Power is not called upon to prevent the export or transport, on behalf of one or other of the belligerents, of arms, munitions of war. . . ."[26]

4.7. Citizens of a Neutral State

The fact that a nation adopts a neutral stance in a conflict does not predetermine the actions of each of its citizens. The rights of a neutral belong to a national of a neutral country only as long as he operates within the bounds of that neutrality. A person cannot avail himself of this neutrality if he commits a hostile act against a belligerent or if he commits an act in favor of a belligerent, particularly if he voluntarily enlists in the ranks of one of the parties. In such cases, the former neutral shall not be more severely treated by the belligerent he opposed than any other national of that belligerent's enemy.[27] There is also in the area of neutral persons a reaffirmation of the principle that the individual does not lose his neutral privileges even though he furnishes loans or supplies to only one side in the war.

4.8. The End of Neutrality as a Legal Status

If "war" is unlawful, then neutrality does not exist, as its very nature

---

[24] Whiteman, *supra* note 7, at 179.
[25] Scott, *supra* note 5, at 535.
[26] *Id.* at 534.
[27] *Id.* at 535.

is to stand outside the purview of a war. The abolition or renunciation of war by treaty or declaration did not stop armed conflicts, it merely changed the labels. To the extent that armed conflicts still take place, neutrality remains a valid concept and its practice should be recognized. Most authorities consider that the United Nations Charter ended neutrality. One of those, Fenwick, refers to it as follows:

> It was to be expected that, with the establishment of the "wider and permanent system of general security" contemplated in the Atlantic Charter and the "general international organization" specifically provided for in the Moscow Declaration of October 30, 1943, the existing international law in respect to the rights and duties of neutral states would no longer be regarded as having legal validity. The adoption of the Charter of the United Nations on June 26, 1945, finally marked the end of neutrality as a legal system. No provision was made for a separate neutral status on the part of the states not invited to participate in the framing of the Charter and not subsequently admitted to membership. In as much, however, as action by the Security Council to enforce the terms of the Charter would not be "war" in the technical sense, it was possible to overlook the technical question as to the rights and duties of states not participating in the action of the Security Council.
>
> *"Neutralism" in relation to the "cold war."* To be sharply distinguished from neutral states under the old, now antiquated, law of neutrality, are the states that have adopted an attitude of neutrality in respect to the obligations of collective security under the Charter of the United Nations. "Neutralism" appears to describe the position of certain states that are unwilling to take a part in the decisions relating not to war in the traditional sense, but to the "cold war" involving the conflicting policies of the Soviet Union and the Western World which, the new neutrals fear, may at any time involve them in a conflict in respect to which they are not prepared to take sides. Justification for the failure to live up to the obligations of the Charter in respect to collective security appears to lie in the fact that the anticipated collective security system broke down from the start, releasing them from their obligations on the principle *rebus non sic stantibus*.[28]

The status of Australia and Switzerland would nonetheless attest to the contrary of such a position. The concept of neutrality as conceived in an epoch when war was still a sovereign right has indeed ended, but so long as armed conflicts continue, the practice of neutrality will always exist and to that extent is bound to be legally recognized and regulated.

[28] Fenwick, *supra* note 1, at 727–28.

CHAPTER VII

UNLAWFUL WEAPONS

Section 1. GENERAL PRINCIPLES

DENISE BINDSCHEDLER-ROBERT

As has already been mentioned,[1] a close connection exists between the principle of delimitation of lawful and unlawful objectives and the weapons which may be used. This topic is one that must be placed within the framework of the regulation of the means of injuring the enemy.

The laws and customs of armed conflicts contain a principle formulated in the Hague Regulations in the following terms: "The right of belligerents to the conflict to adopt means of injuring the enemy is not unlimited."[2] This rule imposes on the belligerents the general obligation to refrain from cruel or treacherous behavior. As far as weapons are concerned, since the nineteenth century this humanitarian principle has been embodied in two rules: one forbids the use of poisons, while the other prohibits the use of weapons capable of causing superfluous injuries. These two principles have in turn been incorporated into the prohibition of particular weapons; the most important conventional instrument on this subject is the Geneva Protocol of 1925 forbidding the use of gases and of bacteriological methods of warfare.[3]

With the appearance of new weapons of mass destruction, the problem has taken on a new aspect. Because the effect of these weapons renders their selective use impossible, they threaten a fundamental norm of the laws of armed conflicts: the distinction between lawful and unlawful objectives. Weapons which by their nature necessarily violate legal rules

[1] See *supra* § 3, ch. VI.

[2] The Hague Regulations, art. 22; the preamble of the Declaration of St. Petersburg of 1868 expresses the same idea.

[3] The other relevant acts are the Declaration of St. Petersburg (explosive projectiles), the Hague Declarations II & III of 1899 (projectiles diffusing asphyxiating or deleterious gases, bullets which expand or flatten in the human body). The Washington Treaty of 1922 Respecting the Use of Submarines and Asphyxiating Gases may also be mentioned. It was never ratified, but it contains stipulations concerning submarines.

may be considered unlawful per se, unless, of course, there has emerged a rule establishing exceptions which make them lawful. A rule legalizing weapons of mass destruction would have the paradoxical result of making all the laws of armed conflicts meaningless by legalizing total war.

Finally, it should be added that the prohibitions contained in the laws and customs of war, in contrast to the law of disarmament, refer only to the use of weapons.

Not only are the rules prohibiting the use of certain weapons valid in regard to specific weapons,[4] but also they supply a test which may be applied generally.[5] Thus, a new weapon is not lawful just because it is new if it is contrary to a general rule governing the use of certain types of weapons. Such a weapon would become lawful only if a rule establishing an exception in its favor has emerged.[6]

Although in the case of weapons of mass destruction the legality of a weapon depends directly on the legality of the objective, it is generally possible to draw a distinction between the weapon and the objective. Thus, the use of certain weapons may be lawful or not, according to the objective to be attacked; simultaneously, the illegality may only consist of the use of the weapon itself.[7] This distinction is an important one.

Section 2. THE LAW OF WAR AND WEAPONS OF MASS DESTRUCTION

Martial Tricaud

2.1. Introduction

In the course of armed conflict, the main objective of the belligerents is to inflict on the enemy the greatest possible harm by all possible means,

[4] *See* U.S. DEPT. OF THE ARMY, FIELD MANUAL, THE LAW OF LAND WARFARE, para. 34 (1956), with respect to weapons causing unnecessary human suffering.

[5] The Austrian army manual defines weapons capable of causing unnecessary injuries as follows: "The means of fighting causing superfluous injuries are those whose use is not absolutely necessary in order to crush the enemy or which cause human suffering out of proportion to the advantage derived from the use of means of fighting considered." 1 KRIEGSVÖLKERRECHT FUR DIE TRUPPE [hereafter cited as Austrian Army Manual] ch. 8 (1965). For the distinction between "superfluous injuries" and "unnecessary human suffering," *see* H. MEYROWITZ, LES ARMES BIOLOGIQUES ET LE DROIT INTERNATIONAL 92 (1968).

[6] E. CASTREN, THE PRESENT LAW OF WAR AND NEUTRALITY 187 (1954); Tucker, *The Law of War and Neutrality at Sea*, NAVAL WAR COLLEGE, INT'L L. STUDIES 45–47 (1957); *The Shimoda Case*, 8 JAPANESE ANNUAL OF INT'L L. 235–36 (1964). In the Shimoda case, the District Court of Tokyo clearly stated, ". . . we cannot regard a weapon as legal only because it is a new weapon. . . ."

[7] MEYROWITZ, *supra* note 5, at 25. Meyrowitz makes the distinction between what he calls the "target aspect" and the "weapon aspect." It has been suggested that napalm be declared unlawful only in respect to certain objectives. *See also Reaffirmation et developpement des lois et coutumes*, REPORT OF THE ICRC, 71 (1969).

except those which are prohibited by the rules of war imposed upon the combatants. As armed conflicts become less and less acceptable to mankind, such limitations and regulations on the conduct of hostilities progressively increase, for they stem from an increased awareness for humanitarian considerations and continue to have as their purpose the elimination of suffering.

Even during the nineteenth century, weapons which were designed to inflict useless suffering had become the subject of some regulation,[1] *e.g.*, explosive or incendiary bullets of small caliber were prohibited under the declaration of St. Petersburg of December 11, 1868, and the use of bullets which may explode or spread out in the human body (known as dumdum bullets) and the use of explosives which spread asphyxiating gases or deleterious substances were prohibited under the Hague Declaration of July 29, 1899.

It may be noted that asphyxiating gases were used for the first time by the Germans during World War I, and the Allies responded in using the same as reprisals. However, the use of gas was formally prohibited by the Treaty of Washington of February 5, 1922, and the Geneva Protocol of June 27, 1925.

One should also recall that both the Fourth Hague Convention of 1907 and the Geneva Convention of 1949 prohibit the attack on or bombing of undefended cities and open cities as well as the infliction of harm upon the civilian population not engaged in the conduct of warfare. In addition, naval bombardment is regulated by the Ninth Hague Convention of 1907 which also prohibits bombardment of open cities or undefended cities. A similar prohibition on bombardment by air is contained in article 25 of the Annex to the Fourth Hague Convention of 1907. It was not, however, until a commission of jurists gathered at the Hague in 1922–23 that a draft for the regulation of aerial warfare was prepared and finally submitted on February 19, 1923. However, this draft of aerial warfare regulations was never transformed into an international agreement, and therefore during World War II aerial warfare was not regulated. As a result, civilian populations were subject to intense bombardment.

Finally, in 1945, the United States used atomic weapons, and since then the world has continued to be concerned with the use of weapons of mass destruction. The concern is not confined to the use of such weapons in the course of combat between armed forces and is especially felt with respect to the effect of such use on the civilian population.

---

[1] For an incisive account of the international regulation of warfare, *see* Mallison, Jr., *The Laws of War and the Juridical Control of Weapons of Mass Destruction in General and Limited Wars*, 36 GEO. WASH. L. REV. 308 (1967).

2.2. Efforts Toward Disarmament Prior to the United Nations

The history of war shows that in its first stages it was a prerogative of each state to arm itself without any restriction whatsoever. And the first efforts during the late nineteenth and early twentieth centuries to impose certain restrictions were without success. One such notable effort that failed was the 1899 Hague Conference, which was initiated at the suggestion of the Czar of Russia to realize the limitations of armaments. But most European countries continued their race for armaments, a race that resulted in World War I with widespread death and destruction.

Following World War I, President Wilson, in his famous fourteen-point message of January 8, 1918, made a succinct statement that armaments should be limited to the extent that it was compatible with a country's internal security. The idea was accepted insofar as the Covenant of the League of Nations provided in article 8(1), that member states of the League recognized that the maintenance of peace required a reduction in national armament, in such a way that it would be the least incompatible with national security and the execution of international obligations as required by collective security action. The Council of the League of Nations was authorized to prepare plans for the reduction of armaments, and member states were supposed to make a complete disclosure of their armaments as well as their future military plans. A permanent commission was to assist the Council in its task.

As the later events showed, the League was unsuccessful in halting the armament race. However, in February 1932, a general conference on disarmament was convened in Geneva, which was attended by fifty-nine states, including several nonmembers of the League, such as the United States and the USSR. The Conference could agree only on the adoption of a resolution known as the Benes Resolution, under which aerial attacks against civilian populations were prohibited. Among other provisions, the resolution recalled the prohibition already established on the use of chemical, bacteriological, and incendiary explosives and limited the individual tonnage of tanks and the caliber of ground artillery, envisaging the possibility of devising a verification and control mechanism.

The conference held two more sessions in the year 1933, but its work had reached an impasse. Germany withdrew from the Conference, denouncing the military clauses of the Treaty of Versailles, and reoccupied the left bank of the Rhine River. From that point on, Europe kept rearming and moving toward World War II.

2.3. Efforts at the United Nations

Under the U.N. Charter, the Security Council is delegated the function of elaborating plans for the regulation of armaments.[2] However, in January 1946, the General Assembly had also established an atomic energy commission,[3] which was composed of representatives of eleven states, then members of the Security Council, and a representative of Canada, then a nonmember but especially invited because of its competence to make a significant contribution in the area.

The commission was charged with insuring the control of atomic energy and eliminating atomic weapons from national arsenals, as well as other weapons of mass destruction. From its inception, however, the commission was presented with two divergent but equally forceful plans to accomplish its objective—that of the USSR, which required the destruction of all atomic weapons in stock, and that of the United States, which proposed the establishment of an international control mechanism prior to the interdiction of manufacturing, stockpiling, and use of atomic weapons.[4]

In addition to the atomic energy commission, established by the Assembly, the Security Council decided to set up a commission on conventional weapons, consisting of representatives of the Council members.[5] However, in January 1952, the General Assembly adopted a resolution to dissolve both the commissions,[6] replacing them by a single commission on disarmament.[7] This conclusion had been reached in view of the fact that it was impossible to limit or to reduce conventional weapons before reaching some kind of agreement on weapons of mass destruction and atomic weapons as well. The new commission was composed of the representatives of the eleven member states of the Security Council and the representative of Canada, essentially the same membership as that of the earlier atomic energy commission. The commission was charged with the preparation of studies to be eventually incorporated in a treaty providing for the regulation, limitation, and reduction of all armed forces and of all armaments, as well as for the effective international control of atomic energy. The objective was to ensure the prohibition of atomic weapons and the use of this energy for peaceful purposes.

The Commission's plan of work consisted of the following item, among others: disclosure and verification of all armed forces and armaments, including atomic armaments.[8] This was to be predicated on the establishment of an international inspection procedure. In addition, a system was

---

[2] Under article 26 of the Charter.

[3] *See* G. A. Res. 1(1) adopted on Jan. 24, 1946.

[4] For a short account, *see* THE UNITED NATIONS AND DISARMAMENT, 1945–1970, at 12–22 (U.N. Publ., Sales No. 70.IX.1., 1970) [hereinafter cited as U.N. AND DISARMAMENT].

[5] *See* Res. 18 of Feb. 13, 1947, U.N. Doc. S/268/Rev.1/corr.1 (1947).

[6] *U.N. and Disarmament, supra* note 4, at 23–24.

[7] *Id.* at 41.

[8] *Id.* at 45.

to be devised which would be capable of uncovering any violations, thus serving as a deterrent and aiding in the accomplishment of the objective of disarmament.

In 1954, the disarmament commission created a subcommittee composed of representatives of five powers namely, Canada, the United States, France, Great Britain, and the USSR.[9] Henceforth, it was the task of this subcommittee to seek agreement on a comprehensive plan of disarmament. Over the next three years there were several proposals presented before the subcommittee as well as the General Assembly by the Western powers on the one hand and the Soviet Union on the other.[10] But the positions were so divergent that no agreement could be reached on a comprehensive disarmament plan. The subcommittee abandoned its efforts and even the General Assembly was reconciled to discussing isolated steps toward disarmament.[11]

However, in November 1958, the General Assembly accepted the Soviet proposal to expand the membership of the disarmament commission. It was to be composed of all members of the United Nations for 1959 and was consituted on an ad hoc basis.[12] Subsequently, a Ten-Nation Committee on Disarmament was established. The committee was composed of five countries, namely the United States, Great Britain, Italy, France, and Canada, and five Eastern European countries, namely the USSR, Poland, Czechoslovakia, Rumania, and Bulgaria. The conference of the committee was convened in Geneva in March, 1960, and ended its deliberations on June 27, 1960, when the five East European delegations withdrew from the conference. In a tense atmosphere, charges and countercharges were exchanged; the Eastern European Powers criticized the Western Powers for allegedly avoiding the question of general and complete disarmament, while the Western Powers criticized the Eastern European Powers for avoiding the question of control and preliminary measures.[13]

During the next eighteen months consultations between the United States and the Soviet Union led to a joint statement of agreed principles as a basis for further negotiations on disarmament and eventually to the adoption of a General Assembly resolution which endorsed the United States-Soviet Union agreement on establishing an eighteen-nation dis-

---

[9] *See* Official Records of the Disarmament Commission, 35th Meeting and Supp. for Apr., May & June 1954, Docs. DC/47, DC/48, and DC/49 (1954).

[10] For a brief report see U.N. AND DISARMAMENT, *supra* note 4, at 51–68.

[11] For the 1957 resolutions, *see* G. A. Res. 1148(XII) & 1149(XII) of Nov. 14, 1957, which were adopted by 56 votes to 9, with 15 abstentions and 71 votes to 9 with 1 abstention, respectively.

[12] G. A. Res. 1252A & D(XIII) adopted by 76 votes to 6, with 2 abstentions.

[13] U.N. AND DISARMAMENT, *supra* note 4, at 81–84.

armament committee (ENDC). The Assembly recommended that the committee, "as a matter of utmost urgency," should undertake negotiations with a view to reaching an agreement on general and complete disarmament under effective international control.[14]

This new committee of eighteen was composed of five states, namely the United States, Great Britain, Canada, Italy, and France; five from the Eastern European Countries, namely the USSR, Poland, Czechoslovakia, Rumania, and Hungary; and eight neutral or nonaligned countries, namely Brazil, Burma, Ethiopia, India, Mexico, Nigeria, the UAR, and Sweden. In fact, it became a seventeen-member committee, as France abstained from participating in the work of the committee.

2.3.1. PARTIAL TEST BAN TREATY. The first major accomplishment of the committee was the Partial Test Ban Treaty, which was signed in Moscow on August 5, 1963.[15] The Treaty banned the testing of nuclear weapons in the atmosphere, the outer space, and under water and was essentially the result of negotiations carried in Geneva outside the ENDC. The major powers primarily responsible for the treaty were the United States, Great Britain, and the USSR. While the treaty did not touch upon the possibility of engaging in underground experimentation, the three signatory states declared in the preamble that they are "seeking to achieve the discontinuance of all test explosions of nuclear weapons for all time," and proclaimed as their aim "the speediest possible achievement of an agreement on total and general disarmament under strict international control in accordance with the objectives of the United Nations. . . ." Each party to the treaty

> . . . undertakes to prohibit, to prevent, and not to carry out any nuclear weapon test explosion, or any other nuclear explosion, at any place under its jurisdiction or control: (a) in the atmosphere; beyond its limits; including outer space; or under water, including territorial waters or high seas. . . .[16]

However, the treaty does not establish any mechanism for control; it merely enunciates a prohibition. Nor is the prohibition contained in the treaty in itself a measure of disarmament, for the nuclear powers continue to conserve their stockpiles of nuclear weapons.

2.3.2. NONPROLIFERATION OF NUCLEAR WEAPONS. The next significant development in the control of nuclear weapons was the Nuclear Nonpro-

[14] G. A. Res. 1722(XVI) of Dec. 20, 1961 (*adopted unanimously*).

[15] For the text of the treaty, *see* U.N. AND DISARMAMENT, *supra* note 4, at 450–52. For similar arrangements entered prior to this treaty, *see* the peace treaties of Feb. 10, 1947, and the treaty on the Atlantic of Dec. 1, 1950.

[16] *See* art. 1.

liferation Treaty.[17] It should be noted that the Moscow Treaty of 1963 had already indicated a willingness on the part of both the United States and the Soviet Union to prevent the proliferation of nuclear weapons. Finally, this willingness on the part of the two Super Powers was given a formal recognition by a General Assembly resolution in June 1968, by which the Assembly commended the Treaty on the Nonproliferation of Nuclear Weapons. It should also be noted that the efforts at the United Nations to prevent the spread of nuclear weapons had continued for almost twelve years before an agreement was reached.[18] Among the nuclear powers, France abstained from voting on this resolution. However, the French representative declared that his government will, in the future, conform its conduct to that of the states which had voted in favor of the resolution.

2.3.3. ANALYSIS OF THE NUCLEAR NONPROLIFERATION TREATY. In the preamble, the parties express their belief that the proliferation of nuclear weapons would considerably increase the danger of nuclear war. They undertake to cooperate in facilitating the application of International Atomic Energy Agency safeguards on peaceful use of atomic energy. They also express their support for research and development efforts toward safeguarding effectively the flow of raw material and fissionable products destined especially for peaceful usage. Furthermore, affirming the principle that benefits of nuclear technology should be available for peaceful purposes to all parties, they declare that it is their intent to cease the nuclear arms race "at the earliest possible date" and urge the cooperation of all states in order to accomplish this objective.

It is important to note that the treaty does not contain a definition of nuclear weapons. Therefore, it is bombs and nuclear warheads and not nuclear reactors or producers of fissionable material which are the object of articles 1 and 2 of the treaty. "Nuclear weapons," however, applies both to offensive and defensive weapons.

The first three articles of the treaty deserve specific mention: article 1 of the treaty imposes an obligation upon every contracting state not to transfer to anyone directly or indirectly nuclear weapons or other nuclear explosive devices or the control of such weapons or devices, nor to aid, encourage, induce in any way, any state which does not have nuclear capability of any sort to manufacture or acquire in any way nuclear weapons or explosive devices.

Under article 2, every state which has no nuclear weapons and is party

[17] The text of the treaty is conveniently contained in U.N. AND DISARMAMENT, *supra* note 4, at 474–78.
[18] *Id.* at 257–306.

to this treaty undertakes not to accept from any transferor, directly or indirectly, any nuclear weapons or other nuclear devices or the control of such weapons or devices, nor to manufacture or acquire in any way nuclear weapons or nuclear devices, nor to seek or receive aid in any manner for the manufacture of nuclear weapons or other nuclear devices.

Under article 3(2) contracting states undertake not to furnish (1) raw material or fissionable products or (2) equipment or material especially designed or prepared for the processing, use or production of fissionable material to a state which does not possess nuclear weapons even for peaceful purposes, unless such raw material or fissionable products are subjected to the safeguards required by the treaty. The safeguards are to be negotiated with the International Atomic Energy Agency, as provided in article 3(1 and 4). Negotiations for these agreements must commence within 180 days from the original entry into force of the treaty, but no later than eighteen months after the commencement of negotiations.

Under article 4(2) all the parties to the treaty undertake to facilitate the exchange of equipment, materials, and technical and scientific information with a view to a maximum utilization of nuclear energy for peaceful purposes.

Article 10 of the treaty grants the right to each state to withdraw from the treaty in the exercise of its national sovereignty if it decides that extraordinary events have jeopardized the supreme interests of its country. Such withdrawal must be notified to the other parties of the treaty as well as to the Security Council three months in advance. Notification must also include a statement of the extraordinary events which led it to consider that its supreme interest had been jeopardized.

The treaty entered into force on March 5, 1970, when it had been signed by ninety-two countries and ratified by forty-seven. On that day, the United States, the USSR, and the United Kingdom simultaneously ratified the treaty. Since then, a noteworthy event has been the initiation of the SALT talks (Strategic Arms Limitation Talks) between the Soviet Union and the United States. The purpose, of course, is to agree upon limitation of armaments, and some progress is being made in that direction.[19]

2.3.4. OTHER ARRANGEMENTS PROHIBITING THE USE OF NUCLEAR WEAPONS. While the idea of nuclear-free zones has been suggested and discussed since 1956,[20] the main accomplishment has thus far been in Latin America

---

[19] However, there are still numerous expressions of concern. *See, e.g.,* "SALT and Reason," Wall Street Journal, May 24, 1971, at 10, Col. 1. *See also* N.Y. Times, June 19, 1971, at 4, col. 5, for a Reader's report, "U.S. Studying a Soviet Proposal for 5-Nation Atom Arms Talk."

[20] For a short account, *see id.* at 327–46.

where a treaty has been successfully negotiated. The Tlateloco Treaty (the Treaty for the Prohibition of Nuclear Weapons in Latin America) was signed in Mexico City on February 14, 1967.[21] Its object is the denuclearization of Latin America. The treaty prohibits the testing, use, manufacture, production, or acquisition of any nuclear weapons by the parties, directly or indirectly, or by anyone on their behalf. The prohibition also applies to the installation and possession of nuclear weapons. The parties further agree to refrain from directly or indirectly engaging in, encouraging, or authorizing the testing, use, manufacture, production, possession, or control of nuclear weapons.

Among other arrangements, special mention should be made of the Antarctic Treaty,[22] Treaty on Principles Governing the Activities of States in the Exploration and Use of Outer Space, Including the Moon and Other Celestial Bodies[23] and the recent agreement prohibiting the emplacement of nuclear weapons and weapons of mass destruction on the seabed.[24]

2.4. Conclusion

As already noted briefly, several agreements have been reached with a view to prohibiting the use of nuclear weapons. But the dream of achieving a general and complete disarmament is still far from realization. Of course, state sovereignty and contending systems of world order pose what seem to be insurmountable hurdles. But the survival perspective demands that these conflicts be subordinated to the common interest of mankind in finding alternatives to the spiraling arms race. The SALT talks might prove to be the first such step in the right direction.

UNITED NATIONS GENERAL ASSEMBLY
RESOLUTION 1653 (XVI) *

The General Assembly . . . declares that:

1. (a) The use of nuclear and thermonuclear weapons is contrary to the spirit, letter and aims of the United Nations and, as such, a direct violation of the Charter of the United Nations;

(b) The use of nuclear and thermonuclear weapons would exceed even the scope of war and cause indiscriminate suffering and destruction to mankind

[21] *Id.* at 459–73.
[22] *Id.* at 441–46.
[23] *Id.* at 453–58.
[24] *See* G. A. Res. 2660 (XXV) of Dec. 7, 1970, adopted by 104 votes to 2, with 2 abstentions.
* Adopted Nov. 24, 1961, by a vote of 55 to 20, with 26 abstentions. The United States, United Kingdom, France, Australia, Canada, China, and Italy were among those voting NO. *See* 16 U.N. GAOR 807 (1961).

and civilization and, as such, is contrary to the rules of international law and to the laws of humanity;

(c) The use of nuclear and thermonuclear weapons is a war directed not against an enemy or enemies alone but also against mankind in general, since the peoples of the world not involved in such a war will be subjected to all the evils generated by the use of such weapons;

(d) Any state using nuclear and thermonuclear weapons is to be considered as violating the Charter of the United Nations, as acting contrary to the laws of humanity and as committing a crime against mankind and civilization. . . .

TREATY BANNING NUCLEAR WEAPON TESTS IN ATMOSPHERE, IN OUTER SPACE, AND UNDER WATER,† SIGNED AUGUST 5, 1963
T.I.A.S. No. 5433; 480 U.N.T.S. 43

Article I. 1. Each of the parties to this treaty undertakes to prohibit, to prevent, and not to carry out any nuclear weapon test explosion, or any other nuclear explosion at any place under its jurisdiction or control:

A. In the atmosphere, beyond its limits, including outer space, or under water including territorial waters or high seas; or

B. In any other environment if such explosion causes radioactive debris to be present outside the territorial limits of the state under whose jurisdiction or control such explosion is conducted. It is understood in this connection that the provisions of this subparagraph are without prejudice to the conclusion of a treaty resulting in the permanent banning of all nuclear test explosions, including all such explosions underground, the conclusion of which, as the parties have stated in the preamble to this treaty, they seek to achieve.

2. Each of the parties to this Treaty undertakes furthermore to refrain from causing, encouraging, or in any way participating in, the carrying out of any nuclear weapon test explosion, or any other nuclear explosion, anywhere which would take place in any of the environments described, or have the effect referred to in paragraph 1 of this article.

Art. IV provides: "This Treaty shall be of unlimited duration.

"Each party shall in exercising its national sovereignty have the right to withdraw from the treaty if it decides that extraordinary events, related to the subject matter of this Treaty, have jeopardized the supreme interests of its country. It shall give notice of such withdrawal to all other parties to the Treaty three months in advance."

TREATY ON NONPROLIFERATION OF NUCLEAR WEAPONS, SIGNED JULY 1, 1968
U.N. Doc. A/RES/2373 (XXII), Annex U.N. Doc. A/7016/Add.1, Annex, June 10, 1968

Article I. Each nuclear-weapon state party to the Treaty undertakes not to transfer to any recipient whatsoever nuclear weapons or other nuclear explosive

† The treaty was signed in triplicate, with the United States, USSR and United Kingdom all functioning as depository governments. The treaty provides for amendments which enter into force for all parties upon the deposit of instruments of ratification of a majority of all the parties, including all three of the United States, USSR, and United Kingdom.

devices or control over such weapons or explosive devices directly, or indirectly; and not in any way to assist, encourage, or induce any nonnuclear-weapon state to manufacture or otherwise acquire nuclear weapons or other nuclear explosive devices, or control over such weapons or explosive devices.

Article II. Each nonnuclear-weapon state party to the Treaty undertakes not to receive the transfer from any transferor whatsoever of nuclear weapons or other nuclear explosive devices or of control over such weapons or explosive devices directly, or indirectly; not to manufacture or otherwise acquire nuclear weapons or other nuclear explosive devices; and not to seek or receive any assistance in the manufacture of nuclear weapons or other nuclear explosive devices.

Article III. 1. Each nonnuclear-weapon state party to the Treaty undertakes to accept safeguards, as set forth in an agreement to be negotiated and concluded with the International Atomic Energy Agency in accordance with the Statute of the International Atomic Energy Agency and the Agency's safeguards system, for the exclusive purpose of verification of the fulfillment of its obligations assumed under this Treaty with a view to preventing diversion of nuclear energy from peaceful uses to nuclear weapons or other nuclear explosive devices. Procedures for the safeguards required by this article shall be followed with respect to source or special fissionable material whether it is being produced, processed or used in any principal nuclear facility or is outside any such facility. The safeguards required by this article shall be applied on all source or special fissionable material in all peaceful nuclear activities within the territory of such state, under its jurisdiction, or carried out under its control anywhere.

2. Each state party to the Treaty undertakes not to provide: (a) source or special fissionable material or (b) equipment or material especially designed or prepared for the processing, use or production of special fissionable material, to any nonnuclear-weapon state for peaceful purposes, unless the source or special fissionable material shall be subject to the safeguards required by this article.

3. The safeguards required by this article shall be implemented in a manner designed to comply with article IV of this Treaty, and to avoid hampering the economic or technological development of the parties or international cooperation in the field of peaceful nuclear activities, including the international exchange of nuclear material and equipment for the processing, use or production of nuclear material for peaceful purposes in accordance with the provisions of this article and the principle of safeguarding set forth in the Preamble of the Treaty.

4. Nonnuclear-weapon states party to the Treaty shall conclude agreements with the International Atomic Energy Agency to meet the requirements of this article either individually or together wih other states in accordance with the Statute of the International Atomic Energy Agency. Negotiation of such agreements shall commence within 180 days from the original entry into force of this Treaty. For states depositing their instruments of ratification or accession after the 180-day period, negotiation of such agreements shall commence not later than the date of such deposit. Such agreements shall enter into force not later than eighteen months after the date of initiation of negotiations.

Article IV. 1. Nothing in this Treaty shall be interpreted as affecting the inalienable right of all the parties to the Treaty to develop research, production, and use of nuclear energy for peaceful purposes without discrimination and in conformity with articles I and II of this Treaty.

2. All the parties to the Treaty undertake to facilitate, and have the right to participate in, the fullest possible exchange of equipment, materials, and scientific and technological information for the peaceful uses of nuclear energy. Parties to the Treaty in a position to do so shall also cooperate in contributing alone or together with other states or international organizations to the further development of the applications of nuclear energy for peaceful purposes, especially in the territories of nonnuclear-weapon states party to the Treaty, with due consideration for the needs of the developing areas of the world.

Article V. Each party to the Treaty undertakes to take appropriate measures to insure that, in accordance with this Treaty, under appropriate international observation and through appropriate international procedures, potential benefits from any peaceful applications of nuclear explosions will be made available to nonnuclear-weapon states party to the Treaty on a nondiscriminatory basis and that the charge to such parties for the explosive devices used will be as low as possible and exclude any charge for research and development. Nonnuclear-weapon states party to the Treaty shall be able to obtain such benefits, pursuant to a special international agreement or agreements, through an appropriate international body with adequate representation of nonnuclear-weapon states. Negotiations on this subject shall commence as soon as possible after the Treaty enters into force. Nonnuclear-weapon states party to the Treaty so desiring may also obtain such benefits pursuant to bilateral agreements.

Article VI. Each of the parties to the Treaty undertakes to pursue negotiations in good faith on effective measures relating to cessation of the nuclear arms race at an early date and to nuclear disarmament, and on a treaty on general and complete disarmament under strict and effective international control.

2.5. Appraisal of Nuclear Weapons in the Law of Armed Conflicts

Denise Bindschedler-Robert

An appraisal of the qualification of nuclear weapons requires certain preliminary data on the effect of these weapons. They not only cause blast effect, but also, on intensive heat explosion, they give off and emit radioactive radiation (initial nuclear radiation); moreover, radioactive fallout, composed of a mixture of products of fission and particles of dust found in the atmosphere as a result of the explosion, creates residual or deferred radiation by direct emission of particles and by eventual contamination of the biological environment.[1] Among other effects on human

[1] *Report of the Secretary-General on the effects of the possible use of nuclear weapons and the security and economic implications for states of the acquisition and further development of these weapons,* U.N. Doc. A/6858, Oct. 10, 1967; *Reaffirmation et developpement des lois et coutumes,* Report of the ICRC (1969); G. Schwarzenberger, The Legality of Nuclear Weapons (1958); *id., Self-Defense under the Charter of the United Nations,* International Law Association Report 192 (1962); Nahlik, *Armes atomiques et droit international,* Annuaire Polonais des Affaires Internationales (*War-*

health, nuclear radiation also has a genetic effect on future generations.[2] Finally, the geographical area of fallout depends on atmospheric conditions; hence, the area of fallout cannot be entirely foreseen, and it considerably exceeds the area of initial destruction.

It does not seem necessary to distinguish here between nuclear and thermonuclear weapons, but one should draw attention to other developments: on the one hand, the production of bombs with ever-increasing explosive force (the Hiroshima bomb was 20 kilotons, but since then the Soviet Union has produced a bomb of 50 megatons), and on the other hand, the "miniaturization" of nuclear explosives down to 1 kiloton ("tactical" nuclear arms).[3] Although the destructive effect of weak nuclear weapons is considerably greater than that of conventional explosives, it is generally conceded that they may be used in the zone of military operations for the destruction of carefully determined military objectives. These weapons have essentially a blast effect and do not cause any radioactive fallout, or, in any case, not beyond the limits of the military objective aimed at. The report of the Secretary-General points out, however, that, in view of the effect of fission, it would be impossible to avoid fallout entirely.[4] This remark applies equally to the more powerful so-called "clean" nuclear weapons, which produce, in addition, a considerable amount of induced radioactivity. Besides, the limitation of the effects of so-called tactical weapons presupposes that the explosion should take place at a well-determined height.[5]

A further distinction may also be possible even with regard to the use of "strategic" nuclear weapons. Such weapons may also be employed at very high altitude to destroy conventional or pilotless aircraft, causing, through the ionization of the atmosphere, the interruption of communications, remote control, or radar; certain nuclear weapons are also designed for the search and destruction of nuclear submarines.[6] If the explosion takes place at a very great height, there may possibly be no radioactive fallout, whereas if it takes place underwater, the contamination is practically inevitable.

---

saw 1961); von der Heydte, *Le Probleme que pose l'existence des armes de destruction massive, supra,* 52 ANNUAIRE, bk. II (1967); and R. Bindschedler, *Das Volkerrecht und die Nuklearwaffen, Melingas Fragistas* 494 (1968).

[2] *Report of the Secretary-General, supra* note 1, annex 2.

[3] The explosive force of the most powerful bomb yet tried is more than 200,000 times greater than that of the smallest nuclear device now in possession of the great powers. The radiation from nuclear devices increases or decreases in proportion to the power of the device.

[4] Report of the Secretary-General, *supra* note 1, at 15–19.

[5] The height is a mathematical function of the explosive force of the device.

[6] Von der Heydte, *Le Problème que pose l'existence des armes de destruction massive, supra* note 1, at 34.

Considering the problem from the point of view of lex lata, one notices, first of all, the absence of any conventional rule specifically prohibiting nuclear weapons. While the General Assembly resolution of November 24, 1961, declares that "the use of nuclear and thermonuclear weapons is contrary to the spirit, letter, and aims of the United Nations and, as such, a direct violation of the Charter of the United Nations," it does not authoritatively establish the law now in force.[7] Since some of the Great Powers (whose attitude is decisive in this case) have refused to declare or admit the illegality of nuclear weapons as such, it is impossible to infer the existence of an *opinio juris* necessary for the formation of a specific rule of prohibition.[8] However, the question arises whether nuclear weapons, or at least some of their uses, are not unlawful on the basis of the general rules described above.

The first of these rules states that not all objectives are lawful. This rule may be expressed as a prohibition of the destruction of nonmilitary objectives, or specifically as a prohibition of mass destruction and indiscriminate warfare, or as a stipulation of the immunity of the civilian population. A weapon whose effects are necessarily indiscriminate is an unlawful weapon. Now, a nuclear bomb, at least one that exceeds a certain size, is such a weapon from two points of view. First, its explosive force is such that it cannot be limited to military objectives; it destroys both lawful and unlawful objectives in an indiscriminate fashion, so that even if it were directed against a lawful objective, the destruction of unlawful objectives would not be purely accidental.[9] Secondly, since fallout is uncontrollable, the nuclear bomb is a blind weapon and hence an indiscriminate one.[10]

---

[7] G.A. Res. 1653 (XVI) of Nov. 24, 1961.

[8] Even those legal scholars who agree that there is an absolute prohibition of nuclear weapons base their argument on preexisting rules and principles.

[9] G.A. Res. 1653 (XVI) of Nov. 24, 1961:

> The General Assembly . . . declares that . . . b) the use of nuclear and thermonuclear weapons would exceed even the scope of war and cause indiscriminate suffering and destruction to mankind . . . c) the use of nuclear and thermonuclear weapons is a war directed not against an enemy or enemies alone but also against mankind in general. . . .

The following scholars have taken this same position in regard to the use of nuclear and thermonuclear weapons: Nahlik, *supra* note 1, at 5; von der Heydte, *supra* note 1, at 50–51; Bindschedler, *supra* note 1, at 499–500; TUCKER, THE LAW OF WAR AND NEUTRALITY AT SEA, NAVAL WAR COLLEGE INT'L LEGAL STUDIES 50 (1957). *See also The Shimoda Case* 8 JAPANESE ANNUAL OF INT'L L. 235, 238–239 (1964) in which the use of nuclear bombs is qualified as "blind aerial bombing."

[10] Because of this aspect of the problem, *Draft Rules* of the International Committee of the Red Cross, art. 14, para. 1, declare nuclear weapons prohibited: ". . . the use is prohibited of weapons whose harmful effects—resulting in particular from the dissemination of incendiary, chemical, bacteriological, radioactive or other agents—could spread to an unforeseen degree. . . ." *See also* Bindschedler, *supra* note 1, at 499–500; *The Shimoda Case, supra* note 9, at 241.

Because the effects of radiation are particularly cruel and out of proportion to any military effect, one may also claim that the nuclear bomb violates the prohibition against causing unnecessary injuries.[11]

An even more explicit link may be established between these same effects and the prohibition of poisonous weapons, if not with respect to the initial nuclear radiation, at least as far as the contamination of the biological environment is concerned, because the absorption of radioactive matter may be assimilated to the absorption of poisonous matters.[12]

Thus, we see that there are numerous grounds for asserting that the use of nuclear bombs is contrary to international law and hence unlawful.

However, if the nuclear weapon is so conceived or used under conditions such that no indiscriminate effects are produced, it appears more difficult to assert its illegality. Thus, nuclear weapons destined to be utilized at great heights and nuclear weapons whose explosive force is sufficiently small to avoid any unlawful effects are often considered as not affected by this prohibition.[13] It should, however, be kept in mind that the explosion must take place under precisely determined conditions. This opinion is, however, criticized because "small" nuclear weapons are alleged to have the same effects as "big ones."[14] This is thus a question of fact which must be decided by experts.

Perhaps the above remarks allow a more precise evaluation of the present legal situation. It clearly follows that if certain types of nuclear weapons are unlawful, there has definitely not emerged any special rule authorizing nuclear weapons in general. On the other hand, certain attitudes may be interpreted in a less categoric fashion. The legality of nuclear weapons has been asserted in debates where the question of illegality or prohibition *de lege ferenda* as been raised in absolute terms; consequently, the replies had to be equally absolute. In reality it seems that the conception

---

[11] This remark applies to all weapons of mass destruction. G.A. Res. 1653 (XVI) of Nov. 24, 1961, refers explicitly to the prohibition of unnecessary suffering and quotes all relevant international instruments. For an interpretation of the preamble of this resolution, *see* von der Heydte, *supra* note 1, at 12; Bindschedler, *supra* note 1, at 498–499; Nahlik, *supra* note 1, at 12.

[12] Schwarzenberger, The Legality of Nuclear Weapons, *supra* note 1; *id., Self-Defense Under the Charter, supra* note 1, at 219; Bindschedler, *supra* note 1, at 499, supports the prohibition of radioactive and poisonous weapons on the basis of the prohibition of cruel and treacherous weapons.

[13] This distinction is made by the following scholars: Bindschedler, *supra* note 1, at 504; Tucker, *supra* note 9, at 55; Castrén, The Present Law of War and Neutrality 206–207 (1954). For a negative view of this concept, *see Reaffirmation et developpement des lois et coutumes applicable dan les conflits armes, Report of the ICRC to the XXIst International Conference of the Red Cross* 59–60 (1969).

[14] *Report of the Secretary General, supra* note 1, at 29, starts with the assumption that, on the average, bombs of 20 kilotons are used. The report does not examine the effect of smaller nuclear devices.

of a relative legality or illegality of nuclear weapons (in the sense indicated above) is nearer to the real intentions of the protagonists of these weapons.[15]

Opinions on the desirability of an explicit and total prohibition of nuclear arms vary.[16] Military interests vary no less. Thus, an explicit prohibition of all nuclear weapons appears to be highly improbable, the more so because it would signify, at least in the opinion of a certain number of states, an extension of the limitations imposed by the law now in force. A partial prohibition basing distinctions on the size and use of nuclear weapons would perhaps have a better chance of implementation,[17] but it would not take into account the great risk of escalation entailed by any use whatsoever of nuclear weapons. Such limited prohibition would therefore be unacceptable to those states which consider nuclear weapons as illegal in all circumstances.

Besides, it is self-evident that in any case it would be impossible to exclude nuclear reprisals against the belligerent who has made first use of nuclear arms. Under these circumstances one might ask whether it would not be advisable to adopt the idea launched by Tucker, *i.e.*, the idea of prohibiting only the first use of nuclear weapons.[18] The obligation not to use nuclear weapons first (which would be tantamount to a prohibition of the use of these weapons, except for reprisals) would eliminate the necessity of expressing an opinion on the lawful or unlawful character of nuclear weapons. It would also be possible to assume this obligation in a simpler form than by way of a treaty.

Such an obligation would, to a point, only reflect the present situation where the balance of terror rests on precisely such a presumption. But

[15] *See* U.S. Army Field Manual, para. 35: "The use of explosive atomic weapons . . . cannot *as such* be regarded as violative of international law. . . ."; *id.,* para. 613: "There is at present *no* rule of international law expressly prohibiting states from the use of nuclear weapons. In the absence of express prohibition, the use of such weapons against enemy combatants and other military objectives is permitted." The Swiss and Austrian manuals make the use of nuclear weapons subject to the restrictions dealing with weapons in general. In fact, the Austrian manual states explicitly that their use against military objectives is not prohibited by international law. 1 Austrian Army Manual, ch. II, para. 10.

[16] It is not necessarily contradictory to consider that nuclear weapons are prohibited by customary law, and at the same time to propose a Convention to record this prohibition explicitly.

[17] This is, basically, the aim of the current efforts to explicitly prohibit weapons of mass destruction.

[18] TUCKER, PROPOSAL FOR NO FIRST USE OF NUCLEAR WEAPONS, PROS AND CONS 1–4 (1963); Falk, *The Claimants of Hiroshima,* in 1 THE STRATEGY OF WORLD ORDER, TOWARD A THEORY OF WAR PREVENTION 309 (R. Falk & S. Mendlovitz eds. 1966): "A tradition of no first use, if seriously supported by the official proclamations of principal governments, would considerably improve the prospects for avoiding nuclear war."

its extension to all nuclear weapons would nevertheless create a new military situation, particularly in Europe, a situation with which NATO could cope only by increasing its conventional armaments. These are, of course, metalegal considerations, but they show the difficulties which must be surmounted.

Section 3. LEGAL LIMITS ON THE MILITARY USES OF THE SEABED AND OUTER SPACE*

Ved P. Nanda

3.1. The Seabed

3.1.1. INTRODUCTION. Coastal states have always considered oceans vital for security purposes, but the ongoing technological revolution has opened new vistas for potential military uses of the sea.[1]

Almost all recent advances in undersea exploration can be effectively utilized for military purposes. Such advances include the Sealab and Tektite projects,[2] the development of deep-sea submersibles,[3] and of un-

---

* Adapted from an earlier article by the author, *Some Legal Questions on the Peaceful Uses of Ocean Space*, 9 Va. J. Int'l L. 343, 396–403 (1969).

[1] *See generally* The Second Report of the President to the Congress on Marine Resources and Engineering Developments, Marine Science Affairs—A Year of Plans and Progress 93–96 (1968) [hereinafter cited as *President's Second Report to the Congress*]; The Third Report of the President to the Congress on Marine Resources and Engineering Development, Marine Science Affairs—A Year of Broadened Participation 81–90, 151–61, 174–75 (1969) [hereinafter cited as *President's Third Report to the Congress*]; Annual Report of the President to the Congress on Marine Resources and Engineering Development, Marine Science Affairs—Selecting Priority Programs 105–79 (1970) [hereinafter cited as *President's 1970 Report to the Congress*]; Annual Report of the President to the Congress on Marine Resources and Engineering Development, together with the Report of the National Council on Marine Resources and Engineering Development, Marine Science Affairs 10–12, 49–61, 71–79 (1971) [hereinafter cited as *President's 1971 Report to the Congress*].

[2] *See, e.g., Aquanauts Will Explore Watery Frontier*, National Observer, Nov. 25, 1968, at 1, col. 4; *id.*, Feb. 24, 1969, at 7, col. 3; *id.*, Mar. 17, 1969, at 1, col. 2; and the following N.Y. Times reports: Apr. 20, 1969, at 78, col. 1; Mar. 10, 1969, at 20, col. 1; *President's Third Report to the Congress* 87–88; *President's 1970 Report to the Congress* 105–13; *President's 1971 Report to the Congress* 10–12.

[3] These are manned vessels designed for working in deep oceans. Submarines are now being equipped with manipulators that can perform important ocean-bottom survey, mapping, and sampling tasks. For various reports *see generally* Oceanology Int'l 16–19 (May/June, 1968); 73 Marine Engr./Log 62, 63 (Aug. 1968); 21 Aerospace Tech. 111 (July 31, 1967); *id.* at 50 (Nov. 6, 1967); 40 Petroleum Engr. 20 (Oct. 1968); 38 Product Engr. 28, 32 (Sept. 25, 1967); 48 Space/Aeronautics 52 (Apr. 1968); 15 Instrumentation Tech. 35 (Mar. 1968); 3 Ocean Industry 29 (Dec. 1968); 66 Oil & Gas J. 48 (Oct. 28, 1968). For a report on the operations conducted by the submersible *Ben Franklin* in 1969, *see President's 1970 Report to the Congress* 119–120; for a report on tests conducted off the submersible *Deep Quest* in May 1970, *see President's 1971 Report to the Congress* 74.

manned systems,[4] the recent extension of ocean observation techniques using laser and sonar systems,[5] and application of improved techniques and instruments to measure and forecast more accurately and expeditiously sea depth, magnetism, wind, waves, currents, and other storm data and sea surface temperature and salinity.[6]

These new developments are likely to change the nature of naval operations. While formerly confined to the surface of the sea or close to it, naval operations in the future may well be primarily undersea, relying heavily upon the effective and efficient use of the depths for their vehicles and weapons. The United States and the Soviet Union have classified information about the nature and extent of the seabed presently being used, and future plans about such uses. Thus, present discussions about the military uses of the sea which are based upon published materials[7] are necessarily speculative in nature and could at best indicate

[4] *See, e.g.,* Snodgrass, *Deep Sea Instrument Capsule,* 162 SCIENCE 78 (Oct. 4, 1968). *See President's 1971 Report to the Congress* 76: "The Deep Submergence Search Vehicle program to develop a manned 20,000-foot-depth submersible has been canceled in favor of development of an unmanned deep-work vehicle program. Current work applying to possible future manned, very deep submersibles is concentrated on fuel cell, buoyancy material, and hull structure technology."

[5] For a technical paper dealing with the Laser system performance over the surface of the oceans, *see* Jelalian, *Sea Echo at Laser Wavelengths,* 56 PROC. INST. ELECTRICAL & ELECTRONIC ENGR. 828 (1968). *See generally Portable Laser for Underwater Use,* 14 ELECTRONICS & POWER 122 (Mar. 1968); *Seeing Under the Sea with Sonar,* 26 WESTINGHOUSE ENGR. 162 (1966); Metherell, *Seeing with Sound,* OCEANOLOGY INT'L 22 (Mar./Apr., 1968). *See Geophysics Probes Deeper, Surveys More Remote Areas,* 167 WORLD OIL 100 (Sept. 1968) for a report on recent improvements in offshore magnetic and gravity exploration and the seismograph, which is the main gas and oil exploration tool. For a recent report on "some examples of opportunities for a broad extension of ocean observation techniques," *see* NATIONAL COUNCIL ON MARINE RESOURCES AND ENGINEERING DEVELOPMENT, UNITED STATES ACTIVITIES IN SPACECRAFT OCEANOGRAPHY (1967). *See also* 40 PETROLEUM ENGR. INT'L 19 (Oct. 1968) for a report on the industry's

> first offshore diving bell designed specifically for crawling along the ocean floor [and] providing its occupants with a close-up view of the ocean bottoms. Just exactly what it sees there is monitored by surface crews and recorded on tape for permanent recording and playback.

McCoy, Jr., *Visual Coring,* 140 OCEANUS 20 (Mar. 1968). A brief report of the latest U.S. activities in this field is contained in *President's 1971 Report to the Congress* 52–54.

[6] *See Effect of Offshore Storms Due Study,* 66 OIL & GAS J. 49 (Oct. 28, 1968); Weiss, *Remote Temperature Sensing,* OCEANOLOGY INT'L 44 (Sept./Oct. 1968); GOFAR [*Global Geological and Geophysical Ocean Floor Analysis and Research*] OPENS NEW HORIZONS, *id.* at 16. For some engineering problems *see Engineers and the Ocean Bed,* 205 ENGINEERING 19 (Apr. 1968). The latest report on U.S. activities is contained in *President's 1971 Report to the Congress* 55–58.

[7] *See generally* Nierenberg, *Militarized Oceans,* in UNLESS PEACE COMES 115–27 (N. CALDER ed. 1968); Nicholson, *A Navy View of Ocean Resources,* 1 NAT. RES. LWYR. 77 (Jan. 1968); Hearn, *The Role of the United States Navy in Formulation of Federal Policy Regarding the Sea,* 1 NAT. RES. LWYR. 23 (June 1968); Gallery, *The Future of Undersea Warfare,* OCEANOLOGY INT'L 59 (Oct. 1966); Pardo, *Who Will Control the Seabed?* 47 FOREIGN AFF. 123, 129–31 (Oct. 1968); HOUSE SUBCOMMITTEE ON INTERNATIONAL ORGANI-

possibilities rather than describe actuality. All that can be said with certainty is that states are presently using the seabed for military purposes.

What follows in this section is a brief outline of some current developments made public about the actual and potential military uses of the ocean depths, and an appraisal of some alternatives to the unrestricted future use of these depths, especially the ocean floor, for military purposes.

3.1.2. POLICIES AT STAKE. The objective of limiting the nuclear arms race gets enthusiastic support from major powers, and almost universal adherence from potential nuclear powers. However, the United States and the Soviet Union disagree on the means to achieve this goal, and "general and complete disarmament" assumes the notoriety of an abused and misused slogan, much like "world peace." The basic question, therefore, is, Is the issue of the peaceful use of the seabed separable from the broader issue of general disarmament? Assuming that a consensus could be reached on the separation of the two issues, the next question would be to agree on the kind of military activities that should be barred from the ocean floor. If the prohibition be extended to "any military purposes whatsoever," it would give rise to an illogical situation permitting a submarine carrying nuclear warheads to use the superjacent waters but barring it from temporarily using the seabed. On the other hand, if a distinction could be made between "peaceful" and "not peaceful"/"not so peaceful" activities, barring only the latter, it will be necessary to establish machinery and identify criteria to make it workable, *i.e.*, to agree upon some international agency to decide whether the activities are peaceful or otherwise, and to set some standards for the agency to decide such questions. A contextual analysis would, of course, be essential: who is using the seabed, for what military purpose, with what objectives, using what strategies, with what outcomes, and what long-range effects?

The U.S. Navy's deep submergence program includes submarine location, escape, and rescue; object location and small-object re-

---

ZATIONS AND MOVEMENTS, INTERIM REPORT ON THE UNITED NATIONS AND THE ISSUE OF DEEP OCEAN RESOURCES, H.R. REP. No. 999, 90th Cong., 1st Sess. [hereinafter cited as H.R. REP. No. 999] 187–215 (1967); Hersh, *An Arms Race on the Sea Bed*, WAR/PEACE REP. 8 (Aug./Sept. 1968); Pardo & Ganci, *The Sea Bed: Common Heritage of Mankind*, id. at 3, 4; Kemp, *The Nuclear Arms Race: Problems of Vertical Proliferation*, TECH. REV. 28 (July/Aug. 1968); Ad Hoc Committee, *The Military Uses of the Sea-bed and the Ocean Floor Beyond the Limits of Present National Jurisdiction*, U.N. Doc. A/AC.135/28, July 10, 1968 [hereinafter cited as *The U.N. Working Paper on the Military Uses of the Sea Bed*]; SECOND REPORT OF THE PRESIDENT TO THE CONGRESS ON MARINE RESOURCES AND ENGINEERING DEVELOPMENT 89–99 (1968); FIRST REPORT OF THE PRESIDENT TO THE CONGRESS ON MARINE RESOURCES AND ENGINEERING DEVELOPMENT 90–96 (1967); *President's Third Report to the Congress* 81–90, 151–60; *President's 1970 Report to the Congress* 105–79; *President's 1971 Report to the Congress* 71–79.

covery; man-in-the sea; a nuclear-powered research and engineering submersible, NR-1; large-object salvage; and deep-submersible biomedicine.
The Advanced Research Projects Agency (ARPS) has initiated an Arctic
Technology Program with a view to "gain a better understanding of the
arctic environment as related to current and potential military operations
such as submarine warfare, ASW, surveillance, logistics, and intelligence,
and to develop technology and operational concepts for critical tactical
and strategic application."[8]

It seems that future developments[9] include further refinements of
modern devices of naval warfare, and other possibilities, *e.g.,* antiballistic
missile systems on the ocean floor; the "surface-effect" submarine hunter,
such as the hovercraft or the captured-air-bubble vessel (CAB), the
oceanographic or submersible airplane; "giant floating bases stationed
against wind and current in a global array that would protect strategic
sites at less long-term cost than the current bases or carriers;"[10] sensor
fields piercing the undersea acoustic barriers; systems including installations and vehicles that may move or crawl around on the seabed, and
may be used both for the purpose of stationing nuclear weapons and
carrying out detection and search operations. Looking ahead, William
Nierenberg, Director of the Scripps Institution of Oceanography, has recently surmised:

> In the 1980's it will no longer be possible to speak meaningfully of anti-
> submarine warfare or even of undersea warfare. . . . We have a vast "no
> man's land" with fleets moving at will through each other and each other's
> installations. Major effort will be expended to obtain up-to-date and meaning-
> ful intelligence because of the shadowy nature of these operations.[11]

3.1.3. DEVELOPMENTS AT THE UNITED NATIONS. It is not hard to imagine
the escalating impact on the nuclear arms race of a combination of two
factors: (1) the disconcertingly rapid rate of current technological development[12] and (2) unrestricted military uses of the oceans. The 1968
report by the Chairman of the U.N. Ad Hoc Committee to Study the

[8] *President's 1971 Report to the Congress* 79.
[9] These observations are based on the authorities cited in notes 7 & 8 *supra.*
[10] Nierenberg, *supra* note 7, at 124.
[11] *Id.* at 125.
[12] *See generally* notes 1–11 *supra* and the accompanying text. *Cf.* Stang, *The Walls Be-
neath the Sea,* 94 U.S. NAVAL INST. PROC. 33, 41 (Mar. 1968): "the military use of the
oceans by all maritime nations is perhaps the most effective deterrent to any one of them
committing high seas aggression. The technological extension beyond that of the missile-
carrying submarine to the use of the seabed itself is one way in which a war-deterring
capability may be strengthened." For a striking example of the use of technological advances
for military purposes, see the projected Navy surveillance satellite program listed in *U.S.
Aerospace Program: Major Projects and Studies as of January 1,* 51 SPACE/AERONAUTICS 33
(Jan. 1969). *See also* N.Y. Times, Apr. 2, 1969, at 9, col. 1.

Peaceful Uses of the Seabed and the Ocean Floor Beyond the Limits of National Jurisdiction[13] reflects this concern:

> There was complete unanimity among all those who participated in the [Committee] debate that the seabed and ocean floor beyond the limits of national jurisdiction should be used exclusively for peaceful purposes.[14]

However, there are inherent ambiguities in the statement, ambiguities caused by a lack of consensus on several key issues. For example: (1) there is no unanimity on the definition of the area covered by the phrase "beyond the limits of national jurisdiction,"[15] (2) the prohibition on the use of the continental shelf (no matter how it is defined)[16] for military purposes would raise serious questions, especially in view of the likelihood that the relatively shallow waters of the shelf will be used first for the deployment of weapons or construction of military installations, and (3) the phrase "exclusively for peaceful purposes" is also subject to varying interpretations.

It is imperative that international agreements be reached on the precise boundary of the "seabed and ocean floor beyond the limits of national jurisdiction."[17] It is equally imperative to resolve the current controversy on the delimitation and status of the continental shelf[18] by a convention. The decision of the U.N. General Assembly to hold a conference in 1973 on the law of the sea[19] is a desirable development and will hopefully lead to a revision of the 1958 Geneva Conventions.

On the question of the peaceful uses of the sea, the Ad Hoc Committee debate in 1968 showed a broad agreement on the highest level of abstraction: states should use the seabed in accordance with the principles and purposes of the U.N. Charter[20] and norms of international law,[21] in the interest of maintaining international peace and security,[22]

[13] The Committee was established pursuant to G.A. Res. 2340(XXII) (Oct. 6, 1967).

[14] *Ad Hoc Committee, Statement by the Chairman of the Ad Hoc Committee at the Seventeenth Meeting on August 23, 1968,* U.N. Doc A/AC.135/32, at 5 (Aug. 23, 1968) [hereinafter cited as *Statement by the Chairman of the Ad Hoc Committee*].

[15] *See generally* Nanda, *Some Legal Questions on the Peaceful Uses of Ocean Space,* 9 VA. J. INT'L L. 343, 350–58 (1969).

[16] *See generally* Nanda, *supra* note 15, at 358–66.

[17] *Id.* at 366–69.

[18] *Id.* at 369–70.

[19] Per G.A. Res. 2750C (XXV), adopted at the Assembly's 1,933d Plenary Meeting on December 17, 1970.

[20] U.N. GAOR, *Report of the Ad Hoc Committee to study the Peaceful Uses of the Seabed and the Ocean Floor Beyond the Limits of National Jurisdiction,* U.N. Doc. A/7230 [hereinafter cited as *Report of the Ad Hoc Committee*], at 52 [Soviet draft resolution], 53 [Indian draft], 55 [U.S. draft], 63 [Working Paper on the Draft Declaration of General Principles].

[21] *See, e.g., id.* at 53 [Indian draft] and 55 [U.S. draft].

[22] *See, e.g., id.* at 52 [Soviet draft], and 53 [Indian draft], and 55 [U.S. draft].

and for the benefit of mankind.[23] However, proposals dealing with the military aspects of the question indicate three distinct positions. First, the United Republic of Tanzania recommended the adoption of a declaration that "the seabed and the ocean floor and the subsoil thereof, underlying the high seas beyond the present national jurisdiction, should not be used by any state or states for any military purposes whatsoever."[24] Second, the Soviet Union pointed to "the need to take steps to prevent the arms race from spreading to the seabed and the ocean floor," and called upon "all states to use the seabed and the ocean floor beyond the limits of the territorial waters of coastal states exclusively for peaceful purposes."[25] Third, the United States stressed the need "to prevent the use of this new environment for the emplacement of weapons of mass destruction."[26]

On the specific question of what concrete steps should be taken to put their recommendations into effect, each of the three states agreed upon referring the question to the U.N. Eighteen-Nation Committee on Disarmament (ENDC), but for different reasons. Under the Tanzanian proposal, the ENDC was requested "to consider, as a matter of urgency, the question of (1) banning the use of seabed and ocean floor beyond the limits of national jurisdiction by nuclear submarines and (2) banning of military fortifications and missile bases on the seabed and ocean floor."[27] The U.S. draft requested the ENDC "to take up the question of arms limitation on the seabed and ocean floor with a view to defining those factors vital to a workable, verifiable, and effective international agreement which would prevent the use of this new environment for the emplacement of weapons of mass destruction."[28] The Soviet draft requested the ENDC "to consider, as an urgent matter, the question of prohibiting the use for military purposes of the seabed and the ocean floor beyond the limits of the territorial waters of coastal states."[29]

Two obvious difficulties in regard to restricting the use of the seabed to military activities are those of verification and enforcement. The CCD [the Conference of the Committee on Disarmament, as the ENDC is now called], which is already examining various aspects of disarmament, is best suited to study these questions and recommend measures that would promote the objective of restraining the nuclear arms race from extending to the seabed.

[23] *See, e.g., id.* at 52 [Soviet draft] and 58 [Belgian draft].
[24] *Id.* at 56–57.
[25] *Id.* at 52.
[26] *Id.* at 54.
[27] *Id.* at 56–57.
[28] *Id.* at 54.
[29] *Id.* at 52.

As an initial step, however, two salutory developments should be noted. First, the General Assembly at its twenty-fifth session has adopted a declaration of principles governing the seabed and the ocean floor.[30] In its operative paragraph 8, the Declaration states:

> The area [the seabed and ocean floor, and the subsoil thereof, beyond the limits of national jurisdiction] shall be reserved exclusively for peaceful purposes, without prejudice to any measures which have been or may be agreed upon in the context of international negotiations undertaken in the field of disarmament and which may be applicable to a broader area. . . .

Second, the General Assembly had on December 7, 1970, commended a Treaty on the Prohibition of the Emplacement of Nuclear Weapons and Other Weapons of Mass Destruction on the Seabed and the Ocean Floor and in the Subsoil Thereof.[31] The Treaty, which opened for signature in London, Moscow, and Washington on February 11, 1971, was called by President Nixon a "modest step among many in the field of control of armaments," but nonetheless "an indication of progress that has been made and continues to be made toward the goal that we all seek: the control of instruments of mass destruction so that we can reduce the danger of war."[32] President Nixon considered the treaty as "only one step toward a greater goal: the control of nuclear weapons on earth and the reduction of that danger that hangs over all the nations of the world as long as those weapons are not controlled."[33]

3.1.4. APPRAISAL OF THE TREATY. The 1971 Treaty suffers from several imperfections and inadequacies. For instance, it does not prevent the installation of conventional weapons on the seabed. Nor does it ban the deployment of submarines and antisubmarine warfare (ASW) weapons and vehicles on the seabed. Also, the lack of adequate verification measures is likely to plague this Treaty more or less the same way as it has tainted the past discussions on the broader question of disarmament.

However, there are certain positive aspects of the Treaty which should not be lightly dismissed. In fact, the Preamble of the Treaty anticipates its significance for the future, for it states that parties are convinced that the Treaty "constitutes a step toward the exclusion of the seabed, the ocean floor, and the subsoil thereof from the arms race," and that it "constitutes a step toward a treaty on general and complete disarmament

---

[30] Per G.A. Res. 2749 (XXV), adopted on Nov. 17, 1970, 108 to 0, with 14 abstentions. *See also* U.N. Doc. A/7623/Add.1, at 3, 4, Nov. 20, 1969, for a report of the U.N. Seabed Committee.

[31] Per G.A. Res. 2660 (XXV), adopted on Dec. 7, 1970.

[32] 64 DEPT. STATE PUB. 289 (1971).

[33] *Id.* at 289–90.

under strict and effective international control, and [states parties are] determined to continue negotiations to this end."

The Treaty has been termed by the U.S. representative as "another building block in the arms-control structure which the world community has been seeking to erect during the past decade."[34] And article 5 of the Treaty provides that the parties "undertake to continue negotiations in good faith concerning further measures in the field of disarmament for the prevention of an arms race on the seabed, the ocean floor, and the subsoil thereof."

Thus, the Treaty is future-oriented, providing a desirable first step for further negotiations of other multilateral agreements toward the peaceful uses of the seabed.

3.1.5. CONCLUSION. The preceding discussion indicates both the enormity and complexity of imposing effective legal limits on the military uses of the oceans. The subject is closely connected with other aspects of disarmament and it is eventually in this broader context that the differences between the major powers, especially the United States and the Soviet Union, will be resolved. At this stage, even a piecemeal approach leading to further agreements on restricting the military uses of the oceans should be welcomed, even though such agreements might be limited in their scope.

3.2. Outer Space[35]

Technological advances in space ventures are presently limited to exploratory devices and even if certain satellites could hypothetically carry nuclear devices, there is no evidence that the two Super Powers have developed any. The exploration and use of outer space remains free from weapons of mass destruction and a treaty has been entered into, in order to preserve this status. Space, like the oceans, is the "common heritage of mankind" and should be preserved as such.

TREATY ON PRINCIPLES GOVERNING THE ACTIVITIES OF STATES
IN THE EXPLORATION AND USE OF OUTER SPACE,
INCLUDING THE MOON AND OTHER CELESTIAL BODIES

Done at Washington, London, and Moscow, January 27, 1967
Entered into force October 10, 1967.
[18 U.S.T. 2410, T.I.A.S. No. 6347]

ARTICLE IV

States parties to the Treaty undertake not to place in orbit around the

[34] U.N. Doc. A/C.1/PV. 1748, at 32.

[35] *See* Cocca, *Some Comments on the Treaty on Principles Governing the Activities of States in the Exploration and Use of Outer Space, Including the Moon and Other Celestial Bodies,* 20 DePaul L. Rev. 581 (1971).

earth any objects carrying nuclear weapons or any other kinds of weapons of mass destruction, install such weapons on celestial bodies, or station such weapons in outer space in any other manner.

The moon and other celestial bodies shall be used by all states parties to the Treaty exclusively for peaceful purposes. The establishment of military bases, installations, and fortifications; the testing of any type of weapons, and the conduct of military maneuvers on celestial bodies shall be forbidden. The use of military personnel for scientific research or for any other peaceful purposes shall not be prohibited. The use of any equipment or facility necessary for peaceful exploration of the moon and other celestial bodies shall also not be prohibited.

Section 4. BIOLOGICAL AND CHEMICAL WEAPONS

DENISE BINDSCHEDLER-ROBERT

4.1. Biological Weapons[1]

By the terms "biological" or "microbiological weapons" we mean the "employment of living organisms, toxic biological products, and chemical plant-growth regulators to produce death or casualties in man, animals, or plants."[2] Frequently this definition includes chemical agents destined to inhibit the growth of plants, but this only obscures the question.

Bacteriological weapons were included in the Geneva Protocol of 1925, prohibiting the use of asphyxiating, poisonous, or other gases and of bacteriological methods of warfare, the latter interdiction being an "extension" of the prohibition of gases.[3] In 1965, the XXth Conference of the Red Cross, in Resolution XXVIII[4] invited the states which had not al-

[1] The Control of Chemical and Biological Weapons, Carnegie Endowment for International Peace (1971); See MEYROWITZ, *infra* note 2; *Reaffirmation et developpement des lois et coutumes, Report of the ICRC to the XXIst International Conference of the Red Cross* 63 (1969).

[2] This definition is that given in the *Dictionary of U.S. Army Terms,* AR 320–5 (Nov. 1958), as quoted in H. MEYROWITZ, LES ARMES BIOLOGIQUES ET LE DROIT INTERNATIONAL 4 (1968). *See also* the Treaty between Belgium, France, Luxembourg, The Netherlands, and the United Kingdom of Great Britain and Northern Ireland for Collaboration in Economic, Social, and Cultural Matters and for Collective Self-defense, Signed at Brussels on Mar. 17, 1948, Protocol III on the Control of Armaments Signed at Paris on Oct. 23, 1954, 211 U.N.T.S., 364. In Annex II, Part III of the Protocol, biological weapons are defined as those expressly designed to use, for military purposes, harmful insects or other living or dead organisms, or their toxic products.

[3] "The high contracting parties . . . agree to extend this prohibition (*i.e.*, the prohibition of the use of asphyxiating, poisonous, or other gases) to the use of bacteriological methods of warfare and agree to be bound as between themselves to the terms of this Declaration." The preamble mentions gases only.

[4] *See* U.N. Docs. A/C.35, Res. 1633, of Dec. 9 and 10, 1968, respectively.

ready done so to accede to the Protocol; that invitation was formulated anew in the Resolution of the United Nations General Assembly of December 5, 1966.[5] At the same time, the General Assembly called for strict observance by all states of the principles of the Protocol and condemned all actions contrary to its objectives. Following this action numerous states acceded to the Protocol; by December, 1969, the states which had adhered to it numbered eighty-four. It is worth noting that neither Japan nor the United States was among them.[6]

One might ask whether the prohibition is limited only to those states which are bound by the Protocol or whether it is a rule of international customary law.[7] It is necessary to recall in this connection that a specific conventional prohibition is not proof of the absence of a rule of international customary law; it may be the confirmation or the source of such a rule. Consequently, it is necessary, as it was with nuclear weapons, either to prove the existence of a special rule of international customary law, or, if such a rule does not exist, to evaluate bacteriological weapons in accordance wth the general rules contained in the laws and customs of war. There are weighty reasons for considering that the prohibition formulated in the Geneva Protocol has been transformed into a rule of international customary law. Bacteriological weapons have never been used, although they could have been, and no state has ever claimed the right to use them.[8] Even if this were not so, the distinction between lawful and unlawful objectives and, hence, the principle of the immunity of the civilian population, the prohibition of poison, and the prohibition of means of warfare capable of causing superfluous injuries would all be applicable in the circumstances. Indeed, the bacteriological weapon is a typical blind weapon; not only are minute quantities sufficient to con-

[5] G.A. Res. 2162 B (XXI), Dec. 5, 1966. This resolution was adopted by 91 votes to 0, with 26 abstentions.

[6] 29 FACTS ON FILE, No. 1518 (Nov. 27–Dec. 3, 1969), at 773. In Nov. 1969, however, President Nixon submitted the Protocol to the Senate for reconsideration.

[7] United Kingdom, *Working Paper on Microbiological Warfare*, U.N. Doc. ENDC/231 (Aug. 6, 1968).

[8] Thus the unproven allegations that the United States has employed bacteriological weapons have been solemnly denied. Moreover, although the United States has not acceded to the Protocol, they have repeatedly declared that they approve of its principles and objectives. Japan, another major nonsignatory state, voted for Res. 2162B (XXI). For analysis of the Protocol as a rule of international customary law see MEYROWITZ, *supra* note 2, at 93; Schwarzenberger, *Self-Defense Under the Charter of the United Nations*, INTERNATIONAL LAW ASS. REP. 219 (1962); *Reaffirmation et developpement des lois et coutumes, Report of the ICRC*, *supra* note 1, at 69. In view of the above, the remarks of Kunz questioning whether there has developed a rule of customary international law prohibiting bacteriological and chemical weapons are not convincing. *See* von der Heydte, *Le Probleme que pose l'existence des armes de destruction massive et la distinction entre les objectifs militaires en general*, 52 ANNUAIRE DE L'INSTITUTE DE DROIT INTERNATIONAL, bk. II, at 124–25 (1969).

taminate large expanses of territory, but also this weapon knows no frontiers, and the victims cannot be identified in advance; if used against crops, it attacks unlawful objectives. In any case, toxins have the characteristics of poison, as they are substances capable of inflicting death or injury to health. Finally, the sufferings and damages caused would seldom be in reasonable proportion to the military aim pursued.[9] The Geneva Protocol prohibits bacteriological methods of warfare unreservedly and, consequently, there is no uncertainty, as there is with respect to chemical weapons, as to the scope of the prohibition.[10] Besides, these weapons are particularly repugnant to the conscience of humanity. Their use must consequently be considered as absolutely prohibited.[11]

The term "bacteriological" used in the Geneva Protocol has raised doubts whether that prohibition also applies to microbiological agents.[12] However, the term "bacteriological" was adapted to the state of knowledge prevailing in 1925 and was certainly not understood in an exclusive sense. We see also that the resolutions and papers referring to the question of the prohibition either continue to use the term "bacteriological" as including all microbiological agents or consider the two terms as interchangeable. There are, therefore, ample grounds for including microbiological weapons in the Geneva Protocol.[13] In any case, the arguments which are favorable to the prohibition of biological weapons or which constitute the basis for such a prohibition are a fortiori valid for microbiological weapons. It might be desirable to modernize the terminology of the Protocol. To insist on this last point would, however, entail the risk of spreading the erroneous idea that all microbiological weapons have not already been prohibited.

One last question concerns reprisals. If it is admitted that bacteriological weapons as such are prohibited, then these weapons cannot be used to sanction such breaches of the law which do not consist in the use of such weapons.[14] Certain states have accompanied their instruments of ratification or accession by a reservation asserting the right to use these weapons against such states who themselves would use them,[15] nevertheless, this could not be interpreted as meaning that without such a

---

[9] See MEYROWITZ, *supra* note 2, at 85.

[10] *See supra* Section 4.1.

[11] CASTREN, THE PRESENT LAW OF WAR AND NEUTRALITY 195 (1954); United Kingdom, *Working Paper*, U.N. Doc. ENDC/231, para. 3 (Aug. 6, 1968).

[12] United Kingdom, *Working Paper*, *supra* note 11, para. 5

[13] MEYROWITZ, *supra* note 2, at 33.

[14] For a discusion of the use of poisonous gases for reprical in the Ethiopian War, *see id.* at 78; and Schwarzenberger, *Self-Defense Under the Charter*, *supra* note 8, at 221.

[15] For a discussion of these reservations and their interpretation, *see* MEYROWITZ, *supra* note 2, at 62.

reservation the use of biological (and chemical) weapons in reprisals would be prohibited.[16]

Besides, the prohibition of the use of biological weapons in reprisal seems as difficult as the prohibition of nuclear weapon reprisals. Biological weapons may have or may acquire considerable efficiency,[17] and a fear of reprisals of the same kind may have a decisive deterrent effect. This fear explains perhaps—at least partly—the fact that up to now this weapon has never been used.

4.2. Chemical Weapons[18]

These weapons have been defined as those which make use of the asphyxiating, toxic, irritant, paralyzing, growth-regulating, antilubricating, or catalyzing properties of any chemical substance.[19] However, the question is whether the prohibition in the Geneva Protocol of the use of "asphyxiating, poisonous, or other gases and of all analogous liquids, materials, or devices," as well as the rule of international customary law of which this Protocol is an expression,[20] includes all the substances mentioned in our definition or only those which are lethal or cause lasting injury to health. This question is a very controversial one, as the French and English texts, both of which are authentic, do not coincide entirely. The French text contains the expression "ou similaires," and the English text says "or other gases."[21]

The question, it seems, should be resolved by reference to the rule of international customary law. This rule prohibits poisons as particularly treacherous and cruel weapons. Besides, it is completed by the rule prohibiting superfluous injuries. This may be interpreted to mean that only gases and other chemical substances which cause lasting damage must be considered as prohibited.[22] Irritant or disabling gases cause only temporary disablement; they do not leave any traces in the body and do not require subsequent medical treatment. Consequently, they would not have the characteristics of poisons, defined as any substance capable of causing death or damage to health, and they would not cause super-

[16] *Id.* at 78.

[17] *Id.* at 11.

[18] *Id.;* Schwarzenberger, *Self-Defense under the Charter,* supra note 8; *Reaffirmation et developpement des lois et coutumes, Report of the ICRC,* supra note 1, at 63; United Kingdom, *Working Paper,* supra note 11.

[19] Protocol III on the Control of Armaments of Oct. 23, 1954, 211 U.N.T.S. 364.

[20] See *supra* notes 3–12 and the acompanying text on bacteriological weapons. The prohibition of gases as a rule of international customary law is considerably older than the Protocol; it rests on the prohibition of poisonous weapons.

[21] *Reaffirmation et developpement des lois et coutumes, Report of the ICRC,* supra note 1, at 67; United Kingdom, *Working Paper,* supra note 11, paras. 1, 2.

[22] MEYROWITZ, *Les Armes biologiques,* supra note 2, at 102.

fluous injuries, as their efficiency is by no means out of proportion to the inconvenience they may cause. Some writers assert that such gases represent a more humane means of warfare than many others.[23]

Such arguments are convincing, provided it is proved that irritant and disabling agents are really not harmful to health. This assertion, however, has been challenged. It has been pointed out that in certain doses, these gases may be toxic and that not all individuals may react to them in the same way.[24] The first argument concerns rather the method of use; it is the same problem as the one concerning nuclear weapons. As to the second argument, one might ask whether it is not justifiable to consider normal reactions rather than marginal cases. Whatever the degree of noxiousness of the gases used up to now (this is a problem for experts to decide), the question remains whether a really innocuous gas is prohibited by the rule of customary international law. In our opinion the reply to this question is negative.[25]

As far as the prohibition of gases is concerned, the Geneva Protocol refers to previous treaties, and parties "recognize" this prohibition. The previous treaties are the Hague Conventions stipulating the prohibition of poison and of poisonous weapons[26] and Hague Declaration II of 1899 prohibiting the use of projectiles "the sole object of which is the diffusion of asphyxiating or deleterious gases." This Declaration is only a concrete expression of the general rule formulated by the Hague Regulations, which have codified international customary law. Hence, the law to which the Geneva Protocol refers is nothing but customary law. To establish that the contracting parties, who explicitly recognize that law, intended to go beyond it, it would be necessary to prove that the signatory states considered the French term "similaires" as equivalent to the English term "other gases" (it is this which has to be proved, not the contrary).[27] The analogy with the prohibition of bacteriological weapons—we have pointed out that this interdiction is absolute—is not convincing because the drafting is different and because these weapons "are generally regarded with even greater abhorrence than chemical methods."[28]

As far as defoliant and crop-destroying agents are concerned, there are two questions: that concerning the innocuousness of these agents for man and that of the legality of the objective. The defoliation of the jungle or of plantations appears to be a lawful means of warfare if it is used to

---

[23] *Reaffirmation et developpement des lois et coutumes*, REPORT OF THE ICRC, supra note 1, at 67.

[24] MEYROWITZ, *supra* note 2, at 49.

[25] *Id.* at 102.

[26] Hague Regulations of 1899 and 1907, art. 23a.

[27] *See* MEYROWITZ, *supra* note 2, at 38.

[28] United Kingdom, *Working Paper, supra* note 11, at 3.

facilitate the operations or to assure the safety of the armed forces.[29] On the contrary, the destruction of crops can be justified only if it is definitely established that they are destined for the enemy army alone.[30] The question of whether the substances utilized are toxic for man pertains only to plantations. The effects of the large-scale use of herbicides are certainly harmful, and consequently it can be said that here, too, the illegality depends on the mode of use; as the substances must be used in large doses in order to be militarily efficient, one may consider that for that reason alone—apart from the character of the objective—the use of defoliant or crop-destroying agents is contrary to law.

One might ask whether the Geneva Protocol should not be completed so as to include all the chemical agents corresponding to the definition given at the beginning of this section. The weightiest argument in favor of this solution is provided by the difficulty of distinguishing the character of substances used and by the danger of escalation resulting therefrom.[31] For the same reasons chemical warfare may lead to biological warfare.

Section 5. THE RED CROSS AND BIOLOGICAL AND CHEMICAL WEAPONS

Jean Mirimanoff-Chilikine[*]

The purpose of this section is to outline the role of the Red Cross in aiding the development of international law in this area. In addition, the efforts of other international organizations in this field will be examined. The section, however, will not attempt to develop or settle the delicate problems arising from the Geneva Protocol of June 17, 1925, for the prohibition of the use in war of asphyxiating, poisonous, or other gases and of bacteriological methods of warfare (*see supra* Section 4).

5.1. ICRC Appeal of February 6, 1918

Far from attenuating the evils of war, progress in the science of aeronautics, ballistics, and chemistry might well be said only to have aggravated suffering and especially to have extended it to all the population, so that war will soon be all destroying and without mercy.

[29] Meyrowitz, *supra* note 2, at 28–29.

[30] See, *e.g.*, *supra* § 3, notes 71–72 and the accompanying text. On this point, the author disagrees with Meyrowitz who considers by analogy with economic warfare that strategic raw materials as well as plantations producing commodities for market are objectives which may legitimately be destroyed. He does, however, make an exception for plantations producing foodstuffs. Meyrowitz, *supra* note 2, at 27.

[31] *Id.* at 50; *see also Reaffirmation et developpement des lois et coutumes, Report of the ICRC, supra* note 1, at 67.

[*] The views expressed herein are those of the author and do not necessarily represent those of the ICRC.

We wish today to take a stand against a barbaric innovation which science is bringing to perfection, that is to say, making it more lethal and more subtly cruel. This innovation is the use of asphyxiating and poisonous gas, which will, it seems, increase to an extent so far undreamed of.

. . .

We now hear of new volatile poisons, large-scale production of which is the more easy as the raw material is ready at hand. We are shown missiles loaded with these poisonous gases spreading death—and a horrible death it is—not only among the fighting forces, but behind the lines among an inoffensive population over a wide area in which all living things will be destroyed. We protest with all the forces at our command against such warfare, which can only be called criminal. And if, as seems likely, the enemy is forced to counterattack or resort to reprisals to compel the perpetrator of this odious practice to give it up, we can only see ahead a struggle which will exceed in barbarity anything which history has known so far.

Such was the International Committee of Red Cross' (ICRC's) appeal to belligerents on February 6, 1918, before the end of hostilities.

5.2. Conventions Before the Geneva Protocol

For the first time in the history of warfare, gas was used on April 22, 1915, at the front at Yser.[1] This was a breach of inchoate laws such as the Saint Petersburg Declaration of 1868, prohibiting the use of weapons which cause unnecessary suffering; the 1899 Hague Declaration concerning the prohibition of using projectiles, the sole object of which is the diffusion of asphyxiating or deleterious gases; and the regulation annexed to the Hague Convention of 1907 (art. XXIII [A] & [E]) prohibiting the use of poison or poisonous weapons.[2]

5.3. Geneva Protocol of June 17, 1925

5.3.1. ORIGIN. With a view to preventing a recurrence of such ghastly events, the ICRC strove to remedy legal shortcomings. On November 22, 1920, the ICRC addressed a letter to the General Assembly of the League of Nations, proposing that various measures should be taken, including "absolute prohibition of the use of asphyxiating gas, a cruel and barbarous weapon which inflicts terrible suffering upon its victims." In 1921, the Tenth International Conference of the Red Cross urged governments to come to an agreement on the absolute prohibition of the use of gas as a

---

[1] Vifluege, a village near Ypres.

[2] The opinion has been expressed that this art. XXIII(a) does not apply to gas:

> It has not been applied generally by states in connection with poison gas. One reason is that art. XXIII(a) was formulated when the experience of mankind did not encompass poison in terms of gas but in terms of poisoned water or food, or poisoned arrows. This codification of custom reflected the past, not the unknown future.

J. Burns Kelly, *Gas Warfare in International Law*, MILIT. L. REV. 44 (1960).

weapon, however delivered, whether by drift, missiles, or otherwise.

This appeal did not go unheeded because four years later, during a Conference convened by the League of Nations on the supervision of international trade in weapons, the participating governments concluded the Geneva Protocol of June 17, 1925. (Despite its title, the Geneva Protocol is not related to the Geneva Conventions, which were drafted by the ICRC with the assistance of international experts.)

5.3.2. TITLE. The Protocol is entitled "Geneva Protocol of June 17, 1925, for the prohibition of the use in war of asphyxiating, poisonous, or other gases and of bacteriological methods of warfare" (Protocole de Genève du 17 juin 1925 concernant la prohibition d'emploi, à la guerre, de gaz asphyxiants, toxiques, ou similaires et de moyens bactériologiques). The authors of the Geneva Protocol were content to repeat the definition given in article 171 of the Treaty of Versailles and article 5 of the Treaty of Washington, the English and French texts of which are equally authentic.

5.3.3. THE BENEFITS OF THE PROTOCOL. The Geneva Protocol is a basic legal instrument because it is devoted entirely to a question which earlier Conventions hardly touched upon, because there is still no similar treaty on biological and chemical weapons and because states parties to the Geneva Protocol are much more numerous than those which are parties to the earlier treaties already mentioned. In practice, apart from the use of reputedly nonlethal gas, held by some to be illicit and by others permissible, the Geneva Protocol has in general been respected by the states parties thereto: no chemical or biological weapons were used during World War II, although the prohibition was violated in an earlier conflict and occasional breaches have been committed since.

5.3.4. TYPES OF BIOLOGICAL AND CHEMICAL AGENTS. What are the biological and chemical agents actually involved? The WHO report "Health Aspects of Chemical and Biological Weapons"[3] defines them generally as follows:

> Chemical agents of warfare include all substances employed for their toxic effects on man, animals or plants. . . . Biological agents include those that depend for their effects on multiplication within the target organism, and are intended for use in war to cause disease or death in man, animals, or plants.[4]

The chemical agents include neurotoxic, asphyxiating, lachrymatory, psychochemical, and other gases. The biological agents include bacteria, viruses, mycetes, and rickettsiae, as well as semisynthetic biological mat-

---

[3] WHO, Geneva, 1970.
[4] *Id.* at 12.

ter. The main difference between the chemical and the biological agents is the latters' ability to multiply.

In military circles,[5] biological and chemical weapons are classified as lethal and nonlethal, but this distinction is subject to controversy and is contested particularly in many scientific circles. An incapacitating, *i.e.,* supposedly nonlethal agent, might be permanently harmful to health. It might even cause the death of certain categories of people, such as young children, the undernourished, the sick, or the aged.

The WHO report[6] divides biological and chemical agents into three types:

> A lethal agent is one intended to cause death when a man is exposed to concentrations well within the capability of delivery for military purposes. An incapacitating agent is one intended to cause temporary disease or to induce temporary mental or physical disability, the duration of which greatly exceeds the period of exposure. A harassing agent (or short-term incapacitant) is one capable of causing a rapid disablement that lasts for little longer than the period of exposure. . . . The above classifications are not toxicological categories, for the effects of a chemical warfare agent depend as much on the way it is used as on its toxicological properties. If too much of an agent intended for harassment is used, it may kill or severely injure. Likewise, if a low concentration of a lethal agent is disseminated, its effects may be only incapacitating or harassing.[7]

5.3.4.1. *Napalm.* The status of napalm, perhaps the most controversial weapon in the Vietnam War, is somewhat nebulous at the moment. Some argue that it is an established permissible weapon provided it is used against military objectives. Others contend that it is illicit on two counts: (1) as an asphyxiant which transgresses the Geneva Protocol and (2) for the atrocious suffering it causes which violates the Saint Petersburg Declaration.

5.3.5. CONTROVERSIES CONCERNING THE INTERPRETATION OF THE GENEVA PROTOCOL. Unfortunately, as a result of trends which have become more evident since the end of World War II, the Geneva Protocol at present gives rise to no little controversy about its interpretation and scope.[8]

Grosso modo, it is generally held in some quarters that the prohibition contained in the Geneva Protocol is absolute, covering all biological and

---

[5] *Cf.* J. Burns Kelly, *supra* note 2, at 59.

[6] *Supra* note 4.

[7] *Id.* at 59.

[8] Res. XXIII of the International Conference on Human Rights (Teheran, Apr.–May 1968), in its fourth preambular paragraph mentions napalm:

> Considering, also, that the widespread violence and brutality of our times, including massacres, summary executions, tortures, inhuman treatment of prisoners, killing of civilians in armed conflicts, and the use of chemical and biological means of warfare, including napalm bombing, erode human rights and engender counterbrutality. . . .

chemical weapons; thus a wide interpretation is given to the Protocol
on the basis of its English title. In other quarters, the view prevails that
the prohibition is relative and does not preclude the use of certain nonlethal weapons; thus the Protocol is construed restrictively on the grounds
of the French title. Yet both the French and the English versions are
equally authentic. However, the French Government, the depositary of
the Geneva Protocol and the first to ratify it, specified in a note in connection with the preparatory work leading to the League of Nations disarmament conference, that it considered the prohibition[9] extended to the
use of lachrymatory agents.[10]

An International Commission of Experts on the Legal Protection of
Civilian Populations Against the Dangers of Chemical Warfare convened
by the ICRC in 1931 determined that "the Geneva Protocol, in a quite
general way, prohibits the use of poisonous and bacteriological weapons.
Such a legal safeguard for the armed forces is a fortiori applicable to
civilian populations."

In a compendium of documents on chemical and air warfare submitted by the ICRC to the members of the Conference for the reduction
and limitation of weapons, the ICRC said:

> The ICRC is certainly convinced of the absolute need to replace war by the
> peaceful settlement of international difficulties, but so long as the possibility
> of recourse to armed force subsists, it is the Committee's duty to bear in mind
> the welfare of all war victims. Restricted today to the terms of reference as-
> signed to it, and with the humanitarian point of view which prompts it to
> action, the ICRC considers that the only way to shelter civilians from some
> of the worst dangers arising from war is *purely and simply to prohibit air
> raids and chemical and bacteriological warfare*, for which it makes a pressing
> appeal to the Conference.

Another current controversial issue is whether the Geneva Protocol prohibits weapons which did not exist or had not been perfected when that
Protocol became operative.[11] There were also, at one time, conflicting
opinions on whether the Geneva Protocol was the expression of customary

---

[9] *Cf.* G. Fischer: *L'emploi des armes chimiques et bacteriologiques,* in LE MONDE
DIPLOMATIQUE (Jan. 1970).

[10] On tear gas, Professor Meselson of Harvard University expressed the following opinion
in the BULLETIN OF ATOMIC SCIENTISTS 31 (Jan. 1970).

> I would like to express the opinion that the question of tear gas might be approached as follows.
> On the one hand, there is no question that there is a danger of escalation when any gas is used.
> On the other hand, it might be felt that tear gas is a useful weapon and under some conditions
> might actually cause less fatalities than other means.
> I would point out that one should expect any gas to be used in conjunction with other weapons,
> and that, therefore, even tear gas, although it is non-lethal, would, under the conditions of war,
> be used to enhance the effectiveness of lethal weapons.

[11] ICRC, DOCUMENTS RELATIFS A LA GUERRE CHIMIQUE ET AÉRIENNE 5 (1932).

law,[12] existing at the time it was drawn up, binding even states which are not parties thereto in view of its basic humanitarian character, its fairly wide diffusion, and the absence of treaty derogations which could permit the use of certain biological and chemical weapons.[13] Resolution 2603 adopted by the U.N. General Assembly in December, 1969, ultimately declared it customary law.[14]

5.3.6. THE LIMITS TO THE GENEVA PROTOCOL. While conferring great advantages, the Geneva Protocol does have limits:

1. It prohibits the use—but not the manufacture and storage—of bacteriological and chemical weapons (it therefore relates to the law of war, but not the law of disarmament).
2. It has not been ratified by a number of states, as is the case of the Geneva Conventions.
3. It does not specifically mention a case of noninternational armed conflict.
4. Accession has often been qualified by reservations. These are generally twofold: (1) that the Protocol is binding on the state making the reservation only in its relations with states which have ratified and adhere to the Protocol and (2) that the Protocol shall cease to be binding on the state making the reservation in its action against an enemy state if the latter's armed forces or allies fail to respect the prohibitions laid down in the Protocol.

Today, consideration is also being given to reservations relating to the contents or interpretation of the text of the Geneva Protocol, and according to which the use of certain specific chemical agents would be "permissible."[15]

[12] "Les armes B étaient, en 1925, à peine connues. On a donc interdit une arme future, et on l'a prohibée sans restriction, sans tenir compte des possibilités de développement dont cette arme était capable, et sachant évidemment qu'il existe des bactéries banales à effet simplement incapacitant." H. MEYROWITZ, LES ARMES BIOLOGIQUES ET LE DROIT INTERNATIONAL 40 (Pedone ed. 1968). *Cf.* J. Burns Kelly, *supra* note 2.

[13] *Cf.* H. Meyrowitz, *supra* note 12, especially at 84.

[14] Likewise, it has been held that the principles of the Hague Conventions and Regulations of 1907 were—and still are—customary law, whereas those of the 1949 Geneva Conventions might have become customary law (*Cf.* U.N. Secretary-General Report *Respect for Human Rights in Time of Armed Conflict*, U.N. Doc. A/7720, Nov. 20, 69; and C. Pilloud, *The Geneva Conventions—an Important Anniversary—1949-1969* in INTERNATIONAL REVIEW OF THE RED CROSS 399 (Aug. 1969).

[15] It is greatly to be hoped that the government(s) concerned will not make such reservations which are to be deplored on many counts: (1) such reservations will throw the door wide open to escalation; (2) they would not cover the fear expressed in certain scientific circles to the effect that the chronic toxicity of certain chemical agents has not yet been sufficiently studied. For example, certain phytotoxic agents (defoliants and others), apparently "benign and permissible," may produce indirectly—through contaminated water or food, effects similar to those of thalidomide (*cf.* the cited WHO report, at 57); (3)

5.4. Red Cross Activities and Biological and Chemical Warfare

The first steps taken by the ICRC in 1918 and 1920, as well as the resolution of the Tenth International Conference of the Red Cross, all of which came before the Geneva Protocol, have already been mentioned. Since then in nearly every International Conference of the Red Cross, states have been cautioned against the use of nondiscriminating weapons and during the interim between the two world wars, particularly against the use of biological and chemical weapons. (By advocating precautions for the protection of civilian populations at the time the Geneva Protocol was being evolved, the ICRC was also, it may be held, an initiator of civil defense). In addition, many resolutions adopted by the International Conferences of the Red Cross,[16] as well as many ICRC memoranda, urge states to accede to the Geneva Protocol.

It would be useful, at this point, to quote from two of the most recent resolutions:

1. *Resolution XXVIII of the XXth International Conference of the Red Cross in Vienna ("Protection of Civilian Populations Against the Dangers of Indiscriminate Warfare")*

> The XXth International Conference of the Red Cross . . . states that indiscriminate warfare consitutes a danger to the civilian population and the future civilization,
> solemnly declares that all governments and other authorities responsible for action in armed conflicts should conform at least to the following principles:
>> a. That the right of the parties to a conflict to adopt means of injuring the enemy is not unlimited.
>> b. That it is prohibited to launch attacks against the civilian populations as such.
>> c. That distinction must be made at all times between persons taking part in the hostilities and members of the civilian population to the effect that the latter be spared as much as possible.

---

they would go against the latest resolution of the U.N. General Assembly No. 2603A (*see below*); (4) they would generalize the tendency of certain military authorities that are unable to utilize nuclear or biological weapons for political or legal reasons and so fall back on chemical weapons with increasing regularity, as if they were conventional means of warfare.

[16] *See* Appendix I for resolutions adopted on this subject by the International Conferences of the Red Cross. The more recent resolutions cover weapons of mass destruction as a whole. On the same subject, the Institute of International Law, at its Edinburgh Session, in September 1969, adopted a resolution entitled "The distinction between military objectives and nonmilitary objects in general and particularly the problems associated with weapons of mass destruction," operative para. 7 of which states:

> Existing international law prohibits the use of all weapons which, by their nature, affect indiscriminately both military and nonmilitary objects, or both armed forces and civilian populations. In particular, it prohibits the use of weapons the destructive effect of which is so great that it cannot be limited to specific military objectives or is otherwise uncontrollable (self-generating weapons) as well as of "blind" weapons.

d. That the general principles of the law of war apply to nuclear and similar weapons.

expressly invites all governments who have not yet done so to accede to the Geneva Protocol of 1925 which prohibits the use of asphyxiating, poisonous, or other gases, all analogous liquids, materials, or devices, and bacteriological methods of warfare. . . .[17]

2. *Resolution XIV of the XXIst International Conference of the Red Cross in Istanbul ("Weapons of Mass Destruction")*

The XXIst International Conference of the Red Cross,
considering that the first and basic aim of the Red Cross is to protect mankind from the terrible suffering caused by armed conflicts,
taking into account the danger threatening mankind in the form of new techniques of warfare, particularly weapons of mass destruction,
confirming the resolutions adopted by the International Conferences of the Red Cross as well as the United Nations General Assembly Resolutions Nos. 2162 (XXI), 2444 (XXIII), and 2454 (XXIII) and the Resolution No. XXIII of the International Conference on Human Rights of 1968,
considering that the adoption of a special agreement on the prohibition of weapons of mass destruction would be an important contribution to the development of international humanitarian law,
requests the United Nations to pursue its efforts in this field,
requests the ICRC to continue to devote great attention to this question, consistent with its work for the reaffirmation and development of humanitarian law and to take every step it deems possible,
renews its appeal to the governments of states which have not yet done so to accede to the 1925 Geneva Protocol and to comply strictly with its provisions,
urges governments to conclude as rapidly as possible an agreement banning the production and stock-piling of chemical and bacteriological weapons.

The ICRC appeal on July 27, 1966,[18] was followed by resolutions adopted at the U.N. General Assemblies of the same year and of 1968. The effect of these measures was to induce a score of states to accede. This was an appreciable success, since before 1966, no more than forty-nine states had been parties to the Protocol.

The ICRC has recently drawn the attention of the governments of those states that are not yet parties to the Geneva Protocol once again to Istanbul Resolution XIV and in particular to operative paragraph 3. Official steps have been taken in a few countries to bring about their accession to the said Protocol in the near future.

---

[17] It should be noted that the first three of these four principles were subsequently included in Res. 2444 of the 23d Session of the U.N. General Assembly dated January 13, 1969, entitled "Respect for Human Rights in Armed Conflicts."

[18] *See* INTL. REV. RED CROSS 59 (Feb. 1967) & Jan. 3 (1968).

5.5. Activities of International Organizations

5.5.1. UNITED NATIONS ORGANIZATION. The question of the adoption of a special agreement prohibiting the production and storage (and use?) of biological and chemical weapons is now being dealt with by the United Nations (in particular by the Conference of the Committee on Disarmament), which is carrying on the work in this field started by the League of Nations.

A number of resolutions on this subject were adopted by the General Assembly.[19] The last of these directed the Secretary-General to draw up, with expert assistance, a report on chemical and biological weapons. In this report,[20] published in July 1969, U Thant urged member states to take the following steps:

1. To renew the appeal to all states to accede to the Geneva Protocol of 1925.
2. To make a clear affirmation that the prohibition contained in the Geneva Protocol applies to the use in war of all chemical, bacteriological, and biological agents (including tear gas and other harassing agents) which now exist or which may be developed in the future.
3. To call upon all countries to reach agreement to halt the development, production, and stockpiling of all chemical and bacteriological (biological) agents for the purpose of war, and effectively to eliminate them from their arsenals.

This important document was followed by a resolution adopted on December 16, 1969, at the General Assembly.[21] It recognizes the existence of an international customary law standard[22] prohibiting the use of all forms of biological and chemical weapons in international armed conflicts. On the grounds of a broad interpretation, and irrespective of whatever technical developments may be evolved, it condemns the use

---

[19] These resolutions were adopted as follows:
Res. 2162 B: For 91; against 0; abstentions 26.
Res. 2444: Unanimously.
Res. 2454: For 107; against 0; abstentions 26.
Res. 2603 A: For 80; against 3; abstentions 36.
[20] Report of the Secretary-General on Chemical and Bacteriological (Biological) Weapons and the Effects of their Possible Use, UN Doc. A/7575, July 1, 1969.
[21] Res. 2603 A.
[22] According to the ICRC Press Release No. 829, of June 2, 1967:

> . . . the ICRC doctors, on arrival at the site, immediately gave treatment to some of the wounded and collected indications pointing to the use of *poison gas.* Extremely disturbed and concerned by these methods of warfare which are absolutely *forbidden by codified international and customary law,* the ICRC at once communicated its delegates' reports to all authorities concerned . . . requesting them to take the solemn engagement not to resort in any circumstances whatsoever to the use of asphyxiating gases or any other similar toxic substances.

of all chemical and biological weapons in international armed conflicts as being contrary to international law.

Two main draft Conventions were submitted to the Disarmament Conference: a Soviet draft entitled "Draft Convention on the Prohibition of the Development, Production, and Stockpiling of Chemical and Bacteriological (Biological) Weapons and on the Destruction of Such Weapons,"[23] and a British "Draft Convention for the Prohibition of Biological Methods of Warfare."[24]

The question of noninternational armed conflicts remains unsolved. It is to be hoped that studies on that subject will not be abandoned, particularly as this type of conflict has increasingly occurred since World War II. The Special Committee on Disarmament of the Nongovernmental Organizations did pass a resolution in Geneva on February 19, 1970, in operative paragraph 2 of which it invites governments to apply the Geneva Protocol in all armed conflicts, *i.e.*, in both international and noninternational armed conflicts.

5.5.2. WORLD HEALTH ORGANIZATION. WHO has just made a significant contribution to the study of the chemical and biological warfare problem generally in the shape of a recently published report in 1970 by a group of consultants, entitled "Health Aspects of Chemical and Biological Weapons." This study offers a more specialized treatment of the subject than does the report of the U.N. Secretary-General, and supplements an interim report that the Director of WHO had transmitted to U Thant. This final report,[25] incorporates part of the information contained in the earlier report.[26]

Aware of the fact that the use of biological and chemical agents for military purposes could sufficiently disturb ecological processes to threaten the very existence of civilization as we know it, the delegates of the Twenty-third World Health Assembly, May 1970, adopted a resolution concerning these weapons.[27] The resolution stressed the importance of prohibiting the development, manufacture, and stockpiling of biological and chemical weapons as swiftly as possible under the auspices of the United Nations and to destroy existing stockpiles as a measure indispensable to the success of the efforts being made to improve man's health situation.

WHO will perhaps be called upon in the future to play a vital and practical supervisory role:

[23] U.N. Doc. A/7685.
[24] U.N. Doc. CCD/255 Rev. 1.
[25] U.N. Doc. A/7575.
[26] *See* Appendix II.
[27] U.N. Doc./WHA 2353.

Finally, there is the possibility that WHO might be called upon by the United Nations to help deal with allegations of use of chemical and biological weapons between nations and to assist in the limitation of chemical and biological weapons, and disarmament. The technical resources of WHO could contribute greatly to the resolution of many of the difficulties that are associated with these problems and are now being discussed within the framework of the United Nations.[28]

5.6. Conclusion

Thus, while the United Nations continues its work[29] the Red Cross continues to devote keen attention to the question of chemical and biological warfare. It is for the United Nations to proscribe the production, storage, and use of specific weapons, and as in the past, for the Red Cross to continue to uphold the rules that protect the individual during armed conflicts. Above all, the Red Cross must insure the protection, respect, and humane treatment of all persons *hors de combat* or not participating in the hostilities and spare them from needless suffering. But its diverse goals may sometimes oblige the Red Cross to express its views on a given weapon, whether indiscriminate or not. The National Red Cross, Red Crescent and Red Lion and Sun Societies, the ICRC, the League and the International Conference of the Red Cross will continue to support, with all their authority, the struggle against biological and chemical warfare by negotiations with governments and by better informing the world public opinion.

It is to be hoped that the forty-fifth anniversary of the Geneva Protocol will provide those states that have not yet acceded, an excellent opportunity to do so, and that it will also be a solemn reminder to all states that the customary law rules it embodies must be respected at all times, in all places, and under all circumstances.

APPENDIX I. LIST OF RESOLUTIONS RELATIVE TO NONDISCRIMINATING WEAPONS, ADOPTED BY INTERNATIONAL CONFERENCES OF THE RED CROSS.

Conference	Place	Date	Resolutions
Xth	Geneva	1921	XII/I/ 1 & 2
XIIth	Geneva	1925	V/ 1, 2 & 3
XIIIth	The Hague	1928	V/VI

[28] *Health Aspects of Chemical and Biological Weapons* 20–21.

[29] It would be unjust not to mention the remarkable studies carried out by the Stockholm International Peace Research Institute (SIPRI), which will shortly be bringing out a 6-volume publication THE PROBLEM OF CHEMICAL AND BIOLOGICAL WARFARE: Part I—History; Part II—Weapons, Military Doctrines, National Policies; Part III—CBW at the League of Nations and the United Nations 1920–1969; Part IV—Verification; Part V—International Law; Part VI—Possible Steps to Avoid CB Warfare.

XIVth	Brussels	1930	V/I, 2 & 3 (4)
XVth	Tokyo	1934	(XVIII) XXXVI
XVIIth	Stockholm	1948	XXIV
XVIIIth	Toronto	1952	XVII/XVIII
XIXth	New Delhi	1957	XVIII
XXth	Vienna	1965	XXVIII
XXIst	Istanbul	1939	XIV

Other, similar resolutions have also been adopted by the Board of Governors of the League, of which the most important was unanimously adopted at the XXIIIrd Session in Oslo, 1954.

APPENDIX II. WHO CONCLUSIONS

(Report "Health Aspects of Chemical and Biological Weapons" 10–11).

The following main conclusions emerge from the WHO analysis:

1. Chemical and biological weapons pose a special threat to civilians because of the often indiscriminate nature of such weapons, and because the high concentrations in which they would be used in military operations could lead to significant unintended involvement of the civilian population within the target area and for considerable distances downwind.

2. The large-scale, or with some agents, even limited use of chemical and biological weapons could cause illness to a degree that would overwhelm existing health resources and facilities.

3. Large-scale use of chemical and biological weapons could also cause lasting changes of an unpredictable nature in man's environment.

4. The possible effects of chemical and biological weapons are subject to a high degree of uncertainty and unpredictability, owing to the involvement of complex and extremely variable meteorological, physiological, epidemiological, ecological, and other factors.

5. Although advanced weapons systems would be required for the employment of chemical and biological agents on a militarily significant scale against large civilian targets, isolated and sabotage attacks not requiring highly sophisticated weapons systems could be effective against such targets in certain circumstances with some of these agents.

These conclusions are in harmony with the conclusions of the U.N. Group of Consultant Experts on Chemical and Bacteriological (Biological) Weapons and with the hope for further action to deal with the threat posed by the existence of these weapons, as expressed by the Secretary-General, U Thant, in the foreword to the United Nations' report.

CHAPTER VIII

HUMANITARIAN LAW OF ARMED CONFLICTS

Section 1. A COMMENTARY ON THE GENEVA CONVENTIONS OF
AUGUST 12, 1949

PERRY GULBRANDSEN[*]

> "Fortune strikes or smiles at will: I was free; now I am a slave.
> I was riding high, now I am in dust. I commanded yesterday; today
> I am in bondage."[1]

1.1. Background and General Principles

Man has obligated himself to observe certain humanitarian rules of
war, even toward an enemy. These rules are principally set forth in the
four Geneva Conventions of August 12, 1949. The Conventions constitute
both an emphatic statement of humanitarian principles and a significant
contribution to the development of the modern law of war.

The First Convention, entitled the "Geneva Convention for the Amelioration of the Condition of the Wounded and Sick in Armed Forces in
the Field," was a revision of the 1929 Convention having a similar name.
The Second Convention, the "Geneva Convention for the Amelioration
of the Condition of Wounded, and Sick and Shipwrecked Members of
Armed Forces at Sea," revised the Tenth Hague Convention of 1907,
which had adapted the Geneva Convention of 1906 to maritime warfare.
The Third Convention, the "Geneva Convention Relative to the Treatment of Prisoners of War," revised the 1929 Convention of the same
name, and the Fourth Convention, the "Geneva Convention Relative to
the Protection of Civilian Persons in Time of War,"[2] is perhaps the most
important of the conventions.

All four Conventions came into force in October 1950 and are now
part of the laws of war. The International Committee of the Red Cross

---

[*] With grateful recognition for the assistance of Professor M. Cherif Bassiouni.
[1] PLAUTUS, CAPTEIVEI II, at 301–303.
[2] Yingling & Ginnane, *The Geneva Conventions of 1949*, 46 A.J.I.L. 393 (1952) [herein-
after cited as Yingling & Ginnane].

368

reports that as of April 1969, 121 countries have, to all intents and purposes, accepted the provisions as binding. Some authorities point out that:

> . . . although the first three Geneva Conventions of 1949 are spoken of in the official documents as "revisions of prior conventions on the same subjects, this may be misleading, as the older conventions have been almost entirely rewritten in the light of intervening experience, particularly in World War II, and not only have many of the provisions of the older conventions been changed, but some of the basic concepts as well.[3]

A distinction must be made between the Law of Geneva and that of the Hague. This body of law was the result of the two peace conferences held in the Hague in 1899 and 1907. The Hague Law relates to the use of weapons and the methods of warfare, codifying the rules of war in all matters outside the scope of the Geneva Conventions. Both the Law of Geneva and the Law of the Hague were inspired by humanitarian principles and aim at restricting violence. The Geneva Conventions, however, more specifically concern the protection of the individual against the abusive use of force, while the Hague Conventions enforce interstate rules on the employment of such force.

There will be occasion during the course of this paper to return to this distinction, but emphasis can already be placed on the purely humanitarian aspects of the Geneva Conventions, originating beyond any political considerations and whose two dominant ideas were the elimination of unnecessary suffering and respect for the individual.[4]

The historical development of, and the events leading to, the Geneva Conventions of 1949 throw some light on their nature and significance and must briefly be referred to here.

Credit must be given to Jean-Jacques Rousseau as being a pioneer of some of the salient principles of the Conventions. In 1762, he wrote the following:

> The object of war being the destruction of the enemy state, one has the right to kill its defenders only when they leave weapons in their hands; but immediately they put them down and surrender, thus ceasing to be enemies or agents of the enemy, they once more become ordinary men and one no longer has any right to their life. Sometimes one can extinguish a state without killing a single member of it; moreover, war confers no right other than that which is necessary for its purpose. These principles . . . flow from the nature of things and are founded upon reason.[5]

This statement is indicative of a changing attitude establishing general protection for war victims, but concrete attempts to achieve such pro-

---

[3] Yingling & Ginnane, at 394.

[4] H. COURSIER, COURSE OF FIVE LESSONS ON THE GENEVA CONVENTIONS 5 (1962) [hereinafter cited as Coursier].

[5] ROUSSEAU, SOCIAL CONTRACT, bk. I, ch. 4.

tection are primarily a development of the second half of the nineteenth century. The first efforts were directed toward the wounded. The campaigns of Napoleon, conscript armies, and increased development of artillery, all played a part in increasing the number of the suffering and the wounded on the battlefield.[6] At the battle of Solferino, during the French and Sardinian campaign against the Austrians in June 1859, some 42,000 men were killed in a matter of hours, and within two months this figure doubled because of wounds received.[7]

Many of the wounded could have been saved had medical care been available. A witness to this slaughter on the battlefield was Henry Dunant, a citizen of Geneva, who became the primary pioneer in humanitarian work for those wounded in war. Dunant's pamphlet, "A Memory of Solferino," gave an account of what he had seen, and offered two practical proposals. The first was that each country should set up a relief society to aid the army medical services in time of war. The second was that the nations of the world should enter into a convention acknowledging the status and function of the national relief societies.[8] In Geneva, on August 22, 1864, Dunant's humanitarian proposals led to the signing of the "first" Geneva Convention for the "Alleviation of the Suffering of Soldiers Wounded on the Battlefield." Field and other military hospitals, medical personnel and materials, civilian ambulance drivers, and the wounded were declared neutral. They were placed under the protection of the belligerent countries, without distinction of nationality, and were to wear the reversed colors of the Swiss Flag (red on a white background) as a protecting symbol.[9]

At the close of the nineteenth century, in 1899, the Hague Peace Conference assembled and extended the terms of the Geneva Convention of 1864 to include war at sea. It detailed provisions for the treatment of prisoners of war—in particular, that they should be treated in a manner similar to that of the troops of the Detaining Power. At the Hague in 1906, the Geneva Convention for the Alleviation of the Suffering of Soldiers Wounded on the Battlefield was considerably enlarged and its application more clearly defined: wounded and sick soldiers, ambulance units and medical establishments, personnel, materials, and transport were brought under its protection. It was at this Convention that the symbol of the Red Cross was chosen in honor of Switzerland. Its use and the use of its designations were restricted to the terms of the Convention. In 1907, again at the Hague, the terms of the revised Geneva Conven-

---

[6] G.I.A.D. DRAPER, THE RED CROSS CONVENTIONS 2 (1958) [hereinafter cited as Draper].

[7] H. DUNANT, A MEMORY OF SOLFERINO 59–60 (1959).

[8] Draper, at 3.

[9] ICRC, SOME PHASES IN THE EVOLUTION OF THE RED CROSS 21 (1943).

tion of 1906 were extended to naval warfare and for the first time contained directions for the treatment of prisoners of war, military internees, and wounded soldiers in neutral countries.

It is the 1906 Convention which governed the treatment of the wounded and sick during World War I and remained in operation until replaced by the 1929 Geneva Convention. The 1929 Geneva Conventions, referring both to the sick and wounded and the prisoners of war, were framed in light of the experience gained in World War I and contained precise directions with regard to conditions of captivity: organization of camps, provisions for vital needs, legal position of prisoners, repatriation of wounded and sick prisoners, death during detention, and prisoners' relief institutions.[10]

Owing to the conditions which developed in conjunction with World War II both conventions executed in 1929 were considered to be in need of substantial revision. Preliminary drafts were prepared, and a diplomatic conference convened in Geneva in 1949. The twofold task of this conference was the revision of the two Conventions and that of the Tenth Hague Convention of 1907 and the preparation of a completely new convention for the protection of civilians. This was achieved within five months.[11]

1.2. Underlying Principles of the Conventions

The essential principles underlying the Geneva Conventions, as compared to their detailed provisions, can best be appreciated by an examination of the so-called "Common Articles," *i.e.*, those articles of a general character that are common to all four Conventions,[12] having been drafted for the most part in the same words and generally speaking inserted at the beginning of each of the four Conventions.[13]

Article I, which is common to all four Conventions, provides that "the contracting parties undertake to respect and to insure respect for the present Convention in all circumstances." This single sentence appears to leave the effect of a unilateral legal obligation not dependent upon corresponding observance by other contracting parties. The words "to insure respect" are by no means redundant or rhetorical.[14]

In effect, their meaning indicates that states are not only required to

[10] *Id.* at 21–22.
[11] The Diplomatic Conference was in continuous session from Apr. to Aug. 1949. The transactions of the Conference are contained in the Final Record of the *Diplomatic Conference of Geneva,* 1949, published by Federal Political Department (Berne, 1950–51).
[12] Yingling & Ginnane, at 394.
[13] *Id.* at 394.
[14] Reference to Commentary and text of the Conventions are to Jean Pictet, at 25 (ICRC, Geneva 1952) (2d 1960, 3d 1960, 4th 1958).

issue instructions to the various departments of the state but additionally to insure their compliance.[15] It may be reasonably stated that "in all circumstances" indicates that the Conventions must be respected in peace as well as in war. Article 2 states that the Conventions "apply to all cases of declared war or any other armed conflict which may arise between two or more of the contracting parties, even if the state of war is not recognized by one of them." Cumulatively, this means that when the conditions for the application of the Convention enumerated in article 2— namely, war declared or undeclared, armed conflict, or occupation— come into play, no party to the Convention can legitimately raise an excuse for their nonobservance.[16]

The fact that aggressive war is illegal by virtue of the Treaty for the Renunciation of War of 1928 and the United Nations Charter, does not exclude the application of these Conventions. It applies to aggressor and victim alike.

The earlier Geneva Conventions were considered to apply only in war, declared or recognized by either belligerent as amounting to a state of war in international law. Certain states have been aware of the advantages that flow from a refusal to treat a conflict as a war. (A case in point is the Korean "war.") The phrase "armed conflict" in article 2, seems to cover such a situation and removes the rather artibrary determination of a state of war from the judgment of the conflicting parties.[17]

The consensus of the authorities researched by this writer concerning the application of the Conventions by a noncontracting party in conflict with a contracting party is that the contracting party should begin by acting in accordance with the provisions "which would lead the opponent to do likewise."

Article 3 evidences the purpose of regulating conflicts not of an international character, *e.g.*, civil wars and insurrections by the establishment of a legal duty to observe certain minimum standards of conduct. The article establishes the minimum obligations of "each party to the conflict." The general principle underlying the specific prohibitions such as "murder, mutilation, cruel treatment, and torture" is that those persons taking no part in the hostilities, including those surrendered, wounded, and sick, are "in all circumstances to be treated humanely, without adverse distinction founded on race, color, religion or faith, sex, birth or wealth, or any other similar criteria." The Red Cross may offer its ser-

[15] Draper, at 8.

[16] Yingling & Ginnane, at 394.

[17] Report on the Work of the Conference of Government Experts for the Study of the Convention for the Protection of War Victims, at 8 (1947).

vices, but the article avoids placing any obligations on the contracting party to accept such services. The parties are encouraged to enter into agreements to apply the Conventions, but the application of article 3 "shall not affect the legal status of the parties." Such a development has been described by one authority in these words: "The observance of fundamental human rights has, in so far as it is the subject matter of legal obligations, ceased to be one of exclusive domestic jurisdiction of states, and has become a matter of legitimate concern for the United Nations and its members."[18] But article 3 and the Conventions in general appear to make few provisions for the case of relations between a state and its own nationals.

Article 3 was the most debated of all the articles considered by the Geneva Conference, and three general positions were advanced: (1) in all cases of internal conflict, the Conventions should be applicable; (2) the Conventions should not be applicable at all in such conflicts, and (3) they should apply only when certain proportions and characteristics had been reached in the conflict. The present article was adopted as a compromise.[19]

Articles 4, 5, and 6 define the persons to be protected and contain provisions for the application of the Conventions by Neutral Powers and the possible conclusion of special agreements between the conflicting parties.[20]

Article 7 in the First, Second, and Third Conventions (art. 8, in the 4th Convention) directs itself to the inalienable character of the rights of the protected persons and purports to prevent any renunciation of the rights secured under the Conventions. It appears that the experiences of World War II are directly responsible for its introduction, *i.e.*, the biological "experiments" in the concentration camps were allegedly carried out with the "consent of the prisoners." Quite clearly, prisoners and internees are not sufficiently "at liberty" to make any genuine waiver of their rights. The article specifies that "in no circumstances" may prisoners renounce in whole or in part the rights secured to them thereunder.[21]

A significant cornerstone of the Conventions concerns the role of the protecting power in article 8.[22] It sets forth the principle that the Conventions will "be applied with the cooperation and under the scrutiny of the protecting powers." In effect, the neutral powers are intrusted with safeguarding the interests of the belligerent powers in enemy countries.

[18] 2 Oppenheim, International Law 740 (8th ed. 1955)
[19] Yingling & Ginnane, at 395.
[20] Coursier, at 29.
[21] *Id.* at 397.
[22] *See* art. 9, Fourth Convention.

It is incumbent upon the contracting parties to facilitate to "the greatest extent possible" the work of the delegates or representatives of the protecting parties. Such cooperation, it is noted, can be terminated temporarily by reasons of "imperative military necessity."

Article 9[23] sanctions the activities of the International Committee of the Red Cross (ICRC) and its right to intervene. It should be added that delegates of the ICRC enjoy the same privilege as representatives of the protecting powers.[24] The fundamental problem, which was how to provide for replacement of the protecting powers in the event that they were unable to exercise their office, is discussed in article 10.[25] The purpose is to assure protected persons of impartial assistance and continuous application of the Conventions. Under article 10, in cases where for any reason prisoners of war are deprived of a protecting power, the detaining power is to request the services of a neutral state or humanitarian organization to assure the function of the protecting power.

Article 11[26] relates to the optional submission of disputes to the International Court of Justice. It further provides that the protecting power "shall lend their good offices with a view of settling this disagreement."

The Common Articles[27] that concern themselves with the imposition of penal sanctions for infractions are significant, and it may be fairly said that upon the success or failure of these Articles rests the success or failure of the Conventions. As indicated before, the Geneva Conventions now form a large part of the laws of war, violations of which are war crimes. War crimes are, by definition, "such hostile or other acts of soldiers or other individuals as may be punished by the enemy on capture of the offenders."[28]

The system proposed in these Articles imposes essentially three obligations on states: (1) a duty to enact legislation to provide penal sanctions for those who order or commit "grave breaches," (2) a duty to search for all persons, regardless of nationality, alleged to have committed such crimes, and (3) a duty to try alleged offenders observing customary judicial safeguards or to turn such offenders over to another contracting-party plaintiff.[29] These duties appear to be quite formidable; however, the optional extradition legislation permitted by the terms of the articles permits an international loophole governable primarily by political considerations.

[23] *See* art. 10, Fourth Convention.
[24] Coursier, at 31.
[25] *See* art. 11, Fourth Convention.
[26] *See* art. 12, Fourth Convention.
[27] First Convention, arts. 49 & 50; Second Convention, arts. 50 & 51; Third Convention, arts. 129 & 130; Fourth Convention, arts. 146 & 147.
[28] Oppenheim, *supra* Note 18, at 566.
[29] Draper, at 21.

The last of the common articles to be considered here are those that permit denunciation of the Convention but which expressly preserve certain basic duties even after denunciation—namely, those principles of the law of nations as they result from the public conscience, the laws of humanity, and the customs and usages of civilized peoples.[30]

The total effect of the ideas of Geneva has been an attempt to create and preserve a balance between humanitarian principles and the cruelties of war. How each of the Geneva Conventions of 1949 has addressed itself to this attempt is the next subject of examination.

1.3. The Wounded and Sick of Armed Forces in the Field and at Sea

This topic is covered by the first two conventions. The Geneva Convention for the Amelioration of the Condition of Wounded and Sick in Armed Forces in the field; and The Geneva Convention of Wounded, and Sick and Shipwrecked Members of Armed Forces at Sea.

Respect for soldiers fallen in battle dates back to before Christ. From the Egyptians, Greeks, and Romans to the Moors and Christians, and from the pre- and post-Renaissance Europeans to the time of the nineteenth century colonial powers, history is replete with incidents of battlefield humanity. Such conduct, however, was an exception and usually formed no pattern.

The First Geneva Convention of 1864, as previously noted, played an important role in the development of humanitarian law and was considered "unique since it aimed at regularizing in a permanent manner, a situation which until then had only been haphazard."[31]

The 1864 Convention, signed by representatives of twelve countries,[32] established the principle that "wounded or sick combatants, to whatever nation they may belong, must be collected and cared for."[33] It further safeguarded and conferred respect for military hospitals, ambulances[34] and related personnel and equipment[35] and recognized the Red Cross emblem as a protective sign for those persons and objects.[36]

The Convention was revised in 1906, again in 1929 in light of the experience of World War I, and again in 1949, forming the Convention for the Wounded and Sick, thus becoming the First Geneva Convention of 1949 (land).[37]

[30] *Id.* at 24.

[31] Louis Renault, Acts of the Geneva Conference 243 (1906).

[32] Boden, Belgium, Denmark, France, Hesse, Italy, Netherlands, Portugal, Prussia, Spain, Switzerland, and Wurtemburg.

[33] Geneva Convention of 1864, art. 6.

[34] *Id.*, art. 1.

[35] *Id.*, art. 2.

[36] *Id.*, art. 7.

[37] Commentary, First Convention, 9–16.

While undertaking the 1949 revision, participants decided to reincorporate in the Geneva Laws, with the necessary amendments and additions, the Hague Convention of 1907 for the Adaption to Maritime Warfare of the Principles of the Geneva Convention of 1906, which thus became the Second Geneva Convention of 1949 (sea).[38] Generally speaking, this convention is a replica of the First Convention. The same principles govern the two texts, and the same rules apply to the persons and objects covered, taking into account the different conditions prevailing on land and on sea. They therefore can justifiably be examined in the same section, each independently and, where possible, comparatively.[39]

The first article of importance is that which defines the class of persons protected by the Conventions. In both Conventions, article 12 lays down that "members of the Armed Forces and other persons mentioned in the following articles who are wounded, sick, or shipwrecked" shall be respected and protected in all circumstances. Article 12 first specifies the nature of the protection afforded and logically is then followed by an enumeration of the various categories of wounded and sick to which the Convention applies in article 13. These categories include first of all those who follow the Armed Forces without directly belonging to them, such as civilian members of military aircraft crews, journalists, war correspondents, contractors, members of military aircraft crews, journalists, war correspondents, contractors, members of labor units or of war services responsible for the welfare of soldiers or sailors. But to enjoy this protection, these persons must have been authorized by the Armed Forces to accompany them. Armed civilians, generally known as "partisans," and those inhabitants of nonoccupied territory who spontaneously take up arms in irregular units to fight the invading forces also come under the Convention, provided they carry arms openly and respect the laws and customs of war. These persons are substantially the same as those entitled to prisoner-of-war status under the Third Convention (prisoners of war). It appears that these categories are specifically listed in article 13 to preclude the possibility of a state being a party to the First Convention without necessarily being a party to the Third Convention. The practical importance of article 13 is that it determines under which Convention the wounded man is to be cared for, not whether he is to receive care. In other words, it determines status, not treatment.[40]

Definitions of the terms "wounded" and "sick" are given in the Commentary on the First Convention. It refers to persons who have fallen by reason of a wound or sickness of any kind or who have ceased to

---

[38] Yingling & Ginnane, at 398.
[39] Coursier, at 42.
[40] *Id.* at 43.

fight and laid down their arms as a consequence of what they themselves think about their health. Cases are frequent of soldiers who have heroically continued to fight in spite of serious wounds and, in so doing, have renounced any claim to protection under the Convention. It is the fact of falling or laying down of arms which constitutes the claim to protection. It is only the soldier who is himself seeking to kill who may be killed. The abandonment of all aggressiveness should put an end to aggression.[41]

Article 14 provides that all wounded and sick soldiers falling into enemy hands are prisoners of war.[42]

Thus, articles 13 and 14 and the First, Second, and Third Conventions are complementary. In other words, the care and protection to which individuals are entitled as wounded and sick is not altered by the fact that they become prisoners of war. The wounded and sick members of the Armed Forces must, as noted in article 12, be treated with respect and protected *in all circumstances,* without distinctions based upon nationality, sex, race, religion, political opinion, or similar criteria. All attempts on ther lives or violence to their persons is strictly forbidden. In particular, they must not be "murdered, or exterminated, or subjected to biological experiments or willfully left without medical assistance and care or exposed to the risk of contagion or infection."[43] In summary, they must receive humane treatment.

Articles 15, 16, and 17[44] may be considered together. According to article 15 (as in article 18 of the 2d Convention), the parties to the conflict must "at all times and particularly after an engagement take all possible measures to search for and collect the wounded, protect them against pillage and maltreatment, give them adequate care, search for the dead and prevent their being despoiled." Here the general obligation to care for the wounded is significant in view of the modern techniques available for on-the-spot treatment of the wounded. If these methods are employed in time, the chance for survival of the victim is substantially increased. Diligent search and rapid treatment have shown their positive effects. Statistics afford proof of the effectiveness of these measures. In the Crimean War, 60 per cent of the wounded died. In World War I, 7.5 per cent died. In World War II, 2.3 per cent died.[45] This record reflects undeniable progress.

Article 16 makes detailed provisions for the recording and forwarding

[41] Commentary, First Convention, at 136.
[42] Similar provision in Second Convention, art. 16.
[43] First Convention, art. 12.
[44] Corresponding provision in Second Convention, arts, 18, 19, & 20.
[45] Commentary, First Convention, at 153.

of information concerning the wounded and sick to the National Information Bureau established by the Third Convention.[46] This provision acknowledges the value of standardizing the use of, and the data contained on, identification tags.

Article 17 relates to the dead and the method of their burial and provides for the establishment of a graves' registration service at the opening of hostilities. The dead are to be honorably interred. Bodies are not to be cremated except for imperative hygienic reasons or the religion of the deceased. These reasons must be stated in the death certificate.[47] It appears that a proper burial, preferably not of a mass-grave nature, is the only method which may permit future exhumation for absolute identification in the interest of the family. It should be noted that the above provisions do not appear to be compulsory if circumstances do not permit.

Article 18 enables the military authorities to appeal to the local inhabitants to collect and care for the wounded under its direction. Civilians and relief societies can do so spontaneously and on their own initiative, but must do so respecting the terms of the laws of war and the Geneva Conventions. Violations of this duty may merit trial, conviction, and punishment. A problem occurs with the provision that "no one may ever be molested or convicted for having nursed the wounded or sick," when contrasted with possible charge of "giving aid and succour to the enemy." It has been submitted that any such person may be prosecuted for the concealment but not for the tending. The same applies in maritime warfare to neutral merchant vessels, yachts, or other craft "which take on board and care for the wounded or shipwrecked persons or collect the dead."[48]

It is interesting to note that the following protective clause was provided in the Geneva Convention of 1864: "All wounded collected and nursed in a house shall serve as its safeguard." No such protection is provided for in the Geneva Convention of 1949.[49]

The military may appeal to the inhabitants but are not bound to. If they do so appeal, any compliance by the civilians is under the control of the military. The latter is not the case when the civilians take the wounded into their houses, they may not display the Red Cross emblem thereon or on their persons. The right to use that symbol is closely regulated.[50]

Articles 19 through 23 refer to the protection of personnel and medical

[46] Draper, at 77.
[47] *Id.* at 78.
[48] Second Convention, art. 21.
[49] Commentary, First Convention, at 14 & 15.
[50] Draper, at 79.

equipment. Medical personnel are not considered as part of the fighting force. They enjoy special protection and are designated as *protected personnel*. Members of the medical corps are to carry an identity card, wear an armband with the Red Cross emblem and may be armed for their own defense and that of the wounded. Fixed establishments and mobile units of the medical service "may in no circumstances be attacked" and must be respected at all times by parties to the conflict. If captured, the personnel must be free to continue their duties as long as the detaining power has not taken such activity over. These medical establishments and units must be placed as far away as possible from military objectives—correspondingly, Red Cross vehicles are to travel at different times and via different routes than military convoys. According to article 21, this protection will not cease until the facilities or mobile units are used for harmful acts to the enemy.[51]

Articles 24 through 32 deal with the position of medical personnel and chaplains as part of the armed forces in the field. If they are civilians or members of the forces at sea, their position and protection are governed by the Fourth and Second Convention, respectively. Article 24 relates to the permanent medical personnel and chaplains of the Armed Forces, who must be protected and respected in "all circumstances," but who also must be employed exclusively on specific medical or religious duties. Auxiliary medical personnel specially trained as hospital orderlies, nurses, or stretcher bearers are protected under article 25, if they are carrying out related duties at the time of capture. This article provides that such auxiliary personnel must be members of the armed services.[52] Civilian medical or religious personnel who are employed in the same duties as their military equivalent fall under the protection of article 26, if the staff of any society providing such civilian personnel is subject to military law.

Article 28 appears to be one of the more controversial provisions in the Convention. Under the 1929 Convention, medical personnel, upon capture, could not be detained and had to be returned.[53] Under the 1949 Convention, permanent medical personnel, chaplains and personnel of the National Red Cross Society can be detained "in so far as the state of health, the spiritual needs, and the number of prisoners of war require."[54] During their detention, they are to have all the benefits provided in the prisoner of war Convention; however, they are not considered prisoners of war and are permitted to carry out their respective

---

[51] Coursier, at 47.
[52] Draper, at 81.
[53] Commentary, First Convention, at 436–46.
[54] First Convention, art. 28.

duties, preferably with the prisoners of their own armed forces. When their detention is dispensable, they are to be returned as soon as a road is open and military requirements permit.[55]

The selection of personnel to be returned is to be objective, consistent with the date of capture and the state of health. The percentage of such personnel to be returned is open to the determination of the conflicting parties, consistent with the numerical proportion of prisoners and distribution of personnel in various camps.[56] Personnel of a recognized medical society of a neutral country who have fallen into the hands of an adverse party are to be treated by the adverse party in a manner corresponding to and consistent with treatment of their own armed forces.

Article 33 asserts the essential principle that the materials of a mobile medical unit must, upon capture, be reserved for the care of the wounded and sick. Supplies, buildings, and material are subject to the regulations of the Hague, but must not be diverted from their purpose if they are needed for the care of the sick and wounded. Such material, equipment, and stores are not to be intentionally destroyed[57] but may be used if previous arrangements, consistent with the needs of the wounded and sick, have been made.

By article 34, the reality and personality of the Red Cross and other equivalent societies are regarded as private property but are subject to the right of requisition, as is set forth in the Hague Regulation, in cases of urgent necessity, after the welfare of the wounded and sick has been safeguarded. Medical vehicles transporting wounded or sick persons or medical equipment are to be respected and protected—as long as they are used solely for the transportation of the wounded and sick and for medical personnel equipment. Conversely, military vehicles, or for that matter any suitable vehicles, can be used temporarily for the transporting of the wounded, and during this time they are entitled to protection subject to the display of the distinctive emblem. When not in use for medical purposes, such emblem must be removed.[58]

Provision is made in articles 36 and 37 for the protection of medical aircraft when used exclusively for the evacuation of wounded and the transport of medical personnel. Such aircraft must be clearly marked both with their national colors and with the Red Cross emblem. (Similar provision is made in articles 38 and 39 of the Second Geneva Convention concerning medical aircraft and chartered ships.) Such aircraft are protected only when flown at heights, times, and on routes specifically agreed

[55] *Id.* art. 30.
[56] *Id.*, art. 31.
[57] *Id.*, art. 33.
[58] *Id.*, art. 34.

upon by the conflicting parties.[59] Military hospital ships built or equipped especially to treat and transport the wounded, sick, and shipwrecked are protected by article 22 of the Second Convention and are exempt from capture. The same applies to hospital ships of Red Cross societies or other recognized relief societies or private persons. This privileged position is evidently explained by the fact that such ships are exceedingly rare, and the destruction or internment of such a vessel would be harmful to the victims. Hospital ships, as well as their lifeboats,[60] small craft for coastal operations, and vessels which might be employed by the Red Cross for evacuation purposes,[61] enjoy this immunity. All the above hospitals, transport vehicles, equipment, and personnel protected in this manner by the Geneva Convention have the right to wear the Red Cross emblem.

Articles 38 through 43 relate to the distinctive emblem of the Red Cross. What is now noted as a compliment to Switzerland appears not to have been a "conscious intention" of the representatives of the 1864 Convention.[62] In some countries, the Red Crescent, the Red Lion, the Sun, and the Red Shield of David have all been viewed as acceptable, though the original idea was the association of the Red Cross from particular religions or philosophies. The emblem is to be clearly visible to obviate the possibility of any hostile action, and any abuse of the emblem constitutes a breach of the laws of war. Its use is prohibited for private, public, and/or commercial use by any other society not authorized by the terms of the Convention. Parties to the Convention are to exercise whatever measures necessary for the prevention and repression of any abuses.

1.4. Prisoners of War: The Third Geneva Convention Relative to the Treatment of Prisoners of War

The captors refuse to list the prisoners. They have made propaganda by releasing a few, but little or nothing has been said about the barbarous treatment the released men have disclosed.

The captors have refused inspection of prisoner camps by the Red Cross or any other neutral authority, except for visits by highly uncritical groups for propaganda purposes. The men in camps are almost entirely isolated. Isolation appears to be a key tactic in an effort to wear down the spirit of the prisoners, who are often kept in solitary confinement for months.

Prisoners frequently are subjected to brutal interrogation, being forced to stand up for forty-eight hours, without food or water under blinding lights. Many are beaten. Some have been hung by their arms for long periods. Others

[59] Yingling & Ginnane, at 399.
[60] Second Convention, art. 26.
[61] *Id.*, art. 27.
[62] Commentary, First Convention, at 298.

have been burned by cigarets or have their finger-nails pulled out. All, even the wounded have been paraded thru streets to be stoned and spat upon by the populace.

Food is poor and barely enough to sustain life. Medical care is inadequate. No known deaths have been reported, but when prisoners are named no one can say whether any have died from beating, neglect, starvation, and improper medical care.

Mail is handled at the whim of the captors. Some packages were allowed at Christmas time, but this was mainly for propaganda purposes. Packages were searched and many items removed. A few were allowed to speak on the radio, and only a few families have received even a card from any of the prisoners.

There is no general mixing or exercise. Torture is common. Punishments are meted out at the whim of the captors.

The article above concerns the treatment of American prisoners in the hands of Vietcong and North Vietnamese and is condensed from an article in the *Chicago Tribune* dated October 12, 1969. Such maltreatment constituted a prominent part of the indictments proffered against the Germans and Japanese before the International Military Tribunal at Nuremburg and Tokyo.

The future developments that may result from the experiences of Vietnam and Biafra are yet to be determined. This writer is guardedly optimistic insofar as the historical development of the Geneva Convention has evidenced a pattern of developing remedies out of experiences which have exposed the inadequacies of the then existing rules of war.

After World War I, the vagaries and loopholes of the preceding Conventions were cleared up to a significant degree by the Geneva Convention of 1929. After the inhumane abuses of World War II, the Geneva Conventions of 1949 attempted to expand the sometimes fragmentary and incomplete provisions of 1929 by a more specific and definitive statement on the humanitarian principles required of nations in their treatment of prisoners of war.

It is to that Convention that this writer now turns. The Convention of 1949 is first and foremost a code of legal rules, both fundamental and detailed, for the protection of prisoners of war throughout the period of their captivity. Secondly, these rules are based upon and are designed to prevent a recurrence of the tragic events of World War II. Thirdly, the principle underlying all the articles is that humane and decent treatment is a right and not a favor conferred on individuals captured in war, recognizing that prisoners are the victims of events and are not criminals. Fourthly, it is clear that prisoners of war owe no allegiance to their captors and are entitled to legal status as prisoners of war not dissimilar to that of the members of the Armed Forces of their captors. Finally, a more comprehensive role is provided for by the protecting power, the Red Cross, and other relief organizations.[63]

Apart from the common articles which have already been considered, the first article that demands attention is article 4, which defines prisoners of war under the Convention.

An individual entitled to the status of prisoner of war must not only have "fallen into the power of the enemy" but must also belong to one of the categories, specified by the article. If not in one of these categories, he will, as will be indicated later, generally be entitled to protection under the Fourth Convention. If the individual is not entitled to prisoner of war status and engaged in the hostilities, there exists the possibility of treatment as a war criminal.[64] Over and above the members of the regular and auxiliary Armed Forces, the article includes "members" of organized resistance movements, provided they fulfill four conditions: (1) they are commanded by a person "responsible" for his subordinates; (2) they have a fixed distinctive emblem; (3) they openly carry arms, and (4) they conduct their operations in accordance with the customs of the laws of war.[65] This last provision, it appears, has aroused substantial debate. The farmer-by-day, assassin-by-night type of "partisan" was not to be condoned by international law, whatever other justification circumstances might give him.[66]

It may be thought that the effectiveness of any resistance movement that complies with these requirements will be reduced if not destroyed. This writer concurs with those who do not hold this position. There will always be patriots who will act as, for lack of a more accurate word, "outlaws" under the knowledge that they do so at the peril of their lives. Heroism necessarily implies this risk.[67]

Article 4 also confers the status of prisoners of war on employed civilians who accompany the armed forces, including "members of crews" of the merchant marine and crews of civil aircraft of the parties to the conflict, who do not benefit by more favorable treatment under any other provisions of international law.[68]

Also entitled to prisoner-of-war status are those inhabitants of an unoccupied country who, on the approach of the enemy, spontaneously take up arms to resist the attackers without time to organize themselves, if

[63] Draper, at 50.

[64] Draper, at 52.

[65] Art. I, Hague Rules of Land Warfare.

[66] Yingling & Ginnane, at 402.

[67] Coursier, at 66.

[68] *See* Yingling & Ginnane, at 404, for a brief summary of the Development of Crews of Merchant Vessels.

they carry arms openly and respect the laws of war. This is known as a *levee en masse.*[69] Curiously, such protection is not extended to such an uprising *after* the enemy has occupied the national territory concerned. Those members of the civil population who, in the area occupied by the enemy, do not form part of the organized resistance groups operating openly in accordance with the laws of war and who participate in hostilities become "unprivileged belligerents."[70] As such, they are liable to be charged with violations of the occupying power's penal law but are still entitled to limited legal protections provided by the Fourth Convention.[71] As previously indicated, a requirement for all persons entitled to prisoner-of-war status is that they "have fallen into the power of the enemy." Those who desert their own forces and give themselves up to the enemy as defectors do not, it is thought, "fall into the power of the enemy," for they have voluntarily put themselves in his power and have never been captured.[72] On the other hand, those who are captured in the ordinary way and who then defect while in captivity are still entitled to rights of prisoners of war. Humanitarian considerations, however, urge a policy of broadening the application of article 4 so that no disparity of treatment is made between combattants on the basis of indiscriminate labels, such as "civil strife" and "guerilla warfare."

Article 5 provides that the Convention applies to a prisoner from the time of capture until final release and repatriation. The reader can immediately see the difficulty ahead in the interpretation of "time of capture" and "final release and repatriation." The Korean peace talks were substantially delayed for eighteen months over the compulsory or voluntary repatriation of prisoners from South to North Korea. Additionally, there have been reports concerning instances of commanders capriciously deciding when enemy troops had been captured and when they should be treated as prisoners of war.[73]

Secondly, article 5 provides that if any doubt should arise as to whether persons who have committed a belligerent act and later fall into the hands of the enemy are or are not prisoners of war as defined in article 4, they are to enjoy the protection of the Convention until their status has been determined by a "competent tribunal."[74] This appears to be a fine and necessary idea, but exceedingly difficult to apply. Admittedly, the purpose of the tribunal is to determine status, not guilt, but as long

[69] Draper, at 53.
[70] Baxter, in 27 Brit. Y.B. Int'l L. 235–266 (1950).
[71] Fourth Convention, arts. 64–78.
[72] R.J. Wilhelm, *Can the Status of Prisoners of War Be Altered?* Revue Internationale de la Croix-Rouge 28–31 (July & Sept. 1956).
[73] Yingling & Ginnane, at 406.
[74] Third Convention, art. 5.

as "a competent tribunal" remains undefined and the limits of its function remain so uncertain, it can provide great latitudes for abuse under the mantle of the Convention.

The general principle underlying the legal protection of prisoners of war, as indicated in article 12, is that they are in the hands of the enemy power, not of the individuals or units who have captured them.[75] Thus the detaining power has the ultimate legal responsibility for their proper treatment.

> In no circumstances may a prisoner of war be transferred to a power which is not a party to the Convention . . . the transferring party must satisfy itself of the willingness and ability of the transferee power to apply the Convention . . . and the transferring power, upon being informed by the protecting power that the transferee power is failing to carry out the Convention, must take effective measures to correct the situation or have the prisoners returned to it.[76]

Article 13 provides in general for the humane treatment of prisoners at all times. It adds: "In particular, no prisoner of war may be subjected to physical mutilation or to medical or scientific experiments of any kind which are not justified as being in his interest. Prisoners are likewise to be protected at all times against acts of violence or intimidation and against insult and public curiosity. Among the general principles to be observed for their protection are the following: they are not to be uselessly exposed to danger pending their evacuation from the fighting men; they can be interned only in premises located on land and affording every guarantee of hygiene and health; and they may not at any time be sent to, or detained in, areas where they may be exposed to the fire of the fighting zone nor used to render certain points or areas immune from military operations owing to their presence.

Article 14 underlines that prisoners of war are entitled in all circumstances to respect of their persons and their honor and that they retain in full the civil capacity which they enjoyed at the time of their capture. They, therefore, continue to hold their civil rights as in their mother country within the restrictions imposed by captivity.[77]

According to article 16, all prisoners must be treated alike, considering age, rank, sex, health, and professional qualifications, without adverse distinction based on belief, political opinion, or like criteria.

Upon capture, a prisoner is required to give his name, rank, date of birth, and armed forces serial number. That is all. He is to be in possession of an identity card issued by his commanding authority. He must

[75] Coursier, at 67.
[76] Yingling & Ginnane, at 406–407.
[77] Coursier, at 67.

produce the card on demand, but he is entitled to its return. No physical or mental torture or any other forms of coercion "may be exercised to obtain information" of any kind and no unpleasant treatment may be meted out for refusal.[78] The prisoner may be deprived only of arms and military equipment. Only officers may remove money from prisoners, and receipts must be given.[79] Evacuation from the battle area must be carried out as swiftly and safely as possible and under humane conditions.[80] In particular, prisoners must receive food, water, and medical attention.[81]

Articles 21 through 48 of the Convention contain provisions relating to the internment of prisoners. Under this heading are included such matters as the citing of camps,[82] the prisoners' quarters,[83] food,[84] clothing,[85] canteen,[86] hygiene and medical treatment,[87] and their religious, intellectual, and physical activities.[88]

Particular attention should be focused on article 26, which provides that the basic daily rations shall be sufficient in quantity, quality, and variety to keep the prisoners in good health and to prevent loss of weight or the development of nutritional deficiencies. This abandons the 1929 Convention principle that the prisoners should receive the same rations as the detaining-power forces do. "This article was strongly advocated by the United States in view of the suffering and deaths of its personnel held as prisoner of war in Asiatic countries during World War II on account of their inability to subsist healthily on the native diet."[89]

Article 41 requires copies of the Convention to be posted in the camps in the prisoners' own language. Article 42 provides that the use of weapons against prisoners, especially against those who are trying to escape, shall constitute an extreme measure, always to be preceded by warnings appropriate to the circumstances.

Articles 49 through 68 of the Convention contain provisions relating to the type and conditions of work of the prisoners of war. The 1929 Convention simply stipulated that prisoners must not be engaged in work with any direct connection with the operation of war. It may be said

---

[78] Third Convention, art. 17.
[79] *Id.*, art. 18.
[80] *Id.*, art. 19.
[81] *Id.*, art. 20.
[82] *Id.*, arts. 22–24.
[83] *Id.*, art. 25.
[84] *Id.*, art. 26.
[85] *Id.*, art. 27.
[86] *Id.*, art. 28.
[87] *Id.*, arts. 29–32.
[88] *Id.*, arts. 34–38.
[89] Yingling & Ginnane, at 407.

that any work aids the enemy in some respect, and the 1949 Convention has taken a definitive approach, *i.e.*, enumerating the classes of work in which prisoners may be used. In particular, the removal of mines is prohibited unless prisoners volunteer for it. As to wages and salaries, prisoners are to receive a monthly advance pay, based on the Swiss franc according to their rank, to be not less than one quarter of a Swiss franc per full working day. This section also covers the receipt and sending of mail, parcels, and clothing, which may not be withheld for disciplinary reasons.

Section VI of the Convention, containing articles 78 through 108, treats complaints, prisoners-of-war representatives, and the very important area of penal and disciplinary sanctions. Quite clearly, a conferring of rights upon prisoners of war entails the necessary corollary that they should have complete freedom to complain of violations of these rights to the detaining power. This freedom has been established by Article 78, which permits complaints to be directed to both the detaining power and the protecting power. Articles 79 through 81 relate to prisoners-of-war representatives, who act as intermedaries between the prisoners and the camp authorities. In the case of officers, their representative is the senior officer holding the highest rank, in accordance with the custom observed in all military forces. In the case of noncommissioned officers or other ranks, the representative is elected by his comrades every six months by free and secret ballot and is eligible for reelection. These representatives may visit premises where prisoners are held, and every prisoner has the right to consult his representative. Their part in securing the proper application of the Convention cannot be underestimated.[90]

The subject of penal and disciplinary sanctions is governed by articles 82 through 108. "In general, the provisions are better arranged and more extensive than the provisions on the same subject in the 1929 Convention."[91] These articles are of considerable importance when considering the penal law to which prisoners of war should be subjected during captivity and the type of court that can properly exercise jurisdiction over them for offenses committed either before or after capture.

Article 82 prohibits all proceedings or punishments contrary to the Convention. Also, if any act is punishable when committed by a prisoner, but not when committed by a soldier of the detaining power, the prisoner may be punished only summarily (not more than thirty days) and may not be brought to trial for that conduct. Under article 83, the detaining power is required to insure that "the competent authorities exercise the greatest leniency" in determining whether to institute disciplinary or ju-

[90] Draper, at 61.
[91] Yingling & Ginnane, at 408.

dicial proceedings against a prisoner of war—where possible, the former is preferred. According to article 84, a prisoner must be tried only by a military court, unless the laws of the detaining power expressly permit the civil courts to try the troops of the detaining power for a similar offense.

> However, in no circumstances may the prisoner be tried by a court which does not offer essential guarantees of independence and impartiality as generally recognized, and procedure of which does not accord to the accused the basic rights and means of defense prescribed by Article 105.[92]

Article 85 provides that "prisoners of war prosecuted under the laws of the detaining power for acts committed prior to capture shall retain, even if convicted, the benefits of the Convention." This appears to mean that prisoners of war charged with war crimes which include "grave breaches" of the Geneva Conventions have to be tried in the same way as those tried for postcapture offenses. This position is a reversal of the law established in the U. S. Supreme Court decision *In re Yamashita.*[93] In this case, it was held that articles 45 through 67 of the Geneva Convention of 1929, relating to the trial of prisoners of war, did not apply to trials of prisoners for offenses (war crimes) committed before capture.

The application of article 85 acts as a bar to the practice, which was adopted at the close of World War II, of discharging prisoners of war and then trying them as civilians before special war-crime tribunals. As previously indicated, a prisoner cannot be deprived of his status, even with his consent, because he cannot renounce his rights according to the "common articles," in particular article 7, of this Convention. It was in relation to article 85, that the Soviet Bloc entered a reservation that a prisoner of war convicted of war crimes shall be excluded from the benefits of the Convention during the period that they are serving their sentence. Certain Western Powers have found this position unacceptable, questioning in part the absence of intention by the Soviet Bloc to reapply the convention upon completion of the sentence.[94]

Under article 87 the courts and military authorities of the detaining powers may not impose sentences or punishments different from those imposed on members of their own forces for the same acts. Collective punishment for individual acts, corporal punishment, imprisonment in places without daylight, and any form of torture or cruelty are forbidden.[95] The summary punishments are limited to confinement of not more than thirty days—and in no case shall punishment be inhuman, brutal,

[92] Yingling & Ginnane, at 408.
[93] 4 War Crimes Trials 1–95 (1946); Yingling & Ginnane, at 410.
[94] Pilloud, Revue Internationale 20–24 (Aug. 1957).
[95] Third Convention, art. 87.

or dangerous to the health of prisoners of war.[96] A prisoner who has attempted to escape, helped another to escape or in an attempt to escape can receive only summary punishment even if it is a repeated offense.[97] A prisoner's escape is considered complete (1) when he has joined his own forces or his allies; (2) when he has left the territory of his captors or their allies, or (3) when he has boarded a ship of his own Power or an ally which is at liberty.[98]

Under article 93, offenses committed "with the sole intention of facilitating the escape and which do not entail violence against life or limb" are only punishable summarily. If anyone, even a fellow prisoner, is injured during an escape by conduct of the prisoner, the prisoner attempting the escape may be subject to judicial measures.

The Convention appears to be silent concerning espionage actions and whether or not spies are inside the protection of the Convention. It seems reasonable, considering the discussion of the "partisan" situation, that as a matter of custom spies would not be considered prisoners of war. The requirements of article 4 are inconsistent with conferring protection under the Convention on spies, yet the legality of belligerents employing spies is virtually unquestioned. Capture may mean trial and execution. To this writer there exists a curious relationship regarding the international legality of espionage and the serious nature of the punishment under municipal law.[99]

Articles 99 through 108 contain significant judicial safeguards concerning the trial of prisoners of war and operate with the aid of the protecting power. The prisoners' representatives and the protecting power are to be told as soon as possible of the offenses punishable by death under the law of the detaining power.[100] No prisoner may be forced into confessing guilt or denied a right to prepare and present his defense with the aid of counsel.[101] Additionally, six months must elapse between notification of the death sentence to the protecting power and execution.[102]

Under article 102, a prisoner can be validly sentenced only if the sentence has been pronounced by the same courts, by the same procedure applied to the armed forces of the detaining power, and are in observance of the Convention. Three weeks' notice of the particulars of an

[96] *Id.*, arts. 89 & 90.
[97] *Id.*, arts. 92 & 93.
[98] *Id.*, art. 91.
[99] Oppenheim, *supra* Note 18 at 422–425, 574–575 (8th ed. 1955); Baxter, 27 Brit. Y.B. Int'l L. 235–266 (1950).
[100] Third Convention, art. 100.
[101] *Id.*, art. 99.
[102] *Id.*, art. 101.

upcoming trial of a prisoner is to be given to the protecting power. Such trial will be adjourned for lack of proof of receipt of such notice; and if it appears that there is no protecting power, there will be no trial,[103] except after notice the trial is *in camera* on grounds of state security.[104] The prisoner is further entitled to the same right of appeal as the armed forces of the detaining power;[105] and if the sentence becomes final or a death sentence was imposed in the first instance, the particulars are to be sent to the protecting power.[106] Finally, sentence must be served in the same establishments and under the same conditions as in the case of members of the armed forces of the detaining power.[107]

A prisoner's captivity may, under the Convention, be ended by (1) direct repatriation of those sick or seriously wounded; but such repatriation shall not be against the individual's will during hostilities.[108] (2) accommodation in neutral countries until close of hostilities.[109] (3) successful escape, (4) death; or (5) release and repatriation after close of hostilities.[110] The Convention specifically states that prisoners must be released and repatriated without delay after the cessation of active hostilities.

At the time of the Korean War, the negotiating parties had diametrically opposed conceptions of the conditions under which repatriation was to be effected. Thousands of prisoners detained by the U.N. Forces, in fact, refused to be repatriated. It is curious that at the time neither the Sino-Koreans nor the United States had yet ratified the 1949 Convention,[111] yet the discussions revolved around article 118 already stated and article 7, which stipulated that "prisoners of war may in no circumstances renounce in part or in entirety the rights secured to them by the present Convention." According to the Sino-Koreans, prisoners of war were still under military discipline and were not free agents. Therefore repatriation should take place even if against the wishes of the prisoners.[112]

The U.N. Forces answered that the Convention was a "decree of human rights for the prisoners" and that "forced repatriation would be in complete contradiction to the humanitarian principle on which the

[103] *Id.,* art. 104.

[104] *Id.,* art. 105.

[105] *Id.,* art. 106.

[106] *Id.,* art. 107.

[107] *Id.,* art. 108.

[108] *Id.,* arts. 109 & 110.

[109] *Id.,* art. 111.

[110] *Id.,* art. 118.

[111] Jaro Mayda, *The Korean Repatriation Problem and International Law,* 47 A.J.I.L. 424 (1953).

[112] Coursier, at 70.

Geneva Convention is based, the principle of protection for the individual.[113]

As stated in the Commentary of the International Committee of the Red Cross:

> Apart from articles 118 and 7, the Convention, especially in articles 13 and 14, expresses very general principles prescribing humane treatment and respect for the person in all circumstances. For this reason, where the repatriation of a prisoner would be manifestly contrary to the general principles of international law for the protection of the human being, the detaining power may, so to speak, grant asylum.[114]

It appears that the representatives to the Convention considered the likelihood of large numbers of prisoners refusing repatriation so remote that it did not justify an express provision.[115] The refusal of prisoners to accept repatriation, as in Korea, is exceptional, but considering the ever-increasing governmental turnovers, it is entirely possible that changes in government may create good reasons to fear that measures affecting a prisoner's life and liberty may be taken against him upon his return. In the Fourth Convention, provision is made for similar cases: the transfer of a protected person to a country where he may have reason to fear persecution for his political opinion or religious beliefs is forbidden.

At the start of a conflict, each party involved must establish an official information bureau for the prisoners in its power and must within the shortest possible time give information to the bureau concerning all salient particulars relating to each prisoner of war in its custody, including name, identification number, next of kin, and notification of transfer, release, escape, or any change in status. This information must then be transported to the powers concerned through the protecting power and the Central Prisoners of War Information Agency.[116] The latter is, according to article 123, to be established in a neutral country, and its function is to collect information as indicated above and forward it to the powers on whom the prisoners depend.

In the closing provisions of the Convention, it is required that representatives of the protecting power and of the ICRC are to have permission to go to all the places where prisoners may be, to points of departure and arrival, and to interview prisoners without witness.[117] It is

---

[113] *Seventh General Assembly of the United Nations*, Publication of the European Center of the Carnegie Foundation, at 15.

[114] Commentary, Third Convention, at 547–548.

[115] 2 Oppenheim, at 613–615 (7th ed. 1955); STONE, LEGAL CONTROLS OF INTERNATIONAL CONFLICT 680–683 (1954).

[116] Third Convention, arts. 122 & 123.

[117] Draper, at 71.

also required that the high contracting parties undertake in both peace and war to disseminate the text of the present Convention as widely as possible.[118]

Several prominent political and legal commentators have summed up the achievements of this Convention, optimistically referring to it as a document which has insured that prisoners are to be treated as human beings who have become victims of events.

The report in the *Chicago Tribune* dated October 12, 1969, should be noted here.

1.5. The Geneva Convention Relative to the Protection of Civilian Persons in Time of War

Auschwitz, Treblinka, Buchenwald are now history. The number of civilians exterminated in the territories occupied by the Third Reich has never been fully calculated.

The figure "6,000,000" is often cited when the extermination of Jews is being discussed in ordinary conversation; therefore, estimates which double this figure may not be far from wrong, particularly considering the Fuehrer's special efforts in Poland and the USSR.[119] One clear lesson which can be learned from this tragic experience is that war crimes caused more loss of life than military operations, yet violations of this type continue to occur in Southeast Asia and in Israeli held territory.[120]

The Geneva Civilians Convention, which contains 159 Articles, is a statement of fundamental and detailed rights for civilians in time of war. It attempts to extend to civilians those rights and protections that have been established for prisoners of war and the sick and wounded of the Armed Forces.

The Convention is divided into four parts and is completed by three annexes. Parts I and IV contain those articles which are common to all four Conventions. Part II, comprising articles 13 through 26, deals with the general protection of civilians against certain consequences of war. Part III, which consists of articles 27 through 141, is divided into four sections. Section I contains the provisions relating to the territories of the parties to the conflict and to occupied territories. Section II governs

---

[118] Third Convention, arts. 126 & 127.

[119] Judgment of the International Military Tribunal, Nuremburg, Cmd. 6964, at 50–53 (1946).

[120] *See* U.N. Doc./HR. 10 (XXVI) Mar. 23, 1970; U.N. GAOR, Res. 2792 (XXVI) Dec. 6, 1971, and Res. 2799 (XXVI) Dec. 13, 1971; U.N. Doc./H.R. E/CN.4/L. 1195 Mar. 22, 1972 which in Para 7 states: "*Considers* that grave breaches of the Fourth Geneva Convention committed by Israel in the occupied territories constitute war crimes and an affront to humanity."

aliens in the territory of a party to the conflict. Section III relates to occupied territories. Section IV contains regulations for the treatment of internees, whether held in the territory of a party to the conflict or in occupied territory.[120a]

As in each of the four Conventions, it is important to determine at the outset the class of persons who are protected. That class in this instance is broad, covering most persons who find themselves in enemy hands, but certain exceptions exist and are important when determining if a "grave breach" has been committed.[121] Grave breaches can occur only in regard to persons or property protected by the Convention. Excluded from protection are all nationals of a party not bound by the Convention. Similarly, certain nationals of a contracting party may be excluded from the protection of the Convention; for example, nationals of a neutral state in the territory of a belligerent state or nationals of a co-belligerent state are not protected as long as the state of which they are nationals has normal diplomatic representation in the state in whose hands they are. Finally, also excluded are those who are protected under any one of the other three Conventions.[122] It is curious to the writer that the Hungarians who were separated by their own government to be sent to Germany to develop work camps would not have been covered when subsequently sent to Auschwitz because their government shared "normal" diplomatic representation with the German Government.

Article 5 operates as a limitation of the protection under the Convention by providing an allowance for the operation of security requirements within strictly prescribed limits. A person normally protected in the territory of the enemy who is "definitely suspected of or engaged in activities hostile to the security of the state is barred from asserting the rights of the Convention which if exercised in his favor would be prejudicial to the security of such state." This portion of the Convention in particular seems to place the rights and privileges of the protected party under the Convention in a precarious position by permitting the state to be the arbiter of its own security interests at the possible expense of the Convention rights.[123]

Part II of this Convention, consisting of articles 13 to 26, deals with civilians generally.[124] Article 13 specifies that the Convention applies to the whole population of countries in conflict, regardless of race, nationality, religion, or political opinion. It appears to this writer that such an

---

[120a] Yingling & Ginnane, at 411–427; Draper, at 27.
[121] Fourth Convention, art. 147.
[122] Draper, at 29.
[123] Fourth Convention, art. 4: Draper, at 29.
[124] Yingling & Ginnane, at 411.

article is an expansion of article 4 in an attempt to cover all civilians provided the civilians are physically in the territory of a party to the conflict that is bound by the Convention.

Article 14 introduces a subject of new and considerable interest in view of the potential use of nuclear weapons. In peacetime and after an outbreak of hostilities, the contracting parties may establish, in their own or occupied territories, hospital or safety zones organized to protect the wounded and sick, the aged, children under fifteen, expectant mothers, and mothers of children under seven. The Draft Agreement found in Annex I to the Convention[125] and in particular article 11[126] of this Draft provides: "In no circumstances may hospital and safety zones be the object of attack. They shall be protected and respected at all times by the parties to the conflict." To this writer, these provisions by the very wording "[i]n no circumstances . . . and at all times" indicate a breakthrough for the possible limitation of nuclear warfare. Additionally, if attacks by such weapons would involve damage to life and health of these safety zones, then it may well be that such an attack is condemned by international law on this point, irrespective of any other criterion that may exist for assessing the lawfulness of the use of such weapons and methods of attack.[127]

On a smaller scale, neutral zones may, by agreements under article 15, be established in the regions where fighting is taking place. "Articles 18, 20, 21, and 22 are noteworthy in that for the first time they permit the use of the Red Cross emblem by civilian hospitals, hospital and first-aid personnel, and the vehicles and aircraft transporting civilians, sick, and wounded."[128] Article 23 provides that shipments of foodstuffs, clothing, and medical supplies needed by civilian populations will not be blockaded if the blockading power is satisfied that the supplies are for civilian use and not directly or indirectly for the use of the enemy. Articles 24, 25, and 26 refer to the welfare of children, intrafamily communication of personal information and the duties of the contracting parties to facilitate renewed contact and reuniting of members of the family who may have been separated because of the conflict.[129]

Section I, Part III, consisting of articles 27 through 34, concerns itself with the status and treatment of protected persons in the sense of article 4. Article 27 appears basic in that it carries on the theme of fundamental principles of the laws of Geneva, *i.e.,* respect for the human person and

[125] 75 U.N.T.S. 402 (1950).
[126] 75 U.N.T.S. 406 (1950).
[127] Willhelm, 3 Revue Internationale de le Croix-Rouge 60 (Supp., Mar. 1951).
[128] Yingling & Ginnane, at 410.
[129] Coursier, at 85.

the inalienable nature of his fundamental rights. Persons, honor, family rights, religious convictions and practices, and their manners and customs are protected against threats or acts of violence, insult, or public curiosity. Women are protected against rape, enforced prostitution, and any force of indecent assault. Article 28 prohibits the use of protected persons to make certain areas "immune" from military operations. Article 29 states that infraction of these prohibitions engages state responsibility and ultimately agents of the state. Article 30 provides that protected persons "shall have every facility for making application to the protecting powers, the ICRC, the national Red Cross (Crescent, Lion, and Sun), or any other organization that may assist them." Physical and moral coercion to obtain information (art. 31), murder, torture, mutilation, and medical or scientific experiments not necessary for the health of the person (art. 32) are prohibited. Similarly, collective punishments, terrorism, pillage, and reprisals against protected persons and their property (art. 33) are prohibited. Article 34 clearly and simply states, "The taking of hostages is prohibited."

Section II, which includes articles 35 to 46, deals with the position of aliens in the territory of the enemy belligerent. All aliens who are protected persons must be allowed to leave the territory at the start of the conflict unless it is "contrary to national interests."[130] Query: Shall draft-age men, scientists, skilled technicians, tradesmen be detained in the national interest? Such detention is subject to the examination of "regularly established procedures." Those who leave may take the necessary funds and reasonable quantities of their effects and personal items.[131] Article 36 provides that such departures, however, should be carried out in satisfactory conditions concerning safety, hygiene, sanitation, and food. Articles 37 and 38 generally impose the duty on the belligerent to treat protected persons humanely. Article 39 provides that protected persons who have lost their employment as a result of the war are to be given an opportunity to find paid employment. If they are unable to support themselves because of regulations or security controls, the controlling Power has the obligation to support them. Article 40 provides that protected parties may be compelled to work only to the same extent as nationals of state they are in. Such work cannot be directly related to the conduct of military operations.

Article 41 provides that if the methods of control as indicated in this Convention are inadequate, the belligerent power shall have no measure of control more severe than that of assigned residence or internment; and then, as indicated in article 42, only if the security of the detaining power makes it absolutely necessary. Such internment is to be reviewed by a

[130] Draper, at 36.
[131] Fourth Convention, art 35.

court or board and must continue to be reviewed at least twice a year; and information as to internments must be given the protecting power unless the interned persons object (art. 42). This appears consistent insofar as not all aliens need be interned, but those that have been should have the opportunity for review and reconsideration.

It appears strange that while certain aliens have the right to leave, others may be expelled at the discretion of the conflicting party. Nowhere does provision appear for the protection of those expelled. "A belligerent may consider it convenient to expel all enemy subjects residing or temporarily staying within his territory. And, although such a measure may be very hard and cruel, the opinion is general that such expulsion is justifiable."[132] There may be some among these expelled enemy aliens in the territory of a party to the conflict who have a particular problem, namely refugees. Article 44 provides that refugees shall not be treated as enemy aliens solely on the basis of de jure nationality of the enemy state if they, in fact, do not enjoy the protection of any government.

Article 45 expressly prohibits the transfer of protected persons in the domestic territory of a contracting party to a power which is not a party to the Convention. In fact, these provisions are virtually identical to article 12 of the prisoners of war Convention concerning the transfer of protected persons.

Section III, which includes articles 47 to 78, is in some respects the most important of the civilian Conventions insofar as it determines the rights and dutes of the occupying power and of the protected persons in that occupied territory. It is here that the majority of the crimes against humanity occurred. "An occupant having military authority over the territory, the inhabitants are under his martial law and have to render obedience to his commands.[133] This latitude is dangerous.

Articles 42 to 56 of the Regulations annexed to the Hague Conventions respecting the Laws and Customs of War on Land of 1899 and 1907 established rather general and limited rules for the protection of inhabitants of occupied territory.[134] Two world wars proved their grave inadequacies. It is against this background that articles 47 through 78 were developed. A summary of the general principles may briefly be referred to here: (1) the occupation is of a limited and temporary nature; (2) sovereignty is not vested in the occupant; (3) the prime duty is the establishment of order in the occupied area; (4) the existing administration, economy, legal system, and general life of the occupied community should be subject only to

---

[132] 1 Oppenheim, at 693 (7th ed. 1955).
[133] *Id.,* at 438–439.
[134] Yingling & Ginnane, at 416.

minimum alteration, and (5) this minimum is to be determined by the restrictions and changes properly imposed for the security of the occupant's military and civil administration.[135]

One of the most important provisions expressed in article 49 is that which prohibits individual or mass transfers and deportation of protected persons from occupied territory to that of the occupant or to that of any other power, occupied or not, "regardless of their motives."[136] It was this practice of deportation which added years to the Nazis' war effort when Germany's own resources were virtually exhausted. This same article allows the occupant to evacuate protected persons in the interest of the safety of the population, for imperative military reasons, or because such areas cannot adequately be supplied. All transfers must be humanely conducted and the protecting power must be informed of them as soon as they have taken place. Conversely, this article prohibits the detention of protected persons in danger areas and, additionally, prevents the occupying power from moving parts of its own population into the occupied territory.

As far as children are concerned (art. 50), it is stipulated that the occupying power will facilitate, with the cooperation of the national and local authorities, the proper working of all institutions which concern themselves with the care, maintenance, and education of children. Identification and parental registration are also to be facilitated.[137]

Article 51 absolutely prohibits the compulsory service of protected persons in the armed forces of the occupant and limits the class of work that the inhabitants may be forced to do. In particular, they cannot be forced to undertake any work which would require them to partake in or contribute to military operations. Article 52 generally provides that the labor legislation of the occupied territory is to apply.[138]

It appears that article 53 made a significant advance in the protection of both public and private property. It provides that destruction of such property by the occupying power is prohibited "except where such destruction is rendered absolutely necessary by military operations."

By article 54, judges and public officials are to have their status maintained, even though the occupying power may remove them from their positions. If, however, they wish to resign for reasons of conscience, they may not be coerced into remaining in office. Article 55 appears both important and curious. It is stipulated that the occupying power insure "to the fullest extent" the sufficiency of the food and medical supplies of the population. And when necessary, *after* the needs of the population have

[135] Draper, at 39.
[136] *Id.*, at 40.
[137] Coursier, at 91.
[138] Draper, at 41.

been considered, the occupying power may import those supplies required when resources are inadequate within the occupied territory for its own armed forces and administration.

Articles 56 through 62 may briefly be summarized as establishing detailed provisions for hospitals, public health, and relief shipments operated under the supervision of the protecting power.

Detailed provisions relating to penal legislation are laid down with a view toward maintaining order in the occupied territory while assuring the protection of individuals against arbitrary measures by the occupying power. In principle, the penal legislation in force prior to occupation remains valid, except as it might constitute a threat to the security of the occupying power, in which case it can be replaced or suspended. The occupying power may subject the inhabitants to regulations necessary in carrying out its duties under the Convention, in maintaining an orderly government, and in insuring the security of the occupying forces and the administration of their establishments and lines of communication.

The occupying power clearly may enact penal laws; however, such law does not have force and effect until it is published and brought to the notice of the inhabitants in their own language and shall not be made retroactive (art. 65). Offenses against this penal law may result in the occupying power handing over the accused to its "properly constituted nonmilitary courts," provided the courts sit in occupied territory (art. 66). According to article 67, these courts may only apply those laws which were applicable before the offense was committed and which "are in accordance with general principles of law, in particular that the penalty is proportionate to the offense."[139]

Protected persons who commit an offense against the occupying power which does not constitute an attempt on the life and limb of members of the occupying forces or administration, nor a grave collective danger, nor involve serious damage to the occupant's property or installation shall be liable to imprisonment or internment as the maximum penalties. The death penalty may be imposed only for case of espionage, serious sabotage, or international offenses causing death, provided that such offenses were punishable by death under the law of the occupied territory before the occupation began. Protected persons under the age of eighteen when the offense was committed are exempted from the death penalty.[140] Query: How many nations of the world have abolished the death penalty?

According to article 70, protected persons may not be tried by the occupying power for acts committed before the occupation, except for "breaches of the laws and customs of war." Article 71 provided that no

---

[139] *Id.*, at 43.
[140] Fourth Convention, art. 68; Draper, at 43.

sentence may be pronounced by an occupation power except after a regular trial, while articles 72 through 77 insure safeguards before, during, and after such a trial.

The protecting power shall be informed of proceedings involving the death penalty or imprisonment for two years, and has the right on request to be advised as to the particulars of current or pending proceedings.[141] The protective power has the right to attend the trial of a protected person, unless, for security reasons, the trial as an exceptional measure is to be *in camera*.[142] Article 75 provided that the result of the trial or any appeal must be forwarded to the protecting power, and, in particular, no death sentence may be carried out before the expiration of at least six months from the date of notifying the protecting power. Article 76 provides that those accused or convicted shall be, in effect, treated humanely. After occupation, such protected persons accused or convicted shall be turned over, with relevant records, to the authorities of the liberated territory (art. 77).

The final article in this section deals with those protected persons who, for reasons of security, may be assigned residences or interned. Such assignment or interment is to be governed by a regular, prescribed procedure and is subject to review at six-month intervals.

Section IV of the Convention, extending from article 79 to 135, is a detailed statement of rights for internees, whether interned in domestic or in occupied territory, and appears clearly to transform internment from what may previously have been a punishment into a safety measure for the public authorities with safeguards for the individual. This section is similar to provisions governing the treatment of prisoners of war in the Third Convention.

The general principles found within this section clearly appear to reflect a rather somber pragmatism. There exist detailed provisions governing the places of internment; food and clothing; hygienic and medical attention; religious, intellectual, and physical activities; personal property and financial resources; administration and discipline; relations with the exterior; penal and dsciplinary sanctions; transfers of internees, wills, death certificates, burials, reports of death to the protecting power; and release, repatriation, and accommodation in neutral countries. It appears that these Articles pinpoint the areas of brutal abuse discovered in the German and Japanese concentration camps.

Finally, Section V provides for the establishment of National Information Bureaus as similarly provided for in the Third Convention, relating to prisoners of war.

The fact that a convention exists exclusively for the protection of civil-

[141] Fourth Convention, art. 71; Draper, at 44.
[142] Fourth Convention, art. 74.

ians is noteworthy in that it represents a substantial step in humanitarian progress. The machinery available within the four corners of its provisions can provide justice and humanity where previously there had been injustice and human suffering. Whether civilized nations will avail themselves of this machinery remains an unknown factor.

1.6. Conclusion

These four Geneva Conventions, consisting of 427 articles, bind 121 countries of the world. As a group, they constitute the major portion of the laws of war. The wounded and sick of the armed forces, both in the field and at sea, prisoners of war, and civilians are now protected by a comprehensive charter. The legal protection which previously existed for members of the armed forces prior to 1949 has been extended and defined to a remarkable degree, while for the civilian population, both in occupied territory and in that of the belligerent, an innovative legal code has been established.[143]

It has been over one-hundred years since the First Geneva Convention was submitted to the nations of the world, and since then there have been thousands of violations. In future wars, such as "wars of liberation," experience indicates that some nations will acknowledge but disregard in fact; others will acknowledge and observe "where applicable," and others will ignore their demanding principles entirely. However, no student of humanitarian progress can afford to lose sight of the thousands of lives that have been spared misery, suffering, and death because of the application of the Conventions.

The common article making dissemination and instruction of the Conventions obligatory to military forces and when possible to civilians is significant. Rights are valueless unless known, and for prisoners of war and internees, they are critical. The signatory nations have pledged themselves to make the Conventions as widely known as possible, in time of peace and in time of war. It is easy to object that the provisions of the Conventions are utopian and unworkable. War has always existed and "primitive peoples" have frequently resorted to force to settle their differences, but we should be aware that in man's development he has sought an avoidance of force and attempted to submit his differences to the arbitration of the state.

[143] Draper, at 115.

Section 2. INDIVIDUAL RESPONSIBILITY FOR MISTREATMENT OF PRISONERS OF WAR

ANDREW LEE

2.1. Captivity, Its Historical Background

During the early part of the Middle Ages, prisoners of war could be killed or enslaved, but the advent of the second half of the Middle Ages witnessed the gradual disappearance of these barbaric atrocities. However, prisoners continued to be treated as criminals and as objects of personal revenge. It was even considered lawful for captors to ransom their prisoners. During the seventeenth century, the concept of considering prisoners to be in the power of their captors dissipated and was replaced by the belief that the sovereign should have full control. But still no rules of international law were in existence regarding the treatment of prisoners of war. It was not until the eighteenth century, that a conviction became general that captivity should be confined to preventing prisoners from returning to their army, and should, as a matter of principle, be distinguished from imprisonment as a punishment for crimes.[1] The Treaty of Friendship concluded in 1785 between the United States of America and Prussia was among the earliest that stipulated proper treatment for prisoners of war.[2] In the nineteenth century, it was generally recognized that prisoners of war should be treated by their captor in a manner analogous to that meted out to his own troops.[3] At the invitation of the Swiss Government in July, 1929, forty-seven nations met at Geneva, to consider the revision of the then existing rules on the treatment of prisoners of war. However, the effectiveness was materially impaired by the so called "General Participation Clause" which made its provisions binding only between the signatories, and inapplicable in the event that a non-contracting power became a belligerent. For example, the 1929 Convention was practically disregarded during World War II by Japan and the Soviet Union, since neither had ratified the Convention. Hence, representatives of many nations reconvened in Geneva to draft another document to guarantee prisoners of war certain rights. Three other Conventions were drafted at the time: (1) The Geneva Convention Relative to the Protection of Civilian Persons in Time of War, (2) The Geneva Convention for the Amelioration of the Condition of the Wounded and

---

[1] 2 OPPENHEIM, INTERNATIONAL LAW, ch. III, § IV (8th ed. 1955).
[2] MARTENS, pt. ii, iv, at 37. Art. 24: Prohibiting confinement in convict prisons and the use of irons, and insisting upon their confinement in a healthy place, where they may have exercise, and kept and fed as troops.
[3] Hague Regulations: Art. 4–20.

Sick in Armed Forces in the Field, and (3) The Geneva Convention for
the Amelioration of the Condition of Wounded, Sick, and Shipwrecked
Members of the Armed Forces at Sea. In the Korean War, none of the
belligerents had ratified the Convention, but they all announced that
they would adhere to the standards of the Convention. At present, over
eighty nations, including the United States, the Soviet Union, North and
South Vietnam, and the Vietcong are signatories of the Convention.[4]

2.2. Who May Claim to Be a Prisoner of War?

The 1949 Convention enumerates, in article 4, the categories of persons,
who, after they have fallen into the power of the enemy, must be treated
as prisoners of war.

> 1. Members of the armed forces of a party to the conflict as well as members
> of militias or volunteer corps forming part of such armed forces;
> 2. Members of other militias and members of other volunteer corps, including
> those of organised resistance movements, belonging to a party to the conflict
> and operating in or outside their own territory, even if this territory is occupied,
> provided that such militias or volunteer corps, including such organised resis-
> tance movements, fulfil the following conditions:
>   a. that of being commanded by a person responsible for his subordinates.
>   b. that of having a fixed distinctive sign recognisable at a distance.
>   c. that of carrying arms openly.
>   d. that of conducting their operations in accordance with the laws and
>   customs of war.
> 3. Members of regular armed forces who profess allegiance to a government
> or an authority not recognised by the detaining power.
> 4. Persons who accompany the armed forces actually being members thereof,
> such as civil members of military aircraft crews, war correspondents, supply
> contractors, members of labour units or of services responsible for the welfare
> of the armed forces, provided that they have received authorization from
> the armed forces which they accompany, who shall provide them for that
> purpose with an identity card similar to the annexed model.
> 5. Members of crews, including masters, pilots, and apprentices of the
> merchant marine and the crews of civil aircraft of the parties to the conflict
> by more favourable treatment under any other provisions of international law.
> 6. Inhabitants of a nonoccupied territory who, on the approach of the
> enemy, spontaneously take up arms to resist the invading forces without
> having had time to form themselves into regular armed units, provided they
> carry arms openly and respect the laws and customs of war.[5]

In addition, the same article includes two other categories of persons that are entitled to be treated as prisoners of war: (1) members of the armed forces of the occupied country if the occupying

[4] Kutner, *International Due Process of Prisoners of War: The Need for a Special Tribunal of World Habeus Corpus*, 21 MIAMI L. REV. 721, 728–29 (1967).
[5] OPPENHEIM, *supra* note 1.

power considers it necessary to intern them—even though it has originally liberated them—while hostilities were proceeding outside the territory now occupied by it and (2) persons who have been received by neutral or nonbelligerent powers on their territory and whom they are required to intern under international law.

2.3. Rights of Protection of Prisoners of War

2.3.1. GENERAL PROVISIONS OF 1949 GENEVA CONVENTION. The 1949 Convention established a minimum standard of treatment for prisoners of war, and it applies not only to cases of declared war but also to any other armed conflicts which may arise between the contracting parties (even if the state of war is not recognized by one of them). It also applies to cases of partial or total occupation of territory, even if such occupation meets with no armed resistance.[6] The Convention expressly prohibits, under all circumstances, the following acts with regard to persons not taking part in the hostilities:

   a. violence to life and person: in particular, murder of all kinds, mutilation, cruel treatment, and torture.
   b. taking of hostages.
   c. outrages upon personal dignity: in particular, humiliating and degrading treatment.
   d. the passing of sentences and the carrying out of executions without previous judgement pronounced by a regularly constituted court affording all the judicial guarantees which are recognised as indispensable by civilised peoples.

Article 2(3) also provides:

Although one of the powers in conflict may not be a party to the present Convention, the powers who are parties thereto shall remain bound by it in their mutual relations. They shall furthermore be bound by the Convention in relation to the said power, if the latter accepts and applies the provision thereof.

This provision clearly emphasizes the legislative, as distinguished from the purely contractual, character of the Convention, for a state which ratifies the Convention assumes an obligation to observe it should a nonsignatory, after the outbreak of hostilities, formally accept and apply it. So, the General Participation clause is expressly excluded in the Convention.

It is also stated in the Convention[7] that no special agreements shall adversely affect the situation of prisoners of war nor restrict the rights which it confers upon them. Correspondingly, the prisoner is precluded

[6] Art. 2, 1949 Convention.
[7] Art. 6, 1949 Convention.

from renouncing the rights which the Convention accords him, *i.e.*, from joining the armed forces of the detaining power,[8] or returning to civilian status.

The Convention describes a protecting power[9] as a neutral state entrusted by a belligerent with the protection of its nationals who are in the power of a capturing state. Since it is the protecting power's duty to safeguard the interests of the parties to the conflict, the Convention dictates that it shall be applied with the cooperation and under the scrutiny of such powers. Besides its diplomatic or consular staff, the protecting power, in fulfilling its function, may appoint delegates from among its nationals or the nationals of other neutral powers, with the approval of the power with which they are to carry out their duties. The Convention, however, clearly states[10] that none of its provisions constitutes an obstacle to the humanitarian activities which the International Red Cross or any other impartial humanitarian organizations may undertake for the protection of the prisoners of war and their relief—subject always to the consent of the belligerents. In fact, article 10 of the Convention authorizes the parties, by agreement, to entrust such functions to an organization which offers all guarantees of impartiality and efficacy in case a neutral power is not available.[11] The functions of a protecting power include, among others, the transmission of correspondence and information, the inspection of facilities, the supervision of the distribution of relief, and the representation of prisoners in judicial proceedings.

2.3.2. PROTECTIONS OF PRISONERS OF WAR. Part II of the 1949 Convention provides for the general protection of prisoners of war. It enacts the principle that the ultimate responsibility for the treatment of prisoners rests with the belligerent nation which captures them. (After World War II, the United States of America enacted a law—Public Law 896—which provided for the payment of claims filed by any prisoner of war for the violation by the enemy government of its obligation for furnishing him with the quantity or quality of food to which he was entitled as a prisoner of war under the terms of the Geneva Convention of July 27, 1929.) It is a fundamental principle that the prisoners of war must at all times be humanely treated. Any act or omission of the

[8] Art. 7, 1949 Convention.
[9] Arts. 8–10, 1949 Convention.
[10] Art. 3, together with arts. 125–126, 1949 Convention.
[11] *Supra* note 4, at 734 n. 28.

A serious defect of the Geneva Convention of 1949 (Draper contends) is that it was framed on the classical assumption that modern armies are natural entities, whereas in our modern age it is more common to have different national contingents of troops operating under a unified command such as the United Nations or NATO.

detaining power which results in death or seriously endangers the health of a prisoner of war is prohibited and shall be regarded as a serious breach of the Convention.[12] Prisoners must also be protected from the curiosity, violence, intimidation, and insults of the local population. (In a judgment given in 1948, the International Military Tribunal of the Far East condemned the Japanese military officers' practice of parading prisoners of war through cities and exposing them to ridicule and insults.) The person and honor of a prisoner must be respected in all circumstances. Reprisals against prisoners of war are prohibited. Medical care of sick and wounded prisoners is to be provided by the detaining power.[13] Articles 19 and 20 provide that prisoners must be given food and water, and all suitable precautions must be taken to insure their safety. Apart from exceptions based on sex, rank, health, or professional qualifications, all prisoners are to be treated alike. A prisoner may be required to give only his surname, first name, rank, date of birth, and army, regimental, personal, or serial number. (art. 17, 1949 Convention.) Failure to give this information may render a prisoner liable to restriction of the special privileges due to him because of his rank or status. But in no case can a prisoner be deprived of any of his basic privileges. However, no physical or mental torture or any other form of coercion may be inflicted on prisoners to compel them to give information.

2.3.3. INTERNMENT. Prisoners of war may be either interned or released on parole. The latter provision is an innovation of the 1949 Convention. The terms of a release on parole are to be determined in accordance with the laws of the prisoner's state. The same article also provides that the internment shall take place only on premises located on land and should afford every guarantee of hygiene and healthfulness. Prisoners should not be accommodated in penitentiaries; nor may they be held in close confinement except as a disciplinary or health measure. Shelters are to be provided for the prisoners against the hazards of war and aerial bombardment,[14] and belligerents must be informed of the location of prisoners' camps.[15]

[12] By art. 129 of the Geneva Convention, 1929, the parties to the Convention undertake to enact legislation necessary to provide effective penalties against persons committing or ordering to be committed any grave breach of the Convention. Grave breaches are enumerated in art. 130 as being willful killing, torture or inhuman treatment, including biological experiments, willfully causing great suffering or serious injury to body or health, compelling a prisoner of war to serve in the forces of a hostile power.

[13] Art. 15. Art. 4 of the Convention of 1929 was silent on the question of which power was liable for the cost of this care. It is clearly laid down that the prisoners of war are entitled to this care free of charge.

[14] Art. 23.

[15] Art. 24.

Prisoners of war must be treated as favorably as the troops of the detaining power quartered in that area, especially as to the dormitories and provisions of bedding and blankets, etc. The camps must be dry, heated, lighted, and afford protection against fire. There must be a sufficient supply of drinking water and food so prisoners can maintain good health and prevent loss of weight or the development of nutritional deficiences. Collective disciplinary measures affecting food are prohibited.[16] The detaining power must insure that prisoners are and remain properly clothed.[17] The detaining power is bound to take all necessary sanitary measures, including the provision and maintenance of clean toilets, baths, and showers. In addition, each camp must have an adequate infirmary where special care and diet can be provided, and there must exist facilities for surgical care. Prisoners should not be prevented from presenting themselves for medical examination. Prisoners who are qualified to act as doctors or dentists may be required to act in these capacities, and in that case, they are not to be considered as prisoners of war. [18] There must be complete freedom of religious belief and worship. If no detained chaplain or prisoner-of-war minister is available, a minister may be appointed with the concurrence of the detaining power.[19]

2.3.4. DISCIPLINE. Articles 43 through 45 of the Convention provide that the maintenance of discipline in the prisoner-of-war camps is to be the responsibility of a regular officer of the forces of the detaining power. It is his duty to insure that its provisions are known to the camp staff and guards. Regulations must be posted where prisoners can read them. Officer prisoners need salute only officers of a high rank of the detaining power. All prisoners must be treated with due regard to age and rank.

Transfer of prisoners is permissible, but must be effected humanely. The sick and the wounded must not be transferred if their recovery might be jeopardized by the journey. Prisoners must be notified in advance of their transfer, and mails must be forwarded to them. They may carry with them limited personal belongings.[20]

2.3.5. EMPLOYMENT. The detaining power may utilize the labor of physically fit prisoners of war. Officers may not in any circumstances be compelled to work; however they may request it. Prisoners may be asked or even compelled to perform such work that may have no direct

---

[16] Art. 26.
[17] Art. 27.
[18] Art. 33.
[19] Art. 38.
[20] Arts. 46, 47, 48.

connection with the operations of the war.[21] Prisoners, however, must not be forced to work in conditions that are worse than those experienced by nationals of the detaining power employed in similar work. Under no circumstances shall conditions of labor be rendered more arduous by disciplinary measures.[22] Prisoners must not, unless they volunteer, be employed on labor which is humiliating, unhealthy, or dangerous.[23] The hours of their daily work must not be longer than the maximum permitted for local civilian workers. Prisoners of war are entitled to one hour's rest in the middle of each day, one day in each week, and eight consecutive days in each year.[24] They are entitled to be paid a fair working rate.[25] The detaining power may decide the maximum amount of money which a prisoner may have in his possession.[26] The excess is to be deposited in the name of each prisoner.[27] However, the prisoners' right to free medical treatment and the duty of the detaining power to provide it remain unimpaired.[28]

2.3.6. RELATIONS BETWEEN PRISONERS AND DETAINING POWER AUTHORITIES. Articles 78 through 86 provide in elaborate detail the relations between prisoners and authorities. Prisoners are permitted to make complaints about the conditions of their captivity; even if such complaints may be unfounded, they must not give rise to punishment. The complaints may be made directly to the protecting powers or through the prisoners' representatives. The representatives must have the same nationality, language, and customs as the prisoners they represent. They must not be held responsible, merely by reason of their duties, for any offenses committed by prisoners of war. The detaining power may take judicial or disciplinary measures with respect to any offense committed against any law by a prisoner of war. But the Convention emphasizes that the competent authorities are to exercise the greatest leniency and to adopt wherever possible disciplinary, as opposed to judicial, measures.

Trials of prisoners must be conducted by courts offering the essential guarantees of justice. The prisoner is entitled to defend himself or to be given defense counsel. He may have an interpreter.[29] No prisoner may be punished more than once for the same act. Any prisoner, for acts committed under the laws of the detaining power, shall continue to be

[21] Art. 50.
[22] Art. 51.
[23] Art. 52.
[24] Art. 53.
[25] Art. 62.
[26] Art. 58.
[27] Art. 61.
[28] Arts. 66, 67, 68.
[29] Art. 105.

entitled, even if convicted, to the benefits of the Convention. The penalties, and the conditions in which they are forced, must not differ from those prescribed for forces of the detaining power. Torture, corporal punishment, imprisonment in premises without daylight, and collective punishment for individual acts are forbidden. Prisoners of war who have undergone punishment, judicial or disciplinary, may not be treated differently from other prisoners of war. Generally, prisoners must not be kept in confinement pending the hearing. No single punishment may last more than thirty days. The period between the sentence awarding disciplinary punishment and its execution must not exceed one month. Judicial proceedings may be brought against a prisoner of war only for alleged violations of international law or the law of the detaining power in force at the time the act was committed.[30] The prisoner and his representative must be notified of the sentence, and the protecting power must be given details of the finding and the sentence, of the investigation and trial, and of the establishment where the sentence is to be served. The prisoner and the protecting power must be informed of the offenses which are punishable by death under the laws of the detaining power. Other offenses must not be punished by death except when concurrent of the state to which the prisoner belongs.[31] Finally, the prisoner has the right to appeal.

2.3.7. PRISONERS' FREEDOM. Captivity may be terminated by release either during the hostilities or with the conclusion of hostilities. Article 110 of the 1949 Convention provides specifically that prisoners who are incurably wounded or sick, or who are not likely to recover within a year, or whose mental and physical fitness seems to have been gravely and/or permanently diminished must be returned directly to their country. As to repatriation after the cessation of hostilities,[32] practically no actual steps need be taken by a defeated belligerent, because frequently the victorious power will release their own troops upon the cessation of hostilities. As the past trends show, the prisoners of the defeated power (or powers) will not be released immediately. The Convention provides for their repatriation, without delay, and regardless of their wishes.[33] The U.N. General Assembly on December 3, 1952, adopted a resolution asserting that forcible repatriation of prisoners who, because of fear

[30] Arts. 101, 102, 104. Unlawful trial of prisoners of war has given rise to several charges and convictions of war crimes. Trial of Sawada *et al.* (1946) included a former commander of a Japanese army for their part in the unlawful trial and in sentencing to death, by a Japanese Military Tribunal, of captured American airmen in mainland China.
[31] Arts. 100, 107.
[32] Arts. 108, 109.
[33] Art. 118.

of punishment for ideological reasons, reject repatriation, would be incompatible with the spirit of the Geneva Convention. In fact, this "nonforcible repatriation" provides an asylum for prisoners who may seek it.

There is no doubt that the 1949 Geneva Convention on the protection of rights of prisoners of war sets a high standard of treatment for such prisoners. However, the enforcement of proper treatment of prisoners of war remains a problem. To punish such violators as war criminals after the cessation of hostilities is no solution. However, the first desirable step to insure adequate protection to prisoners of war may be the establishment of an effective world war-crime tribunal.

2.4. Individual Responsibility for Mistreatment of Prisoners of War

Article 6 of the International Military Tribunal Charter defines war crimes and crimes against humanity as follows:

> War Crimes: namely, violations of the laws or customs of war. Such violations shall include, but not be limited to, murder, ill treatment, or deportation to slave labour, or for any other purpose of civilian population of or in occupied territory, murder or ill treatment of prisoners of war or persons on the seas, killing of hostages, plunder of public or private property, wanton destruction of cities, towns, or villages, or devastation not justified by military necessity.
>
> (c) Crimes against Humanity: namely, murder, extermination, enslavement, deportation, and other inhumane acts committed against any civilian population before or during the war, or persecutions on political, racial, or religious grounds in execution of or in connection with any crime within the jurisdiction of the Tribunal, whether or not in violation of the domestic law of the country where perpetrated.

One of the most controversial issues in modern international law is the problem of the individual responsibility for mistreatment of prisoners of war. This problem involves two main questions: (1) Does international law apply to individuals as well as to states? (2) For what acts may an individual be held criminally responsible under international law?

Arguments, pro and contra, are discussed below.

2.4.1. PRO. The International Military Tribunal at Nuremberg stated that individuals could be held responsible for war crimes and crimes against humanity. It declared: "Crimes against international law are committed by men, not by abstract entities, and only by punishing individuals who commit such crimes can the provisions of international law be enforced."[34]

[34] 22 INTERNATIONAL MILITARY TRIBUNAL 565-66.

The law of nations may be primarily a law between states, but states themselves operate by virtue of the will of individuals. Thus, the individual is the ultimate source of authority and, in a broad sense, international law has already been applied to individuals. Indeed, many authors have strongly advocated the development of modern international law toward formal recognition of the international legal position of the individual.[35] The opinion of the Permanent Court of International Justice clearly stated in the case of *Danzing* (Jurisdiction of the Courts)[36] that although international law may in most spheres be applicable to states, there is nothing inherent in the character of international law to exclude its application to individuals.

Assuming the above, the problem still remains to determine what acts may constitute an international crime for which an individual may be held responsible. According to Oppenheim, the essence of a crime in national law is that "it injures not only the party at whom it is directed, but the community as a whole."[37] An international crime is, in other words, an act which affects international community. If the act is a war crime, an individual can be held responsible for it under international law. For, in accordance with the verdict of International Military Tribunal at Nuremberg, it would indeed be a great injustice if individuals were not held criminally responsible for their act or acts which cause grave harm to humanity or to international community.[38]

2.4.2. CONTRA. Arguments against holding the individual responsible are based on the premise that traditionally international law placed duties and responsibilities on states, and not on individuals, and that basically the law remains unaltered. The breach of an international duty gives rise to the collective responsibility of the delinquent state, and a person cannot be punished for an act which he committed in pursuance of government or military orders. A subordinate simply cannot be expected to shoulder the awesome burden of scrupulously weighing the legal merits of every order. And it must be remembered that a "good soldier" does not question a superior. Furthermore, the rules of warfare are often controversial, and an act otherwise amounting to a war crime may have been executed in obedience to orders conceived as a

---

[35] Aufricht, *Personality in International Law*, 37 AM. POL. SCI. REV. 217 (1943); P. JESSUP, MODERN LAW OF NATIONS 15 (1948).

[36] Jurisdiction of the Courts of Danzig Case [1928], P.C.I.J., ser. B, No. 15.

[37] OPPENHEIM, *supra* note 1.

[38] The International Military Tribunal at Nuremberg declared:

> It is not essential that a crime be specifically defined and charged in accordance with a particular ordinance, statute or treaty if it is made a crime by international convention, recognized customs, and usages of war, or the general principles of criminal justice common to civilized nations generally.

measure of reprisals.[39] It is no secret that some Allied nationals in World War II were just as guilty of certain war crimes as the defeated nations, but they were not tried before any tribunals.

2.4.3. CONCLUSION. Many writers[40] are of the opinion that an individual can be held responsible under national or international law for an act branded as a crime in a statute or convention or law. Although it seems proper to consider "taking orders from a superior" in defense of any person standing trial for international crimes, especially if the accused had to act under pain of death,[41] under no circumstances should it be regarded as an absolute justification for criminal acts. In fact, military laws of many civilized nations contain express provisions to the effect that a subordinate must obey only lawful orders, *e.g.*, Amendment 34 to the British Manual of Military Law. It should be noted that article 8 of International Military Tribunal Charter provides that "[t]he fact that the defendant acted pursuant to order of his government or of a superior shall not free him from responsibility, but may be considered in mitigation of punishment if the Tribunal determines that justice so requires." Hence, the plea of "respondent superior" cannot be considered as an absolute defense. It has already been mentioned that some Allied nationals in World War II were just as guilty of certain war crimes as the Axis, but it is certainly no defense for an individual to claim that a war crime for which he is being tried has also been committed by opposing belligerents. However, it is a great injustice that only nationals of the defeated nations who committed war crimes were brought to be tried and punished.[42]

It seems then that none of the contrary arguments would constitute sufficient legal basis for denying individual responsibility for international crimes. It may be concluded, therefore, that if an act is adjudged to be a crime according to international custom, international conventions, or the general principals of justice, then an individual may be held responsible for it under international law.[43]

2.5. World Court for International Crimes

Although the Geneva Convention provides a detailed account of rights of prisoners of war, the enforcement of proper treatment of prisoners of war still remains a problem. The procedural defect of the Geneva

---

[39] OPPENHEIM, *supra* note 1, at 659.

[40] Ehard, *The Nuremberg Trials Against the Major War Criminals and International Law*, 43 A.J.I.L. 223, 231 (1949).

[41] R. WOETZEL, THE NUREMBERG TRIALS IN INTERNATIONAL LAW 118 (1962).

[42] A. LEE, INTERNATIONAL LAW, CASES AND OTHER MATERIALS 542 2nd ed. 1969).

[43] WOETZEL, *supra* note 41, at 121.

Convention for enforcing its provisions is an inability to bring such cases before an international tribunal. It was true that in the past the deterrent to abuse of such prisoners was due to the fear of punishment at the end of hostilities, should the offending state be the loser. As Oppenheim states: "The combination of the question of the punishment of war crimes by an international organ with the question of international criminal jurisdiction is probably calculated to complicate a problem which in itself is of considerable difficulty."[44] And it seems true that in an international society in which war, notwithstanding the fundamental prohibitions against recourse to it, "continues in fact as a manifestation of the power of sovereign state, there is no guarantee that any international institution, or international law as a whole, will survive the onslaught of lawlessness."[45] But, this does not suffice to be a legal argument against the establishment of an international tribunal in the nature of a world court for international crimes. It is the duty of the international community that it must struggle toward achieving human dignity by establishing an impartial world court for international crimes for the protection of prisoners of war from cruel and inhuman treatment during their wartime confinement. Professor Luis Kutner[46] has wisely suggested that a world habeas corpus tribunal under U.N. auspices be established by treaty between the nations of the world. This world tribunal (or court) should have criminal jurisdiction over international crimes, and it is of little consequence whether it existed as a separate entity, or whether its functions were entrusted to the International Court of Justice as a whole, or even if one or more of the International Court of Justice chambers were especially created for that purpose. The point is that such a tribunal should be created, that it be impartial, and that it be empowered to hear the writs of world habeas corpus, and that it consist of justices who have "severed all of their national ties, and are, so to speak, citizens of the world."[47] The prisoners of war should be entitled to petition for the writ of world habeas corpus and it is again immaterial as to what procedures are devised, *i.e.,* do they petition through protecting power or Red Cross? But the point is that once such a writ is granted, the detaining power must produce the prisoners before the court, and the court must then proceed to determine whether the prisoners' detention was a violation of the provisions of the Geneva Convention. The proposed court should have the power to convict and

---

[44] OPPENHEIM, *supra* note 1, at 585.

[45] OPPENHEIM, *supra* note 1, at 586.

[46] Kutner, *World Habeus Corpus, Human Rights and World Community,* 17 DE PAUL L. REV. 3 (1967).

[47] Kutner, *supra* note 4.

punish a criminal for war crimes committed during or after the cessation of hostilities.[48] It is realized that perhaps the Court's verdict may not be enforced in some instances, especially during the hostilities, but the very fact that an impartial world court for international crimes has come into being and has pronounced on such a significant issue will be a major advance toward creating a world order of human dignity.

Section 3. WAR CRIMES BY IRREGULAR AND NONGOVERNMENTAL FORCES*

ROBERT K. WOETZEL

Article 6 of the Charter of the International Military Tribunal at Nuremberg defines war crimes as

> violations of the laws or customs of war. Such violations shall include, but not be limited to, murder, ill-treatment, or deportation to slave labor or for any other purpose of civilian population of or in occupied territory, murder or ill-treatment of prisoners of war or persons on the seas, killing of hostages, plunder of public or private property, wanton destruction of cities, towns, or villages, or devastation not justified by military necessity.

Since war crimes are closely related to crimes against humanity involving actions by a government against its own citizens, it is well to cite the definition of such crimes in the same article:

> . . . murder, extermination, enslavement, deportation, and other inhumane acts committed against any civilian population, before or during the war; or persecutions on political, racial, or religious grounds in execution of or in connection with any crime within the jurisdiction of the Tribunal, whether or not in violation of the domestic law of the country where perpetrated.[1]

The laws and customs of war are generally regarded as binding on nations. As the IMT at Nuremberg stated, "by 1939 these rules . . . were recognized by all civilized nations, and were regarded as being declaratory of the laws and customs of war . . ."[2] They were contained in such agreements as the Hague Convention of 1907 and the Geneva Conventions of 1949. To the extent that they are codified in the Nurem-

---

[48] LEE, *supra* note 42, at 479.

* This section was discussed at the Panel on Humanitarian Problems and International Law of the American Society of International Law (1971–72).

[1] INTERNATIONAL MILITARY TRIBUNAL, XXII TRIAL OF THE MAJOR WAR CRIMINALS BEFORE THE INTERNATIONAL MILITARY TRIBUNAL 496 (1948) [hereafter referred to as IMT]. *See also* ROBERT K. WOETZEL, THE NUREMBERG TRIALS IN INTERNATIONAL LAW 172–174 (1962).

[2] *Id.* at 497.

berg principles they were unanimously endorsed by the United Nations in Resolution 95 (1) of December 11, 1946.[3]

The Geneva Conventions provide that the laws of war shall be applicable to different types of war, declared and undeclared. Article 2 of the Geneva Convention Relative to the Protection of Civilian Persons in Time of War of August 12, 1949, states that "the present Convention shall apply to all cases of declared war or any other armed conflict which may arise between two or more of the high contracting parties, even if the state of war is not recognized by one of the . . . ."[4] And article 3 lists provisions which are binding, "as a minimum," in the case of armed conflict not of an international character.[5]

The laws of war may also apply to civil wars. As Josef Kunz writes, "civil war is a crime under municipal law, yet often the rules of war are applied."[6] And he adds, "rules of war, including rules of combat, are essential . . . even in time of peace."[7] To paraphrase Philip Jessup, they represent not a matter of sentiment, but of military necessity[8]—regardless of whether a conflict is legal or illegal from the standpoint of crimes against peace.[9]

The question arises to what extent irregular and nongovernmental forces are protected by the laws of war. According to Oppenheim-Lauterpacht,

> There is in modern conditions no justification for the tendency, which was predominant in the nineteenth century which found to some extent expression in the compromise reached at the Hague Conference in 1899 on the subject, to brand as illegal the activities of guerrilla troops. . .[10]

The pronouncement of the IMT and other similar statements on recognized rules of war are relevant. For example, the Fourth Hague Convention of 1907 provided in its so-called "general participation clause" that the rules contained in it and the annexed Regulations did "not apply except between contracting powers and then only if all the belligerents are parties to the Convention." However, if the Hague Conventions

[3] "The General Assembly, recognizing the obligations laid upon it by art. 13 . . . taking note of the Law of the Charter of the Nuremberg Tribunal of Aug. 8, 1945, for the prosecution and punishment of the major war criminals; (1) reaffirms the principles of international law recognized by the Charter of the Nuremberg Tribunal (of Aug. 8, 1945), and the Judgments of the Tribunal. . . ."

[4] ICRC, *Fourth Geneva Convention (civilian)*, in THE GENEVA CONVENTIONS OF AUGUST 12, 1949, at 153 (1950).

[5] *Id. at* 59.

[6] J. KUNZ, *The Chaotic Status of the Laws of War*, 45 A.J.I.L. 57 (1951).

[7] *supra* note 4, at 59.

[8] P. JESSUP, A MODERN LAW OF NATIONS 188–89 (1948).

[9] Kunz, *supra* note 6, at 55.

[10] II OPPENHEIM, INTERNATIONAL LAW 213 (7th ed. Lauterpacht, ed 1955).

are now considered part of customary international law, the general participation clause loses its limiting effect.[11] In the Regulations the concept of "enemy" might be viewed as being broader in scope than the concept of privileged combatant or belligerent. Finally, article 23(b) which protects all "individuals belonging to the hostile nation" certainly provides greater coverage than the definitions in Article I of the Regulations and in the Geneva Conventions.[12]

However, these interpretations could in turn be questioned by the qualifications listed in the opening article which provides that "the laws, rights, and duties of war" apply to persons who fulfill certain specified conditions. Difficulties of interpretation notwithstanding irregular and nongovernmental forces are offered some measures of protection and are considered responsible under existing rules and regulations. As Oppenheim-Lauterpacht states, the right to be treated in accordance with the Hague Regulations, applies, in particular, to cases "in which the resistance movement against the enemy, while lacking military cohesion, is authorized by and acts in accordance with the orders of the lawful government."[13]

Recently Anthony D'Amato *et al.* wrote "both combatants and noncombatants are entitled to prisoner-of-war status."[14] Referring specifically to the case of Vietnam, they added, that "while the law is less certain with respect to partisan guerrillas, the grounds for uncertainty do not seem applicable [there] . . . ."[15] The General Assembly has taken up the question of the legal position of guerrillas in recent sessions and has given the indication that under certain conditions and in specific situations certain additional rights should be granted to guerrillas. Four resolutions adopted by the General Assembly at its twenty-third session are indicative of this trend.[16]

For example, in Resolution 2446 on measures to achieve the rapid and total elimination of all forms of racial discrimination in general and the policy of *apartheid* in particular, the General Assembly confirmed the views of the Teheran International Conference on Human Rights, which recognized and supported the legitimacy of liberation movements in southern Africa and in colonial territories. Also con-

[11] U.N. General Assembly, "Respect for Human Rights in Armed Conflicts," *Report of the Secretary General* (A/7720) Nov. 20, 1969, at 22.

[12] U.N. General Assembly, "Respect for Human Rights in Armed Conflicts," *Report of the Secretary General* (A/8052) Sept. 18, 1970, 32–33.

[13] L. Oppenheim, *supra* note 10, at 213.

[14] A. D'AMATO, H. GOULD, & L. WOODS, *Ware Crimes and Vietnam: The Nuremberg Defense and the Military Service Register*, 57 CAL. L. REV. 1075 (1969).

[15] *Id.* at 1075.

[16] U.N. General Assembly, *supra* note 11, at 5.

firmed was the decision of the Conference to recognize the right of free-dom fighters in southern Africa and in colonial territories to be treated when captured as prisoners of war under the Geneva Conventions of 1949.[17]

Communist writers like I. P. Trainin have supported the rights of guerrillas on the grounds of "justifiable war":

> A truly people's war is one for the basic interests of the people, for its rights, honor, freedom, and independence. Such a war is a justifiable war, in con-tradistinction to an unjustifiable war, i.e., a war directed to the seizure of foreign territories, to the enslavement and subjugation of peoples, to the destruction of their independence as a state. . . .[18]

And a recent publication from Hanoi entitled "U.S. War Crimes in Vietnam" insists that "the mere killing of one countryman of ours, *whether combatant or not,* even with a rifle shot, the mere destruction of a hut, of a bush in our countryside is enough to turn the American pirate into a criminal . . . ."[19] The implication is that irregular forces, combatants, and noncombatants are protected by the laws of war, and violations may be branded as war crimes.

The problem that arises is whether a member of an irregular force may be regarded as a common criminal if he commits acts which are prescribed under municipal law. The issue became particularly relevant when extradition of criminals was involved. As Robert G. Neumann states,

> In the majority of states it is stipulated that persons accused of political crimes or of offenses connected therewith shall not be surrendered. Where this principle is not further modified, as for instance in the Anglo-American countries, a fugitive who could prove that his deed was actually connected with a political element could not be extradited.[20]

The question presents itself whether ordinary acts of murder and robbery when committed with political motives assures an individual status different from that of the ordinary criminal. Neumann explains that

> since 1930, some attempts have been made to exclude socalled acts of ter-rorism from consideration as political offenses or acts connected therewith, but

[17] G.A. Res. 2383 (XXIII) on the question of Southern Rhodesia; 2395 (XXIII) on the question of territories under Portuguese administration; 2396 (XXIII) on the policies of *apartheid* of the Government of South Africa; 2446 (XXIII) on measures to achieve the rapid and total elimination of all forms of racial discrimination in general and the policy of *apartheid* in particular.

[18] I. Trainin, *Questions of Guerilla Warfare in the Law of War,* 40 A.J.I.L. 554 (1946).

[19] JURIDICAL INSTITUTE, U.S. WAR CRIMES IN VIET NAM 203 (1968).

[20] R. Neumann, *Neutral States and the Extradition of War Criminals,* 45 A.J.I.L. 504 (1951).

only a few countries have adopted these rules, and the ambitious attempts of the League of Nations to create a general convention providing, among other things, for the extradition of terrorists did not obtain ratification.[21]

It would seem that this area is fraught with political pitfalls; should a group like the Revolutionary Action Force which has been involved in a bank robbery and murder of a policeman in Boston be regarded as an irregular nongovernmental force? Would their socalled declaration of war on the United States qualify the conflict as "not of an international character"? A consequence might be to bring in an impartial humanitarian body, such as the ICRC, which according to article 3 of the Geneva Convention Relative to the Protection of Civilian Persons, "may offer its services to the parties to the conflict."[22]

It is clear that these problems are not as academic as they may seem when one considers the asylum granted as a political refugee to Bernardine Dohrn of the Weatherman faction by Algeria. Similarly, members of the Black Panther Party have been granted political asylum. The problem is not confined to the United States; members of the Quebec Liberation Front or for that matter the Jewish Defense League might claim rights as irregular forces and invoke the laws of war, and prisoner-of-war status.

Lester Nurick and Roger Barrett conclude:

> the legality of guerrilla forces is likely to be affected by two counterbalancing factors. One is the desire to end as quickly as possible enemy resistance which has no chance of success. The other is the reluctance to treat as war criminals any large body of men who continue to fight solely for patriotic reasons of their own. The answer in a close case may well be dictated by *political* and *military*, rather than legal, considerations.[23]

This represents a highly unsatisfactory solution, since it leaves the area of conflict with irregular forces without guidelines and tends to remove all restraint.

As a matter of fact, the Geneva Conventions of 1949 do provide criteria for recognizing irregular forces under the protection of the laws of war. They must be subject to a responsible authority; they must wear distinctive insignia and carry weapons openly and they must abide by the laws and customs of war.[24] In particular they are bound to respect the prohibition of "grave breaches" defined in article 147 of the Civilian Convention as

[21] *Id.* 504.

[22] ICRC, *supra* note 4, at 56.

[23] L. Nurick & R. Barrett, *Legality of Guerilla Forces under the Laws of War*, 40 A.J.I.L. 583 (1946).

[24] ICRC, *supra* note 4, at 56.

wilful killing, torture, or inhuman treatment, including biological experiments, wilfully causing great suffering or serious injury to body or health, unlawful deportation or transfer or unlawful confinement of a protected person, compelling a protected person to serve in the forces of a hostile power, or wilfully depriving a protected person of the rights of fair and regular trial prescribed in the present Convention, taking of hostages and extensive destruction and appropriation of property, not justified by military necessity and carried out unlawfully and wantonly.[25]

The application of these provisions is limited, however; as Raymund Yingling and Robert Ginnane write,

> . . . these "grave breaches" do not constitute restrictions upon the use of modern combat weapons. For example, modern warfare unfortunately and often may involve the killing of civilians in proximity to military objectives, as well as immense destruction of property. Rather, these provisions cover only persons protected by the conventions, *e.g.*, prisoners of war and the inhabitants of occupied territory. Similarly, the only property protected against destruction or appropriation is property located in occupied territory (by virtue of art. 53 of the Civilian Convention).[26]

Richard Baxter contends that "except to the extent to which the power to impose the death penalty has been removed by the Geneva Civilians Convention of 1949, the offended state may employ that measure in dealing with clandestine hostile conduct." He confirms the right of a capturing state to punish war crimes, and

> although it may be foreseen that in time of war bandits who live by pillage may attempt to contend that they are guerrillas fighting for the defense of their country, the degree to which they comply with the law of war generally applicable to the armed forces will afford the best indication of their purpose, and particularly of their adhesion to one of the belligerents in the conflict rather than to *motives of private gain*.[27]

It would appear that irregular forces are bound to respect the laws of war and that they may be punished for grave breaches. According to articles 129 and 130 of the Civilians Convention, parties are obligated to seek out offenders and to bring them to trial. In the words of Sir Hersch Lauterpacht, "no more emphatic affirmation of the principle of universality of jurisdiction with regard to the punishment of war crimes could be desired."[28]

The problem that remains is what treatment to accord members of irregular forces that do not qualify as protected persons under the Ge-

---

[25] *Id.* at 211.

[26] *Id.* at 174.

[27] R. Baxter, *So-called Unprivileged Belligerency: Spies, Guerillas and Saboteurs*, 28 Brit. Y.B. Int'l L. 323 (1951).

[28] H. Lauterpacht, *The Problem of the Revision of the Law of War*, 29 Brit. Y.B. Int'l L. 362 (1952).

neva Conventions. Should they be subject to ordinary criminal law strictures, or should they enjoy some measure of protection under the laws of war? An incentive to find some accommodation would lie in modifying the methods of warfare and preventing grave breaches by so-called unprivileged belligerents. Expectations of reciprocity may figure strongly in the determination of modes of conflict; the harsher the treatment, the more severe methods are likely to be.

At this time it is clear, as Juerg Schmid explains, the irregular enjoys less protection than the regular combatant.

> Die Verletzung des Kriegsrechts, in genere konstitutiv fuer den Tatbestand des Kriegsverbrechens, muss die kriegsrechtliche Anerkennung des Irregulaeren, die im Gegensatz zu derjenigen der regulaeren, nationalen Streitkraefte dem Voelkerrecht allein entfliesst, zwangslaeufig zunichtemachen. Der Irregulaere kontrastiert hier in augenfaelliger Weise mit dem Soldaten, dessen Kriegsgefangenenstatus weder durch den Kriegsrechtsbruch noch durch Verurteilung als Kriegsverbrecher angetastet wird.[29]

Similarly Walter Meier interprets the Geneva Conventions to deny irregulars the same privileges as regular prisoners of war. "Ein minutioeser Vergleich der beiden Verfahrensrechte ergibt aber einige Abweichungen zum Nachteil des Angeklagten ohne Kriegsgefangenstatus."[30] Irregular forces may still be prosecuted as ordinary criminals, except in specific cases, *e.g.*, in occupied territory. To deny a country jurisdiction except in such instances would be contrary to practice and law.

The loophole of which irregulars may avail themselves lies in article 3 of the Civilians Convention already referred to. It states that "the application of the . . . provisions shall not affect the legal status of the parties to the conflict."[31] It affirms that

> . . . persons taking no active part in the hostilities, including members of armed forces who laid down their arms and those placed *hors de combat* by sickness, wounds, detention, or any other cause, shall in all circumstances be treated humanely, without any adverse distinction founded on race, color, religion or faith, sex, birth or wealth, or any other similar criteria.

The article forbids

> (1) violence to life and person, in particular murder of all kinds, mutilation, cruel treatment, and torture, (2) taking of hostages, (3) outrages upon personal dignity, in particular humiliating and degrading treatment, (4) the passing of sentences and the carrying out of executions without previous judgement pronounced by a regularly constituted court, affording all the judicial guarantees which are recognized as indispensable by civilized peoples.

[29] J. Schmid, Die Volkerrechtliche Stellung der Partisanen im Kriege 134 (1956).
[30] W. Meir, Die Bestimmungen uber das Kriegsverbrechens und Besetzungsstrafrecht in den Cenfer Abkommen zum Schutze der Kriegsopfer von 1949, Winterthur.
[31] ICRC, *supra* note 4, at 154.

To this end the ICRC might be called in to supervise treatment accorded to prisoners, etc. It would seem that the judgment of whether a need for such services arises lies with both the impartial body, *i.e.,* Committee, and the parties to the conflict. A refusal to allow the Committee to inspect U.S. Federal Prisons, for example, where members of the Black Panther Party are held could be regarded as *prima facie* evidence of guilt. In any event, suspicions would be heightened as to the treatment accorded to prisoners, whether it is in accordance with the provisions of the Geneva Conventions.

If protected status is granted to guerrillas, some countries may conclude that such persons no longer owe allegiance to their official government. It is conceivable that they may incur the loss of their citizenship. Such a development would not involve a deprivation of human rights, alien residents being entitled to the ordinary protection of the laws. Unlike protected status under the European Convention on Human Rights which usually involves conflicts of a limited nature, *i.e.,* between a person's action and a specific law or regulation, guerrilla forces represent in their activity an attack upon the system itself. The international nexus is achieved through open conflict between persons owing allegiance to different constituencies.

A more far-reaching remedy to the problems of guerrillas lies in finding institutions which command general respect and that can adjudicate claims of irregular as well as regular forces. With regard to extradition of alleged war criminals who claim political asylum, Neumann points to the need for an international criminal court, "because a state which may hesitate to deliver an officer of a vanquished state to the courts of the victors, would feel fewer qualms in seeing justice administered by an impartial international tribunal."[32]

No authority claims the right to commit war crimes, even those who most vehemently support the rights of partisans and irregulars. Thus Trainin writes that "guerrilla troops take the norms of international law into account in their activities. Such a demand is a dominating one for all defending their freedom, honor, and independence."[33] An international tribunal might be empowered to deal with war crimes committed by persons with contested legal status above and beyond the universal jurisdiction now awarded to states over war crimes under the Geneva Conventions.[34]

It might be suggested, therefore, that as a *minimum,* the services of

[32] R. Neumann, *supra* note 20, at 508.
[33] I. Trainin, *supra* note 18, at 560.
[34] By Res. 485 (V) & Res. 877 (VII) the General Assembly made arrangements for the preparation of one or more preliminary draft conventions and proposals relating to the

the ICRC might be utilized to guarantee fair treatment to irregulars, according to existing Conventions. A more far-reaching proposal would envision the creation of an international criminal court which would take jurisdiction over war crimes by persons with contested legal status. In the words of the late Quincy Wright, this "would demonstrate by acts louder than words that human rights can be vindicated and inhuman offenses can be punished."[35]

Connected with the international criminal court would be an organization, a secretariat, for example, similar to that which services the European Commission and Court of Human Rights, to examine complaints and supply a prosecutorial staff. The structure to be envisaged might comprise (1) supervision through an agency, *e.g.*, the ICRC, over protected persons, (2) examination of relevant cases by an international organization, and (3) indictment and trial of offenders by an international criminal court.[36]

As a practical implementation of the foregoing, it is suggested that each nation (1) reaffirm its intention to live up to its international obligations by consenting to allow the ICRC to supervise persons judged to be members of "irregular" or nongovernmental forces in their treatment according to article 3 of the Geneva Civilians Convention,[37] (2) endorse suggestions for strengthening the ICRC and establishing a new international organization and (3) create an international criminal court to try offenses against international law whether committed by regular or "irregular" forces. The first step should be the holding of an international conference of experts to define guidelines and procedures to be followed.[38]

---

establishment of a statute for an international criminal court. Two committees, the 1951 and the 1953 Committees on International Criminal Jurisdiction submitted drafts of a statute for an international criminal court.

[35] Q. Wright, *War Criminals*, 34 A.J.I.L. 285 (1945). *See also*, J. STONE & R. WOETZEL, TOWARDS A FEASIBLE INTERNATIONAL CRIMINAL COURT (1970).

[36] *The Report of the Secretary General* (A/7720) comments on the need for measures to improve and strengthen the present system of international supervision and assistance to parties to armed conflicts in their observance of humanitarian norms of international law. Suggestions are made for strengthening the institution of "Protecting Power," the use of international organizations, existing or newly created, to act as a substitute for "Protecting Powers" and development of the ICRC to assume a larger role in the present system.

[37] This may be in the form of a declaration of state or resolution by pertinent legislative or judicial institutions.

[38] Such a conference is now in its planning phases co-sponsored by the Foundation for the Establishment of an International Criminal Court and the Johnson Foundation of Racine, Wisconsin.

Section 4. **SOME PROBLEMS OF HUMANITARIAN LAW IN NONINTER-
NATIONAL CONFLICTS AND GUERRILLA WARFARE**

MICHEL VEUTHEY[*]

4.1. Historical Aspects

From the outset, the Red Cross was founded essentially to help the
victims of conflicts between states, and the various Geneva Conventions
since 1863 have been relevant to conflicts of that kind. But it must also
be recognized that internal conflicts have given rise to hundreds of
thousands of victims who, all too often, could not be effectively helped
because of legal or political barriers to Red Cross action. The Red Cross
could not be true to its mission and at the same time indifferent to the
plight of victims of such conflicts, the horror and ferocity of which frequently exceed those of the usual international wars.

Even before the 1949 Diplomatic Conference adopted provisions dealing with internal conflicts, the Red Cross was concerned with what were
still known as civil wars. As early as 1912, one National Society suggested
the drawing up of an international law to enable National Red Cross
Societies to help the victims of internal conflicts. This project was ahead
of its time and was rejected. Five years later, however, following the
Russian Revolution, an International Conference of the Red Cross delegate, after a personal interview with Lenin, obtained agreement for a
group of neutral Red Cross Societies, in concert with the Russian Red
Cross, to create a "Political Red Cross." This group was so known because
it was assigned the mission of visiting political prisoners to provide them
with relief and transmit news on their behalf.

This occurrence was not an isolated instance; rather, it reflected an
underlying interest which was to find clear expression in 1921 at the
Tenth International Conference of the Red Cross which adopted the
following principles:

> The Red Cross, transcending all political, social, religious, racial, class, and
> national competition, affirms its right and duty to take action to provide relief
> in civil war, social disturbances, and revolutions.
> The Red Cross recognizes that all victims of civil war or conflicts of the type
> mentioned are without exception entitled to assistance, pursuant to the general
> principles of the Red Cross.

Stressing the important role of the National Red Cross Society in any

[*] The opinions and conclusions presented herein are those of the author and do not necessarily represent the views of the ICRC, although they are largely based on recent ICRC
researches.

country where civil war breaks out, in impartially assisting the victims, the Conference entrusted the ICRC with the "mandate of intervening in the work of relief in the event of civil war."[1] In addition, that same Conference, "motivated by the grievous experience acquired by the Red Cross in countries where civil war had raged," launched a stirring appeal for the law of nations to be respected even in time of civil war.

Thus it has been almost fifty years since expression was first given to principles which may be considered basic for Red Cross action for the benefit of victims of conflicts which are not international. The adoption of these principles, it is interesting to note, followed closely on the Hungarian Revolution in 1919 during which ICRC delegates intervened (1) to obtain authorization from the new government to enable the National Red Cross Society to carry out its humanitarian work without hindrance and (2) to give attention to the plight of political prisoners and foreigners. Only two months after its adoption, the 1921 Resolution was thoroughly tested in Upper Silesia. Later, the war in Spain entailed intervention by the Red Cross (described by one of its delegates, Dr. Junod, in his book *Warrior Without Weapons*) to such effect that in 1937 a commsision of governmental experts convened by the ICRC unanimously recognized that the Red Cross principles should be respected in all circumstances even when the Geneva Conventions were not applicable. This opinion was reiterated by the Sixteenth International Conference of the Red Cross in 1938.

The Red Cross Conference in Geneva in 1946 (Pre-Conference Meeting of National Red Cross Societies for the Study of the Conventions and the Various Problems Related to the Red Cross) voted the following recommendation: In the event of armed conflict within a state, the Convention shall be applied equally by each of the opposing parties, unless one of them expressly refuses to do so."

Other resolutions were adopted by governmental experts and by the Stockholm Conference in August 1948. At the Diplomatic Conference to revise the Geneva Conventions in 1949, the adoption of one clause relating to internal conflict gave rise to lengthy discussions.[2] It was only after three months that agreement was reached on the text of article 3 which is common to all four Conventions:

> In the case of armed conflict not of an international character occurring in the territory of one of the high contracting parties, each party to the conflict shall be bound to apply, as a minimum, the following provisions:
>
> 1. Persons taking no active part in the hostilities, including members of armed

[1] Agenda XIV "Civil War," IIId Comm'n, meetings of Apr. 6 & 7, 1921.
[2] See *inter alia* PICTET, THE GENEVA CONVENTIONS OF AUGUST 12, 1949. Commentary published under the general editorship of Jean S. Pictet, under art. 3.

forces who have laid down their arms and those placed *hors de combat* by sickness, wounds, detention, or any other cause, shall in all circumstances be treated humanely, without any adverse distinction founded on race, colour, religion or faith, sex, birth or wealth, or any other similar criteria.

To this end, the following acts are and shall remain prohibited at any time and in any place whatsoever with respect to the above-mentioned persons:

(a) violence to life and person, in particular murder of all kinds, mutilation, cruel treatment, and torture;

(b) taking of hostages;

(c) outrages upon personal dignity, in particular humiliating and degrading treatment;

(d) the passing of sentences and the carrying out of executions without previous judgment pronounced by a regularly constituted court, affording all the judicial guarantees which are recognized as indispensable by civilized peoples.

2. The wounded and sick shall be collected and cared for.

An impartial humanitarian body, such as the International Committee of the Red Cross, may offer its services to the parties to the conflict.

The parties to the conflict should further endeavor to bring into force, by means of special agreements, all or part of the other provisions of the present Convention.

The application of the preceding provisions shall not affect the legal status of the parties to the conflict.

This article was a triumph for the Red Cross because it no longer left to the arbitrary decision of parties to an internal conflict the respect and securing of respect for humanitarian principles; it gave official confirmation to certain basic rules and at the same time authorized the ICRC to take action. Since the adoption of article 3, sometimes called the mini-convention, because it summarizes the essential principles of the Geneva Conventions, the Red Cross in general and the ICRC in particular have endeavored to secure application of its provisions which, often with other articles of the Conventions, have been accepted in such conflicts as those in Algeria, Cuba, Lebanon, and Yemen.

However, experience has shown article 3 to be inadequate. Consequently, three meetings of experts were convened in Geneva to consider the question in 1953, 1955, and 1962,[3] while International Conferences of

---

[3] Commission of Experts for the Examination of the Question of Assistance to Political Detainees, Geneva, June 9–11, 1953 (Printed publication of the ICRC No. 453, Geneva, 1953, 8 pp.). Commission of Experts for the study of the question of the application of humanitarian principles in the event of internal disturbances, Geneva, Oct. 3–8, 1955 (Printed publication of the ICRC No. 481, Geneva 1955, 8 pp.). Commission of experts for the study of the question of aid to the victims of internal conflicts, Geneva, Oct. 25–30, 1962 (Printed publication of the ICRC No. 577, Geneva 1962, 11 pp.).

the Red Cross since 1957 have stressed how topical the problem is and how necessary it is to exert constant effort to improve the application of humanitarian law in internal conflicts.

At the Istanbul Conference in 1969, the ICRC submitted a special report "Protection of Victims of Non-International Conflicts."[4] It also dealt with the problem in one chapter of its report on "The Reaffirmation and Development of Laws and Customs Applicable in Armed Conflicts."[5] The fact that the main ICRC conclusions on noninternational conflicts were endorsed in the U.N. Secretary-General's report on "Respect for Human Rights in Time of Armed Conflict"[6] shows clearly that Red Cross action in this field is in keeping with widely felt concern.

As is clear from these reports, the experience of the twenty years following the adoption of article 3 seems to point up the following shortcomings:

1. Respect for the sign of the Red Cross, hospitals, military and civilian medical personnel, and the personnel of National Red Cross Societies, is not expressly laid down in article 3. As a result, the bombing of hospitals clearly marked with the red cross and the molesting of doctors for having treated or given medicines to an enemy have been too frequent for the omission from positive law of safeguards against such events to be allowed to continue.

2. Combatants taken prisoner in internal conflicts are hardly better protected; although provision is made for their "humane treatment" (forbidding murder, torture, humiliation, and degrading treatment) and for at least minimum legal guarantees, there is nothing to prevent the execution of such combatants merely for having borne arms against the enemy. It can readily be understood that the slaughter of prisoners with or without legal proceedings can hardly satisfy humanitarian conscience, nor, it can be said, the political cause of those responsible.

3. Relaxation of blockade for the benefit of enemy civilian population is another provision—similar to that of article 23 of the Fourth Geneva Convention—which could be added to article 3. This would permit the free passage of medical supplies, food, clothing, and essential tonics for children and expectant mothers.

4. Persons detained in internal conflict should, as in international con-

---

[4] XXIst International Conference of the Red Cross, Istanbul, Sept. 1969—Protection of victims of noninternational conflicts—Report submitted by the ICRC, Geneva, May 1969. 11 pp.

[5] Report submitted by the ICRC to the XXIst International Conference of the Red Cross, Istanbul, 1969. *See especially* pp. 97 to 121 and 077–078 (Bibliography).

[6] A/7720, Nov. 1969.

flict, be entitled to correspond with their families and receive relief parcels.

5. Assistance by a neutral body to help parties to an internal conflict to apply the humanitarian principles and provisions is needed. The ICRC under article 3 may do no more than offer its services. Fortunately, in several internal conflicts both the government and the insurgents have recognized the usefulness of such cooperation which in no way affects the legal status of parties to a conflict but does greatly improve the application of the humanitarian principles and provisions and hence the chances of restoring peace.

A further problem which has not yet been mentioned, the solution to which in 1970 will differ from what it would have been at the beginning of the century, and even at the time the 1949 Geneva Conventions were signed, that being the applicability of humanitarian law in noninternational conflicts. The idea is by no means new, for in the eighteenth century a well known European legal expert, Vattel, advocated the application of humanitarian principles to the treatment of rebels. Article 3 itself states that parties to a conflict "should endeavor to bring into force, by means of special agreements, all or part of the other provisions" of the 1949 Geneva Conventions. But in what cases will belligerents—government or insurgent—recognize that article 3 is applicable? All too often the authorities tend to deny its applicability. The tenor of article 3 is clear, yet at the same time, its terms are not very explicit: "armed conflict," "hostilities," "armed forces," suggest operations on no small scale and lasting for some time (past or predictable future), a sizeable number of victims, and possibly (an idea also implied in some proposed amendments in 1949) a territory in the hands of the insurgents.

The Expert Commission to examine the question of aid to the victims of internal conflicts, meeting at Geneva in 1962, concluded that the existence of an armed conflict within the meaning of article 3 could not be denied if the hostile action directed against the government were collective and, to at least a minimum degree, organized. In the opinion of that Commission, account had to be taken of such factors as the duration of the conflict, the number of rebel groups, the extent to which they were under officer supervision, their entrenchment or action in part of the territory, the prevailing tension, the existence of victims, and the efforts made by the government to restore order. Other experts convened by the ICRC at Geneva in February, 1969, reiterated these criteria, but stressed that they should not be too narrowly interpreted.

The U.N. Secretary-General's report on "Respect for Human Rights in Time of Armed Conflict" to the Twenty-Fourth General Assembly went even further. In paragraph 104 it stressed:

In situations of armed conflict which occurred in recent times the determination whether the conflict was or was not of an international character was often difficult to make. While, from the point of view of other branches of international law, *e.g.*, from the point of view of the rights and obligations of neutral powers, this distinction may be of great importance, this may not be so as far as the questions under consideration are concerned, *i.e.*, the securing of minimum humanitarian standards under circumstances of armed conflict.

Such remarks are in keeping with the Twenty-Third U.N. General Assembly's unanimous Resolution 2444 of December 1968, recognizing the "necessity of applying the basic humanitarian principles in all armed conflicts."

In conclusion, there are no political or legal barriers to humanitarian law and it is to be hoped that a statement of principles like Resolution 2444 (XXIII) will lead to regulations applicable to this kind of conflict, and especially to more complete Red Cross action. As Profesor Siotis wrote in the conclusions to his *Le droit de la guerre et les conflits armés d'un caractère non international*:

> Internal armed conflicts are steadily taking on the features of a struggle between the great social and national currents, and nothing short of regulations with a solid foundation in objective bases can subordinate the high feeling which they generate to respect for the principles of humanity and law.[7]

4.2. Factual Aspects: A Study in Typology of Warfare Situations

To strengthen and develop humanitarian law, the facts and situations arising today in guerilla warfare (international or otherwise) and internal disorders must be taken into consideration. Factors in this category are, for example:

1. Types of "internal conflict" (the qualification of which is often disrupted).
2. Combatants (whose status is not always recognized in prevailing law).
3. Civilians (whose claim to have no part in hostilities is sometimes contested, if not in law, at least in practice).
4. Methods of warfare (which, although contrary to the dictates of public conscience are frequently resorted to and which some people consider, at times, justified by the necessities of the fighting).

4.2.1. TYPES OF NONINTERNATIONAL CONFLICTS. Internal conflict is understood to mean conflict between political forces which have recourse to weapons within the jurisdiction or geographic boundaries of a state. The word "guerrilla" is not intended to signify a category of conflict, but a

---

[7] J. SIOTIS, LE DROIT DE LA GUERRE ET LES CONFLITS ARMÉS D'UN CARACTÈRE NON INTERNATIONAL, 248 (1958).

particular method of waging war which may be used in international or internal conflict by persons who in general do not fulfill the conditions required of combatants under the Geneva Conventions to qualify for prisoner-of-war status but who have at their command a logistic and political infrastructure supported by some or all of the population.

4.2.1.1. *Mixed Conflict.* This species of conflict is internal in certain respects and international in others, sometimes being called international civil war (internationaler Bürgerkrieg).[8] Schwarzenberger writes on this situation:

> In a sociological view, the distinction between international and internal armed conflicts is artificial and, at most, one of emphasis. In any age, the areas of international society and those of its constituent national or multinational communities do not constitute self-contained compartments; they interact. The more widespread and protracted an internal struggle, the more it tends to affect other members of the international society, and the more likely is it that they will find it necessary to intervene.[8a]

It is held in some quarters that the determining factor in the international aspect is foreign intervention; that is to say, assistance provided by one or more foreign states to one of the parties to the internal conflict. Such assistance may take several forms:

1. Military assistance (the sending of regular troops, "volunteers," or tolerance of their recruitment, the sending of special antiguerrilla troops, "advisors," instructors, technicians, heavy material, light weapons, etc.).
2. Political assistance (at the United Nations, or a unilaterally favorable attitude to one of the parties to a conflict, such as recognition by a state).
3. Economic and financial assistance (depending on its extent and nature, such assistance may be decisive for the party which benefits from it).

4.2.1.2. *Civil War Between Two Quasi-States.*[9] By "quasi-state" we refer to an organization having certain elements of a state in fact (government, territory, population, armed forces) and even in law (recognition by foreign states) which confer on hostilities a more classical form in which

---

[8] *See* Schindler, *Die Anwendung der Genfer Rotkreuzabkommen seit 1949,* 22 Annuaire suisse de droit international 85 (1965).

[8a] Schwarzenberger, *International Law as Applied by International Courts and Tribunals,* vol. 2, The Law of Armed Conflicts (1968).

[9] The best example of such a situation would perhaps be the Spanish Civil War of 1936–1939. By "quasi-states" we could, for example, mention Biafra or the Southern Confederation during the American Civil War.

the full application of the Geneva Conventions, particularly the first three, is a practical possibility.

To the notion of "civil war" is given the narrow meaning of conflict between regular armed forces within a state.[10]

4.2.1.3. Armed Conflict in Which One of the Parties Does Not Have Effective or Extensive Territorial Domination.

Territorial domination, which was not accepted at the 1949 Diplomatic Conference as a criterion justifying the application of article 3, is not without importance in the application of the provisions of the Conventions as a whole, the Third and Fourth in particular. So far as the notion of "armed conflict" is concerned, the 1962 Commission of Experts for the study of the question of aid to the victims of internal conflicts, which met in Geneva October 25–30, 1962, had this to say:

> The existence of an armed conflict, within the meaning of article 3, cannot be denied if the hostile action, directed against a legal government, is of a collective character and consists of a minimum amount of organization. In this respect and without these circumstances being necessarily cumulative, one should take into account such elements as the length of the conflict, the number and framework of the rebel groups, their installation or action on a part of the territory, the degree of insecurity, the existence of victims, the methods employed by the legal government to reestablish order, etc. (*Cf.* definition of armed conflict within the meaning of article 3 contained in the ICRC report on Reaffirmation, D.S. 4 a, b, e, Geneva, May 1969, pp. 99–100.)[11]

4.2.1.4. Internal Disturbances.[12]

What we qualify as "internal disturbances" are situations in which the following elements are apparent:

---

[10] For this narrow meaning of "civil war" see the excellent study by Charles Zorgbibe, *La Guerre civile,* 6 *Annales de la Faculté de Droit et des Sciences Economiques de l'Université de Clarmont* (1969).

[11] It may be of some interest to quote the following paragraph:

> The experts as a whole regretted the absence of a definition of the non-international conflict adapted to the conditions and requirements of modern warfare. One expert, on the grounds of personal experience, called attention to all the difficulties involved in problems raised by internal conflicts. There are numerous causes for these; they may originate from particular political, social, economic or then religious situations. A war of liberation, the uprising of a minority against the lawful government and a class war: all constitute internal conflicts; the situation is particularly complicated when there are no longer two parties to a conflict, but three, even four parties who are trying to eliminate each other. He, however, suggested possibly defining the non-international conflict as follows: "the internal armed conflict is a means of expression, a deadly form of dialogue when none other is any longer possible."

[12] For this problem, *see Reaffirmation* at 108–111, and the report by the Commissioners of Experts for the study of the question of the application of humanitarian principles in the event of internal disturbances, which met in Geneva Oct. 3–8, 1955. In the first quoted report we could read:

> In situations of serious internal tension which may be considered potential conflicts though they do not necessarily develop into an open struggle between two factions, the conditions of the uprising and the large numbers of victims have made it desirable to apply a minimum of humanitarian rules.

> Owing to the fact that lawful governments and their police forces dispose of means of repression

1. Acts of violence reaching a certain degree of gravity.
2. Events lasting an appreciable length of time (an occasional riot is not significant).
3. Struggle between two or more organized groups.
4. Existence of victims.

4.2.1.5. Internal Tension.[13] This may be described as follows:

1. Sequel to a civil war or internal disturbances.
2. State of serious political, religious, racial, or social tension.
3. The suspension of legal guarantees, recourse to emergency measures and procedures as a result of which the rule of law normally guaranteeing individual freedom under the state constitution is not or is no longer applied.
4. Administrative internment or deportation of persons considered a danger to state security.
5. Particularly heavy penalities for relatively minor offenses.
6. Apparently justified complaints of inhuman treatment.

4.2.1.6. Infiltrations. This is a situation in which one state, while not openly at war with another, surreptitiously introduces people, generally members of its armed forces, into the other state to organize an uprising or the overthrow of the government, with recourse, if need be, to sabotage or terrorism.

4.2.2. COMBATANTS. Examples are quoted below of combatants who might be involved in strictly internal conflicts and in guerrilla warfare, and hence also in international conflicts. It is not claimed that the categories mentioned are clear-cut, completely accurate, or cover all combatants who might be involved in such conflicts.

4.2.2.1. Members of the Regular Armed Forces of the Established Government. The composition of armed forces varies from state to state depending on the organizational structure given to each under national legislation.

4.2.2.2. Members of the Insurgent Armed Forces. These are the regular

---

which often make armed insurrection almost impossible, the conditions have modified. As a result there are now situations of internal tension which are characterized by the government authorities complete control of events and wholesale internment of individuals considered dangerous for their security.

Although these situations fail to fulfill the conditions of a non-international conflict under the terms of Art. 3, the ICRC has for a long time concerned itself with this problem. (*Reaffirmation* at 108).

[13] The present situation in Greece, for example, could meet some of these criteria and therefore be qualified as "internal tension."

armed forces of insurgent movements having quasi-state features, or well-established guerrilla forces. Such forces are organized in a manner comparable to that of a regular army.

4.2.2.3. *Mercenaries.* These are individuals, generally foreigners, who take part in fighting for their own private gain.

4.2.2.4. *Infiltrators.* These may be members of the regular armed forces who have infiltrated (i.e., entered surreptitiously) a country at loggerheads with their own country but not officially at war. Such infiltrators have been known to carry out their activities in uniform or in civilian clothing.

4.2.2.5. *Special Governmental Antiguerrilla Forces.* These are units or combatants specially trained to combat guerrillas, using guerrilla methods and generally operating under an autonomous command separated from the rest of the standing army of the government or state to which they belong.

4.2.2.6. *Guerrillas Fulfilling the Conditions of Article 4 of the Third Geneva Convention.* Guerrillas are organized, with successive grades of command, wear uniforms (or a fixed distinctive sign), respect the laws and customs of war, and belong to one of the parties to the conflict. Such combatants would mainly be resistance fighters in occupied territory during an international conflict.

4.2.2.7. *Guerrillas Not Fulfilling Certain Article 4 Conditions.* These men fight without uniform or distinctive sign, usually in isolation, without being under the orders of a responsible chief.

4.2.2.8. *Guerrillas Operating in the Territory of Neutral States.* In several recent conflicts guerrillas have been known to attack enemy targets, or targets which they claimed to belong to the enemy, in the territory of neutral states. They have attacked military bases, diplomatic representatives, and civilian aircraft belonging to the power with which they were in conflict.

4.2.2.9. *Deserters and "Transfugees."* Deserters (soldiers absconding from the army) and "transfugees" (persons abandoning one side and joining the other) are usual in internal conflicts and guerrilla warfare.

Although forbidden by the Conventions, "brainwashing" of prisoners is not infrequent and is followed by enlistment in the army or administration of their former enemy (see below).

4.2.2.10. *Saboteurs.* According to the *Manuel des Lois et Coutumes de la Guerre* (a Swiss army manual published in 1963):

Sabotage means action within the territory held by an enemy and intended to destroy military installations and depots or to disrupt the supply, transport, and communications systems.

Such action is generally undertaken by individuals or groups brought in secretly by ship or aircraft by the fifth column or the partisan forces.

4.2.2.11. *Spies and Informers.* According to article 29 of the Regulations respecting the Laws and Customs of War on Land annexed to the Hague Convention of 1907:

A person can only be considered a spy when, acting clandestinely or on false pretenses, he obtains or endeavors to obtain information in the zone of operations of a belligerent, with the intention of communicating it to the hostile party.

The term "informer" has also been used more widely to cover a whole range of persons who provide an enemy with information and, consequently, liable to prosecution and punishment in the event of their being discovered.

4.2.2.12. *Terrorists.* This term has given rise to much controversy. Its definition covers all persons acting in isolation in a struggle who violate the laws and customs of war. According to the French dictionary *Robert,*[14] a terrorist is a "member of a political organization who uses terror as a weapon; who carries out acts of terrorism." The same dictionary defines terrorism as "all acts of violence (individual or collective attacks against life, destruction . . .) on the part of a political organization, to impress the population and create an atmosphere of insecurity."

4.2.3. CIVILIANS

4.2.3.1. *Political Opponents.* The only persons embraced by this term are those who are in need of humanitarian assistance because of conditions of house arrest, detention by administrative decision or a court ruling, or maltreatment. The term "political detainees" although of imprecise interpretation, would certainly cover a large part if not all of the persons referred to as political opponents.

4.2.3.2. *Senior Officials and Civil Servants.* These terms refer to people in the political hierarchy (both in the established government and in the insurgent organization in an armed conflict; in guerrilla warfare it may be the political hierarchy of the state or of the resistance movement). These persons have often been the object of attack or systematic threats in recent conflicts.

4.2.3.3. *Administrative Services.* This category includes employees of nonpolitical services such as the postal service, social serivce, teaching pro-

[14] *Robert,* LE DICTIONNAIRE ALPHABÉTIQUE ET ANALOGIQUE DE LA LANGUE FRANCAISE (1966).

fession, and the highway departments. Such employees in the past have not always been able to avoid becoming involved in internal conflicts and guerrilla warfare, one objective of several guerrilla movements having been to disrupt the state's communication system and the country's administration in order to act with impunity.

4.2.3.4. *Police.* This is a term of varied meaning, since it is not infrequent that a state has several types of police forces, each for a different function (road traffic, aliens control, internal state security, criminal investigation, etc.). In case of war, some countries detach part of the police to the armed forces; in others, the police per se not infrequently go into action against internal guerrilla movements. Whether the police as a whole fits into the civilian category, and therefore in principle is spared for attack, is a moot point. It should be mentioned, however, that some police associations are endeavoring to obtain noncombatant status in the event of armed conflict.

4.2.3.5. *Displaced and Resettled Persons.* Both in guerrilla warfare and internal conflicts, the population is not infrequently "resettled" so that it can be better controlled, removed from the sphere of guerrilla operations, and even removed to areas where bombing and shooting on sight are permitted (free-bombing zones, free-fire zones). Even when resettlement operations are not conducted systematically, the hostilities themselves (air raids, threats from parties to the conflict) cause a spontaneous exodus of the population.

4.2.3.6. *Population Intermittently Under the Control of Guerrillas and Their Enemies.* This "intermittence" may refer to the alternating control by guerrillas at night and their enemies during the day, or it might be the result of vicissitudes in the fighting, *e.g.*, the guerrillas or their enemies might occupy a village or a town previously held by their enemies for a matter of days or hours. What is the plight of a civilian population subject to this constantly changing authority, with the hardships which it entails (abduction or execution of sympathizers with the enemy, the commandeering of primary necessities)? In this respect, reference may be made to the first paragraph of article 70 of the Fourth Geneva Convention relative to the protection of civilian persons in time of war, according to which:

> Protected persons shall not be arrested, prosecuted, or convicted by the occupying power for acts committed or for opinions expressed before the occupation, or during a temporary interruption thereof, with the exception of breaches of the laws and customs of war.

4.2.3.7. *Populations Under the Permanent Control of Guerrilla Forces (in an Internal Conflict).* Permanent control is intended to mean several months or years of control without interruption. Communications with the rest of the country become difficult or are in a general state of disruption, for the situation may be the result of a blockade or semiblockade (see below under § 4.2.4.4). In addition, the government or the forces opposing the guerrillas will generally tend to consider the controlled population as an enemy and subject it to bombardment (*c.f.* id.)

4.2.3.8. Persons Supplying Passive (Failure to Denounce) or Active (Provision of Transport, Shelter, Information, etc.) Assistance to the Guerrillas or Combatants in an Internal Conflict. Many experts believe guerrilla forces could not long continue without support from the civilian population. That support may be passive (negative), the population refusing, for example, to inform the enemy of guerrilla movements, or it may be active (positive), providing asylum, transportation, or direct assistance, sometimes going so far as involving occasional participation in operations and terrorism, the manufacture of weapons, and the building of fortifications.

4.2.3.9. Persons Refusing to Obey the Injunctions of Guerrillas. Guerrillas sometimes exert pressure on persons refusing to obey them, as would a regular army in the field or in occupation of a territory.

4.2.4. METHODS OF WARFARE

4.2.4.1. Bombardment and Other Indiscriminate Attacks on Civilian Population. Recent conflicts have shown that World War II was but the beginning of large-scale or indiscriminate attacks against civilian populations by air raids or artillery.

In fighting against guerrilla movements, it has often been noticed that guerrillas find refuge and assistance among the civilian population. When unable to attack combatants themselves, there is sometimes a tendency to resort to large-scale bombardment of population centers and even of crops in order to deprive the guerrilla forces of shelter and sustenance. On the basis of the proposition that guerrillas are in their element among the population, "like a fish in water," an attempt is made to deprive the fish of water.

Apart from the humanitarian problems which such indiscriminate attacks can hardly fail to raise, it has often been observed that they are ineffective from military points of view and indeed may be "counterproductive" in that they galvanize the threatened population's determination to resist and even act as a stimulus to recruiting for the guerrilla movement.

4.2.4.2. Terrorism. Unlike indiscriminate bombing, which is intended to strike at combatants even at the risk of harm to civilians, terrorism's first and almost sole objective is to harass the civilian population.

The methods employed include the detonation of explosives in public places frequented essentially by civilians (markets, shops, meeting places, etc.), destruction of civilian living quarters, districts, and whole villages, and even the outright slaughter of civilians.

Such acts of terrorism may be perpetrated by regular troops or by guerrillas.

4.2.4.3. *Political "Attentats" and Executions.* The word "attentat" is used here in the sense of attack or attempted attack against civilians (such as mentioned above) or against property belonging to the civilian population (means of transport, communications, supplies, administrative buildings, etc.). Such attacks may result in nonfatal injuries to civilians or damage to property. Terrorists also kill specific civilian persons for political reasons. Here again, such acts are not confined to guerrilla or insurgent movements during internal conflict.

4.2.4.4. *Blockade Against the Civilian Population.* According to the *Robert* French dictionary, a blockade is "the investment of a town, port, coast-line, or entire country to isolate it, to cut off all communications with the outside world." Several recent conflicts have shown how this can be an effective and dangerous weapon. A blockade, of course, may be selective and may assume the form, for example, of a prohibition on the sale of certain primary necessities to the civilian population, generally for fear that the guerrillas or insurgents will be supplied through them. Measures of this kind have even been taken as regards medicines, in breach of Red Cross and humanitarian law principles. Perhaps rationing and requisition of primary necessities, and even the destruction of crops, livestock, and medical supplies for the civilian population, should come under this heading.

4.2.4.5. *Torture.* The same dictionary defines torture as "violence to a person to compel him to admit what he refuses to reveal, and by which physical suffering is inflicted in such a manner that he is forced to yield in order to put a stop to his suffering." Threats of torture or indirect moral pressure, *e.g.*, threat of reprisals against the prisoner's family, have the same objective, *i.e.*, "securing by any form of coercion . . . information of any kind whatever," to use the phraseology of the Geneva Conventions.

In view of the surreptitious and often terrorist nature of guerrilla warfare, it is sometimes claimed that the use of torture is justified to obtain information on enemy plans, networks, location of fighting units and stores of weapons, the identity of leaders, etc. It has even been claimed that there is a humane aspect to torture, that "some maltreatment to discover a terrorist network or the location of a bomb was preferable to the death of tens of innocent victims." Fortunately, public opinion and many responsible authorities have reacted vigorously against this point of view.

4.2.4.6. "Brainwashing" of Detainees. Pressure and maltreatment may not only be intended to obtain military information but also to exact admissions of guilt, a favorable attitude toward the detaining power, and even the enlistment of prisoners into that power's own forces. These methods are not infrequently used by both parties in internal conflicts and particularly in guerrilla warfare, with special camps for that purpose even being set up. Although the effectiveness and duration of this "brainwashing" is outside our subject, the humanitarian aspect of such "brainwashing" and the methods used are questionable.

4.3. Legal Aspects

Useful in analyzing the legal aspect of noninternational conflicts and guerrilla warfare is the classification used in respect of their "factual aspects":

1. Types of conflict (scope of application for the Geneva Conventions as a whole, including Article 3).
2. Civilians (application of the Fourth Geneva Convention).
3. Combatants (Article 4 of the Third Geneva Convention).
4. Methods of warfare (rules for the conduct of hostilities and the use of weapons).

These matters shall be examined from two points of view: (1) the protection which the Geneva Conventions afford to human beings involved in a conflict and (2) the legal status, according to international law, particularly the Hague Convention of 1907, of such persons and the organizations of which they are members.

Added to this list of problems have been some suggestions on possible lines of action likely to strengthen and develop the law of armed conflicts. In this respect, the unanimously adopted Resolution XIII at the Twenty-first International Conference of the Red Cross (Istanbul, 1969) underlined

> . . . the necessity and the urgency of reaffirming and developing humanitarian rules of international law applicable in armed conflicts of all kinds, in order to strengthen the effective protection of the fundamental rights of human beings, in keeping with the Geneva Conventions of 1949.

4.3.1. TYPES OF CONFLICTS

4.3.1.1. *Scope of Application of Humanitarian Law*

  a. *General Questions*

    (1) *Procedure.* This is a delicate problem. Must some machinery or body (existing or to be formulated) be assigned the duty of deciding when Article 3, or even the Geneva Conventions as a whole, are applicable in an armed conflict? Suggestions have been made that this decision be assigned to a regional or worldwide collective security organization, such as the United Nations, to a private committee of internationally renowned persons, or even to the ICRC. The real question, however, is whether such a procedure, whatever organ chosen, would really make the application of humanitarian law any easier.

    Another problem to be resolved is how to construe the obligation contained in article 1, common to the four Geneva Conventions, according to which "the high contracting parties undertake to respect and to insure respect for the present Convention in all circumstances." It has been asked whether this declaration implies that states are obliged to enforce respect for the Conventions by other states (and by insurgent and guerrilla movements). In this connection, Resolution XXIII of the International Conference on Human Rights, at Teheran in 1968, approved unanimously, with one abstention, (see Annex VIII, Report on "Reaffirmation," pp. 024–026) contained a most revealing paragraph:

> States parties to the Red Cross Geneva Conventions sometimes fail to appreciate their responsibility to take steps to insure the respect of these humanitarian rules in all circumstances by other states, even if they are not themselves directly involved in an armed conflict.

According to the report issued by the Commission of Experts for the study of the question of aid to the victims of internal conflicts (ICRC, Geneva, Oct. 25–30, 1962), the first article of the four Geneva Conventions affirms that "the high contracting parties undertake to respect and to ensure respect for the present Convention in all circumstances." The government directly concerned is, of course, the first to be obligated to note the existence of an internal conflict. The states parties to the Geneva Conventions also have the right and obligation, however, to have their provisions respected—especially article 3. Finally, the ICRC, the report declares, is entitled "to offer its services to the parties to the conflict, and is necessarily bound, in the exercising of its right of initiative, to appreciate without partiality the existence of the conditions required for the application of article 3."

    (2) *Definition.* Article 3 does not define or even mention situations

to which it is applicable other than by the following clause: "In the case of armed conflict not of an international character occurring in the territory of one of the high contracting parties . . . ." It has therefore been asked whether it would not be of benefit to redress this apparently deliberate omission of 1949, which has had the advantage of leaving a free hand for an interpretation which—at least by writers on international law—over the intervening twenty years has grown increasingly liberal.

In 1949, for instance, article 3 was deemed applicable especially to the conventional type of "civil war" (conflict between the regular forces of quasi-state organizations). In 1962, the Commission of Experts for the study of the question of aid to the victims of internal conflicts wrote:

> In the Commission's opinion, the existence of an armed conflict, within the meaning of article 3, cannot be denied, if the hostile action, directed against the legal government, is of a collective character and consists of a minimum amount of organization.

Likewise, the report of the 1962 Commission of Experts offers examples of situations in which article 3 should be applied (*cf.* previous quotation under § 4.2.1.3).

It is held in some quarters that such fundamental rights and guarantees as are implied in article 3, and which must be heeded whenever force is used to repress political or social disorders, should not be subordinate to any conditions whatsoever, and that there should be no controversy about what constitutes "armed conflict."

b. *Particular Points*

(1) *Application of International Humanitarian Law as a Whole and Especially the Geneva Conventions.* The Red Cross, of course, would like to see all humanitarian law applied in all conflicts, irrespective of what legal and political qualification is attributed to them. This is not a new proposal; it was put forward as long ago as 1949 and the work of a number of writers since, and even several actual cases (recent conflicts), might lead one to hope for a fresh examination of the problem.

As is mentioned below (in relation to the Fourth Convention), the full application of the Geneva Conventions in a conflict which is not international is not without its problems, both practical and theoretical. But a de facto limitation should not be taken as a pretext not to apply the law: it is quite clear that guerrillas or insurgents (or their adversaries) will not always be in a position to respect all articles of the Geneva Conventions to the letter, but that does not absolve them from their obligation to observe at least basic principles.

The cases set forth below should be viewed as a demonstration of the practical possibilities for the full application of humanitarian law in present-day conflicts.

(a) When the insurgent party has certain quasi-state features, such a conflict is de facto of a conventional international type, so that even the most detailed provisions of the Third Convention could, for example, be applied. The only obstacle presented—and herein lies the key problem—is the attitude of the legal government, which could advance legal or political arguments, to refuse to apply provisions which could otherwise be applied.

(b) Where there is foreign intervention, it must be determined whether this intervention, the frequent occurrence of which can no longer be denied, does not increase the number of victims, aggravate their plight, and, in a word, make the application of international humanitarian law increasingly necessary.

(c) At the meeting of experts, at Geneva in February 1969, on the reaffirmation and development of the laws and customs applicable in armed conflicts (see Report on "Reaffirmation," pp. 101–102), some experts considered (on the grounds of the U.N. G. A. Res. 1514 (XV), "Declaration on the Granting of Independence to Colonial Countries and Peoples," Dec. 14, 1960) that the right to self-determination conferred an international character on any struggle by a people for its independence.

It should be noted that the U.N. General Assembly passed a series of resolutions claiming prisoner-of-war status for combatants taken prisoner during any struggle against the authorities in Southern Africa and urging the application of the Geneva Convention of August 12, 1949, relative to the treatment of prisoners of war. Some experts asked why this concept of war of national liberation, this struggle of a people to exercise its right of self-determination, should be limited only to anticolonial conflicts recognized in a U.N. General Assembly resolution, and why other movements struggling in an analogous context should not have the same rights. This question was to be given special attention at the twenty-fifth U.N. General Assembly, the U.N. Secretary-General having been requested in Resolution 2597 (XXIV):

> [t]o continue the study initiated by General Assembly Resolution 2444 (XXIII) giving special attention to the need for protection of the rights of civilians and combatants in conflicts which arise from the struggles of peoples under colonial and foreign rule for liberation and self-determination and to the better application of existing humanitarian international conventions and rules to such conflicts.

(2) *Application of article 3*

(a) Article 3 as written applies only to "armed conflict not of

an international character." The following considerations have led us to
question whether it could also be applied to internal disturbances, and
even internal tension:

> First, the oft-underlined fact that the guarantees recognized by article 3
> (nondiscrimination, prohibition on murder, torture, taking of hostages, in-
> flicting of humiliating or degrading treatment, passing sentences and carrying
> out execution without proper trial) are so basic that, as said at the 1949
> Diplomatic Conference, they could be applied even to common law criminals.
>
> The words "armed conflict" lend themselves to too many restrictive inter-
> pretations, it being an easy matter for the state in question to pretend that the
> conflict is merely a matter of maintaining order even when the police have
> capitulated to the army.
>
> In addition, even without recourse to armed intervention camouflaged as
> "maintenance of order," it cannot be denied that most noninternational con-
> flicts have not reached the stage of "armed" conflict, that is to say, occasioned
> open hostilities, but they may still rightly be described as conflicts, since
> hundreds or thousands of persons are detained for acts hostile to the govern-
> ment or even for no more than their attitude or political opinions.
>
> Several of the experts meeting in February 1969 were warmly in favor of
> an internationally recognized statute conferring on the Red Cross the right to
> act in such cases (see Report on "Reaffirmation," at 110) and even recom-
> mending that the U.N. General Assembly should adopt a resolution asking the
> ICRC to carry out its humanitarian function in places where internal distur-
> bances and tensions prevail, and recommending the governments to appeal
> to it (*id.* at 110–111).

The ICRC has in the past endeavored to assist victims of such situations
with the agreement of the authorities concerned. A study carried out by
the ICRC established the fact that over the last eleven years, forty-two
governments had authorized the ICRC to visit nearly 100,000 persons
detained as a result of situations which did not strictly speaking come
within the purview of article 3 (*id.* at 109). The assistance provided by
the ICRC was mainly in the form of visits to the detainees or deportees;
relief was sent to them and to their families. When necessary, the ICRC
forwarded family news between detainees and their families. ICRC
visits are concerned only with the treatment of detainees. Its reports on
these visits are sent only to the detaining power. The ICRC issues no
pronouncement on the reasons and duration of detention; these are
considerations with which other organizations not subject to the same
conditions as the ICRC may concern themselves.

(b) *Human Rights.* One advantage of article 3 is that it is an
instrument of positive law accepted by all states parties to the Geneva
Conventions (of which there are 125). It specifies that an impartial humanitarian body may offer its services to the parties to the conflict. Even
if more precise and far-reaching instruments of human rights enter into
force, article 3, as it stands, or supplemented, will lose nothing of its

value. Recent situations, in Latin America and Europe, have shown what specific roles may be fulfilled both by organizations created to insure respect for human rights and by the Red Cross.

(c) *The likelihood of Bringing Article 3 and Human Rights into Line.* Some instruments relating to Human Rights contain provisions similar to those of article 3. For example, torture and inhuman or degrading treatment are condemned by article 5 of the Universal Declaration of December 10, 1948, and by article 7 of the unfortunately not yet ratified International Covenant on Civil and Political Rights of December 16, 1966.

A parallel has been drawn between article 3 of the Geneva Conventions and article 4(2) of that Covenant which prohibits any derogation from certain fundamental rights even "in time of public emergency which threatens the life of the nation and the existence of which is officially proclaimed." Two of those basic guarantees, the prohibition already mentioned on torture and the restrictions on applying capital punishment (art. 6), are to be found in article 3. Similarly, a parallel may be drawn between the prohibition in article 3 on "murder of all kinds," with article II of the Convention on the Prevention and Punishment of the Crime of Genocide.

Any attempt to "bring into line" article 3 and legislation on human rights must take into account that, of the main universal human rights texts, the only ones today valid are the U.N. Charter and the Genocide Convention. Article 3, as mentioned earlier, is positive law. It is, moreover, an inseparable part of the Geneva Conventions system and not only confers rights but also imposes obligations (the main one being assistance to the wounded and sick). Although the aim of both systems is to protect human beings, the human rights texts were obviously drafted for application in time of peace, whereas the Geneva Conventions have established a specific system for implementation during armed conflicts. The question therefore arises whether it is not advisable that article 3 be brought in line with other provisions applicable in time of armed conflict, first and foremost with the articles or principles of the Geneva Conventions of 1949 (as the penultimate paragraph of article 3 actually specifies), rather than with human rights legislation. It remains to be seen how the two systems—human rights and Geneva Conventions—may be reconciled to avoid any "no man's land" in the "brink" situations between war and peace which nowadays are increasingly frequent.

4.3.1.2. *The Content of Applicable Law*

a. *Development of Article 3*

The advisibility of developing article 3 has been the subject of several reports and resolutions. The Twenty-first International Conference of the

Red Cross (Istanbul, 1969) adopted several resolutions implicitly in favor of such development. For instance, Resolution XIII (Reaffirmation and Development of the Laws and Customs Applicable in Armed Conflicts)

> . . . underlines the necessity and the urgency of reaffirming and developing humanitarian rules of international law applicable in armed conflicts of all kinds, in order to strengthen the effective protection of the fundamental rights of human beings, in keeping with the Geneva Conventions of 1949.

Resolution XVII (Protection of Victims of Non-International Armed Conflicts) states that "experience has brought out certain points on the basis of which this article (article 3) could be made more specific or supplemented" and "asks the ICRC to devote special attention to this problem within the framework of the more general studies it has started, to develop humanitarian law, in particular with the cooperation of government experts."

All of this development may be carried out without impairing the rule, considered essential, in the last paragraph of article 3, that "the application of the preceding provisions shall not affect the legal status of the parties to the conflict."

b. *More Extensive Protection of the Wounded and the Sick*

The present version of article 3 does no more than restate, in general terms, the principle underlying the first 1864 Geneva Convention, namely: "[t]he wounded and sick shall be collected and cared for."

Article 3 makes no specific provision for respect of the Red Cross sign; of hospitals, military, and civilian personnel, or the personnel of National Societies. The report submitted to Istanbul on "the Protection of Victims of Non-International Conflicts" refers to situations in which Red Cross or medical personnel contingents have hesitated to intervene for fear of not being protected against hostilities or of being subsequently reproached for relief activity on behalf of enemy wounded or sick. Although this is a point on which experts may be consulted at some later date, its importance cannot be ignored.

c. *Plight of Captured Combatants*

This question is quite accurately described in the ICRC Report "Protection of Victims of Non-International Conflicts":

> In spite of several attempts in 1949, it has not been possible to introduce into article 3 any provision that those who fight fairly in the regular armed forces shall not be punished for having done so. As things are at present, a government, consistent with national legislation, may punish those who bore arms against it in an insurrection, even if they served in regular units and were perhaps obliged to enlist. This does not encourage combatants to fight openly

for fear of being punished for having fought even if they have committed no other offense.[15]

The problem will be dealt with at greater length under the heading "Combatants," but at this point in the discussion, it should be proposed that captured enemy combatants be granted immunity for having espoused the cause of one party to a conflict and be given a status appoaching that of prisoners of war under the Third Geneva Convention.

d. *Deferment or Even Annulment of Capital Punishment During Hostilities*

This is a wider proposition than the previous one, but as recent conflicts have shown, the two are closely connected. Any capital punishment in time of conflict, related to the conflict, cannot fail to bring about an increase in tension, vigorous reaction from the enemy, or even reprisals.

e. *Family News and Relief to Detainees*

People have been deprived for long periods of all contact with their family, of all moral comfort and all material relief. Whatever is granted to a captured enemy, consistent with international law, the Third Geneva Convention should not be denied to detained nationals. Security requirements and repression can never justify such severe measures. Experience with prisoners of war and the many political prisoners visited by the ICRC has shown that, in this field as in others, state security and humanity are not incompatible.

f. *Relief to Noncombatants*

As already mentioned in the section on questions of fact, the blockade is a legitimate method of warfare. As stated in the "Commentary on the Fourth Geneva Convention Relative to the Protection of Civilians in Time of War":

> [t]he blockade has become a most effective weapon. A ban on all trade with the enemy or with any country occupied by the enemy, strict regulations governing trade with neutral countries, and an extension of the idea of "war contraband" are measures whose object is to place the adverse party in a state of complete economic and financial isolation; such measures cause suffering to the population as a whole as they affect combatants and noncombatants indiscriminately.[16]

Some relief for noncombatants must be provided.

---

[15] XXIst International Conference of the Red Cross (Istanbul, Sept. 1969), *Protection of Victims of Non-International Conflicts*, Report submitted by the ICRC, Geneva, May 1969, at 7.

[16] Res. XIX *Relief in the Event of Internal Disturbances*, adopted by the XIXth

Provision has been made to allow in international conflicts "the free passage of all consignments of medical and hospital stores and objects necessary for religious worship intended only for civilians. . . ." (art. 23 of the Fourth Convention). The text of article 23 of the fourth Geneva Convention relative to the Protection of Civilian Persons in Time of War, of August 12, 1949, is as follows:

Article 23

Each high contracting party shall allow the free passage of all consignments of medical and hospital stores and objects necessary for religious worship intended only for civilians of another high contracting party, even if the latter is its adversary. It shall likewise permit the free passage of all consignments of essential foodstuffs, clothing, and tonic intended for children under fifteen, expectant mothers, and maternity cases.

The obligation of a high contracting party to allow the free passage of the consignments indicated in the preceding paragraph is subject to the condition that this party is satisfied that there are no serious reasons for fearing:

(a) that the consignments may be diverted from their destination,

(b) that the control may not be effective, or

(c) that a definite advantage may accrue to the military efforts or economy of the enemy through the substitution of the above-mentioned consignments for goods which would otherwise be provided or produced by the enemy or through the release of such material, services, or facilities as would otherwise be required for the production of such goods.

The power which allows the passage of the consignments indicated in the first paragraph of this article may make such permission conditional on the distribution to the persons benefited thereby being made under the local supervision of the protecting powers.

Such consignments shall be forwarded as rapidly as possible, and the power which permits their free passage shall have the right to prescribe the technical arrangements under which such passage is allowed.

It has been suggested that such a provision should be inserted or at least expressly referred to in a supplemented article 3.

g. Penal Prosecutions Against War Criminals

Just as the Geneva Conventions (and other international laws) have defined the legal framework for the repression of breaches of the laws and customs of war in international conflicts, so it has been thought,

---

International Conference of the Red Cross (1957) should be referred to here:

The XIXth International Conference of the Red Cross, considering it necessary to ensure maximum efficiency and equity in the distribution of relief supplies in the event of internal disturbances, declares that relief supplies of all types must be distributed equitably among the victims by the National Red Cross Society, without hindrance on the part of the local authorities; considers that, in the event of the National Red Cross Society being unable to come to the assistance of the victims, or whenever it may be deemed necessary or urgent, the International Committee of the Red Cross should take the initiative for the distribution of relief supplies, in agreement with the authorities concerned; requests authorities to grant the Red Cross every facility in carrying out relief actions.

would it be useful in noninternational conflicts to have specific provisions or reference to other legal instruments. That provision or reference should cover both the punishment of offenders and the requisite judicial guarantees. Included in the methods proposed—disregarding any hypothetical international jurisdiction—is the appointment of international observers.

h. *General Amnesty at the End of Hostilities*

Such amnesty was discounted, by implication, at the 1949 Diplomatic Conference. Several delegates went so far as to say that article 3 would not prevent the taking of proceedings against captured or defeated insurgents. However, several noninternational conflicts have since demonstrated that the proposition is topical. Although several victorious governments have taken severe repressive actions against insurgents reduced to their mercy by force of arms (insurrectionist or secessionist movements), others have been wise in declaring general amnesties to restore national unity through an appeal to feeling and reason.[17]

i. *ICRC Activity*

In many internal conflicts the ICRC has been able to carry out its relief work for the victims. The question arises, however, whether it would not be useful to give this tradition the force of law in a supplemented article 3. The experts meeting in February 1969 expressed the hope that governments would thereby be bound to accept ICRC intervention with a view to the implementation of humanitarian regulations ("Reaffirmation," at 107 [e]).

Article 126 of the Third Convention[18] lays down the prerogatives of delegates of the protecting powers, including the right to visit places of their choice; it grants the same prerogatives to delegates of the ICRC.

[17] The recent examples of Nigeria (after the defeat of the secessionist movement) and Iraq (at the end of the Kurds' insurrection) could prove the practical interest of such a proposition.

[18] The text of art. 126 of the IIId Geneva Convention relative to the Treatment of Prisoners of War, of Aug. 12, 1949, reads as follows:

Article 126

Representatives or delegates of the Protecting Powers shall have permission to go to all places where prisoners of war may be, particularly to places of internment, imprisonment and labour, and shall have access to all premises occupied by prisoners of war; they shall also be allowed to go to the places of departure, passage and arrival of prisoners who are being transferred. They shall be able to interview the prisoners, and in particular the prisoners' representatives, without witnesses, either personally or through an interpreter.

Representatives and delegates of the Protecting Powers shall have full liberty to select the places they wish to visit. The duration and frequency of these visits shall not be restricted. Visits may not be prohibited except for reasons of imperative military necessity, and then only as an exceptional and temporary measure.

The Detaining Power and the Power on which the said prisoners of war depend may agree, if necessary, that compatriots of these prisoners of war be permitted to participate in the visits.

The delegates of the International Committee of the Red Cross shall enjoy the same prerogatives. The appointment of such delegates shall be submitted to the approval of the Power detaining the prisoners of war to be visited.

Those prerogatives which are by no means too far-reaching are designed only to insure genuine protection for victims, and they are a guarantee for both parties to the conflict that the ICRC is enabled to carry out its essential humanitarian duties. Several governments have admitted these prerogatives during noninternational conflicts, and experts have expressed the desire to see them recognized in any new regulations which might be adopted.

4.3.2. APPLICABILITY OF ARTICLE 4 OF THE THIRD CONVENTION TO COMBATANTS[19]

4.3.2.1. Applicability of Article 4 in Noninternational Conflicts. It is true that article 3 protects "members of armed forces who have laid down their arms and those placed *hors de combat* . . . ." It guarantees them certain minimum fundamental rights, but as we have seen earlier, it does not forbid the passing of sentences and the carrying out of executions of combatants (subject, it is true, to certain preliminary guarantees).

It will be recalled that the Twenty-first International Conference of the Red Cross at Istanbul, in Resolution XVIII, "Status of Combatants in Non-International Armed Conflicts," considered "that combatants . . . who conform to the provisions of article 4 of the Third Geneva Convention of August 12, 1949, should, when captured, be protected against any inhumanity and brutality and receive treatment similar to that which that Convention lays down for prisoners of war."

That resolution advocates (1) that the provisions of article 4 apply equally in internal conflicts and (2) that captured combatants complying with the requirements of those provisions be entitled to treatment similar to that afforded to prisoners of war. However, the Conference itself was well aware that it had not resolved all problems by that statement, but that it was a provisional solution pending more thorough study. It requested the ICRC "to make a thorough study of the legal status of such persons and take the action in this matter that it deems necessary."

It is still to be determined, as the resolution makes (at least not ex-

---

[19] Para. A (2) of this article lists several conditions with which combatants not belonging to the armed forces of a party to a conflict must comply in order to claim prisoner-of-war status in the event of capture or surrender. Those conditions are as follows:

    a. they must be commanded by a person responsible for his subordinates;
    b. they must have a fixed distinctive sign recognizable at a distance;
    c. they must carry arms openly;
    d. they must conduct their operations in accordance with the laws and customs of War.

In addition to these four conditions which are also laid down in art. 1 of the 1907 Hague Regulations Concerning the Laws and Customs of War on Land, the same art. 4 implies the obligation for the resistance movement to be organized and to "belong to a party to the conflict" (with at least *de facto* liaison with a belligerent state).

pressly) no provision therefor, whether captured combatants should be exempted from legal proceedings merely for having taken up arms.

4.3.2.2. Amendment or Elimination of Some Conditions of Article 4. The various possibilities may be summarized as follows:

The maintenance and reaffirmation of the conditions listed.

Maintenance and wide interpretation of those conditions (e.g., "carrying arms openly").

Maintenance of those conditions but not requiring all to· be fulfilled.

Choice of one or more conditions deemed essential, the others to be eliminated.

In this respect, the following remarks should be made:

a. The requirement of "a person responsible for his subordinates" would seem quite compatible with the very nature of guerrilla warfare; it is, in a way, a guarantee that the armed struggle is legal. The experts convened by the ICRC in February 1969 considered this requirement essential (*see* "Reaffirmation" at 114–121 and especially at 116).

b. The questions of the distinctive sign and the open display of weapons should at least be examined anew in the light of the development of combat and particularly of camouflage techniques as well as of case law since World War II in connection with the wearing of enemy uniform, which is admitted prior to combat (*see* "Reaffirmation" at 116–117).

c. The condition of membership of one of the parties to the conflict, introduced in 1949 to cover resistance movements in occupied territories, should be reexamined in the context of internal conflict. It would in fact be an obstacle to any legal protection for most guerrillas of today.

d. The condition of conforming with the basic principles of the laws and customs of war, on the other hand, seems to be one which is essential and should be retained.

It has been stressed that the conditions were to be fulfilled by the organization and that individual lapses would only entail consequences for the individuals and not involve the loss of guarantees by other members of the organization. A wide interpretation of these conditions does credit to belligerents who follow it: it is also in their own interest. Guerrillas who may count on prisoner-of-war treatment and even status are more inclined to surrender and to give more favorable treatment to enemy combatants whom they capture.

It might be useful to bear in mind that the conditions mentioned above have been accepted only in the context of the Marten's clause:

> . . . in cases not included in the Regulations adopted by them, the inhabitants and the belligerents remain under the protection and the rule of the principles

of the law of nations as they result from the usages established among civilized peoples, from the laws of humanity, and the dictates of public conscience.

Although it may sometimes be difficult for a government to agree to grant prisoner-of-war treatment to insurgents (particularly at the outbreak of disturbances), the Minimum Rules for the Protection of Non-Delinquent Detainees, drawn up by the *Commission medico-juridique de Monaco*[19a] do lay down standards of extensive and acceptable humanitarian treatment even during situations of internal tension (*see also,* on these Regulations, "Reaffirmation," at 111).

4.3.3. APPLICATION OF THE FOURTH CONVENTION TO THE CIVILIANS. It will be recalled that the final paragraph of a draft Convention for the protection of civilian persons in time of war, submitted by the ICRC to the Seventeenth International Red Cross Conference (Stockholm, 1948) provided:

> In all cases of armed conflict which are not of an international character, especially cases of civil war, colonial conflicts, or wars of religion, which may occur in the territory of one or more of the high contracting parties, the implementing of the principles of the present Convention shall be obligatory on each of the adversaries. The application of the Convention in these circumstances shall in nowise depend on the legal status of the parties to the conflict and shall have no effect on that status.

It is certain that this provision, by itself, would not have been enough, for it is not possible to apply, without serious adaptations, the Fourth Convention—the whole system of which is based on nationality—to an internal conflict. It is true that the provisions of Part II ("General Protection of Populations Against Certain Consequences of War," arts. 13 to 26), and of section I of Part III ("Status and Treatment of Protected Persons," "Provisions Common to the Territories of the Parties to the Conflict and to Occupied Territories," arts. 27 to 34) can be applied to all civilian persons. On the other hand, for interned persons (detained or sentenced) a special system of rules must be provided. Perhaps it might thus be possible to consider that persons detained or prosecuted for acts or attitudes in relation to the conflict should benefit, by analogy, from the provisions applicable in that field to the inhabitants of occupied territories.

4.3.4. METHODS OF WARFARE—RULES RELATING TO THE CONDUCT OF HOSTILITIES AND THE USE OF WEAPONS

4.3.4.1. *Noninternational Conflicts.* Unless there is a declaration of recog-

[19a] These Rules were drafted in June 1966 at the request of the ICRC and are reproduced in a Report to the XXIst International Conference of the Red Cross (Istanbul, 1969) entitled "Implementation and Dissemination of the Geneva Conventions."

nition of belligerency, the rules relating to the conduct of hostilities and to the use of weapons are not, in law, applicable in noninternational conflicts.[20] When one thinks of the ferocity of such conflicts and the extent of the means employed on either side, which are no less than in interstate conflicts, one cannot help finding this situation abnormal. Many voices have been raised to insure respect for the rules in noninternational conflicts. As Vattel wrote in the eighteenth century:

> A flatterer, or a cruel ruler, is quick to say that the rules of war are not made for rebels deserving of extreme penalties. . . . But whenever a large group believes itself entitled to resist the sovereign, and finds itself in a position to take up arms, war between them should be conducted in the same way as between two different nations.

The question, therefore, arises whether the principle of article 3, with automatic entry into force, as soon as certain conditions are objectively fulfilled, cannot equally well be adopted for the rules relating to the conduct of hostilities and the use of weapons.

4.3.4.2. Guerrilla Warfare. This question is of a complicated nature. On one hand, the guerrillas and the population which supports them have recourse to all sorts of methods ranging from a trap to a terrorist attempt on life. On the other hand, such methods are going to encourage the guerrillas' opponents to act similarly. Imagination will devise new weapons, often terribly murderous, and will find a pretext for the use of other weapons and methods which one believed had been finally outlawed by the rules and practice of international law (*e.g.*, gas and torture).

4.4. Recommendations

4.4.1. Reaffirmation of Existing Law. Below are listed some examples of suggested procedures:

> . . . that existing humanitarian texts be interpreted. (By Resolutions of International Conference of the Red Cross, and by the General Assembly or some other organ of the United Nations, for example.)
> *Resolution XVIII* ("Status of Combatants in Non-International Armed Conflicts") of the Twenty-first International Conference of the Red Cross (Istanbul, 1969), asking for treatment similar to that of prisoners of war for combatants captured in an internal conflict, can be regarded as an extensive interpretation of article 3. Similarly, Resolution XXVIII, "Protection of the Civilian Popula-

---

[20] It should be pointed out, however, that art. 3 requires respect for "persons taking no active part in the hostilities," which already implies certain limitations in the conduct of hostilities and the use of weapons. Res. 2444 (XXIII) confirmed that interpretation and recognized "the need for additional humanitarian international conventions or for other appropriate legal instruments to ensure the better protection of civilians, prisoners and combatants *in all armed conflicts* and the prohibition and limitation of the use of certain methods and means of warfare."

tion Against the Dangers of Indiscriminate Warfare," of the Twentieth International Conference of the Red Cross (Vienna, 1965) which was largely embodied in Resolution 2444 (XXIII). "Respect For Human Rights in Periods of Armed Conflict," unanimously adopted by the Twenty-third General Assembly of the United Nations on December 19, 1968, comes entirely under this heading.

. . . that the Parties to a conflict be encouraged (by appeals or by official approaches of the ICRC, for example) to apply extensively and even unilaterally, the existing humanitarian law.

Two requests to belligerents should be recalled in this regard:

> On June 11, 1965, the ICRC sent a communication to the governments of the Republic of Vietnam, the Democratic Republic of Vietnam, the United States of America, and to the National Liberation Front of South Vietnam, calling on them to apply all the Geneva Conventions of 1949, in view of the fact that "the hostilities raging at the present time in Vietnam—both North and South of the 17th parallel—have assumed such proportions recently that there can be no doubt that they constitute an armed conflict to which the regulations of humanitarian law as a whole should be applied.
> On April 4, 1968, in a written approach to the governments engaged in the conflict in the Middle East, the ICRC noted that "no protecting power has as yet been appointed in the conflict between Israel and the neighboring states," adding "[t]hat is a regrettable fact, for the system of the Geneva Conventions is based on the existence of protecting powers, of which the action constitutes an essential guarantee of their strict observance, in particular in the occupied territories," and concluding: "However, the International Committee of the Red Cross will continue, to the full extent of its means and of the possibilities offered to it, to bring its humanitarian aid to the victims of the events."
> . . . that the Parties to the conflict be encouraged to conclude agreements to apply all or part of the four Geneva Conventions (in accordance with the penultimate paragraph of article 3) and even the law of The Hague. Model agreements might be of help in having this suggestion put into effect.

4.4.2. DEVELOPMENT OF THE LAW. There is no doubt that even if much remains to be done to enforce the existing law, and to have it applied, an effort at least as great should be made to remedy its shortcomings even if only its most obvious ones. It has been very rightly observed that the application of the existing law was often hindered by the striking disparity between the present rules and those, still to be codified, which "public conscience" demands ("Reaffirmation," at 7, where the ICRC emphasizes and deplores the considerable "disproportion" between the Law of Geneva and the rules relating to the conduct of hostilities). The best known example of this discrepancy is that of the pilot of a bomber, who, in case of capture, is protected by the Third Geneva Convention, and the civilian population who are the victims of bombardment and are practically without any effective legal protection. That does not mean that there is no legal protection at all, but that it is neither sufficiently precise, nor sufficiently well-known, nor, above all, sufficiently observed. (See the Fourth Hague Convention of 1899 and 1907). One can be certain that the establishment and the application of law protecting the civilian population would help to promote the application of existing rules of protection to captured pilots.

The order in which the three suggestions (listed below) have been set out is no chance matter. It would be possible, on the basis of a model agreement applied in a specific conflict, to induce governments to sign codicils to the Geneva Conventions of 1949 which might serve as valuable bases for new Conventions.

4.4.2.1. *Model Agreements.* A model agreement is of a flexible nature. It can be drafted by a small number of specialists and does not call for the usual ratification procedure required for the adoption of treaties. Such an agreement can also be the subject of discussion and be adapted to each particular case, without thereby laying open to question one or more provisions of the Conventions as a whole. The model agreement does, however, have the disadvantage of leaving the application of its rules to the discretion of the parties, whereas certain humanitarian obligations should be binding on the parties in any situation.

4.4.2.2. *Codicils.* Consideration might be given to a codicil to article 3 making certain articles of the Geneva Conventions applicable in non-international conflicts (such as article 4, as was implicitly proposed in Resolution XVIII at Istanbul). Similarly, one might envisage a protocol embodying the "Vienna principles," possibly supplemented and developed, as formulated in Resolution XXVIII of the Twentieth International Conference of the Red Cross or in Resolution 2444 (XXIII) of the United Nations General Assembly.[21]

4.4.2.3. *New Conventions.* New conventions should eventually be formulated. In speaking of new conventions, no doubt is cast on the value of the texts adopted in 1949, which, in spite of certain gaps or imperfections,

---

[21] The text of these "principles" reads as follows:

   a. the right of the parties to a conflict to adopt means of injuring the enemy is not unlimited;
   b. it is prohibited to launch attacks against the civilian population as such;
   c. distinction must be made at all times between persons taking part in the hostilities and members of the civilian population to the effect that the latter be spared as much as possible;
   d. the general principles of the Law of War apply to nuclear and similar weapons.

It may be interesting to note that the fourth principle (letter d) was omitted in Res. 2444 adopted by the U.N. General Assembly at its 23d session on Dec. 19, 1968.

represent a body of law of great significance of which a complete recasting is not contemplated for the time being.[22]

[22] *See, e.g.,* ICRC's Report to the Istanbul Conference, *Protections of Victims of Non-International Conflicts,* (*supra* note 15, at 11) which states:

> Revision of the Geneva Conventions hardly seems possible for the moment, but consideration could be given to a protocol or other document for approval by the International Conference of the Red Cross which, whilst not having the force of law, would have an important value as a guide.

> As it is stated elsewhere, the ICRC, without waiting any more, will draw up, possibly with expert assistance, standard proposals for the application of the essential provisions of the Geneva conventions.

PART FOUR

COMMON CRIMES AGAINST MANKIND

CHAPTER IX

PIRACY AND TERRORISM

Section 1.   PIRACY: AIR AND SEA[°]

Jacob W.F. Sundberg

1.1. An Introduction to Piracy

The Greek word *peirates* simply meant an adventurer. Adventurers are often no angels and, indeed, such a famous adventurer as Ulysses did, in perfect innocence, many things which today seem criminal.[1] Roman law-books deal only with the pirates' position as outlaws, depriving them of the position of the lawful enemy—*justus hostis*—who made the vanquished his slaves.[2] There is no special text in the Corpus Juris for the punishment of piracy. However, Cicero once said, "pirata non est ex perduellium numero definitus, sed communis hostis omnium."[3] This maxim, normally phrased "pirata est hostis generis humani," has definitely done much to sway judges and lawyers generally against the accused, although more lucid minds have suggested that the assertion was made "not in a way to suggest so much a constituent element of the offence as an epithet of opprobrium which the offence deserves."[4] "Hostis humani generis," observed Tindall, 1693, "is neither a definition, or as much a description of a pirate, but a rhetorical invective to show the odiousness of that crime."[5] Stiel calls it outright nonsense: "nicht mehr als ein Flosk."[6]

A famous pirate named Dionides was caught and brought before Alexander the Great. Alexander asked him why he had arrogated to himself the empire of the seas. Dionides threw the question back, "Why do you yourself sack the earth?" "I am King," said Alexander, "while you are

---

[°] This article was written for this book, but was published first in 20 DePaul L. Rev. 337 (1970) and is reprinted herein in part.

[1] *See* Homer, The Odyssey, bk IX, at 40.

[2] Digest 49.15.19.2; 49.15.24; 50.16.118.

[3] Cicero, De Officiis, lib. III, 29.

[4] Dickinson, *Is the Crime of Piracy Obsolete?*, 38 Harv. L. Rev. 334, 351 (1925) [*citing* Coke, Inst. III, ch. 49; 1 Wynne, Life of Jenkins, 86; Molloy, De Jure Maritimo, Book I, ch. 4, § 1 (6th ed.); 1 Kent Comm. 171–172].

[5] 12 How. St. Tr. 1269, at 1271 n. (1693).

[6] Der Tatbestand der Piraterie Nach Geltendem Völkerrecht, Staats—und völkerrechtliche Abhandlungen bd IV heft 4 (Leipzig, 1905) 42.

455

only a pirate." "What matters the name," replied Dionides. "The business
is the same for both of us. Dionides ravages the ships and Alexander the
empires. If the Gods had made me Alexander and had made you Dionides,
perhaps I would be a better prince than you would be a good pirate."[7]

This story from antiquity has a message for the modern world—it reveals
the razor-thin edge which may separate piracy from other acts of violence.
Indeed, as already noted, Homer shows clearly in his *Odyssey* that he
found nothing criminal in the fact that seafarers descended on the city
of Ismarus, sacked the place, destroyed the males and carried off the
women and the plunder. As was pointed out by Stiel in 1905,[8] the attitude
of the Malayan pirates sentenced to death by the British authorities in
Singapore in 1858 differs little from that of King Agron of Illyria in
229 B.C.—piracy was customary and lawful under the laws of both their
lands. In a certain state of innocence, there is little difference between
piratical behavior and the feuds between princes and city states.[9]

Dionides, perhaps, knew his Odyssey only too well. Even under modern
conditions, it is of limited value to approach the problem of piracy only
from the side of modern, orthodox criminal law. It may be worthwhile
to start from the law of warfare, although more than two thousand years
separate us from Alexander and Dionides.

Articles 14 through 22 of the 1958 Geneva Convention on the High
Seas[10] crowned a number of efforts, which had been initiated during the
days of the League of Nations, to arrive at an international conventional
regulation of piracy. However, the term "piracy" was used in earlier international agreements, such as the so-called antipiracy agreements, which
were entered into in Nyon in 1937.[11] These accords denounce as "piratical"
the acts of submarines, aircraft, and surface vessels in violation of the
rules of naval warfare laid down in the London Naval Treaty of 1930
and the Protocol of November 6, 1936,[12] setting forth the rules as to
the actions of submarines with regard to merchant ships in time of war.
Still earlier, the term "piracy" was used in the so-called Root Treaty of
1922, sometimes also referred to as the Washington Rules.[13] Article III

---

[7] As told in SESTIER, LA PIRATERIE DANS L'ANTIQUITÉ 268 (1880).

[8] *Supra* note 6, at 30 n.1.

[9] A fascinating discussion of the notion of war in the late Middle Ages is offered by Keen,
The Laws of War in the Late Middle Ages, 72–218 (1965).

[10] 450 U.N.T.S. 11.

[11] International Agreement for Collective Measures Against Piratical Attacks in the Mediterranean by Submarines, *signed* Sept. 14, 1937, 181 L.N.T.S. 135; and International Agreement for Collective Measures Against Piratical Attacks in the Mediterranean by Surface
Vessels and Aircraft, *signed* Sept. 17, 1937, 181 L.N.T.S. 149.

[12] Protocol concerning Rules of Submarine Warfare, 173 L.N.T.S. 353.

[13] Treaty on the Use of Submarines and Noxious Gases in Warfare, *signed* Feb. 6, 1922,
in Washington, 1 *Papers Relating to Foreign Relations of the U.S.* 267 (1922). The name
is derived from the American delegate and initiator, Mr. Elihu Root.

denounced certain areas of attack upon and the seizure and destruction of merchant ships and sought to provide for their punishment "as if for an act of piracy." It has been noted that "piracy" in these rules did not mean the same thing as in the Nyon Agreements fifteen years later.[14] The agreement never came into effect, since France refused to ratify it.

The preoccupation with the term "piracy" in these international agreements must, of course, be seen in the context of the British struggle for naval power as well as in the older context of the efforts to make European powers accept having their ships visited and searched on the high seas. In the struggle for naval power, Great Britain had slipped considerably[15] by accepting international law obligations through the Paris Declaration of 1856[16] and the London Declaration of 1909.[17] Attempting to free herself from the fetters thus cast upon her, she had no interest in allowing her enemies to make efficient use of the submarine which had turned out to be a commerce destroyer even more dangerous than the privateer once was and the suppression of privateering was part of the *quid pro quo* which England had gained in hammering out the Paris Declaration. The absence of a right to visit and search vessels of other nations was much regretted by the British when they wanted to implement the recommendation of the Vienna Peace Congress of 1815 that the slave trade be suppressed.[18] As no similar obstacles were raised in relation to the suppression of piracy because the pirate of old was classed as an outlaw, it was realized that whatever could be classed as "piracy" meant rights of visit and search for British men-of-war, hence, the assimilations of slave trading to piracy during the nineteenth century. To use the notion of "piracy" to achieve results which had nothing to do with classical piracy at all became an established international practice.

Historically—both in the treaties and national legislation[19]—while unlawful privateering has been the mainstay of piracy, there are few inherent restrictions on the use of the term. Mutiny was as easily included as excluded and whenever a nation hoped to gain extra advantage, it never hesitated except by the formula "as if" to apply the term to such bizarre things as slave trading or submarine warfare. Also, there is

---

[14] *Supra* note 12. *Piracy in Modern International Law*, 43 Trans. Grotus Soc. 63, 84 (1957).

[15] *See generally* Mahan, *Naval Warfare* in Selections from the Writings of Rear Admiral Alfred T. Mahan 328–41 (A. Westcott ed. 1919).

[16] 15 Nouveau Recueil Général 791.

[17] 7 Nouveau Recueil Général, 3me Série 39.

[18] 165 Eng. Rep. 1464 (1817).

[19] For compilation of national legislations *see generally* 26 A.J.I.L. pt. V (Supp. 1932); Working Draft No. 744–1, Nov. 17, 1969, prepared for the 17th session of the Legal Committee of the International Civil Aviation Organization (ICAO).

nothing inherent in the term which restricts the notion to the sea; it is equally applicable in the skies.

1.2. Capture and Piracy

Historically, the term "capture" applies to seizures, while "piracy" applied to seizure by pirates. Oppenheim stated that "private vessels only can commit piracy. . . . A man-of-war or other public ship, as long as she remains such, is never a pirate. If she commits unjustified acts of violence, redress must be asked from her flag state."[20] Similarly W.E. Hall stated: " 'Piracy' includes acts differing much from each other in kind and in moral value; but one thing they all have in common: they are done under conditions which render it impossible or unfair to hold any state responsible for their commission."[21] And Roxburgh, who edited Oppenheim's treatise after his death, explained that "piracy is a crime which cannot be committed by the authority of any state" because only thereby is it avoided that piracy will "give rise to diplomatic complications."[22] There are, in addition, several reasons why this should be so, apart from the argument put forward by Roxburgh.

One is the idea that international law, in general, and war, in particular, are matters between states only. This was the temporarily successful idea of the enlightenment to which, as Talleyrand explained it to Emperor Napoleon I (Bonaparte), "Europe is indebted for the maintenance and increase of its property even amidst the frequent wars that have divided it."[23] As furthered by Jean Jacques Rousseau and others[24] this was the idea which made the more humane treatment of prisoners of war possible.[25] Consequently, redress for acts of war should be sought from the belligerent country and not from the individuals, and this principle applied a fortiori when violent acts short of war were ordered by one state against another. In this context it is easy to understand the American attitude in the *McLeod* case of the 1840's.

In that case, the American authorities had allowed the gathering, in 1837, on American territory of what later came to be known as a filibuster

---

[20] 1 OPPENHEIM, INTERNATIONAL LAW 341, § 273 (2d ed. 1912).

[21] HALL, INTERNATIONAL LAW 310 § 81 (8th ed. 1924).

[22] Roxburgh, *Submarines at the Washington Conference*, 3 BRIT. Y.B. INT'L L. 150, 155 (1923).

[23] Moniteur Universel, Dec. 5, 1806, No. 339, at 1462, col. 2 (*signed* Berlin, Nov. 20, 1806) (as translated by Bartlett, *Liability for Official War Crimes*, 35 Law Q. Rev. 178 (1919).

[24] 1 CONTRAT SOCIAL.

[25] It is a peculiar twist of history that today, when war is as total as the government being fought against, and consequently the basis of the privileged treatment of prisoners of war has totally disappeared, the privilege as such is still capable to rally enthusiastic support in countries of the Western, non-Communist type.

expedition into Canada which at that time was in a state of rebellion against the British rule. The filibusters planned to enter Canada by means of a tiny steamer called *Caroline* and British forces kept matters under supervision from the Canadian shore. On the night commencing December 29, an expeditionary force under the command of Captain Drew surprised the filibusters on the American side, cut loose the steamer from the dock, set her on fire, and sent her over Niagara Falls. The filibusters and their sympathizers grew wildly indignant about this energetic action in violation of the sanctity of American soil and when, in 1840, Alexander McLeod visited New York on business and happened to boast about his participation in the British expedition, he was arrested and indicted for the killing of the two Americans who had lost their lives in the nightly affray. The diplomatic exchange between Great Britain and the United States which resulted from this incident prompted Daniel Webster, the American Secretary of State, to explain the American attitude to be that "after the avowal of the transaction (*i.e.*, Captain Drew's expedition) as a public transaction, authorized and undertaken by the British authorities, individuals concerned in it ought not . . . to be holden personally responsible in the ordinary tribunals for their participation in it."[26]

The doctrine that a state conduct purges the act committed of its criminality under the laws of the state claiming grievance was restated even after World War II in treatises[27] and cases—among the latter, the case of *Hanswolf von Herder*, decided by the Swedish Supreme Court in 1946.[28] Von Herder was a German citizen and was called up for military service during World War II. As an ordinary soldier he was assigned to the German "Abwehr" in occupied Norway and was there given military intelligence work directed against Sweden. When Germany lost the war, von Herder took refuge in Sweden, was arrested and tried for espionage. Eventually, he was acquitted but expelled from Sweden. Lotika Sarkar explains the outcome of the case in terms of the court "adhering to the territorial principle," referring thereby to the fact that the intelligence work had been carried out in Norway.[29] Professor Gihl, however, considers it difficult to find any reason for the acquittal other "than the fact that von Herder was an officer and had carried out the activity in question in the course of his duties." Having this for a point of departure, Gihl

---

[26] GIHL, *Who is a Spy?*, LEGAL ESSAYS—A TRIBUTE TO FREDE CASTBERG, 230, 235 (1963). For a detailed account of the case, *see* Jennings, *The Caroline and McLeod Cases*, 32 A.J.I.L. 82 (1938).

[27] *See, e.g.,* VERDROSS, VÖLKERRECHT 235 (5th ed. 1964); KELSEN & TUCKER, PRINCIPLES OF INTERNATIONAL LAW 358 (2d ed. 1966).

[28] Von Herder v. Public Prosecutor, Nytt Juridiskt Arkiv 65 (1946); [1946] Ann. Dig. 95.

[29] Sarkar, *The Proper Law of Crime*, 11 INT'L & COMP. L.Q. 446, 452 (1952); *also published in* MUELLER & WISE, INTERNATIONAL CRIMINAL LAW 50, 56 (1965).

indeed considers that it was unlawful for the Russians to convict Francis Powers in September, 1960, for espionage consisting of his flying over Russian territory with an American military U-2 plane for the purpose of collecting information.[30] Powers came down in uniform, his aircraft had United States markings, and the United States officially announced that he had been flying under U.S. orders. Consequently, there was no question about the United States not being responsible for the violation of Soviet territory. But, concludes Professor Gihl: "The United States Government and Powers could not both be responsible at the same time."[31]

A position such as that which Webster took in the *McLeod* case also fits in well with the general expositions of the so-called "act of state" doctrine as stated in the American case *Underhill v. Hernandez.*[32] The doctrine means that "every sovereign state is bound to respect the independence of every other sovereign, and the courts of one country will not sit in judgment on the acts of another government done within its own territory." Indeed, the national court lacks competence to pronounce upon the legality of an act performed by a foreign state and unless the foreign state consents to such a pronouncement, the act must be taken as a fact.[33]

This attitude toward foreign states, however, has not fared well in the development which has taken place in this century.[34] Indeed, the general return, to the idea of a *bellum justum* has dispelled the classic European notion of the *justus hostis* and the fatefully total victories of the one side in the two world wars have allowed the new doctrine to work unfettered of the restraint which the resources of the opposing nations otherwise normally will impose on the victors. The inclination has been to view the world at large in the light of the law as conceived back home and to inflict upon the individuals revenge for lawbreaking which could not be satisfied by dealing with the state. One of the principal instruments in so doing has been the setting aside of the defense of *obedience to superior orders.*[35] It is ironic that most countries which

[30] *Supra* note 26, at 234, 235. Before he was charged with the Chair in International Law in Stockholm, Professor Gihl was legal counsel to the Swedish Foreign Office and served in that capacity during World War II. It is probably a complete mistake to ascribe the outcome of the Herder Case to "the territorial principle" and the reasons will be set out more fully below.

[31] *Id.* at 240.

[32] 168 U.S. 250 (1897).

[33] *See generally* Zander, *The Act of State Doctrine,* 53 A.J.I.L. 826 (1959); Van Panhuys, *In the Borderland Between the Act of State Doctrine and Questions of Jurisdictional Immunities,* 13 INT'L & COMP. L.Q. 1193 (1964).

[34] For previous criticism of the idea that an act cannot be piratical if done under state authority, see Magellan Pirates, 1 SPINK'S ECCL. & ADM. REP 81 (1965) (*decided by* Lushington).

[35] *See* DINSTEIN, THE DEFENCE OF 'OBEDIENCE TO SUPERIOR ORDERS' INTERNATIONAL LAW (1965).

have participated in this turning of the tables, are given to proclaim, as a matter of course, that in case of an unavoidable conflict between a rule of the law of nations and the municipal law of the country in question, the courts should defer to the supreme authority from which they derive their own powers and apply the municipal law. Indignation over enemy warfare and the conviction that the enemy's governmental officials would escape punishment if it were left to their own governments to try them, have contributed to the opposite conclusion in matters of political conflict: international law as interpreted back home takes precedence over the municipal law and orders of the government which the accused had to obey.

The development in this direction was particularly spurred on by pronouncements by the victors' tribunals after World War II and the support which these pronouncements subsequently received from the United Nations, at that time reorganized as a world organization.

1.3. Is Capture by Insurgents Piratical in Character?

Turning now to the case of insurgents, we find that theirs is a case of ever growing importance as the likely disorders of the future are not war or military attack between states but subversion, revolution, insurrection, and civil war.[36]

There have been few uprisings in the course of which the legitimate government has not attempted to brand the insurgent vessels as pirates. There is not much difference to be seen between the British Parliament declaring, on the outbreak of the American revolution, all ships operating in the service of the rebels to be pirates, and the Spanish legitimate government decreeing on July 27, 1936, the Nationalist cruiser *Almirante Cervera* to be a pirate ship which should be treated according to the international law of piracy.[37] Indeed, even the tiny little steamer *Caroline*, active in the abortive American filibuster expedition against Canada of 1837, was branded by the British to be of "piratical character."[38]

A useful example of this development is offered by the American Civil War. When the war broke out, practically the whole regular navy was in

[36] The United Nations Charter bars conquest from the outside (art. 2, para. 4) but—like traditional international law—it does not bar or even address itself to revolution within, whether by constitutional means or by force. *See* Henkin, *Force, Intervention, and Neutrality in Contemporary International Law*, (1963) PROCEEDINGS OF THE AMERICAN SOCIETY OF INTERNATIONAL LAW, 154. It is but natural that tactical and political experts of governments, anticipating a pay-off of lip service to the Charter, will advise force to be applied in furtherance of political aims in the manner not outlawed by the Charter.

[37] Gaceta da Madrid for July 27, 1936, *reproduced in* GENET, DROIT MARITIME POUR LE TEMP DE GUERRE 185 n.270 (1937) (some excerpts translated to English will be found in Genet, *The Charge of Piracy in the Spanish Civil War*, 32 A.J.I.L. 253, 260 (1938).

[38] *Id.* Genet.

Union hands. The Confederates, consequently, had to rely on privateering on the high seas and the American Civil War grew into the last outburst of large-scale privateering.[39] The Union originally charged the prisoners taken from Confederate privateers with piracy,[40] but soon abandoned this policy when it led to retaliatory action on the part of the Confederates. By an order of January 31, 1862, all "pirates" were transferred to military prisons for the purpose "of exchanging them as prisoners of war."[41] The charges were no more successful in neutral courts. In the French *Alabama* Case, decided by the Tribunal de Commerce de Bordeaux on August 8, 1863, the owners of the cargo of the American vessel *Olive Jane*, which had been sunk by the famous Confederate privateer steamer *Alabama* under the command of Captain Semmes, maintained that the *Alabama* was a pirate. The court rejected the claim: "L'Alabama, armé en guerre, portant le pavillon de la Conféderation du Sud, faisant uniquement la guerre au profit du pavillon arboré à bord, ne saurait être considérée comme un pirate."[42]

The conclusion of this state of affairs is drawn by W.E. Hall: "It is impossible to pretend that acts which are done for the purpose of setting up a legal state of things, and which may in fact have already succeeded in setting it up, are piratical for want of an external recognition of their validity, when the grant of that recognition is properly dependent in the main upon the existence of such a condition of affairs as can only be produced by the very acts in question."[43]

The main point in the case of insurgents, however, is not the treatment prepared for the rebels by their adversary, the legitimate government. It is, rather, the attitude taken by third powers. Third powers may consider their own interests only or they may be manipulated to a greater or lesser extent by the parties to the conflict. If a third power were to recognize the parties as belligerents, that would, under the laws of war, imply that both parties have the right of capture on the high seas and above them vis-à-vis the sea and airborne commerce of the recognizing states and can proclaim blockades on the high seas to the detriment of such commerce, not to mention establish war or risk zones on the high

---

[39] The importance of this type of warfare may best be judged by the award of 3,200,000 pounds granted to the United States by the Arbitration Tribunal in Geneva, on Sept. 15, 1872, for Confederate privateers having been permitted the use of British neutral waters. *See generally* 1 Moore, International Arbitration 495–682 (1898), and 4 4057–4178. Scott, Cases on International Law 713–20 (1960) (gives the award).

[40] Calvo, *Examen des trois règles de droit international proposées dans le traité de Washington*, 1874 Rev. Dr. Int. Lég. Comp. 453, 454.

[41] 10. Scott, *supra* note 39, at 350.

[42] Simmonet, Convention sur la haute mer 155 (1966).

[43] *Supra* note 21, at 310.

seas. Often a state is not willing to do this.[44] It is then more tempting not to recognize belligerency, since that confers an illicit character upon naval action against foreign sea or airborne commerce. One main example of this was the attitude of Western nations toward Governmental and Nationalist action in the Spanish Civil War of the 1930's. Some of these nations were happy to outlaw as "piratical" naval action, aimed at preventing the adversary party's importation of contraband.[45] A more recent example has been the United States' attitude toward the war between Communists and Nationalists in China. For political reasons, neither the Chinese (Nationalist-legitimate) government, nor the American government, wanted to concede to the Communist insurgents the prestige and status of belligerents. As a consequence, the Nationalists were deprived of the right to interfere with the sea and airborne commerce of the Communists except within the limits of the Chinese territorial waters.[46] The American Civil War offers an example of the opposite attitude. Great Britain and France almost immediately granted recognition to the contestants in the war as belligerents and this, indeed, made possible the Confederate warfare by means of privateers. The Union government made sophisticated moves to have this weapon outlawed. It proposed a convention with the two powers mentioned by which the United States would accept the Declaration of Paris, 1856, as it stood. The Union interest melted away, however, when the British and French governments intimated that they would attach to their signatures of the convention a declaration which would prevent the convention from having any effect on the warfare of the Confederates.[47]

If the insurgents have *not* been recognized as belligerents, what is the status of their ships cruising the high seas? During the nineteenth century it became a fairly well settled practice in international law that insurgents who interfered with the shipping of a third nation on the high seas (presumably in the exercise of some right equivalent to the right of angary belonging to a belligerent), if apprehended by the warships of such a nation, could be treated as pirates. Instructions to this effect were given to British naval forces in 1873, to American naval forces in 1876,

[44] For a reasoned view, *see* Wilson, *Insurgency and International Maritime Law,* 1 A.J.I.L. 46, 60 (1907).

[45] *Cf.* Genet, *The Charge of Piracy in the Spanish Civil War, supra* note 37, at 262. It may be added that the action by the nations in question appears to have been most efficient inasmuch as the attacks by unknown submarines and aircraft ceased almost immediately. de la Pradelle, *La piraterie aérienne: notion et effets,* REV. GÉN. AIR 299 (1969).

[46] Woolsey, *Closure of Ports by the Chinese Nationalist Government,* 214 A.J.I.L. 350, 354 (1950).

[47] Malkin, *The Inner History of the Declaration of Paris,* 8 BRIT. Y.B. INT'L L. 1, 42 (1927); Hall, *Should the Declaration of Paris, 1856, be revised?* U.S. NAVAL WAR COLLEGE–INTERNATIONAL LAW TOPICS AND DISCUSSIONS 107, 116 (1905).

and to Imperial German naval forces in 1903.[48] Even if Castrén submits that "it seems neither right nor fair to equate insurgents with pirates,"[49] there was little authority until 1958 which seriously challenged this legal qualification of insurgents' naval action against third country shipping.[50] The Harvard Draft (1932) attempted to exclude insurgents' acts from the definition of piracy.[51] This solution, though, would have afforded the insurgents no protection from charges of piracy brought by the affected third country, but only the satisfaction that nonaffected states could not be called upon to hunt them down on the basis of the universal jurisdiction over piracy.[52] When the Convention on the High Seas of 1958 was being prepared, largely on the basis of the Harvard Draft, the debate did not focus on the unrecognized insurgents. A vote was taken to determine whether the words "for private ends" in what is now article 15 of the Convention should be retained. The affirmative vote at least brought about the same result as would have followed from the Harvard Draft. At present, then, the situation would seem to be as follows: A state which does *not recognize* the insurgents as belligerents cannot, under the general international law of piracy, call upon other states to assist in suppressing the naval action of the insurgents against the sea or airborne commerce of the first state; it will have to do so on its own under general principles of self-defense, and even if "the right of self-defense on the high seas in time of peace has at no time received universal approval"[53] the risk would seem minimal to exercise it against ships not flying the flag of any recognized state.[54] But states which do recognize the insurgents as belligerents, on the other hand, need not apply the principles of the Geneva Convention of 1958 to their deeds. If the insurgents' acts are in excess of the law of naval warfare, their captures can be treated as piracy and the law of piracy can be invoked against them.

A complication which ought not to be left out of sight concerns the lower limit of insurgency. The anarchists raised the issue when they

[48] The British directions to the Admiralty of July 24, 1873, are partly reproduced in Stiel, *supra* note 6, at 96 n.1; the United States Navy Regulations of 1876 may be found in 2 MOORE, DIGEST OF INTERNATIONAL LAW 1108 (1904); and the Imperial German "Bestimmungen für den Dienst an Bord" of Nov. 21, 1903, are partly reproduced in Stiel, *supra* note 6, at 96 n.2.

[49] Castrén, *Civil War*, 142 ANNALES ACADEMIAE SCIENTIARUM FENNICAE 2, 131 (1966).

[50] Lauterpacht summarizes the 1947 situation under British and American law as follows: "The preponderant practice of governments, weighty judicial decisions, as well as the majority of writers, seem to favour the view that unrecognized insurgents, if they interfere with the ships of third states or their subjects, may be treated as piratical." RECOGNITION IN INTERNATIONAL LAW 298 (1947).

[51] Art. 16; 26 AJIL Suppl. pt. V (1932).

[52] *Cf.* McDOUGAL & BURKE, THE PUBLIC ORDER OF THE OCEANS 817 (1962).

[53] Brownlie, *The Use of Force in Self-Defense*, 37 BRIT. Y.B. INT'L L. 183, 252 (1961).

[54] *Supra* note 51.

started to appear toward the end of the nineteenth century. They wanted to terrorize society but did not want to govern it. It is presumably with an eye toward this phenomenon that W.E. Hall is unwilling to grant any rights of insurgency to an individual exercising violence upon his neighbor and his neighbor's property, which would raise him above being a pirate, unless he belongs to a group which somehow forms "a politically organized society."[55] Lately, this point has been again stressed by Fenwick commenting upon the *Santa Maria* party of Captain Galvao: "The status of insurgency is not one to be conceded to any and every citizen who believes that the government of his country is tyrannical and should be overthrown."[56] Whether malicious killing, wounding, or destruction is done for "private ends" or not, when the activity is rather individual than collective or when it is rather the expression of discontent with life than of a constructive political message, does not seem to have received any authoritative answer in the Geneva Convention.[57] It is difficult to see that the Convention has added such new elements to the classical problem so that this type of activity must now be privileged. Although in an era characterized more by the absence than by the presence of solidarity between states, the classification is no act of great significance. Obviously this type of activity *can* be piracy under the Geneva Convention.

When the freedom of the sea took form during the seventeenth century, there arose also the problem of whether the sea was simply the arena for all to fight in or, somehow, the framework for orderly cooperation and competition.[58]

Privateering having its heyday in the eighteenth century[59] and needing nothing more than a letter of marque from a belligerent sovereign, the high seas were nearly always affected by whatever war was going on in whatever corner of the earth. Of course, no nation was willing to offer

---

[55] *Supra* note 21, at 311, 312, 313.

[56] Fenwick, *"Piracy" in the Caribbean*, 55 A.J.I.L. 426, 427 (1961).

[57] A survey will be found in McDougal & Burke, *supra* note 52, at 810–12.

[58] *See generally* Nussbaum, A Concise History of the Law of Nations 97 (1950). Grotius' arguments of that day—he was born 1583 and consequently only 22 years old—were perhaps rather cheap: he confused the feudal title of the Spanish with the ownership notion of the Digests and was thereby able to conclude that Alexander Borgia no more than anyone else "plus iuris a alium transferre potest quam ipse habet." *See* Staedler, *Hugo Grotius über die "donatio Alexandri" von 1493*, 1941 Zeitschrift für Völkerrecht 258. De jure praede was left unpublished: publication did not take place until 1868, *see* Schmitt, Der Nomos der Erde im Völkerrecht des Jus Publicum Europaeum 151 (Köln, 1950).

[59] von Martens, Versuch Uber Caper, Feinliche Nehmungen und Insonderheit Wiedernehmungen. Nach Den Gesetzen, Vertragen und Gebrauchen der Europäischen Seemächte (Gottingen, 1795), at 46, concludes from the amount of regulation of privateering in contemporary statutes and treatises that "die 2te Hälfte des 17ten Jahrhunderts die Zeit sey, von welchen der ausgebreiteste und allgemenste Gebrauch der Caper anfängt."

its merchantmen as the prey of the greedy and violent who furthermore, if they exceeded the pattern of lawful privateering, were often held to be pirates. The result was that each nation tried to protect its shipping by arms. In these days, as put by Commander Burdick H. Brittin, "all nations employed substantial portions of their naval forces in efforts directed towards this end," that is to say "as the guardians of the freedom of the seas" and having the suppression of piracy as one of their primary concerns.[60]

Behavior on the high seas thus could be considered from two aspects: (1) what to do when a foreign ship approached and (2) how to approach a foreign ship. The former problem was mainly the one of the merchantman; the second, of the man-of-war. But it might well be the other way around as was illustrated by Lieutenant Colonel A.J. Wrangel commanding the Swedish frigate *Fröja* escorting the famous brig *Maria*.[61]

1.4. The Legal Effects of the Flag: The National Flag

The basic rule of the international law of the sea is that the national flag of a recognized state is a matter of extensive protection by that very state. In times of peace, this general principle forbids any interference with ships of another nationality upon the high seas. In the famous controversy about the Canadian registered rum-running ship *I'm Alone*, which was sunk on the high seas in the Gulf of Mexico by the American revenue cutter *Dexter* on March 22, 1929, the Commissioners appointed by the United States and Canada jointly held that the sinking of the ship "by officers of the United States Coast Guard was . . . an unlawful act" and recommended that the United States apologize to the Canadian Government and pay a material amend in respect of the wrong.[62]

Acts of interference, however, may be justified under powers conferred by treaty.[63] Customary law is believed to accept a general exception to the rule, that a warship is entitled to verify the nationality of any merchant ship it meets at sea.[64] But many countries make the unlawful use of their flag a criminal offense,[65] and it does not seem to be a well-considered solution that foreign warships should have powers to police such a regulation. In the Geneva Convention on the High Seas (art. 22(1)(C)), this

---

[60] BRITTIN, INTERNATIONAL LAW FOR SEAGOING OFFICERS, 85 (1956).

[61] 1 C. Rob. 340 (1799).

[62] 29 A.J.I.L. 329 (1935).

[63] *See, e.g.,* Convention for Regulating the Police of the North Sea Fisheries. 1882, and the Convention Respecting the Liquor Traffic in the North Sea.

[64] Smith, THE LAW AND CUSTOM OF THE SEA 64 (3d ed. 1959).

[65] Under the British Merchant Shipping Act of 1894, § 64, the illegitimate use of the British flag rendered the ship liable to forfeiture, *see* Smith, *supra* note 14, at 64.

right applies only if "there is reasonable ground for suspecting . . . that . . . the ship is, in reality, of the same nationality as the warship."[66]

In times of war, every belligerent warship has the right of visit and search. Every ship on the high seas is subject to this right, however small the conflict upon which the right is based. The only case which may be an exception to the general rule concerns the armed convoy. Although the British in the old days were powerful enough to also insist upon visiting neutral merchantmen in a convoy of neutral warships, and the relative weakness of the neutrals barred them from successfully opposing the practice, it does not require much common sense to see in what situations these practices upon the armed neutrals will doubtless be ending.[67]

The basic rules on the territorial sea is that the warships and public vessels of the littoral state can interfere as they please with foreign ships, unless the latter have a right of innocent passage, a right regulated in the Geneva Convention on the Territorial Sea and the Contiguous Zone, 1958.[68] Under article 14(2) "passage" means any navigation which traverses the territorial sea, to and from the high seas, and to and from internal waters. The passage must not be hampered by the littoral state if it is innocent (art. 15), but it ceases to be so (and to be privileged) if it is prejudicial to the peace, good order, or security of the coastal state (art. 14(4)). The privilege also expires if the littoral state wants to exercise its criminal jurisdiction on board the foreign merchantman if the behavior which is classed as "criminal" by the littoral state "is of a kind to disturb the peace of the country or the good order of the territorial sea" (art. 19(1)) or if it has consequences which extend to the littoral state (art. 19 (1) (a)).

1.5. The Unrecognized Flag: The Jolly Roger

If we turn to the ships sailing under the famous "Jolly Roger" or under the less well known flags of some unrecognized insurgents, we get into the area of the unregistered ships—ships without nationality. The case of the *Asya* is the celebrated illustration of the principle prevailing.[69] In the days of the British mandate of Palestine, the *Asya* made a trip between La Ciotat Bay in France and a port north of Tel

---

[66] This solution partly supports the position advocated by the American Attorney General in the *Virginius Case*, partly derogates from it inasmuch as a suspicion of identical nationality will permit what the Attorney General considered a violation of the American flag. In the latter respect, indeed, as noted by Simonnet: "ce n'est pas une exception, mais une application do le régle qu'en haute mer les narviars ne relèvant que de l'Etat du pavillon." See Simmonet, *supra* note 42, at 181.

[67] *Cf.* Tucker, *The Law of War and Neutrality at Sea*, U.S. NAVAL WAR COLLEGE—INTERNATIONAL LAW STUDIES 334 (1955).

[68] 516 U.N.T.S. 205.

[69] The *Asya*, [1948] Ann. Dig. 115.

Aviv with 733 immigrants to support the Zionist cause in Palestine. Approached on the high seas by the British destroyer *Chequers* on March 27, 1946, the *Asya* hoisted after first showing false colors, the Zionist flag. *Chequers* sent a boarding party which forced the *Asya* to put into Palestine territorial waters. In the subsequent criminal proceedings against her owners, part of the defense to charges of violating a local immigration ordinance was based on the fact that the visit by the *Chequers* was an illegal interference with the freedom of the seas. When the case reached the Privy Council, this defense was brushed aside on the strength of a quote from Oppenheim: "a vessel not sailing under the maritime flag of a state enjoys no protection whatever, for the freedom of navigation on the open sea is freedom for such vessels only as sail under the flag of a state."[70]

The Geneva Convention on the High Seas, 1958, has interfered slightly with this rule. Under article 22(1)(c) of that Convention, a warship is not even entitled to approach an unregistered ship except if there is reasonable ground to suspect that the ship has a nationality which is the same as that of the warship.[71] It is clear, nonetheless, that the unregistered ship is at a loss, since nobody will press its case against the interfering government. This dilemma has repeatedly been illustrated in the course of government attacks on piratical broadcasting installations in European waters in response to their challenge of governmental radio monopolies. Furthermore, it is easy to perceive a tendency to return, by way of "contiguous zones" and the like, to the terrestrian view of the sea. That return means, of course, that the notion of the "international sea" loses out proportionately in the process.[72]

1.6. Policing the Skies

Turning now to aircraft, it is clear that the very technical conditions of flight are such that interference *in flight* is a method of very restricted usefulness. The aircraft has been aptly described as "a tin can in the sky" —you cannot force that tin can to open, you cannot even force it to come down against the will of the pilot in command except by shooting it down. The famous *Maydeck* case[73] arose when a Bulgarian fighter aircraft fired at an El Al airliner which was, by mistake, out of Air Lane Amber 10 between Belgrade and Saloniki (the lane assigned to it under the flight plan) and intruding upon Bulgarian air space: total loss, fifty-eight victims. Sending up fighter aircraft is, therefore, one way

[70] *Id.* at 124; 1 Oppenheim, International Law 546 (8th ed. 1955).
[71] Wright, *Legal Aspects of the U-2 Incident*, 54 A.J.I.L. 836 (1960).
[72] McDougal & Burke, *supra* note 52, at 595.
[73] Revue francais droit aérien 106 (1964); 232 (1965).

to enforce orders to the man in command of the airliner in flight, but it is a kind of brinksmanship. As against a pilot with responsibility for his passengers, it works well. As against a hijacker, it hardly works at all, since he rightly assumes that the fighter pilot will be more considerate to the passengers-hostages than the hijacker intends to be. Perhaps it should be added, too, that the Tokyo Convention of 1963 obliges the contracting states to restore control of the hijacked aircraft to the lawful commander and this cannot reasonably be done by destroying the aircraft with its captive commander.

At this point it may be wise to say a few words on *buzzing* as a means of interfering with aircraft in flight. It is certainly no success. When Trans World Airlines flight 840 was captured by Arab commandos, Israeli fighter aircraft took to the air to buzz it down at Lydda airport (Tel Aviv), and when LOT flight 247 was hijacked by East Germans attempting to escape into West Berlin, two Soviet MIGs tried to buzz it down on the Eastern side of the Iron Curtain. In both cases the technique was of absolutely no avail. The prime concern of the airliner pilots was to keep the hijackers happy and the buzzing simply meant extra difficulties in achieving that goal.

It is clear, then, that the type of police interference discussed in relation to the high seas is largely academic in relation to the skies above them. It is, indeed, difficult to find a case which illustrates problems of *such* interference with aircraft. The only case which has been disputed in aviation concerns the immunity which a charter party would confer upon an aircraft flying over the high seas in relation to the state of registry. This point was raised in the famous *Ben Bella* case in 1956. Here, a French-registered airliner was chartered by a Moroccan airline (Morocco at that time being a French protectorate). On October 22, 1956, in flight over the Mediterranean en route between Rabat and Tunis with Ben Bella and other important Algerian rebels as passengers, the French pilot received orders from the French authorities in Algiers (at that time part of France) to land in Algiers for control. He complied, and the Algerian rebels were seized by the French. Morocco protested against the seizure of a Moroccan plane over the high seas, and an international commission of inquiry and conciliation was set up in Geneva. However, when Morocco became convinced that she could not win, she withdrew her delegation and the commission efforts broke down.[74]

It does not seem altogether unreasonable that the charter party should confer some immunity upon the aircraft over the high seas, particularly if a change of colors of the aircraft is involved. A time-chartered plane

[74] de la Pradelle, *L'enlèvement Aérien des Chefs Fellagah,* 1965 REV. GÉN. AIR, 232–38; Anonymous, *L'affaire du F.OABV,* A.F.D.I., 282–95 (1958).

is often repainted in the colors of the charterer. Lord Wilberforce, explaining the Tokyo Convention Bill to the House of Lords on June 12, 1967, points out that the British criminal jurisdiction under the new legislation extends to "both British registered aircraft and what are known as inter-changed aircraft—that is to say, foreign registered aircraft chartered on demise charter to British operators."[75] It seems reasonable to allow immunity against foreign interference along similar lines. If registry is different from ownership, it seems perfectly clear that the aircraft should be immune from interference by the state of ownership. This is so because the responsibility for the maintenance of the operating quality of the plane stays, under present treaty regulations, with the state of registry, and here, as always in civil aviation, air safety should be the overriding consideration.

What remains to be discussed, then, is simply the right to interfere with the aircraft when it has landed. That problem can be stated in much the same way as its counterpart relative to the territorial sea: To what extent do aircraft have a right to continue the journey without interference from the state of landing?

Recent history is replete with cases showing that under these conditions aircraft enjoy no jurisdictional immunity whatsoever. When an Aeroflot flight on October 31, 1966, made an involuntary stop at Prague because of technical defects, the Czech authorities felt entitled to remove one of the passengers, sought by the Czechs, and to force him to stand trial in Czechoslovakia. When Pan American flight 150 New York-Nairobi made an unannounced refueling stop at Accra on October 29, 1966, the Ghanaian authorities felt entitled to remove from among the passengers the Guinean foreign minister, Luis Benavogui, and his entourage, in order to hold them as hostages. When Air Hanson's air taxi was hijacked, on June 30, 1967, and taken with its passenger Moishe Tshombe to Algiers, the Algerian authorities felt entitled to put him to trial in order to determine whether he should be extradited to the Congo and to detain him until his death two years later.

1.7. The Problem of Jurisdiction

In the *Lotus* case, the Permanent Court of International Justice stated that "the territoriality of criminal law . . . is not an absolute principle of international law and by no means coincides with territorial sovereignty." It further added that international law did not contain any "general prohibition to states to extend the application of their laws and

---

[75] Hansard Parliamentary Debates (5th Ser.) (1967). For a discussion of the notion of *demise* in Anglo-American law, *see* SUNDBERG, AIR CHARTER—A STUDY IN LEGAL DEVELOPMENT, 276–282 (Stockholm, 1961).

the jurisdiction of their courts to persons, property, and acts outside their territory."[76]

The *Lotus* case only crowned a general process toward more extra-territorial application of the criminal law. Even the Anglo-Saxon powers, long shielded by their geographical positions from the rivalries and strains so prevalent on the European Continent, had experienced a need to follow suit. The United States first saw the need to protect its economic structure and competitive system of free enterprise by the extra-territorial application of its antitrust laws.[77] An intent of Congress to encompass acts committed abroad by foreigners was found in the Sherman Act and in section 1546 of the Federal Criminal Code.[78] Indeed, the claims came to be so extensive that even Swedish lawyers, in turn, felt entitled to protest on the basis of international law.[79] An inclination toward greater restraint has lately made itself felt inasmuch as an anti-Lotus Convention was signed in Brussels in 1952.[80] When this convention turned out to be unsuccessful, Article 11 was included in the Convention on the High Seas (1958) in order to reverse the specific holding of the *Lotus* case. These developments, however, have not affected the more general significance of the *Lotus* decision.

The evolution of the attitudes toward piracy during the formative nineteenth and early twentieth centuries shows a divergence of views on the part of the then major actors on the international scene. To the British, for example, the chief problem was to overcome the basic void which they faced when venturing outside the British lands or outside the British ships. Their natural response to the challenge was to rely upon international law for assistance. Others saw it quite differently. The Scandinavians, particularly, had difficulty finding any problem of international law. Their perspective was dominated by a criminal law problem and they saw no reason why this problem should not be mastered in the same way that other criminal law problems were normally mastered: hence the disappearance of piracy as a special crime. It will not be denied that the split opening up between the criminal law proper and the international law rules relating to state jurisdiction made it possible

[76] S.S. "Lotus," [1927] P.C.I.J. ser. A, No. 9.

[77] United States v. Sisal Sales Corp., 274 U.S. 268 (1927); United States v. Aluminum Co. of America, 148 F.2d 416 (2d Cir. 1945).

[78] United States v. Aluminum Co. of America, *supra* note 76; United States v. General Electric Co., 82 F. Supp. 753 (D.N.J. 1949); United States v. Rodriguez, 182 F. Supp. 479 (S.D.Cal. 1960).

[79] *Nordström, Folkrättsliga aspekter pa kontroll av linjekonferenser,* HANDELS-HÖGSKOLAN GÖTEBORG SKRIFTER 6, at 19 (1965).

[80] International Convention for the Unification of Certain Rules Relating to Penal Jurisdiction in Matters of Collision or Other Incidents of Navigation, *signed at* Brussels May 10, 1932, 439 U.N.T.S. 233.

to hold that, as a corollary to the state's obligation to fight piracy, international law exacted a standard of criminal law.[81] Once this standard was met, however, international law ceased to be relevant in the criminal law context.

Today, the extraterritoriality of the international sea commands no excessive respect. Nobody claims that the relations between states be based on some implied Full Faith and Credit Clause. On the contrary, the scene is dominated by concurrent jurisdictions. The high seas themselves are being turned into an arena for conflicts between concurrent jurisdictions; and as to the national air space of the various states, the 1963 Tokyo Convention has done much to include them in that arena. The conflicts to be faced have indeed brought about much adverse comment on the Convention. For instance, Professor Johnson observes: "Whereas in the past there has sometimes been insufficient jurisdiction with regard to crimes committed on board aircraft, there may in the future be too much."[82] Others indicate more pleasure with the aphorism: "Strangely enough, the greater number of ratifying states, the less will be the degree of uniformity accomplished."[83] Indeed, after four centuries with Grotius' idea which tended to blow to pieces the closed community approach, inherited from the Romans, strange results have been arrived at. One may well wonder what those nations which organize their criminal law to be enforced within their narrow state borders but draft it to apply to the world at large are doing. Oblivious to the existence of their neighbors, it appears, each of them lies brooding like a Roman Empire in miniature over its universal rule!

1.8. Is There a Need for a Crime of Piracy?

The problem, thus defined, may be puzzling. After all, it seems a matter of course that it should be criminal to intentionally kill and rob others on the high seas or in the skies above. The problem will, therefore, have to be restated: Is there reason to have a special crime of piracy besides the special provisions against killing, stealing, etc. which are the cardinal points of most penal codes?

This brings us down into that part of legal science which deals with the establishment of crime notions. Is there any element which sets the totality of piracy apart from the total of its parts?

[81] Schwarzenberger, *The Problem of an International Criminal Law*, 3 Curr. Leg. Prob. 263, 269 (1950).

[82] Johnson, Rights in Air Space 79 (1965).

[83] Gutierrez, *Should the Tokyo Convention of 1963 Be Ratified?* 31 J. Air L. & Com. 1, 10 (1965).

Two points here require attention. One is the usefulness of the very word "piracy" with its possible sociopsychological appeal. The other is the international element in the crime of piracy as it appears in most texts, national and international. Let us treat them one at a time.

Obviously, a stigma attaches to the word "pirate", for we need only recall here the efforts at the Washington Conference, in 1922, and at the Nyon Conference, in 1937. It is apparent that the stigma which follows from being branded as a "pirate" is useful for propaganda purposes. But is that not enough to secure its use also when municipal law fights crime?

Name-calling performs an important function in structuring society to abide by the law. This function is known in most of the Western World by the title of the "stigma" theory.[84] The general public indeed tends to look at the label or name of the "crime" and the penalty affixed thereto rather than its elements or the offender. To that extent, there is justification for a separate crime of "piracy."[85]

The second point which would seem to set piracy apart from the sum of its parts is the *international element* which it encompasses. It is a fair guess that the idea which made all nations accept that any one of them could assume the right to visit and punish a pirate ship, when the doctrine of the freedom of the seas was consecrated, was the desire to protect the freedom of navigation to which the pirate constituted a threat. Today's expression of this idea is to be found in article 14 of the Geneva Convention of 1958, requiring all states to cooperate to suppress piracy. The idea that all states have a vested interest in freedom of navigation turns the creation of the crime of piracy into the protection of an interest other than the ones which are protected by such criminal provisions as those relating to killing, robbing, stealing, coercion, etc. To the extent that the crime can be identified by the interest it protects, there exists a case for a separate crime of piracy.

One may wonder, though, if the notion of piracy as defined in the Geneva Convention really coincides with the international element it is believed to protect. Unlike the interest in freedom of navigation on the high seas the interest in civil aviation extends far beyond the activities which take place on the international sea, occasionally overflown by civilian airliners. If piracy is associated with aviation it is consequently hard to explain why it should be limited to the airspace above the international sea. Such a limitation is highly artificial, for after all, the speed

---

[84] *See generally* Shoham, Crime and Social Deviation, ch. 3 (1966).
[85] de la Pradelle, *Les Detournements d'aéronefs et le droit international*, 1969 Revue Générale Aerienne 249.

of modern aircraft is such as to render it almost ridiculous to attach decisive weight to the fact that an incident took place on this or that side of an invisible state border in the air. The flight, as such, is the natural unit: whether the hijackers entered the cockpit while the aircraft was over Sorrento or the Mediterranean; whether the shooting started while the aircraft was still in Spanish air space or outside of it, seems immaterial to a layman.

Air safety, not the freedom of navigation, is the interest which should be protected in civil aviation. The extent to which that interest is threatened by aerial hijacking has been a central point in public discussion lately.[49] The risks which go with a hijacking are very real indeed. A recent example is the hijacking on March 17, 1970, of an Eastern DC-9 in the shuttle service between Newark and Boston. After a cockpit struggle that left the copilot dead and a passenger seriously wounded, the pilot shot in both arms, landed the craft. An even more evil end was put to Cubana Airways flight Miami-Havana on November 3, 1958, at the time when the Batista rule of Cuba was drawing to a close. Castro supporters hijacked the plane and forced the pilot to land on a strip of the beach at Panto Cigarro which resulted in the airliner crashing into the Bay of Nipe. There were seventeen deaths.[86]

The manifest risks which accompany hijacking (whether considered as piracy or something else) are a matter of international concern. At the present stage of international travel, passengers of any nationality fly with aircraft of any nationality. The multitude of nationalities among the passengers using a modern commercial airliner, whether in international or in domestic aviation, makes every safety hazard a matter of international concern. This concern found early expression in article 12 of the Chicago Convention in 1944.[87] This article calls upon all contracting states to "insure the prosecution of all persons violating the regulations," *e.g.* the rules and regulations relating to the flight and maneuver of the aircraft. Incidentally, this article calls for prosecution of hijackers as well. It is difficult to imagine a hijacker taking command of the aircraft without violating, in the course of his action, the pilot-in-command's obligation to stick to his prefiled flight plan.[88]

Two elements have thus been found which set the totality of piracy apart from the total of its parts—a perfect name and an international element. There is no reason why these two elements should not be combined into a new notion of air piracy which would effectively combat the extraordinary hijacking fad which the world has experienced lately.

---

[86] *Time Magazine* 28 (Nov. 10, 1958); 190 Revue Francaise de droit Aerien 123.

[87] 15 U.N.T.S. 295 (1944).

[88] Chicago Convention, *supra* note 87, Annex 2; 2.3.1; 3.3.1.1.1., & 3.5.2.1.

1.9. Crimes Committed in Foreign Jurisdictions or Affecting Foreign Interests and National Policy

The state of hostility which marks the present age may not be peculiar to this age alone. One may doubt whether any previous age really was free from it. Still, it appears in retrospect that the late nineteenth century Europe was markedly different even in that particular respect.

Those were the days of optimistic and semipacifist liberalism. There was a firm belief in the steady progress of mankind toward some kind of Utopia. To the delegates at the contemporary peace conferences it seemed "that all European governments were fundamentally the same and differed only in details. War, even if it could not be altogether avoided, was in essence a regrettable interruption of the normal order."[89] Countries were not regarded as enemy countries when no war was in progress. A citizen was normally free to leave his country and start a fresh life in another. Indeed, the whole immigration to the United States was built upon this assumption.

Such a state of things, of course, should be congenial to the ideas of solidarity between states and, in particular, to solidarity in carrying on the universal fight against crime. A foreign crime was an evil just as much as a domestic one: "une collaboration entre etats pour la réalisation de la justice" was the matter called for.[90] Universal fight against crime must mean that crime is punished where possible and that overlapping of jurisdiction is not allowed to disturb the working of the penal law. As a technical matter, it meant some variation of the principle *aut dedere aut punire*.[91] This makes the principle of political asylum much of a test case in the evolution. The evolution, however, has been most complicated because simplicity is marred by numerous crosscurrents from other sources.

Solidarity between states was marred already at the outset by minor political differences. The difference between monarchism and republicanism is an example. Republican Switzerland, for instance, was unable to appreciate that the Emperor of France needed particular criminal law protection of his life and, consequently, refused to accept the Belgian *attentat clause*.[92] The solidarity between the states was also dis-

---

[89] Smith, Book Review, 7 INT'L COMP. L.Q. 792 (1958).

[90] PAPADATOS, LE DÉLIT POLITIQUE, 66 (Genève, 1954).

[91] *See* BASSIOUNI, *International Extradition and World Public Order: A Conceptual Evaluation*, AKTUELLE PROBLEME DER INTERNATIONALEN STRAFRECHT (Oehler & Potz eds. 1970); BASSIOUNI, *Rapporto di sintezi*, PRE-CONGRESSO DI DIRITTO PENALE INTERNAZIONALE DI SIRACUSA (Siracusano ed. 1969); Wise, *Some Problems of Extradition*, 3–4 REVUE INTERNATIONALE DE DROIT PENAL 518 (1968), reprinted in 15 WAYNE L. REV. 709 (1968); Bassiouni, *International Extradition in the American Practice and World Public Order*, 36 TENN. L. REV. 1 (1969).

[92] PAPADATOS, *supra* note 90, at 68.

turbed by the odd effects of the principle of nonintervention. Nonintervention, of course, means that one state will not organize rebel movements
in neighboring countries. But it also means that one state will not apply
domestically the legislation of a foreign country. Extradition proceedings
invariably involve the expression, even if only indirectly, of an opinion
on the internal affairs for the foreign state; an outright application of
foreign legislation would of necessity do so even more. The more political the legislation is, the greater the potential risk of such an opinion.
It can be argued that avoiding the expression by suppressing extradition
altogether is a tribute to the sovereignty of the foreign state.

In the nineteenth century, the right to seek and be granted asylum
abroad for political crimes was formulated as a general rule: "ce fut par
la Révolution de juillet 1830 en France que l'asile politique trouva pour
la première fois sa consécration définitive en Europe."[93] In a way, however, the exceptions to this rule reveal the state of solidarity between
nations. The Belgian *attentat clause* was considered by Hudson to be
one of the expressions of "the common interest of all peoples of the modern world in the administration of criminal justice."[94] It arose from the
attempt to kill Emperor Napoleon III which was made by Celestin Jacquin in September, 1854. Jacquin escaped to Belguim;[95] this led to a
treaty between Belgium and France of March 22, 1856, establishing this
so-called *clause belge d'attentat.* Belgium, born out of the 1830 revolutions and being, not unnaturally, the very first country to give the principle of political asylum statutory form (1833), undertook by that treaty
to except from the notion of the political crime the attempt upon the
life of a head of state or a member of his family.[96] The solidarity between states in this respect, perhaps, reached its summit with the signing in 1937 of the convention for the prevention and punishment of acts
of political terrorism.[97] The signatory states were prepared to reject the
idea of foreign crime as a national asset vis-à-vis a wide spectrum of
acts. By that time, however, most of the earlier assumption of a common
culture was no longer true.

New forces had been brought to life when democracy spread to the
masses and perverted into totalitarianism, a totalitarianism which placed
militant faith in its economic system, whatever happened to be its contents. Not all of these systems survived World War II. The one which
did reflects profound transformation of the issues at stake. "La loi du

---

[93] Papadatos, *supra* note 90. *Id.* at 64; *cf. also* 1 Oppenheim, International Law 697
(8th ed. Lauterpacht 1955).

[94] Hudson, *The Proposed International Criminal Court*, 32 A.J.I.L. 553 (1938).

[95] *See generally* 1 Oppenheim, *supra* note 59, at 709.

[96] Law concerning extradition, Oct. 1, 1833. On the "attentat clause," *see, e.g.,* H. Lam-
masch, Das Recht der Auslieferung Wegen Politscher Verbrechen 74–81 (1884).

[97] L.N. Doc./C.546/M.383 (1937).

régime sociétique"—said an authoritative Soviet textbook on criminal procedure of 1936—"est une directive politique, et le rôle du juge [est] . . . de l'appliquer d'une manière vigoureuse comme l'expression de la politique du parti et du gouvernement."[98] In perfect harmony with this view, the Soviet Penal Code contains 105 articles on political crime and only forty-five for crimes affecting individuals only.[99] Among the crimes peculiar to the Soviet political order are to be found economic crimes,[100] such as the production of defective goods. Nearly every criminal activity is thus, according to one opinion, political in character. This is coupled with a renaissance of the principle of intervention. It is misleading to attach too much significance to such denunciations of active interventions as were made in the 1930's—the acceptance of the United States (with qualifications) of the principle of nonintervention at the Montevideo Conference in 1933, or the signing of the League of Nations sponsored Convention for the Definition of Aggression in London during the same year.[101] Nor is the experience under the United Nations much different. "Today everyone still persists in asserting that nations must not intervene in the internal affairs of other nations, and governments continue to accept this principle as law . . . but in regard to the fundamental and dramatic issues of political change, there is no indication that these principles have much relation to the conduct of nations."[102] Not only are the super-sovereign powers apt to intervene in other states' affairs shielded by the power of veto in the Security Council, but even the semi-sovereign, medium and small powers are also inclined to play the game if only they can avoid the censure of the superpowers. On various grounds, immune against judicial review, it is possible even for a professedly neutral country like Sweden (which furthermore is allied with Portugal in the European Free Trade Area) to openly support the formation of rebel movements for warfare in the Portuguese territories in Africa.[103]

[98] PAPADATOS, *supra* note 90, at 107.

[99] *Id.* at 106.

[100] By "economic crimes" appears to be meant "toutes les activités pouvant compromettre directement ou indirectement l'ordre économique et la réalisation des plans quinquennaux." PAPADATOS, *supra* note 90, at 117.

[101] 147 L.N.T.S. 79, 211. The latter said in an annex to art. 3 that no act of aggression could be justified on the grounds of the internal conditions of a state.

[102] Henkin, *Force, Intervention and Neutrality in Contemporary International Law*, 1963 PROCEEDINGS OF THE AMERICAN SOCIETY OF INTERNATIONAL LAW 156.

[103] According to a letter of Feb. 6, 1970, received from the Information Unit of the Swedish International Development Authority, the Swedish Government has allotted about $90,000 to aid the civilian part of the FRELIMO organization during each of the accounting years 1968–69 and 1969–70. According to the same letter another rebel movement, PAIGC, in Guinea-Bissay will receive during the latter accounting year support in the form of goods worth about $200,000.

1.10. Hijacking: An International Crime

In such an atmosphere, it is misleading to view criminality in general
and hijackings in particular only in the context of grave offenses which
it is the common interest of all nations to suppress. Too often foreign
crime is viewed as a national asset to be encouraged rather than suppressed. It is, in particular, considered of benefit to one state to lure defectors from another state and it is logical to offer such defectors asylum.
Thus, even the taking of ships or aircraft in the course of such defections
may be overshadowed by the political context. Indeed, it was a hijacking
case which brought the change out into the open.

On October 17, 1951, a Yugoslav airliner was hijacked in flight between
Ljubljana and Belgrade by one of its pilots cooperating with one of the
passengers. Having forced the radio operator to continue regular traffic
and having fired a gun at the mechanic to keep him out of the cockpit,
they flew the aircraft to Zurich-Kloten in Switzerland. Yugoslavia demanded their extradition and could hope for a favorable reply under
a strict interpretation of the Serbian-Swiss extradition treaty of November
28, 1887.[104]

It should be noted that the Swiss extradition practice is of special
significance, for even Oppenheim admits that "the firm attitude" of
Switzerland contributed to the result that the principle of nonextradition
of political criminals "conquered the world."[105] The Extradition Act which
Switzerland passed in 1892 attempted a new departure in determining
whether a common crime was political or not. Article 10 of the act refuses to grant political asylum in case the chief feature of the offense
wears more the aspect of an ordinary than of a political crime,[106] but
abstains from further definition or description and leaves the matter with
the Federal Tribunal (*Bundesgericht*, the highest Swiss court). In the
hammering out of the Swiss attitude, and probably with a keen eye
toward the anarchist ways of terrorizing society without wanting to
govern it, the Swiss court had arrived at the rather restricted view that
the crime, if political, must have been committed in the framework of
a struggle for political power and been directed toward the immediate
realization of political ends.[107] Apparently, the hijackers could not meet
such a test. The Court then deviated from the prior case law and emphasized the fact that there were states in which all opposition was so ruth-

[104] *In re* Kavic, Bjelanovic & Arsenijevic 78(1) BGE 39; (1952).
[105] OPPENHEIM, *supra* note 93, at 706.
[106] *Id.* at 709.
[107] German original: "[D]ass die Handlung in Beziehung zu einer unmittelbar auf die Ver-
wirklichung gewisser politischer Ziele gerichteten allgemenen Aktion stehe." *Cf. In re* Ficorilli,
59(1) BGE 136, 146 (1933), [1933] ANN. DIG. 369; *In re* Ockert, 77(1) BGE 57, 62 (1951),
7 I.L.R. 345 (1951).

lessly suppressed that there could be no struggle for political power in the sense of the prior case law and that in such states escape for political reasons must be equalized with participation in a political struggle.

This Swiss case set the pattern for subsequent extradition decisions. The escape of seven members of the crew of a Polish trawler, fishing in the North Sea, to Whitby, England, in September, 1954, by means of seizing the vessel, resulted in asylum being granted to the sailors—although it is not easy to identify the exact grounds for the court's refusal to extradite. From this case[108] J.A.C. Gutteridge says, "there has emerged an adaptation of the conception of an offense of a political nature to the circumstances of a world in which there exist states where all opposition is so ruthlessly suppressed that there can be no question of two parties in the state in open competition with each other."[109] The German Federal Constitution of 1949 provides (Art. 16[2]) that "the politically persecuted shall enjoy the right of asylum." On February 4, 1959, the German Constitutional Court was called upon to interpret this rule in relation to a Yugoslav seeking to avoid extradition to his home country. (Not without reason, since he had, during his sojourn in West Germany, joined a Royalist Serbian organization, and, furthermore, cooperated with Wehrmacht during the war.) The Court found that the protection "is not confined to so-called political offenders . . . [but] applies also to persons who are being persecuted for nonpolitical offenses 'where such persons, if extradited, would be liable in their home country to suffer measures of persecution involving danger to life and limb or restrictions of personal liberty for political reasons.' "[110]

In 1961, however, the Swiss Court retreated slightly in the *Ktir* case[111] concerning the extradition of an Algerian rebel who had murdered a supposed adversary ("traitor"). The gravity of the crime was heavily weighted, and the Court, failing to find some positive political interest, held the crime was extraditable. "It had not been shown that the interests of the FNL were so gravely impaired by the alleged treason that to 'suppress' him was the only means to safeguard these interests."

What, then, does the political context, reinforced by the state of hostility now surveyed, mean to the legal hijacking problem? It may be wise at first to estimate the relative importance of the political element. Looking at the nature of hijackings, it is natural to distinguish between classical robbery, guerilla warfare acts, and escape cases. The great majority

[108] R. v. Governor of Brixton Prison *ex parte* Kolczynski, [1955] 1 All E.R. 31 I.L.R. 240 (1954).

[109] J.A.C.G., *The notion of Political Offences and the Law of Extradition*, 31 BRIT. Y.B. INT'L L. 430, 434 (1954).

[110] 9 BVerfG 174, 180; 28 I.L.R. 347, 349–50 (1959).

[111] Ktir v. Ministère Public Fédéral, 1961(1) BGE 134 (1961), 34 I.L.R. 143 (1961).

of cases belong to the last category. Even with due allowance for a great number of mental cases among them, the hijackers' choice of destination infects all these escape cases with a political element. The hijackers always select a political adversary of the state to which the victimized airline belongs. The political element is therefore one of the most important in the hijacking problem.[112]

Let us first approach the problem of *unlawfulness*. It is often assumed, *e.g.* in the Geneva Convention on the High Seas, that there exists a body of law common to all nations: indeed the existence of a world law doctrine of universal application, and that the test of "unlawfulness" is a mere "technicality." Unfortunately, this assumption by no means always holds true. To take such an abstract view of the requirement of unlawfulness tends only to obscure some very real conflicts in a world where there is no Full Faith and Credit Clause to control the attitude of nations toward one another. In some legal areas the applicable laws are in such direct conflict that there can be no question of common fight against crime: There is no area of overlapping penal provisions and no area of double incrimination.

This statement calls for illustrations. An excellent example is provided by the Tschombe hijacking in 1967. For all that we know, Tschombe was a murderer and thief in the eyes of the Algerian Supreme Court.[113] It is an almost universal rule that persons other than officials of criminal justice have the right to make an arrest under certain circumstances. In some places, the gravity of the crime determines a private person's powers of arrest.[114] In other places, the existence of a general arrest warrant opens up the opportunity for private enterprise.[115] It may be assumed that the Algerian law followed similar principles. But if so, the Algerian authorities had every reason to look favorably upon the hijacker who had, upon his own initiative, arrested a murderer and thief and brought him, together with some of his presumed accomplices—the British pilots—to justice. The hijacking would thus be part of a lawful arrest of a criminal.

[112] Bassiouni, *Ideologically Matured Offenses and the Political Offence Exception in Tradition—A Proposed Judicial Standard for an Unruly Problem,* 19 DE PAUL L. REV. 217 (1969).

[113] The extradition proceeding against Tshombe before the Algerian Supreme Court was secret, the decision was never published, and only more or less informed press reports as to the views taken are available. *See generally* KEESING'S CONTEMPORARY ARCHIVES 1967, at all. 22.187; TIME MAGAZINE 47 (July 28, 1967).

[114] BASSIOUNI, CRIMINAL LAW AND ITS PROCESSES 348 (1969); DEVLIN, THE CRIMINAL PROSECUTION IN ENGLAND 14 (1960).

[115] The SWEDISH CODE OF PROCEDURE, ch. 24, § 7, provides that if a person is "wanted for an offense" every private person is entitled to apprehend him. Tshombe was sentenced to death *in contumaciam* by a Congolese court and presumably was "wanted" by the Congolese state.

It has been countered that "a state's powers of law enforcement are part of its territorial sovereignty and, like its territorial sovereignty, they come to an end at the state's frontiers." The argument goes on to say that abductions in aeroplanes "are, in principle, no different from abductions on board ships and are subject to the same legal rules as if they had occurred on foreign territory."[116] Since the Tokyo Convention, 1963, has destroyed even the very modest attempt made in the Transit Agreement of 1944 to establish some sort of jurisdictional immunity for aircraft this argument is more of an *avant garde* lawmaking venture than a true rendering of the law as it stands. The argument also suffers from the failure of the English law, as interpreted in *R. v. Martin*, to provide a complete legal regime for aircraft over the high seas. That may have made it difficult even for the British to find the Tschombe hijacking criminal.[117]

Consequently, in such areas of direct conflict between two legal systems, it is impossible to express any opinion of unlawfulness except in relation to one chosen legal system. This view places a certain premium upon the state which, for political reasons, is willing to promulgate, as an accessory to its criminal law, legislation for the capture of airliners (or people or property in them), outside of the state's territory. Unless one is prepared to accept the international sea and the airspace above it as an expanse of lawlessness, it seems hard to deny that this is a theoretical possibility.

Let us now turn to the area of double (multiple) incrimination, that is to say, where the legal systems involved are overlapping and all brand the hijacking as criminal conduct.[118] The crime thus created should, of course, be punished wherever committed and jurisdictional issues should not be allowed to disturb the working of the penal law. Indeed, this is the area of the universal fight against crime. As a technical matter, however, this fight remains related to the parcellisation of jurisdiction in a system of concurrent jurisdictions. The classical and indeed the only practical way to carry it out is by application of some variant of the principle *aut dedere aut punire*. When the criminal is apprehended, the apprehending government is liable either to extradite him to the country the laws of which he has violated initially, or to punish him within its own jurisdiction.

At this stage it may be useful to consider briefly how political control is exercised over law enforcement. In many countries, if not most, there

---

[116] 1967 BULLETIN OF THE INTERNATIONAL COMMISSION OF JURISTS, NOS. 24 & 32.

[117] *Id.*

[118] Bassiouni, *International Extradition in American Practice and World Public Order*, 36 TENN. L. REV. 1 (1969).

is something equivalent to the power of the British Attorney General to enter a *nolle prosequi* and it is an accepted principle that the rule is not that the suspected criminal offense should automatically be the subject of prosecution, but that there should be ample room for considerations affecting public policy.[119] While Sweden is one of the relatively few countries which adhere to the opposite principle, this adherence is more lip service than hard fact. Prosecution for a crime committed outside of Sweden may—with certain exceptions—be instituted only pursuant to an order from the King or from someone authorized by the King to give such order.[120] The very purpose of this provision is to allow considerations of general policy to prevail.

Returning to the principle *aut dedere aut punire* it is apparent that within the sphere of application of that principle there is no room for any political control over law enforcement. This is what creates the problem: The state has tied its own hands.

Until December 16, 1970, the only system suppressing hijacking which had progressed into a signed convention—indeed, it even received one ratification (India) before it was swept out of the area of interest by World War II—was the one which is found in the Convention for the Prevention and Punishment of Terrorism, 1937.[121] True, it only included rare types of hijackings (such as Operation Abu Thalaat) because it was more directed against armed attacks on aircraft and aircraft sabotage

[119] See DEVLIN, *supra* note 115, at 17–20.

[120] PENAL CODE ch. 2, §§ 2 & 5.

[121] This convention was intended to cover terrorist acts which compromised the safety of the air traffic of several contracting states, provided that the enterprise operating the traffic was owned by the state or at least franchised by it. The greatest limitation of the area of application would seem to follow from the requirement of an intent behind the terrorist act to "create a state of terror in the minds of particular persons, or a group of persons or the general public" (art. 1, para. 2). Outside the area of the guerilla warfare of the Palestinian commandos, it would seem comparatively rare to find acts of hijacking which are covered by this requirement. On the scope of the Convention in respect to franchised air services, see art. 2, para. 2, and the comments thereto by Donnedieu de Vabres (de Vabres, *La Répression International du Terrorisme*, 1938 REV. DR. INT. LÉG. COMP. 37, 46). The ICAO draft convention on hijacking proceeded on the assumption that no absolute obligation to prosecute should be imposed on the contracting states (see Legal Committee minutes from 17th session, ICAO Doc. 8877-LC/161 at 69, cf. 51 & 52). At the Hague Diplomatic Conference in Dec. 1970, attempts by, in particular, the American Delegation to have an absolute obligation to prosecute substituted for this assumption finally ended in the compromise twenty-seven nations formula which recurs in art. 7 of the Convention for the Suppression of Unlawful Seizure of Aircraft (Dec. 16, 1970): "to submit the case to its competent authorities for the purpose of prosecution." This formula is believed to move the possible decision *not* to prosecute to the level of the grand jury in the United States and to the level of the Attorney General in England. The formula seems to entail a less strict obligation to prosecute than the formula in art. 9 of the Terrorism Convention: "shall be prosecuted and punished in the same manner as if the offence had been committed on that territory." For some information on the Inter-

and only hijackings *ejusdem generis* were covered.[122] It did, however, come to grips, energetically, with the political element in the crime picture and it was, at the time when it was opened to signature, able to rally the support of states which have since become very important in the hijacking picture, namely Cuba and Egypt, and furthermore Greece, Turkey, the Soviet Union, and France. In many respects, it is therefore more profitable to deal with this Convention than with the Hague Convention for the Suppression of Unlawful Seizure of Aircraft, signed on December 16, 1970. The latter closes its eyes to the problems resulting from the political element.[123] Its chances of success are for practical reasons dependent upon the favorable attitudes of the states in the target areas into which most hijackings go. But such attitude can be forthcoming only if you can teach these states to believe that the political problems do not exist.

Under the Terrorism Convention, the terrorist activities, as defined in the Convention, were to be made extraditable crimes between the contracting states, but the state asked to extradite was entitled to make the

---

national Air Transport Association, *see e.g.,* Sheehan, *The IATA Traffic Conferences,* 7 Sw. L. J. 135-84; Guinchard, *International Air Transport Association,* 2 ANNUAIRE FRANCAIS DE DROIT INTERNATIONAL 602–72 (1956); Rinck, *Interessengemeinschaften und Kartelle im Luftverkehr,* FESTSCHRIFT FÜR OTTO RIESE (Karlsruhe, 1964). The Civil Aeronautics Board attitude to the IATA Conference Resolutions is evidenced in 1949 U.S. Av. R. 362 and 1950 U.S. Av. R. 310. For a more general critical view of the organization, *see* PILLAI, THE AIR NET: THE CASE AGAINST THE WORLD AVIATION CARTEL (1969).

[122] Art. 1, para. 2: "In the present Convention, the expression 'acts of terrorism' means criminal acts directed against a state and intended or calculated to create a state of terror in the minds of particular persons, or a group of persons, or the general public." Under art. 2, contracting states undertook to make a criminal offence of the following acts, if they were directed against another contracting state and if they constituted acts of terrorism: "Wilful destruction of, or damage to, public property belonging to or subject to the authority of another high contracting party." As already noted by Donnedieu de Vabres (*La repression internationale du terrorisme,* 37 REVUE DE DROIT INTERNATIONAL ET DE LÉGISLATION COMPARÉE 46 (1938)) the convention covered terrorist acts which compromised the safety of the air traffic or several contracting states, provided that the enterprise operating the traffic was owned by the state or at least franchised by it. Among recent cases of armed attacks on aircraft which would be per se subject to the convention, if in force, may be mentioned the attacks in Athens, Dec. 26, 1968, and in Zürich, Feb. 18, 1969, both against El Al aircraft. Among recent cases of aircraft sabotage likely to fall under the same convention if in force, may be mentioned the sabotaging of Swissair flight 303 and Austrian Airlines flight 402 on Feb. 21, 1970; as well as the sabotaging of Iberia flights 411, 423, & 511 on May 10, 1970.

[123] The text in art. 7 of the Hague Convention was most carefully drafted (avoiding a previously discussed formula which allowed the alternative decision *not* to prosecute) so as to prevent the exercise of a discretionary power of *Nolle prosequi.* When Schmidt-Räntsch, *Die internationale Luftrechtskonferenz in der Haag und das Abkommen zur Bekämpfung der widerrechtlichen Inbesitznahme von Luftfahrzeugen,* 20 Zeitschrift für Luftrecht und Weltramrechtsfragen 63, at 92 (1971)—as well as the draftsmen behind the corresponding Government Bills in Norway and Sweden-advance the opposite thesis, this may reflect sentiment in certain delegate groups but certainly was not voiced openly at the Conference.

extradition subject to any conditions and limitations recognized by the law or the practice of that state (art. 8). Should extradition fail by reason of such condition or restriction, the state concerned undertook to punish the perpetrators of the criminal acts as if they had been committed within the state territory (arts. 9 & 10).

Donnedieu de Vabres has characterized the Convention on Terrorism as "réaliste et transactionnel".[124] He based this judgment on the way in which the political issue was confronted and mastered. It was anticipated that mutually hostile states participating in this joint fight against crime, at times, must be very embarrassed. Such embarrassment could easily follow from the hard choice between, in the case of extradition, "soumettre l'inculpé à des juridictions étrangères dont il redoute la partialité", and, in the case of a domestic trial, "s'exposer . . . à l'aléa d'une sentence grosse, peut être, de complications: acquittement scandaleux, condamnation injustement sévère que dictera à des juges populaires une opinion ignorante et surexcitée."[125] The solution here provided, indeed the feature which substantiates the characterization just made, was the faculty to refer the whole proceeding to an international penal court, set up under a twin convention.[126] Donnedieu de Vabres' point may be found in the obvious parallel to Pontius Pilate facing the tumultuous crowd. Getting rid of the embarrassing case the government in trouble can say, as the old Roman when he washed his hands before the multitude: "I am innocent of the blood of this just person." (Matthew 27:24.)

Relating this to present-day conditions, it may be seen that the problem has two sides—extradition and domestic trial. As to *extradition*, the situation has been surveyed some pages ago, and unless the hijacking has included some especially grave crime with vicious motives, most countries which are likely to get involved in this type of criminality are inclined to grant asylum. As to *punishment*, following trials in the state's own courts, a recent sequence of European cases displays a rising reaction against aerial hijackings. There are several contemporary cases wherein the issue of asylum and the political offense exception arise. These cases do not challenge either of these principles, but reveal that punishability can exist notwithstanding these principles. These cases do not relate to special crime of air hijacking, or air piracy, but rather to a combination of other crimes, the sentences for them during the mid-1960's were fairly uniformly reached at the level of two years imprisonment or more. The Olympic hi-

---

[124] *Donnedieu de Vabres, supra* note 121, at 61.

[125] *Id.* at 60.

[126] Convention for the Creation of an International Criminal Court, 1937. For English text, see 7 HUDSON, INTERNATIONAL LEGISLATION 878 No. 500. *Cf* Hudson, *The Proposed International Criminal Court*, 32 A.J.I.L. 549 (1938); note in 19 Brit. Y.B. Int'l L. 216 (1938).

jackers, Panichi Maurizio and Giovine Umberto, who forced an Olympic plane to return to Orly on November 8, 1968, as part of their fight against the Greek Government, were tried by a local French court and found guilty of intentional violence and illegal possession of firearms and were sentenced to five and eight months imprisonment, respectively.[127] Only one year later, the LOT hijackers, Peter Klmt and Hans Ulrich von Hof, who forced the aircraft to come down at Tegel airport in the French sector of Berlin on October 19, 1969, were tried by the French military court for the French occupation sector, found guilty of having compromised the security of the working of an air lane, of having endangered the lives of the people on board, and of unlawful coercion, and were each sentenced to two years imprisonment.[128] Subsequently, Romuald Zolotucho and Wieslaw Szymankiewicz, who hijacked another LOT aircraft on November 20, 1969, and forced it to land in Vienna, were tried by a local Austrian court, found guilty of similar crimes under Austrian law, and sentenced to two years, and two years and three months imprisonment, respectively.[129] In June 1970, two decisions by a Greek and a Swedish court followed the lead. The three Palestinians, Sami Abboud, Issam Doumid, and Maha Abu Khalil, who attempted to hijack TWA flight 841 on December 21, 1969, but failed, were each sentenced on June 25 by a local Greek court to two years imprisonment.[130] A dissident Greek, Giorgios Flamourides, who hijacked Olympic flight 944 on January 2, 1969 and forced the pilot to land in Cairo instead of Athens, was sentenced on June 30 by a Swedish city court to one year and ten months imprisonment.[131]

After Operation Abu Thalaat the picture changed. Rudolf Cihac, who with his wife and seven more hijacked a Czech C.S.A. airliner (flight OK 098) on June 8, 1970, and forced it to Nuremberg instead of Prague, was sentenced to two years and six months imprisonment in Bavaria on September 16. Zbigniew Iwanicki, who hijacked a LOT airliner on June 5, 1970, and forced it to land at Kastrup, Denmark, instead of Gdansk, Poland, was sentenced to six years imprisonment on October 5, 1970, by a local Danish court.[132] Raphaele Minichiello, the U.S. Marine, who on October 31, 1969, succeeded in forcing TWA flight 85 to take him for a 6,900 mile ride to Rome, was sentenced by a local Roman court to seven and a half years imprisonment on November 11, 1970.

These cases, however, do not display much of the political element.

---

[127] 1969 Revue générale de l'air et de l'Espace 358.

[128] Tribunal du governement militaire français de Berlin, *decision* 4486 (Nov. 20, 1969).

[129] Landgericht für Strafsachen Wien, judgment (Mar. 11, 1970) (6 c Vr 8513/69).

[130] As reported in International Herald Tribune, June 25, 1970, at 4 col. 6 & 7.

[131] Stockholms rådhusrätt, avdeling 17, judgment DB 523. *Affirmed on appeal.*

[132] Taarnby Ret, judgment in case 169/70. The Court of Appeal reduced the sentence to 3 years and 6 months, but the Danish Supreme Court reinstated the six-year's verdict.

Only in the first French case (the Olympic hijacking) was there any political agitation in connection with the trial.[133] The central problem with which the drafters of the twin conventions on terrorism were concerned is better revealed by the *Tsironis* case in Sweden. This case, which eventually, in June 1971, was tried in the City Court of Stockholm, provides excellent illustrations of the problems feared.

On August 16, 1969, en route between Athens and Jannina, domestic Olympic DC-3 flight 500/I, under command of Captain George Georgis, was hijacked by passengers Dr. Tsironis, his wife, and their two boys. Tsironis pointed a gun at the pilots and said: "I am Dr. Tsironis. In the name of freedom and humanity, I have taken this aircraft and from now on you shall obey to my orders and to those of my colleagues with regard to the course we are going to follow." Thereupon Tsironis forced the pilots to land in Albania. Being subsequently allowed to leave Albania, Dr. Tsironis sought entry into Italy and France but was refused, and finally he arrived in Sweden were he received permission to take up residence.

Pursuant to the Swedish Penal Code, ch. 2, § 2, an alien who has committed a criminal act outside of Sweden which was punishable under the law in force at the place of the crime should be tried according to Swedish law and in a Swedish court, if after having committed the crime he has acquired domicile in Sweden; and even if he is only found in Sweden, provided that in such case the crime is punishable according to Swedish law by imprisonment for more than six months. By the very act of seeking sanctuary in Sweden, Dr. Tsironis had brought the possibility of prosecution for the hijacking upon himself. Although Sweden had nothing to do with the hijackings as such—it was not the state of registry nor the state of landing, nor the state within which the crime had taken place— it claimed jurisdiction over the crime committed by way of the hijacking. Inasmuch as jurisdiction is established, the Swedish experience would seem to be instructive also in other cases in which jurisdiction to prosecute out of state hijacking may be asserted (although pursuant to other rules of jurisdiction) and political complications cloud the horizon. The Swedish Chief State Prosecutor, on November 12, 1969, ordered a preliminary police inquiry.

This police inquiry immediately split into two channels. As to the state of landing, Albania, with which friendly relations were entertained, the inquiry proceeded by means of diplomatic channels. They did not yield more, however, than a cable reproducing the Albanian official news agency's bulletin of the day Tsironis landed in Albania. Relating to Greece, being the state of registry and the *locus delicti*, with which relations were hostile, it was decided to avoid the diplomatic channel which would involve

[133] See J.C.P. 1969. 16 023, note by *de Juglart & du Pontavice.*

political embarrassment, as well as the slightly more technical ICAO channel. Instead, it was decided to rely on the Interpol routine which functioned pursuant to the European Convention on mutual assistance in criminal matters, signed in Strassbourg, April 20, 1959.[134] The local police authority initiated such a request for assistance on November 27, 1969. After about one year, the request had produced almost no results. The only thing that happened was that on May 20, 1970, the Swedish police received a Greek record of prior convictions. Indeed, until Operation Abu Thalaat, the only evidence against the hijacker which the Swedish police succeeded in collecting was a translation of the flight report which had been turned in to Air Traffic Department of Olympic Airways by Captain Georgis, and this piece of evidence was volunteered to the police from private quarters.[135] It is a fair guess that the very slight Greek response to the Swedish police requests was connected with Greek realization of what political embarrassment the situation meant to the Swedish Government. The Greeks were in no way inclined to diminish this embarrassment.

Even the general public might find it "unfair to proceed against men who came to Sweden with official help and were treated by the authorities not as criminals but rather as honored guests."[136] Not until after Operation Abu Thalaat, on Ocober 16, 1970, was it decided by the King in Council to direct a prosecution against Dr. Tsironis and to take the risk of an acquittal that might be denounced as scandalous, on the one hand, and an excessive sentence in a bending-over-backward reaction, on the other.[137]

On February 5, 1969, military policeman, Leonardo Dominguez Fuentes, secured his escape from Colombia to Cuba by hijacking a domestic DC-4 flight of Sociedad Aeronautica Medellin. After three months in camp in Cuba, he was denied immigration entry. With Cuban identity papers he was then sent to seek entry in Switzerland via Prague. Being rejected by the Swiss, he spent the rest of the year in Prague at the expense of

[134] 472 U.N. Treaty Series 185 (Art. 15, para. 5).

[135] On Nov. 25, 1970, the Greek Embassy in Stockholm made a request for extradition, and this request was accompanied by affidavits made by crew members of the hijacked Olympic aircraft. On July 28, 1971, the Swedish Supreme Court advised against extradition and the request was subsequently denied by the Swedish Government.

[136] International Herald Tribune 1, at col. 6. (Nov. 21, 1969); *id.* at 5, col. 4 (Mar. 12, 1970). When Dr. Tsironis arrived in Sweden, he referred to his previous (in fact rather modest) position as a politician in Greece and asked for treatment similar to that enjoyed by his predecessor, the Greek politician Andreas Papandreou, who had been given a Chair in Stockholm by the Swedish Government in order to lead from there the PAK fight in Greece. This request by Tsironis was very favorably received and it appears that Tsironis, during the initial period, received about $2,000 per month in governmental support.

[137] On July 7, 1971, Dr. Tsironis was sentenced by the city court in Stockholm to imprisonment for 3 years and 6 months.

the Cuban consulate and a Latin American student organization. When he found out that the Czech authorities probably would send him back to Colombia once the Cuban consulate decided to support him no more, he flew to Sweden and asked for asylum on January 18, 1970.

The *Fuentes* case is very similar to the *Tsironis* case, the main difference being that Fuentes does not claim to be a politician and that the Swedish Foreign Policy has not singled out Colombia as a chief enemy comparable to Greece. While Tsironis' is an odd case, Fuentes' is not: There are scores of hijackings in Latin American which have produced closely similar cases. In view of the idolization of Latin American revolutionaries in Sweden (the Guevara cult) the embarrassment of making Fuentes stand trial in Sweden will be the same, if not worse, as that which would surround prosecution of Dr. Tsironis.

But the embarrassment to be felt in connection with the entry of hijackers is not exclusively a Swedish phenomenon. Other countries may expect to experience it as well. Italy is on its way to that end in the *Minichiello* case. Raphael Minichiello, it will be recalled, was the U.S. Marine who succeeded, on October 31, 1969, in forcing Trans World Airlines flight 85 to take him for a 6,900 mile ride to Rome. Minichiello's deed was immediately exploited locally. Melito Irpino, Minichiello's Italian home town, made his American counsel an honorary citizen, and film magnate Carlo Ponti announced that he wanted to make a film out of his deed.

Minichiello was sentenced to seven and a half years imprisonment by the District Court of Rome; but on appeal, the sentence was reduced to three and a half years. On May 1, 1971, he was released from jail on parole.

The embarrassment to be expected in such hijacking cases is very much of the same kind as that which was anticipated by the drafters of the twin conventions on terrorism of 1937. The Convention on the Creation of an International Criminal Court was opened to signature on November 16, 1937. It was signed by Twelve European powers, among them France and the Soviet Union, and by Cuba.[138] This court was to be set up for the trial of persons accused of an offense dealt with in the Convention on Terrorism. Instead of punishing these offences in its own courts, or extraditing accused persons, a party to the convention might refer the accused for trial to the court, but it would be under no obligation to do so. The court was to be permanent with its seat at the Hague. The court was to consist of five judges and five deputy judges of different

---

[138] Convention for the Creation of an International Criminal Court, 1937, 1938, REV. DR. INT'L LÉG. COMP. 68. *Cf.* Hudson, *The Proposed International Criminal Court*, 32 A.J.I.L. 549 (1938).

nationality. The judges would be jurists of competence in criminal law, chosen by the World Court from among persons nominated by the parties, and the regular term of the judges would be ten years. Only five members of the court would sit in any case. The Registry of the World Court would be asked to serve the new court also. The salaries of the judges, on a fixed scale, would be payable by the states of which they were nationals.

The conflict-of-laws problems which the court would encounter were, insofar as punishment was concerned, solved by resort to a dual system of law: the lex loci delicti and the law of the state which had committed the accused for trial. *In casu*, the penalty was to be controlled by the more leninent of the two systems (art. 21). Otherwise, the court itself was sole master of the conflict-of-laws questions. If this meant the application of a legal system not represented among the judges on the bench, a consultative assessor specializing in that system could be joined to the court. Arrest and detention of the accused during trial was decided by the court but execution was left to the state in which the court was sitting. Letters rogatory could be sent by the court itself and the court could on its own motion call witnesses and experts. The costs thus incurred were to be met by a common fund. Penalties imposed were to be executed by the state which the court, at its discretion, had selected for this purpose, provided that it assented thereto. The same state could pardon the criminal, after consulting with the court. Money received by way of fines could be disposed of by the court in its discretion.

The apparent merit of this system of law enforcement lies in the fact that it establishes a *modus vivendi* for a world which is more deeply split than is generally officially acknowledged. It never entered into force because of World War II. After the war, interest has not focused so much on this very practical international criminal court which was to deal with everyday crimes under national law, but rather turned toward rather impractical courts for exceptional crimes of the type with which the multinational Nuremberg Military Tribunal was confronted. It should be recalled, however, that as late as at the Tenth Congress of International Criminal Law, in 1969, it was resolved to recommend that disputes relating to the extradition aspects of international criminal law should "be referred compulsorily, or at least optionally, to an international criminal court."[139] In the context of the upsurge of hijackings with im-

---

[139] The idea was presented at the Freiburg Colloquium on Extradition held in 1968 at the Max-Planck Institute for International and Comparative Criminal Law by Professor Bassiouni. *See* Bassiouni, *International Extradition in the American Practice and World Public*, 36 TENN. L. REV. 1 (1968); Bassiouni, *International Extradition: An American Experience and a Proposed Formula*, 3–4 REVUE INTERNATIONALE DE DROIT PENAL 494 (1968), reprinted in 15 WAYNE L. REV. 733 (1959); Bassiouni, *La Estradizione Inter-*

portant political elements involved, I view the creation of an international criminal court along the lines delineated in the 1937 conventions
as the most promising way to cope with the difficult law enforcement
problem here met. The only hesitation I have relates to the geographical
jurisdiction of such a court. It may not be too practical to have only
one such court. Even such a worldwide organization as IATA finds it
useful to split the aviation world into three regions; I believe that one
court for each region is a better model to follow. Once created, of course,
an international court of this type could be charged with other types
of business as well. I believe that the development of this international
court system is the means of effectively dealing with the problems of
piracy and hijacking.

Section 2.   CRIMES OF TERRORISM* AND INTERNATIONAL CRIMINAL LAW

Tran-Tam

2.1. Introduction

This section is concerned with terrorist activities and the problems
such activities pose for the world order. To state the obvious, not only
do terrorist crimes threaten the life and property of individuals, they
concurrently constitute a danger to the whole world and its civilization,
for by their very nature they are likely to jeopardize simultaneously
social order, international public order, and the broader interest of
humanity.[1]

For sometime past, terrorism has been acknowledged as a political
instrument, either domestic or international. Many a political body has
made use of authentic terrorist methods against civilian populations with
the aim of seizing power and imposing a dictatorship on them. Other
governments and regimes base their foreign policies on terrorist activities.
Using them as blackmail, they might foment civil war or provoke limited
international or regional conflicts. The problem of international terrorism
is extremely complex and must be recognized and dealt with as such.

---

nazionale: *Riassunto della Prassi Americana Contemporaneo, ed. uno schema di porposte
per il sinnovanmente dell'istituto,* 10 Rivista del diritto matrimoniale e dello stato
delle persone 418 (1968).

    * The Terrorism Convention of 1935 referred to by the author throughout this article has
not entered into force since its elaboration.

    [1] *See* A. Sottile, *Le Terrorisme International,* Receuil des Cours de l'Academie de
droit international 5 (1939).

The starting point here will be to examine criminal law and international law as they apply to terrorism.

2.2. Juridical Doctrine

The definition of terrorism is still in the process of being formulated. Such difficulty for a commonly acceptable juridical definition is partly due to the fact that, despite continuous efforts, terrorism can only be defined tautologically as terror and barbarity, or in the words of some, fright intimidation. The difficulty is also due to the fact that "terrorism" is a generic term, comprising a whole series of varied acts comprising violence and terrorism. Thus, criminologists have yet to agree on a universally acceptable definition. Apart from the implied tautology that seems to be unavoidable, the suggested definition lacks precision and the result is incomplete and vague, as will be evidenced by a study of the following selected definitions offered by publicists.

According to Professor Givanovitch, terrorism is considered as "[a]cts whose nature is to make one obsessed with an eventual threat or act that is to be performed by intimidation by all means possible and by every method available."

To Dr. Lemkin, terrorism means, largely, intimidation by means of violence.

Mr. Quintillano Saldana conceives that, broadly speaking, "terrorism denotes all crimes and political or social offenses, the execution or warning of which causes dread and constitutes a collective danger to the population." He adds that terrorist attempts are international acts of crime that are committed chiefly and especially for the purpose of giving alarm—"subjective element"—and that are accomplished by any means capable of creating a common danger—"objective element."

Some authors have suggested that terrorism must be treated as an international crime, *i.e.*, an offense, the execution or even warning of which sows general dread and creates a special danger to the community. Being unable to avoid a certain tautology, we regard that, generally speaking, terrorism means an international *modus operandi* of crime characterized by terror and violence, seeking to achieve an intended goal. Thus, terrorism may be defined as acts of international crime committed by means of terror, violence, and intimidation, with a goal of obtaining predetermined goals and purposes.

2.3. Terrorism and "Political Delictum"

In the fight against terrorism, one needs to overcome the difficulty in terminology to establish a line of demarcation between terrorist acts and crimes properly called *political delictum* (political crimes).

There are certain offenses against the state which by their nature not only impair the order of a state but also the social order as a whole. Whatever the motive that determines the commission of such offenses, including a political motive, the possible consequences would make it so apparent that cooperation among states to suppress such offenses is desirable.[2]

The International Law Institute adopted the following resolution, which should be mentioned here:

> . . . not to be deemed political unlawful acts that are directed against all bases of social organization and not only against a certain determined state or a certain form of government. . . . Article 4—Deemed to be political offences those breaches of law that are complex or connected with political offences unless they are the most dangerous crimes in the viewpoint of moral or common law such as murder, kidnapping, explosions, attempts on property by means of fire . . . and those committed by the use of arms and violence. . . .[3]

Article 13 of the same rules of the Institute enumerates the acts that can be subjected to extradition; such acts include crimes against moral and common law such as murder, killing, poisoning, mutilation, and serious wounds.

The American branch of the International Law Institute has also mentioned, in its project No. 15, that acts qualified as anarchic by the laws of two nations would not be considered as political crimes.[4]

According to the *Belge* Clause of 1856, recognized by a great number of treaties, regicide is an offense against the common law calling for extradition. Under Italian and German legislation, many terrorist acts are considered offenses against the common law.

According to a Resolution adopted by the International Law Institute in 1892, the project of the American Branch of the International Law Institute, and the Resolution of the International Conference of 1935 for the Unification of the Penal Law, acts of terrorists are not considered as *political delictum*.

This brief survey suffices to indicate that it is often difficult to distinguish between *political delictum* and terrorist acts. But, in any case, in view of the current trend, terrorist acts of a serious nature are not considered as political offenses. Moreover, the *Belge* Clause, though limited to a particular case, and other treaties which have adopted it since 1856, all agree on the exclusion of regicide from the category of

---

[2] *See* Tran-Tam, 1 REVUE DE DROIT INTERNATIONAL (1967).

[3] *Cf.* V. Pella, *La cour Penale internationale et la Repression du Terrorisme*, 17 REVUE DE DROIT PENAL ET DE CRIMINOLOGIE (Apr. 1938).

[4] *See* A. Sottile, *supra* note 1, at 14.

political offenses. An argument can be made that the Convention for the Prevention and Repression of Terrorism enumerates the terrorist acts for which an extradition is agreed upon by the contracting parties when they do not try the accused in their respective tribunals. It studies many aspects of terrorism—social, political, juridical—and defines that an act is considered as a terrorist offense when it is directed by a criminal factor, when as explicitly set forth in articles 2 and 3, it puts on an international character, and when the method used is clearly terroristic.[5]

The Inter-Governmental Conference has also adopted the principle that terrorism is not a *political delictum* so far as it concerns extradition, a position which is in conformity with the principles of the *Belge* Clause and the Resolutions of (1) the 1892 International Law Institute, (2) the branch of the American International Law Institute, and (3) the 1935 International Conference for the Unification of the Penal Law. This position is also in consonance with the current juridical trends in the legislation of many civilized countries.[6]

2.4. The Sui-Generis Character and Definition of the Crime of Terrorism

Terrorism is an international crime which threatens human tranquility and security, injures the universal conscience, and impairs human dignity.

It is proper to say that the crime of terrorism is of a sui-generis character in most instances. Very few exceptions exist where ordinary individuals act on their own initiative. Terrorism is directed, in the first instance, directly against chiefs of state and other state officials, by any method capable of producing a collective danger. The *modus operandi* includes fires, explosives, and destruction that imperils human life and property.

These acts are generally committed by "secret institutions" or bands created precisely for the purpose of the imposition of their will by means of terror for the advancement of certain doctrines. Since the end does not justify the means, the use of violence and its companion, terror, constitutes a serious breach of ICL. It makes the offense lose its political characteristics.

2.5. A General Survey of International Collaboration for the Repression of the Crime of Terrorism

If the expression "terrorism" is rather novel, the facts that constitute the offense and violence contained in the methods of terror are far from being recent. As it is proven true through the *Belge* Clause since 1856, the trend

[5] *Id.* at 15–18.
[6] *Id.* at 17–18.

has been to exclude certain offenses against the state as political offenses.

For this reason, writes Professor V.V. Pella recently, laws were passed in a number of European nations repressing stated instances that constituted terrorist acts. This was noticeable in France, Italy, Great Britain, Germany, Austria, Spain, Switzerland, and Belgium.

In the twentieth century, the intensification of terrorism can be regarded as an indication of new social and political doctrines that regularly use terror and intimidation. The most striking growth of terrorism, though, dates from the end of World War II; primarily this is due to the advent of new facilities in communications, to the creation of new states, to the recognition of minority problems, and to ideological reasons.[7]

In his important work, published in 1925, *The Collective Criminality of States*, Professor V.V. Pella considered not only the penal responsibility of states, but also the international penal responsibility of the individual, more particularly the responsibility of instigators of worldwide terrorist offenses. He foresaw a plan of international collaboration and even the creation of an international penal court.[8]

The first Conference for the unification of penal law, held in Warsaw, 1927, dealt with terrorism, while not using this precise term. It adopted a text that concerned those offenders who might be subject to extradition and anticipated the universality of repression under the title: "International use of means capable of bringing forth a common danger."

One of the subjects dealt with at the Third Conference, held in Brussels, 1930, was terrorism. At this Conference, Professor Gunzburg presented a report along with a draft resolution of four articles concerning the use of proper means to confront terrorism. For lack of time, the proposals of the Commission were not submitted to the Assembly. At the Fourth Conference, taking place in Paris in December, 1931, the problem of terrorism was discussed by Professor Radulesco and Doctor Lemkin. They both suggested concerted international action for the repression of terrorism. Their suggestions were carried over to a future conference.

The Fifth Conference for the Unification of Penal Law in Madrid, 1934, again studied terrorism and the use of international law as a vehicle capable of confronting this common danger. A text composed of four articles was produced at the Conference, and adopted in a resolution.

At the Sixth International Conference for the Unification of Penal Law in Copenhagen, meeting in August-September, 1935, the problem of terrorism was again at the forefront. Four reports were prepared by

---

[7] *Id.* at 19.

[8] *See* Tran-Tam, *Criminologie et Politique internationale,* 3 REVUE DE DROIT INTERNATIONAL DE SCIENCES DIPLOMATIQUES ET POLITIQUES (1962).

Professors Thomas Givanovitch, Niko Gunsburg, Quintillano Saldana, and Rafael Lemkin.[9]

After examining these reports, the Conference adopted a text of eighteen Articles, preceded by a Preamble and followed by a vow. Let us review some excerpts from the text:

> . . . to be embodied on the Penal Code or in the Penal Law a section or a chapter entitled, "Attempts That Have Created a Danger of Terror." This is to be conceived as follows:
>
> *First Article.* . . . the one who, by his intentional acts directed against the life, corporal integrity, health, or freedom of a head of state or his spouse or any person holding the prerogatives of a head of state as well as crown princes, members of governments, people enjoying diplomatic immunity, and members of the constitutional, legislative, or judicial bodies would create a common danger or a state of terror that might incite either a change or raise an obstacle to the functioning of public bodies or trouble in international relations . . . [would be sentenced severely].
>
> *Second Article.* . . . the one who would create the same common danger or state of terror: (1) by intentional deed aimed either at causing a catastrophe by hindering the normal functioning of air, river, sea, and railways transportation and interruption of public services or services of public utilities; or producing a calamity by means of explosives, incendiaries, gas, or deleterious products; or bringing forth pollution, corruption, or poisoning of drinking water and food products; or spreading epidemic or contagious diseases as well as any other intentional deed whose nature imperils human life; (2) by intentional deed aimed at destroying or impairing public buildings, water supply, power plants belonging to services of public facilities; (3) by the intentional use of explosives in a public place; and (4) by another intentional deed that imperils human lives and endangers the public . . . [would be sentenced severely].
>
> *Fourth Article.* . . . is to be punished he who would organize an association or set up an agreement with the intent of committing an offence already stated in Article 1 or 2, or he who would take part in such an association or agreement.
>
> *Fifth Article.* . . . is to be punished any direct provocation aimed at committing one of the offences already stated in Article 1 or 2.
>
> *Sixth Article.* . . . is to be punished he who would manufacture, keep, or export materials or objects that they know are destined for the preparation or execution of an offence stated in Articles 4 and 2.
>
> *Eighth Article.* If deeds foreseen in the previous Articles are committed in different countries, then each of them must be considered as a distinct offence.
>
> *VOW.* The Sixth International Conference for the Unification of Penal Law formulated the vow that when extradition is not granted, the delinquents can be deferred to an international penal jurisdiction unless the state concerned prefers to have them tried by its own law courts.

[9] V. Pella, Recueil de cours de l'Academie 703 (1930).

Later, in 1937, in a meeting that was called by the League of Nations resolution of May 27, the Council of the League of Nations asked the Secretary-General to invite nonmembers as well as members to consider the problem. Thirty-five countries were represented at the Conference. The Conference gathered together not only diplomats but also eminent jurists. It elected Baron Carton de Viart president; J. Basdevant, vice-president, and Professor V.V. Pella committee reporter general.[10]

On the basis of a rough draft of the Convention, drawn by an eleven-member committee, the Conference adopted, on November 16, 1937, along with the final Act, two Conventions: one for the prevention and repression of terrorism and the other for the creation of an International Criminal Court.[11]

As for the United Nations, it also took terrorism seriously. For example, the draft code of offenses against the peace and security of mankind enumerates the following offenses, among other:

> *Article 4.* The incursion into the territory of a state from the territory of another state by armed bands acting for a political purpose.
> *Article 5.* The undertaking or encouragement by the authorities of a state activities calculated to foment civil strife in another state or the toleration by the authorities of a state of organized activities calculated to foment civil strife in another state.
> *Article 6.* The undertaking or encouragement by the authorities of a state of terrorist activities in another state or toleration by the authorities of a state of organized activities calculated to carry out terrorist acts in another state.

2.6. States' Duty to Repress Terrorism

It is evident that international law imposes on every state rigid duties to be fulfilled: (1) the duty of abstaining from all deeds destined to encourage and incite, directly or indirectly, terrorist activities against other countries and (2) the duty of these countries of suppressing such activities within their own territory.[12]

Being unanimously recognized as a norm of international law, this obligation, having a universal significance, has been reaffirmed directly in the "Convention for the Repression of Terrorism." (art. 1 § 1).

[10] *Cf.* A. Sottile, *supra* note 1, at 27.

[11] Acts de la VIe conference pour l'Unification du droit Penal, Copenhague, 1935.

[12] On the First Convention there have been already twenty-four signatory governments as follows: Afghanistan, Albania, Argentina, India, Bulgaria, Cuba, Dominican Republic, Egypt, Ecuador, Spain, Estonia, France, Greece, Haiti, Monaco, Norway, Netherlands, Peru, Roumania, Czechoslovakia, Turkey, Venezuela, Yugoslavia. On the Second Convention there have been already thirty signatory governments as follows: Afghanistan, Albania, Argentina, Belgium, the United Kingdom, Bulgaria, Denmark, Egypt, Ecuador, Spain, Estonia, Greece, Finland, France, Hungary, India, Lithuania, Monaco, Czechoslovakia, Norway, Netherlands, Peru, Poland, Turkey, USSR, Venezuela, Yugoslavia, Roumania, Switzerland, Uruguay.

World order could be seriously threatened by unlawful acts and acts of violence by states, groups, and individuals. These include, but are not limited to, acts such as piracy, hijacking, terrorism, aggression, and crimes against humanity which even when carried out by a state must not remain unpunished. A regime guilty of perpetration of international crimes endangering peace, security, and justice for mankind, or the authorities of a regime which perpetrates such offenses should not be able to commit crimes with impunity while individuals committing breaches of law in the common sense are dealt with severely. Hopefully, when ICL becomes effective, it will prescribe norms and regulate state conduct toward strengthening world order.

2.7. World Criminal Law in Brief

For a long time, criminal law in each country has responded to the special characteristics of its people: religion, race, history, custom, and climate, for instance. However, a century ago, efforts were initiated by scholars to harmonize the penal legislation of various states. These efforts are now bearing fruit, for the realization is rapidly growing that world order would be strengthened if the states were willing to submit their actions and conduct to the scrutiny of worldwide ICL.

"A civilian process," wrote the French scholar Professor H. Donnedieu de Vabres, "most often regards only pecuniary interests." But, he added, "on the contrary, in a criminal process, it is the freedom, life, and honor of man that is at stake."[13] Thus, we must regard penal law as the most important branch of law.

Penal law, the embodient of rules to safeguard order, includes the following:

1. Common law or penal law.
2. National political penal law.
3. International penal law (classical and modern).

Corresponding to these three categories of penal law are the three fields of crime to be handled: (1) crime under common law, (2) political crime, and (3) crime of an international nature.

2.7.1. COMMON LAW. This covers rules designed for the suppression of acts disturbing the peace, security, and order common to every civilized nation. It follows that there can be no social organization if members are not bound to respect human life, personal freedom, and perhaps the right of property.

[13] *See* V. Pella, *La Guerre crime et les criminels de Guerre*, REVUE DE DROIT INTERNATIONAL); A. Sottile, *supra* note 1.

Murder, wanton destruction, theft, and fraud are examples of crimes subject to punishment regardless of the nation involved. The subject of inadmissability attached to these crimes does not vary from one country to another.

That there exists crime when the common right is threatened is a universally accepted concept. Safeguards are called for by elementary social morality. Consequently, he who offends the Common Law not only violates his national law but threatens the prevailing international social life.[14] Perhaps it can now be asserted that there is a dominant current of thought which considers infractions of the common law as supranational and not merely simple violations of national law. These infractions are acts of an antisocial nature which offend universal morality and call for general repression by all countries with similar punishment.[15]

2.7.2. NATIONAL POLITICAL PENAL LAW. Here consideration is given to the control of illicit acts directed against the form of government and the political order of a given country. In general, such repression concerns only the country in question. This concept postdates the French Revolution. In earlier times the political accusation of *criminal majestatis* was severely punished.

In most cases, political crime is aimed at modifying or changing national political structure, the imposition of a new political doctrine, which invariably requires a change in authority structure within a state.

According to the classical theory, *political delictum* does not have the same criminal intent as crimes against the common law. These crimes are not those of an individual, but are collective in nature. In the perpetration of such acts, the individual plays only the role of an instrument rather than an agent.[16]

Under traditional international law each state determines its own competence to prescribe and apply its criminal laws to events and people in various settings. However, in 1924 Professor V.V. Pella pioneered a draft "Code of Crimes Against Peace and the Security of Mankind" and at the Inter-Parliamentary Conference held in Berne, Switzerland, suggested recognition of the concept of international criminal jurisdiction. He also proposed the creation of a new legal discipline, an international

[14] H. DONNEDIEU DE VABRES, TRAITE ELEMENTAIRE DE DROIT CRIMINEL ET DE LEGISLATION COMPAREE 132 (1938).

[15] *See* GAROFALO, THE SOLIDARITY OF NATIONS IN THE STRUGGLE AGAINST CRIMINALITY. *See also* Pella, *Proposal Made to the League of the Nations in View of Organizing a General System Calculated to Eliminate Dangerous Criminals and Habitual Offenders*, 2 REVUE DE DROIT PENAL (1952).

[16] *Supra* note 14, at 3.

penal law, with a view toward guaranteeing effective peaceful relations among nations.[17]

The Legal Commission of the Inter-Parliamentary Union which met in Paris in April 1925 and the Washington Inter-Parliamentary Conference which met in October 1925 accepted Professor Pella's proposals. The latter meeting adopted a resolution admitting "the responsibility of a collective criminality of states."

Two decades later, in a report prepared by the United States Supreme Court Justice Jackson for the U.S. President, and presented on October 19, 1946, the following commentary appears on the Nuremberg war-crimes trials:

> Of course, it would be extravagant to claim that agreements at trials of this character can make aggressive war or persecution of minorities impossible, just as it would be extravagant to claim that our federal laws make federal crime impossible. But we cannot doubt that they strengthen bulwarks of peace and tolerance. The four nations, through their representatives on the Tribunal, have enunciated standards of conduct which bring new hope to men of good-will and from which future statesmen will not lightly depart.[18]

Subsequently, the International Law Commission has commented on the Nuremberg principles in a similar vein.[19] And, according to Professor Pella:

> International penal law is the embodiment of rules of essence and form which preside over the use of repression against acts committed by the state or group of states, or individuals, to disturb public international order and the harmony existing among peoples; and finally, this legal discipline is just like the branch of international law which determines the infractions, establishes punishment, and fixes the conditions of the international penal responsibilities of the state, or groupings of states, and individuals.[20]

Although there is much common ground between international penal law and the national penal law, especially on the principles administering penal responsibility, there are equally significant differences, which stem from the horizontal nature of the international community.

We recognize that international penal law is still in a formative state. However, significant developments are presently taking place. For example article 7 of the Charter of the Nuremberg Tribunal lays down the basic principles of international competency: "The official position of

---

[17] *See* Clark, Jr., 1909, Proceedings of the American Society of International Law, Supp. III at 98.

[18] *See* V. Pella: Aperçu de la Criminalite de la Guerre et la creation d'un droit repressif des nations (Debat geneal, seance du 25 Aout compte rendu de la 22e conference Inter-parlementaire 335 (335).

[19] *See*, V. PELLA, LA CRIMINALITE COLLECTIVE DES ETATS ET LE DROIT PENAL DE L'AVENIR (1949).

[20] International Law Commission, Session of May 24, 1949, U.N. Doc. A/CN4/SR/P.4.

defendants, whether as head of state or responsible officials in government departments, shall not be considered as freeing them from responsibility or mitigating punishment."

For this reason, the Draft Code of Offenses Against the Peace and Security of Mankind reads:

> The fact that a person acted as head of state or as responsible government official does not relieve him of responsibility for committing any of the offenses defined in this Code [art. 3]. The fact that a person charged with an offense defined in this Code acted pursuant to an order of his government or of a superior does not relieve him of responsibility in international law if, in the circumstances at the time, it was possible for him not to comply with that order [Art. 4].

However, this draft code is still in the draft stage, primarily because of contradictions and conflicting interpretations as to the definition of "crime of aggression."[21]

Another significant development is the entering into force of several humanitarian Conventions. The following provisions should be specifically mentioned: Articles 49 to 52 of the First Geneva Convention Relative to the Treatment of Prisoners of War; articles 50 to 53 of the Second Geneva Convention for the Amelioration of the Conditions of Wounded, Sick, and Shipwrecked of Armed Forces at Sea; articles 129 to 131 of the Third Geneva Convention Relative to the Treatment of Prisoners of War, and articles 146 to 149 of the Fourth Geneva Convention Relative to the Protection of Civilian Persons in Time of War.[22]

Among other developments should be mentioned the 1954 Hague Convention on the Protection of Cultural Property in the Event of Armed Conflict.

While customary international law confers universal jurisdiction pertaining to certain crimes, such as piracy on the high seas, traffic in narcotics, white slavery, and counterfeiting, it is reasonable and logical to include war crimes, crimes of aggression, crimes against humanity, and crimes of terrorism among such crimes.

2.8. Conclusion

If international law is to play an important role in human affairs, its first task must be to prevent war and to deter international crimes; and its second task, to develop principles of international justice and procedures.[23]

[21] V. Pella, le code des crimes contre la Paix et la Sécurité de l'Humanité 35 (1951).

[22] See ICRC, The Geneva Conventions of August 12, 1949, at 4, 16 (2d. rev. ed. 1950) and Gulbrandsen, *A Commentary on the Geneva Conventions of August 12, 1949, supra* pt. III, ch. III, § 1.

[23] See Q. Wright, The Role of International Law in the Elimination of War 86–87 (1961).

The Draft Code of Offenses Against the Peace and Security of Mankind is a desirable first step in this direction. International penal law will hopefully become a reality in the near future.

2.9. Draft Convention on Terrorism and Kidnapping of Persons for Purposes of Extortion—Organization of American States[*]

IN VIEW of the increasing frequency and seriousness with which acts of terrorism are occurring in this hemisphere, especially the kidnapping of persons for purposes of extortion; and

CONSIDERING:

That the General Assembly of the Organization, in Resolution 4, adopted at its first special session, held from June 25 through July 8, 1970, strongly condemned such acts and declared that they constitute serious common crimes characterized by flagrant violation of the most elemental principles of the security of the individual and community as well as offenses against the freedom and dignity of the individual; and

That it is advisable to establish general standards for international cooperation in the prevention and punishment of terrorism and especially of the kidnapping of persons, extortion, and other assaults against them, when such acts have international significance,

The governments of the member states of the Organization of American States

HAVE AGREED ON THE FOLLOWING:

ARTICLE 1. The contracting states undertake to cooperate mutually, by taking all the measures that they may consider effective, within their domestic legal systems, and particularly those that are set forth in this Convention, to prevent and apply punishment for acts of terrorism, especially the kidnapping of persons and extortion in connection with that crime, carried out within their respective territories, when such acts have international significance.

ARTICLE 2. (*First Alternative*). Kidnapping or any other offense against the life, the person, or the freedom of a foreign diplomatic or consular agent who enjoys inviolability under international law, or a member of the family of such a person protected by that prerogative, constitutes a common crime of international significance, whatever the motive for which it was committed.

ARTICLE 2. (*Second Alternative*). Kidnapping or any other offense against the life, the person, or the freedom of any person to whom the state has a duty to extend special protection in accordance with international law constitutes a common crime of international significance, whatever the motive for which it was committed.

ARTICLE 3. The acts of terrorism to which this Convention refers, including the kidnapping of persons for purposes of extortion, do not constitute political offenses or common crimes connected with political offenses. Such acts shall be considered to have international significance in any of the following cases:

    a. When the act is committed in the territory of a contracting state and is di-

[*] Organization of American States, 3d. Special Session, OAS/Off. Rec./ser. P./AG/Doc. 68, Jan. 13, 1971, signed in Rio de Janeiro, Sept. 26, 1970.

rected against a person or persons within he territory of another contracting state;

b. When the person or persons indicted or sentenced for such an act, perpetrated in the territory of one of the contracting states, are found within the territory of another contracting state.

ARTICLE 4. For the purposes of this Convention, an act shall be considered an act of terrorism when it is defined or expressly classified as such by the law of the state in whose territory the act was committed and by the law of the state in whose territory the person who has been indicted or sentenced for that act is located.

If the legislation of any of the contracting states does not contain the definition or classification referred to in the preceding paragraph, for the purposes of this Convention, and regardless of the legal terminology the national laws may use to describe them, the following shall be considered to be acts of terrorism: those that produce terror or intimidation among the inhabitants of a state or sector of the inhabitants thereof and create a common threat to the life, health, physical integrity, or freedom of persons by the employment of a method or device that by its nature can cause, or does cause, great damage, a serious disturbance of public order, or a public calamity, or by the taking over, the violent seizure, or the wrecking of a ship, aircraft, or other means of collective transport.

ARTICLE 5. Persons who take part in the conception, preparation, or execution of the criminal acts mentioned in this Convention shall not be protected by territorial or diplomatic asylum and shall be subject to extradition. In every case, the determination in this regard is to be made by the state under whose jurisdiction or protection such persons are located.

ARTICLE 6. The contracting states undertake to deliver to each other reciprocally, in accordance with the procedures established by the extradition treaties in force, or in their absence in conformity with the requirements set forth in their respective laws, the persons who are in their territory and whose extradition is requested because of their being tried for or their having been convicted of any of the criminal acts to which this Convention refers.

ARTICLE 7. If, when extradition is applicable, a state should not deliver the requested person because of some impediment, the state receiving the request shall be obligated to try the person referred to for the deed imputed to him just as if he had committed it in the territory of that state, and the said state shall inform the state that requested the extradition of the sentence handed down.

ARTICLE 8. In order to cooperate in the prevention and punishment of the acts of terrorism to which this Convention refers, the contracting states accepts the following obligations:

a. To take all measures within their power to prevent the preparation of acts of terrorism that are intended to be executed in the territory of another contracting state;

b. To exchange information and to consider effective administrative measures in the matter of individual security;

c. To make provisions in their respective criminal laws regarding the criminal acts to which this Convention refers if those acts are not already covered therein;

d. To comply in the most expeditious manner with any request from another contracting state in regard to any of the criminal acts to which this Conventions refers;

e. To provide for expeditious extradition procedures in their respective laws.

ARTICLE 9. Each contracting state may, in serious and exceptional circumstances, decide whether or not it would be correct to authorize departure from its territory by, or to deport, as the case may be, any person who is detained or in prison, under the jurisdiction of that state.

The interested contracting states may reach an agreement, in cases of the specific type referred to in the preceding paragraph, regarding the legal status of the persons involved.

ARTICLE 10. This Convention shall remain open for signature by the member states of the Organization of American States, as well as by any other state that is a member of the United Nations, or any other state that may be invited to sign it by the General Assembly of the Organization of American States.

ARTICLE 11. This Convention shall be ratified by the signatory states in accordance with their respective constitutional procedures.

ARTICLE 12. The original of this Convention, the English, French, Portuguese, and Spanish texts of which are equally authentic, shall be deposited in the General Secretariat of the Organization of American States, which shall send certified copies to the signatory governments for purposes of ratification. The instruments of ratification shall be deposited in the General Secretariat of the Organization of American States, which shall notify the signatory governments of such deposit.

ARTICLE 13. This Convention shall enter into force among the states that ratify when they deposit their respective instruments of ratification.

ARTICLE 14. This Convention shall remain in force indefinitely, but may be denounced by any of the contracting states by giving notice one year in advance, after which it shall cease to be in force for the denouncing state, but shall continue to be in force for the other contracting states. The denunciation shall be transmitted to the General Secretariat of the Organization of American States, which shall notify the other contracting states thereof.

CHAPTER X

SLAVERY, GENOCIDE, AND RACIAL DISCRIMINATION

Section 1. SLAVERY* AND SLAVE TRADE: STEPS TOWARD ERADICATION

VED P. NANDA AND M. CHERIF BASSIOUNI

1.1. The "Human Rights Program"

Since the adoption of the Universal Declaration of Human Rights by the U.N. General Assembly in 1948,[1] the common aspirations of mankind have been symbolized by an extraordinary and unprecedented outpouring of concern for increased protection of all basic human rights. This activity set in motion demands for the codification of human rights law, to be accompanied by effective measures of implementation. As a result, there is today an impressive catalog of human rights recognized in various conventions, treaties, agreements, and protocols, covering almost every aspect of mankind's basic values.[2] However, there are few tasks which have been less fulfilled than the realization of these basic values of mankind, for the formulation of world community aspirations is a far cry from their translation into authoritative prescriptions, which are effectively implemented and enforced throughout the world.[3]

The lack of progress, however, is due in no small part to the latent ambiguities contained in the very concept of human rights,[4] and those inherent in its formulation and actuation as a social process with its roots in ascertainable individual (psychological) and collective (sociopsychological) basic values. But the uneven progression or nonprogression in some areas of the U.N. Human Rights Programs should not obscure the fact that some advances have been made. The recognition and at least

---

* Reprinted in part with permission, 12 *Santa Clara Lawyer* 424 (1972).

[1] G.A. Res. 217A (III), 3 U.N. GAOR 71, U.N. Doc. A/810 (1948).

[2] *See generally* United Nations, *Human Rights: A Compilation of International Instruments of the United Nations,* U.N. Doc. A/CONF.32/4 (1967).

[3] Nanda, *The United Nations and Regional Arrangements to Implement Human Rights,* a working paper presented at the Bangkok Conference on World Peace Through Law, Sept. 1969, Conf. Doc. 7/PP-E-9 (1969).

[4] M. MOSKOWITZ, THE POLITICS AND DYNAMICS OF HUMAN RIGHTS 98–99 (1968) succinctly poses the problem:

 [I]nternational human rights is still waiting for its theoretician to systematize the thoughts and

limited application of authoratitive prescriptions in specific areas, such as slavery, confirms the need to avoid these ambiguities and instead, to narrow the scope of the inquiry to specifics by applying means which are commensurate with the gradual development of human aspirations. The pioneering attempt of Professors Myres McDougal, Harold Lasswell, and Lung-Chu-Chen[5] to undertake a systematic examination of the concept of human rights and to present a theoretical framework for applying the concept in specific instances provides the first solid basis for conducting further research and inquiry.

The minimum indispensable requirements for a dignified human existence[6] are the rights to life, liberty, and equality. These three rights have already found their tangible expression in specific conventions prohibiting genocide, slavery, forced prostitution, and racial discrimination.[7] In addition, the International Covenant on Civil and Political Rights and the optional protocol thereto, and the International Covenant on Economic, Social, and Cultural Rights, adopted by the U.N. General Assembly in

---

speculations on the subject and to define desirable goals. Intelligent truisms do not necessarily add up to a theory. No one has yet arisen to draw together into a positive synthesis the facts and fancies which emerge daily from events of bewildering complexity and to carry on an authentic debate. International concern with human rights is still very much a theme begging for a writer. And the scholar has not yet appeared to redress the distortions through a calm and systematic application of facts, to ground abstractions in the specific, and to define the limits of discourse. In the absence of a definite body of doctrine, as well as of deeply rooted convictions, international human rights have been dealt with on the basis of the shifts and vagaries of daily affairs and of evocations of daily events. There is a great need for technical resources and ability to channel the facts to greater effect. Human rights as a matter of international concern is an untrodden area of systematic research. But still a greater need is for superlative virtuosity to deal with international human rights in their multiple human dimensions.

[5] McDougal, Lasswell, & Chen, *Human Rights and World Public Order: A Framework for Policy-oriented Inquiry*, 63 A.J.I.L. 237 (1969).

[6] *Id.* at 267:

Let it be said immediately that a certain minimum of values indispensable to a dignified human existence must be prescribed as immune from all claims of derogation at all times. Notably among these are the right to life, freedom from torture and inhuman treatment, freedom from involuntary human experimentations, freedom from slavery, the slave trade servitude, freedom from imprisonment for debt, freedom from retroactive application of criminal punishment, the right to recognition as a human being, and freedom of thought, conscience and religion. These rights and freedoms are indispensable to a dignified human existence and must remain wholly intact from derogation upon grounds of crisis. In terms of our basic postulation, it can never be necessary to encroach upon these rights and freedoms, even in time of emergency. Nor would their deprivation ever be proportional. If the emerging concept of *jus cogens* is to be given rational meaning in the context of a world public order of human dignity, its bedrock must be in this minimal protection of human rights.

[7] For the Convention on Genocide, *see* G.A. Res. 96(I), Dec. 11, 1946; Res. 260A(III), Dec. 9, 1948, 78 U.N.T.S. 277. Slavery and Prostitution are discussed *infra. See also* McDougal & Leighton, *The Rights of Man in the World Community Constitution*, 3 VAND. L. REV. 683 (1950). The International Convention on the Elimination of all Forms of Racial Discrimination adopted by G.A. Res. 2106A (XX) of Dec. 21, 1965, is contained in United Nations, *Human Rights: A Compilation of International Instruments of the United Nations*, U.N. Doc. A/CONF.32/4 (1967).

December 1966,[8] offer an even wider spectrum of protections in securing life, liberty, equality, and human dignity.

This article is devoted to the prohibition of "slavery." Its approach is not philosophical, but descriptive of the efforts of the world community in counteracting and controlling this form of behavior. The relative success obtained in this area is probably a unique experiment in the application of the world community prescriptions where without resorting to repressive measures and sanctions, the outcome has been to a very large extent satisfactory. Since the enforcement mechanism adopted in this case was more dependent on voluntary compliance than on sanctions, it suggests that the most effective means for combating internationally prohibited conduct is the stimulation of commonly shared basic values. Such a stimulation is likely to lead to voluntary compliance, and to the gradual elimination of the origins and causes of the offensive conduct by the transformation of those values which tolerate such conduct into values which reject it. To maximize the opportunity of accomplishing this goal, an enforcement mechanism should be established which does not have to resort to the type of sanctions traditionally characterized as repressive.[9]

1.2. Development of the Movement to Abolish Slavery and Slave Trade

That slavery existed in various ancient civilizations is well known,[10] but it may be hard to believe that it still persists in different forms in almost forty countries.[11] A stark fact of history is that notwithstanding the existence of this inhumane institution, until the nineteenth century, no collective international agreement or action had been attempted to abolish even the slave trade, not to speak of slavery. The first concerted efforts to suppress slave trade were made in the Peace Treaties of Paris of 1814 and 1815, and the 1815 Congress of Vienna. At the Congress of Vienna, a declaration, signed by eight powers—Austria, France, Great Britain, Portugal, Prussia, Russia, and Sweden—stated that

> The commerce, known by the name of the "Slave Trade" (Traité des Nègres d'Afrique) has been considered, by just and enlightened men in all ages, as repugnant to the principles of humanity and universal morality; [that] at length the public voice, in all civilized countries, calls aloud for its prompt

---

[8] The conventions and the protocol are contained in G.A. Res. 2200A (XXI), 21 U.N. GAOR, Supp. 16, at 49.

[9] On the theories of punishment, *see, e.g.* Bassiouni, CRIMINAL LAW AND ITS PROCESSES ch. I (1969).

[10] *See, e.g.*, R. BARROW, SLAVERY IN THE ROMAN EMPIRE xvi (1928); O. SHERRARD, FREEDOM FROM FEAR—THE SLAVE AND HIS EMANCIPATION 11 (1959).

[11] *See supra* notes 70, 101, and the accompanying text.

suppression [and] several European governments have virtually come to the resolution of putting a stop to it.[12]

This seemingly forceful plea for the "prompt suppression" of slave trade was qualified by the acknowledgment that the declaration could not "prejudge the period that each particular Power may consider as most advisable for the definitive abolition of the Slave Trade."[13]

A similar declaration was signed in 1822 by five powers—Austria, France, Great Britain, Prussia, and Russia.[14] In addition, several multilateral and bilateral treaties were concluded during the nineteenth century which called for specific measures to arrest and search ships allegedly transporting slaves and, in some instances, even provided for adjudicatory machinery to decide such cases.[15] The 1841 Treaty of London and the 1862 Treaty of Washington are the most notable treaties of this period.

The first significant effort to suppress slave trade on the international level was made in 1890 when the representatives of seventeen nations meeting in Brussels concluded a convention "to put an end to the crimes and devastations engendered by traffic in African slaves." Thereafter, efforts have continued under the auspices of the League of Nations and subsequently the United Nations to eradicate slave trade and slavery. But somehow the remnants of slavery, slave trade, and their analogous practices have not been completely eradicated. The United Nations is currently studying the "Question of Slavery and Slave Trade in All Their Practices of *Apartheid* and Colonialism."[16] The following discussion will mainly focus on the U.N. deliberations on slavery and slave trade.

1.3. International Agreements Concerning Slavery and Slave Trade Prior to the Establishment of the United Nations

The 1890 Brussels convention was a most significant international agreement on the subject of slave trade; although the convention was particularly concerned with the African continent, the General Act of the convention

---

[12] Cited in U.N. ECOSOC, Ad hoc Committee on Slavery, *The Suppression of Slavery* (*Memorandum submitted by the Secretary General*), U.N. Doc. ST/ SOA/ 4 (1951), at 3 [hereinafter cited as 1951 Memorandum].

[13] *Id.* at 4.

[14] *Id.* at 4–5.

[15] *See generally id.* at 5–11.

[16] For recent reports submitted by the Special Rapporteur on "Question of Slavery and the Slave Trade in All their Practices and Manifestations, Including the Slavery-like Practices of *Apartheid* and Colonialism," *see* U.N. ECOSOC, Commission on Human Rights, Sub-Commission on Prevention of Discrimination and Protection of Minorities, 23rd Session, Item 5 of the Provisional Agenda, U.N. Doc. E/CN.4/Sub. 2/312, 1 July 1970 [hereinafter cited as 1970 Report of the Special Rapporteur]; *id.,* 24th Session, Item 5 of the Provisional Agenda, U.N. Doc. E/CN. 4/ Sub 2/ 322, 16 July 1971 [hereinafter cited as 1971 Report of the Special Rapporteur].

was a comprehensive document containing one hundred articles.[17] It obligated the contracting parties to undertake a number of economic, legislative and military measures toward the suppression of the slave trade in Africa. Of special note are the following:

1. The mutual right of visit and search over vessels of less than 500 tons within a defined maritime zone in which the slave trade was still in existence.[18]
2. Pledges by contracting parties to whose territories "slaves are sent [and] whose institutions recognize the existence of domestic slavery,[19] especially those by the Ottoman Empire, Persia, and Zanzibar.
3. The establishment of institutions to secure the execution of the General Act—an International Maritime Office at Zanzibar[20] to centralize all documents and information sent by signatory states, and international bureau at Brussels[21] for the exchange and circulation of documents and information relating to the slave trade.

The Brussels convention was followed, at the end of World War I, by the convention of St. Germain-en-Laye, signed on September 10, 1919, by Belgium, the British Empire, France, Italy, Japan, Portugal, and the United States and subsequently ratified by all the signatory states. Article 11, paragraph 1, of the convention provides:

> The signatory Powers exercising sovereign rights or authority in African territories will continue to watch over the preservation of the native populations and to supervise the improvement of the conditions of their moral and material well-being. They will, in particular, endeavor to secure the complete suppression of slavery in all its forms and of the slave trade by land and sea.[22]

The convention, however, made no provision for creating appropriate machinery to effectuate the objective expressed in article 11(1). This lacuna was aptly considered by many observers to be an unfortunate occurrence, since article 13 of the convention has been interpreted to abrogate the implementing provisions covering slavery in the Brussels Act.[23]

Although the Covenant of the League of Nations did not contain any

[17] The translated text of the General Act for the Repression of African Slave Trade is contained in 1951 Memorandum, at 46–68.
[18] Arts. 20–29 of the Act.
[19] Ch. IV (arts. 62–73).
[20] Ch. V, § 1 (arts. 74–80).
[21] Ch. V, § 2 (arts. 81–85).
[22] Cited in 1951 Memorandum, at 12.
[23] *See generally* C. Greenidge, Slavery 178–79 (1958).

specific reference to slavery except for those countries within the Mandates System,[24] in 1922 the League undertook the task of examining the question of worldwide slavery. Two years later the Council of the League established a Temporary Slavery Commission, which the following year reported on the following eight topics:[25]

1. Legal status of slavery.
2. Slave raiding and similar acts.
3. Slave acts.
4. Slave dealing.
5. Practices restrictive of the liberty of the person.
6. Domestic or praedial slavery (serfdom).
7. Compulsory labor, public or private, paid or unpaid.
8. Transition from servile or compulsory labor to free-wage or independent production.

The Commission report was based on state responses to the two questionnaires the Secretary-General had sent to governments as well as on communications the Commission has received from nongovernmental sources.

A majority of the Commission recommended that an international convention on slavery be concluded and suggested the inclusion of specific topics in the proposed convention. The League Council and the Assembly acted favorably on this recommendation and the Slavery Convention was approved by the Assembly in its resolution of September 25, 1926.[26] The legal definitions of slavery and slave trade, contained in article 1 of the Convention are among its lasting achievements. Slavery is defined as "the status or condition of a person over whom any or all of the powers attaching to the right of ownership are exercised."[27] The slave trade includes "all acts involved in the capture, acquisition, or disposal of a person with intent to reduce him to slavery; all acts involved in the acquisition of a slave with a view to selling or exchanging him; all acts of disposal by sale or exchange of a slave acquired with a view to being sold or exchanged, and, in general, every act of trade or transport in slaves."[28]

Although the convention, as finally adopted, did not incorporate the proposal that engaging in the slave trade at sea should be declared piracy, it did contain specific measures for the suppression of slave trade at

[24] For specific provisions, *see* 1951 Memorandum, at 27–28.
[25] Report of the Temporary Slavery Commission, July 25, 1925, League of Nations Doc. A. 19. 1925. VI.
[26] The resolution is contained in 1951 Memorandum, at 35–36.
[27] Art. 1(1) of the Convention.
[28] Art. 1(2) of the Convention.

sea.[29] In another article, the convention attempted to limit the employment of forced labor.[30]

Subsequently, in 1931, the Council of the League appointed a Committee of Experts on Slavery to conduct an appraisal of the effectiveness of the Slavery Convention "in putting an end to slavery."[31] Pursuant to the Committee's recommendation, an Advisory Committee of Experts on Slavery was set up in 1934 to study and examine the documents received by the League Secretariat. The advisory committee continued annual sessions until 1938 when it discontinued its work because of the outbreak of World War II. Included in its report to the Council was a chapter dealing with institutions analogous to slavery, such as (1) debt slavery, pawning, and peonage, (2) Mui-Tsai system, (3) quasi-adoption of children, and (4) serfdom.[32]

Among the notable achievements of the League's efforts were (1) the legal abolition of slavery in Afghanistan (1923), Iraq (1924), Nepal (1926), Transjordania and Persia (1929),[33] (2) a pledge by the government of Ethiopia that it would abolish slavery as a condition for admission to membership of the League,[34] and (3) the establishment of the International Commission of Enquiry to investigate allegations pertaining to conditions of slavery and forced labor in Liberia.[35] The League also made some progress in dealing with the subject of compulsory or forced labor.[36]

1.4. The Role of the United Nations in the Abolition of Slavery and Slave Trade

Although the U.N. Charter did not contain any specific reference to slavery, there was no doubt that the United Nations would confront the problem squarely, for one of the U.N. objectives is to achieve international cooperation in "promoting and encouraging respect for human rights, and for fundamental freedoms for all without distinction as to race, sex, language, or religion."[37] Thus, it was no surprise when the Universal Declaration of Human Rights, adopted by the General Assembly on December 10, 1948, proclaimed in article 4: "No one shall

[29] See art. 3 of the Convention.

[30] See art. 5 of the Convention.

[31] A brief reference to the committee's work is contained in 1951 Memorandum, at 39–41.

[32] See League of Nations Doc. 1937. VI. B. 2; C. 188. M. 173. 1937. VI. Ch. IV dealt with "Other Institutions."

[33] Noted in 1970 Report of the Special Rapporteur, at 4.

[34] *Id.*

[35] For its report, *see* League of Nations Doc. C. 658.M. 272. 1930. VI; 1930. VI. B. 6.

[36] *See generally* 1951 Memorandum, at 44–45.

[37] Art. 1(3) of the U.N. Charter.

be held in slavery or servitude; slavery and the slave trade shall be prohibited in all their forms."[38]

The first specific action undertaken by the United Nations was the establishment of an ad hoc committee of experts to investigate into the field of slavery and other institutions or customs resembling slavery and to suggest methods of combating these problems. The committee was appointed by the Secretary-General pursuant to the 1949 decisions of the General Assembly and the Economic and Social Council respectively.[39] On the advice of the committee, a protocol was concluded in 1953 by which the 1926 Slavery Convention was placed under the care of the United Nations. The committee also recommended that the 1926 convention be supplemented by a new instrument, since the earlier convention had not covered all institutions and practices similar to slavery. The outcome was the convocation in Geneva of a special conference in August-September 1956, which was attended by members of the United Nations and of the specialized agencies. The Conference adopted the Supplementary Convention on the Abolition of Slavery, the Slave Trade, and Institutions and Practices Similar to Slavery.[40]

The 1956 Supplementary Convention was meant to strengthen the 1926 Slavery Convention by including the following "institutions and practices, where they still exist and whether or not they are covered by the definition of slavery contained in article 1 of the [1926 Slavery Convention]:[41] Debt bondage, serfdom, the sale of women into marriage without their consent and the sham adoption of a child with a view to the exploitation of the child . . . or of his labor."[42]

Subsequently, in July 1963, the Economic and Social Council discussed the question of slavery; several delegates remarked that slave trade was still in existence, and the Council adopted a resolution[43] requesting the Secretary-General to appoint a special rapporteur on slavery so as to bring up to date an earlier report.[44] In February 1964, the Secretary-General appointed Mohamed Awad as the special rapporteur; his final

[38] U.N. Office of Public Information, *The Universal Declaration of Human Rights—A Standard of Achievement* 34 (U.N. Publ. No. 62. I. 9).

[39] For a summary report, *see* 1951 Memorandum, at 1.

[40] *See* United Nations Conference of Plenipotentiaries on a Supplementary Convention of the Abolition of Slavery, the Slave Trade, and Institutions and Practices Similar to Slavery (Held at Geneva, Switzerland from Aug. 13, to Sept. 4, 1956)—Final Act and Supplementary Convention, U.N. Doc. E/CONF. 24/23. The Convention was adopted by 40 votes in favor, none against, and 3 abstentions.

[41] *Id* at 19 (art. 1).

[42] *Id.* at 19–20 (art. 1).

[43] Res. 960 (XXXVI), entitled "Slavery."

[44] 19 U.N. ECOSOC Off. Rec., Annexes, Agenda item No. 8, U.N. Doc E/2673 (1963). The earlier report of 1955 was prepared by Hans Engen, pursuant to the Council resolution 525 (XVII).

report was submitted in July 1966.[45] The report was based on the responses of state and specialized agencies as well as several nongovernmental agencies in consultative status to a questionnaire on slavery formulated and dispatched by the Secretary-General in September-October 1964.[46] It also contained the following recommendations, among others, for possible action by the United Nations:[47] (1) that the U.N. program of technical assistance be expanded in order to bring about economic, social, and cultural reforms "for the elimination of all aspects of slavery and servitude"[48] and (2) that the assistance of regional organizations be sought in combating slavery and slave trade.[49]

The responses to the Secretary-General's questionnaire contained several useful suggestions, only a few of which will be noted here. Senegal asked for an international investigation of slave-trade networks;[50] Iran suggested the conclusion of international agreements, providing for "judicial assistance and cooperation for the elimination of slavery;"[51] Laos called for the holding of regional meetings to combat trafficking in women "which is rife in the Southeast of Indo-China;"[52] Nepal urged that the governments concerned be persuaded to undertake legislative and administrative measures "for abolishing slavery in their respective lands;"[53] Nigeria stressed the importance of an international covenant which would provide "means of international supervision;"[54] the Soviet Union urged the ratification of the 1956 Supplementary Convention;[55] and several nongovernmental organizations advocated the establishment of a special U.N. committee of experts and the holding of regional meetings and seminars.[56]

Pursuant to the rapporteur's recommendations, the Economic and Social Council called upon all member states to ratify the 1926 Slavery Convention and the 1956 Supplementary Convention.[57] It also decided to refer the question of "slavery and the slave trade in all their practices and manifestations, including the slavery-like practices of *apartheid* and colonialism," to the Commission on Human Rights for making "specific

---

[45] Mohamed Awad, *Report on Slavery*, U.N. Doc. E/4168/ Rev. 1 (1966) [hereinafter cited as 1966 Slavery Report].

[46] The questionnaire is contained in *id.* at 2–6.

[47] *Id.* at 299–314.

[48] *Id.* at 301–303.

[49] *Id.* at 301.

[50] *Id.* at 275.

[51] *Id.* at 282.

[52] *Id.* at 301.

[53] *Id.* at 302.

[54] *Id.*

[55] *Id.* at 303.

[56] *Id.* at 304–305.

[57] Per Res. 1126 (XLI) of July 26, 1966. The text is contained in *id.* at 313–14.

proposals for effective and immediate measures which the United Nations could adopt" to put an end to slavery and similar practices.[58]

Since the Commission, in turn, referred the question to its subcommission on Prevention of Discrimination and Protection of Minorities, the Economic and Social Council adopted a resolution in May 1968 authorizing the subcommission

> . . . to undertake a study of the measures which might be taken to implement the International Slavery Convention of 1926 and the Supplementary Convention of 1956 on the Abolition of Slavery, the Slave Trade, and Institutions and Practices Similar to Slavery and the various recommendations included in the resolutions of the General Assembly, the Economic and Social Council and the Commission on Human Rights relating to the slavery-like practices of *apartheid* and colonialism.[59]

The subcommission was further authorized to "initiate a study of the possibilities of international police cooperation to interrupt and punish the transportation of persons in danger of being enslaved, taking into account, as appropriate, the views of the competent international organizations."[60] Former special rapporteur Mohamed Awad was designated to be the special rapporteur to carry out a study under the terms of the Council resolution, and the Council sought the assistance of the Secretary-General and the cooperation of specialized agencies and regional intergovernment and nongovernmental organizations in the proposed study.[61]

Meanwhile, on December 16, 1966, the General Assembly adopted the International Covenant on Civil and Political Rights,[62] which would transform the proclamation of the Universal Declaration into a legal obligation, when the Covenant enters into force. Article 8 of the Covenant provides

> 1. No one shall be held in slavery; slavery and the slave trade in all their forms shall be prohibited.
> 2. No one shall be held in servitude.[63]

The Covenant also provides for the establishment of a Human Rights Committee,[64] whose function would be to consider reports on measures

---

[58] *Id.*

[59] Resolution of May 31, 1968. The relevant Part of the resolution is contained in U.N. ECOSOC, *Preliminary report submitted by the* Special Rapporteur, Mr. Mohamed Awad, U.N. Doc. E/CN.4/Sub. 2/304, Aug. 18, 1969, at 1–2. [hereinafter cited as 1969 Report of the Special Rapporteur].

[60] *Id.* at 2.

[61] Per Res. 1419 of June 9, 1969.

[62] *See* Resolutions Adopted by the General Assembly During Its 21st Session, Sept. 20–Dec. 20, 1966, 21 U.N. GAOR Supp. No. 16, at 49, 52; U.N. Doc. A/6316 (1966).

[63] *Id.* at 54.

[64] Arts. 28–45. See *id.* at 56–58.

adopted by states to give effect to the rights recognized in the Covenant. In certain circumstances, the proposed Human Rights Committee would also consider communications from a state party claiming that another state party is not fulfilling its obligations under the Covenant. Under the Optional Protocol to the Covenant,[65] the Committee would also be entitled to receive, in certain circumstances, communications from individuals alleging violations of any of the rights granted by the Covenant.

1.5. The 1971 Special Report

Within three months after his designation as Special Rapporteur, Mohamed Awad presented a preliminary report to the subcommission for its consideration at its 22nd session.[66] After noting that the presently available machinery for the implementation of the 1926 Slavery Convention was inadequate,[67] he observed that "further measures are [clearly] required" to implement these conventions. He considered it "his primary task to study such measures, and to make suggestions regarding them to the subcommission."[68]

The rapporteur noted his disappointment that the states parties to the 1956 Supplementary Convention had not communicated to the Secretary-General the measures they had undertaken to implement the convention.[69] He specially mentioned the two suggestions made by the Secretary-General:[70] (1) that "the techniques used to suppress the illicit trade in narcotics might be adopted to suppress the illicit trade in slaves," and (2) that "the articles of the Single Convention (on Narcotic Drugs of 1961), dealing with the measures to insure the execution of its provisions, might serve as a model for future conventions in the field of slavery in all its forms." He also examined the possibility of cooperation with the International Criminal Police Organization (Interpol) to suppress slavery.[71] The subcommission considered the preliminary report and resolved to widen the scope of the rapporteur's investigation so as to include "measures for combating the manifestations of the slavery-like practices akin to *apartheid* which exist in Southern Rhodesia and Nambia, especially the practice of forced, sweated African labor and the total denial of trade union rights to Africans in those territories."[72]

---

[65] For the text, *see id.* at 59.

[66] *See* 1969 Report of the Special Rapporteur, *supra* note 50.

[67] *Id* at 2–5.

[68] *Id.* at 6.

[69] *Id.* at 7–8.

[70] Contained in U.N. Doc. E/CN. 4/Sub. 2/280, at 33, 42 and cited in 1969 Report of the Special Rapporteur, at 10.

[71] *See* 1969 Report of the Special Rapporteur, at 13–24.

[72] Per Res. 4(XXII) of Sept. 10, 1969, contained in 1970 Report of the Special Rapporteur, at 8–9.

Subsequently the rapporteur consulted with officials of the International Labor Organization (ILO),[73] the United Nations' High Commissioner for Refugees (UNHCR),[74] the Commission on Narcotic Drugs,[75] the International Criminal Police Organization (Interpol),[76] UNESCO,[77] and the Anti-Slavery Society.[78]

On the present state of slavery and slavery-like practices, the rapporteur noted that the Anti-Slavery Society "has reason to believe that chattel slavery, serfdom, debt bondage, the sale of children, and servile forms of marriage survive today to the extent that they constitute a recognizable element in the pattern of society" in several countries.[79]

The rapporteur's discussions with the officials of the International Labor Office caused him to explore the possibilities of further cooperation between ILO and the United Nations. He was impressed with the great variety of ILO programs "that contribute to the achievement of personal freedom for persons who have suffered as a result of living in servitude."[80] Specifically, he observed that (1) in seeking further state ratifications of the 1926 and 1956 conventions, the United Nations could adopt some of the ILO's informal methods of encouraging governments to ratify the latter's international labor conventions;[81] (2) the United Nations could appeal to member states to ratify certain ILO conventions dealing with matters closely related to slavery and servitude,[82] and to give effect to certain ILO recommendations concerning "the improvement of conditions of life and work of tenants, sharecroppers, and similar categories of agricultural workers;"[83] and (3) the United Nations may recommend to the ILO to continue and expand its assistance to persons "who escape from countries or territories where they have suffered from slavery, the slave trade, or any of the slavery-like practices of *apartheid* or colonialism."[84]

The rapporteur's discussions with officials of the Division of Narcotic Drugs in Geneva were primarily directed to studying the Secretary-General's suggestions made in 1967 that[85] (1) the same techniques might be used to suppress the illicit trade in slaves as is being used to suppress the

[73] For the rapporteur's account, *see id.* at 12–23.
[74] *See id.* at 24–26.
[75] *See id.* at 26–32.
[76] *See id.* at 32–39.
[77] *See id.* at 39–42.
[78] *See id.* at 42–43
[79] *Id.* at 43. *See also* 1971 Report of Special Rapporteur, at 29.
[80] 1971 Report of the Special Rapporteur, at 15.
[81] *Id.*
[82] *Id.*
[83] *Id.* at 16.
[84] *Id.*
[85] *See supra* note 61 and the accompanying text.

illicit trade in narcotics and (2) the articles of the Single Convention on Narcotic Drugs of 1961, dealing with measures of implementation, might serve as a model for future conventions on slavery. While he did not reach any conclusion on the latter question,[86] terming it "essentially political in character," the rapporteur discussed the possibilities of adapting the two basic techniques used by the Division of Narcotic Drugs:[87] (1) periodic publication of seizures and illicit transactions of narcotics and (2) promotion of technical cooperation in narcotics control.

The rapporteur favors the publication of periodic summaries of illicit traffic in persons, especially since

1. states parties to the Supplementary Convention of 1956 are obligated, pursuant to article 3(3) of the Convention, to exchange information on the subject, both as to measures taken by them in combating slave trade and as to cases of slave trade and of attempts to engage in slave trade; and
2. the Economic and Social Council has, in its Resolution 1593 (L) of May 21, 1971, requested the Secretary-General to assist the state parties to the 1956 Convention for the purpose of exchanging such information, and has authorized him to supplement such information by information available from official sources, including international organizations and states not parties to the 1956 Convention.[88]

Although the rapporteur foresees the possibility of adapting the program of technical cooperation in narcotics control, by utilizing the advisory services of the U.N. human rights program in such activities as offering expert advice, or training of national officers and arranging regional seminars and meetings, he warns of two problems:[89] (1) the fear of states that their request for technical assistance to eliminate slavery and servitude might lead to the charges that they are "harboring persons in a servile status" and (2) "a lack of general interest in the immediate eradication of institutions and practices which exist, for the most part, only clandestinely and without legal sanction."[90]

In connection with the rapporteur's consultations with various organizations, it should also be noted that Interpol officials indicated their willingness to cooperate with the United Nations in its efforts to eliminate slavery and slave trade.[91] Specifically, Interpol was willing to furnish annually to the appropriate U.N. body the information it might have on

[86] 1971 Report of the Special Rapporteur, at 22.
[87] *Id.* at 20–22.
[88] Noted in *id.* at 21.
[89] *Id.*
[90] *Id.*
[91] *Id.* at 26. On consultations with Interpol, *see id.* at 22–27.

the international traffic in persons.[92] Subsequently, on May 20, 1971, the U.N. Economic and Social Council approved an arrangement for the exchange of information between the United Nations and Interpol.[93]

The rapporteur offers the following specific suggestions:

1. Since Interpol has already indicated that its machinery for cooperation "can function as effectively for slavery as for fraud, counterfeiting, or theft," its facilities should be utilized to stimulate international police cooperation "in order to enable the police forces in
   different countries to coordinate their work effectively in order to
   enforce the existing laws relating to slavery and the slave trade and
   to prevent and suppress crimes in this field."[94] Interpol's willingness
   to furnish information on the international traffic in persons has
   already been noted.[95] Furthermore, Interpol could stimulate government interest by taking certain measures such as organizing international seminars for police officers who are responsible for combating
   slavery trade, and encouraging research and publication in the
   field.[96]

2. Regional activities should be encourged to explore effective ways
   to eradicate the problem. Regional intergovernmental and nongovernmental organizations should arrange conferences and seminars
   for the exchange of ideas,[97] and regional agreements could perhaps
   be reached on common standards and programs for the solution of
   these problems.[98]

3. States should take the following steps to implement the principles
   embodied in the Slavery Conventions of 1926 and 1956:

   a. Criminal laws should be enacted, providing for harsh penalties in
      cases of slavery, slave trade, and slavery-like institutions and
      practices;[99] more specific legislation outlawing such practices and
      institutions, making them penal offenses and establishing the
      necessary administrative machinery for eradicating them, may be
      necessary in some states.[100]

   b. Steps should be taken to prepare the people to accept effective
      state enforcement action. "Massive educational efforts" may be
      necessary to accomplish this objective, as well as that of pro-

[92] *Id.* at 27.
[93] Per Res. 1579 (L) of May 20, 1971, which is conveniently contained in *id.* at 79–80.
[94] *Id.* at 29.
[95] *See supra* notes 83 & 84 and the accompanying text.
[96] 1971 Report of the Rapporteur, at 30.
[97] *Id.* at 39–40.
[98] *Id.* at 39.
[99] *Id.* at 30, 37–38.
[100] *Id.* at 37.

moting fundamental economic and social change in some states. Presumably, a planned effort would be made to make available technical assistance to states from international intergovernmental organizations, such as UNESCO and the U.N. Development Program, and nongovernmental organizations, especially religious organizations.[101]

c. Adequate assistance should be provided "to those freed from a state of slavery or servitude to facilitate their integration as free persons into the social life of their community."[102] ILO and UNESCO, among other international organizations, could provide useful service, the former in training people freed from slavery and slavery-like institutions for industrial employment, and the latter, through its educational programs, for the benefit of such persons.[103]

d. Legislation should be enacted where needed to abolish bondage.[104]

e. Measures should be taken to offer expanded land reform and vocational guidance programs,[105] benefiting from the successful ILO and FAO experiences in this regard.[106]

f. States which have not yet ratified the Slavery Conventions of 1926 and 1956 and the Convention on Consent to Marriage, Minimum Age for Marriage and Registration of Marriage of 1962 should ratify these conventions.[107]

1.6. Efforts Toward the Suppression of White Slavery

A related question which is of sufficient importance to be included in a discussion of slavery and slave trade is that of white slavery. It needs no emphasis that the forced use and trade of women and girls in and for the use of prostitution and other immoral purposes is a reprehensible form of human degradation and deprivation of freedom. Control of this practice has been attempted by regulation, prohibition, and abolition, a brief sketch of which follows here.

The first international agreement on the subject was reached in 1904 in the form of an International Agreement for the Suppression of White Slave Traffic.[108] It was essentially a scheme for the coordination of

[101] *Id.* at 30, 47.
[102] *Id.* at 31, 38–39, 47–49.
[103] *Id.* at 47–48.
[104] *Id.* at 44–45.
[105] *Id.* at 41–44.
[106] *Id.*
[107] *Id.* at 36–37.
[108] The text is contained in 2 A.J.I.L., Supp., 363 (1908).

information relative to the procurement of women and girls for prostitution and immoral purposes by abuse or compulsion or for those women and girls under age. Six years later the International Convention for the Suppression of the White Slave Traffic[109] went beyond the measures contained in the 1904 agreement and bound the parties to criminal punishment of the offenders. The subject matter, however, remained within the exclusive domain of nation-states, and the emphasis still was primarily on regulation.

Subsequently, in 1921, the International Convention for the Suppression of the Traffic in Women and Children[110] was adopted, followed in 1933 by the International Convention for the Suppression of the Traffic in Women of Full Age.[111] The model was now prohibitionist instead of being regulatory. Criminal sanctions were to be applied and extended to violations beyond the actual conduct to include attempt, preparation, as well as acts of enticing and leading away persons beyond the boundaries of a given state with intent to use them for such purposes as defined by the Convention. However, the enforcement mechanism still rested on the notion that while the treaty had established an obligation, its implementation was to be national in scope, with the role of the international machinery being confined to providing information and insuring cooperation among member states.

Finally, in 1949, an all-inclusive Convention for the Suppression of the Traffic in Persons and the Exploitation of the Prostitution of Others was adopted.[112] This convention, referred to as the Consolidated Convention, attempts to abolish white slavery, while still relying on the enforcement mechanism embodied in the earlier conventions. All these efforts have failed to accomplish the set objective, for the emphasis was on penal sanctions without giving adequate consideration to the endemic social and psychological reasons for the existence of the problem and without any serious attempts to changing subjectivities and mores.

The persistence of the malady led the U.N. Economic and Social Council to study the problem and prepare a report in 1959 on Traffic in Persons and Prostitution,[113] wherein an action program was proposed. While the report noted that "the abolitionist system can be considered a necessary prerequisite to any programme of action to combat the traf-

[109] The text is contained in Parliamentary Papers, 1912–13 (CMD. 6326).
[110] The text is contained in 18 A.J.I.L., Supp., 130 (1924).
[111] Submitted to the U.S. Senate on Mar. 18, 1935, but no action was taken. *See* 4 Treaties, Conventions, Int'l Acts, Protocols, and Agreements between the U.S. and other Powers, 1923–31, at 5728.
[112] The text is contained in United Nations, *Human Rights: A Compilation of International Instruments of the United Nations* 48 (1967).
[113] U.N. Doc. ST/SOA/SD/8 (1959).

fic in persons and commercialized prostitution," it recommended that the

> adoption of this system is, however, insufficient by itself and should be accompanied by measures aimed at the prevention of prostitution, the rehabilitation of persons engaged in prostitution, the repression of the traffic in persons and of the exploitation of the prostitution of others, and the prevention of venereal disease. From an organizational point of view, this requires effective coordination of the corresponding programmes, policies, and services.[114]

This report reveals that the prior emphasis on sanctions is inappropriate and concludes that like any other social problem,

> prostitution is caused by factors which, although often of a general character, are shaped by national, regional, and even local social and economic conditions. In the development of policies and the organization of programmes these conditions should be kept constantly in mind. Flexibility and adaptability, therefore, should be two main characteristics of such policies and programmes.[115]

The suggestion should be made that in an effective international control scheme the emphasis should be along the lines of social attitudinal changes by a transformation of the basic values which support or tolerate the behavior sought to be altered. This is what accounts for the relative success of the eradication of slavery and slave trade and the relative failure of the abolition of white slavery.

1.7. Appraisal and Recommendations

It has already been noted that the Sub-Commission on Prevention of Discrimination and Protection of Minorities of the U.N. Commission on Human Rights, which has been assigned the task of studying the question of slavery and slave trade, has recently added colonialism and apartheid to be studied along with slavery and slave trade. However, the decision of the Sub-Commission should not be interpreted to mean that slavery and slave trade, which had been until recently the focus of international attention, no longer deserve the primary attention, or that the battle against such practices has been won.[116] For while a recent

---

[114] *Id.* at 32–33.

[115] *Id.* at 38.

[116] *See, e.g.,* S. O'CALLAGHAN, THE SLAVE TRADE TODAY (1962). On comparative approach to slavery, *see* D. DAVIS, THE PROBLEM OF SLAVERY IN WESTERN CULTURE (1966); SLAVERY IN THE NEW WORLD (L. Foner & E. Genovese eds. 1969). For an incisive study, *see* S. ELKINS, SLAVERY: A PROBLEM IN AMERICAN INSTITUTIONAL AND INTELLECTUAL LIFE (1959); for good historical accounts *see,* AMERICAN NEGRO SLAVERY (A. Weinstein & F. Gatell eds. 1968); J. INGRAM, A HISTORY OF SLAVERY AND SERFDOM (1895); E. COPLEY, A HISTORY OF SLAVERY AND ITS ABOLITION (1969). In the post World War I era, *see* J. HARRIS, SLAVERY OR "SACRED TRUST"? (1926); K. SIMON, SLAVERY (1929). On the anti-slavery movement in Great Britain, which roughly covered the period 1770–1833,

report from Afghanistan indicates that the practice of forced labor and serfdom, caused mainly by debt bondage, persists in that country,[117] the antislavery society claims that debt bondage, serfdom, chattel slavery, servile forms of marriage, and the sale of children still constitute "a recognizable element in the pattern of society" in thirty-eight countries.[118]

The rapporteur has noted that "the international traffic in persons for the purpose of reducing them to a servile status may no longer be a problem of worldwide proportions and that such slave trade as may continue to exist has been forced underground and in most cases out of sight.[119] But it is our conclusion that because of the clandestine nature of the slave trade at present, effective measures which are worldwide and internationally coordinated are necessary to destroy the remaining vestiges of the institution.

Any international control scheme must ultimately rely, in the absence of an international coercive body, and even then, on the willful compliance and cooperation of states. World community proscriptions will, therefore, be effective if the participants in that process share the value-oriented goals of the program and are committed to its effective implementation. Admittedly, there will seldom be a uniform or completely homogeneous set of basic values for the world community, but the objective must be that of coalescing different standards and approaches so as to attain an identifiable set of basic human values. Concurrent with that systematic process, efforts should be made to check the prohibited activity.

A key problem lies with the lack of adequate national implementation and enforcement of the existing international legislation. As of June 30, 1971, a large number of states had yet to ratify the Supplementary Convention. These included fourteen Latin American states, twelve Asian states, and twenty-five African states.[120] Efforts to secure these ratifications should be the top priority item on the ECOSOC's agenda. Second, further measures should be taken to encourage the exchange of information, called for under article 3(3) of the Supplementary Convention. Third, simultaneous efforts on all fronts should be taken to prevent, deter, and suppress these practices, while at the same time taking the necessary steps

---

voluminous literature is available. *See generally,* F. KLINGBERG, THE ANTI-SLAVERY MOVEMENT IN ENGLAND (1926); O. SHERRARD, FREEDOM FROM FEAR (1959); R. COUPLAND, THE BRITISH ANTI-SLAVERY MOVEMENT (1933). For a recent study on Africa, *see* A. FISHER & H. FISHER, SLAVERY AND MUSLIM SOCIETY IN AFRICA (1970).

[117] Reported in Lake, *Afghanistan Peasant "Slavery" Described,* The Denver Post, Dec. 1, 1971, p. 13, col. 1. Lake published his report for Britain's Anti-Slavery Society in June 1971.

[118] 1970 Report of the Rapporteur, at 43.

[119] *Id.* at 44.

[120] Noted in 1971 Report of the Rapporteur, at 3.

to rehabilitate those freed from servitude. The rapporteur's reports, which have been extensively discussed in this section, offer several useful recommendations for states, intergovernmental, and nongovernmental organizations.

Finally, further studies should be conducted on the questions of enacting adequate international legislation and providing effective international machinery for implementation. Although it can be argued that the conventions of 1926 and 1956 provide the necessary legislation internationally to cope with the problem of slavery, perhaps a case can still be made for the codification of the existing multilateral conventions and protocols dealing with slavery into a single convention,[121] as in the case of the Single Convention on Narcotic Drugs, 1961 (notwithstanding its many shortcomings). A single convention which provides for the enactment of penal laws, coordination of "preventive and repressive action against clandestine forms of slavery and servitude," mutual assistance, and exchange of information and legal documents among the states as well as the United Nations, and the establishment of a permanent body of independent experts, which would have responsibility for ensuring the execution of its provisions,[122] might prove more effective in combating slavery than present measures. Similarly, the question of the establishment of an international slavery board on the model of the International Narcotics Control Board should be given serious consideration.[123]

Finally, since the eradication of this type of behavior depends in large measure on the changing mores of the human society, efforts at the prohibition of slavery, slave trade, as well as other forms of human rights violations must place the highest priority on those programs which lead to attitudinal changes rather than coercive-repressive measures.

Section 2.   GENOCIDE AND RACIAL DISCRIMINATION

M. CHERIF BASSIOUNI

2.1. Introduction

A quarter of a century has elapsed since Lemkin said, "New conceptions require new terms," and a new word entered the legal vocabulary: *genocide*. It was intended

> to signify a coordinated plan of different actions aiming at the destruction of essential foundations of life of national groups. . . . The objectives of such a plan would be the disintegration of the political and social institutions of culture, language, national feelings, religion, and the economical existence of

[121] *See id.* at 22; 1970 Report of the Rapporteur, at 47.
[122] *See* 1970 Report of the Rapporteur, at 48; 1971 Report of the Rapporteur, at 77–78.
[123] *See* 1971 Report of the Rapporteur, at 49-50.

national groups, and the destruction of personal security, liberty, health, dignity, and even lives of the individuals belonging to such groups.[1]

The standards of mankind's common morality improved with each tragic advent of human atavism. As more people considered all wars to be fratricide, and human dignity the most sacred value of civilization, "Genocide" acquired more meaning to more people.[2]

At Nuremberg the distinction was drawn between the murder of anti-Nazi Germans and German Jews, and anti-Nazi non-Germans and non-German Jews.[2] The tribunal concerned itself with crimes committed in war times or connected with war, excluding peacetime atrocities.[3]

Thus, "crimes against humanity" were considered either part of "war crimes" or separate crimes connected to the conduct of war. Nuremberg provided, to that extent, a weak precedent for international individual responsibility for crimes which were not war connected. The world community realized the need to legislate the prohibition and punishment of peacetime conduct which amounts to the mass destruction of human lives. This was one of the objectives of the International Law Commission's "Draft Code of Offenses against the Peace and Security of Mankind" of 1954 which was tabled by the General Assembly.[4] In 1948, the Genocide Convention was passed and almost a decade later one of its themes was embodied in the "Convention on the Elimination of all Forms of Racial Discrimination."[5]

2.2. The Genocide Convention[6]

The scope of the Convention is not limited to crimes committed during war. Its preamble and substantive articles read as follows:

[1] LEMKIN, AXIS RULE IN OCCUPIED EUROPE 79 (1944).

[2] Lemkin, *Genocide as a Crime under International Law* 41 A.J.I.L. 145 (1947).

[3] I OPPENHEIM, INTERNATIONAL LAW 279–80 (Lauterpacht ed. 1958), & Schwelb, *Crimes Against Humanity,* BRIT. Y.B. INT'L L. 178 (1946).

[4] Johnson, *The Draft Code of Offences against the Peace and Security of Mankind,* 4 INT'L & COMP. L.Q. 445 (1955).

[5] *See infra* § 2.

[6] U.N. GAOR Res. 96 (I), Dec. 11, 1946; Res. 260 A (III), Dec. 9, 1948; 78 U.N.T.S. 277. The vote on the Convention was 55 votes to 0, with Costa Rica, El Salvador, and the Union of South Africa absent. For statement by Ernest A. Gross, Legal Advisor, Department of State, and Alternate U.S. Representative to the General Assembly, made before the General Assembly on Dec. 9, 1948, *see* XIX Bulletin, Department of State, No. 493, at 755–56 (Dec. 12, 1948).

On the background in the United Nations of the Genocide Convention *see* I Whiteman, DIGEST OF INTERNATIONAL LAW 217–220 (1963). Much has been written concerning the Convention on the Prevention and Punishment of the Crime of Genocide, including, among other writings, the following: Sohn, *United States Senate Action in 1949 on Convention as to Genocide,* a comment in 58 YALE L. J. 1142 (1949); Kuhn; *The Genocide Convention and State Rights,* 43 A.J.I.L. 498; McDougal & Leighton, *The Rights of Man in the World Community: Constitution,* 3 VAND L. REV. 683–709 (1950).

The Contracting Parties,

Having considered the declaration made by the General Assembly of the United Nations in its resolution 96(I) dated 11 December 1946 that genocide is a crime under international law, contrary to the spirit and aims of the United Nations and condemned by the civilized world;

Recognizing that at all periods of history genocide has inflicted great losses on humanity; and

Being convinced that, in order to liberate mankind from such an odious scourge, international cooperation is required,

Hereby agree as hereinafter provided:

Article I

The Contracting Parties confirm that genocide, whether committed in time of peace or in time of war, is a crime under international law which they undertake to prevent and to punish.

Article II

In the present Convention, genocide means any of the following acts committed with intent to destroy, in whole or in part, a national, ethical, racial, or religious group, as such:

(a) Killing members of the group;

(b) Causing serious bodily or mental harm to members of the group;

(c) Deliberately inflicting on the group, conditions of life calculated to bring about its physical destruction in whole or in part;

(d) Imposing measures intended to prevent births within the group;

(e) Forcibly transferring children of the group to another group.

Article III

The following acts shall be punishable:

(a) Genocide;

(b) Conspiracy to commit genocide;

(c) Direct and public incitement to commit genocide;

(d) Attempt to commit genocide;

(e) Complicity in genocide.

Article IV

Persons committing genocide or any of the other acts enumerated in article III shall be punished, whether they are constitutionally responsible rulers, public officials, or private individuals.

Article V

The Contracting Parties undertake to enact, in accordance with their respective Constitutions, the necessary legislation to give effect to the provisions of the present Convention and, in particular, to provide effective penalties for persons guilty of genocide or of any of the other acts enumerated in article III.

Article VI

Persons charged with genocide or any of the other acts enumerated in article III shall be tried by a competent tribunal of the State in the territory of which the act was committed, or by such international penal tribunal as may have jurisdiction with respect to those Contracting Parties which shall have accepted its jurisdiction.

Article VII

Genocide and the other acts enumerated in article III shall not be considered as political crimes for the purpose of extradition.

The Contracting Parties pledge themselves in such cases to grant extradition in accordance with their laws and treaties in force.

Article VIII

Any Contracting Party may call upon the competent organs of the United Nations to take such action under the Charter of the United Nations as they consider appropriate for the prevention and suppression of acts of genocide or any of the other acts enumerated in article III.

Article IX

Disputes between the Contracting Parties relating to the interpretation, application, or fulfilment of the present Convention, including those relating to the responsibility of a State for genocide or for any of the other acts enumerated in article III, shall be submitted to the International Court of Justice at the request of any of the parties to the dispute.[7]

The main principles established by the Convention are the following:

1. Contracting states are bound to enact the laws needed to give effect to the provisions of the Convention, in particular to provide effective penalties.
2. States undertake to try persons charged with these offenses in their competent national court.
3. Parties to the Convention agree that the acts listed shall not be considered as political crimes. Therefore, they pledge to grant extradition in accordance with their laws and treaties.

The Convention also envisages trial by an international penal tribunal should one be set up and should the contracting parties accept its jurisdiction.

If there is any dispute between one country and another on the interpretation, application or fulfilment of the Convention, the dispute must be submitted to the International Court of Justice at the request of any of the parties to the dispute.

Article IV of the Convention declares that those guilty of genocide and the other acts listed shall be punished "whether they are constitutionally responsible rulers, public officials, or private individuals." This clause makes it impossible for a person to plead immunity because he was the head of a state or other public official.

Under article VIII of the Convention, any contracting party may call upon the competent organs of the United Nations to take such action under the Charter of the United Nations as they consider appropriate for the prevention and suppression of acts of genocide or any of the related acts. The related acts are (1) conspiracy to commit genocide, (2) direct and public incitement to commit genocide, (3) an attempt to commit the crime, and (4) complicity in its commission.

During discussion by the Legal Committee in 1948, the question of international penal jurisdiction was considered carefully. As a result, the idea is envisaged and provided for in article VI of the Convention. Further, along with the Convention, the Assembly adopted a resolution which made three provision:

1. It recognized that "in the course of development of the international community there will be an *increasing need* of an international judicial organ for the trial of certain crimes under international law".
2. It invited the International Law Commission to study both the desirability and the possibility of establishing such an international judicial organ "for the trial of persons charged with genocide, or other crimes over which jurisdiction will be conferred upon that organ by international conventions."
3. It required the International Law Commission, in carrying out its task, to pay attention to the possibility of establishing a Criminal Chamber of the International Court of Justice.

After studying the question, the International Law Commission concluded that an international criminal court was both possible and desirable but recommended that it be a separate institution rather than a Criminal Chamber of the International Court. Subsequently, the Committee on International Criminal Jurisdiction submitted a draft statute for a separate court. The General Assembly agreed that the problems raised by this matter are closely related to the question of defining aggression and to the Proposed Draft Code of Offenses Against the Peace and Security of Mankind. It therefore postponed consideration of an international criminal jurisdiction until it could consider all other reports on these related questions.[7]

---

[7] U.N. GAOR, IX, supp. 12 (A12695)23–26 (1954). For summary of the matter, *see Historical Survey of the Question of International Criminal Jurisdiction* (memorandum submitted by the Secretary-General) A/CN 4/7 Rev. 1, at 30–46 (1949).

2.3. Advisory Opinion by the International Court of Justice on Reservations to the Convention on Genocide[8]

On May 28, 1951, the International Court of Justice, on request from the General Assembly of November 16, 1950, delivered an advisory opinion, by a vote of 7 to 5, on three questions concerning reservations to the Genocide Convention.

First, the Court declared that a state having made and maintained a reservation which has been objected to by one or more of the parties to the Convention, but not by others, can be regarded as being a party to the Convention if the reservation is compatible with the object and purpose of the Convention; otherwise, that state cannot be regarded as being a party.

In reply to the General Assembly's second question concerning the effect of the reservations with respect to parties objecting to a reservation and parties accepting it, the Court held that if a party to the Convention objects to a reservation which it considers to be incompatible with the object and purpose of the Convention, it can in fact consider that the reserving state is not a party to the Convention. If, on the other hand, a party accepts the reservation as being compatible with the object and purpose, it can in fact consider that the reserving state is a party.

Third, the Court stated that an objection made by a signatory state which has not yet ratified the Convention can have legal effect only upon ratification; until that moment the objection merely serves as a notice to the other states of the eventual attitude of the signatory state. Further, an objection made by a state which is entitled to sign or accede, but which has not yet done so, is without legal effect.

2.4 The Eichmann Case: Attorney General of Israel v. Eichmann[9]

36 Intl. L. Rep. 5 (Israel, Dist. Ct. Jerusalem 1961)

[Adolf Eichmann, a Nazi functionary of German or Austrian nationality, who was concerned in the Nazi murders in Germany and Austria of large numbers of Jewish persons of German, Polish, and other nationalities prior to the 1945 defeat of Germany, escaped to Argentina. There he was tracked down by Israeli nationals (it was doubtful whether officials or private persons), seized, and abducted to Israel. Argentina complained to the Security Council, which, while disclaiming any condonation of the crimes of which Eichmann was accused, declared that "acts such as that under consideration, which affect the sovereignty of a Member State and therefore cause international friction, may, if repeated, endanger international peace and security." It requested the Government of Israel "to make appropriate reparation in

[8] 1951 I.C.J. REF. 15: *See also* U.N. Doc., N.O.A. 1517; *see* 45 A.J.I.L. (Supp. 13, (1951).

[9] Excerpted in 56 A.J.I.L. 805 (1962).

accordance with the Charter of the United Nations and the rules of international law."[10] Argentina d'd not, however, demand the return of Eichmann, and by a joint communiqué issued August 3, 1960, by the Argentine and Israeli governments, they resolved "to regard as closed the incident which arose out of the action taken by citizens of Israel, which infringed the fundamental rights of the State of Argentina."

[Eichmann was tried in Israel under Israel's Nazi Collaborators (punishment) Law, enacted after Israel became a state in 1948; convicted, and executed after the judgment was confirmed by the Supreme Court of Israel on appeal in 1962. In a long opinion, the trial court said in part:]

[The Court found that national law would prevail over international law in an Israel court, but examined the international law questions at length.]

From the point of view of international law, the power of the State of Israel to enact the Law in question or Israel's "right to punish" is based, with respect to the offences in question, on a dual foundation: the universal character of the crimes in question and their specific character as intended to exterminate the Jewish people. . . .

12. The abhorrent crimes defined in this Law are not crimes under Israel law alone. These crimes, which struck at the whole of mankind and shocked the conscience of nations, are grave offenses against the law of nations itself (*delicta juris gentium*). Therefore, so far from international law negating or limiting the jurisdiction of countries with respect to such crimes, international law is, in the absence of an International Court, in need of the judicial and legislative organs of every country to give effect to its criminal interdictions and to bring the criminals to trial. The jurisdiction to try crimes under international law is *universal*. . . .

[Here the Court discussed piracy, and instances of universality jurisdiction over war crimes. It also referred to genocide as having become a crime under customary international law prior to the Genocide Convention; but held that the limitation in the Genocide Convention, Article 6, to trial before the court of the territory, was a treaty rule only, applicable only to offences committed after the Genocide Convention entered into force in 1951.]

26. . . . It is superfluous to add that the "crime against the Jewish people," which constitutes the crime of "genocide," is nothing but the gravest type of "crime against humanity" (and all the more so because both under Israel law and under the Convention a special intention is requisite for its commission, an intention that is not required for the commission of a "crime against humanity"). Therefore, all that has been said in the Nuremberg principles about "crimes against humanity" applies a fortiori to "crime against the Jewish people". . . .

27. . . . It is indeed difficult to find a more convincing instance of a just retroactive law than the legislation providing for the punishment of war criminals and perpetrators of crimes against humanity and against the Jewish people, and all the reasons justifying the Nuremberg Judgments justify *eo ipse* the retroactive legislation of the Israel legislator. . . . The accused in this case is charged with the implementa-

---

[10] See U.N. Docs. S/4334 & S/4336; for Israeli reply, see S/4342. For Security Council Resolution of June 23, 1960, see S/4349. See also 15 U.N. SCOR, 867th and 868th meetings (June 23, 1960) and 15 U.N. SCOR, Supp. (Apr.-June 1960), at 24. Concerning trial of persons brought within the jurisdiction by force or fraud, see p. 577 *infra*. See also Cardozo, *When Extradition Fails, Is Abduction the Answer?* 55 A.J.I.L. 127 (1961); Silving, *in re* Eichmann: *A Dilemma of Law and Morality*, id at 307. PAPADATOS, THE EICHMANN TRIAL (1964).

tion of the plan for the "final solution of the problem of the Jews." Can anyone in his right mind doubt the absolute criminality of such acts. . . .?

28. . . . The contention of learned counsel for the defence that it is not the accused but the State on whose behalf he had acted, who is responsible for his criminal acts is only true as to its second part. It is true that under international law Germany bears not only moral, but also legal, responsibility for all the crimes that were committed as its own "acts of State," including the crimes, attributed to the accused. But that responsibility does not detract one iota from the personal responsibility of the accused for his acts. . . .

The repudiation of the argument of "act of State" is one of the principles of international law that were acknowledged by the Charter and Judgment of the Nuremberg Tribunal and were unanimously affirmed by the U.N. Assembly in its Resolution of December 11, 1946. . . .

30. We have discussed at length the international character of the crimes in question because this offers the broadest possible, though not the only, basis for Israel's jurisdiction according to the law of nations.

41. It is an established rule of law that a person being tried for an offence against the laws of a State may not oppose his trial by reason of the illegality of his arrest or of the means whereby he was brought within the jurisdiction of that State. The courts in England, the United States, and Israel have constantly held that the circumstances of the arrest and the mode of bringing the accused into the territory of the State have no relevance to his trial, and they have consistently refused in all instances to enter upon an examination of these circumstances. . . .

50. Indeed, there is no escaping the conclusion that the question of the violation of international law by the manner in which the accused was brought into the territory of a country arises at the international level, namely, the relations between the two countries concerned alone, and must find its solution at such level. . . .

52. . . . According to the existing rule of law there is no immunity for a fugitive offender save in the one and only case where he has been extradited by the asylum State to the requesting State for a specific offence, which is not the offence for which he was being tried. The accused was not surrendered to Israel by Argentina, and the State of Israel is not bound by any agreement with Argentina to try the accused for any other specific offence, or not to try him for the offences being tried in the present case. The rights of asylum and immunity belong to the country of asylum and not to the offender, and the accused cannot compel a foregin sovereign State to give him protection against its will. The accused was a wanted war criminal when he escaped to Argentina by concealing his true identity. Only after he was kidnapped and brought to Israel was his identity revealed. After negotiations between the two governments, the Government of Argentina waived its demand for his return and declared that it viewed the incident as closed. The Government of Argentina thereby refused conclusively to grant the accused any sort of protection. The accused has been brought to trial before the Court of a State which charges him with grave offences against its laws. The accused has no immunity against this trial and must stand trial in accordance with the indictment.

2.5. Racial Discrimination

The multivalue deprivatory conditions which affect specific groups led to the gradual realization that such conditions are threatening to minimum world order. Events that preceded World War II and experiences during that period, revealed that a rational nexus exists between such deprivatory conditions and what came to be recognized as an international crime such as genocide. The realization, however, that a process of systematic human destruction is not only limited to physical extermination but also extends to other forms of dehumanization led to the enunciation of "human rights" guarantees under the U.N. Charter and subsequent human rights covenants, treaties, and conventions.

The Convention on the Elimination of All Forms of Racial Discrimination[11] is the culmination of a historical development which characterizes this type of conduct as a form of international deviance requiring the formulation of a legal norm to impede it.

The Convention was adopted December 21, 1965, and went into effect March 31, 1969. It defines racial discrimination in article I as follows:

> . . . [A]ny distinction, exclusion, restriction, or preference based on race, colour, descent, or national or ethnic origin which has the purpose or effect of nullifying or impairing the recognition, enjoyment, or exercise, on an equal footing, human rights and fundamental freedoms in the political, economic, social, cultural, or any other field of public life.

The specific rights guaranteed and protected by the Convention are set out in detail in article 5. The basic policy of article I applies essentially to citizens and is ambiguous in its application to noncitizens (Para. 2). It does not, for example, affect municipal laws on nationality, citizenship, or naturalization, as long as they do not discriminate against a particular nationality (para. 3).

Paragraph 4 states:

> Special measures taken for the sole purpose of securing adequate advancement of certain racial or ethnic groups or individuals requiring such protection as may be necessary in order to ensure such groups or individuals equal enjoyment or exercise of human rights and fundamental freedoms shall not be deemed racial discrimination, provided, however, that such measures do not, as a consequence, lead to the maintenance of separate rights for different racial groups and that they shall not be continued after the objectives for which they were taken have been achieved.

The exclusion stated therein is reiterated in article II (1) (e) and article II (2) as well as in article VI.

As Professor Reisman states it:

> For all of its breadth, article I does have defects. Even when paragraph 1 is balanced with paragraph 4, the predominant conception of racial discrimina-

[11] *See infra*, pt. III, ch. 5 § 4, VOGLER, THE DEFENSE OF SUPERIOR ORDERS IN INTERNATIONAL CRIMINAL LAW, & DINSTEIN, THE DEFENSE OF "SUPERIOR ORDERS" IN INTERNATIONAL LAW (1965).

tion continues to be one of severe repression of the vigorous demands of a subjugated group. Discrimination may start in this manner, but at some point it becomes a reciprocal process. The great wound of continuing discrimination is its internalization in the target; the discriminated person who has, after years and perhaps generations of alien acculturation, begun to adopt the image the discriminators hold of him and to doubt his own and his group's worth will always lack sufficient self-awareness and self-confidence to avail himself of the formal rights and prerogatives which the law purports to offer him. One of the most arduous and delicate challenges of the elimination of racial discrimination will be the elimination of internalized or self-discrimination. This process may well involve violence to established structures and cultural values within the discriminated group, for the elite of a discriminated group has often reached an accommodation with the surrounding society of discrimination and may view any change as a threat to its own, limited ascendancy. The various claims which will inevitably be raised in a program of elimination of racial discrimination under international auspices will be much more realistically handled if those authorized to apply the Convention operate with a grasp of enormity and complexity of the problems confronting them.[12]

Articles 2 to 7 of the Convention set out the substantive obligations of contracting parties. Three basic undertakings appear in these five articles: (1) a governmental obligation to eliminate, within official processes, all forms of racial discrimination, (2) a governmental obligation to eliminate discrimination by individuals and organizations within the state, and (3) a governmental obligation to undertake a developmental program.

The Convention relies on five jurisdictional authorities as implementation processes: (1) the Security Council, (2) the General Assembly, (3) the International Court of Justice, (4) U. N. agencies (ECOSOC—Commission on Human Rights) and (5) Commission on the Elimination of Racial Discrimination (as a U. N. agency).

This latter is the only new structure created by the Convention.

The Committee's function is to appraise "legislature, judicial administrative, or other measures" adopted by governments and decide on claims submitted. The procedure is quite elaborate and whenever it will be implemented is likely to clarify the general substantive provisions of the Convention while operating as a control mechanism.

2.6. Conclusion

Genocide is an international crime imposing individual responsibility upon its perpetrator who cannot claim the defense of "act of state" or "superior orders."[13]

---

[12] *See infra*, pt. V, ch. II, DAUTRICOURT, THE CONCEPT OF AN INTERNATIONAL CRIMINAL JURISDICTION, & Drost, *supra* note 2.

[13] *E.g.*, McDougal & Feliciano, LAW AND MINIMUM WORLD PUBLIC ORDER (1960).

This responsibility extends to principles and accessories, before and after the fact as in the case of any common crime regardless of whether such individual is a public official, scientist, writer, or anyone who instigates, plans, prepares, conspires, contributes, or executes the crime in whole or in part. This responsibility also extends to "popular spontaneous" acts of masses who may commit such acts as are prohibited by the Convention.

The repression of genocide can be effective only if in addition to municipal legislation an international criminal court can be established with effective means of exercising its jurisdiction and implementation of its judgments.[14] In addition, the Convention must be supplemented with collective sanctions.

The collective aspect of genocide is to be seen in the protected groups under the Convention. According to the definition of the crime, the element of collectivity is to be found in the special intent to destroy a particular human group. It is argued that fundamentally genocide is but mass homicide with a special intent directed toward a special category of people but ultimately perpetrated on a particular person belonging to such group. The definition of genocide leads also to the conclusion that it amounts to an offense against the fundamental human rights of the individual.

The realization that no genocide can be committed without a state's commission or omission of any or all of the elements of the crime should be given careful consideration. Such acts should be repressed not only because their apparent and immediate victims are human beings but also because they impair the peace and security of mankind and threaten minimum world order.[15]

---

[14] The Declaration on the Elimination of All Forms of Racial Discrimination was adopted in 1963, E/CN.4/815, para. 176; the General Assembly adopted the proposed draft convention Dec. 21, 1965, Res. 1904 (XVIII); it was ratified by 42 states in 1969 and went into effect that year; A/PV 1406; Res. 2106 A (XX).

On the Convention's history and background, *see* Schwelb, *The International Convention on the Elimination of All Forms of Racial Discrimination,* 15 INT'L & COMP. L.Q. 996 (1966).

[15] Reisman, *Responses to Crimes of Discrimination and Genocide: An Appraisal of the Convention on the Elimination of Racial Discrimination,* 1 DENVER J. INT'L L. & Pol. 29 (1971).

CHAPTER XI

THE INTERNATIONAL NARCOTICS CONTROL SYSTEM*

M. CHERIF BASSIOUNI

Section 1. INTERNATIONAL CONTROL OF COMMON CRIMES AND NARCOTICS

Any international scheme must ultimately rest, in the absence of an international coercive body, on the willful compliance and cooperation of member states of the world community. World community proscriptions will therefore be as effective as world-community participants are desirous of implementing them. The *will* to participate in a global system of control is the only alternative to die-hard imperatives of the old self-serving international politics. Such a commitment can be attained only after the types of activity and conduct sought to be regulated by world-community proscriptions have attained a certain level of opprobrium in the common morality of mankind. Admittedly there will seldom be a uniform level or homogeneous sense of values among all peoples of the world, consequently a minimum threshold must be found.

The dangers of drug abuse and particularly dangerous drugs are too well recognized scientifically to be debated, and the effects of drug abuse on the user and consequently on society are also well established. Such a commonly recognized individual and social harm constitutes, therefore, such a minimum common denominator warranting if not compelling cooperation between nation-states to combat this type of activity.

The obligations which derive from the existence of the contemporary situation of drug abuse are twofold: (1) effective national controls and (2) international cooperation to maximize national efforts. This type of international responsible participation in world-community processes is by no means limited to those nation-states particularly affected by the consequences of the harmful activity but extends to all world-community

* Adopted in part from an article by the author in 46 St. John's L. Rev. 713 (1972).

participants. A direct consequence of this concept is the development of an international obligation to combat such criminality in compliance with the maxim *aut dedere aut punire*.[1]

1.1. The Development of an International Control System

It should be stated at the outset of any study on narcotics that there is no uniformly recognized definition of the term. Certainly there are numerous writings which provide a pharmacological or psychological classification of substances in terms of their effect on the natural organism. This is the main reason why municipal legislation and international treaties refer to specific substances and drugs rather than attempt a broad definitional classification. The categories of narcotic substances and dangerous drugs covered by international agreements are (1) *opium* and its derivative morphine, produced from the poppy seed; (2) *cocaine*, produced from the coca bush; (3) *Cannabis sativa*, or Indian hemp, known as hashish, marijuana, bhang, and other names, depending on its geographic location, and (4) *psychotropic substances*, which are chemically manufactured drugs and not agriculturally produced.

Not all of these categories have always been the subject of international control and even among these categories only a limited number were included in the original measures which are confined to opium and its derivatives. In 1931, a system of international legislation was established under which new narcotic drugs could be added by decision of an international organ, which would be binding upon all signatory states. This mandatory system applied originally only to certain derivatives of opium and of the coca leaf, but a protocol adopted on November 19, 1948, extended it to all narcotic drugs of whatever chemical structure, including drugs which are made synthetically; the *Cannabis sativa* drugs were, however, not included.

The 1961 Single Convention took over these classifications and included *Cannabis sativa*, but failed to cover psychotropic substances and that is the reason for the 1971 Convention on psychotropic substances.

The international control of narcotic drugs scheme is founded upon twelve multilateral treaties concluded between 1912 and 1972; the most important is the Single Convention of 1961, which came into effect on December 15, 1964 to which proposed amendments were signed in March 24, 1972.[2] The operation of this system of international control rests on

---

[1] *See* Bassiouni, *International Extradition and World Public Order*, 36 TENN. L. REV. 1 (1969).

[2] *See* U.N. Doc. E/Conf. 63/8 (1972) and Waddell, *International Narcotics Control*, 64 A.J.I.L. 310 (1970); *see also* for a list of treaties and signatories between 1912–1961, a note by the Secretary-General, U.N. Doc. E/CN.7/504, Annex I, and LOWES, THE GENESIS OF INTERNATIONAL NARCOTICS CONTROL (1966).

national controls to be established and supervised by individual states within their territorial jurisdiction and subject to their constitutional limitations. The narcotics treaties provide that the signatory states are to adopt appropriate legislation, introduce necessary administrative and enforcement measures and cooperate with international control organs as well as with other countries in compliance with treaty provisions.

More than one hundred countries are parties to one or more of the conventions and are therefore participants in the international control system; even countries and territories not bound by any or some of these treaties nonetheless abide by them (to some extent) in practice. As a result, universal acceptance of an international control system has been attained, even though the exercise of effective control measures still leaves much to be desired as witnessed by large volume of illicit traffic. A sense of historic continuity in international cooperation has, however, been achieved and progress toward more effective controls is developing consistently. Each Narcotic Convention benefited from the experience of its predecessor and filled certain gaps while improving previously existing devices. The object of the system is not to eliminate narcotic substances and drugs, because of their medical and scientific importance, but to restrict their use to these purposes. Thus the dilemma of control and difficulty of enforcement lies in finding a way to produce some of these substances and drugs which are necessary for medical and scientific purposes but also to control their production, limit their use, and curb their abuse.

The international control scheme is predicated on an indirect method whereby each state exercises and administers its own control system without interference by an international agency. This is so far necessitated by the xenophobic attitudes of most nations toward the concept of sovereignty. In fact, because of such attitudes only an indirect scheme of international control could have ever developed. This control scheme is predicated almost entirely on the cooperation of governments and has two essential characteristics: (1) it depends almost entirely on voluntary international cooperation, and (2) it has no coercive powers, only the ability to denounce a violator to the international community and therefore produce a moral deterrent to insure compliance.

Although each international narcotic agreement will be discussed separately in this article, the ensuing remarks will encompass several of these agreements to illustrate the two above-mentioned characteristics of the control scheme.

1.1.1. The Estimate System. The system of estimates was introduced by the 1931 Convention and administered by the Permanent Central Opium Board and the Drug Supervisory Body which were merged by the 1961

Single Convention in the International Narcotics Control Board INCB. They all provided for measures of quantitative control extending to signatory as well as nonsignatory states. The estimate system is intended to limit the narcotics supplies of every country and territory in the world to the amounts needed for medical and scientific purposes. Every state, regardless of whether or not it is a party to any of these Conventions when they were in force, and presently under the 1961 Single Convention, is required to furnish its estimates of narcotics needed for the coming year. If a state fails to send such an estimate, then the competent international body may make the estimate and it is on that basis that the maximum amount importable by that country is established. Though the international body that examines the estimates submitted by governments has never had the power to change them unilaterally, it may make inquiries with respect both to the estimates as a whole and to a particular drug. The record of these international bodies shows that governments generally cooperate in furnishing the requested explanations. Shipments of drugs can be made to a state only within the limits of the estimates furnished by the importing country or made by the international body. The INCB and its predecessor the Permanent Central Opium Board (PCOB) can make a determination that the limit of shipments to any country has been reached and accordingly notify the exporting states, which are then bound not to make any further shipments to that state.

Both the PCOB and presently the INCB control the quantities of narcotics supplied to countries by controlling stockpiling. If it finds that a dangerous quantity of drugs is accumulating in any country, it may recommend that other states temporarily or permanently stop shipments of drugs to that country. It may also make this recommendation if, in comparing the estimates and the statistics furnished by governments, it finds that a country has violated its treaty provisions relating to the maximum amount of narcotic drugs which it may manufacture or import, computed on the basis of the estimates. Although no such recommendation was ever made by the PCOB or INCB, its authority to do so has nevertheless occasionally influenced governments to comply more fully with the relevant treaty provisions.

The 1961 Single Convention continues the practice of the PCOB to request any state, whether party or not party to the 1925 and 1931 Conventions, to explain a condition which, in the view of the Board, indicates an improper accumulation of narcotic drugs.

1.1.2. The Import-Export Certification System. The import certificate and export authorization system constitutes one of the most important institutions of international narcotics control. According to this system, no legitimate shipments can be sent from one country to another without an import authorization from the government of the receiving country and a corresponding export authorization from the government of the sending country. Thus, by controlling the movements of legal drugs, this provision enables detection of any country's exceeding its import maximum.

1.1.3. THE DISCLOSURE AND DISSEMINATION OF INFORMATION. Governments provide the international control organs with data and information on which the system depends. These governments maintain an import certificate and export authorization system for foreign trade, furnish annual reports and texts of laws and regulations enacted by them to implement the narcotics treaties, and report seizures of narcotic drugs from the illicit traffic and other relevant data. They notify the United Nations of newly developed substances with possible addiction-producing properties, and are pledged to place under control, drugs which are found by international control organs to have such properties or to be convertible into drugs having such properties. The discovery of new chemicals such as LSD/LSD25 resulted in the 1971 Convention on Psychotropic Substances (discussed below). General compliance has always been the goal of the narcotics control system, but until all countries are bound by the conventions and implement them in good faith, illicit traffickers will operate from the territory of nonconforming states and thus prevent the effective operation of the system. The effectiveness of international narcotics control, however, lies in world public opinion, thus "publicity" will foster compliance with international obligations according to the terms of the various narcotics treaties. While overdramatization by information media of drug addiction, illicit traffic, and other aspects of narcotics control has often been found harmful to the efforts of national and international authorities, publicity given to the lack of governmental cooperation has a salutary effect. Governments are extremely sensitive to any public outcry that they have failed to cooperate in such a social humanitarian activity. Such publicity is intended to be provided by published reports of the organs of international control based on information furnished by governments (annual reports, laws, statistics, estimates, seizure reports) and by discussions in various United Nations bodies and dissemination of general information.

1.1.4. THE ROLE OF INTERNATIONAL ORGANIZATIONS. The League of Nations and the United Nations have been closely associated with these efforts and the administration of this system of indirect control.

The organs presently functioning under U.N. auspices are the Commission on Narcotic Drugs and the International Narcotics Control Board (INCB).

The Commission is a policy-making one which succeeded the League of

Nations Advisory Committee on Traffic in Opium and other Dangerous Drugs, which was then a general organ of control. The INCB was established by the 1961 Single Convention and replaced two specialized administrative organs, the Permanent Central Opium Board and the Drug Supervisory Body, charged particularly with the supervision of provision of the narcotics treaties dealing with measures of quantitative control (statistics and estimates).

The Economic and Social Council and the Commission on Narcotic Drugs formulate policies, coordinate activities and supervise the implementation of international conventions and agreements. They make particular or general recommendations to governments on these matters from the World Health Organization.

The technical assistance programs of the United Nations and such specialized agencies as the World Health Organization (WHO) and the Food and Agriculture Organization (FAO) are made available to governments seeking to cope with their particular problems in this area.[3]

1.1.5. THE OVERALL CONCEPT. These observations reveal the degree of reliance of the international control system on the good will of cooperating states, and its gradually developed structures attest to the patience and persistence of those who for years nurtured its acceptance by generally reluctant states. The inarticulate premise of the entire system which spans all of half a century (from 1909 to this date) is to reach agreement by as many nations as possible on attainable objectives. This accounts for the gradualist development of the system and also for some apparent loopholes and known weaknesses which still exist. The conclusion to be drawn is that the process of international compromise is neither easy nor satisfactory but ultimately it is far better than none.

Section 2. A CHRONOLOGY OF INTERNATIONAL EFFORTS TO CONTROL NARCOTICS

2.1. Narcotics Control Prior to the League of Nations

2.1.1. THE SHANGHAI OPIUM COMMISSION OF 1909. Thirteen powers with interests in the Far East appointed an Opium Commission which met at Shanghai in 1909. The delegates to the Commission had no power to draw up or sign any treaty, the primary motive for convening the Commission

---

[3] 520 UNTS 204; proposed amendments U.N. Doc. E/Conf. 63/18, 24 March 1972; *See also* INTERNATIONAL CONTROL OF NARCOTIC DRUGS, U.N. Publications Office of Public Information, N.Y. (1965).

being to discuss the international ramifications of the Chinese opium problem. It led, however, to the signing of the first treaty three years later.[1]

2.1.2. THE HAGUE CONVENTION OF 1912. The first international narcotics convention was concluded at The Hague in 1912[2] and established international cooperation in the control of narcotic drugs.

2.2. Narcotics Control under the League of Nations

Article 23 of the League of Nations Covenant provided that the members of the League should "entrust the League with the general supervision over agreements with regard to . . . the traffic in opium and other dangerous drugs." The first League Assembly created the Advisory Committee on Traffic in Opium and Other Dangerous Drugs to assist and advise the League's Council in these tasks. Among other duties, the Committee initiated various international legislative actions under the auspices of the League.

2.2.1. THE GENEVA CONVENTION OF 1925. The Geneva Convention of February 19, 1925, was a great step forward in the control of narcotic drugs.[3] Governments were required to submit to the newly created Permanent Central Opium Board annual statistics concerning production of opium and coca leaves; the manufacture, consumption, and stocks of narcotic drugs, and quarterly reports on the import and export of such drugs (including opium and coca leaves). It also established the system of import certificates and export authorizations requiring governmental approval of each import and export.

2.2.2. CONVENTION FOR LIMITING THE MANUFACTURE AND REGULATING THE DISTRIBUTION OF NARCOTIC DRUGS OF 1931. The aim of this Convention, signed at Geneva on July 13, 1931, is to limit world manufacture of drugs to its medical and scientific needs.[4] It contains provisions to restrict the quantities of drugs available in each country and territory. Countries bind themselves not to exceed in their manufacture and imports certain maxima computed on the basis of estimates of their narcotics requirements.

---

[1] Until that period, trade in narcotics was legal and encouraged by England, but when by 1909 it was estimated that China had ten million opium smokers, England, strongly pressured by the United States and religious groups, closed the opium trade between China and India. See House of Commons Resolution of May 30, 1906, in 158 PARL. DEB., H.C. (4th ser.) 494, 516 (1906). See also, Renborg, *International Control of Narcotics,* 22 LAW & CONTEMP. PROB. 86 (1957).

[2] 8 L.N.T.S. 187; 38 U.S. Stat. L. 1912; 6 A.J.I.L. 177 (Supp. 1912).

[3] 81 L.N.T.S. 317; 23 A.J.I.L. 135 (Supp. 1929).

[4] 139 L.N.T.S. 301; 48 Stat. 1543; T.S. 863; 28 A.J.I.L. 21 (Supp., 1934), & Q. Wright, *The Narctics Convention of 1931,* 28 A.J.I.L. 475 (1934).

2.2.3. THE CONVENTION FOR THE SUPPRESSION OF THE ILLICIT TRAFFIC IN DANGEROUS DRUGS OF 1936. The Convention for the Suppression of the Illicit Traffic in Dangerous Drugs was signed in Geneva June 26, 1936, and came into effect in October 1939.[5] It was the last treaty on narcotics concluded under the auspices of the League of Nations. The parties undertook to enact measures to prevent offenders from escaping prosecution for technical reasons and to facilitate extradition for drug offenses.

2.3. Narcotics Control Under the United Nations

The United Nations considered it an urgent task to take the initiative in a control system which had broken down during World War II. The initiative was taken when, at its first session in 1946, the Economic and Social Council created the Commission on Narcotic Drugs to carry out the functions entrusted to the League's Committee on Traffic in Opium and Other Dangerous Drugs. It was by the Protocol of 1946 that the functions previously exercised by the League under the various narcotics treaties concluded before the Second World War were transferred to the United Nations. The next steps were the Paris Protocol of 1948, which authorized WHO to place under international control any addiction-producing drug, and the Opium Protocol of 1953, which limited the use of and trade in opium to medical and scientific needs.

2.3.1. THE GENEVA PROTOCOL OF 1946. A protocol signed on December 11, 1946, transferred to the United Nations the functions previously exercised by the League under the various narcotics treaties concluded before the Second World War.[6]

2.3.2. THE PARIS PROTOCOL OF 1948. The Commission on Narcotic Drugs, at its first session in November–December 1946, initiated a study of the procedures necessary for bringing new synthetic drugs under control.[7] This resulted in the preparation of an instrument known as the Paris Protocol of 1948. The Protocol was signed at the Palais de Chaillot on November 19, 1948, and came into force on December 1, 1949. It authorizes WHO to place under full international control any new drug (including synthetic drugs) which could not be placed under such control by application of the relevant provisions (art. 11) of the 1931 Convention and which it finds either to be addiction-producing or convertible into an addiction-producing drug.

---

[5] 198 L.N.T.S. 229, & Starke, *The Convention of 1936 for the Suppression of the Illicit Traffic in Dangerous Drugs*, 31 A.J.I.L. 31 (1937).

[6] 12 U.N.T.S. 180, T.I.A.S., 1671 and 1859; 61 Stat. (pt. 2) 2230, 62 Stat. (pt. 2) 1796. See also, Gregg, *The United Nations and the Opium Problem*, 13 INT'L & COMP. L. Q. 96 (1964).

[7] 44 U.N.T.S. 277, T.I.A.S. 2308.

2.3.3. The Protocol for Limiting and Regulating the Cultivation of the Poppy Plant, the Production of, International and Wholesale Trade in, and Use of Opium of 1953. With the aim of limiting the production of opium to the quantities needed for medical and scientific purposes, the Commission on Narcotic Drugs endeavored to bring about an international opium monopoly with quotas allocated to the various opium-producing countries and with a system of international inspection.

The principal opium-producing and drug-manufacturing countries, however, could not reach agreement on several important questions, such as the price of opium and international inspection. Consequently, the Economic and Social Council turned to an alternative plan, proposed in the Commission by France, which formed the basis of a protocol adopted by the United Nations Opium Conference held in New York in May–June 1953. The protocol came into force on March 8, 1963.[8]

The 1953 Protocol limits the use of opium and the international trade in it to medical and scientific needs and eliminates legal overproduction of opium through the indirect method of limiting the stock of the drug maintained by individual states.

2.3.4. The Single Convention on Narcotic Drugs, 1961. The Single Convention of 1961 went into effect December 13, 1964.[9] This convention is a milestone in the history of international narcotics control. More than half the members of the United Nations ratified the Convention and a greater number apply its provisions.

The first objective of this Convention was the unified codification of existing multilateral treaties in this field, with the exception of most provisions of the 1936 Convention on illicit traffic which are to be continued. As among parties to the Single Convention, all the other eight treaties cease to exist, and even in the case of the 1936 Convention, its article 9, relating to extradition, is terminated as between parties to both conventions, and replaced by a provision in the Single Convention.

The new treaty simplified the international control machinery and changed the Permanent Central Opium Board and the Drug Supervisory Body into a single unit, the International Narcotics Control Board.

[8] U.N. Doc. E/N.T. 18 T.I.A.S. 5273, 14 U.S.T. 10; *see also* Lowes, The Genesis of International Narcotics Control (1966) and Gregg, *infra* note 9.

[9] U.N. Doc. E/Conf. 34/22 (1961); 520 U.N.T.S. 204; T.I.A.S. 6298, 18 U.S.T. 1407. For its background, *see* Engel, *Integration of International Legislation*, 45 A.J.I.L. 770 (1951); for an analysis, *see* Waddell, *International Narcotics Control*, 64 A.J.L.L. 310 (1970); Gregg, *The Single Convention*, 16 Food, Drug & Cosm. L. J. 187 (1961); Lande, *The Single Convention*, 16 Int'l Organization 776 (1962); for a U.S. position report by the U.S. Dept. of State, *see* 61 A.J.I.L. 802 (1967). For the Convention's effect on marijuana, *see* Kingsley, *Effects of the Single Convention on Narcotic Drugs on the Regulation of Marijuana*, 19 Hastings L. J. 848 (1968).

2.3.4.1. *The Functions of the Commission on Narcotic Drugs.* The Commission (1) assists the Council in exercising such powers of supervision over the application of international conventions and agreements dealing with narcotic drugs as may be assumed by or conferred on the Council, (2) carries out such functions entrusted to the League of Nations Advisory Committee on Traffic in Opium and Other Dangerous Drugs by the international conventions on narcotic drugs as the Council has found necessary to assume and continue, (3) advises the Council on all matters pertaining to the control of narcotic drugs and prepares such draft international conventions as may be necessary, (4) considers what changes may be required in the existing machinery for the international control of narcotic drugs and submits proposals to the Council, and (5) performs such other functions relating to narcotic drugs as the Council may direct.

A division of the Secretariat of the United Nations, transferred in 1955 from New York to Geneva, is in charge of administrative and research duties in the field of narcotics. It includes a laboratory, which is entrusted with scientific research and coordinates research carried on by scientists of individual countries. The Commission is composed of twenty-four members.

2.3.4.2. *The Functions of the INCB.* Unlike the Commission this is not a U.N.-created board but is a product of the narcotics treaties, and its incumbents consist of eleven persons. The INCB (1) enforces the provisions of the Convention, (2) secures estimates of drug requirements, existing stocks, production and consumption statistics, and statistics on seizures of unlawfully held drugs and publishes results, (3) requests information, explanations, and public declarations by governments, (4) recommends embargoes on imports and exports, (5) gathers and publishes texts of laws and regulations concerning narcotics from signatory states.

2.3.4.3. *Weaknesses of the Single Convention.* These weaknesses can be summarized in the following areas: (1) it rests essentially upon faithful cooperation by all parties in the context of their national decisions rather than upon effective international measures; (2) the limited authority given the international control bodies—the Commission on Narcotic Drugs and the International Narcotics Control Board—is apparently inadequate to halt or even to slow down the increasing illicit traffic; (3) the Convention lacks a precise obligation, machinery, and incentives for preventing overproduction of drugs; (4) it fails to clearly prohibit production of certain medically and scientifically unnecessary substances and drugs; (5) it has no direct controls over the execution of any treaty provision, particularly with respect to production controls which are very indirect; (6) it has no assignment of production quotas or production ceilings; (7) it does not prevent countries from entering into the production market; (8) the denunciation of the Convention is rather facile and operation outside its ambit is possible (to wit the People's Republic of China); (9) there is no international enforcement machinery (Interpol has no jurisdictional authority); and (10) there are no international sanctions applicable to individual offenders.

2.3.5. CONVENTION ON PSYCHOTROPIC SUBSTANCES, 1971. Strict international controls over LSD, mescaline, and similar substances—including regulations more rigorous than existing controls for other drugs, such as morphine—are provided for in this new international agreement adopted by a United Nations Conference in Vienna, February 19, 1971.[10]

The agreement, known as the Draft Protocol on the Control of Psychotropic Drugs Outside the Scope of the Single Convention on Narcotic Drugs of 1961, covers thirty-two substances having hallucinogenic effects on the human organism, including "pep pills," which stimulate the central nervous system, and barbiturate-type sleeping pills and tranquilizers, which are depressants.

The substances are listed in four schedules annexed to the Convention, which provides for varying degrees of control over the substances in each schedule.

2.3.5.1. *Analysis of the Provisions of the Convention and a Brief Comparison with the 1961 Single Convention.* The Convention relies on the same scheme contemplated by the 1961 Single Convention, and in fact its provisions are almost alike. It relies on the element of notice by a party that a substance previously uncontrolled should be subject to:

(i)   require licenses for manufacture, trade, and distribution as provided in article 8 for substances in Schedule II;
(ii) require medical prescriptions for supply or dispensing as provided in article 9 for substances in Schedule II;
(iii) comply with the obligations relating to export and import provided in article 12, except in respect to another Party having given such notice for the substance in question; (art. 7 (a))

It makes, however, more use of the expertise of WHO particularly:

If the World Health Organization finds:
(a) that the substance has the capacity to produce
    (i)   (1) a state of dependence, and
          (2) central nervous system stimulation or depression, resulting in hallucination or disturbances in motor function or thinking or behaviour or perception or mood, or

[10] E/Conf. 58/6–19 Feb. 1971; see for its history the records of the Commission which, at its 23rd session, Jan. 13,–1969, adopted a draft protocol thereafter submitted to governments for comment by June 30, 1969. For text of draft (U.N. Doc. E/4606/Rev. 1, Annex IV (May 1969), *see* 8 INT'L LEGAL MATERIALS 769 (July, 1969).

(ii) similar abuse and similar ill effects as a substance in Schedule
I, II, III, or IV, and

(b) that there is sufficient evidence that the substance is being or is likely to
be abused so as to constitute a public health and social problem warranting the placing of the substance under international control, the World
Health Organization shall communicate to the Commission an assessment
of the substance, including the extent or likelihood of abuse, the degree
of seriousness of the public health and social problem and the degree of
usefulness of the substance in medical therapy; together with recommendations on control measures, if any, that would be appropriate in the
light of its assessment (art. 2(4)).

Providing for special means of controlling such preparations, the Convention relies on the same indirect method of the previous narcotics
treaties, but some of the escape clauses are however quite noticeable.
One such clause is article 3 (2) which exempts countries from certain
requirements under articles 8, 11, 13, 15, 16, and 22 whenever the:

. . . preparation containing a phychotropic substance other than a substance
in Schedule I is compounded in such a way that it presents no, or a negligible,
risk of abuse and the substance cannot be recovered by readily applicable
means in a quantity liable to abuse, so that the preparation does not give
rise to a public health and social problem . . . .

Such a finding is made unilaterally by a party seeking the exemption
for one or more of the measures of control. Such a party shall notify
the Secretary-General of any such decision, of the name and composition
of the exempt preparation, and of the measures of control from which it
is exempted. The Secretary-General shall transmit the notification to the
other parties, to the World Health Organization, and to the Board, who
may, however, make a different finding and advise the Secretary-General,
and the Commission shall decide if the substance should be controlled.

The method of record keeping and control, from manufacture to consumption, via distribution warehousing and shipment, is left to each signatory without international control and is, therefore, likely to prove nonexistent or, at best, ineffective. The Commission and the Board undertake
essentially the same functions as they do with respect to the 1961 Single
Convention. Secretary of State William Rogers in his letter of submission
to the President transmitted to the Senate with the request that the Convention be ratified by the United States stated:

There are a number of significant differences between the two Conventions,
including the following. The new Convention does not undertake to control
the cultivation of plants from which psychotropic substances may be derived as in the case of the Single Convention with respect to narcotic drugs.
Provision is made in the new Convention that assessments by the World Health
Organization are determinative as to medical and scientific matters with re-

spect to psychotropic substances. Decisions by the United Nations Commission on Narcotic Drugs to place a new psychotropic substance under control or to change existing controls over a substance must be by a two-thirds majority of members of that Commission as compared with a simple majority of members with respect to controls over narcotic drugs, and such decisions regarding narcotic drugs under the Single Convention are binding immediately upon receipt by the parties of notification thereof. Corresponding decisions under the new Convention regarding phychotropic substances are not binding until 180 days after their receipt; a party may take an exception to such a decision and apply a lower category of controls to the substance. The manufacture, export, import, and use of substances in Schedule I of the new Convention are much more restricted than drugs in the comparable Schedule of the Single Convention. No annual estimates of quantities of psychotropic substances are necessary under the new Convention as in the case of narcotic drugs under the Single Convention. Under the Single Convention preparations containing a drug under control are subject to all the controls to which the drug itself is subject except where lesser controls may be applied after the preparation has been included in Schedule III to that Convention, but under the new Convention a party need apply only certain limited controls to a preparation if the party exempts the preparation, such exemption being subject to replacement by a decision of the Commission to terminate the exemption, subject to further decision of the Commission to terminate the exemption of the preparation from any or all control measures.

The difference between the two Conventions arises basically from the fact that the world community has had over half a century of experience in the application of international controls to narcotic drugs beginning with the Hague Convention of 1912, and has had no such experience with respect to the psychotropic substances; the production of narcotic drugs is of far more economic and social significance to countries that cultivate the opium poppy and the coca bush than the manufacture of the psychotropic substances is to the manufacturing countries; there are a great many more kinds of psychotropic substances than there are of narcotic drugs, and the quantities of psychotropics manufactured are much greater than the quantities of narcotics manufactured.[11]

2.3.5.2. The Penal Provisions and Sanctions Approach in the Convention on Psychotropic Substances and the Single Convention. The "territorial principle" of jurisdiction is invoked in both Conventions as it is throughout all of the narcotics treaties, but concurrently, signatories are urged to prosecute or alternatively extradite individual violators on the additional theory of "universality" because violation of the narcotics treaties constitutes an international crime. Article 22 of the Convention on Psychotropic Substances and article 36 of the Single Convention relate to the penal provisions of their respective Conventions. Both articles are identical and state:

[11] Message from the President of the United States, transmitting a copy of the Convention on Psychotropic Substances, signed at Vienna February 21, 1971, to the Senate. 92d. Cong., 1st Sess., June 29, 1971, G.O.P. 65–118, at VII.

2. Subject to the constitutional limitations of a Party's legal system and domestic law:

    (a) (i) if a series of related actions constituting offenses under paragraph 1 has been committed in different countries, each of them shall be treated as a distinct offense;

       (ii) intentional participation in; conspiracy to commit and attempts to commit, any of such offenses, and preparatory acts, and financial operations in connection with the offenses referred to in this article, shall be punishable offenses as provided in paragraph 1;

     (iii) foreign convictions for such offenses shall be taken into account for the purpose of establishing recidivism; and

     (iv) serious offenses heretofore referred to committed either by nationals or by foreigners shall be prosecuted by the Party in whose territory the offense was committed, or by the Party in whose territory the offender is found if extradition is not acceptable in conformity with the law of the Party to which application is made, and if such offender has not already been prosecuted and judgement given.

    (b) It is desirable that the offenses referred to in paragraph 1 and paragraph 2(a)(ii) be included as extradition crimes in any extradition treaty which has been or may hereafter be concluded between any of the Parties, and, as between any of the Parties which do not make extradition conditional on the existence of a treaty or on reciprocity, be recognized as extradition crimes; provided that extradition shall be granted in conformity with the law of the Party to which application is made, and that the Party shall have the right to refuse to effect the arrest or grant the extradition in cases where the competent authorities consider that the offense is not sufficiently serious.

The two provisions are identical even in their paragraph and subparagraph numbering. They impose a duty upon the signatory state to punish violations of this Convention by making such violations a crime under municipal law, but do not disallow multiple prosecutions and repeated punishment in every territory or state in violation of the principle of double jeopardy (*ne bis in idem*).[12] Significantly, they make conspiracy a crime even though that type of offense is peculiar only to the Anglo-American legal system and those countries which have been inspired by the common law. The penal provisions further provide for a partial recognition of foreign penal judgments with respect to recidivists without regard for the rights of the offender in such cases and fails to set forth the basis for such cooperation between states with respect to the recognition and consequences of foreign penal convictions. The most astonishing observation is that these penal provisions do not require states to include the offense of illicit narcotic traffic (cultivation, manufacturing, sale, transportation, and their derivative operations in their extradition treaties or

---

[12] Bassiouni, Criminal Law and Its Processes 126–36 (1969).

reciprocal practices). Even when a state agrees to extradite such offenders, the provisions have an astounding escape clause which is that
if in the opinion of the state of refuge the offense is "not sufficiently
serious," it does not have to extradite the accused offender. Recognizing
the principle "universality" by allowing any state wherein the offender may
be found to prosecute for the offense as an alternative to extradition, it
nonetheless only suggests the "desirability" to make it an extraditable
offense. No wonder so few treaties contain such violations in their list of
extraditable offenses.[13]

A particularly laudable feature which appears in the Psychotropic Convention is its concern with treatment of drug abusers, even though the
promise is likely to remain hollow and its implementation very doubtful in
the case of many signatories.

Article 22–1

(b) Notwithstanding the preceding sub-paragraph, when abusers of psychotropic substances have committed such offenses, the Parties may
provide, either as an alternative to conviction or punishment or in addition to punishment that such abusers undergo measures of treatment,
education, after-care, rehabilitation, and social reintegration in conformity with paragraph 1 of article 20.

Article 20 deals with measures against the abuse of psychotropic substances
and requires that:

1. The Parties shall take all practicable measures for the prevention of abuse
of psychotropic substances and for the early identification, treatment,
education, after-care, rehabilitation, and social reintegration of the persons involved and shall co-ordinate their efforts to these ends.
2. The Parties shall as far as possible promote the training of personnel
in the treatment, after-care, rehabilitation, and social reintegration of
abusers of psychotropic substances;
3. The Parties shall assist persons whose work so requires to gain an understanding of the problems of abuse of psychotropic substances and of its prevention, and shall also promote such understanding among the general
public if there is a risk that abuse of such substances will become widespread.

Such humane understanding has not been prevalent in other treaties,
but suggests that overemphasis on punitive and retributive conceptions
of narcotics control are giving way to a more scientific approach. This
is a major difference in the sanctions orientation of both Treaties since
the provision dealing with treatment of addicts in the single convention
states, article 38:

---

[13] For a list of U.S. Treaties, *see* Bassiouni, *International Extradition and World Public
Order,* 36 TENN. L. REV. 1 at 3 (1969).

1. The Parties shall give special attention to the provision of facilities for the medical treatment, care, and rehabilitation of drug addicts.
2. If a Party has a serious problem of drug addiction and its economic resources permit, it is desirable that it establish adequate facilities for the effective treatment of drug addicts.

The approach is recommendatory, as in the advisability clause on extradition mentioned above, and not mandatory. In a decade there has been no change in the language of the penal provisions and its extradition clause, only the concern over addiction took a more positive tone.

It should be noted that WHO suggested since the fifties that the term "addiction" and "habituation" be replaced by that of "dependence" and has since sponsored many studies on this subject. It had also initiated the use of the term "abuser" instead of "addict." This new terminology was not used in the 1961 Single Convention, but appears in the Convention on Psychotropic Substances and it is not clear if the reason for it was dictated by the differences between the types of drugs covered in the 1961 Single Convention as distinguished from Psychotropic Substances or because of popular acceptance of the conceptual significance of both terms.

The results of scientific tests and pharmacological distinctions between *Cannabis sativa* drugs, opium-morphine, and cocaine are not reflected in either of these Conventions (other than in the schedules) which are primarily penal sanctions oriented and only secondarily treatment-rehabilitation conscious. In this respect the Psychotropic Convention is more attuned to contemporary scientific research findings than its 1961 predecessor. One reason may well be the decade of scientific research that separates both of these conventions.

2.3.6. THE 1972 GENEVA PROTOCOL AMENDING THE 1961 SINGLE CONVENTION ON NARCOTIC DRUGS.[14] On May 20, 1971, ECOSOC called a plenipotentiary conference to consider proposed amendments to the 1961 Single Convention. All signatories were eligible to participate, as well as all members of the United Nations and its specialized agencies. The conference was convened at Geneva and 97 participants were registered, of which 3 were observers.

The amendment process had been initiated by the United States in March, 1971 (as discussed earlier in the text), and in October, 1971, France, Peru and Sweden proposed additional amendments. The amendments proposed were revised and sponsored by 19 nations but shortly before the conference convened, an additional 11 nations became sponsors.

The conference adopted the Amending Protocol by a vote of 71 in favor, none against, and 12 abstentions and is now open for signatures to

[14] U.N. Doc. E/Conf. 6318 (1972)

all parties to the Single Convention (or parties adhering thereto) and will enter into force upon adhesions by 40 nations. (Thirty-six have adhered as of June, 1972.)

The Amending Protocol continues to rely on the indirect scheme of control depending too significantly on governmental cooperation without direct enforcement sanction or ever independent fact-finding machinery. Nonetheless, it did make certain notable improvements in the present system: 1) Increased competence of the Board; 2) Reorganization of the Board; 3) The Estimate System; 4) Informational Input; 5) Informational Output; 6) Control and Sanctions; 7) Extradition; 8) Technical Assistance; 9) Treatment and Rehabilitation; 10) Preventive Measures.

Section 3. THE SUPPRESSION OF ILLICIT TRAFFIC IN DANGEROUS DRUGS AND NARCOTICS UNDER THE PRESENT SCHEME OF INTERNATIONAL CONTROL

The illicit traffic in drugs and the criminal activities of smugglers are of concern to the world community without distinction. The top organizers of the international illicit traffic do not in most cases physically handle any drugs themselves, but instigate, finance, and direct these operations which are carried out by underlings and then diffused to the users by pushers who perpetuate and disseminate these drugs as part of an organized snowballing system.

The international nature of the offense ideally requires the application of the principle of universality of jurisdiction in national criminal legislation and calls for punishment of violators irrespective of their nationality or the place of their crime. Thus, where international traffickers cannot be prosecuted in the country in which they are found, they should be extradited to a country which is willing to try them, but this is not accomplished by a "desirability" clause in narcotics treaties, but by a mandatory clause coupled with a multilateral extradition treaty as part of the international control scheme.

The 1936 Convention for the Suppression of the Illicit Traffic in Dangerous Drugs introduced the optional principle of universality for adoption by municipal penal legislation to insure that illicit traffickers would not escape prosecution because of lack of criminal jurisdiction. The adoption of municipal uniform penal sanctions, however, is a very difficult task because of ideological and political divergences and different cultural traditions on which this type of legal control ultimately depends. The 1936 Convention limited itself to the formulation of rather vague provisions, accompanied by escape clauses, in order to secure adherence by countries which would otherwise never accept stipulations basically different from their national standards. The 1961 Single Convention, besides expressing the *desirability* of making narcotic crimes subject to extradition (a provision it takes over from the 1936 treaty), requires parties to it to take action against the illicit traffic and to provide for the punishment of narcotic offenses but does not distinguish between international traffickers, local pushers (dealers), users, and addicts. It requires that parties should make arrangements at the national level for coordinating preventive and repressive action against illicit traffic by setting up special agencies for such coordination and to assist each other in fighting the illicit traffic by exchanging information and legal papers for the purpose of prosecuting offenders. The way these obligations are worded they are no more than a "best efforts" clause. Governments are required to furnish the Secretary-General particulars of each important case of illicit traffic, the source from which drugs are obtained for such illicit traffic and the methods employed by illicit traffickers. This type of data report is wholly ineffective in practice, even though in theory it is perfectly laudable. If the 1972 Amendments enter into force some of these shortcomings may be alleviated.

Governments have recognized after decades of narcotics treaties that, in order to be effective, penalties imposed on traffickers must have a deterring effect in which the penalty overweighs in the eyes of the potential offender the benefits of the prohibited activity. Only recently, however, have all countries enacted prison terms rather than fines for such violations. Some countries have even introduced capital punishment for certain crimes in the illicit traffic of narcotic drugs, especially when minors are exploited or led into addiction. But these measures have largely proved to be ineffective as the number of narcotics users and abusers is on the increase throughout the world.

Prevention and enforcement of narcotics violations are still the most cloak-and-dagger undercover activities in existence. They are often the result of years of work involving many persons, some of whom need to maintain their secret identity. Such activities are, therefore, not likely to be printed in the United Nations Secretary-General's Report on "the last catch," and invaluable cooperation which should be institutionalized is relegated to personal exchange of confidences betwen agents or agencies who have developed some form of working relationship.

The Commission on Narcotic Drugs reviews annually the general problem of illicit trade in individual drugs as well as the situation of the international traffic on a country-by-country basis. This review is based on information supplied by governments and such other sources as Interpol. Although the seizure reports furnished by governments may show here and there a decrease in the quantity of drugs seized in illicit trade as indicating effective control, the recent surveys of the Commission indicate that, on the whole, the illicit traffic remains at a high level and remains well organized.

The most important drugs in the illicit traffic (both international and local) are still opium and the opiates (principally morphine and heroin) which continue to present the greatest problem to national and international authorities. Opium originates mainly in the Middle East, in a well-defined triangle area in Southeast Asia along the borders of Burma, Thailand, and Laos and in the Peoples Democratic Republic of China, which is producing and exporting an unknown quantity of drugs, since it is outside the international control scheme. In the Middle East, some opium seems to escape local control where it is licitly cultivated, but most of it comes from illicit cultivation, whether in Turkey or in other parts of the world, such as Mexico—notwithstanding these countries' efforts to control it, the profit is so great that it will be impossible for them to be wholly successful. Adding to it the volume of individual travelers makes it at best haphazard. There is no system of international customs cooperation or data bank for international exchange of information. Interpol, however, maintains a reference operation and signals individuals to customs or police officials, but their activity is naturally limited.

Opium, as is well known, is used in clandestine factories for the manufacture of morphine, which is then converted into heroin. Morphine and particularly heroin are much more potent than opium and much less bulky, thus much easier to smuggle to countries such as the United States, Canada, Thailand, and Vietnam, where addiction, especially to heroin, has become a serious problem as it is also in other countries such as in Iran and Hong Kong. The United States, for example, has an estimated addiction population of half a million addicts, but its breakdown as to typology of drug users is very uncertain. An estimated 3.5 billion dollars is spent on illicit drugs in the United States annually. Smuggling heroin is very profitable and not easily detectable. At a time when world-trade expansion requires the reduction of administrative and customs controls and the volume of international trade is so great, the task of customs detection is extraordinary. On June 30, 1971, Prime Minister Erim of Turkey declared:

> We cannot allow Turkey's supreme interests and the prestige of our nation to be further shaken. Our government has decided to apply a clear and firm solution. It forbids completely the planting of poppies. . . .
>
> Poppies will not be planted in Turkey beginning next year. . . .

This laudable step is not likely to prevent illicit production, since wherever cultivation was permitted it had always been government controlled. Some illicit cultivation is still expected to take place until modern techniques can be used such as aerial and ground inspection as well as the maintenance of a permanent governmental control structure. Hopefully, Turkey will continue to be vigilant even if the decree abolishing any licit cultivation is likely to take the heat off its public agencies. It is also noteworthy that Thailand started a pilot program of crop substitution to curtail the extent of traditionally legal opium growing.

Cannabis sativa in its various forms, such as marijuana and hashish, continues to be in quantitative terms the biggest narcotic substance in the international illicit traffic; financially heroin is still the largest money producer. Cannabis-type plants grow in many parts of the world with great ease and represent, therefore, a particularly difficult problem to enforcement agencies. In the Middle East, Asia, Africa, and Latin America this drug crosses frontiers in bulk; although in some countries it is mainly a domestic problem. Cocaine from coca leaves grown mainly in Latin America appears in the international traffic on a smaller scale than opium and heroin, but the traffic in this drug seems to be spreading through Latin America and to other parts of the world. The reason is that it is in much less demand, which confirms the idea that priority should be given to curtailing demand and curbing the profit motive. Analysts of these problems tend to look at them more in terms of law enforcement than of user demand. This is why the international concern as well as that of most states is with repressive penal sanctions rather than curtailing user demand by scientific means and developing a method of direct control over production and manufacturing of all such drugs and curbing the profit incentive of those engaged in this type of illicit activity.

It is true by and large that the illicit traffic is unable to obtain any significant supplies of drugs from legally manufactured channels except for synthetic drugs wherein seizures have been seriously increasing in recent years and are often retraceable to licit channels of manufacturing, particularly amphetamines and other stimulants and depressants stolen in the course of trade.

The means of transportation in the international illicit traffic are not limited to ships and their crew members, as governments' seizure reports point to a growing use of commercial and private aircrafts by traffickers. In 1952, the Economic and Social Council recommended that the Secretary-General compile and bring up to date at regular intervals a list of merchant seafarers and members of the civil air crews who have been convicted on narcotic offenses on or after January 1, 1953. Such crew members are to be blacklisted and not employed again on board ships or aircraft, as the case may be, but little ever came of that device. Another method of transportation is the ordinary tourist and the unwitting courier. The extraordinary increase in tourism and business travel makes thorough individual customs inspection a practical impossibility. Customs agencies are on the horns of a dilemma: should they ease their inspections to make the tourist feel welcome or be thorough and catch the smuggler? Economic realism makes most countries opt for the former measure. Another channel must not be discounted and that is the regular shipment of goods in international trade. Most narcotic drugs are easily concealable and can be shipped with goods and merchandise without too much fear of discovery in customs. The only reason it is not used so much is not fear of customs seizure but that intermediate handlers of the legitimate merchandise may find it and take it.

Valuable help in combating illicit traffic and activities of traffickers is rendered by Interpol, which acts as a clearing house for national law enforcement agencies. The organization, whose headquarters is in Paris, provides information on illicit traffic to the organs of international and national narcotics control and usually participates, through an observer, in the Commission's meetings. It organizes conferences and seminars for national police forces and other services, such as customs. Interpol remains, however, an agency without supranational power and is not as the name suggests a true international police.

The Division of Narcotic Drugs of the United Nations Secretariat carries out research in its laboratory in Geneva, and national laboratories and individual scientists in various parts of the world also participate in the United Nations program of drug research. The laboratory helped to coordinate opium research that was carried out by scientists throughout the world and arranged for the distribution of opium samples for this work. Some of the laboratory research is on the analysis of government-authenticated samples of opium which originated or were discovered in that country. Several scientific methods have been developed and after extensive testing are now conclusively applied to determine the geographical origin of samples of opium seized in illicit traffic and thus help to pinpoint its illicit origin.

The United Nations, cognizant of the importance of curbing user demand for illicit drugs, instituted a program of drug abuse control in March 1971. In an *Aide-Memoire* released by the Secretary-General, it was stated:

> 3. The demand for drugs comes from large numbers of addicts and habitual abusers in many parts of the world, and it stimulates both production and the illicit traffic. To diminish demand, addicts and abusers must be treated and reintegrated as productive members of society. This treatment and reintegration cannot follow a wholly uniform pattern everywhere, but must be based on studies which take full account of social and economic conditions, cultural traditions, etc., in each country or region. Moreover, demand must also be reduced by preventive measures, which include education, particularly of young people, in the dangers of drug-taking and addiction. In developing countries, measures

to reduce the demand require the help of developed countries. If such help is not forthcoming, there is a serious risk that addiction will spread from new sources of contagion, and that new centres for the illicit traffic wil come into being.

4. The repression of the illicit traffic requires the strengthening of enforcement action in many countries of the world. No country can defend itself against the illicit traffic without the co-operation of other countries, and common efforts will have to be undertaken on the international level to deal with this aspect.

5. The purpose of the United Nations Fund for Drug Abuse Control will be to develop short-term and long-term plans and programmes along the lines indicated above, and to provide assistance in the execution of those plans and programmes. During the initial stages of the Fund, pending the completion and submission of a proposed long-term policy and plan of action which would deal with all aspects of the problems related to drug abuse control, the voluntary contributions to the Fund will be used for specific projects to be included in a short-term programme without prejudice to ongoing projects. The short-term programme will consist of projects to expand the research and information facilities of United Nations drug-control bodies; to plan and implement programmes of technical assistance in pilot projects for crop substitution purposes, the establishment and improvement of national drug-control administrations and enforcement machinery, the training of personnel, ad in setting up or expanding research and training centres which could serve national or regional needs; to enlarge the capabilities and extend the operations of United Nations drug-control bodies and their secretariats; to promote facilities for the treatment, rehabilitation, and social reintegration of drug addcts; and to develop educational material and programmes suitable for use on high-risk populations.[1]

The Fund shall be financed through voluntary national contributions and after one year of interim administration, it will be placed under the direction of the Division of Narcotic Drugs.

Section 4. RECOMMENDATIONS FOR A NEW SYSTEM*

The indirect method of control bears its endemic weakness in that its control scheme relies on the willingness and effectiveness of multiple participants in a process in which not all share the same degree of concern and interest. These weaknesses, discussed throughout this article, are only some of those which persons concerned with the problem have identified over the years. The general scheme of the alternative proposed is as follows: (1) a direct control scheme whereby an international agency would have, in the case of the opiates, the monopoly of production, distribution, warehousing, and sale; in the case of cocaine and *Cannabis sativa*-type drugs, the powers of indirect supervision, and in the case of psychotropic sub-

[1] SG/SM/1442 SOX/NAR/104, Mar. 30, 1971.

* Bassiouni, *The International Narcotics Control Scheme: A Proposal*, 46 St. John's L. Rev. (1972) and Bassiouni, Transnational Control of Narcotics, 1972 Proceedings of the American Society of International Law.

stances the power of supervising local controls devices and (2) minimum standards of treatment of abusers applicable indirectly by each state, but subject to the international agency's supervision with an international financial subsidy scheme wherever needed.

4.1. The Direct Control Scheme

The direct control scheme would entail the following:

1. Establishing an international monopoly agency which would select one or more locations for growing opium and manufacturing morphine necessary for medical and scientific purposes.
2. Subsidizing countries presently producing the poppy in order to allow alternative crops to be grown by individuals who would be economically adversely affected by the scheme.
3. Vesting the agency with control powers to regulate with competent local agencies the manufacturing and distribution of psychotropic substances and supervising local agencies in their controlling activities to insure compliance with the regulating scheme.
4. Continuing the system of reporting, certification, and estimates already in operation but with direct sanctions power in the agency.
5. Vesting Interpol with the characteristics of a true international police with the necessary technical and scientific means to carry out this function, endowing it with the right to participate with local authorities in arrests, searches and seizures, and other techniques of law enforcement along the model of a federal police system, and having it function as one of the supervisory bodies of the international agency.
6. Establishing uniformity in all national penal laws on this subject on the basis of a proposed model treaty-statute.
7. Distinguishing between (a) international traffickers, (b) local pushers and dealers, (c) users, and (d) addicts and treating each category differently for purposes of prevention, enforcement, repression, and treatment-rehabilitation legislation.
8. Categorizing narcotic drugs as follows:
   a. Opium and its derivatives and cocaine.
   b. Psychotropic substances.
   c. *Cannabis sativa* and its derivatives.
   The distinction would be based on scientific data on the addiction-dependence properties of these categories and their harmful effects in comparison with legal substances, granting WHO the authority to add or to remove any drug or substance from any of these categories.
9. Having a multilateral treaty-statute on extradition with right of re-

view before the international court of justice with equal standing for individual recourses as well as states and the international agency.[2]

4.2. The Minimum Standards of Abuser Treatment

The minimum standards would require the following:

1. The recognition that abuse of drugs is a disease and that as such, whether its cause is psychological or physiological, it is better controlled by treatment than by imprisonment.
2. The setting of international standards for the following:

    a. The delineation of what constitutes addiction-dependence.
    b. The best-suited treatment for each category of abusers.
    c. The maner in which treatment should be given.
    d. The agreement of each state that such a program be conducted under U.N. supervision but implemented by each state for better rehabilitative-treatment result.
    e. The giving of international subsidies to developing states unable to absorb the high costs of rehabilitation-treatment or in the alternative, whenever certain states do not have the necessary scientific resources to set up regional compacts under international sponsorship to provide such services.

It is the opinion of this writer that the present international scheme served its purpose so far but must give way to a direct international control system; that there is no alternative to a concurrent program of curtailing user demand and curbing the profit incentive in illicit traffic and trade. The President's Commission on Marijuana is presently undertaking studies on this subject; and its preliminary results favored "decriminalization" of the *Cannabis sativa*. Such conclusions should also apply to other substances now deemed narcotic. The modest proposal outlined herein may hopefully trigger an interest in the development of an alternative international control scheme to the present one which proved so ineffective judging by increased rate of addiction everywhere in the world, even though that system was achieved arduously and over the span of half a century. It remains nonetheless, as it always was, one step behind the needs it is to serve.

[2] This proposal was made by this author to the Xth International Law Congress of Rome in 1969 in the American National Report; Bassiouni, *A Summary of International Extradition in the American Practice and a Proposal*, 39 REVUE INTERNATIONALE DE DROIT PENAL 494 (1968), reprinted in 15 WAYNE L. REV. 733 (1969).

PART FIVE

THE PROSECUTION OF INTERNATIONAL CRIMES
AND THE CREATION OF AN
INTERNATIONAL CRIMINAL COURT

CHAPTER XII

THE PROSECUTION OF WAR CRIMES

Section 1. WAR CRIMES: HISTORY AND DEFINITION

REMIGIUSZ BIERZANEK

1.1. The Period to World War I

The concept of war crimes is a corollary of the law regulating the recourse to and conduct of war. Hence, the development of the concept of
war crimes and responsibility for them is intimately connected with the
history of the law of war.

Rules prohibiting the use of certain means of warfare, imperfect as
they were, developed in ancient Greece, which consisted of a community of small states with the same cultural traditions. Later, in
much greater quantity, in the medieval "Family of Christian Nations."
Like much of the law of those times, these prohibitions of certain means
of warfare were rooted in religious patterns of behavior and supported by
religious sanctions. Thus the Amphictyons of ancient Greece swore not
to poison springs and wells: those who violated such rules were considered perjurers. In the Middle Ages ecclesiastic synods imposed numerous restrictions on the action that belligerents might take against the
enemy, either prohibiting violence against particular categories of population (clergy, students, peaceful peasants) or specifying special periods
(feast days, Lent) when Christians were not permitted to wage war.
Sometimes the synods tried to ban certain specific means of warfare which
were held to be unbecoming a Christian, *e.g.*, the Lateran Council of 1139
forbade the use of crossbows, though only in wars waged between
Christians. In the seventh century Islam developed new rules.

As far as the concept of unlawful war is concerned, its roots go back
to the Roman idea of *bellum injustum*, a war that has not been declared
in conformity with the formalistic *jus fetiale*. The notion of *bellum injustum* assumed a completely different meaning in the Christian doctrine
of the Middle Ages as developed first by St. Augustine and then by St.
Thomas Aquinas and the other *canonists*. In this view, war was permissible only if there existed *causa justa*. Such "just cause" could arise

only if it were undertaken either against an unlawful attack by an enemy (war of defense) or in pursuit of a legitimate claim which an enemy refused to satisfy voluntarily (war of execution). Thus the concept of *bellum justum* contained the elements of a punitive action, since such a war was a means to rectify a breach of law.

The canonists' interpretation was adopted by Grotius and the other *naturalists*. They believed that although natural law and the law of nations did not forbid all wars, conflicts which violated the rights of others could not be sanctioned. The only cause which could justify war was *injuria*,[1] a "state of claiming one's rights."[2] This was the theoretical foundation on which criminal responsibility for breaches of the law in relations between states was elaborated, particularly by Grotius. He maintained that a community as well as individuals was liable for actions and omissions, and that one community was obliged, on the demand of another, either to punish offenders or comply with any request for their extradition (*aut puniendi aut dedendi*).[3] Thus, we have here a concept of the concurrent jurisdiction of states in respect to punishing crimes of an international character.

The close connection between peace and criminal responsibility for waging war was perceived by some writers. In the thirteenth century in particular, when plans for assuring permanent peace in Europe were widely discussed, the view could be found that offenders against peace should be tried and punished. History has, in fact, recorded a case of a ruler who was placed on trial and sentenced to death for initiating an unjust war (Conradin von Hohenstaufen in Naples in 1268).

While the canonists and the naturalists placed their main emphasis on the distinction between just and unjust war and attached less importance to the question of the means of legitimate and illegitimate warfare, the *positivists* opposed the distinction between just and unjust war and conceded states an *unqualified* right to resort to war (*jus ad bellum*). Hence, they directed their attention to the conduct of war (*jus in bello*). It was, of course, the positivist school of thought which dominated international law in the eighteenth and nineteenth centuries.

In the second half of the eighteenth century, under the impact of the Enlightenment, a new and more humanitarian concept of warfare appeared, the so-called Rousseau-Portalis doctrine. They maintained that hostilities should not extend beyond members of armed forces or encroach upon private property. In the words of Jean Jacques Rousseau: "War is not a relation of man to man but a relation of state to another

---

[1] *See* H. Grotius, De Jure Belli ac Pacis, Bk. II, ch. II.
[2] *See* E. Vattel, Le Droit des Gens, bk. III, paras. 1 & 26 (1887).
[3] *See* H. Grotius, *supra* note 1, at ch. XXI.

state in which individuals are becoming enemies to say incidentally, not as men, not even as citizens, but as soldiers, [and] not as members of their countries but as their defenders."[4] The same idea was expressed in a speech made by Portalis on Floreal 14 of the year VIII at the inauguration of the Maritime Tribunal.

The ideas of Rousseau and Portalis significantly influenced the first major restrictions on warfare which developed in the second half of the nineteenth and at the beginning of the twentieth century. The Treaty of Paris of 1856 outlawed privateering. The first Red Cross Convention concerning the amelioration of the conditions of the wounded and sick in armed forces in the field was concluded in Geneva in 1864. It was followed by many other conventions which have done much to curb the inhumaneness of war and to protect the wounded and the sick as well as medical personnel, hospitals and their means of transportation. The rules of land warfare codified at the Second Hague Conference in 1907 and other Hague Conventions concerning particular fields of the law of warfare and neutrality, form a fairly comprehensive body of rules imposing on belligerents numerous restrictions in dealing with enemy armies and civilian populations. According to some of these conventions the state whose armies have violated the laws of warfare is bound to make reparations or to punish persons guilty of those violations.[5]

As far as individual responsibility for breaches of the laws and customs of warfare is concerned, the status of the individual in the course of history was certainly far from satisfactory. Individual offenders ran the risk of being punished by the enemy in the event of being captured. It was generally accepted that international law permitted the trial of persons charged with breaches of the customs of war if they fell into the hands of the country whose citizens had been the victims of their offenses. For this purpose special courts might be set up. The right of a victorious power to bring to trial individual members of enemy armies accused of violating the laws of war was recognized by international custom.[6] However, it was the general practice to insert in peace treaties an amnesty clause for persons guilty of wrongful acts during the war. Since waging war had for centuries been one of the sovereign rights of every state—like the power to conclude treaties or sending and receiving diplomatic envoys (*jus belli, jus tractatuum, jus legationis*)—it was not

[4] J. Rousseau, Contrat Social, bk. I, ch. IV.

[5] *See* art. 3 of the IV Hague Convention of 1907, art. 56 of the Rules appendixed to this Convention, & art. 21 of the X Hague Convention of 1907; also Part IV, this volume.

[6] In the report of the Commission on the Responsibility of the Authors of the War, submitted in 1919, it was said that every belligerent has, according to international law, the power and authority to try individuals alleged to be guilty of crimes against the laws and customs of war. *See* C. Fenwick, International Law 672 (1948).

itself considered an unlawful act, even in cases in which the war was an aggressive one lacking any *justa causa*. However, rulers did sometimes make special commitments not to resort to war. Violation of these obligations raised the problem of responsibility for waging war. Such was the case with Napoleon I, who after his abdication and retirement to Elba returned to break the treaty pledges he had given. After his subsequent defeat and capture, the possibility of placing him before a tribunal for prosecution of war crimes was considered. But the English government chose a political rather than a legal solution, and deported him to the island of Saint Helena.

1.2. The Period of World War I

World War I marked a new phase in the historical development of criminal responsibility for war crimes. The number and the gravity of war crimes therein committed, though not so appalling to a generation which lived through World War II, horrified contemporaries because of the flagrancy of their violation of the laws of war.

The German aggression itself was accompanied by the cynical reference of Chancellor Bethman-Hollweg to the treaty on the neutralization of Belgium as a "scrap of paper." The rules of warfare were not observed and their violations were cruel. Massacres, torture, the arrest and execution of hostages, artillery and aerial bombardments of open towns, sinking of merchant ships without any regard for the safety of passengers and crew, collective penalties, use of shields formed of living human beings, attacks on hospitals, looting and wanton destruction of public and private property, methodical and deliberate devastation of private industries, disregard of the rights of the wounded, prisoners of war, and women and children, all these took place.

Under the pressure of public opinion which demanded the trial and punishment of war criminals, the Paris Peace Conference appointed on January 25, 1919, a Commission to inquire into and report violations of international law alleged against Germany and her Allies.

Each of the five big powers—the United States, the British Empire, France, Italy, and Japan—had two representatives. Each of the five smaller countries—Belgium, Greece, Poland, Roumania, and Serbia— had one representative on the Commission. That Commission appointed three subcommissions: one on criminal acts, one on the responsibility for the war, and a third on the responsibility for the violation of the laws and customs of war.

In March 1919, the Commission adopted a report in which it recommended that the Treaty of Peace should require the enemy governments to recognize the jurisdiction of the national tribunals and the High

Tribunal and surrender war criminals for trial. As far as the definition of war crimes was concerned, the Commission laid down a list of crimes or groups of crimes as a basis for the future collection of information concerning such offenses. This list specified offenses in violation of the laws and customs of war:

1. Murders and massacres; systematic terrorism.
2. Putting hostages to death.
3. Torture of civilians.
4. Deliberate starvation of civilians.
5. Rape.
6. Abduction of girls and women for the purpose of forced prostitution.
7. Deportation of civilians.
8. Internment of civilians under inhuman conditions.
9. Forced labour of civilians in connection with the military operations of the enemy.
10. Usurpation of sovereignty during military occupation.
11. Compulsory enlistment of soldiers among the inhabitants of occupied territory.
12. Attempts to denationalize the inhabitants of occupied territory.
13. Pillage.
14. Confiscation of property.
15. Exaction of illegitimate or exorbitant contributions and requisitions.
16. Debasement of currency and issue of spurious currency.
17. Imposition of collective penalties.
18. Wanton devastation and destruction of property.
19. Deliberate bombardment of undefended places.
20. Wanton destruction of religious, charitable, educational, and historic buildings and monuments.
21. Destruction of merchant ships and passenger vessels without warning and without provision for the safety of passengers and crew.
22. Destruction of fishing boats and relief ships.
23. Deliberate bombardment of hospitals.
24. Attack on and destruction of hospital ships.
25. Breach of other rules of the Red Cross.
26. Use of deleterious and asphyxiating gases.
27. Use of explosive or expanding bullets, and other inhuman appliances.
28. Directions to give no quarter.
29. Ill-treatment of wounded and prisoners of war.
30. Employment of prisoners of war on unauthorized work.

31. Misuse of flags of truce.
32. Poisoning of wells.[7]

Nevertheless, in its inquiry into war crimes, the Commission also took note of the atrocities committed on the territory of the Central Powers against their own nationals such as the massacres of Armenian population perpetrated by the Turkish authorities and the crimes of Austrian troops against the Italian national minority. These acts were qualified as coming within the meaning of violations of the "laws of humanity."[8] It should be added, however, that the American members of the Commission objected in the Memorandum of Reservations to the phrase "laws and principles of humanity" as included in the report, arguing that in contradistinction to the laws and customs of war, the former principles were not a sufficiently reliable standard of conduct and that "war was and is by its very nature inhuman [and even] acts consistent with the laws and customs of war, although . . . inhuman [were] nevertheless not subject to punishment by a court of justice," for "the laws and principles of humanity are not certain, varying with time, place and circumstance, and accordingly, it [must] be [left] to the conscience of the individual judge."[9]

As far as the responsibility of war criminals was concerned, the Commission concluded that four categories of offenses were to call for prosecution in an international tribunal:

1. Offenses against civilians and soldiers of Allied nations such as atrocities committed in prison camps in which citizens of several countries were confined.
2. Offenses by persons of authority whose orders were executed not only in one area or on one battle front, but which affected the conduct of operation against several of the Allied armies.
3. Offenses by civil or military authorities without distinction of rank who ordered or abstained from preventing violations of the laws or customs of war.
4. Charges against such other persons belonging to enemy countries as, having regard to the character of the offense of the law of any belligerent country, it may be considered advisable not to proceed before a court other than the High Tribunal.

The report of the Commission recommended that other war crimes not

[7] HISTORY OF THE UN WAR CRIMES COMMISSION 34 (1948).
[8] In a declaration issued by France, Russia, and Great Britain on May 28, 1918, the massacres of the Armenian population were described as new crimes of Turkey against humanity and civilization.
[9] HISTORY OF THE U.N. WAR CRIMES COMMISSION 36 (1948).

covered in these four points should be prosecuted and tried before national courts.

The Commission insisted that in the hierarchy of persons in authority, there was no reason why rank, however exalted, should in any circumstances protect the holder of it from responsibility when that responsibility had been determined before a properly established tribunal. All persons belonging to enemy countries, however high their positions (including chiefs of states), who had been guilty of offenses against the laws and customs of war or the laws of humanity would be held liable, the Commission affirmed, to criminal prosecution.

The Commission advised the establishment of a "High Tribunal" to conduct trials of war criminals falling within international criminal jurisdiction. The High Tribunal was to be composed of members nominated by the Allied governments. Each of the five Great Powers was to appoint three members, and each other government, one member. The procedure to be employed by the High Tribunal was to be determined by the Tribunal itself. The Prosecuting Committee, consisting of five members designated by the Great Powers, was to be charged with selection of cases for trial and direction of prosecutions.

The Allied Powers ultimately followed the recommendations of the Commission only to a limited extent in drafting the Treaty of Versailles. Even when adopted, such recommendations often proved ineffective. Under Article 227 of the Treaty, Wilhelm II Hohenzollern, former German Emperor, was to be publicly arraigned "for a supreme offense against international morality and the sanctity of treaties," and to be tried before a specially constituted international tribunal. Under Article 228 of the Treaty, the Allied and Associated Powers had the right to bring before military tribunals persons accused of having committed acts in violation of the laws and customs of war. This right was recognized by the German Government which was required by the Treaty to hand over to the Allied and Associated Powers all such accused who were to be specified by name or by rank, office or employment which they held under the government authorities. Those found guilty were to be sentenced to punishments laid down by law. Article 229 provided for the trial of war criminals before military tribunals of the state against whose nationals the alleged crimes had been committed. According to Article 230, the German Government was obliged to furnish all documents and information of any kind which might be considered necessary "to ensure full knowledge of the incriminated acts, the discovery of offenders, and the just appreciation of responsibility." It should be emphasized that the provisions of the Treaty of Versailles followed both of the lines taken by the historical development of the concept of war crimes. Though stress was generally laid on crimes committed in violation of the laws and customs of war, *jus in bello,* Article 227 also recognized the responsibility of a person guilty of waging an unlawful war. (See Appendix I).

But as before mentioned, efforts made to prosecute and punish the war criminals of World War I on the strength of the provisions of articles 227 to 230 of the Treaty of Versailles, were far from successful. The Government of the Netherlands refused to surrender ex-Kaiser Wilhelm II, and the Allied Powers failed to undertake any concerted action to persuade the Dutch Government to change its decision. As far as the legal aspect of its refusal is concerned, that decision was based on the argument that Netherlands was not a party to the Treaty of Versailles and therefore was not bound by articles 227 and 228. Moreover, it was declared that the extradition of Wilhelm II would not be consistent with Dutch law and the tradition of asylum.[10]

In accordance with Article 228 of the Treaty of Versailles, a joint list of war criminals was drawn up from the names supplied by France, Belgium, Great Britain, Poland, Rumania, Italy, and Yugoslavia. The joint list, naming 901 war criminals—mostly German with a few Turks—was presented to the German Government on February 3, 1920.

As soon as the Treaty of Versailles was ratified, the Germans embarked on diplomatic action to prevent the surrender of their war criminals and to this end emphasized the danger of a political and social revolution.[11] The Allies were informed that . . .

> the entire German Volk, without regard to class and party, [was] of the conviction that it [was] impossible to deliver up the so-called war criminals; if, despite this, the Reich Government [would] attempt to carry out their extradition, it would encounter the strongest opposition; no German official would lend a hand to the arrest of a German in order to deliver him up to the justice of the Entente. . . . The mere proposal of an order of this kind would create such a storm of indignation that the entire peace structure would be gravely threatened.[12]

The President of the German Peace Delegation, Baron von Lersner, reported an "immense movement that [had] covered all Germany" with numerous mass meetings held in churches and in the streets, in which

[10] Texts and notes of the Allied and Associated Powers of Jan. 15 & Feb. 14, 1920, the notes of the Dutch Government of Jan. 21, 1920, & Mar. 2, 1920, and of the note of the German Peace Delegation of Feb. 3, 1920. *See* Berber, Diktat von Versailles 1195 (1939).

[11] It has been said in the note of the German Peace Delegation from Jan. 25, 1920, that the demand of extradition by the Allied and Associated Powers undoubtedly must give rise to convulsions in political as well as in economical field. *See* Berber, *supra* note 10, at 1207.

[12] Von Lersner, Die Auslieferung der deutschen Kriegsverbrecher in Zehn Jahre Versailles vol. 1, at 22 (H. Schnee & H. Draeger eds. 1929).

thousands of people protested in the sharpest manner against the claim of extradition.[13]

Different positions were taken by each of the Allied Powers in the Peace Conference Commission with respect to the trial of war criminals. The Japanese delegates considered the question "whether international law recognize[d] a penal law as applicable to those who [were] guilty," and indicated "the consequences which would be created in the history of international law by the prosecution for breaches of the laws and customs of war of enemy heads of states before a tribunal constituted by the opposite party. The American delegates refused to give their assent to "creating an international criminal court for the trial of individuals, for which a precedent [was] lacking and which appear[ed] to be unknown in the practice of nations." Instead they favored "the mere assemblage of the existing national military tribunals or commissions . . . bringing with them the law to be applied, namely the laws and customs of war, and the procedure, namely the procedure of the national commissions or courts."

Conscious of the lack of consensus among the Allies, the Germans were able, in the words of von Lersner, "to present an energetic front and to leap into the breach . . ." and as a result of the German action "the first great demand which the Entente Governments presented to [the Germans] by virtue of the *Dikat von Versailles* was broken, like glass upon stone, on the unity of the German people."[14]

In 1920, the Allied governments accepted the German proposal, submitted as a compromise, to have all persons accused by the Allies of war crimes tried before the Supreme Court of Germany in Leipzig. In this respect, the German Government declared as a new token of its earnest will to punish Germans guilty of a war crime or misdemeanor and that "Germany would give all conceivable guarantees of the impartial and firm execution of the proceedings, especially through the assistance of official representatives of the interested opposition states." However, the Allies reserved their right to consider whether Germany, as a result of those trials and punishments, had complied with her obligations under articles 228 to 230 of the Treaty of Versailles, and, if they were not satisfied, to try the war criminals before their own tribunals. This right was explicitly acknowledged in a German letter of reply.

The trial of the German war criminals began in May, 1921, and lasted until June, 1922. It involved only an abridged test list containing no more than forty-five of the names originally supplied by the Allies to the German Government. In the majority of cases, the prosecution considered it

[13] *Id.* at 26.
[14] *Id.* at 26, 27.

impossible to proceed as "evidence has been found insufficient," "misdeeds were not covered by German laws," or because of other formal requirements, *e.g.*, the whereabouts of some war criminals were unknown.

The trials took place in an atmosphere of "patriotic indignation" against the humiliation of Germany: applause and bouquets greeted the appearance of "national heroes" "unjustly" accused and sentenced. Some of the criminals given the heaviest sentences, like Lieutenant Bold, who was convicted of having torpedoed a hospital ship, succeeded in escaping from prison, and their feat was hailed by many German newspapers as the flight of "U-boat heroes."

The result of the Leipzig trials was that of the 901 persons on the list of war criminals accused of the most appalling crimes, 888 were either not tried, acquitted or summarily released, and only thirteen were convicted to sentences ranging from six months to four years and even they were not made to serve their terms; several escaped and the prison wardens who engineered their escape were publicly congratulated.[15]

At the beginning of 1922, the Commission of Allied Jurists, established to inquire into the Leipzig trials, unanimously found them unsatisfactory as "some of the accused who were acquitted should have been convicted and . . . in any case the sentences were not adequate." It recommended to the Allies, that rather than send new cases to Leipzig, the German Government should be compelled to extradite war criminals as required by article 228 of the Treaty of Versailles.

In the vigorous protest issued by the Conference of Ambassadors, it was stated that the German Government "ha[d] not kept its promise to administer justice objectively and loyally" and in consequence the Allies would "completely disregard the German proceedings taken by the Leipzig Court against future defendants and . . . would resume and reserve to themselves all rights belonging to them by virtue of the Treaty of Versailles at present and in the future, in particular the right to prosecute the war criminals themselves, if necessary, in absentia."[16] This laudable protest, however, was not followed up by any efforts to impose on Germany fulfillment of the provisions contained in articles 228 to 230 of the Treaty of Versailles.

The British had expressed mildly approving opinions of the formal correctness of the Leipzig proceedings. Thus the German government responded to Poincaré's note with an expression of its surprise that all the principal Allied Powers doubted the trials, since "foreign witnesses of the highest juristic repute, among them the English Solicitor General Sir Ernest Pollock, the English Attorney General Sir Gordon Hew-

---

[15] *See* History, *supra* note 9, at 48.
[16] *Note of Protest of Poincaré*, Aug. 23, 1922. *See* Berber, *supra* note 10, at 1217.

art . . . ha[d] acknowledged the impartiality of the Reichsgericht."[17] At the same time, truculent protest meetings organized by nationalist groups were taking place in Germany in which war criminals were presented as "national heroes" and resolutions were passed to prevent their deliverance to the "justice of the Entente."

In summary, attempts to punish the war criminals of World War I in accordance with the provisions of the peace treaties came to nothing. As recapitulated by the authors of the *History of the UNWCC*, this failure had its roots in the fact that "the sanctions came too late, when public opinion no longer upheld them," that "the Allies were no longer united when the war was over," that "the world in 1919–1920 was not internationally mature [enough] to understand the consequences of failure to ensure respect of the provisions of the Treaty," and that "articles 228–230 were hastily and imperfectly framed, so that it would have been impossible to carry them out."[18]

As far as other peace treaties of this period are concerned, attention should be drawn to article 230 of the treaty concluded by the Allied Powers with Turkey at Sèvres in 1920 which was not ratified and which was replaced by the Treaty of Lausanne of 1923, which did not contain any provision on the subject of war crimes. According to that article, Turkey undertook to hand over to the Allied Powers the persons whose surrender would have been required by the latter as being responsible for the massacres committed during the continuance of the state of war on territory which formed part of the Turkish Empire on August 1, 1914. The Allied Powers reserved to themselves the right to designate the Tribunal which would try the persons so accused, and the Turkish Government agreed to recognize such a Tribunal once constituted. This article, referring to the massacres of Turkish citizens of Armenian and Greek origin, constituted a precedent which the more recent treaty provisions concerning the punishment of crimes against humanity could follow.

1.3. The Interwar Period

Following World War I the trend in international law was directed toward outlawing war (see Supra Part II for Crimes Against Peace), and the continued effort to restrict the freedom of states in their choice of means of warfare.

In the Covenant of the League of Nations, any war or threat of war was declared to be a matter of concern for the whole League. The member states agreed to submit to arbitration or to judicial settlement or to refer to the Council of the League any dispute between them that might

[17] BERBER, *supra* note 10, at 1217; JOURNAL DU DROIT INTERNATIONAL (1922).

[18] HISTORY, *supra* note 9, at 52.

lead to rupture, and undertook not to resort to war except under conditions specified in the Covenant. A member state acting in violation of the Covenants provisions for maintenance of peace was subject to sanctions. Although the Covenant did not eliminate war and even conceded its legality, in certain cases, the traditional *jus ad bellum* was considerably curtailed.

In this respect, certain other international documents of the interwar period went further than the terms of the Covenant. Thus in article 1 of the Draft Treaty of Mutual Assistance discussed by the League in 1923, the contracting parties solemnly declared that "aggressive war is an international crime" and in article 2 agreed "in no case to resort to war, either with one another or against a state which, if the occasion arises, accepts all obligations hereinafter set out, except in case of resistance to aggression." The Protocol, unanimously recommended by the Assembly of the League, was not ratified by the states. It was not until the Paris Pact of 1928 that the principle of outlawing war was recognized as a part of binding international law. The parties to the Pact solemnly declared on behalf of their respective peoples that "they condemn[ed] recourse to war for the solution of international controversies and renounce[d] it as an instrument of national policy in their relations with one another" (art. 1) and agreed that "the settlement or solution of all disputes or conflicts of whatever nature or of whatever they [might] be, which [might] arise among them, [would] never be sought except by pacific means" (art. 2).

Apart from this, a number of nonaggression treaties were concluded by the Soviet Union and its neighbor states. These were supplemented by the Convention on the Definition of Aggressor signed in London in 1933. The American states at the Sixth Pan-American Conference which met in Havana in 1928 adopted a resolution according to which "a war of aggression constitute[d] an international crime against the human species" and "aggression was considered illicit and as such was declared prohibited." In the Anti-War Treaty of Non-aggression and Conciliation signed in Rio de Janeiro in 1933 (Saavedra Lamas Treaty), five Latin American states condemned "wars of aggression in their mutual relations or in those with other states."

In this same interwar period, some progress was achieved in the law regarding the rules of warfare. To be noted here are the Protocol banning the use of asphyxiating, poisonous, and other gases and bacteriological warfare, signed in Geneva in 1925; the International Conventions on the amelioration of the condition of the wounded and sick in armies in the field and on treatment of prisoners of war, signed in Geneva in 1929, and the Procés-verbal relating to the rules of submarine warfare, signed in London in 1936. Other international instruments described violations of certain rules of warfare as "acts of piracy" (art. 3 of the Washington Treaty of 1922 and the Preamble to the Nyon Agreement of 1937).

Some aspects of responsibility for committing war crimes were discussed by unofficial international bodies at this time. Thus at the thirty-fourth Conference of the International Law Association, held in Vienna in 1926, where one of the topics on the agenda was proposals for the creation of an International Criminal Court, the crimes to be included in its jurisdiction were put up for discussions. Among them were violations of treaty law "which regulate[d] the methods and conduct of warfare" as well as "violations of the laws and customs of war generally accepted as binding by civilized nations." The thirty-ninth Conference of the same Association, held in Paris in 1936, issued a declaration aimed at invoking the speedy jurisdiction of the Permanent Court of International Justice in the case of any violation of the Paris Pact.

1.4. The Period of World War II

Although the idea of punishing war criminals has deep roots in history, it took the events of World War II to see it given real effect. "It was not until World War II with its tragic lessons," Professor Pella has written, "that the rulers of states finally decided to cast off the old armor of prejudice which had led them to declare any international penal justice impossible," as "the idea of repressing acts committed by states as well as by individuals endangering, directly or indirectly, the supreme legal good, *i.e.*, peace, was often regarded as the manifestation of a dangerous revolutionary sentiment."[19]

The war crimes committed by the Axis Powers during World War II reached dimensions unprecedented in history. The conduct of the war by Germany and, above all, its treatment of the population of the occupied countries were not only glaring violations of the laws of warfare but also, where Eastern Europe was concerned, an outright bid to exterminate whole nations. In actual fact, the attempted extermination was directed against Jewish national groups and large sections of the Polish people and the peoples of the Soviet Union.

In this situation, while the war was still in progress, statesmen of the Allied Powers in many occasions solemnly declared their intention of prosecuting and punishing persons guilty of war crimes and inhuman atrocities. The first official denunciation of the German war crimes was made by the governments of Poland and Czechoslovakia in a joint statement issued in November, 1940, which itemized the violence and bru-

---

[19] V. Pella, La Guerre-Crime et les Criminels de Guerre 16 (1946).

tality to which their countries had been subjected. There followed the separate declarations on the subject made by President Roosevelt and Prime Minister Churchill on October 25, 1941, and the Soviet note of November 7, 1941, on the atrocities committed against war prisoners. In a joint declaration signed at Saint James Palace in London on January 13, 1942, the governments of the nine countries occupied by Germany—Belgium, Czechoslovakia, France, Greece, Luxembourg, the Netherlands, Norway, Poland, and Yugoslavia—placed among their principal war aims "the punishment, through the channel of organized justice, of those guilty of or responsible for war crimes whether they have ordered them, perpetrated them, or participated in them." They resolved "to see to it in a spirit of international solidarity that all those guilty or responsible, whatever their nationality, [were] sought out, handed over to justice and judged, [and] that the sentences pronounced [were] carried out." As far as the definition of war crimes was concerned, the Declaration referred to the international law in force and particularly to the Convention signed at The Hague in 1907 on the laws and customs of warfare in the field, and stated that the acts of violence against civilian populations prohibited by that Convention had nothing in common with the conceptions of an act of war or a political crime as understood by civilized nations. The Declaration endorsed the principle that neither national legislation nor orders given in keeping with this legislation could be regarded as legitimating the activities of persons who acted against the laws and customs of warfare. "It would be useless," said the Luxembourg Minister for Foreign Affairs on signing the Declaration, "when the day of victory comes for the torturers of our people to claim that they only did what they were ordered to do and acted according to their laws; these laws and the application of them are now stigmatized by the Declaration of the Governments of the occupied countries as being contrary to law."[20]

In the Declaration of Moscow of November 1, 1943, the governments of the Soviet Union, the United Kingdom, and the United States, "speaking in the interests of the thirty-three United Nations" warned the Germans of their intention" to pursue persons responsible for war crimes to the uttermost ends of the earth and deliver them to the accusers in order that justice [would] be done." All those guilty of atrocities, massacres and executions in any country were put on notice that they would "be sent back to the countries in which their abominable deeds were done in order that they [could] be judged and punished according to the laws of those liberated countries," while "the major criminals" whose offenses had no particular geographical location "would be punished by the joint decision of the governments of the Allies.

[20] *See* HISTORY, *supra* note 9, at 91.

Other declarations by the governments and statesmen of the Allied Powers during the war delivered similar warnings, serving notice that war criminals would be punished. Thus it was reiterated that war criminals "[would] have to stand in courts of law in the very countries they [were then] oppressing and answer for their acts."[21] and "that those guilty of the vile system of hostages and the massacre of civilian population, whose names [were] known to tens of thousands of tortured persons [would] not escape the terrible punishment which await[ed] them,"[22] that they would not be permitted to acquire a right of asylum in other countries,[23] and again, that "none who participate[d] in these acts of savagery [would] go unpunished."[24]

In the Joint Declaration of December 17, 1942, the governments of the United Kingdom, the Soviet Union, and the United States reaffirmed their solemn resolve to insure that war criminals responsible for crimes against persons of the Jewish race would not escape retribution.[25] After the end of the war in Europe, the heads of the same Great Powers declared in the Potsdam Agreement that "war criminals and those who ha[d] participated in planning and carrying out Nazi enterprises involving or resulting in atrocities or war crimes [would] be arrested and brought to judgment," that "stern justice [would] be meted out to all war criminals" and that the major war criminals would be brought to swift and sure justice.

Heeding all these declarations, the Allied governments took certain preparatory steps toward organizing the postwar prosecution and punishment of war criminals. On October 20, 1943, it was decided at a diplomatic conference to set up a U.N. Commission for the investigation of war crimes. The Commission contributed much to the solution of the legal issues raised by the prosecution and punishment of war criminals and of the problems connected with investigating and recording the facts involved. Its inquiries were preceded by some preparatory work done by such semiofficial bodies as the London International Assembly, set up in 1941 under the auspices of the League of Nations Union, and the International Commission for Penal Reconstruction and Development established in 1943.

In its approach the Commission was strongly influenced by memories of World War I and particularly by the failure to punish German and

[21] *See* the reply given by President Roosevelt on July 30, 1942 to representatives of the Netherlands, Yugoslavia, and Luxembourg, HISTORY, *supra* note 9, at 93.

[22] *See* the speech made by the U.K. Lord Chancellor on Oct. 7, 1942.

[23] *See* the speech made by Marshall Stalin on Nov. 6, 1942.

[24] *See* the statement made by President Roosevelt on Mar. 24. 1944. DEPARTMENT OF STATE BULLETIN, No. 248, at 277.

[25] HISTORY, *supra* note 9, at 106.

Turkish war criminals. As has been noted in the History of the UNWCC, "the German offer to try the war criminals before their own courts was in complete opposition with the letter and with the spirit of the Treaty" and "the fact that only about ten accused were sentenced to punishments which were quite out of proportion with the gravity of [their] crimes, and that th[o]se penalties were never really served, showed the German public that the provisions of the Treaty of Versailles concerning retribution were being flouted, and led them to believe that the other provisions of the Treaty could be just as easily disregarded."[26]

The inquiries of the Commission proceeded in three directions: (1) investigation of facts and evidence, (2) enforcement of the law on the punishment of war criminals, and (3) the drafting of legal opinions on war crimes and the penal responsibility of criminals. The Legal Committee dealing with this third subject paid much attention to the definition of war crimes.

The term "war crimes" was understood by the Commission, in a narrow sense, as violations of the laws and customs of warfare, and in a broad sense, as also covering crimes against humanity and crime against peace. As far as war crimes *sensu stricto* were concerned, the Committee set out to draw up a list of offenses. Following discussions of the catalogue of war crimes established by the 1919 Commission on Responsibilities,[27] it was recognized that there were, or at least might be, war crimes not included in this register. In its report, the Legal Committee recommended extending the list issued in 1919 in keeping with the Preamble to the Fourth Hague Convention in which the contracting parties declared that "in cases not covered by the rules adopted by them, the inhabitants and the belligerents remain under the protection and governance of the principles of the law of nations, derived from the usages established among civilized peoples, from the laws of humanity, and from the dictates of the public conscience." The Commission followed the recommendation of the Legal Committee and supplemented the 1919 list of war crimes by adding "indiscriminate mass arrests" and declared that the above-mentioned Preamble would at all times be taken into account and would make possible the extensions suggested. At the same time the Legal Committee introduced a very general definition by recommending to the Commission to "proceed upon the footing that international law recognizes the principle that a war crime is a violation of the laws and customs of war, and that no question can be raised as to the right of the United Nations to put on trial as a war criminal in

[26] *See* HISTORY, *supra* note 9, at 51.
[27] *Supra* note 7.

respect of such violations any hostile offender who may fall into their hands."[28]

As far as crimes against humanity were concerned, there was a strong feeling within the Commission that the concept of war crimes should be extended to cover atrocities committed on racial, political, or religious grounds in enemy territory, which did not fall strictly within the definition of war crimes. However, the suggestion made by the American delegation and supported by the Czechoslovak and Dutch delegations, to use the term "laws of humanity," met with serious objections. A definite solution of the problem was not reached until the London Agreement of 1945.

With regard to the question whether aggressive war amounted to a crime, the Legal Committee wanted to include among war crimes "the crimes committed for the purpose of preparing or launching the war, irrespective of the territory where those crimes had been committed" and "crimes that were committed in order to prevent the restoration of peace." This proposal, however, was not adopted by the Commission. After long discussions the majority report expressed the view that "acts committed by individuals merely for the purpose of preparing for and launching aggressive war [were] *lege lata*, not war crimes"; nevertheless, the acts and outrages "perpetrated by the responsible leaders of the Axis Powers and their satellites in preparing and launching [World War II] were of such gravity that they should be made the subject of a formal condemnation in the peace treaties." This viewpoint was opposed by the delegations of Czechoslovakia, Poland, Australia, China, New Zealand, and Yugoslavia. The matter was referred to the Enforcement Committee which recommended that "any person in the service of any state who ha[d] violated any rule of international law forbidding the threat or use of force . . . [should] be held individually responsible and . . . be brought to trial and punishment."[29]

In pursuance of all the previous declarations regarding war criminals, the four Powers, namely France, the Soviet Union, the United Kingdom, and the United States, "acting in the interests of all the United Nations," signed the London Agreement of August 8, 1945, setting up an International Military Tribunal for the trial of war criminals of the European Axis whose offenses had no particular geographical location, defining the law it was to administer and laying down rules for the proper conduct of the trial. As far as the war criminals of Japan were concerned, the Supreme Commander of the Allied Forces in the Far East, on the

[28] *See* HISTORY, *supra* note 9, at 171.
[29] *See* HISTORY, *supra* note 9, at 170–87.

authority of the Great Powers, established, by a Proclamation of January 19, 1946, the International Military Tribunal for the Far East.

In article 6 of the Charter annexed to the London Agreement, three categories of crimes were defined as coming within the jurisdiction of the International Military Tribunal: (1) crimes against peace (planning, preparation, initiation, or waging of a war of aggression; or a war in violation of international treaties, agreements, or assurances; or participation in a common conspiracy for the accomplishment of any of the foregoing), (2) war crimes (violations of the laws and customs of war), and (3) crimes against humanity (murder, extermination, enslavement, deportation, and other inhumane acts committed against any civilian population, before or during the war, or persecutions on political, racial, or religious grounds in execution of or in connection with any crime within the jurisdiction of the Tribunal, whether or not in violation of the domestic law of the country where perpetrated). These three categories were similarly defined in Order No. 10 promulgated by the Control Council for Germany (art. 2) and in the Charter of the Tokyo Tribunal (art. 5).

The peace treaties signed with Italy, Finland, Hungary, Bulgaria, and Roumania obliged these countries to insure the apprehension and surrender for trial of (1) persons accused of having committed, ordered, or abetted war crimes, or crimes against peace and humanity and (2) nationals of any Allied or Associated Power accused of having violated their national law by treason or collaboration with the enemy during the war.

The London Agreement on the prosecution and punishment of the major criminals of the European Axis, concluded in the same year as the U.N. Charter, was founded on the premise that violation of the principles of international law entails, even where there are no specific provisions defining the implications of such a breach, liability in international law. Taking its lead from this Agreement, the International Military Tribunal stated in the Nuremberg Judgment that the chief Nazi criminals were subject to criminal responsibility for violation of the principle of renunciation of war as an instrument of national policy embodied in the Paris Pact of 1928 to which the State of Germany was a party, even though the Pact did not specify the precise sanctions involved and did not contain any express provisions regarding the enforcement of this principle. The Tribunal gave these grounds for its ruling:

> The nations who signed the Pact or adhered to it unconditionally condemned recourse to war for the future as an instrument of policy and expressly renounced it. . . . But it is agreed that the Pact does not expressly enact that such wars are crimes, or set up courts to try those who make such wars. To that extent the same is true with regard to the laws of war contained in the

Hague Conventions. . . . In interpreting the words of the Pact, it must be remembered that international law is not the product of an international legislature, and that such international agreements as the Pact of Paris have to deal with general principles of law, and not with administrative matters of procedure.[30] (See Appendix I to Section 2 of this chapter).

In the light of this declaration there can no longer be any doubt that violation of the principles of international law prohibiting recourse to war or regulating the methods of warfare is a war crime in the same way as a breach of the other rules of international law in this field.[31]

The London Agreement on the prosecution and punishment of the criminals of the European Axis and the Nuremberg Judgment did much to crystallize and clarify the concept of principles of international law. Although the distinction between principles of international law and the other rules in this area had appeared in the doctrine earlier[32] and had also been frequently invoked in international agreements,[33] it was only in the U.N. system and the international documents issued in connection with the termination of World War II that the concept of international principles assumed a more precise definition.

In the U.N. Charter, the principles of international law were made separate from the general body of provisions contained in this document. Article 2 specifies the principles which should be followed by the United Nations and its members. The distinction between the principles and the other stipulations of the Charter was reflected not only in their separate formulation but also in the special legal importance attached to these principles. In the words of article 2(6): "the Organization shall ensure that states which are not members of the United Nations act in accordance with these principles so far as may be necessary for the maintenance of international peace and security." Thus, unlike the other provisions, the applicability of the Charter is extended beyond the community of members to embrace all existing states. From this it follows that violation by a nonmember state of the principles of the Charter regarding the maintenance of international peace and security may lead to action being taken by the United Nations to persuade or even compel a nonmember state to observe these principles. The approach adopted by

---

[30] *See* Trial of the Major War Criminals Before the International Military Tribunal 220 (1947).

[31] A few years later the subcommission of the International Law Commission cogently made this same point: "A violation of international law may be an international crime even if no legal document has defined it as such."

[32] *Cf.* A Alvarez, Exposé des Motifs et Declaration des Grands Principes du Droit International Moderne (1938).

[33] *See, e.g.,* the preamble to the IV Convention concluded in The Hague in 1907, the preamble to the London Declaration of 1909, the Treaty of Peace with Turkey concluded in Lausanne in 1923, certain treaties of arbitration, and certain governmental declarations.

the Charter was without a doubt influenced by the idea that peace is indivisible. In accord with this concept it is thought necessary (1) that certain principles be observed by all states and (2) that the Organization whose chief task is the maintenance of international peace and security have legal powers to enforce sanctions even against nonmember states.

1.5. Postwar Development by the United Nations

From the very outset, the United Nations paid much attention to the problems connected with war crimes. In one of its first resolutions, Resolution 3/I of February 13, 1946, the General Assembly took note of the definition of war crimes and crimes against peace and humanity contained in the Charter of the Nuremberg International Tribunal, urged the member states to cause the arrest of war criminals and extradite them to the countries where their abominable deeds were committed and called on the governments of other states to take all necessary measures for the apprehension of such criminals with a view to their immediate removal to the site of the crimes. The recommendation concerning the surrender and trial of war criminals was reiterated in Resolution 170/II of October 31, 1947.

But it was primarily by its endorsement and formulation of the so-called "Nuremberg principles" that the General Assembly most contributed to the development of international law in our field. In Resolution 95/I of December 11, 1946, following a proposal submitted by the U.S. delegation, the General Assembly affirmed "the principles of international law recognized by the Charter of the Nuremberg Tribunal and the judgment of the Tribunal" and initiated the explicit drafting of these principles. The International Law Commission which was charged with this task adopted a report at its second session in 1950, containing a formulation of principles of international law recognized in the Charter of the Nuremberg Tribunal and in the judgment of the Tribunal. Principal I asserts: "Any person who committed an act which constitutes a crime under international law is responsible therefor and liable for punishment." In a comment, it was said that this principle is based on the general rule that international law may impose duties on individuals directly, without any interposition of internal law. And the following passage of the judgment of the Nuremberg Tribunal was referred to: "That international law imposes duties and liabilities upon individuals as well as upon states has long been recognized. . . . Crimes against international law are committed by men, not by abstract entities, and only by punishing individuals who commit such crimes can the provision of international law be enforced."[34]

[34] TRIAL OF THE MAJOR WAR CRIMINALS, *supra* note 30, at 223.

According to Principle II, the fact that internal law does not impose a penalty for an act which constitutes a crime under international law does not relieve the person who committed the act from responsibility under international law. Similarly the fact that a person who committed an act which constitutes a crime under international law acted as head of state or as a responsible government official does not relieve him from responsibility under international law, nor does the fact that a person acted on the orders of his government or of a superior excuse his actions provided a moral choice was in fact open to him (Principles III and IV).

Principle VI contains a definition of the three categories of crimes: (1) crimes against peace, (2) war crimes, and (3) crimes against humanity, as formulated in the Charter annexed to the London Agreement of 1945. The comment explained that in the opinion of the Nuremberg Tribunal, the definition of crimes against peace was "the expression of international law existing at the time of its creation"; and the Tribunal refuted the case made by the defense that aggressive war was not an international crime. As far as crimes against humanity were concerned, it was emphasized in the comment that the Tribunal did not exclude the possibility that such crimes might also be committed before a war and for this reason the Commission had omitted the phrase "before or during war" which was contained in the Charter.[35]

The postwar period has seen still further progress in the development of antiwar law, the law of warfare and humanitarian law.

In the U.N. Charter, the member states made a solemn pledge to concert efforts "to maintain international peace and security, and to ensure, by acceptance of principles and the institution of methods, that armed force shall not be used, save in the common interest" and conferred on the Security Council, which was to act on the basis of unanimity of the Great Powers, the primary responsibility for the maintenance of international peace and security. In later years the General Assembly adopted resolutions recommending the drafting of a definition of aggression[36] and formulation of a principle that states should refrain in their international relations from the threat or use of force against the territorial integrity and political independence of any state, or act in any other manner inconsistent with the purposes of the United Nations.[37]

More successful were efforts to give greater precision to some categories

[35] *See* Y.B. Int'l L. Comm'n 374 (1950).

[36] See U.N. GAOR, 1st Comm., 385th meeting; 2 Y.B. Int'l L. Comm'n (1951), Doc. A/1858, and Res. 378/V, 599/VI, 688/VII, & 1181/XII.

[37] *See the Report of the Special Committee on principles on international law concerning friendly relations and cooperation among States* [Doc.A/7326]. In the committee there was agreemen on the statement that "such a threat or use of force constitutes a violation of international law and the Charter of the United Nations" and that "a war of aggression constitutes a crime against peace, for which there is responsibility under international law."

of crimes against humanity and war crimes. In 1948, the General Assembly approved the text of a Convention on the prevention and punishment of the crime of genocide which was ratified by a considerable number of states. The Convention contains a definition of genocide (art. II) and states that persons charged with such a crime "shall be tried by a competent tribunal of the state in the territory of which the act was committed, or by such international penal tribunal as may have jurisdiction with respect to those contracting parties which shall have accepted its jurisdiction" (art. VI). According to the provisions of the Convention, genocide is not to be considered a political crime as far as extradition is concerned, and the contracting parties are pledged to grant extradition in accordance with their laws and the treaties in force (art. VII).[38]

Outside the United Nations, a considerable progress in developing the laws of warfare and in adapting them to modern conditions was achieved by the four Geneva Conventions of 1949 concerning the victims of war.[39]

While the first three were revised versions of the earlier conventions on amelioration of the wounded and sick in armed forces in the field and at sea, and on the treatment of prisoners of war, the Fourth Convention concerning protection of civilians in time of war made a signal contribution to safeguarding the elementary rights of the civilian population which previously had been abandoned to the mercy of belligerents. Each of the four Conventions stipulated that states have a duty to insure in their legislation effective penal sanctions against persons committing or ordering any grave breaches of the convention's provisions. Among these grave breaches were included the following acts: (1) willful killing, (2) torture or inhuman treatment including biological experiments, (3) willfully causing great suffering or serious injury to body or health, and (4) extensive destruction and appropriation of property not justified by military necessity and carried out unlawfully and wantonly.

As far as national legislation is concerned, in many countries since World War II, laws or regulations related to war crimes have been enacted. Most of these countries are parties to one or more of the relevant international conventions. The definitions given in their legislation mostly invoke international law either in the general terms of "laws and customs of war," "law of nations" or in the form of particular conventions. In other countries, national legislation does not refer to "war crimes" as such, but finds grounds in the provisions of general criminal law—*e.g.*, those relating to murder, arbitrary deprivation of liberty, the infliction of bodily harm—for the punishment of persons responsible for war crimes. These countries are also parties to one or more of the relevant

---

[38] *See* Bassiouni, Part Four, Chapter X, Section 2, on Genocide.
[39] *See* Gulbrandsen and Lee, Part Two, Chapter VIII, on the Geneva Conventions of 1949.

international conventions. In many other nation-states, mostly in Asia and Africa, such an offense as "war crimes" is unknown to their legislation. Moreover, those countries are not parties to any international convention on the subject. Their governments have never in practice encountered the problem of punishing persons responsible for such crimes, but this lack of statutory definition does not necessarily mean that war crimes, as defined in international law, would not be punishable under general criminal law.[40]

A very important contribution to the international character of war crimes has been made by the conclusion of the Convention on Non-Applicability of Statutory Limitations to War Crimes and Crimes against Humanity of 1968 (Appendix III).

The official wartime declarations announcing the postwar punishment of war criminals, the texts of the charters of the Nuremberg and Tokyo Tribunals, and Control Council Order No. 10 for Germany made no mention of any period of limitation beyond which such criminals could no longer be tried; nor did the judgments of the international military tribunals and national courts acting on the basis of C.C.O. 10. There is no such reference either in the subsequent international conventions (Genocide Convention, the Geneva Conventions of 1949). The fact is that unless otherwise stated these offenses are to be considered as not subject to limitation,[41] particularly since statutory time limitation in criminal law is far from being a principle universally recognized. Thus it was thought superfluous to include specific provisions on this subject in postwar international relations. "We participants at the Nuremberg trials," said General Rudenko, the Soviet Chief Prosecutor at the Nuremberg Trial, "would never have believed that it could ever occur to someone to absolve the Hitlerite criminals of legal responsibility."[42] This question became an issue when West Germany's statute of limitations applicable to murder could have benefitted war criminals not yet apprehended. Public opinion in many countries came out strongly in favor of nonapplicability

[40] More detailed information on the national legislation in this respect is to be found in the Study on Insuring the Arrest and Punishment of Persons Responsible for War Crimes and Crimes Against Humanity and the Exchange of Documentation Relating to It [U.N. Doc. E/CN.4/983] as well as in the documents containing the observations of particular governments, referred to in the Study.

[41] International law does not contain any provisions whereby the obligations of one state toward another arising out of the liability of the former for its acts or omissions lapse after a passage of time. In some cases, international arbitration courts have explicitly stated that no period of statutory limitations can be invoked under international law. The only conclusion that might be drawn from the judgment of these courts is that the lapse of a longer period of time might indicate some kind of presumption of the abandonment of certain claims. However, without any express treaty provisions to this effect, it cannot be argued that there is any period of limitation on the prosecution of war crimes.

[42] *See* III (8) SOVIET DOCUMENTS 13 (1965).

of statutes of limitations to war criminals,[43] and in countries recognizing statutory limitations in criminal law, special legislation was passed specifically excluding war crimes from their provisions.

In 1965, the U.N. Commission for Human Rights agreed, on the recommendation of the Polish Government, to put this question on its agenda. Accordingly, a draft of a Convention was prepared. In Resolution 2391/XXIII of December 9, 1968, the General Assembly adopted and invited signature of a Convention on Non-Applicability of Statutory Limitations to War Crimes and Crimes against Humanity. In this Convention, states agree that no statutory limitation will apply—irrespective of the date of commission of those crimes—to the following categories of crimes:

1. War crimes as they are defined in the Charter of the International Military Tribunal, Nuremberg, and confirmed by relevant resolutions of the General Assembly, particularly the "grave breaches" enumerated in the Geneva Conventions of August 12, 1949, for the protection of war victims.
2. Crimes against humanity whether committed in time of war or in time of peace and inhuman acts resulting from the policy of apartheid and the crime of genocide, even if such acts do not constitute a violation of the domestic law of the country in which they were committed.

The provisions of the Convention will apply to representatives of the state authority and private individuals who, as principals or accomplices, participate in or who directly incite others to the commission of any of these crimes, or who conspire to commit them, irrespective of the degree of completion, and to representatives of the state authority who tolerate their commission (art. II). The states parties to the Convention undertake to adopt the necessary domestic measures, legislative or otherwise, to insure that statutory or other limitations will not apply to the crimes mentioned above and make possible the extradition in accordance with international law of the criminals mentioned in article II (arts. III & IV).

It should be added that in the Covenant on Civil and Political Rights of 1969 it was stipulated that the principle, according to which "no one will be held guilty of any criminal offense on account of any act or omission which did not constitute a criminal offense, under national or international law, at the time when it was committed" would not preju-

---

[43] See J. Graven, *Les crimes contre l'humanité peuvent-ils bénéficier de la prescription*, 2 Revue penale suisse (1965); Report of the Third Committee of the General Assembly of 8 Dec. 1965, Doc. A/6143, para. 61–66.

dice "the trial and punishment of any person for any act or omission which, at the time when it was committed, was criminal according to the general principles of law recognized by the community of nations" (art. 15).

1.6. Conclusions

From a historical viewpoint, we can see that until World War I the concept of war crimes, an idea inherent in the customary treaty restrictions on warfare, was only a general notion without any practical legal consequence. It was not until the peace treaties which were concluded after World War I, that the first efforts were made to bring about the punishment of war criminals. Those attempts ended, however, in complete failure as far as both Wilhelm II of Hohenzollern and ordinary war criminals were concerned. This failure undoubtedly was one important factor that was taken into consideration by major war criminals of World War II when they made their criminal decisions. Hitler in his speech delivered to military commanders on August 22, 1939, said brutally, "Who is concerned now with the extermination of Armenians?"[44]

Two factors contributed significantly to the growing importance attached to the problem of effective punishment of war criminals. On the one hand, the development of antiwar law and, to a lesser extent, on the law of warfare in the interwar period required more effective sanctions against persons who committed crimes against peace and war crimes. On the other hand, the crimes of the Germans and Japanese during World War II, which reached dimensions unparalleled in human history, so immensely shocked world public opinion that the punishment of war criminals came to be regarded among the most urgent problems to be solved after the war. The futility of the attempts to punish war criminals of World War I guided the formulation of the new law on war crimes. The idea of having those individuals prosecuted and punished by the tribunals of their own countries, proved ineffective by World War I experience, was abandoned. As a result, for the first time those responsible for waging a war of aggression or guilty of other crimes under international law were subjected to real penalties. This was a turning point in the history of international criminal law. According to the provisions of the Moscow Declaration, the "major criminals" were to be judged and punished by a joint decision of the Allied governments (as was ultimately done by the international military tribunals of Nuremberg and Toyko), while all other war criminals were to "be sent back to the countries in which their abominable deeds were done in order that they [could] be judged and punished according to the laws

---

[44] Nurnberg Trial Documents, Doc. L–3.

of th[o]se liberated countries." The concept of war crimes was defined more precisely in the Charter annexed to the London Agreement of 1946 which extended it to cover crimes against peace and humanity.

The arguments invoked in order to paralyze the effectiveness of the punishment of war criminals, based either on principles recognized in the internal criminal law of some countries or on traditionalist legal concepts, *e.g.*, the nonresponsibility of heads of states or those acting on the orders of a superior, the nonretroactivity of criminal laws, the nonextradition of nationals and criminals acting "for political purposes," were dismissed by the new rules of responsibility of war criminals of World War II. Because of these decisions a much greater degree of effectiveness in punishing war criminals could be achieved than that accomplished after World War I. In particular, the recognition of the right of the country where war crimes were committed to punish their tormentors helped to make the punishment of war criminals more effective than in any other period of history, though the reluctance of certain countries to hand over war criminals enabled a considerable number of criminals to escape with impunity.

It is true that some have regarded these innovations as nothing more than a unilateral imposition of the will of the victorious powers on the vanquished, and thus violating the principle of penal nonretroactivity. However, it was only by overruling such objections that the punishment of war criminals could be meaningfully undertaken to the satisfaction of the victims and the demand of world public opinion to see justice done. On the other hand, it should be emphasized that the victors, anxious to assure the war criminals a fair trial, rejected proposals advocating either a "purely police solution" or a "political and not legal solution" of the problem of the war criminals of World War II.

In the postwar period, the so-called "Nuremberg principles" have been expressly recognized as a part of international law. Moreover, the attempt to dilute these principles through statutory limitations has been frustrated by the Convention of 1968 on nonapplicability of statutory limitations to war crimes and to crimes against humanity. Further progress has been achieved in defining war crimes, *e.g.*, Convention on Genocide, the Geneva Conventions of 1949. As regards the definition of aggression, a concept closely linked with the system of international security, that problem has been under consideration at the United Nations, but no positive results have yet been achieved.

In discussions of the development of law on prosecution and punishment of war crimes, it is sometimes claimed that the expansion of this law is superfluous or even unrealistic in light of present political conditions. One of the arguments used in support of this claim is that today it is necessary to concentrate all legal efforts on the development of anti-war law in order to prevent wars. The whole question of the laws of war thus becomes of secondary importance. Modern warfare and progress in military technologies, it is hypothesized, make it doubtful whether it is feasible to observe the rules of either traditional or modern war law which cannot keep pace with rapid advances in the means of warfare. Furthermore, the likelihood that weapons of mass destruction will be used in a future war makes irrelevant the question of responsibility for disregard of the law in force in time of war. This nihilistic contention, from a legal point of view, cannot be accepted on the following grounds. First, apart from all-out nuclear wars, there is a possibility, as the years since World War II have shown, of other wars of a more limited nature. Secondly, war crimes are a natural consideration in the formulation of not only war law, but also of antiwar law which prohibits recourse to war: the creation of an international system insuring as effective as possible prosecution and punishment of war criminals is a key factor in preventing both the crime of waging war and violation of the laws of warfare.

Another argument which is sometimes advanced is that all proposals connected with the law of warfare should be shelved until a basic reform of the existing international law has been effected. This argument is not tenable since it calls for unnecessary delays. There can be no doubt that results can be achieved within the framework of the law presently in force. A case in point is the Geneva Conventions of 1949.

Rather than not to act, it would be more logical to act more effectively under today's international law. In particular it would be useful to specify more precisely in future international agreements the obligations of states with regard to extradition of war criminals,[45] and to stipulate which of the violations of the laws of warfare are "grave breaches" involving the international responsibility of the persons guilty of their commission.

The question of the effective prosecution and punishment of war criminals is often linked with, and made contingent on, the creation of permanent international criminal courts and sometimes upon structural changes in international relations. It seems indisputable that an essential aspect of all criminal responsibility is the existence of criminal courts. The presence of permanent courts has certain advantages. The historical experience at the close of World War II indicates, of course, that the existence of permanent international criminal courts is not the only medium of effective international penal justice, and that there is another alternative: the appointment of ad hoc courts and the extradition of criminals

[45] *See Raport présenté par R. Bierzanek au X*e *Congrès de l'Association International de Droit Pénal*, 39 REVUE INTERNATIONALE DE DROIT PÉNAL 699 (1968).

to the countries in which their crimes were committed. Historical experience also goes to show that even in circumstances of opposed ideologies and different political and social systems it is possible to give effect to international penal justice which is of crucial importance in maintaining peace and implementing the most fundamental principles of humanitarian law.

APPENDIX I.

TREATY OF PEACE BETWEEN THE ALLIED AND ASSOCIATED POWERS AND GERMANY

Versailles, June 28, 1919*

Part II. Penalties

Article 227

The Allied and Associated Powers publicly arraign William II of Hohenzollern, formerly German Emperor, for a supreme offence against international morality and the sanctity of treaties.

A special tribunal will be constituted to try the accused, thereby assuring him the guarantees essential to the right of defence. It will be composed of five judges, one appointed by each of the following Powers: namely the United States of America, Great Britain, France, Italy, and Japan.

In its decision the tribunal will be guided by the highest motives of international policy, with a view to vindicating the solemn obligations of international undertakings and the validity of international morality. It will be its duty to fix the punishment which it considers should be imposed.

The Allied and Associated Powers will address a request to the Government of the Netherlands for the surrender to them of the ex-Emperor in order that he may be put on trial.[1]

Article 228

The German Government recognizes the right of the Allied and Associated Powers to bring before military tribunals persons accused of having committed acts in violation of the laws and customs of war. Such persons shall, if found guilty, be sentenced to punishments laid down by law. This provision will apply notwithstanding any proceedings or prosecution before a tribunal in Germany or in the territory of her allies.

* Treaties, Conventions, International Acts, Protocols, and Agreements between the United States of America and Other Powers, 1910–1923 (Redmond ed. 1923) Vol. 3, at 3329. In force Jan. 10, 1920.

[1] In fact, the Dutch Government refused to surrender the Kaiser on the ground that it had no duty "to associate itself with this high act of policy of the powers," and the trial was not proceeded with. *See* Garner 2 International Law and the World War 488–495 (1920).

The German Government shall hand over to the Allied and Associated Powers, or to such one of them as shall so request, all persons accused of having committed an act in violation of the laws and customs of war, who are specified either by name or by the rank, office, or employment which they held under the German authorities.

Article 229

Persons guilty of criminal acts against the nationals of one of the Allied and Associated Powers will be brought before the military tribunals of that Power.

Persons guilty of criminal acts against the nationals of more than one of the Allied and Associated Powers will be brought before military tribunals composed of members of the military tribunals of the Powers concerned.

In every case the accused will be entitled to name his own counsel.

Article 230

The German Government undertakes to furnish all documents and information of every kind, the production of which may be considered necessary to ensure the full knowledge of the incriminating acts, the discovery of offenders, and the just appreciation of responsibility.[2]

APPENDIX II.

REPORT OF THE INTERNATIONAL LAW COMMISSION
U.N. G.A.O.R. V, SUPP. 12 (A/ 1316) 11–14 (1950).

Part III. Formulation of the Nuremberg Principles

Principles of International Law Recognized in the Charter of the Nuremberg Tribunal and in the Judgment of the Tribunal

Principle I. Any person who commits an act which constitutes a crime under international law is responsible therefor and liable to punishment.

Principle II. The fact that internal law does not impose a penalty for an act which constitutes a crime under international law does not relieve the person who committed the act from responsibility under international law.

Principle III. The fact that a person who committed an act which constitutes a crime under international law acted as Head of State or responsible government official does not relieve him from responsibility under international law.

[2] The Allies submitted a demand to Germany for the trial of 901 persons under arts. 228–230 of the Versailles Treaty. Germany refused to accept the list; as a compromise measure, the Allies accepted an offer by Germany to try a selected number of individuals before the Criminal Senate of the Imperial Court of Justice of Germany. Of 45 names selected, only 13 were actually tried, and of these 6 were acquitted. The trials dealt almost exclusively with the treatment of the shipwrecked survivors of submarine activity and with the treatment of prisoners of war. The heaviest sentence imposed was four years' imprisonment. See MULLINS, *The Leipzig Trials* (1921); *The Dover Castle Case* (No. 231); *The Llandovery Castle Case*, No. 235 in (1923–1924) *Annual Digest*.

Principle IV. The fact that a person acted pursuant to order of his government or of a superior does not relieve him from responsibility under international law, provided a moral choice was in fact possible to him.

Principle V. Any person charged with a crime under international law has the right to a fair trial on the facts and law.

Principle VI. The crimes hereinafter set out are punishable as crimes under international law:

a. Crimes Against Peace:

  (i) Planning, preparation, initiation or waging of a war of aggression or a war in violation of international treaties, agreements or assurances;

  (ii) Participation in a common plan or conspiracy for the accomplishment of any of the acts mentioned under (i).

b. War Crimes:

  Violations of the laws or customs of war which include, but are not limited to, murder, ill-treatment or deportation to slave-labour or for any other purpose of civilian population of or in occupied territory, murder or ill-treatment of prisoners of war, of persons on the seas, killing of hostages, plunder of public or private property, wanton destruction of cities, towns, or villages, or devastation not justified by military necessity.

c. Crimes Against Humanity:

  Murder, extermination, enslavement, deportation and other inhuman acts done against any civilian population, or persecutions on political, racial or religious grounds, when such acts are done or such persecutions are carried on in execution of or in connexion with any crime against peace or any war crime.

Principle VII. Complicity in the commission of a crime against peace, a war crime, or a crime against humanity as set forth in Principle VI is a crime under international law.

APPENDIX III

CONVENTION ON THE NONAPPLICABILITY OF STATUTORY LIMITATIONS TO WAR CRIMES AND CRIMES AGAINST HUMANITY
(G.A. Res./2391 (XXIII) Dec. 9, 1968)

Article 1

No statutory limitation shall apply to the following crimes, irrespective of the date of their commission:

a. War crimes as they are defined in the Charter of the International Military Tribunal, Nuremberg, of August 8, 1945 and confirmed by Resolutions 3 (I) of February 13, 1946, and 95 (I) of December 11, 1946, of the General Assembly of the United Nations, particularly the "grave breaches" enumerated in the Geneva Conventions of August 12, 1949, for the protection of war victims;

b. Crimes against humanity whether committed in time of war or in time of peace as they are defined in the Charter of the International Military Tribunal, Nuremberg, of August 8, 1945, and confirmed by resolutions 3 (I) of February 13, 1946, and 95 (I) of December 11, 1946, of the General Assembly of the United Nations, eviction by armed attack or occupation and inhuman acts resulting from the policy of *apartheid,* and the crime of genocide as defined in the 1948 Convention on the Prevention and Punishment of the Crime of Genocide, even if such acts do not constitute a violation of the domestic law of the country in which they were committed.

Article II

If any of the crimes mentioned in article I are committed, the provisions of this Convention shall apply to representatives of the state authority and private individuals who, as principals or accomplices, participate in or who directly incite others to the commission of any of those crimes, or who conspire to commit them, irrespective of the degree of completion, and to representatives of the state authority who tolerate their commission.

Article III

The states parties to the present Convention undertake to adopt all necessary domestic measures, legislative or otherwise, with a view to making possible the extradition, in accordance with international law, of the persons referred to in article II of this Convention.

Article IV

The states parties to the present Convention undertakes to adopt, in accordance with their respective constitutional processes, any legislative or other measures necessary to insure that statutory or other limitations shall not apply to the prosecution and punishment of the crimes referred to in articles I and II of this Convention and that, where they exist, such limitations shall be abolished.

Article V

This Convention shall, until December 31, 1969, be open for signature by any state member of the United Nations or member of any of its specialized agencies or of the International Atomic Energy Agency, by any state party to the Statute of the International Court of Justice, and by any other state which has been invited by the General Assembly of the United Nations to become a party to this Convention.

Article VI

This Convention is subject to ratification. Instruments of ratification shall be deposited with the Secretary-General of the United Nations.

Article VII

This Convention shall be open to accession by any state referred to in article V. Instruments of accession shall be deposited with the Secretary-General of the United Nations.

Article VIII

1. This Convention shall enter into force on the nineteenth day after the date

of the deposit with the Secretary-General of the United Nations of the tenth instrument of ratification or accession.

2. For each state ratifying this Convention or acceding to it after the deposit of the tenth instrument of ratification or accession, the Convention shall enter into force on the ninetieth day after the date of the deposit of its own instrument of ratification or accession.

Article IX

1. After the expiry of a period of ten years from the date on which this Convention enters into force, a request for the revision of the Convention may be made at any time by any contracting party by means of a notification in writing addressed to the Secretary-General of the United Nations.

2. The General Assembly of the United Nations shall decide upon the steps, if any, to be taken in respect of such a request.

Section 2.　THE NUREMBERG AND THE TOKYO TRIALS IN RETROSPECT

BERT V.A. RÖLING[*]

To see things and their real significance one needs the correct distance. Too close, and one is struck only by the details, one does not see the forest for the trees. Too far away, and one may have a good view on the whole, but one misses the particulars and their impact on the direct surroundings; that impact has often more to do with details than with the general structure.

Do we already have enough distance to evaluate the Tokyo Trial, in which after World War II Japanese statesmen and military leaders were sentenced? To give a balanced judgment directly after the war is almost impossible, beyond human capacity. War propaganda—one of the unavoidable tools of warfare—has brought about hatred and anger. This propaganda may have been somewhat careless of the truth—but people are too angry and too indignant to care. In war it is only a question of black and white, and nowadays every one is involved. War does not stop with the ending of hostilities. It rages on in the minds of men. A young Dutch author wrote in a remarkable war novel: "War ceases only when the last one who participated in it has died.[1]

Still we need an evaluation of the Nuremberg and Tokyo trials now that almost twenty-five years have passed. We need an evaluation, because they stand in history as a fact. On the facts of the past, starting from history, we have to build the future.

---

[*] Ed.: Judge, International Military Tribunal for the Far East (Tokyo trials).
[1] Harry Mulish, HET STENEN BRUIDSBED 95 (1959).

At the time, participating in the Tokyo trial as one of the judges, the words of Macbeth alarmed me:

"that he but teach Bloody instructions, which being taught, return
To plague the inventors" (*Macbeth,* Act I, Sc. 7)

Are the "bloody instructions," as formulated in the charters and executed in the judgments to plague us? Or to guide us? Will they be an asset, or a liability in the shaping of the future? Reappraisal of what happened in the postwar trials may contribute to the answers on that question.

The essence of the postwar judgments was not that war criminals were tried and sentenced. War criminals were tried also during and after World War I. If nothing but conventional war crimes had been brought before tribunals, the mass scale of it would have been remembered, and perhaps the fact that only the vanquished was brought to account for his criminal behavior. That one-sidedness indeed annoys the lawyer and is repulsive to the defeated. Every army commits war crimes. On the allied side one needs only to remember the mass bombings (Dresden, Tokyo). As a matter of fact, from World War II above all two things are remembered: the German gas chambers and the American atomic bombings.

Still one might say that one-sided prosecution of war criminals is better than no prosecution at all. Providud, of course, that the victor does not claim as a right, what is charged against the vanquished as a crime. *Quod licet Jovi non licet bovi* has factual, not normative, validity. The principle of *tu quoque* was introduced by the defendants, in Nuremberg as well as in Tokyo. It was partly recognized in this way, that from the list of war crimes, drawn up by the Commission on Responsibilities of the Paris Peace Conference in 1919, some were deleted by the U. N. War Crimes Commission "as these refer to acts which, in the present war, the forces of the United Nations have themselves been obliged to commit."[2]

Moreover, some crimes, *e.g.* mass bombing of civilian population, were not inserted in the indictment. Lastly, it occurred that the Tribunal, after having heard the Allied practice, refused to base its judgment on similar acts, charged as crimes.[3]

More important was the introduction of the concept of the crime against humanity, formulated in view of German behavior toward German Jews. Persecution of a group of people, on the basis of race or religion, in occupied territory would already have been covered by the concept of the

---

[2] Report of the Subcommittee, consisting of Sir Cecil Hurst, de Baer, Eoer, de Moor and Glaser.

[3] The Nuremberg Tribunal, having heard of the Allied submarine warfare, declared: "[T]he sentence of Doenitz is not assessed on the ground of his breaches of the international law of submarine warfare" (JUDGMENT NUREMBERG 109 (Brit ed. 1946).

conventional war crimes. Consequently, in most cases the indictment for crimes against humanity amounted only to a charge of qualified war crimes, committed on a large scale, on the ground of a specific policy. German atrocities against German Jews compelled the Allies to prosecute for a specific internal policy. This amounted to a new concept of the place of the national state, of the individual within his national state, and of the role of humanity as a guardian of a minimum standard of state decency. The Genocide Convention, 1948, has consolidated this new concept, and has recognized its validity, in peace and in war. For the Pacific theatre this new concept of the crime against humanity has had less importance than it had in Europe. In the Tokyo indictment the defendants were accused of a mass-annihilation policy toward China (opium policy) and the white population of Asia. It seems to me that this charge was not proved, notwithstanding the fact that out of anger and hate many crimes against the Chinese and Europeans were committed. From shortsightedness, incompetence, and greed, many grave faults were committed in the opium policy. The effort to dethrone European authority easily led to the impression that Japan aimed at the annihilation of the European population.

More important still was the new concept of the crime against peace. This concept of the crime of aggressive war slowly developed out of the European-American world. Until recently traditional international law had regarded the *jus ad bellum* as one of the prerogatives of the sovereign state.[4] The development of the techniques of war gradually caused war to be considered an unbearable institution. Hence the quest for peace, the more desirable since in centuries of fighting gradually states had settled, borders were fixed, aspirations had become conservative. The same applied for the United States of America. In the imperialist period of the Theodore Roosevelt era, the United States succeeded in rounding off its territory and in securing its strategic position. Joseph C. Grew, the former U.S. Ambassador to Japan, could write: "We have now attained the desired maximum of our national entity as well as adequate national strength. International morality, including, respect for legal commitments and permanent abandonment of force as an instrument of national policy, has become for us at once a watchword and a religion."[5] The latecomers— Germany, Russia, and Japan—consequently were to be kept in check. The strivings, as formulated in the 1928 Pact of Paris, were not at all adequate

---

[4] *Cf.* Oppenheim INTERNATIONAL LAW, vol. I1 DISPUTES, WAR AND NEUTRALITY 145 (6th ed. Lauterpacht 1944); C. FENWICK, INTERNATIONAL LAW 441 (2d ed. 1943): "This right was, indeed, so well established that it was used as a sort of final test of a 'sovereign' as distinguished from a semisovereign or dependant state."

[5] J. GREW, TEN YEARS IN JAPAN 300 (1944).

to the uncertain relations in the Asian world, in which the instability of nations and power concentrations, and the newly awaked self-confidence, hardly provided a theater for the application of European peace principles. As it was clearly formulated by Stimson: "The peace treaties of modern Europe made out by the Western nations of the world no more fit the three great races of Russia, Japan, and China, who are meeting in Manchuria, than . . . a stovepipe hat would fit an African savage."[6]

The European quest for peace, combined with the deeply felt indignation about Nazi-German criminality led to the Nuremberg Trial, one great indictment of the Nazi regime, not only related to the waging of the war but also comprising the Nazi-methods of warfare. The combination of the two charges made it possible to bring about the prosecution of individuals for the crime against peace. The conscience of the world was at rest because both charges were made. It is an open question if public opinion would have easily approved of a trial only related to the crime of aggression. A confusion did exist in the public mind between the violations of the *jus ad bellum* and the *jus in bello*. Max Radin justly remarked:

> It is impossible to determine with certainty whether public opinion at the present time supports the doctrine of individual guilt for crimes against peace. The impossibility is due to the fact that the three types of crimes are inevitably fused in the public mind by being combined in a single trial. To regret any one of the three creates the impression of defending men whose vicious actions seem to place their guilt beyond the reach of any sort of clemency.[7]

The unheard-of Nazi atrocities have been one of the reasons that individuals were indicted for the crime of aggression. Looking back at the postwar trials it becomes more and more clear that the German issue played the central role. The German situation was decisive, and in its wake followed the Japanese solution. The Nuremberg trial is the central problem, if one tries to explain what happened after World War II. It is for that very reason that something more should be said about it.

Public opinion approved of the triple charges made against the German defendants. But why was it that the "crime of aggressive war" was created and the indictment of the German major war criminals concentrated on aggressive war? We know that England did not want a criminal prosecution for the crime against peace. In an aide memoire of April 23, 1945, the British Government expressed that it was not at all clear that unprovoked attacks could properly be described as crimes under international law.[8] The French Government expressly declared that it did not consider

[6] H. STIMSON: I ON ACTIVE SERVICE IN PEACE AND WAR 233 (1947).

[7] Max Radin, *Justice at Nuremberg*, 24 FOREIGN AFFAIRS 381 (1946).

[8] *Cf. Report of Robert H. Jackson, U.S. Representative to the International Conference on Military Trials*, London 1945, Dep't of State Publication 3080, at 19 (1949). The

aggressive war to be a crime,[9] and that it wished to prosecute the Nazi leaders for the cruelties committed during their illegal war. Russia, though Marshall Stalin himself had introduced the concept of the crime of aggressive war in his speech of November 6, 1943,[10] followed the French line. The Russian representatives feared endless discussions on the causes of the war,[11] and probably disliked the chance that Soviet-Russian policy as to Finland and Poland and the role of its neutrality pacts with Germany and Japan would be dealt with in court. That the Nuremberg trial took place and that the Charter of Nuremberg contained the "crimes against peace" are due to the attitude of the United States, so ably defended and brought to victory by Justice Jackson. Jackson was disarmingly honest on this point: the United States entering the war, had violated the existing laws of neutrality on the ground that the German aggression was criminal. A public trial should prove that the American attitude had been correct and justified. To quote his own words:

> Our attitude as a nation, in a number of transactions, was based on the proposition that this was an illegal war from the moment that it was started, and that therefore, without losing our rights as neutrals and nonbelligerents, it was our right to extend aid to the nations under illegal attack, and the lend-lease program, the exchange of bases for destroyers, and much of American policy was based squarely on the proposition that a war of aggression is outlawed. . . . Therefore, our view is that this is not merely a case of showing that these Nazi-Hitlerite people failed to be gentlemen in war; it is a matter of their having designed an illegal attack on the international peace, which to our mind is a criminal offense by common-law tests, at least, and the other atrocities were all preparatory to it or done in execution of it. . . .[12] Now we come to the end and have crushed her aggression, and we do want to show that this war was an illegal plan of aggression. We want this group of nations to stand up and say, as we have said to our people, as President Roosevelt said to the people,

---

British intended to kill the major war criminals without trial. The same opinion was shared by influential statesmen in the U.S., *e.g.,* Cordell Hull—The Memoirs of Cordell Hull, vol. II, at 1289 (1948). Against these opinions Justice Jackson reacted in his famous "Report to the President," June 7, 1945, in justification of the Nuremberg Trial: "To free them without a trial would mock the dead and make cynics of the living. But undiscriminating executions or punishments without definite findings of guilt, fairly arrived at, would violate pledges repeatedly given, and would not set easily on the American conscience or be remembered by our children with pride" [hereinafter cited as Report of Robert H. Jackson].

[9] Report of Robert H. Jackson, at 293, 334, 385.

[10] "In conjunction with our Allies we shall have to take measures to ensure that all the fascist criminals who are responsible for this war and the suffering the peoples have endured shall meet with stern punishment and retribution for all the crimes they have committed, no matter in what country they may hide," J. Stalin, On The Great Patriotic War of the Soviet Union (1946).

[11] Report of Robert H. Jackson, at 298.

[12] Report of Robert H. Jackson, at 299.

as members of the Cabinet said to the people, that launching a war of aggression is a crime and that no political or economic situation can justify it. If that is wrong, then we have been wrong in a good many things in the policy of the United States which helped the countries under attack before we entered the war.

The United States wanted the Germans and anybody else to know that as far as the United States is concerned it regards any attack on the peace of the world as an international crime. It may become necessary to abandon the effort to try these people on that basis, but there are some things worse for me than failing to reach an agreement, and one of these is reaching an agreement which would stultify the position which the United States has taken throughout.[13]

The political reasons for having a trial in which Germans would be tried for the crime against peace are very clear. The U.S. Government had acted on the assumption that launching any attack on the peace was an international crime, and it wanted to prove by charter and judgment that launching a war of aggression constituted a criminal violation of the law of nations. It is beyond doubt that before World War II there had been no question of individual criminal responsibility for a violation of the Kellogg-Briand pact. Neither this treaty nor the resolutions of the League of Nations or the abortive treaties in which it was stated that aggressive war was an international crime had the effect of creating international criminal law.

It is at this moment a practically undisputed thesis that before World War II positive international law did not recognize the crime of aggressive war for which individuals could be punished.[14] No wonder that the U.N. War Crimes Commission did not consider aggressive war an international crime. A minority opinion to the contrary (Dr. Ecer) did not find support, until after the Charter of Nuremberg had been formulated. The UNWCC was unanimous in its opinion that aggressive war should be made a crime in the future. This opinion was communicated to the San Francisco Conference. Only in its Resolution of January 30, 1946, did it recognize the "crime against peace.[15]

The initiative to punish the individuals responsible for the aggressive war was taken by Marshall Stalin in his speech of November 6, 1943. Some authors had suggested similar ideas.[16] Benes proposed in 1941 "political

---

[13] Report of Robert H. Jackson, at 384.

[14] *Cf.* Q. Wright, A Study of War 893 (1944); Hans Wehberg: Die völkerrechtliche Verantwortlichkeit von Individuen wegen Friedensbruchs im Zeitalter des Volkenbundes, Festschrift für Rudolf Laun, 379–394 (1952); C.A. Pompe, Aggressive War an International Crime 277 (1953).

[15] *Cf.* History of the UNWCC and the Development of the Laws of War 180–187 (1948).

[16] H. Mannheim, War and Crime 171 (1941) G. Schwarzenberger, International Law and Totalitarian Lawlessness, (1943) p. 65.

punishment of those who are responsible for this war,"[17] and Dr. Ecer defended the same opinion in the UNWCC. But these suggestions had not met with any response. After Stalin's statement, the London International Assembly changed its former opinion and inserted in its December, 1943, report the "crime of war," "in accordance with Stalin's views as expressed on November 6, 1943."[18] The suggestion of Stalin was elaborated in the book of Professor A.N. Trainin: "The criminal responsibility of the Hitlerites" (Moscow, 1944).[19] Against the doubts and misgivings of international lawyers and many statesmen—Stimson considered the concept "a little in advance of international thought"[20]—the new idea gradually won acceptance. Growing indignation about ever more gruesome atrocities prevented the sharp distinction between the law as it stood and the law as it should be in view of the factual development of warfare. Mass bombing and atomic warfare made war into something that should be prevented by all means, including the attribution of criminal responsibility for launchng it.

Even before the atomic bombs fell on Hiroshima and Nagasaki, the United Nations had come to the conclusion that war should be outlawed in the future. The Covenant of the League of Nations had not forbidden waging war. The Pact of Paris had maintained the freedom to start war in self-defense, and from its *travaux préparatoires* it appears that it left to every state the right to determine whether a case of self-defense existed. In the Charter of the United Nations the parties renounced the right to use armed force (art. 2 (4), except in case of an armed attack (art. 51).

The Tokyo Trial was a natural and unavoidable consequence of the Nuremberg Trial. As a matter of fact, in many quarters there was little inclination to apply "the advanced thought" to the Asian world. In the past, Europe had conquered Asia in forceful actions that hardly could be called defensive wars. Japan, a century ago compelled to enter into the family of nations, rising as a big power, was out to gain the position of world supremacy. It wished to expel Europe from Asia, to liberate the colonies, and to gain with the realization of the principle of "Asia for the Asians" undisputed might in the Far East. If it had been able to continue the policy, outlined by Hirota and pursued by Konoye, to stir up independence movements, to conclude pacts of mutual assistance with every Asian people which had declared itself independent—in the meantime making itself so strong militarily that no European nation would dare to start fighting—

[17] THE PUNISHMENT OF WAR CRIMINALS: RECOMMENDATIONS OF THE LONDON INTERNATIONAL ASSEMBLY 7.

[18] *See* Q. Wright, *War Criminals*, 39 A.J.I.L. 260 (1945).

[19] Trainin was one of the Soviet-Russian delegates to the London Conference which formulated the Charter of Nuremberg.

[20] *Supra* note 6, vol. II, at 587.

it would have developed into the most powerful nation in the world. But it needed a strong army, and when the strong army was built, the government was unable to keep it under control. Hence the Manchurian Incident and the Marco Polo Bridge Incident, which led inevitably to the Pacific War. The Japanese military, especially the army, has indeed an enormous responsibility. They set the conditions for the fateful development. But to approach Japan's "war of liberation" with the concept of the crime of aggression was for Europe not self-evident at all.

As a matter of fact only little inclination existed in high American circles to bring Japanese leaders before a Court charging them with the crime against peace. One wish did exist in American military and political circles, and that was to revenge the attack on Pearl Harbor, the surprise attack which had crippled the American Pacific Fleet, taking 4000 American lives. For the United States, Pearl Harbor was the symbol of Japanese guile, if not of Japanese criminality. For this attack without declaration of war the responsible leaders should be punished exemplarily. That was the opinion of General Douglas MacArthur, as he told me personally.

Political reasons for such a charge and such a punishment were many. In the United States, heated debate was going on about the question of who was responsible for the catastrophe of Pearl Harbor—one of the most disgraceful episodes in the history of the United States, as it was called— the local commanders or the central Government in Washington? The commanding officers had obeyed the order "to take appropriate measures against sabotage," and rumor circulated that in Washington the attack had been less unexpected than in Pearl Harbor itself. Military investigating committees were set up, but they did not advise to court-martial Admiral Kimmel and General Short. Neither did the Congressional investigation, begun November 15, 1945, clear the air. In view of mutual accusation, accusations with strong political implications, it is easily understood that prosecution of the Japanese for this "treacherous attack"[21] in violation of the laws of war was a relief for every one. The more it would appear that this undeclared attack amounted to a criminal outrage, the more American negligence or even guilt might diminish. How much Washington, in November and December, 1941, knew of the imminent danger is not known at this moment,[22] but it was more than the government later was inclined to admit. One cannot escape the impression that the urge to punish the Japanese for the unexpected attack on Pearl Harbor, was nourished by the

[21] As President Roosevelt had called it in his special message to Congress, Dec. 15, 1941; Secretary Hull's statement of Dec. 7, 1941 read: "Japan has made a treacherous and utterly unprovoked attack on the United States."

[22] With the Nov. 26 Memorandum, Hull was aware of having ended the negotiations with Japan. 'I have washed my hands of it and it is now in the hands of you and Knox-

wish to show Japan's action as perfidious and treacherous to such an extent that scarcely anybody had the duty to reckon with such unheard-of knavery.

The Tokyo indictment has extensively dealt with the attack on Pearl Harbor in an undeclared war. This part of the indictment was not very strong from the legal point of view. For, a Convention on the declaration of war did exist,[23] but it did not ask for a specific period between the declaration of war and the opening of hostilities. The Netherlands' proposal in 1907 to insert a time limit of twenty-four hours was rejected because the powers were not prepared to sign away the possibility of a surprise attack. According to the treaty provision, it was permitted to declare war at Washington at 12:00 and to start hostilities at Pearl Harbor at 12:01. It is a fact that a Japanese declaration of war was not delivered in clear terms and in due time. Formally, the attack on Pearl Harbor was in violation of the provisions of international law. But for the very reason that it had not been the intention of the Hague Convention to eliminate the possibility of a surprise attack, this violation cannot be compared in viciousness with other acts committed by the Axis Powers as well as by the Allied armies.

The American urge to organize a big trial against Japan was intrinsically based on Pearl Harbor. Since, however, the precedent of Nuremberg was set, it was hardly possible to avoid prosecuting Japanese leaders for the crime against peace. Restricting the Japanese indictment to the undeclared attack on Pearl Harbor would have amounted to the repudiation of the Nuremberg principles. Thus developed from different roots the Tokyo Trial, "the biggest trial in recorded history."

The Tokyo Charter, drawn up by General MacArthur, and except for some deviations of little significance, similar to the Charter of Nuremberg, demanded a fair trial for the accused. Has there been a fair trial? Is a fair trial conceivable, humanly possible, just after a cruel war? An American newspaper wrote: "We'll give them a fair trial and then hang them." During the years that the trial lasted, the American occupation policy was based on the assumption that Japan had started an aggressive war. In the directive prepared by the Department of State, containing the basic post-surrender policy for Japan, "the aggressions of past decades" were men-

---

the Army and the Navy," he remarked Nov. 27 to Secretary Stimson. At the Nov. 25 White House Conference, Roosevelt had brought up the event that the U.S. was likely to be attacked by the Japanese perhaps as soon as next Monday. "The question was how we should maneuver them into the position of firing the first shot without allowing too much danger to ourselves" (Diary of Stimson for Nov. 25, 1941). The actual attack brought a feeling of relief, to Stimson, according to his Diary for Dec. 7. The moral conflict had come to an end.

[23] Hague Convention, 1907, on the opening of hostilities.

tioned, and it states: "Every effort shall be made to bring home to the Japanese people that part played by those who have deceived and misled them into embarking on world conquest, and those who collaborated in so doing."[24]

The main issue before the International Military Tribunal for the Far East was the external policy of Japan, from 1929 up till 1945. What were the causes of the Pacific War? And who were the principal actors in this tragedy? An American historian wrote in 1946[25]:

> Should the thesis of responsibility for World War II be so formulated as to lay a share of blame on other nations or on the three aggressors, an examination of its validity would assume Herculean proportions. It would involve, first of all, an informed judgment on the most perplexing questions of historical interpretation, including the issues connected with "causation" and "free will" in the making of history, national and universal. It would also raise special questions of challenging intricacy, *e.g.*, at what point in time should history of the "blameworthy" nations be taken up in search for the characteristics to which war guilt is to be ascribed? Or again, for instance, how did Japan, after clinging to a hermitlike foreign policy for more than two hundred years, rather suddenly acquire, near the end of the nineteenth century, the propensities of a rabid imperialism and crusade against "white" supremacy in the Far East? Moreover, an inquiry so broad in scope would call for a mastery of languages, documentation, and philosophic thinking which few, if any, students of history or political science command.

It is very difficult indeed in such a case of world history to determine individual guilt of one nation, and the guilt of individuals within that nation. Do individuals shape history, or are they merely "les étiquettes de l'histoire" as Tolstoi so forcefully argued?[26] There is another question: are perhaps the events too big, too colossal, to bring individuals to account for them? In Roman times the rule existed: *de minimis non curat praetor.* Has the present time room for a similar kind of principle *de maximis non curat lex?*[27] The adoption of such a principle might be defended with the argument that it is an almost superhuman task to decide, just after the war, about individual war guilt, and that applies to guilt of individual nations as well as to guilt of individual persons.

Has there been a fair trial? Only the victor nations were represented in the Court, including Soviet Russia, which had concluded a neutrality pact

---

[24] Text in E.G. Lewe van Aduard, Japan, from Surrender to Peace 317 (1953).

[25] C. Beard, American Foreign Policy in the Making, 1932–1940, A Study in Responsibilities 42 (1946).

[26] Leo Tolstoi, II La guerre et la paix, ch. IV.: "Les pretendus grands hommes ne sont que les étiquettes de l'Histoire: ils donnent leurs noms aux évenements, sans même avoir, comme les étiquettes, le moindre lien avec le fait lui-même". Decisive is, according to Tolstoi, "la marche générale de l'histoire et de l'humanité".

[27] *Cf.* E. Cohn, *The Problems of War Crimes Today* 26 Trans. Gro. Soc'y, 141 (1940).

with Japan. That neutrality pact was one of the reasons that Japan at the time dared to start the war. There were no neutrals or Japanese on the bench. This was a grave error. Neutrals and even the vanquished should have been represented. It would have prevented in the verdict the generalities which the tribunal too easily adopted. Neutrals and Japanese judges might have formed a counterpoint against the prevailing, and at the time almost undisputed, official attitudes of the victors.

How is the situation? War propaganda is used by both sides. Exaggerations, distortions, and one-sidedness are needed to make the people and the army morally capable of using the means of destruction available in warfare. The masses need to be made fanatical, to make them willing to use and to tolerate the modern weapons of destruction. No one can escape the influence of such systematic war propaganda and everyone gets used to living in a world of black and white. Trials after the war are the unavoidable consequence of the scientifically cultivated moral indignation of the victor.[28] As such, postwar trials are the by-product of total war in which the masses of the contesting nations are involved. It is easily understood that the chance is tempting to use the trials for making good the war propaganda, for obscuring the misbehavior of the victor, for enlarging on the crimes of the vanquished. It is certainly incorrect to hold that the trials were organized only to distort history.[29] But it cannot be denied that distortions of history did take place in the postwar trials. Neither Nuremberg nor Tokyo needed very much such distortion. But where it suited the victors, it took place. That it happened only on such a small scale is easily explained from the circumstance that the victors begrudged one another some distortions.

One example of the one-sidedness of the Tribunal may suffice. The defendants claimed to have acted in China against the menace of communism. The majority of the Tribunal ruled "that no evidence of the existence or spread of communism or of any other ideology in China or elsewhere is relevant in the general phases."[30] Later development in China and elsewhere shows that this exclusion was incorrect.

From the majority judgment and the dissenting opinions it appears that considerable difference of opinion existed among the Tokyo judges. The dissenting opinion of the French judge Bernard partly discloses the consequences these conflicting opinions had with regard to the cooperation of the judges in chambers.

[28] This postwar attitude may explain that in the Tokyo judgment all the accused were found guilty. In my Dissenting Opinion, I showed that Shigemitsu, Togo, Hirota, Kido, and Hata should have been acquitted.

[29] This was the main thesis of M. Belgion's Epitaph on Nuremberg (1947). *See also* his very critical Victors' Justice.

[30] *See* Transcript of Proceeding 21081; *compare also* 22451.

As to the law of the case, one need only compare the majority judgment and the dissenting opinion of the Indian judge R.B. Pal[31] to note the wide difference on fundamental points. The majority judgment holds that "the law of the Charter is decisive and binding on the Tribunal." It observes that victorious powers, creating tribunals and formulating a law to be applied by these tribunals, may act only within the limits of international law. But, expressing its unqualified adherence to the relevant opinions of the Nuremberg Tribunal, it mentioned especially from the Nuremberg Judgment the phrase "The Charter is not an arbitrary exercise of power on the part of the victorious nations but is the expression of international law existing at the time of its creation," and "In the opinion of the Tribunal, the solemn renunciation of war as an instrument of national policy necessarily involves the proposition that such a war is illegal in international law; and that those who plan and wage such a war, with its inevitable and terrible consequences, are committing a crime in so doing." Further on, the majority judgment states: "Aggressive war was a crime at international law long prior to the date of the Declaration of Potsdam." It does not specifically repeat the sentence from the Nuremberg Judgment: "To initiate a war of aggression, therefore, is not only an international crime; it is the supreme international crime differing only from other war crimes in that it contains within itself the accumulated evil of the whole." But this strong statement in the Nuremberg Judgment is covered too by the "unqualified adherence."

In his elaborate "Dissentient Judgment," Judge Pal discusses the several opinions about the criminality of aggressive war, and comes to the conclusion "no category of war became a crime in international life up to the date of commencement of the world war under our considerations."[32] The general conclusion of Pal's Judgment reads: "For the reasons given in the foregoing pages. I would hold that each and everyone of the accused must be found not guilty of each and every one of the charges in the indictment and should be acquitted of all those charges."[33]

It is indeed a real contrast: the supreme international crime, in the opinion of Nuremberg and the majority Tokyo judgment—no crime at all according to the dissenting opinion of Judge Pal.

However, this opinion of the majority about the supreme international crime is not borne out by the verdicts. In the Nuremberg Judgment, those defendants found guilty of the crime against peace, who were not, or only to a limited degree, found guilty of conventional war crimes, were given

[31] The DISSENTIENT JUDGMENT OF JUSTICE PAL is the only part of the judgment that appeared in print (1953).

[32] *Id.* at 70.

[33] *Supra* note 31, at 697.

only prison sentences (Hess, Doenitz, Raeder, Funk, von Neurath). The same we find in the Tokyo verdict. Nobody is sentenced to death for having committed the crime against peace only. The death sentences are pronounced against the accused found guilty of considerable war crimes. For Tokyo is valid what Stimson observed with regard to the Nuremberg verdicts: "Certainly, then, the charge of aggressive war has not been established in international law at the expense of any innocent lives."[34] This leniency with regard to the "supreme crime," *e.g.*, Shigemitsu was found guilty of the crime against peace and sentenced to seven years imprisonment, has been explained by the newness of the crime. But it might also be that a difference existed between the verdict and its reasoning.

The very mild verdicts pronounced for the "supreme crime" are remarkable. Remarkable, too, is the fact that so very few people were accused of and sentenced for the crime against peace. In the Pacific theater only the Tokyo trial dealt with the charge of aggressive war. In Europe[35] tribunals were very reluctant to declare individuals guilty of the crime of aggressive war. Minor figures, such as Fritsche, were found too small for so great a crime. Industrialists and military people were considered not to belong to the group who "waged" aggressive war, unless they contributed to shaping the aggressive policy.[36] In the I.G. Farben trial this thought is further elaborated: "To depart from the concept that only major war criminals—*i.e.*, those persons in the political, military, and industrial fields, for example, who were responsible for the formulation and execution of politics—may be held liable for waging wars of aggression would lead far afield. Under such circumstances there could be no practical limitation on criminal responsibility. . . ."[37] In the Krupp trial all accused were acquitted from the charge of having committed crimes against peace.[38]

As already indicated above, aggression was not considered a true "crime"

---

[34] H. Stimson, *The Nuremberg Trial, Landmark in Law,* 25 FOREIGN AFF. 188 (1947).

[35] I leave aside the Helsinki-trial, in which Finnish statesmen were punished for having waged an aggressive war against Soviet Russia; in this trial the punishments amounted to prison terms of some years.

[36] In the High Command Case all accused were acquitted from the charge of "aggressive war." The sentence reads: "If and as long as a member of the armed forces does not participate in the preparation, planning, initiating, or waging of aggressive war on a policy level, his war activities do not fall under the definition of Crimes Against Peace. It is not a person's rank of status, but his power to shape or influence the policy of his state, which is the relevant issue for determining his criminality under the charge of Crimes Against Peace." THE GERMAN HIGH COMMAND TRIAL, XII LAW REPORTS OF TRIALS OF WAR CRIMINALS 69 (1949).

[37] *I.G. Farben Trial* 10 L.R. 38.

[38] *Krupp-Trial,* 10 L.R. 103.

before and during a good part of the last war. The dreadfulness of World War II made us realize the necessity of preventing wars in the future. It was the irony of history that the horror of the atomic bombings contributed to the recognition of the criminality of Japanese aggression. On the wave of indignation, mixed with a conscious or unconscious feeling of guilt about Allied behavior, the conviction was carried that to plan and initiate aggressive war was a crime. This conviction signified a revolution in legal thought. It introduced in international law the concept of individual criminal responsibility for the maintenance of a minimum standard of human behavior, as formulated in some essential rules of the law of nations.

In this respect Nuremberg and Tokyo were a turning point, or—to use the words of the French judge Donnedieu de Vabres—"un oeuvre révolutionaire,"[39] a revolution in law. In the words of the judgment in the Justice Trial[40] "the force of circumstances, the grim fact of worldwide interdependence, and the moral pressure of public opinion" resulted in international recognition that certain activities constituted criminal violations of common international law.

The factors brought about the emotional and revolutionary considerations and declarations about the "supreme crime." If we are compelled to make a distinction between postwar sentences and their reasoning, it will be easily understood that the moral indignation, together with "the felt necessities of the time," led to the expression that the crime against peace was the supreme crime comprising all the lesser evils.

However, with this moral indignation the real punishments meted out are hardly compatible. These punishments, not giving death sentences for the supreme crime, need a separate explanation.

There is no doubt that powers victorious in a *bellum justum*, and as such responsible for the frail peace, have, according to international law, the right to counteract elements consitituting a threat to the newly established order, and that they are entitled, as a means of preventing the recurrence of gravely offensive conduct, to seek and retain the custody of the pertinent persons. Napoleon's elimination offers a precedent. The responsible powers felt entitled to take, in political action, "les mesures de précaution, que le repos et le salut public peuvent exiger à son égard."[41] Napoleon was eliminated from the European scene "comme ennemi et perturbateur du repos du monde," as the Vienna Congress had called him.

After World War I the responsible powers tried to achieve the same

[39] Donnedieu de Vabres, *Le procès de Nuremberg devant les principes modernes du droit pénal internation*, Recueil des Course de l'Académie de Droit International de l'Hague 481 (1947).

[40] 6 L.R. 45.

[41] Decision of the Congress of Aix la Chapelle, 1810. *Cf.* H. Hale Bellot, *The Detention of Napoleon Bonaparte*, 39 L.Q. Rev. 170 (1923).

against the German emperor in judicial action. The Treaty of Versailles (art. 227) provided for an international tribunal of five members to try the Emperor "for a supreme offense against international morality and the sanctity of treaties." Not stern justice in a criminal trial would be meted out, but the tribunal would be guided "by the highest motives of international policy." The Allied Powers, requesting from the Netherlands Government the Emperor's extradition, emphasized "the special character of their demands, which contemplate, not a juridical accusation, but an act of high international policy."[42] It need not cause surprise that lawyers did not consider the contemplated trial as a criminal trial. Garner wrote (*op cit.* II at 494): "Since he was not charged with a crime, he would hardly seem liable to the penalties prescribed for the violations of the criminal law. . . ." The refusal to extradite William II prevented the realization of the trial. As contemplated, the trial would have amounted to the taking of political measures of security, after judicial inquiry and judgment about the politic dangerousness of the accused and the adequate sanctions.

The duty of the victors to take adequate measures of security was, after World War II, emphasized in the Potsdam Declaration:

> There must be eliminated for all time the authority and influence of those who have deceived and misled the people of Japan into embarking on world conquest, for we insist that a new order of peace, security and justice will be impossible until irresponsible militarism is driven from the world.

In his opening statement, the Chief Prosecutor in the Tokyo Trial stressed this point of danger:

> For the accused in the dock are no contrite penitents. If we are to believe their claims as already asserted in this trial, they acknowledge no wrong and imply that if they were set free they would repeat their aggression again and again. So that from the sheer necessity for security they should be forever restrained.[43]

The same thought was expressed by the Russian prosecutor:

> The accused have not laid down arms. . . . they continue actively advocating their criminal aggressive policy which brought innumerable calamities and suffering to millions of people. The conspirators now in the dock are also dangerous because around them rally the most reactionary elements in Japan represented by former generals, intelligence agents and diplomats who appearing in this court as witnesses are doing their best to shield their former bosses.[44]

Mere political action could have achieved the same goal for protection.

[42] *Cf.* J.W. GARNER, II INTERNATIONAL LAW AND THE WORLD WAR 493 (1920).
[43] Official Transcript of the Tokyo Trial, at 469.
[44] *Id.* at 39738.

That the judicial way was chosen to select those who had been and who were the driving forces of aggression is a novelty that marks a difference with the past.

The concept of crime in international law is applied to different phenomena. It ranges from the really immoral act, such as the wanton killing of prisoners of war, to the merely hostile action, like the "illegal action" of the "freie Heldentum" which was denied protection by the Hague Conventions. The crime against peace—described in the *reasonings* of the postwar judgments as the "supreme crime," as the utmost immorality—might also be conceived as indicating an act comparable to merely political crimes in domestic law. The *punishments* delivered in the post war judgments indicate that they were based on this concept of the political crime, where the decisive element is the political danger rather than the criminal guilt, where the "criminal" is considered an enemy rather than a villain, and where the sanction emphasizes the *mesure de sureté* rather than the judicial retribution. In this sense the crime against peace, as formulated in the Charters, was in perfect accordance with existing international law. Consequently, there seems to be a divergence between the verdicts of the judgments, and their reasoning. Where the judgment of Nuremberg stresses the point that the Charter is "the expression of international law existing at the time of its creation"[45]—a pronunciation reiterated in the Tokyo verdict[46]—it might be suggested that such opinion holds good only with regard to the concept of international crime handled in the verdicts.[47]

Different motives brought about the postwar trials and the indictment for the crime of aggressive war. Different lines of thought were followed by the victorious powers, which at the same time organized trials to decide whether the wars waged were aggressive, and based their postwar policies on the assumption that the vanquished nations had been out for military conquest of the world. Different opinions were held by the individuals who sat in judgment. Different concepts were at the basis of the reasonings of the judgments and of the verdicts pronounced and the sanctions applied. Anger and hate played their role, as did sincere moral indignation and practical policy. The multitude of motives and intricacy of their interplay are apt to confuse the mind. Elements of foul play are easily exaggerated, dishonesty in official statements easily too much stressed. Altogether Nuremberg and Tokyo amounted to a revolution in law, and revolutions are usually the outcome of many factors, in which good and bad are intermingled. As in every revolution the new concepts were based on the conscience of the people. The world conscience was aroused by the

[45] JUDGMENT NUREMBERG 38 (Brit. ed. 1946).

[46] JUDGMENT TOKYO 27.

[47] The "Dissenting Opinion" I delivered is based on this concept of the crime of aggression.

International Criminal Law

horrors of the war and by the experience of the new weapons. In an emotional outburst the world demanded that war should be outlawed to the extent that individual warmakers should be made criminally responsible. This world sentiment was carried in the general *considerations and reasonings* of the judgments. The Charter was, according to the Nuremberg Judgment, at the same time "the expression of international law existing at the time of its creation" and "itself a contribution to international law."[48] One might say that the Charters were not decisive. It was the judgments that made the crime against peace enter into positive law.[49] The judgments stand in history as indelible facts. They form a precedent. They have the power of the beaten path.

It need not cause surprise that the revolutionary character of Nuremberg and Tokyo is emphasized by German and Japanese scholars. It should not be denied. But there is no sense in measuring the significance of a revolution with the standards it intended to destroy. It is nonsense to judge a revolution by the laws it abolished. Its worth is determined by its value for the future.[50]

It need also not cause surprise that German and Japanese scholars enlarge on the negative aspects of Nuremberg and Tokyo. These aspects too should not be denied. But one should never forget that new law often is created with mixed motives and out of mixed reasons. It holds good for the growth of law, in the national as well as in the international field, that sometimes the birth of law appears as the consequence of rape. New legal thoughts often find strange ways to realization, good ideas often take advantage of bad intentions. As Whitehead put it: "Great ideas often enter into reality with evil associates and with disgusting alliances."[51] That criticism on Nuremberg and Tokyo is warranted does not imply that the principal idea materialized in these trials would necessarily be wrong.

Stimson, in 1944, considered the concept of individual criminal responsibility for the crime against peace "a little in advance of international thought.[52] Later he called the Nuremberg Trial "Landmark in Law."[53] It is a landmark that indicates the beginning of international law of the atomic era. One might say that, after World War II, in a hurricane of emotion the world swept aside obsolete conceptions of national sovereignty and established new law. As such the law of Nuremberg and Tokyo signifies an outpost of legal development. It is law "in advance" of actual legal

[48] *Supra* note 45.

[49] *Cf.* C.A. POMPE, AGGRESSIVE WAR AN INTERNATIONAL CRIME 281 (1954).

[50] In this sense Otto Kranzbühler, *Nürnberg als Rechtsproblem, in* FESTGABE FÜR ERICH KAUFMANN 219 (1950).

[51] A.N. WHITEHEAD, ADVENTURES OF IDEAS 28 (1948).

[52] *Supra* note 6, vol. II, at 587.

[53] *Supra* note 34.

concepts and juridical situations. But this new law on the maintenance of peace is not at all in advance of the facts of international relations. The world needs new law, to prevent universal catastrophe. The natural law of the atomic age includes as a matter of course the criminal responsibility of the individual bent on aggressive war. It is therefore the task of the United Nations to implement the revolution of Nuremberg and Tokyo, and one may doubt whether the United Nations is living up to that responsibility.[54] That many other legal developments belong to "the necessities of the time" is beyond question. It is also beyond question that on many other points the law of international relations has to change if criminal individual responsibility is to become the keystone of an effective law on peace. To maintain the outpost, the legal forces of the rear will have to advance.

Lawyers know that law is not logic. Some parts occasionally may leap forward pushed by special emotions and by special interest. Often it takes a long time to arrive at a closed system of legal provisions. However, *to arrive at a stage of legal development in which this individual criminal responsibility is but the logical consequence of the international juridical situation may be the precondition of the survival of civilization.*

For our time some principles applied in the Nuremberg and Tokyo trials are of paramount importance. The first is *that aggressive war is illegal and criminal.* It seems to me that the post war world has not lived up to this principle. If one looks at the postwar legal development, it might seem that more and more exceptions are recognized.[55]

A second principle should be mentioned: *that individuals are criminally responsible for the crime against peace.* It means that the individual is called upon to disobey his national government in case this government is out on aggression. According to the judgments some rules of world law, expressing the loyalty that everyone should have to humanity as a whole, prevail upon national obligations. The Nuremberg Judgment expressed this fundamental idea when it explained the intrinsic significance of its Charter: "[T]he very essence of the Charter is that individuals have international duties which transcend the national obligations of obedience imposed by the individual state."[56] This principle is also relevant in connection with conventional war crimes.

[54] Compare the present writer's: *The United Nations and the Development of International Criminal Law,* in The United Nations, Ten Years' Legal Progress (1956). At its XIIth Session (1954) the General Assembly adopted Res. 1187 (XII) shelving for the time being the agenda item "Code of Offences against the Peace and Security of Mankind." As the Netherlands representative, I voted, as a token of protest, against this Resolution, which was adopted with 74 votes in favor and 1 against.

[55] An enumeration of these exceptions is given in B. Roling, *Hat das Kriegsverbot noch einen Sinn?* in Jahrbuch für Internationales Recht 74 (1969).

[56] *Supra* note 45, at 42.

With respect to the violation of the laws and customs of war, the conventional war crimes, the Tokyo Judgment made an essential contribution. In the Judgment of Nuremberg punishments were only meted out to those who themselves had committed war crimes or had ordered them to be committed.[57] In Japan the main question was in how far the accused were responsible for the crimes which were committed in the field—regularly and on a mass scale—but which had not been ordered by them. The Tokyo Judgment acknowledged this responsibility for not having acted, for not having prevented the violation of the laws of war, in case the accused knew of the crimes, and were in a command position which made it possible for them to stop the criminal practice.[58] This responsibility for omission to act seems at present to be totally disregarded.

APPENDIX I.

EXCERPTS FROM JUDGMENT OF THE NÜRNBERG TRIBUNAL
SEPTEMBER 30, 1946*

*Nazi Conspiracy and Aggression—Opinion
and Judgment (1947)*

On the 8th August 1945 the Government of the United Kingdom of Great Britain and Northern Ireland, the Government of the United States of America, the Provisional Government of the French Republic, and the Government of the Union of Soviet Socialist Republics entered into an Agreement establishing this Tribunal for

[57] *See, e.g.,* the discussions with respect to the responsibility of Admiral Donitz in relation to his Laconia-order. The question of his responsibility for not having prevented the practice of the killing of survivors was not even mentioned (*Supra* note 45, at 109).

[58] Count 55 of the Tokyo Indictment charged the accused that they "being by virtue of their respective offices responsible for securing the observance of . . . the Laws and Customs of War in respect of the armed forces . . . and in respect of many thousands of prisoners of war and civilians then in the power of Japan . . ., deliberately and recklessly disregarded their legal duty to take adequate steps to secure the observance and prevent breaches thereof." In the Judgment this question of negligence in the duty to enforce the rules of war is discussed with regard to each of the defendants. With respect to the scope of this responsibility differences may exist. According to the Majority Judgment in Tokyo, Hata, Hirota, and Shigemitsu were guilty of negligence (pp. 1155, 1160, 1195). In my Dissenting Opinion, I discussed the guiding principles concerning "responsibility for omission" (p. 54–61) and came to the conclusion that Hata, Hirota, and Shigemitsu were to be acquitted on this score (pp. 189, 203–210, 238–242), applying the legal principles adopted by the Supreme Court of the United States *in re* Yamashita, 327 U.S.1 (1946) also Reel, the case of General Yamashita (1949). For a more contemporary appraisal see Taylor, Nuremberg and Vietnam: An American Tragedy 1970 and Bassiouni, The War Power and the Laws of War: Theory and realism, 18 DePaul L. Rev. 188 (1968).

* Full text also in 22 *Proceedings in the Trial of the Major War Criminals Before the International Military Tribunal* 411–589; 41 A.J.I.L. 172 (1947); 6 F.R.D. 69 (1946); 20 Temp. L.Q. 167 (1947).

the trial of war criminals whose offenses have no particular geographical location. In accordance with Article 5, the following Governments of the United Nations have expressed their adherence to the agreement: Greece, Denmark, Yugoslavia, the Netherlands, Czechoslovakia, Poland, Belgium, Ethiopia, Australia, Honduras, Norway, Panama, Luxembourg, Haiti, New Zealand, India, Venezuela, Uruguay, and Paraguay.

By the Charter annexed to the agreement, the consititution, jurisdiction, and functions of the Tribunal were defined. . . .

Four hundred and three open sessions of the Tribunal have been held; 33 witnesses gave evidence orally for the prosecution against the individual defendants, and 61 witnesses, in addition to 19 of the defendants, gave evidence for the defense.

A further 143 witnesses gave evidence for the defense by means of written answers to interrogatories.

The Tribunal appointed commissioners to hear evidence relating to the organizations, and 101 witnesses were heard for the defense before the commissioners, and 1,809 affidavits from other witnesses were submitted. Six reports were also submitted, summarizing the contents of a great number of further affidavits.

Thirty-eight thousand affidavits, signed by 155,000 people, were submitted on behalf of the Political Leaders, 136,213 on behalf of the SS, 10,000 on behalf of the SA, 7000 on behalf of the S.D., 7000 on behalf of the General Staff and OKW, and 2000 on behalf of the Gestapo.

The Tribunal itself heard 22 witnesses for the organizations. The documents tendered in evidence for the prosecution of the individual defendants and the organizations numbered several thousands. A complete stenographic record of everything said in court has been made, as well as an electrical recording of all the proceedings.

Copies of all the documents put in evidence by the prosecution have been supplied to the defense in the German language. The applications made by the defendants for the production of witnesses and documents raised serious problems in some instances, on account of the unsettled state of the country. It was also necessary to limit the number of witnesses to be called, in order to have an expeditious hearing, in accordance with Article 18(c) of the Charter. . . .

I. The Charter Provisions

The individual defendants are indicted under Article 6 of the Charter.

IV. Violations of International Treaties

The Charter defines as a crime the planning or waging of war that is a war of aggression or a war in violation of international treaties. The Tribunal has decided that certain of the defendants planned and waged aggressive wars against 10 nations, and were therefore guilty of this series of crimes. This makes it unnecessary to discuss the subject in further detail, or even to consider at any length the extent to which these aggressive wars were also "wars in violation of international treaties, agreements, or assurances." Thsee treaties are set out in Appendix C of the indictment. Those of principal importance are the following:

(A) Hague Conventions

In the 1899 Convention the signatory powers agreed: "before an appeal to arms. . . to have recourse, as far as circumstances allow, to the good offices or mediation of one or more friendly powers." A similar clause was inserted in the Convention for Pacific Settlement of International Disputes of 1907. In the accompanying Convention Relative to Opening of Hostilities, article I contains this far more specific language: "The Contracting Powers recognize that hostilities between them must not commence without a previous and explicit warning, in the form of either a declaration of war, giving reasons, or an ultimatum with a conditional declaration of war."

Germany was a party to these conventions.

(B) Versailles Treaty

Breaches of certain provisions of the Versailles Treaty are also relied on by the prosecution—not to fortify the left bank of the Rhine (art. 42–44); to "respect strictly the independence of Austria" (art. 80); renunciation of any rights in Memel (art. 99) and the Free City of Danzig (art. 100); the recognition of the independence of the Czecho-Slovak State; and the Military, Naval, and Air Clauses against German rearmament found in part V. There is no doubt that action was taken by the German Government contrary to all these provisions, the details of which are set out in appendix C. . .

(C) Treaties of Mutual Guarantee, Arbitration, and Non-Aggression

It is unnecessary to discuss in any detail the various treaties entered into by Germany with other powers. Treaties of Mutual Guarantee were signed by Germany at Locarno in 1925, with Belgium, France, Great Britain, and Italy, assuring the maintenance of the territorial status quo. Arbitration treaties were also executed by Germany at Locarno with Czechoslovakia, Belgium, and Poland.

Conventions of arbitration and conciliation were entered into between Germany, the Netherlands, and Denmark in 1926; and between Germany and Luxemburg in 1929. Nonaggression treaties were executed by Germany with Denmark and Russia in 1939.

(D) Kellogg-Briand Pact

The Pact of Paris was signed on the 27th August 1928 by Germany, the United States, Belgium, France, Great Britain, Italy, Japan, Poland, and other countries; and subsequently by other powers.

It is to be noted that on the 26th January 1934, Germany signed a Declaration for the Maintenance of Permanent Peace with Poland, which was explicitly based on the Pact of Paris, and in which the use of force was outlawed for a period of ten years. . . .

(E) The Law of the Charter

The jurisdiction of the Tribunal is defined in the Agreement and Charter, and the crimes coming within the jurisdiction of the Trbunal, for whch there shall be individual responsibility, are set out in Article 6. The law of the Charter is decisive, and binding upon the Tribunal.

The making of the Charter was the exercise of the sovereign legislative power by the countries to which the German Reich unconditionally surrendered; and the undoubted right of these countries to legislate for the occupied territories has been recognized by the civilized world. The Charter is not an arbitrary exercise of power on the part of the victorious nations, but in the view of the Tribunal, as will be shown, it is the expression of international law existing at the time of its creation; and to that extent is itself a contribution to international law.

The Charter makes the planning or waging of a war of aggression or a war in violation of international treaties a crime; and it is therefore not strictly necessary to consider whether and to what extent aggressive war was a crime before the execution of the London Agreement. But in view of the great importance of the questions of law involved, the Tribunal has heard full argument from the prosecution and the defense, and will express its view on the matter.

It was urged on behalf of the defendants that a fundamental principle of all law—international and domestic—is that there can be no punishment of crime without a preexisting law. "*Nullum crimen sine lege, nulla poena sine lege.*" It was submitted that ex post facto punishment is abhorrent to the law of all civilized nations, that no sovereign power had made aggressive war a crime at the time the alleged criminal acts were committed, that no statute had defined aggressive war, that no penalty had been fixed for its commission, and no court had been created to try and punish offenders.

In the first place, it is to be observed that the Maximum nullum crimen sine lege is not a limitation of sovereignty, but is in general a principle of justice. To assert that it is unjust to punish those who in defiance of treaties and assurances have attacked neighboring states without warning is obviously untrue, for in such circumstances the attacker must know that he is doing wrong, and so far from it being unjust to punish him, it would be unjust if his wrong were allowed to go unpunished. Occupying the positions they did in the government of Germany, the defendants, or at least some of them must have known of the treaties signed by Germany, outlawing recourse to war for the settlement of international disputes; they must have known that they were acting in defiance of all international law when in complete deliberation they carried out their designs of invasion and aggression. On this view of the case alone, it would appear that the maxim has an application to the present facts.

[It] is argued that the pact does not expressly enact that such wars are crimes, or set up courts to try those who make such wars. To the extent the same is true with regard to the laws of war contained in the Hague Convention. The Hague Convention of 1907 prohibited resort to certain methods of waging war. These included the inhumane treatment of prisoners, the employment of poisoned weapons, the improper use of flags of truce, and similar matters. Many of these prohibitions had been enforced long before the date of the Convention; but since 1907 they have certainly been crimes, punishable as offenses against the laws of war; yet the Hague Convention nowhere designates such practices as criminal, nor is any sentence prescribed, nor any mention made of a court to try and punish offenders. For many years past, however, military tribunals have tried and punished individuals guilty of violating the rules of land warfare laid down by this Convention. In the opinion of the Tribunal, those who wage aggressive war are doing that which is equally illegal, and of much greater moment than a breach of one of the rules of the Hague Convention. In interpreting the words of the pact, it must be remembered that international law is not the product of an international legislature, and that such international agreements as the Pact of Paris have to deal with general principles of law, and not with administrative matters of procedure. The law of war is to be found not only in treaties, but in the customs and practices of states which gradually obtained universal recognition, and from the general principles of justice applied by jurists and practiced by military courts. This law is not static, but by continual adaptation follows the needs of a changing world. Indeed, in many cases treaties do no more than express and define for more accurate reference the principles of law already existing.

. . . The principal objection appeared to be in the difficulty of defining the acts which would constitute "aggression," rather than any doubt as to the criminality of

aggressive war. The preamble to the League of Nations 1924 Protocol for the Pacific
Settlement of International Disputes, ("Geneva Protocol"), after "recognising the
solidarity of the members of the international community," declared that "a war
of aggression constitutes a violation of this solidarity and is an international crime."
It went on to declare that the contracting parties were "desirous of facilitating the
complete application of the system provided in the Covenant of the League of Nations
for the pacific settlement of disputes between the states and of ensuring the repression
of international crimes." The Protocol was recommended to the members of the
League of Nations by a unanimous resolution in the Assembly of the 48 members
of the League. These members included Italy and Japan, but Germany was not
then a member of the League.

Although the Protocol was never ratified, it was signed by the leading statesmen
of the world, representing the vast majority of the civilized States and peoples,
and may be regarded as strong evidence of the intention to brand aggressive war
as an international crime.

[Many] expressions of opinion, [and declarations] solemnly made, reinforced the
construction which the Tribunal placed upon the Pact of Paris, that resort to a war
of aggression is not merely illegal, but is criminal. The prohibition of aggressive war
demanded by the conscience of the world, finds its expression in the series of Pacts
and Treaties to which the Tribunal has just referred.

It is also important ot remember that Article 227 of the Treaty Versailles provided
for the constitution of a special tribunal, composed of representatives of five of the
Allied and Associated Powers which had been belligerents in the First World War
opposed to Germany, to try the former German Emperor "for a supreme offence
against international morality and the sanctity of treaties." The purpose of this trial
was expressed to be "to vindicate the solemn obligations of international undertakings, and the validity of international morality." In Article 228 of the Treaty, the
German Government expressly recognized the right of the Allied Powers "to bring
before military tribunals persons accused of having committed acts in violation of the
laws and customs of war."

It was submitted that international law is concerned with the actions of sovereign
States, and provides no punishment for individuals; and further, that where the act
in question is an act of State, those who carry it out are not personally responsible,
but are protected by the doctrine of the sovereignty of the State. In the opinion of
the Tribunal, both these submissions must be rejected. That international law imposes
duties and liabilities upon individuals as well as upon states has long been recognized.

The principle of international law, which under certain circumstances, protects
the representatives of a State, cannot be applied to acts which are condemned as
criminal by international law. The authors of these acts cannot shelter themselves
behind their official position in order to be freed from punishment in appropriate
proceedings. Article 7 of the Charter expressly declares: "The official position of
defendants, whether as heads of State, or responsible officials in government departments, shall not be considered as freeing them from responsibility, or mitigating
punishment."

On the other hand the very essence of the Charter is that individuals have international duties which transcend the national obligations of obedience imposed by the
individual State. He who violates the laws of war cannot obtain immunity while
acting in pursuance of the authority of the State if the State in authorizing action
moves outside its competence under international law.

It was also submitted on behalf of these defendants that in doing what they did they were acting under the orders of Hitler, and therefore cannot be held responsible for the acts committed by them in carrying out these orders. The Charter specifically provides in Article 8: "The fact that the defendant acted pursuant to order of his Government or of a superior shall not free him from responsibility, but may be considered in mitigation of punishment."

The provisions of this Article are in conformity with the law of all nations. That a soldier was ordered to kill or torture in violation of the international law of war has never been recognized as a defense to such acts of brutality, though, as the Charter here provides, the order may be urged in mitigation of the punishment. The true test, which is found in varying degrees in the criminal law of most nations, is not the existence of the order, but whether moral choice was in fact possible.

V. The Law as to the Common Plan or Conspiracy

In the previous recital of the facts relating to aggressive war, it is clear that planning and preparation had been carried out in the most systematic way at every stage of the history.

Planning and preparation are essential to the making of war. In the opinion of the Tribunal aggressive war is a crime under international law. The Charter defines this offense as planning, preparation, initiation, or waging of a war of aggression "or participation in a common plan or conspiracy for the accomplishment . . . of the foregoing." The indictment follows this distinction. Count one charges the common plan or conspiracy. Count two charges the planning and waging of war. The same evidence has been introduced to support both counts.

In the opinion of the Tribunal, the evidence establishes the common planning to prepare and wage war by certain of the defendants. It is immaterial to consider whether a single conspiracy to the extent and over the time set out in the indictment has been conclusively proved. Continued planning, with aggressive war as the objective, has been established beyond doubt. . . .

VI. War Crimes and Crimes Against Humanity

The Tribunal proposes, therefore, to deal quite generally with the question of war crimes, and to refer to them later when examining the responsibility of the individual defendants in relation to them. Prisoners of war were ill-treated and tortured and murdered, not only in defiance of the well-established rules of international law, but in complete disregard of the elementary dictates of humanity. Civilian populations in occupied territories suffered the same fate. Whole populations were deported to Germany for the purposes of slave labor upon defense works, armament production and similar tasks connected with the war effort. Hostages were taken in very large numbers from the civilian populations in all the occupied countries, and were shot as suited the German purposes. Public and private property was systematically plundered and pillaged in order to enlarge the resources of Germany at the expense of the rest of Europe. Cities and towns and villages were wantonly destroyed without military justification or necessity. . . .

(F) The Law Relating to War Crimes and Crimes Against Humanity

The Tribunal is of course bound by the Charter, in the definition which it gives both of war crimes and crimes against humanity. With respect to war crimes, however, as has already been pointed out, the crimes defined by Article 6, section (b), of the Charter were already recognized as war crimes under international law. They were covered by Articles 46, 50, 52 and 56 of the Hague Convention of 1907, and Articles 2, 3, 4, 46, and 51 of the Geneva Convention of 1929. That violation of these provisions constituted crimes for which the guilty individuals were punishable is too well settled to admit of argument.

But it is argued that the Hague Convention does not apply in this case, because of the "general participation" clause in Article 2 of the Hague Convention of 1907. That clause provided: "The provisions contained in the regulations (rules of land warfare) referred to in Article I as well as in the present convention do not apply except between contracting powers, and then only if all the belligerents are parties to the convention." Several of the belligerents in the recent war were not parties to this convention.

In the opinion of the Tribunal it is not necessary to decide this question. The rules of land warfare expressed in the convention undoubtedly represented an advance over existing international law at the time of their adoption. But the convention expressly stated that it was an attempt "to revise the general laws and customs of war," which it thus recognized to be then existing, but by 1939 these rules laid down in the convention were recognized by all civilized nations, and were regarded as being declaratory of the laws and customs of war which are referred to in Article 6(b) of the Charter.

With regard to crimes against humanity, there is no doubt whatever that political opponents were murdered in Germany before the war, and that many of them were kept in concentration camps in circumstances of great horror and cruelty. The policy of terror was certainly carried out on a vast scale, and in many cases was organized and systematic. The policy of persecution, repression, and murder of civilians in Germany before the war of 1939, who were likely to be hostile to the Government, was most ruthlessly carried out. The persecution of Jews during the same period is established beyond all doubt. To consitute crimes against humanity, the acts relied on before the outbreak of war must have been in execution of, or in connection with, any crime within the jurisdiction of the Tribunal. The Tribunal is of the opinion that revolting and horrible as many of these crimes were, it has not been satisfactorily proved that they were done in execution of, or in connection with, any such crime. The Tribunal therefore cannot make a general declaration that the acts before 1939 were crimes against humanity within the meaning of the Charter, but from the beginning of the war in 1939 war crimes were committed on a vast scale, which were also crimes against humanity; and insofar as the inhumane acts charged in the indictment, and committed after the beginning of the war, did not constitute war crimes, they were all committed in execution of, or in connection with, the aggressive war, and therefore constituted crimes against humanity.

VII. *The Accused Organizations*

. . . A criminal organization is analogous to a criminal conspiracy in that the essence of both is cooperation for criminal purpose. There must be a group bound together and organized for a common purpose. The group must be formed or used in connection with the commission of crimes denounced by the Charter. Since the declaration with respect to the organizations and groups will, as has been pointed out, fix the criminality of its members, that definition should exclude persons who had no knowledge of the crminal purposes or acts of the organization and those who were drafted by the State for membership, unless they were personally implicated in the commission of acts declared criminal by Article 6 of the Charter as members of the organizations. Membership alone is not enough to come within the scope of these declarations.

APPENDIX II

EXCERPTS FROM THE JUDGMENT IN THE TOKYO WAR CRIMES TRIAL, 1948°

(Excerpt from main judgment)

CHAPTER I. ESTABLISHMENT AND PROCEEDINGS OF THE TRIBUNAL

The Tribunal was established in virtue of and to implement the Cairo Declaration of the 1st of December, 1943, the Declaration of Potsdam of the 26th of July, 1945, the Instrument of Surrender of the 2nd of September, 1945, and the Moscow Conference of the 26 of December, 1945. . . .

The Declaration of Potsdam . . . was made by the President of the United States of America, the President of the National Government of the Republic of China, and the Prime Minister of Great Britain and later adhered to by the Union of Soviet Socialist Republics. Its principal relevant provisions are:

"Japan shall be given an opportunity to end this war.

"There must be eliminated for all time the authority and influence of those who have deceived and misled the people of Japan into embarking on world conquest, for we insist that a new order of peace, security and justice will be impossible until irresponsible militarism is driven from the world. . . .

"We do not intend that the Japanese people shall be enslaved as a race or destroyed as a nation, but stern justice shall be meted out to all war criminals including those who have visited cruelties upon our prisoners."

[Twenty-eight Japanese were indicted, all but one pleaded guilty—seven were sentenced to death, 16 imprisoned for life, 2 prison sentences—Emperor Hirohito was not indicted, nor was any industrialist.]

(a) Jurisdiction of the Tribunal

In our opinion the law of the Charter is decisive and binding on the Tribunal. This is a special tribunal set up by the Supreme Commander under authority conferred on him by the Allied Powers. It derives its jurisdiction from the Charter. In this trial its members have no jurisdiction except such as is to be found in the Charter. The Order of the Supreme Commander, which appointed the members of the Tribunal, states: "The responsibilities, powers, and duties of the members of the Tribunal are set forth in the Charter thereof. . . ." In the result, the members of the Tribunal, being otherwise wholly without power in respect to the trial of the accused, have been empowered by the documents, which constituted the Tribunal and appointed

°The 1218-page judgment and individual opinions rendered Nov. 4–12, 1948, are quoted in the U.S. NAVAL WAR COLLEGE, INTERNATIONAL LAW DOCUMENTS, 1948–1949, at 71–107 (1950) *See also* Horowitz, The Tokyo Trial, l Intl. Conc. No. 465 (1950); KEENAN & BROWN, CRIMES AGAINST INTERNATIONAL LAW (1950); Comyns-Carr, *Tokyo War Crimes Trial,* 18 Far East. Surv. 109 (1949).

them as members, to try the accused but subject always to the duty and responsibility of applying to the trial the law set forth in the Charter.

The foregoing expression of opinion is not to be taken as supporting the view, if such view be held, that the Allied Powers or any victor nations have the right under international law in providing for the trial and punishment of war criminals to enact or promulgate laws or vest in their tribunals powers in conflicts with recognized international law or rules of principles thereof. In the exercise of their right to create tribunals for such a purpose and in conferring powers upon such tribunals belligerent powers may act only within the limits of international law.

The substantial grounds of the defence challenge to the jurisdiction of the Tribunal to hear and adjudicate upon the charges contained in the Indictment are the following:

(1) The Allied Powers acting through the Supreme Commander have no authority to include in the Charter of the Tribunal and to designate as justiciable "Crimes against Peace" (Article 5(a));

(2) Aggressive war is not per se illegal and the Pact of Paris of 1928 renouncing war as an instrument of national policy does not enlarge the meaning of war crimes nor constitute war a crime;

(3) War is the act of a nation for which there is no individual responsibility under international law;

(4) The provisions of the Charter are "ex post facto" legislation and therefore illegal;

(5) The Instrument of Surrender which provides that the Declaration of Potsdam will be given effect imposes the condition that Conventional War Crimes are recognized by international law at the date of the Declaration (26 July 1945) would be the only crimes prosecuted;

(6) Killings in the course of belligerent operations except in so far as they constitute violations of the rules of warfare or the laws and customs of war are the normal incidents of war and are not murder;

(1) Several of the accused being prisoners of war are triable by court martial as provided by the Geneva Convention of 1929 and not by this Tribunal.

Since the law of the Charter is decisive and binding upon it this Tribunal is formally bound to reject the first four of the above seven contentions advanced for the Defence but in view of the great importance of the questions of law involved the Tribunal will record its opinion on these questions.

After this Tribunal had in May 1946 dismissed the defence motions and upheld the validity of its Charter and its jurisdiction thereunder, stating that the reasons for this decision would be given later, the International Military Tribunal sitting at Nuremberg delivered its verdicts on the first of October 1946. . . .

Prisoners taken in war and civilian internees are in the power of the Government which captures them. This was not always the case. For the last two centuries, however, this position has been recognized and the customary law to this effect was formally embodied in the Hague Convention No. IV in 1907 and repeated in the Geneva Prisoners of War Convention of 1929. Responsibility for the care of prisoners of war and of civilian internees (all of whom we will refer to as "prisoners") rests therefore with the Government having them in possession. This responsibility is not limited to the duty of mere maintenance but extends to the prevention of mistreatment. In particular, acts of inhumanity to prisoners which are forbidden by the customary law of nations as well as by conventions are to be prevented by the Government having responsibility for the prisoners.

In the discharge of these duties to prisoners Governments must have resort to persons. Indeed the Governments responsible, in this sense, are those persons who direct and control the functions of Government. In this case and in the above regard we are concerned with the members of the Japanese Cabinet. The duty to prisoners is not a meaningless obligation cast upon a political abstraction. It is a specific duty to be performed in the first case by those persons who constitute the Government. In the multitude of duties and tasks involved in modern government there is of necessity an elaborate system of subdivision and delegation of duties. In the case of the duty of Governments to prisoners held by them in time of war those persons who constitute the Government have the principal and continuing responsibility for their prisoners, even though they delegate the duties of maintenance and protection to others.

In general the responsibility for prisoners held by Japan may be stated to have rested upon:

(1) Members of the Government;

(2) Military or Naval Officers in command of formations having prisoners in their possession;

(3) Officials in those departments which were concerned with the well-being of prisoners;

(4) Officials, whether civilian, military, or naval, having direct and immediate control of prisoners.

It is the duty of all those on whom responsibility rests to secure proper treatment of prisoners and to prevent their ill-treatment by establishing and securing the continuous and efficient working of a system appropriate for these purposes. Such persons fail in this duty and become responsible for ill-treatment of prisoners if:

(1) They fail to establish such a system.

(2) If having established such a system, they fail to secure its continued and efficient working.

Each of such persons has a duty to ascertain that the system is working and if he neglects to do so he is responsible. He does not discharge his duty by merely instituting an appropriate system and thereafter neglecting to learn of its application. An Army Commander or a Minister of War, for example, must be at the same pains to ensure obedience to his orders in this respect as he would in respect of other orders he has issued on matters of the first importance.

Nevertheless, such persons are not responsible if a proper system and its continuous efficient functioning be provided for and conventional war crimes be committed unless:

(1) They had knowledge that such crimes were being committed, and having such knowledge they failed to take such steps as were within their power to prevent the commission of such crimes in the future, or

(2) They are at fault in having failed to acquire such knowledge.

If such a person had, or should, but for negligence or supineness, have had such knowledge he is not excused for inaction if his Office required or permitted him to take any action to prevent such crimes. On the other hand it is not enough for the exculpation of a person, otherwise responsible, for him to show that he accepted assurances from others more directly associated with the control of the prisoners if having regard to the position of those others, to the frequency of reports of such crimes, or to any other circumstances he should have been put upon further enquiry as to whether those assurances were true or untrue. That crimes are notorious, numerous and widespread as to time and place are matters to be considered in imputing knowledge.

A member of a Cabinet which collectively, as one of the principal organs of the Government, is responsible for the care of prisoners is not absolved from responsibility if, having knowledge of the commission of the crimes in the sense already discussed, and omitting or failing to secure the taking of measures to prevent the commission of such crimes in the future, he elects to continue as a member of the Cabinet. This is the position even though the Department of which he has the charge is not directly concerned with the care of prisoners. A Cabinet member may resign. If he has knowledge of ill-treatment of prisoners, is powerless to prevent future ill-treatment, but elects to remain in the Cabinet thereby continuing to participate in its collective responsibility for protection of prisoners he willingly assumes responsibility for any ill-treatment in the future.

Army or Navy Commanders can, by order, secure proper treatment and prevent ill-treatment of prisoners. So can Ministers of War and of the Navy. If crimes are committed against prisoners under their control, of the likely occurrence of which they had, or should have had, knowledge in advance, they are responsible for those crimes. If, for example, it be shown that within the units under his command conventional war crimes have been committed of which he knew or should have known, a commander who takes no adequate steps to prevent the occurrence of such crimes in the future will be responsible for such future crimes.

Departmental Officials having knowledge of ill-treatment of prisoners are not responsible by reason of their failure to resign; but if their functions included the administration of the system of protection of prisoners and if they had or should have had knowledge of crimes and did nothing effective, to the extent of their powers, to prevent their occurrence in the future then they are responsible for such future crimes. . . .

Under the heading of "Crimes Against Peace" the Charter names five separate crimes. These are planning, preparation, initiation and waging aggressive war or a war in violation of international law, treaties, agreements or assurances; to these four is added the further crime of participation in a common plan or conspiracy for the accomplishment of any of the foregoing. The Indictment was based upon the Charter and all the above crimes were charged in addition to further charges founded upon other provisions of the Charter.

A conspiracy to wage aggressive or unlawful war arises when two or more persons enter into an agreement to commit that crime. Thereafter, in furtherance of the conspiracy, follows planning and preparing for such war. Those who participate at this stage may be either original conspirators or later adherents. If the latter adopt the purpose of the conspiracy and plan and prepare for its fulfillment they become conspirators. For this reason, as all the accused are charged with the conspiracies, we do not consider it necessary in respect of those we may find guilty of conspiracy to enter convictions also for planning and preparing. In other words, although we do not question the validity of the charges we do not think it necessary in respect of any defendants who may be found guilty of conspiracy to take into consideration or to enter convictions upon Counts 6 to 17 inclusive.

A similar position arises in connection with the counts of initiating and waging aggressive war. Although initiating aggressive war in some circumstances may have another meaning, in the Indictment before us it is given the meaning of commencing the hostilities. In this sense it involves the actual waging of the aggressive war. After such a war has been initiated or has been commenced by some

offenders others may participate in such circumstances, as to become guilty of waging the war. This consideration, however, affords no reason for registering convictions on the counts of initiating as well as of waging aggressive war. We propose
therefore to abstain from consideration of Counts 18 to 26 inclusive.

Counts 37 and 38 charge conspiracy to murder. Article 5, sub-paragraphs (b)
and (c) of the Charter, deal with Conventional War Crimes and Crimes against
Humanity. In sub-paragraph (c) of Article 5 occurs this passage: "Leaders, organizers, instigators and accomplices participating in the formulation or execution of a
common plan or conspiracy to commit any of the foregoing crimes are responsible
for all acts performed by any person in execution of such plan." A similar provision appeared in the Nuremberg Charter although there it was an independent
paragraph and was not, as in our Charter, incorporated in sub-paragraph (c). The
context of this provision clearly relates it exclusively to sub-paragraph (a), Crimes
against Peace, as that is the only category in which a "common plan or conspiracy"
is stated to be a crime. It has no application to Conventional War Crimes and Crimes
against Humanity as conspiracies to commit such crimes are not made criminal by
the Charter of the Tribunal. The Prosecution did not challenge this view but submitted that the counts were sustainable under Article 5(a) of the Charter it was
argued that the waging of aggressive war was unlawful and involved unlawful
killing which is murder. From this it was submitted further that a conspiracy to
wage war unlawfully was a conspiracy also to commit murder. The crime triable
by this Tribunal are those set out in the Charter. Article 5(a) states that a conspiracy to commit the crimes therein specified is itself a crime. The crimes, other
than conspiracy, specified in Article 5(a) are "planning, preparation, initiating or
waging" of a war of aggression. There is no specification of the crime of conspiracy
to commit murder by the waging of aggressive war or otherwise. We hold therefore that we have no jurisdiction to deal with charges of conspiracy to commit
murder as contained in Counts 37 and 38 and decline to entertain these charges.

Section 3. THE DEFENSE OF "SUPERIOR ORDERS" IN INTERNATIONAL CRIMINAL LAW*

THEO VOGLER

3.1. Introduction

The question of whether, and under what conditions, the defendant
in a criminal proceeding can effectively assert as a defense the fact that he
acted pursuant to the command of a superior is authoritatively answered
in almost every national legal system. However, the significance of this
question is not limited to national law. The development of a scientific
ICL requires an answer to the same question based on international law
principles,[1] since the principle of the preeminence of international law
precludes recourse to justifications which are valid in the national legal

---

* Translated by John St. Clair; J.D., (Chicago).
[1] Regarding the development of an objective international criminal since Nuremberg,
see also O. TRIFFTERER, DOGMATISCHE UNTERSUCHUNGEN ZUR ENTWICKLUNG DES MATERI-
ELLEN VÖLKERSTRAFRECHTS SEIT NÜRNBERG (1966).

systems insofar as such justifications do not agree with international law. Accordingly, the criminal responsibility for an act which is punishable according to ICL be avoided only if the ICL itself contains exculpatory factual situations precluding punishment.[2]

Despite the history of interest in this issue, one cannot view it as solved within the context of international law. This conclusion is dictated not only by the fact that the question cannot be limited to a determination of the extent to which the defense of superior orders is relevant but also by the fact that it is first necessary to demonstrate that international law contains rules applicable to this issue. It is only when the existence of such international law rules can be proven that it will be possible to limit the inquiry more narrowly to a determination of the content of such applicable rules. The present state of the discussion makes an interim assessment fitting; however, it is only after a sober examination of that which has already been accomplished that one is able to separate the concrete legal realities from political value judgments and illusory wish conceptions. Such an examination simultaneously clears the way for new approaches to a solution of the problem.

The concept of "acts in obedience to orders" in this connection concerns only the illegal order,[3] and the judgment of the illegality of an order is based exclusively on the criteria of international law. The consideration of the legal order need not be taken up here.[4] In making this judgment the lawfulness *vel non* of the order according to national law is not considered.[5] An order is illegal according to international law if it violates an international law principle (*i.e.* international law resulting from treaties, custom, or widely accepted general legal principles).

Hence, valid solutions to the question regarding the existence and content of an international legal norm governing the superior orders defense can be developed only by referring to well-established sources for the recognition of international law. Therefore, one must consider the international legal rules found in international treaties, those developed by international legal customs, and those derived from the general principles

---

[2] *Compare* the text *with* the numerous monographs and treatises reviewed in this periodical (collected by A. de Ripainsel in the review of Dinstein, *The Defense of Obedience to Superior Orders in International Law,* in VII (1) Revue de Droit Pénal militaire et de Droit de la Guerre 143 (1967).

[3] The issue of the relationship between the illegality of an order and its legally binding force is discussed by H.-H. Jescheck, *Befehl und Gehorsam in der Bundeswehr,* in Bundeswehr und Recht 63, 77 (1965) (with extensive citations).

[4] *Compare the text with* Dinstein, The Defense of 'Obedience to Superior Orders' in International Law 69 (1965) [hereinafter cited as Y. Dinstein].

[5] P. Fuhrmann, Der höhere Befehl als Rechtfertigung im Völkerrecht 19 (1963) [hereinafter cited as P. Fuhrmann].

of law recognized by the majority of civilized nations.[6] The organizational structure of this inquiry follows this tripartite division of international law sources.

3.2. International Treaties

Although the superior orders defense did in fact play a role in the preparation, following World War I, of the Paris Peace Treaties, which included criminal sentences against nationals of the Central Powers for war crimes,[7] it was not mentioned in the treaties themselves.[8] Further, special commission,[9] established for the purpose of clarifying the political and legal questions of the proceedings against the leaders of the Central Powers, discussed the problem of the superior orders defense without attaining agreement on the issue[10] beyond a statement that a superior's declared guilt for an offense did not absolve other civilian or military authorities of responsibility for the same offense. The special commission left it to the court in the individual case to determine whether or not the defense of superior orders was sufficient to release the defendant from criminal responsibility for the act.[11]

The so-called Washington Agreement of February 6, 1922,[12] which concerned the use of U-boats and poisonous gases in war and was signed by the United States, Great Britain, France, Japan, and Italy should be mentioned as another attempt at codifying this area of international law. Although limited to the use of U-boats in war, article 3 of this treaty[13] contained a regulation covering the question of the criminal culpability of a subordinate whose acts are committed pursuant to a superior's order. According to this article, every violation of the rules of the agreement was punishable as piracy regardless of whether or not it was committed pursuant to the orders of a superior. However, this agreement was not ratified by the signing powers and, thus, never came in force.[14]

[6] *Compare* the text *with* G. Dahm, I VÖLKERRECHT 37 (1962); & W. Wengler, I VÖLKERRECHT 171 (1964).

[7] *Cf.* arts. 227 *et. seq.* of the Versailles Treaty (*Supra* Appendix I to Section 1. of this chapter).

[8] *Cf.* Y. Dinstein, supra note 4, at 96. Concerning the criminal provisions of the Versailles Treaty, *cf.* H.-H. JESCHECK, DIE VERANTWORTLICHKEIT DER STAATSORGANE NACH VÖLKERSTRAFRECHT 59 (1952) [hereinafter cited as H.-H. Jescheck].

[9] Regarding the work and report of the Commission in detail, *see also* H.-H. Jescheck, at 51; Y. Dinstein, *supra* note 4, at 93.

[10] *Compare* the text *with* the different possible interpretations given in Y. Dinstein, at 94.

[11] *Cf.* P. Fuhrmann, at 36; Y. Dinstein, at 94. The report of the Commission is printed in 14 A.J.I.L. 95, 117 (1920).

[12] Printed in 16 A.J.I.L. 58 (Supp., 1922); *cf.* H.-H. Jescheck, at 92; Y. Dinstein, at 97; P. Fuhrmann, at 48.

[13] The text is printed in H.-H. Jescheck, at 92.

[14] *Cf.* Y. Dinstein, at 98; P. Fuhrmann, at 49.

The Four-Power Agreement of August 8, 1945, among the United States, the USSR, France, and Great Britain, establishing the International Military Tribunal (IMT)[15] and regulating the prosecution and punishment of the principal war criminals, can also be viewed as an attempt to solve the problem of the superior orders defense through contractual international law. It was this Agreement which formed the legal basis for the Nuremberg Trials of war criminals. Regarding the defense of having acted pursuant to a superior's orders, article 8 of the IMT Statute provided: "The fact that the defendant acted pursuant to order of his government or of a superior shall not free him from responsibility, but may be considered in mitigation of punishment if the Tribunal determines that justice so requires." However, one cannot attribute to the Four-Power Agreement and the IMT Statute the general effect of a contractual source of international law precisely because this treaty was drafted with reference to the sentencing of a particularly defined group of persons in regard to specific acts which had already been committed.[16] As a result of the inter pares effect of treaties, this Four-Power Agreement legally could have bound only the signing parties[17] who, in this instance, wished not to be bound by the agreement in regard to this question.[18] The Ratification of the Nuremberg Principles by the United Nations General Assembly on December 11, 1946, similarly provides no basis for a different assessment of the Agreement.[19] This Ratification can be excluded *ab initio* as a source of international contractual law. As a result of the lack of international legal norm-establishing competence, such resolutions of the General Assembly are basically mere recommendations and certainly are not sources of international law in the sense of article 38 of the statute of the ICI.[20]

---

[15] *Compare* the text *with* the detailed exposition in H.-H. Jescheck, at 140; Y. Dinstein, at 104.

[16] *Cf.* H.-G. Mähler, Die völkerrechtliche Bedeutung des Kriegs- und Gewaltverbots durch Kellog-Pakt und UN-Satzung insbesondere im Hinblick auf das Neutralitätsrecht, die Bestrafung von Staatsorganen wegen "Verbrechen gegen den Frieden" und das Recht des Gebietserwerbs 86 (1965) [hereinafter cited as H.-G. Mähler].

[17] *Cf.* H.-H. Jescheck, at 151.

[18] H.-H. Jescheck, at 154. Regarding the legal nature of the IMT Statute, *see id* at 177.

[19] H.-H. Jescheck, *Gegenwärtiger Stand und Zukunftsaussichten der Entwicklungsarbeiten auf dem Gebiet Völkerstrafrechts*, in Erinnerungsausgabe für Max Grünhut (1893–1964), at 47, 52 n.37 [hereafter cited as H.-H. Jescheck, *Gegenwärtiger Stand*), gives an extensive collection of the controversial views regarding the meaning of the Resolution along with the source citations. *See also* H.-G. Mähler, *supra* note 16, at 87; O. Triffterer, *supra* note 1, at 18.

[20] A. Verdross, *supra* note 6, at 349 [hereinafter cited as A. Verdross]; P. Fuhrmann, at 103. In regard to the broad question of whether the General Assembly of the U.N. can develop further international law in general, *cf.* O. Asamoah, The Legal Significance of the Declarations of the General Assembly of the United Nations (1966); O. Triffterer, *supra* note 1, at 18; A. Verdross, *Kann die Generalversammlung der Vereinten Nationen das Völkerrecht weiterbilden?* 1966 ZaöRV 690.

Similarly, various attempts of the International Law Commission (ILC) to codify the Nuremberg principles have not led to the adoption of an international law agreement.[21] As a result of a resolution of the United Nations General Assembly of November 27, 1947, the ILC in 1950 proposed a draft that contained seven basic principles which allegedly were recognized by the judgments of and the statute establishing the IMT. Concerning the problem of culpability resulting from actions taken pursuant to superior orders, this draft stated: "The fact that a person acted pursuant to order of his government or of a superior does not relieve him from responsibility under international law, provided a moral choice was in fact possible to him."[21a] The formulation of this principle remained disputed, however, and the General Assembly has yet to make a binding decision among the conflicting phrasings.[22]

In the process of later work on the draft of a Code of Offenses Against the Peace and Security of Mankind,[23] the ILC again was concerned with this problem. As originally proposed, article 4 of this draft corresponded literally to the formulation in the Nuremberg basic principles. To counter criticism directed at the lack of clarity in the concept of "a moral choice," article 4 of the draft of 1954 was worded to state:

> The fact that a person charged with an offense defined in this code acted pursuant to an order of his government or of a superior does not relieve him of responsibility in international law if, in the circumstances at the time, it was possible for him not to comply with that order.[24]

The work of the ILC has not advanced beyond the drafting stage, and none of the *projets* has yet been concretely taken up by the General Assembly. Because the ILC is purely an advisory commission lacking competence to establish binding legal norms, their draft proposals do not constitute a source for authoritative international law principles. Moreover, a concurrence of the General Assembly to such a draft would not alter this situation; authoritative international law could be created only by a ratified treaty or multilateral convention. The prospects for such an agreement in the near future appear slim.[25]

[21] Regarding the work of the ILC in detail, *see* H.-H. Jescheck, *Die Entwicklung des Völkerstrafrechts nach Nürnberg,* in 1957 SCHWEIZERISCHE ZEITSCHRIFT FÜR STRAFRECHT (REVUE PÉNALE SUISSE) 217, 222 [hereinafter cited as H.-H. Jescheck, *Entwicklung*]; Y Dinstein, at 226; P. Fuhrmann, at 106; O. Triffterer *supra* note 1, at 16, 75.

[21a] Printed in Y. Dinstein, at 237.

[22] For a legal evaluation of the principle, *see* H.-H. Jescheck, at 155; O. Triffterer, *supra* note 1, at 76.

[23] *See* H.-H. Jescheck, at 155; H.-H. Jescheck, *Entwicklung,* at 222, 242; H.-H. Jescheck, *Gegenwärtiger Stand,* at 48, 54; Y. Dinstein, at 241; P. Fuhrmann, at 107; O. Triffterer, *supra* 1, at 16, 76.

[24] Printed in Y. Dinstein, at 251.

[25] *Compare* the text *with* the "outlook" in H.-H. Jescheck, *Gegenwärtiger Stand,* at 58. For a legal evaluation of the work of the ILC other than by Jescheck, *cf.* P. Fuhrmann, at 110; O. Triffterer, *supra* note 1, at 16, 76, 222.

Other attempts to deal with this issue have been equally futile. The Genocide Convention of 1948[26] did not include a provision governing the defense of superior orders. A corresponding proposal which would have added to article 5 of the Agreement a second paragraph stating that "command of law or superior orders shall not justify genocide" was rejected.[27]

Similarly, the efforts of the four Geneva Conferences of 1948–1949[28] to draft regulations concerning criminal penalties, which also were to include the issue of acts done pursuant to superior orders, came to naught.[29] An expert committee had formulated the following proposal:

> Le fait pour l'inculpe, d'avoir agi sur l'ordre d'un supérieur ou en exécution d'une, prescription officielle, ne constitue pas une excuse légale si l'accusation établit que, d'après les circonstances, l'inculpé pouvait raisonnablement se rendre compte qu'il participait à une violation de la présente Convention. Toutefois, si les circonstances le justifient, la peine pourra être atténuée ou exclue à son égard . . .[30]

This proposed addition to the draft, however, met strong opposition, and the rules concerning the culpability of a subordinate acting pursuant to the orders of a superior were not included in the final version of the four Geneva Conventions.

The proposed military law of the European Defense Community (EDC) constitutes a recent interesting attempt to codify the international law rules governing the problem of acts performed pursuant to orders.[31] In the course of the preparatory work on a common EDC military penal code, a regulation was proposed according to which the fact that the act was done under orders would be a defense to criminal culpability only if the command was lawful and issued by an "autorité qualifiée." An act performed pursuant to an illegal order would not be considered as a defense to criminal culpability. As a consequence of the collapse of the EDC, the plan for a common military criminal code never became a reality.

In spite of numerous attempts to codify the international law of the superior orders defense, one must reach the following conclusion: *There do not exist international law principles derived from treaties which govern the issue of the defense of having acted pursuant to a superior's orders.*

---

[26] Konvention vom 9. Dezember 1948 über die Verhütung und Bestrafung des Völkermordes, BGB1. 1954 II S. 729.

[27] *See* Y. Dinstein, at 217, for a detailed account of the history of the origin of the formulation.

[28] Genfer Abkommen zum Schutz der Kriegsopfer, BGB1 1954 II S. 783, 813, 838, 917.

[29] *Compare* the text *with* Y. Dinstein, at 223; P. Fuhrmann, at 116; and J.-P. Maunoir, LA RÉPRESSION DES CRIEMS DE GUERRE DEVANT LES TRIBUNAUX FRANCAIS ET ALLIES 233 (1956) [hereinafter cited as J.-P. Maunoir].

[30] Printed in P. Fuhrmann, at 116.

[31] *Cf.* J.-P. Maunoir, *supra* note 29, at 236.

3.3. Customary International Law

According to the criteria of international customary law, a determination that definite rules have been uniformly and continuously observed by the concerned parties under the conviction that such behavior was legally required by these rules is required for the proof of the existence of binding customary rules of law. The primary sources for the recognition of international customary law are generally international legal doctrine and the judgments of international law courts.

Given these obviously wide parameters, it should be noted at the outset that the attempt in this article to present a survey of the expressed opinions in the international legal doctrine and jurisprudence concerning the defense of having acted according to superior orders makes no claim to completeness; further, instead it is limited to the writings of selected authors. Because the question relevant here is the presently valid international law, one can forego an extended analysis of historical development.[32]

The examination of the relevant doctrinal literature, in the main, finds no definitive solution to the superior orders defense. Each of the major commentators takes a different position.

For example, Guggenheim states that fundamentally an assertion of having acted pursuant to orders in no way eliminates the personal criminal culpability of the subordinate individual.[33] However, whether or not there existed a possibility for choice on the part of the individual is to be determined for the purpose of exemption from or mitigation of the sentence. Guggenheim continues by noting that it also must be determined whether the subordinate could believe "in good faith" that the criminal act committed by him followed as retaliation for an unlawful act of the party.[34]

Verdross takes a somewhat different approach. Although he presumably represents the basic viewpoint present in article 8 of the IMT Statute, Verdross concedes that there could exist situations in which opposition by the subordinate to the command of a superior is objectively impossible. The decisive question for him, therefore, is not whether a command existed but rather "whether a moral choice was in fact possible."[35]

Dahm seems to adopt the position that the soldier does not personally incriminate himself when acting pursuant to a superior's command unless he either knows or should be able to recognize the illegality of the order according to international law. Thus, the limited answerability Dahm gives to the subordinate would be circumscribed by the possibility of recognizing the *injustice* of the order. He does point out, however, that many laws are

[32] *Cf.* P. Fuhrmann, at 24, 52.
[33] P. Guggenheim, II LEHRBUCH DES VÖLKERRECHTS 551 (1951).
[34] *Id.* at 551–552 n.118.
[35] A. Verdross, at 219.

more lenient in restricting culpability to only those cases in which the order is obviously illegal.[36] Moreover, in Dahm's analysis the further question of whether the subordinate was in a situation in which he could have avoided obeying the order must be answered. In other words, one must know whether or not a condition of subjection existed in which no action except obedience to the order was possible (situation of necessity).[37]

According to the view of Berber,[38] the primary liability for war offenses committed pursuant to orders should not be placed on the individual army member but instead should fall on his commanding superior and the enemy state. However, if it were to appear obvious to a subordinate of reasonable intelligence that the commanding superior had suddenly become crazed or that the ordered action was criminal, the order could not be obeyed without criminal culpability.

Regarding the superior orders defense from the viewpoint of ICL, Jescheck writes:

> An illegal command cannot justify the deeds—apart from trivialities—of the subordinate but is to be considered only as excluding his guilt. The subordinate acts not only illegally, but also—except in situations of necessity—criminally if he recognized positively the illegality of the order . . . . The illegal command does have the effect of an excuse if the subordinate might reasonably rely on its legality. Such reliance is not to be protected if the order was obviously illegal.[39] Decisive for his criminal responsibility is thus, first, whether or not the subordinate knew the felonious nature of the command, or, secondly, whether the criminal nature of the order was so obvious that the subordinate's ignorance of its unlawfulness renders him criminally responsible. In the case of such culpable ignorance, however, one should consider as a cause for mitigation of the sentence the fact that the subordinate was bound by a relationship of obedience.[40]

Kelsen, who considers the superior orders defense as an aspect of the act-of-state doctrine,[41] explains his position thusly:

> From the point of view of general international law, the difference between an act performed at superior command and an act performed on the own initiative of the acting individual is irrelevant. Only the question whether the act is or is not an act of state is decisive. An act performed at superior command may or may not be an act of state. It is not an act of state, if the command is not an act of state. The responsibility for acts performed at superior command is a specific problem of criminal law, not of international law.[42]

[36] G. Dahm, III VÖLKERRECHT 311 (1961)
[37] *Id.* at 312.
[38] F. Berber, II LEHRBUCH DES VÖLKERRECHTS 246 (1962)
[39] H.-H. Jescheck, at 261.
[40] H.-H. Jescheck, II WÖRTERBUCH DES VÖLKERRECHTS 375.
[41] *Contra,* Y. Dinstein, at 57.
[42] H. KELSEN, PRINCIPLES OF INTERNATIONAL LAW 136 (1952).

Lauterpacht, the editor of Oppenheim's treatise *International Law,* substituted in the sixth edition a viewpoint which differed from the earlier position of the work:[43]

> The fact that a rule of warfare has been violated in pursuance of an order of the belligerent government or of an individual belligerent commander does not deprive the act in question of its character as a war crime: neither does it, in principle, confer upon the perpetrator immunity from punishment by the injured state. . . . Members of the armed forces are bound to obey lawful orders only and. . . . cannot therefore escape liability if, in obedience to a command, they commit acts which both violate unchallenged rules of warfare and outrage the general sentiment of humanity.[44]

This survey of extracts from the relevant doctrinal literature justifies the observation that in the scientific literature of international law a uniform view of the solution to the superior orders defense issue simply does not exist. The only positive statement now possible is an expression of the opinion that the unconditional unaccountability of the subordinate is no longer followed. Likewise, the principle of unqualified criminal responsibility of the actor in such situations is predominantly rejected in the modern doctrine. In the wide area lying between these extremes, there is basically very little agreement. Even the more narrow issue of using reliance on the fact of having acted pursuant to order as a defense receives no consistent answer in the current doctrinal literature.[44a]

In attempting to use international court opinions as recognition sources for international customary law, referral is often made, for lack of other examples, to the decisions in proceedings against war criminals following both world wars. The use of these opinions is invalid according to the now prevailing opinion because none of these proceedings involved a genuine international law tribunal.

With regard to the German *Reichsgericht*—which after World War I and in opposition to the concept of article 228 *et. seq.* of the Versailles Treaty was declared competent in this area on the basis of the contrary view of the *Reichsregierung*—one need go no farther to demonstrate its purely national character. The same can be said for the German courts in which the war crimes proceedings after World War II were held.

---

[43] The consistently unchanged view of Oppenheim in the first five editions had stated:

> Violations of rules regarding warfare are war crimes only when committed without an order of the belligerent government concerned. If members of the armed forces commit violations by order of their government, they are not war criminals and may not be punished by the enemy; the latter may, however, resort to reprisals.

[44] Oppenheim-Lauterpacht, II INTERNATIONAL LAW § 253 (8th ed. 1955); *accord,* Lauterpacht, *The Law of Nations and Punishment of War Crimes,* 1944 BRIT. Y.B. INT'L L. 58, 69.

[44a] *Accord,* P. Fuhrmann, at 126; G. Stratenwerth, *Verantwortung und Ghoersam* 43 (1958).

In spite of the misleading characterization as an international court, the IMT in Nuremberg was purely a court of the Occupying Powers, primarily because there was absent the prerequisite agreement by the parties involved to establish a court of international law.[45] As a military court of the four Occupying Powers, the IMT exercised national rather than international jurisdiction. Therefore, the decisions of this court without more cannot be considered direct sources for the recognition of international law.

For the same reasons, one can exclude as a potential source of international law the judgments in the twelve subsequent proceedings before American military tribunals in Nuremberg. The twelve U.S. judges in the Nuremberg proceedings likewise were purely *national judges*.[45a] Similarly, the proceedings, after termination of the war, against German nationals or collaborators of their own nationality in numerous other countries (*e.g.,* Great Britain, France, Belgium, the Netherlands, Denmark, Norway, Austria, Poland, and Czechoslovakia) occurred exclusively before national courts.[46]

The circumstance that all of the above instances involved the exercise of national jurisdiction by national courts certainly does not totally exclude the usefulness of the opinions as a means for discovering applicable international law principles. Although such decisions of national courts themselves are in no way sources of international law, they, like the judgments of international courts, can provide data about the contemporary position of international law and can contribute to the proof of customary international law. The value of such decisions as a means for the determination of customary international law is dependent upon whether such courts apply international law in addition to the applicable national law in their decisions and upon the extent of any such application.

Based upon this analysis, the statements of the German courts in the war crimes proceedings regarding the culpability of acts performed pursuant to the command of a superior contribute little to the solution of the international law question. In the proceedings following World War I concerning the sinking of the two military hospital ships "Dover Castle" and "Llandovery Castle,"[47] in which the superior orders defense played a role, the German *Reichsgericht* applied exclusively German substantive and procedural law.[48]

---

[45] F. Berber, I *Lehrbuch des Völkerrechts* 147 (1962); H.-H. Jescheck, at 150; P. Fuhrmann, at 85; O. Triffterer, *supra* note 1, at 40; G. Hoffmann, *Strafrechtliche Verantwortung im Völkerrecht* 161 (1962).

[45a] H.-H. Jescheck, at 156; Dinstein, at 163.

[46] With regard to the war crimes trials outside Germany, *see* P. Fuhrmann, at 92; J.-P. Maunoir, *supra* note 29, at 233.

[47] *Cf. Anhang zu den Verhandlungen des Reichstags*, Wahlperiode 1920, Bd. 368, Aktienstück Nr. 2584, 2577 (The official Whitepaper concerning the trials before the *Reichsgericht*).

[48] Y. Dinstein, at 13, 19; P. Fuhrmann, at 37; H.-H. Jescheck, at 64.

Further, insofar as German courts have conducted war crime proceedings after World War II on the basis of control council order 10,[49] they have applied[50] the principle of article II 4(b) of this statute, which literally corresponds to the rule of article 8 of the IMT Statute.[51] There is now extensive agreement concerning the legal nature of the IMT statute. The oft-found earlier claim, advanced by the IMT itself, that the London Agreement with the IMT statute only reflected the existent international law position on the superior orders defense is not tenable. A brief discussion on this point will clarify the matter.

In order for the assertion that the IMT Statute reflected the state of customary international law of that time to be persuasive, it would be necessary to prove, among other premises, both that exclusion of the superior orders defense as an exculpation in favor of the view that it could operate only to mitigate the sentence within the court's discretion and that the identical treatment of obviously illegal and apparently lawful orders in fact corresponded to the majority legal opinion. Objective support for such premises cannot be shown. The rule of the IMT Statute was not consistent with the position of the national law in the United States,[52] nor was it supported by the international doctrinal literature of the pre-World War II period.[53] The absolute exclusion of the superior orders defense as a ground of exculpation represents an exception to the general legal position.[54] The international law significance of the IMT Statute does not extend beyond the obligations of the signatories to try the principal war criminals according to the criminal offenses defined in the statute. These described criminal offenses, including the rule regarding the superior orders defense, have not become general international law by virtue of inclusion in the IMT Statute but instead represent the particular law of the occupying forces in relation to Germany.[55]

Through the reception of the IMT Statute into Control Council Order 10 of December 10, 1945, the particular substantive rule of the criminal law of the occupying forces was merely included in the general code of occupational law.[56] It was this Control Council Order 10, which was the legal basis for the twelve subsequent proceedings before American military

---

[49] *Cf.* Amtsblatt des KR in Deutschland Nr. 3 vom 31. Januar 1946, S. 52.

[50] *Cf.* Die Entscheidungen OGHBrZ I, 49 (51), 91 (94), 198 (200), 229 (232), 310 (312); II, 269 (277); OLG Kiel DRZ 1946–47 S. 158; Bay. ObLG NJW 49, S. 758.

[51] "The fact that one acted pursuant to one's regime or one's superior does not free him from the responsibility for the crime; it can, however, be considered as cause for mitigation of punishment."

[52] *See* text, *infra*, corresponding to note 71. *Cf.* H.-H. Jescheck, at 262; P. Fuhrmann at 56.

[53] P. Fuhrmann, at 51; G. Hoffmann, *supra* note 45, at 130.

[54] H.-H. Jescheck, at 262.

[55] *Id.*

[56] *Id.* at 178.

tribunals in Nuremberg. The superior orders defense rule of this law in article II (4) (b) was exactly identical with the provision of article 8 in the IMT Statute.

The legal nature of the IMT Statute was not altered by either the addition of other nations to the London Agreement or the resolution of agreement by the U.N. General Assembly on December 11, 1946. Further, the fact that only nineteen nations have signed the London Agreement prevents one from speaking of the consensus of the "predominate majority" of civilized nations which is a prerequisite for the creation of customary international law.[57] The assumption that the London Agreement at least acquired the status of general customary international law by virtue of the U.N. resolution of agreement is fundamentally opposed to the fact that a binding declaration from the national representatives as agents of these states "to submit themselves to these norms and to make them the applicable rules of conduct in all future similarly situated cases" neither could be given nor was in any degree intended to be the result of the resolution of agreement to the principles of the London Agreement.[58] The simultaneously drafted resolution to have the principles of decision which were developed in the Nuremberg proceedings codified by a committee and the subsequent fate of this codification attempt[59] demonstrates the aptness of assessing these events as mere political sanctions of the Nuremberg proceedings.[60]

The other national courts which conducted trials of war criminals applied exclusively their own domestic rules of law almost without exception.[61] These decisions, therefore, cannot elucidate an international law solution to the question of the superior orders defense. As one example, the trials of Germans before the English judges were based on a "Royal warrant, regulations for the trial of war criminals" of June 14, 1945. Because this warrant contained no specific provision regarding the problem of the superior orders defense, the usual rules of English law were applied.[62] The judgments in the other foreign proceedings likewise were based on the respective domestic substantive and procedural laws which, however, beforehand were made harsher by the enactment of specific statutes. For example, the normal rules applying to criminal acts performed

---

[57] *Id.* at 153.

[58] Id. O. Triffterer, *supra* note 1, at 18.

[59] *See* text, *supra* corresponding to notes 15–20.

[60] For the present state of the opinions, *see* H.-H. Jescheck, *Gegenwärtiger Stand*, at 52 n.37. *See also* P. Fuhrmann, at 102; G. DAHM, ZUR PROBLEMATIK DES VÖLKERSTRAFRECHTS 66 (1956); O. Triffterer, *supra* note 1, at 1, 15.

[61] Y. Dinstein, at 13, 19.

[62] P. Fuhrmann, at 92.

pursuant to a command, insofar as they provided a defense to the criminal charge, were repealed in whole or part.[63]

These modifications of the domestic law rules were primarily for the purpose of incorporating the rule of article 8 of the IMT Statute into the national law. Nonetheless, this incorporation of article 8 into the domestic laws of such nations as well as the application of the rule therein in the war criminals proceedings cannot be asserted to be the recognition of it as a customary international law principle. Disregarding the fact that no later agreement of these states concerning either the principles in the London Agreement or those later drafted by the IMT could be achieved,[64] these modifications of domestic law through the specific statutes were meant to apply only for a limited time and only to a narrow class of individuals. The generally valid domestic law rules regarding the superior order defense were not changed by these provisional modifications. This circumstance alone prevents one from considering these modifications as a change of the prevailing legal opinion. Moreover, the individual rules which were adopted were not themselves in accord.[65]

Although national determinations of the applicable legal rule have been excluded as direct sources for the recognition of international law, one cannot exclude in this connection the special development of the handbook rules of military law which are valid for the British and American armed forces.[66] Even though these lack the force of national law in the two legal systems, they can be considered the authoritative opinions of the war departments of the two countries regarding the authoritative international rules of law. In the British *Manual of Military Law* of 1914, edited by Oppenheim and Edwards, the superior orders defense was governed by the rule stated in article 414:

> It is important, however, to note that members of the armed forces who commit such violations of the recognized rules of warfare as are ordered by their government, or by their commander, are not war criminals and cannot, therefore, be punished by the enemy. He may punish the officials or commanders responsible for such orders if they fall into his hands, but otherwise he may only resort to the other means of obtaining redress. . . .

Even broader was the contemporaneous statement of the *United States Basic Field Manual* "Rules of Land Warfare":

> Individuals of the armed forces will not be punished for these offenses in case

[63] The individual laws and changes in the existing statutes, insofar as they affect the superior orders defense, are collected in G. Lummert, *Die Strafverfahren gegen Deutsch, in Ausland wegen "Kriegsverbrechen"* 89 (1949); P. Fuhrmann, at 92.

[64] *See* text *supra* corresponding to note 21.

[65] *Cf.* P. Fuhrmann, at 100; G. Stratenwerth, *supra* note 44a, at 43.

[66] *Compare* text *with* H.-H. Jescheck, at 299. *See also* Y. Dinstein, at 46; M. GREENSPAN, THE MODERN LAW OF LAND WARFARE 490 (1959).

they are committed under the orders or sanction of their government or commanders. The commanders ordering the commission of such acts, or under whose authority they are committed by their troops, may be punished by the belligerent into whose hands they may fall.

Both rules were redrafted during the years 1943–1944, rejecting their former position on this question. The English *Manual of Military Law* stated in the amended article 34:

> The fact that a rule of warfare has been violated in pursuance of an order of the belligerent government or of an individual belligerent commander does not deprive the act in question of its character as a war crime; neither does it, in principle, confer upon the perpetrator immunity from punishment by the injured belligerent. Undoubtedly, a court confronted with the plea of superior orders adduced in justification of a war crime is bound to take into consideration the fact that obedience to military orders, not obviously unlawful, is the duty of every member of the armed forces and that the latter cannot, in conditions of war discipline, be expected to weigh scrupulously the legal merits of the order received. The question, however, is governed by the major principle that members of the armed forces are bound to obey lawful orders only and that they cannot therefore escape liability if, in obedience to a command, they commit acts which both violate unchallenged rules or warfare and outrage the general sentiment of humanity.[67]
>
> In November 1944, the U.S. Rules of Land Warfare were changed. The text of article 345(1) became the following: Individuals and organizations who violate the accepted laws and customs of war may be punished therefor. However, the fact that the acts complained of were done pursuant to order of a superior or government sanction may be taken into consideration in determining culpability, either by way of defense or in mitigation of punishment.[68] The person giving such orders may also be punished.

It is difficult to assess exactly the effect on these basic changes in the provisions of the military handbooks of the preparations for the planned trials of war criminals following World War II. The inference is repeatedly drawn from the temporal connection that the modifications represent less the expression of a new prevailing legal opinion than a fundamentally political phenomenon.[69] Equally striking could be judged the further reformulations in these military manuals again in the years 1956 and 1958 respectively. Although section 627 of the *Manual of Military Law*, published by the British War Office in 1958, in principle retained the viewpoint of the 1944 edition, and thus followed the rule of article 8 in the IMT statute, the 1956 edition of the *United States Basic Field Manual*, "The Law of Land Warfare," did not follow the principle of the London Statute, but instead section 409 ("Defense of Superior Orders") was changed to conform to the majority opinion of the American common

[67] Printed in M. Greenspan, *supra* note 66, at 491.

[68] *Id.* at 490.

[69] *Cf.* P. Fuhrmann, at 76; H.-H. Jescheck, at 260; A. V. Knieriem, Nürnberg 265 (1953).

law.[70] This circumstance—in combination with the fact that the extreme positions of the manuals from 1914 regarding the absolute irresponsibility of the ordered subordinate originated in the acceptance of Oppenheim's doctrine and were not in accord with the domestic law positions up to that time—makes it appropriate to question the conclusions drawn from the repeatedly changed manuals.

Principles of customary international law which would allow a judgment to be made with regard to this issue based on a common doctrinal opinion thus cannot be derived from the legislation providing for trials of war crimes nor from the actual trials based on such legislation. In addition, the legal rules governing the superior orders defense developed in the military manuals cannot serve as the foundation for customary international law. Other indications of the practice of nations are not evident.

3.4. General Principles of International Law

The only remaining sources of international law which might be able to provide legal rules governing the superior orders defense are the general legal doctrines which, in the sense of article 38(I)(c) of the U.N. Charter, are followed by the great majority of civilized nations. There exist such principles which are more or less similarly recognized by the legal systems of all nations and which thus can be characterized as the supranational common law of civilized states.[71] In recognizing such principles as sources of international law, reference is made to the national laws of the members of the international community. However, it is clear that by this effect of article 38 international law does not incorporate these basic rules of national laws as such but rather derives from them general legal doctrines.[72] A prerequisite for the determination of such general principles which might serve as a source of international law is their recognition by the principal legal systems of the world.

A comparative law analysis of the domestic legal positions in the various countries of necessity would far exceed the boundaries of this investigation. To this extent a reference to the existing summaries must suffice.[73] If the examples from foreign legal systems considered in these summaries also can make no claim to being complete or representative in the sense of a supranational common law, a supplementary discussion at this point indeed seems superfluous. The more or less limited selections from the national legal systems,[74] which include the like or comparable legal insti-

---

[70] *Cf.* P. Fuhrmann, at 121.

[71] *Cf.* G. Dahm, I VÖLKERRECHT 36 (1958).

[72] *Cf.* F. Berber, *supra* note 45, at 69.

[73] *Cf.* P. Fuhrmann, at 127; H.-H. Jescheck, at 255; G. Stratenwerth, *supra* note 44a, at 27.

[74] The particular statutes mentioned on p. 117 *supra* should not be considered because they are purely exceptional rules.

tutions of the vast majority of nations, show that a general, consistent agreement does not exist. Inclusion of other legal systems would presumably further elucidate the differences among the legal rules. The only result one may infer from the review of domestic legal provisions governing this issue is that, on the one hand, none of the legal orders recognized the unconditional nonresponsibility of the subordinate performing the command of a superior while, on the other hand, none of the national systems completely ignored as a defense the fact that the deed was done pursuant to an order.

3.5. Conclusion

If, at this point, one may be allowed the statement that the defense of having acted pursuant to an order is definitely relevant in international law, the sources do not establish clearly to what extent it is to be weighed. Similar to the majority of legal systems, international law seems to be moving toward an intermediate solution lying between the extremes of unconditional freedom from responsibility of the subordinate and the total irrelevance of the defense of superior orders. In result, both international law and the national legal systems seem to agree with the predominant opinion in the doctrinal literature that the decisive criterion for the culpability or blamelessness of the subordinate is whether or not he could rely on the legality of the command. From this principle of good faith reliance,[75] it follows "that criminal punishment of the subordinate comes into consideration only if he had in reality recognized the criminal nature of the order, or if the fact of its criminality was obvious." Notwithstanding the presumed lawfulness of the acts of statutorily competent authorities, the foundation for this reliance disappears if the subordinate either knew the criminal nature of the order or if its criminality was so obvious that his failure to recognize it renders him culpable.[76] It is in this sense that Greenspan summarizes his research with the conclusion:

> In summary, the present legal position regarding the plea of superior orders apears to be as follows: Superior orders do not offer a defense where they are obviously illegal; or where the person executing the orders knows they are criminal. . . .[77]

If, as a result of the impression of universal uncertainty in an admittedly small but certainly important area of international law, this conclusion appears discouraging, it does permit recognition of the beginnings of a satisfactory solution to the problem of the superior orders defense. The difficulties which stand in the way of the materialization of such a solu-

[75] *Cf.* G. Stratenwerth, *supra* note 44a, at 42.
[76] *Cf.* H.-H. Jescheck, *supra* note 40, at 375.
[77] M. Greenspan, *supra* note 66, at 495.

tion—as is the case with the development of international criminal law in general[78]—may be more political than doctrinal in nature. One can only hope that future relaxation of political tensions will make possible a continuation of the international law work in this area which has begun within the United Nations.

[78] *Compare* the text *with* the outlook of O. Triffterer, *supra* note 1, at 222.

CHAPTER XIII

THE INTERNATIONAL CRIMINAL COURT:

THE CONCEPT OF INTERNATIONAL CRIMINAL JURISDICTION—DEFINITION AND LIMITATION OF THE SUBJECT

J.Y. DAUTRICOURT

The following two questions, which seem basic, will be discussed in this section: (1) Why could or should permanent international criminal jurisdiction be created? (2) On what conditions could a permanent international criminal jurisdiction become a useful international institution and an effective guarantee for peace?

Thus, we consider that the following subjects do not pertain to our topic: (1) the Historical Survey of the Question of International Criminal Jurisdiction which was already made in the Memorandum of the Secretary-General of the United Nations,[1] (2) the discussion and the criticism of the advice of the International Law Commission, in its second session 1950, where it decided that the International Criminal Jurisdiction was both "desirable" and "possible,"[2] (3) the discussion of the reports of the 1951 and 1953 Committees on International Criminal Jurisdiction which was the topic of Fannie J. Klein and Daniel Wilkes,[3] and (4) the discussion of the organization of an international criminal court— though, as representative of our country, Belgium, in the 1953 Committee, we made, concerning that point, some relevant suggestions.

We believe that the case for and against the creation of international criminal jurisdiction is not yet sufficiently ripe to give the problems of organization their due consideration and thus we will confine ourselves to the two above-stated questions.

---

[1] U.N. Doc. A/CN.4/7/Rev.1, May 27, 1949.

[2] 5 U.N. GAOR, Supp. 12, at 18, U.N. Doc. A/1316 (1950).

[3] Klein & Wilkes, *United Nations Draft Statute for an International Criminal Court; an American Evaluation,* in Mueller and Wise (eds.) INTERNATIONAL CRIMINAL LAW, 513, 526 (1965) [Hereinafter cited as MUELLER & WISE].

Section 1. A CONTEMPORARY GENERAL VIEW ON CRIME AND CRIMINALS

1.1. A Division as to the Public Order that Crimes and Criminals Offend

On the basis of the nature of the public order that crimes and criminals offend, they may now be divided into *three classes:*

1. The crimes and criminals *against the domestic or municipal public order.* These crimes and criminals are tried and punished in pursuance of the domestic penal law by the courts and the tribunals of the state.

2. The crimes and criminals *against the international public order,* which appear to be the sum of all the domestic public orders of all the states concerned with the crime and of the state in the territory of which the criminal took refuge or was arrested. Such a criminal may be judged by the municipal courts of the country which holds him either on the grounds that that country is directly concerned by his crime or on the principle of universal jurisdiction. He may also be extradited to one of the other concerned countries provided that that country demands it and is willing to put him on trial within its own jurisdiction. Also, he might, from a more theoretical point of view, be put on trial before an international criminal jurisdiction.

It is obvious that in cases with some political feature and in cases which depend on the quality of the belligerence of the offender, the most impartial or, at least, the alternative subject to the least suspicion would be an international criminal jurisdiction.

3. The crimes and criminals *against the universal or world public order* which cannot be efficiently and impartially put on trial except before an international or universal court or tribunal even though the national state still claims jurisdiction over those crimes or criminals.

1.2. Crimes and Criminals Against the Municipal Public Order

It is a presumption of the municipal law of almost all modern states, and of the classic law of nations as well, that the natural judge of any offender is his municipality or nation. And, indeed, that principle is inscribed in many constitutions. But the state does not limit its jurisdiction to its nationals. It also claims jurisdiction over any foreigner who has committed an offense on its territory. Moreover, it may summon before its penal courts anyone who has broken its laws abroad, regardless of nationality, if the offender inflicted injury to it or to one of its nationals.

The presumption and claims of jurisdiction take root, on the one hand, in the old principle of allegiance and in the belief that the subject belongs to his prince and, on the other hand, in the trend of modern states to protect their interests and their policy as far as they may possibly reach. That these widespread claims of jurisdiction serve the policy of nation-states, and, not the least, the policy of the Great Powers, is obvious; but whether they really serve justice as well, seems rather doubtful.

Even if we admit that that presumption and these claims are justified as far as they concern offenses and offenders of the municipal law, we may wonder whether such a continuous expansion of competence, based on political grounds, is still compatible with effectiveness. At the root of that trend, we find, on the one hand, a strong decision of the state to extend the competence of its courts as far as possible and, on the other hand, an incurable reluctance to submit offenses and offenders to foreign courts, even when guarantees are given that the judges, sitting in those courts, are as impartial and as independent as its own.

1.3. Crimes and Criminals Against the International Public Order

Some crimes and some criminals break not only the law and the municipal public order of one particular state but the law and order of two or more states at the same time. Frequently, the criminals are not arrested in the territory of the state where they have committed, planned, or prepared their crime or in the countries whose nationals have been affected, because they seek refuge in another country, as far away and as friendly as possible, where criminal law sanctions are the mildest. Many of these crimes are well defined and known as *delicta juris gentium*, crimes against the law of nations, or against the international law and order. They are defined as "breaches of criminal common law, which were prepared, executed, patronized, or fulfilled in different countries." The "mafia" and the "cosa nostra" are just the best known examples of international organizations devoted to crime, but there are many others.

The evolution of common law criminality toward internationalism seems to us both inevitable and irrepressible. It is certainly a problem to cope with, and international jurisdictions may well be the means by which to challenge international crime.

Although international common law criminality is indeed a matter which deserves due consideration, we are much more concerned with the increase of international criminal violence with political features. Unfortunately, more and more people seem to admit that sanctity of the goal means condonation of the means, and—what is worst of all—the states set an example by waging war not directly but by third person. For example, trade in weapons and traffic in war material should surely be booked among the crimes of the law of nations. Governments not only permit their nationals, private persons, or companies and firms to sell, at high profit, armaments and war material to foreign countries or to the revolutionary movements which they favor, but they openly do it themselves. Trade in weapons is, in fact, regarded by the governments and especially those of the Great Powers as a lawful means to accomplish their policy.

More and more international crimes of common law are acquiring a political character which strongly influences not only their prevention but their repression. The same result follows when such crimes are committed in places which escape the jurisdiction of any particular state, such as the high sea, the air, the cosmos, and the polar territories.

These crimes may be divided into three classes:[4]

1. Crimes against human persons and against the rights of men.
   a. Terrorism.
   b. Slavery.
   c. Slave trade.
   d. Traffic in women and children.
   e. Traffic in drugs and narcotics.
2. Crimes against public morality—circulation of obscene and pornographic books, publications, prints, films, and records.
3. Crimes against the international good faith, the international trade, and the international means of communication.
   a. Piracy on the high seas.
   b. Air piracy.
   c. Currency counterfeiting.
   d. Destruction of and damage to submarine cables.

These crimes are the adopted and classified international crimes, but more and more offenses are being included in this categorization.

Both international crime of common law and international political crime have become a scourge of our time. As international transportation and communication improve, murder, robbery, racket, and fraud are more and more organized on an international scale. Among these crimes, we may note political terrorism, political guerrilla fighting, and political sea and air piracy or hijacking.

The criminals who commit crimes against the international public order may be divided into two classes. The first class includes common law criminals of the most vulgar and dangerous type. Their low moral standards, the means they resort to, their boldness, the scale on which they act, their savage and merciless struggles for power make them the hard core of the underworld and an increasing threat to both domestic and international law and order. The second class comprises men of another type: political fighters, soldiers of fortune, mercenaries, fanatics,

---

[4] Quoted by Saldana Quintiliano, in ACTS OF THE 1ST CONGRESS ON PENAL LAW 642 (1926).

and desperados, acting alone or as commandos, who commit their crimes by order, on a prepared plan of action, on behalf of states, revolutionary organizations, movements, or groups, or who at least pretend to do so. This class poses a two-part inquiry: (1) Are they or are they not political criminals and if so to what extent? (2) Are they or are they not "belligerents" in the sense of the Geneva Conventions, August 12, 1949?

Generally speaking, the obvious increase of grave international criminality is abetted by national particularisms and by the differences of the law systems and of the policies of the states. Even in federal unions, the differences between legal systems of the states or provinces which belong to the Federation are a great boon to the accused, to the suspects, and to their lawyers. They know very well in what country, in what state, in what province they should seek refuge, not only because the law is milder or the punishment is less harsh because the police department is weaker, less vigilant, or even corrupt but because of the political regime and policy of that state. It is a fact that the more severe states, governments, and their statutes are against the opponents to their regime, the more lenient they become to the opponents of the political regime of other countries which they are struggling against. The condition has deteriorated so badly that today whether terrorists or air capers will be punished as criminals or welcomed as heroes depends entirely on the policy of the country where they were arrested or where they took refuge. If that country favors the cause for which the terrorists or air capers are fighting, the more their crimes were bold and cruel, the more they will be excused and welcomed. On the contrary, if the terrorists or air capers were taken prisoner in the country which opposes their cause or which is really neutral, they will be put on trial and possibly suffer severe punishment.

We note today, all over the world, in a questionable climate of apathy, laxity and benevolence, under the false pretenses of both policy and war, the rise of an almost insurmountable tide of violence which spares nobody and nothing, neither innocent nor neutral, even on neutral soil. The taking and execution of neutral civilian hostages, the blowing up of civilian planes with the loss of neutral passengers and aircraft, and air piracy are the contemporary shapes of that political international criminality which is growing daily. Young men and even children are instructed and trained to drop bombs and plastics and to commit sabotage, on neutral soil, at the loss of or danger to neutral persons and neutral property, on the pretense of making war.

"So long as air piracy is regarded by some countries as a glorious weapon to strike the enemy, there is no solution in view."[5] Acts of piracy

[5] Schneider, *Kapen & Kapers van vliegtuigen,* in Streven, Antwerp, Mar. 1970, p. 554.

and terrorism are common law crimes. Should their political motive or the quality of belligerence of the culprits in any case excuse them? As long as the law of nations recognizes war as lawful violence, much depends on the personal status of the offender. Is he or is he not a political offender? Is he or is he not a belligerent? As long as the answers to those questions are left to national jurisdictions or governments, there is little chance of an effective punishment or of a fair trial for the accused. These questions should be presented to and settled by international, or at least, neutral jurisdictions.

A second question to be posed before an international or neutral jurisdiction is whether the political motive of the criminal deed invoked by the accused is a real or a pretended one? The third question is whether and to what extent the invoked political motive covers and excuses the criminal act under the given circumstances. The same questions apply to pretended war crimes. Does an actual state of international war exist between the country the accused is fighting for or, at least, pretending to fight for, and one or more other countries? And if not, is the accused really engaged in an actual civil war? If the accused is really belligerent and recognized as such, did he lawfully act as such under the law and customs of war? In our opinion, acts of war committed in a neutral country or onboard neutral aircraft, at the loss of neutral property and innocent neutral lives can never be lawful under the law of war and ought to be punished without mercy whatever the motive.

To palliate to a certain extent the danger of international criminality, two legal procedures have been applied. The first is extradition. Extradition is the delivery of an accused by one state to another state, to be judged, on request of the latter, according to a treaty concluded between the two powers, on the basis of reciprocity. But extradition of nationals or political offenders should never be granted and, in any case, depends on a political or judicial decision of the state which holds the prisoner and on the state of relations between the requested and requesting states.

However,

> . . . offenses with some political features may be extraditable; namely those involving political terrorism, genocide, or war crimes. The Genocide Convention of 1948 expressly provided that genocide should not be considered as a political offense for the purpose of extradition. In 1946, the General Assembly of the United Nations adopted a resolution to the effect that war criminals should be extradited to the countries in which their abominable deeds were done.[6]

---

[6] M. SORENSEN, MANUAL OF PUBLIC INTERNATIONAL LAW 524 (1968).

That resolution is but a repetition of the Declaration of Moscow, October 30, 1943.

Extradition in any case is a slow, complicated, uncertain procedure which usually leads to tardy trials. It seems to us primitive, questionable, and doubtful justice, in any case, to deliver prisoners to their enemies for revenge rather than to try them on the political value of the cause for which they fought.

The second procedure to deal with international crime is universal jurisdiction or jurisdiction upon the principle of universality.

> Universal jurisdiction over piracy has long been widely recognized both under customary international law and treaty; whatever the nationality of the offender or of the victim, and wherever on the high seas the offense was committed, any state which catches the pirate has jurisdiction to prosecute and punish for acts that amount to piracy by international law.[7]

Under the Geneva Conventions of August 12, 1949,

> . . . each contracting state is obliged either to try "grave breaches" of the Conventions of 1949, before its own courts [which means universal jurisdiction] or, if it prefers, to hand over the offenders for trial, to another contracting state concerned, provided the latter has made out a prima facie case against him.

But universal jurisdiction grants, in fact, a privilege to the offender or to the criminal in that he can choose the country and the authorities to which he surrenders. A famous example is the *Santa Maria* case.[8]

Unfortunately, it was an example also to our contemporary air pirates, who, at the rate of one or two a week, capture and force civilian planes to fly wherever they want to go, on political motives, or, at least, on political pretenses. As long as states admit those motives and those pretenses as legitimate, we see no means to stop the hijackings. Encouraged by the lack and the weakness of repression, the air capers will continue to carry on air piracy.

The security of international communications is nowadays an essential feature of international law and order. If it is not effectively protected, the social conscience will react in some way and demand that protection. The political pretext will wear thin rapidly. We recognize the reluctance of the states and of governments to set up international courts or tribunals. We think, however, that it should not be the only one, but one among the many means used to check and to stop the tremendous increase of international criminality. There is no fundamental juridical objection to the attribution of jurisdiction by two or more states in an

[7] *Id.* at 365.

[8] Franck, *To Define and Punish Piracies—The Lesson of the Santa Maria,* in M. SORENSEN, *supra* note 6, at 218.

international permanent court or tribunal, provided that the state which keeps the accused under arrest was party to the treaty which created the court and granted jurisdiction to it to try those cases, provided, above all, that the state is really willing to bring the accused to trial before that court. But the example of the International Court for the Repression of Terrorism, the only one we find in history, demonstrates the weakness and the ineffectiveness of a court whose jurisdiction is not both compulsory and universal.

The murder of King Alexander of Yugoslavia and of the French Minister of Foreign Affairs, Louis Barthou, in Marseille, France, on October 9, 1934, deeply concerned the world and the French Government. In pursuance of a proposal made by the French Government, the Council of the League of Nations "took steps to prepare an international convention for the prevention and the punishment of acts of political terrorism."[9] Two conventions were opened to signature of the powers which took part in the diplomatic conference of Geneva on November 16, 1937. With the first, "the contracting parties undertook to treat as criminal offenses, acts of terrorism, including conspiracy, incitement, and participation in such acts and, in some cases, to grant extradition for such crimes."[10] The second called for "the creation of an international court to try the individuals accused of an offense punished by the first Convention." In pursuance of article 2, any contracting party, instead of placing any person accused of one of the crimes mentioned in articles 2, 3, 9, and 10 of the Convention, before its domestic courts or of extraditing him to another country, could defer him to that international court. That court would be permanently organized, but would meet and sit only if an offender were put on trial before it (art. 3). The criminal law which the court would enforce would be the least severe of the domestic laws of both involved countries, the one on whose territory the breach was committed and the other which had deferred the accused to the court (art. 21).[11]

The scholars of the period between the two world wars called the convention which they had sponsored "a step toward international justice" and even an "historical event." Although inspired by the rules of the most classical law of nations, though respectful of the sovereignty of the contracting parties, to the extent that the jurisdiction of the court was a mere possibility and entirely dependent on the convenience of the party which detained the accused, the convention was signed by only a small number of powers and was never used. But, ineffective and illusory as it

[9] Doc. on International Affairs 111 (1934).

[10] L.N. Doc. C546 Virgule M383.

[11] United Nations Secretariat, Historical Survey of the Question of International Criminal Jurisdiction, U.N. Doc. A/CN.4/7/Rev.1, at 18 (1949).

was—and probably precisely for that reason—that Convention on the International Criminal Court for the Repression of Terrorism inspired the two committees on international criminal jurisdiction of 1951 and 1953.

1.4. Crimes and Criminals Against the Universal or World Public Order

By their nature, by their dimension, and by the fact that they were committed by persons acting as heads, rulers, or agents of a state, some major crimes shatter all the provisions of the municipal criminal law with such force that universal social conscience demands the prosecution and punishment of the perpetrators, even if under domestic law and the classical law of nations they are justifiable, because the deed or the omission is an act of state. The concept of crimes against the universal or world public order contains both major and comparatively minor crimes. The major crimes are (1) aggressive war and conspiracy to wage such a war and (2) genocide. The minor crimes are (1) war crimes and (2) crimes against humanity.

Anyone who tried war criminals quickly realized that persons accused of waging a war of aggression or committing genocide, war crimes, or crimes against humanity are generally of a different breed than the ordinary offenders of municipal and international criminal law. Many were well educated and responsible men, entrusted with the most important public offices of their state and from the top ranks in the armed forces. Nevertheless, they were charged with the deliberate murder of hundreds, thousands, and millions of innocent people.

Under the famous definition of Clausewitz, "war is but the continuation of policy, by other means." And the same applies to genocide. It would have been impossible to carry out those crimes as private citizens. It was done by use, or rather misuse, of the power and of the means with which they were entrusted by the state. The war criminals all claimed to have been but agents of the policy of the state and of the orders of its government. They all pretended that these crimes committed by order and on behalf of the state were "acts of state" and presented a plea of superior order.[12] The charter annexed to the London agreement August 8, 1945, suspended the pleas of "act of state" (art. 7) and of "superior order" (art. 8), but only within the limits of the jurisdiction of the International Military Tribunal. Professor Luis Jimenez de Asua, in his masterly *Tratado de Derecho penal* expresses the view that crimes against the peace are not a matter of criminal law, but belong to the public respon-

---

[12] Dautricourt, J. Y., *L'Orientation moderne des Notions d'Auteur de l'Infraction et de Participation à l'Infraction; rapport au VIIe Congrès international de Droit pénal Athènes,* REVUE INTERNATIONALE DE DROIT PÈNAL 107 (1957); Jimenez de Asua, Luis: Rapport général, *id.* at 534.

sibility of the state and cannot be punished unless directly by the people, as the Italians did with Mussolini. He does not deny that during World War II, atrocities and common law crimes were actually committed, including some of unusual cruelty. But those which should be tried were already qualified, he affirms, by the common domestic criminal law of any state.[13]

In the same *Tratado*, the author also remarks that "genocide," although it is characterized by the intention to destroy a national, racial, or religious group, as such, does not cease, for that reason, to be a crime against humanity.[14] We believe that "genocide," unlike ordinary crimes against humanity, cannot be committed against individuals but only against human groups; that it involves deliberate and willful assassination of thousands or millions of victims; that it cannot be perpetrated, unless by abuse of the public authority, and that, like war of aggression, it is an act of state, and, in pursuance of the principal assertion by Professor Jimenez himself, it ought to fall within the political, noncriminal category of acts of the tyrants. What is the use of criminal law, if the major and the worst crimes on earth cannot be punished? Criminal responsibility of the state is but a delusion, because states—being corporate bodies—are fictions. They have no moral conscience but only a policy. Why should the Italian people bear the responsibility of Mussolini's war?

States are nevertheless responsible in international law and are subject to civil liability for damages caused by their rulers or their agents. But why should these rulers or agents escape personal criminal responsibility for mass crimes on the pretense that these crimes shatter the usual dimensions of crimes punished by municipal penal law?

The Convention of the Prevention and Punishment of Genocide, December 9, 1948, prescribes that "Persons charged with genocide, shall be tried by a competent tribunal of the state in the territory of which the act was committed or by such international penal tribunal as may have jurisdiction with respect to those contracting parties, which shall have accepted its jurisdiction."[15]

But what if those persons, instead of being the losers, subverted and driven out by their foreign or municipal enemies, become the winners and remain the victors; what if the crime was committed by the authorities and the agents of the state in which the act was committed? Because trial and punishment of genocide by national courts make little sense, Professor Henri Donnedieu de Vabres, French judge of the I.M.T. of Nuremberg, wanted to establish an international criminal jurisdiction

---

[13] JIMENEZ DE ASUA, LUIS, II TRATADO DE DERECHO PENAL 902, 1300.
[14] *Id.*
[15] 78 U.N.T.S. 277.

under the auspices of the United Nations. However, very few governments sincerely favored or wanted the creation of an international criminal court, even to try genocide: neither those of the Communist group which considered the "definition of aggression" as "crucial" before taking further action and were not even willing, on that pretense, to sit in the 1951 and 1953 committees on international criminal jurisdiction; nor those of the Western group which feared a judicial conviction of colonialism; nor the nonaligned, being proud and jealous of their newly won independence and sovereignty, and not wanting to yield to international authority, judicial or otherwise. Later on, most of the states, far from giving jurisdiction to their municipal courts and tribunals to try genocide, did not take steps to ratify the Convention on genocide. Thus, the genocide convention became one more of the many solemn declarations and pacts which are unenforcible.

Unlike war of aggression and genocide, which can only be tried and punished by an international jurisdiction, war crimes and crimes against humanity can be brought before municipal jurisdictions, whether military or not. After World War II, the accused were, in pursuance of the Declaration of Moscow, October 30, 1943, "sent back to the countries in which their abominable deeds were done, in order that they could be judged and punished according to the laws of these liberated countries and of the free governments that were created therein." We can agree with J.B. Herzog, quoted by Jimenez de Asua when he declares that "a war crime [and why not a crime against humanity committed in the same circumstances?] is but a crime of common law, perpetrated on the occasion and on the pretext of the state of war," and when he states that they [war crimes] can easily be brought under the provisions of the yet existing municipal penal law,[15a] but we cannot admit that it is the best of justice, or even justice at all to extradite suspects or accused of war crimes and of crimes against humanity to the enemy countries, in which they committed their crimes. How could the court-martial procedure of a country escape the prejudice or at least the suspicion of revenge and partiality when the accused, charged with crimes on fellow soldiers or citizens, are put on trial before it?

The four Humanitarian Conventions of Geneva, August 12, 1949, in their Articles 49, 50, 129, and 146, concerning the search for the suspected persons and for the repression of grave breaches against the Conventions, adopted the principle of universal jurisdiction, in the following terms: "Each high contracting party shall be under the obligation to search for persons alleged to have committed or to have ordered to be

---

[15a] *Supra* note 13.

committed such grave breaches and shall bring such persons, regardless of their nationality before its own Courts."

We regret that the high contracting parties bound themselves only "to undertake to enact any legislation necessary to provide effective penal sanctions for persons committing or ordering to be committed, any of the grave breaches of the present convention, defined in the [above-said] articles," instead of drafting a law, which could have been adopted by the parties offering to all of the accused the guarantee of the same law and of the same sanctions, whatever their nationality and whatever the country in which they should have been prosecuted and put on trial. That could have been a first step toward the trial of persons charged with war crimes or crimes against humanity, by international or, at least, by neutral courts.

The Commission which was entrusted by the Belgian Government with the task of adapting the Belgian municipal criminal law to the requirements of the Geneva Conventions drafted a bill which was conceived and worded as an international statute and was utterly independent of the Belgian municipal law and which could have been adopted by all parties and enforced by an international court or military jurisdiction and by municipal jurisdictions as well. We presented that type of law at the meeting of experts organized by the International Committee of the Red Cross in Geneva, October 8–12, 1956. As it appears from the introductory speeches, the ICRC ardently favored such a type of act, and Mr. Siordet assigned it as a goal of the meeting.[16] Unfortunately, the countries which had already passed the statutes to modify and to adopt their municipal law in order to enforce the Geneva Conventions appeared not to be willing to amend them anew (although they did it previously in various and often most questionable ways)[17] nor to submit the judgment of grave breaches of those Conventions to international courts or tribunals.

The extradition or the delivery of persons suspected or accused of war crimes and crimes against humanity to the country in which they committed their crimes or to the country of which the victims were the nationals is surely not the best mode of attaining justice, because there is a strong suspicion of revenge. But on the other hand, the trial of these persons before their own national jurisdiction arouses a suspicion of benevolence and laxity. No matter how impartially they administer justice, they are subject to the criticism that they were created by the victors to

[16] ICRC, Meeting of Experts Consulted on the Question of the Repression of Grave Breaches of the Geneva Conventions 1 & 2 (1956).

[17] Dautricourt J. Y., *La Protection Penale des Conventions internationales Humanitaries—Une Conception de la Loi-type*, R.D.P. 191 (1953–54).

crush the vanquished. In contrast, a court composed of neutral judges would be less questionable, and an international jurisdiction would be the best of all solutions.

Through quoting John Maktos our American colleague on the 1953 Committee on International Criminal Jurisdiction, we may conclude as follows:

> A presently existing, permanent, international court, whose judges have been elected before a case arises, according to accepted impartial procedures, not only escapes such criticism, but has, as an important precedent, on the civil side, the International Court of Justice.
> . . . While it is to be hoped that proscribed force and the threat of force would not be resorted to in international relations, states do not allow this fact to deter them from necessary military preparedness. The question then arises: why should there not be also preparedness in the international legal field, with a view to meet such contingences as might arise.[18]

In our opinion, what the judges and prosecutors of Nuremberg desired (and surely Judges Biddle and Donnedieu de Vabres and Justice Jackson) and the scholars and the peoples really wanted was an international criminal court which could "deter the states from necessary military preparedness" and could become an effectual support of peace.

Section 2. OBSTACLES TO THE CREATION OF A PERMANENT INTERNATIONAL CRIMINAL COURT

2.1. Introduction

In his report on the question of international criminal jurisdiction to the International Law Commission of the United Nations at its second session (1950), Ricardo J. Alfaro, special rapporteur, stated: "During that time [the last thirty years] the public opinion of the world, official and unofficial entities representing the world's legal and political thought, have strongly advocated the creation of an international criminal jurisdiction."[1] Today, the statement seems to us only partially true because it is rather doubtful whether such entities really, as Alfaro contended, represent world public opinion and world political thoughts. There is, on the contrary, a strong reluctance of statesmen and of politicians to set up a permanent international criminal court, and public opinion is still not prepared to demand it.

To support their point of view, statesmen and politicians put forward a number of problems to the creation of the court, some of which are rather formal but can openly be discussed, while the real ones, less available

---

[18] J. Maktos, Letter, Apr. 30, 1963, in MUELLER & WISE, at 580, 582.
[1] Alfaro Ricardo, U.N. Doc. A/CN.4/Ser.A/1950/Add.1, at 15.

to world public opinion, remain hidden. All the pros and cons have been developed in a succession of documents by some of the best scholars of our time, who are named in our bibliography. But, in our opinion, these writers have not fully explored the subject. We believe that the cons deserve more consideration than the pros because the former still prevail. The formal obstacles are based on the structure of the United Nations and on the impossibility to amend the Charter, at least, at the present time.

The real arguments proceed from the concept of national sovereignty, from the mistrust of the state of anything which is foreign and international, and finally, from the classical law of nations.

2.2. The Formal Obstacles

The International Law Commission at its second session, in 1950, under the chairmanship of Professor Georges Scelle, decided "that the establishment of an international judicial organ for the trial of persons charged with genocide or other crimes over which jurisdiction will be conferred upon that organ by international convention is desirable" and "that the establishment of the above mentioned international judicial organ is possible. . . ."[2]

The two alternatives to the creation of that organ are as follows:

1. The establishment of an international jurisdiction, outside the framework of the United Nations, by any group of states. With reference to this type of tribunal, a selective approach would be to deal with a single subject. However, governments whose members could be charged with genocide or other crimes would certainly not be willing to be parties to the Convention which would set up the court and, if they were, even more certainly would not be willing to put themselves on trial before that court. Depending upon the crime chosen, that court could remain inefficient and powerless and would probably, like the proposed court for terrorism, never convene.

2. The establishment of a judicial organ within the framework of the United Nations by a resolution of the General Assembly.

Professor Roling made such a proposal in the 1953 Committee on International Criminal Jurisdiction. In his report to the International Law Commission, Professor Sandstrom correctly states:

> The difficulties arise only when the question is raised of establishing a judicial organ within the framework of the United Nations, with a view to establishing a jurisdiction universal in principle. Considering that the request to study this problem came from the General Assembly and in view of the

[2] U.N. Doc. A/CN/ Ser.A/1950/Add.1, at 379.

circumstances in which the request was made, the latter alternative must be considered as the correct interpretation of the terms of reference.[3]

To be efficient, however, in cases of genocide and of aggressive war, the jurisdiction of that court must not only be "universal in principle" but universal in fact, and compulsory. In the present state of the law of nations that seems to be impossible.

Professor Sandstrom also poses the question whether it is possible to establish an international judicial organ having competence in criminal matters within the framework of the United Nations. His answer is Yes if it is a subsidiary organ (art. 7(2) of the Charter), but No if it is a principal organ of the organization, unless there is first an amendment of the Charter (art. 7(1)) (which implies a special majority).

In the 1953 Committee, the argument raised for the waiving of the latter requirement was that after the war in Korea and under the circumstances of the cold war, no special majority could possibly be found and that, even if it were found, at least one of the great powers would veto the amendment. Indeed, from the beginning, the position of the Soviet Union was that no international criminal jurisdiction could be created if "aggression" were not previously defined. Therefore the members of the Soviet Bloc refused to sit either on the 1951 or on the 1953 Committees on International Criminal Jurisdiction. And by binding the whole of international criminal justice to the previous definition of aggression, the General Assembly, in 1957, shared that view. It was on the same ground, *i.e.*, the impossibility of amending the Charter, that the one plausible solution to the problem of the creation of the Court, the attribution of criminal jurisdiction to a criminal chamber of the International Court of Justice, although recommended by most of the scholars, was dismissed without further examination.

Of the seventeen representatives of Western and nonaligned countries, only three, namely the Netherlands, France, and Israel, advocated the creation of the Court. The others were not only reluctant but seemed prone to reject the International Law Commission's conclusion that an international judicial organ for the trial of persons, charged with genocide and other crimes, was both desirable and possible. Some of the representatives even expressed the view that an International Criminal Jurisdiction was not desirable at all and asked the opinion be noted in the report. They emphasized "the need of a political screening which should let the U.N.O. prevent that a case should be put before the Court."[4] The 1953 Committee dampened the hope of the judges and prosecutors

---

[3] E. Sandstrom, U.N. Doc. A/CN.4/15, at 19.
[4] Report of the 1953 Committee, 9 U.N. GAOR, Supp. 12, at 5, U.N. Doc. A/2645 (1954).

of the Nuremberg trial (Francis Biddle, Henri Donnedieu de Vabres,/ Justice Jackson, Telford Taylor, and Sir David Maxwell Fyfe) and of prominent scholars such as Vespasian V. Pella, Georges Scelle, Stefan Glaser, Jean Graven, Antonio Quintano Ripolles, Quincy Wright, and others that, on the principles of Nuremberg, some universal law and order could be built, by means of a universal, permanent criminal jurisdiction.[5] The five characteristics which the 1953 Committee enumerated for international criminal jurisdiction—(1) stability, (2) permanence, (3) independence, (4) efficacy, and (5) universality[6] (provided that the last two characters should also mean "compulsory jurisdiction") still remain valid and useful.

2.3. American Obstacles

Fannie F. Klein and Daniel Wilkes, after an elaborate analysis of the 1953 draft statute of the Court, have produced an American evaluation of the problem, pointing out that "written analysis of the United Nations draft statutes by American international law scholars has been disappointingly meager. . . ."[7] They ascribe that inertia to the absence of a committee for study and discussion of the draft statue, although the late George M. Morris, chairman of the 1953 Committee, recommended such a procedure. The same lack of interest also applies to Europe. But this may be attributed to a different cause: the obvious disappointment of the supporters of the Law of Nuremberg.[8]

Klein and Wilkes point out three general problem areas relating to the protection of the accused under the Tribunal's statute. The first is the fear of submitting American citizens abroad to antitrust laws and unlawful confiscations.[9] Americans "are unwilling to agree that solely overt military conquest is an invalid means of diplomacy, unless covert subversion be equally impermissible."[10] The second area of contention is compulsory jurisdiction and "no obligation without conferment," not only for jurisdiction but also for obligation to cooperate.[11] The third is the problem of whether the American Constitution permits the United States to surrender someone on American soil, to trial before an international criminal court.[12]

[5] J. Y. Dautricourt, *La Justice Criminelle universelle aux Nations-Unies—Reflexions sur un Abandon*, R.I.D.P. 1954.

[6] Report 1953 Committee, at 4.

[7] J. Klein & D. Wilkes, *United Nations Draft Statute for an International Criminal Court: an American Evaluation*, in MUELLER & WISE, at 572.

[8] S. Glaser, *Introduction a l'Etude du Droit international penal* 145 (1954).

[9] *Supra* note 7, at 572.

[10] *Id.* at 576.

[11] *Id.* at 575.

[12] *Id.* at 576.

The authors themselves refute these contentions:

> It would be truly ironic if immunity from or denial of an impartial international trial were accorded [to] those who destroyed whole peoples or committed offenses in regions not susceptible of national control, simply because of unstated, yet as real as they are irrelevant, objections to antitrust laws and unlawful confiscations.
>
> The American laws themselves recognize the need of extraterritorial reach for special offenses, whether based on citizenship or on the special need itself.[13]

The authors conclude in note 157 cite a number of federal criminal statutes which are expressly extraterritorial and a number of offenses, many of which are crimes under international law.

As to the second and third groups of contention, the authors point out (1) that there are many criminal acts upon which there is agreement and for which Americans surrender their nationals for extradition, (2) that despite the tie between a definition of aggression and the creation of an international criminal court, it should be possible to recognize that there are other areas (a) in which agreement can already be obtained as to the substantive offenses (crimes of international law or crimes against the U.N. personnel or property) and (b) in which the need for an impartial international criminal court is already recognized, *e.g.*, for war crimes and crimes against humanity, and (3) that the ability to submit, at least with ad hoc conferment (*e.g.*, the Eichmann case) to a nonnational tribunal, would certainly reduce international tension.

2.4. The Real Obstacles

In the present state of the international community, there are but two real obstacles to the creation of an international criminal court. The two are tied to the roots of the matter and their importance cannot be overrated. The first is the lack of an organization for bringing the accused before the Court and for executing the judgment. The second is the stubborn unwillingness of the governments to submit themselves, their policy, and their power to moral standards, to the commonweal of mankind, and to the needs of its future on the basis of what is asserted to be ideology but which in actuality is nationalism.

In an address to the Royal Academy of Moral and Political Sciences of Belgium on "the Possibilities of International Criminal Law," the late Leon Cornil, former attorney general of the realm, quoting the French novelist Anatole France, stated that "the judge is but a poor dreamer, without the policeman."[14] The U.N. actions in Korea and in the Congo

---

[13] *Id.* at 575.

[14] L. CORNIL, LES POSSIBILITÉS DE DROIT INTERNATIONAL PÉNAL, 41(5) BULLETIN DE L'ACADÉMIE 256 (1955).

against the secession of Katanga, which are sometimes invoked as precedents, enforcing resolutions of the Secretary Council and of the General Assembly, were, in fact, political and nonjudicial actions. Sandstrom states that "as a fact, there is no international means for the purpose of bringing accused before the Court or of enforcing criminal sentences. . . ."[15] "There is of course, at least in theory, a possibility of creating the necessary machinery by amending the charter, even if it is difficult to see how it would be organized and who would consent to act as the policeman. . . ."[16]

But why not employ the permanent members of the Security Council in this role? They could serve well indeed if their governments were not involved in a struggle for world dominion, world supremacy, or at least world leadership, but were working on behalf of the commonweal of the human race for the maintenance of the world public order.

Speaking of the "desirability" of an international criminal jurisdiction, Professor Sandstrom reaches the heart of the matter:

> If one keeps in mind that the criminal jurisdiction exercised by a state within its territory is a product of a long development whereby the state has gained sovereignty within that territory, it cannot be taken for granted that in the actual organization of the international community, an effective interstate criminal jurisdiction can be established. . . .
>
> But a very important group of states—say the majority—are still of the opinion that the repression of crimes which have an interstate character is a matter within the exclusive competence of the state and not a matter to be dealt with by the international community.[17]

Section 3. THE CONDITIONS OF A UNIVERSAL CRIMINAL JURISDICTION

3.1. Introduction

The classic law of nations, on the one hand, and, the immaturity and the unpreparedness of the social conscience of mankind on the other, in demanding the submission of the leaders to the rules of the international ethic and to the needs of the world public order are the major assets of the governments in their resistance to any kind of international justice and a universal jurisdiction. The time is coming when the concept of public order will no longer be confined within the state and be dependent entirely upon it. That concept must expand to a higher universal level. World public order, universal public law, and international crimi-

[15] E. Sandstrom, *supra* note 3, at 21.
[16] *Id.* at 20.
[17] *Id.*

nal jurisdiction are but aspects and names for the one major problem of our time: international peace.

Heads of states; members of governments; officers, organs, and agents of the state still rely on the privileges which were granted to the kings by "God's will," by three basic provisions of the classical law of nations:

1. Waging war at will.
2. The act of state doctrine.
3. The defense of superior order.

Why should leaders willingly waive these protections in ruling their peoples and consent to stand trial at some future time before an international criminal court, for criminal deeds or omissions? Only the demand and the pressure of an awakening universal social conscience will force them to submit. In our opinion, the real struggle for peace will probably not be fought on the battlefields of a third nuclear world war but will be waged within the states and the nations, within the Great Powers, by the people who already admit that their loyalty to mankind will not permit them to surrender to the countervailing aims of a national policy as dictated by government and even supported by a majority. The dangers which threaten the human race at present are not simply the weapons of mass destruction which are stored in overabundant quantities in the arsenals of the Atomic Powers, but the law and the institutions which make their explosion possible.

Unfortunately, we do not foresee that the rapidly approaching struggle for peace within the state will be any shorter, less violent, or less cruel than an international war. It will pit those who are forced to fight against those who get profit and power of war and of its preparation. It will set youth against the seniors; the poor against the rich. It implies a fundamental modification of the traditional law of nations, by a revision and limitation of the very concept of sovereignty. Fortunately, the final outcome of that struggle cannot be doubted. Some kind of universal society, of universal institutions, and of universal law will be the ultimate goal of an expanded human social conscience and mankind's salvation.

The elements of a universal or world public order can be summarized in the following manner:

1. A definition of peace.
2. Substantial revision of the classic law of nations.
3. Promotion of the universal social conscience.
4. Conception and creation of universal institutions.

It appears that the last among these institutions to be created, organized, and put into action will be the permanent international criminal court, for it is not, as some scholars after World War II expressed, an ad hoc means to achieve peace, but a means of enforcing the peace once it is achieved.

3.2. A Definition of Peace

It is indeed a rather surprising fact that there is no tenable definition of peace. The most common definition seems to be "absence of armed warfare." But, defining peace by using its antithesis, "war," seems to be a questionable method of definition.

Under "polemology," many competent and devoted scholars have united their efforts in studying all kinds of war to achieve a viable definition of peace, but in vain, for peace cannot be defined as a mere negative concept. World public order is indeed a very positive one. The fact is that our scientific, modern minds are so accustomed to the experimental methods that we become confused when challenged by problems of creative imagination. Peace is neither observable nor measurable. It has never existed in history. We are thus forced to imagine peace and no effort seems to us more distressing or incomprehensible.

We believe that "starting" is useless, when the goal is neither located nor defined. It is thus necessary to express what we really mean by "international or universal peace" and to propose a definition which will meet the criticisms of scholars and of students. Peace is

> . . . a world public order by which, through universal institutions and statutes, based on ethic and inspired by the pursuance of the commonweal and the future of mankind, as a whole, the peoples and the states, could find a solution of the conflicts which oppose them and the human person or, at least the human communities, a resort against abuse of power, committed by the rulers of the states.[1]

Although we grant that the science of peace is based on the contributions of all the sciences and mainly of the social sciences, we do, however, believe that the synthesis of all these contributions is a legal one. Reducing the problem of peace to its political, economic, or social dimensions seems to us, both wrong and dangerous. We do not pretend that adjudication is the only means to settle disputes and conflicts among states and human communities, but we do believe that it is the best alternative to violence. It is obvious that once a world could be conceived, achieved, and expressed in universal statutes, the task of the International Court of Justice, and principally of its criminal chamber, would be prominent.

A few statesmen, some people, and many scholars dwell on such slo-

---

[1] J. Y. DAUTRICOURT, *Les Conditions du Droit criminel universel*, REVUE DE DROIT PÉNAL ET DE CRIMINOLOGIE 107 (1966–67).

gans as "Peace through law." But what law? If law means the classic law
of nations, we say No because that law is still the *jus belli ac pacis* of
Grotius and of the kings of "God's will"; it fosters war and violence, as
the lawful means of policy and actually foments among the states permanent insecurity and anarchy. If law means preservation of the
greatest Powers' selfish, national interests, of the demands of their establishment, or of one political party, in the name of which, they condemn
and sap all attempts of the peoples to free themselves of economic domination and nationalistic ideology, we still say No. But if "law" means a
renewed international public law, deserving of its name and concerned
with the defense of the supreme values of mankind, *i.e.* the human
being, on the one hand, and the commonweal and destiny of mankind
conceived as a nascent universal society, on the other, we would fully
agree.

3.3. Objections to the Classical Law of Nations

There are many grievances against the classical law of nations, but even
throughout the centuries, wars, and major crises, it survived with little
change. It is still presented by many as the best of all possible laws, as if no
alternative could possibly be conceived or achieved. We wish to review the
most important of these objections against the classical law of nations:

1. Outdatedness.
2. Discrepancy with the social facts.
3. Overrating of the state.
4. Contempt of the supreme values of mankind.
5. Bitter fruits.
    a. Permanent international anarchy.
    b. The heavy burden of armament and the balance of terror.

3.3.1. OUTDATEDNESS. The classic law of nations was drawn up in the
sixteenth and seventeenth centuries not by moralists or scholars, like
Vitorria, Suarez, Grotius, or Gentilis but by diplomats or statesmen such
as Machiavelli, Vattel, and Martens, who were remunerated by monarchs to formulate and to strengthen their absolutism. What we call the
law of nations was not conceived to insure the commonweal of the nations, international morality, natural law and peace, but to legalize the
greed and the power of the monarch. The kings, founders of the modern
European national states claimed the absolute "imperium" of the Roman
emperors, under the name of "sovereignty." The country was the king's
heritage and the inhabitants were his subjects. *Cujus regio, illius religio.*

Ability to declare war at will and inviolability of his person were his privileges.

From the peace of Westphalia (1648), the kings in order to carry out their policies and their conquests, on the one hand, and to insure their security and the defense of those conquests against their enemies, on the other, were forced to rely on a system of agreements, "the European balance of powers." The revolutions which dethroned the kings insured the rights of some peoples, within the municipal frame of the state, on a democratic basis, but had very little impact on the system of international relations. The most important historical events of the two past centuries—the wars of Napoleon and the two world wars—left that system of the international relations basically untouched. A coalition defeated Napoleon; other coalitions defeated Wilhelm II and Adolf Hitler. The single change was from a European to a world balance of power. Neither the League of Nations nor the United Nations Organization altered the system, because they were founded on the principle of the "sovereign equality of their members" (art. 2(2) of the Charter). This is so in an everchanging world at a stage of culture and civilization which is more and more characterized by tremendous worldwide moral and social problems, by fantastic progress in the sciences of nature and material things, by an awakening sense of the unity of mankind and of his common future, by the international ethic and the international customs, and by the system of international relations. The laws of nations still remain classical and basically unchanged since the seventeenth century.

3.3.2. DISCREPANCY WITH THE UNIVERSAL SOCIAL FACTS. One of the most lucid scholars of our time, Professor Georges Scelle, chairman of the second session of the International Law Commission of the United Nations, sees "the source of the rules of law in the social fact and in the conjunction of ethic and power, produces of social solidarity."[2] In analyzing the social facts on a world scale, the discrepancy between those facts and the classical law of nations becomes obvious. These facts are (1) the unity of the earth, (2) the unity of mankind, (3) the unity of the human ethic, and (4) the unity of the commonweal and of the future of mankind. Is it necessary to prove the unity of the earth, that globe suspended in the cosmos? What frontier is more natural than the border of space? The landing of men on the moon and the exploration of other planets of the solar system demonstrate that unity and the unity of the genuine conditions which permitted that life to evolve and ultimately to produce that unique animal: man. The unity of the human race was pro-

[2] G. SCELLE, MANUEL DE DROIT INTERNATIONAL PUBLIC 843 (1948).

claimed in Articles 1 and 2 of the Universal Declaration of Human Rights. The *Courrier de l'UNESCO* (Apr., 1965) published a report signed by a large staff of scientists of all countries of the world who certify that all men belong to one species called *Homo sapiens*. When and how the different human groups became different remains a controversial question. Racism as such and in its form of "apartheid" is frequently condemned by all the organs of the United Nations. It may thus be concluded that the human race is one. It is a natural human community which awaits self-conscience to become some day, in some kind, an organized society whose powers would be supreme because, if based on democracy, no superior powers could be conceivable. Distance, lack of communication and knowledge, exploitation of the differences between races and peoples by the monarchs and the governments on their own behalf, and natural boundaries divided mankind into nations and states in the past, but today the conscience of the fundamental unity of the human race is secure by the world's youth.

The unity of the moral standards which should govern the conduct of men, their deeds and their omissions, is obvious despite some slight differences. The basic principles of ethic—one should not kill, one should not steal, one should not cheat—are very much the same among all the peoples of the world and they oblige the whole of mankind. There seems to be but one exception: that of the heads and the governments of states who pretend that international policy and diplomacy have nothing to do with ethic and that Machiavelli was right when he described what should be the conduct of the prince in the state of complete political anarchy which characterized the early Renaissance in Italy. In fact, the poor Machiavelli is still the victim of much slander. He does not approve; he simply states. He demonstrates that anarchy forces the prince to govern by violence, by terror, by fraud, and by treason and that the end justifies the means. Machiavelli was but the prophet who announced the evils which, a century later, the classic law of nations, also based on fundamental anarchy, would bring first to the peoples of Europe, and later to all the peoples of the world. Statesmen and too many scholars dwell on international morals and natural law as if they were Heaven granted. Because they were inscribed in treaties, in pacts, and in the most solemn declarations, such men affirm these ethics as being the law. But, as long as they are not confirmed by facts and by international custom, that touchstone of international law, as long as they remain sanctionless, they are not valid.

The outlawry of aggressive war, subscribed to in the pacts of Locarno and of Paris, in the Covenant of the League of Nations, in the Charter of the United Nations, in the judgments of Nuremberg and of Tokyo, never belonged to customary law and failed in 1953 (with the definition of aggression) to become statutory law. The Convention for the Prevention and the Repression of Genocide cannot be enforced because of the lack of international jurisdiction. The principles of Nuremberg, the Draft Code of Offenses Against the Peace and Security of Mankind, though formulated, still remain useless and unenforcible and even the Universal Declaration of the Rights of Men and other declarations of which the United Nations is so proud, however eloquent and generous in their terms, they may be, still remain impotent because of the restriction of state "sovereignty."

It is daring to pretend that aggressive war is an international crime, since waging of war is still an attribute of sovereignty under the customary law.*

That the major Nazi criminals were put on trial before an ad hoc tribunal, charged with offenses defined in an ad hoc statute, that they were sentenced and hanged, changed matters very little. It was no more than a historical event which is now closed, except of the work of some classic scholars who took, too early, their wishes for a reality.[3] Could the pacts of Locarno and Paris, could the judgments of Nuremberg and Tokyo prevent or stop one single war since the termination of World War II? Could the convention on genocide ever prevent or stop slaughter of civilian populations which were very much like genocide, with weapons furnished by states, some of which are members of the Security Council? Customary international law is not to be found in the books of many good scholars who are prone to invoke the custom to support their doctrines, but in fact, the repeated comportment of states and governments often disprove what these scholars consider to be the law.

In summing up, it can be stated that all pretenses of fundamental change in the international morals and of the classic law of nations, after Nuremberg, are denied by the facts. It is no less sad to consider that the concept of the commonwealth of mankind and any concern about its common future are completely absent from the law of nations. In our so-called enlightened time, the whole of it is still based on the interests and needs of state policies and on the fiction of sovereignty. It is "fiction," because in our contemporary world, only three states can be said fully sovereign, although some others still try to make of that fiction, a reality. Most states have been forced to give up more or less of· that sovereignty to a group of states and the Great Power which took the leader-

---

* Editor's note: This assertion is questionable under the Law of the United Nations Charter. *See* Kelsen, The law of the United Nations (1964) and Goodrich and Hambro, Charter of the United Nations (1958).

[3] S. GLASER, INTRODUCTION À L'ETUDE DU DROIT INTERNATIONAL PÉNAL (1954); R. QUINTANO, 1 & 2 TRATADO DE DERECHO PENAL INTERNACIONAL & INTERNACIONAL PENAL (1955 & 1958). *See also* G. Scelle, *supra* note 36.

ship of that group, as the price for their security. These minor powers would see no objection to resigning some of their sovereign rights and part of their jurisdiction to international courts, provided that, in doing so, they could find an effective protection of their rights and, above all, a recourse against potential excesses of the exercise of power, by the Great Three. But ultimately the strongest rampart of the classic law of nations today rests not so much upon the will of power and of domination of the Great Powers, but in their mistrust and in their fear of one another. Hopefully, someday a world order will be built on the four unities herein described.

Meanwhile, it is clear that we are bound to live, to suffer, and to die together. We simply cannot afford a nuclear war. That war would mean mass destruction and a recession of all the standards of life for centuries. What use of being the winner, if it is to reign over corpses and ruins? But it is obvious that the governments of the Great Powers are still determined to pay the full price rather than to give up both the classic law of nations and war as the ultimate means of achieving their policy.

3.3.3. OVERRATING OF THE STATE. The state is surely of lasting and real value. It was born over the centuries, not only from the will of power or power of the monarchs, but ultimately from the will of a human group to live together independently and freely, under the same institutions and under the same law. The state is still, within its boundaries, a source of law and order, a conserver of its culture and its own way of life. From the outside it appears a rampart of freedom and independence, but that value must not be considered supreme to the extent that the welfare and the policy of the state might endanger the commonweal and the future of the whole of mankind, the rights of other nations who also want to be free and the lives of millions of human beings.

Why should mass murders such as war and genocide remain unpunished because they were committed on behalf of the state, in pursuit of a state, value which could not be supreme?

Although the concept of criminal responsibility of individuals in the field of international law has made some progress, heads of states, members of governments, commanding officers, and agents of the state still consider themselves not penally responsible for the criminal deeds or omissions which they ordered or committed in the pursuit of their function, for they were acts of state. Members of the armed forces still plead superior order for war crimes and crimes against humanity, though that plea is limited in the case of crimes which took place during World War II, and were committed by members of the forces of the Axis Powers, or by members of the Nazi Party.

3.3.4. BITTER FRUITS. One of the bitter fruits of the classic law of nations is its contempt for the supreme values of mankind, as has already been emphasized. There are at least two others: (1) organization of permanent international anarchy and (2) the heavy burden of armaments to maintain the balance of terror. Law which is not founded on the needs and the aims of the whole human race, but on the interests and the policies of the parts, namely the states, cannot but produce and foster lasting and permanent anarchy, and what many sensible human beings think of is an international community which condemns even the wealthiest and most powerful powers. All the costly discoveries in the field of the material sciences applied to armament and means of mass destruction, in order to maintain a balance of terror which, by definition, is frail and always questionable?

3.3.5. CONCLUSION. The outdatedness, the discrepancy with the social facts, the overrating of the state, the contempt of the supreme human values, the organization of lasting anarchy, the failure to define and to set up a world public order, the fostering of war as a means of law, the inability to insure peace, the heavy cost, are more than enough reasons to condemn or, at least, to challenge the classic law of nations.

Matters have gone so far that, today, mankind is urgently challenged with the problem of deciding whether it can rely on that law to insure its survival and its future; whether that law standing alone may be a danger which threatens it so as to force it to think earnestly of some other international public law which might better guarantee its survival.

It is time to realize that the aim of international public law is not to legalize the dominion and the leadership of the Great Powers over the rest of the world, but to insure on a world scale the protection of the human person against the dangers of war and genocide by reason of state action and to insure the survival and the future of the whole human race.

Will mankind go on, entrusting that future to professional statesmen, prisoners of the state from which they received their power and their privileges, who, taking advantage of the ignorance, the blindness, and the national prejudice of their fellow citizens, present as being peace and world public order, their own political conception of order and their own pretenses of dominion and leadership of the world; who would wage everything, even a nuclear war, rather than give up power and the classic law of nations which backs it? The answer to this question depends entirely on the lucidity and on the maturity of the world social conscience.

Returning to international criminal jurisdiction, it must be simply stated that such international jurisdiction is utterly inconsistent with the very principles of the classic law of nations. At the present, the king makes law but cannot be liable to it. Why and how should heads of states, members of governments, or top-ranking officers surrender and stand trial for alleged crimes, before a universal criminal court, unless forced to do so, either by a victor or by the social conscience of their people whose demand could become irrespressible?

3.4. Promotion of the Universal Social Conscience

We could define social conscience, that touchstone of the law, as "the will of the members of a human group of organizing it into a legally defined structure or institution." Natural communities are the family, the tribe, the nation, the race and, last but not least, the entire human race. Some political groups are more or less artificial. They were not forged out of the ties of blood or of common values but were built on a community of needs and interests, or on constraint and conquest which time has changed into consent. In any case, it is the degree of that social conscience within the community which provides its cohesion, its strength and the social value of the group.

In the absence of or weakening of social conscience within the community, the grouping crumbles and disintegrates.

As a rule, social conscience, which in its early stages is rather restricted and restrictive, tends, in later stages, to expand to still larger communities and that expansion depends on the development and the culture of the group concerned.

We are familiar with races and peoples whose social conscience is still tribal and not yet national. We know of others where that conscience is fully national or is presently awakening to a national feeling. Among the peoples of Europe, the Arabian nations, or the black peoples of Africa, we can see a real sense of communion founded upon culture, religion, and race.

Social conscience is so real that, when frustrated, it may lead to bitterness, to despair, and even to rebellion, as with the black people in the United States. Everything seems to indicate that, generally speaking, social conscience expands from small groups to larger ones and that the ultimate goal of its evolution may be a sense of all-human community, the all-encompassing society whose powers should be supreme because no higher or larger society can yet be conceived.

We strongly believe that some day—and that day may not be so far— some lucid and responsible persons and, later on, a majority of the human race, taking conscience of the four unities that have been described above, will consider mankind not only as a community of peoples and of individuals but as a possible society and demand that the states whose citizens they are should willingly give up part of their sovereign rights which have already been waived in part in the interest of security, to achieve the largest society which can possibly be conceived: the universal society of men and of peoples.

A universal social conscience could be the source and the basis of *a new public order,* no longer confined within the narrow boundaries of a state or a group of states, but broadened to the whole and put on a superior level, above the states, and of *a new universal public law* which could replace the outdated, ineffective, and dangerous law of nations and oblige obedience to the standards of ethics, of commonweal and the future of mankind of not only all human beings as individuals, not only of all human groups and communities, but of the states and their rulers as well. Much more than the power of the victors over the defeated Nazi German state, it was the social conscience of mankind which backed the law of Nuremberg. For the one universal public law is the law of peace and not the law of nations.

It is beyond the scope of this section to determine how universal social conscience could be awakened, promoted, and ripened among the peoples of the world. It is certain that social conscience first begins to become effective when it is adult and responsible, and the facts already reveal some trends in that direction both on a general level and among the youth.

One of the grievances of youth against the older generation is that, having furnished the victims and the killers of the two world wars, the seniors have failed to achieve a lasting peace. As an alternative to insecurity, fear, and deep anguish, we can offer them but material comfort, the society of consumption, the religion of material science and material progress, all values which many youth despise, contest, and oppose. And, truly, there is no reason for self-complacency or conceit, nor for persisting in proposing our standards, our ideals, our goals, our way of life, and our law as a model to the younger generation.

We have already set forth the opinion that the combat for peace, for world public order, for universal public law and universal criminal jurisdiction, is not to be fought on international battlefields, but within the states themselves and between the greatest powers, the two generations. As a fact, that combat has already started; it is continuing and expanding at this very moment.

The youth strongly oppose war, all kinds of war, all causes and sources of war, all the pageantry and the brass of war. Why should they be urged to kill and to be killed on behalf of policies which they neither share nor approve. To be understood, scholars and professors should put the problem of war and peace to the students, sincerely, correctly, earnestly, and before it is too late, without pretending that they have the solution or even *one* solution because in fact, at this very moment, there is none.

Shortly after World War II, the late Dutch scholar W.P.J. Pompe wrote: "Since that war, a criminal law also came into being, above the states; as if it were in a first primitive stage."[4] He was right. But today that first primitive stage almost belongs to history, and we have returned to the bare classic law of nations.

The classic law of international relations and the law of international institutions should be taught in our universities and law schools as before but in a much more critical sense. Far too many professors and scholars hold them in too high esteem. If we contemplate the present condition of the world, its needs and the dangers which threaten the human race, it would be dishonest not to show the students that one of the causes of these evils is the law itself. If they come to discover that themselves, they could react in their own, negative way.

Mankind should not feel itself doomed to bear that classic law of nations as a cross to the bitter end, as if no better law, either more sensible or more humane, could be conceived or put into action. The main problem is to pose the question before it is too late.

World public order should not be described as a static mold which can undergo neither change nor progress. One major fault of our generation is conservatism and lack of imagination. We obstinately retain outdated and backward values: profit in our Western countries, monopoly of the party in the Communist countries. If the young would win their way, nothing could stop progress toward a universal social conscience based on universal public law.

The search for a world public order, the scientific search for peace has started. Our modest part should be to interest and to enlist the youth of the world in that search upon which depends both the future and the survival of mankind. The harvest ripens; it may be abundant, but the workers are too few.

Section 4. CONCEPTION AND CREATION OF WORLD INSTITUTIONS, WORLD STATUTES, WORLD POWER AND OF THE CRIMINAL JURISDICTION

What kind of institutions? In any case, not the United Nations, as it is now, having been inspired by and founded on the classic law of nations, neither universal, nor validly representative of the human race, nor effi-

---

[4] W. P. POMPE, HANDBOOK VAN HET NEDERLANDSE STRAFRECHT, Zwolle Tjeenk Willink, 5e uitg., bl. 13 (1959).

cient. It is not universal because regardless of its motives, some of the most important and numerous peoples of the world are still absent, *e.g.*, Germany. It does not validly represent the human race, because it is based on the sovereign equality of all the member states, a fictional concept and not on the realities of the unity of mankind and the equality of all human beings. Diplomats accredited as representatives represent their governments and not the peoples of the states which they are supposed and presumed to represent.

Resolutions of the Security Council and recommendations of the General Assembly do not bind the member states and, even less so the states which are not members. Resolutions are subject to the "veto" of the Great Powers, permanent members of the Security Council. The United Nations recently proved to be inefficient and powerless, in such instances as the Biafra rebellion, the Middle-East conflict, and the war in Vietnam. Its condemnations of Portugal, South-Africa, Rhodesia, and Israel remain a dead letter.

The United Nations could win prestige and authority if it were to become a union of representatives of the legislative assemblies of the member states, mandated by their peoples to draw up compulsory universal statutes, criminal ones among them and to create the necessary jurisdictions to carry out the law and to organize the necessary police forces to enforce the sentences. But in the present state of things, it is more an international political tribunal, than a universal institution.

Some politicians, most of them American, dwell on the idea of a world federation on the model of the United States which could replace the United Nations. That idea is based on the rather naive assumption that no better constitution, no better political system could be thought of than a federal union. But it is much too soon to decide that the federal solution is the best one or even any solution at all. The federal solution should, of course, be considered, but other ones may appear to the social conscience of mankind which offer more opportunity and more possibilities among peoples and states whose political, economical, sociological, cultural, and philosophical systems are so vastly different and do not cast them into the same mold.

Looser ties might be more desirable, for peoples are unhappy having order imposed upon them as a pillory. What men want on a world scale is exactly what they want on a national scale: the most liberty which is compatible with exactly that degree of public order which appears to be essential to suppress, to avoid, and to prevent anarchy. A unitary world-state, on the other hand, inspired and governed by a totalitarian ideology, could—whether federal or not—produce the worse tyranny mankind ever knew.

It is obvious that an institution, based on the sovereign equality of all its member states, does not and cannot meet mankind's desperate need for order on a world scale. Some other institution is needed which, on a democratic basis, could validly represent all the peoples of the world, create a power above the states, and oblige them to yield to the supreme values of mankind which are, on the one hand, the human person and, at least, human life, and on the other, the commonweal and future of mankind as a nascent political society. The chosen institution should exert the three fundamental powers of any political body: the legislative, the executive, and the judicial function of which the last should not be put first, for peace is a world public order of which a criminal jurisdiction may be the tutor, but cannot be the creator.

Whether that wanted world-institution will be created by evolution of the United Nations or by revolution depends completely on mankind's wisdom and on the progress of the universal social conscience. We are convinced that the roots of the United Nations Organization are so questionable and so weak that, just as the League of Nations could not survive World War II, the United Nations could not survive a third world war.

The idea, cherished by Pella, Donnedieu de Vabres, John Maktos, B. Roling, and others, that the mere existence of a permanent international criminal court, despite the absence of definition of aggression, regardless of the absence of criminal statutory law, a Code of Offenses against Peace and Security of Mankind, and regardless of the absence of all preliminary conditions or structures which give substance to world public order, could offer the possibility or an opportunity for creating judicial repressive solutions for international crimes, for working out a jurisprudence and for promoting peace, seems to us, at the moment, quite chimerical. For states, and chiefly the Great Powers, are less than ever willing to give up their municipal jurisdiction which they still try to expand or to put persons suspected or accused of international crimes with some political implications on trial before an international court. They would yield only to an irresistible pressure of the awakening universal social conscience of their young people.

If thinkers, scholars, strategists, economists, and mainly politicians and statesmen persist in pretending that the nation-state and its policy are the supreme values and in teaching that war is a natural phenomenon, a component of the state, a necessary factor of its progress and, in fact, its very life, the human race is indeed, at this critical period of evolution, very much in danger.

The lightning progress of the material and natural sciences, the compulsory utilization of all their discoveries and applications in the production of armaments, as a consequence of the principles of the classic law of nations and of the maintenance of the balance of power, have made the governments gradually lose control of the situation.

Rather than wage war as the ultimate means of their policy, the Great Powers continue to accumulate an arsenal of nuclear weapons sufficient to destroy several times the whole of mankind and to improve and develop it beyond reasonable limits.

Ad hoc Courts such as the International Military Tribunals of Nuremberg and of Tokyo are but occasional and questionable jurisdictions, being set up by the victors to try the vanquished and being exceptional. The quality of the judges, the fairness of the proceedings, and above all, the consent of the social conscience, which is the very basis of the law of Nuremberg, might approve and support the sentences. But could an incident in the history of mankind which is almost closed create customary law?

Optional international criminal jurisdictions, such as the court against terrorism and the court whose project was drawn up by the 1951 and 1953 Committees, may be concessions to the nascent social conscience of some peoples or groups of peoples, but not to the universal social conscience of mankind. But their concept is but a caricature of the permanent universal criminal court, whose jurisdiction, to enforce the universal law and order, should be both universal and compulsory. In spite of the advice of the International Law Commission in its second session (1950), the one criminal jurisdiction which could suit the purpose of declaring and protecting world public order would be a criminal chamber, created in the international arena, not as a prelude to, but as a consecration of, peace.

APPENDIX I OF CHAPTER XIII.

DRAFT STATUTE FOR AN INTERNATIONAL CRIMINAL COURT[*]

CHAPTER I. GENERAL PRINCIPLES

Article 1. Purpose of the Court

There is established an International Criminal Court to try natural persons accused of crimes generally recognized under international law.

Article 2. Law to Be Applied by the Court

The Court shall apply international law, including international criminal law, and where appropriate, national law.

[*] From Report of the 1953 Committee on International Criminal Jurisdiction, 9 U.N. GAOR, Supp. 12, at 23, U.N. Doc. A/2645 (1954).

Article 3. Permanent Nature of the Court

The Court shall be a permanent body. Sessions shall be called only when matters before it require consideration.

CHAPTER II. ORGANIZATION OF THE COURT

Article 4. Qualifications of Judges

The Court shall be composed of a body of independent judges, elected regardless of their nationality from among persons of high moral character, who possess the qualifications required in their respective countries for appointment to the highest judicial offices, or are juriconsults of recognized competence in international law, especially in international criminal law.

Article 5. Number of Judges

The Court shall consist of fifteen judges.

Article 6. Nationality of Judges

1. Judges may be elected from candidates of any nationality or without nationality.
2. No two judges may be nationals of the same state. A person who, for the purpose of membership in the Court, could be regarded as a national of more than one state shall be deemed to be a national of the state in which he ordinarily exercises civil and political rights.

Article 7. Nomination of Candidates

Alternative A	*Alternative B*
1. Judges shall be elected from a list of candidates nominated by the states which have conferred jurisdiction upon the Court.	1. Judges shall be elected from a list of candidates nominated by members of the United Nations and by those non-member states which have conferred jurisdiction upon the Court.

2. Each state may submit the names of not more than four candidates.

Article 8. Invitation to Nominate

1. The date of each election shall be fixed by the Secretary-General of the United Nations.

Alternative A	*Alternative B*
2. At least three months before this date, he shall address a written request to the states which have conferred jurisdiction upon the Court, inviting them to undertake, within a time specified, the nomination of qualified persons in a position to accept the duties of a judge.	2. At least three months before this date, he shall address a written request to the states referred to in article 7 (*alternative B*), inviting them to undertake, within a time specified, the nomination of qualified persons in a position to accept the duties of a judge.

Article 9. List of Candidates

Alternative A	*Alternative B*
The Secretary-General of the United Nations shall prepare a list, in alphabetical order, of all candidates. He shall	The Secretary-General of the United Nations shall prepare a list, in alphabetical order, of all candidates. He shall

submit the list to the states which have conferred jurisdiction upon the Court.

submit the list to the states referred to in article 7 (*alternative B*).

Article 10. Representative Character of the Court

The electors shall bear in mind that the judges, as a body, should, as far as possible, represent the main forms of civilization and the principal legal systems of the world.

Article 11. Election of Judges

Alternative A

1. The judges shall be elected, at meetings of representatives of the states which have conferred jurisdiction upon the Court, by an absolute majority of those present and voting. The Secretary-General of the United Nations shall, after due notice to each of such states, convene these meetings.

Alternative B

1. The judges shall be elected, at meetings of the states referred to in article 7 (*alternative B*), by an absolute majority of those present and voting. The Secretary-General of the United Nations shall, after due notice to each of such states, convene these meetings.

2. In the event of more than one national of the same state obtaining a sufficient number of votes for election, the one who obtains the greatest number of votes shall be considered as elected and if the votes are equally divided, the elder or eldest candidate shall be considered as elected.

Article 12. Terms of Office

1. The judges shall be elected for nine years and may be reelected; provided, however, that of the judges elected at the first election, the terms of five judges shall expire at the end of three years and the terms of five more judges shall expire at the end of six years.

2. The judges whose terms are to expire at the end of the initial periods of three and six years shall be chosen by lot drawn by the Secretary-General of the United Nations immediately after the first election has been completed.

3. Each judge whose term of office has expired shall continue to discharge his duties until his place has been filled. Though replaced, he shall finish any case which he may have begun.

4. In the case of the resignation of a judge, the resignation shall be addressed to the President of the Court, who shall transmit the resignation to the Secretary-General. This transmission shall make the place vacant.

Article 13. Solemn Declaration

Each judge shall, before taking up his duties, make a solemn declaration in open court that he will perform his functions impartially and conscientiously.

Article 14. Privileges and Immunities

Each judge, when engaged on the business of the Court, shall enjoy diplomatic privileges and immunities.

Article 15. Occupations of Judges

1. No judge shall engage in any occupation which interferes with his judicial function during sessions of the Court. Nor shall he engage in any occupation which is incompatible with his functions as a judge.

2. Any doubt on this point shall be settled by the decision of the Court.

Article 16. Disability of Judges

1. No judge may participate in proceedings relating to any case in which he has previously taken part in any capacity whatsoever.

2. Any doubt on this point shall be settled by the decision of the Court.

Article 17. Disqualification of Judges

1. If, for some special reason, a judge considers that he should not participate in a particular proceeding, he shall so inform the President.

2. Any party to a proceeding may submit that a judge should not participate in that proceeding. Such submission shall be addressed to the President.

3. If the President, upon receipt of such submission or of his own motion, considers that a judge should not participate in a particular proceeding, the President shall so advise the judge.

4. If the President and the judge disagree on the issue, the Court shall decide.

Article 18. Dismissal of Judges

1. No judge shall be dismissed unless, in the unanimous opinion of the other judges, he has ceased to fulfil the conditions required for his continuance in office.

2. Formal notification of such unanimous opinion shall be made to the Secretary-General of the United Nations by the Registrar.

3. This notification shall make the place vacant, and thereupon the dismissed judge shall immediately cease to perform all functions as a member of the Court.

Article 19. Vacancies

1. Vacancies shall be filled by the same method as that prescribed for the first election, except that the Secretary-General of the United Nations shall, within one month of the occurrence of a vacancy, issue the invitations provided for in article 8.

2. A judge elected to replace a judge whose term of office has not expired shall hold office for the remainder of his predecessor's term.

Article 20. Officers

1. The Court shall elect its President and Vice-President for three years; each may be reelected.

2. The Court shall appoint its Registrar and shall provide for the appointment of such other officers as may be necessary.

Article 21. Seat of the Court

The permanent seat of the Court shall be established at ———. The Court may, however, sit and exercise its functions elsewhere whenever the Court considers it desirable.

Article 22. Emoluments

Each participating judge shall be paid travel expenses, and a daily allowance when the Court is in session. Each judge shall be paid an annual remuneration.

Article 23. Finances

The states which have conferred jurisdiction upon the Court shall create and maintain a fund to be collected and administered in accordance with regulations adopted by the parties. From this fund shall be paid the costs of maintaining and operating the Court and the Board of Clemency and Parole, and the expenses for the defence as provided in article 38 (2) (*c*), and as approved by the Court.

Article 24. Rules of the Court

1. The Court shall adopt rules for carrying out its functions. In particular, it shall prescribe rules of procedure and such general principles governing the admission of evidence as the Court may deem necessary.
2. These rules and any amendments thereto shall be published without delay and shall not be altered so as to affect pending proceedings.

CHAPTER III. COMPETENCE OF THE COURT

Article 25. Jurisdiction as to Persons

The Court shall be competent to judge natural persons, whether they are constitutionally responsible rulers, public officials, or private individuals.

Article 26. Attribution of Jurisdiction

1. Jurisdiction of the Court is not to be presumed.
2. A state may confer jurisdiction upon the Court by convention, by special agreement, or by unilateral declaration.
3. Conferment of jurisdiction signifies the right to seize the Court, and the duty to accept its jurisdiction subject to such provisions as the state or states have specified.
4. Unless otherwise provided for in the instrument conferring jurisdiction upon the Court, the laws of a state determining national criminal jurisdiction shall not be affected by that conferment.

Article 27. Recognition of Jurisdiction

No person shall be tried before the Court unless jurisdiction has been conferred upon the Court by the state or states of which he is a national and by the state or states in which the crime is alleged to have been committed.

Article 28. Withdrawal of Jurisdiction

A state may withdraw its conferment of jurisdiction. Such withdrawal shall take effect one year after the delivery of notice to that effect to the Secretary-General of the United Nations.

Article 29. Access to the Court

Alternative A

Proceedings before the Court may be instituted by a state which has conferred jurisdiction upon the Court over such offences as are involved in those proceedings.

Alternative B

1. Proceedings before the Court may be instituted by a state which has conferred jurisdiction upon the Court over such offences as are involved in those proceedings.
2. In the interest of the maintenance of peace, a United Nations organ to be designated by the United Nations may stop the presentation or prosecution of a particular case before the Court.

Article 30. Challenge of Jurisdiction

1. The jurisdiction of the Court may be challenged by the parties to any proceeding or by any state referred to in article 27.

2. Such challenge made at the beginning of trial shall be decided by the Court at once.

3. Such challenge made after the beginning of trial shall be decided by the Court at such time as the Court thinks fit.

Article 31. Assistance of States

1. The Court, including the Committing Chamber, may request national authorities to assist it in the performance of its duties.

2. A state shall be obliged to render such assistance only in conformity with any convention or other instrument in which the state has accepted such obligation.

Article 32. Penalties

The Court shall impose upon an accused, upon conviction, such penalty as the Court may determine, subject to any limitations prescribed in the instrument conferring jurisdiction upon the Court.

CHAPTER IV. COMMITTING CHAMBER AND PROSECUTING ATTORNEY

Article 33. Committing Chamber

1. The Committing Chamber shall be composed of five judges appointed annually for one year, at a sitting of the whole Court by a majority of the members present. Retiring members of the Chamber shall not be eligible for immediate reappointment. No judge who has participated in committing a case may adjudicate on the substance thereof.

2. The function of the Chamber shall be to examine the evidence offered by the complainant to support the complaint.

3. The complainant shall designate an agent or agents who shall present the evidence before the Chamber.

4. If the Chamber is satisfied that the evidence is sufficient to support the complaint, the Chamber shall so certify to the Court and to the complainant.

5. Before issuing any such certificate, the Chamber shall give the accused reasonable opportunity to be heard. If necessary and, in particular, to ensure that the accused shall have a fair trial, the Chamber may order further inquiry or the investigation of specific matters.

6. The Court shall determine the rules of procedure of the Committing Chamber.

Article 34. Prosecuting Attorney

1. A jurisconsult appointed by the complainant or complainants shall assume the functions of Prosecuting Attorney.

2. The Prosecuting Attorney shall file with the Court an indictment of the accused based on the findings certified by the Committing Chamber and shall be responsible for conducting the prosecution before the Court.

CHAPTER V. PROCEDURE

Article 35. Indictment

1. The indictment shall contain a concise statement of the facts which constitute

each alleged offence and a specific reference to the law under which the accused is charged.

2. The Court may authorize amendment of the indictment.

Article 36. Notice of the Indictment

1. The Court shall bring the indictment to the notice of the accused, of the state or states of which the accused is alleged to be a national, of the state in which the crime is alleged to have been committed and, as far as possible, of the state of which the victims are nationals.

2. The Court shall not proceed with the trial unless satisfied that the accused has had the indictment and any amendment thereof served upon him and has sufficient time to prepare his defence.

Article 37. Jury

Trials shall be without jury, except where otherwise provided in the instrument by which jurisdiction has been conferred upon the Court.

Article 38. Rights of the Accused

1. The accused shall be presumed innocent until proved guilty.

2. The accused shall have a fair trial and, in particular:

(*a*) The right to be present at all stages of the proceedings;

(*b*) The right to conduct his own defence or to be defended by counsel of his own choice, and to have his counsel present at all stages of the proceedings;

(*c*) The right to have reasonable expenses of his defence charged to the fund referred to in article 23 in so far as the Court is satisfied that the accused is unable to engage the services of counsel;

(*d*) The right to have the proceedings of the Court, including documentary evidence, translated into his own language;

(*e*) The right to interrogate, in person or by his counsel, any witness and to inspect any document or other evidence introduced during the trial;

(*f*) The right to adduce oral and other evidence in his defence;

(*g*) The right to the assistance of the Court in obtaining access to material which the Court is satisfied may be relevant to the issues before the Court.

3. The accused shall have the right to be heard by the Court but shall not be compelled to speak. His refusal to speak shall not be relevant to the determination of his guilt. Should he elect to speak, he shall be liable to questioning by the Court and by counsel. He shall not be compelled to take an oath.

4. If the Court considers it impossible to ensure a fair trial, the Court may, by a decision supported by reasons, suspend the proceedings and, if they are not resumed within a time limit determined by the Court, dismiss the case. If the case be dismissed, the accused shall be automatically released.

Article 39. Publicity of Hearings

1. The Court shall sit in public unless there are exceptional circumstances in which the Court finds that public sittings might prejudice the interests of justice.

2. The deliberations of the Court shall take place in private and shall not be disclosed.

Article 40. Warrants of Arrest

The Court shall have power to issue warrants of arrest related to crimes over which the Court has jurisdiction.

Article 41. Provisional Liberty of Accused

The Court shall decide whether the accused shall remain in custody during the trial or be provisionally set at liberty, and the conditions under which such provisional liberty shall be granted.

Article 42. Authority of the Court

The Court shall have the authority necessary to the proper conduct of the trial, including the authority to require the attendance of witnesses and the production of documents and other evidentiary material, to rule out irrelevant issues, evidence, and statements, and to maintain order at the trial.

Article 43. Withdrawal of Prosecution

If the complainant state withdraws the complaint, the Court alone shall decide whether the accused shall be discharged; if the complaint is not substantiated, the Court shall acquit the accused.

Article 44. Quorum

The participation of seven judges shall suffice to constitute the Court.

Article 45. Required Majority

1. All questions shall be decided by a majority of votes of the judges participating in the trial.
2. With the exception of a decision to impose the death penalty or life imprisonment, in the event of an equality of votes, the presiding judge shall have a casting vote.

Article 46. Contents and Signature of Judgment

1. The judgment shall state, in relation to each accused, the reasons upon which it is based.
2. The judgment shall contain the names of the judges who have taken part in the decision. It shall be signed by the President and the Registrar.

Article 47. Separate Opinions

If the judgment of the Court does not represent the unanimous opinion of the judges, any judge shall be entitled to deliver a separate opinion.

Article 48. Delivery of Judgment

The judgment shall be read in open Court.

Article 49. No Appeal

The judgment shall be final and without appeal.

Article 50. Double Jeopardy

No person who has been tried and acquitted or convicted before the Court shall be subsequently tried for the same offence in any court within the jurisdiction of any state which has conferred jurisdiction upon the Court with respect to such offence.

Article 51. Execution of Sentences

Sentences shall be executed in accordance with conventions relating to the matter.

Article 52. Revision of Judgment

1. An accused who has been found guilty may apply to the Court for revision of the judgment.

2. An application for revision shall not be entertained unless the Court is satisfied:

(*a*) That a fact was discovered of such a nature as to be a decisive factor; and

(*b*) That that fact was, when the judgment was given, unknown to the Court and the applicant.

3. Revision proceedings shall be opened by a judgment of the Court expressly recording the existence of the new fact and recognizing that it has such a character as to lay the case open to revision.

CHAPTER VI. CLEMENCY AND PAROLE

Article 53. Board of Clemency and Parole

Alternative A	*Alternative B*
1. The states which have conferred jurisdiction upon the Court, shall, at the meetings and in the manner provided in article 11, elect a Board of Clemency and Parole consisting of five persons.	1. The states referred to in article 7 (*alternative B*) shall designate a Board of Clemency and Parole.

2. Subject to the provisions of the instruments by which states have conferred jurisdiction upon the Court, the Board shall have the powers of clemency and parole.

3. Before deciding on a petition for clemency or parole, the Board shall request the advice of the Court.

4. The Board shall adopt its own rules of procedure.

CHAPTER VII. FINAL PROVISIONS

Article 54. Special Tribunals

Nothing in the present statute shall be taken to prejudice the right of two or more states which have conferred jurisdiction upon the Court jointly to set up special tribunals to try the perpetrators of crimes over which each of such states has jurisdiction according to the general rules of international law.

CHAPTER XIV

THE ENFORCEMENT MACHINERY OF INTERNATIONAL CRIMINAL LAW

Section 1. **THE ROLE OF AN INTERNATIONAL CRIMINAL·POLICE IN THE CONTEXT OF AN INTERNATIONAL CRIMINAL COURT AND POLICE COOPERATION WITH RESPECT TO INTERNATIONAL CRIMES**

JEAN NEPOTE

1.1. Introduction

When I came to consider the subject assigned to me as part of this collective work, it seemed to me that it involved two quite separate considerations.

The first is purely hypothetical: If there were an international criminal court, what would be the role of the international criminal police force attached to this court?

The second is, in contrast, quite concrete: In what way do the police already cooperate at the international level in cases of international crime?

It would perhaps have been more logical to take these two subjects in reverse order and deal with the present before the future. But I am sure there will be no confusion between the abstract study of possible developments in the first section and the concrete facts of the second.

1.2. The Role of an International Criminal Police in the Context of an International Criminal Court

All communities need a minimum amount of order and collective discipline if they are to survive, but in none of them are the police an end in themselves; they always act on behalf of someone or something, and any action they take is the result of an order received from some "authority," whether political or judicial. It is obvious that the role and activities of an international criminal court would have a decisive influence on the role of an international police force; there is no doubt that there would be true interaction between the two.

Since we are in the realm of theory, let us take as our starting point a

676

series of questions which would have to be answered if, having established an international criminal court, we were about to create an international criminal police force and make it operational.

1.2.1. How Could an International Criminal Police Force Be Responsible for Detecting and Investigating "International" Offenses? Such offenses would, of course, have to be defined, and the jurisdiction of the international police force in such cases could be established in three different ways:

1. Laws could be passed by a supranational legislative and political body: One day, the U.N. General Assembly, the European Parliament in Strasbourg, the O.A.U. in Addis Ababa, the Organization of American States in Washington, or the Arab League in Cairo may well pass criminal laws which would have effect in all countries of the community. It is possible to imagine, for example, a European penal code. To a certain extent this is what happens in the United States when a federal law defines a particular action or behavior as a federal offense; *e.g.*, a federal law has recently made it an offense to make an attempt on the life of an American President. This kind of offense is outside the jurisdiction of local authorities.

2. Alternatively, a number of countries could agree to adopt a convention with an international court controlling its application. It is easy to foresee the day when offenses defined by international conventions (the 1961 Narcotics Convention, the 1924 Obscene Publications Convention, and the 1970 Convention on Aircraft Hijacking) will, by agreement between the countries concerned, be referred to the jurisdiction of an international criminal police force.

3. It might even be possible to pass national laws to deal with offenses which, by some form of mutual agreement, would be termed "international." In this case, a certain number of common denominators would be found in the legislations of different countries which would allow intervention by an international criminal police force.

The jurisdiction of an international criminal police force both *ratione loci* and *ratione materiae* would be determined by the answer to this first, basic question.

1.2.1.1. *Jurisdiction Ratione Loci.* An international criminal police force could of course act only in those territories or regions where international laws applied. In the first of the three alternatives given above, there is no particular problem; once a supranational body has passed supranational laws, these laws would be applicable over the entire territory of the international community concerned. And analogous to federal police forces of the United States, the international police force and not the state police would have the duty to enforce these international laws.

However, under the second alternative, areas of jurisdiction would be much more difficult to determine. It could, and indeed does, happen that the same international texts are not adopted by all: One convention might be ratified by countries A, B, C, and D, another by countries B and D, a third by countries A, B, and C. Territorial jurisdiction of the international criminal police force would then vary according to the law in question, and before taking action, the police would have to check that a country had in fact adopted the convention concerned. Obviously, in such circumstances the situation would be much less clear than in the case of the first alternative. But the problem would not be insoluble, for the experts would soon know exactly which texts had been ratified by which countries.

The third alternative could have almost the same results as the second, but it would certainly cause much more confusion and conflict. It would entail interpreting national laws in order to decide whether or not the offenses they cover correspond exactly, and in this field, questions of case law would have as much importance as legislation proper.

1.2.1.2. Jurisdiction Ratione Materiae. In considering the three alternatives mentioned above in this respect, there would seem to be no serious problems involved in the first two. Since here the provisions of the law apply to the various parts of a whole, it would be relatively easy for an international criminal police force to decide which acts were covered by international law. Gradually, a series of precedents would become available to help the courts clarify difficult cases and interpret the law whenever necessary.

In the third alternative, however, a large number of problems arise. In this case, the legislation of each nation would define the acts which that particular nation would be willing to classify as international crimes coming under the jurisdiction of an international court. It is impossible to expect that definitions laid down in the various national legislations would suggest exactly the same actions to everyone. When actual cases had to be dealt with, there would inevitably be conflicting interpretations, just as there are at the present time when dealing with cases involving the extradition of offenders. One particular action may be considered fraud in a certain country, and fraud can give rise to extradition; but is the same action considered fraud in another country?

In such circumstances, there would undoubtedly be many cases of two countries refusing permission for the international criminal police to take action on the grounds, for example, that their interpretation of the national law was inaccurate or too free. There might even be real conflict between the country's own case law and that of the international court. Would the latter then take priority? Should we consider setting up a tribunal to settle such disputes and solve problems? International police officers having to work under such conditions would not be envied.

Any attempt to draw up a list of "international crimes" at the present time would be a foolhardy enterprise. Many people would put genocide— which is already considered an international crime—at the top of the list. Other crimes which could be included are drug trafficking and currency counterfeiting. Aircraft hijacking could be added too. If the principle of supranational law enforcement were accepted, the list would probably grow suprisingly quickly.

1.2.2. TO WHAT AUTHORITY WOULD AN INTERNATIONAL CRIMINAL POLICE FORCE BE RESPONSIBLE? As stated earlier, a police force always comes under political or judicial authority. An independent police force not answerable to any higher authority would be unthinkable. Different systems have been adopted in different countries. In the majority, the police are answerable to the political authorities (Ministry of the Interior). In others, they are answerable to the judicial authorities who delegate the power of tracing criminals to them. In most countries, the police are merely the secular arm of the law. A typical example is that of Belgium, where, from the administrative point of view, the criminal police come under the Attorneys General and the Ministry of Justice. In the same way, an international criminal police force would have to be subordinate to an international criminal court.

It is difficult to imagine an international police force existing in limbo. On the other hand, it is easy to conceive of an international criminal court delegating work to, and controlling the activities of, a police force placed under its direct authority. In conclusion, there is, in my opinion, only one possible and logical solution: an international criminal police force which is an offshoot of an international criminal court and which is attached to it for administrative purposes.

With regard to personnel, should the chief of this police force be a magistrate or a serving police officer? It is quite logical to conclude that the head of a criminal police force—especially an international one— should be a police officer. I wish to emphasize this point as it is not always the case in national forces today.

1.2.3. WHAT PROCEDURE SHOULD BE FOLLOWED BY THIS INTERNATIONAL CRIMINAL POLICE FORCE IN ITS LAW ENFORCEMENT ACTIVITIES? By and large there are two main types of procedure. In one, the police act, except when the offender is caught redhanded, on the authority and orders of the judicial authorities, which remain responsible for the prosecution of offenders. In the other, the police are entirely responsible for preparing the case

for the prosecution. It is then for the court to decide whether this evidence
constitutes proof of guilt.

If an international criminal police force were established, it would of
course be necessary to decide which procedural system it should adopt.
Countries have come to adopt one or other of these procedural systems
as a result of circumstances and historical influences which they have undergone. The second system would seem to be preferable for several
reasons peculiar to the problem we are considering: An international criminal police force would inevitably be highly mobile and be dispersed over
a very wide area. How could a magistrate, permanently based in one place,
control the police officers' activities? The system of "delegated authority"
would create obstacles which would be difficult to overcome. They could,
of course, be avoided by asking magistrates to accord what is sometimes
called a general delegation of authority. If this were granted, however, it
would reduce the magistracy's control to a mere pretense, an ineffective
facade.

It would therefore be both simpler and more logical to adopt the British-
type system, but would a country with the "judicial investigation" system
of criminal procedure, where police work is directed by the examining
magistrate, allow a police force, even an international one, to act on its
territory with more freedom than its own national police? It is extremely
doubtful. Perhaps it would in fact be best to disregard preferences for one
or other of the systems and to opt for a compromise whereby the international police would comply with the procedure in force in each country
where they operate. This would mean that the procedure followed by the
international criminal court would itself have to be unusually flexible and
versatile. Whatever solution is adopted, the statutes of an international
criminal court would have to define the criminal procedure governing
international police operations.

1.2.4. WOULD AN OFFICER OF THE INTERNATIONAL POLICE FORCE HAVE INDE-
PENDENT POWERS? Another question, directly related to the previous one,
comes to mind: Would international police officers have independent
powers, in other words, would they be able to make arrests, search premises, question persons, etc. on their own initiative? Or would officers
of national forces have to act on the orders or at the request of the international police on their behalf? This is an all-important question.

Today, a police officer is "commissioned"—to use the British term—only
in his own country. Once outside that country, he has no authority at all.
Would this situation remain unchanged if an international criminal police
force were set up? The following situation is easy to imagine: The international criminal police force would carry out and direct investigations on

the basis of orders received and information obtained. They would be helped by local officers who would be responsible for drawing up documents concerning hearings, findings, seizures, etc. In such a situation, the international officers would be to a large extent dependent on the goodwill of the local police officers, and numerous conflicts would undoubtedly arise in the handling of cases—some of which may be extremely important.

Finally, therefore, although we may be reluctant to give international police officers supranational powers, we shall probably have to do so if we wish to set up an international police force.

1.2.5. WHAT WOULD BE THE SCOPE OF THE INTERNATIONAL POLICE OFFICERS' POWERS OF ARREST? Of all the powers invested in international police officers, surely the power of arrest is the one most likely to give rise to controversy and resistance. Whenever a person is arrested and until he has been tried, there is always a certain amount of doubt as to his guilt, even under those systems whose procedures safeguard human rights and individual liberty the most. There comes a moment when, whether we wish to do so or not, we literally have to lay hands on an offender and bring him before a judge in order to answer for his criminal activities.

Would it be possible for an international police officer to detain a suspect for twenty-four or forty-eight hours prior to arrest, with a view to questioning him and to clarifying some point of an inquiry as is the practice in many countries? The officer would have to have premises available for this detention but what sort of premises? Would they belong to the international police or to the police in the country where he is operating? Could the national police, whose premises he is to use, decline to help and refuse him access?

Of course, there would be a general desire to limit to the absolute minimum the powers of arrest given to international police officers. All arrests made by them would have to be followed by the suspect's immediate appearance before the international criminal court or any other judicial authority appointed by the court.

1.2.6. PROBLEMS OF COST AND ADMINISTRATION. This is, in fact, several questions in one, and they are all important: Do we realize just how much an international criminal police force would cost? Its officers would always be traveling, inevitably giving rise to very high costs, which would be difficult to check. What personnel would make up the international criminal police force? Would it be staffed by officers with proven experience in their own country's police organization who would be transferred to the international force, or by specifically recruited personnel with no special experience at either the national or local level? These are questions of a purely practical nature, but they would have a far-reaching effect on the functioning of this international criminal police force. These are the basic considerations—and the list is far from complete—confronting anyone who wishes to set up an international criminal police force.

In addition to the problems of practical organization mentioned above, for which there are no easy solutions, there is the problem of structural organization. For example, would an international criminal police force be a centralized unit? Or would it be made up of a number of regional or national units, each having jurisdiction over a given geographical area? The structure of an international criminal court would obviously have a considerable influence on that of an international criminal police force.

This study of basic questions, although by no means exhaustive, clearly shows that establishing an international criminal court would pose serious problems which will never be solved while countries continue to cling to traditional principles of national sovereignty.

1.3. International Police Cooperation with Regard to International Crime

At the present time, international police cooperation is based on traditional principles and relies on traditional ideas of cooperation between states. The concept of national sovereignty is, in fact, the cornerstone of international relations. It is the basis of the relationships between states; it is also the basis of the relationships between the law and international crime.

It is common knowledge that at the present time the powers of Law and Police extend only to the borders of a country and that it is only possible to prosecute offenders at the international level if the states concerned have a reciprocal agreement. From the legal standpoint, action against criminals at the international level takes the form of extradition or diplomatic requests to a nation to prosecute on behalf of another.

This fundamental principle—the respect of national sovereignty—has a determining influence on police cooperation regarding international crimes. The very words used are significant; since we speak of "cooperation," we can only mean that equal effort is made in the common cause by all concerned. Since police cooperation respects national sovereignty, it will, by definition, be concentrated on ordinary law crimes or, in other words, those acts universally considered as offenses. Political interests very rarely coincide; consequently, police cooperation in political crimes is inevitably delicate, problematic, and limited. In such cases, national sensitivity is close to the surface, and the situation can rapidly degenerate into conflict. Furthermore, police cooperation is useful only if it is followed up by action on the part of judicial authorities. This is not usually the case for political offenses, since extradition agreements do not apply to political crimes.

"Common crimes," however, are more germane to our topic. This expression, which is part of the vocabulary of all legal experts, covers offenses which are universally recognized as constituting breaches of what could be called the natural laws of any society: murder, theft, fraud, drug traffic, counterfeiting of documents (including currency), traffic in human beings, etc. From time to time, of course, there is discussion and even controversy over the contents of such a list. The same acts committed in different contexts may not always have the same significance. With the passing of time, it has become noticeable that crimes of violence are becoming concomitant with certain political actions, and it is not always easy to distinguish between what may be labelled "political" and what is merely wanton crime. Care should therefore be taken not to qualify as "political" acts of violence which can have no direct effect on the political life of a country. Common crimes are sometimes related to "fiscal" crimes. In India, for example, traffic in gold is a very serious problem.

All these possible interpretations of common crimes reveal the true importance of the principle of respecting national sovereignty. Each state has the absolute right and complete freedom to decide whether or not to cooperate. It can therefore be seen that, basically, police cooperation is confined to combating common crime within the framework of national sovereignty. This of course has a number of consequences which have become the principles on which any international police cooperation must be based:

1. Each country will collaborate with other countries through its own police forces, using the existing and often very complex structures of these forces.
2. When cooperating at the international level, the police forces of the various countries will not apply "international" laws. For any action they take, the police of a given country will apply that country's own laws, and will conform to the procedure dictated by them.
3. There is no international police force, nor are there any international police officers in the strict sense of the word; lovers of "thrillers" will be disappointed to learn that there is no such person as James Bond, international agent.

Admittedly, this may not seem a very constructive approach to the problem of international cooperation in the international law enforcement field, but the positive results are to be found in what has been built up on the basis of these principles, taking them as a pivot around which to construct international police cooperation. This has been the work of the International Criminal Police Organization, Interpol.

1.3.1. ICPO—INTERPOL. Interpol's philosophy has always been based on the following considerations:

1. The age of supranationality has not yet been reached.
2. National sovereignty must be scrupulously respected.
3. The structures of each country must be adapted for close international cooperation.
4. Anything likely to cause conflict or division (*e.g.*, political cases) must be avoided at all costs, and all countries wishing to collaborate on an international scale should be allowed to do so.

A few years ago, when General de Gaulle was President of France, the Press frequently reported him as saying that he was in favor of "a Europe of nations" as opposed to a "United States of Europe." To paraphrase this, we can say that the international police of 1970 are the "police of nations" and not a kind of "supranational police force." Once the governments of two countries have given their necessary permission, then in theory no special form of organization is needed for their police forces to cooperate from time to time. In practice, however, an organizational structure is necessary for a number of reasons:

1. Police cooperation, if it is to be effective, cannot remain bilateral. Most cases call for multilateral cooperation, which of course complicates matters.
2. To cooperate effectively, the police need a rapid communications system; the establishment and the maintenance of such a system call for a series of choices which can be made only by joint decision.
3. Police cooperation needs to be reinforced and followed up by direct contact between the persons responsible for it.

In short, if we wish to develop really effective international cooperation, it is essential to decide on organizational structures and working methods, to establish collective discipline and to reach agreements on a number of problems.

The ICPO-Interpol has gradually built up these organizational structures, which are embodied in its Constitution, adopted in 1956 and completed by two appendices added subsequently: the Financial Regulations in 1957 and the Regulations Concerning National Central Bureaus in 1965.

1.3.1.1. *National Central Bureaus* (NCBs). In no two countries of the world are the police organized in the same way. In some cases there is a single national force (e.g., Israel, Nigeria, and Japan), and in others there are a large number of forces with regional jurisdiction (*e.g.*, the U.S.A. and Germany). In some countries the police come under the Ministry of Justice, and in others the Ministry of the Interior. The police may be paramilitary or civilian; they may carry out all activities connected with public order, or there may be a separate body responsible for crime investigation. Because of this complexity, it is not—and never has been—a question of all police services in all countries being able to cooperate with each other. Neither has there ever been any question of asking those countries who wish to participate in a widespread movement of police cooperation to set up new departments, which would serve only to complicate still further organizational structures and therefore give rise to added expense.

The solution adopted by ICPO-Interpol was as follows: In each country a central department is appointed by the national authorities to function as a kind of relay station, an operations base for international co-operation. This department becomes a sort of permanent correspondent at the national level. It is in permanent touch with its counterparts in other countries and with the local services in its own country. This is what in international jargon is known as an Interpol National Central Bureau.

The ICPO-Interpol Constitution fixes the role of the NCBs as follows:

Article 32

In order to ensure the above co-operation, each country shall appoint a body which will serve as the National Central Bureau. It shall ensure liaison with:

 a) The various departments in the country.
 b) Those bodies in other countries serving as National Central Bureau.
 c) The Organization's General Secretariat.

Provision is made for certain exceptions:

Article 33

In the cases of those countries where the provisions of article 32 are inapplicable or do not permit of effective, centralized co-operation, the General Secretariat shall decide, with these countries, the most suitable means of co-operation.

Examples of "National Central Bureaus" are the following:

1. The Commissariat Général aux Délégations Judiciaires (Belgium)
2. New Scotland Yard (United Kingdom)
3. The Headquarters of the Royal Canadian Mounted Police (Canada)
4. The Policia Federal (Argentina)
5. In the United States, the NCB is located within the U.S. Treasury Department.

These NCBs are, of course, responsible to the national authorities.

1.3.1.2. *The General Secretariat.* It is obvious that a permanent organization grouping together a large number of members (105 affiliated countries) needs a center to coordinate its activities. This role is fulfilled by
the General Secretariat. It is an international body, independent of all
governments and working on behalf of all.

1.3.1.3. *Communications System.* A permanent communications system
(by post, telegram, and Telex) exists between these "structures." One invaluable instrument is the radio network, which links together about forty
of the 105 NCBs. In 1969, 134,558 messages were sent over this network.
This figure shows not only how useful the network is but also how active
the cooperation is.

Periodically, direct personal contacts are made, which strengthen these
permanent links: These take place at the Organization's annual General
Assembly. Such contacts help to improve the Organization's efficiency.

Before explaining the aims of the Organization, some idea of the extent
of its activities can be obtained by quoting some figures taken from the
Progress Report: For the period of June 1968 to June 1969:

Cases handled by the General Secretariat	7,908
International notices issued about persons	349
Items of information exchanged between National Central Bureaus	184,529

The daily activities of the NCBs and the General Secretariat involve contacts with almost all Interpol-affiliated countries; for example, in 1968
Peru and Japan were in touch with forty-nine and sixty-one countries
respectively.

1.3.2. SPHERES IN WHICH INTERNATIONAL POLICE COOPERATION OPERATES. It
must be emphasized that everything depends on the *will* to cooperate
at the international level—this is essential. Nothing and no one can bring
about cooperation by force. But the will to do what? To do all that the
police have the power and the right to do under their national laws.
Within the limits of these laws, cooperation between police authorities
can take the following forms: exchange of information, checking of suspects' statements, forwarding of documents, circulation of offenders' descriptions, investigations of certain circles, etc. The range is enormous.

The following are just some examples of this daily cooperation:

Example 1. In August 1968, an international wanted-notice concerning a
swindler was circulated at the request of the Lebanese authorities. The
offender was arrested in Caracas, Venezuela, in June 1969 and extradited
to Lebanon in March 1970.

Example 2. In February 1970, a body was found washed up on the shore in Gibralter. A general message was broadcast over the Interpol radio network and the Spanish authorities replied that the body could be that of a seaman reported missing from a Spanish ship. Identity particulars were exchanged and the body was identified in April 1970 as that of the missing seaman.

Example 3. In 1968, a dangerous Indian criminal wanted by the Indian police was arrested in France as a result of information supplied by the United States and Australia. The offender was extradited to India to stand trial.

International police cooperation is necessarily limited in cases where the police cannot act without the intervention of magistrates. This is often the case with regard to the searching of premises and the seizure of property. It is also true for the holding of a person in detention for an extended period of time. Before taking action, the police officer must consult the magistrate, who will be guided in his decisions by the rules and principles of judicial cooperation which are often fixed by diplomatic treaties. Moreover, in many cases, the police set in motion the machinery of judicial cooperation when they approach the judicial authorities.

It is impossible to situate exactly the dividing line between direct, independent police cooperation and police cooperation which needs the authorization of the judicial authorities in order to become effective. Everything depends on the distribution of powers between police and judicial authorities, on the type of procedure, and on the judicial system. It is obvious that the allocation of powers will not be exactly the same in countries where there are examining magistrates as it is in countries where the police have sole responsibility for conducting investigations. Consequently, one of the basic rules of the "cooperation game" is acceptance of the fact that certain things can be done in some countries, but not in others.

1.3.3. ARREST AND EXTRADITION. Any legal expert who is concerned about individual liberty may wonder whether international police cooperation does not make a mockery of the traditional rules and whether, by circumscribing the laws and/or rules of procedure, it does not result in arbitrary measures being taken. On the contrary, international police cooperation has actually helped to add to the reputation of the extradition process by allowing it to function efficiently. It has also meant that certain measures—more expeditious perhaps, but much more likely to threaten human rights—are now little or no longer used.

In ordinary national law, the police have certain powers of arrest. Under the Anglo-Saxon system, the suspect must immediately be brought before the judge after evidence has been obtained. Under the "continental" system, the police may check the suspect's identity and activities for a strictly controlled period of twenty-four hours. After this, the suspect must either be released or transferred to the legal authorities. In the case of extradition, international police cooperation basically consists of the following:

1. Tracing the wanted person and establishing his whereabouts.
2. Informing immediately the judicial authority which requested the search that the person has been found.
3. Placing the suspect under surveillance or holding him in police custody in accordance with national regulations (*"garde á vue"* in France), to prevent an escape before the legal documents arrive. (The first of these documents is a telegram giving details of the arrest warrant; according to most extradition treaties, this telegram authorizes the judicial authorities to detain the suspect while the rest of the extradition papers are sent through diplomatic channels.)

In the field of extradition, police cooperation is involved only in the preparatory stages. It opens the way to the implementation of treaties. The police do not try to supplant the judicial authorities, nor emasculate the rules of judicial procedure. Article 16 of the European Convention on Extradition allows telegraphic notices of arrest warrants to be sent through ICPO-Interpol channels. This constitutes actual state and legal recognition of the role played by international police cooperation. In 1968, the police of twenty-one countries arrested 2,271 offenders with a view to extradition, using the procedures described above. It is obvious that such results could never have been achieved if police cooperation had not been so organized.

1.4. Interpol and the Evolution of Criminal Law

1.4.1. AT THE NATIONAL LEVEL. The exchanges of views and information which have taken place at General Assemblies and through the General Secretariat have made it possible for several countries to learn from the experience of others, and thus remedy faults and gaps in their own national legislations. For example, it was the adoption of resolutions by the ICPO-Interpol General Assembly which induced a number of countries to take administrative or statutory measures to make the fitting of anti-theft devices on new cars compulsory. With regard to drug-trafficking, the range of penalties has been modified in several European countries following recommendations made by that Organization.

With regard to another aspect of extradition, the role of the Organization—in the absence of an international convention linking all states—has been to encourage countries to adopt national laws outlining the broad principles of extradition and extradition procedure which the agencies of that country must follow when dealing with a request for extradition from a foreign country. The existence of such laws facilitates the extradition procedure between countries not linked by an extradition treaty. Several countries have implemented the recommendation made at the Interpol General Assembly on these lines; for example, several states, such as India, Ghana, and Malawi, passed such laws when they became independent. In order to assist them, Interpol recently circulated the texts of the national extradition laws of forty-four countries.

1.4.2. AT THE REGIONAL LEVEL. At the end of World War II, a considerable number of regional organizations were established. Interpol collaborates at the regional level with several of these. Since the founding of the Council of Europe, it has taken part in the work of drawing up several European conventions. A number of existing texts, including the draft general convention on extradition drawn up by Interpol in 1948 in conjunction with the then International Penal and Penitentiary Commission, were used as a basis for the European Convention on Extradition. The ICPO observers at the Council of Europe contributed notably to the drafting of clauses fixing conditions of provisional arrest.

The ICPO also collaborated actively in the European Convention on the Punishment of Road Traffic Offenses. To help the Council of Europe in its work, the ICPO carried out an inquiry among those countries which are members of both the Council of Europe and Interpol, in order to establish the volume of road traffic offenses; the idea of a "Common Schedule of road traffic offenses," adopted by the Convention, was advanced by the Interpol observer who took part in the drafting of this Convention.

Apart from collaboration in the drafting of conventions, the ICPO contributes to the development of ideas in the scientific field, notably by participating in the work of associations specializing in penal matters, and by cooperating with the European Committee on Crime Problems (Council of Europe). In 1963, for example, the Organization submitted a report to the European Committee on Crime Problems, in which it emphasized the need to establish international machinery for restoring property which was the subject of offenses when the offender and the victim were in two different countries.

The League of Arab States attaches particular importance to problems of social defense and crime prevention and has set up a specialized body known as the Pan-Arab Social Defense Organization (PASDO). The ICPO and the PASDO have collaborated on several occasions, in particular in drug traffic cases. Interpol also cooperates with the Organization of African Unity in the field of law enforcement by publishing reports or memoranda stressing the need for an inter-African convention on extradition or for national extradition laws.

1.4.3. AT THE WORLDWIDE LEVEL. Interpol's contribution to the evolution of ICL was very effective from the first years of its existence (as the International Criminal Police Commission). Indeed, it was police cooperation among member countries of the ICPO which revealed the fact that a certain number of offenses were typically international and could be combated only by international agreement between the countries concerned.

Within the framework of the League of Nations, Interpol observers took an active part in the drafting of the Convention for the Suppression of Counterfeiting Currency of April 29, 1929, after our national representatives had drawn the attention of their governments to this offense. Although the Convention itself does not refer to the ICPO, it is interesting to note that the central offices mentioned in articles 12, 13, and 14 were set up in many countries in the Interpol NCBs. Article 15 makes provision for international conferences to be held periodically between central authorities and also for the organization of an international central office of information. The setting up of an international central office is now no longer necessary because Interpol serves and has always served this function in accordance with a recommendation (No. 9) attached to the Convention. Moreover, all the international conferences which have been held in accordance with article 15 of this Convention have met on the initiative and under the auspices of Interpol. The latest such conference, the fifth, was held in Mexico City in October 1969 under the auspices of ICPO.

A complex international legal problem arose in connection with the 1929 Geneva Convention for the Suppression of Counterfeiting Currency and also with other conventions which were signed at the time of the existence of the League of Nations. It was solved partly by later international police cooperation which revealed how difficult it was for new states to adhere to conventions adopted at the time of the League of Nations. Following a resolution adopted by the ICPO at its 1962 General Assembly session in Madrid, and its communication to the United Nations, the U.N. General Assembly, after a report from the International Law Commission, decided to simplify the procedure for adhesion of new states to the Convention for the Suppression of Counterfeiting Currency and also to a number of other conventions.

At the meeting in New York in March 1961 of the U.N. plenipotentiary conference for the adoption of a Single Convention on Narcotic Drugs, the main purpose of the ICPO's collaboration was to introduce certain amendments to articles 44 to 46 of the draft convention.

I.C.L., which has greatly developed in the last few years, took another step forward in 1963 with the Tokyo Convention on Offenses and Certain Other Acts Committed on Board Aircraft. Interpol played an active part as an observer on the ICAO legal committee in the drafting of this convention which came into force on December 4, 1969. The ICPO's position was that the range of the convention should be extended to apply to criminal offenses committed on board aircraft and not only to those actions considered as endangering the security of the aircraft, as provided for in the original draft convention. The text which was eventually adopted as article 1 of this convention took into account, for the most part, Interpol's views which had been set out at the meeting of the ICAO Legal Committee in Rome in 1962; and in 1970, Interpol collaborated on the drafting of an international convention referred to as the 1970 Hague Convention on Unlawful Seizure of Aircraft.

It would be impossible to draw up a complete list of the direct or indirect action taken by Interpol in order to bring about an evolution in the law. However, the few examples given here demonstrate that such action can, and does, often produce positive results.

1.5. The Legal Status of International Police Action

As we reach the end of this study the following questions arise: At what level in international law should police cooperation be situated? Should it be considered as cooperation at governmental level, at administrative level, or merely on an unofficial basis?

This extremely complex question can be analyzed in the light of the sustained and ever-increasing action in which Interpol has been engaged for nearly fifty years (since 1923) and which has brought about a slow but sure evolution in the legal status of international police cooperation.

In theory, there are only two main types of international organizations: intergovernmental and nongovernmental (N.G.O.).

An intergovernmental organization can be defined as a body which has a certain kind of organizational structure (such as a plenary assembly, an executive committee, and a permanent secretariat) and which is adhered to by governments. Almost all such organizations are established by treaties between states, and countries are represented within these organizations by delegates appointed by their governments. The financial resources are also provided by the governments. This is not always the case, for in so empirical a field it is impossible to apply to the various types of international organizations legal rules as rigid as those applied to national associations within countries.

There are approximately 250 intergovernmental organizations of different types. Some are truly international, whereas others have only regional jurisdiction. Their legal competence varies according to the nature of their functions and the powers with which they are invested.

The United Nations is the most important intergovernmental organization; it has worldwide competence and political powers. The U.N. special agencies (13 in all) deal with economic and social matters such as health, education, labor, transport, and communications.

The other intergovernmental organizations are technical bodies with fairly limited scope such as the International Coffee Organization and the International Bureau of Weights and Measures, or regional organizations such as the Council of Europe, the Organization of African Unity, or the Organization of American States.

What then are nongovernmental organizations? In theory, they are private international associations, adhered to by national associations whose members work in the private sector; the state has no part in these associations. They are nonprofitmaking and their legal statutes are in no sense "public" since they are not founded on national laws or international treaties. They are private organizations grouping together private individuals with common interests, and financed by them.

What is the position of the ICPO-Interpol according to these definitions? It is true that Interpol is not founded on an international convention, in the usual diplomatic tradition. There is no parchment, red ribbon, or official seal. But its most recent constitution was adopted (in 1956) by an assembly composed of government-appointed delegates. Moreover, this constitution was sent at the time to the ministries of foreign affairs of all affiliated countries, and these authorities were given a period of six months to raise objections to any of the clauses of the constitution, on behalf of their country. Since no objections were raised, it can reasonably be argued that the organization's constitution was approved by the foreign ministries of all the governments involved.

Despite the fact that the ICPO-Interpol was not founded in the same way as the traditional kind of intergovernmental organization, it has the characteristics of such organizations. For example:

1. Cooperation is carried out at the level of official police agencies. There is, in fact, little difference from the point of view of hierarchy between the international cooperation carried out within the special U.N. agencies and that carried out between these government-appointed police agencies. In both cases, cooperation is between national administrations.

2. Its financial resources are provided by governments. The annual contribution to Interpol is included in each government's national budget.

3. The International Telecommunications Union maintains close relations with the ICPO. The International Frequency Registration Board allocates the radio network "the frequencies necessary for the international exchange of information intended to assist in the arrest of offenders."* This international allocation of frequencies to Interpol is carried out through the intermediary of governments which are members of both organizations.

4. Since the adoption of the present constitution in 1956 almost all the countries which have joined Interpol have done so by means of a written application signed by the chief of state or by a minister, and referring to a cabinet decision in most cases. Because of the national importance of such decisions, some countries adopted national laws authorizing their government to participate in Interpol activities. The United States became a member in this way, with the passing of a Congressional law which was adopted by Congress and signed by President Eisenhower on August 28, 1958. Also, Argentina, Morocco, and Bolivia—to quote just a few examples—all confirmed their affiliation to the organization by governmental decrees adopted on January 22, 1962; June 30, 1962, and April 19, 1963, respectively.

5. The "official" character of the ICPO is seen very clearly from the composition of its plenary body, the general assembly. According to article 7 of the constitution, the head of each country's delegation to the assembly "shall be appointed by the competent governmental authority of that country."

The only difference between the traditional kind of intergovernmental organization and the ICPO arises from a point of procedure: the form of the organization's constitution. The ICPO was not founded by a convention, but by a text adopted unanimously by an assembly of governmental delegates.

Moreover, it is interesting to note that during negotiations about relations between the ICPO and the Council of Europe, the letter stated in a memorandum dated August 12, 1958, that "unquestionably, it (the ICPO) is not an international nongovernmental organization." As a result, in 1959, relations between the Council of Europe and the ICPO-Interpol

---

* See para. 279 of the Radiocommunications Regulations, appended to the International Telecommunications Convention, signed in Atlantic City in 1947.

were fixed by an exchange of letters constituting a cooperation agreement.

Even more conclusive is the position adopted by the United Nations.

Between 1947 and 1972, relations between the United Nations and Interpol were based on the "consultative status granted to nongovernmental organizations." However, on May 20, 1971, at its fiftieth session, the U.N. Economic and Social Council adopted a resolution setting out the terms of "special cooperation arrangements" between the United Nations and the ICPO-Interpol (U.N. doc E/RES/1579L (June 3, 1971)).

This text came into force following its approval by the Interpol General Assembly in September 1971.

In the U.N.'s view, the ICPO-Interpol, "formerly a nongovernmental organization in consultative status with the council is now to be regarded as an intergovernmental organization" (U.N. ECOSOC Doc. E/4961, at 3 (Mar. 8, 1971)).

From this it can only be concluded that among the various international organizations, the ICPO-Interpol is a true international public service of the intergovernmental type, recognized as such by governments and operating according to the methods and principles in force in intergovernmental organization. Interpol operates on an official and clearly defined basis.

1.6. Conclusion

How can international police cooperation as it exists today be developed to bring it closer to some of the more idealistic expectations?

As long as the concept of national sovereignty remains, there can be no hope of any drastic change in the present situation.

In spite of this, international police cooperation *can* make progress and become even more effective. How? By more united efforts on the part of the countries concerned, by an ever-increasing centralization of information at national level, by still greater and more rapid international exchange of information, and by greater collective discipline. These are the concrete tasks which in the years ahead face those who have the great responsibility of promoting international police cooperation.

Section 2. PERMANENT OR TEMPORARY UNITED NATIONS PEACE-KEEPING FORCES—A WORLD POLICE FORCE

S.K. AGRAWALA

Section 2.1. Introduction

The prohibition of war as an instrument of national policy under the General Treaty for the Renunciation of War, 1928,[1] and the subsequent ban on the use of force in general under the provisions of the U.N. Char-

[1] 94 L.N.T.S. 57; 4 Hudson, INTERNATIONAL LEGISLATION 2522 (1929).

ter[2] make it incumbent upon the international community to establish a universal and comprehensive system of international control that could keep a constant watch over the observance and application of this new obligation by the states. In other words, if threats to international peace and security have to be effectively counteracted, and if acts of aggression or other breaches of the peace have to be suppressed[3] and peace restored, a permanent world police force superior in strength to the forces of any state or a group of states for enforcement action under Chapter VII of the Charter is indispensable.[4] If because of the present state of international relations and lack of consensus among the Big Five, unanimity on the creation of such a force does not exist, the next best alternative to creating a Permanent U.N. Force for the limited purpose of "peace-keeping" must be pursued.[5]

However, thus far only temporary forces whether in the forms of observation groups, or a military force like the one in Korea, or a "peace-keeping" force like the U.N. Emergency Force (UNEF) in the Middle East or the U.N. Operations in the Congo (ONUC) have operated on behalf of the United Nations with varying degrees of success. Each one of these military operations has also been an exercise in improvisation with all its attendant drawbacks.

These operations have thrown to the fore legal problems of great significance, many of which had to be solved by the U.N. Secretariat particularly, and by others concerned with the operations. The U.N. practice in the field is by now sufficiently extensive and the legal problems that the organization of and the operation by such a force generates are identifiable.

An attempt has been made in this section to briefly examine the legal competence of the Security Council and the General Assembly to establish a force of this nature, to survey the U.N. experience with respect to the organization and operation of such forces, to build on that experience, and to determine the general outlines on which a future Permanent U.N. Peace-keeping Force could be established.

2.2. Raising of Forces Under Chapter VII of the Charter[6]

Under the U.N. Charter, when a dispute or situation brought to the

[2] Art. 2(4) & 2(3); also the preamble "to ensure . . . that armed forces shall not be used, save in the common interest . . . ."

[3] Art. 1(1) of the U.N. Charter.

[4] See CLARK & SOHN, WORLD PEACE THROUGH WORLD LAW 11 *passim* (2d. rev. ed. 1962) [hereafter cited as Sohn].

[5] *See id.* at 42-59.

[6] On the interpretation of these articles, *see* KELSEN, LAW OF THE UNITED NATIONS 724 *passim* (1964) [hereinafter cited as Kelsen]. *See also* GOODRICH & HAMBRO, CHARTER OF THE UNITED NATIONS (1949).

attention of the Security Council either by a state (art. 35) or by the Secretary-General (art. 99) cannot be resolved by peaceful methods under Chapter VI of the Charter, and the necessity of some coercion or application of force is indicated, the Security Council has to first make a determination under article 39. It determines "the existence of any threat to the peace, breach of the peace, or act of aggression . . .", and can call upon the parties to comply with certain provisional measures (art. 40), or it can make recommendations (art. 39). Sometimes, the recommendations of the Security Council authorize full-fledged military action by individual members, as in Korea, or they initiate a U.N. peace-keeping operation, including the setting up of appropriate mechanisms for that purpose, as in Cyprus in 1964 and after.[7] The Security Council can also employ measures not involving the use of armed forces (art. 41) and as a last resort can even use force (art. 42), for "it may take such action by air, sea, or land forces as may be necessary to maintain or restore international peace and security. Such action may include demonstrations, blockades, and other operations by air, sea, or land forces of members of the United Nations." The Charter thus leaves the way open for the Security Council to compose its forces either of national contingents contributed by member states or by other methods, such as individual enlistment.

The implementation of this Charter scheme called for agreements between the Security Council and member states for making available to the Security Council, on its call, armed forces, assistance, and facilities, including rights of passage, necessary for the purpose of maintaining international peace and security (art. 43[1]).[8] Article 47(1) of the Charter provided for the establishment of a Military Staff Committee "to advise and assist the Security Council on all questions relating to the Security Council's military requirements for the maintenance of international peace and security, employment, and command of forces placed at its disposal, the regulation of armaments, and possible disarmament." "The strategic direction of any armed forces placed at the disposal of

---

[7] *See* M. Sorensen, Manual of Public International Law 786, 787 (1968).

[8] *See also* arts. 43(2) & 43(3). Finn Seyersted, however, takes the view that there appears to be no basis in the text of art. 42 or in the *travaux preparatories* for assuming that the article can be applied only in the circumstances laid down in Art. 43. Art. 42 does not even provide that the force must necessarily consist of national contingents, but leaves the way open, for example, also for individual enlistment by the organization. Still less does art. 42 require that any national contingents must be provided under obligations undertaken pursuant to art. 43, rather than voluntarily. *See* F. Seyersted, United Nations Forces in the Law of Peace and War 29–30, 130–32 [hereinafter cited as Seyersted]. *See also* Brit. Y.B. Int'l L. 438–39, 463–64 (1961) by the same author.

the security council" was also to be entrusted to it (art. 47[3]). The Military Staff Committee was to consist of the chiefs of staff of the permanent members of the Security Council or their representatives (art. 47[2]). The Security Council in 1946 directed the Military Staff Committee as its first task "to examine from the military point of view the provisions contained in article 43 of the Charter, and to submit the results of the study and any recommendations to the Council in due course."[9] The Committee failed to arrive at any agreement regarding the basic principles which were to be embodied in the agreements to be concluded under article 43. Basic disagreements soon arose among the members (mainly between the Soviet Union and the United States) on the size of the force, relative sizes of the contributions of the five permanent members, their location, bases, logistical support, and other matters.[10] The effort was virtually abandoned in August 1948; consequently, the agreements contemplated in article 43 were never concluded. The Committee did, however, present to the Council in its report, a set of "General Principles[11] governing the organization of the armed forces made available to the Security Council by member nations of the United Nations."

2.3. U.N. Guard, U.N. Legion, Truce and Military Observation Groups, etc.

The first proposal[12] for any sort of U.N. force came in 1948 from the Secretary-General, who pleaded for the establishment of a U.N. Guard[13] composed of from 800 to several thousand uniformed, lightly armed men recruited by the Secretary-General as a unit of the Secretariat, but it had to be abandoned because of lack of support by the big powers. His

---

[9] 1 U.N. SCOR, No. 1, at 369a (1946).

[10] *See* Report of the Military Staff Committee of Apr. 30, 1947. 2 U.N. SCOR, Special Supp. 1., at 1–32 U.N. Doc. S/336, (1947). For comments on the report, *see* ROSNER, THE UNITED NATIONS EMERGENCY FORCE 217–219 (1963); R. Russell, *United Nations Experience with Military Forces*, Institute for Defence Analyses, Research Paper, at 15–23 (May 1963).

[11] For text, *see* 2 REPERTORY OF PRACTICE OF U.N. ORGANS 396; 2 U.N. SCOR, Special Supp. 1 (1947). These were not in all cases agreed principles, and on certain articles two or more alternative texts were given, recording the extent and nature of the disagreement. The Security Council adopted provisionally the articles agreed by the committee and then turned to those not agreed, after the failure to agree on art. 11. The remaining articles were not discussed. For a brief review of these "General Principles," *see* BOWETT, UNITED NATIONS FORCES 14–17 (1964) [hereinafter cited as Bowett]. *See also*, Frye, A UNITED NATIONS PEACE FORCE 52–55 (1957) [hereinafter cited as Frye]; Seyersted *supra* note 8, at 30–31.

[12] For previous history before the establishment of U.N., *see* Frye, *Supra* note 11, at 46 *passim;* Bowett, *supra* note 11, at 3–11; Rosner, *supra* note 10, Historical Appendix, at 207–22.

[13] 3 U.N. GAOR, p. 2, Annexes, at 6 *passim* (1948); Schwebel, *A United Nations Guard and a United Nations Legion,* in Frye, *supra* note 11, at 412 *passim.*

proposal for a U.N. legion composed of volunteers recruited and trained on a national basis suffered the same fate.

However, a small U.N. Headquarters Guard Force and Headquarters Security Service, uniformed but unarmed was established early for the purpose of maintaining order and security at the U.N. headquarters. In 1948, a special force of some fifty U.N. guards was sent to Palestine to assist the military truce observers. In 1949, the General Assembly authorized the Secretary-General to establish a U.N. Field Service on the basis of a secretariat proposal.[14] This force of 300 men recruited individually as part of the Secretariat, wearing U.N. uniforms and carrying only side arms in special cases, was created. Their functions are entirely civilian and consist of providing technical services for U.N. missions as well as doing guard duties at headquarters. The Field Service has been utilized in several troubled areas, including Palestine, Kashmir, and Korea. It can in no sense be considered to be an armed force under article 43, nor could it be used for enforcement action under Chapter VII.

Another example of U.N. forces consists of truce observation groups and other military observation missions which the U.N. has employed in Palestine,[15] Kashmir,[16] Lebanon,[17] etc. The members of these groups are not recruited as members of the Secretariat. They are taken on an individual and temporary basis from national armies. Their functions are to observe military events, and to mediate and persuade when hostile actions or other violations of a truce occur. They do not themselves perform military operations, and may carry arms only for self-defense. The military observation groups are established ad hoc in each case, but the General Assembly has also created a U.N. Panel of Field Observers to give the system some sort of permanency.

The temporary and entirely civilian force established for the clearance

[14] See 5 REPERTORY OF PRACTICE OF U.N. ORGANS, at 266–68. See also Bowett supra note 11, at 18–21.

[15] The U.N. Truce Supervision Organization (U.N.T.S.O.) was established by the U.N. Mediator for Palestine under the authority of the Security Council Resolutions of May 29 and July 15, 1949, to observe the truces ordered by the Council. It was also called upon to observe the armistices established by the Armistice Agreement between Israel and Egypt of Feb. 24, 1949, and such other agreements with the other Arab States. (42 U.N.T.S. 251 passim). See also Hurewitz, The U.N. Conciliation Commission for Palestine, INTERNATIONAL ORGANIZATION 484–97 (1953).

[16] The U.N. Military Observer Group in India and Pakistan was established by the Security Council Resolution of Apr. 21, 1948 (para. 17) and was authorized to station observers where it deemed necessary by the cease-fire-line agreement of July 27, 1949, U.N. Doc. S/1430, Annex 26. See also Louri, The Military Observer Group in India and Pakistan, 9 INTERNATIONAL ORGANIZATION 19–51 (1955).

[17] The U.N. Observation Group in Lebanon (U.N.O.G.I.L.) was established by the Security Council Resolution of June 11, 1958 and comprised of 592 officers from 21 countries. See the reports of the Group in U.N. SCOR 3, 24, 33, 79, 127, & 157 (1958).

of the Suez Canal in 1957[18] is also sometimes mentioned as another illustration of the constituting of a U.N. force.

2.4. U.N. Action in Korea

Only in the case of Korea in 1950 was an international force set up against an aggressor, and it still stands as the solitary occasion on which enforcement action was taken by the United Nations. The Security Council was unable to invoke the duty of member states under articles 43 *et seq.* to contribute national contingents, or to establish a force by individual enlistment. So the Security Council without referring to any article of the Charter, but apparently basing itself upon article 39, recommended by the resolution of June 27, 1950, that member states furnish assistance and, subsequently, made basic provisions for the command of contingents offered voluntarily by member states pursuant to this recommendation.[19] The validity of the action of the United States which instructed its sea and air forces to render assistance to South Korea on June 27 but before the Resolution of that date was passed, has been rightly questioned.[20]

The Resolution of July 7 also recommended the establishment of a unified command[21] under the United States to which the members were to provide military forces and other assistance. The United States was requested to designate the commander of such forces; the command was to be authorized to fly the U.N. flag and the United States was requested to report to the Security Council on the course of action taken by the Unified Command.

The representative of the Soviet Union returned to the Council table on August 1, 1950, and no further action could be possible by the Security Council because of the lack of unanimity among the permanent

---

[18] *See* Seyersted, *supra* note 8, at 24–25. *See also* 257 U.N.T.S. 75 for the texts of letters exchanged between the U.N. and Egypt.

[19] U.N. Doc. S/1501, adopted on June 25, 1950, by 9 votes with 1 abstention (Yugoslavia) and 1 member absent (USSR); S/1511, adopted on June 27, 1950 by 7 votes to 1 (Yugoslavia) with 1 member absent (USSR) and 2 abstaining (Egypt & India). India subsequently accepted the resolution (S/1520). S/1588, adopted on July 7, 1950, by 7 votes with 3 abstentions (Yugoslavia, Egypt, India) and one member absent (USSR). For a detailed discussion of the constitutional bases of these three Security Council resolutions, *see* Bowett, *supra* note 11, at 30–36; Seyersted, *supra* note 8, at 32–40, 129–32; BRIT Y. B.L. INT'L 362 *passim*, 437–40 (1961). *See also* Potter, *Legal Aspects of the Situations in Korea* 44 A. J. I. L. 709, 712 (1950).

[20] See Bowett, *supra* note 11, at 32. *See also United States Policy in the Korean Crisis*, Dept. of State Publication 3922; STONE, LEGAL CONTROLS OF INTERNATIONAL CONFLICT 231 n.13 (1959). Stone suggests collective self-defense as justification for U.S. action.

[21] For the views on the legality of the establishment of a U.N. Command, *see* KELSEN, RECENT TRENDS IN THE LAW OF UNITED NATIONS 931 *passim* (1951); Stone *supra* note 20, at 232; Bowett, *supra* note 11, at 33, 34–36.

members. Subsequently, the official U.N. action was taken only by the General Assembly but only on political, relief, and other matters of wider scope. Military matters were left to the U.S. Government as the Unified Command. The armistice negotiations lasting for about two years were also conducted by the U.N. Command under instructions from the U.S. Government.

Bowett has observed that the principal defects of the Korean experience were the following:

1. Uncertainty as to the legal basis for the Security Council Resolutions.
2. The dominant role of the United States, which assumed the major military burden.[22]
3. The inadequacy of the system of political control over the military command (which in practice worked under the orders of the U.S. Government).

Nevertheless, the parties involved on the U.N. side commonly spoke of the forces and the action in terms of U.N. forces and U.N. action,[23] which suggests the recognition of the action as a collective action within the framework of the United Nations.

2.5 The Uniting for Peace Resolution—and the Collective Measures Committee

The Korean experience soon demonstrated that no enforcement action could be possible by the Security Council in the future because of the absence of unanimity among the permanent members. It was, therefore, proposed that the General Assembly be put in a position to recommend collective measures in the face of the inactivity of the Security Council. The General Assembly, therefore, adopted by 52 votes to 5 and with 2 abstentions the Uniting for Peace Resolution on November 3, 1950.[24]

---

[22] It has been estimated that numerically the United States contributed 50.32 per cent of the ground forces, 85.89 per cent of the naval forces and 93.38 per cent of the air forces. The Republic of Korea contributed 40.10 per cent, 7.45 per cent, and 5.65 per cent, respectively, while 15 other members contributed the remainder. *See* Frye, *supra* note 11, at 188; Goodrich, 494 INTERNATIONAL CONCILIATION 114–19, 178–81 (1953).

[23] *See* Bowett. *supra* note 11, at 45–47; Seyersted, *supra* note 8, at 39–41.

[24] G.A. Res. 377 A(V), 5 U.N. GAOR, Supp. 20, at 10–12, U.N. Doc. A/1775 (1950); 45 A.J.I.L. (Supp. 1 1951). *See* Petersen, *The Uses of the Uniting for Peace Resolution Since 1951,* 13 INTERNATIONAL ORGANIZATION 219 (1959); Sohn, *The Authority of the United Nations to Establish and Maintain a Permanent United Nations Force,* 52 A.J.I.L. 233–34 (1958); Kelsen, *supra* note 6, at 953; Andrassy, *Uniting for Peace,* 50 A.J.I.L. 563 (1956); GOODRICH and SIMONS, THE UNITED NATIONS AND THE MAINTENANCE OF INTERNATIONAL PEACE AND SECURITY 406–23, 430–33 (1955); Goodrich, *Development of the General Assembly,* 471 INTERNATIONAL CONCILIATION 267, 274 (1951).

The Resolution provided for the following important changes in organization and procedure:

1. The authority to transfer a peace and security issue to the General Assembly if the security council was blocked by veto.
2. The capacity to call emergency sessions of the Assembly, if necessary, for this purpose.
3. A recommendation that member states maintain special U.N. designated units in their respective national armed forces.
4. The creation of the following:

    (a) A Peace Observation Commission.
    (b) A Collective Measures Committee.
    (c) A Panel of Military Experts.

Thus it was believed that the central problems of the maintenance of peace and security could be solved by advance warning through the Peace Observation Commission; by expeditious shifting of the dispute from the stymied Council to the veto-less Assembly; by use, if necessary, of voluntarily and unilaterally earmarked forces, and by further long-range planning through the Collective Measures Committee.[25]

2.6. Legality of the Uniting for Peace Resolution and the Power of the General Assembly with Respect to the Operation of the U.N. Collective Security System

Though the Charter confers on the Security Council "primary responsibility for the maintenance of international peace and security,"[26] it does not confer on it exclusive jurisdiction in respect thereof. Under article 11(1), the General Assembly could adopt regulations defining the principles which should govern the establishment, training, organization command, and use of any forces put at the disposal of the United Nations. It could then recommend to the members that they take such steps as may be necessary to implement these principles. But the General Assembly has only the power to make recommendations and any member state can refuse to comply with a recommendation that it contribute personnel, arms, bases, or assistance to a U.N. Force. But Professor Sohn is of the view that their discretion to refuse compliance is always limited by their duty under article 2(2) of the Charter "to fulfill in good faith the obligations assumed by them" in accordance with the Charter.[27]

Article 10 gives the General Assembly the wide power of making recommendations on any questions or matters within the scope of the pres-

[25] Petersen, *supra* note 24, at 219, 220.
[26] Art. 24.
[27] Sohn, *supra* note 4, at 231, n.11.

ent Charter or relating to the powers and functions of any organs provided for in the present Charter . . . ." The competence to adopt recommendatory resolutions comprises in particular "any questions relating
to the maintenance of international peace and security" (art. 11[2])
and "measures for the peaceful adjustment of any situation, regardless of
origin . . . ." (art. 14).

It is under these Charter provisions that the power of the General Assembly with respect to the operation of the U.N. Collective Security system and the legal validity of the Uniting for Peace Resolution is sought
to be justified. But this interpretation of Charter provisions is not universally accepted by U.N. members. According to the Soviet view, apart
from article 106, the Security Council has the exclusive jurisdiction to act
when there is a threat to or breach of peace or act of aggression. The
General Assembly cannot act as a substitute for the Security Council in
matters covered by Chapter VII of the Charter. The Assembly's power
to make recommendations is restricted not only by article 12 but also by
articles 11 and 106. The United Nations can resort to force only through
the Security Council—under articles 41, 42, and 94(2). Kelsen[28] takes
the view that articles 5, 50, 53(1), and 99 can be properly explained
only when it is assumed that enforcement measures can be taken exclusively by the Security Council. It may be submitted, however, that it is
too restrictive an interpretation of a constitutional document like the
U.N. Charter, and does not at all encompass the new facts of present
international relations, *e.g.*, the impotence of the Security Council because of the unscrupulous use of veto, and the changed political role of
the General Assembly as a result of its changed composition due to the
admission of several newly independent Afro-Asian states. A constitutional document in order to be enduring must be so interpreted as to
satisfy the growing aspirations and the changing character of the society
which it is meant to regulate. It is interesting to note that despite its
above stand, the Soviet Union did not find itself constrained to support
the General Assembly action in the Suez Affair of 1956 and the Middle
Eastern Crisis of 1968.

2.7. The Collective Measures Committee

The Collective Measures Committee consisted of fourteen states and
was directed "to study and make a report on . . . methods, including
those in section C of the Uniting for Peace Resolution, which might be
used to maintain international peace and security . . . ." In section C,
each member was invited to survey its resources in order to determine
the nature and scope of the assistance it may be in a position to render

[28] Kelsen, *supra* note 6, at 973–74.

in support of any recommendation of the Security Council or of the General Assembly. It further recommended to the members to "maintain within its national armed forces elements so trained, organized, and equipped that they could promptly be made available in accordance with its constitutional processes, for service as a U.N. unit or units . . . ." The Committee presented three reports[29] to the General Assembly. It was the first systematic attempt by the United Nations to study the whole field of collective action, but produced only a set of guiding principles for future action and nowhere proposed actual steps to be taken to create an embryonic U.N. force in advance.[30] The military measures suggested by the Committee are ones which could be used pending the conclusion of agreements provided for in article 43 of the Charter.

The first report was more or less a faithful reproduction of the system adopted in the Korean conflict. The Second Report (1952) reproduces and recommends for study certain proposals of the Secretary-General which go beyond the procedure adopted in Korea.[31] He had proposed that states which were not in a position to contribute self-contained combat or ancillary units could organize in advance combatant or auxiliary units to be later integrated into a U.N. force. In addition, individual volunteers could be enlisted and trained on a part-time basis on behalf of the United Nations by the states willing to do so. They too could be mobilized for service by the United Nations in case of need, either as part of a national force contributed by the state concerned or as a separate unit. The cost of recruiting, equipping, and training such U.N. volunteer reservists was proposed to be met by cooperating states as part of their overall advance contribution to collective security under the United Nations.

The recommendations of the Collective Measures Committee were not made in categorical terms and they were never adopted by the General Assembly, but merely noted. They do not, therefore, constitute any binding directives.

The third and the last reports of the Collective Measures Committee mentioned that the Secretary-General had himself withdrawn his proposal for the time being, and as such, no further study or action was required.

The reports of the Committee were wholly guided by the Korean ex-

---

[29] First Report, 6 U.N. GAOR, Supp. 13, U.N. Doc. A/1891 (1951); Second Report, 7 U.N. GAOR, Supp. 17, U.N. Doc. A/2215 (1952); Third Report, 9 U.N. GAOR, Annexes, Agenda Item No. 19, U.N. Doc. A/2713, S/3283 (1954). For further details, *see* A. Katzin, *Collective Security: The Work of the Collective Measures Committee*, ANNUAL REVIEW OF THE U.N. AFFILRS (1952); Frye, *supra* note 11, at 62–64; Bowett, *supra* note 11, at 21–28.

[30] Bowett, *supra* note 11, at 22.

[31] Seyersted, *supra* note 8, at 44.

perience. Very little thought, if at all, was given to problems of financing the operations, status and privileges of the forces, withdrawal of consent by the host state and the contributing state, problems which had to be faced in the subsequent operations. In the 1956 crisis, therefore, no existing practical scheme, which would have insured an effective and efficient U.N. force, was available and the task became one of sheer improvisation.[32]

It is interesting to note, however, that the Secretary-General had considered the creation of a permanent force as administratively, financially, and militarily impractical at that time, and the Collective Measures Committee had endorsed it in full.[33]

2.8. The U.N. Emergency Force (UNEF) and The U.N. Operations in the Congo (Organisation des Nations Unies au Congo) (ONUC)

Since Korea, the U.N. forces have been used on a relatively large scale in the Middle Eastern Crisis in 1956, in the Congo in 1960, in West New Guinea in 1961,[34] and in Cyprus in 1963.[35] However, the UNEF and the ONUC offer the richest experience for the composition of any U.N. force in the future. They have, therefore, been studied (within the limitations of space) under the following subheadings:

1. Circumstances in which the forces were created.
2. The constitutional bases.
3. Functions and powers.
4. Composition, organization, and control.
5. Status in international law.
6. Claims for and against the force and its members, jurisdiction.
7. Consent for the presence of a U.N. force.
8. Withdrawal of national contingents.
9. Financing the force.

2.8.1. CIRCUMSTANCES IN WHICH THE FORCES WERE CREATED. In October, 1956, Israeli armed forces crossed the Armistice Demarcation line, entered the territory of Egypt, and proceeded toward the Suez Canal. The United Kingdom and France soon joined Israel. The Security Council being unable to act because of the negative votes of France and the United Kingdom, called an emergency session of the General Assembly, as provided in the Uniting for Peace Resolution. By Resolutions 998 (ES-I) of November 4, 1000 (ES-I) of November 5, and 1001 (ES-I) of Novem-

---

[32] Bowett, *supra* note 11, at 28.
[33] Report of the Collective Measures Committee 12 (1952).
[34] Bowett, *supra* note 11, at 255–61.
[35] *Id.* at 552–60.

ber 7, 1956, the General Assembly without a negative vote established the U.N. Emergency Force (UNEF).

The Republic of Congo achieved independence from Belgium on June 30, 1960. Soon after certain units of Congolese forces mutinied, and Belgian troops were reintroduced into the territory on July 12 for the stated purpose of protecting lives and property. The province of Katanga seceded from the new republic. The President of the new republic immediately cabled the Secretary-General condemning the Belgian invervention as aggression and requesting the urgent dispatch of military assistance. The Secretary-General, acting expressly under article 99 of the Charter, called a meeting of the Security Council on July 13 which initiated the operations (ONUC). Successive resolutions were passed by the Security Council and the General Assembly as complex events in the Congo developed.

2.8.2. THE CONSTITUTIONAL BASES OF THE U.N. EMERGENCY FORCE (UNEF). In the resolutions of the General Assembly no reference is made to its legal basis. However, its creation by the General Assembly can be more than justified under the wide powers and functions entrusted to the General Assembly by articles 10, 11, and 14[36] of the Charter, to discharge "a residual responsibility." The General Assembly was exercising a power which it had claimed for itself under the Uniting for Peace Resolution. Though it was hardly the armed force to be used against an aggressor, its validity seems to be based on the premise that "the right to establish such a smaller force is implicit in the right to establish a large fighting force."[37]

In the words of the Secretary-General it was to be considered as a "subsidiary organ of the General Assembly,"[38] because it had been established in accordance with Article 22 of the Charter.[39] Rosner[40] also justified its creation under the "implied powers"[41] of the General Assembly.

The International Court of Justice, too, in the *Expenses* case,[42] after examining the General Assembly resolutions creating the force, has held

[36] *See* Goodrich and Hambro *Supra* note 6.

[37] Sohn, *supra* note 4, at 234.

[38] U.N. Doc. A/3943 at 24. *See* ROSNER, THE UNITED NATIONS EMERGENCY FORCE 40–44 (1963) for a detailed discussion of this point. See also UNEF Reg. 6, Regulations enacted by the Secretary-General on Feb. 20, 1957, 271 U.N.T.S. 169; Status Agreement with Egypt, Introduction para. 23, 260 U.N.T.S. 61 & 271, *id.* at 145.

[39] *Report of the Secretary-General on Arrangements Concerning the Status of the UNEF in Egypt*, U.N. Doc. A/3526; 11 U.N. GAOR, 2, 3, Annexes, Agenda Item No. 66, at 52–53 (1956–57).

[40] Rosner, *supra* note 10, at 44.

[41] *Reparations for Injuries Suffered in the Service of the U.N.*, I.C.L. REP. 182–183 (1949).

[42] *Case Concerning Certain Expenses of the U.N.*, I.C.J. REP. 151, 164–165, 172 (1962).

that "action" under article 11(2)[43] did in fact refer to "enforcement action" and that the General Assembly's action was not of this character. It really constituted "measures" within article 14. The Court did not rest the constitutionality of UNEF on the Uniting for Peace Resolution either.

Whereas the overwhelming majority of the General Assembly members have continued to accept its establishment to be perfectly legal, the Soviet Union has taken the stand that its creation by the General Assembly was illegal because Chapter VII of the Charter empowers only the Security Council to set up an international armed force, and they have, therefore, refused to pay their assessments for UNEF's expenses. It led the General Assembly ultimately to request an advisory opinion from the International Court of Justice. It is, however, interesting to note that the Soviet Union only abstained from voting, and did not cast a negative vote on resolutions 1000 and 100 (ES-I)., establishing the force. Earlier the Soviet Union had even voted for the transfer of the question to the General Assembly.

2.8.3. U.N. OPERATIONS IN THE CONGO (ONUC). Neither the Security Council nor the General Assembly specifically stated the Charter provisions upon which particular resolutions were based. The creation of ONUC was accomplished by the Secretary-General under the express authorization of the Security Council by its resolution of July 14, 1960,[44] ". . . authorizes the Secretary-General . . . to provide the government with such military assistance as may be necessary . . . ." Schachter[45] has taken the view that decision was taken under Chapter VII of the Charter and more specifically under article 40. Though there was no initial determination under article 39, and the Security Council did not use the phrase, "threat to international peace and security," until its Resolution of February 21, 1961, the International Court of Justice,[46] in its opinion of July 20, 1962, holds that the Resolution of July 14 was clearly adopted with a view to maintaining international peace and security. Though the court did not consider it necessary to express an opinion as to which article of the Charter was the basis of the Resolution, it added that the operation did not involve preventive or enforcement measures against any state under Chapter VII.[47] Since the force was limited to the specific purposes of preventing civil war and expelling mercenaries, it

---

[43] Art. 11(2) of the Charter: "Any such question on which action is necessary shall be referred to the Security Council by the General Assembly . . ."

[44] U.N. Doc. S/4387.

[45] Schachter, *Legal Aspects of the United Nations in the Congo*, 55 A.J.I.L. 1 (1961); *see also* Jennings, *The United Nations Force and the Congo*, THE LISTENER (Oct. 19, 1961).

[46] I.C.J. REP. 175 (1962).

[47] *Id.* at 151.

was not a force created under article 42. The principle of nonintervention and article 2(7) of the Charter were constantly insisted upon. Article 40, coupled with the power to establish subsidiary organs in article 29, therefore seems to be the proper constitutional basis of the decision to create the force. The Secretary-General has himself cited this article when addressing the Security Council.[48]

The various types of instructions given to states could be justified under articles 40, 41, 25, and 49; or even under the general obligation contained in article 2(5) of the Charter. With regard to nonmembers, the United Nations has the general power of article 2(6), and the action of the Security Council under articles 39 and 40 is not limited to acting in relation to member states only.

The legal basis for instructions to the secessionist and other factors within the Congo, the nonstate entities, can be found under articles 39 and 40.

The General Assembly Resolutions were mostly endorsements of the actions of the Security Council and the Secretary-General, and were not concerned with the creation of the force. But the unusual decision contained in the Resolution of April 14, 1961,[49] that all Belgian and other foreign military, paramilitary personnel, mercenaries, etc. shall be completely withdrawn and evacuated, can be taken as the one not addressed to the states but to the ONUC; and the constitutional authority for the same may be found under article 14.[50]

In the case of the force created to meet the West New Guinea situation and also the Cyprus situation, no clear indication of the constitutional basis of the U.N. action was given in the resolutions.

2.9. Functions and Powers of UNEF and ONUC

2.9.1. UNEF. The purpose, organization, status, functioning, and financing of the force are laid down in a number of documents.[51] (General Assembly resolutions, Reports of the Secretary-General, basic agreements with participating states, status of forces agreement with Egypt, Secretary-General's Regulations, etc.).

[48] 15 U.N. SCOR, 884th meeting, at 4; 920th meeting, at 19. However, Draper finds art. 29 itself a satisfactory basis. See *The Legal Limitation Upon the Employment of Weapons by the U.N. Force in the Congo*, 12 INT'L & COMP. L.Q. 392 (1963). Halderman relies on art. 1(1). See *Legal Basis for the U.N. Armed Forces*, 56 A.J.I.L. 971 (1962). Bowett relies on art. 39, *see supra* note 11, at 178–80 for the reason that while the supervision of compliance with the call for provisional measures was a major part of ONUC's function, it was not the entire function.
[49] G.A. Res. 1599 (XV).
[50] Bowett, *supra* note 11, at 182.
[51] See *The United Nations Emergency Force, Basic Documents*, a collection prepared by E. Lauterpacht (1960). See *also* Seyersted, *supra* note 8, at 46–47.

The purpose of the force[52] was not to fight an aggressor, as in Korea, but to secure and supervise the cessation of hostilities. It entered the areas occupied by the invading forces as they withdrew, to turn them over to Egypt, and after the complete withdrawal of the invading troops, the force was stationed on the Egyptian side of the armistice line and the international border south of the Gaza strip, patrolling these lines in order to prevent incidents across them, and apprehending infiltrators and turning them over to the local police.

The troops had a right to fire in self-defense,[53] but they were never to take the initiative in the use of arms.

The force, in a sense was an extension of the functions of the General Assembly with respect to the pacific settlement of disputes, and not an instrument of enforcement.[54]

The scope of the actual tasks undertaken by the force in the field was determined by these principles. A series of sensitive questions have been settled de facto, if not de jure, since the mission of the UNEF was not completely clarified by the Assembly resolutions.[55]

2.9.2. ONUC. The Security Council Resolution of November 24, 1961,[56] restated the policies and purposes of the United Nations with respect to the Congo:

1. To maintain the territorial integrity and the political independence of the Republic of the Congo.
2. To assist the Central Government of the Congo in the restoration and maintenance of law and order.
3. To prevent the occurrence of civil war in the Congo.
4. To secure the immediate withdrawal and evacuation from the Congo of all foreign military, paramilitary, and advisory personnel not under the U.N. command, and all mercenaries.

The ONUC had to perform a number of tasks in the Congo in order to fulfill its mandate.[57] But in the complex situation operating there because of the secessionist movements, competition for political power within the Central Government and foreign intervention through troops and mercenaries, at times, involved the force in military operations on a large scale. Active measures by the United Nations to arrest and expel

---

[52] *See* Seyersted *supra* note 8, at 47–49; Bowett, *supra* note 11, at 105 *passim;* Rosner, *supra* note 10, at 66–115.

[53] *See* Rosner, *supra* note 10, at 70; Frye, *supra* note 11, at 15.

[54] Bowett, *supra* note 11, at 106.

[55] Rosner, *supra* note 10, at 112–15.

[56] U.N. Doc. S/5002.

[57] See Seyersted *supra* note 8, at 67–68; Bowett, *supra* note 10, at 186 *passim.*

foreign military personnel and mercenaries provoked attacks by the Katangese forces. Numerous incidents of warfare also occurred between the U.N. forces and the Central Congolese forces, but these encounters were localized and short-lived.

Like the UNEF, the ONUC was never intended to carry out active military operations. However, when the threat of a full-scale civil war between the rival governments in the various provinces became imminent after the murder of Prime Minister Lumumba, the Security Council passed a resolution on February 21, 1961,[58] urging even "the use of force, if necessary, in the last resort," to prevent the occurrence of civil war.

The force did not engage in offensive operations even after the above resolution of the Security Council. But this defensive policy was not pressed to the point where the force could not act to reestablish its own positions and freedoms when these had been temporarily overthrown by larger contingents of Congolese troops.

At a later stage, in its attempt to evacuate foreign military personnel and mercenaries, the ONUC took important preventive measures; attacks on its positions involved the United Nations in hostilities in the latter half of 1961 and forced it to take preventive offensive action in several respects, *e.g.*, aerial bombardment of military installations and communication lines. This provoked strong protests to the United Nations from certain states, though the Security Council Resolution of November 24, 1961,[59] fully justified this action.

In accordance with its mandate the ONUC maintained absolute neutrality in internal conflicts,[60] confining its efforts to the prevention of offensive civil war operations, through persuasion, mediation, neutral zones, or if necessary, armed resistance. But the ONUC took effective action when foreign activities were involved.

2.10. Composition, Organization, and Control of UNEF and ONUC

2.10.1 UNEF. Unlike Korea, the United Nations did not entrust the task of organizing the force and directing its operations to one of its members, but performed these functions itself. The General Assembly appointed a

---

[58] U.N. Doc. S/4741.

[59] U.N. Doc. S/5002. The Council:

   4. Authorizes the Secretary-General to take vigorous action, including the use of the requisite measure of force, if necessary, for the immediate apprehension, detention, deportation of all foreign military and paramilitary personnel and political advisers not under the U.N. command, and mercenaries. . . .

   5. Further requests the Secretary-General to take all necessary measures to prevent the entry or return of such elements under whatever guise and also of arms, equipment, or other material in support of such activities.

[60] *See* Seyersted, *supra* note 8, at 68–76; Bowett, *supra* note 11, at 196–204, for a criticism of the principle of nonintervention and military action only in self-defense.

commander of the force as a regular U.N. official to organize the force in consultation with the Secretary-General as regards size and composition.[61] He was given full authority and responsibility for command, operations, and deployment, to be exercised in consultation with the Secretary-General. The Secretary-General in consultation with the Advisory Committee issued regulations for the force.[62]

The field forces, as in Korea, were supplied by various member states mostly as self-contained national contingents commanded by their own officers. The national contingents generally retained their identity and organizational unity. The commanding officers of the national contingents, however, took their orders from the UNEF commander and through him from the Secretary-General and the General Assembly. The contingent commanders were free to communicate with their home governments on all matters affecting their units, but the governments had no right to instruct the contingent commander in matters falling under the authority of the UNEF commander.

The Secretary-General and the commander decided what states to ask for contingents and what offers to accept.[63] In this way the United Nations was able to secure an effective and balanced force.

Contingents and military staff officers from the permanent members of the Security Council and from states which, for geographical or other reasons, might have had a special interest in the conflict, were deliberately excluded. The Secretary-General also avoided such differences in the size of national contingents as might have led to excessive dependence on any one state.

Thus, a truly international force—created, recruited, and led by the United Nations alone—was for the first time brought into being.

The military members of the command were recruited by the commander from the observer corps of the U.N. Truce Supervision Organization for Palestine and directly from the various member states. The Secretary-General was assisted in his task by an advisory committee, with himself as chairman and representatives of five states providing contingents and two states which had offered to do so.[64]

The total size of the force has ranged between 5,000 to 6,000 men, of which little more than half performed active patrolling duty and the rest formed part of the supporting units and services.

---

[61] G.A. Res. 1000 & 1001 (Emer. Sess. I), U.N. GAOR, Supp. 1, at 2, U.N. Doc. A/3354.

[62] Regulations for the UNEF, Feb. 20, 1957, U.N. Doc. ST/SGB/UNEF/1.

[63] *Agreements with "participating" states*, 271 U.N.T.S., para. 8. Some 24 members offered to contribute forces, but 10 of these offers were accepted. (Brazil, Canada, Columbia, Denmark, Finland, India, Indonesia, Norway, Sweden, and Yugoslavia).

[64] G.A. Res. 1001 (Emer. Sess. I), paras. 6–9.

Military reconnaissance aircraft were provided by the Canadian Air Force. Air transportation to the area of operations was provided by the same air force and by the air forces of two nonparticipating member states as well as a civilian airline. Sea transport of troops and material was performed by vessels chartered or owned by UNEF or made available by participating or other governments.

Thus in composition, organization, and leadership, the UNEF established precedents which were bound to influence the organization of a paramilitary task force by the United Nations in the future.

2.10.2. ONUC. The ONUC was constituted on a much more modest basis than the UNEF. The Security Council did not lay down in its resolutions,[65] even the basic principles on which the force was to be organized, as the General Assembly had done in the case of UNEF. The organization of the force, including the appointment of its supreme commander, was left to the Secretary-General. After the split between the President and the Prime Minister of the Congo in September, 1960, when the Security Council was unable to agree on the action to be taken, the matter was referred to the General Assembly under the Uniting for Peace Resolution. But the resolutions of the General Assembly[66] did not concern themselves directly with the force, except for the budgetary aspects.

In the absence of new resolutions, agreements, and regulations, the Secretary-General relied on his summary study of the experience derived from the establishment and operation of the UNEF,[67] and his report to the Security Council detailing the principles he had followed in the organization of the force was commended by the Security Council in its resolution.[68] Following the UNEF precedent, contingents from permanent members of the Security Council were excluded, and the ONUC was built around a hard core of military units from African states, but maintaining the universal character of a U.N. operation. While the views of the host state were taken into consideration, ultimately the United Nations decided on the question of composition.[69]

In addition to national contingents, the force was comprised of a supreme commander with a general staff made up of officers recruited di-

---

[65] U.N. Docs. S/4387, S/4405, S/4426, S/4526, S/4741, S/5502.

[66] G.A. Res. 1583(XV), 1590(XV), 1595(XV), 1619(XV). 1633(XVI). *See also* Res. 1474 (Emer. Sess. IV), 1599 (XV), & 1600 (XV) on certain operational matters.

[67] See *Summary Study*, 13 U.N. GAOR, Annexes, Agenda Item No. 65, at 8 *passim*, U.N. Doc. A/3943 (1958) [hereinafter cited as *Summary Study*].

[68] U.N. Doc. S/4405.

[69] *See* Bowett, *supra* note 10, at 206–207. *See also* Status Agreement of Nov. 27, 1961, U.N. Doc. S/4986, para. 2.

rectly from member governments or transferred from UNEF or UNTSO.[70]
The ONUC, as compared to UNEF, also included an important civilian
operation of technical assistance to the Congo, and the head of the whole
U.N. operation was not the commander of the force but a political officer,
the special representative of the Secretary-General. The chief of the civilian operations was of the same rank and authority as the supreme commander. At the headquarters, the Secretary-General was controlled only
by the political organs of the United Nations and advised by an advisory committee of contributing states (like the UNEF). He was assisted by a military adviser and an adviser on civilian assistance.[71]

National contingents were normally under their own commands, but
certain operational situations occasionally necessitated the detachment of
one or more companies to other areas, functions, or contingents for limited periods.[72] The total strength of the force ranged between 15,000 to
20,000 officers and men. It was also equipped with a considerable number of motor vehicles and aircraft. Unlike the UNEF, this force had to
carry out a variety of tasks[73] throughout a vast territory.

2.11. Status in International Law of UNEF and ONUC

2.11.1. UNEF. The status agreement concluded by the Secretary-General
with Egypt, concerning the status of the force in Egyptian territory[74]
and arrangements between the contributing states and United Nations
embody the essential rules, orders, instructions, and practices governing
the legal status of the force. These arrangements were accomplished by
an exchange of letters on June 21, 1957, in which the Secretary-General
referred to the guiding principles and policies adopted on the status of
the force,[75] the Convention on the Privileges and Immunities of the
United Nations (to which Egypt had acceded on September 17, 1948),[76]
and regulations for the UNEF enacted by the Secretary-General on
February 20, 1957.[77]

2.11.2 UNEF's POSITION AND RIGHTS. Being a subsidiary organ of the
United Nations and in particular of the General Assembly it enjoyed
the status, privileges, and immunities of the organization in accordance
with the Convention on the Privileges and Immunities of the United Nations (art. 22 read with article 105 of the Charter). Provisions of article

[70] *See supra* note 15.
[71] *See* Reports of the Secretary-General SCOR for July-Sept. U.N. Doc. S/4417 (1960).
[72] Press Release SG/1016, Mar. 4, 1961.
[73] Van Horn, Soldiering for Peace (1968).
[74] 260 U.N.T.S. at 61, 145, 271. For the text of the Agreement, *see* U.N. Doc. A/3526.
[75] For the text of the letter, *see* U.N. Doc. A/3943, Annex 1, at 33.
[76] For text, *see* U.N. Doc. A/64, July 1, 1946, at 25–33.
[77] U.N. Doc. ST/SGB/UNEF/1.; 271 U.N.T.S. 169.

II(2) of the General Convention are also declared to apply to "the property, funds, and assets of participating states" used in the host state.[78] The force also had the right to import—free of duty—equipment, provisions, and supplies.

The commander and the staff detailed from the U.N. Secretariat to serve with him were entitled to privileges and immunities under the Convention as officials of the United Nations; the military members of the UNEF command were entitled to privileges and immunities· as experts on missions for the United Nations. Personnel recruited locally enjoyed immunity only in respect to official acts as provided in pargraph 18(a) of the Convention.[79]

Members of national contingents were not covered by the General Convention, but were accorded largely corresponding privileges and immunities, including immunity in respect of official acts in Egypt and complete immunity from criminal jurisdiction under the status agreement.[80]

2.11.3. ONUC Like the UNEF, the basic agreement with the Congo[81] was predicated on the lines of the Aid-Memoire on the Basis for the Presence and Functioning of the UNEF in Egypt.[82] A status agreement partly modeled upon that of the UNEF,[83] regulations for the force,[84] and arrangements with states providing contingents (which were made by correspondence rather than by formal agreements) embody the basic principles governing the legal status of the force.

With respect to the ONUC the Secretary-General based his actions for the most part on his summary study of the experience derived from the establishment and operation of the UNEF.[85]

2.11.3.1. *ONUC's Position and Rights.* It was a subsidiary organ of the Security Council, and Regulation 10 specifically provided that article 105 of the Charter applied. Detailed provisions regarding privileges and immunities, etc. were, however, laid down in the status agreement. They were spelled out in detail and not by reference to the 1946 General Convention on U.N. privileges and immunities, as was the case with the UNEF agreement (since Egypt was a party to that Convention, but the Congo was not). But in substance they provide the same immunities and privileges[86] as in the case of the UNEF.

[78] Status Agreement with Egypt, UNEF Regulation 10, para. 23.
[79] Status Agreement with Egypt, UNEF Regulation 19, paras. 24–25.
[80] *Supra* Note 74.
[81] 27, U.N. Doc. S/4389. SCOR, Supp. July-Sept. 1960.
[82] 11 U.N. GAOR, Annexes, Agenda Item No. 66, at 9.
[83] U.N. Docs. A/4986, S/5004; 414 U.N.T.S. 229.
[84] U.N. Doc. ST/SGB/ONUC/1, July 15, 1963, issued by the Secretary-General.
[85] 13 U.N. GAOR, Annexes, Agenda Item No. 65, at 8 *passim.*
[86] Paras. 15, 16, 18, 20, 24, 27, 30, of the Status Agreement.

2.12. International Character of the Force

2.12.1. UNEF. The international character of the force was stressed in the regulations issued by the Secretary-General. Although members of the UNEF remained in their national service, they were, during the period of their assignment to the U.N. command, international personnel under the authority of the United Nations.[87] They could receive instructions only from the commander, and the chain of command designated by him. They were still subject, however, to the military rules. and regulations of their respective national states, a fact which did not derogate from their responsibilities as components of the force. They were also under a duty to respect the law and regulations of the host state and to refrain from any activities of a political character therein.[88]

The commander-in-chief had general responsibility for the good order of the force. Commanders of national contingents exercised disciplinary authority within their own units. The members of the force, whether serving in national contingents or as part of the U.N. command, wore their national uniforms with U.N. blue helmets, berets, desert caps, and UNEF badges and insignia.[89] They carried U.N. identity cards, flew the U.N. flag,[90] and all means of transportation and equipment bore a distinctive U.N. mark and license.[91]

2.12.2. ONUC. The international character of ONUC was laid down in Regulation 6. The authorization to use the U.N. flag (Reg. 7),[92] the provision requiring a distinctive U.N. mark and license on all transportation of the force (Reg. 9),[93] and the provisions on privileges and immunities of the force (Reg. 10), were all indicative of the international character of ONUC.

2.13. Claims for and Against the Force and Its Members; Jurisdiction

2.13.1. PROTECTION OF THE RIGHTS OF THE FORCE AND ITS MEMBERS. Claims on behalf of UNEF and ONUC were presented and representations were made by the United Nations, not by the states providing contingents. UNEF Regulation 30 clearly provided that members of the force are entitled to the legal protection of the United Nations and shall be regarded as its agents for the purpose. A similar provision was laid down in Regulation 25 of ONUC.

---

[87] UNEF Regulation 6.
[88] UN Doc. ST/SGB/UNEF 1, at 5.
[89] UNEF Regulation 8; Secretary-General's Summary Study, para. 43.
[90] UNEF Regulation 7; Status Agreement with Egypt, para. 20.
[91] UNEF Regulation 9.
[92] *See also* Status Agreement with the Congo, para. 26.
[93] *Id.* para. 32.

An advisory opinion of the International Court of Justice in the Reparations Case[94] has already held that in the event an agent of the United Nations suffered injury in the performance of his duties in circumstances involving the responsibility of a state, the United Nations as an organization has the capacity to bring an international claim against the responsible de jure or de facto government with a view to obtaining the reparation due in respect of the damage caused to the victim or to persons entitled through him. It was also held that the United Nations can base such a claim only upon a breach of obligations due to itself, not upon breach of obligations due to the state of which the agent is a national.

The division of functions and powers between the organization and the national states must equally apply in respect to members of national contingents serving in the U.N. force. In case of the UNEF, it followed clearly from Regulation 30, but it must also apply in other cases, such as the Congo, where the members of the contingents during the period of their assignment to the force were subject to the operational orders of the United Nations.[95]

In cases of violence by Congolese forces against members of national contingents of ONUC, demands and protests have been lodged by the United Nations with the central government and with provincial authorities.[96] Since the acts of the Congolese forces violated both the general obligations of a state concerning the position of aliens and special rules for the protection of the U.N. agents performing functions in the Congo pursuant to the invitation of the Congolese Government, the United Nations was justified in exercising functional protection of its agents, and the contributing state of diplomatic protection of its nationals.

In practice, it is believed that no claims were made against the Congo. U.N. action was confined only to protect about maltreatment or killing of ONUC personnel. Some contributing states also lodged protests, but these were in support of a U.N. protest and not separate claims on the basis of a breach of the Congo's duties toward aliens.

Under the status agreements, the United Nations had assumed protection of the members of national contingents also in matters which were not directly related to their functions for the United Nations, e.g. settlement of civilian claims against them, wide immunity even in respect of nonofficial acts. The agreements concluded with the host state were couched in such wide and general terms that in most or all cases it was possible to base any claims or protests made on behalf of the force or

[94] I.C.J. REP. 181–8 (1949).
[95] Seyersted, *supra* note 8, at 113.
[96] *See e.g.*, 15 SCOR (Supp. July-Sept., 1960) Annex II, at 78, U.N. Docs. S/4417/Add. 8, S/4753; *id.* (Supp. Jan-Mar., 1961) U.N. Docs. S/4780, S/4940/Add. 16, Annex I.

its members on the agreements, even though this was not always done.[97]

Regarding compensation for death, injury, or illness of UNEF troops attributable to service with the force, the Secretary-General in his first report on administrative and financial arrangements for the UNEF assumed that soldiers and their dependents qualified for benefits under their own national service pension or compensation regulations.[98] Benefits were not received directly from the United Nations. However, the Secretary-General subsequently informed the participating states that pending establishment of a compensation system, the United Nations would reimburse indemnities paid by them according to their national regulations.[99]

One may agree with Rosner when she comments that it would even be desirable if UNEF members were given compensation directly by the United Nations in the event of illness, accident, or death attributable to the performance of official duties, as is the procedure with members of the Secretariat.[100]

2.13.2. CLAIMS AGAINST THE FORCE AND ITS MEMBERS. Claims against the UNEF and also the ONUC were settled by the United Nations, not by the participating states. Compensation to dependents of Egyptian nationals accidentally killed by UNEF members was always paid by the United Nations. All members of the UNEF were entitled to the legal protection of the United Nations as agents of the organization.[101] The agreement between the United Nations and Egypt provided that any claim made by (1) an Egyptian citizen in respect to any damages alleged to result from an act or omission of a member of the force relating to his official duties, (2) the Government of Egypt against a member of the force, or (3) the force or the Government of Egypt against one another, shall be settled by a claims commission established for that purpose[102] (excluding claims dealing with the general convention and the status agreement). Egypt and the Secretary-General were to nominate one person each to this commission, and the chairman was to be jointly chosen by them, and in the event of disagreement, by the President of the International Court of Justice.

Such an arbitral procedure with respect to ONUC was also laid down by the United Nations in the status agreement with the Congo.[103] For

---

[97] Seyersted, *supra* note 8, at 116.

[98] U.N. Doc. A/3883 & Rev. 1, Nov. 21, 1956, 11 U.N. GAOR 2–3 Annexes, Agenda Item No. 66, at 15 (1956).

[99] U.N. Doc. A/3694 and Add. 1, at 11.

[100] Rosner, *supra* note 10, at 153–54.

[101] UNEF Regulation 30.

[102] U.N. Doc. A/3526, at 56.

[103] Status Agreement with the Congo, para. 10(b)-11, U.N. Doc. S/5004; *See also* ONUC Regulation 29(d).

"nonofficial" acts, Article 10(c) of the status agreement with the Congo provided that the United Nations would use its good offices to assist the parties in arriving at a settlement. In the absence of settlement, arbitration was the proper remedy, although the United Nations was not presumably to be a party. Claims between the United Nations and non-Congolese civilians, *e.g.* foreign corporations, were not dealt with in the status agreement, and should, in accordance with the U.N. established practice,[104] be dealt with by arbitration.

The host state could seek the good offices of the United Nations in order to obtain satisfaction of judgments by local courts or awards by claims commissions[105] against members of the force.

In Korea, claims were settled not by the United Nations, but by the unified command or by other participating states. No state acted under instructions from the United Nations nor was compensation paid from U.N. funds. The agreements between the United States and the participating states provided that claims of any third government or its nationals against the government or nationals of the participating state or vice versa shall be a matter for disposition between the government of the participating state and the third government or its nationals.[106] However, the agreements did not delimit the respective liability of the parties.[107] There is no evidence of the United Nations' having assumed this responsibility directly or indirectly in the case of Korea.

2.13.3. DISCIPLINARY ACTION, CRIMINAL AND CIVIL JURISDICTION

2.13.3.1. UNEF. Disciplinary action in national contingents was the responsibility of the contingent commander.[108] To confer such authority upon the UNEF commander would probably have required specific legislation in most participating states.[109] However, the UNEF commander could receive reports on disciplinary action and could consult with the contingent commander and the government concerned.[110] The military police provided for the force had the power of arrest insofar as it was necessary to maintain order and discipline among members of the force.

The members of the force were under the criminal jurisdiction of their governments,[111] even in respect to acts performed in their capacity as members of the force.[112] But the host state could present any demand

---

[104] See JENKS, THE PROPER LAW OF INTERNATIONAL ORGANIZATIONS, p. III (1962).
[105] Status Agreement with Egypt, para. 12(i, f,) & 38(b) (i, f,).
[106] *See e.g.*, art. 4 of the Agreement with the Union of South Africa, 177 U.N.T.S. 244.
[107] Seyersted, *supra* note 8, at 110–11.
[108] UNEF Regulation 13; Agreements with Participating States, paras. 6–7.
[109] Secretary-General's Summary Study, para. 139.
[110] UNEF Regulation 13.
[111] *See* the Secretary-General's explanation for this Regulation, U.N. Doc. A/3943, at 26.
[112] *Id.* **Regulation** 34; Status Agreement with Egypt, para. 11.

for such prosecution to the United Nations, not to the state concerned. Each contingent also had the power to arrest its own members.[113] However, the immunity from Egyptian criminal jurisdiction was based on the clear understanding that the contributing states were under an obligation to exercise this jurisdiction and the offenses were not to go unpunished.[114]

It was also provided that no member of the UNEF was subject to the civil jurisdiction of Egyptian courts or to other legal process in any matter relating to his official duties.[115] In those cases where civil jurisdiction was exercisable by Egyptian courts with respect to the members of the force, sufficient opportunity to safeguard their interests was to be provided to them.[116]

There were a number of legal ambiguities which existed with regard to the criminal and civil jurisdiction, but these questions were never fully answered.[117]

2.13.3.2. ONUC. Paragraph 13 of the status agreement provided that the United Nations and the Congo would each exercise a power of arrest over the military personnel of the other only when the competent authorities were unable to act with the necessary speed. The personnel in such cases were to be delivered immediately to the nearest authority to whom the person in question was responsible.

Like the UNEF, paragraph 9 of the status agreement gave complete immunity from criminal jurisdiction of the Congo to all members of the force.[118]

But in contrast to the UNEF Agreement which contemplated a certain amount of civil jurisdiction in the Egyptian courts, paragraph 10 of the Congo Agreement virtually substituted for jurisdiction over "official act[s]." a process of negotiation between the United Nations and the Congo; and failing agreement, it provided for recourse to arbitration. In the case of civil law obligations not arising out of an official act, the United Nations was to use its good offices to assist the parties in arriving at settlement; failing which it was to go to arbitration at the request of either party.

2.13.4. ARBITRAL SETTLEMENT OF DISPUTES. The status agreement between the United Nations and Egypt and the agreements between member states and the Secretary-General provided identically that a dispute

---

[113] *Id.* Regulation 14.
[114] U.N. Doc. A/3943, Annex 1, at 33.
[115] Status Agreement, U.N. Doc. A/3526, at 53.
[116] *Id.* at 53–54.
[117] Rosner, *supra* note 10, at 150–51.
[118] *See also* ONUC Regulation 29(9).

regarding the interpretation or application of the agreements would be settled by a tribunal of three arbitrators, if it could not be settled by negotiation or other means agreeable to both the parties.[119] Almost parallel provisions are incorporated in case of the ONUC.

2.14. Consent if Necessary for the Presence of a U.N. Force

2.14.1. THE AGGRESSOR STATE. The rule does not admit of any doubt, that a state determined to be an "aggressor" by the United Nations, against which preventive or enforcement actions are recommended or decided upon, cannot stultify U.N. action by withholding its consent to the presence of the U.N. force on its territory.[120] By its own conduct, it has forfeited the right to inviolability of its territory.

In Korea, the forces operating under the U.N. command did cross the 38th parallel and the legality of such a step in the absence of the consent of the North Korean authorities has not been questioned. The Secretary-General's statement[121] on the entry of ONUC into Katanga that, had the ONUC been taking enforcement action under Chapter VII, such entry could have been effected by force, reaffirms the above position.

There has been a tendency, however, to obtain the consent even of parties whose actions might have been deemed illegal, though not unequivocally an aggression. The Secretary-General thus felt that UNEF could not be stationed on Israeli territory without the consent of the Israeli Government, which was not in the event forthcoming.[122] But the fact that the UNEF operations were initiated by the Assembly and not the Security Council was of vital significance in this connection.

2.14.2. THE VICTIM STATE OR OTHER "HOST" STATE. If the Security Council decides upon action like the enforcement action under Chapter VII, the victim state is bound to admit and assist the U.N. force in its territory because of its obligations under articles 2(5), 25, and 49 of the Charter.[123]

A mere recommendation that such action be taken would not impose such an obligation.

Peace-keeping operations under Chapter VI, *e.g.*, an observer group or force, would be recommendatory rather than obligatory, thus requiring the consent of the territorial state. This is also supported by practice.[124]

The same would be the position if the U.N. force operating under the authority of the Security Council carries out "peace-keeping operations"

---

[119] U.N. Doc. A/3526, at 56–57; U.N. Doc. A/3943, Annex 1, at 33.

[120] Bowett, *supra* note 11, at 412.

[121] Secretary-General's Second Report, U.N. Doc S/4417/Add.2., para. 9.

[122] U.N. Doc A/3512, para. 5.

[123] This derives from the powers of the S.C. under Chapter VII, *see e.g.* Goodrich and Hambro, *supra* note 6.

[124] Bowett, *supra* note 11, at 67–68.

under Chapter VII, but not actually enforcement action under article 42. Thus, with regard to ONUC, repeated emphasis has been placed on the invitation by the Congo Government to the United Nations.[125] The International Court of Justice has also placed emphasis on the principle of consent inasmuch as the fact that UNEF and ONUC had been set up with the approval of the host state weighed heavily with the Court in the assessment of their status as legal.[126] However, Bowett has taken a different and broader view of Security Council powers.[127]

So far as the General Assembly is concerned, the whole position of an enforcement action taken by it is unclear and it has been doubted if under the Uniting For Peace Resolution, the General Assembly could initiate, even by way of a recommendation, action directed against a state.[128] If the Assembly could lawfully initiate coercive action against an aggressor state by its own conduct, that state would have to forfeit the right to inviolability of its territory, and no consent of that state would be necessary. So far as the victim state is concerned, the obligation to admit a U.N. force into its territory can rest on the general obligation in article 2(5).

However, it seems to be generally agreed[129] that if the General Assembly authorizes a "peace-keeping operation" like the UNEF, such operation could only proceed on the basis of consent of the state upon whose territory the operation is to take place. The limitation arises from the fact that the General Assembly has virtually no power to take decisions binding upon states.

The nonmember states would not be in a position different from member states, and the above observations would also seem to apply to them. In the Congo, a nonmember requested U.N. assistance; therefore, an obligation to consent to the presence of the force was really self-imposed. This involves the further obligation to accept decisions of the Security Council relating to the operations of the force.

2.14.3. THE EFFECT OF THE WITHDRAWAL OF CONSENT TO THE PRESENCE OF THE FORCE BY THE HOST STATE. In case of the UNO GIL (United Nations Group in Lebanon), the group had indicated that its task was completed, but the actual withdrawal was on the basis of a plan accepta-

---

[125] First Report of the Secretary-General on the implementation of Security Council Resolution, U.N. Docs. S/4387 & S/4389, at 2.

[126] I.C.J. REP. 170–1, 175 (1962).

[127] Bowett, *supra* note 11, at 414–16.

[128] *See supra* note 28.

[129] *See Summary Study*, U.N. Doc. A/3943, para. 15; G.A. Res. 503 (VI); Sohn, *supra* note 4, at 238; Seyersted, *supra* note 8, at 166; Rosner, *UNEF*, 11 INTERNATIONAL ORGANIZATION 419 (1957).

ble to the Lebanese Government through the decision of the Secretary-General.[130]

2.14.3.1. UNEF. In the case of the UNEF, the basic agreement with Egypt[131] (Aide-memoire) specifically regulated the question of the withdrawal of the force. Both Egypt and the United Nations agreed to be guided by good faith with respect to the presence and functioning of UNEF by their acceptance of General Assembly Resolution 1000 (ES-I) of November 5, 1956, and the United Nations reaffirmed its willingness to maintain UNEF until its task was completed.

Yet the Secretary-General in response to the demand of the U.A.R.[132] to withdraw the force from Gaza and Sinai complied with the request between May 16 and 18, 1967.[133] The Secretary-General has sought to defend this action on many counts:[134]

1. The forces were on UAR territory with its consent, and when the UAR demanded their withdrawal, they had to be withdrawn.
2. The advisory committee before which the matter was placed and which was competent to request the convening of the General Assembly to consider the situation arising from the UAR's action did not do so.
3. He has also maintained that there was no legal duty on him to take the final decision on withdrawal only after consideration of that question by the Assembly which was in session at that time.
4. He brought the situation to the notice of the Security Council on May 19, the Council met on May 24, but took no action.
5. He was also concerned about the safety of the contingents stationed in UAR, and the threat of India and Yugoslavia to withdraw their contingents.

However, the critics[135] have rightly criticized the action of the Secretary-General in acceding to the unilateral request of Egypt for withdrawal of the forces. In the face of the agreement, Egypt had no such unilateral right, the question should have been taken to the General As-

---

[130] *See* U.N. Docs. S/4113, S/4114.

[131] U.N. Doc. A/3375, Annex.

[132] U.N. Doc. A/6669, May 18, 1967, at 4.

[133] *See* Tandon, *UNEF, the Secretary-General and International Diplomacy in the Third Arab-Israeli War*, 22 INTERNATIONAL ORGANIZATION 529 (1968). For the documents concerning the withdrawal, *see* 6 INTERNATIONAL LEGAL MATERIALS 557–642 (1967).

[134] *See* U.N. Doc. A/6730, Add. 3.

[135] Cohen, *The Demise of UNEF*, 23 INT'L J. 19–37 (1967–68); *see supra* note 31 for a list of principal documents in this regard; Burns, *The Withdrawal of UNEF and the Future of Peacekeeping*, 23 INT'L J. 1–5 (1967–68); Franck, *United Nations Law in Africa, the Congo Operations as a Case Study*, 27 LAW CONTEMP. PROB. 632 (1962); Weissberg, *The International Status of U.N.* 131–40 (1961). *See also Summary Study*, para. 158.

sembly, which was the only competent body to decide if the task of the UNEF was completed. There is, however, no reason to suppose that the Secretary-General's action has set up any precedent in the matter for the future.

2.14.3.2. ONUC. In regard to ONUC, one must go back to the establishment of the force by the Security Council under Chapter VII of the Charter,[136] in response to a request from the Congolese Government for military assistance. The Security Council resolution of July 14, 1960,[137] authorized the Secretary-General to provide military assistance "until . . . the national security forces might be able in the opinion of the government, to meet fully their tasks." But later in the basic agreement the United Nations reaffirmed, "considering it to be in accordance with the wishes of the Government of the Republic of the Congo, that it is prepared to maintain the U.N. force in the Congo until such time as it [the U.N.] deemed the latter's task to have been fully accomplished."[138]

Professor C. W. Jenks[139] has observed that it is reasonable to imply an obligation to give sufficient notice of any such withdrawal of consent to afford the Security Council (and/or the General Assembly)[140] an adequate opportunity to consider the changed condition created thereby; failing such an obligation, uncertainty concerning the continued effectiveness of an international force may be a factor of aggravation rather than stability in a crisis.

2.15. Withdrawal of National Contingents

In the Korean agreements no provision was included for withdrawal. But in the absence of agreements concluded under article 43 of the Charter, the practice that has emerged appears to be that the states retain the right to withdraw their contingents at any time unless they agree to provide troops for a fixed period or restrict their discretion in some other way.

In the case of UNEF the member states were specifically required to give adequate notice of withdrawal, though the right to withdraw was conceded by the Secretary-General.[141] However, the Secretary-General avoided such differences in the size of the national contingents as might have led to excessive dependence on any one state.[142]

---

[136] *Supra,* note 123.
[137] U.N. Doc. S/4387.
[138] U.N. Doc. S/4389, Add. 5.
[139] JENKS, A NEW WORLD OF LAW 38 (1969).
[140] Added by this writer.
[141] Letter of the Secretary-General of June 21, 1957, to states contributing troops to UNEF, *Summary Study,* paras. 8, 50; 271 U.N.T.S., para. 8.
[142] *Summary Study,* para. 17.

In the case of ONUC, though no written agreements were entered into, it seems to have been assumed both by the Secretary-General and the contributing states, that any state had the legal right to withdraw its contingent when it wished. Some governments did at a certain time withdraw their contingents from the force because of their dissatisfaction with the manner in which the force was being deployed. Bowett has, however, taken the view that the principle of good faith and the obligations of articles 2(5), 25, and 49 may suggest some limitations on the absolute right of withdrawal.[143] The dangers of unilateral withdrawal are obvious[144] and even the requirement of reasonable notice may not always save a dangerous situation from arising. It is therefore necessary that whenever U.N. forces are established in the future, the right of withdrawal must be properly regulated through agreements based upon a realistic appraisal of the possible reasons for the withdrawal of contingents by the states.[145]

If the troops withdrawing from the U.N. force choose to remain on the territory and intervene in the situation independently of the U.N. force, as in the case of ONUC, the Secretary-General has rightly taken the position that all troops remaining on Congolese territory, but not under ONUC's command, would become foreign military personnel and therefore liable to expulsion by ONUC under the Security Council resolutions.[146]

2.15.1. WITHDRAWAL OF A NATIONAL CONTINGENT ON THE CALL OF THE UNITED NATIONS. In case agreements under article 43 were entered into, the Security Council would have retained sufficient authority to decide and insure that a particular contingent could be withdrawn, and this decision would have been subject to the concurrent votes of the five permanent members.

Whereas in the case of a force like the UNEF or ONUC, the necessity for withdrawal could arise because there was no longer any need or the task was completed, or because of a demand by the host state for the withdrawal of a particular contingent,[147] or the failure to observe the laws of war or to comply with the orders of the U.N. command. Normally the Secretary-General and the participating state should be able to settle the matter by negotiation. It is only if they have failed and the

[143] Bowett, *supra* note 11, at 208.
[144] *See* the Secretary-General's communication to the Casablanca powers, U.N. Doc. S/4640, Annexes I & II; *See also* U.N. Doc. S/4761, paras. 5, 17.
[145] Bowett, *supra* note 11, at 381–85.
[146] 15 U.N. SCOR, 896th meeting, para. 109, U.N. Doc. S/4668 (1960).
[147] E.g., the Congolese authorities once called for the withdrawal of the UAR contingent, U.N. Doc. S/4639.

state concerned refuses to withdraw, would the Secretary-General need to approach the General Assembly or the Security Council, as the case may be. In case of the UNEF, the agreement specifically provided for the right of the United Nations to order withdrawal subject to adequate prior notice.[148]

2.16. Financing the Force

2.16.1. UNEF

2.16.1.1. *The Apportionment of Expenses Between the United Nations and the Member States Which Provide Contingents.* Expenses in connection with payment of salaries and wages and the cost of normal equipment of the national contingents were to rest upon the participating states, but the United Nations was to make reimbursements for certain items.[149] It was also to bear the cost of the replacement of equipment[150] and all extra and extraordinary costs for making the forces available for UNEF service. However, difficulties of interpretation did arise in actual cases and the Secretary-General decided in the light of the circumstances of each particular case.[151]

Compensation for service-incurred death, injury, or illness was paid by the participating governments according to the national regulations,[152] but reimbursement was later made by the United Nations.[153]

Expenses borne directly by the United Nations included the cost of the upkeep of troops, daily overseas allowance, transport communications, supplies, satisfaction of successful claims against the United Nations, etc.[154]

2.16.1.2. *Apportionment of Expenses of the Organization Between Member States*

1. *Budgetary Arrangements.* The UNEF expenses could not obviously be borne by the normal budget of the organization. For several reasons[155] it was thought preferable to finance the initial expenses of UNEF on an ad hoc basis; therefore, the General Assembly was asked for authority to

---

[148] U.N. Doc. A/3943, Annex I (exchange of letters dated June 21, 1957): "should circumstances render the service of some national contingent with the force no longer necessary, the Secretary-General undertakes to consult with your government and to give adequate prior notification concerning its withdrawal."

[149] U.N. Doc. A/3302, para. 15; 12 U.N. GAOR, Annexes, Agenda Item No. 65, U.N. Doc. A/3694 (1957); G.A. Res. 1001 (Emer. Sess. I.), Res. 1089(XI).

[150] G.A. Res. 1151 (XII).

[151] Bowett, *supra* 11, at 140.

[152] UNEF Regulations 38–40.

[153] 12 U.N. GAOR Annexes, Agenda Item No. 65, at 11 (1957).

[154] U.N. Doc. A/3943, para. 120.

[155] *Id.* para. 108.

raise money to pay for the force. This it did by several resolutions each year.

The General Assembly by its resolution of November 26, 1956,[156] set up a special account for the purpose of accepting and incorporating voluntary contributions from member states, and the contributions to be assessed on the organization's membership as a whole. The wisdom of establishing a special account has been questioned on many grounds,[157] but legally the International Court of Justice rejected the argument that the allocation of the expenses to the special account made any difference to the application of article 17.[158]

2. The Method of Apportionment Adopted. The General Assembly has consistently adopted the principle of assessing the member states according to the scale laid down by the General Assembly for the contributions to the regular budget of the organization. The General Assembly approved this method in case of the UNEF and applied it to the first ten million dollars of expenses,[159] without prejudice to the subsequent apportionment of any expense in excess of that amount.

There have been several lines[160] of attack on this method of allocation. The Soviet Bloc has argued that the total UNEF expenses should be borne by the aggressor states. Others have argued that the primary responsibility for financing should rest with the permanent members, who have been entrusted with primary responsibility for the maintenance of international peace and security. This controversy continued during several sessions of the General Assembly and ultimately the Soviet bloc refused to pay any amount toward its expenses. On December 5, 1959, the General Assembly made a departure when it agreed to apply the voluntary contributions as a credit to reduce by 50 per cent the contributions of as many governments as possible, beginning with those with the minimum assessment.[161]

Later, the question of financing UNEF became involved with the question of financing ONUC, for many states had refused to pay their assessment. The failure to pay led to a financial crisis. The General Assembly in 1962 referred the question to the International Court of Justice, whether these "expenses" constitute "expenses of the organization" within the meaning of article 17(2) of the Charter.[162] The Court distinguished

[156] G.A. Res. 1122 (XI) para. 1.
[157] Rosner, *supra* note 10, at 182.
[158] *Advisory Opinion on Certain Expenses of the U.N.,* I.C.J. REP. 152 (1962).
[159] G.A. Res. 11089 (XII), U.N. Doc. A/3572, paras. 1 & 2 (Dec. 21, 1956); Res. 1151 (XI), para. 4 (Nov. 27, 1957).
[160] Bowett, *supra* note 11, at 146–147.
[161] G.A. Res. 1441 (XIV), U.N. Doc. A/4486 (Sept. 13, 1960).
[162] G.A. Res. 1731 (XVI) (Dec. 20, 1961).

among three questions: (1) the identification of what are the expenses of the organization, (2) the question of apportionment, and (3) the interpretation of the phrase "shall be borne by members" as used in article 17. With respect to the first question, the Court rejected the argument that there existed a distinction between the "administrative" and "operational" budgets of the United Nations so as to bring only the former within the scope of article 17(2). It similarly rejected the argument that the budgetary authority of the Assembly, or the power to portion expenses, did not extend to the expenses resulting from operations for the maintenance of peace and security.[163] The Court, therefore, concluded that UNEF and ONUC expenses were properly regarded as expenses of the organization within the meaning of article 17(2). The General Assembly accepted this opinion in the Resolution of December 19, 1962,[164] and adopted it in its Resolution of June 27, 1963.

The Court did not answer the question whether the adopted method of apportionment was the correct one, nor did it decide whether there was a legal obligation upon the member states to pay. However, Bowett takes the view that since the General Assembly is given the power to make monetary decisions with respect to budgetary matters, it would seem that there is a legal obligation to pay.[165] Though the court has not specifically answered the question, it has stated that: "the exercise of the power of apportionment creates the obligation specifically stated in article 17(2) of each member to bear that part of the expenses which is apportioned to it by the General Assembly."[166]

Further, the opinion of the court was still an opinion and not a judgment, so there were many states which did not regard themselves as legally bound to accept this opinion.

2.16.2. ONUC. With respect to the apportionment of the expenses of the ONUC the General Assembly first[167] adopted the regular scale of assessment, but by the Resolution of April 21, 1961, it also made an appeal to the permanent members to make sizeable additional contributions, to other members to make voluntary contributions, and called upon Belgium to make a substantial contribution. This resolution reflected the criteria which some members were suggesting in determining a different scale of assessments. This was not a decision of the General Assembly but only an appeal for voluntary contributions. However by the Resolution of De-

---

[163] I.C.J. Rep. 158–65 (1962).
[164] G.A. Res. 1854 (XVII).
[165] Bowett, *supra* note 11, at 148.
[166] I.C.J. Rep. 164 (1962).
[167] G.A. Res. 1583 (XV).

cember 20, 1961,[168] the General Assembly introduced a sliding scale reducing by 80 per cent the contributions of members with the lowest budgetary contributions. The deficit was to be made up by additional voluntary contributions. The Resolution of June 27, 1963,[169] further elaborated this system of correlating the exemptions to the less prosperous states with the voluntary contributions.

2.17. Special Committee on the Review of the Questions of Peace-Keeping Operations

At the time of the Ninteenth session of the General Assembly, sixty-two member states were in arrears on one or both of the peace-keeping operations.[170] Strengthened by the opinion of the International Court of Justice that peace-keeping expenses were the expenses of the United Nations for purposes of article 17 of the Charter, the United States insisted that countries who were in arrears in excess of the amount of their assessed contributions for the preceding two years, be stripped of their voting rights under article 19. At one time the controversy threatened the virtual breakdown of the United Nations. The General Assembly later appointed a special committee for a comprehensive review of the whole question of peace-keeping operations in all their aspects, including ways of overcoming the then financial difficulties of the organization.[171] The special committee arrived at a consensus in its report of August 31, 1965, that the question of the applicability of article 19 would not be raised with regard to the UNEF and ONUC operations, and the financial difficulties of the organization should be solved through voluntary contributions by member states. The General Assembly adopted the report of the special committee.[172] Thus, though the momentary crisis was averted, the United Nations was left much weakened, and the financial crisis was unresolved.[173]

The General Assembly on the recommendation of the Special Committee adopted on December 15, 1966, a resolution,[174] proposed by nineteen states, wherein it expressed the opinion that pending the adoption of an alternative system for financing peace-keeping operations. (1) peace-keeping expenditures up to one million dollars, not otherwise covered by

[168] G.A. Res. 1732 (XVI).

[169] G.A. Res. 1876 (Emer. Sess. IV).

[170] Padelford, *Financing Peacekeeping: Politics and Crisis,* 19 INTERNATIONAL ORGANIZATION 444–45 (1965).

[171] U.N. Doc. A/5900, G.A. Res. 2006 (XIX) /Rev. 1 (Feb. 18, 1965).

[172] *See* the *Annual Report of the Secretary-General on the Work of the Organization,* 20 INTERNATIONAL ORGANIZATION 131 (1966).

[173] 22 INTERNATIONAL ORGANIZATION 600 (1968).

[174] U.N. Doc. A/6603.

agreements or in the regular budget, should be apportioned as follows: (a) 5 per cent among the economically less-developed member
states, (b) 5 per cent among the economically developed member states
other than the permanent members of the Security Council, and (c) the
remaining 70 per cent among the permanent members of the Security
Council, and (c) the remaining 70 per cent among the permanent members of the Security Council who vote in favor of the operation, provided
that no member shall be assessed for more than 50 per cent of the net
cost of the operation. Any balance left unassessed by reason of this
proviso shall be apportioned to the second category of states. (2) Ex-
penditure in excess of one million dollars in any one year should be assessed on the second and third category of states. (3) Within each
group the amount to be paid by each member shall be in proportion to
its scale of assessment of regular budget. (4) Voluntary subscriptions may
reduce the amount to be assessed on any or all of the groups.

It may, however, be appreciated that it is not even a recommendation of the General Assembly, but merely an expression of opinion.
Further, it is only an interim suggestion pending the adoption of a more
permanent system of financing peace-keeping operations. However, this
expression of opinion, adopted by 88 to 1 votes with 3 abstentions, is
indicative of the guidelines on which any future system of financing
peace-keeping acceptable to the majority of states could be based.

In another resolution passed the same day, general suggestions regarding the various modes of financing peace-keeping and the equitable sharing of costs in the future were also made.

Member states were invited to communicate to the United Nations information concerning kinds of military or civil forces or services which
they might be in a position to provide for a peace-keeping operation in
the future. Certain recommendations for improving peace-keeping operations of a nonenforcement nature were also made to the Security Council,
including the discharge of its responsibilities by the Security Council under articles 42 and 45 and the negotiation of agreements under article 43.
The special committee was requested to continue its work.

On April 3, 1968, the special committee decided to appoint a working
group to prepare working papers for the study that the special committee was to submit to the General Assembly in accordance with General Assembly Resolution 2308 (xxii).[175] The working group decided

[175] G. A. Res. 2308 (XXII) (Dec. 13, 1967). "Paragraph 3—Considers that the preparation
of a study on matters related to facilities, services, and personnel which member states might
provide, in accordance with the Charter of the U.N. for U.N. peace-keeping operations, would
be appropriate." The resolution requested the Special Committee to prepare its report on the
above subject for the 23rd session of the General Assembly by July 1, 1968.

first to make a study of the U.N. military observers established or authorized by the Security Council for observation purposes. The special committee was requested by the General Assembly[176] to submit at the latest to its twenty-fourth session a comprehensive report on U.N. military observers, as well as the progress report on the work of the special committee.[177]

2.18. Some Basic Lessons of the UNEF and ONUC Experience

The success of the UNEF, ONUC and other forces, has demonstrated the feasibility of organizing an international police and paramilitary force for peace-keeping purposes. A number of basic principles have also emerged from these experiences which can well be followed in the future.

1. A U.N. force can be organized even in the absence of agreements under article 43, *e.g.*, by the Security Council under article 39, by the General Assembly under articles 10, 11, and 14, or article 22; by the Security Council under articles 40 and 29, or even under article 36(1), as in case of the UNFICYP. In none of the cases (other than Korea) was an enforcement action taken, but instruments for the maintenance of peace and/or for pacific settlement were created.

2. The great powers were excluded from the operation in case of UNEF and ONUC as a matter of principle, thus establishing their dispensability in the composition of international forces and giving expression to the change that has occurred in the United Nations over the years regarding peace and security.[178]

3. The UNEF experience has demonstrated that some limited action by the United Nations can be possible even in the face of illegal use of force by some great powers. It exploded the myth of the concept of collective security on which the U.N. system is supposed to be based[179] and proved the capability of the organization as such for peace-keeping.

4. The complete freedom of the organization in the composition of the force and in its organization, regulation, and deployment was established. The participating states have ceded the power to exercise direct legislative and administrative jurisdiction over the contingents in operational matters.

5. Healthy precedents and patterns regarding the command structure, military organization, and leadership of the force have been established. The role of the Secretary-General, his relationship with the commander-in-chief, advisory committee, and military advisors to the Secretary

[176] U.N. Doc. A/7455, G.A. Res. 2451 (XXIII) (Dec. 19, 1968).

[177] *See infra* note 194.

[178] Rosner, *supra* note 10, at 191.

[179] *The United Nations and the Use of Force*, 532 INTERNATIONAL CONCILIATION 325 *et seq.* Claude ed. (1961).

General established in case of the UNEF were also followed at the time of ONUC.

6. The Status Agreements and Regulations laying down the international status of the force, its privileges and immunities, its rights, liabilities, and jurisdiction, vis-à-vis the host state and the participating states, etc., are bound to serve as guidelines for the future.

7. In spite of all possible pressures the ONUC and the UNFICYP (United Nations Force in Cyprus) have kept clearly out of the internal conflict in very trying situations, thus establishing the complete impartiality and independence of the force.

8. The composition of the force, besides its status, has been truly international.

9. The freedom of movement, facilities, and communication within their fields of operation were guaranteed by the host state under the basic agreements.

In spite of these definite gains, it may also be appreciated that in the absence of a Council decision under Chapter VII, the entry of the force into territory of the host state is dependent on its consent. Though there seems to be no escape from this legal position under the present Charter system, there is at the same time no justification for extending the principle of consent to the continued presence of the force in the territory of the host state. The force must withdraw only when its task is completed and determination of this question rests with U.N. organs. Withdrawal of the force on the unilateral request of the host state is most certain to scatter away all the gains that the force might have made during its stay in the area, as the consequences following the UNEF withdrawal have shown.

The question of financing the force still remains as intractable as ever. Perhaps the suggestions of the special committee as incorporated in General Assembly Resolution A/6603 of December 15, 1966,[180] are most equitable and practical, but there is no method of compelling the Great Powers and the developed nations on whom the greatest financial burden would lie under the resolution to pay their suggested shares, except to work on their conscience. The financial difficulties seem to reestablish the nonvulnerability of the idea of a collective security system and to undo all that the General Assembly has been able to achieve thus far.

A permanent U.N. force in a disarmed world under a more integrated world authority may possibly be the only answer to this stalemate. Under that system the question of finances would automatically be worked out, and the Great Powers might also be willing to contribute liberally for the

---

[180] See Frye, *supra* note 11 and *infra* note 194.

maintenance of a U.N. force when substantial funds are released from their defense expenditures.

The difficulties of improvising an ad hoc force on short notice might affect the efficiency, chances of success, and morale of the force. The least that could be done is to maintain on a permanent basis a body like the military advisers to the Secretary-General who may constantly study the problem and keep blueprints for organizing a future force in any troubled area of the world where U.N. action may appear politically feasible. A permanent U.N. force would obviously not suffer from this handicap.

Lastly, however efficient the U.N. force might be, its success or failure depends to a large extent upon the nature of the mandate given to it. If the mission that it has to fulfill is obscure as in case of the ONUC or if its mandate is too limited as in the case of the UNFICYP,[181] the U.N. force could find itself too constrained in its operations; and the subsequent political controversy to which it could lead, either because of its inactivity or because of too much activity in the eyes of others, could be very damaging for the force, both operationally and politically. It is therefore essential that at the time the U.N. political organs pass their first resolutions for raising such a force and the basic agreement and the status agreements are entered into with the host state, the functions of the force and the task that it has to achieve must be stated in the clearest terms and with the widest possible latitude to adopt whatever means might be necessary to achieve the purpose. Professor Jenks adds another caution that its functions must be limited by the degree of agreement which exists concerning its purpose.[182]

Even if a permanent U.N. force is established, it is only when it is called upon to take enforcement action under Chapter VII that the consent of the host or the aggressor state would not be necessary and the political organs of the United Nations would be free to give it any mandate unilaterally within the framework of the Charter. In all other situations, the necessity for a clear, unambiguous, and wide mandate would be there for a permanent U.N. force, too.

2.19. A Permanent U.N. Peace–Keeping Force

A permanent U.N. police force could be set up not only through agreements under article 43 of the U.N. Charter for enforcement action, but also for the performance of noncombatant duties[183] like those entrusted to the UNEF, ONUC, or UNFICYP.

[181] Bowett, *supra* note 11, at 558.
[182] *Supra* note 139, at 36–39.
[183] Frye, *supra* note 11, at 32.

In the past, however, there does not appear to have been much enthusiasm for a permanent U.N. force of any type on the part of the world community. The General Assembly did not accept the Secretary-General's proposals for an individually recruited U.N. guard in 1948 and for a U.N. legion in 1952. And both the Collective Measures Committee and later the Secretary-General[184] have expressed the view that a standing U.N. force would not be necessary or practical.[185] They have instead made proposals for standby arrangements under which it would be possible, by drawing upon national contingents earmarked and prepared in advance, to organize an ad hoc force adapted to the circumstances of each particular case as it might arise.[186] Hammarskjold thought that each case which arises is highly variable, requiring different personnel specialists, and supporting units. The Secretary-General's emphasis on the special circumstances of the UNEF operation was unduly strong,[187] and his outlook for the creation of the nucleus of a permanent force, too pessimistic.

Only the conclusions contained in the Secretary-General's Summary Study were relied upon in case of the ONUC, but the General Assembly never formally approved any of the above proposals. Further, the Scandinavian states on their own initiative have taken steps to prepare national contingents and technical personnel for U.N. service on call, to give effect to the above proposals.[188] Lester Pearson,[189] Sir Leslie Munro,[190] and William Frye[191] among others have been strong advocates of a standing U.N. army. The proposal has also been supported by a number of countries.[192] However, the opponents of a permanent military institution for the United Nations have also been many.[193]

A significant step has nonetheless been taken since both the Soviet Union and the United States have included proposals for a U.N. force in the drafts of a disarmament treaty which they submitted to the U.N. Conference on Disarmament in Geneva in 1962.[194]

[184] *Summary Study* at 8–33 (1958).

[185] *See* Rosner, *supra* note 10 and *infra* note 194.

[186] Seyersted, *Supra* note 8, at 403; U.N. Doc A/3943, at 27 *passim*.

[187] Rosner, *supra* note 10, at 202.

[188] Per Haekkerup, *Peace-keeping Forces for U.N.*, 42 FOREIGN AFF. 674 (1963–64).

[189] Pearson, *Force For U.N.*, 35 FOREIGN AFF. 403 (1957).

[190] Munro, *The Case For a Standing U.N. Army*, N.Y. Times Magazine, July 27, 1958.

[191] Frye, *supra* note 11, at 32.

[192] *Id.* at 69–70 for statements of various delegates.

[193] *See* 13 U.N. GAOR, Special Pol. Comm. 98th meeting, 56–57 (Oct. 31, 1958).

[194] *See Blueprint for the Peace Race*, USACDA Publication 4, gen. ser. May 3, 1962. *See also* U.N. Doc A/4879 (Sept. 20, 1961); Dept. of State Bulletin, Oct. 16, 1961; U.N. Doc. A/4505 (Sept. 23, 1960); U.N. Docs. ENDC/2 (Mar. 15, 1962) and A/C. I/867 (Sept. 24, 1962). Relevant extracts from these documents have been reproduced in BLOOMFIELD, INTER-

Perhaps disarmament and a permanent U.N. force individually recruited, fully trained, and equipped, having permanent bases in the different regions of the world, ready to undertake enforcement action against a state on the call of a reinforced United Nations, is an ideal solution.[195] One cannot deny the fact that the realization of this ideal is not within the realm of practical international politics at the present moment.

It would be more realistic, therefore, to be content at the moment with a permanent force for peace-keeping functions only. It is such a force that ought first to be aimed at. It would be modest in size as compared to a force needed for enforcement action. Situations calling for peace-keeping roles would be more frequent than those calling for enforcement action. The General Assembly could also set up such a force (whose legal competence to authorize an enforcement action as such is in doubt). Above all it is likely to be more acceptable to the states economically and politically.[196]

Such a peace-keeping force would be composed of national contingents, preferably of members other than the permanent members of the Security Council, maintained and supported, when not on U.N. missions, as units of national armed forces.[197] Such a force which, although functioning mainly to secure a cease-fire, maintain law and order, supervise an armistice, patrol a frontier, or oversee a plebiscite, would not be limited to use of weapons solely for purposes of self-defense.[198] It must have wider powers to use arms to bring about an early restoration of peace and security, though peace-keeping functions would not envisage its use directly against a state.

A small nucleus with the commander and his staff appointed by, and subject to the jurisdiction of, the Security Council or the General Assembly could be permanently maintained at U.N. headquarters. Certain military advisers could be there to assist the Secretary-General. It could be the function of this permanent team to keep a constant watch on the troubled areas of the world, to keep plans of military action ready, to survey the operational, logistical, and administrative problems that might be involved in any operation, to formulate model status and basic agree-

---

NATIONAL MILITARY FORCES 12 *passim*, 47 *passim* (1964), *See also* Bowett, *supra* note 11, at 519–21, for a detailed discussion on disarmament and an international force.

[195] Sohn, *supra* note 4, at 19–33.

[196] Bowett, *supra* note 4, at 265, 561–69. *See also* speech of Lord McNair, 246 PARL. DEB., H.L. (5th ser.), 1395 (1963).

[197] *See* Goodrich and Rosner, *The United Nations Emergency Force*, 19 INTERNATIONAL ORGANIZATIONS 429–30 (1957). *See also* Bloomfield *supra* note 194, ch. VII.

[198] Rosner, *supra* note 10, at 203–204.

ments, and regulations for adoption by the political organs of the United Nations and the participating states as, and when, necessary.

The military personnel could assume command responsibilities at times when a force for specific purposes was established out of the pledges made by the member states in advance. The Scandinavian countries have taken the lead in the matter on their own initiative. Some others have shown their willingness in principle to provide contingents for a U.N. force.[199] There is no reason to infer that still others would not be coming forward to emulate their example if a genuine effort is once made in the direction.[200] The success of the UNEF and ONUC operations, though limited, has established the utility and the feasibility of such a force beyond any doubt.

The question of finances could be solved in the light of the General Assembly resolution of December 15, 1966.[201] It places the highst financial responsibility on the permanent members of the Security Council who vote in favor of the operation. Some permanent members would always be there to back up the operation in any crisis. These expenses would hardly mean a fraction of their national defense budgets. They must come forward to give practical shape to the opinion of the General Assembly. On all other matters the experience from the UNEF, ONUC, and other U.N. operations, as discussed earlier, could be relied on with suitable modifications.

In any case, as Claude writes, there is a strong case for probing the limits of consensus among the nations for the creation of a permanent U.N. force. If the probing does not go far enough, the United Nations will be doomed to the underdevelopment of its capabilities for the maintenance of peace and security, one of the main purposes for which it had been established.[202] "The decision as to how far to go should not necessarily be determined by considerations related to the financial health of the United Nations."[203]

It is the view of this writer that the probing to discover the extent of such consensus to date has not gone far enough or seriously enough.

[199] Bloomfield, *supra* note 194, at 77–78; Bowett, supra note 11, at 333.

[200] Professor Sohn has observed that no attempt was made to use the favorable atmosphere which accompanied the adoption of the Uniting for Peace Resolution by 45 votes against 5, with 7 abstentions for its prompt implementation. Though the replies of member states to a request by the Collective Measures Committee for information as regards the action taken under Section C of the Resolution were disappointing (6 U.N. GAOR, Supp. 13, at 37–48, U.N. Doc A/1891 (1951)) but even where conditional pledges were given, no steps were taken by the U.N. to ensure their execution once the conditions had been fulfilled. Sohn, *The Authority of the United Nations to Establish and Maintain a Permanent U.N. Force*, 52 A.J.I.L. 229–33 (1958).

[201] U.N. Doc. A/6603.

[202] *See* Claude, *Supra* note 179, and Art. 1(1) of the Charter.

[203] *See* STOESSENGER, FINANCING THE UNITED NATIONS SYSTEM, ch. I (1964). *See also* Jenks, *supra* note 182, at 38.

INDEX OF NAMES

INDEX OF SUBJECTS

A

Aggression, 159–97, 235, 258–59

aggressive propaganda, 238–72

categories and examples of, 251–55

codes of ethics on, for the media (sample quoted), 271–72

a common law misdemeanor, 250

conferences on radio and press communications and peace, 242–43

defined, 244–47

international documents condemning,

early nineteenth century and post-World War I treaties, 257

(1931) Draft of the General Convention to Improve the Means of Preventing War, 247

(1936) Convention on the Use of Broadcasting in the Cause of Peace, 218, 247, 262–63

(1937 and 1940) South American regional agreements on radiocommunications, 218

(1945) United Nations Charter, on subversive propaganda, 258, 265

(1946) Nuremberg and Tokyo judgments, outlawing aggressive propaganda, 250–51

(1948) Draft declaration of rights and duties of states, 255

(1948) Bogota Charter, 257

(1950) UN General Assembly Resolution, "Peace Through Deeds," 256, 259

(1954) Draft Code of Offences against the Peace and Security of Mankind, 256, 259

(1954) Caracas Declaration of Solidarity, 257–58

(1961) International Covenant on Civil and Political Rights, article 20 (1), 248

(1962) UN ENCD declaration for enforcing declaration condemning aggressive propaganda, 248–49

remedies for, 261–72

aggressive war,

an international crime, 231, 570, 602–603, 608–615

international documents condemning,

(1919) League of Nations Covenant, article 10, 160, 183, 569–70

(1923) League of Nations draft treaty of mutual assistance, and protocol, 570

(1924) draft of Geneva Protocol, 160–61

(1925) Geneva Protocol

(1925–37) interwar treaties, 570 (see also Kellogg-Briand Pact.)

(1928) Resolution of 6th Pan American Conference, Havana, 570

(1933) Anti-War Treaty of Non-Aggression and Conciliation, Rio de Janeiro (Saavedra Lamas Treaty), 570

(1933) Convention on the Definition of Aggression, 570

(1945) United Nations Charter, 596

(1946) Nuremberg and Tokyo judgments, 608–615

crimes against peace, 61–63, 157–291, and *passim*

defined, in Nuremberg Charter (1945), 111, 231, 576, 594–95; in Tokyo Charter (1945), 618

made international crimes by Nuremberg and Tokyo judgments, 606

a new concept, 26, 592–95

"the supreme international crime," 601–605

definition of, 159–81, 235, 258–59

in international documents,

(1933) London conventions for the definition of aggression, 187, 216

(1933) Act Relating to the Definition of the Aggressor (Politis Report), 187, 216

(1934) Protocol Annex to the Pact of the Balkan Entente, 216

(1937) Saadabad Pact, 216

(1971) proposals before the United